The Complete Funky Winkerbean

Volume 5   1984–1986

Black Squirrel Books™ 🐿™

Kent, Ohio

THE COMPLETE

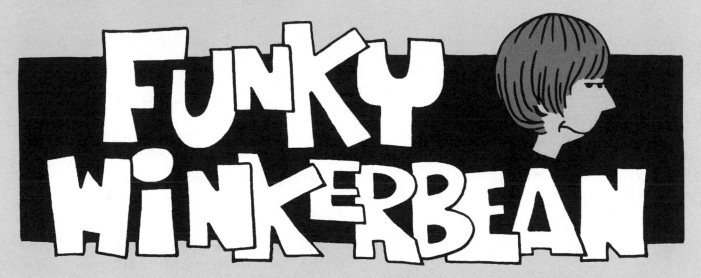

FUNKY WINKERBEAN

VOLUME 5   1984-1986

TOM BATIUK

BLACK SQUIRREL BOOKS™ 🐿™
Frisky, industrious black squirrels are a familiar sight on the
Kent State University campus and the inspiration for Black
Squirrel Books™, a trade imprint of The Kent State University
Press. www.KentStateUniversityPress.com

Library of Congress Catalog Number 2016008091
ISBN 978-1-60635-299-1
Manufactured in the United States of America
Designed by Christine Brooks

Library of Congress Cataloging-in-Publication Data
Names: Batiuk, Tom, author, illustrator.
Title: The complete Funky Winkerbean. Volume 5, 1984-1986 /
    Tom Batiuk.
Description: Kent, Ohio : The Kent State University Press, [2016]
Identifiers: LCCN 2016008091 (print) | LCCN 2016009672 (ebook) |
    ISBN 9781606352991 (hardcover : alk. paper) ∞ |
    ISBN 9781631012426 (ePub) | ISBN 9781631012433 (ePDF)
Subjects: LCSH: High schools--Comic books, strips, etc. | GSAFD:
    Comic books, strips, etc.
Classification: LCC PN6728.F8 B266 2016 (print) | LCC PN6728.F8
    (ebook) | DDC 741.5/6973--dc23
LC record available at http://lccn.loc.gov/2016008091

20 19 18 17 16   5 4 3 2 1

To the girl in a sketchbook

Contents

Savoring *Funky*

Maggie Thompson

You hold in your hands a massive collection of 1,096 comic strips, and you may not even realize what a recent phenomenon this opportunity represents. On the one hand, it's not *that* many years since even the few strip collections that were published were limited to relatively small bites of continuity. Only obsessives cared enough to clip and preserve all their favorite comic strips for rereading.

On the *other* hand, this bounty (an additional day, thanks to Leap Year!) presents a basic complication of publishing the art form known as daily comic strips. Daily comic strips, after all, are not designed to be read in thousand-strip chunks.

On the other other hand: Wow, what a treat!

Those of us who used to clip our favorites every day, filing them in sequence—well, yes, we were a little nuts. But how else were we to savor them? Thanks to the Kent State University Press in this case, we can binge, even while we note the

construction and, yes, evolution of the increasingly complex world of *Funky Winkerbean*.

Previous forewords in this series have addressed the strip from a variety of standpoints. Cartoonist and comics historian R. C. Harvey discussed its beginnings during 1972, 1973, and 1974, placing *Funky Winkerbean* in the context of the history of teen comics and identifying the early signs of what the strip would become. The *Cleveland Plain Dealer*'s Michael Heaton noted the positioning of *Funky Winkerbean* in the world that teens were experiencing from 1975 to 1977. In the 1978–1980 collection, singer, songwriter, performer, and fellow Kent Stater Joe Walsh paid tribute to the growing structure Tom Batiuk was building. And (wow!) Marvel's Stan Lee (after paying tribute to Tom's art and gags) singled out the brilliant characterization on display in the strips from 1981 to 1983.

To top it off, Tom himself has continued to provide wonderful behind-the-scenes background in each volume. This publishing project is a treasure, indeed.

There's another aspect of the strip that you may have noticed, thanks to being able to evaluate more closely what he's done: Tom is clearly One of Us, a pop-culture connoisseur. And he combines his affections and talents with insights concerning the world around him. It might even be time to point out that these still-early years of *Funky Winkerbean*—while fun—have so far provided only the merest hints of the feast that was to come. His stunning *Lisa's Story,* for example . . .

But I'm getting ahead of things. This is only the fifth volume, covering strips published from 1984 to 1986. By this point in its evolution, the feature had long since begun to resonate with readers. Tom was touring and doing interviews to support the selection of strips from 1981 and 1982 published in the slim paperback *Funky Winkerbean: You Know You've Got Trouble When Your School Mascot Is a Scapegoat.* (The foreword to *that* was by Erma Bombeck!) He was becoming better known, high school band members (and directors!) were increasingly paying tribute to band director Harry Dinkle, and appreciation of the popular strip was growing.

Let's be clear about this: Humorous comic strips were introduced to provide a quick, sharp burst of laughter to wrap up the day's reading of a newspaper that might otherwise be a pretty depressing collection of information. A few of the accompanying adventure strips might benefit from being collected in some of *their* ongoing story arcs, because continuity was a major element of their existence, but the funny strips? Those were designed to delight as stand-alones. (Speaking of more serious continuity, by the way, this might be the place to remind Tom's fans that he has often paid tribute to his own pop-culture influences, commenting in admiration on the comics serials that have featured such characters as Flash Gordon, Skeezix, Judge Dredd, Dick Tracy, Little Orphan Annie, Captain Kirk, Luke Skywalker, the Flash, Prince Valiant, Adam Strange, Elric, and members of the Fantastic Four, Alpha Flight, and Teen Titans—you get the idea.)

But back to the funny strips: They have a freestanding socko impact. They're fun to stick to the refrigerator, to pin to bulletin boards, and to exchange with buddies. Tom's challenges in creating those funny strips included the simultaneous necessities of being fresh, of being memorable, and of providing something different every day. And he met those challenges with ingenuity, intelligence, and—yes—wit.

Nevertheless, as we saw in the 1981–1983 collection, he was beginning to add darker shades to his metaphoric palette. In this fifth volume, collecting strips from 1984 through 1986, he was creating entertainment for a world that was not only passing through, it was going beyond, the imaginings of George Orwell. The AIDS virus was identified, Indira Gandhi was assassinated, Ronald Reagan was reelected, the domain name system for the Internet was introduced, Coca-Cola offered New Coke, Nintendo released *Super Mario Bros.* and *The Legend of Zelda,* the first PC virus spread (as did the ability to send and receive email), the *Challenger* space shuttle disintegrated, and there was a disaster at the Chernobyl Nuclear Power Plant.

Major events, oddball events: Every day, as the newspapers reported the events, Tom Batiuk brought readers a daily bonus—

and sometimes reminded those readers of serious topics. Today, if you want to recapture the experience, you can try doling out the contents of this volume at the rate of one strip per day.

But, as you revisit the era, I bet you won't be able to keep from turning page after page to read more strips—and more.

Take a look.

****

Comics historian and essayist Maggie Thompson adds, "If this foreword were about me, I'd mention that this was the era in which my husband, Don, and I helped to turn the weekly *Comics Buyer's Guide* into a newspaper designed to—well—guide people who wanted to buy comics. And *Funky Winkerbean* was one of the pleasures that kept us entertained in the midst of that fascinating job. But this isn't about me." Among many other activities, she coedited that publication for three decades (initially with her husband, who died in 1994) and she now contributes to the *Toucan* blog of Comic-Con International: San Diego and to the *Scoop* newsletter of Diamond Comic Distributors.

Acknowledgments

Special thanks for help with this volume to Bill Sandor, Ashley Sullivan, and Mike "Mr. Media" Olszewski. As ever, thanks to Will Underwood, Susan Cash, Mary Young, and Chris Brooks of the KSU Press.

Prologue

There's an old joke about these parents who have a baby who is perfect in just about every way . . . except that when it came time for him to be able to talk, he didn't. He didn't talk when he was a toddler, when he was in elementary school, when he was in high school, or even when he was in college. His parents sent him to numerous speech pathologists, therapists, and other linguistic experts, and nothing they tried worked. No one was able to determine why this young man who was perfectly fine in every other way was unable to talk. Then one day when he was twenty-six or so, he was having dinner at home with his parents (apparently he was a millennial) when he suddenly said, "The ham is too salty." His parents couldn't believe it, and his astonished mother said, "You can talk! Why haven't you said anything before now?" And he replied, "Up 'til now, everything's been OK."

The Episode Where the Bat Guano Hits the Windmill

Allow me to digress for a moment (I don't know if you can have a digression before you've even written word one of the actual intro, but just work with me here). It was the heart of the winter of January 1966 and there I was sitting in the front row of seats in the TV room of Kent State University's Stopher Hall about a minute away from something that I felt was going to be Earth shattering. Turned out that the only thing shattered that black night would be my belief system and entire philosophy of life. Maybe they weren't exactly shattered, but they were certainly dinged up.

President Johnson was going to be giving a State of the Union address that evening and its implications regarding my future promised to be enormous, but that's not why I was there. I was waiting to catch a new television show that was premiering that night. To make sure I had a front-row seat for the 7:30 program, I had shown up in my dormitory TV lounge

at 5:00. Which meant that I had to sit through *Captain Penny's Fun House* at 5:00, *Yogi Bear* at 5:45, the ABC News at 6:15, *Honey West* at 6:30, the news and weather at 7:00, and Dorothy Fuldheim at 7:15—all to catch the premiere of *Batman* at 7:30. As the appointed hour neared, I was totally psyched and then some. Being a comic book aficionado from almost before I could read,* the prospect of seeing Batman on TV was beyond exciting. I was in heaven, and then the show started. I had anticipated a drama that took the Batman premise seriously and was prepared to tell an exciting and straightforward story framed by that context. What I saw unfolding before me was a horror show. Insipid, foolish writing coupled with garishly colored costumes and sets, and, worst of all, sound effects

*Please see volumes 1, 2, and 3 of this award-winning series for the full details.

that popped up graphically in special effects comic balloons. ABC had decided to turn *Batman* into an exaggerated, Pop Art, silly piece of camp. I guess the calculus was that it would make it amusing for adults. Well, it wasn't amusing to me. As far as I was concerned they had blown it. Completely, irrevocably, without even a silver lining of a saving grace blown it. They treated the art form that I aspired to as some sort of lower caste illegitimate that would only be palatable to adults if you made fun of it. The show turned out to be a smash hit for the network. The American viewing public loved it. Well, they were wrong too.

As long as I'm at it, the whole Pop Art movement was wrong as well. The artists of the Pop Art movement treated the comics as something disposable and shallow even as they tried to emulate them. It's a pick 'em call whether they were reflecting them or critiquing them, but in either case I had a bone to pick with their terms and conditions. It would still be awhile before comics were accepted by institutions of higher learning and elevated to the status of a legitimate art form, but from the get-go, work of genuine quality was always present and appreciated by the cognoscenti twelve years old and up. It never occurred to me that comics should be denied a seat at the art table. It was always my unshakable belief that comics could achieve substance and chronicle like any other art form what it means to be human. I bring all of this up for two reasons. One, I needed a way into this intro, and, two, I wanted to make a couple of points (it's always nice when you can do both). I wanted to clarify my mind-set at the time the strips in this volume were being created. As I mentioned in the previous volume, my work had been slowly edging toward the idea that my characters could evolve. That their perceptions and personalities could be molded by events. In short, I wanted to introduce drama into their lives. But as I also discussed earlier, it would have to be done in the face of prescriptive expectations as well as cultural and editorial resistance. The years contained within this volume are where that process begins to gain purchase. The teen pregnancy series will provide the beginnings of an answer, but I would be tiptoeing into my sixth decade before I would truly seal the bargain I was about to make with myself. To move toward this future, I would need to look to the past with an eye toward reclaiming the full genetic code of the American comic strip.

There were times when I would imagine that I lived in a world where cartoonists were free to write about whatever interested them, that their creations would belong to them and no one else, that the concerns of commerce were not their concerns. In essence, that they were happily free to pursue their art. Then a butterfly would flap its wings and I would find myself back in 1984 (not <u>that</u> *1984,* but close) and the vexing realities of the real world would set in. I was entering a period of bone-rattling changes. My syndicate, Field Enterprises/Publishers-Hall, was about to be sold; my cocreator on *John Darling,* Tom Armstrong, would soon take leave of the strip; I would attempt to syndicate yet another comic strip with a brand-new syndicate; I would coauthor a high school musical; and I would begin taking steps to rectify the draconian contract that I signed in my callow youth. I had been tagged by my syndicate as one of their "quiet" contributors, and that was true because until that point everything had been OK. However, things were becoming less OK by the minute.

The year kicked off with me crisscrossing the country in support of a *Funky* book collection entitled *Funky Winkerbean: You Know You've Got Trouble When Your School Mascot Is a Scapegoat*. You also know you've got trouble when something like that is the title of your book. The ever-expanding repertory company of characters collectively known as *Funky Winkerbean* was never an easy brand to wrap your arms around and market. It lacked the one-cat-fits-all mentality. When you couple that with the direction in which I wanted to take the work, the picture for licensing the strip didn't look rosy. In a period when licensing dollars were falling from the sky like snowflakes in an Alberta clipper, not many stuck to *Funky*. Of course, if I had

Syndicated in over 350 newspapers coast to coast!
FUNKY WINKERBEAN
BY TOM BATIUK
WITH A FOREWORD BY
Erma Bombeck
YOU KNOW YOU'VE GOT TROUBLE WHEN YOUR SCHOOL MASCOT IS A SCAPEGOAT

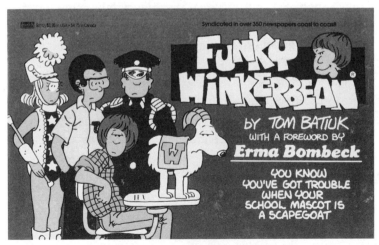

Could we have made Erma Bombeck's name any bigger?

to deal with tons of licensing, the work and time dedicated to that would have splintered my focus and inevitably caused the strip to suffer. When you add to that the fact that a large market presence would have no doubt dictated that the original *Funky* gang remain in high school forever, endlessly repeating their high school hijinks, you would have found me to be quite the unhappy camper. Granted, I'd be camping in a much bigger house on a massive estate with a horse in the Kentucky Derby and whatnot, but unhappy nonetheless. But while the book tour wasn't about to land me on the *New York Times* Best Sellers list, it did have one fascinating spin-off.

I had just finished an interview at a TV station in Atlanta and was in the lobby about to leave when the receptionist called me over. There was a phone call for me from a fan of *Funky* who said that she really enjoyed the strip but that there were two things missing: a school secretary and a school bus driver. I thanked her, made a mental note, and was off and running to the airport. At some point later on the book tour, I found myself with some time on my hands at Sea-Tac Airport in Washington waiting for my next flight. I unpacked my mental notes and remembered the call from Atlanta. I was really glad that I did because I thought that the school secretary idea was a real winner with all the potential in the world. I immediately began jotting down some ideas for the character, and I decided to use a character already extant in the strip. My character Ann Randall had been riffed from her teaching job and had been working as a burger bouncer at McArnolds. While she was there, she made friends with a coworker named Betty. Thanks to Ann's influence, Betty decides to apply for the job of secretary at the high school. I loved how I was able to make it take shape organically out of the strip, and I was excited by the possibilities that the school secretary promised. Before I got on my plane, I had the first two weeks finished with notes jotted down for future weeks. (I should probably at this point send a retroactive shout-out to my unknown benefactor in Atlanta. Much like the fictional Blanche DuBois, I owe much to the kindness of strangers.) Oh, and I had also made a note about the school bus driver. I was going to call him Crankshaft.

While I was flying around the country that frosty March, my syndicate (and me as well if you read the contract carefully) was being sold. I woke up one morning to find that I, and everything I ever created, was now owned paper, pencil, and penholder by Rupert Murdoch. To be fair, I doubt that *Funky Winkerbean* was even on Rupert Murdoch's radar. The primary target in his acquisition was the *Chicago Sun-Times,* and the syndicate just came along for the ride. Nevertheless, I just had this sinking feeling that Rupert and I weren't exactly on the same comics page. In fact, we weren't even reading the same newspaper. It seemed to me that this shotgun marriage was not going to be a happy union. As the grandson of union men and living in a home where as a child the Weavers could be heard on the record player, I came by my progressive leanings honestly. Rupert Murdoch, as far as I could ascertain, was not in the same place, and it didn't seem that this turn of events was going to accrue to my benefit. Just call me "Nostrathomas." Right out of the gate, it cost me one of the biggest papers on the East Coast and a paper that had been a *Funky* cornerstone from the start. When Murdoch decreed that some

of newly christened News America Syndicate's highly valued properties should be moved from the *Boston Globe* to the Murdoch-owned *Boston Herald,* the *Globe* retaliated by dropping their remaining News America features, including *Funky Winkerbean,* and I lost a major presence on the East Coast and one of the bigger clients on my list. Although Murdoch's ownership of the syndicate would be relatively brief (he would be forced to divest himself of it by government mandate due to overlapping media holdings), it was long enough to do some real damage. In fact, down the road, he would still get one more shot at me when the British managing editor he installed at the *Sun-Times* would drop *Funky* over a story about a young woman dying of cancer. A story that violated his obdurate dictum that comics should only be funny. However, I'm getting a bit ahead of myself and that story will have to wait for a future *Funky* volume.* Needless to say, the circumstances I found myself in were a little disquieting. Make that a lot disquieting. Had the gentleman brought in to manage the *Sun-Times* instead been installed as the president of the syndicate, my career trajectory might have taken a far different and downward turn. Just as I approached the cusp of blossoming as an artist, all the buds could have been shorn. But.

The man brought in to be the president of News America Syndicate would turn out to be a surprise to everyone, not the least of whom I'm sure would be Rupert Murdoch. Rick Newcombe came to News America by way of United Press International, where he was an editor, and the Los Angeles Times Syn-

---

*See the future.

dicate, where he was the general manager. Although only a few years younger than me, he seemed much younger and full of energy and enthusiasm. He brought with him a creator-oriented philosophy that was the antithesis of anything I had experienced up to that point. Rick was concerned with the needs of the feature writers and cartoonists and wanted to do whatever he could to help make them more productive and, by extension, his syndicate more successful. In line with that thinking and as time went on, Rick would travel to meet with the syndicate's contributors to introduce himself, to get to know them, and to see how things were going. He came out to visit a couple of times, and, on one of those trips, he stayed overnight with us and the next morning while we were out jogging he asked me if there was anything that was bothering me or that I needed regarding the strip or the syndicate. Having recently been made aware of what a blunt instrument my contract with the syndicate could be in the wrong hands and how fugitive and vaporous the verbal inducements saying it was a "gentlemen's agreement" truly were, my first and only thought was to protect my work. I said that I would like to have complete and absolute editorial control. The rest of the discussion consisted of two words. Rick said, "Done." I said, "Thanks." And a butterfly flapped its wings. Editorially speaking, I was a free man, but freedom can be a tricky concept. While I now felt free to shift the terms of the engagement, I had to decide exactly what it was that I was going to do with that freedom. To paraphrase Stan Lee, with full editorial control comes full responsibility. And, of course, while I was free to create what I wanted, my creations themselves weren't free. Work remained.

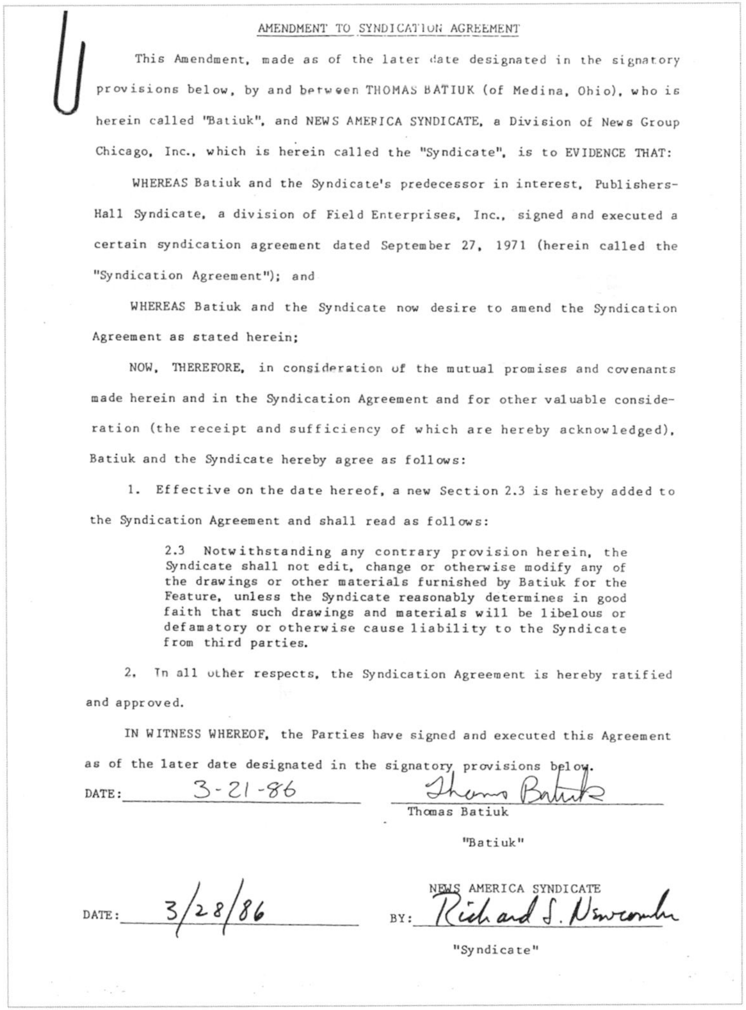

AMENDMENT TO SYNDICATION AGREEMENT

This Amendment, made as of the later date designated in the signatory provisions below, by and between THOMAS BATIUK (of Medina, Ohio), who is herein called "Batiuk", and NEWS AMERICA SYNDICATE, a Division of News Group Chicago, Inc., which is herein called the "Syndicate", is to EVIDENCE THAT:

WHEREAS Batiuk and the Syndicate's predecessor in interest, Publishers-Hall Syndicate, a division of Field Enterprises, Inc., signed and executed a certain syndication agreement dated September 27, 1971 (herein called the "Syndication Agreement"); and

WHEREAS Batiuk and the Syndicate now desire to amend the Syndication Agreement as stated herein;

NOW, THEREFORE, in consideration of the mutual promises and covenants made herein and in the Syndication Agreement and for other valuable consideration (the receipt and sufficiency of which are hereby acknowledged), Batiuk and the Syndicate hereby agree as follows:

1. Effective on the date hereof, a new Section 2.3 is hereby added to the Syndication Agreement and shall read as follows:

> 2.3 Notwithstanding any contrary provision herein, the Syndicate shall not edit, change or otherwise modify any of the drawings or other materials furnished by Batiuk for the Feature, unless the Syndicate reasonably determines in good faith that such drawings and materials will be libelous or defamatory or otherwise cause liability to the Syndicate from third parties.

2. In all other respects, the Syndication Agreement is hereby ratified and approved.

IN WITNESS WHEREOF, the Parties have signed and executed this Agreement as of the later date designated in the signatory provisions below.

DATE: 3-21-86 Thomas Batiuk

"Batiuk"

NEWS AMERICA SYNDICATE

DATE: 3/28/86 BY:

"Syndicate"

Fifty-five words that changed everything.

Meanwhile, back in the funny pages, school bus driver Ed Crankshaft made his first appearance in the strip. I was a city boy at the start of my school experience, so walking back and forth to school every day as I had been, I was my own man. Whether I got home late or early was purely my call. A story long told in our family was of how on one rainy afternoon following school, after I failed to make a timely appearance at home, a search party was dispatched and they found me slowly meandering home in the rain, taking my time to walk around each puddle I encountered along the way. There was apparently something interesting going on there, and I was taking the necessary time to thoroughly examine it. Whatever problems ensued, they were of my own making. In short, I held my destiny in my own hands. When we moved from Akron to a more rural setting, the transition to having to ride a school bus every day was, putting it mildly, traumatic. Suddenly my fate was in the hands of others (anyone else picking up a theme here?). A fact that was exacerbated by the bus driver on my route who was, shall we say, unusual. My normal method when developing a character is to take someone's quirks and personality traits and exaggerate and expand upon them to create the character. In this case, I had to take the personality of my bus driver and tone it down quite a bit to make it believable enough for a comic strip. When I first started riding the bus, I would sit right behind the bus driver, all the better to make sure that he dropped me off at the correct house rather than the wrong house where I would no doubt have to be taken in by strangers for the night. From my vantage point behind the driver, I once watched him pull up so close to a Volkswagen beetle that the car disappeared from view. When you couple incidents like that with frantically hurrying out of school at the end of each day desperate to find the right bus in a field of yellow to ensure it didn't leave without you, or watching for the bus in the morning and then running down the driveway in ice and snow with your books and a trombone case or, worse, a science project consisting of a papier-mâché volcano on a plywood board, it's no small wonder that I came away scarred by these experiences. The comics have always given me a place to go where I could make sense of the world, first as a reader and later as a creator. So it's no surprise that I drew upon these experiences when I created the trauma-inducing Ed Crankshaft. What *was* a surprise is that it appeared I wasn't alone.

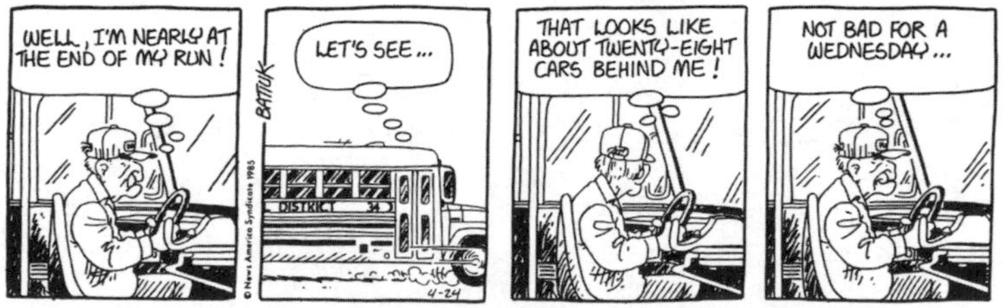
WELL, I'M NEARLY AT THE END OF MY RUN!
LET'S SEE...
THAT LOOKS LIKE ABOUT TWENTY-EIGHT CARS BEHIND ME!
NOT BAD FOR A WEDNESDAY...
BATIUK
© News America Syndicate 1985
DISTRICT 34
4-24
Crankshaft would later drive bus 13, which somehow seemed more appropriate.

I immediately began hearing from readers who recognized that surly old curmudgeon. Apparently I'd come up with another comics character who was unique to the comics page yet familiar to my readers. Not since the introduction of my band director Harry L. Dinkle had I gotten such an enthusiastic response to a new character. And, not being a complete idiot, it made me want to use him all the more. My school secretary,

Betty, would soldier on until I finally sent her off to the cartoon character's retirement home, but Crankshaft was turning out to be a lot of fun. Who knew? I was beginning to see more dimensions to him than I had originally anticipated. Much like John Darling before him, Crankshaft was becoming a strip within a strip. Hmmmm.

Almost unnoticed, another new character appeared quietly and without any fanfare. She didn't even have a name at this point. In fact, she had started out as simply a sketch in a sketchbook. Big hair was becoming a big thing at my old high school where I still went to sketch every week, and I think I put her in the strip as a one-off simply because I liked drawing her hair.

Other changes were afoot on the comics pages. My partner on *John Darling*, Tom Armstrong, had started a new strip of his own called *Marvin* about a young child. The demands on his time were such that he was having trouble keeping up with *John Darling*, and something was going to have to give. I knew the feeling well from my early days on *Funky* and, when Tom called one day saying he was ready to move on and just concentrate on *Marvin*, I gave him my blessing. Tom gave me some time to find a replacement, but I didn't have to look far. I had tried to start a couple of new strips with a terrific local artist from Cleveland, Gerry Shamray, and he was able to jump in on *John Darling* without missing a beat.* Truth be told, however, *John Darling* was beginning to wear a little thin with me. The writing was easy enough, but it was becoming a little

*See the introduction to *The Complete* Funky Winkerbean, *Volume 4, 1981–1983.*

The smoking Lisa sketchbook page.

discouraging to satirize what was happening on TV only to have TV top you with something more outrageous the next week. Broadcast TV was rapidly becoming a bigger joke than any joke you could ever write about it, and reality TV wasn't even on the horizon yet. It was becoming a mugs game. Still, you hate to let one of your characters go, so Gerry and I slogged on, and I'm glad we did. Why? Because John and Jan Darling would soon become the proud parents of a baby girl. A baby girl named Jessica who would grow up to play a prominent role in the life of that as-yet-unnamed girl from the sketchbook I mentioned earlier.

Also in the strips contained within this volume, the *John Darling* and *Funky Winkerbean* strips crossed over for the Fourth of

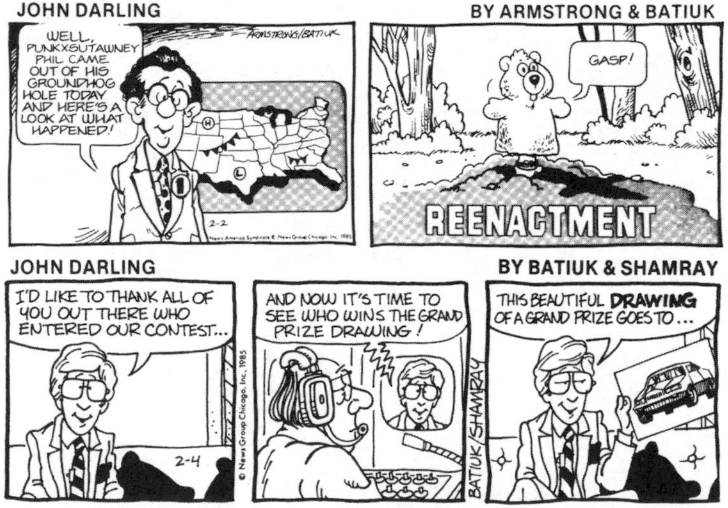
JOHN DARLING
BY ARMSTRONG & BATIUK
WELL, PUNKXSUTAWNEY PHIL CAME OUT OF HIS GROUNDHOG HOLE TODAY AND HERE'S A LOOK AT WHAT HAPPENED!
GASP!
REENACTMENT
JOHN DARLING
BY BATIUK & SHAMRAY
I'D LIKE TO THANK ALL OF YOU OUT THERE WHO ENTERED OUR CONTEST...
AND NOW IT'S TIME TO SEE WHO WINS THE GRAND PRIZE DRAWING!
THIS BEAUTIFUL DRAWING OF A GRAND PRIZE GOES TO...
The artists changed without missing a cue card.

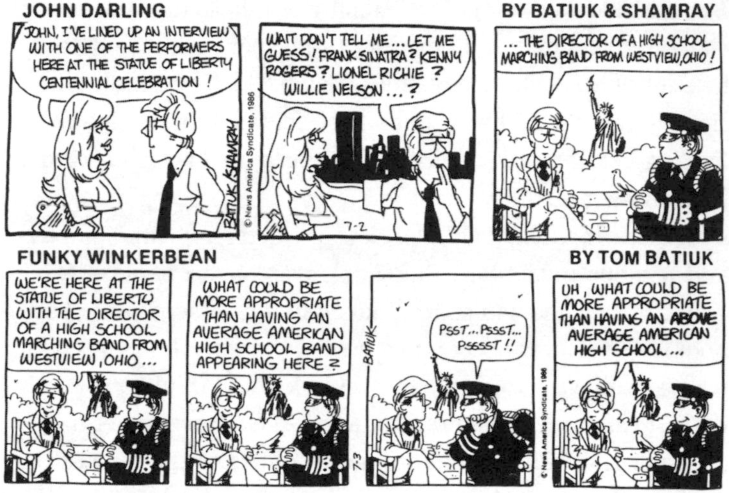
JOHN DARLING
BY BATIUK & SHAMRAY
JOHN, I'VE LINED UP AN INTERVIEW WITH ONE OF THE PERFORMERS HERE AT THE STATUE OF LIBERTY CENTENNIAL CELEBRATION!
WAIT DON'T TELL ME... LET ME GUESS! FRANK SINATRA? KENNY ROGERS? LIONEL RICHIE? WILLIE NELSON...?
...THE DIRECTOR OF A HIGH SCHOOL MARCHING BAND FROM WESTVIEW, OHIO!
FUNKY WINKERBEAN
BY TOM BATIUK
WE'RE HERE AT THE STATUE OF LIBERTY WITH THE DIRECTOR OF A HIGH SCHOOL MARCHING BAND FROM WESTVIEW, OHIO...
WHAT COULD BE MORE APPROPRIATE THAN HAVING AN AVERAGE AMERICAN HIGH SCHOOL BAND APPEARING HERE?
PSST... PSSST... PSSSST!!
UH, WHAT COULD BE MORE APPROPRIATE THAN HAVING AN ABOVE AVERAGE AMERICAN HIGH SCHOOL...
Too many egos for one strip.

July celebrations commemorating the newly refurbished Statue of Liberty. Both Harry L. Dinkle and John Darling were in New York for the festivities, and it seemed only natural for John to interview *Funky*'s resident band director. I'd always loved it when comic book characters would cross over in comic books, so I would jump at the chance to play comic book company any time I could. Not every paper carried both *Funky* and *Darling,* of course, but, for those that did, the crossover was a nice little Easter egg. As I mentioned in a previous volume* whenever a crossover occurs between *Darling* and *Funky* or *Crankshaft* and *Funky,* we'll include the crossover strips as well so that you

*I forget which one.

won't miss a single scintillating moment of monumental merriment (still in comic book mode).

Another milestone contained in this volume is the marriage of Ann Randall and Fred Fairgood. As I mentioned in the last volume,* their relationship was one of my earliest attempts at a longer form narrative, and this story arc brought it to its natural conclusion. The part in the story where Fred forgets to get the marriage license was based on a real event (ahem, mine). Instead of having to have someone hack the courthouse records like Fred does, I was able to take advantage of the fact that our landlord's husband was a judge in Elyria who had the power to waive the usual seven-day waiting period. Sometimes it just pays to be lucky. It also shows how a comic strip forces you to strip-mine your past for material, no matter how embarrassing.

With all of this craziness flying around, I decided to do the only reasonable thing a person could do under the circumstances. I wrote a musical. Put more correctly, I wrote the book for a musical. Andy Clark, the publisher of my band cartoon collections, and I were in Chicago during the holiday season for the Midwest Band and Orchestra Conference, when over dinner at the Berghoff he floated the idea of the two of us creating a musical featuring Funky Winkerbean. It would be a musical designed for high schools to perform. I would write the book and lyrics and Andy would write the music. As they say in the movies, the idea was so crazy that it just might work. And so, along with everything else I was doing, I added writing a musical to my to-do list. It would be called *Funky Winkerbean's Homecoming*. The plot revolved around the fact that through some sort of scheduling quirk, Westview High School's homecoming game had been scheduled as an away game. Everything was thrown into turmoil and comedy ensued. Writing the musical was revelatory in that it confirmed for me the notion that longer form story arcs were the kind of writing that I now preferred to do. Instead of writing stand-alone gags, you could produce a story from which the humor could flow in a more natural fashion. In short, I had more fun writing *Homecoming* than I'd had in a while. Music-wise, there was a song for every major character, including one called "Mean Old Bus Drivin' Man" for my new favorite character, Crankshaft. *Homecoming* turned out to be very successful for us, and Andy and I attended any number of world premieres. Every time we did, we always waited for one special line where the cheerleaders lamented having to cheer for a losing football team by saying that it really tended to dampen their élan. Whether due to poor writing, which I discount, or the performers' inability to really sell the line, which I favor, it never ever ever and I mean ever got a laugh—

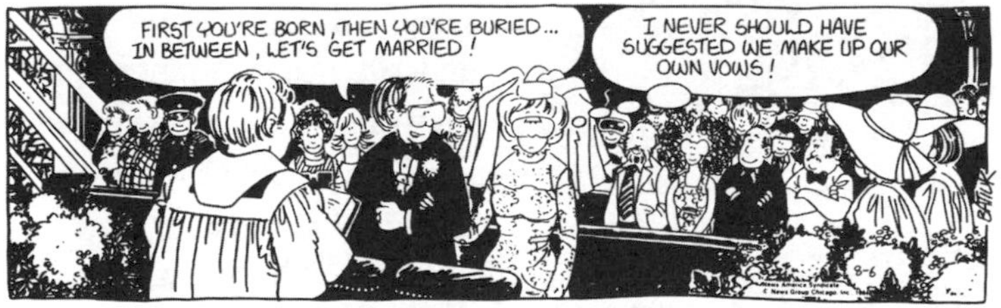
FIRST YOU'RE BORN, THEN YOU'RE BURIED... IN BETWEEN, LET'S GET MARRIED!
I NEVER SHOULD HAVE SUGGESTED WE MAKE UP OUR OWN VOWS!

Funky's first milestone event pretty much says it all.

*See the introduction to *The Complete* Funky Winkerbean, *Volume 4, 1981–1983*.

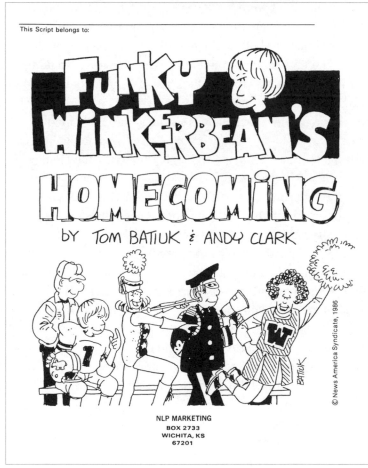

This Script belongs to:

FUNKY WINKERBEAN'S HOMECOMING

BY TOM BATIUK & ANDY CLARK

NLP MARKETING
BOX 2733
WICHITA, KS
67201

Watch out, Broadway!

RESERVED

SEC.	ROW	SEAT
RGT	D	11

ADMIT ONE THIS DATE

NOV 14 1986

MENTOR
THESPIANS
PRESENT
FUNKY
WINKERBEAN'S
HOMECOMING
* * * * *
PREMIERE
MHS THEATRE
NOV 14 1986
FRI 8 00 PM

NO REFUNDS	PRICE	NO EXCHANGES
	$4.00	

SEC.	ROW	SEAT
RGT	D	11

RESERVED

One of the many world premieres.

except, of course, for Andy and me laughing like two loons amid the otherwise deafening silence. One has to wonder at times what the world is coming to.

I was also wondering what the world was coming to back in the fall of 1986 when it was announced that News America Syndicate was to be sold to King Features. Once again, I and my creations were on the block, and once again I was made aware of the tenuousness of my situation. My body of work and my brand were for the second time being sold for a bundle, and all I received from it was a notice that in January of the coming year I should begin sending my finished strips to a new address. I was starting to become a little desperate and in that desperation, an idea occurred. In my craziness, I decided to do the only reasonable thing a person could do under the circumstances and began work on a new strip. The tremendous response I was getting to *Crankshaft* had started me thinking about having my school bus driver drive out on his own, and I had even begun pulling some sample strips together. I got a very positive response to the strips as I showed them around to friends and decided to see if News America Syndicate would want to syndicate *Crankshaft*—which I knew they couldn't do. Why would I do that, you ask (you know, you ask the most prescient questions, which is why writing for you is so much fun). I recalled my previous attempts at syndicating a second strip back in the good old lazy days when I was working on only one, and I remembered that when the syndicate turned them down, I had asked for and received a release allowing me try to syndicate them elsewhere.* I knew that with its pending sale, News America Syndicate was in no position to launch a new comic strip, and, when they turned me down, I'd ask for the usual release I'd gotten several times in the past. So I did and they did, and then I did and they did. I now had a release to take *Crankshaft* somewhere else. There were no guarantees that it would ever lead to anything, but, with the leverage of being able to walk away from any contract offer that wouldn't let me own my own character, I at least had a ray of hope that such a possibility existed. It was a desperate long shot, but that's why they're called desperate long shots. I received news of the release while attending one of the world premieres of *Funky Winkerbean's Homecoming* in Dallas, Texas, and that night even the fact that the "élan" line once again failed to elicit even a snicker didn't bother me nearly as much. Oh, and along with the new strip, I also sent the syndicate a letter from my attorney saying that I wanted to renegotiate my contract.

While all of this was going on, that girl from my sketchbook

*See the introduction to *The Complete* Funky Winkerbean, *Volume 3, 1978–1980.*

had begun little by little to insinuate herself into the strip. In my mind, the students in the strip had reached their junior year and as such the junior/senior prom was looming. Les needed a date for the prom, and this new girl seemed to be the perfect candidate. Along with Les I learned her name—Lisa. They went to the prom together and continued to date. They followed the typical bell curve of a high school relationship and eventually broke up with Lisa transferring to another school. Nice story, that. The problem, however, is that I had really grown to like Lisa and I missed having her in the strip almost as much as Les seemed to. It turned out that my journey with Lisa was only starting. Twice I would banish her from the strip and twice she would return with a new story to tell.

The smell of cut grass drifted through the screen as I sat writing in my studio in the late summer of 1986, contemplating her return. I was leafing through my sketchbook looking for, I don't know what exactly, when I idly turned a page and saw a sketch I'd made of a girl at the high school who was pregnant. I began to explore the idea of doing something with that in the strip. About ten years earlier I had written a single idea dealing with a pregnant teen and was told in no uncertain terms by my syndicate that there was no place for something like that on the comics page. In all fairness, I'm glad they did because the idea was too flippant and too light. No, this time it would be something much different. This time it would be more substantial. Somewhere during that work session, the idea about writing about a pregnant teen and the desire to bring Lisa back joined hands, and so when some time in the strip has passed and Les sees her again, Lisa is pregnant.

Turning a page.

If I may digress for a moment, from the earliest days of the strip I would get together with Cathy and my folks for something we called a gag session wherein I would test a lot of new material. It was a great way to cull only the A-list ideas for the strip and relegate the other ones to notebook purgatory. It seems rare when you can demarcate a clear inflection point in life, but, in hindsight, the teen pregnancy story is where the storm front broke. All of those ideas that I had for the direction in which I wanted to take the work started to coalesce, and going forward—not all at once, but over time—the strip was going to become something different. Lisa had her eye on the bigger picture, so I discontinued the gag sessions and began to follow her lead.

Okay, so I just lied to you. I'd forgotten about the weekend that Cathy and I used her pizza-making skills (one of the reasons I married her, folks) to lure Gerry Shamray over for an evening during which we spread eight weeks of the teen pregnancy story line across the living room floor, and, with a great deal of back-and-forthing and pizza dribbling, selected the four weeks that I eventually used. Not strictly a gag session per se, but more like a soft-rollout-beta test. Just thought I should mention that for the record.

Now all that remained was to convince the syndicate that we could run with this story and that the world wouldn't come to an end, at least I was pretty sure it wouldn't. At Rick Newcombe's invitation, I flew out to California to personally make my case for the story. I knew that this work was something different and I didn't want to sandbag an editor by simply allowing it to show up in the mail unannounced. To his credit, Rick, who had a lot on his plate at that particular moment and who may have had some personal reservations about what sort of reaction we would receive, had my back the whole way. Rather than the typical "no, we don't dare do that because someone might write a letter to the editor of the paper and complain" syndicate reaction, Rick made some suggestions that strengthened the piece, which I happily incorporated. Ironically, just as I had acquired editorial control, I found someone who could work side by side with me to make the strip better. The syndicate also created a lot of sidebar material that editors of newspapers on *Funky*'s client list could use in conjunction with the strip to inform readers and to create a discussion around the issue of teen pregnancy. In essence, the problem of putting this story before the readers was flipped on its head and it was used instead to present a teachable and reachable moment. Rather than saying that work like this didn't belong on the comics page, the syndicate said let's use the comics page to shine a light on this problem, to start a discussion. And it worked, but at first it almost didn't.

The package of supporting materials was intended to go out with the strip's release sheets. When I received my copy of the release sheets in the mail, I eagerly looked for the backing material and found—nothing. All that was in the envelope were the strips, nothing else. In a panic, I called the syndicate and found out that someone in shipping had accidentally forgotten to include the attendant material, which meant that the strips would show up at newspapers across the country unannounced

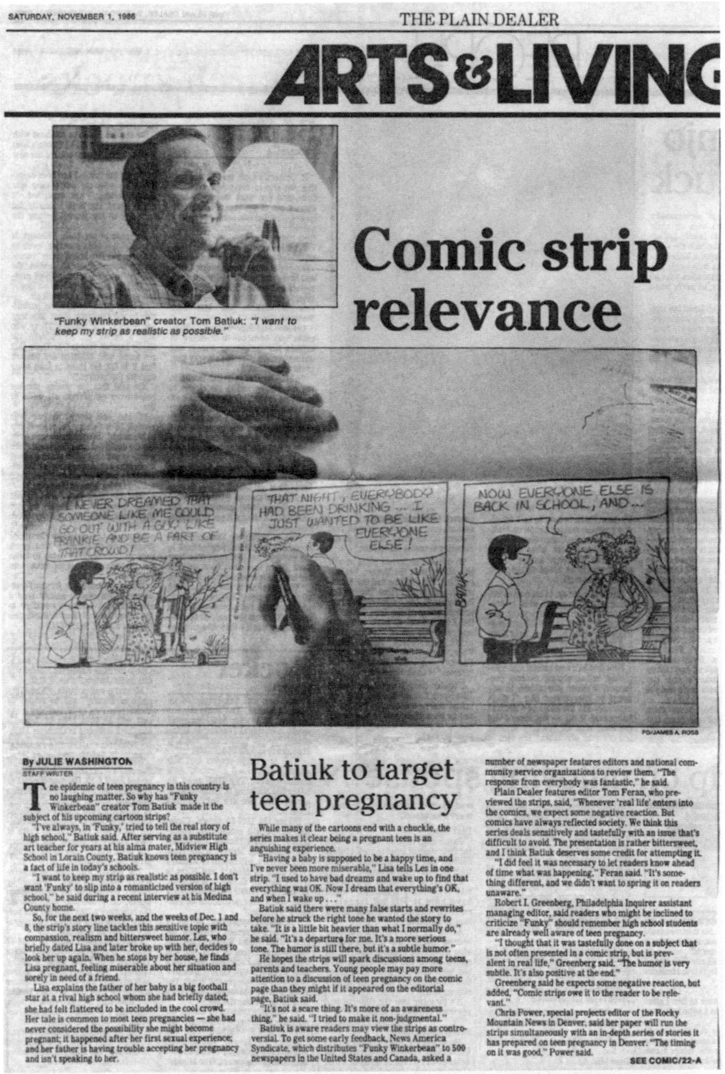

SATURDAY, NOVEMBER 1, 1986 THE PLAIN DEALER

ARTS & LIVING

Comic strip relevance

"Funky Winkerbean" creator Tom Batiuk: *"I want to keep my strip as realistic as possible."*

I NEVER DREAMED THAT SOMEONE LIKE ME COULD GO OUT WITH A GUY LIKE FRANKIE AND BE A PART OF THAT CROWD!
THAT NIGHT, EVERYBODY HAD BEEN DRINKING ... I JUST WANTED TO BE LIKE EVERYONE ELSE!
NOW EVERYONE ELSE IS BACK IN SCHOOL, AND...
BATIUK

PD/JAMES A. ROSS

Batiuk to target teen pregnancy

By JULIE WASHINGTON
STAFF WRITER

The epidemic of teen pregnancy in this country is no laughing matter. So why has "Funky Winkerbean" creator Tom Batiuk made it the subject of his upcoming cartoon strips?

"I've always, in 'Funky,' tried to tell the real story of high school," Batiuk said. After serving as a substitute art teacher for years at his alma mater, Midview High School in Lorain County, Batiuk knows teen pregnancy is a fact of life in today's schools.

"I want to keep my strip as realistic as possible. I don't want 'Funky' to slip into a romanticized version of high school," he said during a recent interview at his Medina County home.

So, for the next two weeks, and the weeks of Dec. 1 and 8, the strip's story line tackles this sensitive topic with compassion, realism and bittersweet humor. Les, who briefly dated Lisa and later broke up with her, decides to look her up again. When he stops by her house, he finds Lisa pregnant, feeling miserable about her situation and sorely in need of a friend.

Lisa explains the father of her baby is a big football star at a rival high school whom she had briefly dated; she had felt flattered to be included in the cool crowd. Her tale is common to most teen pregnancies — she had never considered the possibility she might become pregnant; it happened after her first sexual experience; and her father is having trouble accepting her pregnancy and isn't speaking to her.

While many of the cartoons end with a chuckle, the series makes it clear being a pregnant teen is an anguishing experience.

"Having a baby is supposed to be a happy time, and I've never been more miserable," Lisa tells Les in one strip. "I used to have bad dreams and wake up to find that everything was OK. Now I dream that everything's OK, and when I wake up . . ."

Batiuk said there were many false starts and rewrites before he struck the right tone he wanted the story to take. "It is a little bit heavier than what I normally do," he said. "It's a departure for me. It's a more serious tone. The humor is still there, but it's a subtle humor."

He hopes the strips will spark discussions among teens, parents and teachers. Young people may pay more attention to a discussion of teen pregnancy on the comic page than they might if it appeared on the editorial page, Batiuk said.

"It's not a scare thing. It's more of an awareness thing," he said. "I tried to make it non-judgmental."

Batiuk is aware readers may view the strips as controversial. To get some early feedback, News America Syndicate, which distributes "Funky Winkerbean" to 500 newspapers in the United States and Canada, asked a number of newspaper features editors and national community service organizations to review them. "The response from everybody was fantastic," he said.

Plain Dealer features editor Tom Feran, who previewed the strips, said, "Whenever 'real life' enters into the comics, we expect some negative reaction. But comics have always reflected society. We think this series deals sensitively and tastefully with an issue that's difficult to avoid. The presentation is rather bittersweet, and I think Batiuk deserves some credit for attempting it.

"I did feel it was necessary to let readers know ahead of time what was happening," Feran said. "It's something different, and we didn't want to spring it on readers unaware."

Robert I. Greenberg, Philadelphia Inquirer assistant managing editor, said readers who might be inclined to criticize "Funky" should remember high school students are already well aware of teen pregnancy.

"I thought that it was tastefully done on a subject that is not often presented in a comic strip, but is prevalent in real life," Greenberg said. "The humor is very subtle. It's also positive at the end."

Greenberg said he expects some negative reaction, but added, "Comic strips owe it to the reader to be relevant."

Chris Power, special projects editor of the Rocky Mountain News in Denver, said her paper will run the strips simultaneously with an in-depth series of stories it has prepared on teen pregnancy in Denver. "The timing on it was good," Power said.

SEE COMIC/22-A

The storm front breaks. (*The Plain Dealer,* Nov. 1, 1986. Author's collection)

and naked, and long before we could get the buttressing information to them. That's when two wonderful women in the promotion department, Patti Minassian and Cathy Irvine, stepped up and made lemonade. Since there was no way to get the supporting material to editors in time, they called each and every one of *Funky*'s editors personally to discuss the series and how they could use the strips along with the soon-to-be-arriving sidebar material as a catalyst to draw attention to the issue of teen pregnancy. The editors were impressed with the personal attention, pleased to be included as partners in the enterprise. Like I said, it worked. The response to those four short seminal weeks was greater than any I had received up to that point. There were so many requests for copies of that series that we put together a special booklet collecting the strips, *Life's Lessons Aren't Always Learned in the Classroom,* and sent out more than sixty thousand copies. When the requests continued to come in, we had to go back for a second printing.

With the teen pregnancy story arc, *Funky* started on its path to becoming an outlier on the comics page. I was moving from a very safe position to one that courted failure, but there was an exciting side effect to the whole thing—freedom. There would be praise and condemnation. On the condemnation side were those who felt I was betraying a trust to only provide something funny. One reader even went so far as to state that I was negligent in my fiduciary responsibility under my contract to produce a funny strip. My contract says a lot of things, but it never said that. Others just abhorred any kind of change and wanted me to go back to the way the strip was in the beginning. What they failed to grasp is that the beginning

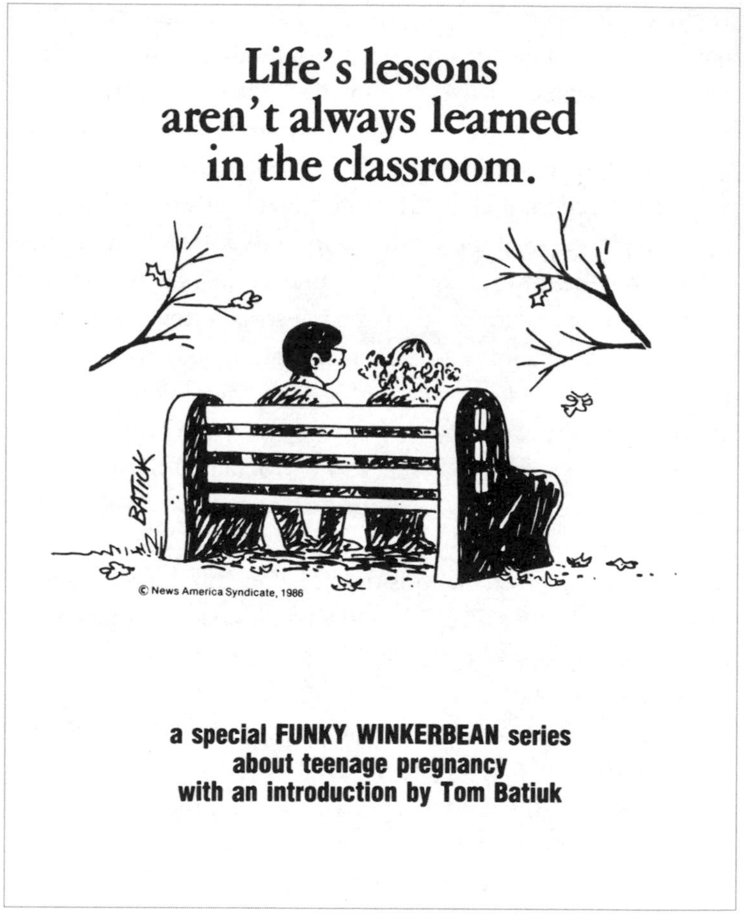
Life's lessons
aren't always learned
in the classroom.
BATIUK
© News America Syndicate, 1986
a special FUNKY WINKERBEAN series
about teenage pregnancy
with an introduction by Tom Batiuk

Just for the record, the branches on the right weren't mine.

strips were just that, only a beginning. From the majority of my readers, however, I received a wonderful gift—their trust. They gave me the space to grow and change and trusted that I wouldn't let them down, at least this time. Someone once said that you have to challenge your audience a little. You can't give them what they think they want, because that's not what they really want. You have to give them something they don't know they want but will once they see it. I think that's true, but that's a very thin and a very high wire to walk.

'Funky Winkerbean' reprint

Pregnant-teen booklet hot item

By NANCY BOSTWICK
C-T Staff Writer

Executives for the News America syndicate are as pleased as Batiuk is: 'The response was absolutley overwhelming.'

ELYRIA — The response to Tom Batiuk's bittersweet portrayal of a teenager's pregnancy in his comic strip, "Funky Winkerbean," has stunned — and pleased — the cartoonist.

"The response is much, much bigger than we expected," said Batiuk, who got his start drawing Funky at the Chronicle-Telegram in 1970. The series about Lisa appeared in newspapers around the country in late November and early December.

REPRINTS of the teen pregnancy strips in booklet form offered free by newspapers which carry "Funky" are going out the doors as fast as they can be made, at the rate of about 10,000 a week, Batiuk said.

After several requests, News America Syndicate, which distributes Batiuk's work to more than 350 newspapers, offered an initial printing of 10,000 copies and Batiuk said they weren't sure there would be a demand for so many.

But requests flooded in from newspapers, school systems and social service agencies. One school district requested — and received — 5,000 copies.

To date, the syndicate has printed 60,000 copies and most of those have been distributed.

The Chronicle-Telegram has been deluged with calls for the booklet and has given out more than 400 copies so far. (The booklet, "Life's lessons aren't always learned in the classroom," is still available from the C-T.)

"It's very gratifying for me, because that means it's going to be around a lot longer and do a lot more good," Batiuk said Thursday by phone from his Medina home.

EXECUTIVES for the News America syndicate are as pleased as Batiuk is. "The response was absolutley overwhelming," said Cathy Irvine, assistant promotions manager. "Requests are coming in, in very large quantities."

Batiuk said he first approached covering the topic of teen pregnancy in his strip with some trepidation.

In the forward to the booklet he wrote, "I decided that I shouldn't let a fear of controversy keep me from discussing a topic that deserves continued attention, and that a comic strip could, in fact, be an excellent way to stimulate healthy discussion."

While Batiuk has heard a few negative comments about touching on such a sensitive issue in the comic pages, the postive responses have far outweighed the negative, he said.

"The people who read the strip were willing to give it a chance," he said.

Now, educators and social workers want to give the booklet a chance to help prevent what is considered an epidemic problem.

THE C-T has been deluged with calls for the reprints and the distribution here has included 20 picked up by Thomas Porter, executive secretary for Children's Services for use by persons who counsel unmarried parents.

Batiuk, a former Elyrian and graduate of Midview High School, still visits Midview regularly for ideas for his lighthearted look at the high school world. He often sits in on art classes and substitutes as a teacher to keep his series in touch with reality, he said.

His strip previously covered a teacher's strike and the open heart surgery of a faculty member. Batiuk said the next sensitive issue that will appear in the strip will be dyslexia, a learning disorder.

It will run this summer and be about students attending summer school.

And although drug abuse prevention is a topic much in vogue in education circles, Batiuk said he won't be touching on it in the near future.

Financial Aid Night set at Midview

GRAFTON — Midview High School will hold a Financial Aid Night for students and their parents Monday at 7 p.m. in room 303.

Paul Boguski, financial aid director for LCCC, will explain federal and state grants as will as other types of financial aid available to students who want a college education.

My readers give me a chance. (The Elyria, Ohio, *Chronicle-Telegram*. Author's collection.)

At the end of the teen pregnancy story, I had Lisa leave the strip to go live with her grandparents in Seattle. To have her continue on in the strip as if nothing had happened just didn't feel right. Likewise, after having been Lisa's confidant and birthing partner, it was going to be impossible to go back to things like having Les being stuck up on the rope in gym class and ending up being repurposed as a decoration for the homecoming dance. A line had been crossed, and my characters now were going to have to grow up. The philosopher Immanuel Kant reasoned that, if you have sequence, then ippso pippso (my words, not his) you have time. Comic strips always had sequence, but then somewhere along the way they slipped into the habit of circling back at the end of each day's strip and restarting the clock. However, inherent in their genetic code was the ability to take that sequence and just keep on going like, oh, I don't know, life does. I wanted that for my characters and I wanted it for me. From the teen pregnancy story forward, I would slowly begin moving them toward graduation and beyond. What that "beyond" was exactly and how I would get there was still a project under construction. Like they say on those little magnetic aphorisms that you stick on the fridge, sometimes you just have to jump off the cliff and build your wings on the way down. I don't recommend this, by the way, unless there are no other options, and Lisa had left me with no other options. In the end, what really happened was that Lisa and the teen pregnancy story opened a door for me and invited me to walk through. But opening doors can be scary, because there's always something on the other side.

1984

FUNKY WINKERBEAN
BY TOM BATIUK ®

1984

SUNDAY	MONDAY	TUESDA
1	2	3
8	9	10
15	16	17

I'VE MADE UP MY MIND!

NINETEEN EIGHTY-FOUR IS GOING TO BE DIFFERENT!

THIS YEAR I'M GOING TO RESOLVE TO DO SOMETHING I'VE WANTED TO DO FOR A LONG TIME!

1-1

I'M GOING TO START TREATING MYSELF RIGHT!

I'M GOING TO GO DOWN TO THE HEALTH SPA...

BATIUK

AND QUIT!

© Field Enterprises, Inc., 1984

19

YOU THOUGHT THEY WERE FINISHED BUT NO SUCH LUCK! FUNKY WINKERBEAN PRESENTS THE RETURN OF THE READERS!
© Field Enterprises, Inc. 1984
WHAT KIND OF CAR DOES YODA DRIVE?
A TOYODA!
1-2
THANKS AND A TIP OF THE DARTH VADER TOPPER TO:
LAURA SHEAHAN - ARLINGTON, VIRGINIA

YOU THOUGHT THEY WERE FINISHED BUT NO SUCH LUCK! FUNKY WINKERBEAN PRESENTS THE RETURN OF THE READERS!
© Field Enterprises, Inc. 1984
WHAT DID MICK JAGGER SAY WHEN AN EWOK JOINED THE ROLLING STONES?
IT'S JUST EWOK AND ROLL TO ME!
1-3
THANKS AND A TIP OF THE DARTH VADER TOPPER TO:
RICHARD W. BENNETT - GREAT BEND, KANSAS

YOU THOUGHT THEY WERE FINISHED BUT NO SUCH LUCK! FUNKY WINKERBEAN PRESENTS THE RETURN OF THE READERS!
© Field Enterprises, Inc. 1984
WHAT KIND OF UPHOLSTERY DOES HAN SOLO HAVE IN HIS MILLENNIUM FALCON?
1-4
SOFT CORELLIAN LEATHER!
THANKS AND A TIP OF THE DARTH VADER TOPPER TO:
GERI & BOB HAMILTON - SEATTLE, WASHINGTON

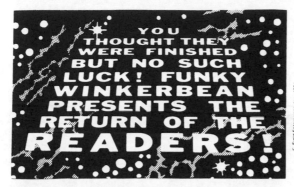

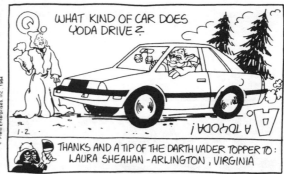

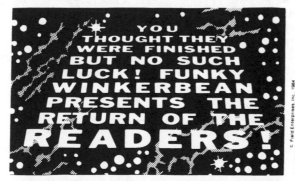

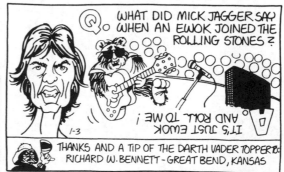

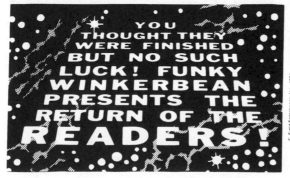

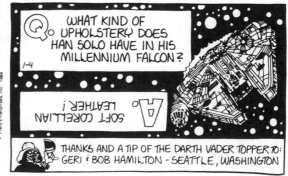

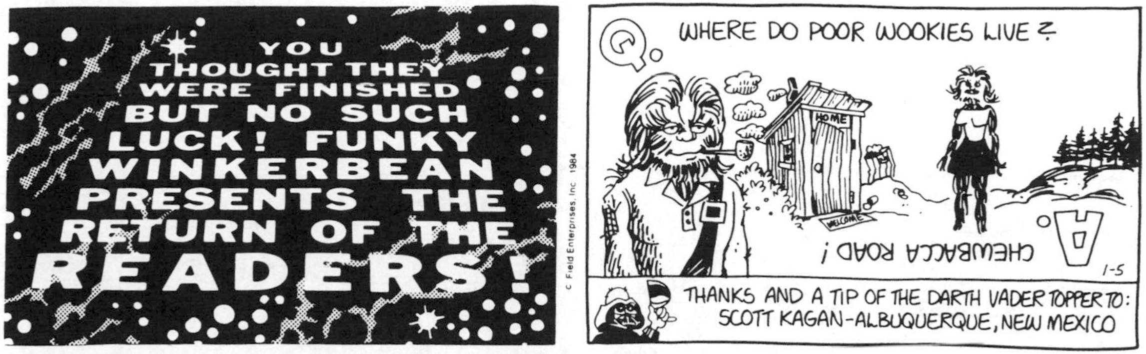
YOU THOUGHT THEY WERE FINISHED BUT NO SUCH LUCK! FUNKY WINKERBEAN PRESENTS THE RETURN OF THE READERS!
© Field Enterprises, Inc. 1984
Q
WHERE DO POOR WOOKIES LIVE?
HOME
WELCOME
A
CHEWBACCA ROAD!
1-5
THANKS AND A TIP OF THE DARTH VADER TOPPER TO:
SCOTT KAGAN-ALBUQUERQUE, NEW MEXICO

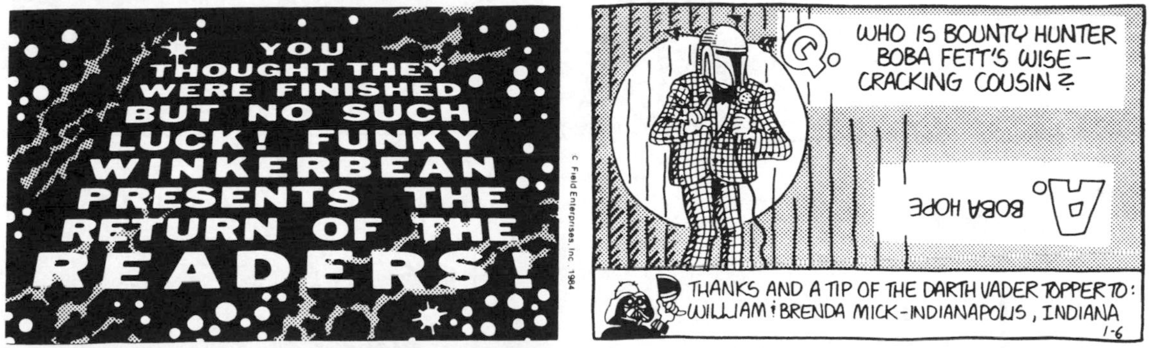
YOU THOUGHT THEY WERE FINISHED BUT NO SUCH LUCK! FUNKY WINKERBEAN PRESENTS THE RETURN OF THE READERS!
© Field Enterprises, Inc. 1984
Q
WHO IS BOUNTY HUNTER BOBA FETT'S WISE-CRACKING COUSIN?
A
BOBA HOPE
THANKS AND A TIP OF THE DARTH VADER TOPPER TO:
WILLIAM & BRENDA MICK-INDIANAPOLIS, INDIANA
1-6

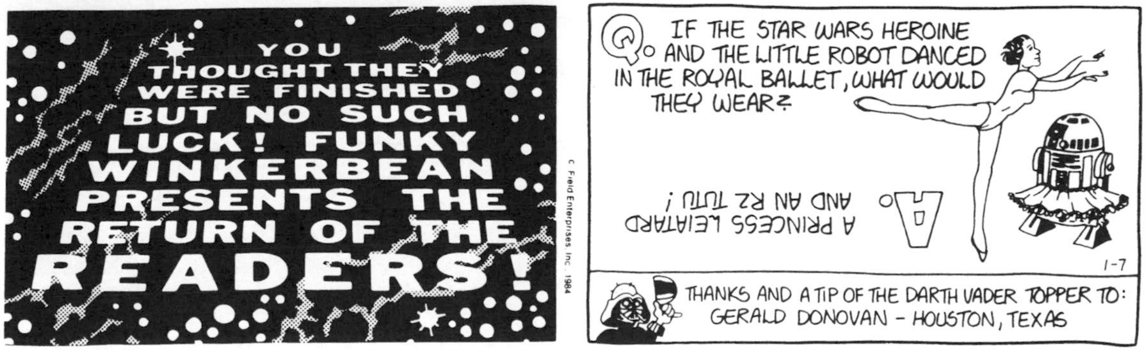
YOU THOUGHT THEY WERE FINISHED BUT NO SUCH LUCK! FUNKY WINKERBEAN PRESENTS THE RETURN OF THE READERS!
© Field Enterprises, Inc. 1984
Q
IF THE STAR WARS HEROINE AND THE LITTLE ROBOT DANCED IN THE ROYAL BALLET, WHAT WOULD THEY WEAR?
A
A PRINCESS LEIATARD AND AN R2 TUTU!
1-7
THANKS AND A TIP OF THE DARTH VADER TOPPER TO:
GERALD DONOVAN - HOUSTON, TEXAS

FUNKY WINKERBEAN
BY TOM BATIUK
HEY, FUNKY... DID YOU HEAR WHAT HAPPENED?
BULL BUSHKA CAUGHT UP WITH LES IN THE PARKING LOT OF MONTONI'S LAST NIGHT!
NO KIDDING! DID BULL BEAT LES UP?
© Field Enterprises, Inc., 1984
BATIUK
1-8
NO, THE MOTORCYCLE GANG SCARED HIM OFF!

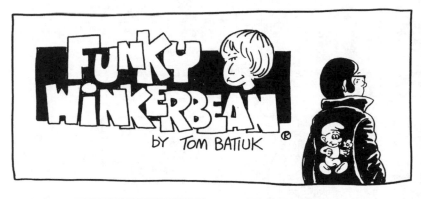

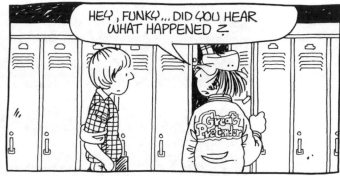

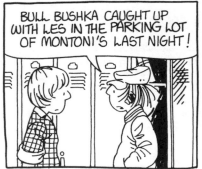

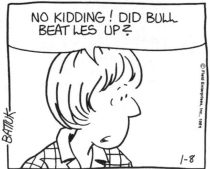

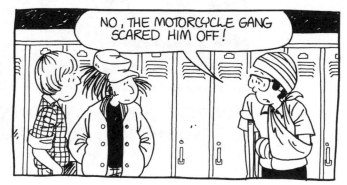

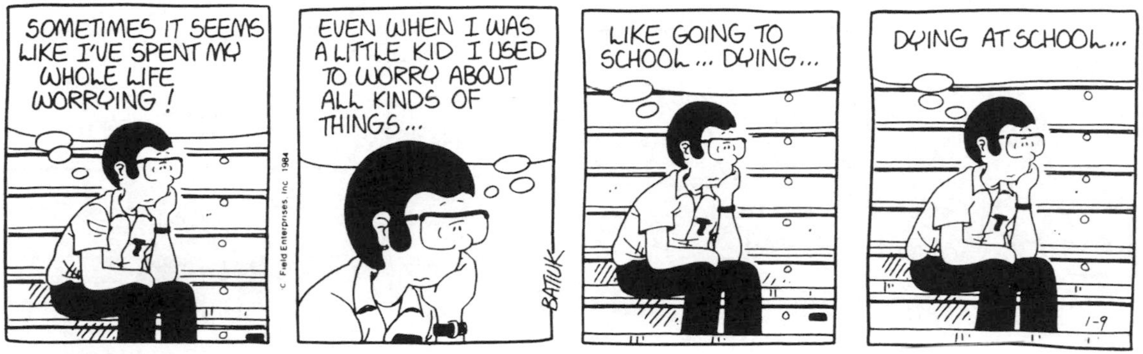
SOMETIMES IT SEEMS LIKE I'VE SPENT MY WHOLE LIFE WORRYING!
EVEN WHEN I WAS A LITTLE KID I USED TO WORRY ABOUT ALL KINDS OF THINGS...
© Field Enterprises, Inc. 1984
BATIUK
LIKE GOING TO SCHOOL... DYING...
DYING AT SCHOOL...
1-9

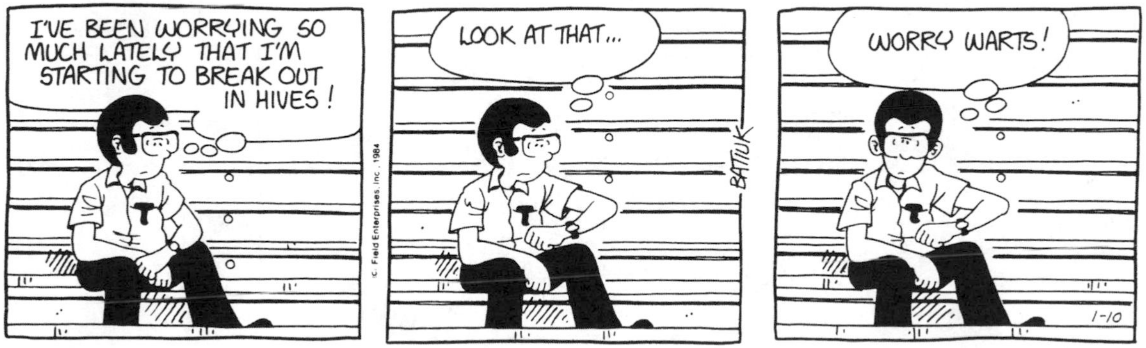
I'VE BEEN WORRYING SO MUCH LATELY THAT I'M STARTING TO BREAK OUT IN HIVES!
© Field Enterprises, Inc. 1984
LOOK AT THAT...
BATIUK
WORRY WARTS!
1-10

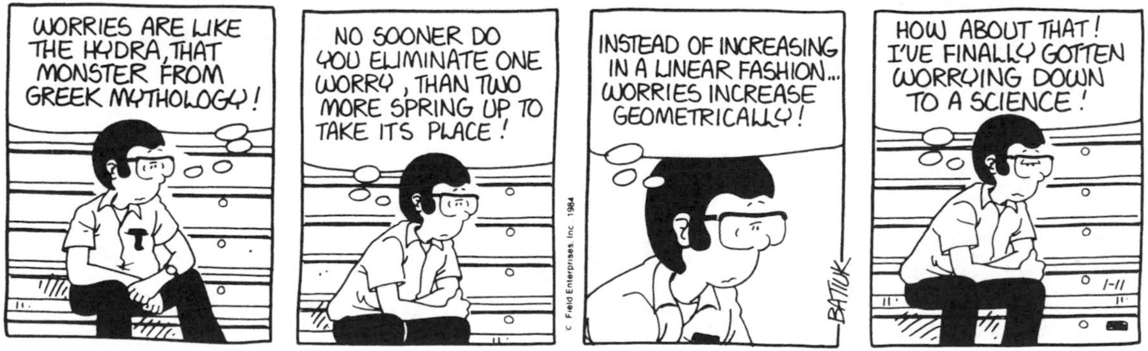
WORRIES ARE LIKE THE HYDRA, THAT MONSTER FROM GREEK MYTHOLOGY!
NO SOONER DO YOU ELIMINATE ONE WORRY, THAN TWO MORE SPRING UP TO TAKE ITS PLACE!
© Field Enterprises, Inc. 1984
INSTEAD OF INCREASING IN A LINEAR FASHION... WORRIES INCREASE GEOMETRICALLY!
BATIUK
HOW ABOUT THAT! I'VE FINALLY GOTTEN WORRYING DOWN TO A SCIENCE!
1-11

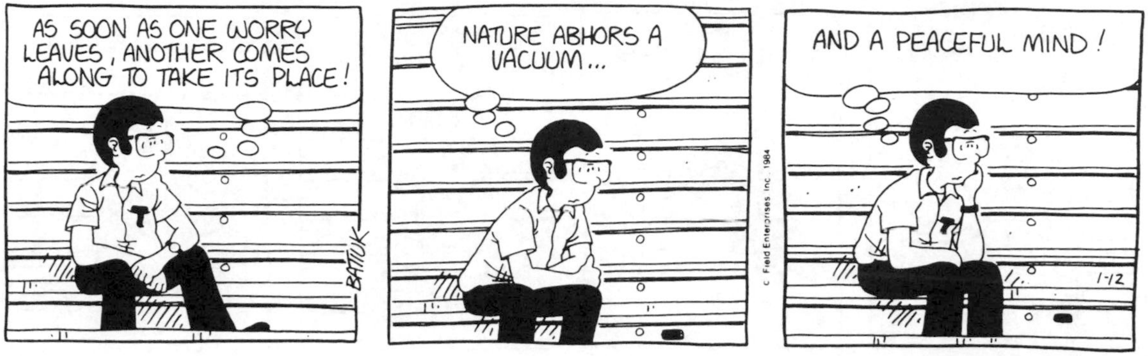
AS SOON AS ONE WORRY LEAVES, ANOTHER COMES ALONG TO TAKE ITS PLACE!
BATIUK
NATURE ABHORS A VACUUM...
© Field Enterprises Inc. 1984
AND A PEACEFUL MIND!
1-12

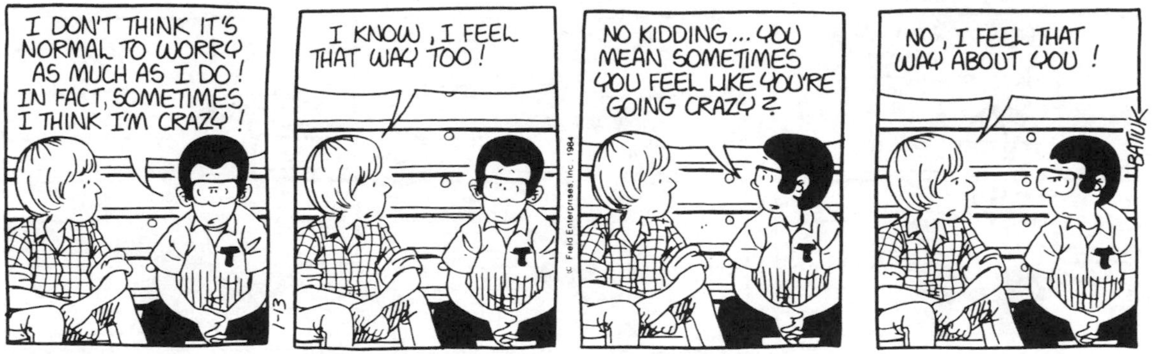
I DON'T THINK IT'S NORMAL TO WORRY AS MUCH AS I DO! IN FACT, SOMETIMES I THINK I'M CRAZY!
1-13
I KNOW, I FEEL THAT WAY TOO!
© Field Enterprises Inc. 1984
NO KIDDING... YOU MEAN SOMETIMES YOU FEEL LIKE YOU'RE GOING CRAZY?
NO, I FEEL THAT WAY ABOUT YOU!
BATIUK

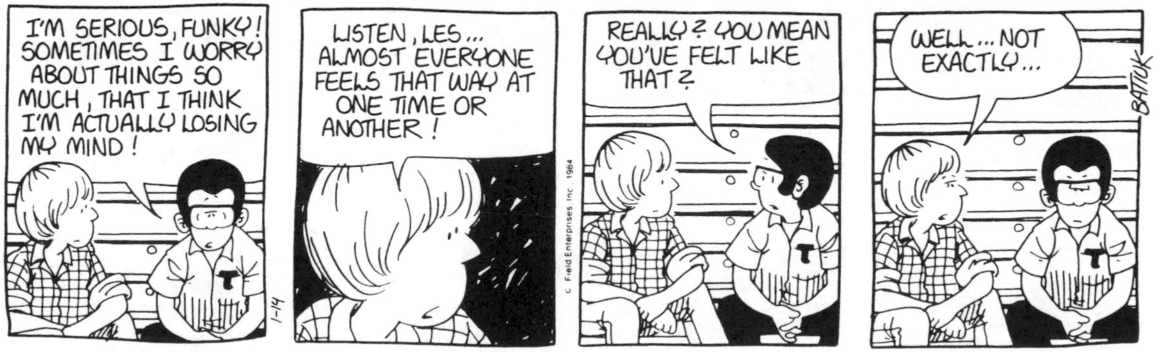
I'M SERIOUS, FUNKY! SOMETIMES I WORRY ABOUT THINGS SO MUCH, THAT I THINK I'M ACTUALLY LOSING MY MIND!
1-14
LISTEN, LES... ALMOST EVERYONE FEELS THAT WAY AT ONE TIME OR ANOTHER!
© Field Enterprises Inc. 1984
REALLY? YOU MEAN YOU'VE FELT LIKE THAT?
WELL... NOT EXACTLY...
BATIUK

FUNKY WINKERBEAN
by TOM BATIUK ®
FORM 1016
WORKM
COMPEN
NAME
(PLEASE PRINT
ADDRESS
YOU MEAN THERE'S NOTHING YOU CAN DO?
I'M AFRAID NOT!
I'M SORRY, NATE, BUT YOUR FOOD POISONING CLAIM JUST ISN'T COVERED!
I'M AFRAID THAT IT DOESN'T REALLY QUALIFY AS AN ON-THE-JOB ACCIDENT!
STVIEW SCHOOL
GIRLS
BALL H
WESTVI HIGH SC OL
BUT THAT'S WHAT IT WAS!
BATIUK
© Field Enterprises, Inc., 1984
1-15
I FORGOT AND ACCIDENTALLY ATE LUNCH IN THE SCHOOL CAFETERIA!

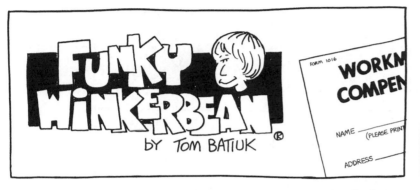

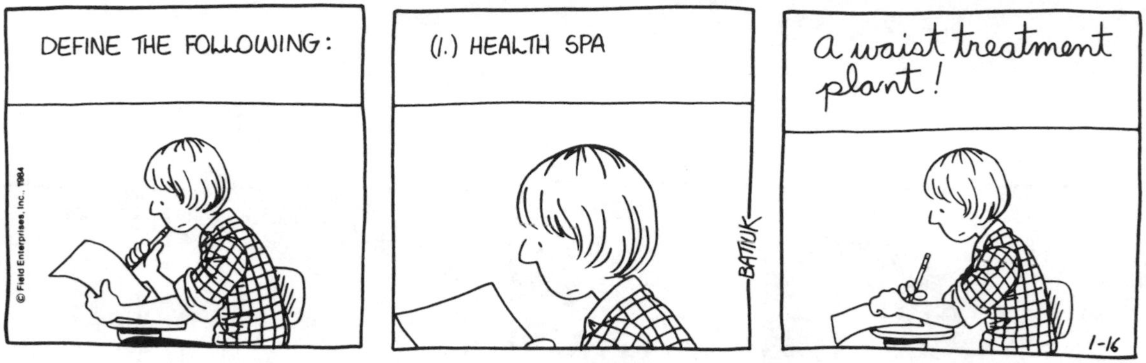
DEFINE THE FOLLOWING:
(1.) HEALTH SPA
a waist treatment plant!
© Field Enterprises, Inc., 1984
BATIUK
1-16

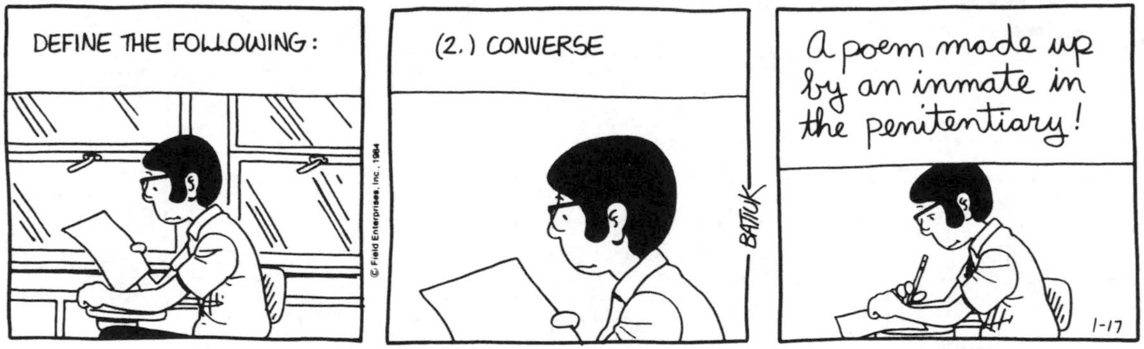
DEFINE THE FOLLOWING:
(2.) CONVERSE
A poem made up by an inmate in the penitentiary!
© Field Enterprises, Inc., 1984
BATIUK
1-17

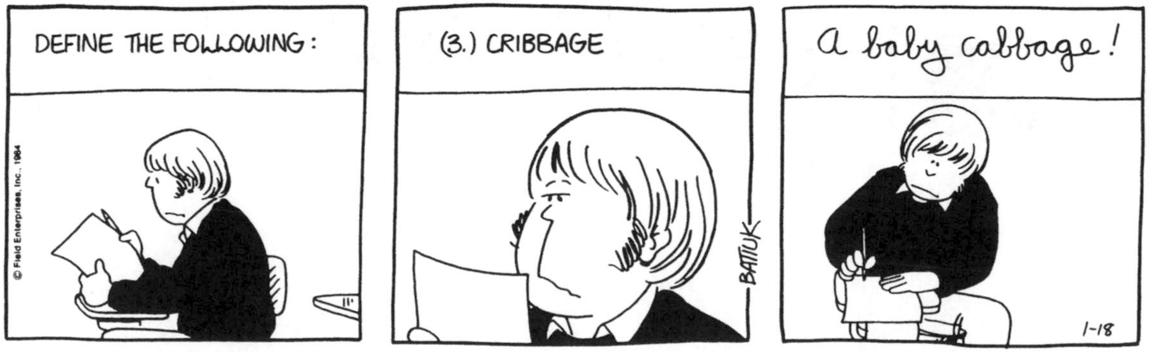
DEFINE THE FOLLOWING:
(3.) CRIBBAGE
a baby cabbage!
© Field Enterprises, Inc., 1984
BATIUK
1-18

DEFINE THE FOLLOWING:	(4.) FINGERNAILS	*What you fix broken fingers with!*

DEFINE THE FOLLOWING:	(5.) COSMIC RAY	*The sole survivor of a nuclear war!*

DEFINE THE FOLLOWING:	(6.) LOGJAM	*A preserve that would be more popular if it weren't for the splinters!*

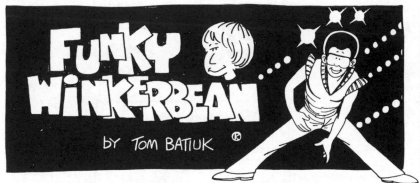

FUNKY WINKERBEAN

BY TOM BATIUK

SIGH!

WHY DO I ALWAYS END UP SITTING HERE ALONE IN THE BLEACHERS DURING MY LUNCH PERIOD?

I'D LIKE NOTHING BETTER THAN TO BE DOWN ON THE GYM FLOOR DANCING AND HAVING FUN LIKE THE OTHER KIDS DO DURING LUNCH!

MAYBE I'M JUST TOO SELF-CONSCIOUS ABOUT THE WAY I DANCE!

EVERY TIME I'M OUT ON THE FLOOR DANCING, I THINK THAT EVERYONE IS LOOKING AT ME ...

AND TAKING PICTURES!

© Field Enterprises, Inc. 1984

1-22

28

I COULDN'T PRACTICE THIS WEEKEND BECAUSE THIEVES BROKE INTO MY HOUSE AND STOLE MY HORN!
© Field Enterprises, Inc., 1984
I'M SORRY TO HEAR THAT! WHAT ELSE WAS STOLEN?
BATIUK
JUST MY HORN! APPARENTLY IT WAS A SURGICAL STRIKE!
1-23

HOW DO YOU EXPECT TO GET ANY BETTER IF YOU **NEVER PRACTICE**?
BATIUK
THE **ONLY** TIME YOU EVER SEE THIS MUSIC IS WHEN YOU SHOW UP FOR YOUR **LESSON**!
© Field Enterprises, Inc., 1984
YEAH, BUT YOU'VE GOT TO ADMIT THAT I'M GETTING TO BE A BETTER SIGHT READER!
1-24

UH... I COULDN'T PRACTICE THIS WEEKEND BECAUSE OF, UH...
MAKE IT GOOD! I'M SAVING THESE FOR A BOOK!
© Field Enterprises, Inc., 1984
HYSTERICAL BLINDNESS!!
BATIUK
NOT BAD! I JUST MAY GIVE YOU YOUR OWN CHAPTER!
1-25

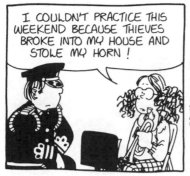

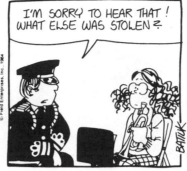

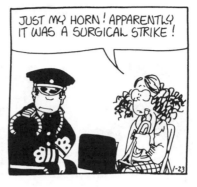

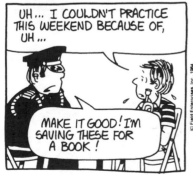

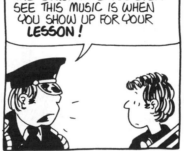

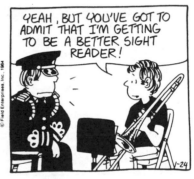

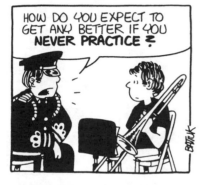

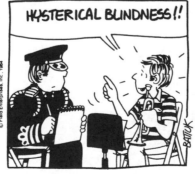

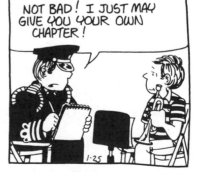

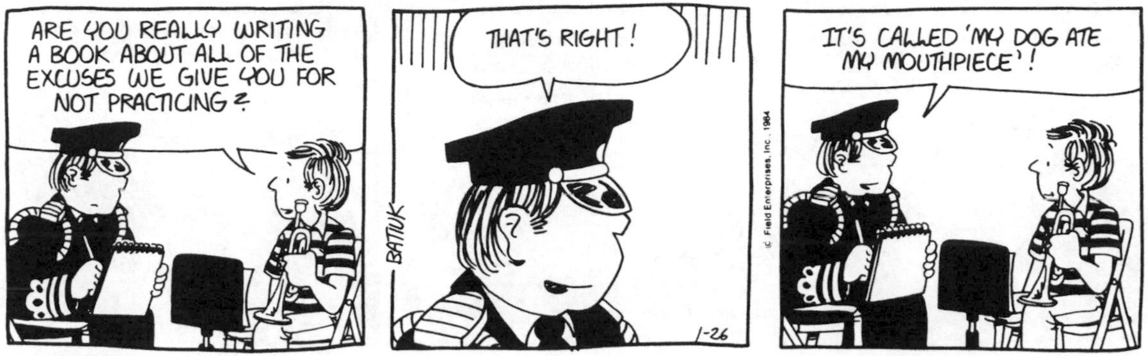
ARE YOU REALLY WRITING A BOOK ABOUT ALL OF THE EXCUSES WE GIVE YOU FOR NOT PRACTICING?
THAT'S RIGHT!
BATIUK
1-26
© Field Enterprises, Inc., 1984
IT'S CALLED 'MY DOG ATE MY MOUTHPIECE'!

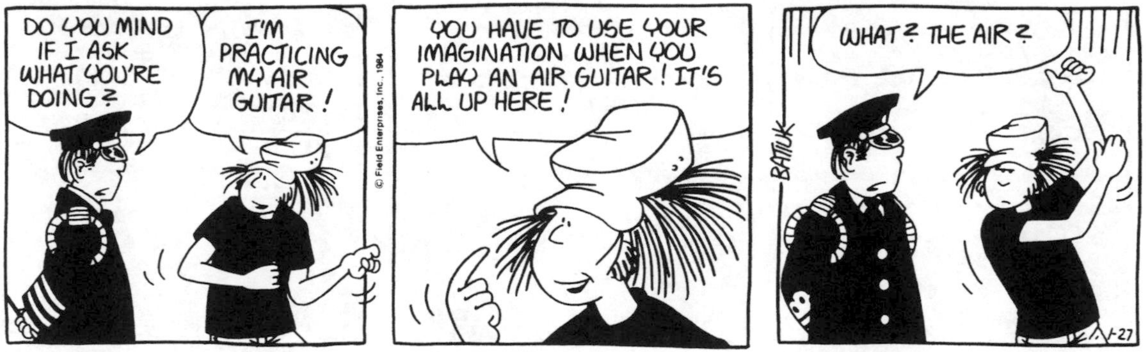
DO YOU MIND IF I ASK WHAT YOU'RE DOING?
I'M PRACTICING MY AIR GUITAR!
© Field Enterprises, Inc., 1984
YOU HAVE TO USE YOUR IMAGINATION WHEN YOU PLAY AN AIR GUITAR! IT'S ALL UP HERE!
WHAT? THE AIR?
BATIUK
1-27

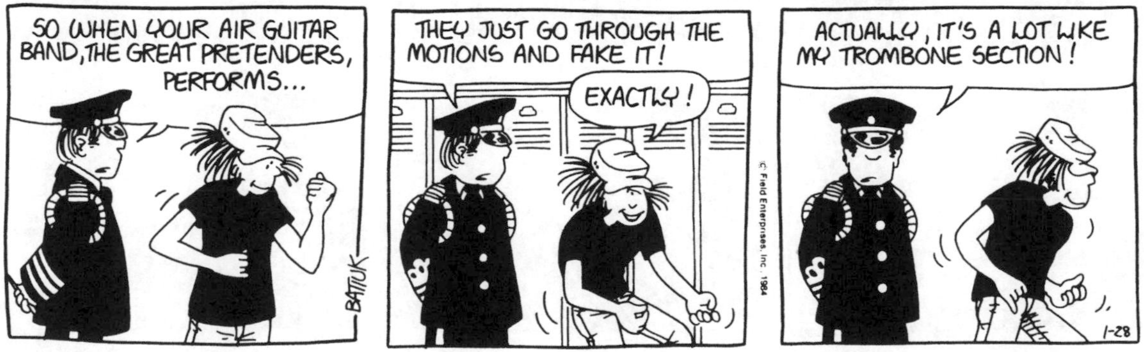
SO WHEN YOUR AIR GUITAR BAND, THE GREAT PRETENDERS, PERFORMS...
BATIUK
THEY JUST GO THROUGH THE MOTIONS AND FAKE IT!
EXACTLY!
© Field Enterprises, Inc., 1984
ACTUALLY, IT'S A LOT LIKE MY TROMBONE SECTION!
1-28

FUNKY WINKERBEAN

by Tom Batiuk

WESTVIEW HIGH SCHOOL — BAND AWARDS BANQUET

AND NOW, THE MOMENT YOU'VE ALL BEEN WAITING FOR...

THE BAND BOOSTER OF THE YEAR AWARD!

© Field Enterprises, Inc., 1984

I DON'T THINK THAT ANYONE HAS EVER WORKED HARDER FOR OUR BAND THAN THIS YEAR'S BAND BOOSTERS PRESIDENT, SUZI BUSHMILLER!

1-29

BATIUK

BEING PRESIDENT REQUIRES A NUMBER OF SACRIFICES! THERE ARE LONG HOURS AWAY FROM HOME ON BAND TRIPS, NOT BEING THERE AT MEALTIMES, LATE MEETINGS AND WEEKENDS SPENT FUNDRAISING...

WESTVIEW HIGH SCHOOL — BAND AWARDS BANQUET

SO IT IS WITH DEEP APPRECIATION THAT WE PRESENT THIS CERTIFICATE OF GRATITUDE!

BAND BOO

AND I'M SURE YOU'LL ALSO BE PLEASED TO HEAR THAT SUZI HAS GOTTEN CUSTODY OF THE CHILDREN!

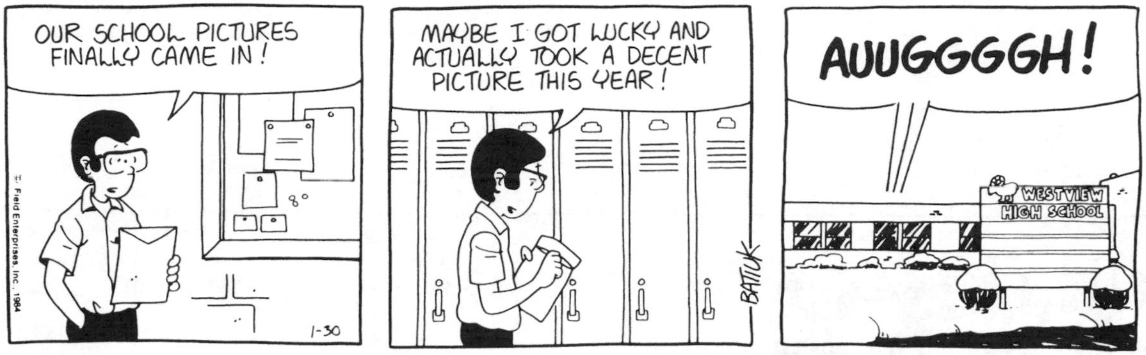
OUR SCHOOL PICTURES FINALLY CAME IN!
MAYBE I GOT LUCKY AND ACTUALLY TOOK A DECENT PICTURE THIS YEAR!
AUUGGGGH!
WESTVIEW HIGH SCHOOL
© Field Enterprises, Inc. 1984
BATIUK
1-30

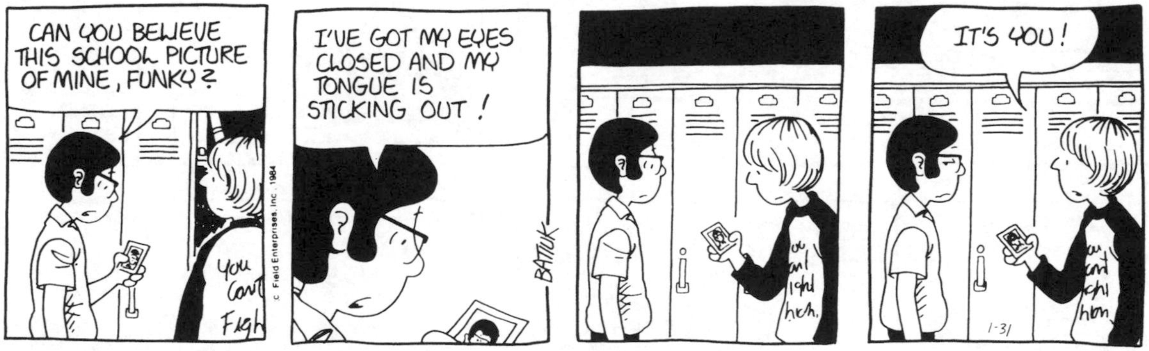
CAN YOU BELIEVE THIS SCHOOL PICTURE OF MINE, FUNKY?
I'VE GOT MY EYES CLOSED AND MY TONGUE IS STICKING OUT!
IT'S YOU!
© Field Enterprises, Inc. 1984
BATIUK
1-31

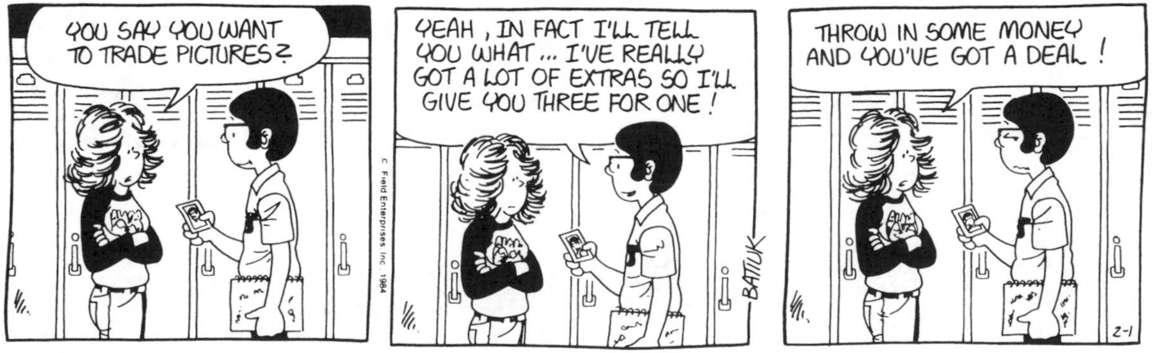
YOU SAY YOU WANT TO TRADE PICTURES?
YEAH, IN FACT I'LL TELL YOU WHAT... I'VE REALLY GOT A LOT OF EXTRAS SO I'LL GIVE YOU THREE FOR ONE!
THROW IN SOME MONEY AND YOU'VE GOT A DEAL!
© Field Enterprises, Inc. 1984
BATIUK
2-1

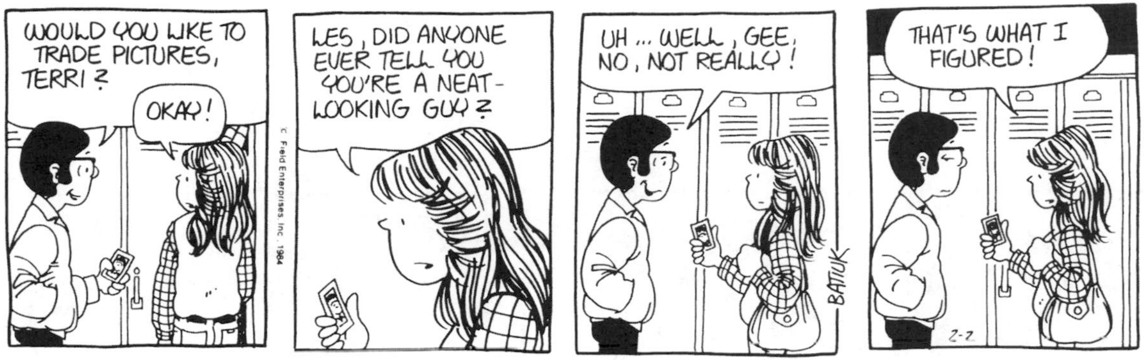
WOULD YOU LIKE TO TRADE PICTURES, TERRI ?
OKAY!
LES, DID ANYONE EVER TELL YOU YOU'RE A NEAT-LOOKING GUY ?
UH ... WELL, GEE, NO, NOT REALLY!
THAT'S WHAT I FIGURED!
BATIUK
2-2

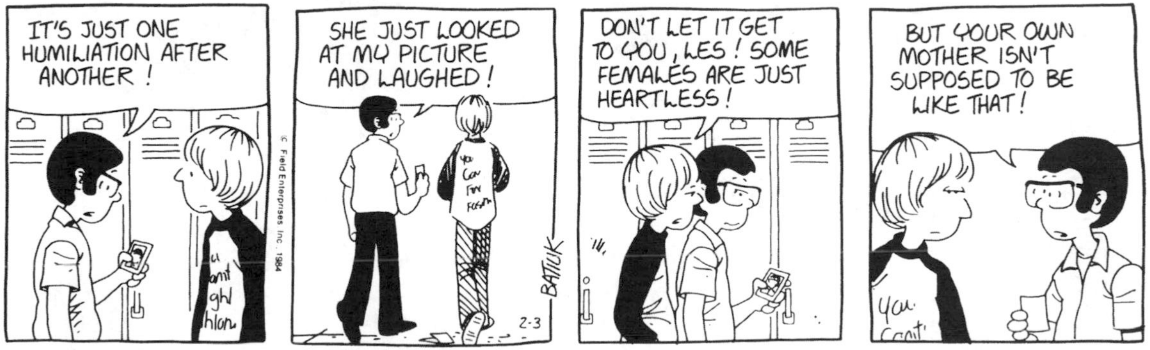
IT'S JUST ONE HUMILIATION AFTER ANOTHER!
SHE JUST LOOKED AT MY PICTURE AND LAUGHED!
DON'T LET IT GET TO YOU, LES! SOME FEMALES ARE JUST HEARTLESS!
BUT YOUR OWN MOTHER ISN'T SUPPOSED TO BE LIKE THAT!
BATIUK
2-3

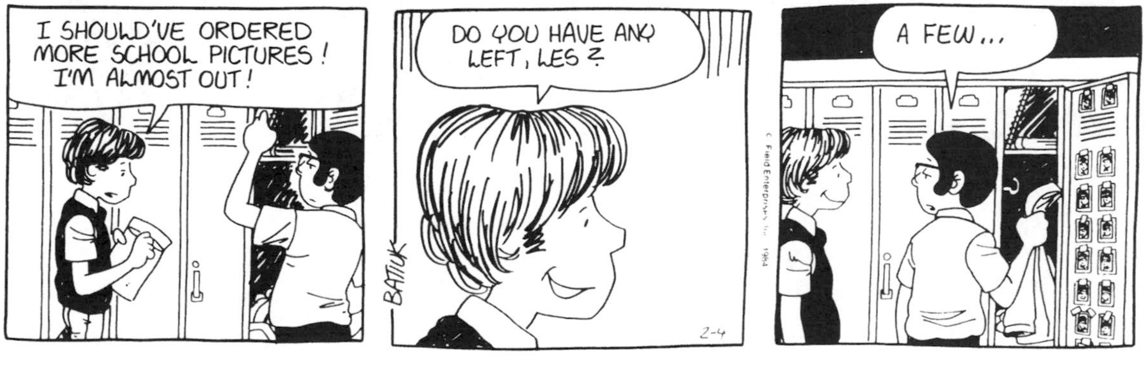
I SHOULD'VE ORDERED MORE SCHOOL PICTURES! I'M ALMOST OUT!
DO YOU HAVE ANY LEFT, LES ?
A FEW...
BATIUK
2-4

FUNKY WINKERBEAN
BY TOM BATIUK
NOTES
THAT WAS CLOSE! I ALMOST RECOGNIZED IT!
DO YOU PLAN TO TAKE YOUR MUSIC FOLDER HOME TO PRACTICE TONIGHT?
YES!
THAT'S GOOD BECAUSE I KNOW SOMEONE WHO'LL BE PRETTY UPSET IF YOU DON'T!
WHO?
A CERTAIN PERSON WHO DRESSES IN BLACK AND WORKS WITH MUSICIANS!
JOHNNY CASH KNOWS WHETHER I PRACTICE OR NOT!?
BATIUK
© Field Enterprises, Inc., 1984
2-5

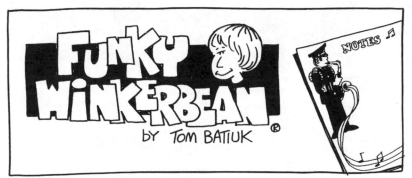

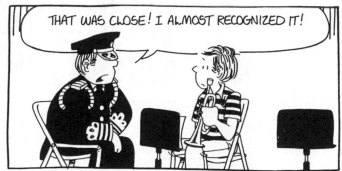

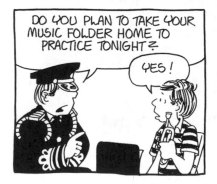

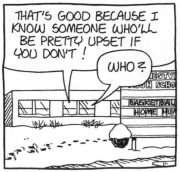

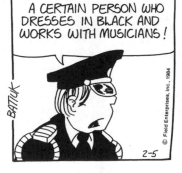

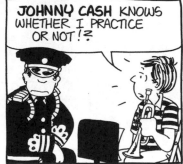

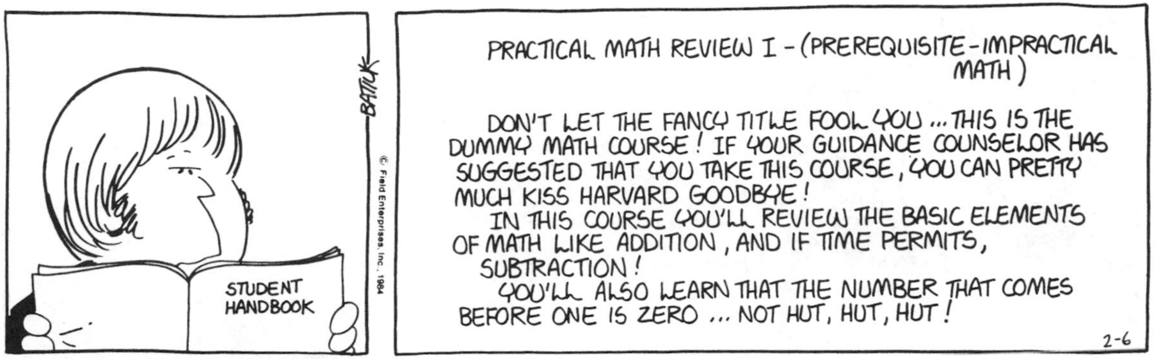
STUDENT HANDBOOK
BATIUK
© Field Enterprises, Inc. 1984
PRACTICAL MATH REVIEW I - (PREREQUISITE-IMPRACTICAL MATH)
DON'T LET THE FANCY TITLE FOOL YOU ... THIS IS THE DUMMY MATH COURSE! IF YOUR GUIDANCE COUNSELOR HAS SUGGESTED THAT YOU TAKE THIS COURSE, YOU CAN PRETTY MUCH KISS HARVARD GOODBYE!
IN THIS COURSE YOU'LL REVIEW THE BASIC ELEMENTS OF MATH LIKE ADDITION, AND IF TIME PERMITS, SUBTRACTION!
YOU'LL ALSO LEARN THAT THE NUMBER THAT COMES BEFORE ONE IS ZERO ... NOT HUT, HUT, HUT!
2-6

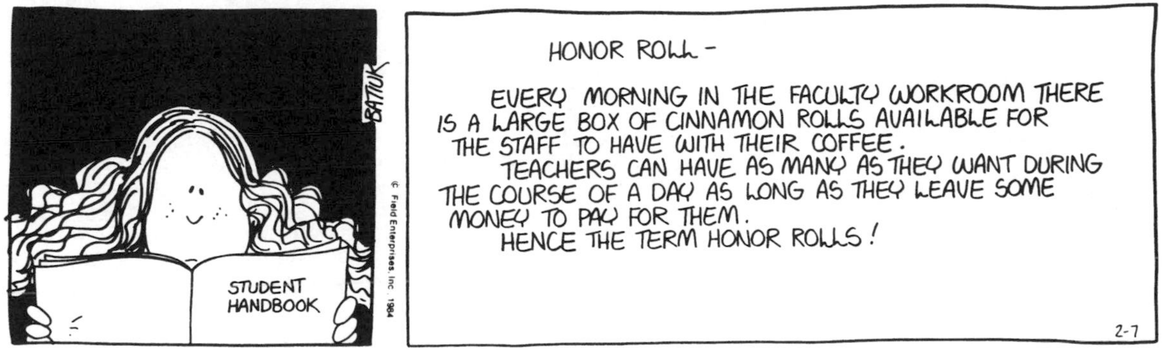
STUDENT HANDBOOK
BATIUK
© Field Enterprises, Inc. 1984
HONOR ROLL -
EVERY MORNING IN THE FACULTY WORKROOM THERE IS A LARGE BOX OF CINNAMON ROLLS AVAILABLE FOR THE STAFF TO HAVE WITH THEIR COFFEE.
TEACHERS CAN HAVE AS MANY AS THEY WANT DURING THE COURSE OF A DAY AS LONG AS THEY LEAVE SOME MONEY TO PAY FOR THEM.
HENCE THE TERM HONOR ROLLS!
2-7

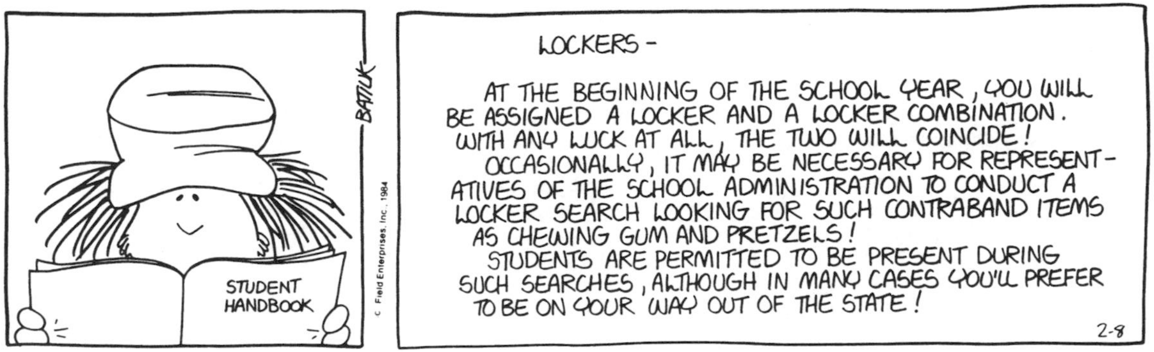
STUDENT HANDBOOK
BATIUK
© Field Enterprises, Inc. 1984
LOCKERS -
AT THE BEGINNING OF THE SCHOOL YEAR, YOU WILL BE ASSIGNED A LOCKER AND A LOCKER COMBINATION. WITH ANY LUCK AT ALL, THE TWO WILL COINCIDE!
OCCASIONALLY, IT MAY BE NECESSARY FOR REPRESENTATIVES OF THE SCHOOL ADMINISTRATION TO CONDUCT A LOCKER SEARCH LOOKING FOR SUCH CONTRABAND ITEMS AS CHEWING GUM AND PRETZELS!
STUDENTS ARE PERMITTED TO BE PRESENT DURING SUCH SEARCHES, ALTHOUGH IN MANY CASES YOU'LL PREFER TO BE ON YOUR WAY OUT OF THE STATE!
2-8

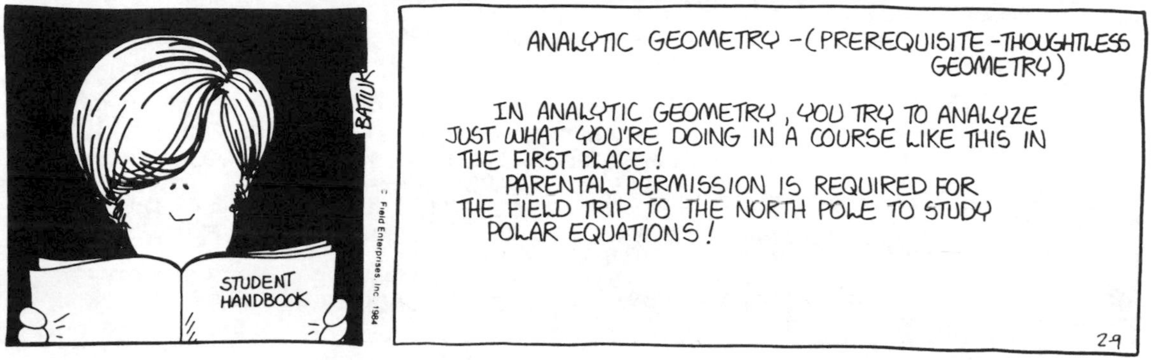
BATIUK
© Field Enterprises, Inc. 1984
STUDENT HANDBOOK
ANALYTIC GEOMETRY -(PREREQUISITE-THOUGHTLESS GEOMETRY)
IN ANALYTIC GEOMETRY, YOU TRY TO ANALYZE JUST WHAT YOU'RE DOING IN A COURSE LIKE THIS IN THE FIRST PLACE!
PARENTAL PERMISSION IS REQUIRED FOR THE FIELD TRIP TO THE NORTH POLE TO STUDY POLAR EQUATIONS!
2-9

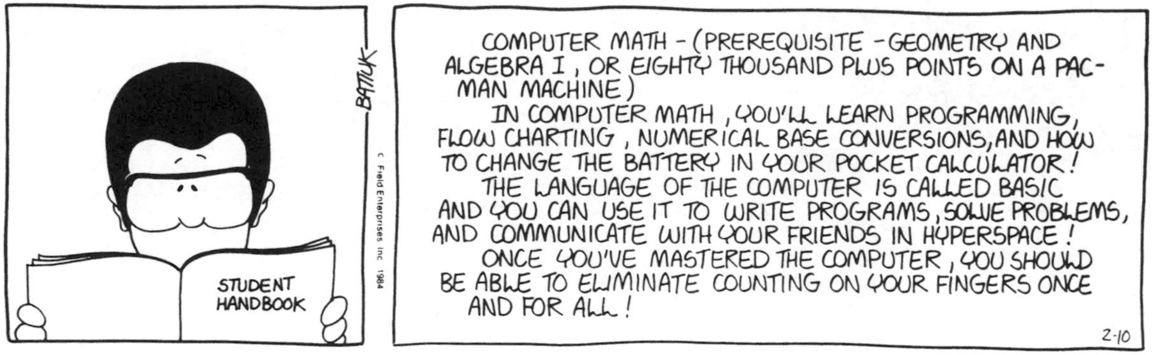
BATIUK
© Field Enterprises, Inc. 1984
STUDENT HANDBOOK
COMPUTER MATH -(PREREQUISITE -GEOMETRY AND ALGEBRA I, OR EIGHTY THOUSAND PLUS POINTS ON A PAC-MAN MACHINE)
IN COMPUTER MATH, YOU'LL LEARN PROGRAMMING, FLOW CHARTING, NUMERICAL BASE CONVERSIONS, AND HOW TO CHANGE THE BATTERY IN YOUR POCKET CALCULATOR!
THE LANGUAGE OF THE COMPUTER IS CALLED BASIC AND YOU CAN USE IT TO WRITE PROGRAMS, SOLVE PROBLEMS, AND COMMUNICATE WITH YOUR FRIENDS IN HYPERSPACE!
ONCE YOU'VE MASTERED THE COMPUTER, YOU SHOULD BE ABLE TO ELIMINATE COUNTING ON YOUR FINGERS ONCE AND FOR ALL!
2-10

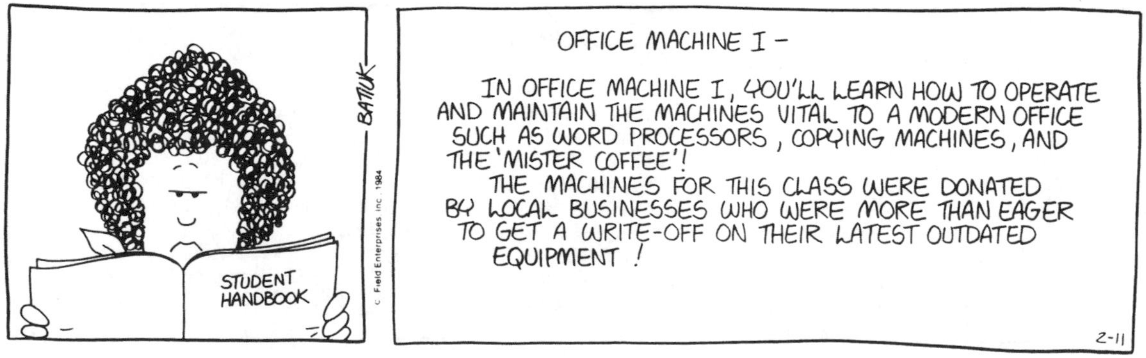
BATIUK
© Field Enterprises, Inc. 1984
STUDENT HANDBOOK
OFFICE MACHINE I -
IN OFFICE MACHINE I, YOU'LL LEARN HOW TO OPERATE AND MAINTAIN THE MACHINES VITAL TO A MODERN OFFICE SUCH AS WORD PROCESSORS, COPYING MACHINES, AND THE 'MISTER COFFEE'!
THE MACHINES FOR THIS CLASS WERE DONATED BY LOCAL BUSINESSES WHO WERE MORE THAN EAGER TO GET A WRITE-OFF ON THEIR LATEST OUTDATED EQUIPMENT!
2-11

FUNKY WINKERBEAN
BY TOM BATIUK ®
HEY!
WHAT'S THIS ?
© Field Enterprises, Inc., 1984
THERE'S ANDREA AND SHE'S ALL BY HERSELF AT HER LOCKER!
BATIUK
I'VE BEEN WANTING TO ASK HER OUT ALL WEEK AND THIS LOOKS LIKE THE PERFECT TIME TO ...
FORGET IT!
SHOOT!
2-12

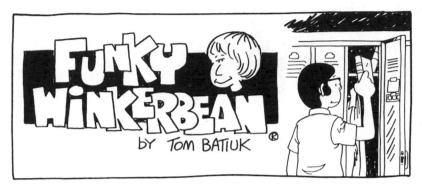

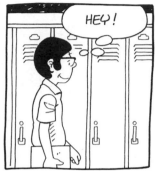

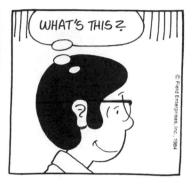

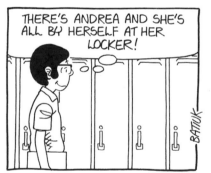

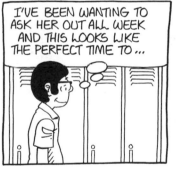

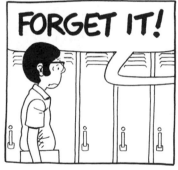

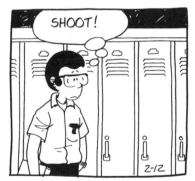

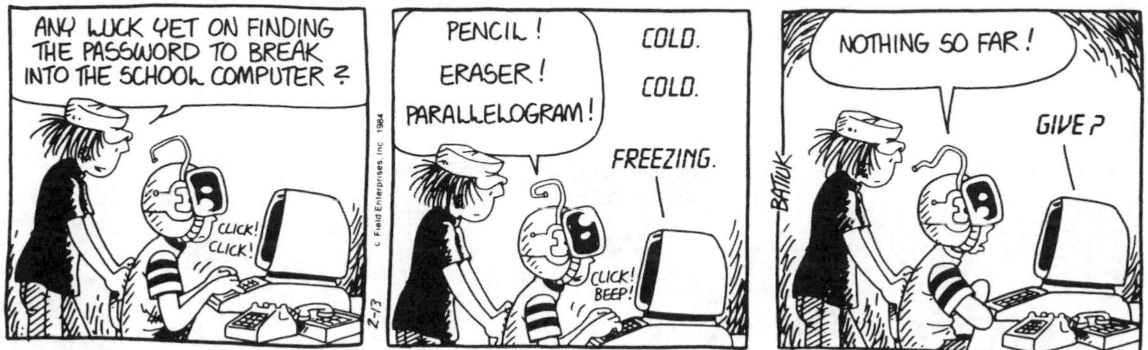
ANY LUCK YET ON FINDING THE PASSWORD TO BREAK INTO THE SCHOOL COMPUTER ?
CLICK! CLICK!
2-13
© Field Enterprises, Inc. 1984
PENCIL! ERASER! PARALLELOGRAM!
COLD. COLD. FREEZING.
CLICK! BEEP!
NOTHING SO FAR!
GIVE?
BATIUK

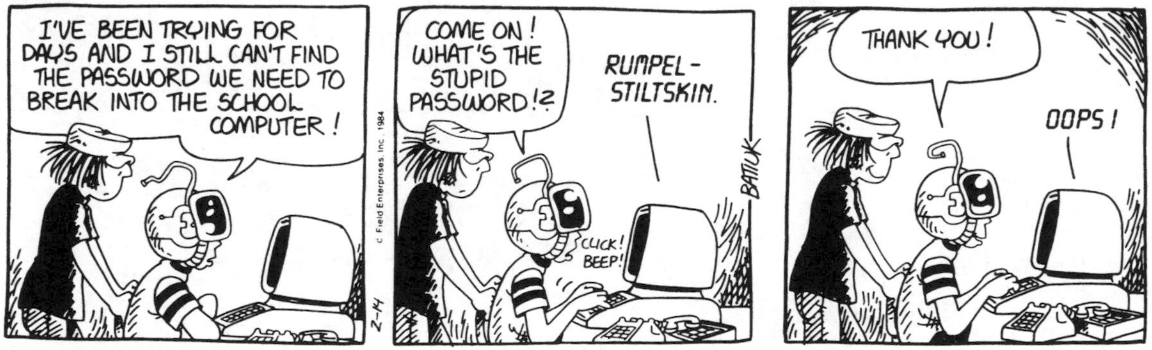
I'VE BEEN TRYING FOR DAYS AND I STILL CAN'T FIND THE PASSWORD WE NEED TO BREAK INTO THE SCHOOL COMPUTER!
2-14
© Field Enterprises, Inc. 1984
COME ON! WHAT'S THE STUPID PASSWORD!?
RUMPEL-STILTSKIN.
CLICK! BEEP!
BATIUK
THANK YOU!
OOPS!

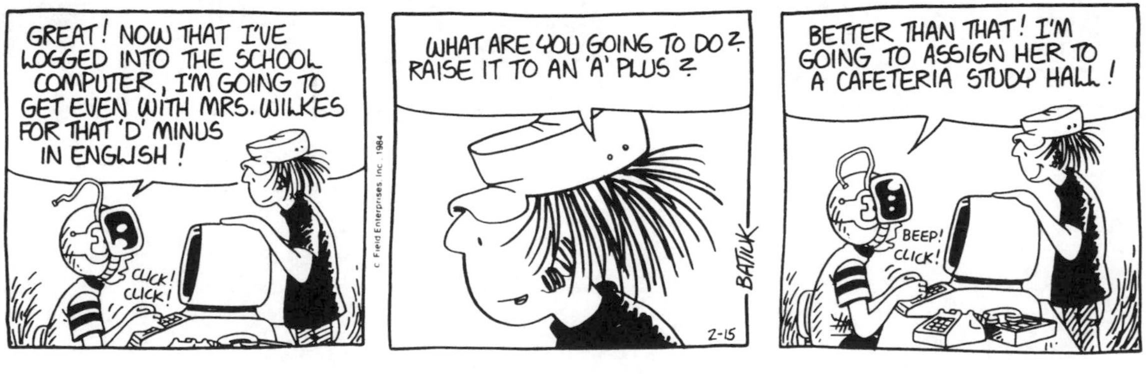
GREAT! NOW THAT I'VE LOGGED INTO THE SCHOOL COMPUTER, I'M GOING TO GET EVEN WITH MRS. WILKES FOR THAT 'D' MINUS IN ENGLISH!
CLICK! CLICK!
© Field Enterprises, Inc. 1984
WHAT ARE YOU GOING TO DO? RAISE IT TO AN 'A' PLUS?
BATIUK
2-15
BETTER THAN THAT! I'M GOING TO ASSIGN HER TO A CAFETERIA STUDY HALL!
BEEP! CLICK!

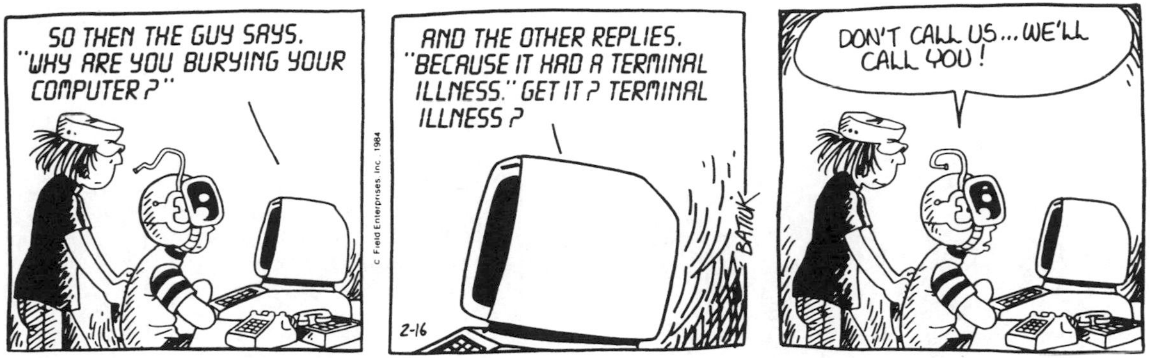
SO THEN THE GUY SAYS. "WHY ARE YOU BURYING YOUR COMPUTER?"
AND THE OTHER REPLIES. "BECAUSE IT HAD A TERMINAL ILLNESS." GET IT? TERMINAL ILLNESS?
DON'T CALL US... WE'LL CALL YOU!

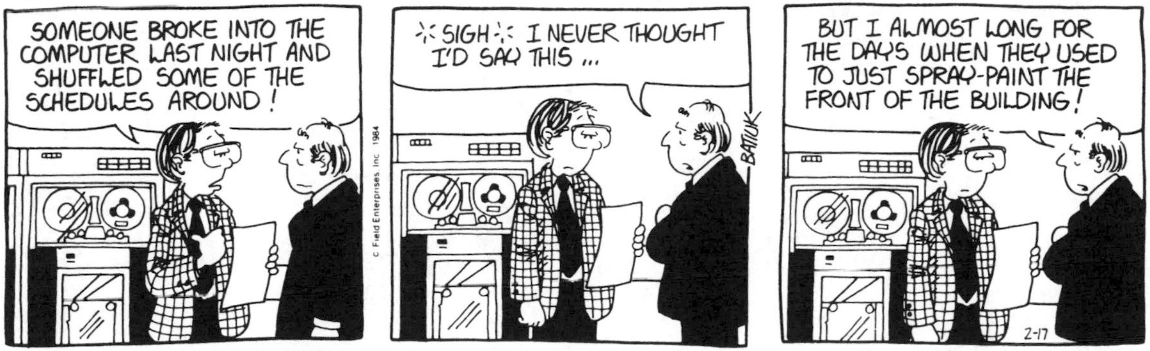
SOMEONE BROKE INTO THE COMPUTER LAST NIGHT AND SHUFFLED SOME OF THE SCHEDULES AROUND!
SIGH I NEVER THOUGHT I'D SAY THIS ...
BUT I ALMOST LONG FOR THE DAYS WHEN THEY USED TO JUST SPRAY-PAINT THE FRONT OF THE BUILDING!

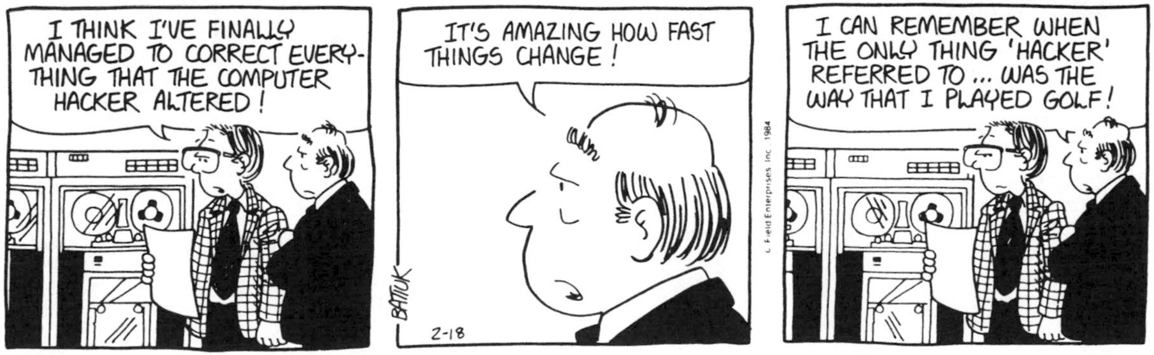
I THINK I'VE FINALLY MANAGED TO CORRECT EVERYTHING THAT THE COMPUTER HACKER ALTERED!
IT'S AMAZING HOW FAST THINGS CHANGE!
I CAN REMEMBER WHEN THE ONLY THING 'HACKER' REFERRED TO ... WAS THE WAY THAT I PLAYED GOLF!

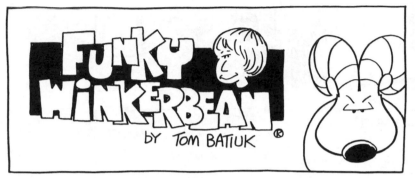

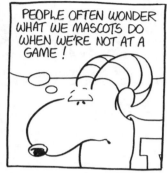

FUNKY WINKERBEAN
BY TOM BATIUK ®
PEOPLE OFTEN WONDER WHAT WE MASCOTS DO WHEN WE'RE NOT AT A GAME!
THE SCHOOL FINDS LITTLE JOBS FOR US!
HALL MONITOR
YOU'RE THE HALL MONITOR? YOU'VE GOTTA BE KIDDING!
I'M JUST GOING ON THROUGH! THERE'S NO WAY I'M GOING TO SHOW MY HALL PASS TO A GOAT!
GO AHEAD...
© Field Enterprises, Inc., 1984
BATIUK
2-19
MAKE MY DAY!!

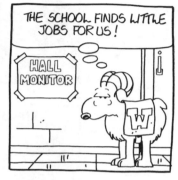

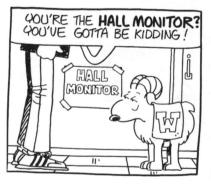

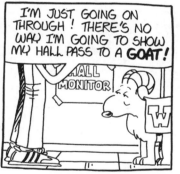

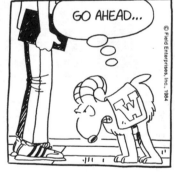

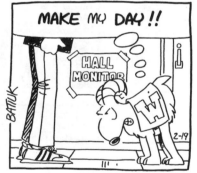

THEY WERE THE BEST OF PUNS AND THE WORST OF PUNS, AND THEY CAME FROM THE REST OF THE
READERS!

Q
IF SANTA CLAUS WAS FLYING WITH LUKE AND HE FELL INTO THE SAND MONSTER'S MOUTH, WHAT WOULD LUKE BECOME?
A
A REBEL WITHOUT A CLAUS!
2-20
THANKS AND A TIP OF THE DARTH VADER TOPPER TO:
ERIC JACOBSON - SKOKIE, ILLINOIS

THEY WERE THE BEST OF PUNS AND THE WORST OF PUNS, AND THEY CAME FROM THE REST OF THE
READERS!

Q
WHAT DO YOU CALL A FEMALE EWOK SOLDIER?
A
AN E-WAC!
2-21
THANKS AND A TIP OF THE DARTH VADER TOPPER TO:
CHRISTINA VASILAKIS - PHOENIX, ARIZONA

THEY WERE THE BEST OF PUNS AND THE WORST OF PUNS, AND THEY CAME FROM THE REST OF THE
READERS!

Q
WHERE DO C3PO AND R2-D2 GET THEIR INSURANCE?
POLICY
A
DROIDS OF LONDON!
2-22
THANKS AND A TIP OF THE DARTH VADER TOPPER TO:
ROBBIE MORAN - SOUTH MILWAUKEE, WI

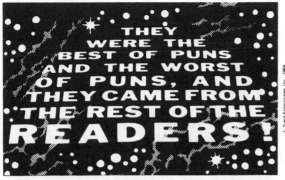

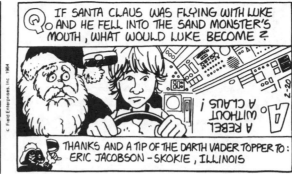

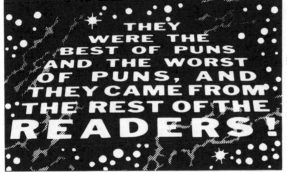

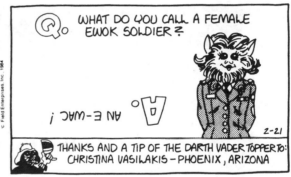

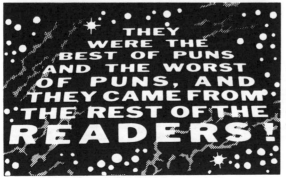

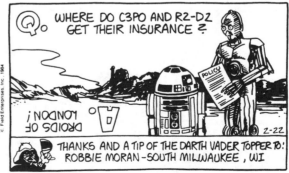

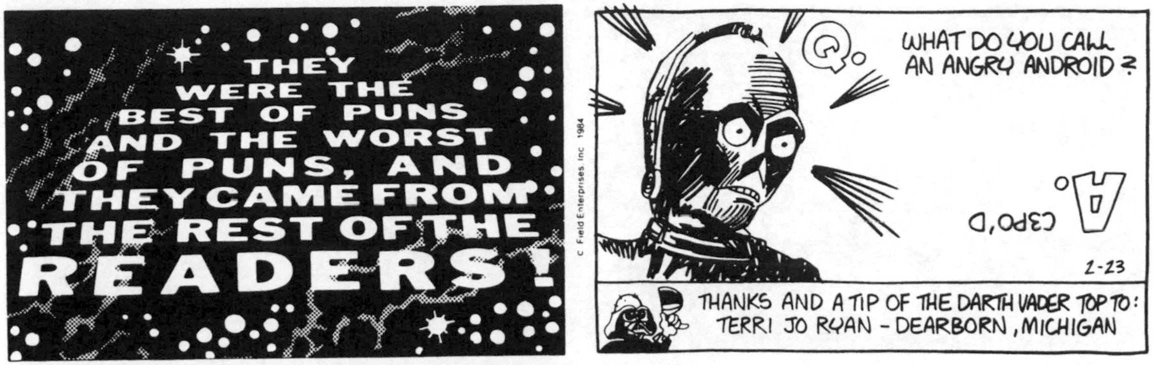
THEY WERE THE BEST OF PUNS AND THE WORST OF PUNS, AND THEY CAME FROM THE REST OF THE READERS!
c Field Enterprises, Inc. 1984
Q
WHAT DO YOU CALL AN ANGRY ANDROID?
A
C3PO'D
2-23
THANKS AND A TIP OF THE DARTH VADER TOP TO: TERRI JO RYAN - DEARBORN, MICHIGAN

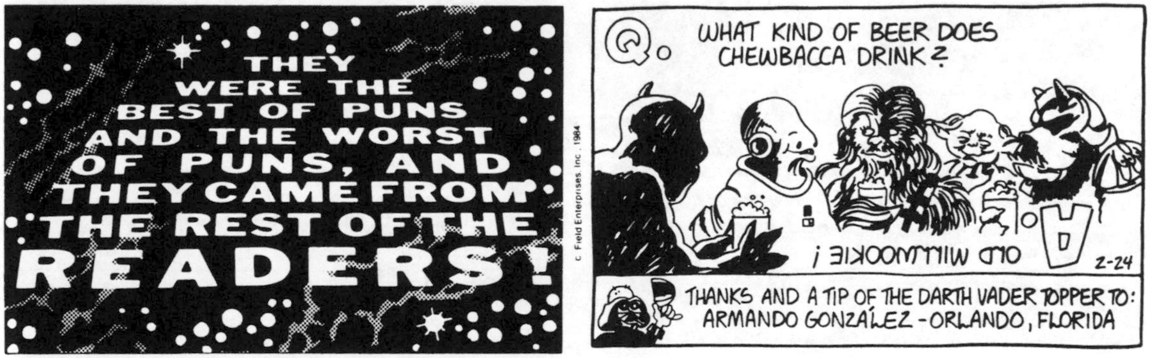
THEY WERE THE BEST OF PUNS AND THE WORST OF PUNS, AND THEY CAME FROM THE REST OF THE READERS!
c Field Enterprises, Inc. 1984
Q
WHAT KIND OF BEER DOES CHEWBACCA DRINK?
A
OLD MILLWOOKIE!
2-24
THANKS AND A TIP OF THE DARTH VADER TOPPER TO: ARMANDO GONZÁLEZ - ORLANDO, FLORIDA

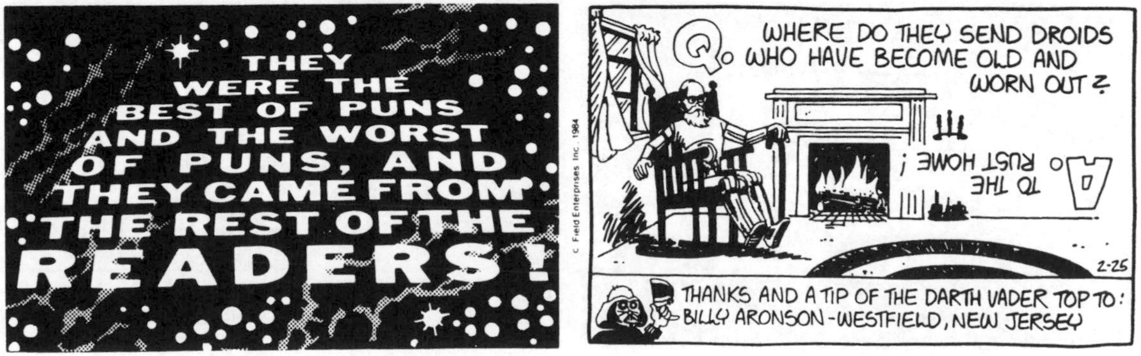
THEY WERE THE BEST OF PUNS AND THE WORST OF PUNS, AND THEY CAME FROM THE REST OF THE READERS!
c Field Enterprises, Inc. 1984
Q
WHERE DO THEY SEND DROIDS WHO HAVE BECOME OLD AND WORN OUT?
A
TO THE RUST HOME!
2-25
THANKS AND A TIP OF THE DARTH VADER TOP TO: BILLY ARONSON - WESTFIELD, NEW JERSEY

FUNKY WINKERBEAN
BY TOM BATIUK
MULTITRON HACKER 3000
THERE!
CLICK! CLICK!
YOU'VE **DONE** IT!
CLICK!
YOU'VE LOGGED INTO THE SCHOOL COMPUTER AGAIN, ELIMINATOR!
CLICK! CLICK!
WOW! WHAT ARE ALL THOSE **HUGE** NUMBERS?
THAT'S THE SCHOOL'S BUDGET FOR THE ENTIRE YEAR!
CLICK! CLICK!
BATIUK
WHAT ABOUT THOSE LITTLE NUMBERS THERE?
2-26
© Field Enterprises, Inc., 1984
THOSE ARE THE TEACHERS' SALARIES!

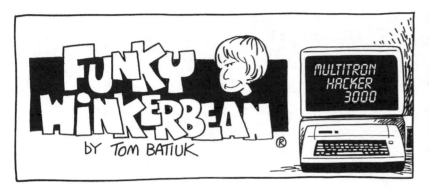

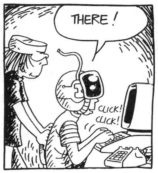

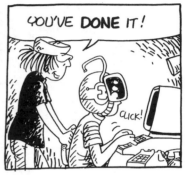

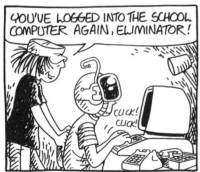

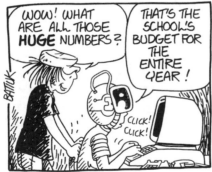

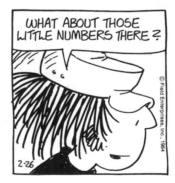

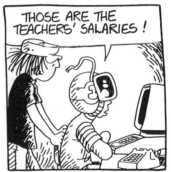

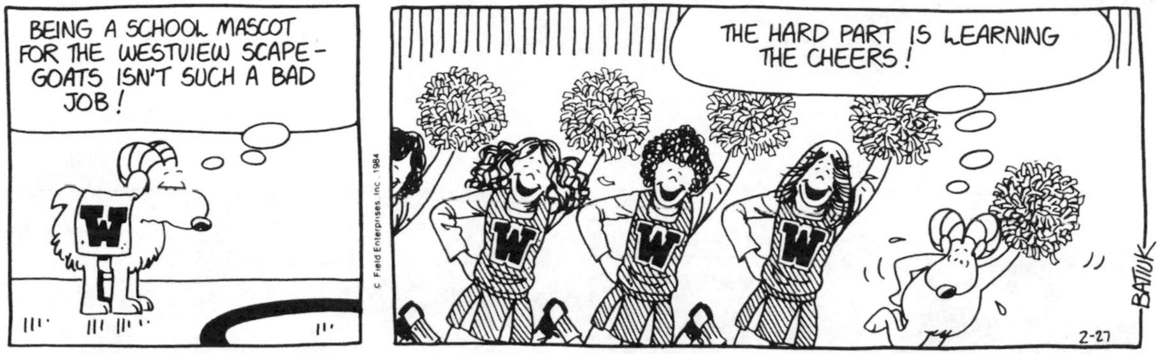
BEING A SCHOOL MASCOT FOR THE WESTVIEW SCAPE-GOATS ISN'T SUCH A BAD JOB!
c Field Enterprises, Inc. 1984
THE HARD PART IS LEARNING THE CHEERS!
BATIUK
2-27

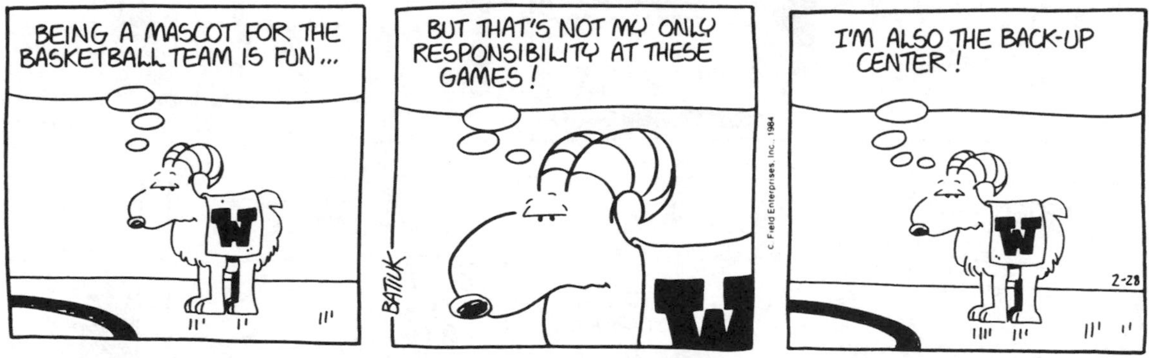
BEING A MASCOT FOR THE BASKETBALL TEAM IS FUN...
BATIUK
BUT THAT'S NOT MY ONLY RESPONSIBILITY AT THESE GAMES!
c Field Enterprises, Inc. 1984
I'M ALSO THE BACK-UP CENTER!
2-28

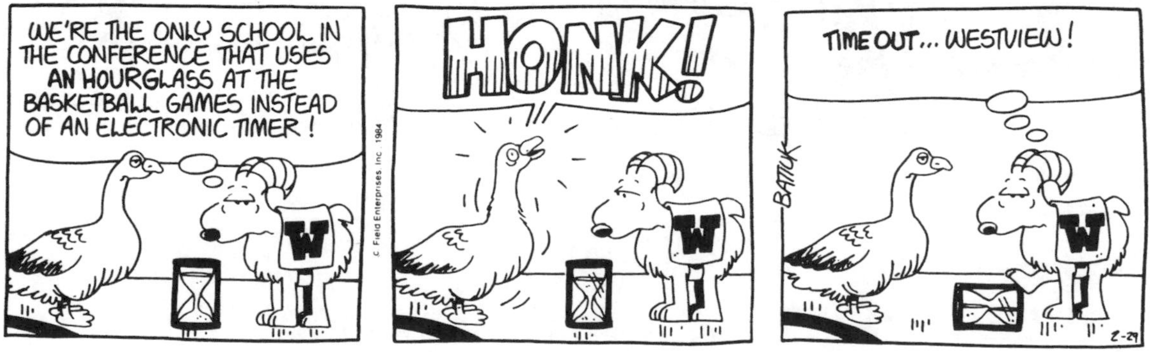
WE'RE THE ONLY SCHOOL IN THE CONFERENCE THAT USES AN HOURGLASS AT THE BASKETBALL GAMES INSTEAD OF AN ELECTRONIC TIMER!
c Field Enterprises, Inc. 1984
HONK!
BATIUK
TIME OUT... WESTVIEW!
2-29

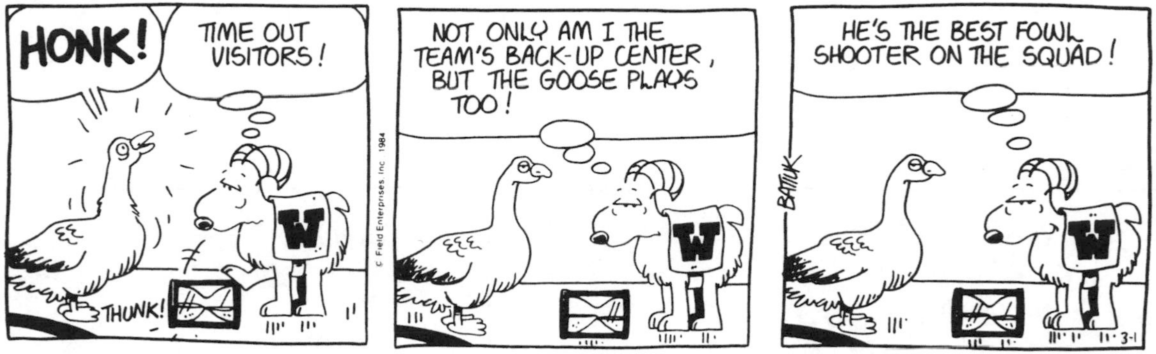
HONK!
TIME OUT VISITORS!
THUNK!
© Field Enterprises, Inc. 1984
NOT ONLY AM I THE TEAM'S BACK-UP CENTER, BUT THE GOOSE PLAYS TOO!
HE'S THE BEST FOWL SHOOTER ON THE SQUAD!
BATIUK
3-1

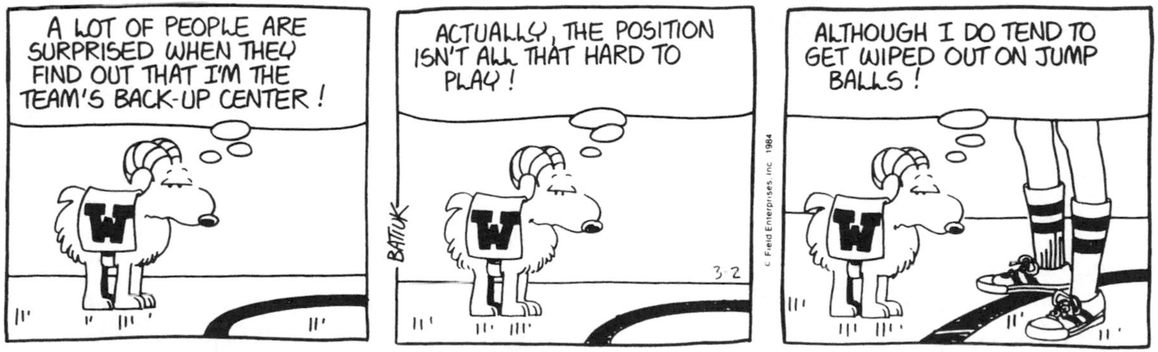
A LOT OF PEOPLE ARE SURPRISED WHEN THEY FIND OUT THAT I'M THE TEAM'S BACK-UP CENTER!
BATIUK
ACTUALLY, THE POSITION ISN'T ALL THAT HARD TO PLAY!
3-2
© Field Enterprises, Inc. 1984
ALTHOUGH I DO TEND TO GET WIPED OUT ON JUMP BALLS!

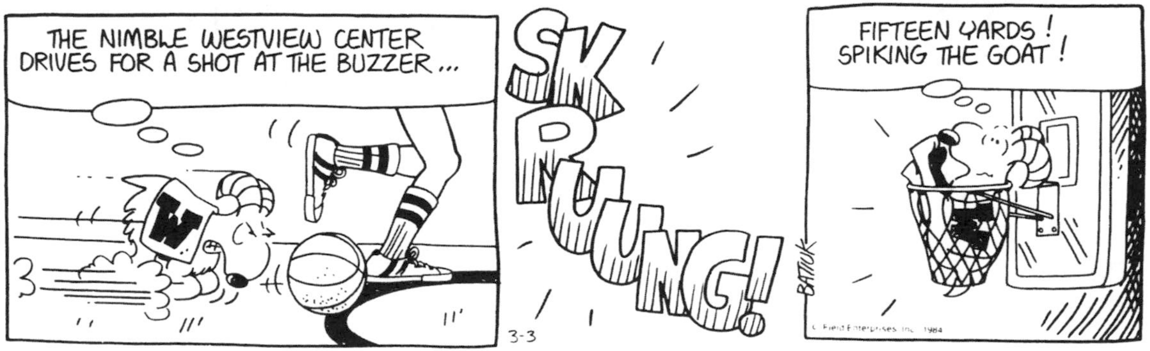
THE NIMBLE WESTVIEW CENTER DRIVES FOR A SHOT AT THE BUZZER...
SKRUUNG!
3-3
FIFTEEN YARDS! SPIKING THE GOAT!
BATIUK
© Field Enterprises, Inc. 1984

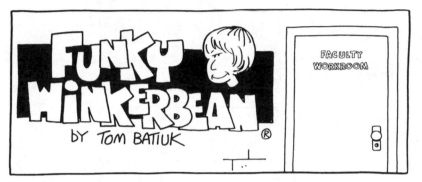

FUNKY WINKERBEAN
BY TOM BATIUK
FACULTY WORKROOM
DID YOU HEAR WHAT HAPPENED TO HARRY?
NO, WHAT?
© Field Enterprises, Inc., 1984
LAST CHRISTMAS THE BAND SOLD FRUITCAKES TO EARN MONEY, AND HARRY ORDERED SO MANY THAT THEY COULDN'T SELL THEM ALL!
WELL, THEY DRIED OUT ON HIM AND NOW HE'S STUCK WITH A GARAGE FULL OF PETRIFIED FRUITCAKES!
BATIUK
NO KIDDING! SO WHAT'S HE GOING TO DO?
HI THERE! WOULD YOU BE INTERESTED IN BUYING A BAND DOORSTOP?
3-4

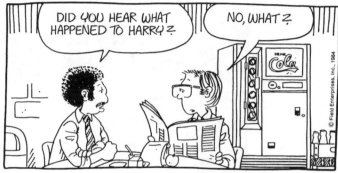

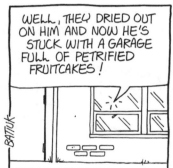

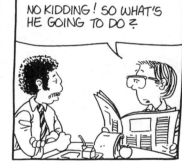

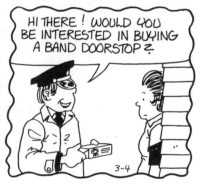

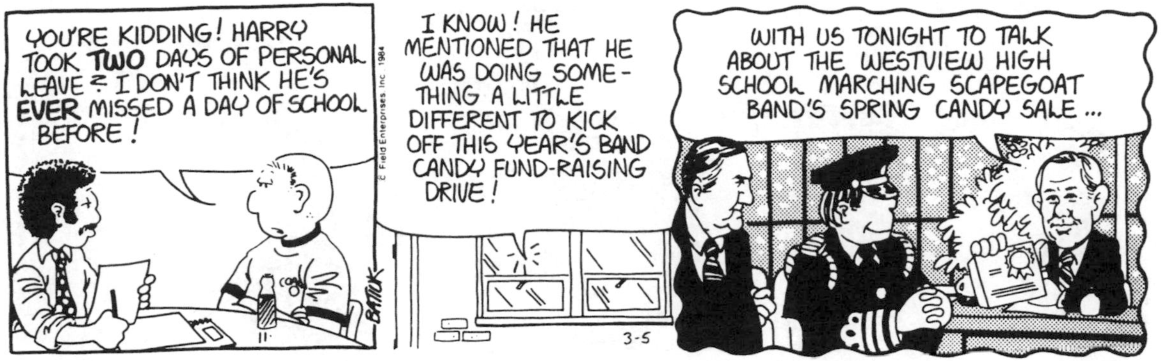
YOU'RE KIDDING! HARRY TOOK **TWO** DAYS OF PERSONAL LEAVE? I DON'T THINK HE'S **EVER** MISSED A DAY OF SCHOOL BEFORE!
I KNOW! HE MENTIONED THAT HE WAS DOING SOMETHING A LITTLE DIFFERENT TO KICK OFF THIS YEAR'S BAND CANDY FUND-RAISING DRIVE!
WITH US TONIGHT TO TALK ABOUT THE WESTVIEW HIGH SCHOOL MARCHING SCAPEGOAT BAND'S SPRING CANDY SALE ...
BATIUK
© Field Enterprises, Inc. 1984
3-5

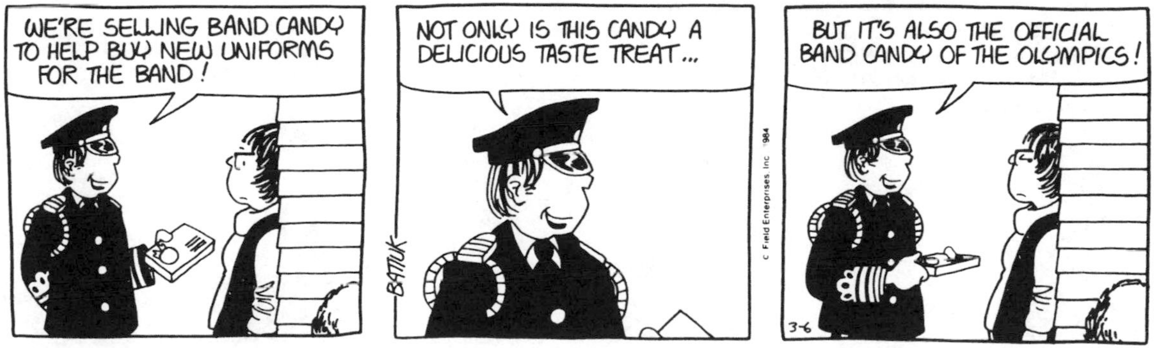
WE'RE SELLING BAND CANDY TO HELP BUY NEW UNIFORMS FOR THE BAND!
NOT ONLY IS THIS CANDY A DELICIOUS TASTE TREAT...
BUT IT'S ALSO THE OFFICIAL BAND CANDY OF THE OLYMPICS!
BATIUK
© Field Enterprises, Inc. 1984
3-6

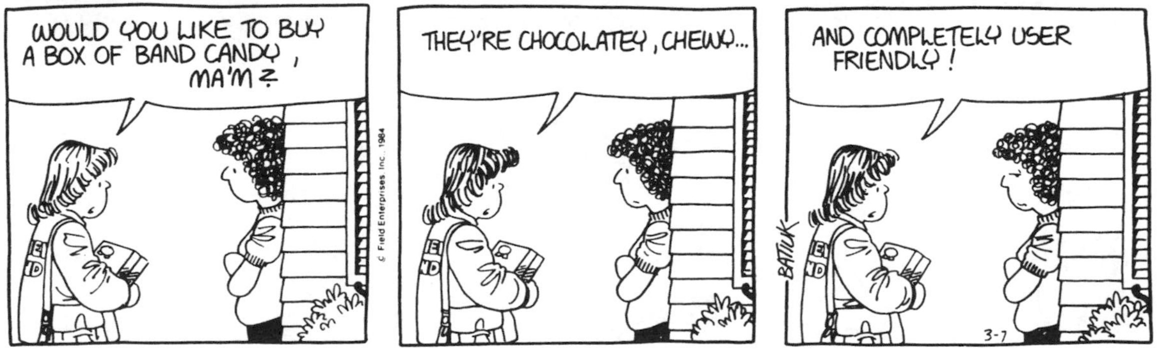
WOULD YOU LIKE TO BUY A BOX OF BAND CANDY, MA'M?
THEY'RE CHOCOLATEY, CHEWY...
AND COMPLETELY USER FRIENDLY!
BATIUK
© Field Enterprises, Inc. 1984
3-7

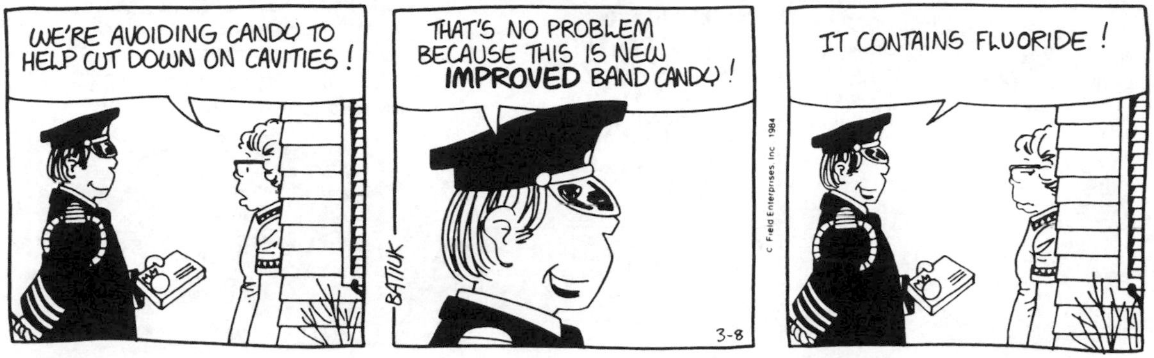
WE'RE AVOIDING CANDY TO HELP CUT DOWN ON CAVITIES!
THAT'S NO PROBLEM BECAUSE THIS IS NEW **IMPROVED** BAND CANDY!
BATIUK
3-8
© Field Enterprises, Inc. 1984
IT CONTAINS FLUORIDE!

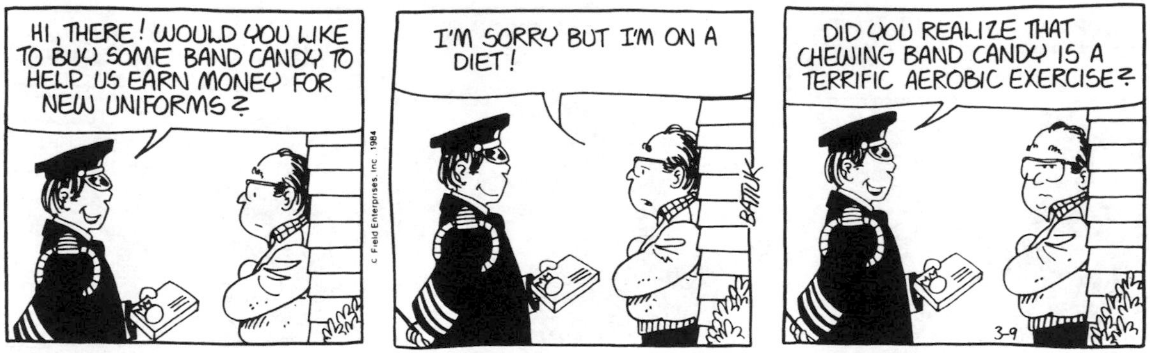
HI, THERE! WOULD YOU LIKE TO BUY SOME BAND CANDY TO HELP US EARN MONEY FOR NEW UNIFORMS?
© Field Enterprises, Inc. 1984
I'M SORRY BUT I'M ON A DIET!
BATIUK
DID YOU REALIZE THAT CHEWING BAND CANDY IS A TERRIFIC AEROBIC EXERCISE?
3-9

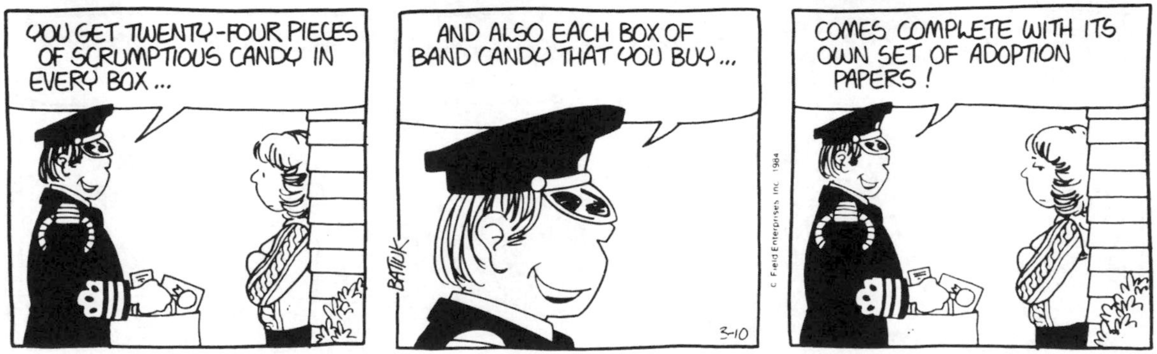
YOU GET TWENTY-FOUR PIECES OF SCRUMPTIOUS CANDY IN EVERY BOX...
AND ALSO EACH BOX OF BAND CANDY THAT YOU BUY...
BATIUK
3-10
© Field Enterprises, Inc. 1984
COMES COMPLETE WITH ITS OWN SET OF ADOPTION PAPERS!

FUNKY WINKERBEAN
BY TOM BATIUK
WESTVIE
HIGH SCHO
FRI HOME
JACKSON
HOLD IT! HOLD IT!!
© Field Enterprises, Inc., 1984
I GIVE UP!!
BATIUK
THAT WAS HORRIBLE!
WHEN IT COMES TO CLASSICAL MUSIC ...
THE BACH STOPS HERE!!
3-11

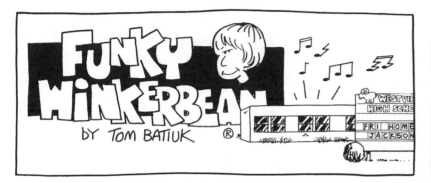

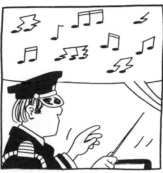

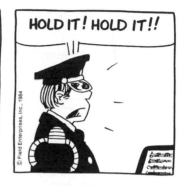

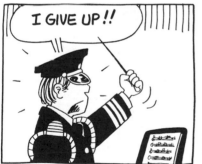

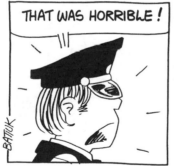

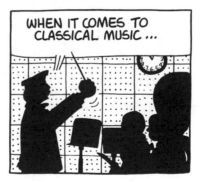

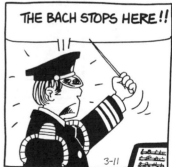

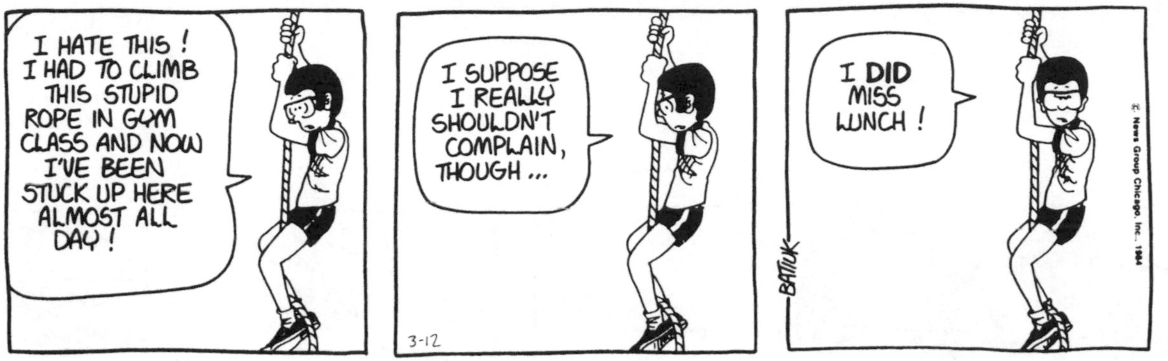
I HATE THIS! I HAD TO CLIMB THIS STUPID ROPE IN GYM CLASS AND NOW I'VE BEEN STUCK UP HERE ALMOST ALL DAY!
I SUPPOSE I REALLY SHOULDN'T COMPLAIN, THOUGH ...
3-12
I **DID** MISS LUNCH!
BATIUK
© News Group Chicago, Inc., 1984

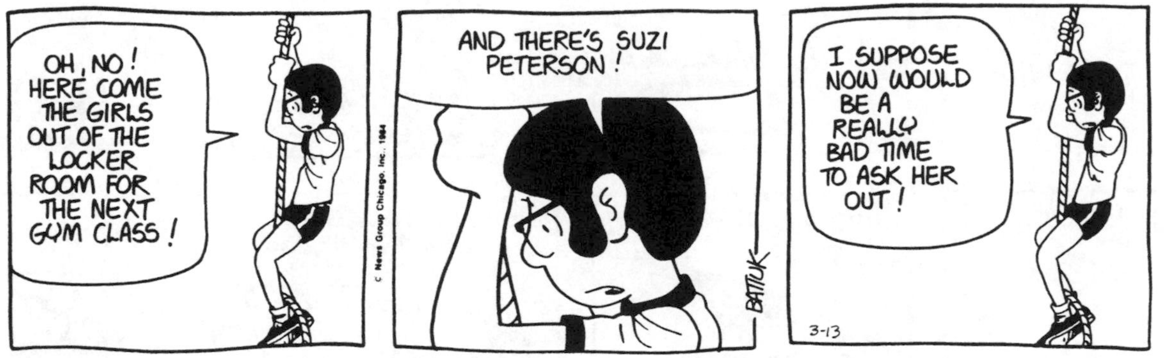
OH, NO! HERE COME THE GIRLS OUT OF THE LOCKER ROOM FOR THE NEXT GYM CLASS!
© News Group Chicago, Inc., 1984
AND THERE'S SUZI PETERSON!
BATIUK
I SUPPOSE NOW WOULD BE A REALLY BAD TIME TO ASK HER OUT!
3-13

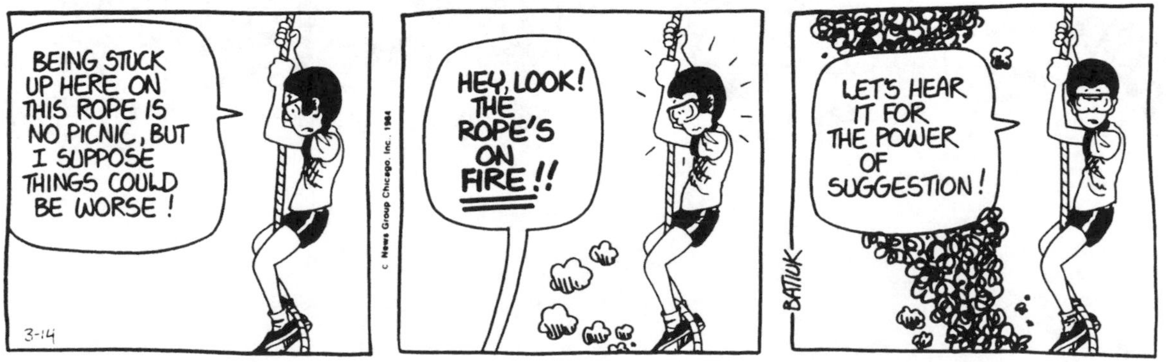
BEING STUCK UP HERE ON THIS ROPE IS NO PICNIC, BUT I SUPPOSE THINGS COULD BE WORSE!
3-14
© News Group Chicago, Inc., 1984
HEY, LOOK! THE ROPE'S ON FIRE!!
BATIUK
LET'S HEAR IT FOR THE POWER OF SUGGESTION!

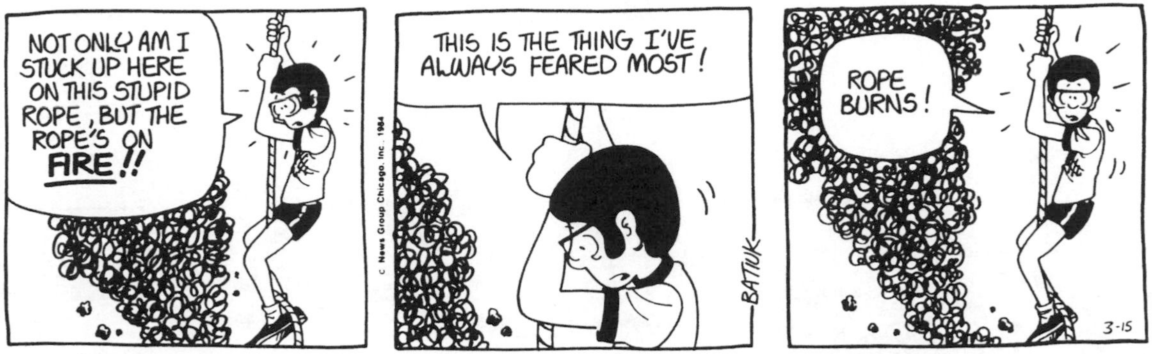
NOT ONLY AM I STUCK UP HERE ON THIS STUPID ROPE, BUT THE ROPE'S ON FIRE!!
© News Group Chicago, Inc. 1984
THIS IS THE THING I'VE ALWAYS FEARED MOST!
BATIUK
ROPE BURNS!
3-15

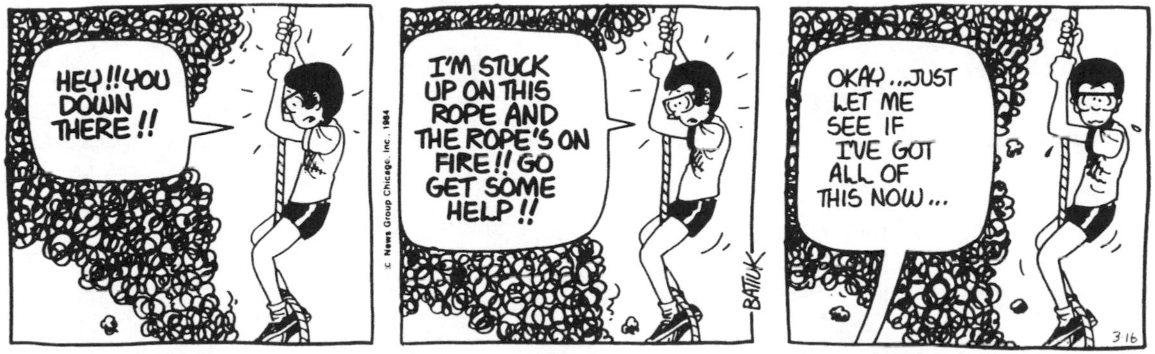
HEY!! YOU DOWN THERE!!
© News Group Chicago, Inc. 1984
I'M STUCK UP ON THIS ROPE AND THE ROPE'S ON FIRE!! GO GET SOME HELP!!
BATIUK
OKAY...JUST LET ME SEE IF I'VE GOT ALL OF THIS NOW...
3-16

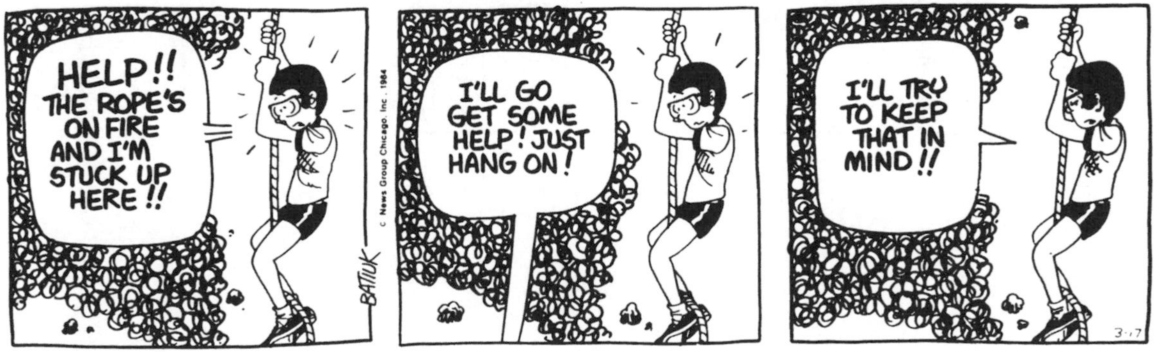
HELP!! THE ROPE'S ON FIRE AND I'M STUCK UP HERE!!
© News Group Chicago, Inc. 1984
BATIUK
I'LL GO GET SOME HELP! JUST HANG ON!
I'LL TRY TO KEEP THAT IN MIND!!
3-17

FUNKY WINKERBEAN
BY TOM BATIUK
WHAT'S YOUR NAME?
BUD!
OH, NO!!
© Field Enterprises, Inc., 1984
DID YOU SEE THE TV ON THAT GUY'S PATIO DOWN THERE!?
BATIUK
THERE'S A FOOTBALL GAME ON! DON'T TELL ME IT'S FALL ALREADY!!
NO, DON'T WORRY! THAT'S THE U.S.F.L.! THEY PLAY IN THE SPRING AND SUMMER!
WHEW! FOR A SECOND THERE, I THOUGHT I WAS A LATE BLOOMER!
3-18

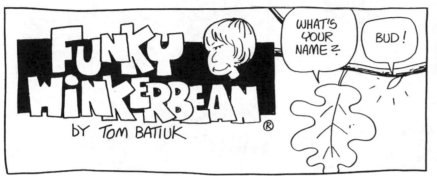

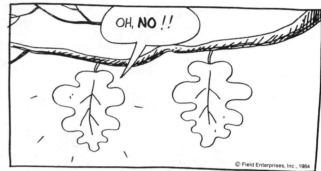

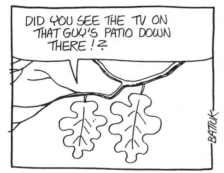

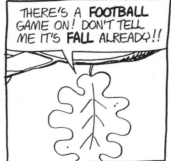

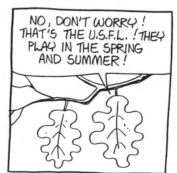

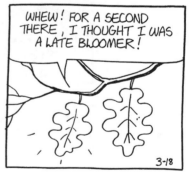

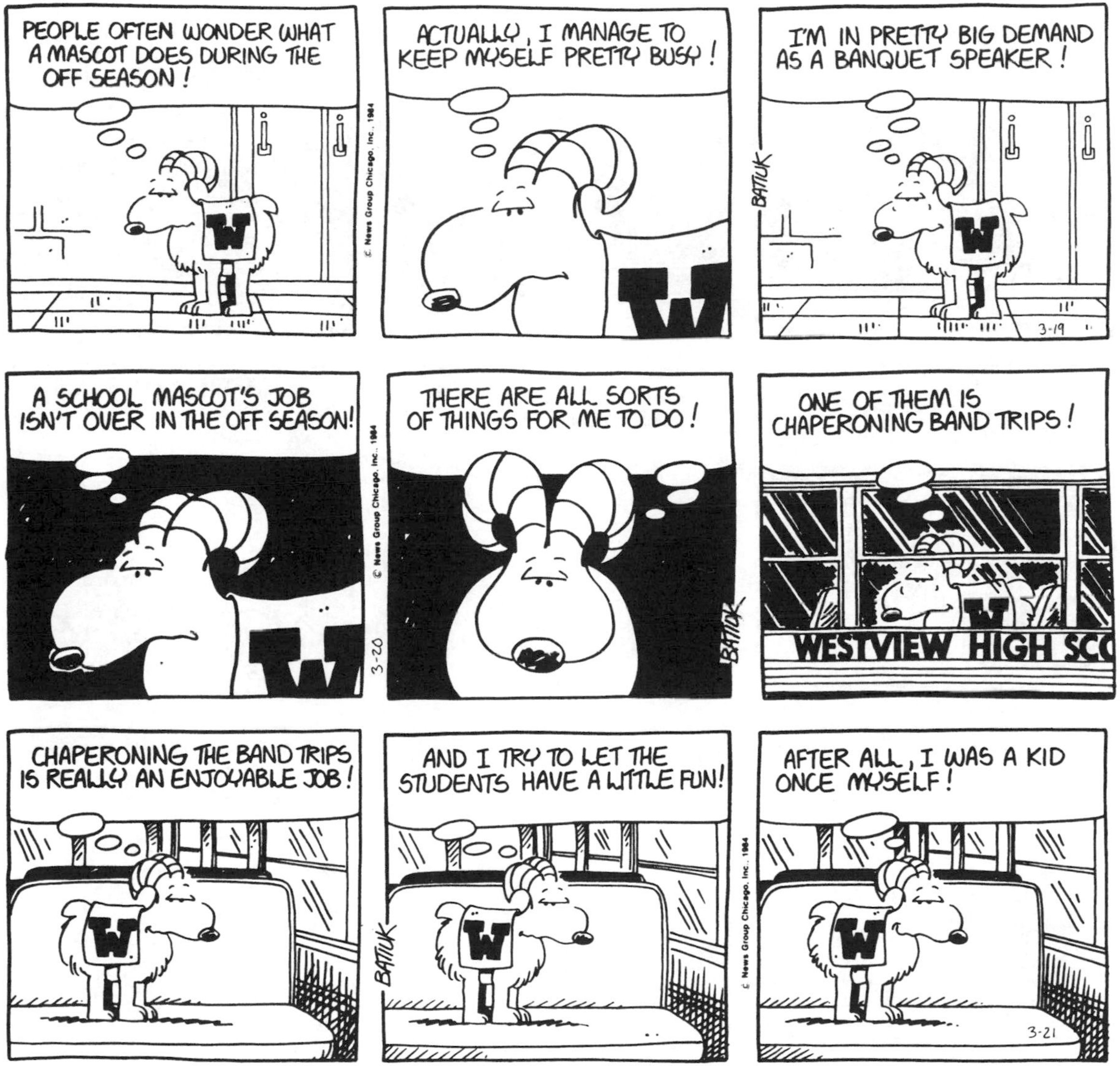
PEOPLE OFTEN WONDER WHAT A MASCOT DOES DURING THE OFF SEASON!
© News Group Chicago, Inc., 1984
ACTUALLY, I MANAGE TO KEEP MYSELF PRETTY BUSY!
BATIUK
I'M IN PRETTY BIG DEMAND AS A BANQUET SPEAKER!
3-19
A SCHOOL MASCOT'S JOB ISN'T OVER IN THE OFF SEASON!
© News Group Chicago, Inc., 1984
3-20
THERE ARE ALL SORTS OF THINGS FOR ME TO DO!
BATIUK
ONE OF THEM IS CHAPERONING BAND TRIPS!
WESTVIEW HIGH SC
CHAPERONING THE BAND TRIPS IS REALLY AN ENJOYABLE JOB!
BATIUK
AND I TRY TO LET THE STUDENTS HAVE A LITTLE FUN!
© News Group Chicago, Inc., 1984
AFTER ALL, I WAS A KID ONCE MYSELF!
3-21

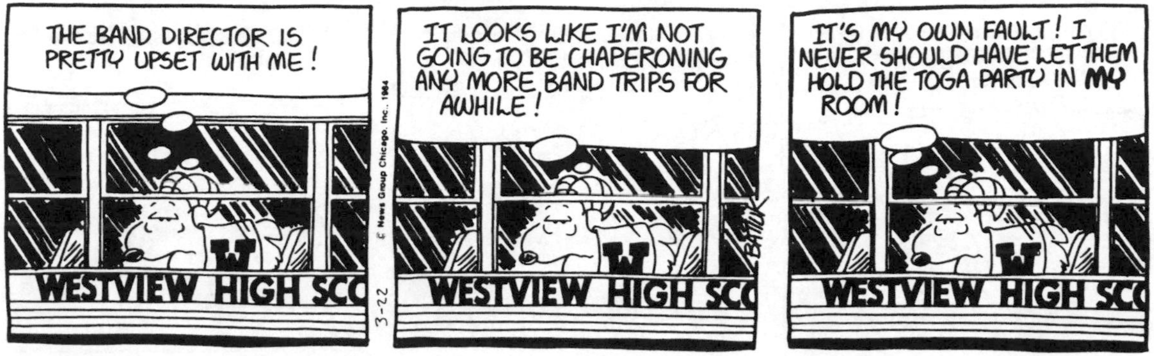
THE BAND DIRECTOR IS PRETTY UPSET WITH ME!
WESTVIEW HIGH SCO
© News Group Chicago, Inc., 1984
3-22
IT LOOKS LIKE I'M NOT GOING TO BE CHAPERONING ANY MORE BAND TRIPS FOR AWHILE!
BATIUK
IT'S MY OWN FAULT! I NEVER SHOULD HAVE LET THEM HOLD THE TOGA PARTY IN **MY** ROOM!

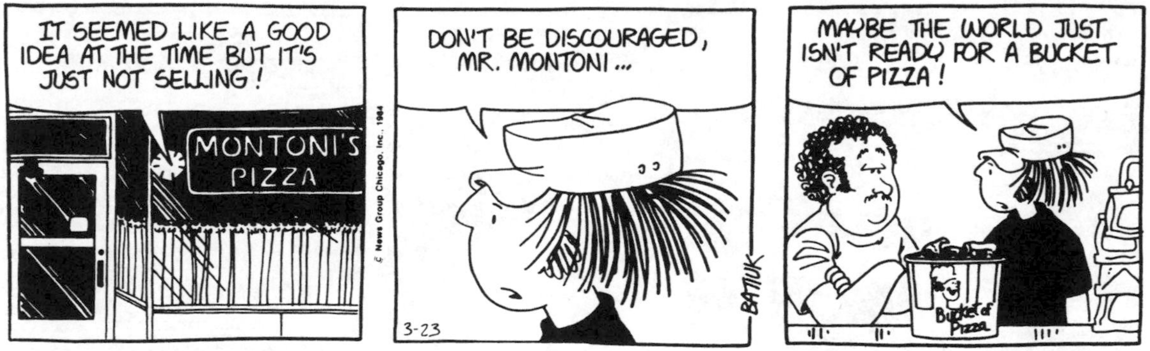
IT SEEMED LIKE A GOOD IDEA AT THE TIME BUT IT'S JUST NOT SELLING!
MONTONI'S PIZZA
© News Group Chicago, Inc., 1984
DON'T BE DISCOURAGED, MR. MONTONI...
3-23
BATIUK
MAYBE THE WORLD JUST ISN'T READY FOR A BUCKET OF PIZZA!
Bucket of Pizza

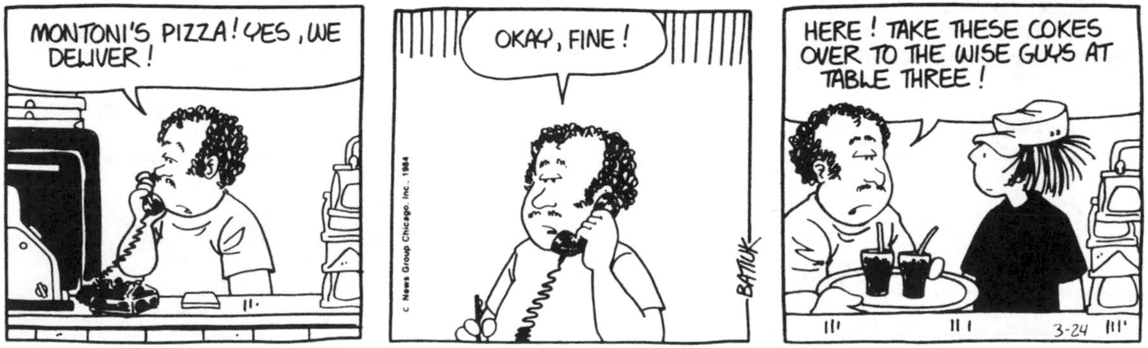
MONTONI'S PIZZA! YES, WE DELIVER!
© News Group Chicago, Inc., 1984
OKAY, FINE!
BATIUK
HERE! TAKE THESE COKES OVER TO THE WISE GUYS AT TABLE THREE!
3-24

COMPUTER ROOM

by Tom Batiuk

sigh...

i just can't get any rest anymore.

almost every night some computer hacker breaks into me...

© Field Enterprises, Inc., 1984

and fudges his grades or shuffles my schedules around.

but i'm finally getting even.

BATIUK

i've started breaking into home terminals and mixing up their checking accounts!

3-25

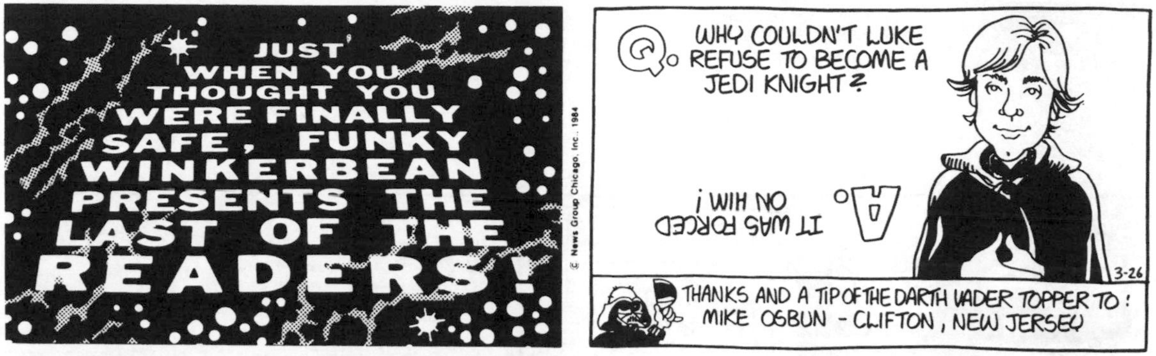
JUST WHEN YOU THOUGHT YOU WERE FINALLY SAFE, FUNKY WINKERBEAN PRESENTS THE LAST OF THE READERS!
© News Group Chicago, Inc. 1984
Q. WHY COULDN'T LUKE REFUSE TO BECOME A JEDI KNIGHT?
A. IT WAS FORCED ON HIM!
3-26
THANKS AND A TIP OF THE DARTH VADER TOPPER TO: MIKE OSBUN - CLIFTON, NEW JERSEY

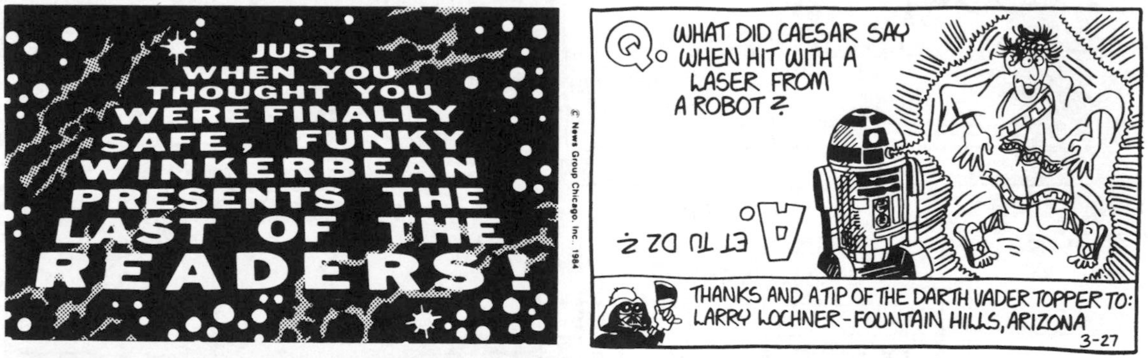
JUST WHEN YOU THOUGHT YOU WERE FINALLY SAFE, FUNKY WINKERBEAN PRESENTS THE LAST OF THE READERS!
© News Group Chicago, Inc. 1984
Q. WHAT DID CAESAR SAY WHEN HIT WITH A LASER FROM A ROBOT?
A. ET TU D2?
THANKS AND A TIP OF THE DARTH VADER TOPPER TO: LARRY LOCHNER - FOUNTAIN HILLS, ARIZONA
3-27

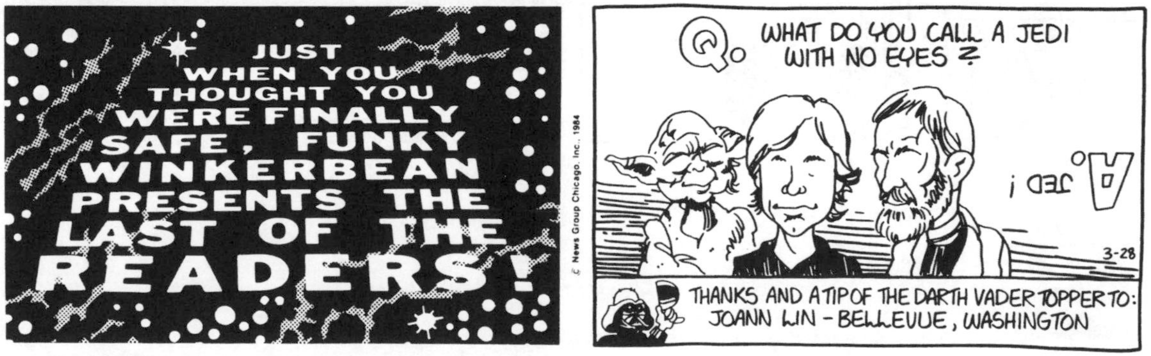
JUST WHEN YOU THOUGHT YOU WERE FINALLY SAFE, FUNKY WINKERBEAN PRESENTS THE LAST OF THE READERS!
© News Group Chicago, Inc. 1984
Q. WHAT DO YOU CALL A JEDI WITH NO EYES?
A. JED!
3-28
THANKS AND A TIP OF THE DARTH VADER TOPPER TO: JOANN LIN - BELLEVUE, WASHINGTON

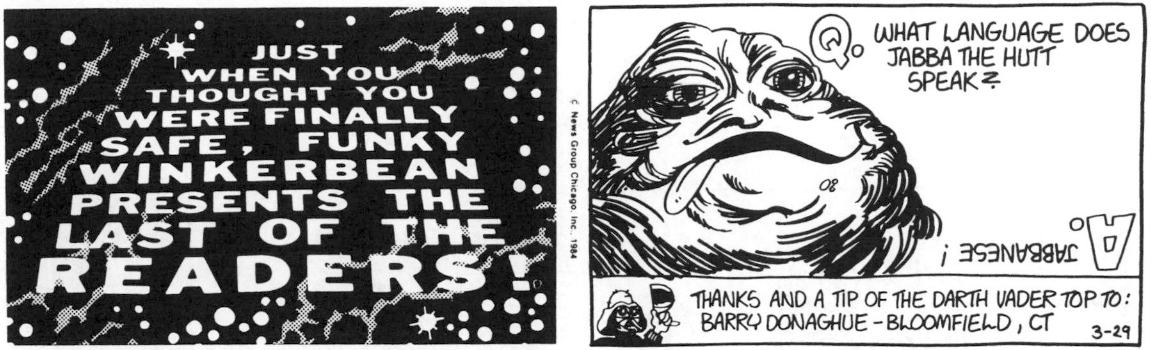

JUST WHEN YOU THOUGHT YOU WERE FINALLY SAFE, FUNKY WINKERBEAN PRESENTS THE LAST OF THE READERS!
Q. WHAT LANGUAGE DOES JABBA THE HUTT SPEAK?
A. JABBANESE!
THANKS AND A TIP OF THE DARTH VADER TOP TO: BARRY DONAGHUE - BLOOMFIELD, CT
3-29

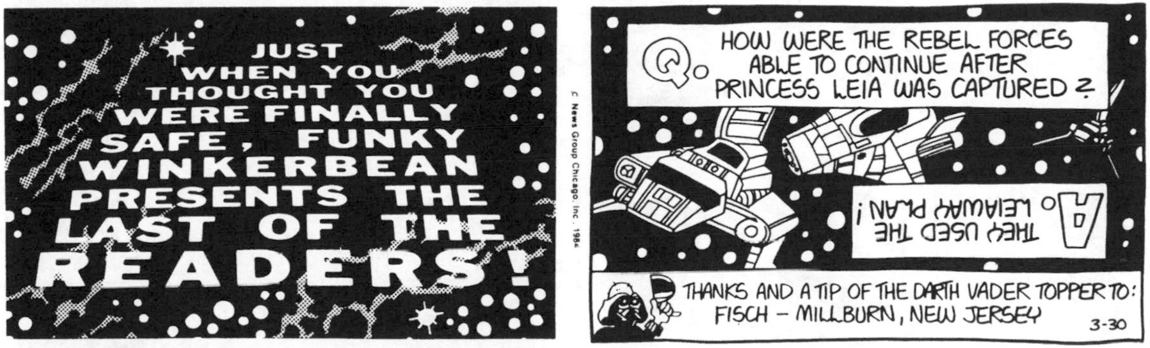

JUST WHEN YOU THOUGHT YOU WERE FINALLY SAFE, FUNKY WINKERBEAN PRESENTS THE LAST OF THE READERS!
Q. HOW WERE THE REBEL FORCES ABLE TO CONTINUE AFTER PRINCESS LEIA WAS CAPTURED?
A. THEY USED THE LEIAWAY PLAN!
THANKS AND A TIP OF THE DARTH VADER TOPPER TO: FISCH - MILLBURN, NEW JERSEY
3-30

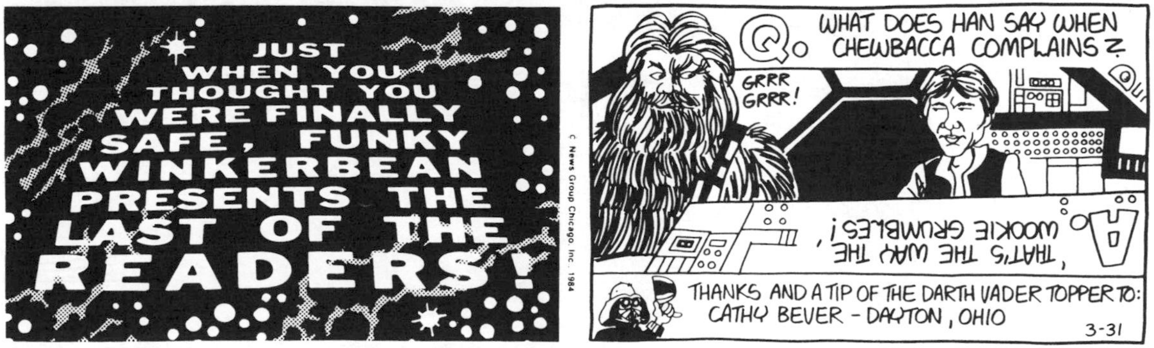

JUST WHEN YOU THOUGHT YOU WERE FINALLY SAFE, FUNKY WINKERBEAN PRESENTS THE LAST OF THE READERS!
Q. WHAT DOES HAN SAY WHEN CHEWBACCA COMPLAINS?
GRRR GRRR!
A. THAT'S THE WAY THE WOOKIE GRUMBLES!
THANKS AND A TIP OF THE DARTH VADER TOPPER TO: CATHY BEVER - DAYTON, OHIO
3-31

FUNKY WINKERBEAN
by TOM BATIUK ®
I DON'T KNOW WHAT TO DO WITH YOU PEOPLE!
YOU PLAYED THAT LIKE YOU WERE SEEING THIS MUSIC FOR THE VERY FIRST TIME!
YOU PLAYED THAT SO BADLY THAT I'M SCHEDULING A THREE-HOUR PRACTICE FOR THE **ENTIRE** BAND ON **SUNDAY** NIGHT!!
AWWWWW!
APRIL FOOL!
IT'S ONLY A **TWO**-HOUR PRACTICE!
BATIUK
4-1
© Field Enterprises, Inc., 1984

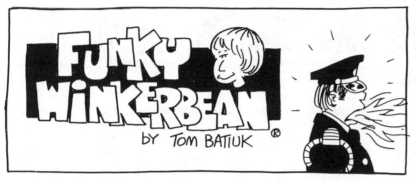

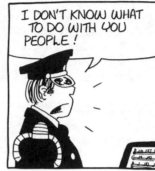

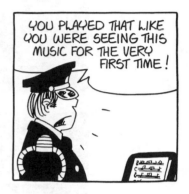

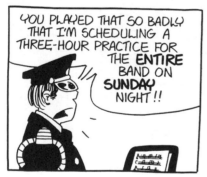

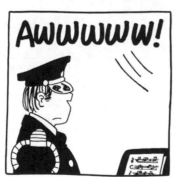

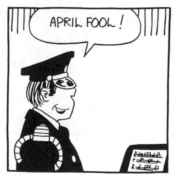

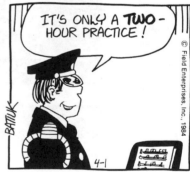

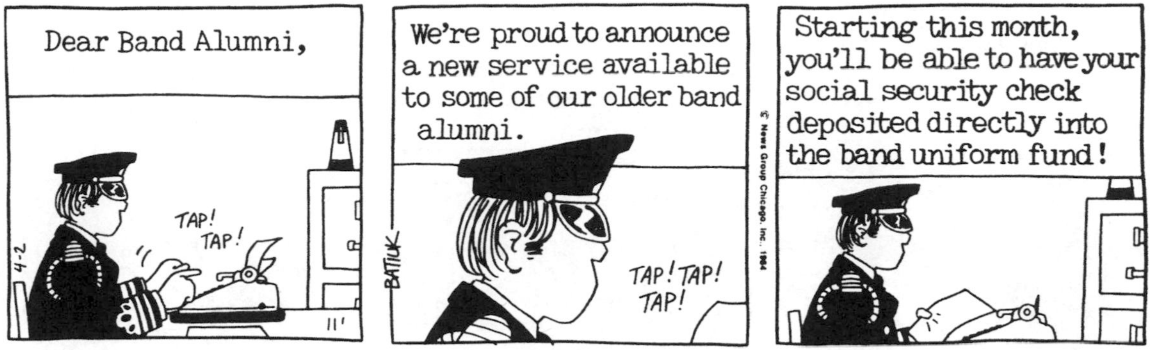
Dear Band Alumni,
TAP! TAP!
We're proud to announce a new service available to some of our older band alumni.
TAP! TAP! TAP!
BATIUK
© News Group Chicago, Inc., 1984
Starting this month, you'll be able to have your social security check deposited directly into the band uniform fund!

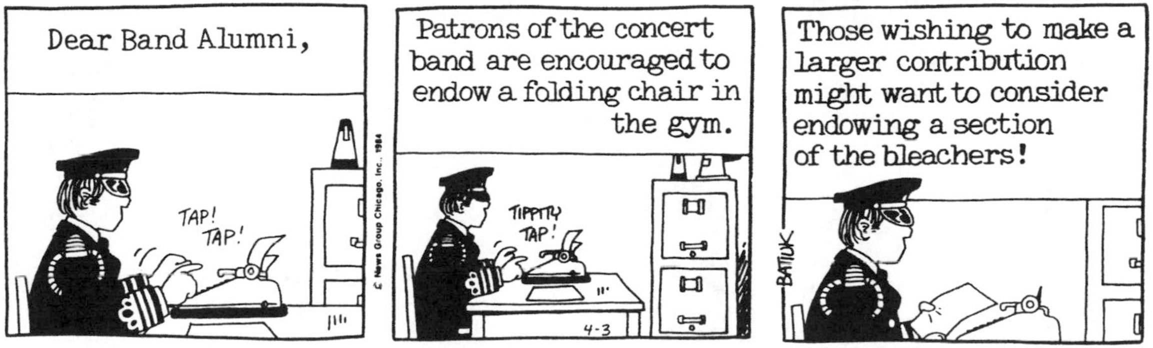
Dear Band Alumni,
TAP! TAP!
© News Group Chicago, Inc., 1984
Patrons of the concert band are encouraged to endow a folding chair in the gym.
TIPPITY TAP!
Those wishing to make a larger contribution might want to consider endowing a section of the bleachers!
BATIUK

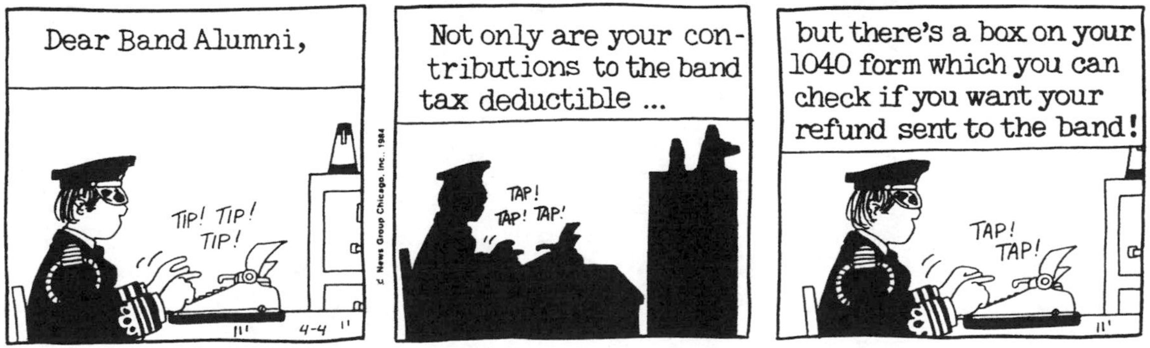
Dear Band Alumni,
TIP! TIP! TIP!
© News Group Chicago, Inc., 1984
Not only are your contributions to the band tax deductible ...
TAP! TAP! TAP!
but there's a box on your 1040 form which you can check if you want your refund sent to the band!
TAP! TAP!

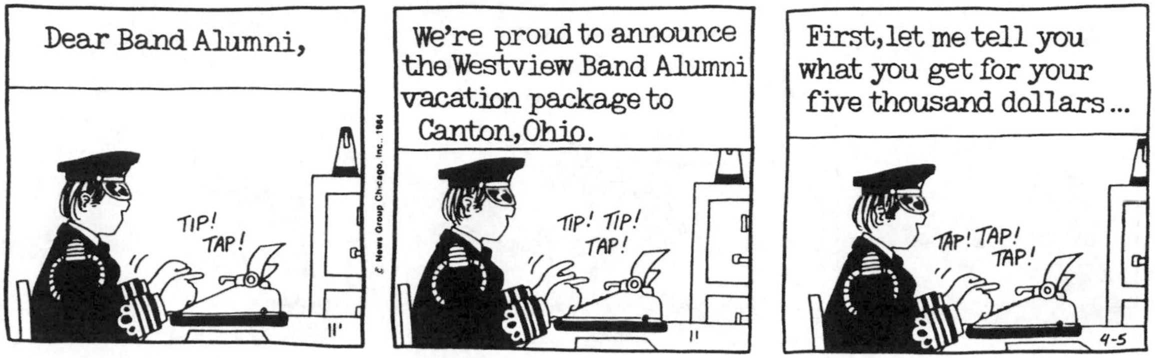
Dear Band Alumni,
TIP! TAP!
We're proud to announce the Westview Band Alumni vacation package to Canton, Ohio.
TIP! TIP! TAP!
First, let me tell you what you get for your five thousand dollars...
TAP! TAP! TAP!
4-5
© News Group Chicago, Inc., 1984

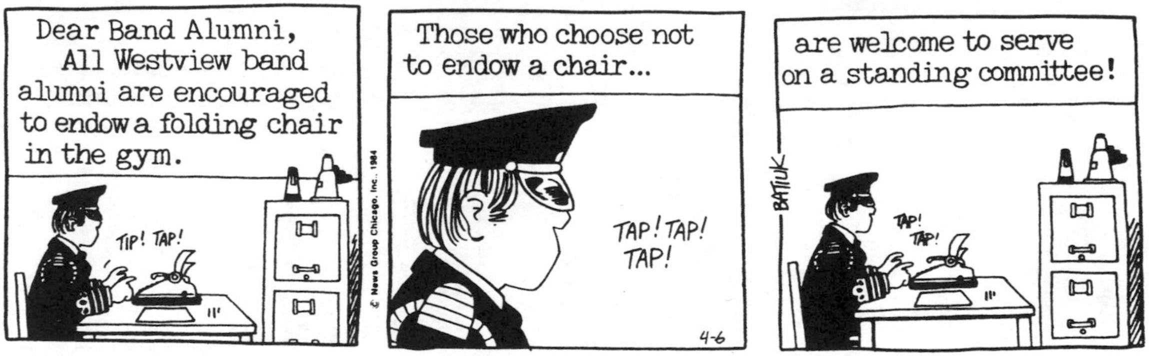
Dear Band Alumni, All Westview band alumni are encouraged to endow a folding chair in the gym.
TIP! TAP!
Those who choose not to endow a chair...
TAP! TAP! TAP!
4-6
are welcome to serve on a standing committee!
TAP! TAP!
BATIUK
© News Group Chicago, Inc., 1984

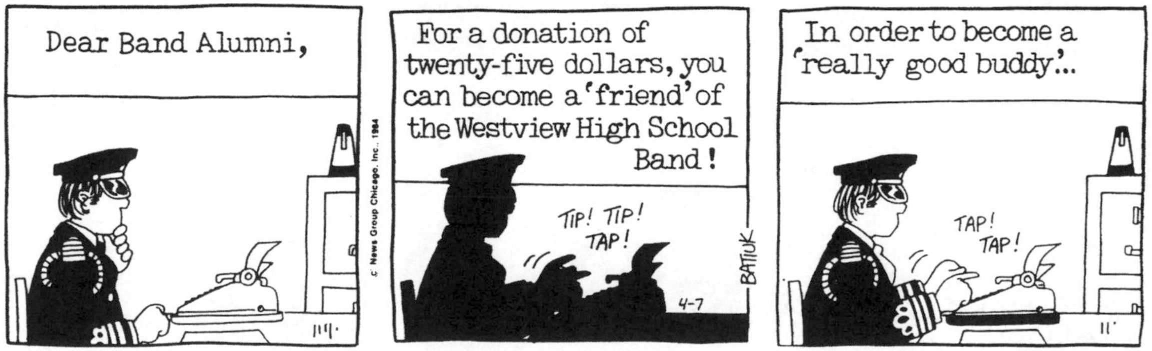
Dear Band Alumni,
For a donation of twenty-five dollars, you can become a 'friend' of the Westview High School Band!
TIP! TIP! TAP!
BATIUK
4-7
In order to become a 'really good buddy'...
TAP! TAP!
© News Group Chicago, Inc., 1984

FUNKY WINKERBEAN
BY TOM BATIUK
I THINK I MAY HAVE IT!
LET'S SEE HOW THIS SOUNDS...
WE THINK THINGS ARE JUST SENSATIONAL...
HERE AT TRI-COUNTY JOINT VOCATIONAL!
JUST BETWEEN YOU AND ME... THIS IS ONE ALMA MATER I NEVER SHOULD HAVE AGREED TO WRITE!
4-8
BATIUK
© Field Enterprises, Inc., 1984

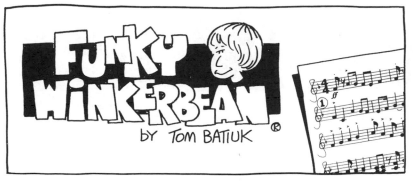

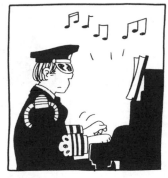

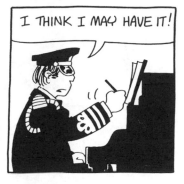

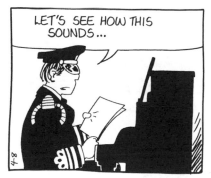

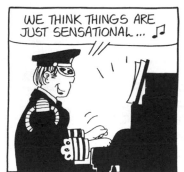

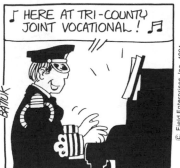

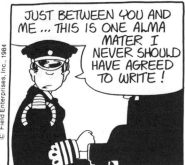

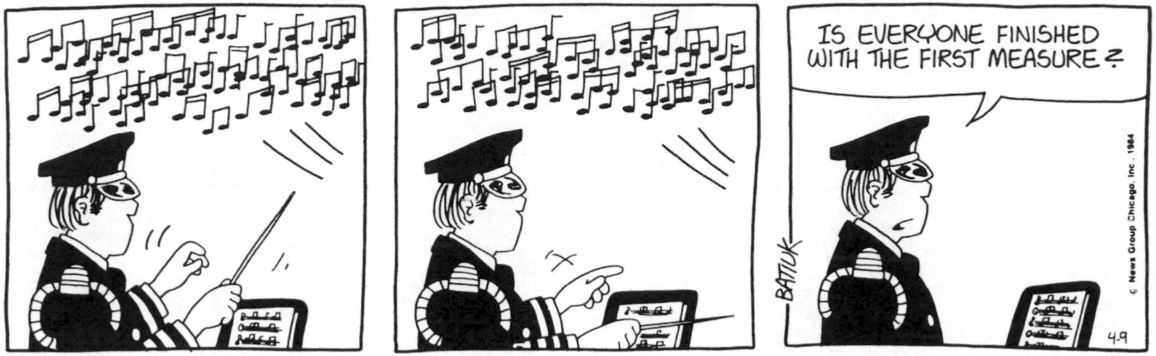
IS EVERYONE FINISHED
WITH THE FIRST MEASURE?
BATIUK
© News Group Chicago, Inc., 1984
4-9

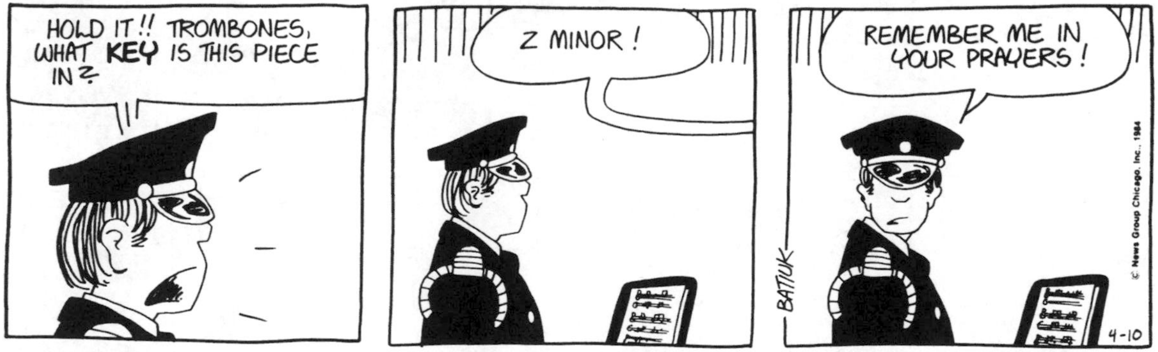
HOLD IT!! TROMBONES,
WHAT KEY IS THIS PIECE
IN?
Z MINOR!
REMEMBER ME IN
YOUR PRAYERS!
BATIUK
© News Group Chicago, Inc., 1984
4-10

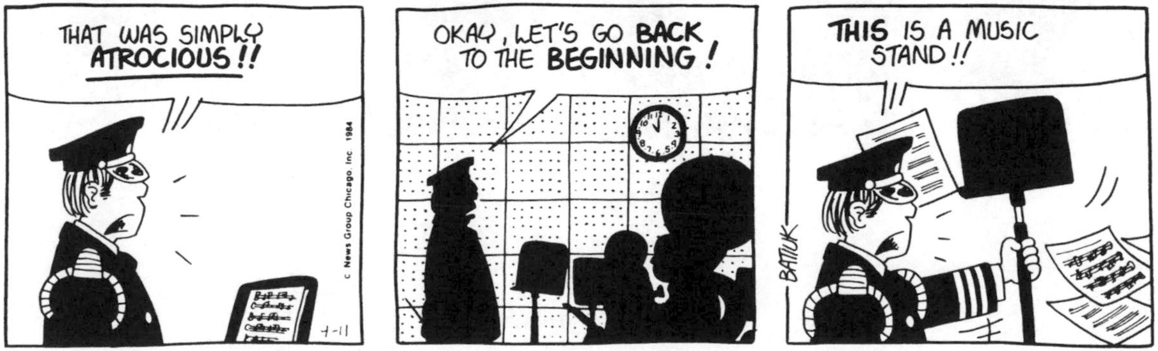
THAT WAS SIMPLY
ATROCIOUS!!
© News Group Chicago, Inc. 1984
4-11
OKAY, LET'S GO BACK
TO THE BEGINNING!
THIS IS A MUSIC
STAND!!
BATIUK

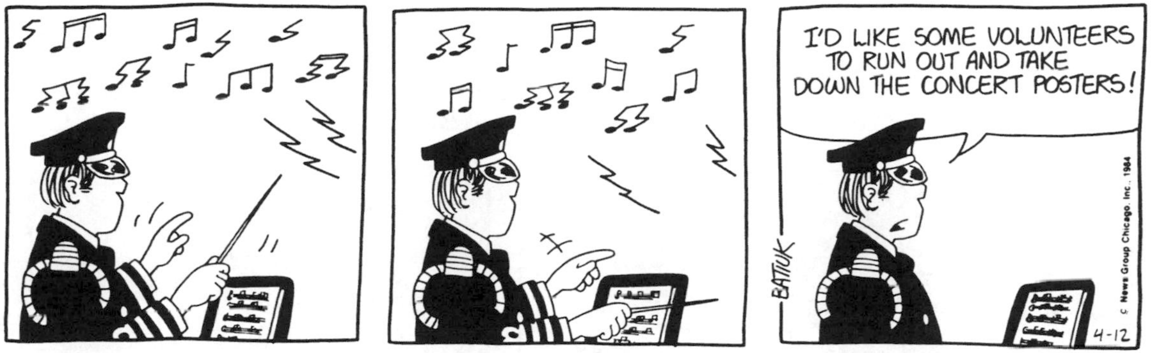
I'D LIKE SOME VOLUNTEERS TO RUN OUT AND TAKE DOWN THE CONCERT POSTERS!
BATIUK
© News Group Chicago, Inc. 1984
4-12

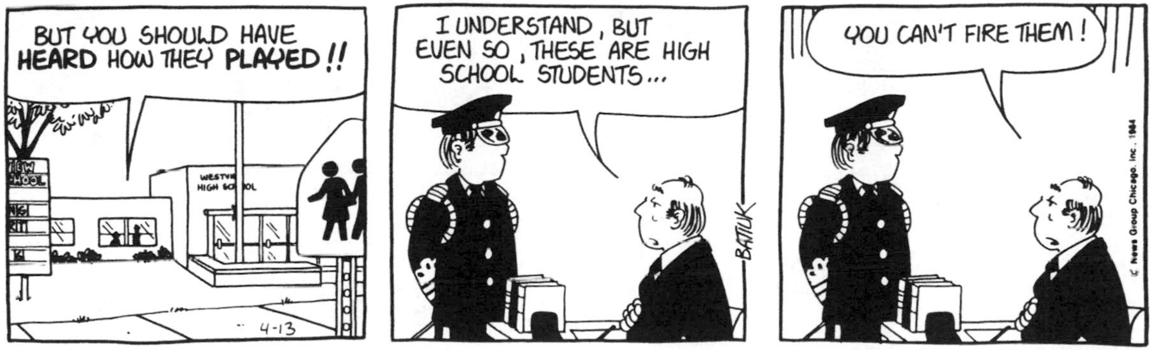
BUT YOU SHOULD HAVE **HEARD** HOW THEY **PLAYED**!!
WESTVIEW HIGH SCHOOL
4-13
I UNDERSTAND, BUT EVEN SO, THESE ARE HIGH SCHOOL STUDENTS...
BATIUK
YOU CAN'T FIRE THEM!
© News Group Chicago, Inc. 1984

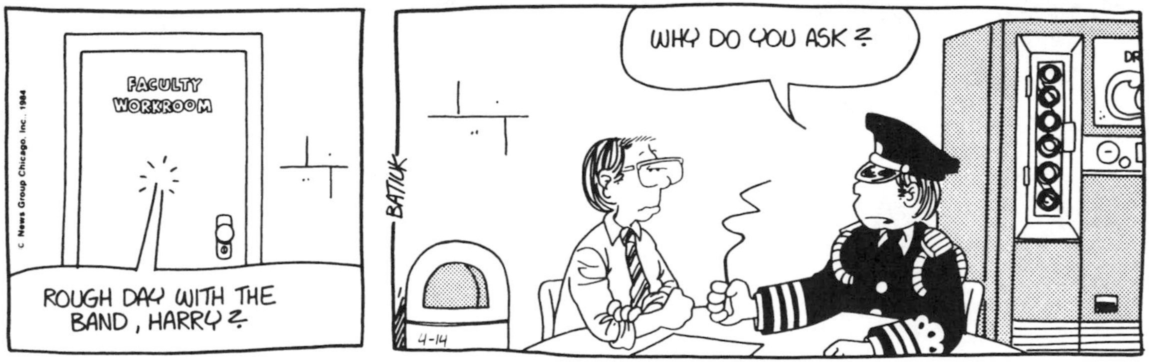
© News Group Chicago, Inc. 1984
FACULTY WORKROOM
ROUGH DAY WITH THE BAND, HARRY?
BATIUK
WHY DO YOU ASK?
4-14

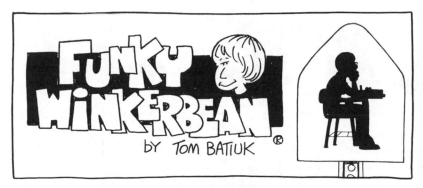

FUNKY WINKERBEAN
BY TOM BATIUK ®
TODAY, HALL MONITOR...
HALL MONITO
CHECK IN HER
TOMORROW, THE WORLD!
HALL MONITOR
CHECK IN HERE
ONE OF THE DUTIES OF A HALL MONITOR...
HALL MONITOR
CHECK IN HERE!
© News Group Chicago, Inc., 1984
IS MAKING SURE THAT NOBODY RUNS IN THE HALL!
BATIUK
HALL MONITOR
CHECK IN HERE!
IT USED TO BE TOUGH TO MAKE A CHARGE LIKE THAT STICK...
BEFORE WE GOT RADAR!
HALL MONITOR
CHECK IN HERE!
4-15

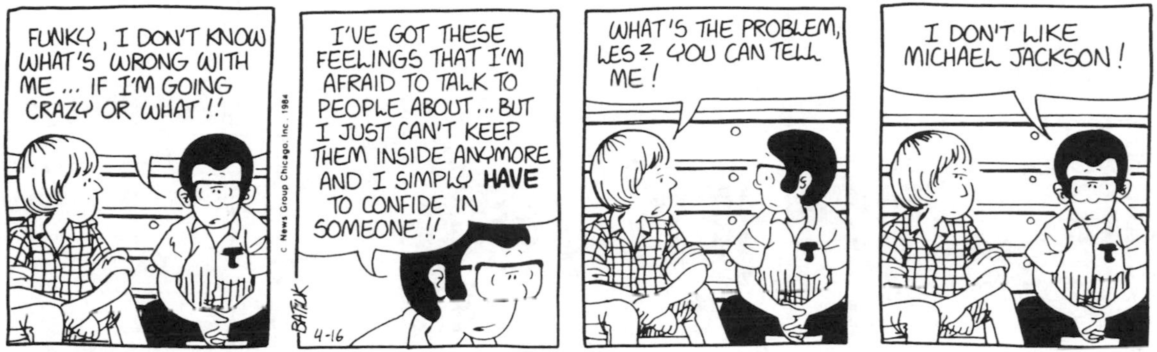
FUNKY, I DON'T KNOW WHAT'S WRONG WITH ME ... IF I'M GOING CRAZY OR WHAT!!
© News Group Chicago, Inc. 1984
I'VE GOT THESE FEELINGS THAT I'M AFRAID TO TALK TO PEOPLE ABOUT... BUT I JUST CAN'T KEEP THEM INSIDE ANYMORE AND I SIMPLY **HAVE** TO CONFIDE IN SOMEONE!!
BATIUK
4-16
WHAT'S THE PROBLEM, LES? YOU CAN TELL ME!
I DON'T LIKE MICHAEL JACKSON!

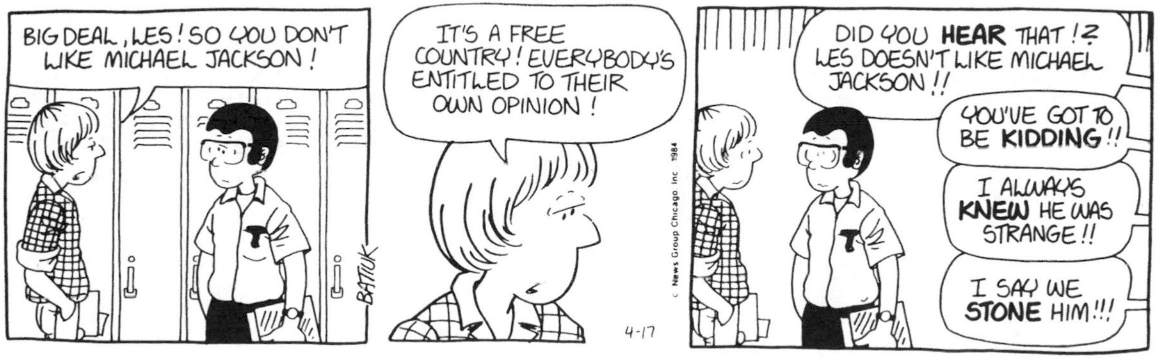
BIG DEAL, LES! SO YOU DON'T LIKE MICHAEL JACKSON!
BATIUK
IT'S A FREE COUNTRY! EVERYBODY'S ENTITLED TO THEIR OWN OPINION!
4-17
© News Group Chicago, Inc. 1984
DID YOU **HEAR** THAT!? LES DOESN'T LIKE MICHAEL JACKSON!!
YOU'VE GOT TO BE **KIDDING**!!
I ALWAYS **KNEW** HE WAS STRANGE!!
I SAY WE **STONE** HIM!!!

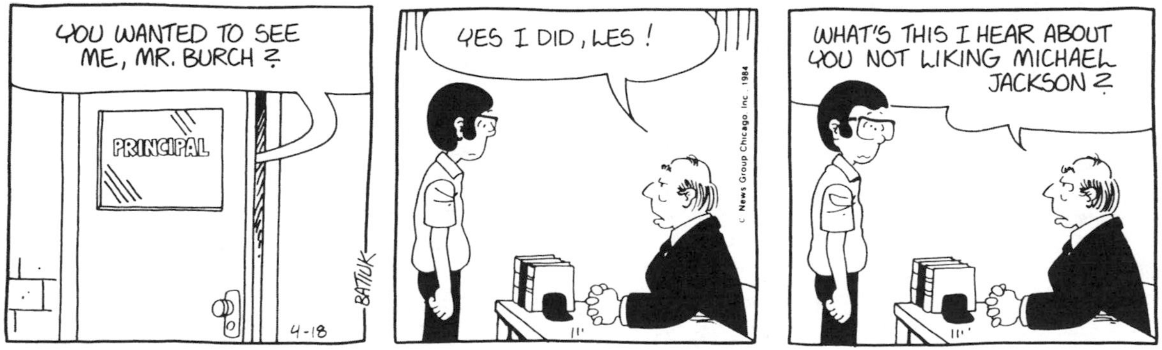
YOU WANTED TO SEE ME, MR. BURCH?
PRINCIPAL
BATIUK
4-18
YES I DID, LES!
© News Group Chicago, Inc. 1984
WHAT'S THIS I HEAR ABOUT YOU NOT LIKING MICHAEL JACKSON?

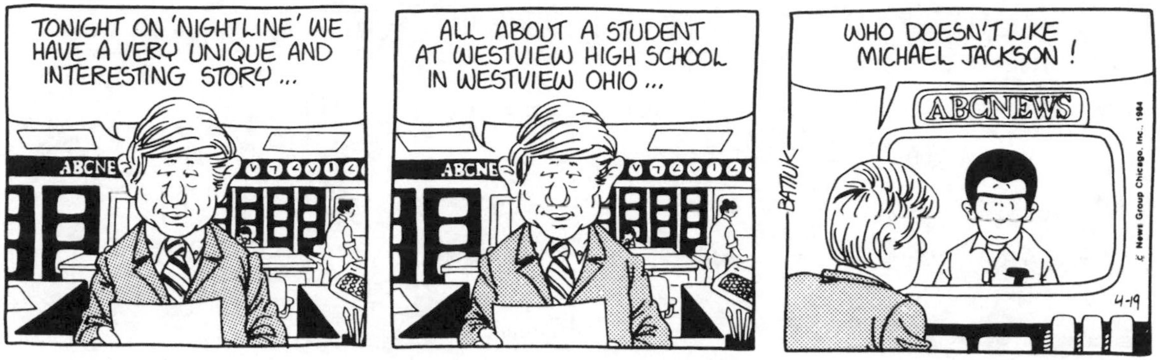
TONIGHT ON 'NIGHTLINE' WE HAVE A VERY UNIQUE AND INTERESTING STORY ...
ALL ABOUT A STUDENT AT WESTVIEW HIGH SCHOOL IN WESTVIEW OHIO ...
WHO DOESN'T LIKE MICHAEL JACKSON !
ABCNEWS
BATIUK
© News Group Chicago, Inc., 1984
4-19

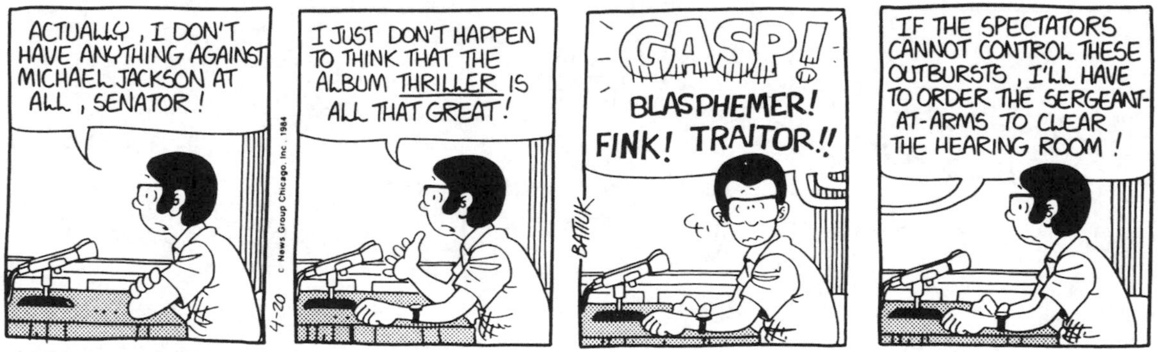
ACTUALLY , I DON'T HAVE ANYTHING AGAINST MICHAEL JACKSON AT ALL , SENATOR !
© News Group Chicago, Inc., 1984
4-20
I JUST DON'T HAPPEN TO THINK THAT THE ALBUM THRILLER IS ALL THAT GREAT !
GASP!
BLASPHEMER! FINK! TRAITOR!!
BATIUK
IF THE SPECTATORS CANNOT CONTROL THESE OUTBURSTS , I'LL HAVE TO ORDER THE SERGEANT-AT-ARMS TO CLEAR THE HEARING ROOM !

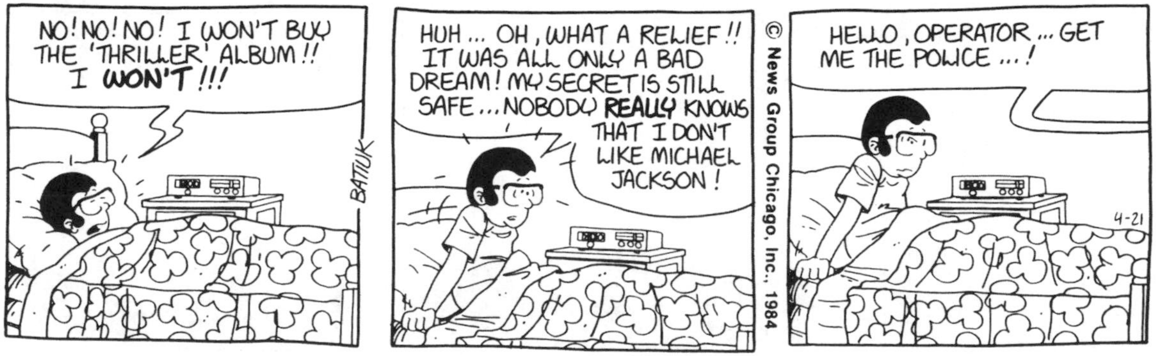
NO! NO! NO! I WON'T BUY THE 'THRILLER' ALBUM !! I **WON'T** !!!
BATIUK
HUH ... OH, WHAT A RELIEF !! IT WAS ALL ONLY A BAD DREAM! MY SECRET IS STILL SAFE ... NOBODY **REALLY** KNOWS THAT I DON'T LIKE MICHAEL JACKSON !
© News Group Chicago, Inc., 1984
HELLO, OPERATOR ... GET ME THE POLICE ... !
4-21

FUNKY WINKERBEAN
by TOM BATIUK
RESERVED FOR THE COACH
I'LL CATCH YOU GUYS LATER!
DRINK Cola
© News Group Chicago, Inc., 1984
THERE GOES THE COACH WITH ANOTHER FILM!
BATIUK
DOES HE SHOW ONE **EVERY** DAY?
4-22
UH, HUH! IF THE ELECTRICITY EVER WENT OUT, HE WOULDN'T BE ABLE TO HOLD CLASS!
DRINK Cola

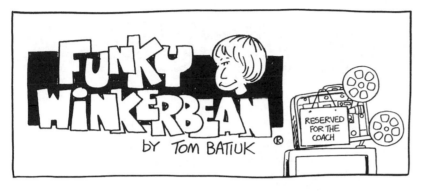

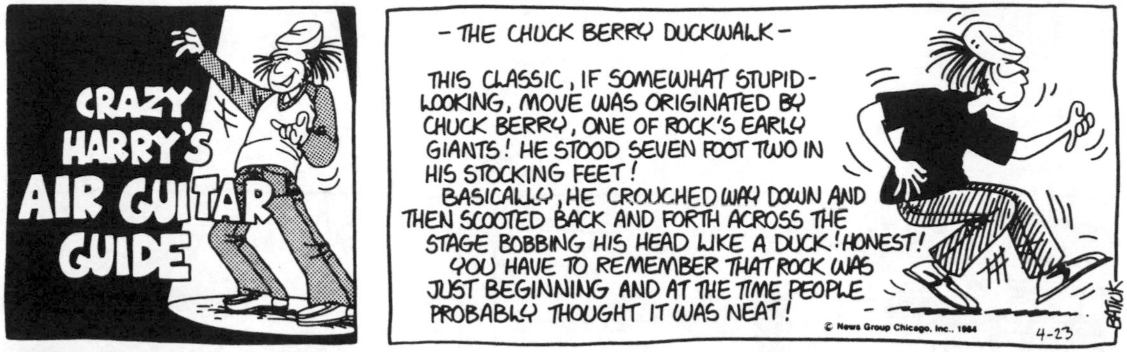

CRAZY HARRY'S AIR GUITAR GUIDE

- THE CHUCK BERRY DUCKWALK -

THIS CLASSIC, IF SOMEWHAT STUPID-LOOKING, MOVE WAS ORIGINATED BY CHUCK BERRY, ONE OF ROCK'S EARLY GIANTS! HE STOOD SEVEN FOOT TWO IN HIS STOCKING FEET!

BASICALLY, HE CROUCHED WAY DOWN AND THEN SCOOTED BACK AND FORTH ACROSS THE STAGE BOBBING HIS HEAD LIKE A DUCK! HONEST!

YOU HAVE TO REMEMBER THAT ROCK WAS JUST BEGINNING AND AT THE TIME PEOPLE PROBABLY THOUGHT IT WAS NEAT!

© News Group Chicago, Inc., 1984   4-23   BATIUK

CRAZY HARRY'S AIR GUITAR GUIDE

- THE TOWNSHEND TWO-STEP -
(A.K.A. THE JOAN JETT JUMP)

THIS EXCITING AIR GUITAR LEAP GETS ITS NAME FROM ITS MOST FAMOUS PRACTITIONER, PETE TOWNSHEND OF THE WHO. WHAT AT FIRST GLANCE APPEARS TO BE A MOST DYNAMIC AND DIFFICULT MOVE BECOMES RELATIVELY SIMPLE ONCE YOU REALIZE THAT IT'S NOTHING MORE THAN THE BASIC CHUCK BERRY DUCKWALK* PERFORMED SEVERAL FEET OFF THE GROUND.

THE PROPER PAINED GRIMACE SHOWS YOU HAVE THE TORTURED SOUL OF A TRUE ARTIST... EITHER THAT OR YOU'VE JUST PULLED A HAMSTRING!

* SEE MONDAY'S STRIP

© News Group Chicago, Inc., 1984   BATIUK 4-24

CRAZY HARRY'S AIR GUITAR GUIDE

- THE SPRINGSTEEN STRADDLE -

THIS MOVE WAS FIRST DEVELOPED BY BRUCE SPRINGSTEEN AT THE ROXY IN L.A. IN 1978. AS HE WAS MOVING ACROSS THE STAGE, THE NECK OF HIS FENDER TELECASTER GUITAR CAME IN CONTACT WITH A LIVE MICROPHONE WITH FRAYED WIRING.

THE AUDIENCE GOT A REALLY BIG CHARGE OUT OF IT, BUT NOT AS BIG AS BRUCE DID!

© News Group Chicago, Inc., 1984   BATIUK   4-25

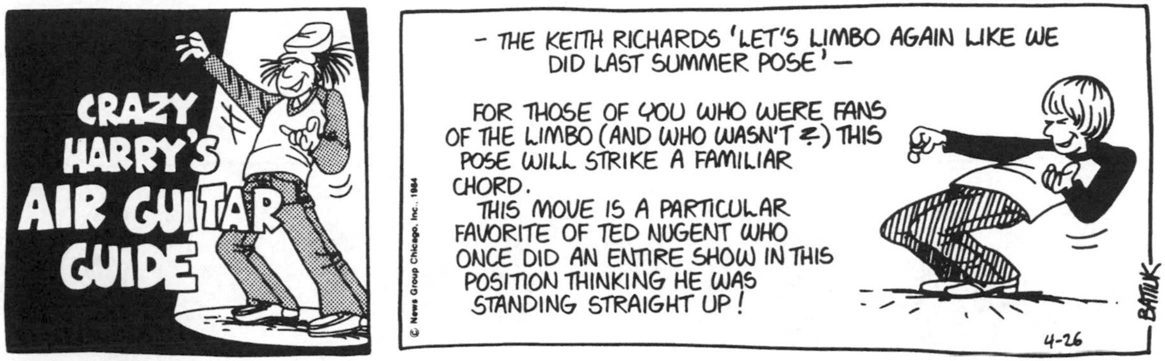
CRAZY HARRY'S AIR GUITAR GUIDE
- THE KEITH RICHARDS 'LET'S LIMBO AGAIN LIKE WE DID LAST SUMMER POSE' -
FOR THOSE OF YOU WHO WERE FANS OF THE LIMBO (AND WHO WASN'T?) THIS POSE WILL STRIKE A FAMILIAR CHORD.
THIS MOVE IS A PARTICULAR FAVORITE OF TED NUGENT WHO ONCE DID AN ENTIRE SHOW IN THIS POSITION THINKING HE WAS STANDING STRAIGHT UP!
© News Group Chicago, Inc., 1984
BATIUK
4-26

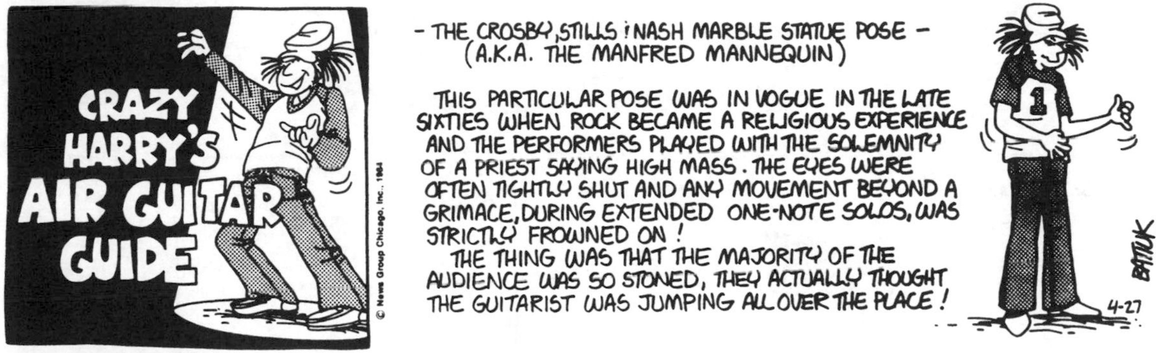
CRAZY HARRY'S AIR GUITAR GUIDE
- THE CROSBY, STILLS & NASH MARBLE STATUE POSE -
(A.K.A. THE MANFRED MANNEQUIN)
THIS PARTICULAR POSE WAS IN VOGUE IN THE LATE SIXTIES WHEN ROCK BECAME A RELIGIOUS EXPERIENCE AND THE PERFORMERS PLAYED WITH THE SOLEMNITY OF A PRIEST SAYING HIGH MASS. THE EYES WERE OFTEN TIGHTLY SHUT AND ANY MOVEMENT BEYOND A GRIMACE, DURING EXTENDED ONE-NOTE SOLOS, WAS STRICTLY FROWNED ON!
THE THING WAS THAT THE MAJORITY OF THE AUDIENCE WAS SO STONED, THEY ACTUALLY THOUGHT THE GUITARIST WAS JUMPING ALL OVER THE PLACE!
© News Group Chicago, Inc., 1984
BATIUK
4-27

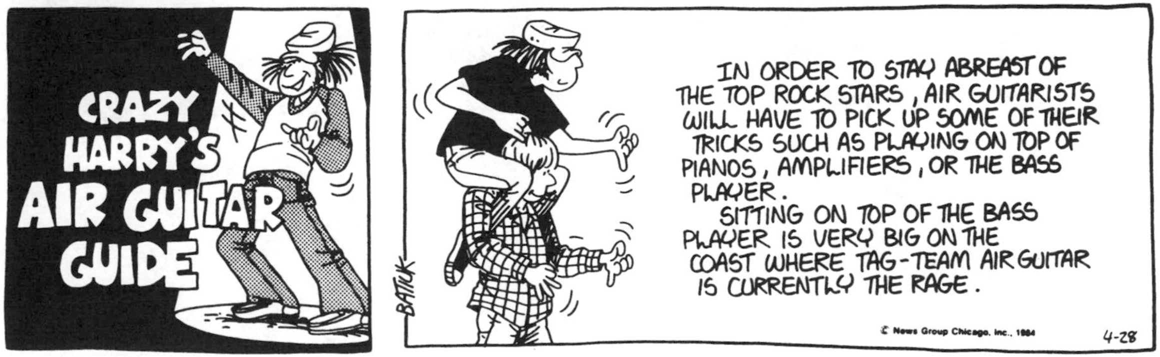
CRAZY HARRY'S AIR GUITAR GUIDE
IN ORDER TO STAY ABREAST OF THE TOP ROCK STARS, AIR GUITARISTS WILL HAVE TO PICK UP SOME OF THEIR TRICKS SUCH AS PLAYING ON TOP OF PIANOS, AMPLIFIERS, OR THE BASS PLAYER.
SITTING ON TOP OF THE BASS PLAYER IS VERY BIG ON THE COAST WHERE TAG-TEAM AIR GUITAR IS CURRENTLY THE RAGE.
BATIUK
© News Group Chicago, Inc., 1984
4-28

FUNKY WINKERBEAN
BY TOM BATIUK
BAND ROOM
© News Group Chicago, Inc., 1984
BATIUK
I THINK CONGRATULATIONS ARE DEFINITELY IN ORDER FOR THE TROMBONES ...
FOR FINISHING FIRST!
4-29

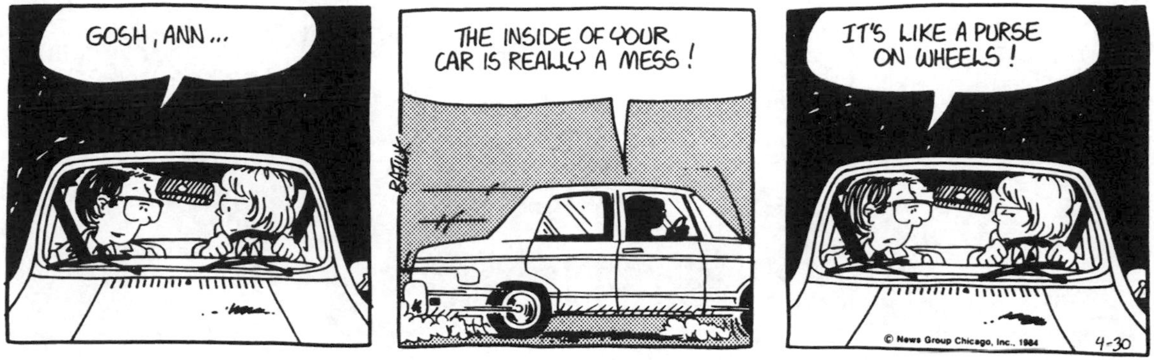
GOSH, ANN...
THE INSIDE OF YOUR CAR IS REALLY A MESS!
BATIUK
IT'S LIKE A PURSE ON WHEELS!
© News Group Chicago, Inc., 1984
4-30

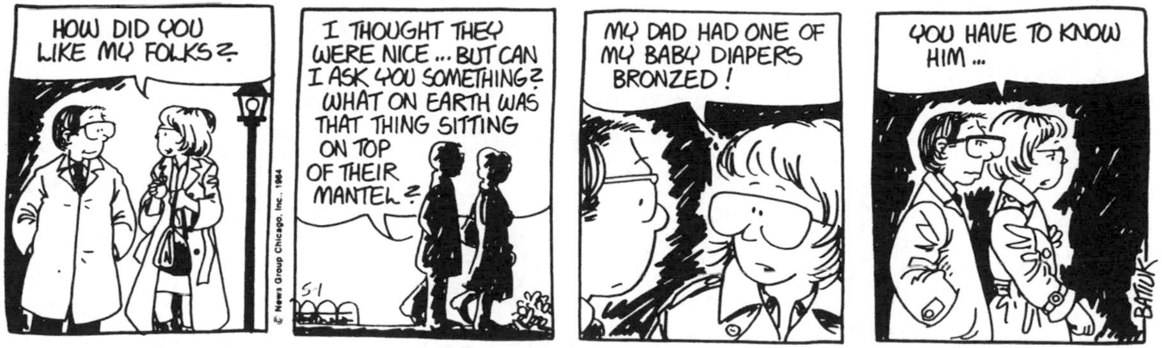
HOW DID YOU LIKE MY FOLKS?
© News Group Chicago, Inc., 1984
I THOUGHT THEY WERE NICE ... BUT CAN I ASK YOU SOMETHING? WHAT ON EARTH WAS THAT THING SITTING ON TOP OF THEIR MANTEL?
5-1
MY DAD HAD ONE OF MY BABY DIAPERS BRONZED!
YOU HAVE TO KNOW HIM...
BATIUK

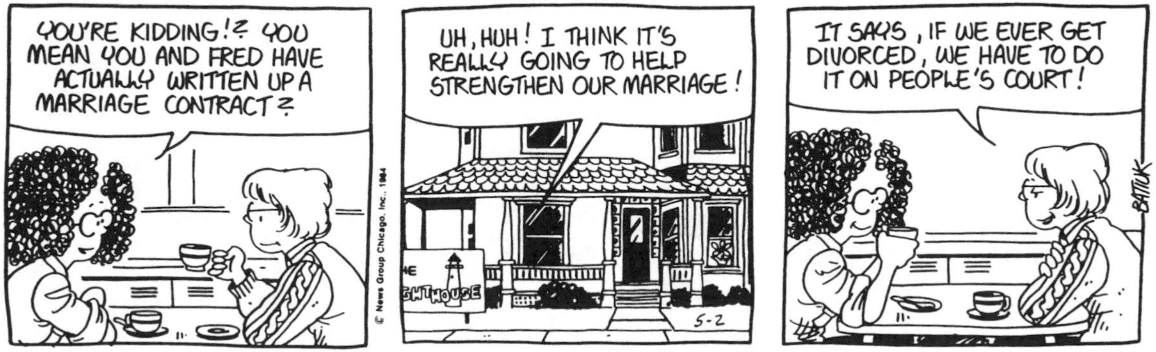
YOU'RE KIDDING!? YOU MEAN YOU AND FRED HAVE ACTUALLY WRITTEN UP A MARRIAGE CONTRACT?
© News Group Chicago, Inc., 1984
UH, HUH! I THINK IT'S REALLY GOING TO HELP STRENGTHEN OUR MARRIAGE!
5-2
IT SAYS, IF WE EVER GET DIVORCED, WE HAVE TO DO IT ON PEOPLE'S COURT!
BATIUK

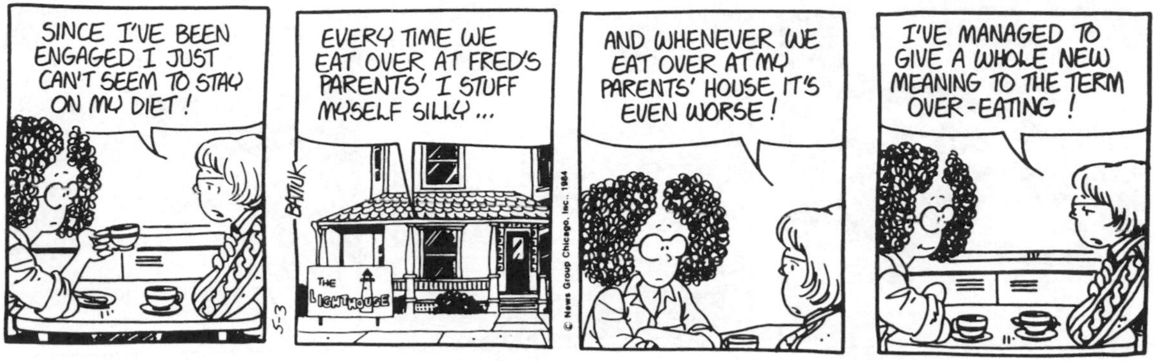
SINCE I'VE BEEN ENGAGED I JUST CAN'T SEEM TO STAY ON MY DIET!
EVERY TIME WE EAT OVER AT FRED'S PARENTS' I STUFF MYSELF SILLY...
THE LIGHTHOUSE
BATIUK
5-3
© News Group Chicago, Inc., 1984
AND WHENEVER WE EAT OVER AT MY PARENTS' HOUSE IT'S EVEN WORSE!
I'VE MANAGED TO GIVE A WHOLE NEW MEANING TO THE TERM OVER-EATING!

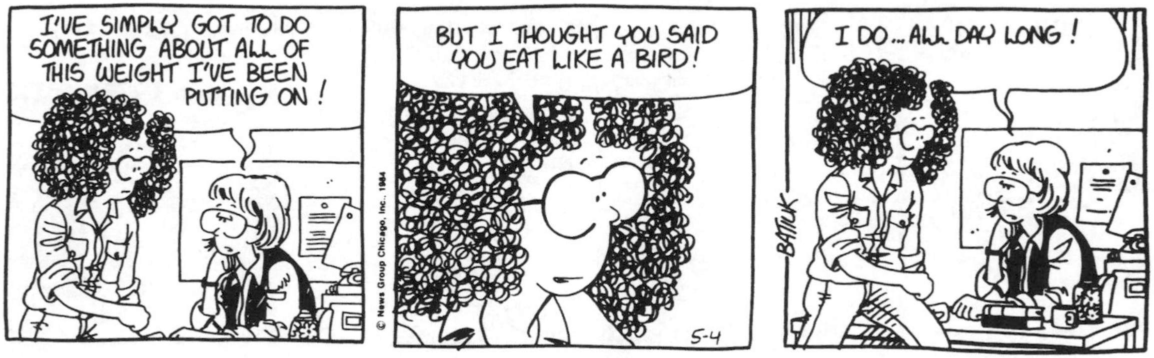
I'VE SIMPLY GOT TO DO SOMETHING ABOUT ALL OF THIS WEIGHT I'VE BEEN PUTTING ON!
© News Group Chicago, Inc., 1984
BUT I THOUGHT YOU SAID YOU EAT LIKE A BIRD!
5-4
I DO... ALL DAY LONG!
BATIUK

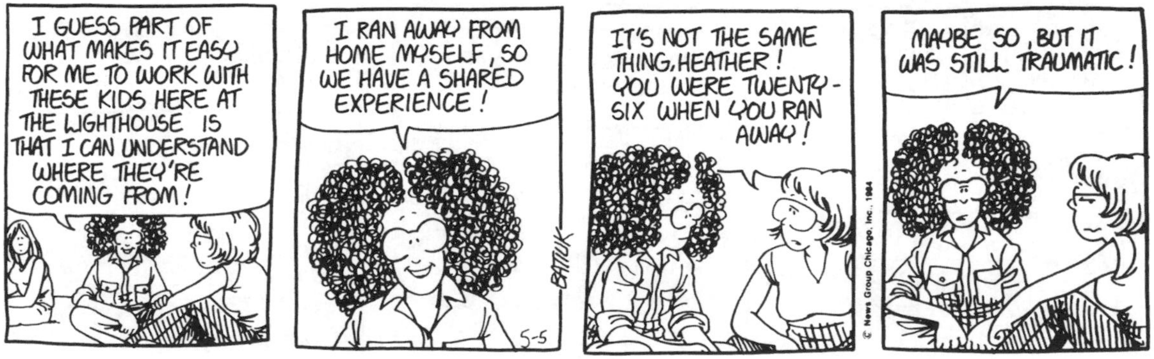
I GUESS PART OF WHAT MAKES IT EASY FOR ME TO WORK WITH THESE KIDS HERE AT THE LIGHTHOUSE IS THAT I CAN UNDERSTAND WHERE THEY'RE COMING FROM!
I RAN AWAY FROM HOME MYSELF, SO WE HAVE A SHARED EXPERIENCE!
BATIUK
5-5
IT'S NOT THE SAME THING, HEATHER! YOU WERE TWENTY-SIX WHEN YOU RAN AWAY!
© News Group Chicago, Inc., 1984
MAYBE SO, BUT IT WAS STILL TRAUMATIC!

FUNKY WINKERBEAN
by TOM BATIUK ®
© News Group Chicago, Inc., 1984
SIGH NOTHING WORKS ON THIS PAINT!
WELL, AT LEAST IT'S IN THE SCHOOL COLORS!
I HATE THE PRINCIPAL
WE'VE TRIED EVERYTHING AND WE STILL CAN'T CLEAN THIS SPRAY PAINT OFF THE FRONT OF THE BUILDING!
5-6
BATIUK
HERE! TRY A LITTLE OF THIS STUFF ON IT!
IT TAKES THE PAINT RIGHT OFF!! WHAT IS IT!?
IT'S SOME OF THE SHAMPOO THE BAND SOLD LAST FALL!
THIS WORKS GREAT!!
I'D APPRECIATE IT IF YOU DIDN'T MENTION THIS TO ANYONE!

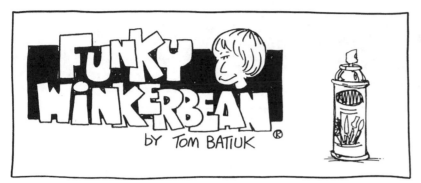

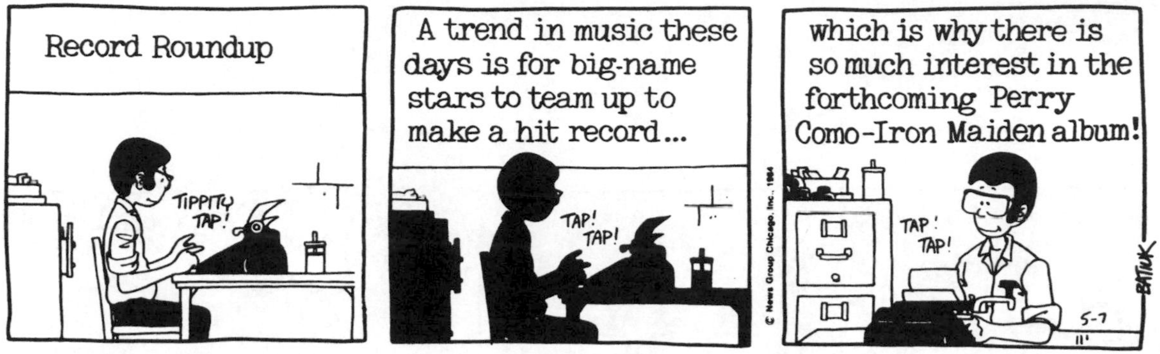
Record Roundup
TIPPITY TAP!
A trend in music these days is for big-name stars to team up to make a hit record...
TAP! TAP!
which is why there is so much interest in the forthcoming Perry Como-Iron Maiden album!
TAP! TAP!
© News Group Chicago, Inc., 1984
BATIUK
5-7

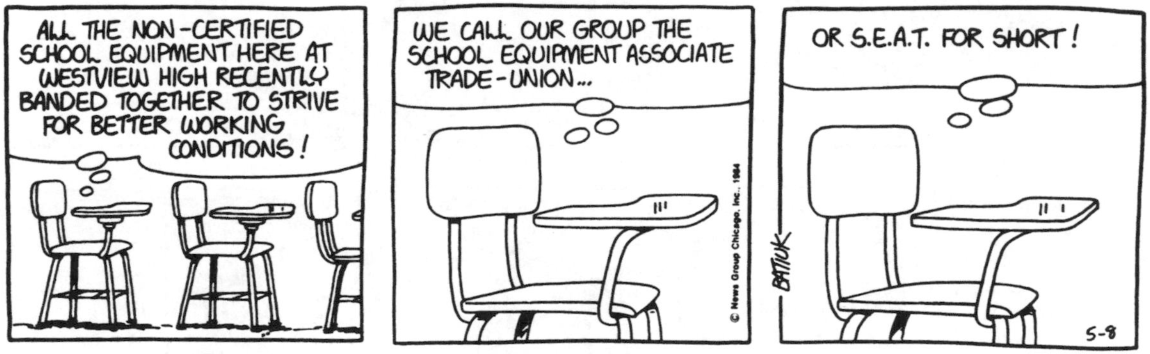
ALL THE NON-CERTIFIED SCHOOL EQUIPMENT HERE AT WESTVIEW HIGH RECENTLY BANDED TOGETHER TO STRIVE FOR BETTER WORKING CONDITIONS!
WE CALL OUR GROUP THE SCHOOL EQUIPMENT ASSOCIATE TRADE-UNION...
© News Group Chicago, Inc., 1984
BATIUK
OR S.E.A.T. FOR SHORT!
5-8

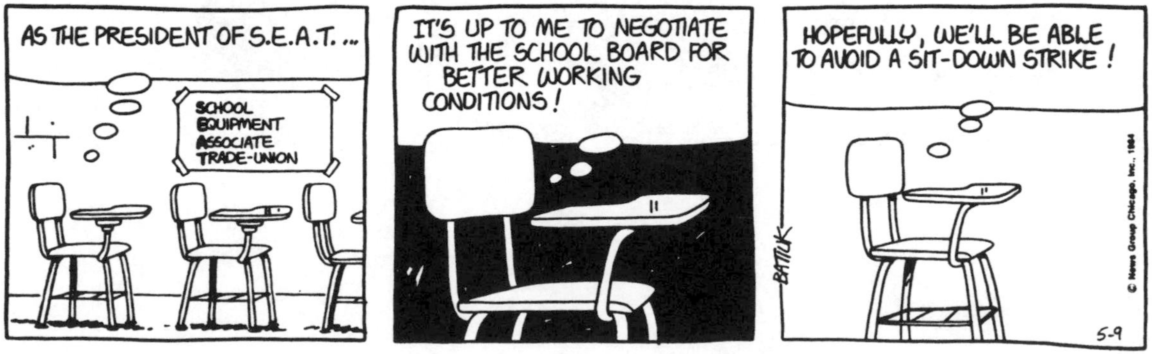
AS THE PRESIDENT OF S.E.A.T. ...
SCHOOL EQUIPMENT ASSOCIATE TRADE-UNION
IT'S UP TO ME TO NEGOTIATE WITH THE SCHOOL BOARD FOR BETTER WORKING CONDITIONS!
BATIUK
HOPEFULLY, WE'LL BE ABLE TO AVOID A SIT-DOWN STRIKE!
© News Group Chicago, Inc., 1984
5-9

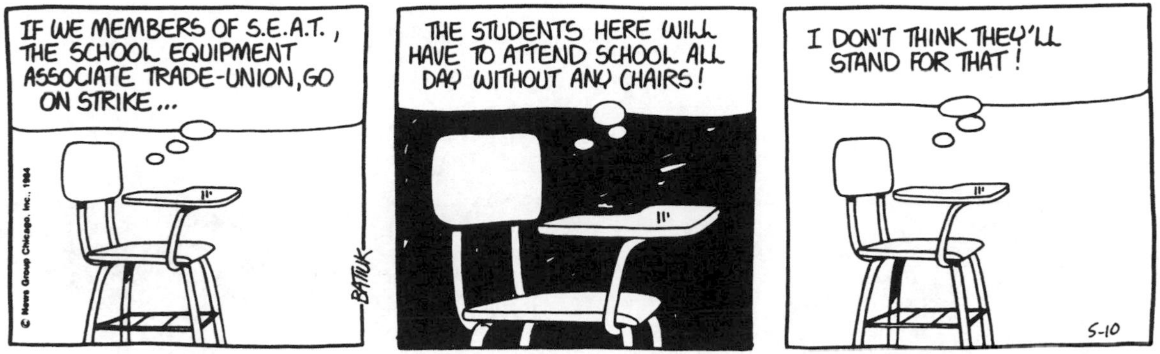
IF WE MEMBERS OF S.E.A.T., THE SCHOOL EQUIPMENT ASSOCIATE TRADE-UNION, GO ON STRIKE...
© News Group Chicago, Inc., 1984
BATIUK
THE STUDENTS HERE WILL HAVE TO ATTEND SCHOOL ALL DAY WITHOUT ANY CHAIRS!
I DON'T THINK THEY'LL STAND FOR THAT!
5-10

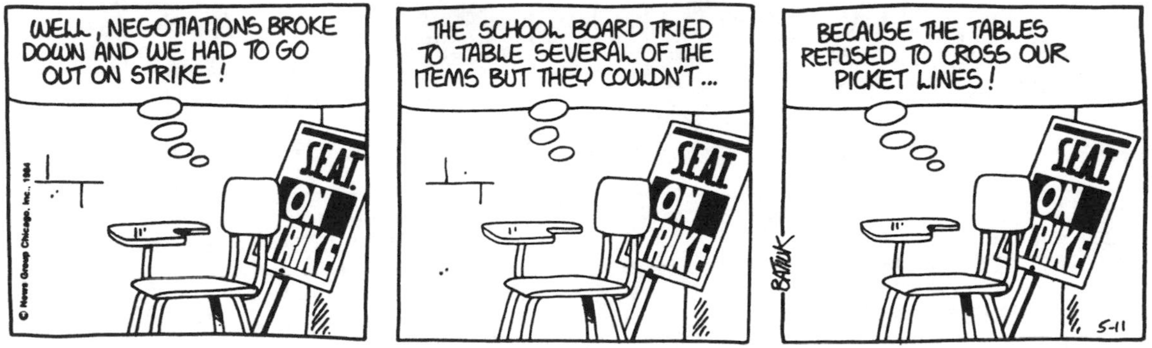
WELL, NEGOTIATIONS BROKE DOWN AND WE HAD TO GO OUT ON STRIKE!
© News Group Chicago, Inc., 1984
S.E.A.T. ON STRIKE
THE SCHOOL BOARD TRIED TO TABLE SEVERAL OF THE ITEMS BUT THEY COULDN'T...
BECAUSE THE TABLES REFUSED TO CROSS OUR PICKET LINES!
BATIUK
5-11

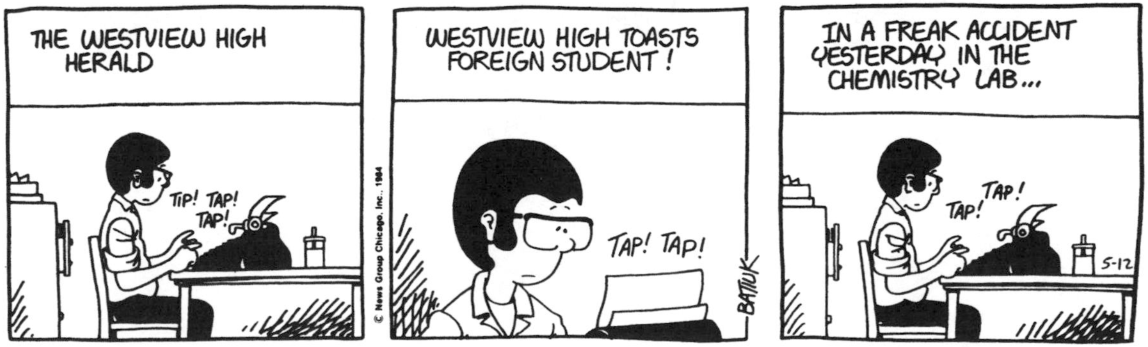
THE WESTVIEW HIGH HERALD
TIP! TAP! TAP!
WESTVIEW HIGH TOASTS FOREIGN STUDENT!
© News Group Chicago, Inc., 1984
TAP! TAP!
BATIUK
IN A FREAK ACCIDENT YESTERDAY IN THE CHEMISTRY LAB...
TAP! TAP!
5-12

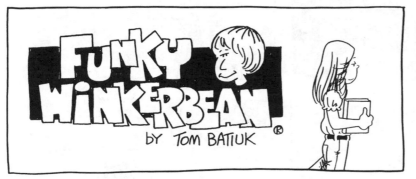

FUNKY WINKERBEAN
BY TOM BATIUK
HI, CINDY!
OH, OH...
HERE COMES LES! I JUST KNOW HE'S GOING TO ASK ME OUT! WHAT SHOULD I DO ?
JUST MAKE UP SOME KIND OF EXCUSE...
BUT, WHATEVER YOU TELL HIM, MAKE SURE YOU DON'T GIVE HIM ANY KIND OF HOPE AT ALL!
HE TAPES EVERYTHING YOU SAY!
CREEM
BATIUK
5-13
© News Group Chicago, Inc., 1984

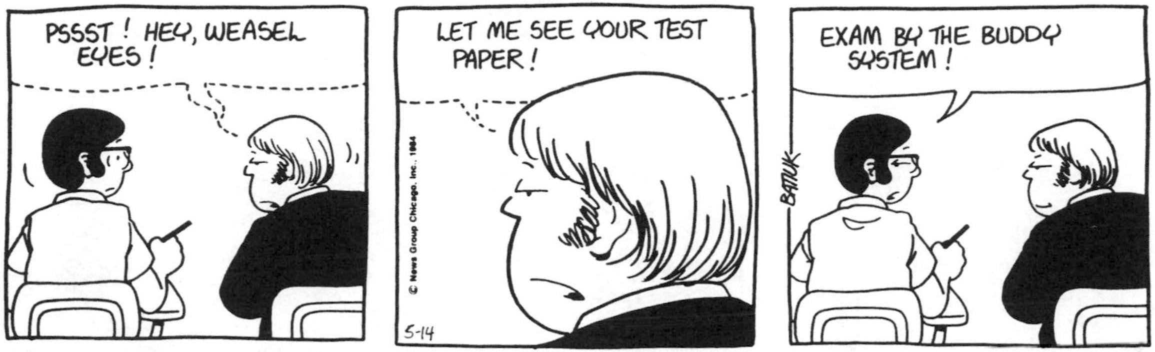
PSSST! HEY, WEASEL EYES!
LET ME SEE YOUR TEST PAPER!
EXAM BY THE BUDDY SYSTEM!

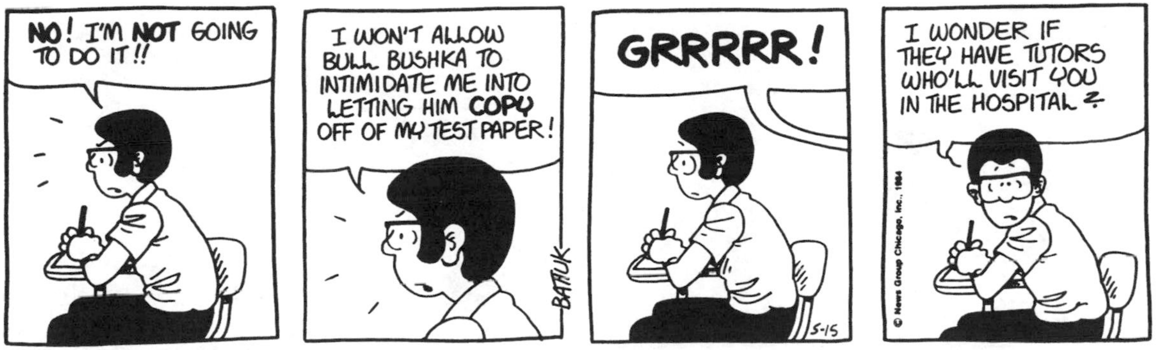
NO! I'M NOT GOING TO DO IT!!
I WON'T ALLOW BULL BUSHKA TO INTIMIDATE ME INTO LETTING HIM COPY OFF OF MY TEST PAPER!
GRRRRR!
I WONDER IF THEY HAVE TUTORS WHO'LL VISIT YOU IN THE HOSPITAL?

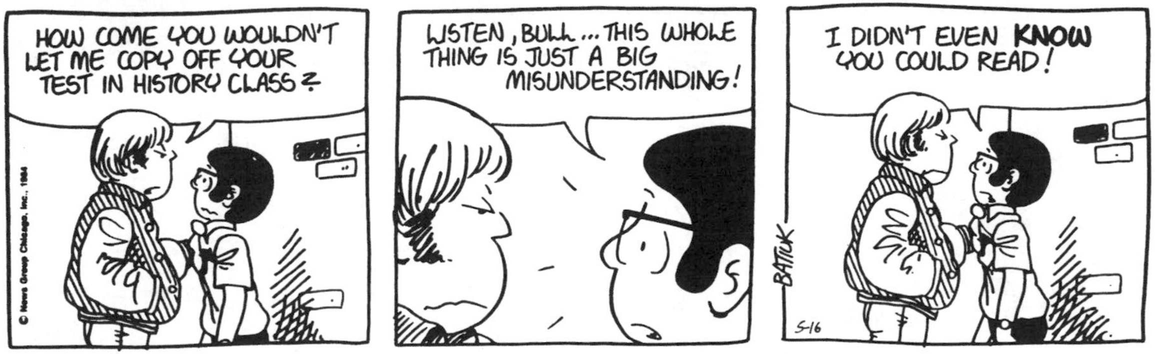
HOW COME YOU WOULDN'T LET ME COPY OFF YOUR TEST IN HISTORY CLASS?
LISTEN, BULL... THIS WHOLE THING IS JUST A BIG MISUNDERSTANDING!
I DIDN'T EVEN KNOW YOU COULD READ!

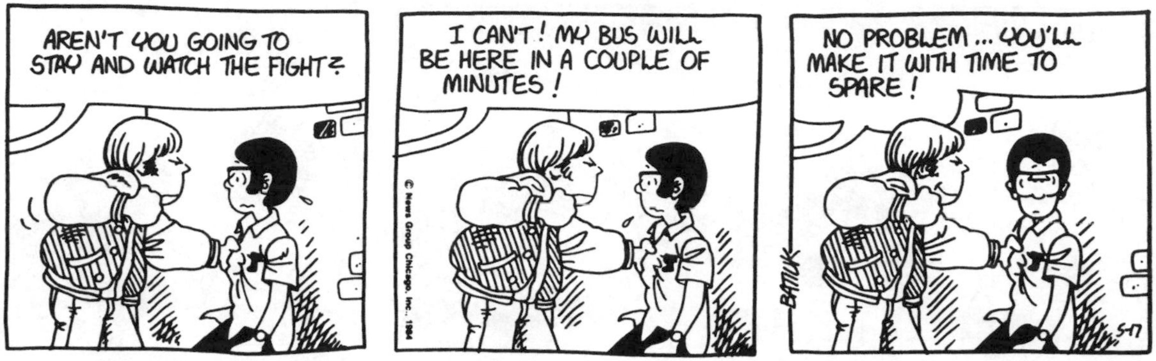
AREN'T YOU GOING TO STAY AND WATCH THE FIGHT?
I CAN'T! MY BUS WILL BE HERE IN A COUPLE OF MINUTES!
© News Group Chicago, Inc., 1984
NO PROBLEM ... YOU'LL MAKE IT WITH TIME TO SPARE!
BATIUK
5-17

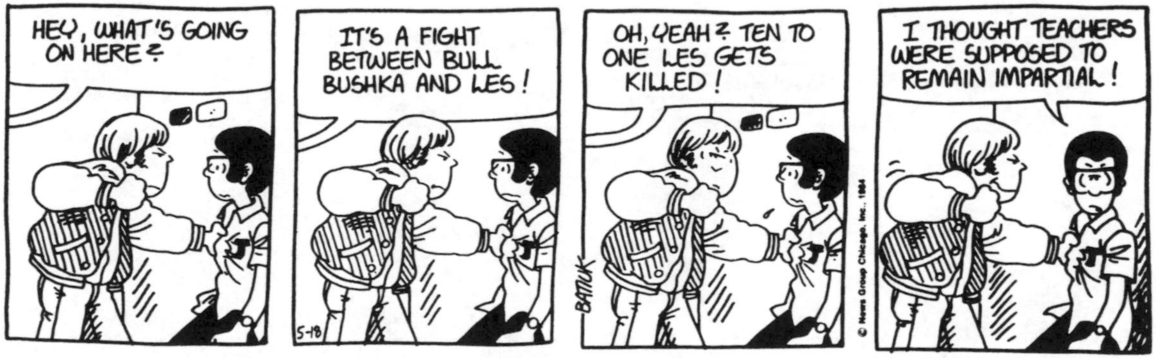
HEY, WHAT'S GOING ON HERE?
IT'S A FIGHT BETWEEN BULL BUSHKA AND LES!
5-18
OH, YEAH? TEN TO ONE LES GETS KILLED!
BATIUK
© News Group Chicago, Inc., 1984
I THOUGHT TEACHERS WERE SUPPOSED TO REMAIN IMPARTIAL!

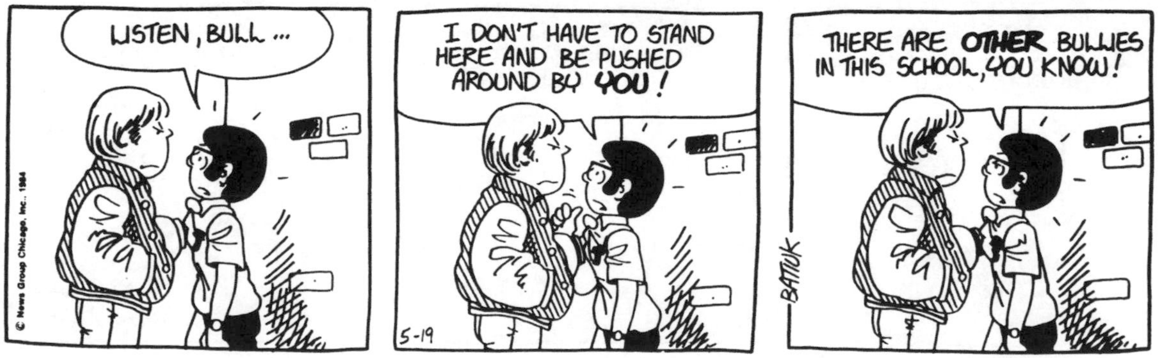
LISTEN, BULL ...
© News Group Chicago, Inc., 1984
I DON'T HAVE TO STAND HERE AND BE PUSHED AROUND BY YOU!
5-19
THERE ARE OTHER BULLIES IN THIS SCHOOL, YOU KNOW!
BATIUK

FUNKY WINKERBEAN ®
BY TOM BATIUK
DISMISSAL SLIP
Name
Date
Dismissed from at
To
at
Dismissed to at
at
Dismissed to
I'M SORRY, BARRY, BUT RULES ARE RULES!
YOU'RE WRITING UP ME ... BARRY BALDERMAN ... FOR NOT HAVING A HALL PASS!!?
BUT I'M THE PRESIDENT OF STUDENT COUNCIL, YEARBOOK EDITOR, SECRETARY OF THE NATIONAL HONOR SOCIETY, CHAIRMAN OF THE PROM COMMITTEE, CAPTAIN OF THE DEBATE TEAM, JUNIOR CLASS OFFICER, TREASURER OF THE PEP CLUB, AND LIBRARY AND OFFICE AIDE!!!
5-20
I KNOW!
BATIUK
© News Group Chicago, Inc., 1984

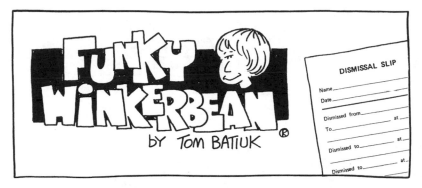

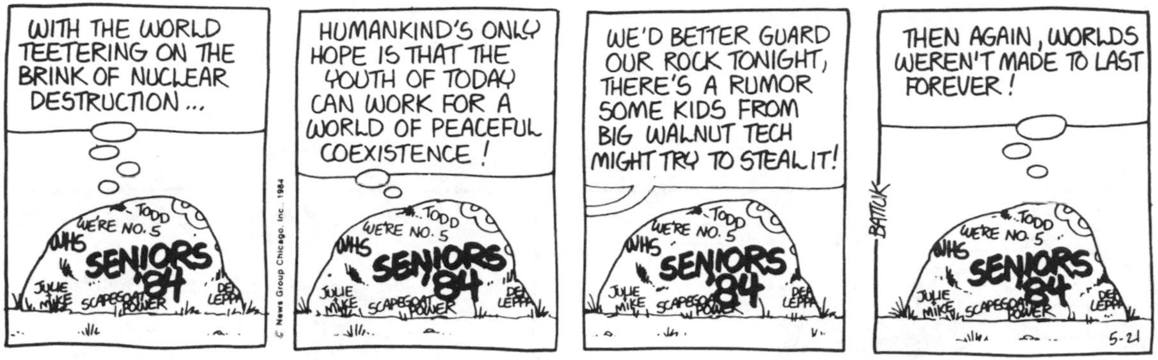
WITH THE WORLD TEETERING ON THE BRINK OF NUCLEAR DESTRUCTION ...
HUMANKIND'S ONLY HOPE IS THAT THE YOUTH OF TODAY CAN WORK FOR A WORLD OF PEACEFUL COEXISTENCE !
WE'D BETTER GUARD OUR ROCK TONIGHT, THERE'S A RUMOR SOME KIDS FROM BIG WALNUT TECH MIGHT TRY TO STEAL IT!
THEN AGAIN, WORLDS WEREN'T MADE TO LAST FOREVER !
BATIUK
5-21

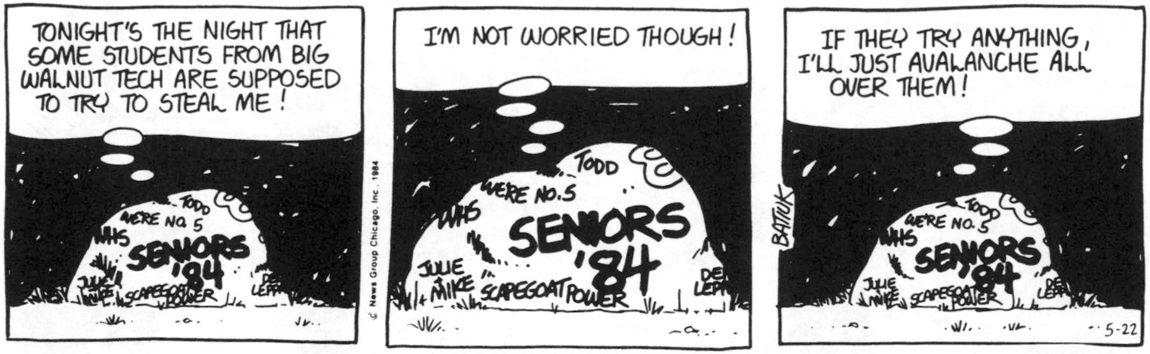
TONIGHT'S THE NIGHT THAT SOME STUDENTS FROM BIG WALNUT TECH ARE SUPPOSED TO TRY TO STEAL ME !
I'M NOT WORRIED THOUGH !
IF THEY TRY ANYTHING, I'LL JUST AVALANCHE ALL OVER THEM !
BATIUK
5-22

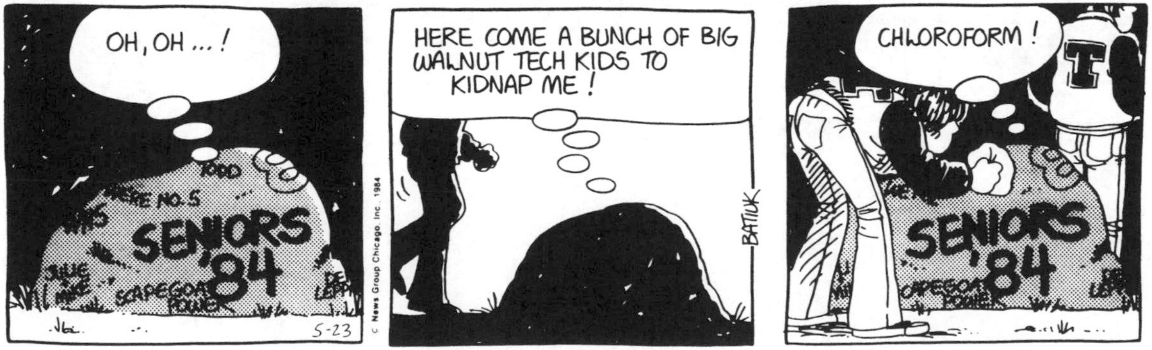
OH, OH ... !
5-23
HERE COME A BUNCH OF BIG WALNUT TECH KIDS TO KIDNAP ME !
BATIUK
CHLOROFORM !

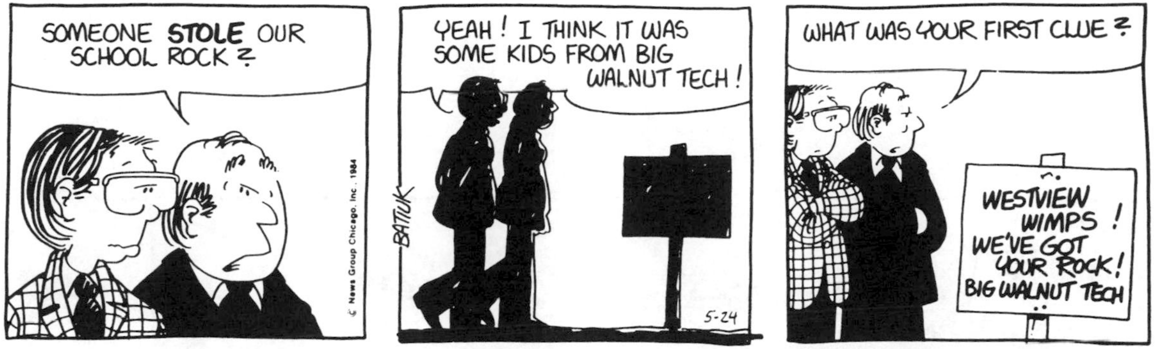
SOMEONE STOLE OUR SCHOOL ROCK?
YEAH! I THINK IT WAS SOME KIDS FROM BIG WALNUT TECH!
WHAT WAS YOUR FIRST CLUE?
WESTVIEW WIMPS! WE'VE GOT YOUR ROCK! BIG WALNUT TECH
© News Group Chicago, Inc. 1984
BATIUK
5-24

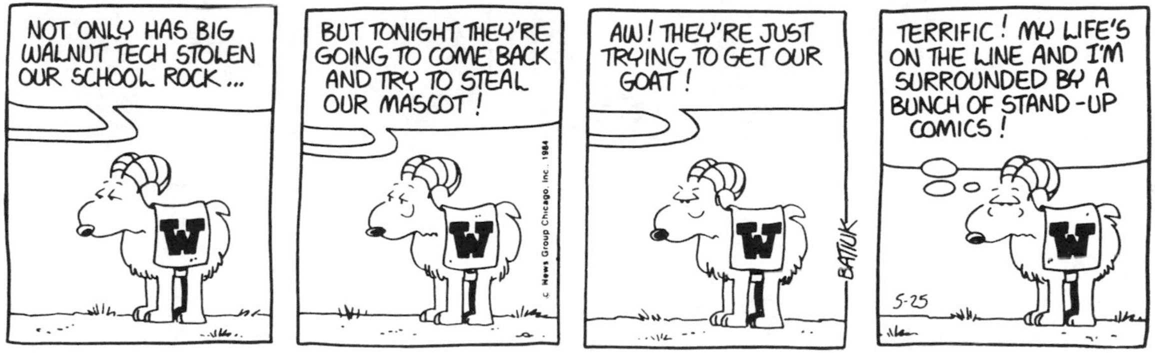
NOT ONLY HAS BIG WALNUT TECH STOLEN OUR SCHOOL ROCK...
BUT TONIGHT THEY'RE GOING TO COME BACK AND TRY TO STEAL OUR MASCOT!
AW! THEY'RE JUST TRYING TO GET OUR GOAT!
TERRIFIC! MY LIFE'S ON THE LINE AND I'M SURROUNDED BY A BUNCH OF STAND-UP COMICS!
W
© News Group Chicago, Inc. 1984
BATIUK
5-25

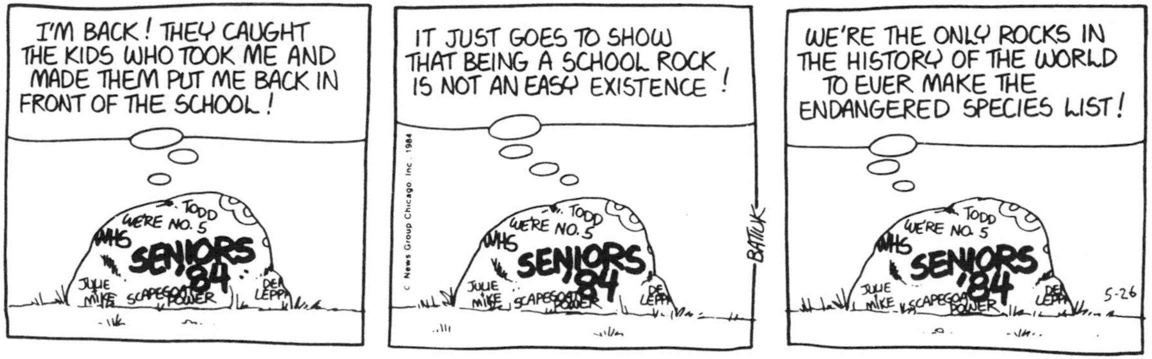
I'M BACK! THEY CAUGHT THE KIDS WHO TOOK ME AND MADE THEM PUT ME BACK IN FRONT OF THE SCHOOL!
IT JUST GOES TO SHOW THAT BEING A SCHOOL ROCK IS NOT AN EASY EXISTENCE!
WE'RE THE ONLY ROCKS IN THE HISTORY OF THE WORLD TO EVER MAKE THE ENDANGERED SPECIES LIST!
TODD
WE'RE NO. 5
WHS
SENIORS '84
© News Group Chicago, Inc. 1984
BATIUK
5-26

FUNKY WINKERBEAN
BY TOM BATIUK
WELL, I CAN SEE YOU'RE HARD AT WORK, HARRY!
WHAT'S THIS NEW PIECE YOU'RE WRITING?
BATIUK
5-27
© News Group Chicago, Inc., 1984
I'M A MARCH!
I PREFER TO LET MY MUSIC SPEAK FOR ITSELF!

DEFINE THE FOLLOWING:	(1.) DODDER	Fodder's little girl!

5-28

DEFINE THE FOLLOWING:	(2.) CONSERVE	The act of putting the ball in play in the prison volleyball game!

5-29

DEFINE THE FOLLOWING:	(3.) BALDERDASH	An annual fun run held each spring in Balder, England.

5-30

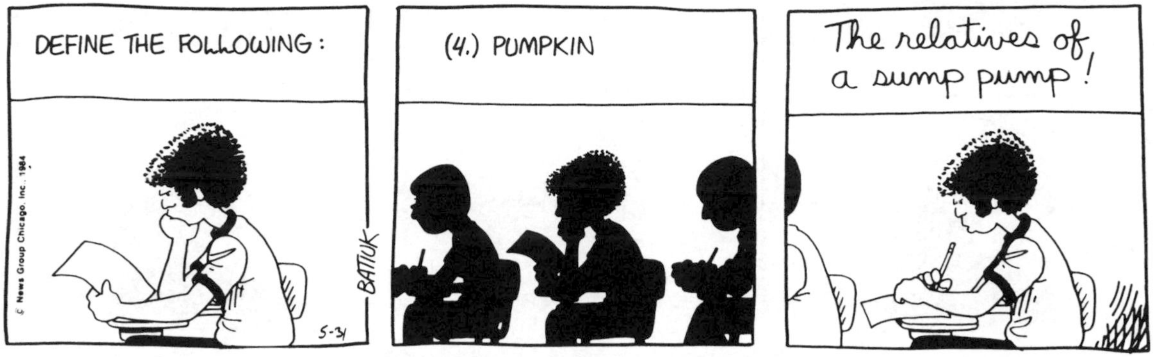
DEFINE THE FOLLOWING:
(4.) PUMPKIN
The relatives of a sump pump!
© News Group Chicago, Inc. 1984
BATIUK
5-31

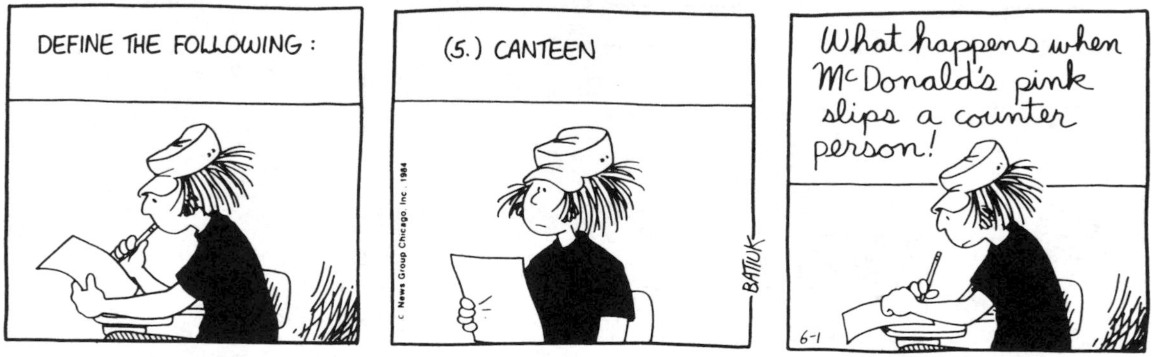
DEFINE THE FOLLOWING:
(5.) CANTEEN
What happens when McDonald's pink slips a counter person!
© News Group Chicago, Inc. 1984
BATIUK
6-1

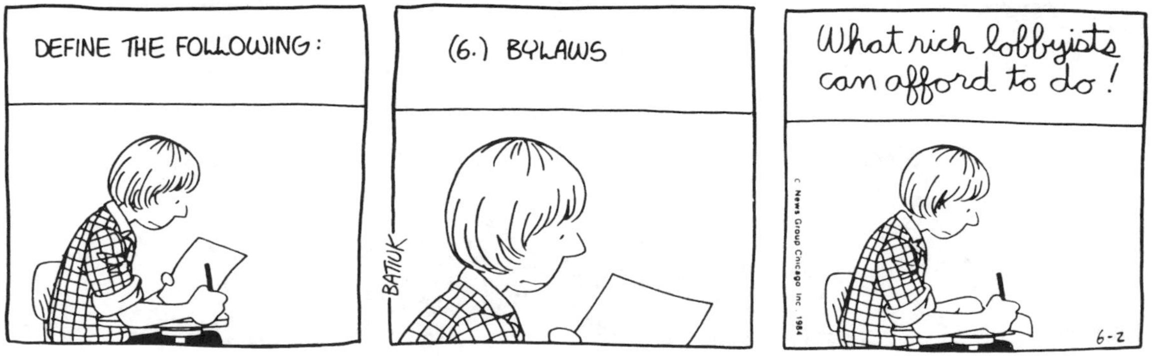
DEFINE THE FOLLOWING:
(6.) BYLAWS
What rich lobbyists can afford to do!
© News Group Chicago, Inc. 1984
BATIUK
6-2

FUNKY WINKERBEAN
by TOM BATIUK ®
TODD
WE'RE NO. 5
WHS
SENIORS '84
JULIE
MIKE
AT TIMES LIKE THIS, I OFTEN QUESTION WHETHER WE AS EDUCATORS HAVE REALLY DONE OUR JOB...
BUT THEN I REMIND MYSELF THAT YOU GET WHAT YOU PAY FOR!
GRADUATING SENIORS, YOU CAN LOOK BACK ON THIS PAST YEAR WITH A GREAT DEAL OF PRIDE!
OUR FOOTBALL TEAM HAD ONE OF ITS BEST SEASONS IN RECENT MEMORY!
PEOPLE ARE STILL TALKING ABOUT THE GAME WHERE WE SCORED!
© News Group Chicago, Inc., 1984
6-3

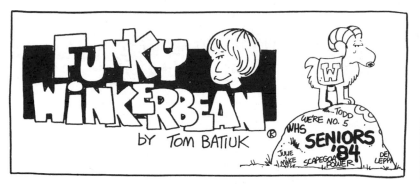

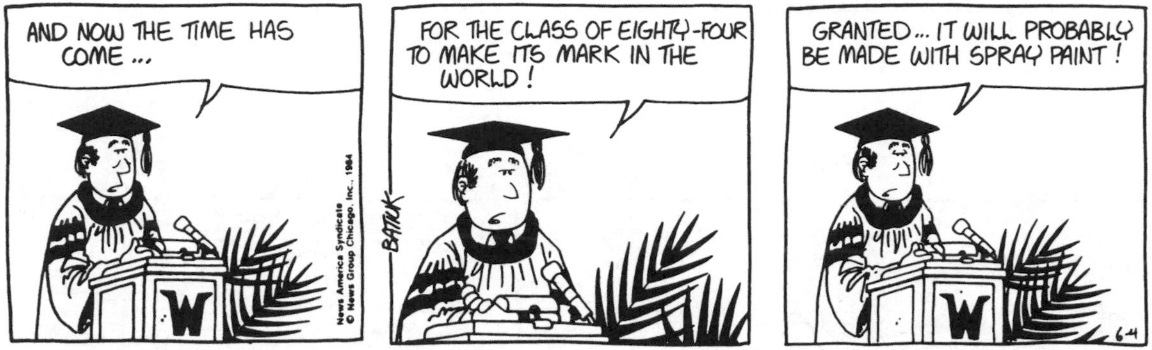
AND NOW THE TIME HAS COME ...
FOR THE CLASS OF EIGHTY-FOUR TO MAKE ITS MARK IN THE WORLD!
GRANTED ... IT WILL PROBABLY BE MADE WITH SPRAY PAINT!
News America Syndicate © News Group Chicago, Inc., 1984
BATIUK
6-4

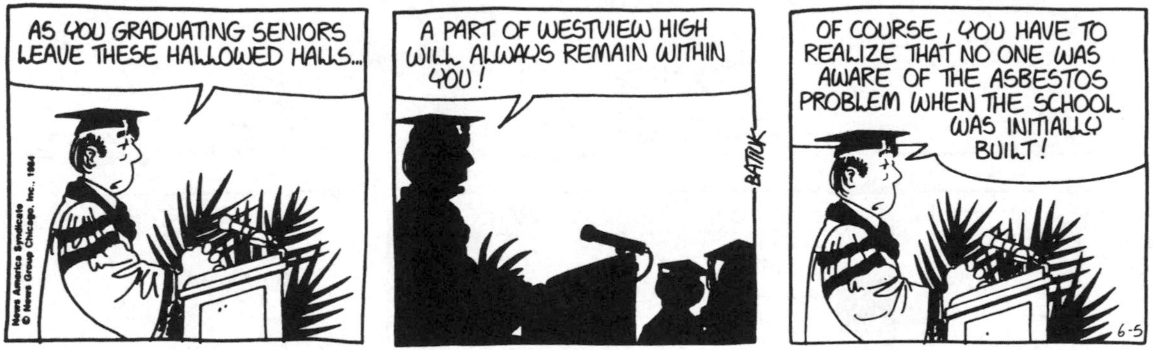
AS YOU GRADUATING SENIORS LEAVE THESE HALLOWED HALLS...
A PART OF WESTVIEW HIGH WILL ALWAYS REMAIN WITHIN YOU!
OF COURSE, YOU HAVE TO REALIZE THAT NO ONE WAS AWARE OF THE ASBESTOS PROBLEM WHEN THE SCHOOL WAS INITIALLY BUILT!
News America Syndicate © News Group Chicago, Inc., 1984
BATIUK
6-5

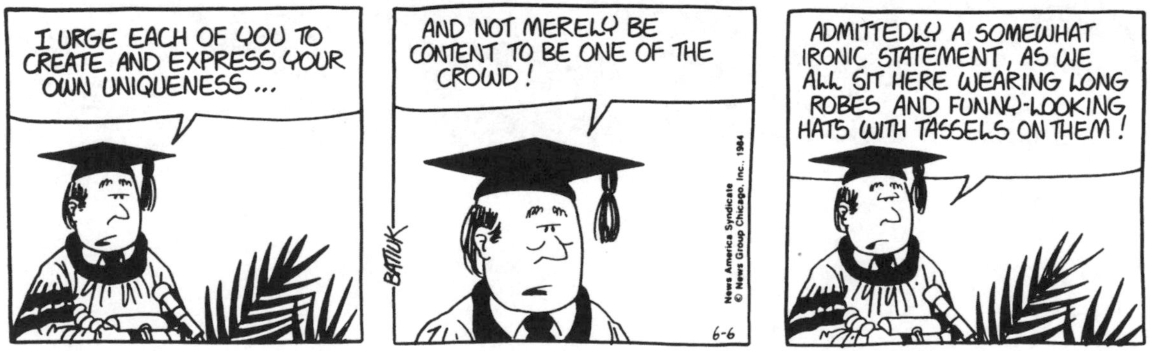
I URGE EACH OF YOU TO CREATE AND EXPRESS YOUR OWN UNIQUENESS ...
AND NOT MERELY BE CONTENT TO BE ONE OF THE CROWD!
ADMITTEDLY A SOMEWHAT IRONIC STATEMENT, AS WE ALL SIT HERE WEARING LONG ROBES AND FUNNY-LOOKING HATS WITH TASSELS ON THEM!
News America Syndicate © News Group Chicago, Inc., 1984
BATIUK
6-6

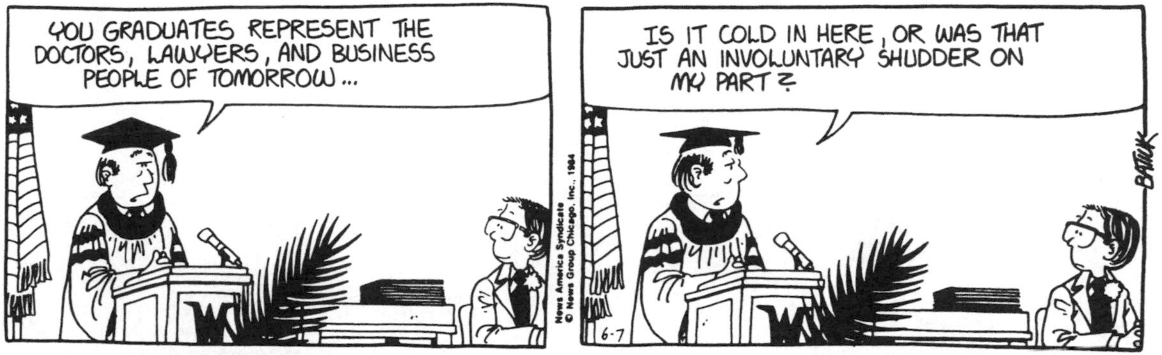
YOU GRADUATES REPRESENT THE DOCTORS, LAWYERS, AND BUSINESS PEOPLE OF TOMORROW...
News America Syndicate © News Group Chicago, Inc., 1984
IS IT COLD IN HERE, OR WAS THAT JUST AN INVOLUNTARY SHUDDER ON MY PART?
BATIUK
6-7

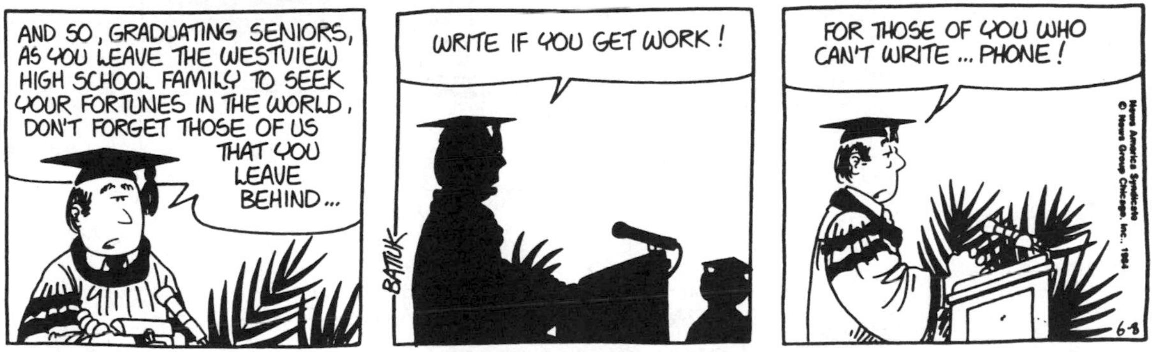
AND SO, GRADUATING SENIORS, AS YOU LEAVE THE WESTVIEW HIGH SCHOOL FAMILY TO SEEK YOUR FORTUNES IN THE WORLD, DON'T FORGET THOSE OF US THAT YOU LEAVE BEHIND...
BATIUK
WRITE IF YOU GET WORK!
FOR THOSE OF YOU WHO CAN'T WRITE... PHONE!
News America Syndicate © News Group Chicago, Inc., 1984
6-8

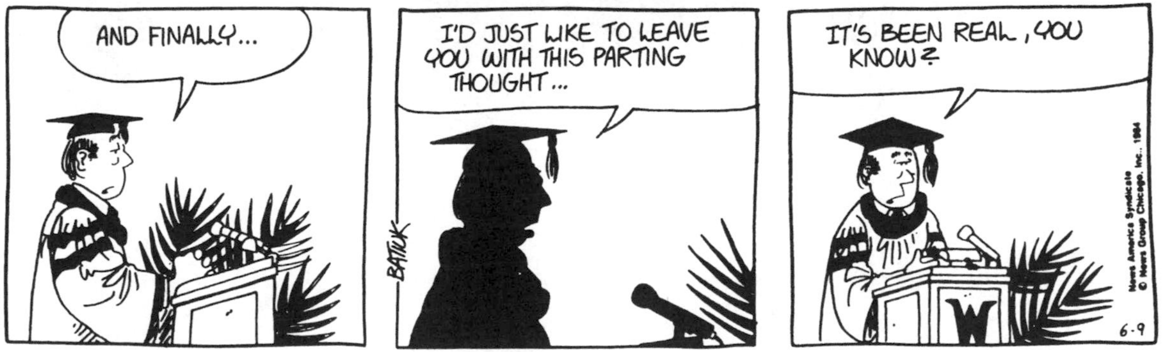
AND FINALLY...
BATIUK
I'D JUST LIKE TO LEAVE YOU WITH THIS PARTING THOUGHT...
IT'S BEEN REAL, YOU KNOW?
News America Syndicate © News Group Chicago, Inc., 1984
6-9

FUNKY WINKERBEAN
BY TOM BATIUK
MONTONI'S PIZZA
RING!
MONTONI'S PIZZA
WE DELIVER
MONTONI'S PIZZA...
WHERE'S MY !! PIZZA!!?
I ORDERED IT OVER TWO HOURS AGO!! IT'S NEARLY ONE A.M. !!!
MONTONI'S PIZZA
WE DELIVER
I'M SORRY, SIR! OUR DELIVERY BOY IS ON HIS WAY AND SHOULD BE THERE ANY MINUTE NOW!
BATIUK
MONTONI'S PIZZA... WHEN IT ABSOLUTELY HAS TO BE THERE TOMORROW!
6-10
© News Group Chicago, Inc., 1984

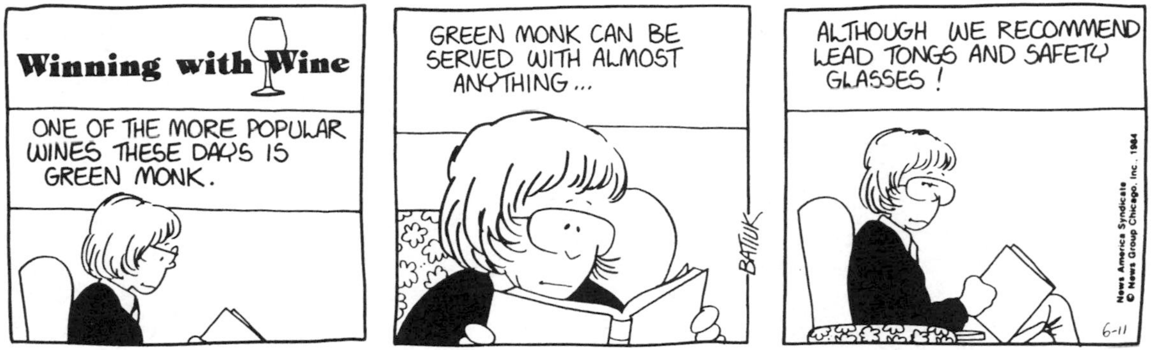
Winning with Wine
ONE OF THE MORE POPULAR WINES THESE DAYS IS GREEN MONK.
GREEN MONK CAN BE SERVED WITH ALMOST ANYTHING...
BATIUK
ALTHOUGH WE RECOMMEND LEAD TONGS AND SAFETY GLASSES!
News America Syndicate © News Group Chicago, Inc., 1984
6-11

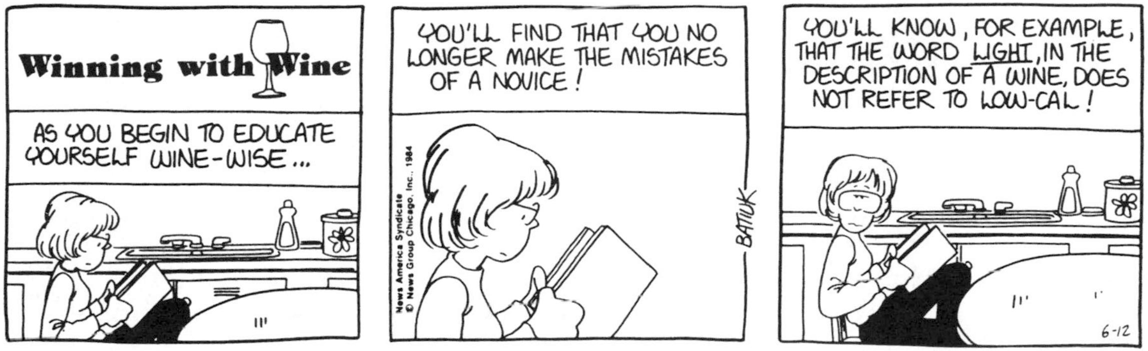
Winning with Wine
AS YOU BEGIN TO EDUCATE YOURSELF WINE-WISE...
YOU'LL FIND THAT YOU NO LONGER MAKE THE MISTAKES OF A NOVICE!
News America Syndicate © News Group Chicago, Inc., 1984
BATIUK
YOU'LL KNOW, FOR EXAMPLE, THAT THE WORD LIGHT, IN THE DESCRIPTION OF A WINE, DOES NOT REFER TO LOW-CAL!
6-12

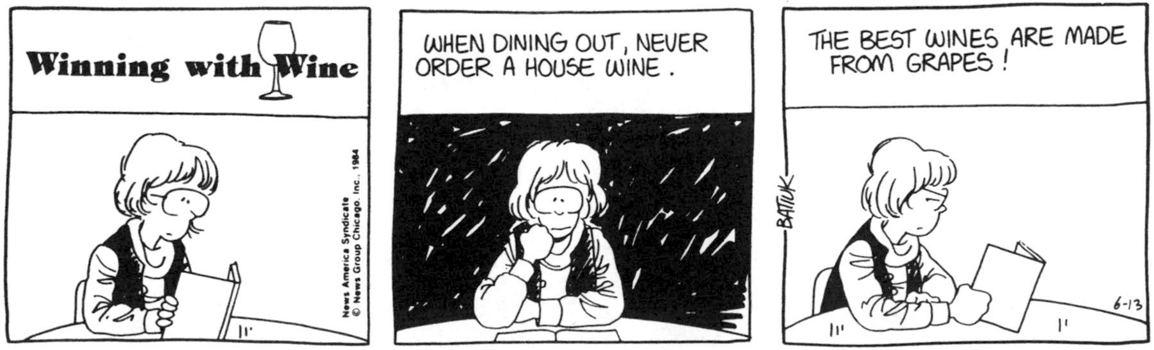
Winning with Wine
News America Syndicate © News Group Chicago, Inc., 1984
WHEN DINING OUT, NEVER ORDER A HOUSE WINE.
BATIUK
THE BEST WINES ARE MADE FROM GRAPES!
6-13

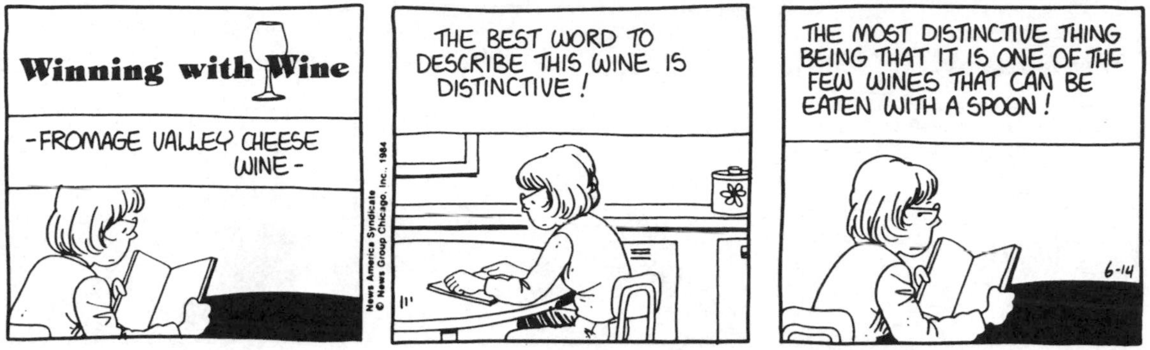
Winning with Wine
-FROMAGE VALLEY CHEESE WINE-
News America Syndicate © News Group Chicago, Inc., 1984
THE BEST WORD TO DESCRIBE THIS WINE IS DISTINCTIVE!
THE MOST DISTINCTIVE THING BEING THAT IT IS ONE OF THE FEW WINES THAT CAN BE EATEN WITH A SPOON!
6-14

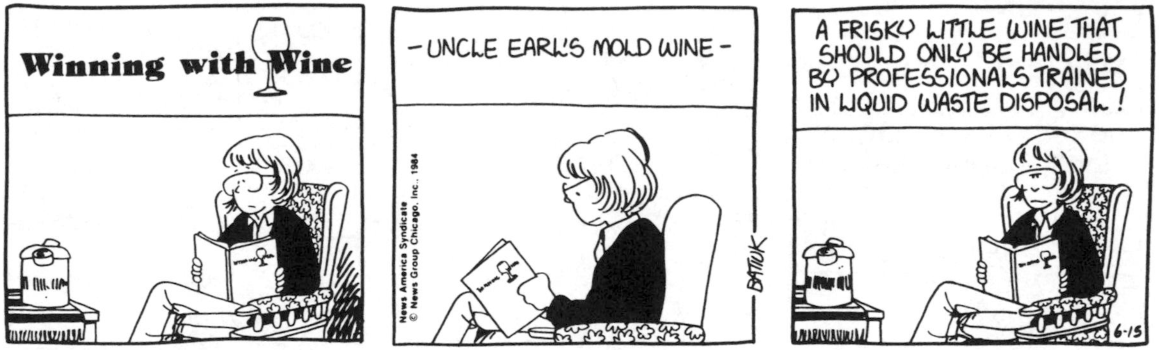
Winning with Wine
News America Syndicate © News Group Chicago, Inc., 1984
-UNCLE EARL'S MOLD WINE-
BATIUK
A FRISKY LITTLE WINE THAT SHOULD ONLY BE HANDLED BY PROFESSIONALS TRAINED IN LIQUID WASTE DISPOSAL!
6-15

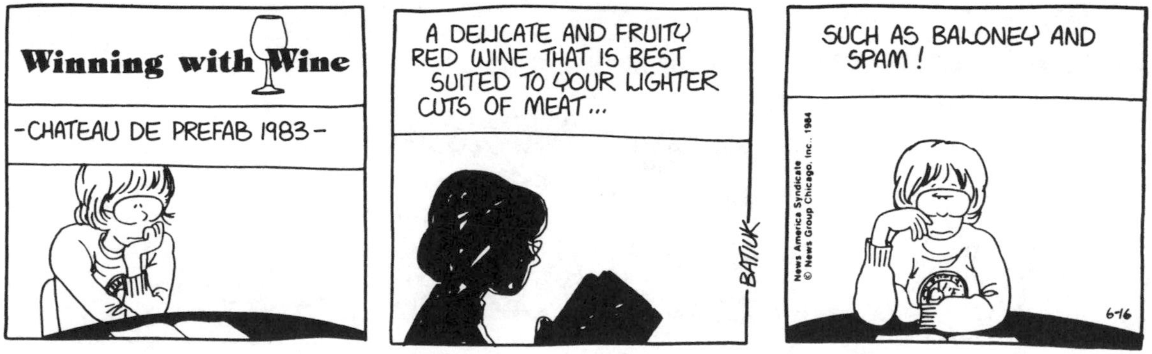
Winning with Wine
-CHATEAU DE PREFAB 1983-
A DELICATE AND FRUITY RED WINE THAT IS BEST SUITED TO YOUR LIGHTER CUTS OF MEAT...
BATIUK
SUCH AS BALONEY AND SPAM!
News America Syndicate © News Group Chicago, Inc., 1984
6-16

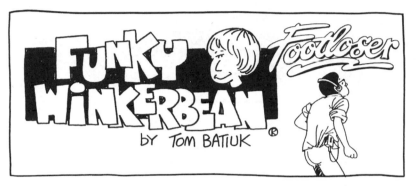

Funky Winkerbean *Footloose*

by Tom Batiuk

LOOK AT THOSE KIDS BREAK DANCING!

THEY SURE LOOK LIKE THEY'RE HAVING FUN!

YOU KNOW, FUNKY... I'LL BET I COULD BREAK DANCE AS WELL AS ANY OF THOSE KIDS OVER THERE!

COME ON, LES... GET SERIOUS!

BATIUK 6-17

© News Group Chicago, Inc. 1984

I AM SERIOUS! IN FACT THE LAST TIME I WENT DANCING, SEVERAL PEOPLE EVEN SUGGESTED IT!

NO, YOU DON'T UNDER-STAND... WHEN THEY SAID, 'GIVE US A BREAK,' WHAT THEY MEANT WAS...

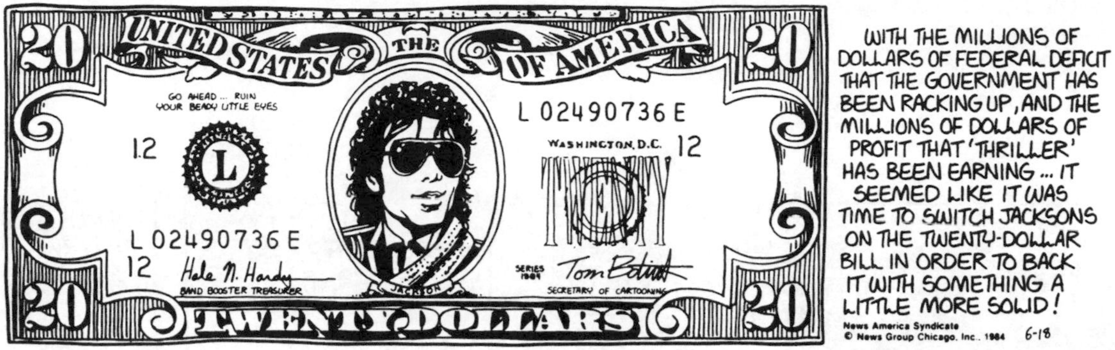
UNITED STATES THE OF AMERICA
20
GO AHEAD ... RUIN YOUR BEADY LITTLE EYES
L 02490736 E
12
WASHINGTON, D.C.
TWENTY
Hale N. Hardy
BAND BOOSTER TREASURER
SERIES 1984
Tom Batiuk
SECRETARY OF CARTOONING
JACKSON
TWENTY DOLLARS
WITH THE MILLIONS OF DOLLARS OF FEDERAL DEFICIT THAT THE GOVERNMENT HAS BEEN RACKING UP, AND THE MILLIONS OF DOLLARS OF PROFIT THAT 'THRILLER' HAS BEEN EARNING ... IT SEEMED LIKE IT WAS TIME TO SWITCH JACKSONS ON THE TWENTY-DOLLAR BILL IN ORDER TO BACK IT WITH SOMETHING A LITTLE MORE SOLID!
News America Syndicate
© News Group Chicago, Inc., 1984
6-18

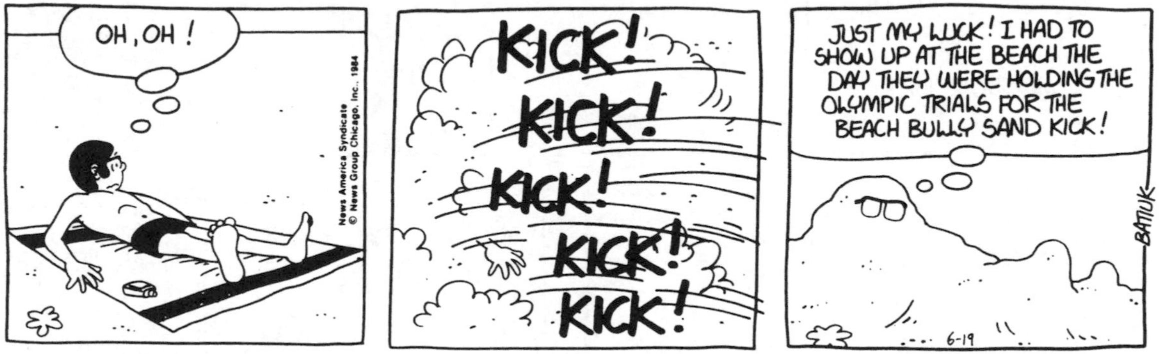
OH, OH!
News America Syndicate
© News Group Chicago, Inc., 1984
KICK!
KICK!
KICK!
KICK!
KICK!
JUST MY LUCK! I HAD TO SHOW UP AT THE BEACH THE DAY THEY WERE HOLDING THE OLYMPIC TRIALS FOR THE BEACH BULLY SAND KICK!
BATIUK
6-19

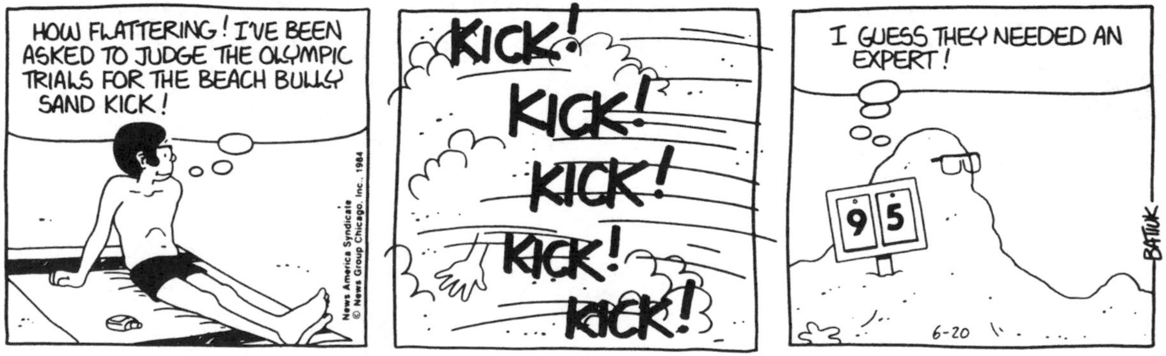
HOW FLATTERING! I'VE BEEN ASKED TO JUDGE THE OLYMPIC TRIALS FOR THE BEACH BULLY SAND KICK!
News America Syndicate
© News Group Chicago, Inc., 1984
KICK!
KICK!
KICK!
KICK!
KICK!
I GUESS THEY NEEDED AN EXPERT!
9 5
BATIUK
6-20

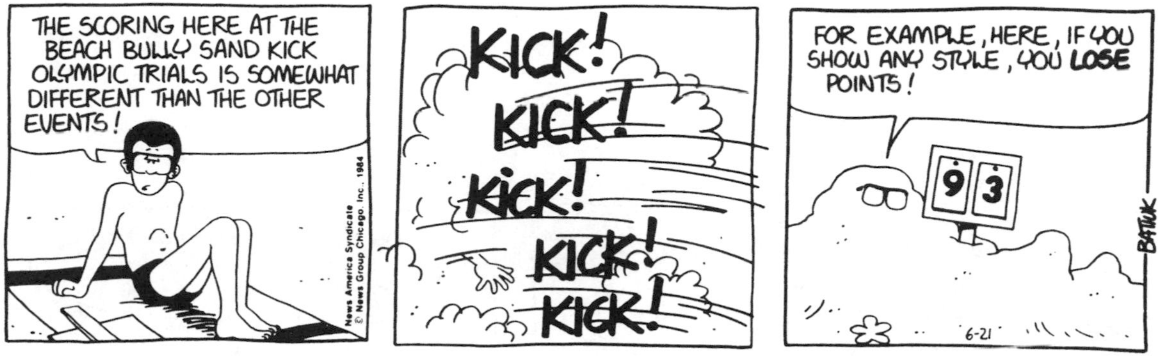
THE SCORING HERE AT THE BEACH BULLY SAND KICK OLYMPIC TRIALS IS SOMEWHAT DIFFERENT THAN THE OTHER EVENTS!
News America Syndicate © News Group Chicago, Inc., 1984
KICK! KICK! KICK! KICK! KICK!
FOR EXAMPLE, HERE, IF YOU SHOW ANY STYLE, YOU **LOSE** POINTS!
9 3
BATIUK
6-21

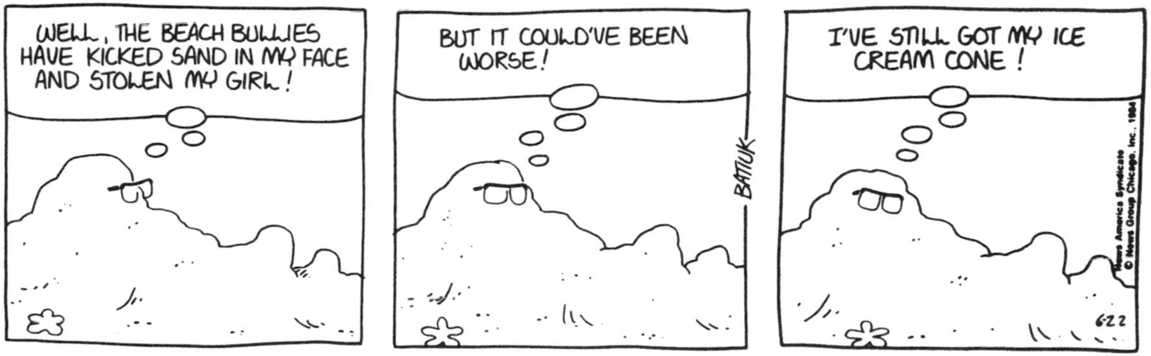
WELL, THE BEACH BULLIES HAVE KICKED SAND IN MY FACE AND STOLEN MY GIRL!
BUT IT COULD'VE BEEN WORSE!
BATIUK
I'VE STILL GOT MY ICE CREAM CONE!
News America Syndicate © News Group Chicago, Inc., 1984
6-22

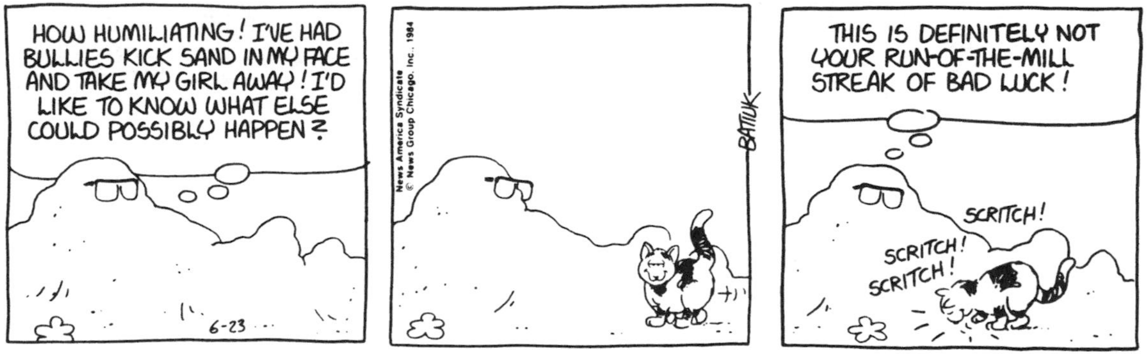
HOW HUMILIATING! I'VE HAD BULLIES KICK SAND IN MY FACE AND TAKE MY GIRL AWAY! I'D LIKE TO KNOW WHAT ELSE COULD POSSIBLY HAPPEN?
6-23
News America Syndicate © News Group Chicago, Inc., 1984
BATIUK
THIS IS DEFINITELY NOT YOUR RUN-OF-THE-MILL STREAK OF BAD LUCK!
SCRITCH!
SCRITCH!
SCRITCH!

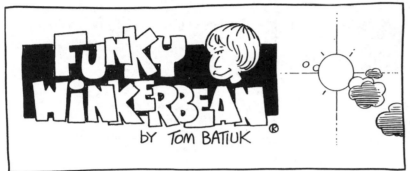

FUNKY WINKERBEAN
by Tom Batiuk

OH, OH! IT LOOKS LIKE WE'RE GOING TO GET SOME RAIN!

RAIN, RAIN, GO AWAY!

COME AGAIN SOME OTHER DAY!

6-24

IF THERE'S ONE THING I CAN'T STAND...

IT'S PEOPLE WHO TELL YOU TO DROP BY SOME DAY, BUT DON'T REALLY MEAN IT!

BATIUK

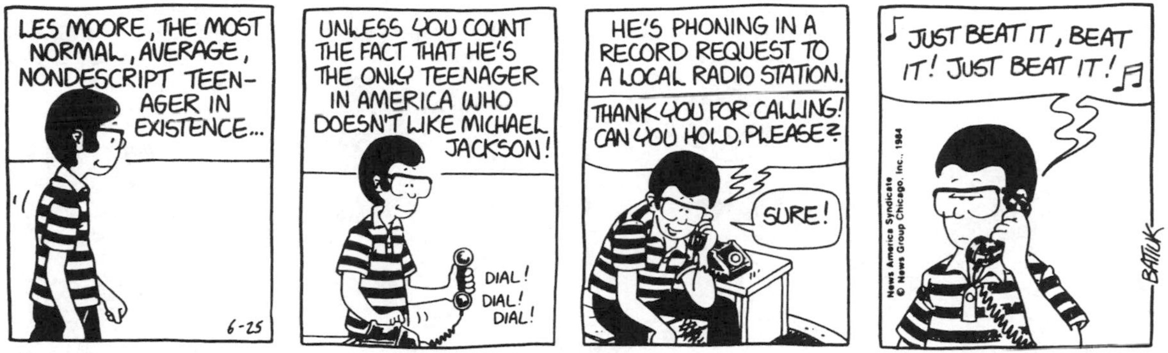
LES MOORE, THE MOST NORMAL, AVERAGE, NONDESCRIPT TEEN-AGER IN EXISTENCE...
6-25
UNLESS YOU COUNT THE FACT THAT HE'S THE ONLY TEENAGER IN AMERICA WHO DOESN'T LIKE MICHAEL JACKSON!
DIAL! DIAL! DIAL!
HE'S PHONING IN A RECORD REQUEST TO A LOCAL RADIO STATION.
THANK YOU FOR CALLING! CAN YOU HOLD, PLEASE?
SURE!
♪ JUST BEAT IT, BEAT IT! JUST BEAT IT! ♫
News America Syndicate © News Group Chicago, Inc., 1984
BATIUK

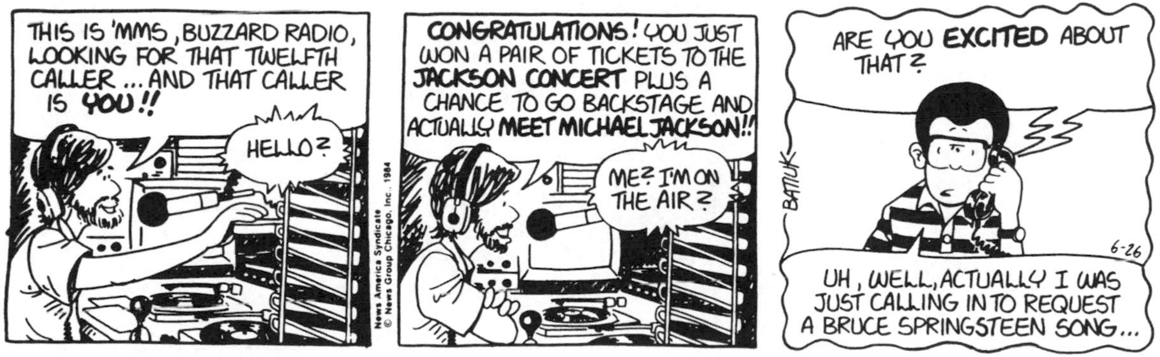
THIS IS 'MMS, BUZZARD RADIO, LOOKING FOR THAT TWELFTH CALLER ... AND THAT CALLER IS **YOU**!!
HELLO?
News America Syndicate © News Group Chicago, Inc., 1984
CONGRATULATIONS! YOU JUST WON A PAIR OF TICKETS TO THE **JACKSON CONCERT** PLUS A CHANCE TO GO BACKSTAGE AND ACTUALLY **MEET MICHAEL JACKSON**!!
ME? I'M ON THE AIR?
ARE YOU **EXCITED** ABOUT THAT?
BATIUK
6-26
UH, WELL, ACTUALLY I WAS JUST CALLING IN TO REQUEST A BRUCE SPRINGSTEEN SONG...

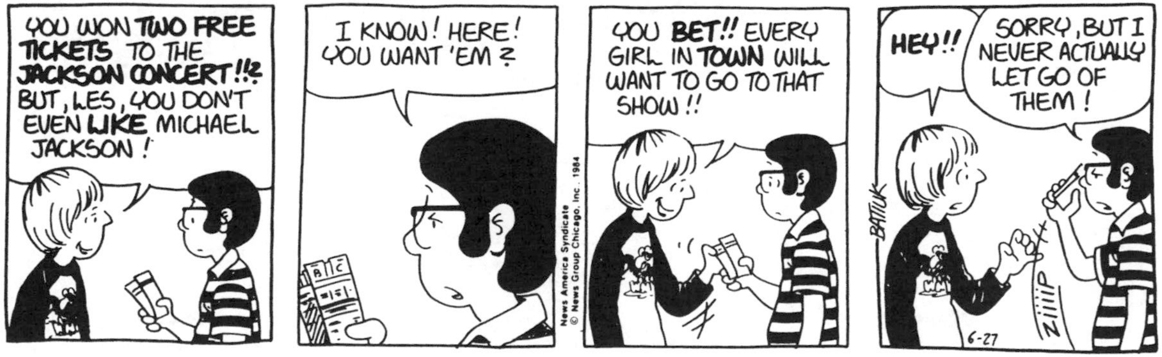
YOU WON **TWO FREE TICKETS** TO THE **JACKSON CONCERT**!!? BUT, LES, YOU DON'T EVEN **LIKE** MICHAEL JACKSON!
I KNOW! HERE! YOU WANT 'EM?
News America Syndicate © News Group Chicago, Inc., 1984
YOU **BET**!! EVERY GIRL IN **TOWN** WILL WANT TO GO TO THAT SHOW!!
HEY!!
SORRY, BUT I NEVER ACTUALLY LET GO OF THEM!
ZIIIIP
BATIUK
6-27

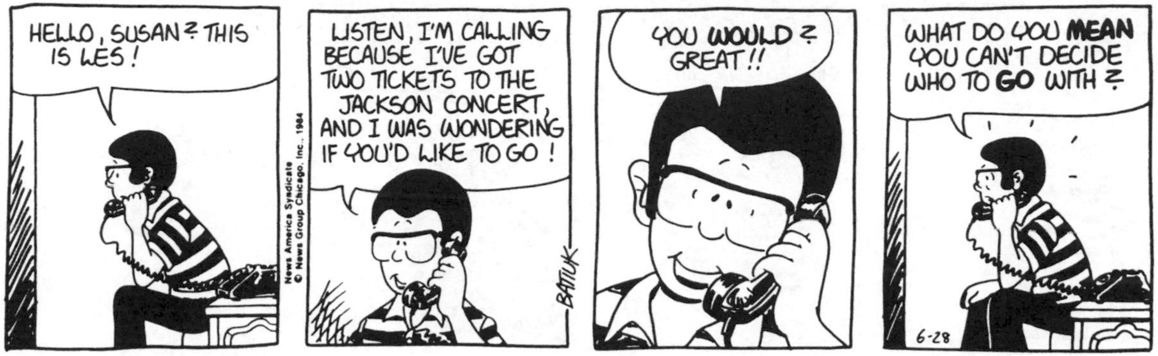
HELLO, SUSAN? THIS IS LES!
LISTEN, I'M CALLING BECAUSE I'VE GOT TWO TICKETS TO THE JACKSON CONCERT, AND I WAS WONDERING IF YOU'D LIKE TO GO!
News America Syndicate © News Group Chicago, Inc., 1984
BATIUK
YOU **WOULD**? GREAT!!
WHAT DO YOU **MEAN** YOU CAN'T DECIDE WHO TO **GO** WITH?
6-28

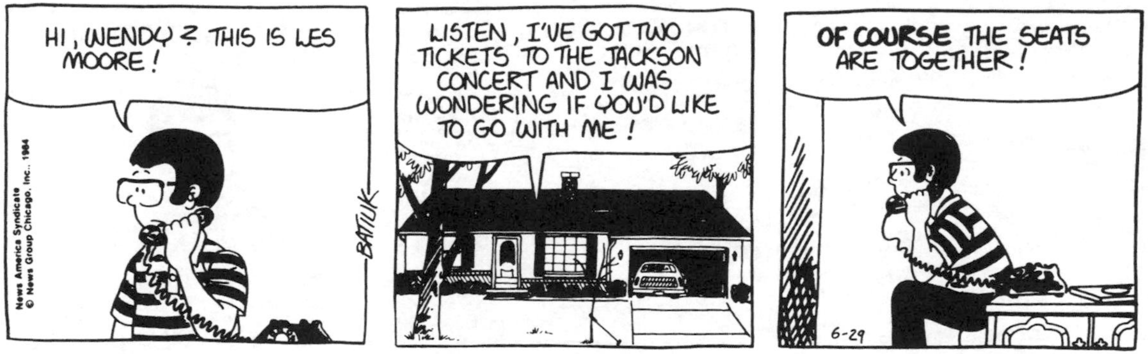
HI, WENDY? THIS IS LES MOORE!
News America Syndicate © News Group Chicago, Inc., 1984
BATIUK
LISTEN, I'VE GOT TWO TICKETS TO THE JACKSON CONCERT AND I WAS WONDERING IF YOU'D LIKE TO GO WITH ME!
OF COURSE THE SEATS ARE TOGETHER!
6-29

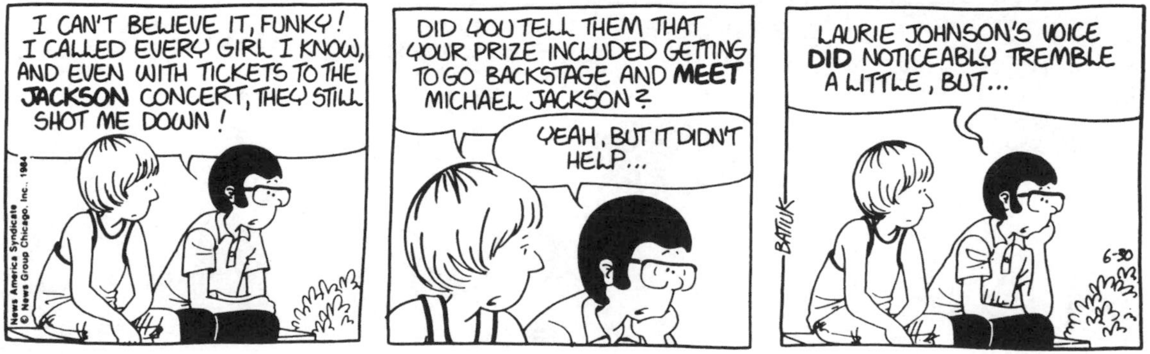
I CAN'T BELIEVE IT, FUNKY! I CALLED EVERY GIRL I KNOW, AND EVEN WITH TICKETS TO THE **JACKSON** CONCERT, THEY STILL SHOT ME DOWN!
News America Syndicate © News Group Chicago, Inc., 1984
DID YOU TELL THEM THAT YOUR PRIZE INCLUDED GETTING TO GO BACKSTAGE AND **MEET** MICHAEL JACKSON?
YEAH, BUT IT DIDN'T HELP...
BATIUK
LAURIE JOHNSON'S VOICE **DID** NOTICEABLY TREMBLE A LITTLE, BUT...
6-30

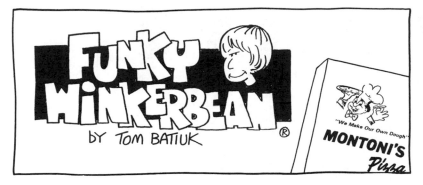

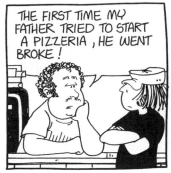

FUNKY WINKERBEAN
BY TOM BATIUK ®
"We Make Our Own Dough"
MONTONI'S Pizza
THE FIRST TIME MY FATHER TRIED TO START A PIZZERIA, HE WENT BROKE!
HE COULDN'T RAISE THE DOUGH!
MONTONI'S PIZZA
MY FATHER TRIED A LOT OF DIFFERENT THINGS BEFORE HE GOT INTO THE PIZZA BUSINESS!
AT ONE TIME HE OWNED A GAS STATION BUT IT NEVER WORKED OUT!
MONTONI'S PIZZA
© News Group Chicago, Inc., 1984
ACTUALLY HE WAS WAY AHEAD OF HIS TIME!
BATIUK
HE WAS THE FIRST ONE TO HAVE A GAS STATION WITH A SALAD BAR!
7-1

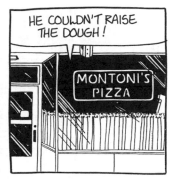

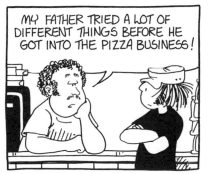

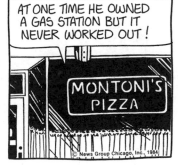

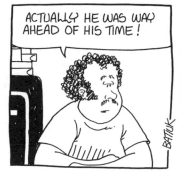

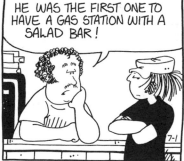

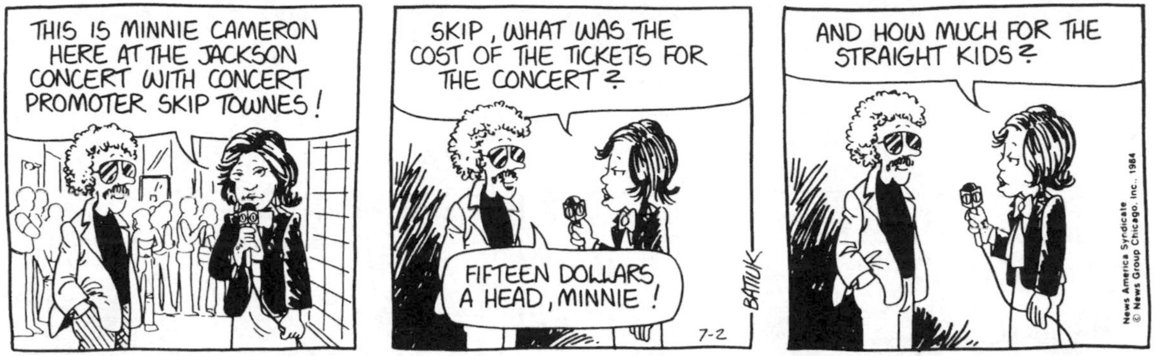
THIS IS MINNIE CAMERON HERE AT THE JACKSON CONCERT WITH CONCERT PROMOTER SKIP TOWNES!
SKIP, WHAT WAS THE COST OF THE TICKETS FOR THE CONCERT?
FIFTEEN DOLLARS A HEAD, MINNIE!
BATIUK
7-2
AND HOW MUCH FOR THE STRAIGHT KIDS?
News America Syndicate © News Group Chicago, Inc., 1984

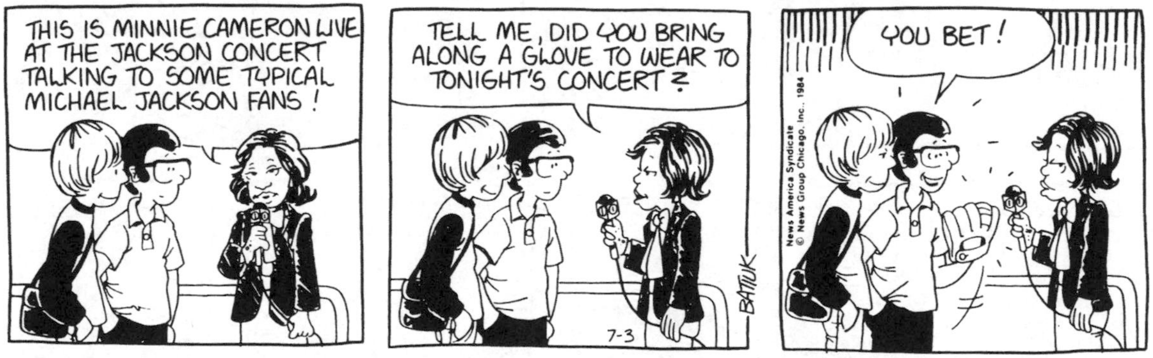
THIS IS MINNIE CAMERON LIVE AT THE JACKSON CONCERT TALKING TO SOME TYPICAL MICHAEL JACKSON FANS!
TELL ME, DID YOU BRING ALONG A GLOVE TO WEAR TO TONIGHT'S CONCERT?
BATIUK
7-3
News America Syndicate © News Group Chicago, Inc., 1984
YOU BET!

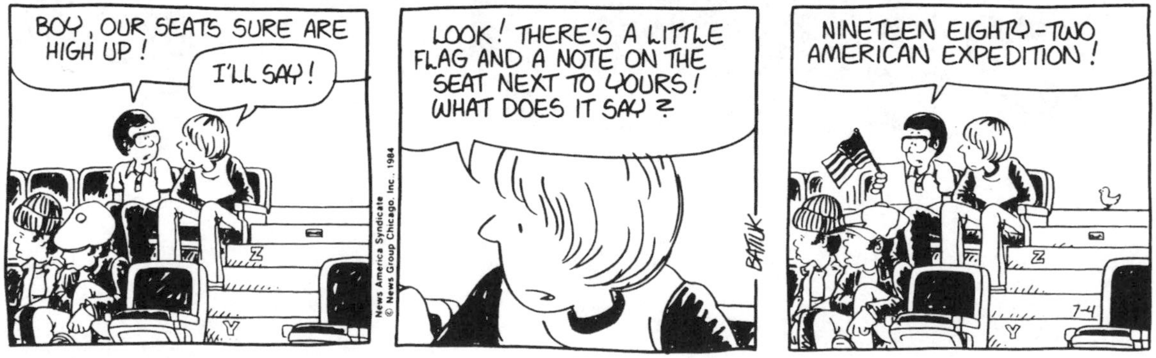
BOY, OUR SEATS SURE ARE HIGH UP!
I'LL SAY!
Z
Y
News America Syndicate © News Group Chicago, Inc., 1984
LOOK! THERE'S A LITTLE FLAG AND A NOTE ON THE SEAT NEXT TO YOURS! WHAT DOES IT SAY?
BATIUK
NINETEEN EIGHTY-TWO AMERICAN EXPEDITION!
7-4

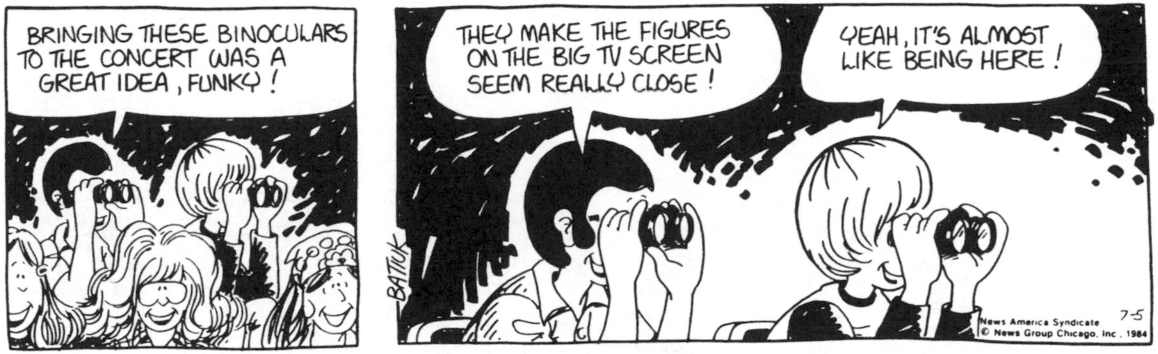
BRINGING THESE BINOCULARS TO THE CONCERT WAS A GREAT IDEA, FUNKY!
THEY MAKE THE FIGURES ON THE BIG TV SCREEN SEEM REALLY CLOSE!
YEAH, IT'S ALMOST LIKE BEING HERE!
BATIUK
7-5
News America Syndicate
© News Group Chicago, Inc. 1984

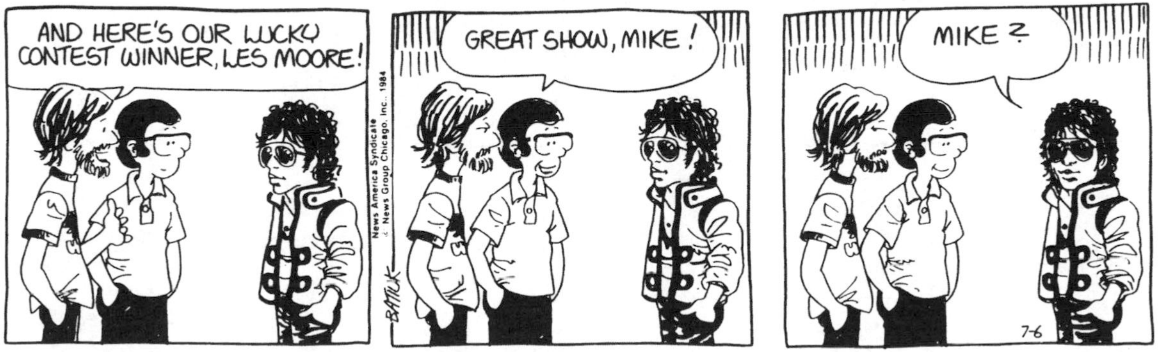
AND HERE'S OUR LUCKY CONTEST WINNER, LES MOORE!
News America Syndicate
© News Group Chicago, Inc. 1984
BATIUK
GREAT SHOW, MIKE!
MIKE?
7-6

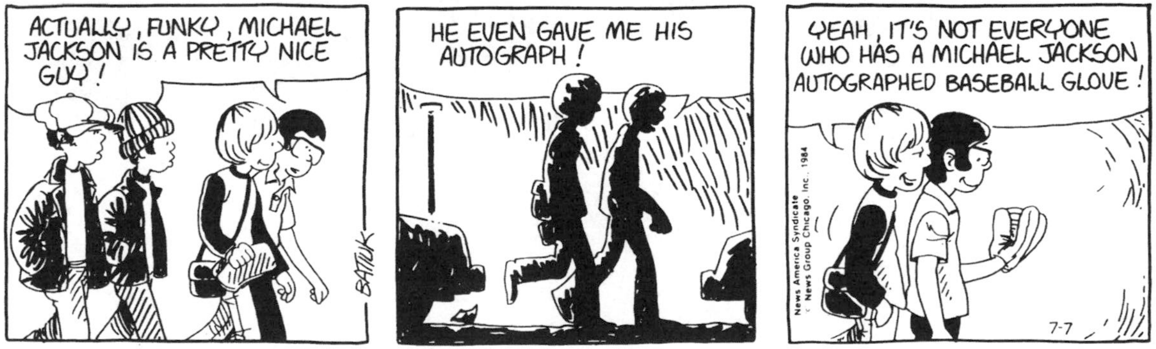
ACTUALLY, FUNKY, MICHAEL JACKSON IS A PRETTY NICE GUY!
BATIUK
HE EVEN GAVE ME HIS AUTOGRAPH!
YEAH, IT'S NOT EVERYONE WHO HAS A MICHAEL JACKSON AUTOGRAPHED BASEBALL GLOVE!
News America Syndicate
© News Group Chicago, Inc. 1984
7-7

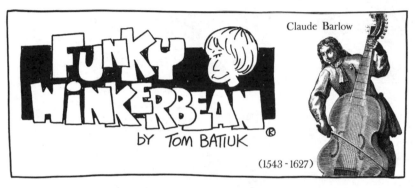

FUNKY WINKERBEAN
by TOM BATIUK ®
Claude Barlow
(1543 - 1627)
Famous Composers
Chapter Ten - Claude Barlow
TAP! TIP! TAP!
One of the most intriguing mysteries surrounding Claude Barlow concerns the suspicion that he was responsible for the death of Mozart!
According to the theory, Claude dropped by Mozart's apartment one day...
TIP! TIP! TAP!
and played his newest composition for the young genius...
News America Syndicate
© News Group Chicago, Inc., 1984
TIP! TAP!
7-8
upon which, the sensitive Mozart is reported to have succumbed to shock!
BATIUK

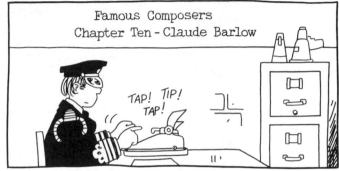

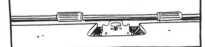

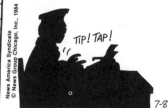

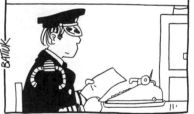

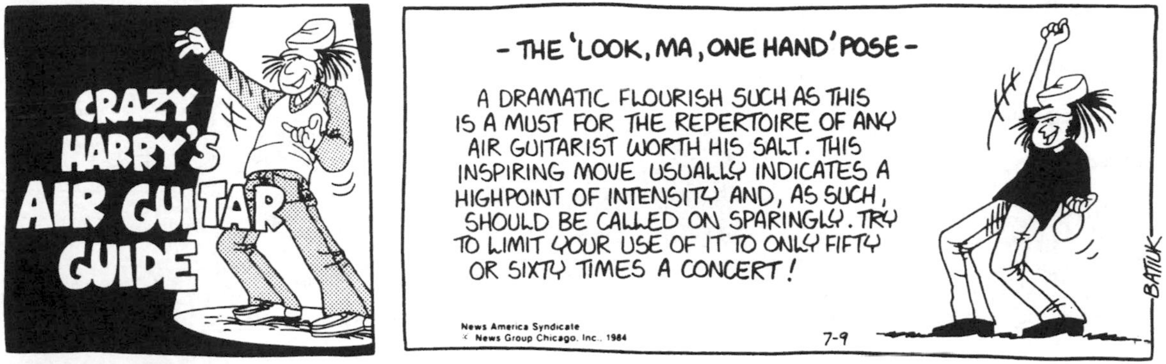
CRAZY HARRY'S AIR GUITAR GUIDE
- THE 'LOOK, MA, ONE HAND' POSE -
A DRAMATIC FLOURISH SUCH AS THIS IS A MUST FOR THE REPERTOIRE OF ANY AIR GUITARIST WORTH HIS SALT. THIS INSPIRING MOVE USUALLY INDICATES A HIGHPOINT OF INTENSITY AND, AS SUCH, SHOULD BE CALLED ON SPARINGLY. TRY TO LIMIT YOUR USE OF IT TO ONLY FIFTY OR SIXTY TIMES A CONCERT!
News America Syndicate
© News Group Chicago, Inc., 1984
7-9
BATIUK

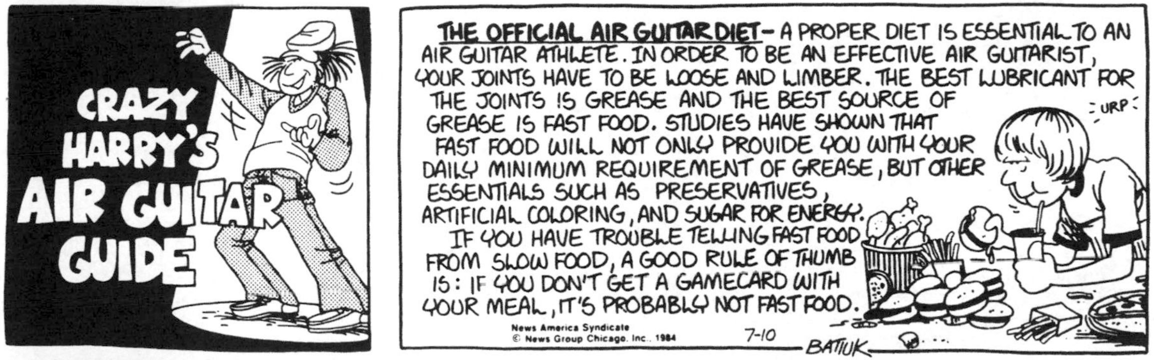
CRAZY HARRY'S AIR GUITAR GUIDE
THE OFFICIAL AIR GUITAR DIET - A PROPER DIET IS ESSENTIAL TO AN AIR GUITAR ATHLETE. IN ORDER TO BE AN EFFECTIVE AIR GUITARIST, YOUR JOINTS HAVE TO BE LOOSE AND LIMBER. THE BEST LUBRICANT FOR THE JOINTS IS GREASE AND THE BEST SOURCE OF GREASE IS FAST FOOD. STUDIES HAVE SHOWN THAT FAST FOOD WILL NOT ONLY PROVIDE YOU WITH YOUR DAILY MINIMUM REQUIREMENT OF GREASE, BUT OTHER ESSENTIALS SUCH AS PRESERVATIVES, ARTIFICIAL COLORING, AND SUGAR FOR ENERGY.
IF YOU HAVE TROUBLE TELLING FAST FOOD FROM SLOW FOOD, A GOOD RULE OF THUMB IS: IF YOU DON'T GET A GAMECARD WITH YOUR MEAL, IT'S PROBABLY NOT FAST FOOD.
URP
News America Syndicate
© News Group Chicago, Inc., 1984
7-10
BATIUK

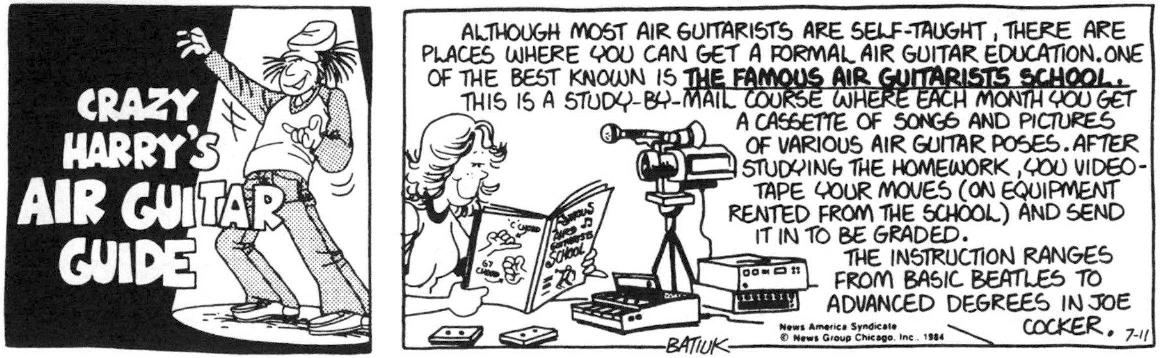
CRAZY HARRY'S AIR GUITAR GUIDE
ALTHOUGH MOST AIR GUITARISTS ARE SELF-TAUGHT, THERE ARE PLACES WHERE YOU CAN GET A FORMAL AIR GUITAR EDUCATION. ONE OF THE BEST KNOWN IS THE FAMOUS AIR GUITARISTS SCHOOL.
THIS IS A STUDY-BY-MAIL COURSE WHERE EACH MONTH YOU GET A CASSETTE OF SONGS AND PICTURES OF VARIOUS AIR GUITAR POSES. AFTER STUDYING THE HOMEWORK, YOU VIDEO-TAPE YOUR MOVES (ON EQUIPMENT RENTED FROM THE SCHOOL) AND SEND IT IN TO BE GRADED.
THE INSTRUCTION RANGES FROM BASIC BEATLES TO ADVANCED DEGREES IN JOE COCKER.
News America Syndicate
© News Group Chicago, Inc., 1984
7-11
BATIUK

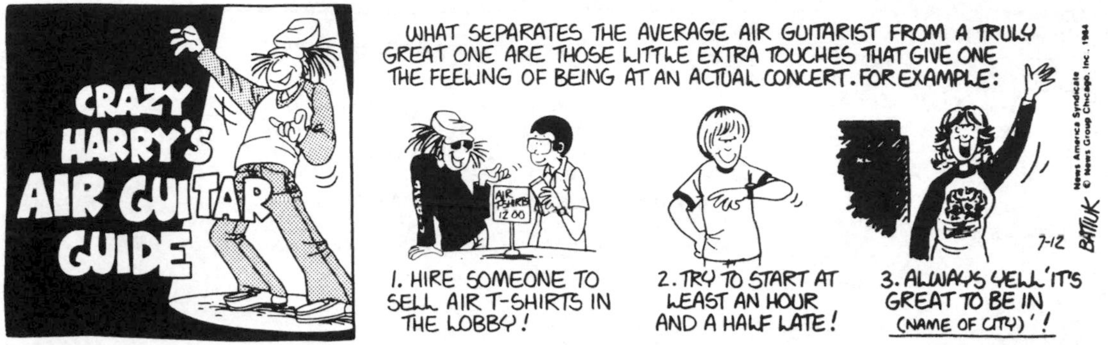
CRAZY HARRY'S AIR GUITAR GUIDE
WHAT SEPARATES THE AVERAGE AIR GUITARIST FROM A TRULY GREAT ONE ARE THOSE LITTLE EXTRA TOUCHES THAT GIVE ONE THE FEELING OF BEING AT AN ACTUAL CONCERT. FOR EXAMPLE:
AIR T-SHIRTS 12.00
1. HIRE SOMEONE TO SELL AIR T-SHIRTS IN THE LOBBY!
2. TRY TO START AT LEAST AN HOUR AND A HALF LATE!
3. ALWAYS YELL 'IT'S GREAT TO BE IN (NAME OF CITY)'!
7-12
BATIUK
News America Syndicate
© News Group Chicago, Inc. 1984

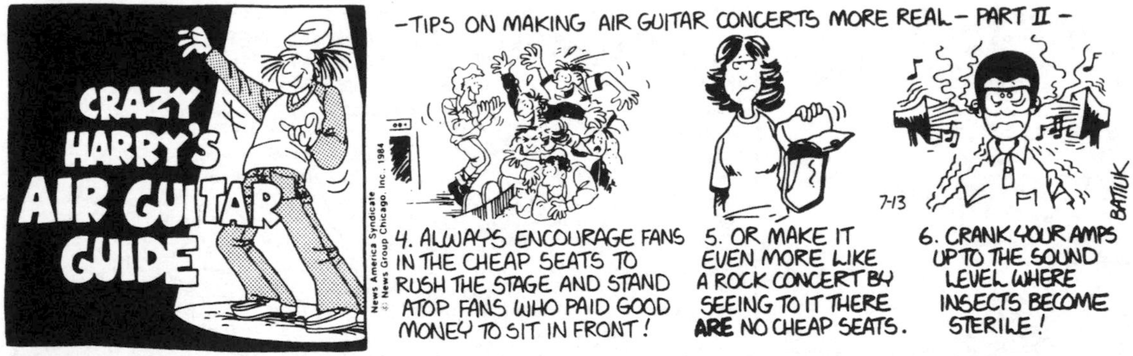
CRAZY HARRY'S AIR GUITAR GUIDE
-TIPS ON MAKING AIR GUITAR CONCERTS MORE REAL - PART II -
News America Syndicate
© News Group Chicago, Inc. 1984
4. ALWAYS ENCOURAGE FANS IN THE CHEAP SEATS TO RUSH THE STAGE AND STAND ATOP FANS WHO PAID GOOD MONEY TO SIT IN FRONT!
5. OR MAKE IT EVEN MORE LIKE A ROCK CONCERT BY SEEING TO IT THERE ARE NO CHEAP SEATS.
6. CRANK YOUR AMPS UP TO THE SOUND LEVEL WHERE INSECTS BECOME STERILE!
7-13
BATIUK

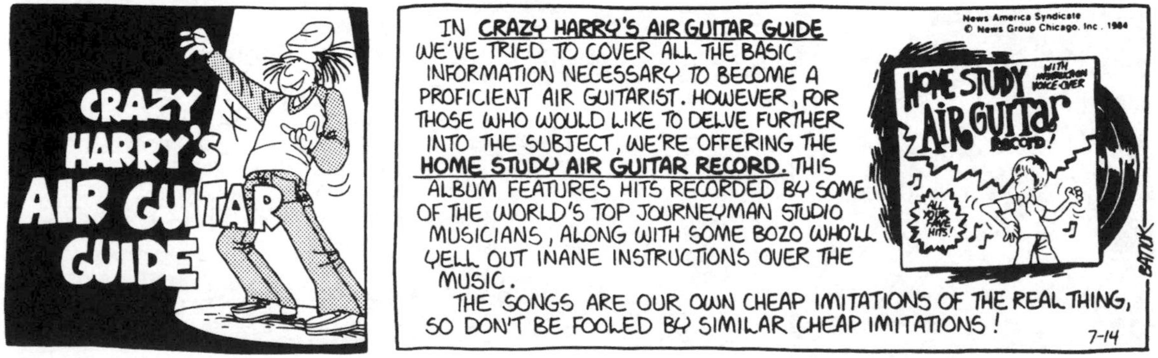
CRAZY HARRY'S AIR GUITAR GUIDE
News America Syndicate
© News Group Chicago, Inc. 1984
IN CRAZY HARRY'S AIR GUITAR GUIDE WE'VE TRIED TO COVER ALL THE BASIC INFORMATION NECESSARY TO BECOME A PROFICIENT AIR GUITARIST. HOWEVER, FOR THOSE WHO WOULD LIKE TO DELVE FURTHER INTO THE SUBJECT, WE'RE OFFERING THE HOME STUDY AIR GUITAR RECORD. THIS ALBUM FEATURES HITS RECORDED BY SOME OF THE WORLD'S TOP JOURNEYMAN STUDIO MUSICIANS, ALONG WITH SOME BOZO WHO'LL YELL OUT INANE INSTRUCTIONS OVER THE MUSIC.
THE SONGS ARE OUR OWN CHEAP IMITATIONS OF THE REAL THING, SO DON'T BE FOOLED BY SIMILAR CHEAP IMITATIONS!
HOME STUDY
VOICE-OVER
Air Guitar RECORD!
ALL YOUR FAVE HITS!
BATIUK
7-14

FUNKY WINKERBEAN
BY TOM BATIUK
Any way you slice it, we'
got the BEST PIZZA
& PASTA in town . . . Tr
AVE $3.00 ON
One Large Pizza
Any Style
at
MONTONI'S
I DON'T KNOW ... BUSINESS HAS REALLY BEEN SLOW LATELY!
WHAT ABOUT A PROMOTION?
WITH BUSINESS THIS BAD, HOW DO YOU EXPECT ME TO GIVE YOU A NEW JOB?
THINGS HAVE CERTAINLY CHANGED AROUND HERE, CRAZY!
WE REALLY USED TO HAVE A BOOMING PIZZA BUSINESS!
7-15
BATIUK
THAT WAS BACK WHEN WE HAD THOSE LEAKY GAS OVENS!
News America Syndicate
© News Group Chicago, Inc., 1984

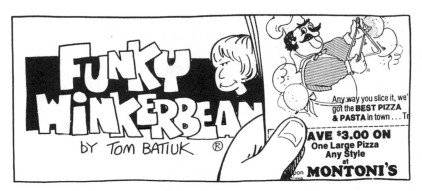

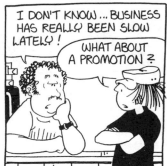

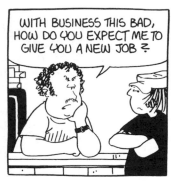

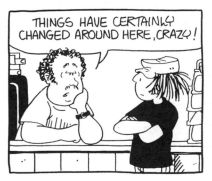

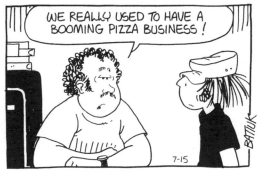

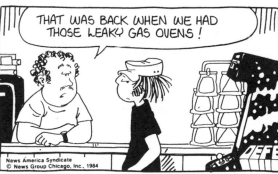

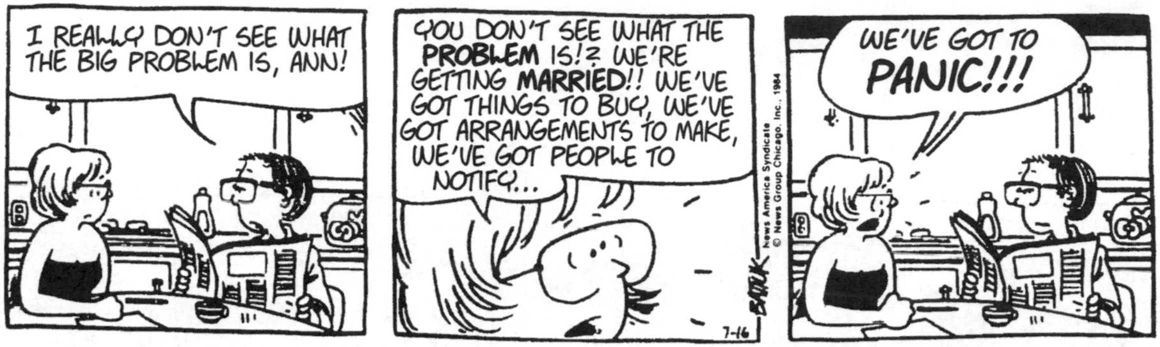
I REALLY DON'T SEE WHAT THE BIG PROBLEM IS, ANN!
YOU DON'T SEE WHAT THE **PROBLEM** IS!? WE'RE GETTING **MARRIED**!! WE'VE GOT THINGS TO BUY, WE'VE GOT ARRANGEMENTS TO MAKE, WE'VE GOT PEOPLE TO NOTIFY...
7-16
BATIUK
News America Syndicate © News Group Chicago, Inc., 1984
WE'VE GOT TO **PANIC!!!**

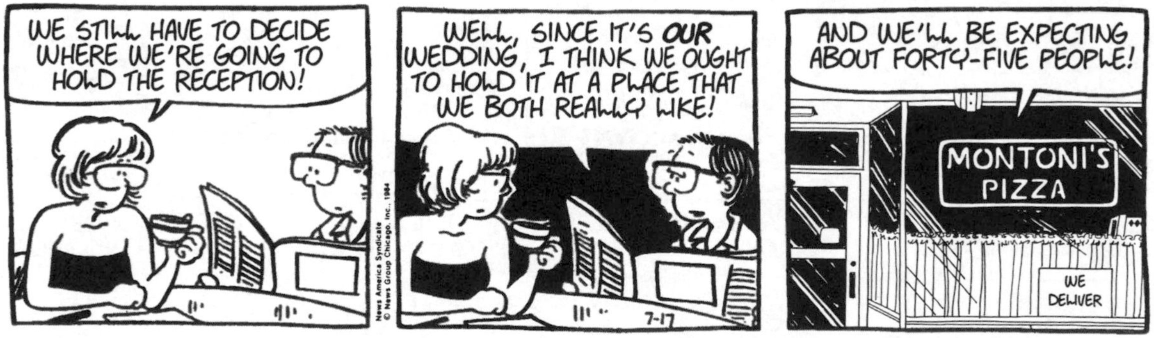
WE STILL HAVE TO DECIDE WHERE WE'RE GOING TO HOLD THE RECEPTION!
News America Syndicate © News Group Chicago, Inc., 1984
WELL, SINCE IT'S **OUR** WEDDING, I THINK WE OUGHT TO HOLD IT AT A PLACE THAT WE BOTH REALLY LIKE!
7-17
AND WE'LL BE EXPECTING ABOUT FORTY-FIVE PEOPLE!
MONTONI'S PIZZA
WE DELIVER

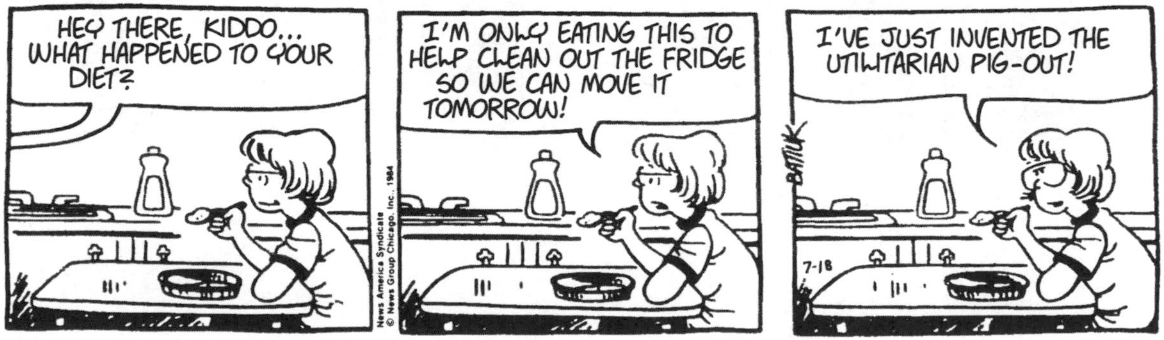
HEY THERE, KIDDO... WHAT HAPPENED TO YOUR DIET?
News America Syndicate © News Group Chicago, Inc., 1984
I'M ONLY EATING THIS TO HELP CLEAN OUT THE FRIDGE SO WE CAN MOVE IT TOMORROW!
BATIUK
I'VE JUST INVENTED THE UTILITARIAN PIG-OUT!
7-18

HONEY, WHAT'S WRONG?
SNIFF!
News America Syndicate © News Group Chicago, Inc., 1984
ARE YOU FEELING SAD ABOUT LEAVING YOUR OLD PLACE?
BATIUK
7-19
NO, I JUST HATE MOVING!

I DON'T UNDERSTAND IT!
U-MAUL
BATIUK
HOW COULD I MOVE INTO THIS APARTMENT WITH TEN BOXES OF STUFF AND LEAVE WITH TWENTY-FIVE?
News America Syndicate © News Group Chicago, Inc., 1984
IT'S A MIRACLE!
7-20

WAIT! I HAVE AN IDEA...
BATIUK
MAYBE IT WOULD JUST BE EASIER TO LEAVE IT HERE...
News America Syndicate © News Group Chicago, Inc., 1984
AND BUILD A NEW SET OF STAIRS SOMEWHERE ELSE!
7-21

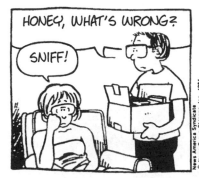

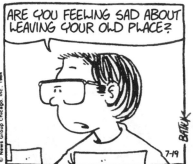

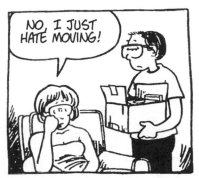

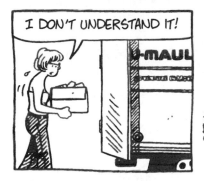

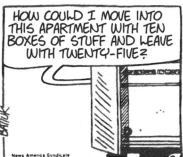

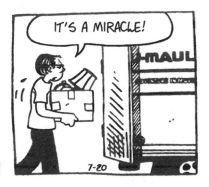

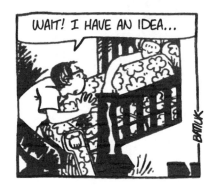

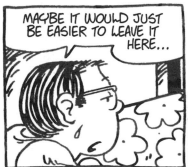

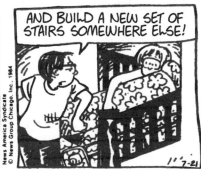

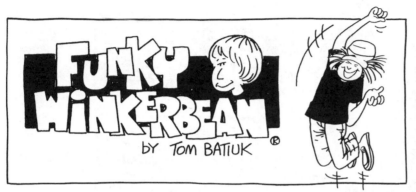

FUNKY WINKERBEAN
BY TOM BATIUK ®
CRAZY HARRY'S AIR GUITAR GUIDE
— THE VERTICAL POSES —
ANY FOOL CAN PLAY AN AIR GUITAR HOLDING IT HORIZONTALLY, BUT IF YOU WANT TO BE RECOGNIZED AS A TRULY GREAT 'AIR-HEAD', THEN YOU'LL NEED TO ADD THE FOLLOWING VERTICAL POSES TO YOUR REPERTOIRE! THE IMPORTANT THING TO REMEMBER IS THAT THESE POSES ARE FOR GUITAR ONLY AND SHOULD NEVER BE ATTEMPTED WITH A PIANO!
BATIUK
THE CLASSIC VERTICAL
THE SIDE VERTICAL
THE EXTENDED VERTICAL
(AND MOST DIFFICULT OF ALL) THE EXTENDED VERTICAL ON ONE LEG
News America Syndicate
© News Group Chicago, Inc., 1984
7-22

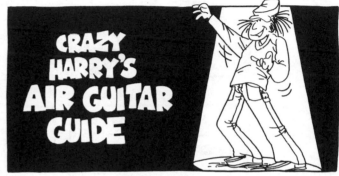

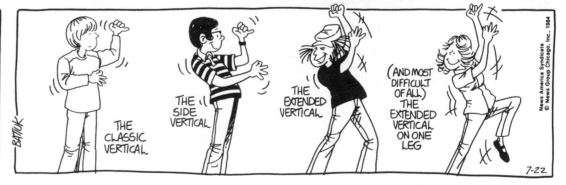

CRAZY, I WANT YOU TO GIVE OUT THESE FREE COUPONS WITH EVERY PIZZA YOU DELIVER!
GREAT! HOW MUCH ARE THEY WORTH?
MONTONI'S PIZZA
WE DELIVER
7-23
NOTHING! THEY'RE JUST FREE COUPONS!
News America Syndicate © News Group Chicago, Inc., 1984
BATIUK

THERE GOES ANGELO'S PIZZA MAKING ANOTHER DELIVERY!
News America Syndicate © News Group Chicago, Inc., 1984
HERE, GO OVER TO THE PAY PHONE AND GIVE ANGELO'S A CALL...
BATIUK
7-24
AND THEN LEAVE IT OFF THE HOOK!

MR. MONTONI! THERE'S A CALL ON THE HOTLINE!
News America Syndicate © News Group Chicago, Inc., 1984
IS THAT A SPECIAL NUMBER FOR RUSH ORDERS?
NO, IT'S JUST THE PHONE NEXT TO THE STOVE!
BATIUK
7-25

THANKS A LOT, MR. MONTONI!
YEAH! SEE YOU NEXT THURSDAY!
MONTONI'S PIZZA
WE DELIVER
News America Syndicate © News Group Chicago, Inc., 1984
`BYE, LADIES!
THEY ALWAYS DROP IN AFTER THEIR AEROBICS CLASS!
BATIUK
7-26

WOW!
News America Syndicate © News Group Chicago, Inc., 1984
A HUNDRED AND SEVENTY-NINE THOUSAND POINTS!
YOU KNOW BUSINESS IS DOWN WHEN MY SCORES GO UP!
BATIUK

WHERE'S MY PIZZA!!? I ORDERED IT OVER THREE HOURS AGO!!!
I APOLOGIZE FOR THE DELAY, SIR! OUR DELIVERY BOY SHOULD BE THERE ANY MINUTE NOW!
News America Syndicate © News Group Chicago, Inc., 1984
BATIUK
NO ONE WILL EVER ACCUSE MONTONI'S OF BEING A FAST-FOOD PLACE!
7-28

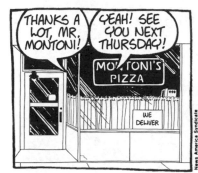

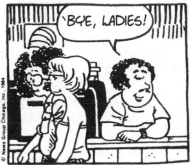

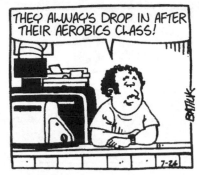

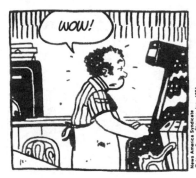

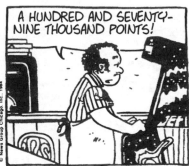

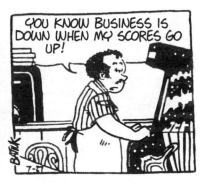

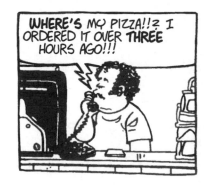

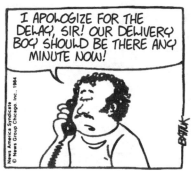

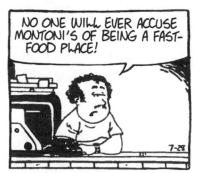

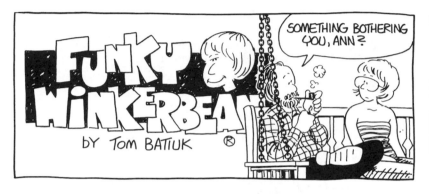

FUNKY WINKERBEAN
BY TOM BATIUK ®
SOMETHING BOTHERING YOU, ANN?
I GUESS I'M A LITTLE NERVOUS ABOUT GETTING MARRIED BEFORE THE RIGHT MOVIE COMES ALONG, NEAL!
THE RIGHT MOVIE?
I FIRST BEGAN TO QUESTION WHAT MY LIFE WAS ALL ABOUT WHEN I SAW 'REBEL WITHOUT A CAUSE' ON THE LATE LATE MOVIE AT A PAJAMA PARTY!
BATIUK
THINGS SORT OF CRYSTALLIZED FOR ME WHEN I SAW 'THE GRADUATE' IN COLLEGE AND, WHEN THE MOVIE 'WOODSTOCK' APPEARED, IT EXPRESSED MY NEW-FOUND SENSE OF FREEDOM!
THOUSE
7-29
BUT THEN THE 'BIG CHILL' CAME ALONG AND THINGS STARTED TO BECOME UNRAVELED AGAIN!
News America Syndicate
© News Group Chicago, Inc., 1984
WHEN I DIE, THEY'LL PROBABLY RUN MY OBITUARY AS A REVIEW IN THE ENTERTAINMENT SECTION!

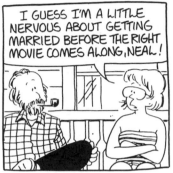

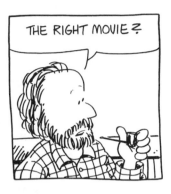

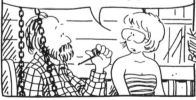

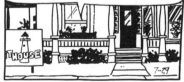

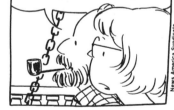

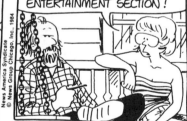

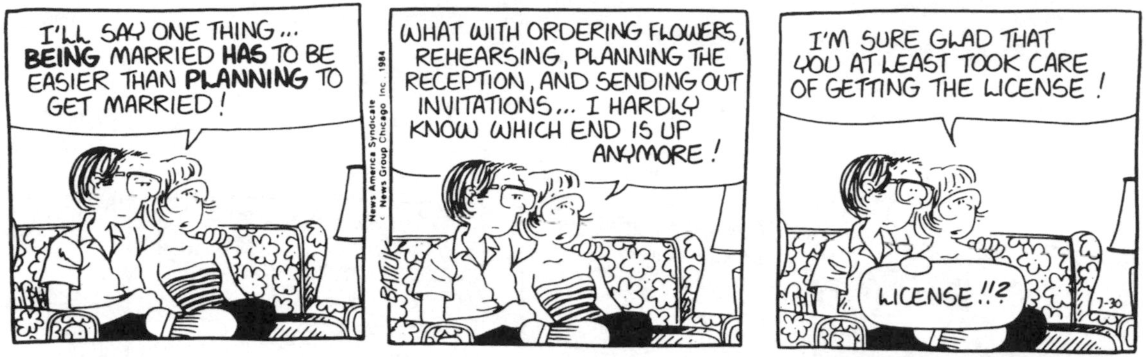
I'LL SAY ONE THING... **BEING** MARRIED **HAS** TO BE EASIER THAN **PLANNING** TO GET MARRIED!
News America Syndicate © News Group Chicago, Inc. 1984
BATIUK
WHAT WITH ORDERING FLOWERS, REHEARSING, PLANNING THE RECEPTION, AND SENDING OUT INVITATIONS... I HARDLY KNOW WHICH END IS UP ANYMORE!
I'M SURE GLAD THAT YOU AT LEAST TOOK CARE OF GETTING THE LICENSE!
LICENSE!!?
7-30

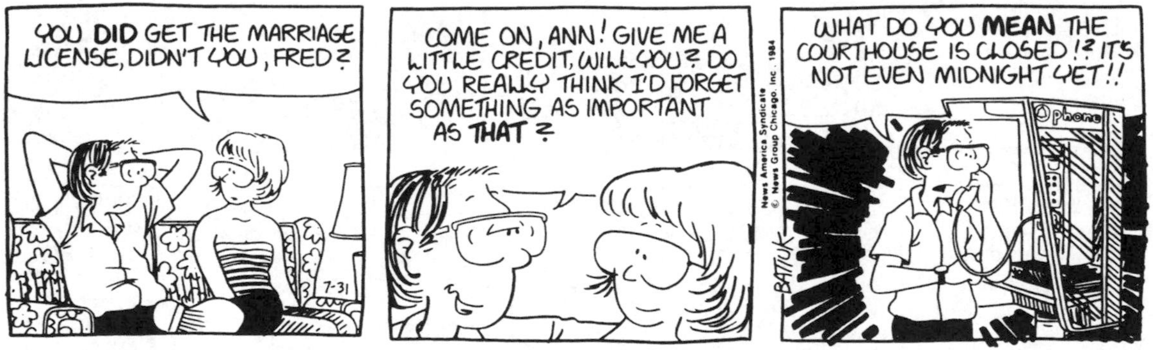
YOU **DID** GET THE MARRIAGE LICENSE, DIDN'T YOU, FRED?
7-31
COME ON, ANN! GIVE ME A LITTLE CREDIT, WILL YOU? DO YOU REALLY THINK I'D FORGET SOMETHING AS IMPORTANT AS **THAT**?
News America Syndicate © News Group Chicago, Inc. 1984
BATIUK
WHAT DO YOU **MEAN** THE COURTHOUSE IS CLOSED!? IT'S NOT EVEN MIDNIGHT YET!!
phone

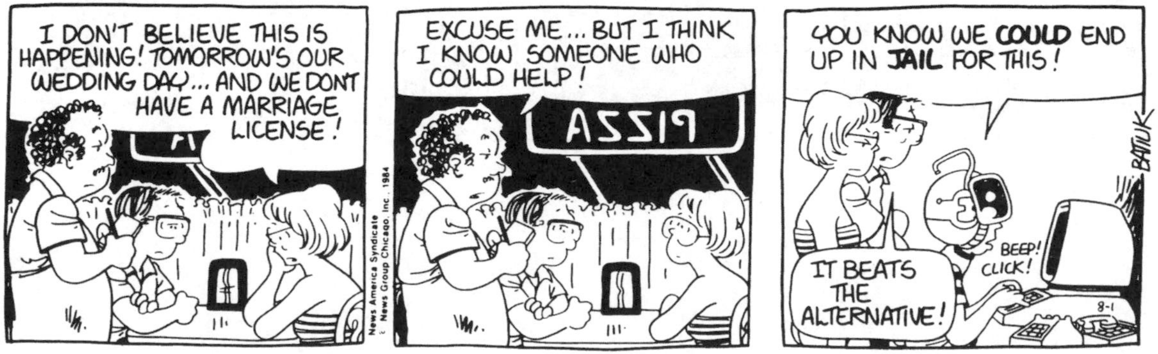
I DON'T BELIEVE THIS IS HAPPENING! TOMORROW'S OUR WEDDING DAY... AND WE DONT HAVE A MARRIAGE LICENSE!
News America Syndicate © News Group Chicago, Inc. 1984
EXCUSE ME... BUT I THINK I KNOW SOMEONE WHO COULD HELP!
PIZZA
YOU KNOW WE **COULD** END UP IN **JAIL** FOR THIS!
BATIUK
IT BEATS THE ALTERNATIVE!
BEEP! CLICK!
8-1

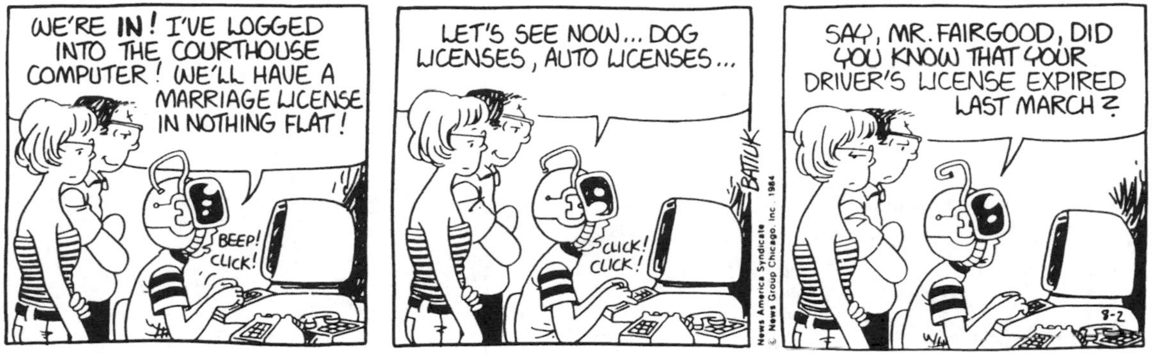
WE'RE **IN**! I'VE LOGGED INTO THE COURTHOUSE COMPUTER! WE'LL HAVE A MARRIAGE LICENSE IN NOTHING FLAT!
BEEP! CLICK!
LET'S SEE NOW... DOG LICENSES, AUTO LICENSES...
CLICK! CLICK!
BATIUK
News America Syndicate
© News Group Chicago, Inc. 1984
SAY, MR. FAIRGOOD, DID YOU KNOW THAT YOUR DRIVER'S LICENSE EXPIRED LAST MARCH?
8-2

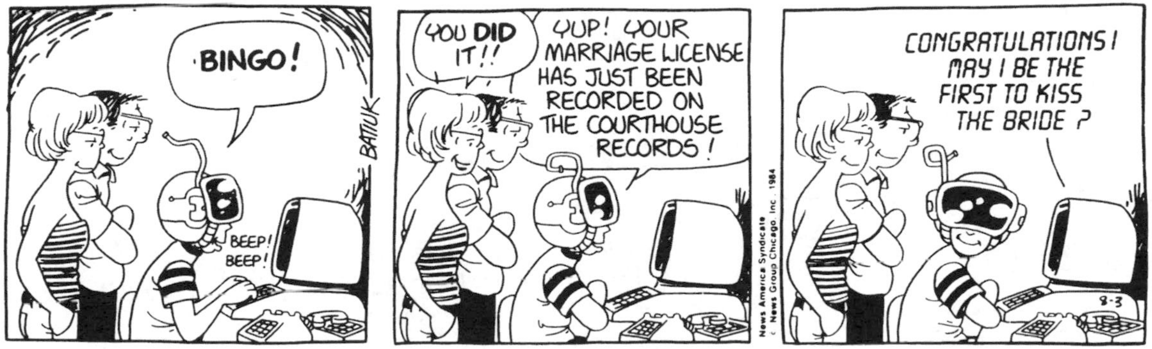
BINGO!
BEEP! BEEP!
BATIUK
YOU **DID** IT!!
YUP! YOUR MARRIAGE LICENSE HAS JUST BEEN RECORDED ON THE COURTHOUSE RECORDS!
News America Syndicate
© News Group Chicago, Inc. 1984
CONGRATULATIONS! MAY I BE THE FIRST TO KISS THE BRIDE?
8-3

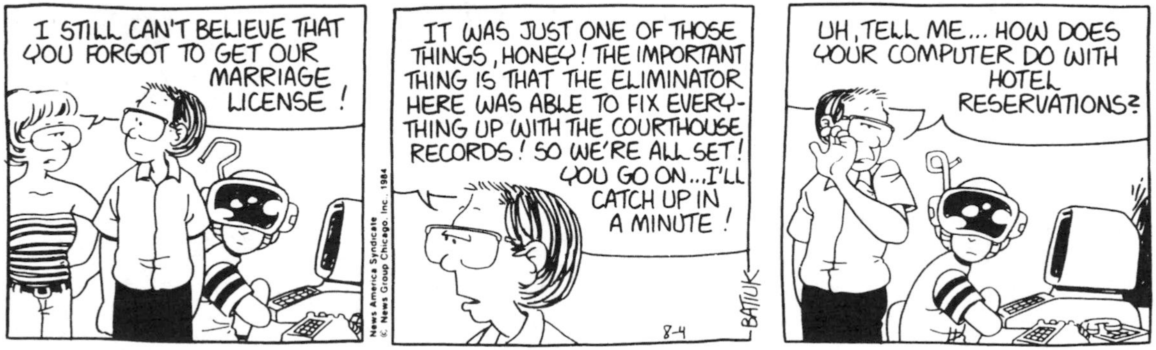
I STILL CAN'T BELIEVE THAT YOU FORGOT TO GET OUR MARRIAGE LICENSE!
News America Syndicate
© News Group Chicago, Inc. 1984
IT WAS JUST ONE OF THOSE THINGS, HONEY! THE IMPORTANT THING IS THAT THE ELIMINATOR HERE WAS ABLE TO FIX EVERYTHING UP WITH THE COURTHOUSE RECORDS! SO WE'RE ALL SET! YOU GO ON...I'LL CATCH UP IN A MINUTE!
8-4
BATIUK
UH, TELL ME... HOW DOES YOUR COMPUTER DO WITH HOTEL RESERVATIONS?

FUNKY WINKERBEAN
BY TOM BATIUK
WHY DO I PUT MYSELF THROUGH THIS EVERY YEAR?
SO WHAT IF I DON'T JUMP OFF THIS HIGH DIVE?
I MEAN LET'S FACE IT! WHO'LL EVER KNOW?
BATIUK
HI, THIS IS JIM McKAY! WE INTERRUPT OUR OLYMPIC COVERAGE TO BRING YOU THIS SPECIAL SPORTING EVENT!
8-5

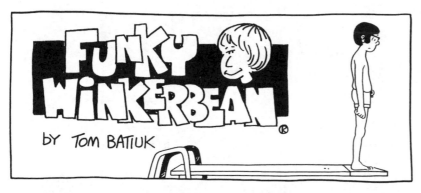

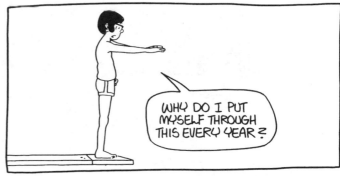

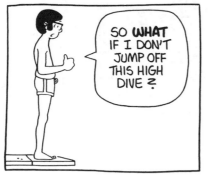

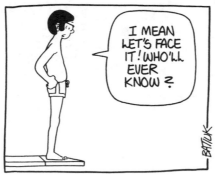

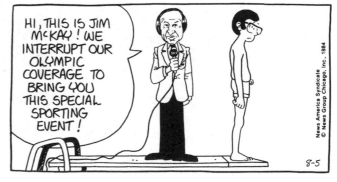

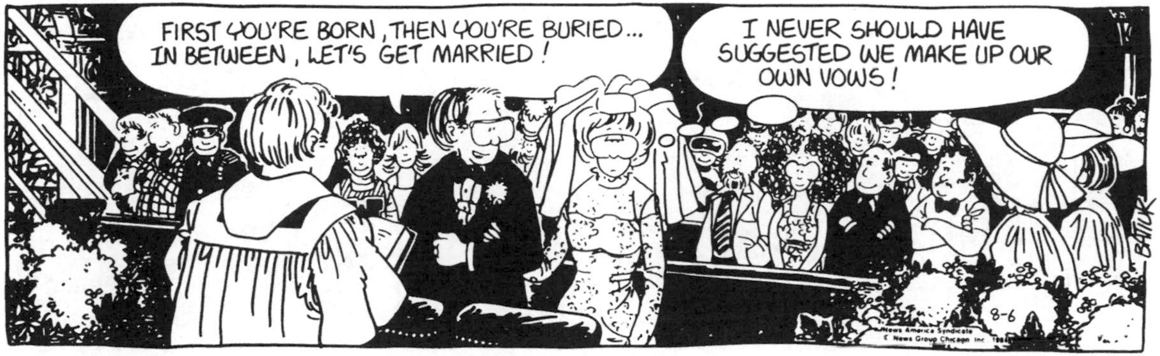
FIRST YOU'RE BORN, THEN YOU'RE BURIED... IN BETWEEN, LET'S GET MARRIED!
I NEVER SHOULD HAVE SUGGESTED WE MAKE UP OUR OWN VOWS!
BATIUK
8-6

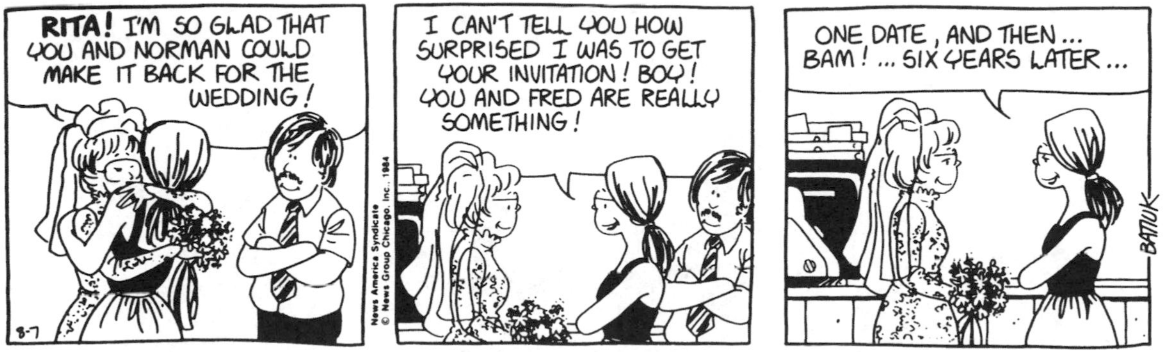
RITA! I'M SO GLAD THAT YOU AND NORMAN COULD MAKE IT BACK FOR THE WEDDING!
8-7
News America Syndicate
© News Group Chicago, Inc., 1984
I CAN'T TELL YOU HOW SURPRISED I WAS TO GET YOUR INVITATION! BOY! YOU AND FRED ARE REALLY SOMETHING!
ONE DATE, AND THEN... BAM! ... SIX YEARS LATER...
BATIUK

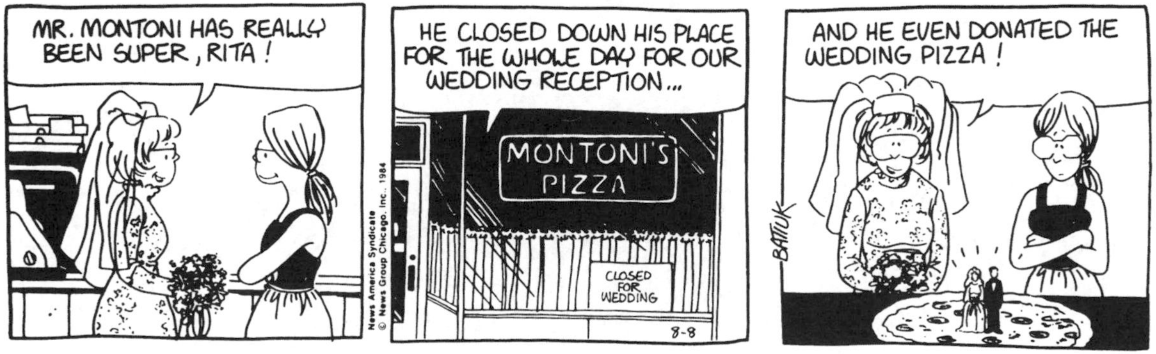
MR. MONTONI HAS REALLY BEEN SUPER, RITA!
News America Syndicate
© News Group Chicago, Inc., 1984
HE CLOSED DOWN HIS PLACE FOR THE WHOLE DAY FOR OUR WEDDING RECEPTION...
MONTONI'S PIZZA
CLOSED FOR WEDDING
8-8
BATIUK
AND HE EVEN DONATED THE WEDDING PIZZA!

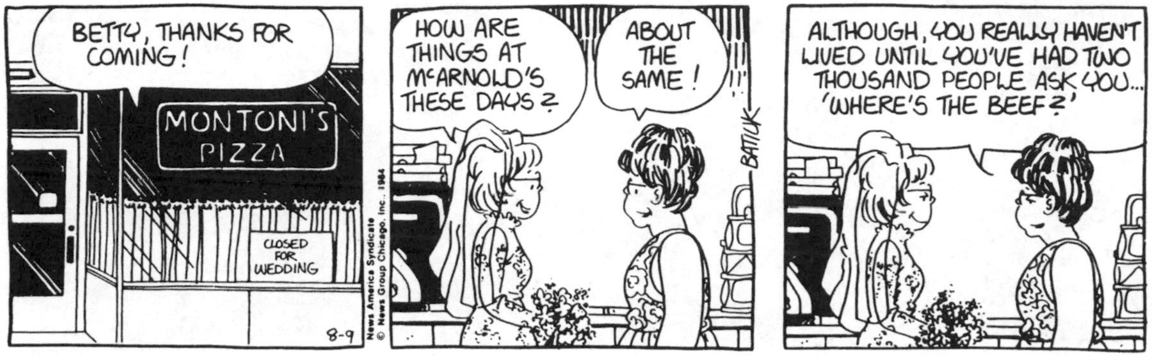
BETTY, THANKS FOR COMING!
MONTONI'S PIZZA
CLOSED FOR WEDDING
8-9
News America Syndicate © News Group Chicago, Inc. 1984
HOW ARE THINGS AT McARNOLD'S THESE DAYS?
ABOUT THE SAME!
BATIUK
ALTHOUGH, YOU REALLY HAVEN'T LIVED UNTIL YOU'VE HAD TWO THOUSAND PEOPLE ASK YOU... 'WHERE'S THE BEEF?'

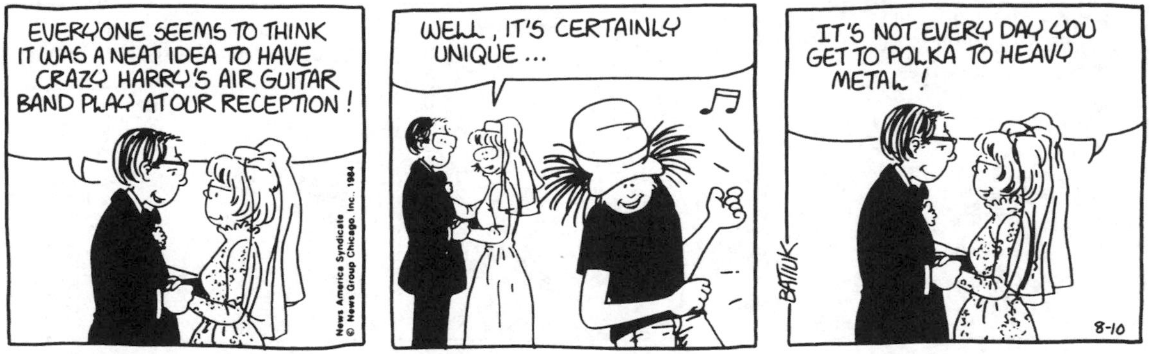
EVERYONE SEEMS TO THINK IT WAS A NEAT IDEA TO HAVE CRAZY HARRY'S AIR GUITAR BAND PLAY AT OUR RECEPTION!
News America Syndicate © News Group Chicago, Inc. 1984
WELL, IT'S CERTAINLY UNIQUE...
IT'S NOT EVERY DAY YOU GET TO POLKA TO HEAVY METAL!
BATIUK
8-10

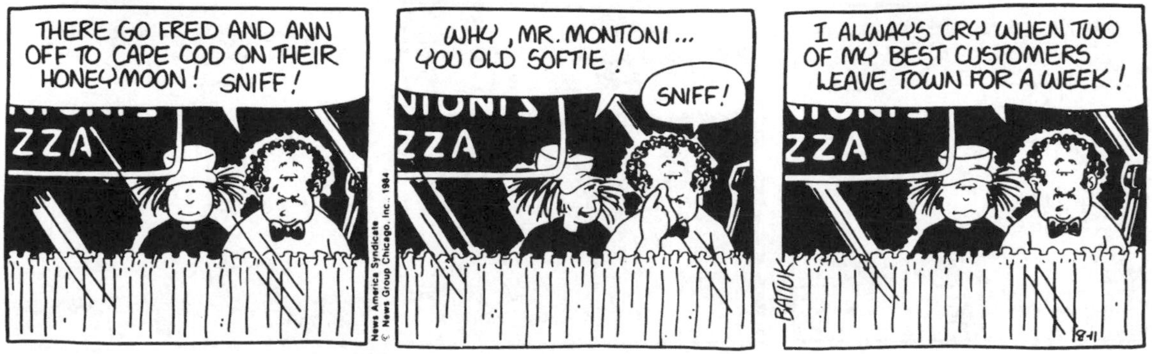
THERE GO FRED AND ANN OFF TO CAPE COD ON THEIR HONEYMOON! SNIFF!
News America Syndicate © News Group Chicago, Inc. 1984
WHY, MR. MONTONI... YOU OLD SOFTIE!
SNIFF!
BATIUK
I ALWAYS CRY WHEN TWO OF MY BEST CUSTOMERS LEAVE TOWN FOR A WEEK!
8-11

FUNKY WINKERBEAN
BY TOM BATIUK
MELODY GROVE BAND CAMP
HOW'S YOUR NEW 'SCRIPT WESTVIEW' ROUTINE COMING?
NOT TOO WELL... IS THERE ANY WAY WE CAN SHORTEN THE NAME OF THE SCHOOL?
OKAY, PEOPLE... LET'S TAKE IT FROM THE TOP...
AND TRY SPELLING OUT THE WORD 'WESTVIEW' ON THE FIELD AGAIN!
AND THIS TIME REMEMBER...
IT'S 'I' BEFORE 'E' EXCEPT AFTER 'C'!!
BATIUK
8-12
News America Syndicate
© News Group Chicago, Inc., 1984

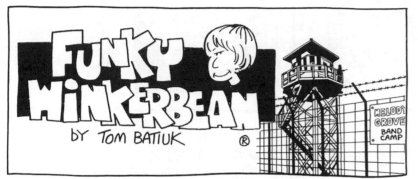

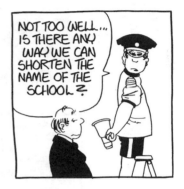

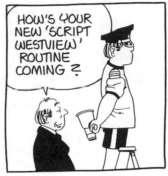

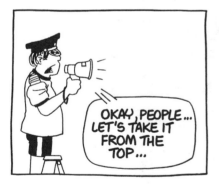

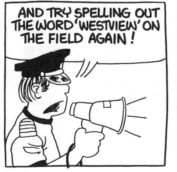

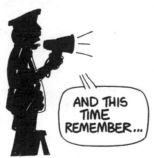

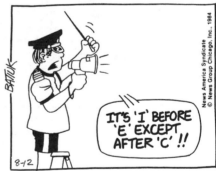

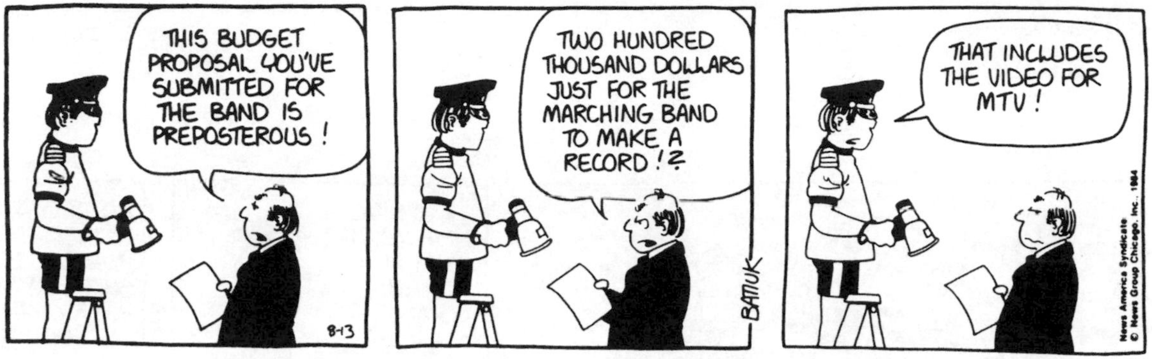
THIS BUDGET PROPOSAL YOU'VE SUBMITTED FOR THE BAND IS PREPOSTEROUS!
8-13
TWO HUNDRED THOUSAND DOLLARS JUST FOR THE MARCHING BAND TO MAKE A RECORD!?
BATIUK
THAT INCLUDES THE VIDEO FOR MTV!
News America Syndicate © News Group Chicago, Inc., 1984

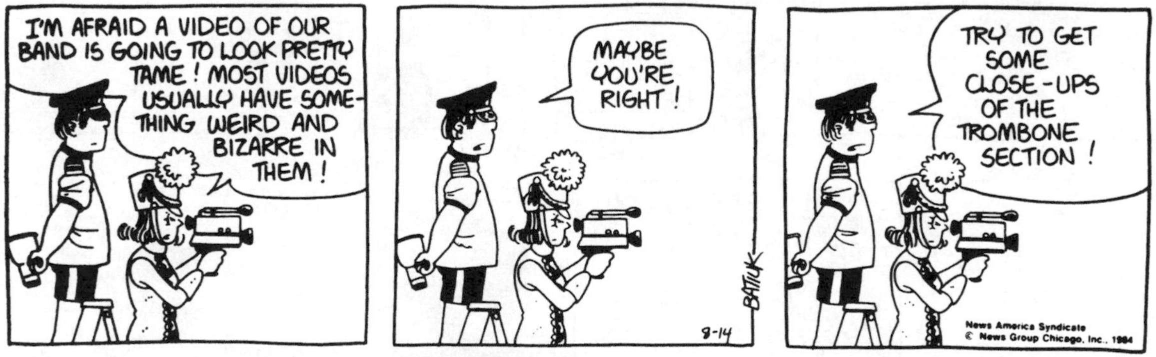
I'M AFRAID A VIDEO OF OUR BAND IS GOING TO LOOK PRETTY TAME! MOST VIDEOS USUALLY HAVE SOMETHING WEIRD AND BIZARRE IN THEM!
MAYBE YOU'RE RIGHT!
BATIUK
8-14
TRY TO GET SOME CLOSE-UPS OF THE TROMBONE SECTION!
News America Syndicate © News Group Chicago, Inc., 1984

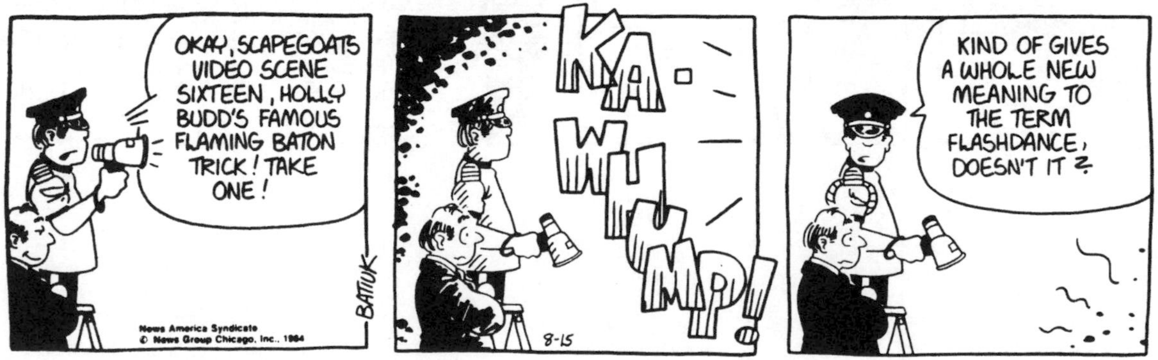
OKAY, SCAPEGOATS VIDEO SCENE SIXTEEN, HOLLY BUDD'S FAMOUS FLAMING BATON TRICK! TAKE ONE!
News America Syndicate © News Group Chicago, Inc., 1984
BATIUK
KA-WHUMP!
8-15
KIND OF GIVES A WHOLE NEW MEANING TO THE TERM FLASHDANCE, DOESN'T IT?

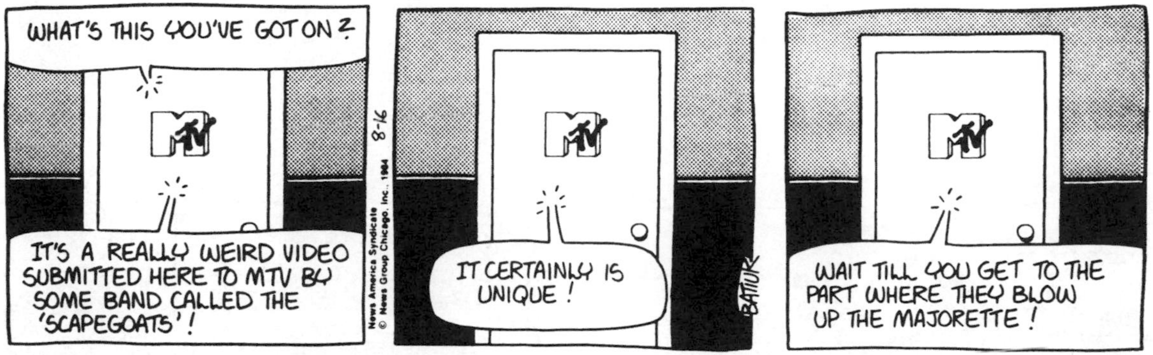
WHAT'S THIS YOU'VE GOT ON?
IT'S A REALLY WEIRD VIDEO SUBMITTED HERE TO MTV BY SOME BAND CALLED THE 'SCAPEGOATS'!
8-16
News America Syndicate
© News Group Chicago, Inc., 1984
IT CERTAINLY IS UNIQUE!
BATIUK
WAIT TILL YOU GET TO THE PART WHERE THEY BLOW UP THE MAJORETTE!

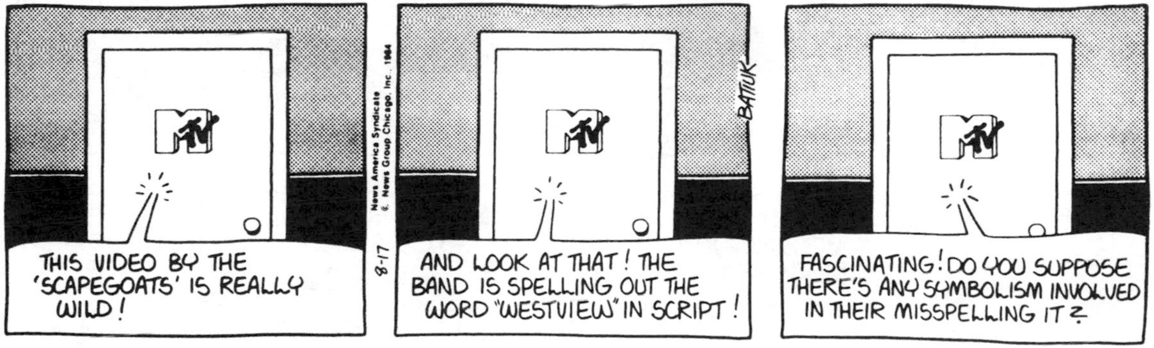
THIS VIDEO BY THE 'SCAPEGOATS' IS REALLY WILD!
News America Syndicate
© News Group Chicago, Inc., 1984
8-17
AND LOOK AT THAT! THE BAND IS SPELLING OUT THE WORD "WESTVIEW" IN SCRIPT!
BATIUK
FASCINATING! DO YOU SUPPOSE THERE'S ANY SYMBOLISM INVOLVED IN THEIR MISSPELLING IT?

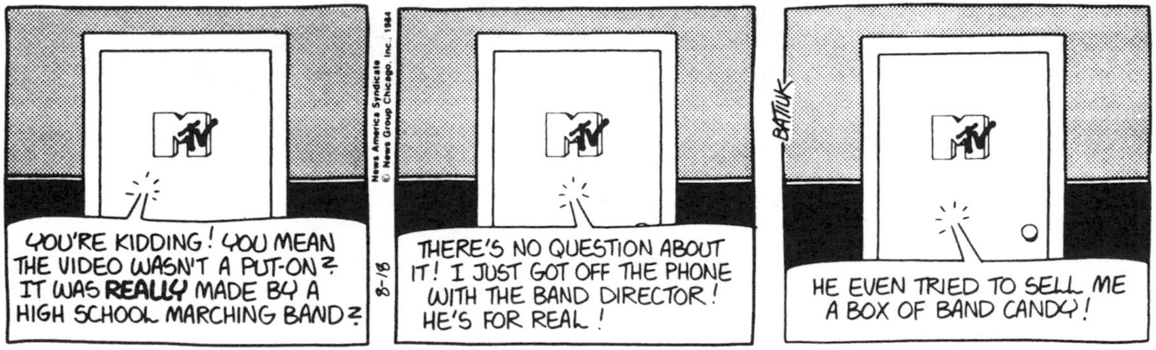
YOU'RE KIDDING! YOU MEAN THE VIDEO WASN'T A PUT-ON? IT WAS **REALLY** MADE BY A HIGH SCHOOL MARCHING BAND?
News America Syndicate
© News Group Chicago, Inc., 1984
8-18
THERE'S NO QUESTION ABOUT IT! I JUST GOT OFF THE PHONE WITH THE BAND DIRECTOR! HE'S FOR REAL!
BATIUK
HE EVEN TRIED TO SELL ME A BOX OF BAND CANDY!

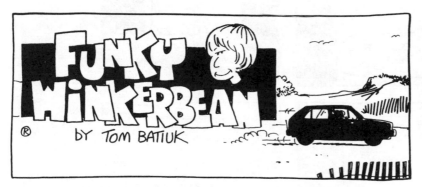

FUNKY WINKERBEAN
®
BY TOM BATIUK
WE'RE HERE!
CAPE COD AT LAST!
JUST MARRIED
THIS PLACE IS REALLY NICE, ISN'T IT, FRED?
8-19
YEAH, BUT I WISH WE'D HAVE BROUGHT OUR REFRIGERATOR WITH US!
MARINE SUPPLIES
OUR REFRIGERATOR!? WHY?
News America Syndicate
© News Group Chicago, Inc., 1984
BECAUSE OUR RESERVATIONS ARE SITTING ON TOP OF IT!
BATIUK

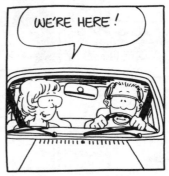

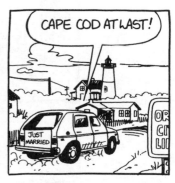

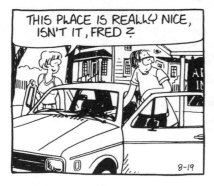

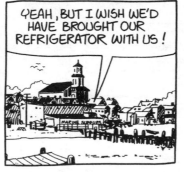

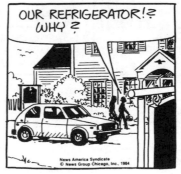

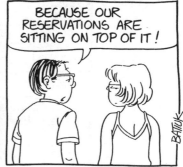

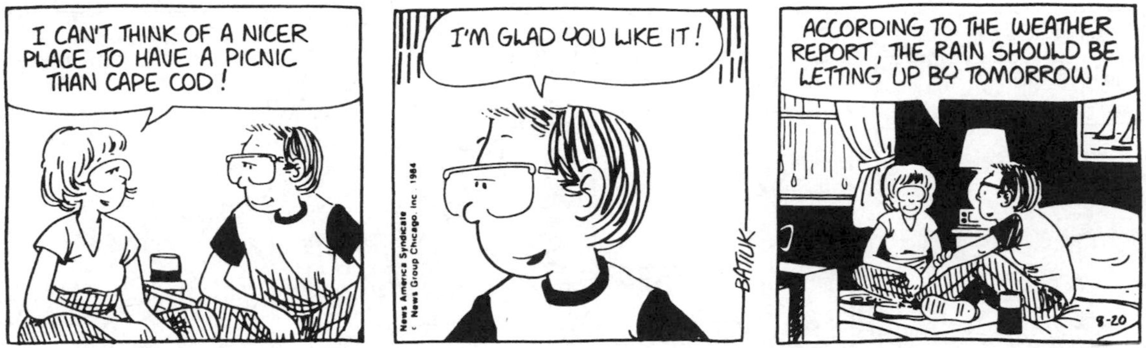
I CAN'T THINK OF A NICER PLACE TO HAVE A PICNIC THAN CAPE COD!
I'M GLAD YOU LIKE IT!
News America Syndicate
© News Group Chicago, Inc. 1984
BATIUK
ACCORDING TO THE WEATHER REPORT, THE RAIN SHOULD BE LETTING UP BY TOMORROW!
8-20

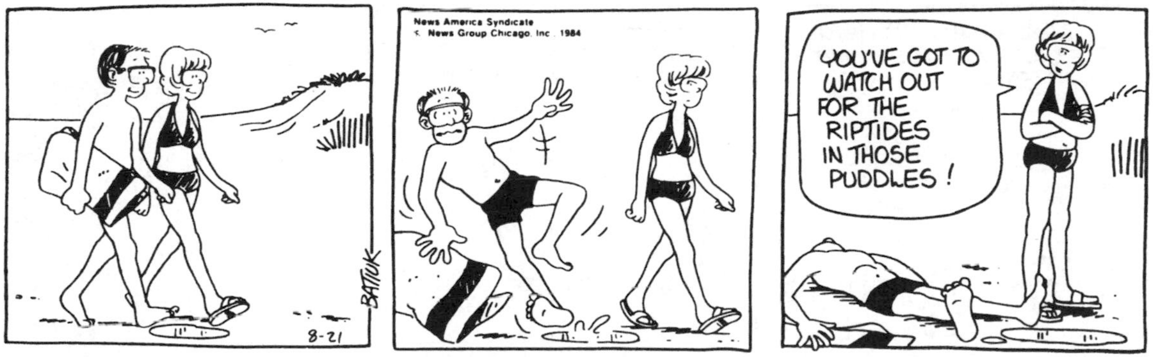
BATIUK
8-21
News America Syndicate
© News Group Chicago, Inc. 1984
YOU'VE GOT TO WATCH OUT FOR THE RIPTIDES IN THOSE PUDDLES!

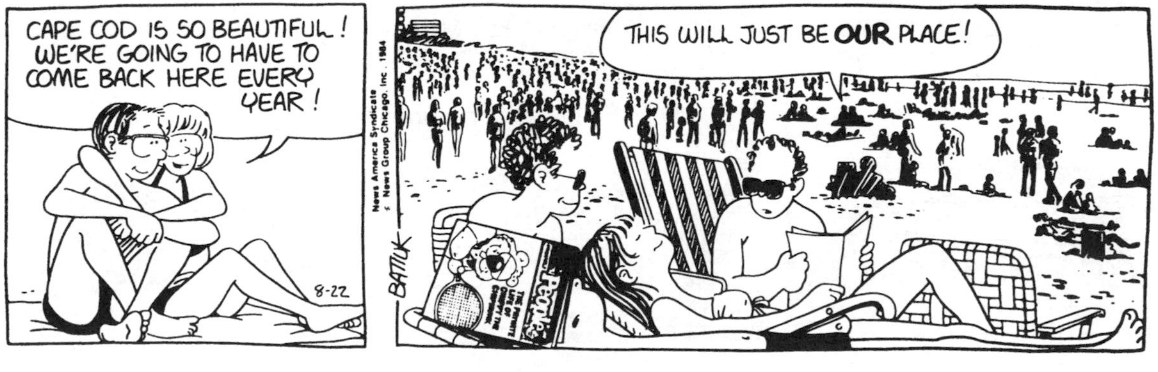
CAPE COD IS SO BEAUTIFUL! WE'RE GOING TO HAVE TO COME BACK HERE EVERY YEAR!
8-22
News America Syndicate
© News Group Chicago, Inc. 1984
BATIUK
THIS WILL JUST BE **OUR** PLACE!
People

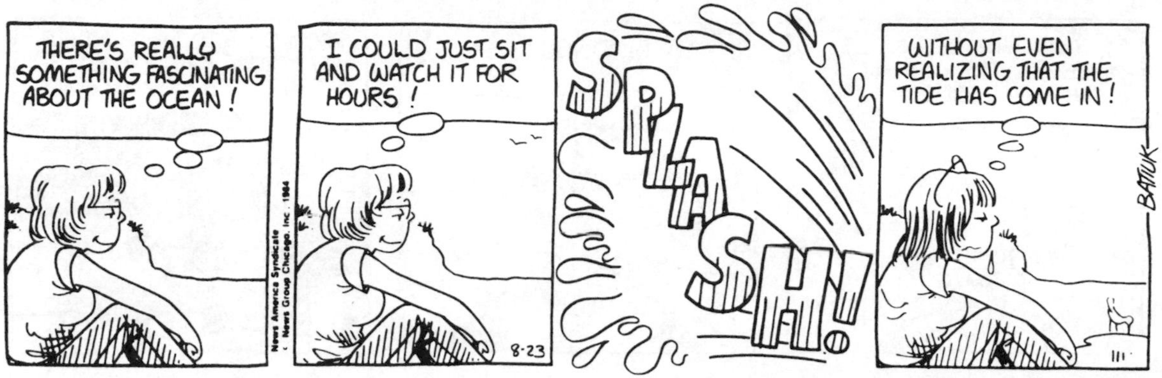
THERE'S REALLY SOMETHING FASCINATING ABOUT THE OCEAN!
News America Syndicate © News Group Chicago, Inc. 1984
I COULD JUST SIT AND WATCH IT FOR HOURS!
8-23
SPLASH!
WITHOUT EVEN REALIZING THAT THE TIDE HAS COME IN!
BATIUK

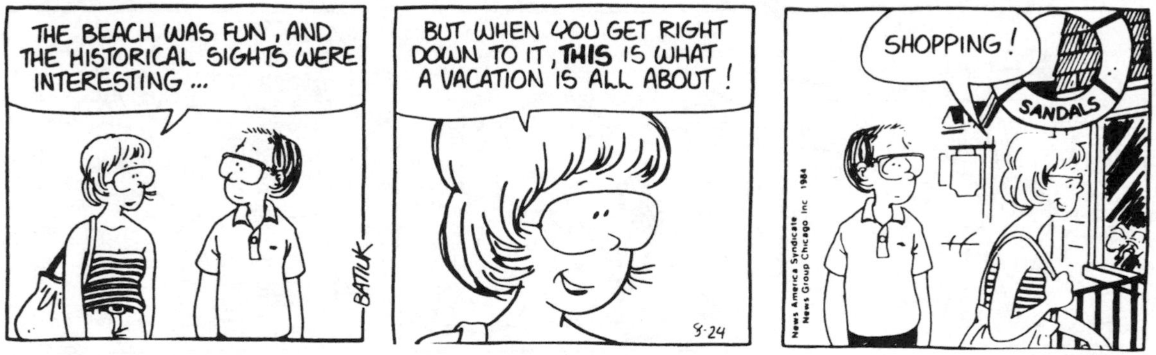
THE BEACH WAS FUN, AND THE HISTORICAL SIGHTS WERE INTERESTING...
BATIUK
BUT WHEN YOU GET RIGHT DOWN TO IT, **THIS** IS WHAT A VACATION IS ALL ABOUT!
8-24
SHOPPING!
SANDALS
News America Syndicate News Group Chicago Inc 1984

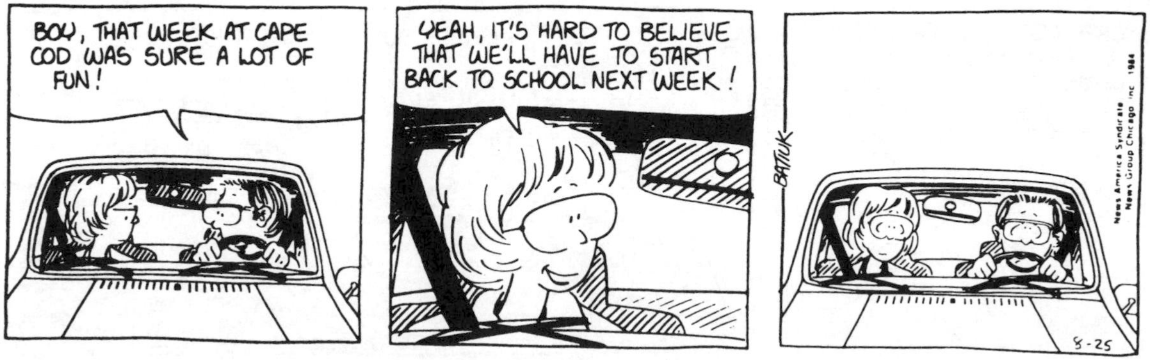
BOY, THAT WEEK AT CAPE COD WAS SURE A LOT OF FUN!
YEAH, IT'S HARD TO BELIEVE THAT WE'LL HAVE TO START BACK TO SCHOOL NEXT WEEK!
BATIUK
News America Syndicate News Group Chicago Inc 1984
8-25

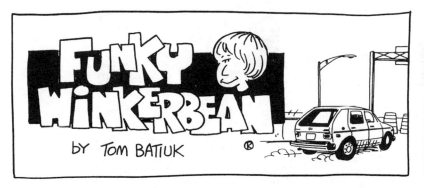

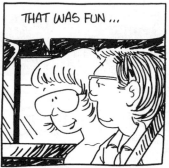

FUNKY WINKERBEAN
by TOM BATIUK ®
THAT WAS FUN ...
BUT IT'S KIND OF NICE TO BE BACK HOME!
WELL, WE'RE BACK AT OUR APARTMENT FOR THE FIRST TIME AS HUSBAND AND WIFE!
8-26
ARE YOU GOING TO CARRY ME ACROSS THE THRESHOLD?
NO PARKIN IN DRIV
BATIUK
News America Syndicate © News Group Chicago, Inc., 1984
OF COURSE!
THIS ISN'T EXACTLY WHAT I HAD IN MIND!

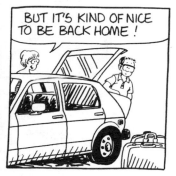

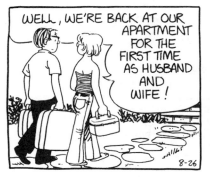

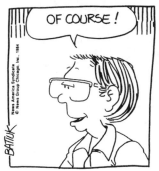

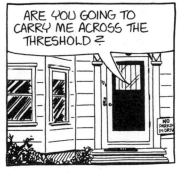

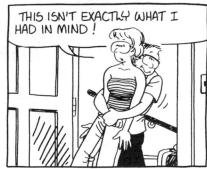

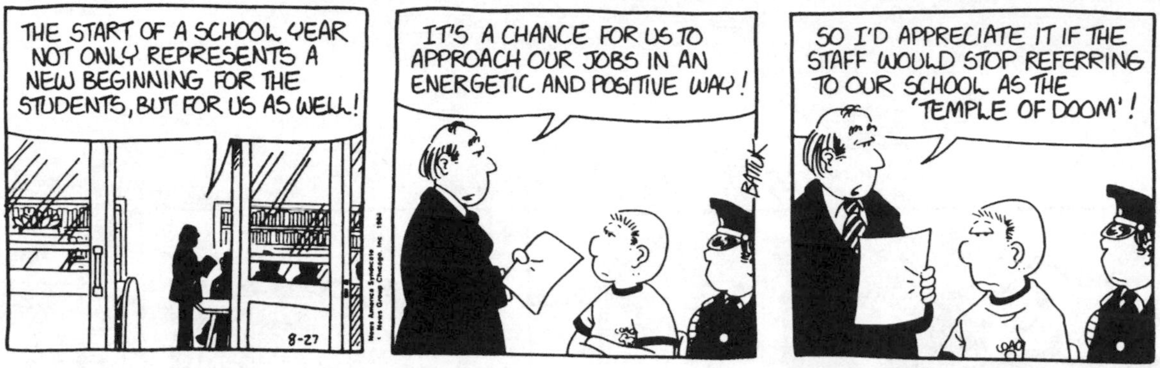
THE START OF A SCHOOL YEAR NOT ONLY REPRESENTS A NEW BEGINNING FOR THE STUDENTS, BUT FOR US AS WELL!
IT'S A CHANCE FOR US TO APPROACH OUR JOBS IN AN ENERGETIC AND POSITIVE WAY!
SO I'D APPRECIATE IT IF THE STAFF WOULD STOP REFERRING TO OUR SCHOOL AS THE 'TEMPLE OF DOOM'!
8-27
BATIUK

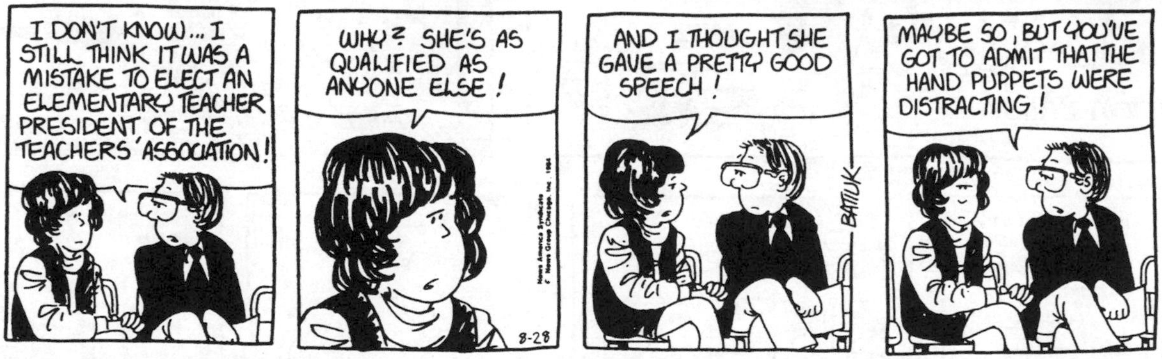
I DON'T KNOW... I STILL THINK IT WAS A MISTAKE TO ELECT AN ELEMENTARY TEACHER PRESIDENT OF THE TEACHERS' ASSOCIATION!
WHY? SHE'S AS QUALIFIED AS ANYONE ELSE!
AND I THOUGHT SHE GAVE A PRETTY GOOD SPEECH!
MAYBE SO, BUT YOU'VE GOT TO ADMIT THAT THE HAND PUPPETS WERE DISTRACTING!
8-28
BATIUK

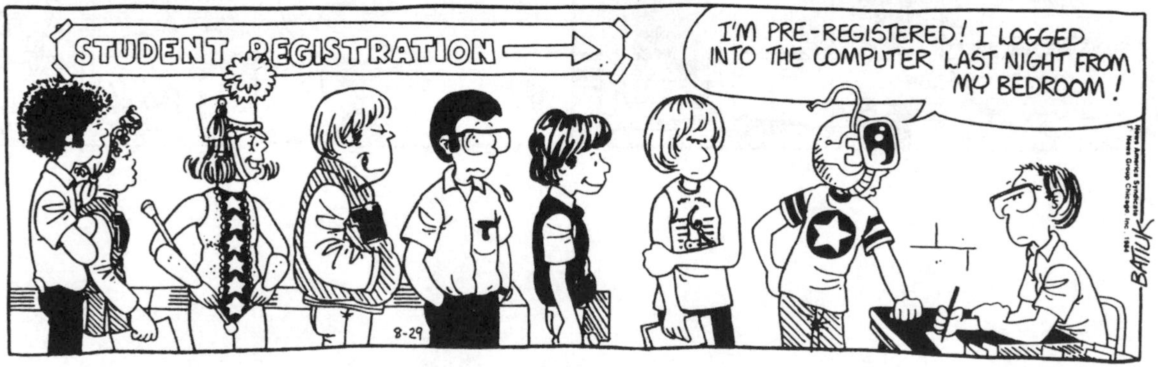
STUDENT REGISTRATION
I'M PRE-REGISTERED! I LOGGED INTO THE COMPUTER LAST NIGHT FROM MY BEDROOM!
8-29
BATIUK

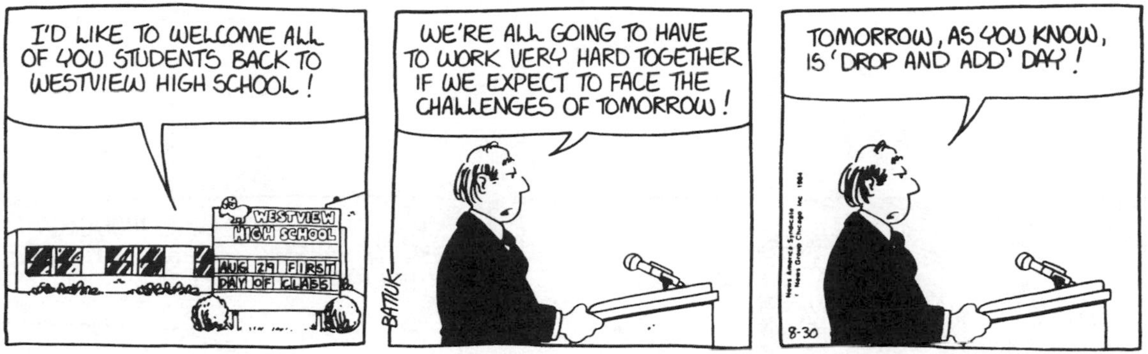
I'D LIKE TO WELCOME ALL OF YOU STUDENTS BACK TO WESTVIEW HIGH SCHOOL!
WESTVIEW HIGH SCHOOL
AUG 29 FIRST DAY OF CLASS
WE'RE ALL GOING TO HAVE TO WORK VERY HARD TOGETHER IF WE EXPECT TO FACE THE CHALLENGES OF TOMORROW!
BATIUK
TOMORROW, AS YOU KNOW, IS 'DROP AND ADD' DAY!
8-30

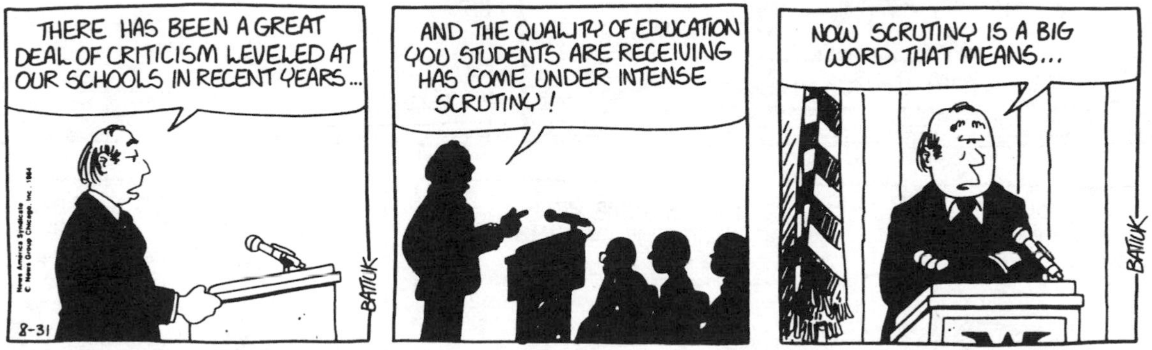
THERE HAS BEEN A GREAT DEAL OF CRITICISM LEVELED AT OUR SCHOOLS IN RECENT YEARS...
8-31
BATIUK
AND THE QUALITY OF EDUCATION YOU STUDENTS ARE RECEIVING HAS COME UNDER INTENSE SCRUTINY!
NOW SCRUTINY IS A BIG WORD THAT MEANS...
BATIUK

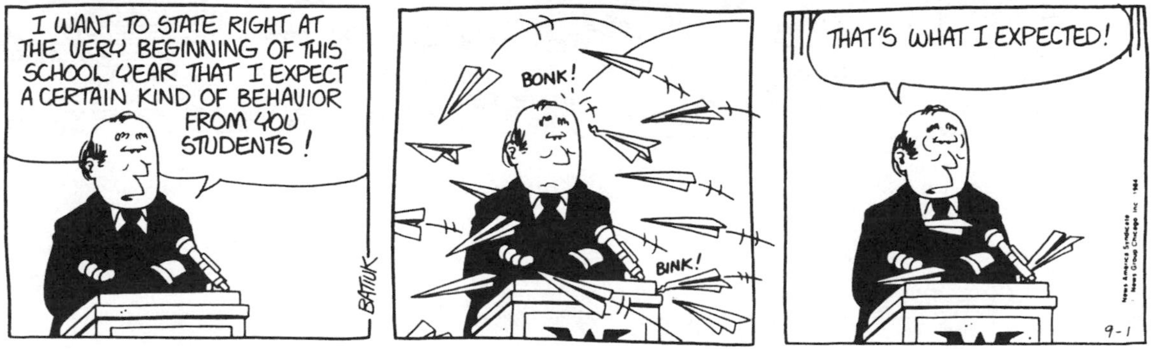
I WANT TO STATE RIGHT AT THE VERY BEGINNING OF THIS SCHOOL YEAR THAT I EXPECT A CERTAIN KIND OF BEHAVIOR FROM YOU STUDENTS!
BATIUK
BONK!
BINK!
THAT'S WHAT I EXPECTED!
9-1

FUNKY WINKERBEAN
BY TOM BATIUK ®
BOY, AM I **BEAT**! WE THUNDERSTORMS REALLY HAVE TO COVER A LOT OF GROUND ON HOLIDAY WEEKENDS!
THERE'S RECENTLY BEEN A SCIENTIFIC BREAKTHROUGH THAT'S BEEN OF REAL INTEREST TO US THUNDERCLOUDS!
IT'S GIVEN US SOME REAL INSIGHT INTO OUR ORIGINS!
BATIUK
News America Syndicate © News Group Chicago, Inc., 1984
THEY'VE PROVEN THAT THUNDERSTORMS ARE THE DIRECT RESULT OF STATIC ELECTRICITY CAUSED BY PEOPLE WAXING CARS!
9-2

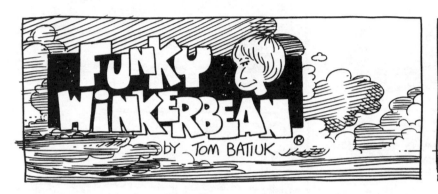

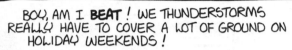

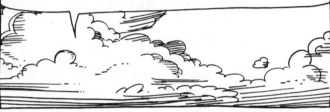

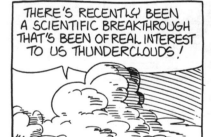

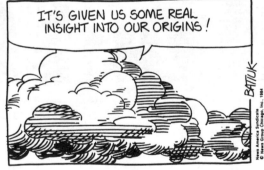

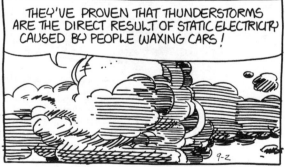

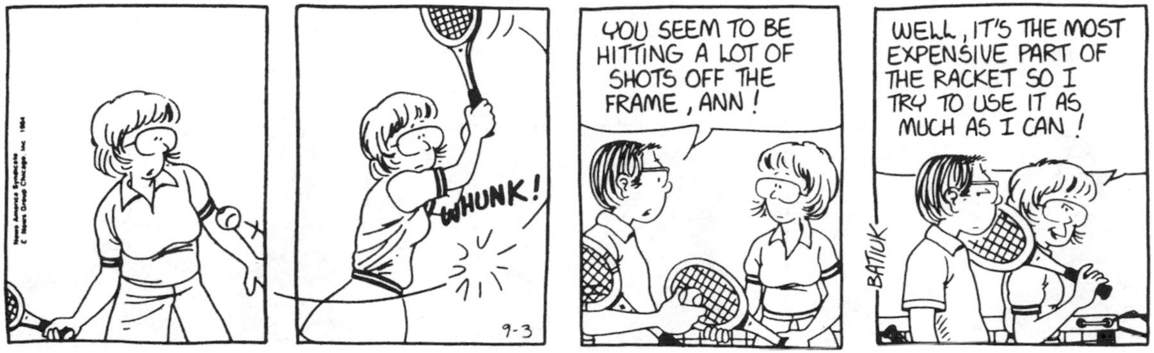
WHUNK!
9-3
YOU SEEM TO BE HITTING A LOT OF SHOTS OFF THE FRAME, ANN!
WELL, IT'S THE MOST EXPENSIVE PART OF THE RACKET SO I TRY TO USE IT AS MUCH AS I CAN!
BATIUK

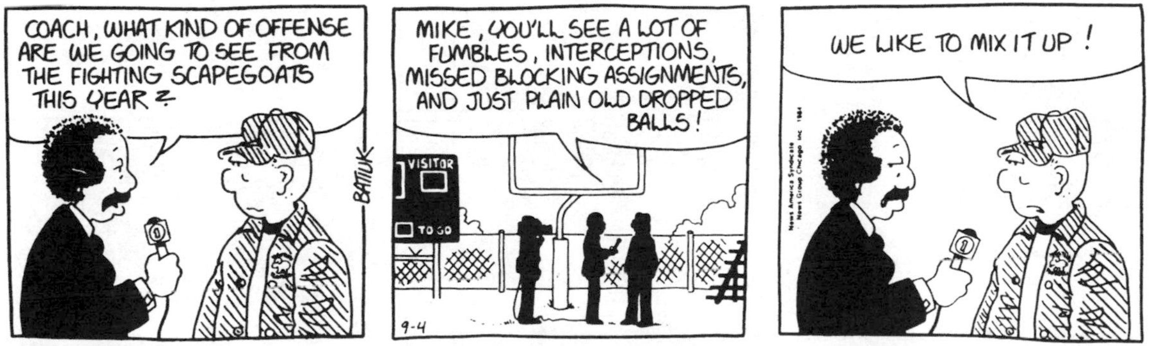
COACH, WHAT KIND OF OFFENSE ARE WE GOING TO SEE FROM THE FIGHTING SCAPEGOATS THIS YEAR?
BATIUK
MIKE, YOU'LL SEE A LOT OF FUMBLES, INTERCEPTIONS, MISSED BLOCKING ASSIGNMENTS, AND JUST PLAIN OLD DROPPED BALLS!
VISITOR
TO GO
9-4
WE LIKE TO MIX IT UP!

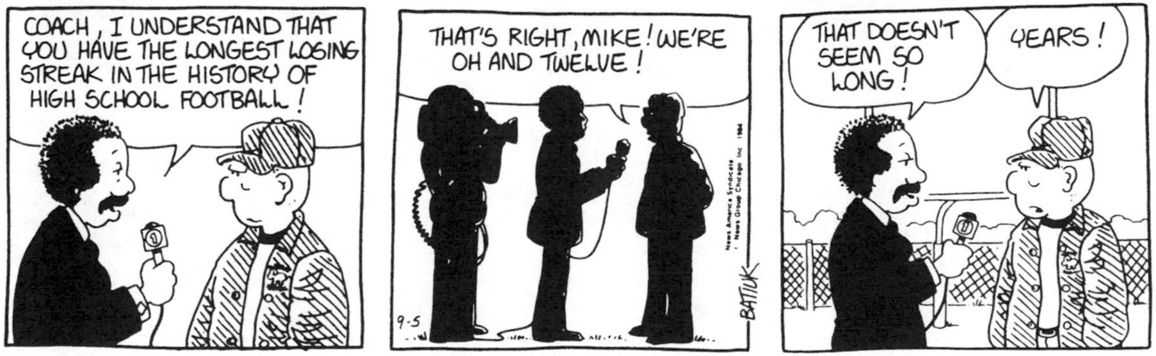
COACH, I UNDERSTAND THAT YOU HAVE THE LONGEST LOSING STREAK IN THE HISTORY OF HIGH SCHOOL FOOTBALL!
THAT'S RIGHT, MIKE! WE'RE OH AND TWELVE!
9-5
BATIUK
THAT DOESN'T SEEM SO LONG!
YEARS!

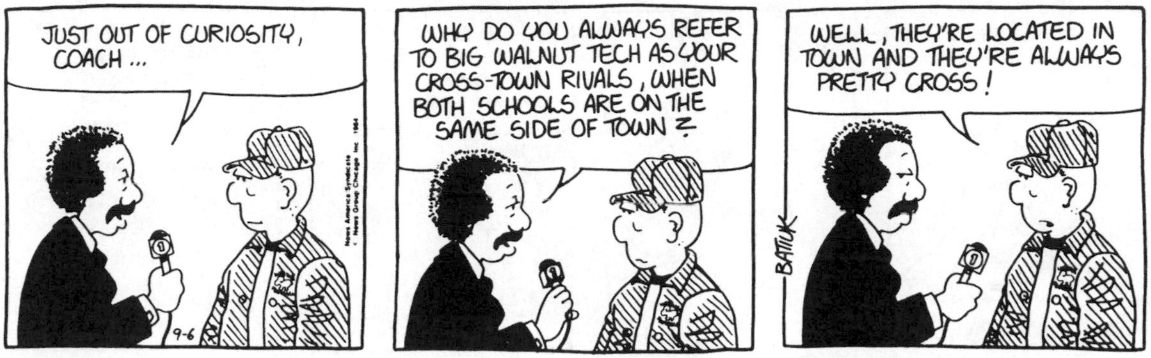
JUST OUT OF CURIOSITY, COACH ...
WHY DO YOU ALWAYS REFER TO BIG WALNUT TECH AS YOUR CROSS-TOWN RIVALS, WHEN BOTH SCHOOLS ARE ON THE SAME SIDE OF TOWN ?
WELL, THEY'RE LOCATED IN TOWN AND THEY'RE ALWAYS PRETTY CROSS !

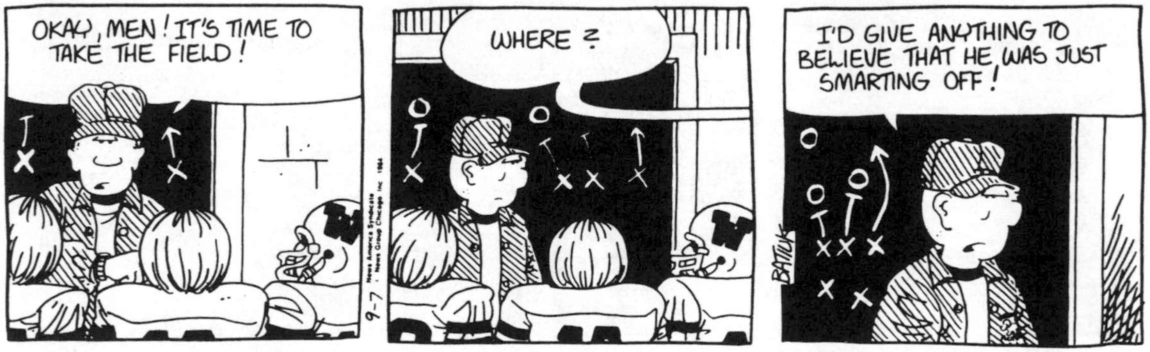
OKAY, MEN ! IT'S TIME TO TAKE THE FIELD !
WHERE ?
I'D GIVE ANYTHING TO BELIEVE THAT HE WAS JUST SMARTING OFF !

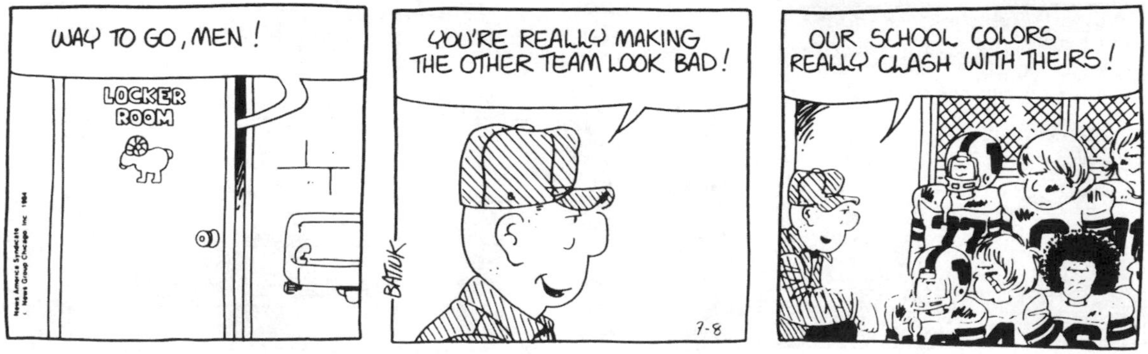
WAY TO GO, MEN !
LOCKER ROOM
YOU'RE REALLY MAKING THE OTHER TEAM LOOK BAD !
OUR SCHOOL COLORS REALLY CLASH WITH THEIRS !

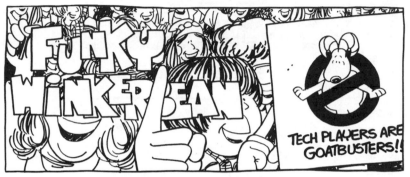

FUNKY WINKERBEAN
TECH PLAYERS ARE GOATBUSTERS!!
LISTEN UP!
LOCKER ROOM
THERE'S ONE LAST THING I WANT TO SAY!
MEN, WHEN YOU TAKE THIS HAT OUT ONTO THE FIELD...
I WANT YOU TO WEAR IT WITH PRIDE!
9-9
AND REMEMBER...
BATIUK
News America Syndicate
© News Group Chicago, Inc., 1984
THE OPEN END GOES TOWARDS THE FRONT!

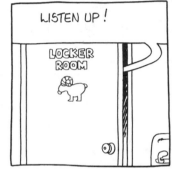

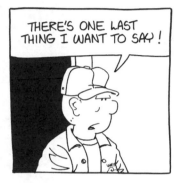

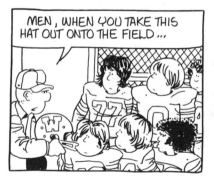

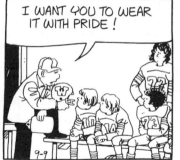

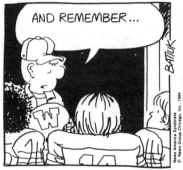

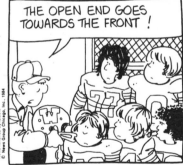

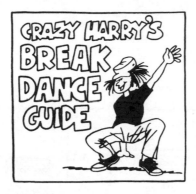

CRAZY HARRY'S BREAK DANCE GUIDE
— COUNTRY BREAK DANCING —
DO-SI-DO AND DOWN YOU GO! YES, COUNTRY BREAK DANCING IS A POPULAR NEW OFFSHOOT OF THIS UNIQUE DANCING STYLE! HOWEVER, IT'S BEST NOT TO TRY IT WITH SPURS ON UNTIL YOU'RE REALLY GOOD AT IT!
THOSE WHO CAUGHT WILLIE NELSON AT THE BREAK DANCE JAMBOREE AT GILLEY'S WILL SURELY REMEMBER THE SIGHT THE REST OF THEIR LIVES!
News America Syndicate
© News Group Chicago, Inc., 1984
9-10

CRAZY HARRY'S BREAK DANCE GUIDE
— BREAK BALLET —
BREAK BALLET HAS BEEN SOMEWHAT SLOWER TO CATCH ON DUE TO THE HIGH COST OF CLEANING TUTUS!
HOWEVER, ITS POPULARITY CONTINUES TO GROW!
PICTURED HERE ARE TWO DANCERS PERFORMING A SCENE FROM THE NOW-CLASSIC 'SWAN LAKE BREAK'!
News America Syndicate
© News Group Chicago, Inc., 1984
9-11

CRAZY HARRY'S BREAK DANCE GUIDE
— POLKA BREAK DANCING —
YES, BREAK OUT THE BARREL, ALL YOU POLKA BREAK DANCERS OUT THERE, BECAUSE HERE COMES THE NEW RAGE!
THE MAN PICTURED HERE, HOWEVER, IS NOT BREAK DANCING! HE SIMPLY FELL OVER AND IS BEING CRUSHED BY HIS ACCORDION! AS ALWAYS, BE SURE TO CHECK WITH YOUR PHYSICIAN BEFORE ATTEMPTING TO BE CRUSHED BY AN ACCORDION!
News America Syndicate
© News Group Chicago, Inc., 1984
9-12

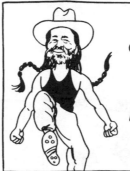

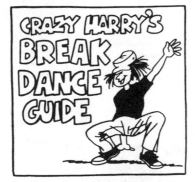

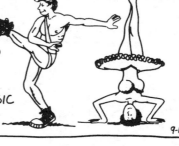

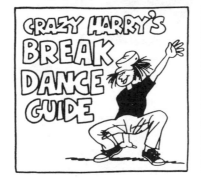

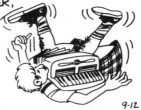

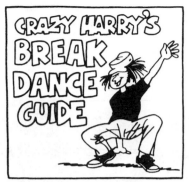

CRAZY HARRY'S BREAK DANCE GUIDE
— FULL CONTACT BREAK DANCING —
FULL CONTACT BREAK DANCING SHOULD ONLY BE ATTEMPTED BY THE MOST ADVANCED BREAK DANCERS! IT IS A TRULY BEAUTIFUL ART FORM THAT COMBINES THE VERY BEST ASPECTS OF FRED ASTAIRE AND BRUCE LEE!
IT BECOMES EVEN MORE EXCITING WHEN YOU GET A HUNDRED OR MORE PEOPLE ON A SIDE, GIVING IT THE VISUAL APPEARANCE OF A JANE FONDA WORKOUT ON AMPHETAMINES!
News America Syndicate © News Group Chicago, Inc. 1984
9-13

CRAZY HARRY'S BREAK DANCE GUIDE
— FAMOUS BREAK DANCERS MAIL INSTRUCTION COURSE —
THIS COURSE GETS YOU OFF THE STREETS AND ALLOWS YOU TO LEARN BREAK DANCING IN THE COMFORT OF YOUR OWN HOME! EACH MONTH YOU GET A NEW CASSETTE OF TOP BREAK DANCE MUSIC, AN INSTRUCTION CHART, AND A CAN OF FLOOR WAX! YOU CAN ALSO DEDUCT THE ENTIRE COST OF THE COURSE FROM YOUR INCOME TAX! YOU'LL END UP IN BIG TROUBLE, BUT YOU CAN DO IT!
OLD STYLE DANCE CHART
NEW BREAK DANCE CHART
News America Syndicate © News Group Chicago, Inc. 1984
9-14

CRAZY HARRY'S BREAK DANCE GUIDE
— WHERE NOT TO BREAK DANCE —
WHEN IT COMES TO BREAK DANCING, IT'S BEST TO AVOID SUCH SITES AS:
(1.) SWAMPS
(2.) ROOFS
(3.) THE TESTING ROOM IN A JACKS FACTORY
(4.) WHEATFIELDS
News America Syndicate © News Group Chicago, Inc. 1984
9-15

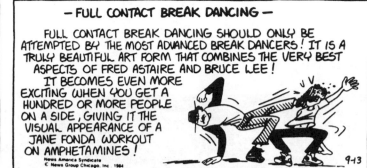

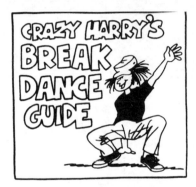

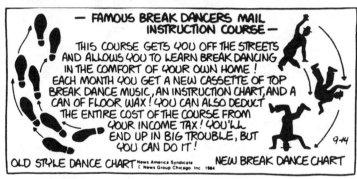

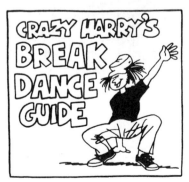

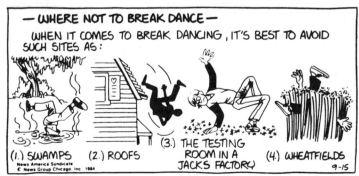

COME ON, DEREK... QUIT COMPLAINING

LOOK, I KNOW THE JACKSONS MADE A LOT OF MISTAKES SETTING UP THIS TOUR... AND I KNOW WE ENDED UP GETTING TICKETS FOR THE WRONG CITY!

BUT THAT'S ALL IN THE PAST! THEY'VE FINALLY GOT THEIR ACT TOGETHER AND WE'RE HERE AT THE SHOW, SO LET'S JUST ENJOY IT!

BATIUK

9-16

News America Syndicate
© News Group Chicago, Inc. 1984

OKAY... HOW MUCH FOR A SMALL COLA?

SIX BUCKS!

SIX BUCKS!!?

AND YOU GOTTA BUY FOUR!

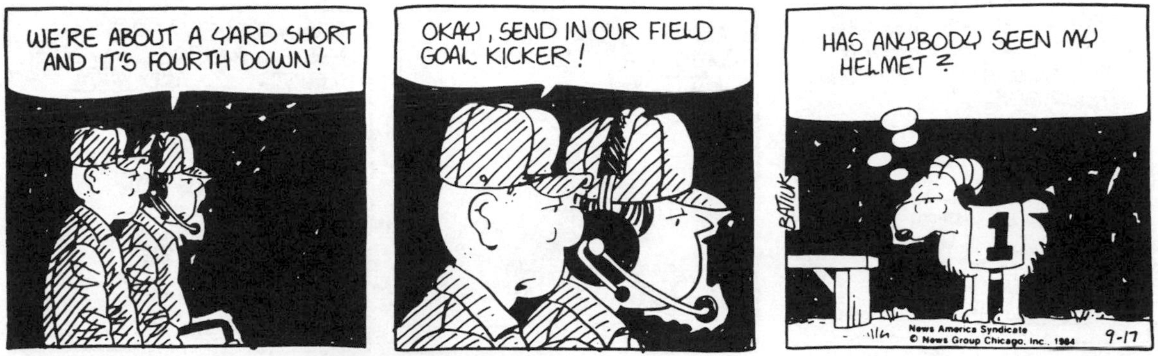
WE'RE ABOUT A YARD SHORT AND IT'S FOURTH DOWN!
OKAY, SEND IN OUR FIELD GOAL KICKER!
HAS ANYBODY SEEN MY HELMET?
BATIUK
1
News America Syndicate © News Group Chicago, Inc. 1984
9-17

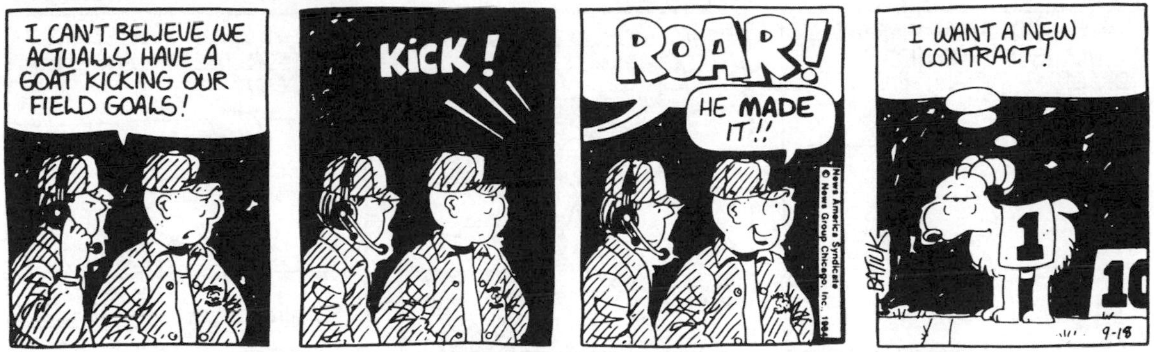
I CAN'T BELIEVE WE ACTUALLY HAVE A GOAT KICKING OUR FIELD GOALS!
KICK!
ROAR!
HE MADE IT!!
News America Syndicate © News Group Chicago, Inc. 1984
I WANT A NEW CONTRACT!
BATIUK
1
10
9-18

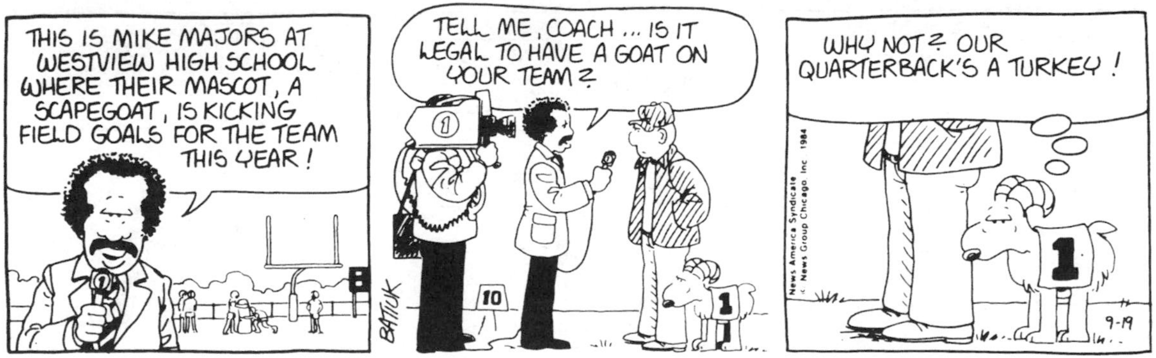
THIS IS MIKE MAJORS AT WESTVIEW HIGH SCHOOL WHERE THEIR MASCOT, A SCAPEGOAT, IS KICKING FIELD GOALS FOR THE TEAM THIS YEAR!
BATIUK
TELL ME, COACH ... IS IT LEGAL TO HAVE A GOAT ON YOUR TEAM?
10
1
WHY NOT? OUR QUARTERBACK'S A TURKEY!
News America Syndicate © News Group Chicago Inc 1984
1
9-19

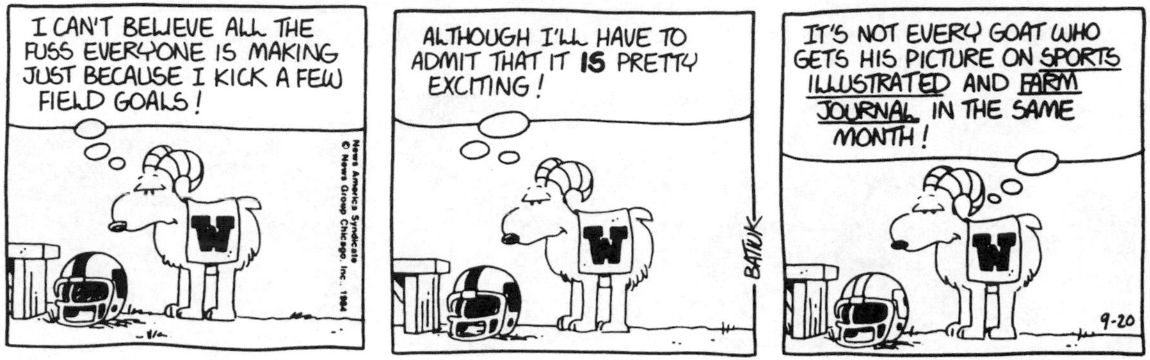
I CAN'T BELIEVE ALL THE FUSS EVERYONE IS MAKING JUST BECAUSE I KICK A FEW FIELD GOALS!
News America Syndicate © News Group Chicago, Inc. 1984
ALTHOUGH I'LL HAVE TO ADMIT THAT IT IS PRETTY EXCITING!
BATIUK
IT'S NOT EVERY GOAT WHO GETS HIS PICTURE ON SPORTS ILLUSTRATED AND FARM JOURNAL IN THE SAME MONTH!
9-20

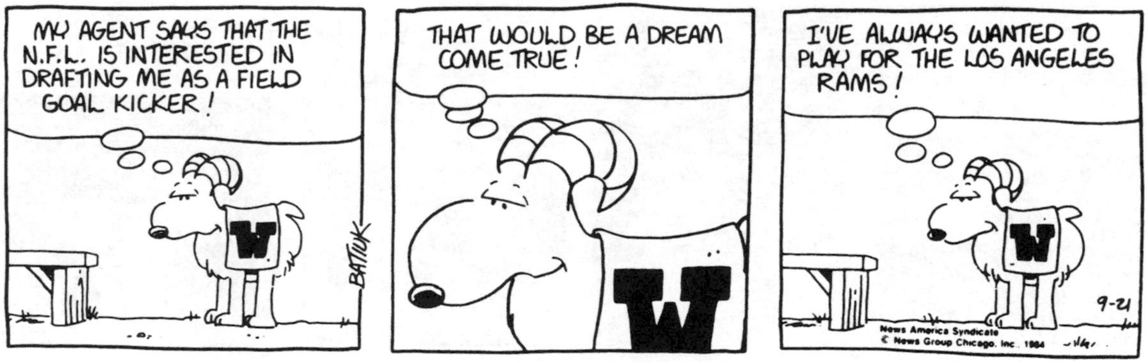
MY AGENT SAYS THAT THE N.F.L. IS INTERESTED IN DRAFTING ME AS A FIELD GOAL KICKER!
BATIUK
THAT WOULD BE A DREAM COME TRUE!
I'VE ALWAYS WANTED TO PLAY FOR THE LOS ANGELES RAMS!
9-21
News America Syndicate © News Group Chicago, Inc. 1984

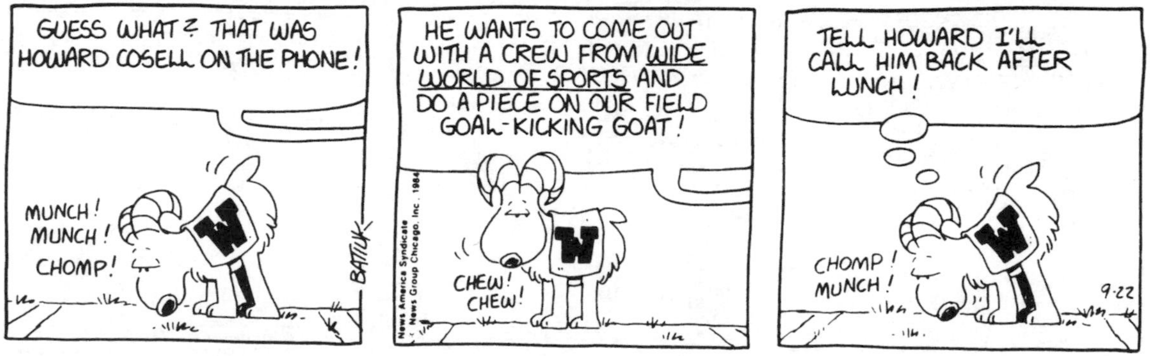
GUESS WHAT? THAT WAS HOWARD COSELL ON THE PHONE!
MUNCH! MUNCH! CHOMP!
BATIUK
HE WANTS TO COME OUT WITH A CREW FROM WIDE WORLD OF SPORTS AND DO A PIECE ON OUR FIELD GOAL-KICKING GOAT!
News America Syndicate © News Group Chicago, Inc. 1984
CHEW! CHEW!
TELL HOWARD I'LL CALL HIM BACK AFTER LUNCH!
CHOMP! MUNCH!
9-22

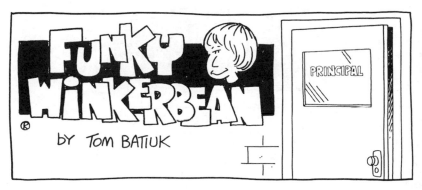

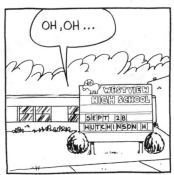

FUNKY WINKERBEAN
BY TOM BATIUK
PRINCIPAL
OH, OH...
WESTVIEW HIGH SCHOOL
SEPT 28
HUTCHINSON H
I DIDN'T REALIZE THAT THIS YEAR'S SCHOOL ADMINISTRATORS' CONFERENCE WAS COMING UP SO SOON!
ALL PRINCIPALS WISHING TO ATTEND THE SCHOOL ADMINISTRATORS' CONFERENCE IN COLUMBUS NEXT MONTH...
ARE URGED TO FILL OUT THE ENCLOSED FORM IMMEDIATELY...
News America Syndicate
© News Group Chicago, Inc., 1984
BATIUK
9-23
AND SEND IN THEIR TWENTY-FIVE DOLLAR REGISTRATION FEE...
ALONG WITH A PERMISSION SLIP SIGNED BY THEIR SCHOOL SECRETARY!

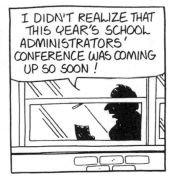

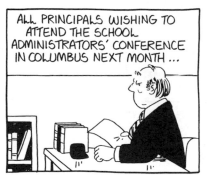

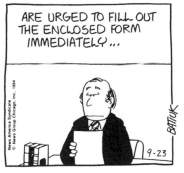

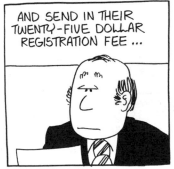

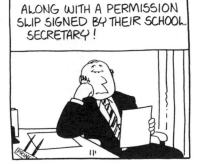

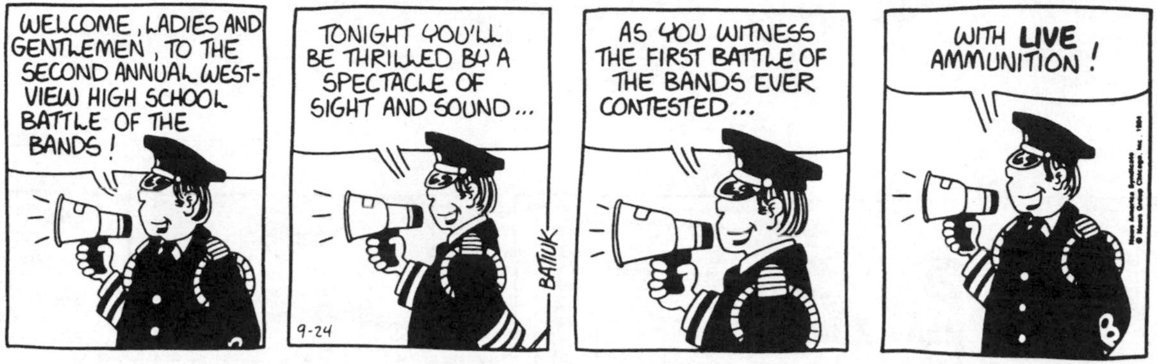
WELCOME, LADIES AND GENTLEMEN, TO THE SECOND ANNUAL WESTVIEW HIGH SCHOOL BATTLE OF THE BANDS!
TONIGHT YOU'LL BE THRILLED BY A SPECTACLE OF SIGHT AND SOUND...
9-24
BATIUK
AS YOU WITNESS THE FIRST BATTLE OF THE BANDS EVER CONTESTED...
WITH **LIVE** AMMUNITION!
News America Syndicate © News Group Chicago, Inc. 1984

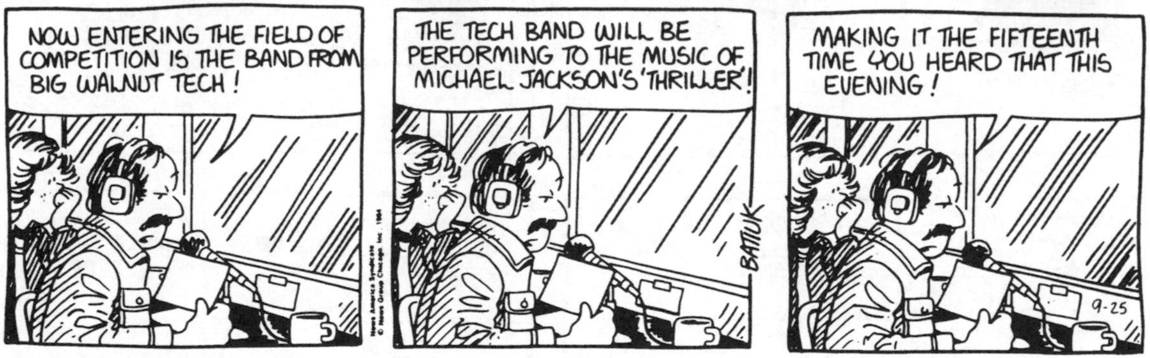
NOW ENTERING THE FIELD OF COMPETITION IS THE BAND FROM BIG WALNUT TECH!
News America Syndicate © News Group Chicago, Inc. 1984
THE TECH BAND WILL BE PERFORMING TO THE MUSIC OF MICHAEL JACKSON'S 'THRILLER'!
BATIUK
MAKING IT THE FIFTEENTH TIME YOU HEARD THAT THIS EVENING!
9-25

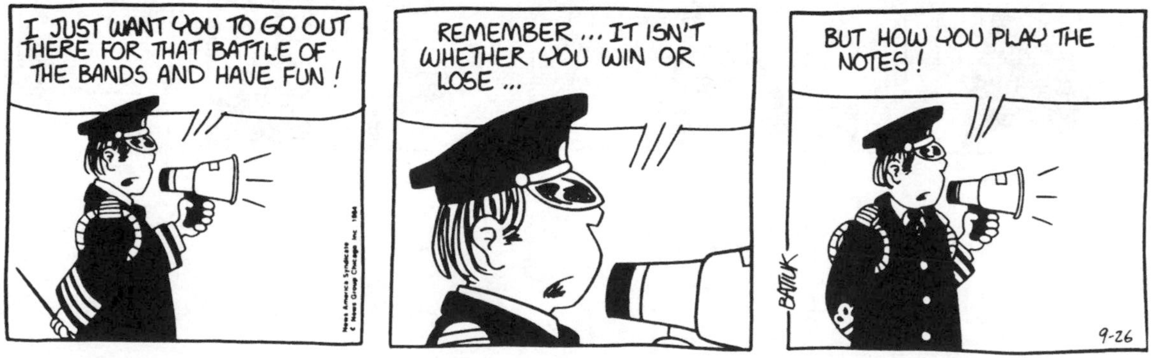
I JUST WANT YOU TO GO OUT THERE FOR THAT BATTLE OF THE BANDS AND HAVE FUN!
News America Syndicate © News Group Chicago, Inc. 1984
REMEMBER... IT ISN'T WHETHER YOU WIN OR LOSE...
BATIUK
BUT HOW YOU PLAY THE NOTES!
9-26

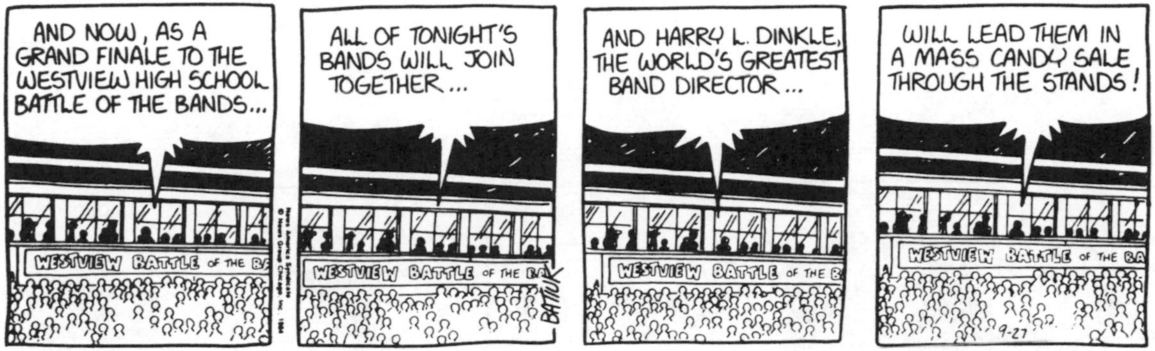
AND NOW, AS A GRAND FINALE TO THE WESTVIEW HIGH SCHOOL BATTLE OF THE BANDS...
ALL OF TONIGHT'S BANDS WILL JOIN TOGETHER...
AND HARRY L. DINKLE, THE WORLD'S GREATEST BAND DIRECTOR...
WILL LEAD THEM IN A MASS CANDY SALE THROUGH THE STANDS!
BATIUK
9-27

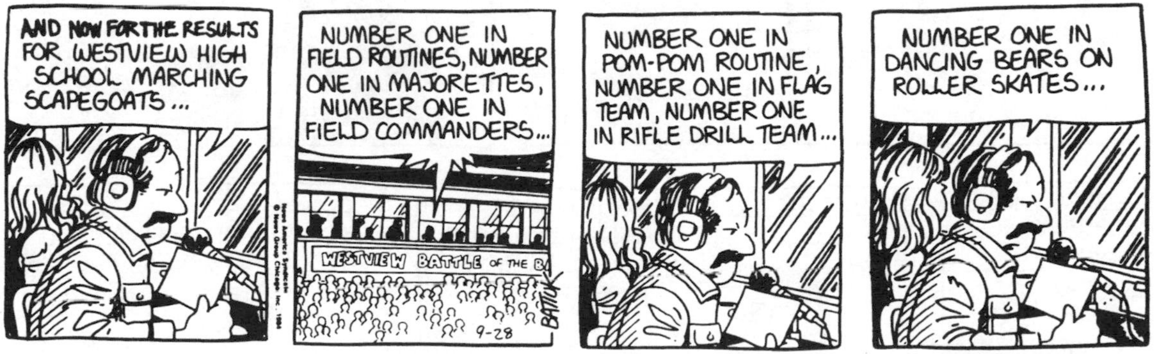
AND NOW FOR THE RESULTS FOR WESTVIEW HIGH SCHOOL MARCHING SCAPEGOATS...
NUMBER ONE IN FIELD ROUTINES, NUMBER ONE IN MAJORETTES, NUMBER ONE IN FIELD COMMANDERS...
NUMBER ONE IN POM-POM ROUTINE, NUMBER ONE IN FLAG TEAM, NUMBER ONE IN RIFLE DRILL TEAM...
NUMBER ONE IN DANCING BEARS ON ROLLER SKATES...
BATIUK
9-28

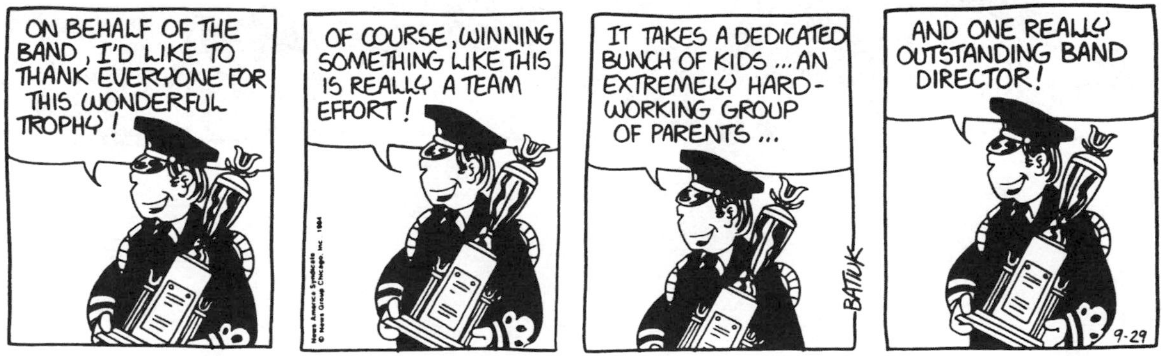
ON BEHALF OF THE BAND, I'D LIKE TO THANK EVERYONE FOR THIS WONDERFUL TROPHY!
OF COURSE, WINNING SOMETHING LIKE THIS IS REALLY A TEAM EFFORT!
IT TAKES A DEDICATED BUNCH OF KIDS ... AN EXTREMELY HARD-WORKING GROUP OF PARENTS ...
AND ONE REALLY OUTSTANDING BAND DIRECTOR!
BATIUK
9-29

FUNKY WINKERBEAN
BY TOM BATIUK ®
F Horn
REPEAT AS DESIRED
News America Syndicate
© News Group Chicago, Inc., 1984
MR. DINKLE, I'VE BEEN HAVING A LOT OF TROUBLE PLAYING FRENCH HORN...
SO I WAS WONDERING IF MAYBE I SHOULD SWITCH TO SPANISH HORN INSTEAD! WHAT DO YOU THINK?
AS MARCUS WELBY WOULD SAY: 'MANY PEOPLE LEAD NORMAL AND MEANINGFUL LIVES, EVEN WITH A HANDICAP SUCH AS YOURS'!
BATIUK
9-30

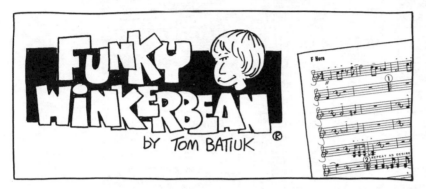

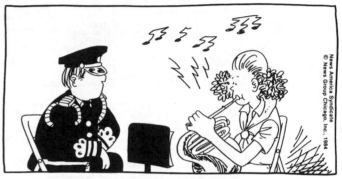

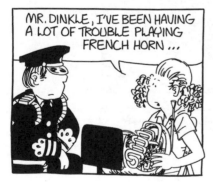

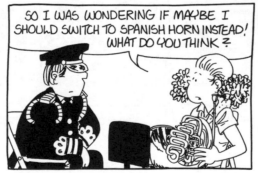

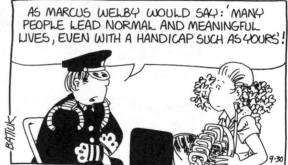

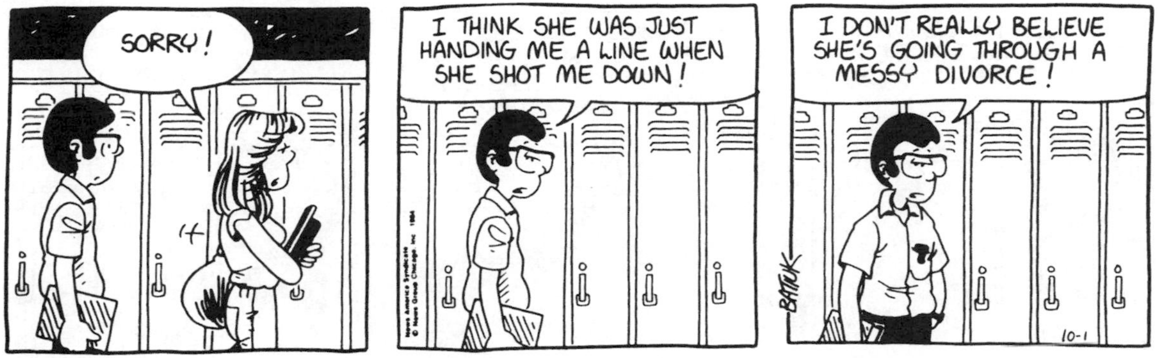
SORRY!
I THINK SHE WAS JUST HANDING ME A LINE WHEN SHE SHOT ME DOWN!
I DON'T REALLY BELIEVE SHE'S GOING THROUGH A MESSY DIVORCE!
BATIUK
10-1

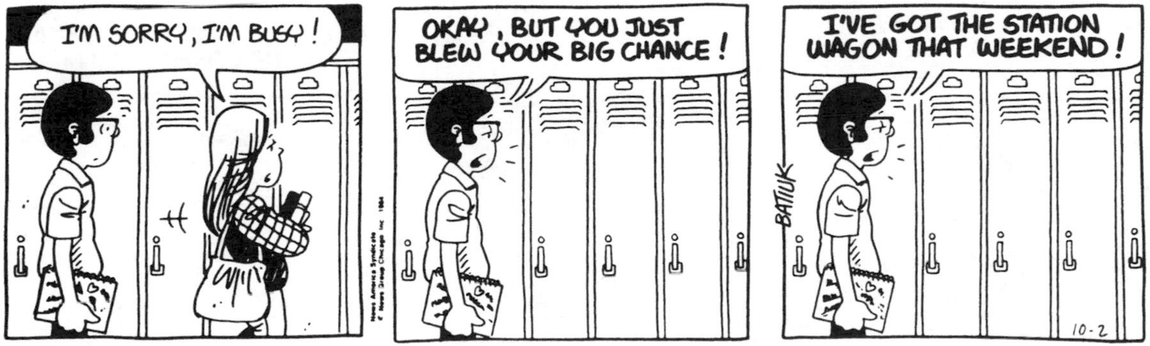
I'M SORRY, I'M BUSY!
OKAY, BUT YOU JUST BLEW YOUR BIG CHANCE!
I'VE GOT THE STATION WAGON THAT WEEKEND!
BATIUK
10-2

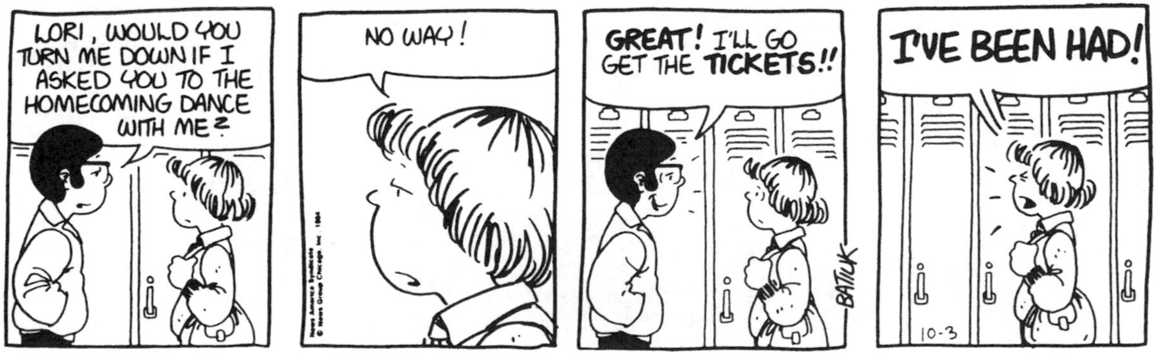
LORI, WOULD YOU TURN ME DOWN IF I ASKED YOU TO THE HOMECOMING DANCE WITH ME?
NO WAY!
GREAT! I'LL GO GET THE TICKETS!!
BATIUK
I'VE BEEN HAD!
10-3

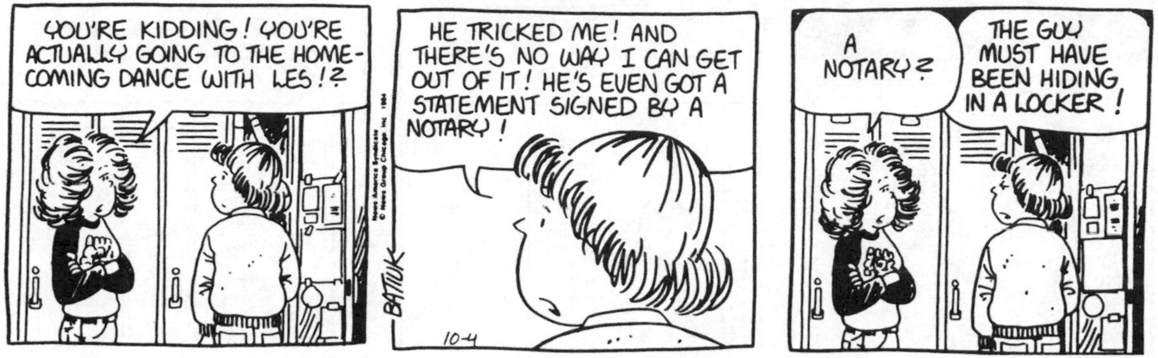
YOU'RE KIDDING! YOU'RE ACTUALLY GOING TO THE HOME-COMING DANCE WITH LES!?
HE TRICKED ME! AND THERE'S NO WAY I CAN GET OUT OF IT! HE'S EVEN GOT A STATEMENT SIGNED BY A NOTARY!
A NOTARY?
THE GUY MUST HAVE BEEN HIDING IN A LOCKER!
BATIUK
10-4

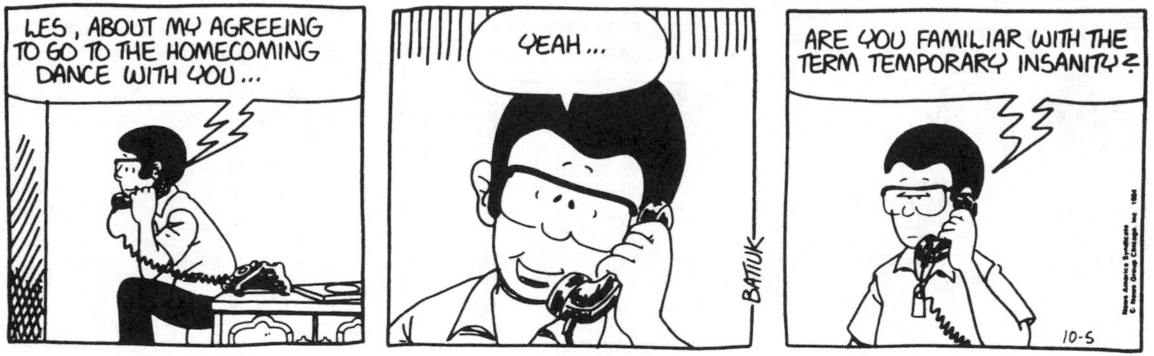
LES, ABOUT MY AGREEING TO GO TO THE HOMECOMING DANCE WITH YOU...
YEAH...
ARE YOU FAMILIAR WITH THE TERM TEMPORARY INSANITY?
BATIUK
10-5

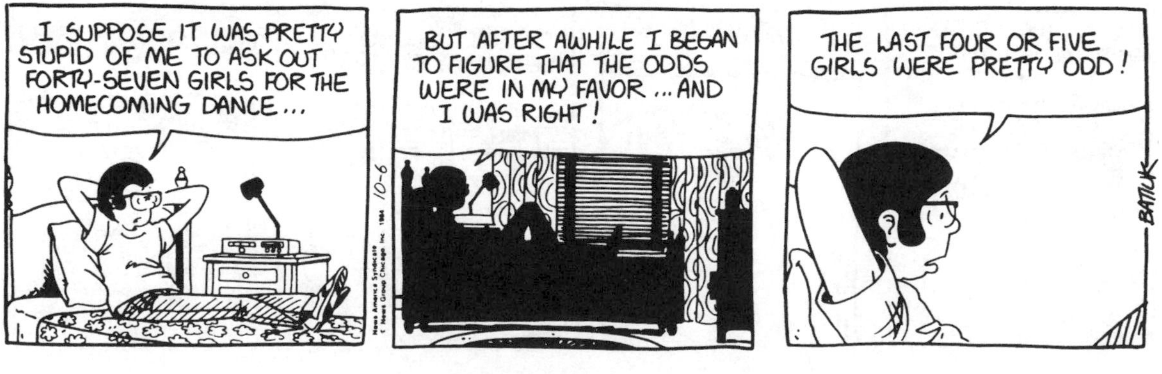
I SUPPOSE IT WAS PRETTY STUPID OF ME TO ASK OUT FORTY-SEVEN GIRLS FOR THE HOMECOMING DANCE...
BUT AFTER AWHILE I BEGAN TO FIGURE THAT THE ODDS WERE IN MY FAVOR ... AND I WAS RIGHT!
THE LAST FOUR OR FIVE GIRLS WERE PRETTY ODD!
BATIUK
10-6

FUNKY WINKERBEAN
BY TOM BATIUK ®
SIGH
FRANKLY, I WISH THAT SUMMER HAD LASTED A LITTLE LONGER!
HOW DO YOU GUYS FEEL ABOUT FALLING FROM THE TREE AND DYING?
BATIUK
News America Syndicate
© News Group Chicago, Inc., 1984
'OF ALL THE WONDERS THAT I YET HAVE HEARD, IT SEEMS TO ME MOST STRANGE THAT MEN SHOULD FEAR, SEEING THAT DEATH, A NECESSARY END, WILL COME, WHEN IT WILL COME.'
WILLIAM SHAKESPEARE
JULIUS CAESAR ACT ii, SC. 2
'I ONLY KNOW THAT WE DON'T LIVE TWICE, THEREFORE SHUN DEATH IS MY ADVICE.'
ROBERT BROWNING
10-7
'THERE ONCE WAS A LEAF FROM NANTUCKET...'
OH SHUT UP!

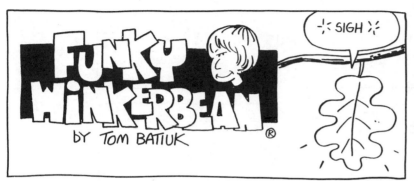

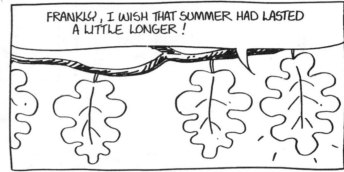

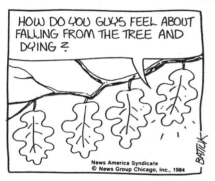

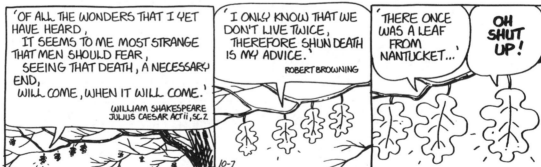

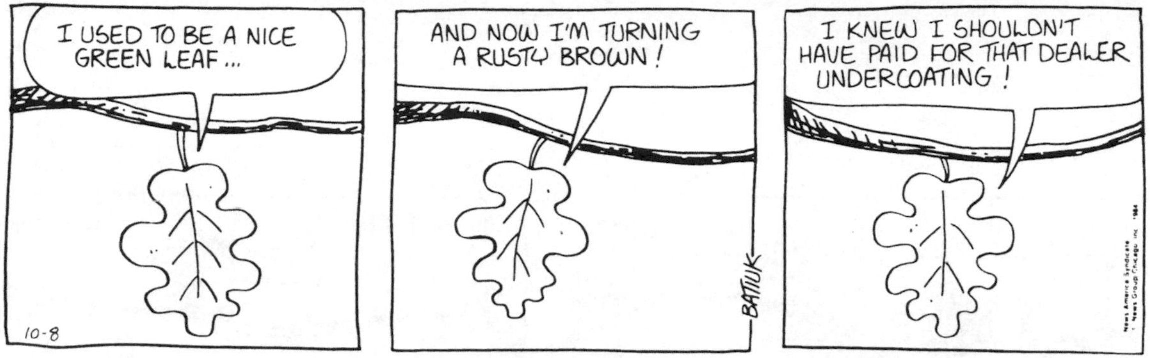
I USED TO BE A NICE GREEN LEAF...
AND NOW I'M TURNING A RUSTY BROWN!
I KNEW I SHOULDN'T HAVE PAID FOR THAT DEALER UNDERCOATING!
10-8
BATIUK

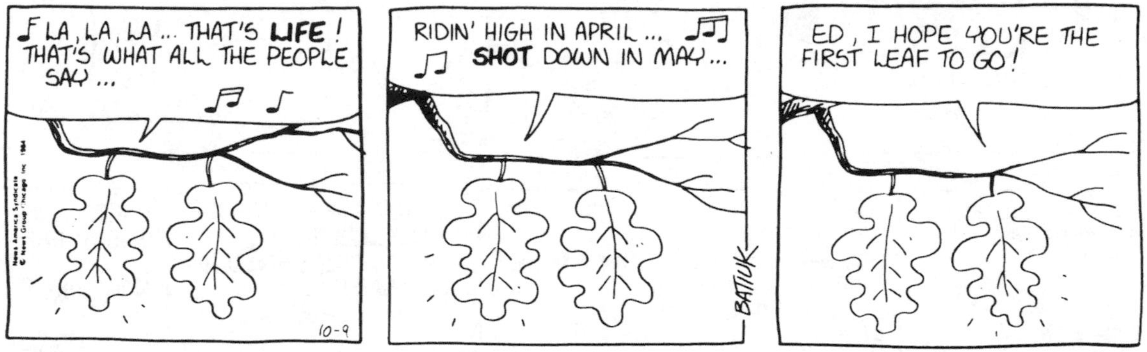
LA, LA, LA... THAT'S **LIFE**! THAT'S WHAT ALL THE PEOPLE SAY...
RIDIN' HIGH IN APRIL... **SHOT** DOWN IN MAY...
ED, I HOPE YOU'RE THE FIRST LEAF TO GO!
10-9
BATIUK

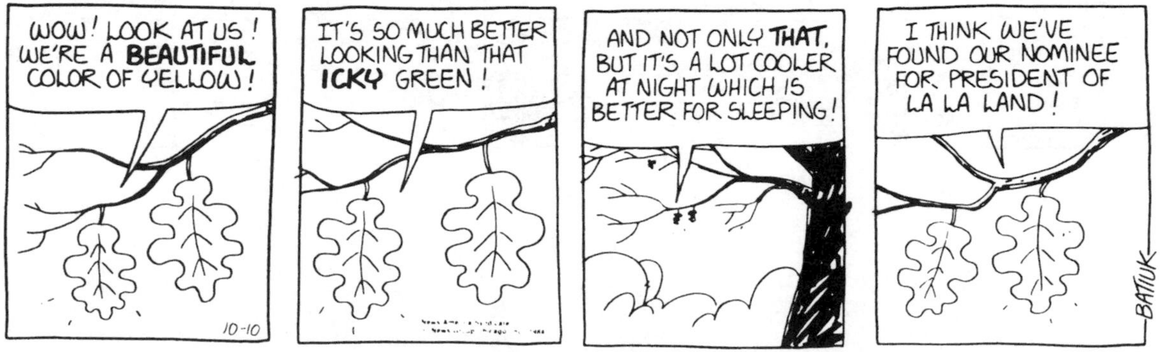
WOW! LOOK AT US! WE'RE A **BEAUTIFUL** COLOR OF YELLOW!
IT'S SO MUCH BETTER LOOKING THAN THAT **ICKY** GREEN!
AND NOT ONLY **THAT**, BUT IT'S A LOT COOLER AT NIGHT WHICH IS BETTER FOR SLEEPING!
I THINK WE'VE FOUND OUR NOMINEE FOR PRESIDENT OF LA LA LAND!
10-10
BATIUK

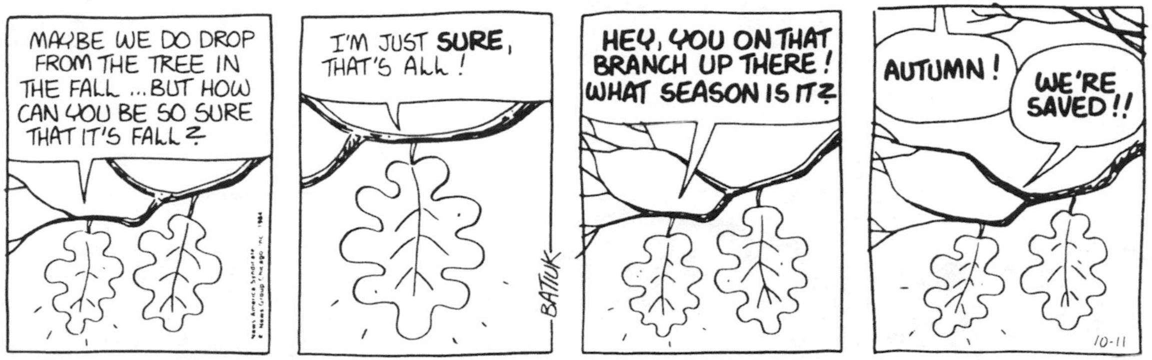
MAYBE WE DO DROP FROM THE TREE IN THE FALL ...BUT HOW CAN YOU BE SO SURE THAT IT'S FALL?
I'M JUST SURE, THAT'S ALL!
BATIUK
HEY, YOU ON THAT BRANCH UP THERE! WHAT SEASON IS IT?
AUTUMN!
WE'RE SAVED!!
10-11

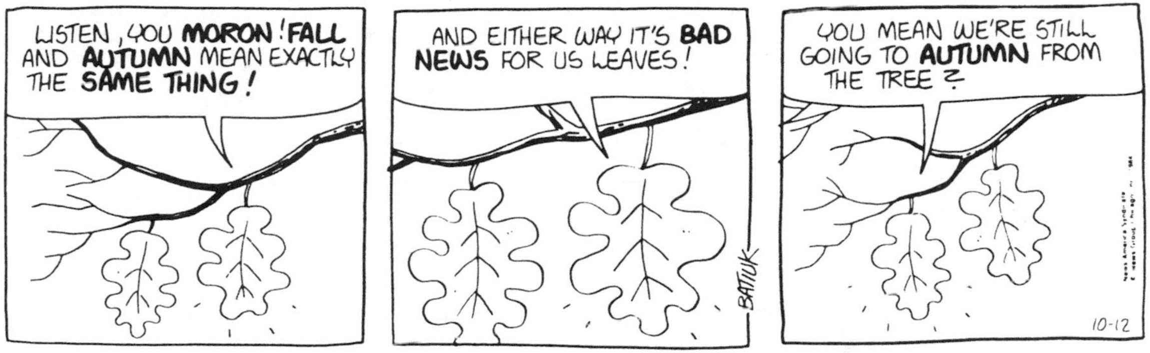
LISTEN, YOU MORON! FALL AND AUTUMN MEAN EXACTLY THE SAME THING!
AND EITHER WAY IT'S BAD NEWS FOR US LEAVES!
BATIUK
YOU MEAN WE'RE STILL GOING TO AUTUMN FROM THE TREE?
10-12

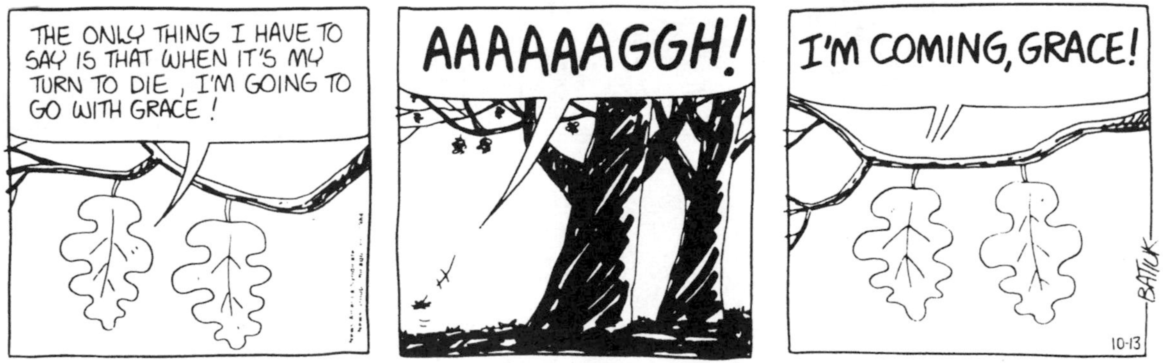
THE ONLY THING I HAVE TO SAY IS THAT WHEN IT'S MY TURN TO DIE, I'M GOING TO GO WITH GRACE!
AAAAAAGGH!
I'M COMING, GRACE!
BATIUK
10-13

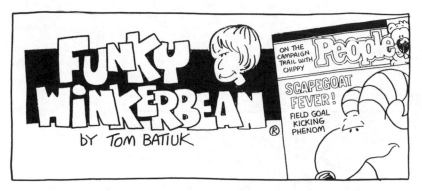

FUNKY WINKERBEAN
BY TOM BATIUK
ON THE CAMPAIGN TRAIL WITH CHIPPY
People
SCAPEGOAT FEVER!
FIELD GOAL KICKING PHENOM
VERY GOOD!
I'LL GET BACK TO THEM THIS AFTERNOON!
I WAS JUST TALKING WITH MY AGENT!
HE SAYS THE UNITED STATES FOOTBALL LEAGUE WANTS TO SIGN ME AS A FIELD GOAL KICKER!
BATIUK
BUT WE'VE DECIDED TO HOLD OUT FOR THE REALLY **BIG** MONEY!
© News America Syndicate News Group Chicago, Inc., 1984
WE'RE GOING FOR A COLLEGE TEAM!
10-14

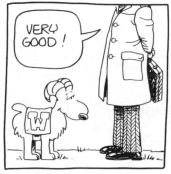

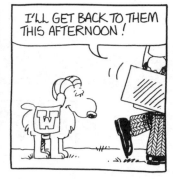

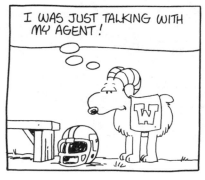

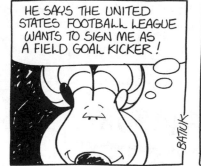

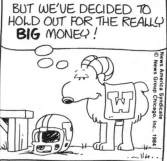

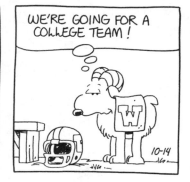

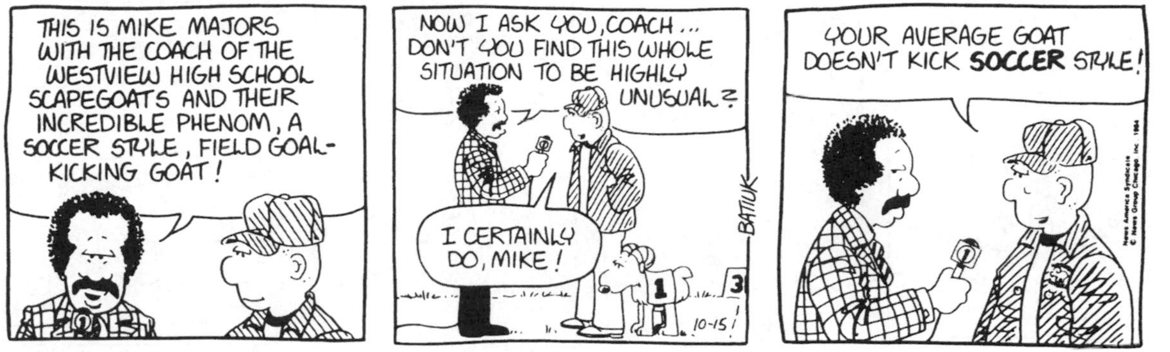
THIS IS MIKE MAJORS WITH THE COACH OF THE WESTVIEW HIGH SCHOOL SCAPEGOATS AND THEIR INCREDIBLE PHENOM, A SOCCER STYLE, FIELD GOAL-KICKING GOAT!
NOW I ASK YOU, COACH... DON'T YOU FIND THIS WHOLE SITUATION TO BE HIGHLY UNUSUAL?
I CERTAINLY DO, MIKE!
BATIUK
10-15
YOUR AVERAGE GOAT DOESN'T KICK **SOCCER** STYLE!
News America Syndicate © News Group Chicago Inc 1984

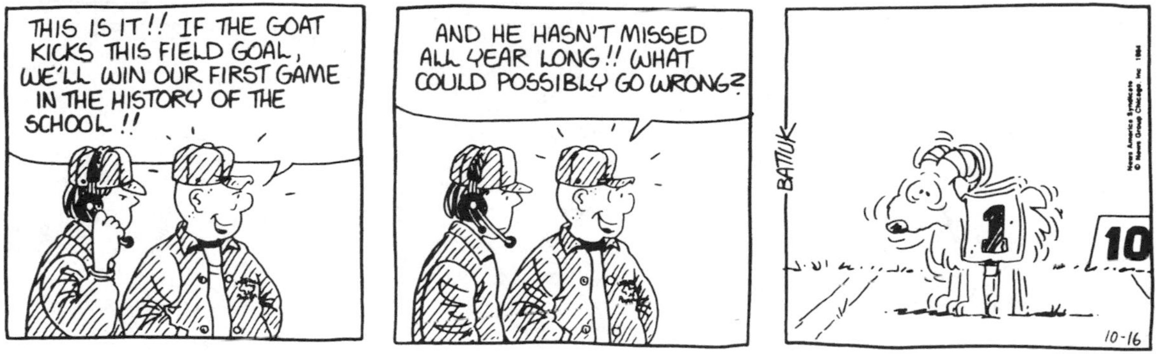
THIS IS IT!! IF THE GOAT KICKS THIS FIELD GOAL, WE'LL WIN OUR FIRST GAME IN THE HISTORY OF THE SCHOOL!!
AND HE HASN'T MISSED ALL YEAR LONG!! WHAT COULD POSSIBLY GO WRONG?
BATIUK
News America Syndicate © News Group Chicago Inc 1984
10
10-16

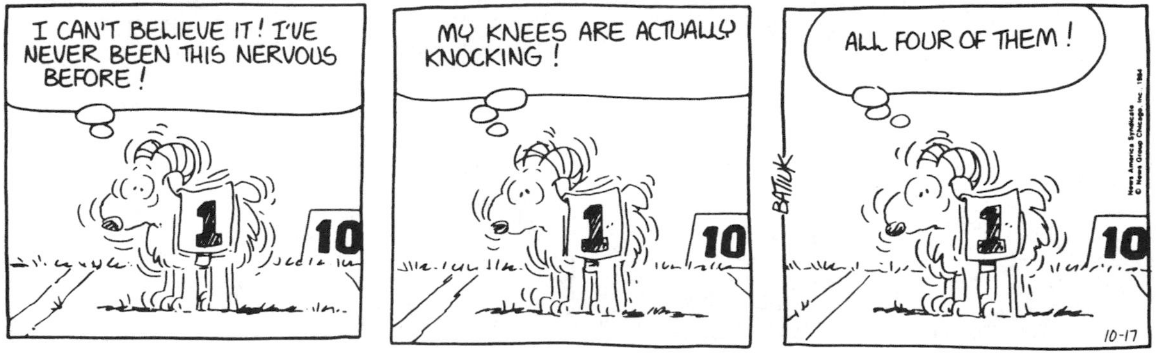
I CAN'T BELIEVE IT! I'VE NEVER BEEN THIS NERVOUS BEFORE!
MY KNEES ARE ACTUALLY KNOCKING!
ALL FOUR OF THEM!
BATIUK
News America Syndicate © News Group Chicago Inc 1984
10-17

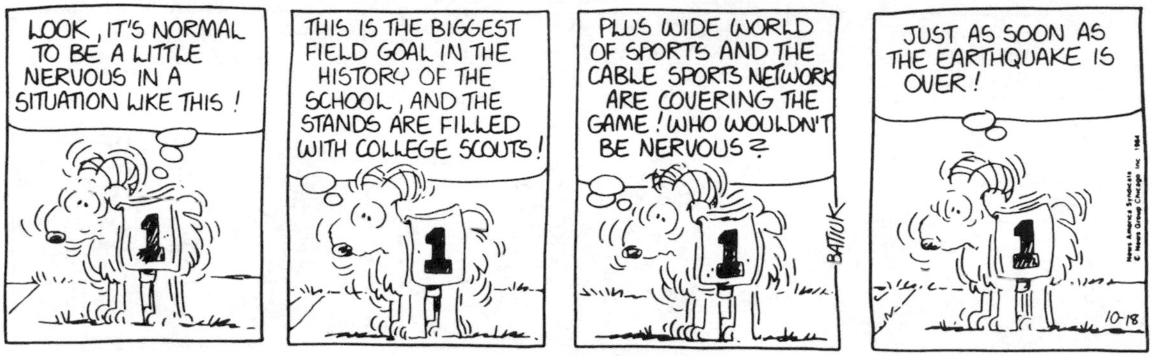
LOOK, IT'S NORMAL TO BE A LITTLE NERVOUS IN A SITUATION LIKE THIS!
THIS IS THE BIGGEST FIELD GOAL IN THE HISTORY OF THE SCHOOL, AND THE STANDS ARE FILLED WITH COLLEGE SCOUTS!
PLUS WIDE WORLD OF SPORTS AND THE CABLE SPORTS NETWORK ARE COVERING THE GAME! WHO WOULDN'T BE NERVOUS?
BATIUK
JUST AS SOON AS THE EARTHQUAKE IS OVER!
News America Syndicate
© News Group Chicago Inc 1984
10-18

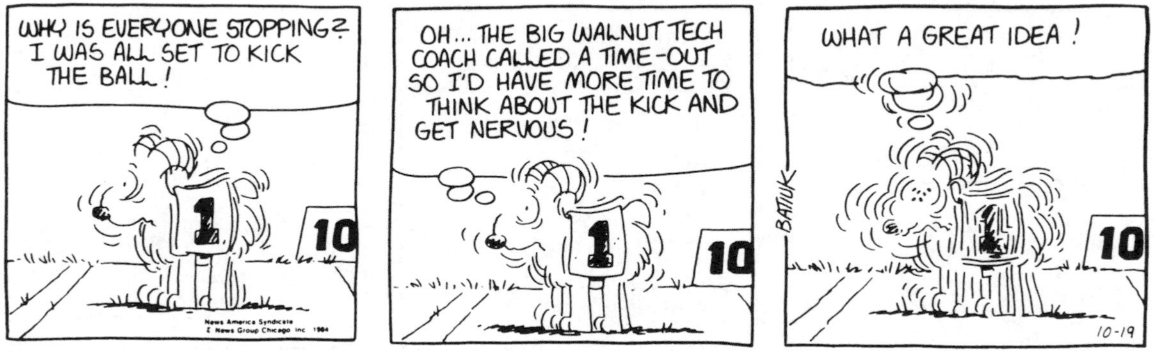
WHY IS EVERYONE STOPPING? I WAS ALL SET TO KICK THE BALL!
10
News America Syndicate
© News Group Chicago Inc 1984
OH... THE BIG WALNUT TECH COACH CALLED A TIME-OUT SO I'D HAVE MORE TIME TO THINK ABOUT THE KICK AND GET NERVOUS!
10
BATIUK
WHAT A GREAT IDEA!
10
10-19

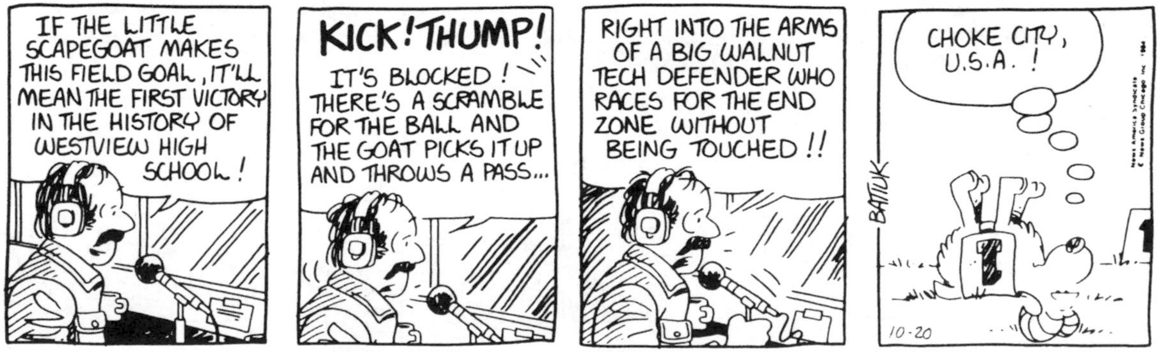
IF THE LITTLE SCAPEGOAT MAKES THIS FIELD GOAL, IT'LL MEAN THE FIRST VICTORY IN THE HISTORY OF WESTVIEW HIGH SCHOOL!
KICK! THUMP!
IT'S BLOCKED! THERE'S A SCRAMBLE FOR THE BALL AND THE GOAT PICKS IT UP AND THROWS A PASS...
RIGHT INTO THE ARMS OF A BIG WALNUT TECH DEFENDER WHO RACES FOR THE END ZONE WITHOUT BEING TOUCHED!!
BATIUK
CHOKE CITY, U.S.A.!
News America Syndicate
© News Group Chicago Inc 1984
10-20

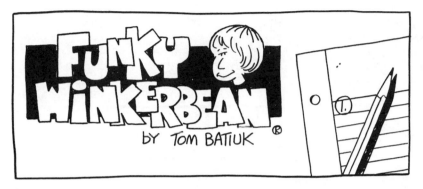

FUNKY WINKERBEAN
BY TOM BATIUK ®
ARE THERE ANY QUESTIONS BEFORE WE START THE TEST ?
YES, WHAT'S THE ANSWER TO NUMBER ONE ?
DEFINE THE FOLLOWING :
News America Syndicate © News Group Chicago, Inc., 1984
(1.) DRAGON
What political campaigns always seem to do !
BATIUK
10-21

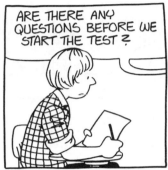

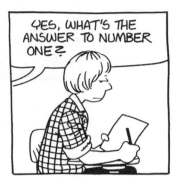

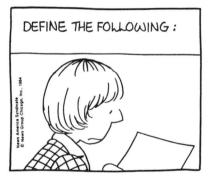

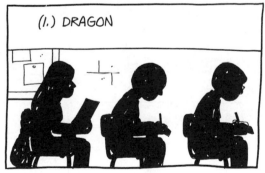

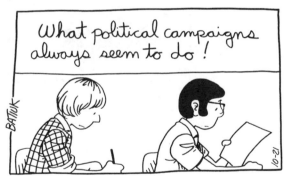

DEFINE THE FOLLOWING:	(1.) HOVERCRAFT	Needlepoint done in a helicopter!

DEFINE THE FOLLOWING:	(2.) DIMINISHED CAPACITY	A broken wine bottle!
	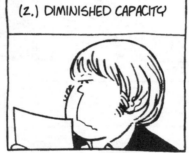	
DEFINE THE FOLLOWING:	(3.) SUBCONSCIOUS	A person whose awareness has been raised concerning submarines!

DEFINE THE FOLLOWING:
(4.) PANORAMA
News America Syndicate © News Group Chicago, Inc., 1984
BATIUK
The largest convention of skillets in the world!
10-25

FUNKY WINKERBEAN'S
CHEERS FOR LOSING FOOTBALL TEAMS!
BATIUK
10-26
THE GAME IS JUST ABOUT TO START,
AND OUR TEAM IS RECEIVING!
News America Syndicate © News Group Chicago, Inc., 1984
THEY'RE LOOKING FIT AND SET TO PLAY,
BUT LOOKS CAN BE DECEIVING!

FUNKY WINKERBEAN'S
CHEERS FOR LOSING FOOTBALL TEAMS!
BATIUK
10-27
WE JUMP AND YELL AND SCREAM AND SHOUT;
WE'RE PEPPY, PERT AND NIMBLE!
News America Syndicate © News Group Chicago, Inc., 1984
BUT WHAT WE KNOW 'BOUT FOOTBALL GAMES
WOULD FIT INSIDE A THIMBLE!

FUNKY WINKERBEAN
BY TOM BATIUK ®
EXCUSE ME ...
COULD I PLEASE HAVE YOUR ATTENTION FOR A MINUTE ?
AS THIS YEAR'S WATERMELON SPOKESPERSON, I'D LIKE TO PERSONALLY CONGRATULATE EVERYONE WHO TOOK OUR ADVICE LAST YEAR AND USED A WATERMELON FOR THEIR HALLOWEEN JACK O'LANTERN!
COMMENDATIONS GO TO THE MAURER FAMILY OF DAVENPORT, IOWA AND S. SAVINO OF MOORESTOWN, NEW JERSEY!
BATIUK
News America Syndicate
© News Group Chicago, Inc., 1984
YESSIREE! THINGS ARE REALLY STARTING TO SNOWBALL!
10-28

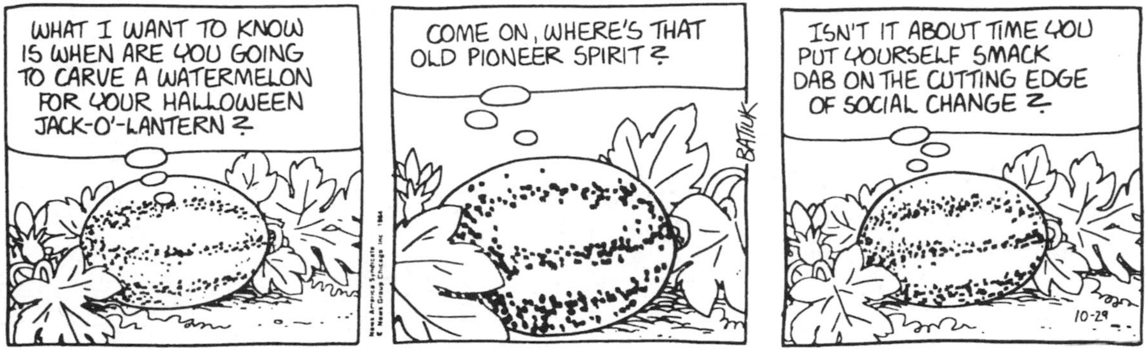
WHAT I WANT TO KNOW IS WHEN ARE YOU GOING TO CARVE A WATERMELON FOR YOUR HALLOWEEN JACK-O'-LANTERN?
COME ON, WHERE'S THAT OLD PIONEER SPIRIT?
BATIUK
ISN'T IT ABOUT TIME YOU PUT YOURSELF SMACK DAB ON THE CUTTING EDGE OF SOCIAL CHANGE?
10-29

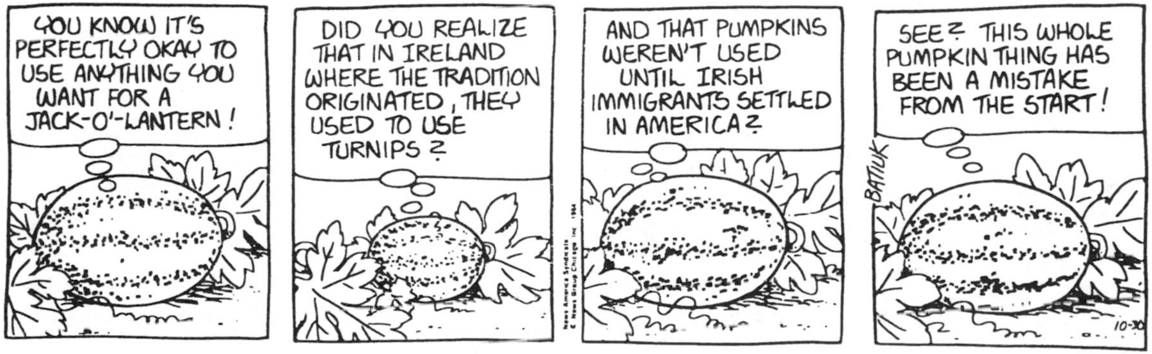
YOU KNOW IT'S PERFECTLY OKAY TO USE ANYTHING YOU WANT FOR A JACK-O'-LANTERN!
DID YOU REALIZE THAT IN IRELAND WHERE THE TRADITION ORIGINATED, THEY USED TO USE TURNIPS?
AND THAT PUMPKINS WEREN'T USED UNTIL IRISH IMMIGRANTS SETTLED IN AMERICA?
BATIUK
SEE? THIS WHOLE PUMPKIN THING HAS BEEN A MISTAKE FROM THE START!

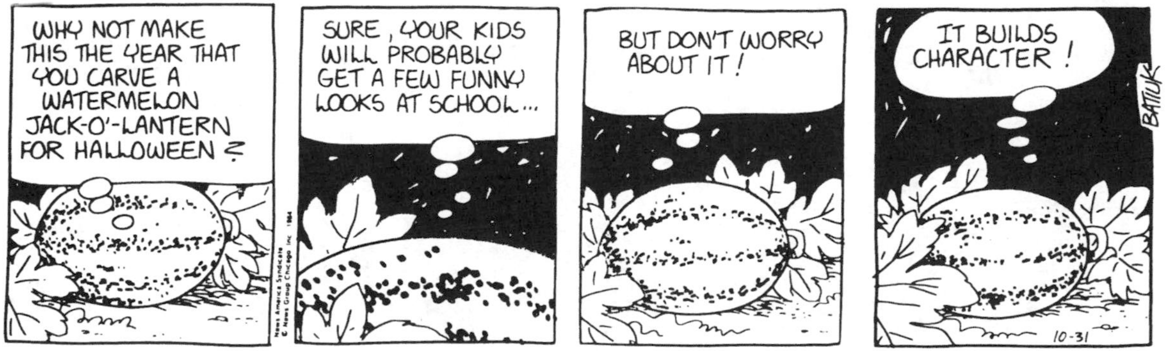
WHY NOT MAKE THIS THE YEAR THAT YOU CARVE A WATERMELON JACK-O'-LANTERN FOR HALLOWEEN?
SURE, YOUR KIDS WILL PROBABLY GET A FEW FUNNY LOOKS AT SCHOOL...
BUT DON'T WORRY ABOUT IT!
IT BUILDS CHARACTER!
BATIUK
10-31

Panel 1: WELL, WE CERTAINLY GOT TO THE HOMECOMING GAME EARLY ENOUGH!

Panel 2: OH, STOP COMPLAINING!

Panel 3: WHEN YOU COME EARLY, YOU GET A GOOD PARKING SPOT, A GOOD SEAT, AND YOU GET TO SEE ALL THE INTERESTING THINGS THAT TAKE PLACE BEFORE THE GAME!

BATIUK

Panel 4: THAT'S TRUE! I'VE NEVER SEEN THEM LINE THE FIELD BEFORE!

11-1

Panel 5: I'M GLAD WE CAME TO THE HOMECOMING GAME, FRED!

Panel 6: IT SORT OF TAKES YOU BACK AND MAKES YOU FEEL YOUNG AGAIN!

Panel 7: DID YOU KNOW THAT THE MOTHER OF ONE OF THE GIRLS ON THE HOMECOMING COURT GRADUATED WITH US?

BATIUK

11-2

Panel 8: THEN AGAIN, I COULD'VE STAYED HOME AND WATCHED DALLAS!

Panel 9: BOY, I SURE WISH SOMEONE HAD BOUGHT A HOMECOMING MUM FOR **ME**!

11-3

Panel 10: THAT'S NOT FAIR, ANN! I TOLD YOU I TRIED TO GET A MUM BUT THEY WERE ALL OUT! BESIDES, I **DID** GET YOU SOMETHING!

BATIUK

Panel 11: THAT'S TRUE! I WONDER IF IT'S POSSIBLE TO PRESS A HIGH SCHOOL SWEATSHIRT IN A SCRAPBOOK?

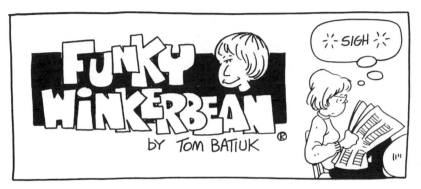

FUNKY WINKERBEAN
BY TOM BATIUK ®
SIGH
THIS IS ALL CONFUSING!
WHAT'S WRONG?
WE HAVE TO VOTE THIS TUESDAY AND I DON'T EVEN KNOW WHAT MOST OF THE ISSUES ARE!
IT'S EMBARRASSING! YOU'D THINK THAT BEING A TEACHER, I'D AT LEAST HAVE A VAGUE IDEA OF WHAT'S GOING ON, BUT I DON'T!
BATIUK
11-4
I WOULDN'T SAY THAT, ANN!
© News America Syndicate News Group Chicago, Inc., 1984
I THINK YOU'VE GOT A **VERY** VAGUE IDEA OF WHAT'S GOING ON!

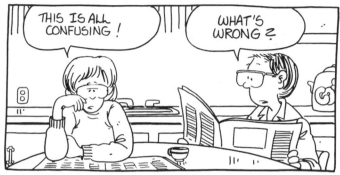

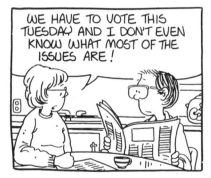

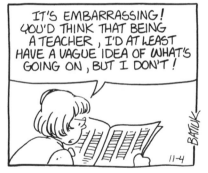

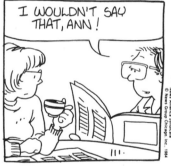

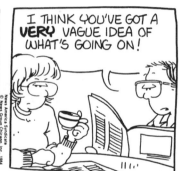

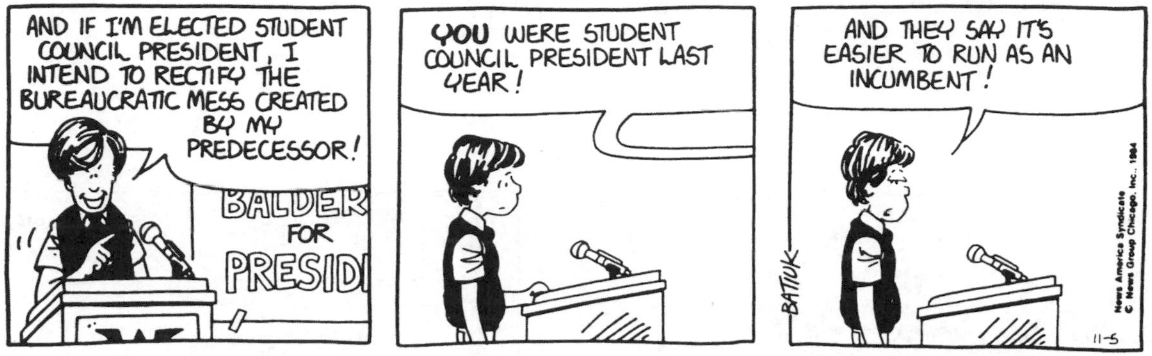
AND IF I'M ELECTED STUDENT COUNCIL PRESIDENT, I INTEND TO RECTIFY THE BUREAUCRATIC MESS CREATED BY MY PREDECESSOR!
BALDER FOR PRESID
YOU WERE STUDENT COUNCIL PRESIDENT LAST YEAR!
AND THEY SAY IT'S EASIER TO RUN AS AN INCUMBENT!
BATIUK
News America Syndicate © News Group Chicago, Inc., 1984
11-5

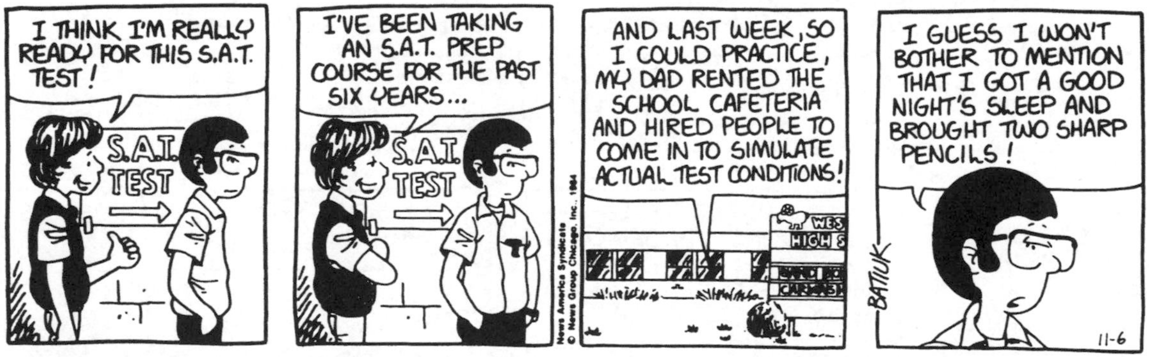
I THINK I'M REALLY READY FOR THIS S.A.T. TEST!
S.A.T. TEST
I'VE BEEN TAKING AN S.A.T. PREP COURSE FOR THE PAST SIX YEARS...
S.A.T. TEST
News America Syndicate © News Group Chicago, Inc., 1984
AND LAST WEEK, SO I COULD PRACTICE, MY DAD RENTED THE SCHOOL CAFETERIA AND HIRED PEOPLE TO COME IN TO SIMULATE ACTUAL TEST CONDITIONS!
I GUESS I WON'T BOTHER TO MENTION THAT I GOT A GOOD NIGHT'S SLEEP AND BROUGHT TWO SHARP PENCILS!
BATIUK
11-6

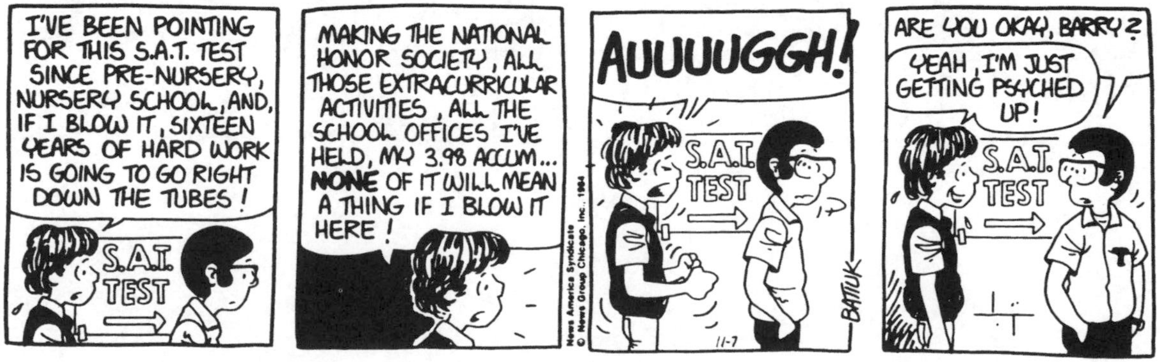
I'VE BEEN POINTING FOR THIS S.A.T. TEST SINCE PRE-NURSERY, NURSERY SCHOOL, AND, IF I BLOW IT, SIXTEEN YEARS OF HARD WORK IS GOING TO GO RIGHT DOWN THE TUBES!
S.A.T. TEST
MAKING THE NATIONAL HONOR SOCIETY, ALL THOSE EXTRACURRICULAR ACTIVITIES, ALL THE SCHOOL OFFICES I'VE HELD, MY 3.98 ACCUM... NONE OF IT WILL MEAN A THING IF I BLOW IT HERE!
News America Syndicate © News Group Chicago, Inc., 1984
AUUUUGGH!
S.A.T. TEST
BATIUK
11-7
ARE YOU OKAY, BARRY?
YEAH, I'M JUST GETTING PSYCHED UP!
S.A.T. TEST

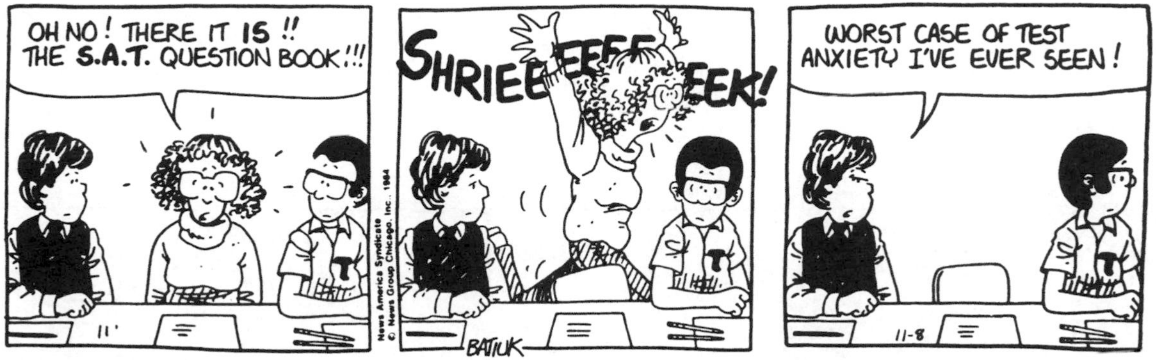
OH NO! THERE IT IS!! THE S.A.T. QUESTION BOOK!!!
SHRIEEEEEEEEEK!
WORST CASE OF TEST ANXIETY I'VE EVER SEEN!
News America Syndicate © News Group Chicago, Inc., 1984
BATIUK
11-8

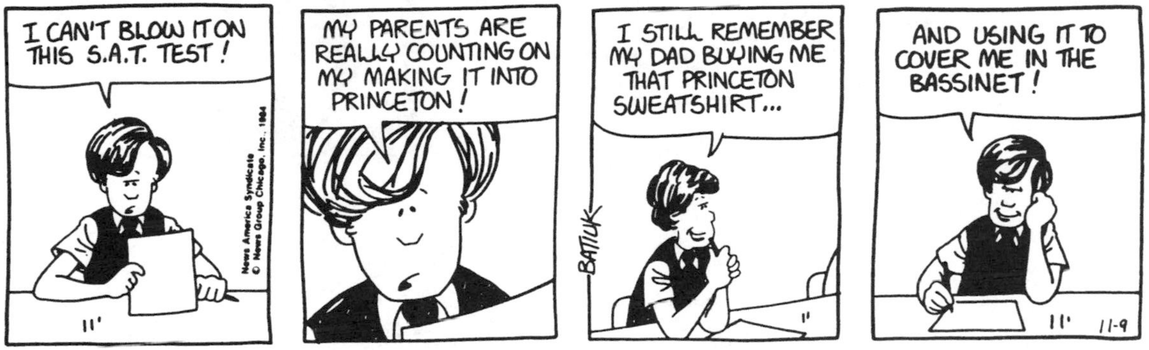
I CAN'T BLOW IT ON THIS S.A.T. TEST!
MY PARENTS ARE REALLY COUNTING ON MY MAKING IT INTO PRINCETON!
I STILL REMEMBER MY DAD BUYING ME THAT PRINCETON SWEATSHIRT...
AND USING IT TO COVER ME IN THE BASSINET!
News America Syndicate © News Group Chicago, Inc., 1984
BATIUK
11-9

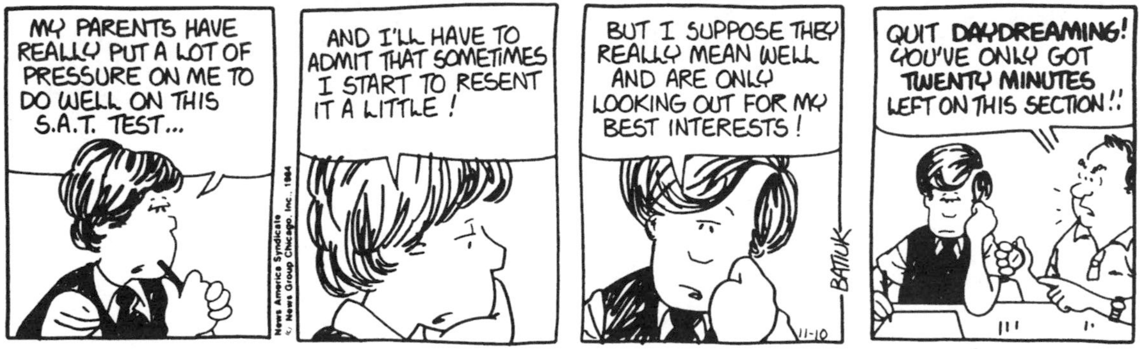
MY PARENTS HAVE REALLY PUT A LOT OF PRESSURE ON ME TO DO WELL ON THIS S.A.T. TEST...
AND I'LL HAVE TO ADMIT THAT SOMETIMES I START TO RESENT IT A LITTLE!
BUT I SUPPOSE THEY REALLY MEAN WELL AND ARE ONLY LOOKING OUT FOR MY BEST INTERESTS!
QUIT DAYDREAMING! YOU'VE ONLY GOT TWENTY MINUTES LEFT ON THIS SECTION!!
News America Syndicate © News Group Chicago, Inc., 1984
BATIUK
11-10

FUNKY WINKERBEAN
by TOM BATIUK
OKAY... HIKE IT ON TWO!
WHAT ABOUT ME?
LES, YOU GO LONG!
EVERY PLAY IT'S 'LES GO LONG'!
BATIUK
I DON'T KNOW WHY! THEY **NEVER** THROW ME THE BALL!
News America Syndicate © News Group Chicago, Inc., 1984
THE OTHER TEAM DOESN'T EVEN **COVER** ME ANYMORE!
EVERYBODY'S YELLING! WE MUST'VE SCORED!
11-11

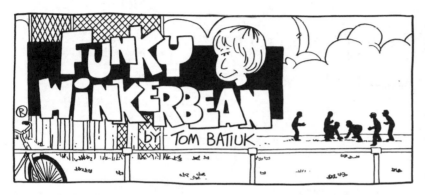

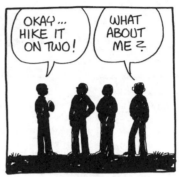

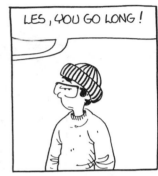

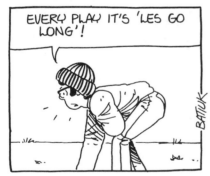

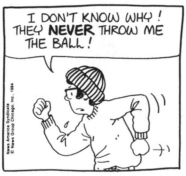

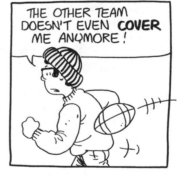

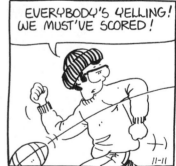

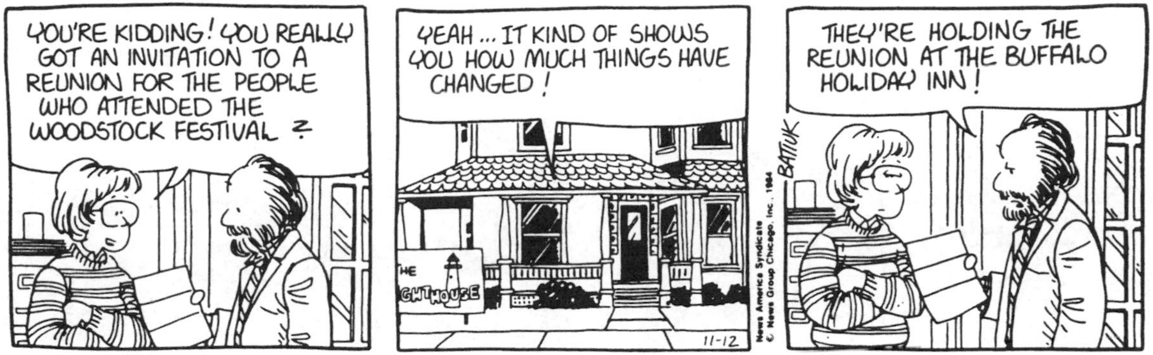
YOU'RE KIDDING! YOU REALLY GOT AN INVITATION TO A REUNION FOR THE PEOPLE WHO ATTENDED THE WOODSTOCK FESTIVAL ?
YEAH ... IT KIND OF SHOWS YOU HOW MUCH THINGS HAVE CHANGED!
THE
GHTHOUSE
11-12
News America Syndicate
© News Group Chicago, Inc., 1984
BATIUK
THEY'RE HOLDING THE REUNION AT THE BUFFALO HOLIDAY INN!

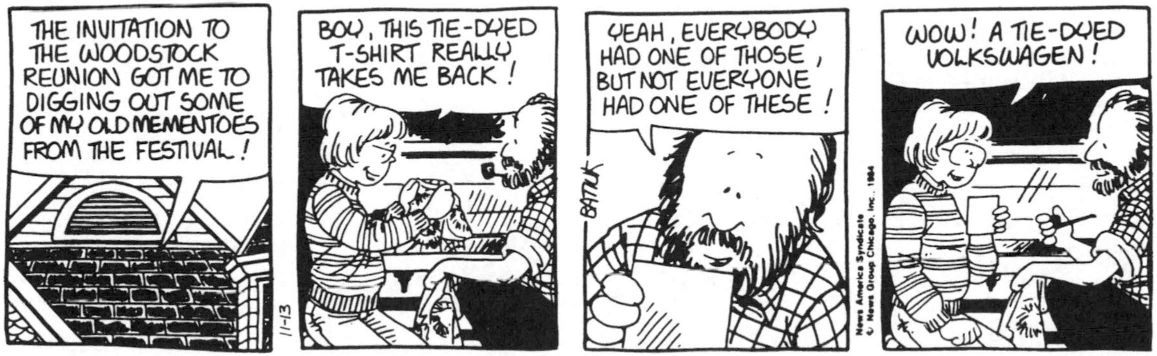
THE INVITATION TO THE WOODSTOCK REUNION GOT ME TO DIGGING OUT SOME OF MY OLD MEMENTOES FROM THE FESTIVAL!
11-13
BOY, THIS TIE-DYED T-SHIRT REALLY TAKES ME BACK!
YEAH, EVERYBODY HAD ONE OF THOSE, BUT NOT EVERYONE HAD ONE OF THESE!
BATIUK
News America Syndicate
© News Group Chicago, Inc., 1984
WOW! A TIE-DYED VOLKSWAGEN!

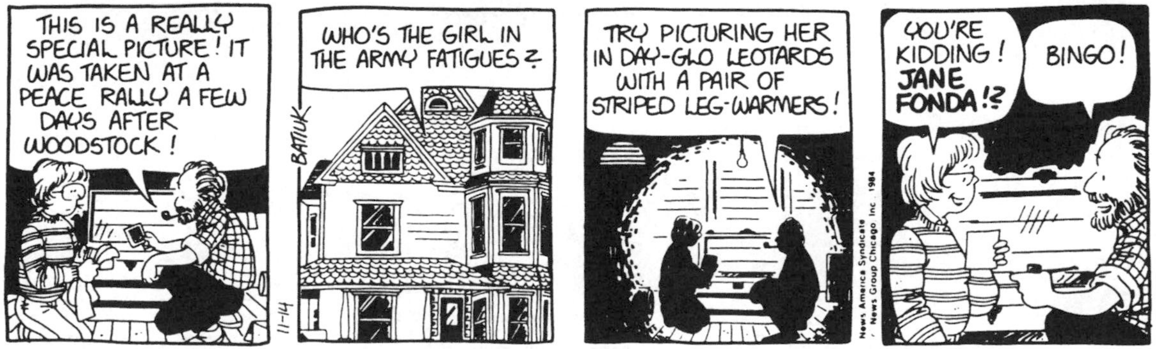
THIS IS A REALLY SPECIAL PICTURE! IT WAS TAKEN AT A PEACE RALLY A FEW DAYS AFTER WOODSTOCK!
11-14
BATIUK
WHO'S THE GIRL IN THE ARMY FATIGUES ?
TRY PICTURING HER IN DAY-GLO LEOTARDS WITH A PAIR OF STRIPED LEG-WARMERS!
News America Syndicate
© News Group Chicago Inc. 1984
YOU'RE KIDDING! **JANE FONDA!?**
BINGO!

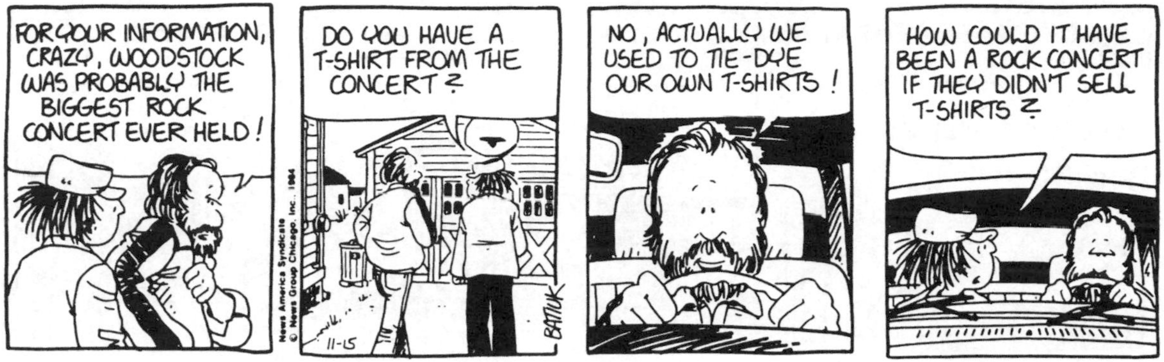
FOR YOUR INFORMATION, CRAZY, WOODSTOCK WAS PROBABLY THE BIGGEST ROCK CONCERT EVER HELD!
DO YOU HAVE A T-SHIRT FROM THE CONCERT?
News America Syndicate © News Group Chicago, Inc. 1984
11-15
BATIUK
NO, ACTUALLY WE USED TO TIE-DYE OUR OWN T-SHIRTS!
HOW COULD IT HAVE BEEN A ROCK CONCERT IF THEY DIDN'T SELL T-SHIRTS?

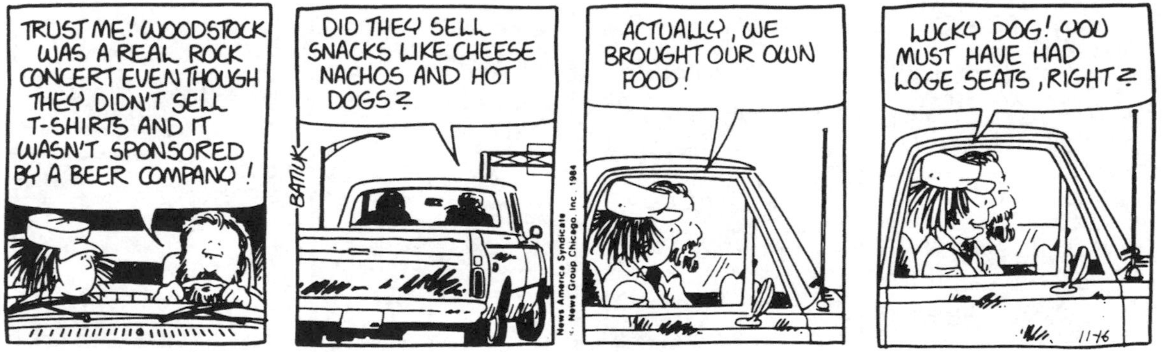
TRUST ME! WOODSTOCK WAS A REAL ROCK CONCERT EVEN THOUGH THEY DIDN'T SELL T-SHIRTS AND IT WASN'T SPONSORED BY A BEER COMPANY!
DID THEY SELL SNACKS LIKE CHEESE NACHOS AND HOT DOGS?
BATIUK
News America Syndicate © News Group Chicago, Inc. 1984
ACTUALLY, WE BROUGHT OUR OWN FOOD!
LUCKY DOG! YOU MUST HAVE HAD LOGE SEATS, RIGHT?
11-16

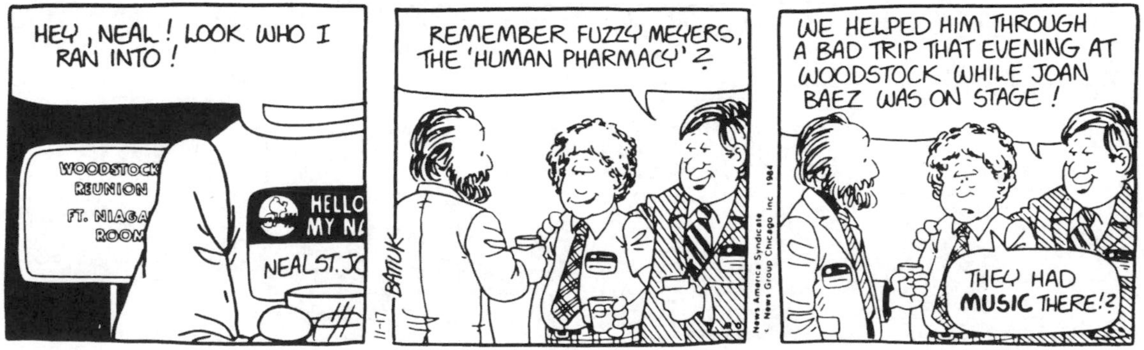
HEY, NEAL! LOOK WHO I RAN INTO!
WOODSTOCK
REUNION
FT. NIAGA
ROOM
HELLO
MY NA
NEAL ST. JO
BATIUK
11-17
REMEMBER FUZZY MEYERS, THE 'HUMAN PHARMACY'?
News America Syndicate © News Group Chicago Inc. 1984
WE HELPED HIM THROUGH A BAD TRIP THAT EVENING AT WOODSTOCK WHILE JOAN BAEZ WAS ON STAGE!
THEY HAD MUSIC THERE!?

FUNKY WINKERBEAN
BY TOM BATIUK ®
HMM ... IT'S STARTING TO SNOW!
NO MATTER! A GOOD SALESMAN NEVER TAKES SNOW FOR AN ANSWER!
HELLO, WOULD YOU LIKE TO HELP OUR BAND EARN MONEY FOR NEW UNIFORMS BY BUYING A BAND TURKEY?
BATIUK
11-18
I'M SORRY, BUT I'M NOT REALLY A BIG FAN OF TURKEY!
News America Syndicate
© News Group Chicago, Inc., 1984
SON OF A GUN! WOULD YOU LOOK AT THAT!!
IT SEEMS I'VE BROUGHT ALONG ONE OF OUR JUMBO ROCK CORNISH HENS BY MISTAKE!!

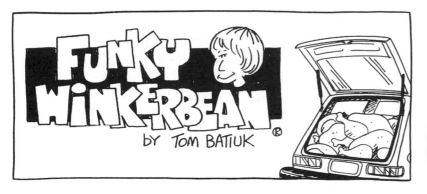

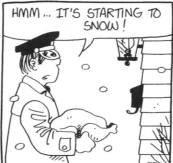

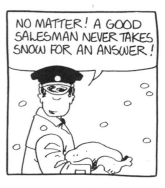

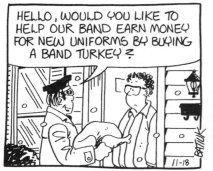

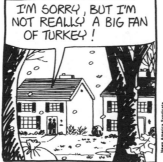

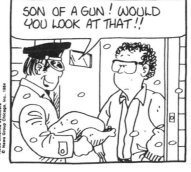

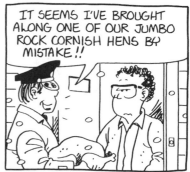

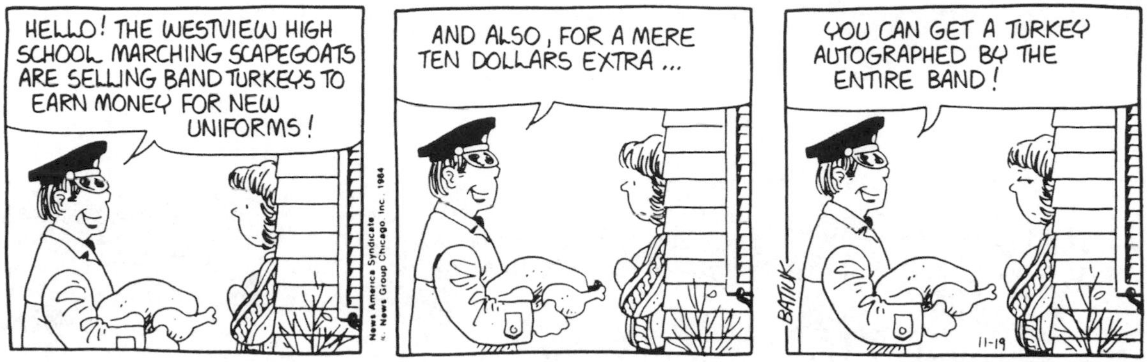
HELLO! THE WESTVIEW HIGH SCHOOL MARCHING SCAPEGOATS ARE SELLING BAND TURKEYS TO EARN MONEY FOR NEW UNIFORMS!
AND ALSO, FOR A MERE TEN DOLLARS EXTRA ...
YOU CAN GET A TURKEY AUTOGRAPHED BY THE ENTIRE BAND!

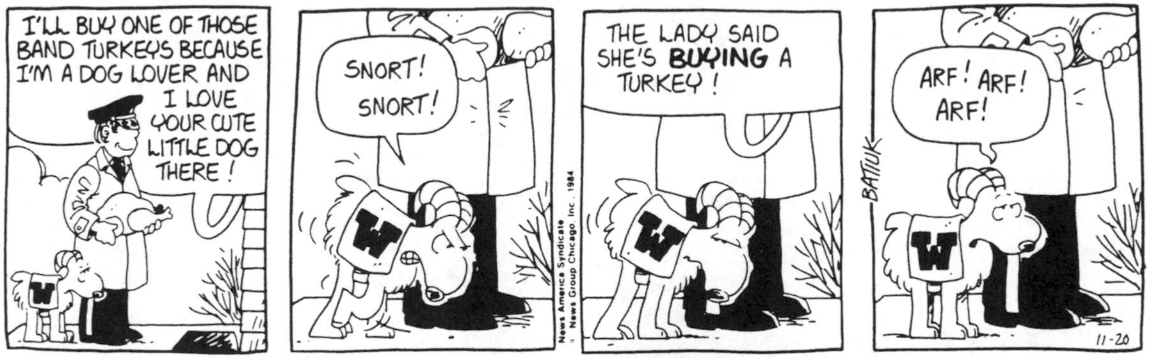
I'LL BUY ONE OF THOSE BAND TURKEYS BECAUSE I'M A DOG LOVER AND I LOVE YOUR CUTE LITTLE DOG THERE!
SNORT! SNORT!
THE LADY SAID SHE'S **BUYING** A TURKEY!
ARF! ARF! ARF!

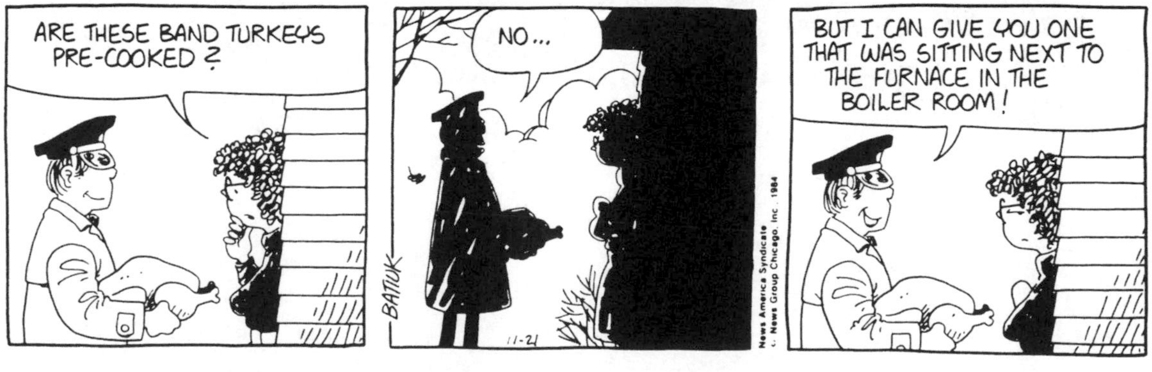
ARE THESE BAND TURKEYS PRE-COOKED?
NO...
BUT I CAN GIVE YOU ONE THAT WAS SITTING NEXT TO THE FURNACE IN THE BOILER ROOM!

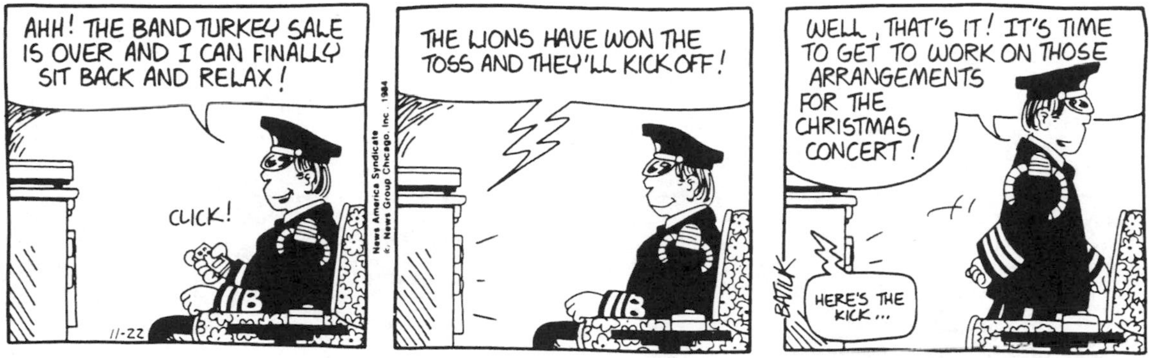
AHH! THE BAND TURKEY SALE IS OVER AND I CAN FINALLY SIT BACK AND RELAX!
CLICK!
11-22
THE LIONS HAVE WON THE TOSS AND THEY'LL KICKOFF!
News America Syndicate © News Group Chicago, Inc. 1984
WELL, THAT'S IT! IT'S TIME TO GET TO WORK ON THOSE ARRANGEMENTS FOR THE CHRISTMAS CONCERT!
HERE'S THE KICK...
BATIUK

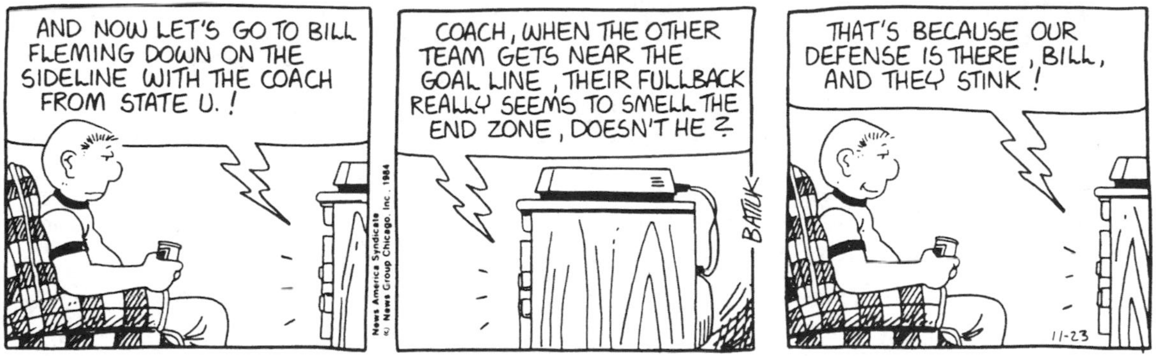
AND NOW LET'S GO TO BILL FLEMING DOWN ON THE SIDELINE WITH THE COACH FROM STATE U.!
News America Syndicate © News Group Chicago, Inc. 1984
COACH, WHEN THE OTHER TEAM GETS NEAR THE GOAL LINE, THEIR FULLBACK REALLY SEEMS TO SMELL THE END ZONE, DOESN'T HE?
BATIUK
THAT'S BECAUSE OUR DEFENSE IS THERE, BILL, AND THEY STINK!
11-23

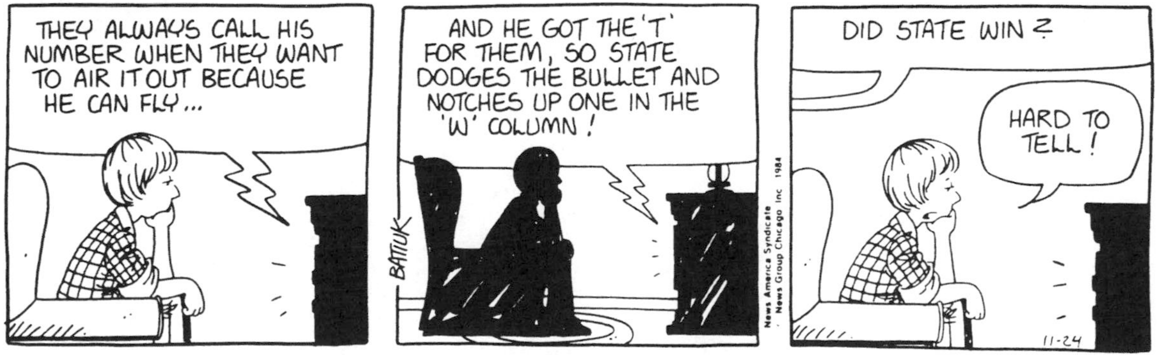
THEY ALWAYS CALL HIS NUMBER WHEN THEY WANT TO AIR IT OUT BECAUSE HE CAN FLY...
BATIUK
AND HE GOT THE 'T' FOR THEM, SO STATE DODGES THE BULLET AND NOTCHES UP ONE IN THE 'W' COLUMN!
News America Syndicate © News Group Chicago Inc 1984
DID STATE WIN?
HARD TO TELL!
11-24

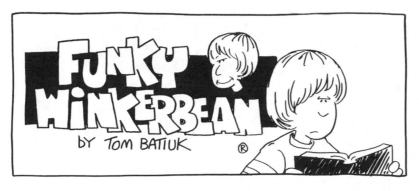

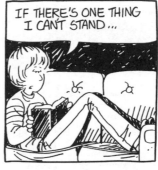

FUNKY WINKERBEAN
BY TOM BATIUK
IF THERE'S ONE THING I CAN'T STAND...
IT'S THESE SUGGESTED PROJECTS AT THE END OF EACH CHAPTER!
HERE'S A NIFTY SCIENCE EXPERIMENT YOU MIGHT WANT TO TRY!
SIMPLY TAKE YOUR MOTHER'S ELECTRIC SWEEPER AND PLACE IT IN THE MIDDLE OF A WIDE-OPEN FIELD DURING A THUNDERSTORM!
News America Syndicate
© News Group Chicago, Inc., 1984
IN A MATTER OF MINUTES, IT WILL BE STRUCK BY LIGHTNING... THEREBY PROVING THAT OLD SCIENTIFIC AXIOM...
BATIUK
THAT NATURE ABHORS A VACUUM!
11-25

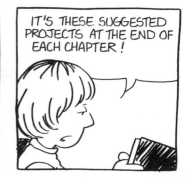

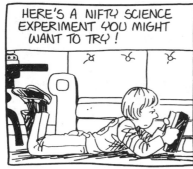

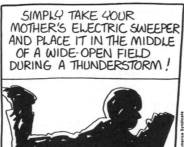

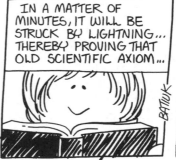

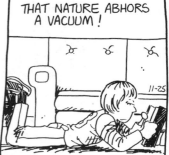

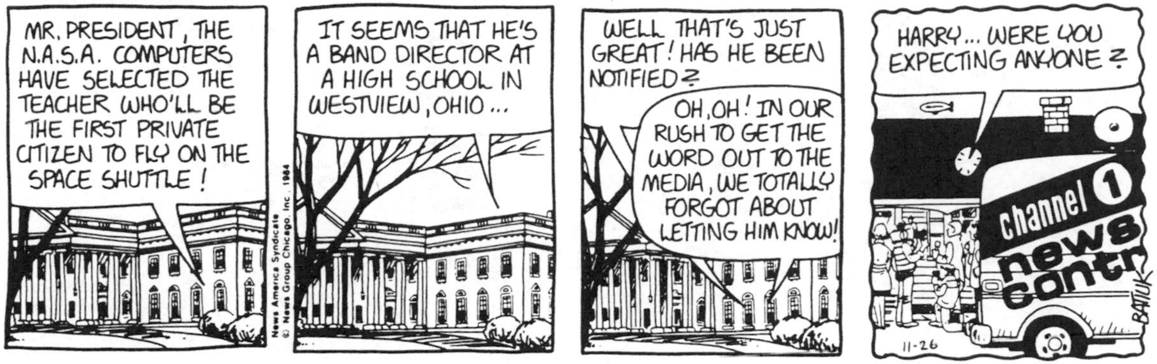
MR. PRESIDENT, THE N.A.S.A. COMPUTERS HAVE SELECTED THE TEACHER WHO'LL BE THE FIRST PRIVATE CITIZEN TO FLY ON THE SPACE SHUTTLE!
News America Syndicate © News Group Chicago, Inc. 1984
IT SEEMS THAT HE'S A BAND DIRECTOR AT A HIGH SCHOOL IN WESTVIEW, OHIO...
WELL THAT'S JUST GREAT! HAS HE BEEN NOTIFIED?
OH, OH! IN OUR RUSH TO GET THE WORD OUT TO THE MEDIA, WE TOTALLY FORGOT ABOUT LETTING HIM KNOW!
HARRY... WERE YOU EXPECTING ANYONE?
channel 1
news
contr
BATIUK
11-26

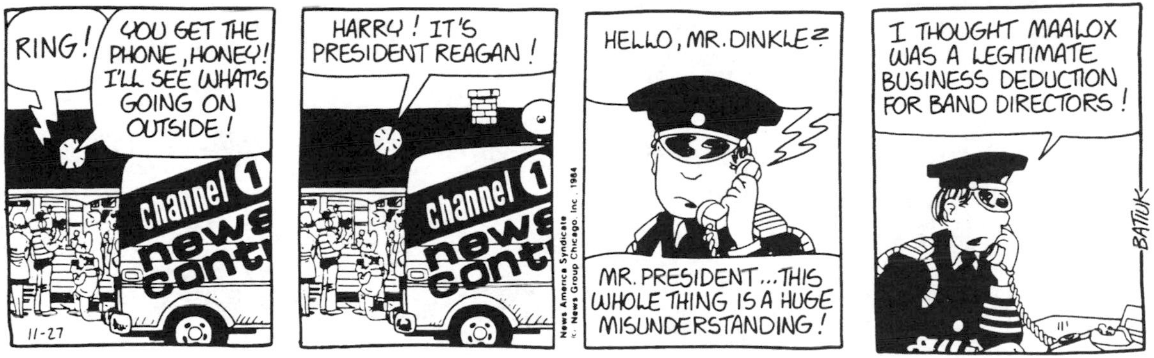
RING!
YOU GET THE PHONE, HONEY! I'LL SEE WHAT'S GOING ON OUTSIDE!
channel 1
news
cont
11-27
HARRY! IT'S PRESIDENT REAGAN!
channel 1
news
cont
News America Syndicate © News Group Chicago, Inc. 1984
HELLO, MR. DINKLE?
MR. PRESIDENT... THIS WHOLE THING IS A HUGE MISUNDERSTANDING!
I THOUGHT MAALOX WAS A LEGITIMATE BUSINESS DEDUCTION FOR BAND DIRECTORS!
BATIUK

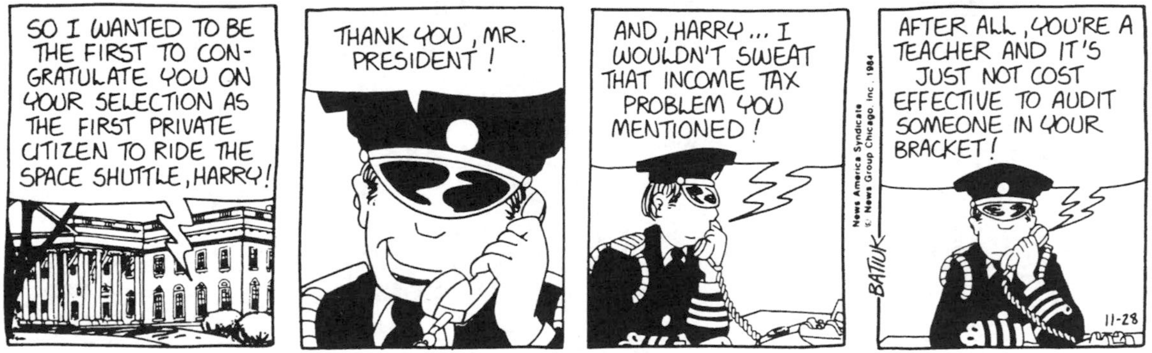
SO I WANTED TO BE THE FIRST TO CONGRATULATE YOU ON YOUR SELECTION AS THE FIRST PRIVATE CITIZEN TO RIDE THE SPACE SHUTTLE, HARRY!
THANK YOU, MR. PRESIDENT!
AND, HARRY... I WOULDN'T SWEAT THAT INCOME TAX PROBLEM YOU MENTIONED!
News America Syndicate © News Group Chicago, Inc. 1984
BATIUK
AFTER ALL, YOU'RE A TEACHER AND IT'S JUST NOT COST EFFECTIVE TO AUDIT SOMEONE IN YOUR BRACKET!
11-28

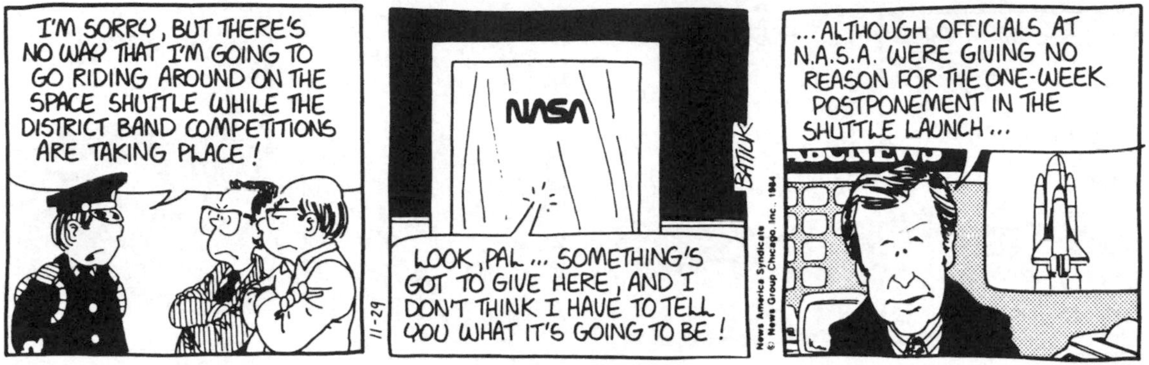
I'M SORRY, BUT THERE'S NO WAY THAT I'M GOING TO GO RIDING AROUND ON THE SPACE SHUTTLE WHILE THE DISTRICT BAND COMPETITIONS ARE TAKING PLACE!
11-29
NASA
LOOK, PAL... SOMETHING'S GOT TO GIVE HERE, AND I DON'T THINK I HAVE TO TELL YOU WHAT IT'S GOING TO BE!
BATIUK
News America Syndicate © News Group Chicago, Inc. 1984
...ALTHOUGH OFFICIALS AT N.A.S.A. WERE GIVING NO REASON FOR THE ONE-WEEK POSTPONEMENT IN THE SHUTTLE LAUNCH...

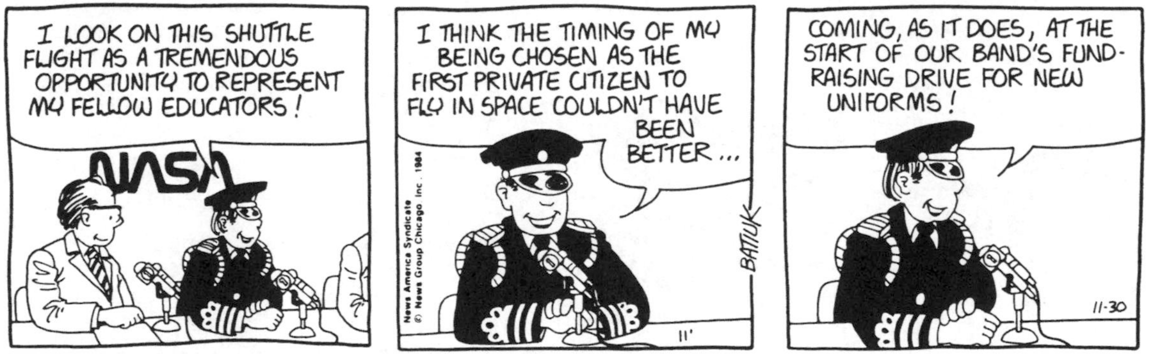
I LOOK ON THIS SHUTTLE FLIGHT AS A TREMENDOUS OPPORTUNITY TO REPRESENT MY FELLOW EDUCATORS!
NASA
News America Syndicate © News Group Chicago, Inc. 1984
I THINK THE TIMING OF MY BEING CHOSEN AS THE FIRST PRIVATE CITIZEN TO FLY IN SPACE COULDN'T HAVE BEEN BETTER...
BATIUK
COMING, AS IT DOES, AT THE START OF OUR BAND'S FUND-RAISING DRIVE FOR NEW UNIFORMS!
11-30

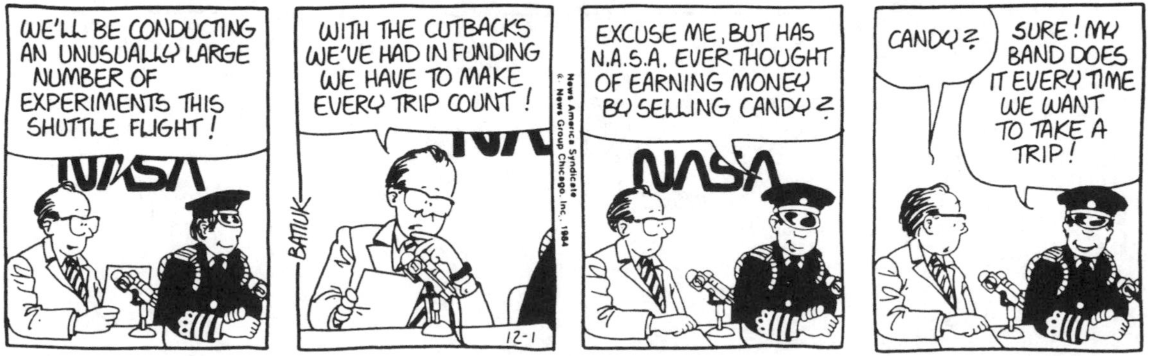
WE'LL BE CONDUCTING AN UNUSUALLY LARGE NUMBER OF EXPERIMENTS THIS SHUTTLE FLIGHT!
BATIUK
WITH THE CUTBACKS WE'VE HAD IN FUNDING WE HAVE TO MAKE EVERY TRIP COUNT!
12-1
News America Syndicate © News Group Chicago, Inc. 1984
EXCUSE ME, BUT HAS N.A.S.A. EVER THOUGHT OF EARNING MONEY BY SELLING CANDY?
NASA
CANDY?
SURE! MY BAND DOES IT EVERY TIME WE WANT TO TAKE A TRIP!

Funky Winkerbean

by Tom Batiuk

FROM YOUR ASSOCIATION...

STAFF MEETING 3:00 IN THE MEDIA CENTER!

AND FINALLY WE HAVE ONE LAST ITEM ON THE AGENDA FOR TONIGHT'S STAFF MEETING!

WE'VE HAD A NUMBER OF QUESTIONS RECENTLY FROM STAFF MEMBERS...

REGARDING THE RESURFACING OF THE MAIN PARKING LOT!

AS YOU'RE ALL AWARE, WE'VE HAD QUITE A LOT OF RAIN THE PAST FEW WEEKS...

12-2

News America Syndicate © News Group Chicago, Inc., 1984

BUT AS SOON AS THINGS DRY OUT A LITTLE BIT, WE EXPECT THE PARKING LOT TO RESURFACE!

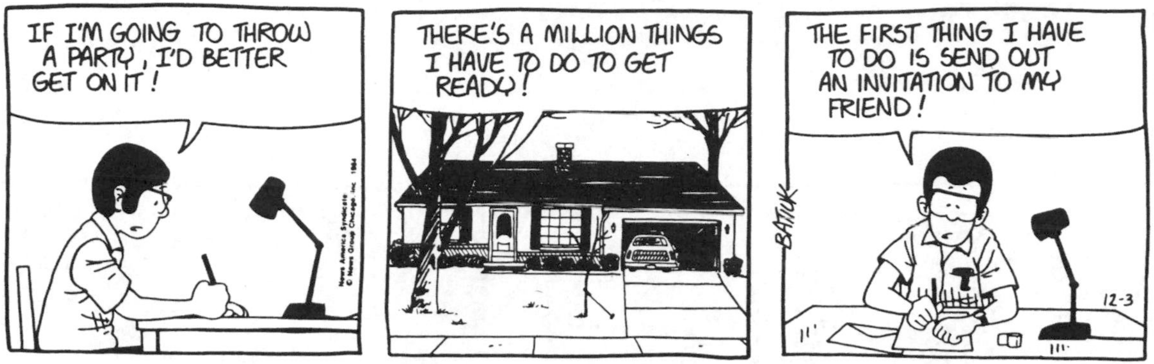
IF I'M GOING TO THROW A PARTY, I'D BETTER GET ON IT!
THERE'S A MILLION THINGS I HAVE TO DO TO GET READY!
THE FIRST THING I HAVE TO DO IS SEND OUT AN INVITATION TO MY FRIEND!
BATIUK
12-3

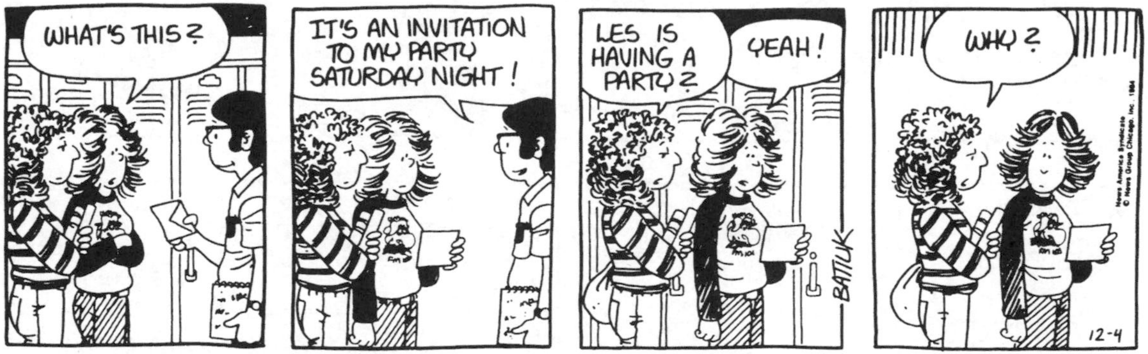
WHAT'S THIS?
IT'S AN INVITATION TO MY PARTY SATURDAY NIGHT!
LES IS HAVING A PARTY?
YEAH!
WHY?
BATIUK
12-4

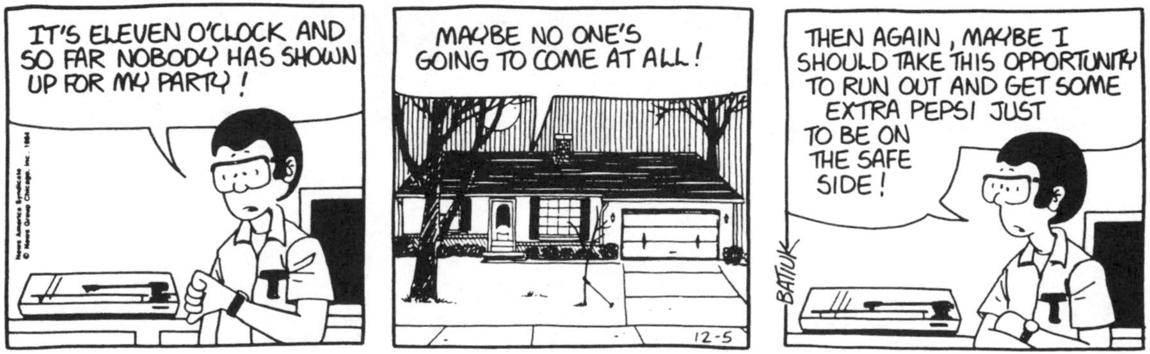
IT'S ELEVEN O'CLOCK AND SO FAR NOBODY HAS SHOWN UP FOR MY PARTY!
MAYBE NO ONE'S GOING TO COME AT ALL!
THEN AGAIN, MAYBE I SHOULD TAKE THIS OPPORTUNITY TO RUN OUT AND GET SOME EXTRA PEPSI JUST TO BE ON THE SAFE SIDE!
BATIUK
12-5

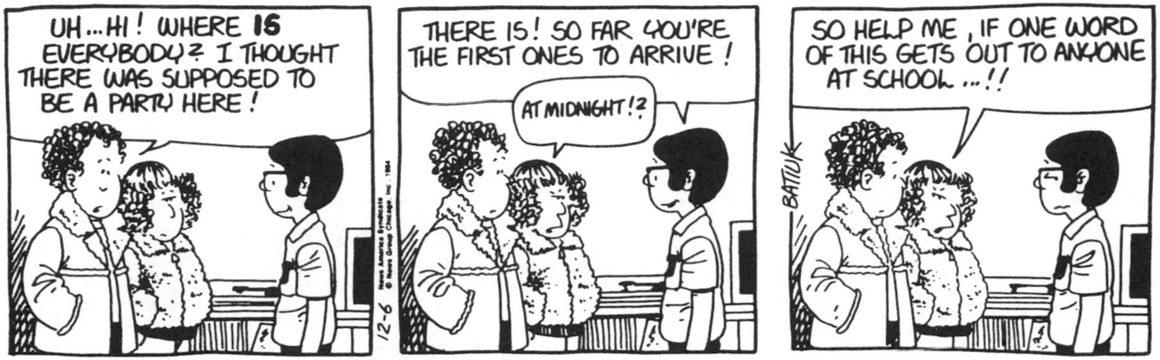
UH...HI! WHERE IS EVERYBODY? I THOUGHT THERE WAS SUPPOSED TO BE A PARTY HERE!
THERE IS! SO FAR YOU'RE THE FIRST ONES TO ARRIVE!
AT MIDNIGHT!?
SO HELP ME, IF ONE WORD OF THIS GETS OUT TO ANYONE AT SCHOOL...!!
BATIUK

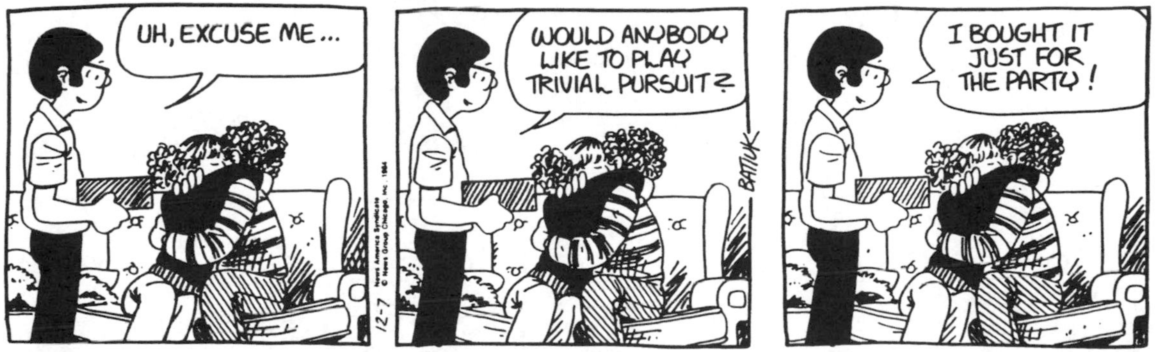
UH, EXCUSE ME...
WOULD ANYBODY LIKE TO PLAY TRIVIAL PURSUIT?
I BOUGHT IT JUST FOR THE PARTY!
BATIUK

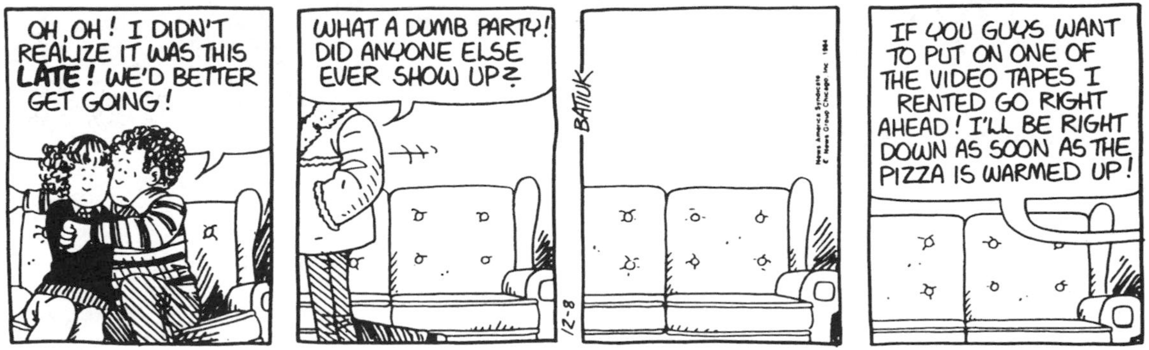
OH, OH! I DIDN'T REALIZE IT WAS THIS LATE! WE'D BETTER GET GOING!
WHAT A DUMB PARTY! DID ANYONE ELSE EVER SHOW UP?
IF YOU GUYS WANT TO PUT ON ONE OF THE VIDEO TAPES I RENTED GO RIGHT AHEAD! I'LL BE RIGHT DOWN AS SOON AS THE PIZZA IS WARMED UP!
BATIUK

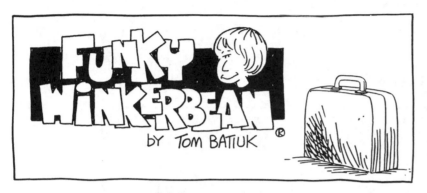

FUNKY WINKERBEAN
by TOM BATIUK ®
SHERLOCK HOLMES' SECRET CASES
SHERLOCK HOLMES
SHERLOCK HOLMES AND THE QUICKIE CAPER!
SHALL I PACK A SUITCASE FOR YOUR TRIP, HOLMES?
I DON'T THINK SO, WATSON!
BATIUK
THIS PARTICULAR PROBLEM SHOULDN'T TAKE TOO LONG!
News America Syndicate © News Group Chicago, Inc., 1984
IN THAT EVENT I'LL JUST PACK YOUR BRIEFCASE!
12-9

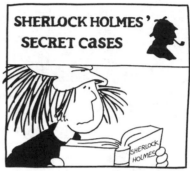

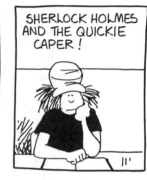

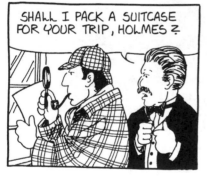

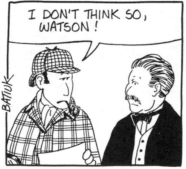

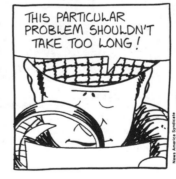

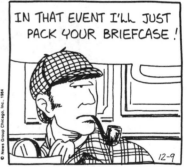

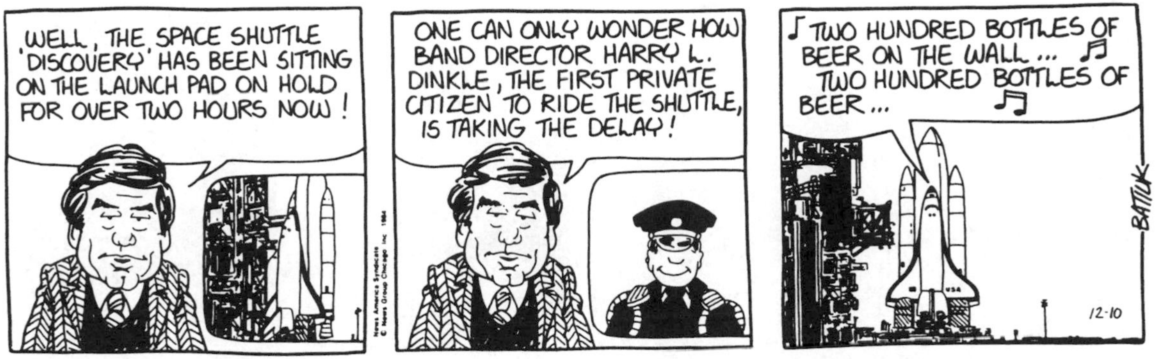
WELL, THE SPACE SHUTTLE 'DISCOVERY' HAS BEEN SITTING ON THE LAUNCH PAD ON HOLD FOR OVER TWO HOURS NOW!
ONE CAN ONLY WONDER HOW BAND DIRECTOR HARRY L. DINKLE, THE FIRST PRIVATE CITIZEN TO RIDE THE SHUTTLE, IS TAKING THE DELAY!
News America Syndicate © News Group Chicago Inc 1984
♩ TWO HUNDRED BOTTLES OF BEER ON THE WALL... ♫ TWO HUNDRED BOTTLES OF BEER... ♫
BATIUK
12-10

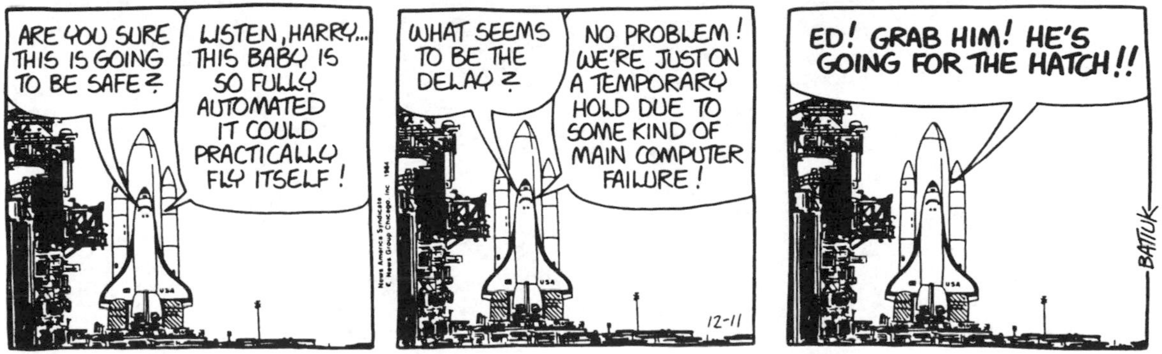
ARE YOU SURE THIS IS GOING TO BE SAFE?
LISTEN, HARRY... THIS BABY IS SO FULLY AUTOMATED IT COULD PRACTICALLY FLY ITSELF!
News America Syndicate © News Group Chicago Inc 1984
WHAT SEEMS TO BE THE DELAY?
NO PROBLEM! WE'RE JUST ON A TEMPORARY HOLD DUE TO SOME KIND OF MAIN COMPUTER FAILURE!
12-11
ED! GRAB HIM! HE'S GOING FOR THE HATCH!!
BATIUK

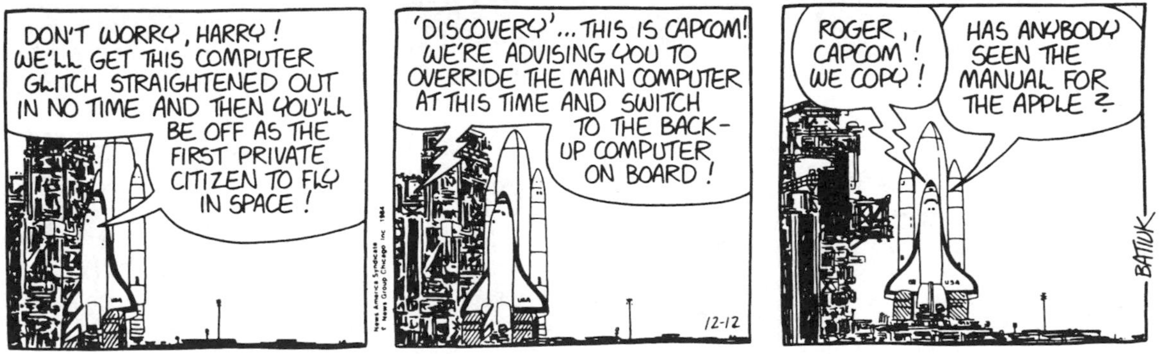
DON'T WORRY, HARRY! WE'LL GET THIS COMPUTER GLITCH STRAIGHTENED OUT IN NO TIME AND THEN YOU'LL BE OFF AS THE FIRST PRIVATE CITIZEN TO FLY IN SPACE!
News America Syndicate © News Group Chicago Inc 1984
'DISCOVERY'... THIS IS CAPCOM! WE'RE ADVISING YOU TO OVERRIDE THE MAIN COMPUTER AT THIS TIME AND SWITCH TO THE BACK-UP COMPUTER ON BOARD!
12-12
ROGER, CAPCOM! WE COPY!
HAS ANYBODY SEEN THE MANUAL FOR THE APPLE?
BATIUK

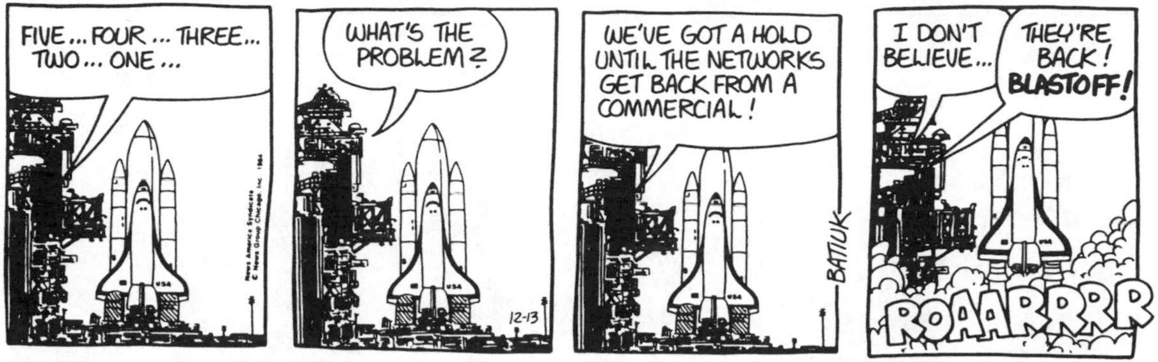
FIVE ... FOUR ... THREE... TWO ... ONE ...
WHAT'S THE PROBLEM?
12-13
WE'VE GOT A HOLD UNTIL THE NETWORKS GET BACK FROM A COMMERCIAL!
BATIUK
I DON'T BELIEVE...
THEY'RE BACK! BLASTOFF!
ROAARRRR

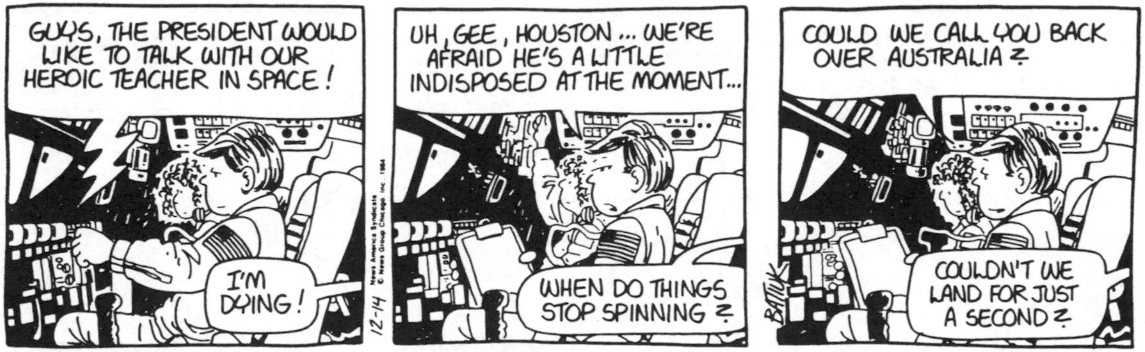
GUYS, THE PRESIDENT WOULD LIKE TO TALK WITH OUR HEROIC TEACHER IN SPACE!
I'M DYING!
12-14
UH, GEE, HOUSTON ... WE'RE AFRAID HE'S A LITTLE INDISPOSED AT THE MOMENT...
WHEN DO THINGS STOP SPINNING?
COULD WE CALL YOU BACK OVER AUSTRALIA?
BATIUK
COULDN'T WE LAND FOR JUST A SECOND?

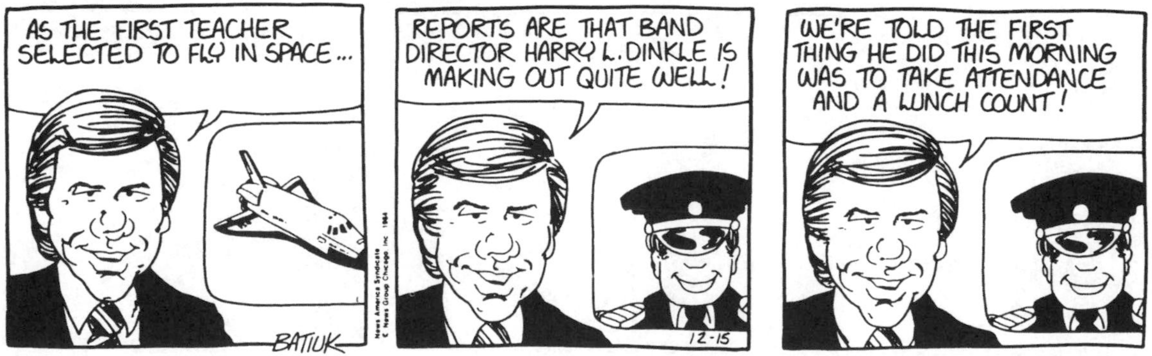
AS THE FIRST TEACHER SELECTED TO FLY IN SPACE...
BATIUK
REPORTS ARE THAT BAND DIRECTOR HARRY L. DINKLE IS MAKING OUT QUITE WELL!
12-15
WE'RE TOLD THE FIRST THING HE DID THIS MORNING WAS TO TAKE ATTENDANCE AND A LUNCH COUNT!

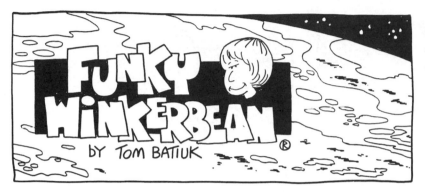

FUNKY WINKERBEAN
BY TOM BATIUK ®
HOW ARE YOU FEELING, HARRY?
MUCH BETTER!
USA
I THINK I'M FINALLY OVER MY SPACE SICKNESS!
GOOD!
IN FACT, I'M KIND OF HUNGRY! WOULD YOU GUYS CARE FOR A SNACK?
SURE!
ME TOO!
UNITED STATES
News America Syndicate
© News Group Chicago, Inc., 1984
SAY, THIS ISN'T BAD! WHAT IS IT?
BATIUK
DEHYDRATED BAND CANDY!
12-16

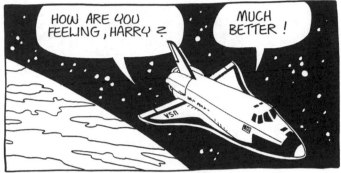

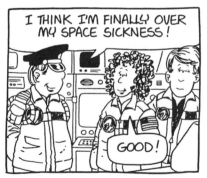

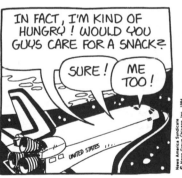

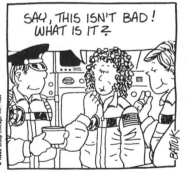

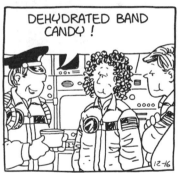

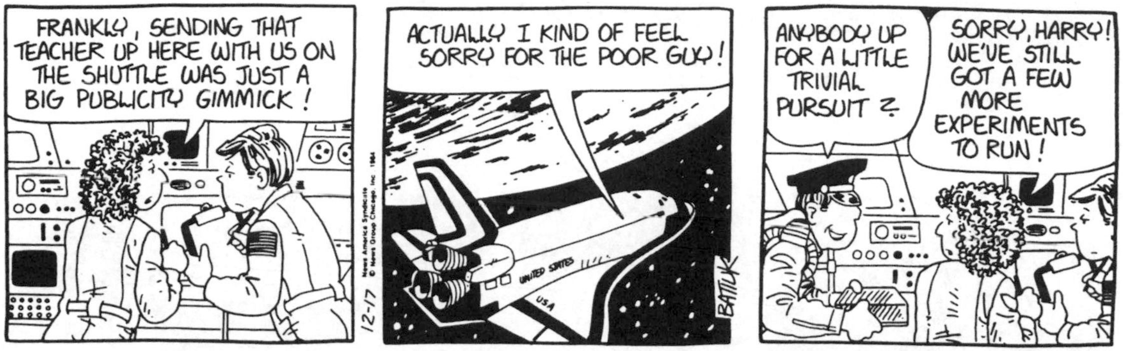
FRANKLY, SENDING THAT TEACHER UP HERE WITH US ON THE SHUTTLE WAS JUST A BIG PUBLICITY GIMMICK!
12-17
News America Syndicate © News Group Chicago Inc 1984
ACTUALLY I KIND OF FEEL SORRY FOR THE POOR GUY!
UNITED STATES
USA
BATIUK
ANYBODY UP FOR A LITTLE TRIVIAL PURSUIT?
SORRY, HARRY! WE'VE STILL GOT A FEW MORE EXPERIMENTS TO RUN!

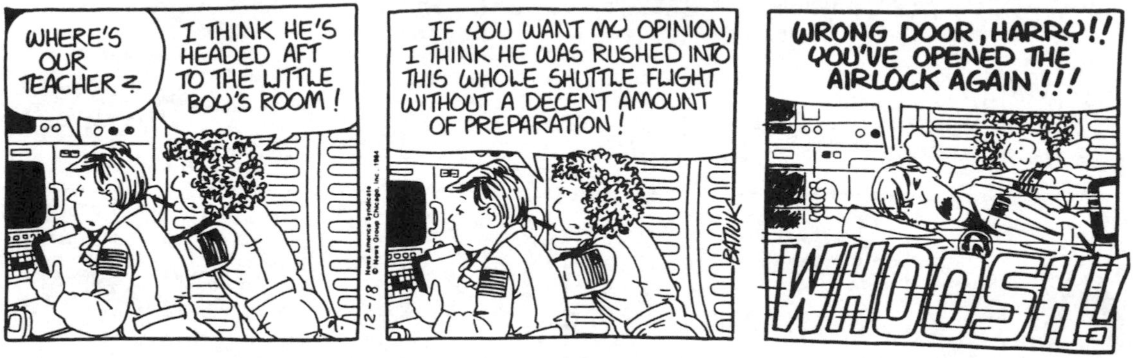
WHERE'S OUR TEACHER?
I THINK HE'S HEADED AFT TO THE LITTLE BOY'S ROOM!
12-18
News America Syndicate © News Group Chicago Inc 1984
IF YOU WANT MY OPINION, I THINK HE WAS RUSHED INTO THIS WHOLE SHUTTLE FLIGHT WITHOUT A DECENT AMOUNT OF PREPARATION!
BATIUK
WRONG DOOR, HARRY!! YOU'VE OPENED THE AIRLOCK AGAIN!!!
WHOOSH!

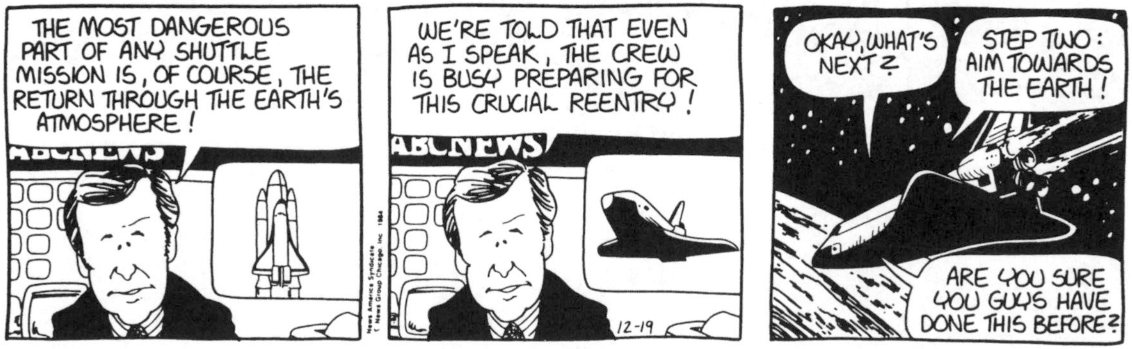
THE MOST DANGEROUS PART OF ANY SHUTTLE MISSION IS, OF COURSE, THE RETURN THROUGH THE EARTH'S ATMOSPHERE!
ABC NEWS
News America Syndicate © News Group Chicago Inc 1984
WE'RE TOLD THAT EVEN AS I SPEAK, THE CREW IS BUSY PREPARING FOR THIS CRUCIAL REENTRY!
ABC NEWS
12-19
OKAY, WHAT'S NEXT?
STEP TWO: AIM TOWARDS THE EARTH!
ARE YOU SURE YOU GUYS HAVE DONE THIS BEFORE?

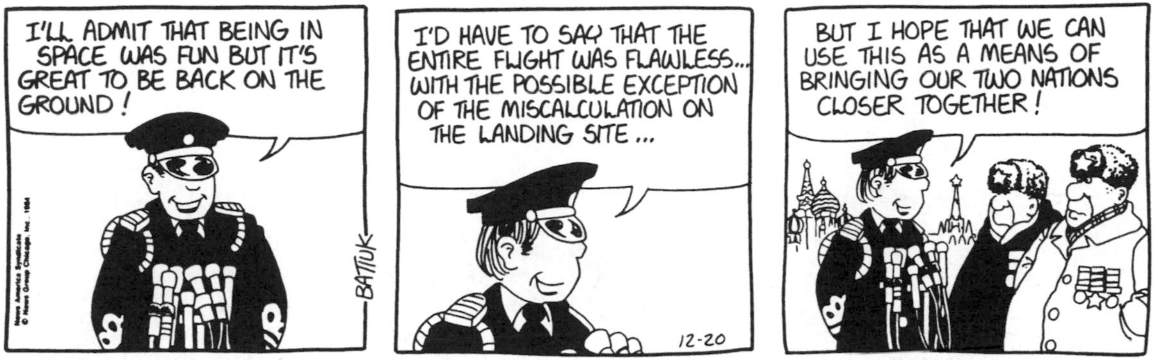
I'LL ADMIT THAT BEING IN SPACE WAS FUN BUT IT'S GREAT TO BE BACK ON THE GROUND!
BATIUK
I'D HAVE TO SAY THAT THE ENTIRE FLIGHT WAS FLAWLESS... WITH THE POSSIBLE EXCEPTION OF THE MISCALCULATION ON THE LANDING SITE...
12-20
BUT I HOPE THAT WE CAN USE THIS AS A MEANS OF BRINGING OUR TWO NATIONS CLOSER TOGETHER!

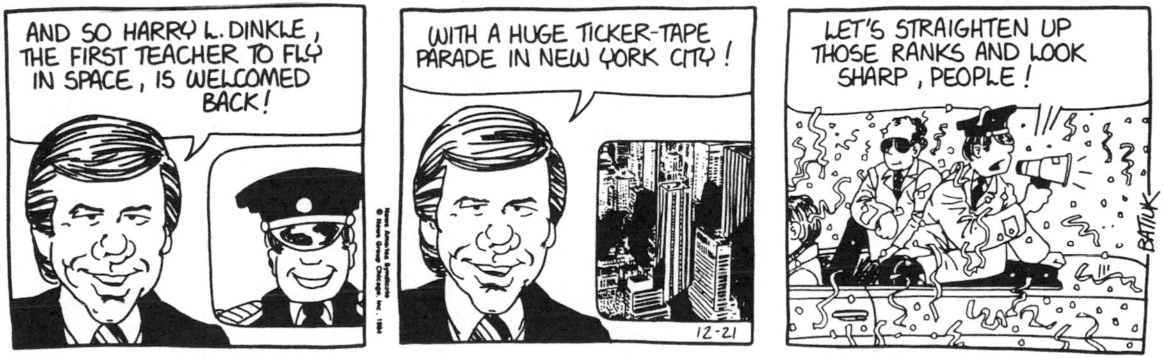
AND SO HARRY L. DINKLE, THE FIRST TEACHER TO FLY IN SPACE, IS WELCOMED BACK!
WITH A HUGE TICKER-TAPE PARADE IN NEW YORK CITY!
12-21
LET'S STRAIGHTEN UP THOSE RANKS AND LOOK SHARP, PEOPLE!
BATIUK

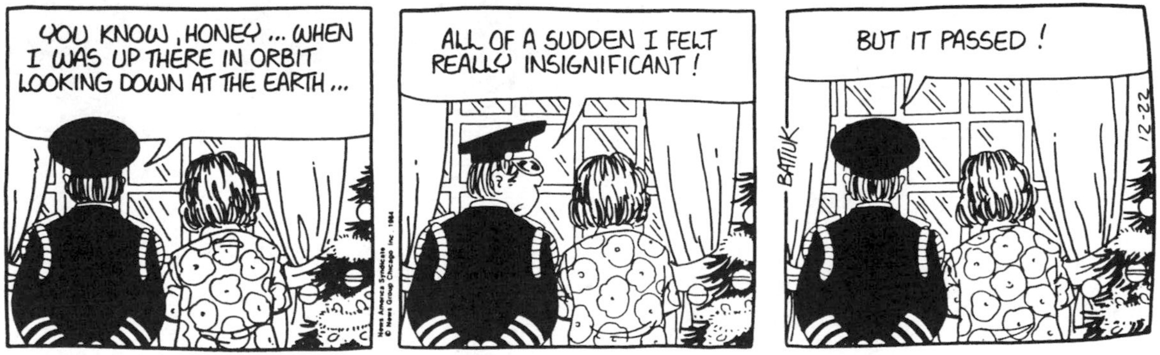
YOU KNOW, HONEY... WHEN I WAS UP THERE IN ORBIT LOOKING DOWN AT THE EARTH...
ALL OF A SUDDEN I FELT REALLY INSIGNIFICANT!
BATIUK
BUT IT PASSED!
12-22

FUNKY WINKERBEAN
BY TOM BATIUK ®
HOLD IT A SECOND!
I'LL HAVE TO ADMIT ONE THING...
YOU PEOPLE HAVE CERTAINLY MANAGED TO CAPTURE THE ESSENCE OF CHRISTMAS IN YOUR PLAYING!
WESTVIEW HIGH SCHOOL
DEC 24 CHRISTMAS CONCERT
BECAUSE IF IT SOUNDS HALFWAY DECENT ON CONCERT NIGHT...
IT'LL BE A **MIRACLE!!!**
BATIUK
12-23
News America Syndicate
© News Group Chicago, Inc., 1984

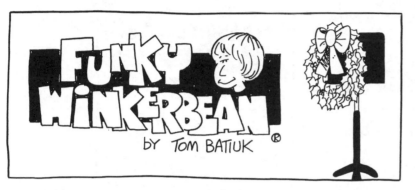

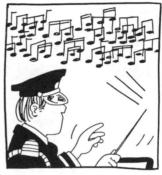

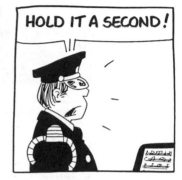

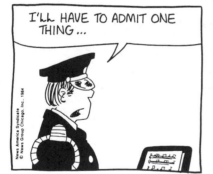

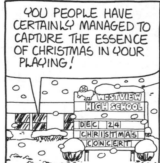

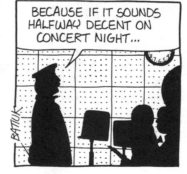

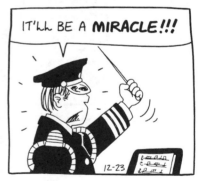

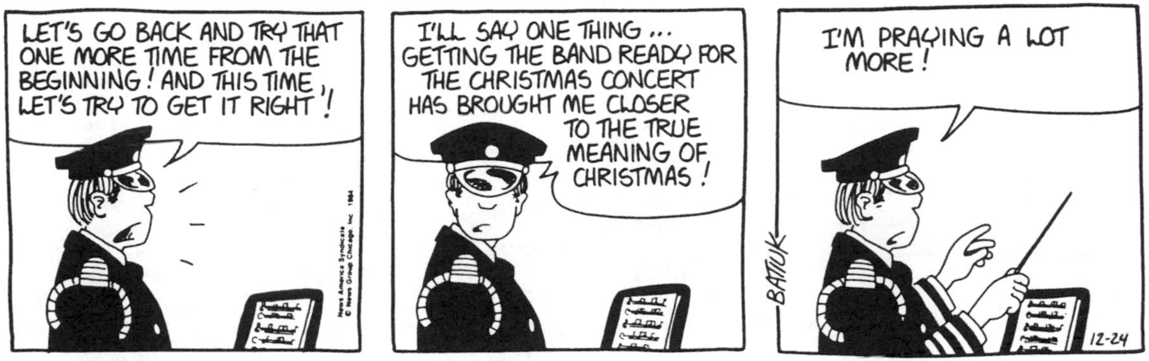
LET'S GO BACK AND TRY THAT ONE MORE TIME FROM THE BEGINNING! AND THIS TIME, LET'S TRY TO GET IT RIGHT'!
I'LL SAY ONE THING... GETTING THE BAND READY FOR THE CHRISTMAS CONCERT HAS BROUGHT ME CLOSER TO THE TRUE MEANING OF CHRISTMAS!
I'M PRAYING A LOT MORE!
BATIUK
12-24

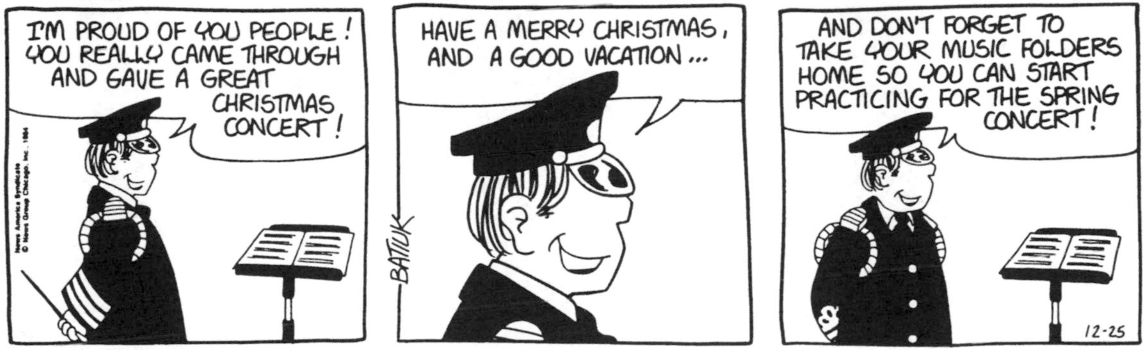
I'M PROUD OF YOU PEOPLE! YOU REALLY CAME THROUGH AND GAVE A GREAT CHRISTMAS CONCERT!
HAVE A MERRY CHRISTMAS, AND A GOOD VACATION...
BATIUK
AND DON'T FORGET TO TAKE YOUR MUSIC FOLDERS HOME SO YOU CAN START PRACTICING FOR THE SPRING CONCERT!
12-25

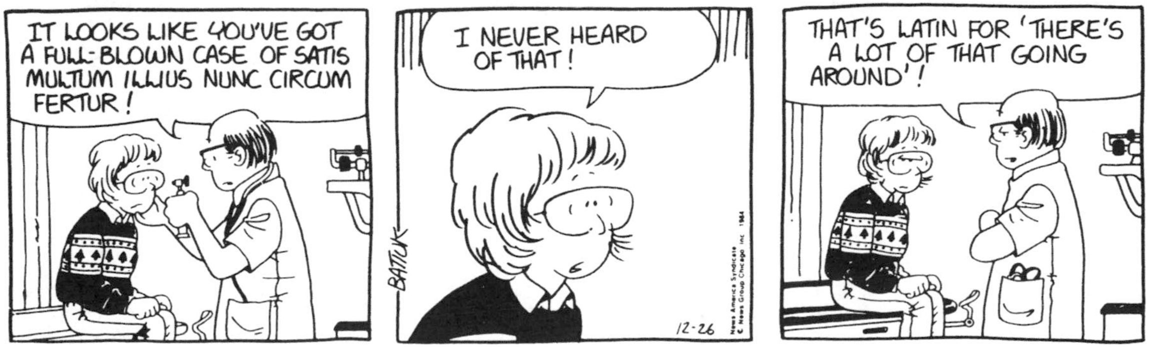
IT LOOKS LIKE YOU'VE GOT A FULL-BLOWN CASE OF SATIS MULTUM ILLIUS NUNC CIRCUM FERTUR!
I NEVER HEARD OF THAT!
BATIUK
12-26
THAT'S LATIN FOR 'THERE'S A LOT OF THAT GOING AROUND'!

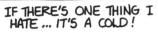

Panel 1: IF THERE'S ONE THING I HATE ... IT'S A COLD!

Panel 2: WELL, YOU'RE IN LUCK!

Panel 3: YOU'VE GOT THE FLU!

Panel 4: IT LOOKS LIKE I'LL HAVE TO OPEN A NEW BOTTLE OF ASPIRIN!

Panel 5: I WONDER WHY THEY ALWAYS PUT COTTON IN THE TOP OF A BOTTLE OF ASPIRIN...

Panel 6: BUT THEY NEVER PUT ANY ASPIRIN IN THE TOP OF A BOX OF COTTON?

Panel 7: MAYBE I'LL TRY THIS COUGH MEDICINE TO SEE IF IT HELPS!

Panel 8: LET'S SEE ... 'SHAKE WELL WITH CAP ON'!

174

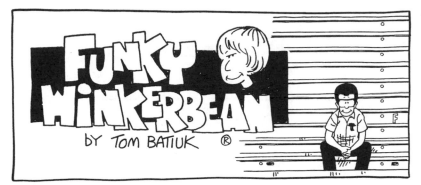

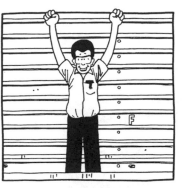

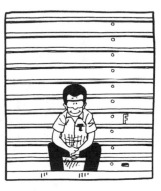

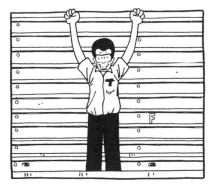

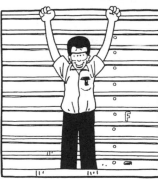

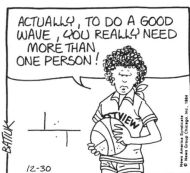

FUNKY WINKERBEAN
BY TOM BATIUK ®
ACTUALLY, TO DO A GOOD WAVE, YOU REALLY NEED MORE THAN ONE PERSON!
BATIUK
12-30
News America Syndicate
© News Group Chicago, Inc., 1984

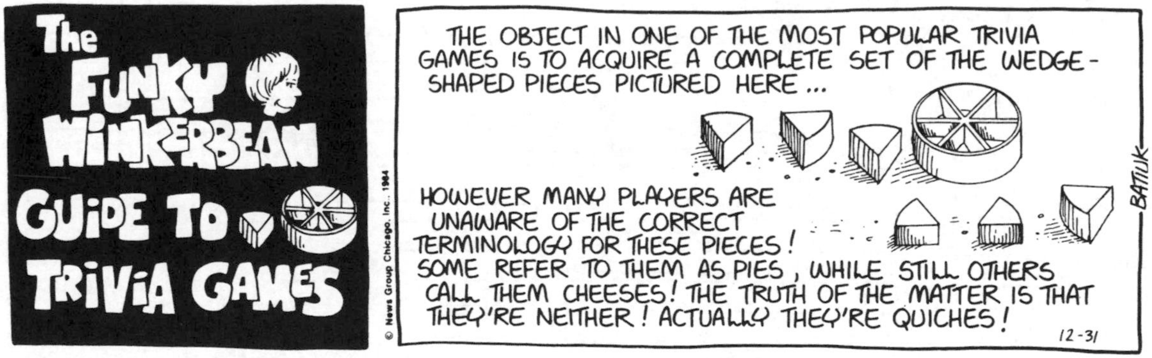
The FUNKY WINKERBEAN GUIDE TO TRIVIA GAMES
© News Group Chicago, Inc. 1984
THE OBJECT IN ONE OF THE MOST POPULAR TRIVIA GAMES IS TO ACQUIRE A COMPLETE SET OF THE WEDGE-SHAPED PIECES PICTURED HERE ...
HOWEVER MANY PLAYERS ARE UNAWARE OF THE CORRECT TERMINOLOGY FOR THESE PIECES! SOME REFER TO THEM AS PIES, WHILE STILL OTHERS CALL THEM CHEESES! THE TRUTH OF THE MATTER IS THAT THEY'RE NEITHER! ACTUALLY THEY'RE QUICHES!
BATIUK
12-31

1985

The Funky Winkerbean Guide to Trivia Games

© News Group Chicago, Inc., 1985

MANY PEOPLE LIKE TO COMBINE THEIR TRIVIAL PURSUIT SETS INTO ONE LARGE GAME FEATURING THE GENUS, BABY BOOMERS, AND SILVER SCREEN EDITIONS!

STILL OTHERS LIKE TO COMBINE THEIR SETS WITH COMPLETELY DIFFERENT GAMES SUCH AS MONOPOLY, SORRY, BINGO, CANDYLAND, AND BOWLING!

I'LL TAKE ONE CHEESE AND A HOTEL AND SEND YOU BACK TO START!

BATIUK

1-1

The Funky Winkerbean Guide to Trivia Games

© News Group Chicago, Inc., 1985

BY CLOSELY OBSERVING THE PLAYERS, YOU CAN OFTEN TELL HOW A TRIVIA GAME IS GOING! FOR EXAMPLE, WHICH PLAYER PICTURED BELOW HAS JUST SUCCESSFULLY TALKED HER TEAM INTO THE WRONG ANSWER?

BATIUK

1-2

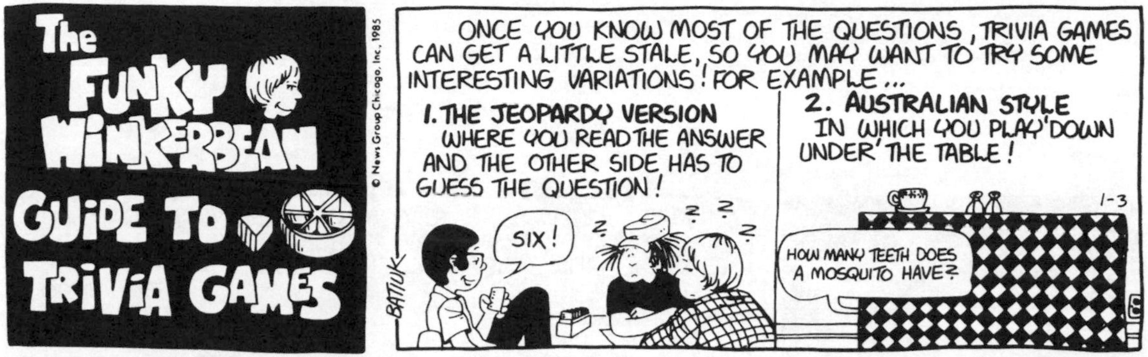
The Funky Winkerbean Guide to Trivia Games
© News Group Chicago, Inc, 1985
ONCE YOU KNOW MOST OF THE QUESTIONS, TRIVIA GAMES CAN GET A LITTLE STALE, SO YOU MAY WANT TO TRY SOME INTERESTING VARIATIONS! FOR EXAMPLE ...
1. THE JEOPARDY VERSION
WHERE YOU READ THE ANSWER AND THE OTHER SIDE HAS TO GUESS THE QUESTION!
SIX!
Z Z Z Z
2. AUSTRALIAN STYLE
IN WHICH YOU PLAY 'DOWN UNDER' THE TABLE!
1-3
HOW MANY TEETH DOES A MOSQUITO HAVE?
BATIUK

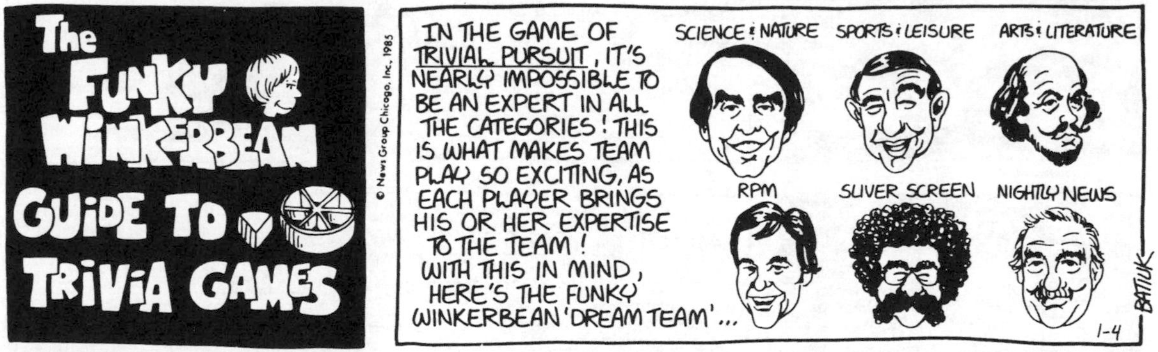
The Funky Winkerbean Guide to Trivia Games
© News Group Chicago, Inc, 1985
IN THE GAME OF TRIVIAL PURSUIT, IT'S NEARLY IMPOSSIBLE TO BE AN EXPERT IN ALL THE CATEGORIES! THIS IS WHAT MAKES TEAM PLAY SO EXCITING, AS EACH PLAYER BRINGS HIS OR HER EXPERTISE TO THE TEAM! WITH THIS IN MIND, HERE'S THE FUNKY WINKERBEAN 'DREAM TEAM'...
SCIENCE & NATURE
SPORTS & LEISURE
ARTS & LITERATURE
RPM
SILVER SCREEN
NIGHTLY NEWS
1-4
BATIUK

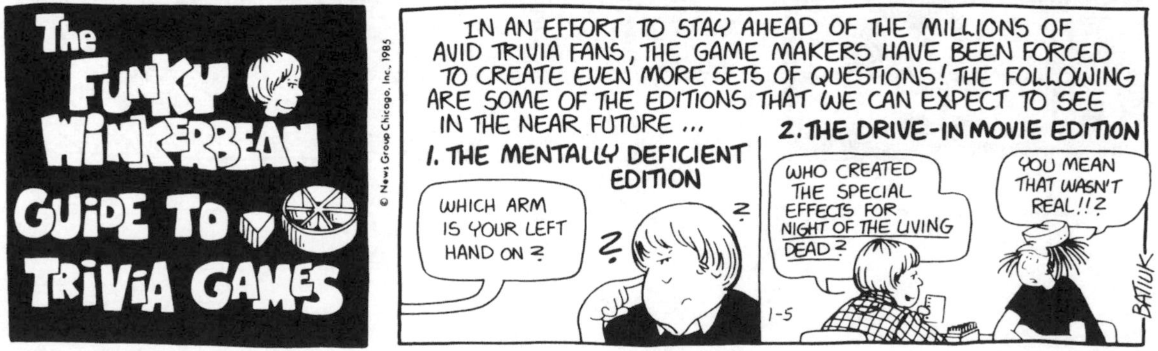
The Funky Winkerbean Guide to Trivia Games
© News Group Chicago, Inc, 1985
IN AN EFFORT TO STAY AHEAD OF THE MILLIONS OF AVID TRIVIA FANS, THE GAME MAKERS HAVE BEEN FORCED TO CREATE EVEN MORE SETS OF QUESTIONS! THE FOLLOWING ARE SOME OF THE EDITIONS THAT WE CAN EXPECT TO SEE IN THE NEAR FUTURE ...
1. THE MENTALLY DEFICIENT EDITION
WHICH ARM IS YOUR LEFT HAND ON?
2. THE DRIVE-IN MOVIE EDITION
WHO CREATED THE SPECIAL EFFECTS FOR NIGHT OF THE LIVING DEAD?
YOU MEAN THAT WASN'T REAL!!?
1-5
BATIUK

FUNKY WINKERBEAN

BY TOM BATIUK

YOU'LL HAVE TEN MINUTES TO DO THESE DEFINITIONS!

DEFINE THE FOLLOWING:
1. FUTILITY

1-6

Companies that have a monopoly on a public need...

and thus are able to charge whatever they want without anyone being able to do a thing about it...

as, for example, an electric futility!

BATIUK

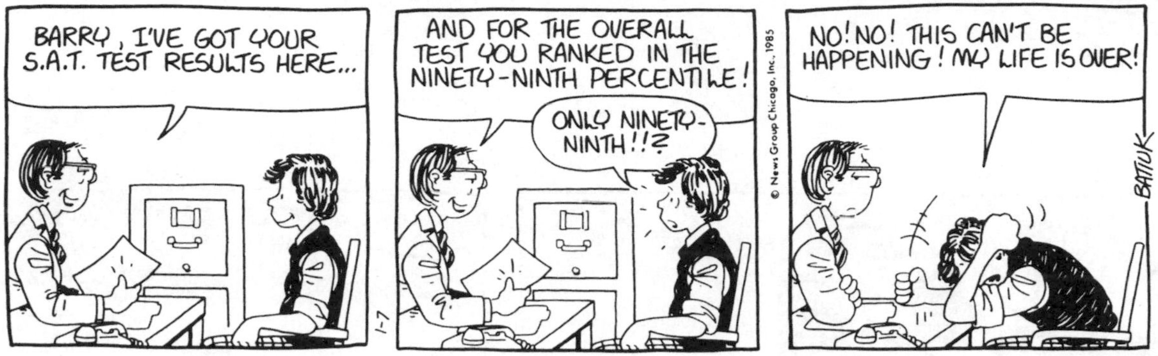
BARRY, I'VE GOT YOUR S.A.T. TEST RESULTS HERE...
AND FOR THE OVERALL TEST YOU RANKED IN THE NINETY-NINTH PERCENTILE!
ONLY NINETY-NINTH!!?
NO! NO! THIS CAN'T BE HAPPENING! MY LIFE IS OVER!
BATIUK
1-7
© News Group Chicago, Inc., 1985

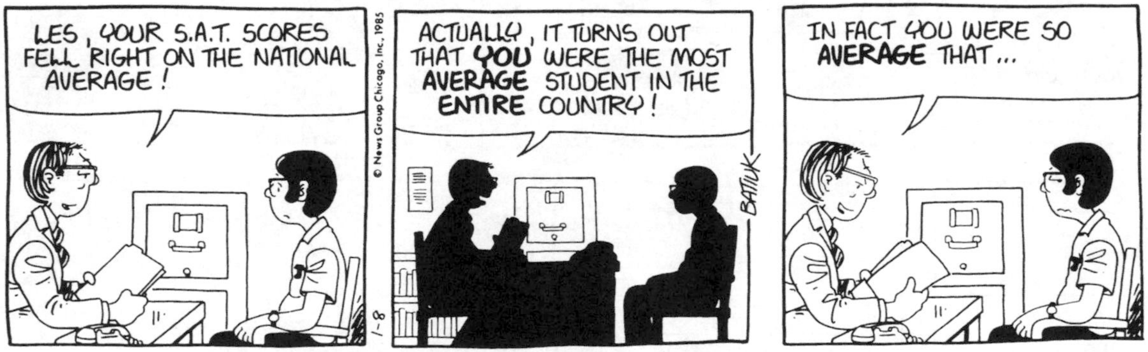
LES, YOUR S.A.T. SCORES FELL RIGHT ON THE NATIONAL AVERAGE!
ACTUALLY, IT TURNS OUT THAT **YOU** WERE THE MOST **AVERAGE** STUDENT IN THE **ENTIRE** COUNTRY!
IN FACT YOU WERE SO **AVERAGE** THAT...
BATIUK
1-8
© News Group Chicago, Inc., 1985

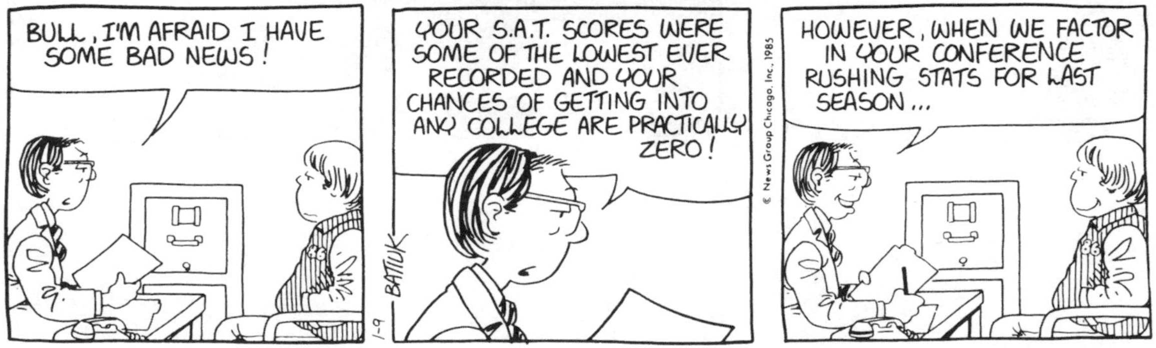
BULL, I'M AFRAID I HAVE SOME BAD NEWS!
YOUR S.A.T. SCORES WERE SOME OF THE LOWEST EVER RECORDED AND YOUR CHANCES OF GETTING INTO ANY COLLEGE ARE PRACTICALLY ZERO!
HOWEVER, WHEN WE FACTOR IN YOUR CONFERENCE RUSHING STATS FOR LAST SEASON...
BATIUK
1-9
© News Group Chicago, Inc., 1985

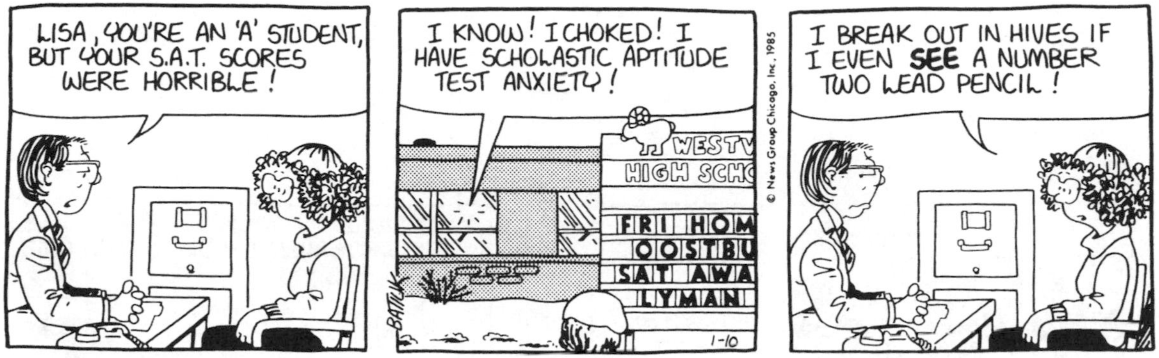
LISA, YOU'RE AN 'A' STUDENT, BUT YOUR S.A.T. SCORES WERE HORRIBLE!
I KNOW! I CHOKED! I HAVE SCHOLASTIC APTITUDE TEST ANXIETY!
WESTV
HIGH SCHO
FRI HOM
OOSTBU
SAT AWA
LYMAN
BATIUK
1-10
© News Group Chicago, Inc., 1985
I BREAK OUT IN HIVES IF I EVEN **SEE** A NUMBER TWO LEAD PENCIL!

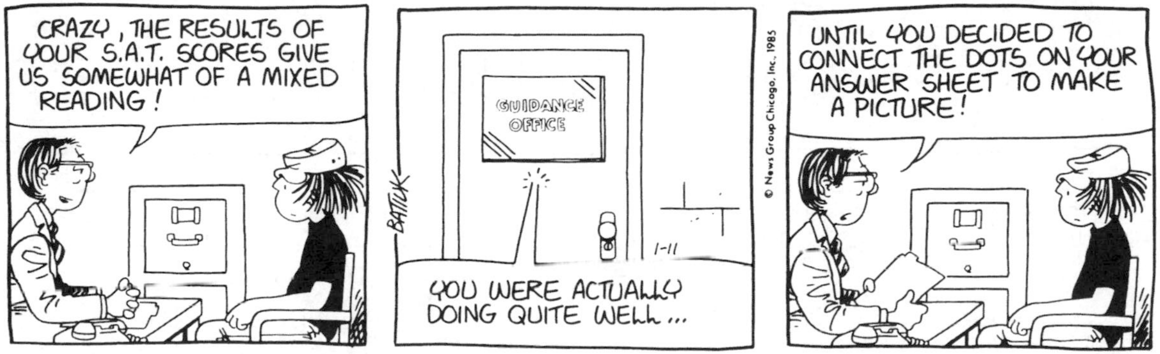
CRAZY, THE RESULTS OF YOUR S.A.T. SCORES GIVE US SOMEWHAT OF A MIXED READING!
GUIDANCE OFFICE
BATIUK
1-11
YOU WERE ACTUALLY DOING QUITE WELL...
© News Group Chicago, Inc., 1985
UNTIL YOU DECIDED TO CONNECT THE DOTS ON YOUR ANSWER SHEET TO MAKE A PICTURE!

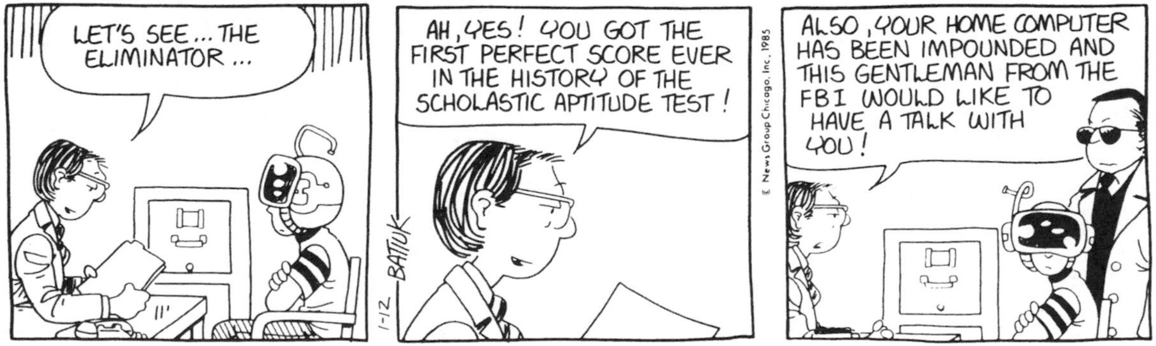
LET'S SEE... THE ELIMINATOR...
BATIUK
1-12
AH, YES! YOU GOT THE FIRST PERFECT SCORE EVER IN THE HISTORY OF THE SCHOLASTIC APTITUDE TEST!
© News Group Chicago, Inc., 1985
ALSO, YOUR HOME COMPUTER HAS BEEN IMPOUNDED AND THIS GENTLEMAN FROM THE FBI WOULD LIKE TO HAVE A TALK WITH YOU!

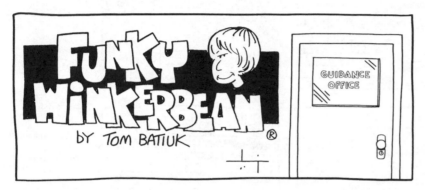

FUNKY WINKERBEAN
BY TOM BATIUK ®
GUIDANCE OFFICE
CONSIDERING YOUR CAREER GOALS, I THINK YOU PROBABLY SHOULD TAKE SOME JOURNALISM COURSES!
I HAVE TO TAKE COURSES IN JOURNALISM?
IF YOU'RE PLANNING TO BECOME A COMMUNICATIONS MAJOR IN COLLEGE, I'D CERTAINLY RECOMMEND IT, BARRY!
WESTVIEW HIGH SCHOOL
FRI JAN 18
WOODWAY H
1-13
BUT I DON'T WANT TO BE A JOURNALIST!
News America Syndicate © News Group Chicago, Inc. 1985
BATIUK
I WANT TO WORK IN TELEVISION!

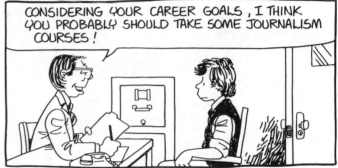

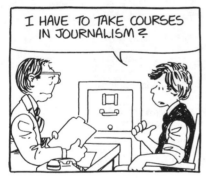

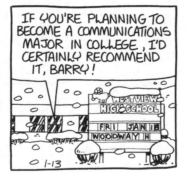

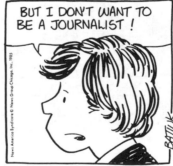

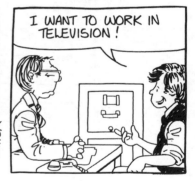

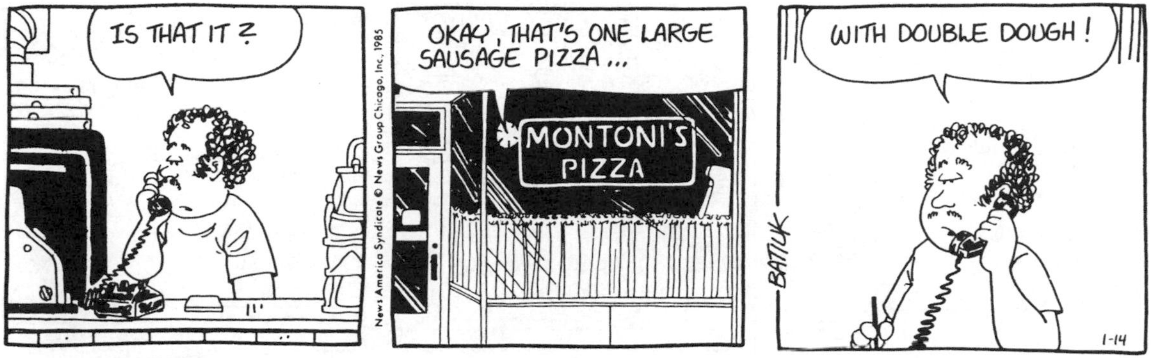
IS THAT IT ?
News America Syndicate © News Group Chicago, Inc., 1985
OKAY, THAT'S ONE LARGE SAUSAGE PIZZA...
MONTONI'S PIZZA
WITH DOUBLE DOUGH!
BATIUK
1-14

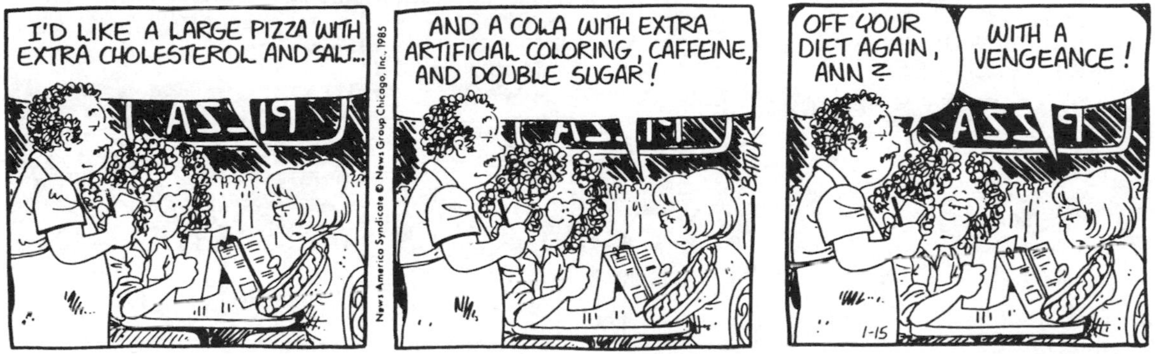
I'D LIKE A LARGE PIZZA WITH EXTRA CHOLESTEROL AND SALT...
News America Syndicate © News Group Chicago, Inc., 1985
AND A COLA WITH EXTRA ARTIFICIAL COLORING, CAFFEINE, AND DOUBLE SUGAR!
BATIUK
OFF YOUR DIET AGAIN, ANN ?
WITH A VENGEANCE!
1-15

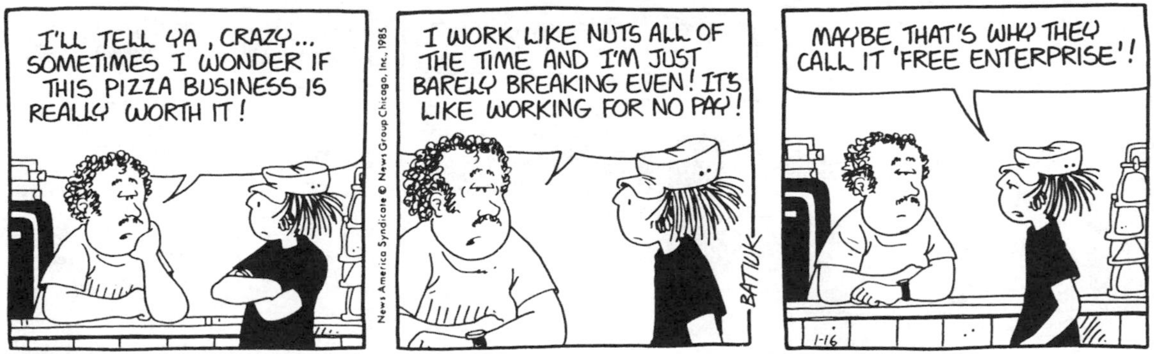
I'LL TELL YA, CRAZY... SOMETIMES I WONDER IF THIS PIZZA BUSINESS IS REALLY WORTH IT!
News America Syndicate © News Group Chicago, Inc., 1985
I WORK LIKE NUTS ALL OF THE TIME AND I'M JUST BARELY BREAKING EVEN! IT'S LIKE WORKING FOR NO PAY!
BATIUK
MAYBE THAT'S WHY THEY CALL IT 'FREE ENTERPRISE'!
1-16

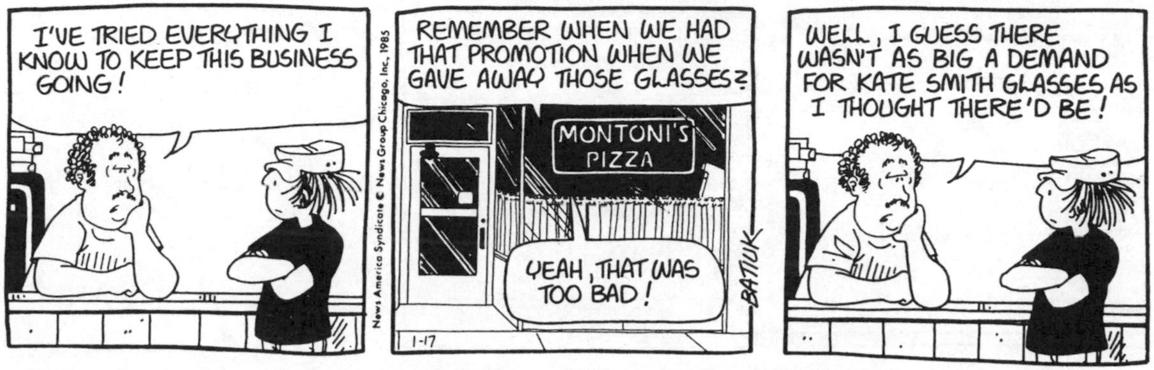
I'VE TRIED EVERYTHING I KNOW TO KEEP THIS BUSINESS GOING!
News America Syndicate © News Group Chicago, Inc., 1985
REMEMBER WHEN WE HAD THAT PROMOTION WHEN WE GAVE AWAY THOSE GLASSES?
MONTONI'S PIZZA
YEAH, THAT WAS TOO BAD!
BATIUK
1-17
WELL, I GUESS THERE WASN'T AS BIG A DEMAND FOR KATE SMITH GLASSES AS I THOUGHT THERE'D BE!

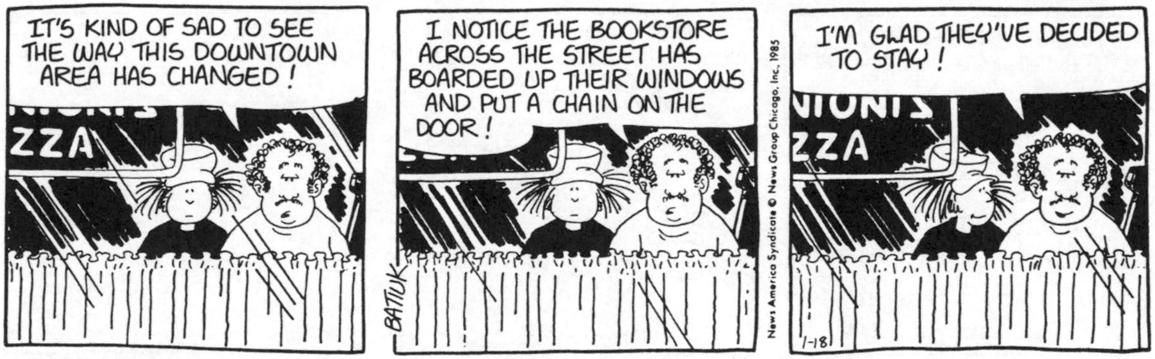
IT'S KIND OF SAD TO SEE THE WAY THIS DOWNTOWN AREA HAS CHANGED!
BATIUK
I NOTICE THE BOOKSTORE ACROSS THE STREET HAS BOARDED UP THEIR WINDOWS AND PUT A CHAIN ON THE DOOR!
News America Syndicate © News Group Chicago, Inc., 1985
I'M GLAD THEY'VE DECIDED TO STAY!
1-18

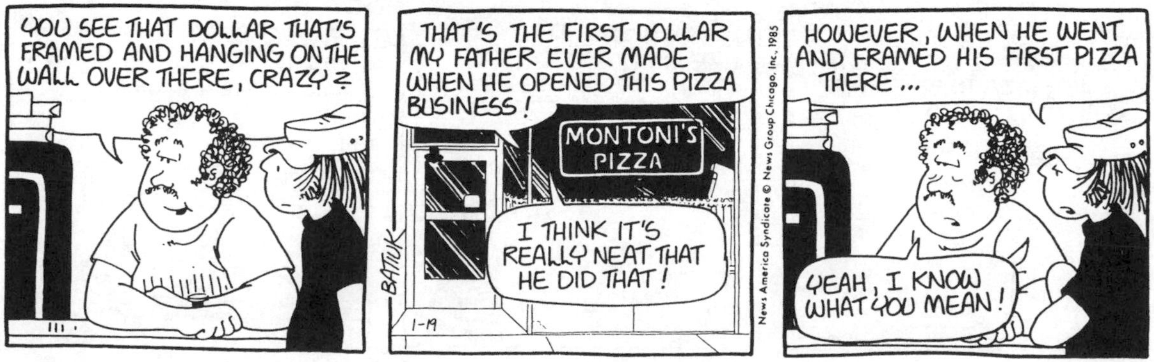
YOU SEE THAT DOLLAR THAT'S FRAMED AND HANGING ON THE WALL OVER THERE, CRAZY?
BATIUK
THAT'S THE FIRST DOLLAR MY FATHER EVER MADE WHEN HE OPENED THIS PIZZA BUSINESS!
MONTONI'S PIZZA
I THINK IT'S REALLY NEAT THAT HE DID THAT!
1-19
News America Syndicate © News Group Chicago, Inc., 1985
HOWEVER, WHEN HE WENT AND FRAMED HIS FIRST PIZZA THERE...
YEAH, I KNOW WHAT YOU MEAN!

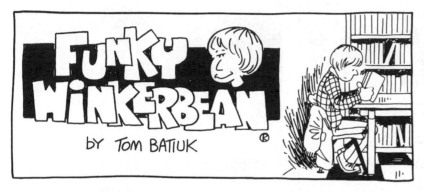

FUNKY WINKERBEAN
BY TOM BATIUK
I'D LIKE TO USE ONE OF THE FILM PROJECTORS!
SORRY, COACH, BUT ALL THE FILM PROJECTORS ARE CHECKED OUT! IT LOOKS LIKE YOU MIGHT HAVE TO TEACH A CLASS TODAY!
LISTEN! IT JUST SO HAPPENS THAT I'M PERFECTLY CAPABLE OF TEACHING A CLASS WITHOUT SHOWING A MOVIE, SO YOU CAN JUST KEEP YOUR CUTE COMMENTS TO YOURSELF, OKAY?
BATIUK
1-20
SORRY! I WAS OUT OF LINE!
News America Syndicate © News Group Chicago, Inc., 1985
WHAT HAVE YOU GOT IN THE WAY OF VIDEOTAPES?

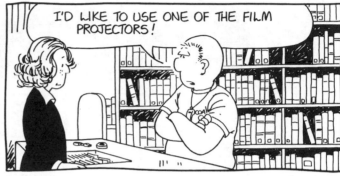

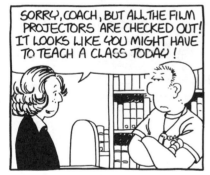

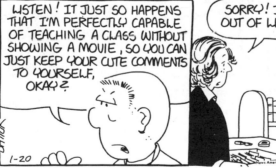

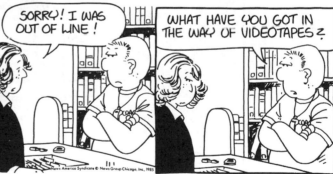

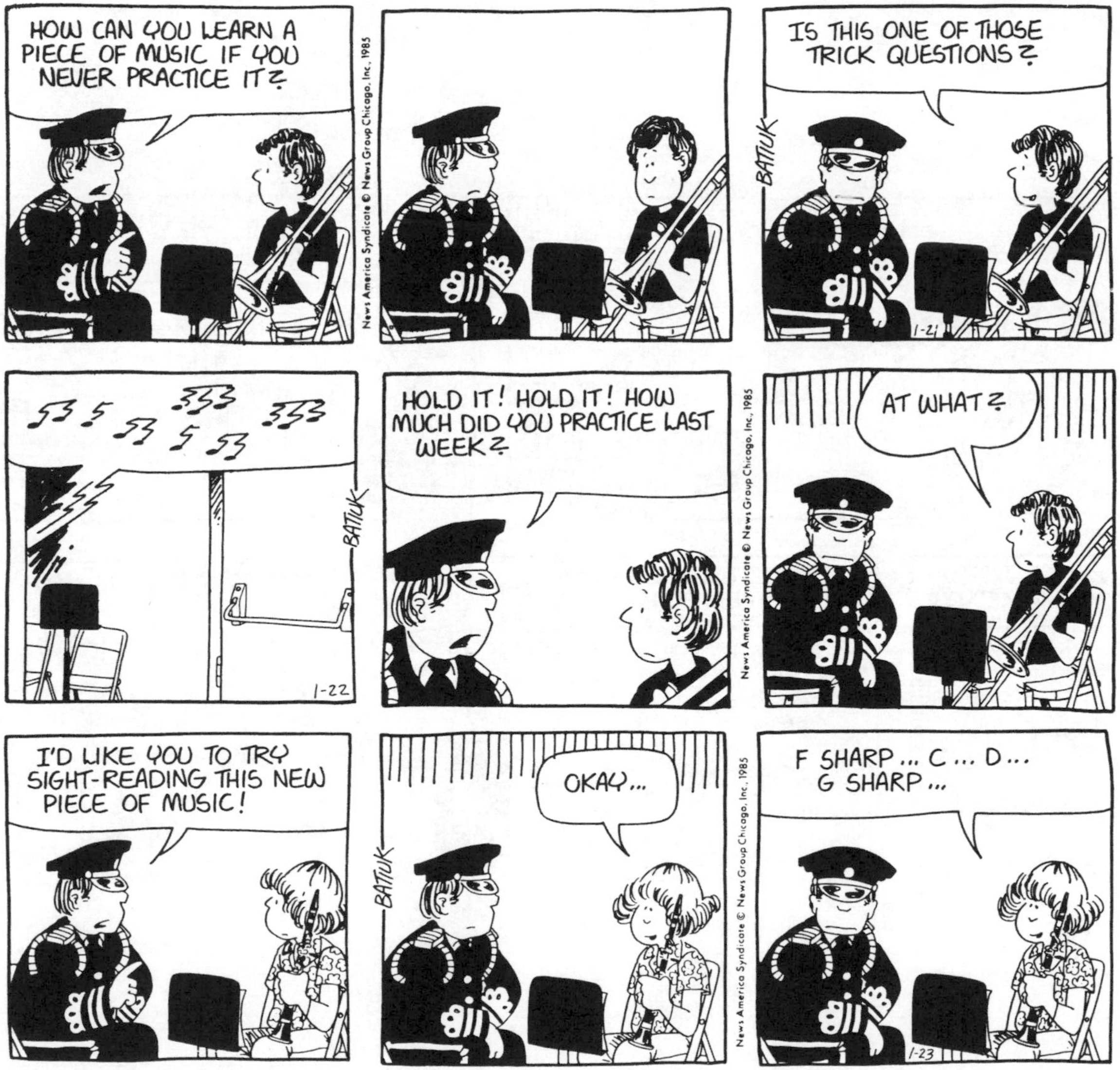
HOW CAN YOU LEARN A PIECE OF MUSIC IF YOU NEVER PRACTICE IT?
News America Syndicate © News Group Chicago, Inc. 1985
IS THIS ONE OF THOSE TRICK QUESTIONS?
BATIUK
1-21
BATIUK
1-22
HOLD IT! HOLD IT! HOW MUCH DID YOU PRACTICE LAST WEEK?
News America Syndicate © News Group Chicago, Inc. 1985
AT WHAT?
I'D LIKE YOU TO TRY SIGHT-READING THIS NEW PIECE OF MUSIC!
BATIUK
OKAY...
News America Syndicate © News Group Chicago, Inc. 1985
F SHARP ... C ... D ... G SHARP ...
1-23

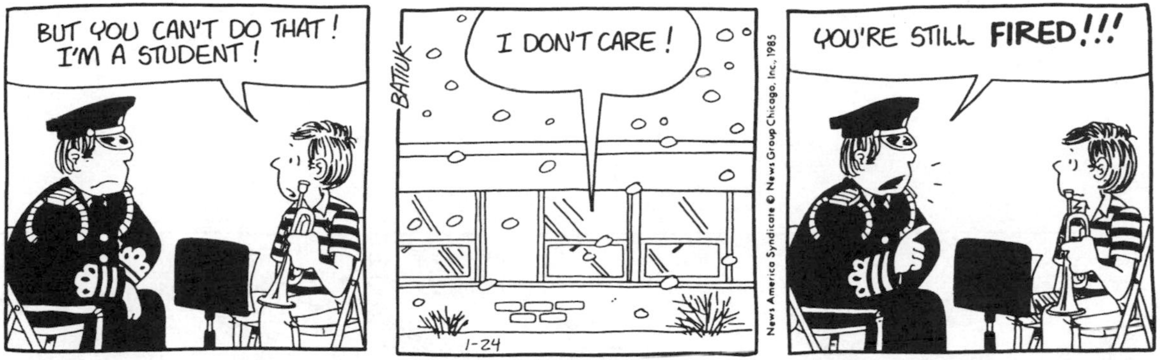
BUT YOU CAN'T DO THAT! I'M A STUDENT!
I DON'T CARE!
YOU'RE STILL **FIRED**!!!
BATIUK
1-24
News America Syndicate © News Group Chicago, Inc., 1985

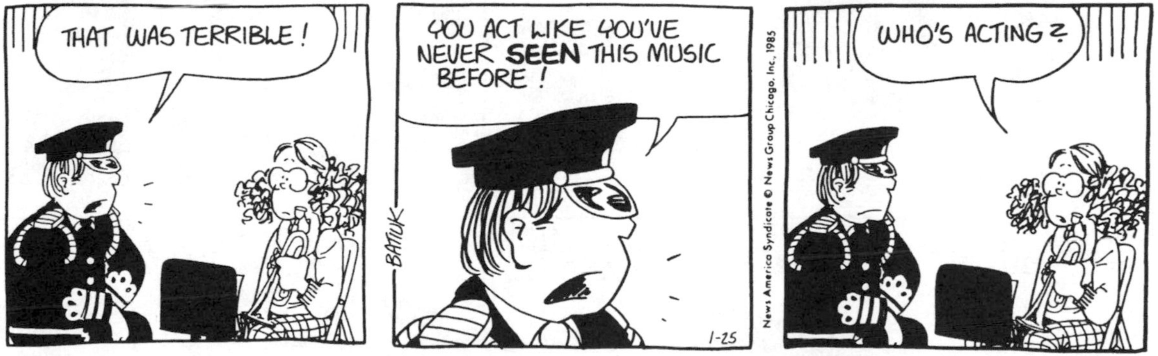
THAT WAS TERRIBLE!
YOU ACT LIKE YOU'VE NEVER **SEEN** THIS MUSIC BEFORE!
WHO'S ACTING?
BATIUK
1-25
News America Syndicate © News Group Chicago, Inc., 1985

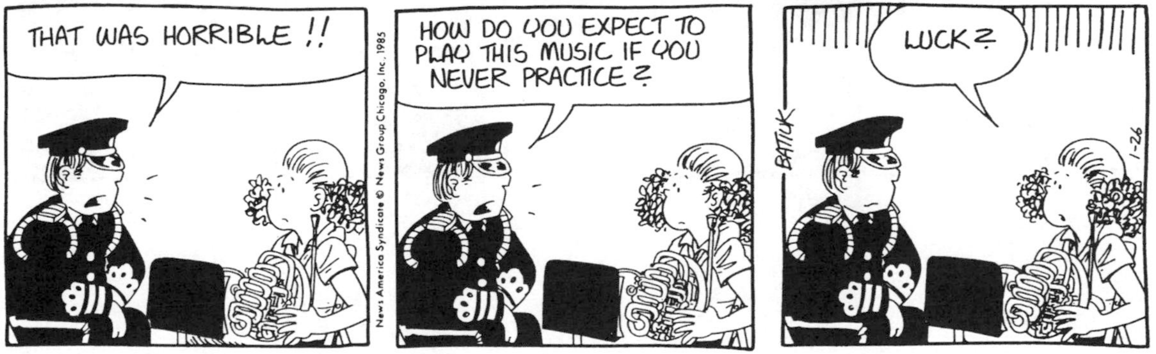
THAT WAS HORRIBLE!!
HOW DO YOU EXPECT TO PLAY THIS MUSIC IF YOU NEVER PRACTICE?
LUCK?
BATIUK
1-26
News America Syndicate © News Group Chicago, Inc., 1985

FUNKY WINKERBEAN
BY TOM BATIUK
HIGH SCHO
FRI HOME
NORTHROP
THAT STUNK!! WHAT'S THE MATTER WITH YOU PEOPLE ?
DON'T YOU HAVE ANY PRIDE OR SELF-RESPECT ?
NO!
HAVE THINGS CHANGED THAT MUCH ?
BATIUK
1-27

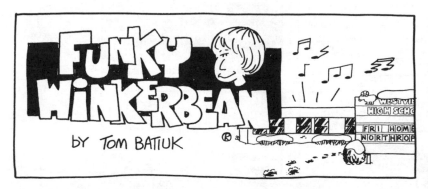

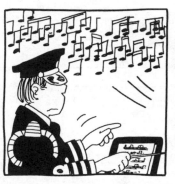

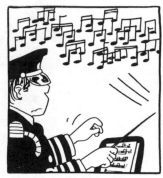

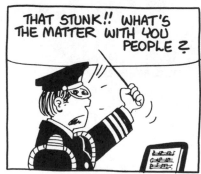

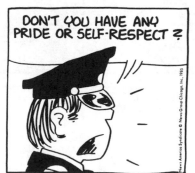

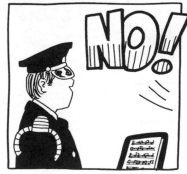

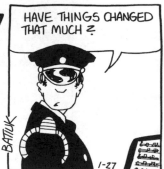

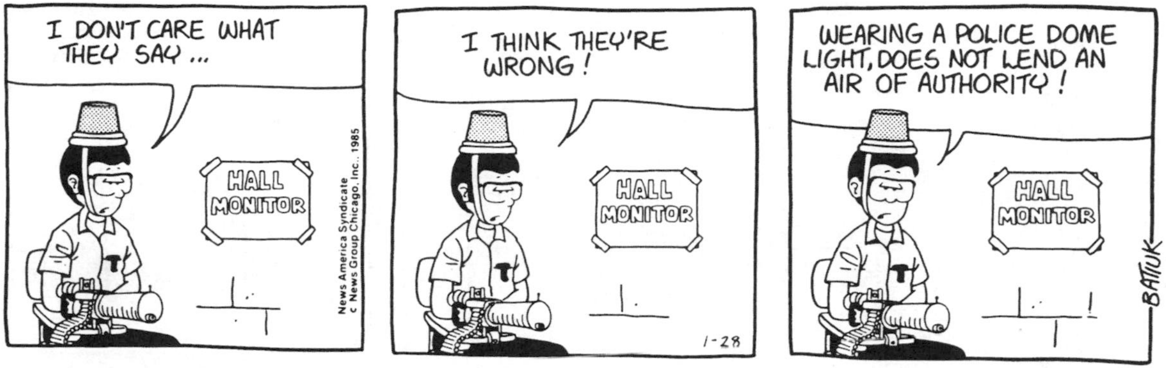
I DON'T CARE WHAT THEY SAY ...
HALL MONITOR
News America Syndicate c News Group Chicago, Inc., 1985
I THINK THEY'RE WRONG!
HALL MONITOR
1-28
WEARING A POLICE DOME LIGHT, DOES NOT LEND AN AIR OF AUTHORITY!
HALL MONITOR
BATIUK

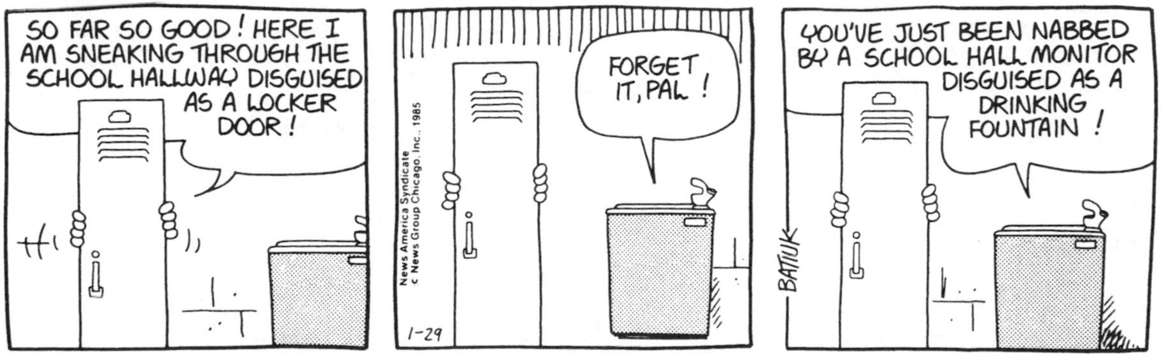
SO FAR SO GOOD! HERE I AM SNEAKING THROUGH THE SCHOOL HALLWAY DISGUISED AS A LOCKER DOOR!
News America Syndicate c News Group Chicago, Inc., 1985
FORGET IT, PAL!
1-29
YOU'VE JUST BEEN NABBED BY A SCHOOL HALL MONITOR DISGUISED AS A DRINKING FOUNTAIN!
BATIUK

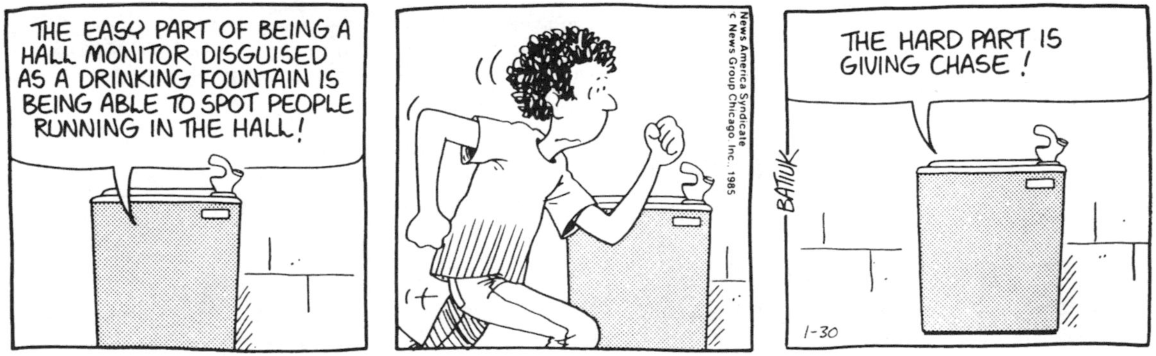
THE EASY PART OF BEING A HALL MONITOR DISGUISED AS A DRINKING FOUNTAIN IS BEING ABLE TO SPOT PEOPLE RUNNING IN THE HALL!
News America Syndicate c News Group Chicago, Inc., 1985
BATIUK
THE HARD PART IS GIVING CHASE!
1-30

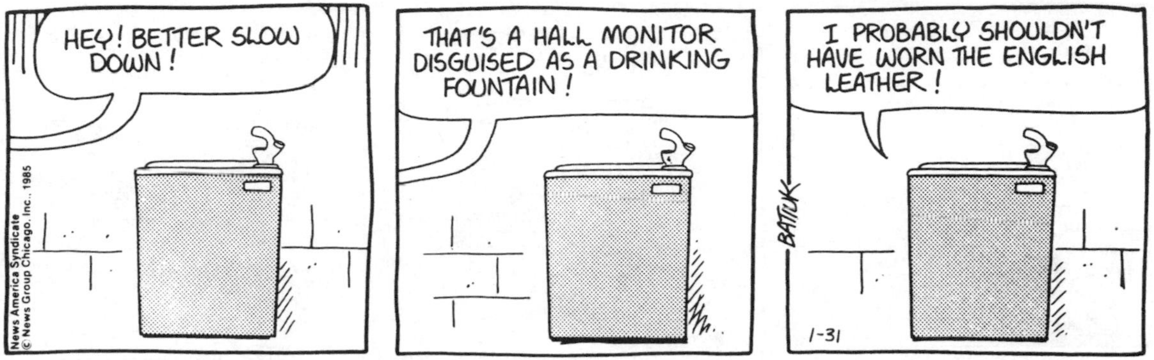
HEY! BETTER SLOW DOWN!
THAT'S A HALL MONITOR DISGUISED AS A DRINKING FOUNTAIN!
I PROBABLY SHOULDN'T HAVE WORN THE ENGLISH LEATHER!
News America Syndicate © News Group Chicago, Inc., 1985
BATIUK
1-31

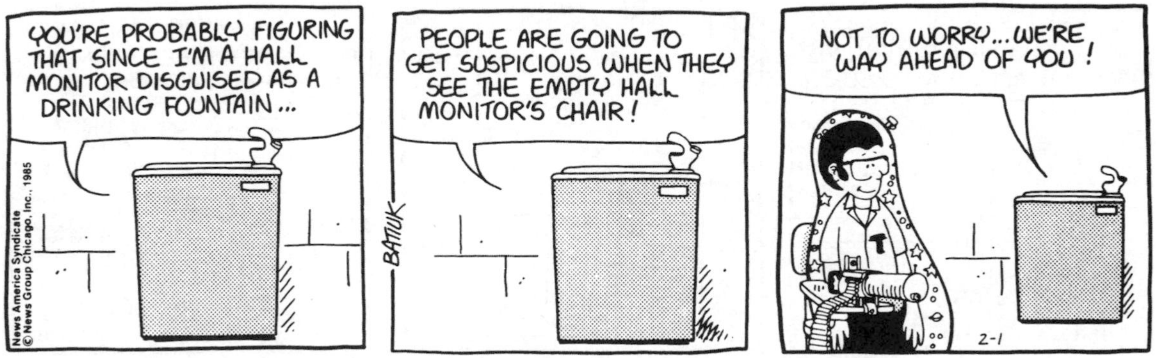
YOU'RE PROBABLY FIGURING THAT SINCE I'M A HALL MONITOR DISGUISED AS A DRINKING FOUNTAIN...
PEOPLE ARE GOING TO GET SUSPICIOUS WHEN THEY SEE THE EMPTY HALL MONITOR'S CHAIR!
NOT TO WORRY... WE'RE WAY AHEAD OF YOU!
News America Syndicate © News Group Chicago, Inc., 1985
BATIUK
2-1

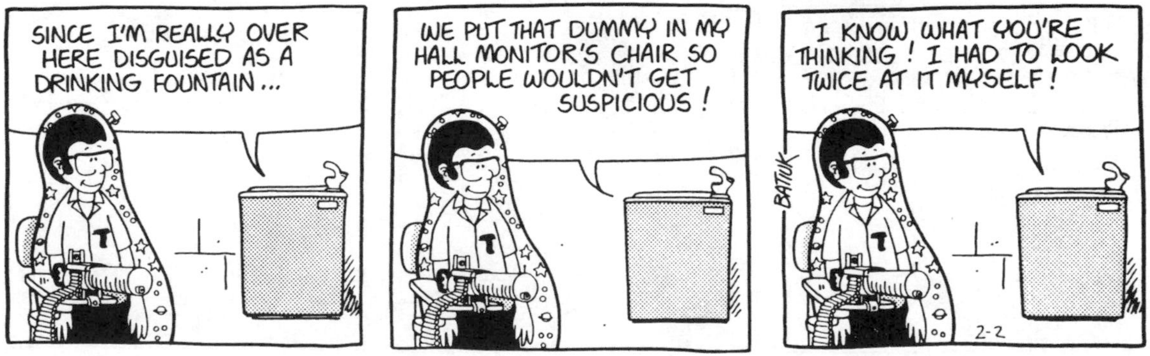
SINCE I'M REALLY OVER HERE DISGUISED AS A DRINKING FOUNTAIN...
WE PUT THAT DUMMY IN MY HALL MONITOR'S CHAIR SO PEOPLE WOULDN'T GET SUSPICIOUS!
I KNOW WHAT YOU'RE THINKING! I HAD TO LOOK TWICE AT IT MYSELF!
BATIUK
2-2

FUNKY WINKERBEAN
by TOM BATIUK
IN JOY STILL FELT THE AUTOBIOGRAPHY OF ISAAC SIMOV, 54-1978
I CHONG
WOODY GUTHRIE A Life by Joe Klein
OGDEN NASH I WOULDN'T HAVE MISSED IT
Side Effects Woody Allen
PLUMPT LION
HMMM... HERE'S A BOOK I HAVEN'T LOOKED AT IN A WHILE...
SAYINGS FROM THE I CHONG ANCIENT BOOK OF CHINESE PHILOSOPHY
THE MASTER SAYS:
© The Times of London Syndicate, 1985
HE WHO RIDES A DOLPHIN...
KENT
IS DOING IT ON PORPOISE!
BATIUK

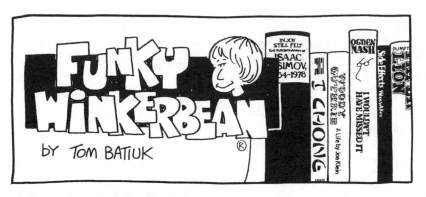

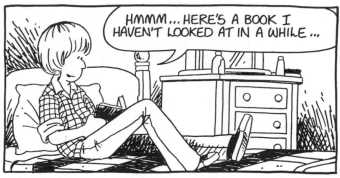

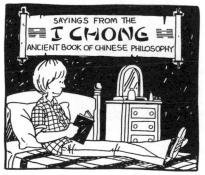

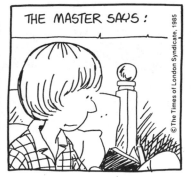

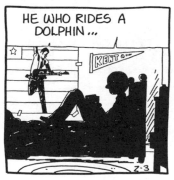

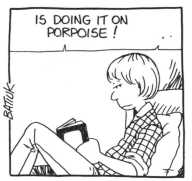

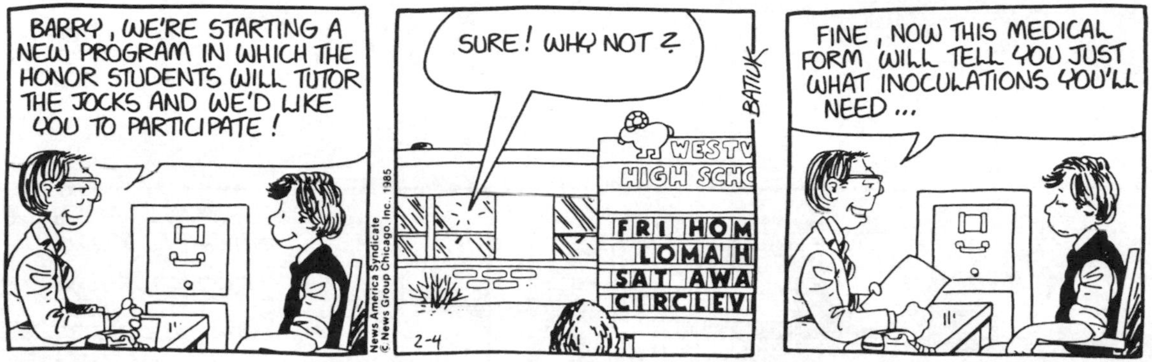
BARRY, WE'RE STARTING A NEW PROGRAM IN WHICH THE HONOR STUDENTS WILL TUTOR THE JOCKS AND WE'D LIKE YOU TO PARTICIPATE!
SURE! WHY NOT?
WESTV
HIGH SCHO
FRI HOM
LOMA H
SAT AWA
CIRCLEV
FINE, NOW THIS MEDICAL FORM WILL TELL YOU JUST WHAT INOCULATIONS YOU'LL NEED ...
BATIUK
2-4
News America Syndicate
© News Group Chicago, Inc., 1985

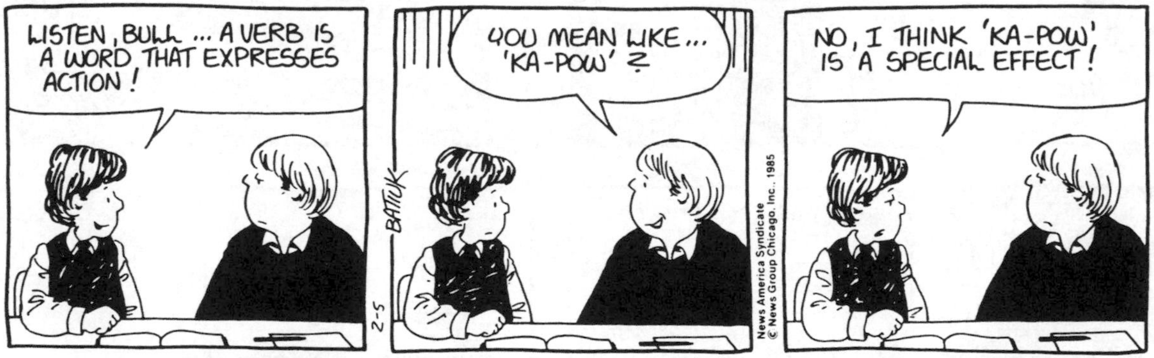
LISTEN, BULL ... A VERB IS A WORD THAT EXPRESSES ACTION!
YOU MEAN LIKE... 'KA-POW'?
NO, I THINK 'KA-POW' IS A SPECIAL EFFECT!
BATIUK
2-5
News America Syndicate
© News Group Chicago, Inc., 1985

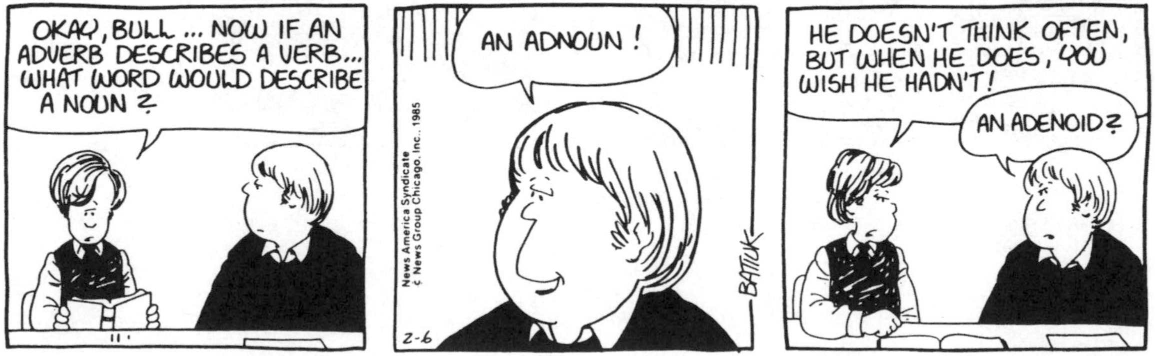
OKAY, BULL ... NOW IF AN ADVERB DESCRIBES A VERB... WHAT WORD WOULD DESCRIBE A NOUN?
AN ADNOUN!
HE DOESN'T THINK OFTEN, BUT WHEN HE DOES, YOU WISH HE HADN'T!
AN ADENOID?
BATIUK
2-6
News America Syndicate
© News Group Chicago, Inc., 1985

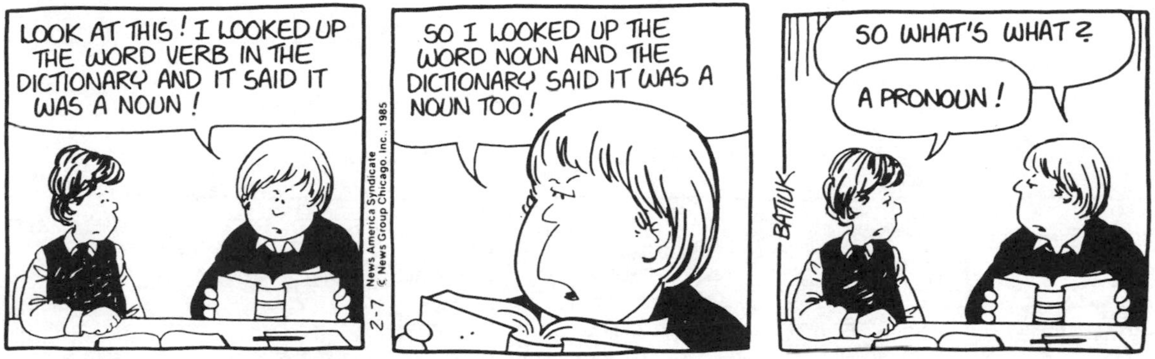
LOOK AT THIS! I LOOKED UP THE WORD VERB IN THE DICTIONARY AND IT SAID IT WAS A NOUN!
2-7
News America Syndicate
© News Group Chicago, Inc., 1985
SO I LOOKED UP THE WORD NOUN AND THE DICTIONARY SAID IT WAS A NOUN TOO!
BATIUK
SO WHAT'S WHAT?
A PRONOUN!

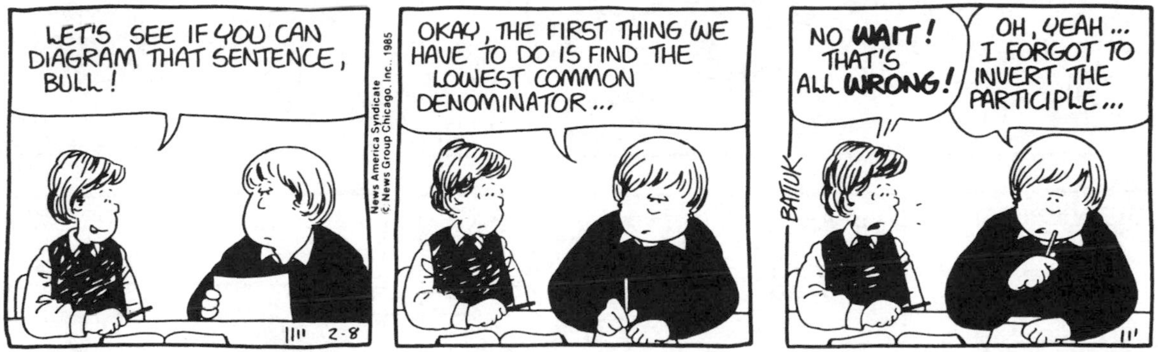
LET'S SEE IF YOU CAN DIAGRAM THAT SENTENCE, BULL!
2-8
News America Syndicate
© News Group Chicago, Inc., 1985
OKAY, THE FIRST THING WE HAVE TO DO IS FIND THE LOWEST COMMON DENOMINATOR...
BATIUK
NO **WAIT**! THAT'S ALL **WRONG**!
OH, YEAH... I FORGOT TO INVERT THE PARTICIPLE...

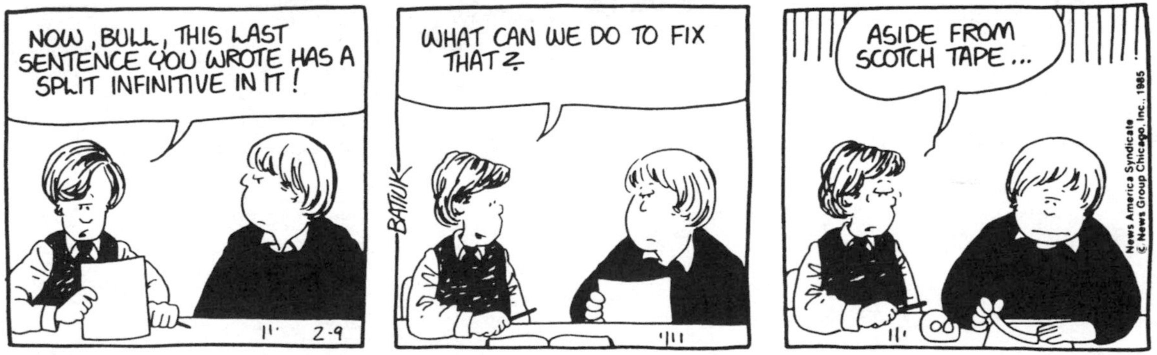
NOW, BULL, THIS LAST SENTENCE YOU WROTE HAS A SPLIT INFINITIVE IN IT!
2-9
BATIUK
WHAT CAN WE DO TO FIX THAT?
ASIDE FROM SCOTCH TAPE...
News America Syndicate
© News Group Chicago, Inc., 1985

FUNKY WINKERBEAN
by TOM BATIUK
I TAKE IT YOU'RE SUBBING TODAY!
USN 17
WHO ARE YOU TODAY?
I'M SUBBING FOR MRS. NASH!
YOU KNOW, WE SUBSTITUTE TEACHERS ARE REALLY LUCKY IN A WAY!
BATIUK
2-10
WE GET TO SAVOR SO MUCH MORE OF LIFE THAN MOST PEOPLE ...
BECAUSE THE DAYS SEEM SO MUCH LONGER!
© The Times of London Syndicate, 1985

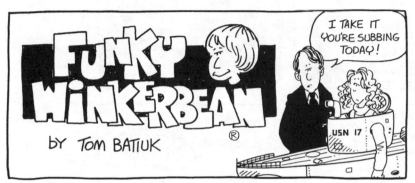

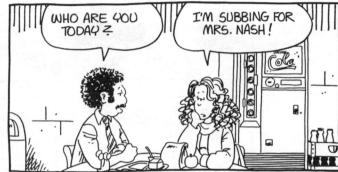

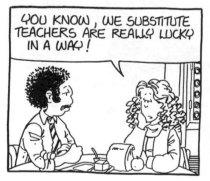

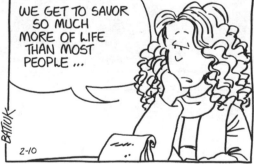

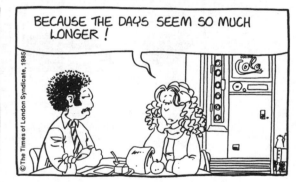

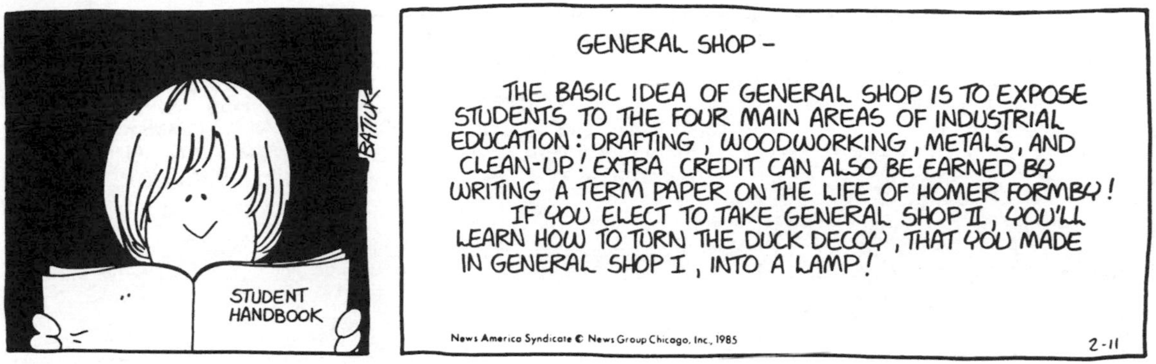
BATIUK
STUDENT HANDBOOK
GENERAL SHOP -
THE BASIC IDEA OF GENERAL SHOP IS TO EXPOSE STUDENTS TO THE FOUR MAIN AREAS OF INDUSTRIAL EDUCATION: DRAFTING, WOODWORKING, METALS, AND CLEAN-UP! EXTRA CREDIT CAN ALSO BE EARNED BY WRITING A TERM PAPER ON THE LIFE OF HOMER FORMBY!
IF YOU ELECT TO TAKE GENERAL SHOP II, YOU'LL LEARN HOW TO TURN THE DUCK DECOY, THAT YOU MADE IN GENERAL SHOP I, INTO A LAMP!
News America Syndicate © News Group Chicago, Inc., 1985
2-11

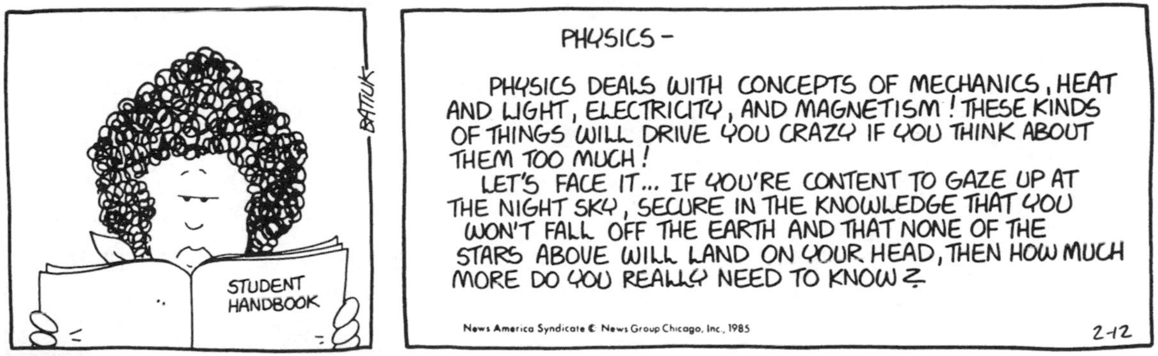
BATIUK
STUDENT HANDBOOK
PHYSICS -
PHYSICS DEALS WITH CONCEPTS OF MECHANICS, HEAT AND LIGHT, ELECTRICITY, AND MAGNETISM! THESE KINDS OF THINGS WILL DRIVE YOU CRAZY IF YOU THINK ABOUT THEM TOO MUCH!
LET'S FACE IT... IF YOU'RE CONTENT TO GAZE UP AT THE NIGHT SKY, SECURE IN THE KNOWLEDGE THAT YOU WON'T FALL OFF THE EARTH AND THAT NONE OF THE STARS ABOVE WILL LAND ON YOUR HEAD, THEN HOW MUCH MORE DO YOU REALLY NEED TO KNOW?
News America Syndicate © News Group Chicago, Inc., 1985
2-12

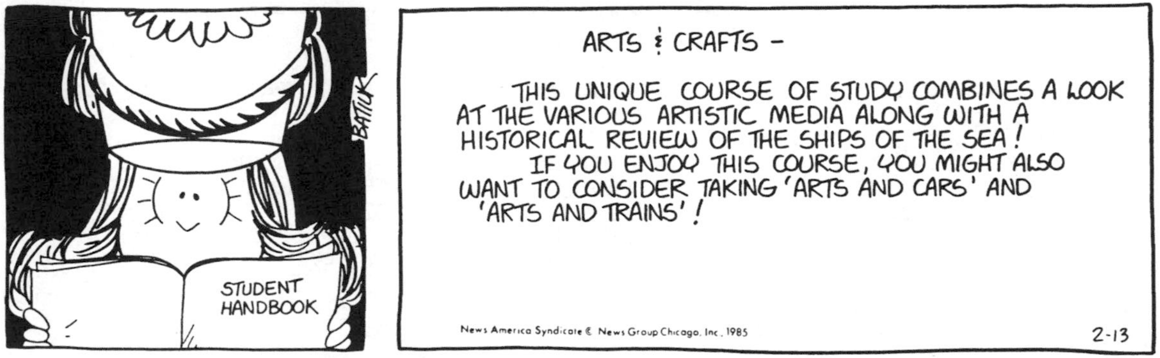
BATIUK
STUDENT HANDBOOK
ARTS & CRAFTS -
THIS UNIQUE COURSE OF STUDY COMBINES A LOOK AT THE VARIOUS ARTISTIC MEDIA ALONG WITH A HISTORICAL REVIEW OF THE SHIPS OF THE SEA!
IF YOU ENJOY THIS COURSE, YOU MIGHT ALSO WANT TO CONSIDER TAKING 'ARTS AND CARS' AND 'ARTS AND TRAINS'!
News America Syndicate © News Group Chicago, Inc., 1985
2-13

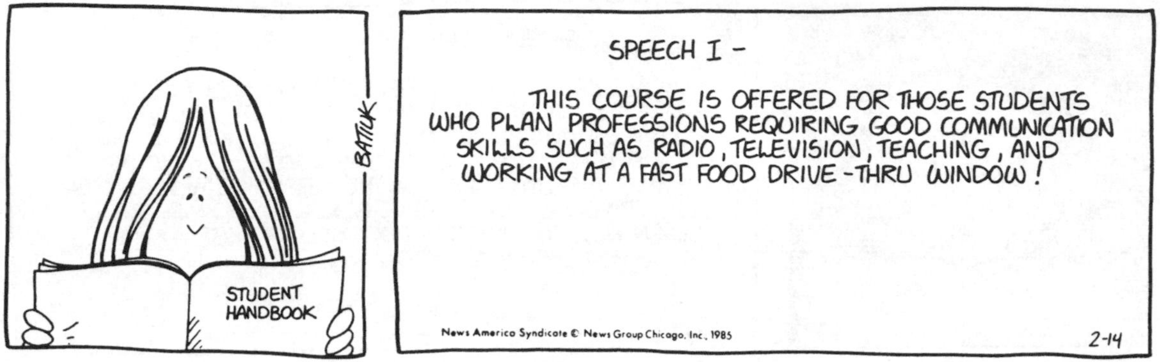
STUDENT HANDBOOK
BATIUK
SPEECH I -
THIS COURSE IS OFFERED FOR THOSE STUDENTS WHO PLAN PROFESSIONS REQUIRING GOOD COMMUNICATION SKILLS SUCH AS RADIO, TELEVISION, TEACHING, AND WORKING AT A FAST FOOD DRIVE-THRU WINDOW!
News America Syndicate © News Group Chicago, Inc., 1985
2-14

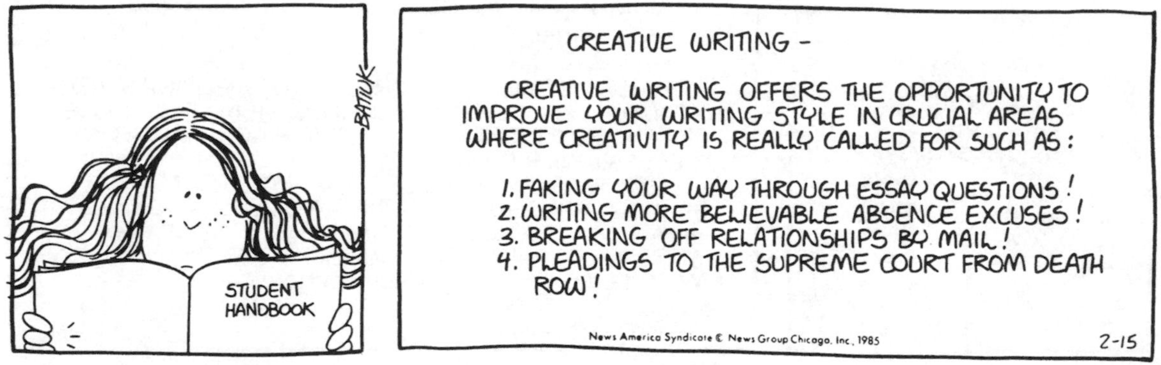
STUDENT HANDBOOK
BATIUK
CREATIVE WRITING -
CREATIVE WRITING OFFERS THE OPPORTUNITY TO IMPROVE YOUR WRITING STYLE IN CRUCIAL AREAS WHERE CREATIVITY IS REALLY CALLED FOR SUCH AS:
1. FAKING YOUR WAY THROUGH ESSAY QUESTIONS!
2. WRITING MORE BELIEVABLE ABSENCE EXCUSES!
3. BREAKING OFF RELATIONSHIPS BY MAIL!
4. PLEADINGS TO THE SUPREME COURT FROM DEATH ROW!
News America Syndicate © News Group Chicago, Inc., 1985
2-15

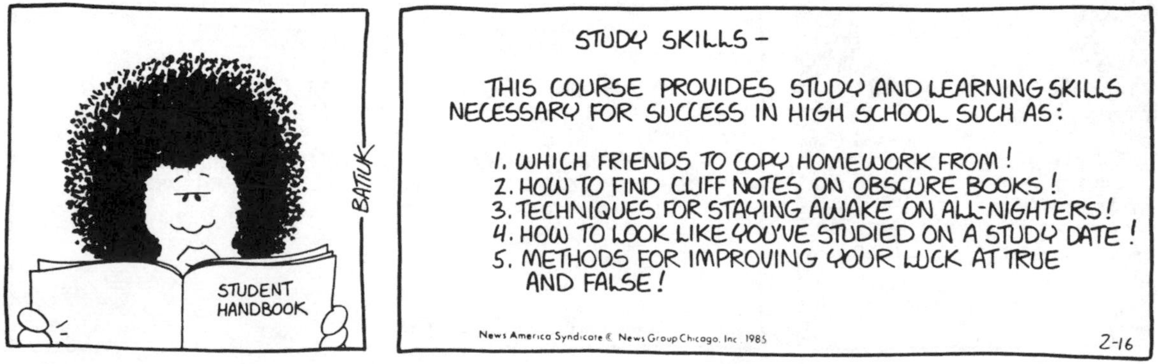
STUDENT HANDBOOK
BATIUK
STUDY SKILLS -
THIS COURSE PROVIDES STUDY AND LEARNING SKILLS NECESSARY FOR SUCCESS IN HIGH SCHOOL SUCH AS:
1. WHICH FRIENDS TO COPY HOMEWORK FROM!
2. HOW TO FIND CLIFF NOTES ON OBSCURE BOOKS!
3. TECHNIQUES FOR STAYING AWAKE ON ALL-NIGHTERS!
4. HOW TO LOOK LIKE YOU'VE STUDIED ON A STUDY DATE!
5. METHODS FOR IMPROVING YOUR LUCK AT TRUE AND FALSE!
News America Syndicate © News Group Chicago, Inc. 1985
2-16

WARNING SIGNS / SCHOOLS

Emphasis has been given to the SCHO CHOSSWALK signs through a new per SCHOOL sign warns a motorist that h school zone, while the SCHOOL CROS tifies established crossings where chil cross a roadway.

SCHOOL

OKAY, YOU CAN USE THE LAST TEN MINUTES OF THE PERIOD FOR A STUDY HALL!

DRIVER'S HANDBOOK

WHEN YOU SEE THIS SIGN IT MEANS...

© The Times of London Syndicate, 1985

(A.) WATCH OUT FOR HORSE-DRAWN CARRIAGES ON THE ROAD.

(B.) THE TRAFFIC IN THAT AREA WILL DRIVE YOU BUGGY!

DRIVER'S HANDBOOK

2-17

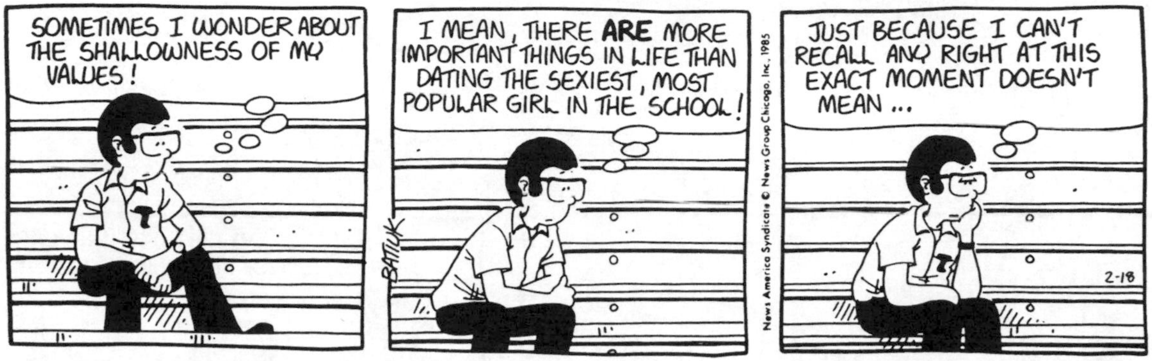
SOMETIMES I WONDER ABOUT THE SHALLOWNESS OF MY VALUES!
I MEAN, THERE **ARE** MORE IMPORTANT THINGS IN LIFE THAN DATING THE SEXIEST, MOST POPULAR GIRL IN THE SCHOOL!
BATIUK
News America Syndicate © News Group Chicago, Inc., 1985
JUST BECAUSE I CAN'T RECALL ANY RIGHT AT THIS EXACT MOMENT DOESN'T MEAN ...
2-18

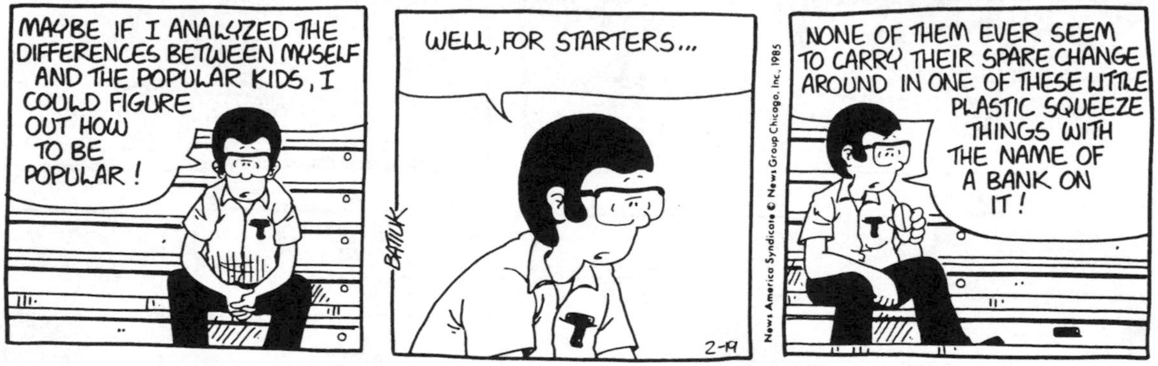
MAYBE IF I ANALYZED THE DIFFERENCES BETWEEN MYSELF AND THE POPULAR KIDS, I COULD FIGURE OUT HOW TO BE POPULAR!
BATIUK
WELL, FOR STARTERS...
2-19
News America Syndicate © News Group Chicago, Inc., 1985
NONE OF THEM EVER SEEM TO CARRY THEIR SPARE CHANGE AROUND IN ONE OF THESE LITTLE PLASTIC SQUEEZE THINGS WITH THE NAME OF A BANK ON IT!

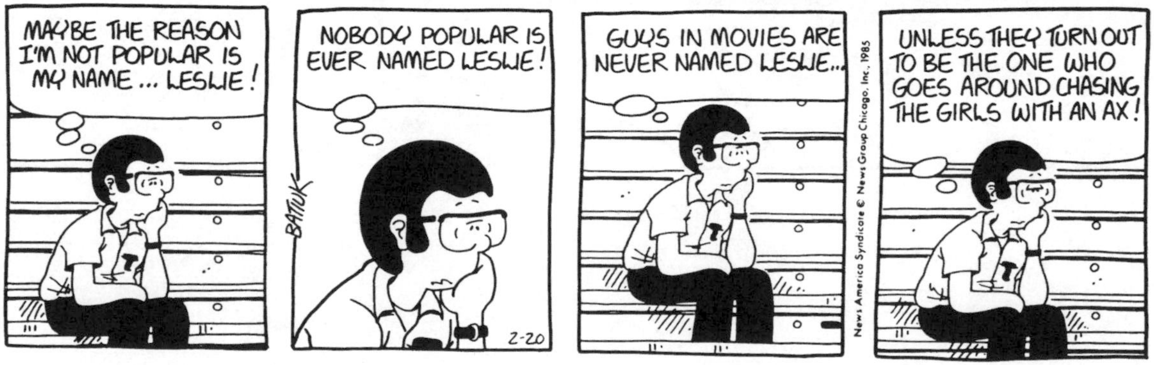
MAYBE THE REASON I'M NOT POPULAR IS MY NAME... LESLIE!
BATIUK
NOBODY POPULAR IS EVER NAMED LESLIE!
2-20
GUYS IN MOVIES ARE NEVER NAMED LESLIE...
News America Syndicate © News Group Chicago, Inc., 1985
UNLESS THEY TURN OUT TO BE THE ONE WHO GOES AROUND CHASING THE GIRLS WITH AN AX!

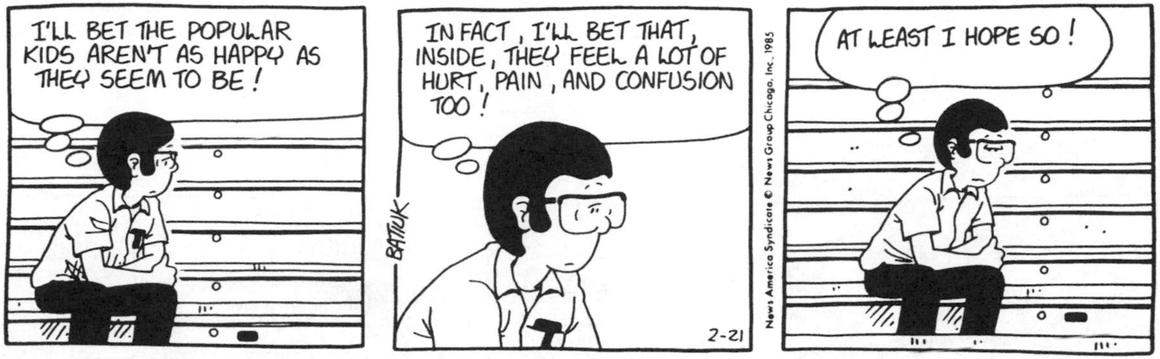
I'LL BET THE POPULAR KIDS AREN'T AS HAPPY AS THEY SEEM TO BE!
IN FACT, I'LL BET THAT, INSIDE, THEY FEEL A LOT OF HURT, PAIN, AND CONFUSION TOO!
BATIUK
2-21
News America Syndicate © News Group Chicago, Inc., 1985
AT LEAST I HOPE SO!

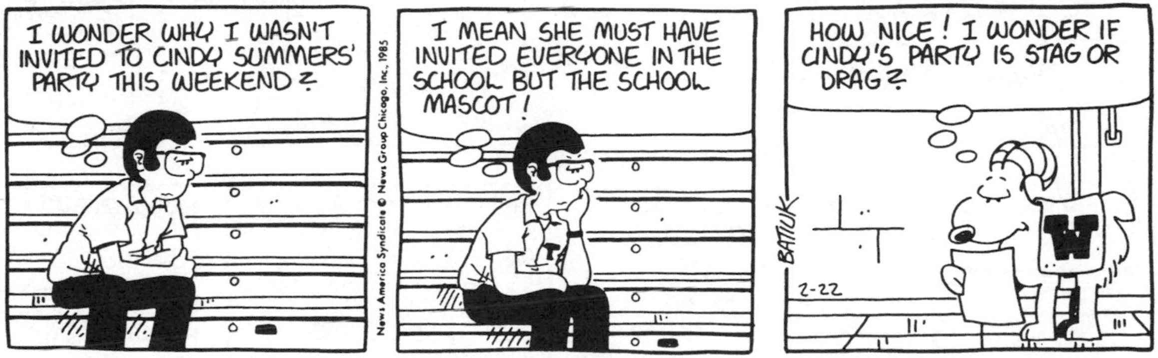
I WONDER WHY I WASN'T INVITED TO CINDY SUMMERS' PARTY THIS WEEKEND?
News America Syndicate © News Group Chicago, Inc., 1985
I MEAN SHE MUST HAVE INVITED EVERYONE IN THE SCHOOL BUT THE SCHOOL MASCOT!
HOW NICE! I WONDER IF CINDY'S PARTY IS STAG OR DRAG?
BATIUK
2-22

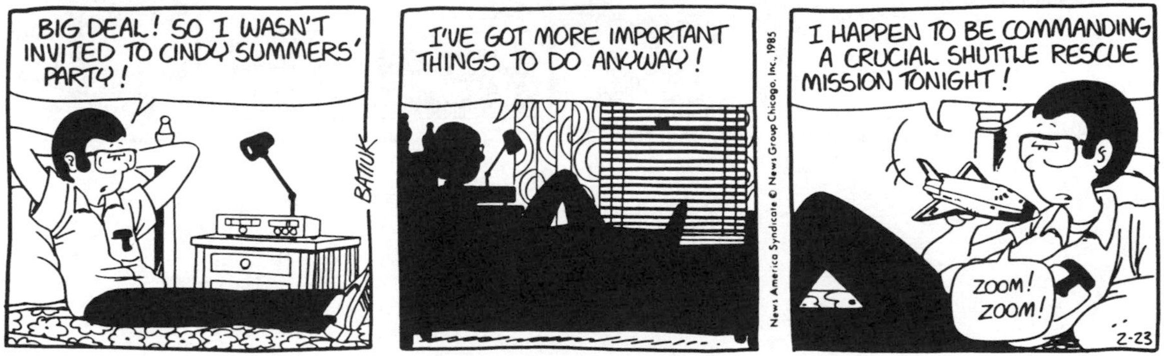
BIG DEAL! SO I WASN'T INVITED TO CINDY SUMMERS' PARTY!
BATIUK
I'VE GOT MORE IMPORTANT THINGS TO DO ANYWAY!
News America Syndicate © News Group Chicago, Inc., 1985
I HAPPEN TO BE COMMANDING A CRUCIAL SHUTTLE RESCUE MISSION TONIGHT!
ZOOM! ZOOM!
2-23

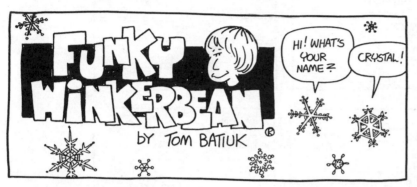

FUNKY WINKERBEAN
by TOM BATIUK ®
HI! WHAT'S YOUR NAME?
CRYSTAL!
WHAT'S THE MATTER WITH THEM?
THE HIGHWAY PATROL HAS ISSUED A TRAVELER'S ALERT...
CAN'T THEY RECOGNIZE A BLIZZARD WHEN THEY SEE ONE?
WHY HAVEN'T THEY CALLED SCHOOL OFF YET?
HIGH WINDS AND DRIFTING SNOW ARE MAKING DRIVING TREACHEROUS...
THERE'S NO WAY THEY CAN HOLD SCHOOL TODAY! THE ROADS ARE IMPASSABLE AND THE WIND CHILL FACTOR WOULD KILL A POLAR BEAR!
NO PARKING IN DRIVE
BATIUK
HERE'S A PARTIAL LIST OF SCHOOL CLOSINGS THAT WE'VE JUST RECEIVED... BIG WALNUT TECH IS CLOSED, WESTVIEW SCHOOLS ARE CLOSED, THE LIGHTHOUSE ALTERNATIVE SCHOOL IS CLOSED...
701
FM 88
AM 54
News Group Chicago, Inc., 1985
ALL RIGHT! IF I HUSTLE I CAN BE UP AT THE MALL BY THE TIME THE STORES OPEN!
NORTHROP SCHOOLS ARE CLOSED...
2-24

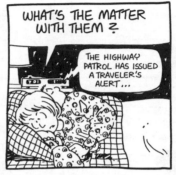

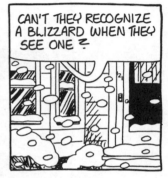

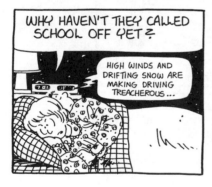

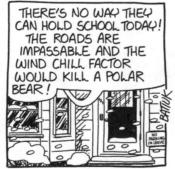

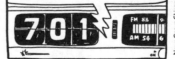

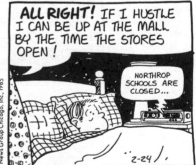

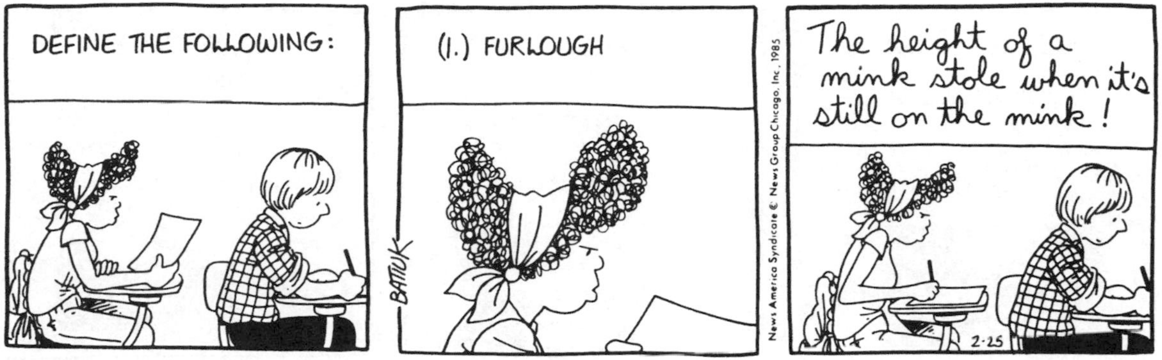
DEFINE THE FOLLOWING:
(1.) FURLOUGH
BATIUK
News America Syndicate © News Group Chicago, Inc. 1985
The height of a mink stole when it's still on the mink!
2-25

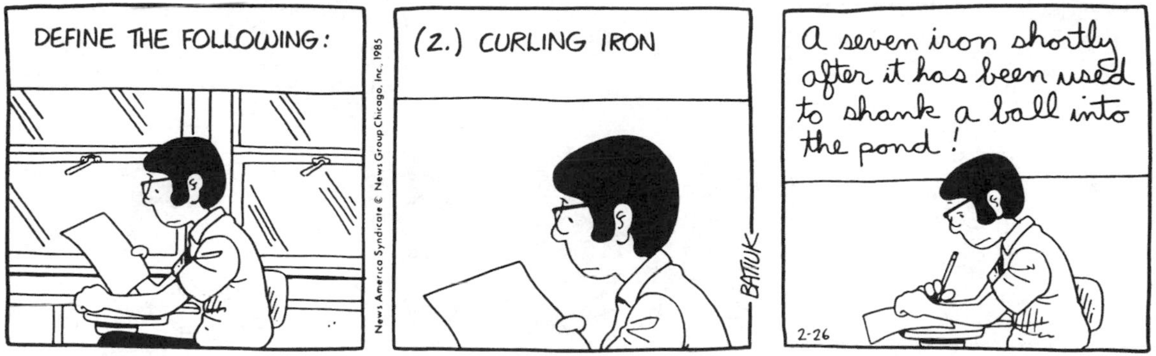
DEFINE THE FOLLOWING:
News America Syndicate © News Group Chicago, Inc. 1985
(2.) CURLING IRON
BATIUK
A seven iron shortly after it has been used to shank a ball into the pond!
2-26

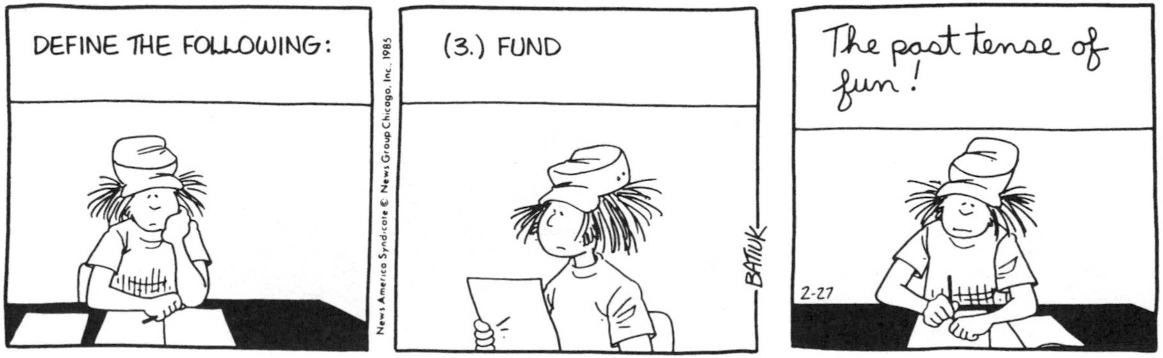
DEFINE THE FOLLOWING:
News America Syndicate © News Group Chicago, Inc. 1985
(3.) FUND
BATIUK
The past tense of fun!
2-27

DEFINE THE FOLLOWING:	(4.) LESION	An injury received while fighting as a mercenary soldier as in: French Foreign lesion!
		 2-28
DEFINE THE FOLLOWING:	(5.) LIMBURGER	A Big Mac made from a tree branch!
		 3-1
DEFINE THE FOLLOWING:	(6.) PACK HORSE	What the wealthy breeder forgot to do when he left for the Kentucky Derby!
 3-2		

FUNKY WINKERBEAN
BY TOM BATIUK
®
SIGH
EVERYONE TAKES ME FOR GRANITE!
JOHN + LAURIE
PURPLE RAIN
SENIORS '85 ROCK
CINDY + BOB
MMS BUZZARDS
RATT
YOU KNOW, WE ROCKS HAVE BEEN AROUND FOR A LONG TIME!
MILLIONS OF YEARS AGO, BACK DURING THE ICE AGE...
© News Group Chicago, Inc., 1985
BATIUK
THIS LAND WAS COVERED BY A HUGE GLACIER!
AS IT MOVED FORWARD, IT SCOOPED UP THE LARGE ROCKS, CARRYING THEM FOR HUNDREDS OF MILES...
AND DEPOSITING THEM AT THE ENTRANCES TO HIGH SCHOOLS ALL OVER THE COUNTRY!
3-3

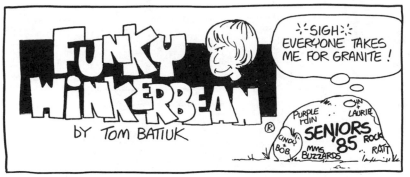

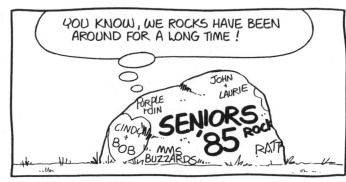

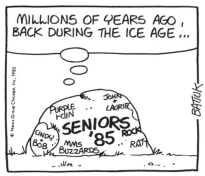

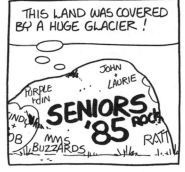

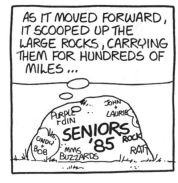

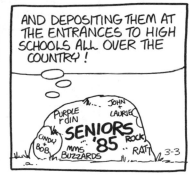

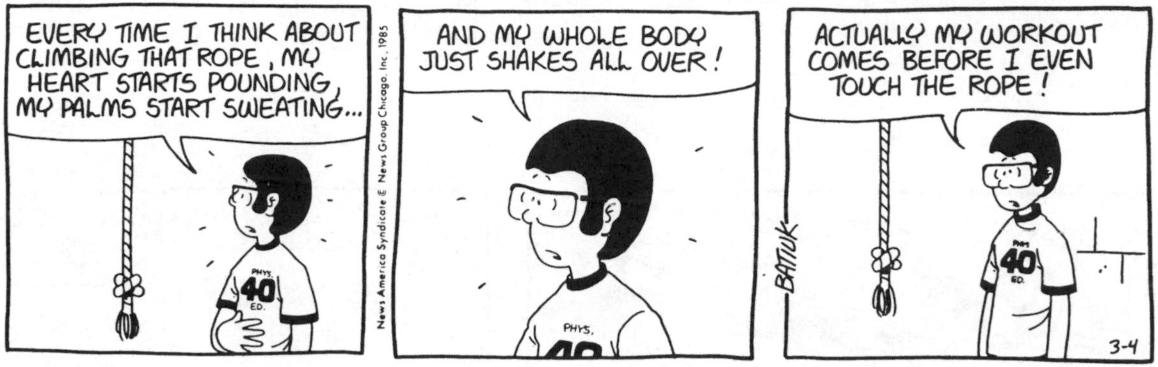
EVERY TIME I THINK ABOUT CLIMBING THAT ROPE, MY HEART STARTS POUNDING, MY PALMS START SWEATING...
AND MY WHOLE BODY JUST SHAKES ALL OVER!
ACTUALLY MY WORKOUT COMES BEFORE I EVEN TOUCH THE ROPE!
News America Syndicate © News Group Chicago, Inc. 1985
BATIUK
3-4

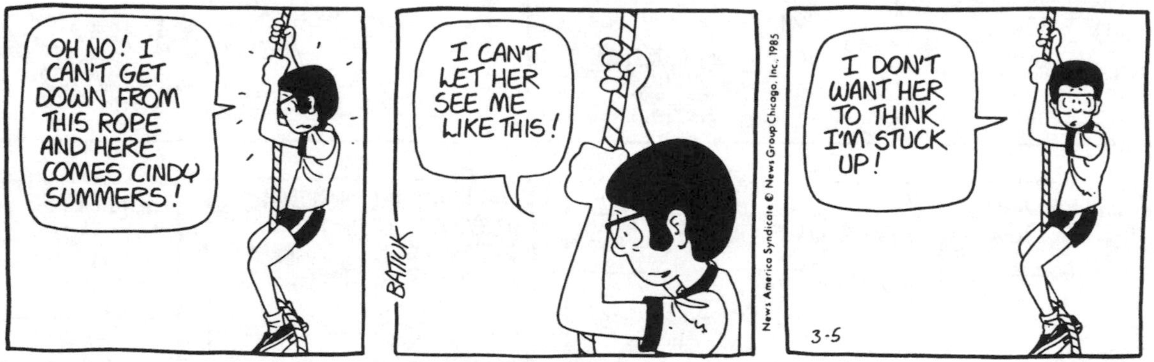
OH NO! I CAN'T GET DOWN FROM THIS ROPE AND HERE COMES CINDY SUMMERS!
BATIUK
I CAN'T LET HER SEE ME LIKE THIS!
News America Syndicate © News Group Chicago, Inc. 1985
I DON'T WANT HER TO THINK I'M STUCK UP!
3-5

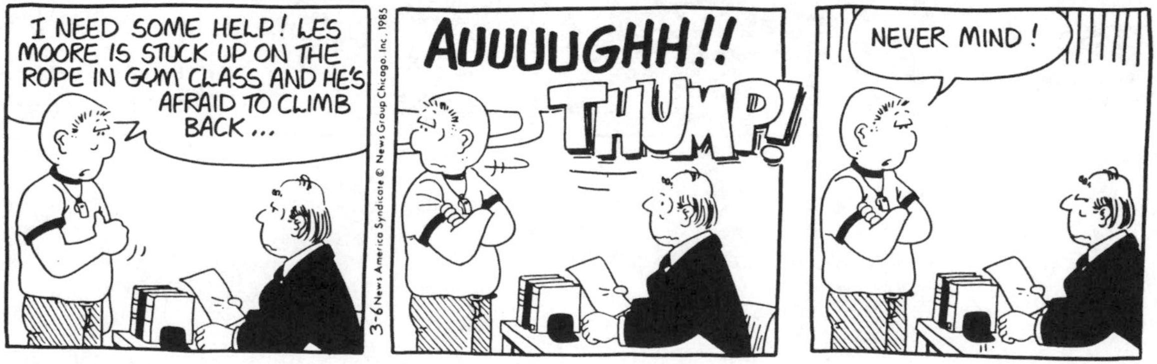
I NEED SOME HELP! LES MOORE IS STUCK UP ON THE ROPE IN GYM CLASS AND HE'S AFRAID TO CLIMB BACK...
3-6 News America Syndicate © News Group Chicago, Inc. 1985
AUUUUGHH!!
THUMP!
NEVER MIND!

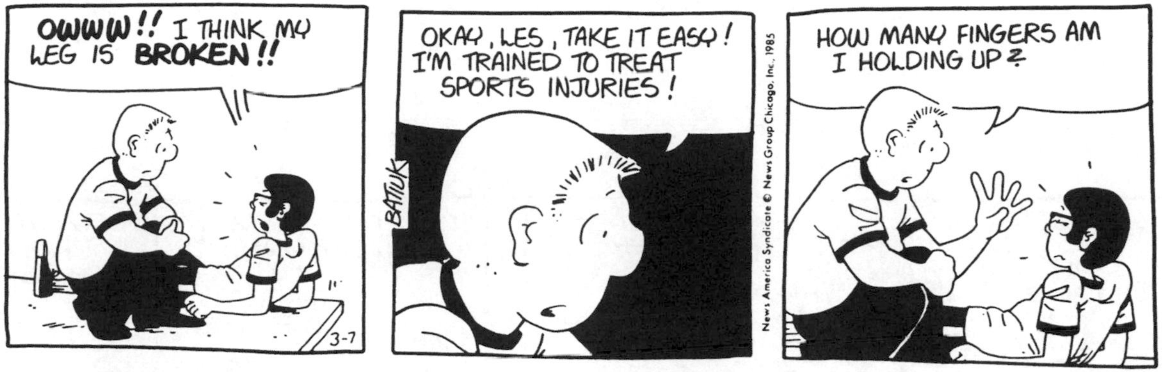
OWWW!! I THINK MY LEG IS BROKEN!!
BATIUK
OKAY, LES, TAKE IT EASY! I'M TRAINED TO TREAT SPORTS INJURIES!
News America Syndicate © News Group Chicago, Inc. 1985
HOW MANY FINGERS AM I HOLDING UP?
3-7

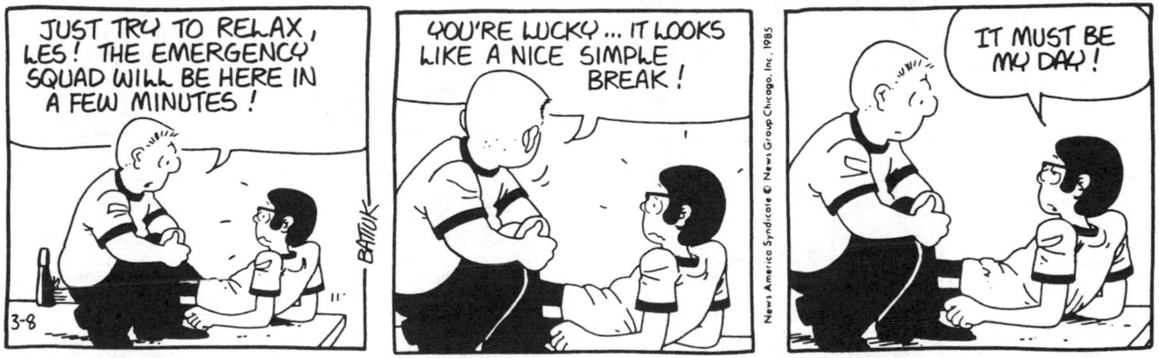
JUST TRY TO RELAX, LES! THE EMERGENCY SQUAD WILL BE HERE IN A FEW MINUTES!
3-8
BATIUK
YOU'RE LUCKY... IT LOOKS LIKE A NICE SIMPLE BREAK!
News America Syndicate © News Group Chicago, Inc. 1985
IT MUST BE MY DAY!

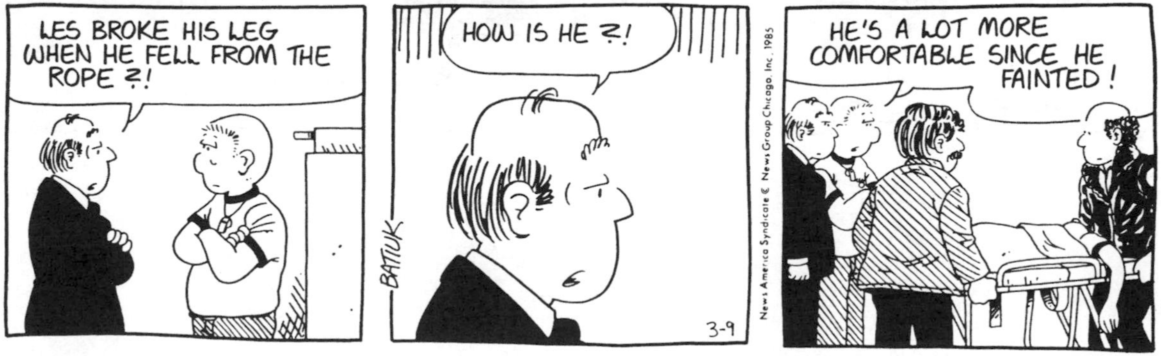
LES BROKE HIS LEG WHEN HE FELL FROM THE ROPE?!
HOW IS HE?!
BATIUK
3-9
News America Syndicate © News Group Chicago, Inc. 1985
HE'S A LOT MORE COMFORTABLE SINCE HE FAINTED!

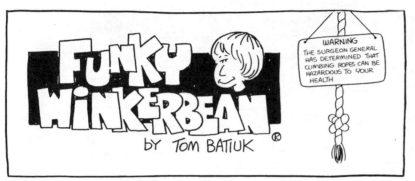

FUNKY WINKERBEAN
BY TOM BATIUK
WARNING
THE SURGEON GENERAL HAS DETERMINED THAT CLIMBING ROPES CAN BE HAZARDOUS TO YOUR HEALTH
IT'S LUCKY THE MATS WERE UNDER YOU WHEN YOU FELL FROM THE ROPE, LES!
YOU COULD'VE REALLY MARRED THE FINISH ON THE GYM FLOOR!
DO YOU THINK MY LEG IS REALLY BROKEN?
OH YEAH, IT'S BROKEN ALL RIGHT!
News Group Chicago, Inc., 1985
DO YOU HAVE ANYTHING FOR PAIN?
BATIUK
3-10
DOESN'T YOUR LEG HURT YOU ENOUGH?

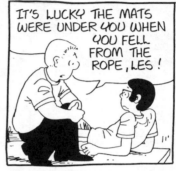

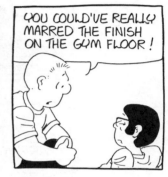

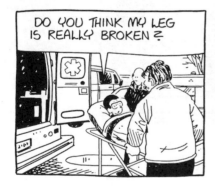

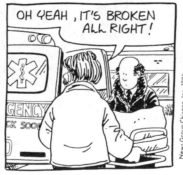

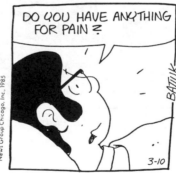

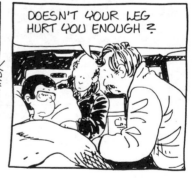

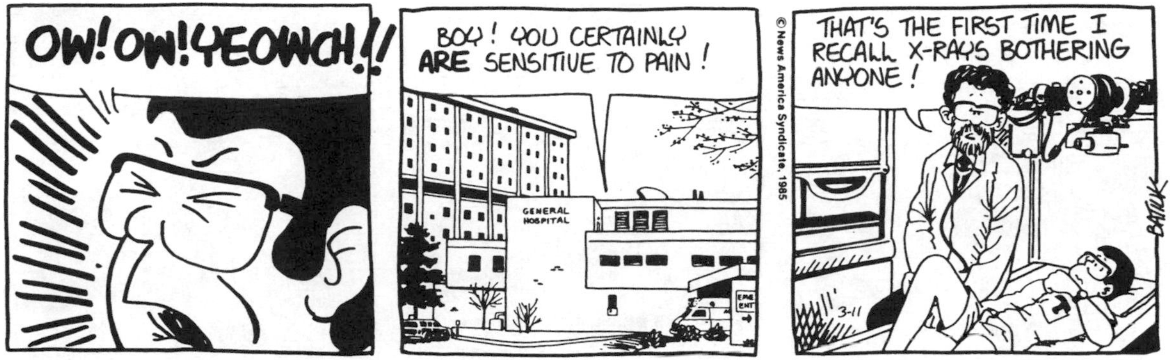
OW! OW! YEOWCH!!!
BOY! YOU CERTAINLY ARE SENSITIVE TO PAIN!
GENERAL HOSPITAL
© News America Syndicate, 1985
THAT'S THE FIRST TIME I RECALL X-RAYS BOTHERING ANYONE!
BATIUK
3-11

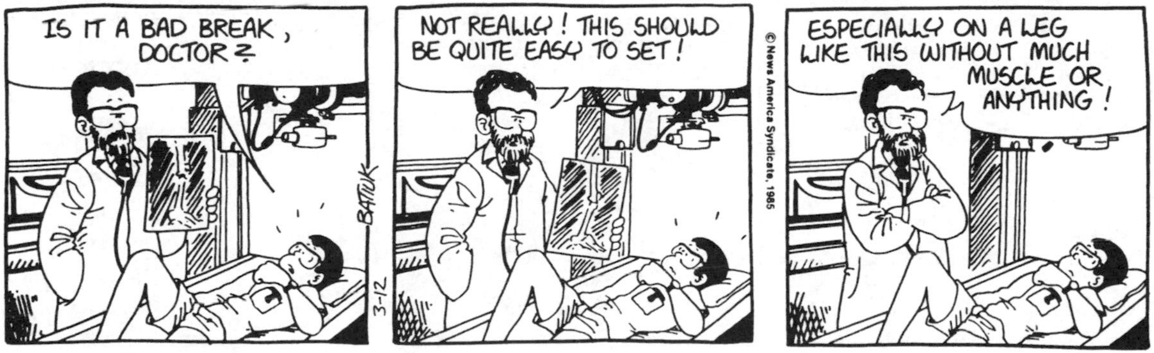
IS IT A BAD BREAK, DOCTOR?
BATIUK
3-12
NOT REALLY! THIS SHOULD BE QUITE EASY TO SET!
© News America Syndicate, 1985
ESPECIALLY ON A LEG LIKE THIS WITHOUT MUCH MUSCLE OR ANYTHING!

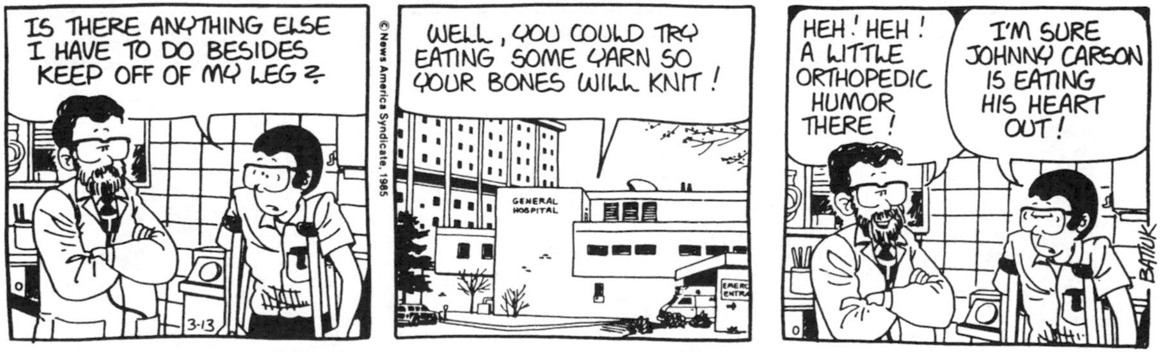
IS THERE ANYTHING ELSE I HAVE TO DO BESIDES KEEP OFF OF MY LEG?
3-13
© News America Syndicate, 1985
WELL, YOU COULD TRY EATING SOME YARN SO YOUR BONES WILL KNIT!
GENERAL HOSPITAL
HEH! HEH! A LITTLE ORTHOPEDIC HUMOR THERE!
I'M SURE JOHNNY CARSON IS EATING HIS HEART OUT!
BATIUK

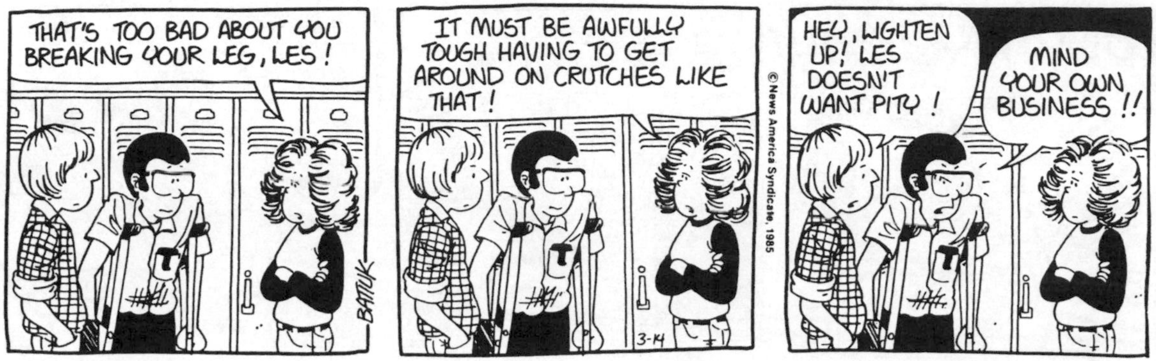
THAT'S TOO BAD ABOUT YOU BREAKING YOUR LEG, LES!
IT MUST BE AWFULLY TOUGH HAVING TO GET AROUND ON CRUTCHES LIKE THAT!
HEY, LIGHTEN UP! LES DOESN'T WANT PITY!
MIND YOUR OWN BUSINESS!!
© News America Syndicate, 1985
BATIUK
3-14

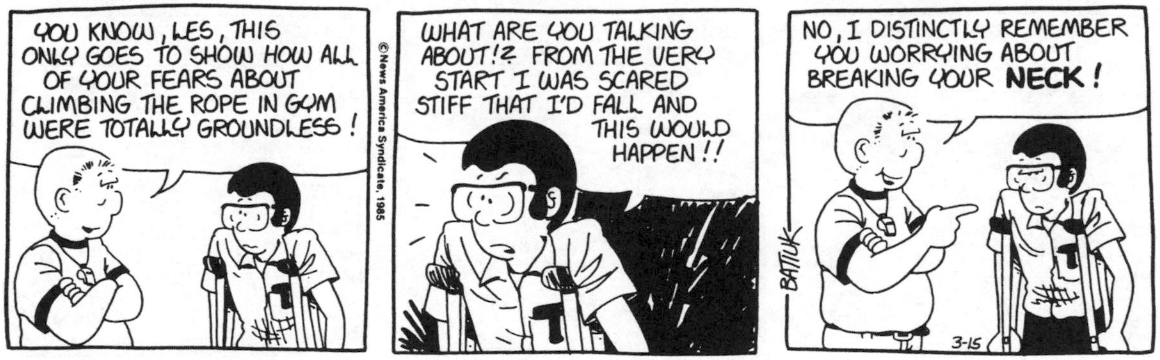
YOU KNOW, LES, THIS ONLY GOES TO SHOW HOW ALL OF YOUR FEARS ABOUT CLIMBING THE ROPE IN GYM WERE TOTALLY GROUNDLESS!
WHAT ARE YOU TALKING ABOUT!? FROM THE VERY START I WAS SCARED STIFF THAT I'D FALL AND THIS WOULD HAPPEN!!
NO, I DISTINCTLY REMEMBER YOU WORRYING ABOUT BREAKING YOUR NECK!
© News America Syndicate, 1985
BATIUK
3-15

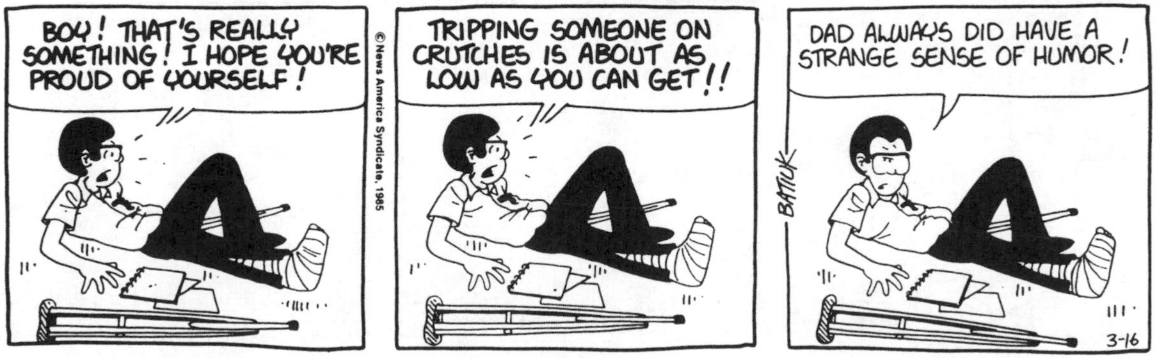
BOY! THAT'S REALLY SOMETHING! I HOPE YOU'RE PROUD OF YOURSELF!
TRIPPING SOMEONE ON CRUTCHES IS ABOUT AS LOW AS YOU CAN GET!!
DAD ALWAYS DID HAVE A STRANGE SENSE OF HUMOR!
© News America Syndicate, 1985
BATIUK
3-16

FUNKY WINKERBEAN
by TOM BATIUK
I MUST HAVE THE WORST LUCK IN THE ENTIRE WORLD!
WHY ME? WHY DOES THIS KIND OF THING ALWAYS HAPPEN TO ME?
BATIUK
SIGH
News America Syndicate © News Group Chicago, Inc., 1985
I SUPPOSE I SHOULD STOP FEELING SO SORRY FOR MYSELF AND TRY TO THINK OF OTHERS!
WHY COULDN'T THIS HAVE HAPPENED TO SOMEBODY ELSE?
3-17

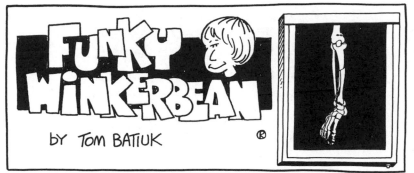

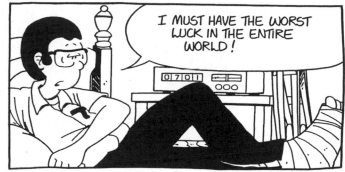

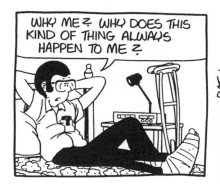

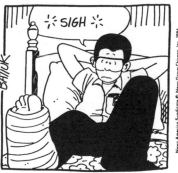

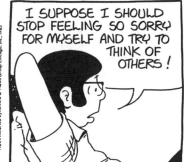

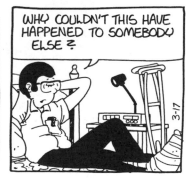

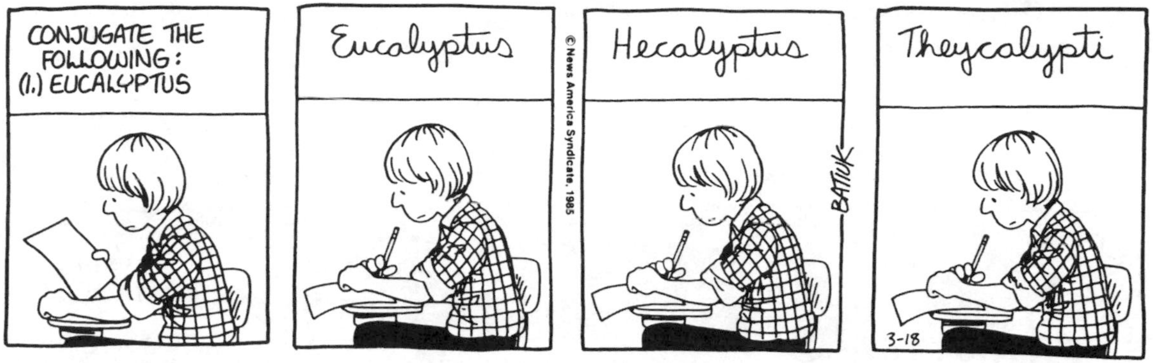
CONJUGATE THE FOLLOWING: (1.) EUCALYPTUS
Eucalyptus
© News America Syndicate, 1985
Hecalyptus
BATIUK
Theycalypti
3-18

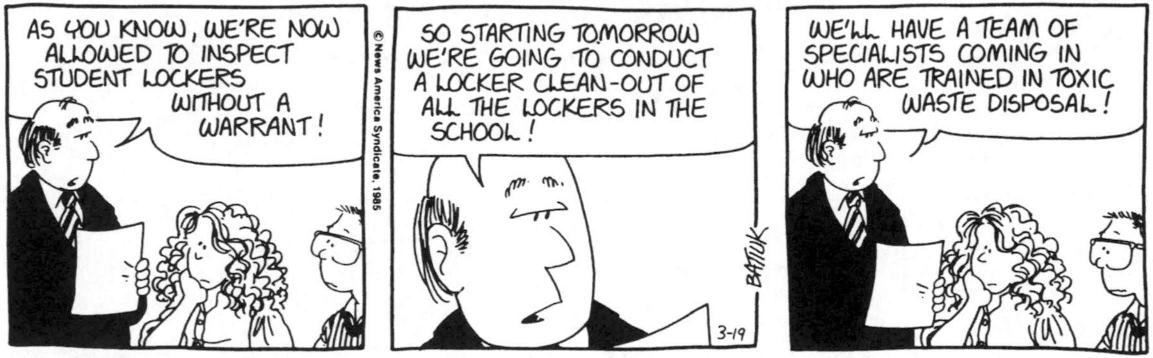
AS YOU KNOW, WE'RE NOW ALLOWED TO INSPECT STUDENT LOCKERS WITHOUT A WARRANT!
© News America Syndicate, 1985
SO STARTING TOMORROW WE'RE GOING TO CONDUCT A LOCKER CLEAN-OUT OF ALL THE LOCKERS IN THE SCHOOL!
BATIUK
3-19
WE'LL HAVE A TEAM OF SPECIALISTS COMING IN WHO ARE TRAINED IN TOXIC WASTE DISPOSAL!

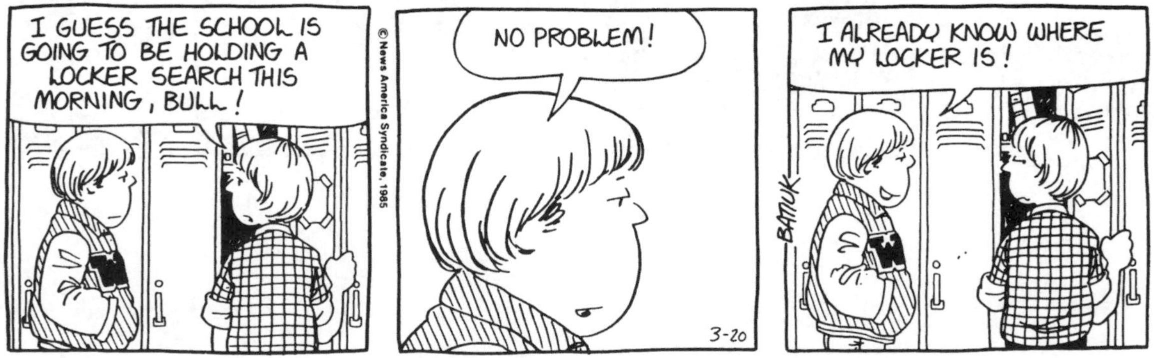
I GUESS THE SCHOOL IS GOING TO BE HOLDING A LOCKER SEARCH THIS MORNING, BULL!
© News America Syndicate, 1985
NO PROBLEM!
3-20
I ALREADY KNOW WHERE MY LOCKER IS!
BATIUK

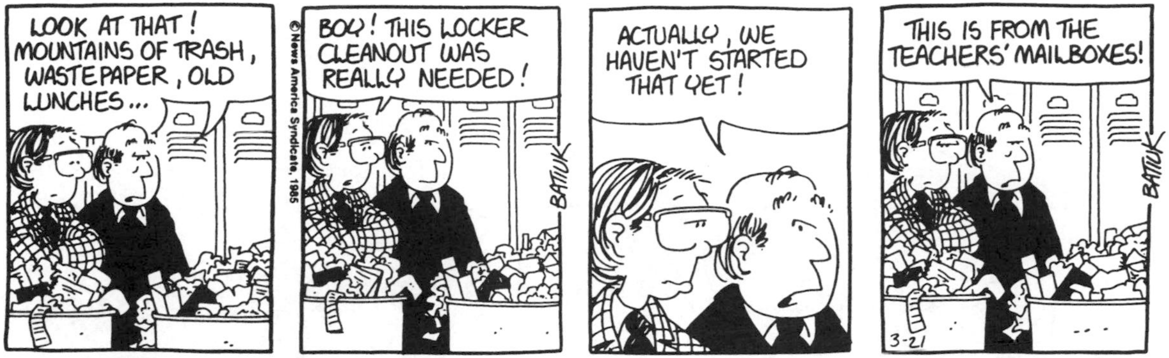
LOOK AT THAT! MOUNTAINS OF TRASH, WASTEPAPER, OLD LUNCHES...
BOY! THIS LOCKER CLEANOUT WAS REALLY NEEDED!
ACTUALLY, WE HAVEN'T STARTED THAT YET!
THIS IS FROM THE TEACHERS' MAILBOXES!
© News America Syndicate, 1985
BATIUK
3-21

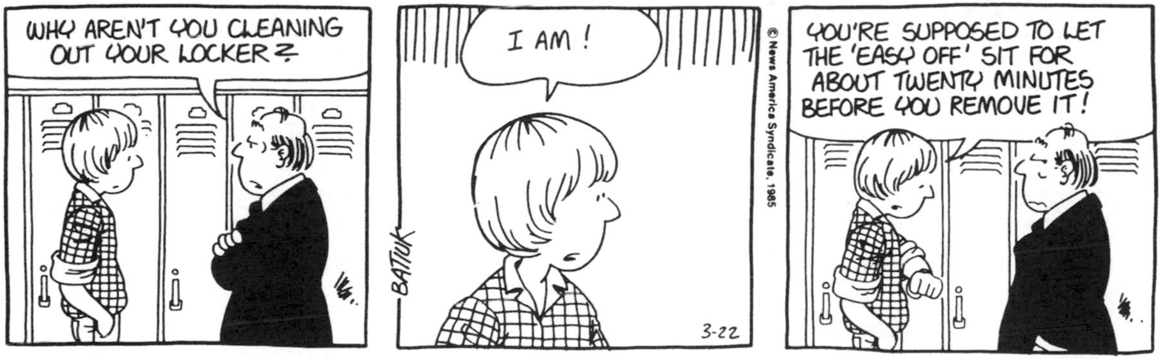
WHY AREN'T YOU CLEANING OUT YOUR LOCKER?
I AM!
YOU'RE SUPPOSED TO LET THE 'EASY OFF' SIT FOR ABOUT TWENTY MINUTES BEFORE YOU REMOVE IT!
© News America Syndicate, 1985
BATIUK
3-22

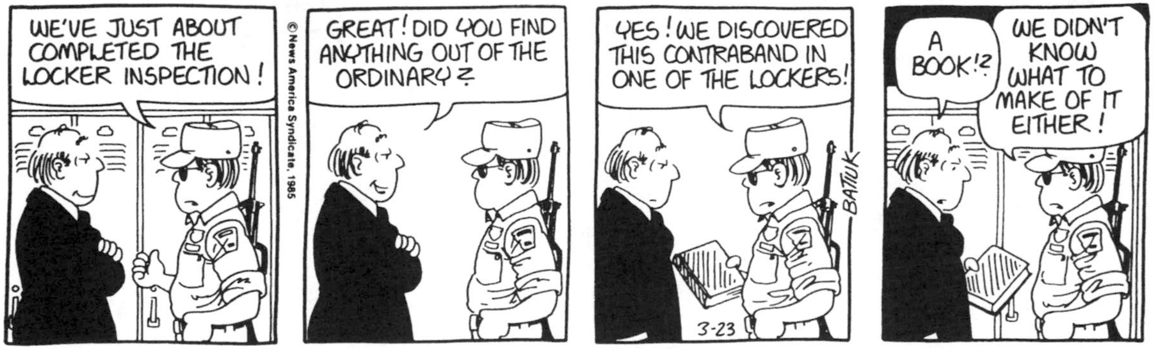
WE'VE JUST ABOUT COMPLETED THE LOCKER INSPECTION!
GREAT! DID YOU FIND ANYTHING OUT OF THE ORDINARY?
YES! WE DISCOVERED THIS CONTRABAND IN ONE OF THE LOCKERS!
A BOOK!?
WE DIDN'T KNOW WHAT TO MAKE OF IT EITHER!
© News America Syndicate, 1985
BATIUK
3-23

FUNKY WINKERBEAN
BY TOM BATIUK ®
SCHOOL
LISTEN ... DON'T GET ME WRONG !
LOOK, I KNOW A BROKEN LEG IS NO PICNIC, LES ... BUT YOU'VE GOT TO STOP FEELING SO SORRY FOR YOURSELF !
HOOL
CLASS '85
I MEAN THINGS COULD BE A LOT WORSE ! YOU COULD'VE BEEN HIT BY A TRUCK OR SOMETHING !
News America Syndicate © News Group Chicago, Inc., 1985
YEAH ... WHEN YOU LOOK AT IT THAT WAY, FUNKY, YOU'RE RIGHT ! THANKS, I'LL SEE YOU TOMORROW !
SCREECH !
THUMP !
BATIUK
3-24

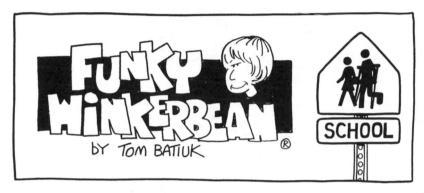

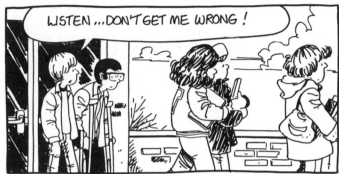

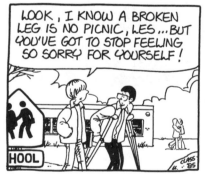

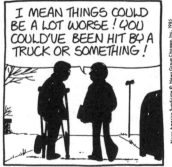

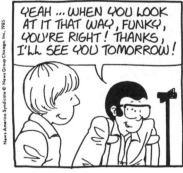

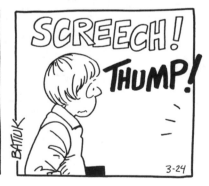

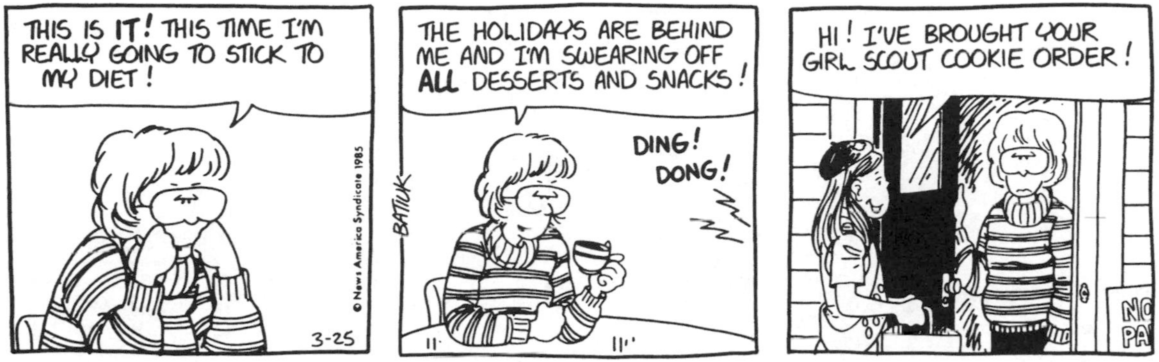
THIS IS IT! THIS TIME I'M REALLY GOING TO STICK TO MY DIET!
THE HOLIDAYS ARE BEHIND ME AND I'M SWEARING OFF ALL DESSERTS AND SNACKS!
DING! DONG!
HI! I'VE BROUGHT YOUR GIRL SCOUT COOKIE ORDER!
© News America Syndicate 1985
3-25
BATIUK

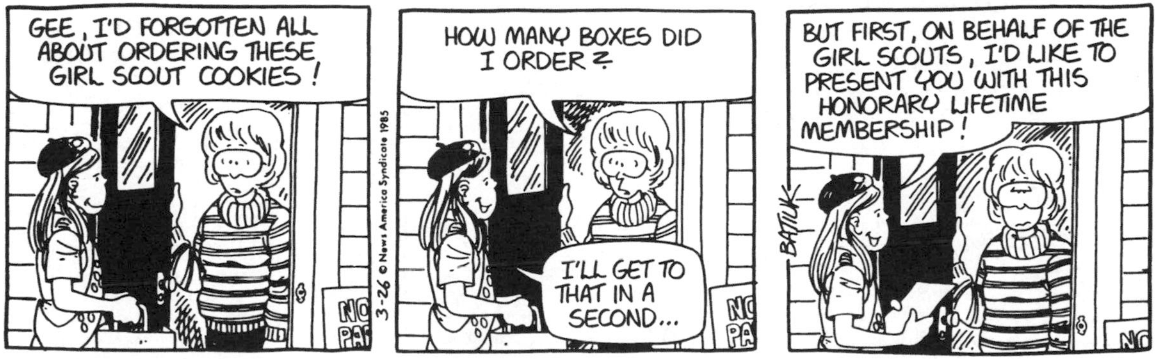
GEE, I'D FORGOTTEN ALL ABOUT ORDERING THESE GIRL SCOUT COOKIES!
HOW MANY BOXES DID I ORDER?
I'LL GET TO THAT IN A SECOND...
BUT FIRST, ON BEHALF OF THE GIRL SCOUTS, I'D LIKE TO PRESENT YOU WITH THIS HONORARY LIFETIME MEMBERSHIP!
3-26 © News America Syndicate 1985
BATIUK

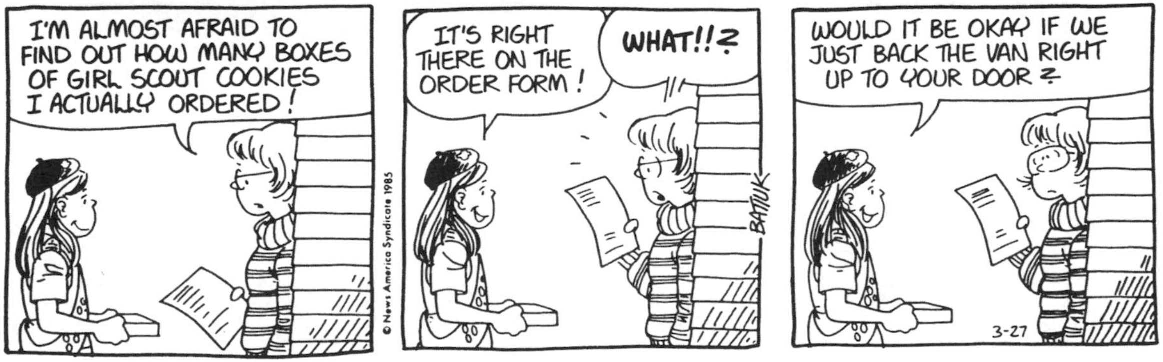
I'M ALMOST AFRAID TO FIND OUT HOW MANY BOXES OF GIRL SCOUT COOKIES I ACTUALLY ORDERED!
IT'S RIGHT THERE ON THE ORDER FORM!
WHAT!!?
WOULD IT BE OKAY IF WE JUST BACK THE VAN RIGHT UP TO YOUR DOOR?
© News America Syndicate 1985
BATIUK
3-27

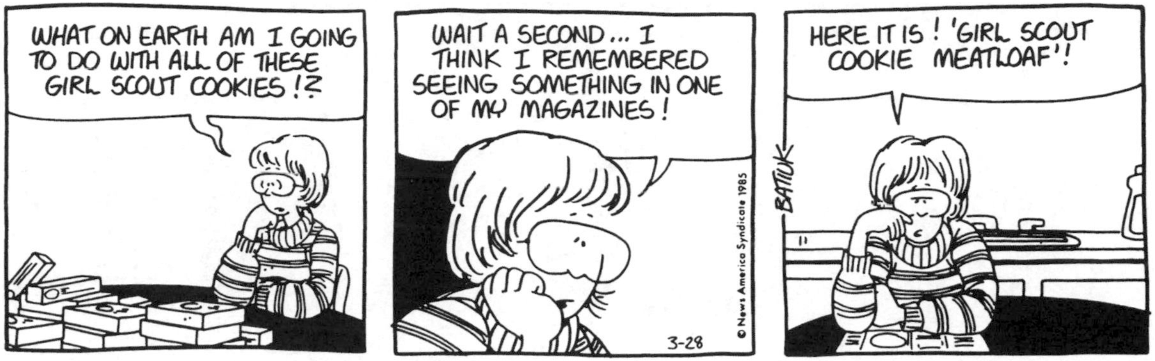
WHAT ON EARTH AM I GOING TO DO WITH ALL OF THESE GIRL SCOUT COOKIES !?
WAIT A SECOND ... I THINK I REMEMBERED SEEING SOMETHING IN ONE OF MY MAGAZINES !
3-28
© News America Syndicate 1985
BATIUK
HERE IT IS ! 'GIRL SCOUT COOKIE MEATLOAF' !

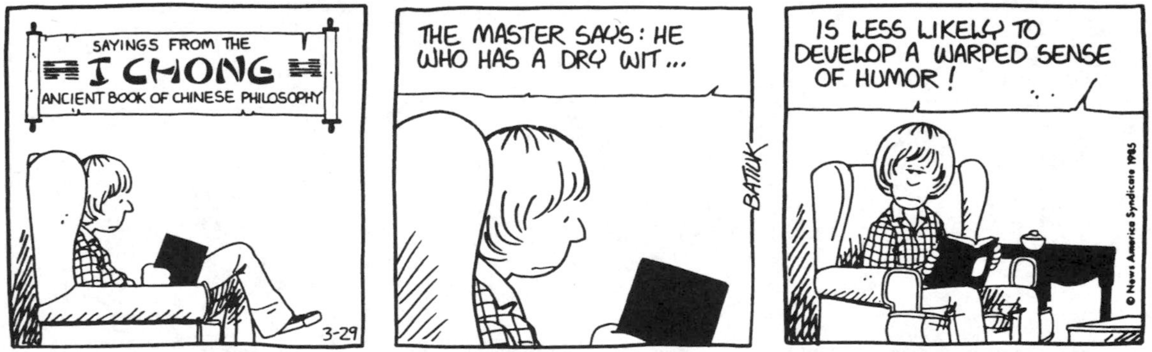
SAYINGS FROM THE
I CHONG
ANCIENT BOOK OF CHINESE PHILOSOPHY
3-29
THE MASTER SAYS: HE WHO HAS A DRY WIT...
BATIUK
IS LESS LIKELY TO DEVELOP A WARPED SENSE OF HUMOR !
© News America Syndicate 1985

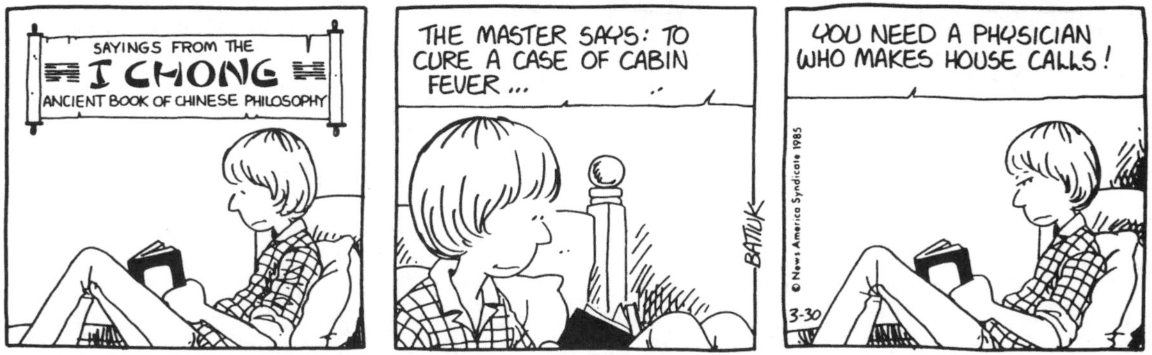
SAYINGS FROM THE
I CHONG
ANCIENT BOOK OF CHINESE PHILOSOPHY
THE MASTER SAYS: TO CURE A CASE OF CABIN FEVER ...
BATIUK
YOU NEED A PHYSICIAN WHO MAKES HOUSE CALLS !
© News America Syndicate 1985
3-30

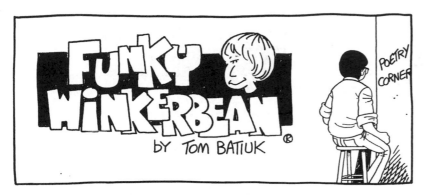

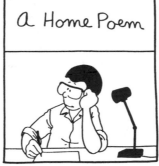

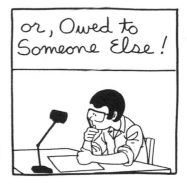

FUNKY WINKERBEAN
BY TOM BATIUK
POETRY CORNER
A Home Poem
or, Owed to Someone Else!
I don't think I shall ever own...
A thing as lovely as a home!
Poets simply moan and groan...
BATIUK
News America Syndicate © News Group Chicago, Inc., 1985
But only banks can make a loan!
3-31

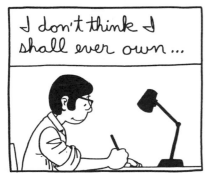

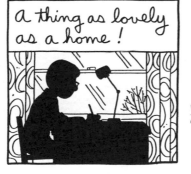

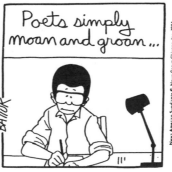

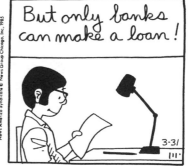

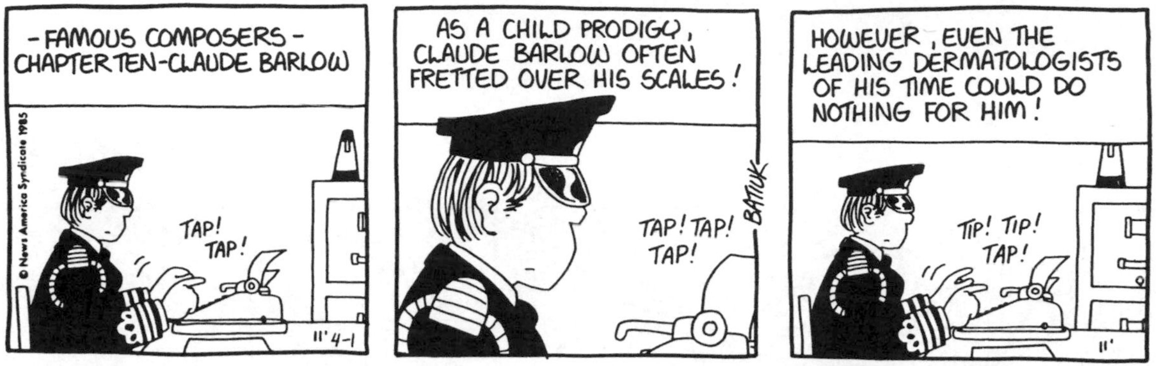

-FAMOUS COMPOSERS-
CHAPTER TEN-CLAUDE BARLOW
© News America Syndicate 1985
TAP! TAP!
AS A CHILD PRODIGY, CLAUDE BARLOW OFTEN FRETTED OVER HIS SCALES!
TAP! TAP! TAP!
BATIUK
HOWEVER, EVEN THE LEADING DERMATOLOGISTS OF HIS TIME COULD DO NOTHING FOR HIM!
TIP! TIP! TAP!

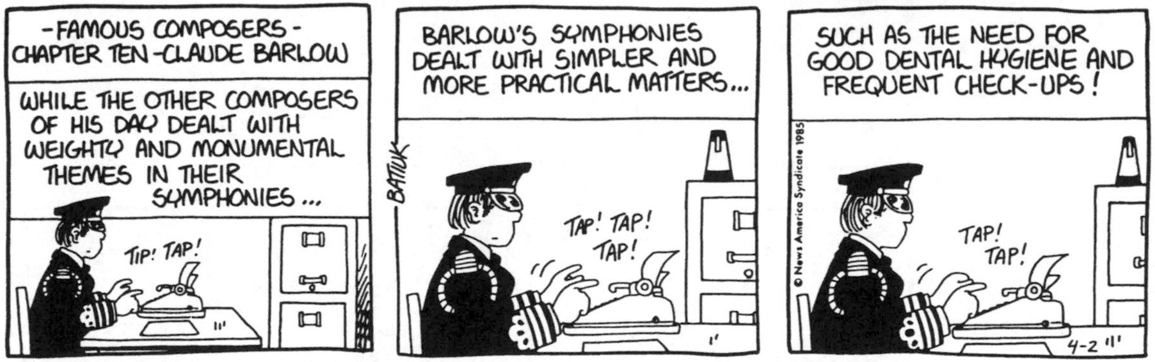

-FAMOUS COMPOSERS-
CHAPTER TEN-CLAUDE BARLOW
WHILE THE OTHER COMPOSERS OF HIS DAY DEALT WITH WEIGHTY AND MONUMENTAL THEMES IN THEIR SYMPHONIES...
TIP! TAP!
BATIUK
BARLOW'S SYMPHONIES DEALT WITH SIMPLER AND MORE PRACTICAL MATTERS...
TAP! TAP! TAP!
SUCH AS THE NEED FOR GOOD DENTAL HYGIENE AND FREQUENT CHECK-UPS!
© News America Syndicate 1985
TAP! TAP!

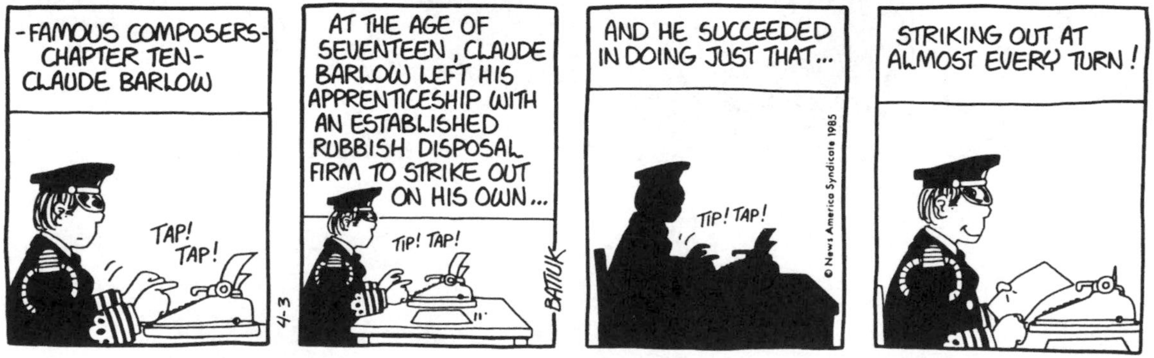

-FAMOUS COMPOSERS-
CHAPTER TEN-
CLAUDE BARLOW
TAP! TAP!
AT THE AGE OF SEVENTEEN, CLAUDE BARLOW LEFT HIS APPRENTICESHIP WITH AN ESTABLISHED RUBBISH DISPOSAL FIRM TO STRIKE OUT ON HIS OWN...
TIP! TAP!
BATIUK
AND HE SUCCEEDED IN DOING JUST THAT...
© News America Syndicate 1985
TIP! TAP!
STRIKING OUT AT ALMOST EVERY TURN!

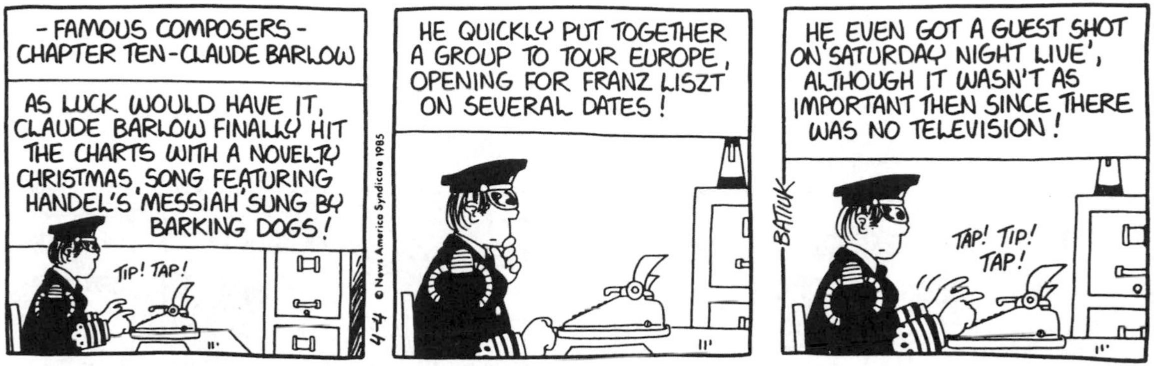
- FAMOUS COMPOSERS -
CHAPTER TEN - CLAUDE BARLOW
AS LUCK WOULD HAVE IT, CLAUDE BARLOW FINALLY HIT THE CHARTS WITH A NOVELTY CHRISTMAS SONG FEATURING HANDEL'S 'MESSIAH' SUNG BY BARKING DOGS!
TIP! TAP!
4-4
© News America Syndicate 1985
HE QUICKLY PUT TOGETHER A GROUP TO TOUR EUROPE, OPENING FOR FRANZ LISZT ON SEVERAL DATES!
HE EVEN GOT A GUEST SHOT ON 'SATURDAY NIGHT LIVE', ALTHOUGH IT WASN'T AS IMPORTANT THEN SINCE THERE WAS NO TELEVISION!
BATIUK
TAP! TIP! TAP!

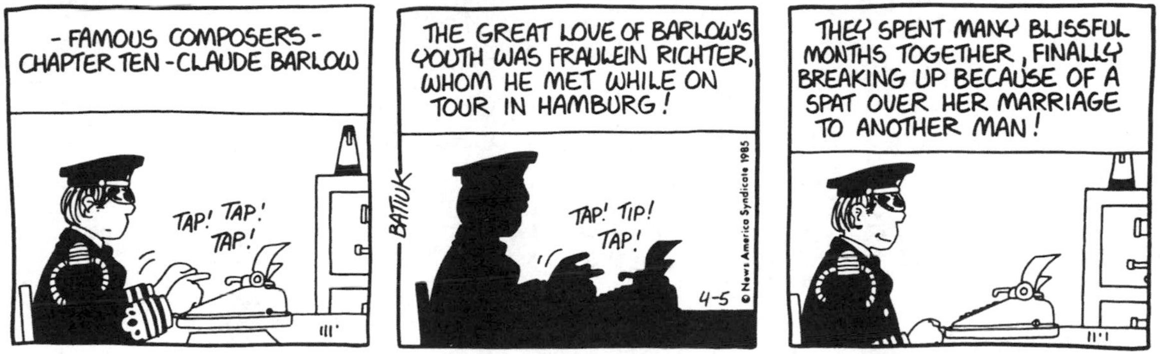
- FAMOUS COMPOSERS -
CHAPTER TEN - CLAUDE BARLOW
TAP! TAP! TAP!
BATIUK
THE GREAT LOVE OF BARLOW'S YOUTH WAS FRAULEIN RICHTER, WHOM HE MET WHILE ON TOUR IN HAMBURG!
TAP! TIP! TAP!
4-5
© News America Syndicate 1985
THEY SPENT MANY BLISSFUL MONTHS TOGETHER, FINALLY BREAKING UP BECAUSE OF A SPAT OVER HER MARRIAGE TO ANOTHER MAN!

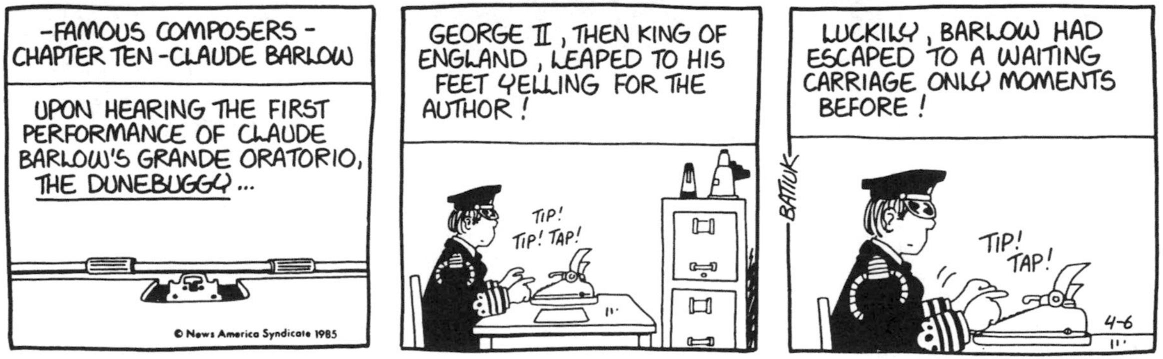
-FAMOUS COMPOSERS -
CHAPTER TEN - CLAUDE BARLOW
UPON HEARING THE FIRST PERFORMANCE OF CLAUDE BARLOW'S GRANDE ORATORIO, THE DUNEBUGGY...
© News America Syndicate 1985
GEORGE II, THEN KING OF ENGLAND, LEAPED TO HIS FEET YELLING FOR THE AUTHOR!
TIP! TIP! TAP!
LUCKILY, BARLOW HAD ESCAPED TO A WAITING CARRIAGE ONLY MOMENTS BEFORE!
BATIUK
TIP! TAP!
4-6

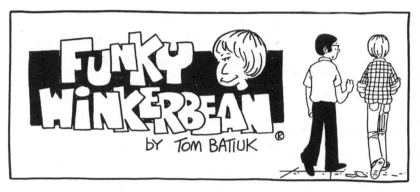

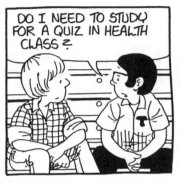

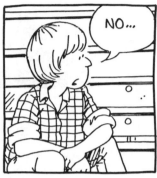

FUNKY WINKERBEAN
BY TOM BATIUK
DO I NEED TO STUDY FOR A QUIZ IN HEALTH CLASS?
NO...
THEY SHOWED A FILM IN HEALTH CLASS THIS MORNING ABOUT DRUGS AND PEER PRESSURE!
©News America Syndicate, 1985
BATIUK
LIKE HOW PEOPLE WILL TRY SOMETHING AT A PARTY JUST BECAUSE EVERYONE ELSE IS DOING IT!
I'LL TELL YOU... THAT'S ONE THING THAT'S NEVER GOING TO HAPPEN TO **ME**!
I NEVER GET INVITED TO ANY PARTIES!
4-7

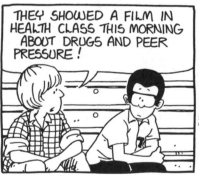

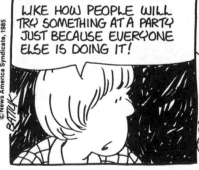

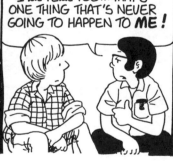

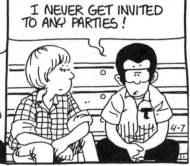

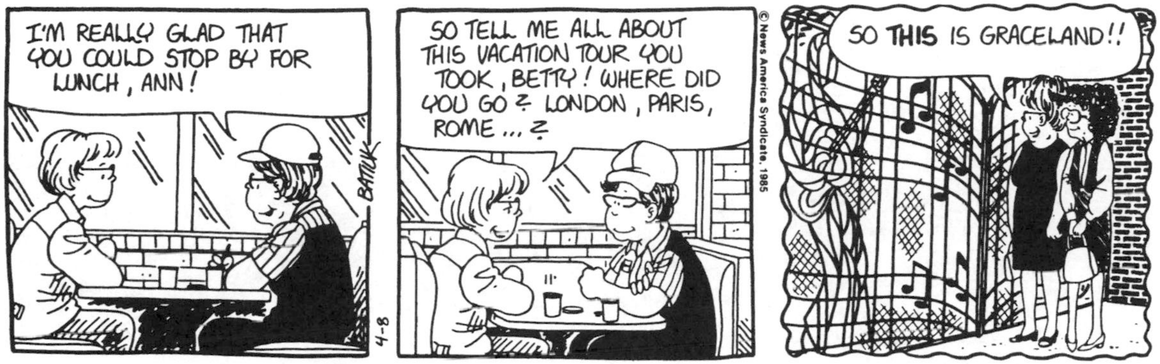
I'M REALLY GLAD THAT YOU COULD STOP BY FOR LUNCH, ANN!
SO TELL ME ALL ABOUT THIS VACATION TOUR YOU TOOK, BETTY! WHERE DID YOU GO? LONDON, PARIS, ROME...?
SO **THIS** IS GRACELAND!!
BATIUK
4-8
© News America Syndicate, 1985

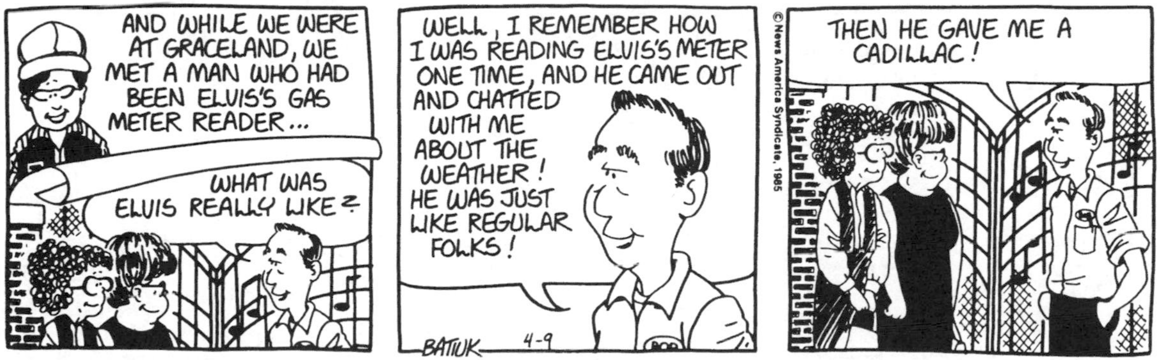
AND WHILE WE WERE AT GRACELAND, WE MET A MAN WHO HAD BEEN ELVIS'S GAS METER READER...
WHAT WAS ELVIS REALLY LIKE?
WELL, I REMEMBER HOW I WAS READING ELVIS'S METER ONE TIME, AND HE CAME OUT AND CHATTED WITH ME ABOUT THE WEATHER! HE WAS JUST LIKE REGULAR FOLKS!
THEN HE GAVE ME A CADILLAC!
BATIUK
4-9
© News America Syndicate, 1985

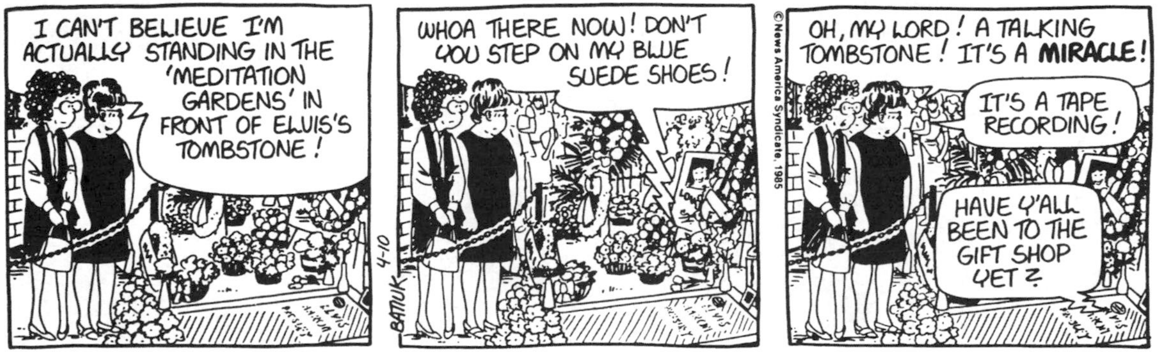
I CAN'T BELIEVE I'M ACTUALLY STANDING IN THE 'MEDITATION GARDENS' IN FRONT OF ELVIS'S TOMBSTONE!
WHOA THERE NOW! DON'T YOU STEP ON MY BLUE SUEDE SHOES!
OH, MY LORD! A TALKING TOMBSTONE! IT'S A **MIRACLE**!
IT'S A TAPE RECORDING!
HAVE Y'ALL BEEN TO THE GIFT SHOP YET?
BATIUK
4-10
© News America Syndicate, 1985

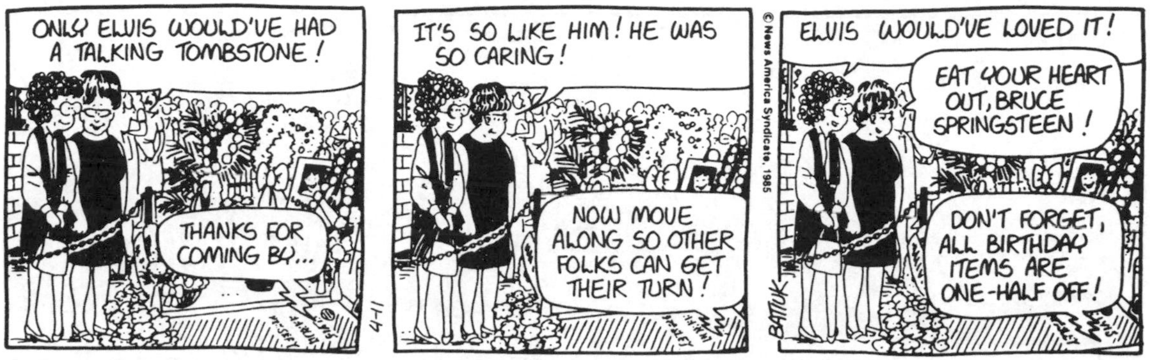
ONLY ELVIS WOULD'VE HAD A TALKING TOMBSTONE!
THANKS FOR COMING BY...
4-11
IT'S SO LIKE HIM! HE WAS SO CARING!
NOW MOVE ALONG SO OTHER FOLKS CAN GET THEIR TURN!
© News America Syndicate, 1985
ELVIS WOULD'VE LOVED IT!
EAT YOUR HEART OUT, BRUCE SPRINGSTEEN!
DON'T FORGET, ALL BIRTHDAY ITEMS ARE ONE-HALF OFF!
BATIUK

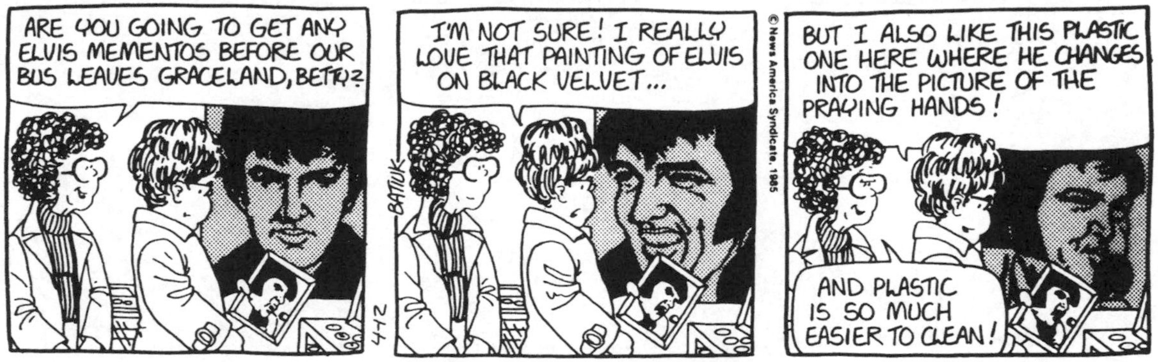
ARE YOU GOING TO GET ANY ELVIS MEMENTOS BEFORE OUR BUS LEAVES GRACELAND, BETTY?
4-12
BATIUK
I'M NOT SURE! I REALLY LOVE THAT PAINTING OF ELVIS ON BLACK VELVET...
© News America Syndicate, 1985
BUT I ALSO LIKE THIS PLASTIC ONE HERE WHERE HE CHANGES INTO THE PICTURE OF THE PRAYING HANDS!
AND PLASTIC IS SO MUCH EASIER TO CLEAN!

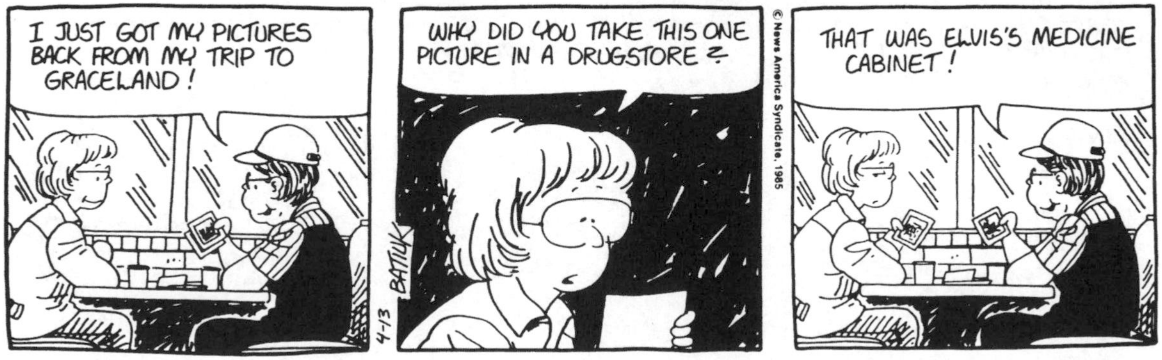
I JUST GOT MY PICTURES BACK FROM MY TRIP TO GRACELAND!
4-13
BATIUK
WHY DID YOU TAKE THIS ONE PICTURE IN A DRUGSTORE?
© News America Syndicate, 1985
THAT WAS ELVIS'S MEDICINE CABINET!

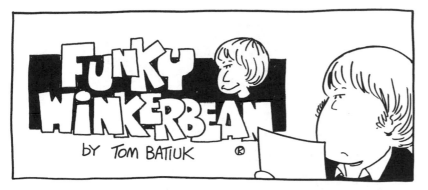

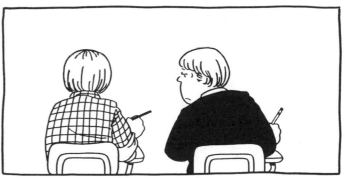

FUNKY WINKERBEAN
BY TOM BATIUK ®
DEFINE THE FOLLOWING:
1. TRANCENDENTALISM
4-14
© News America Syndicate, 1985
BATIUK
A Philosophy that explores life beyond dentistry!

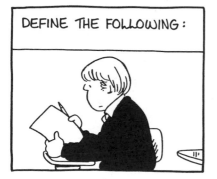

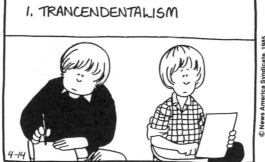

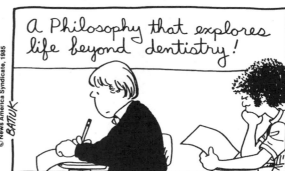

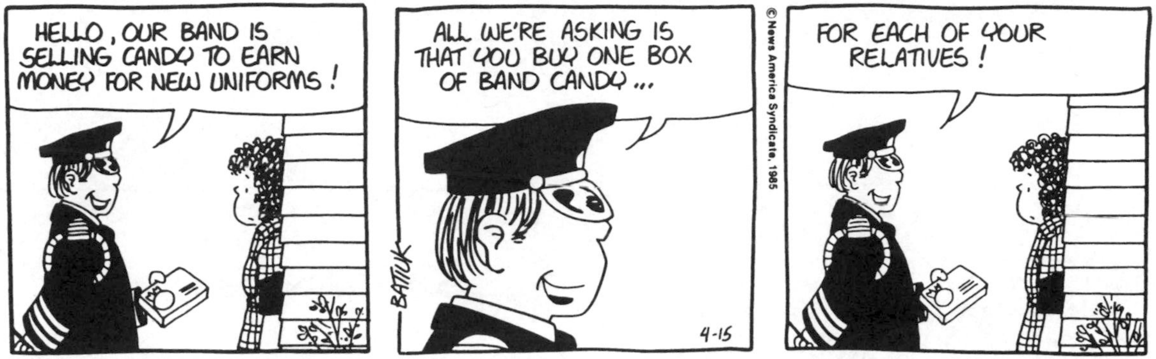
HELLO, OUR BAND IS SELLING CANDY TO EARN MONEY FOR NEW UNIFORMS!
ALL WE'RE ASKING IS THAT YOU BUY ONE BOX OF BAND CANDY...
BATIUK
4-15
© News America Syndicate, 1985
FOR EACH OF YOUR RELATIVES!

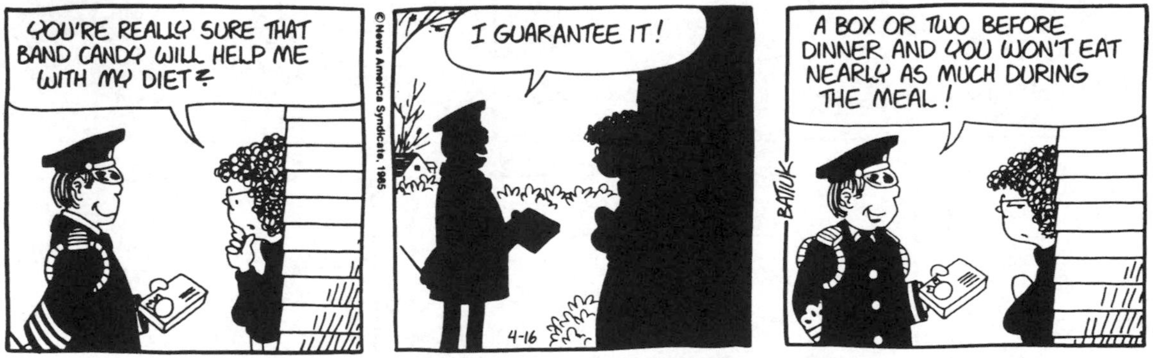
YOU'RE REALLY SURE THAT BAND CANDY WILL HELP ME WITH MY DIET?
© News America Syndicate, 1985
I GUARANTEE IT!
4-16
A BOX OR TWO BEFORE DINNER AND YOU WON'T EAT NEARLY AS MUCH DURING THE MEAL!
BATIUK

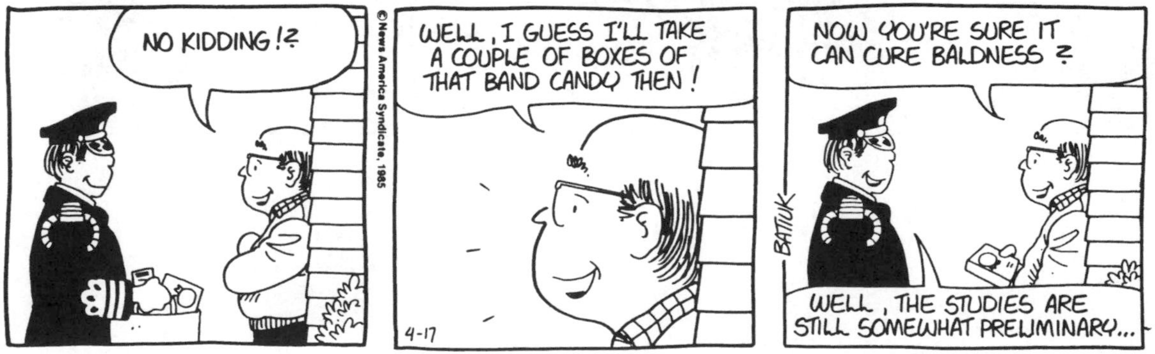
NO KIDDING!?
© News America Syndicate, 1985
WELL, I GUESS I'LL TAKE A COUPLE OF BOXES OF THAT BAND CANDY THEN!
4-17
NOW YOU'RE SURE IT CAN CURE BALDNESS?
BATIUK
WELL, THE STUDIES ARE STILL SOMEWHAT PRELIMINARY...

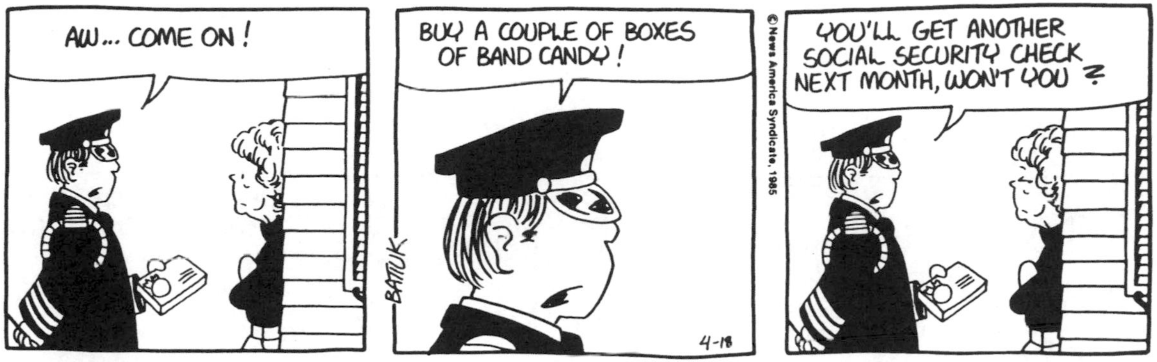
AW... COME ON!
BUY A COUPLE OF BOXES OF BAND CANDY!
BATIUK
4-18
© News America Syndicate, 1985
YOU'LL GET ANOTHER SOCIAL SECURITY CHECK NEXT MONTH, WON'T YOU ?

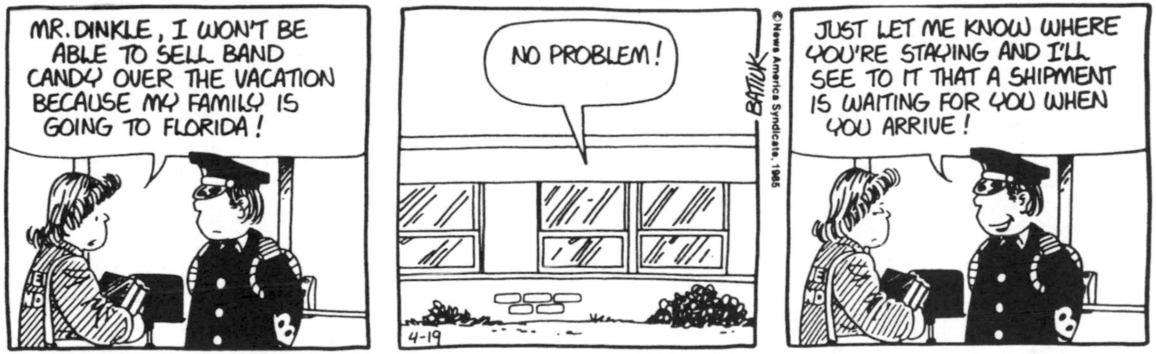
MR. DINKLE, I WON'T BE ABLE TO SELL BAND CANDY OVER THE VACATION BECAUSE MY FAMILY IS GOING TO FLORIDA!
NO PROBLEM!
4-19
BATIUK
© News America Syndicate, 1985
JUST LET ME KNOW WHERE YOU'RE STAYING AND I'LL SEE TO IT THAT A SHIPMENT IS WAITING FOR YOU WHEN YOU ARRIVE!

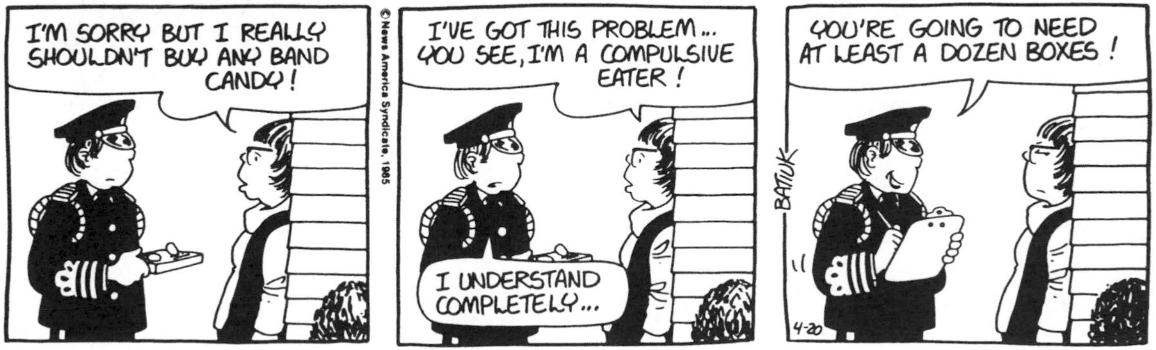
I'M SORRY BUT I REALLY SHOULDN'T BUY ANY BAND CANDY!
© News America Syndicate, 1985
I'VE GOT THIS PROBLEM... YOU SEE, I'M A COMPULSIVE EATER!
I UNDERSTAND COMPLETELY...
YOU'RE GOING TO NEED AT LEAST A DOZEN BOXES!
BATIUK
4-20

FUNKY WINKERBEAN
BY TOM BATIUK ®
OLD BAND DIRECTORS NEVER DIE ... THEY JUST SLOWLY DECOMPOSE !
IT SOUNDS LIKE THIS IS THE FIRST TIME YOU'VE EVER LOOKED AT THIS MUSIC !
THAT'S NOT SO !
I PRACTICED THIS PIECE ALL WEEKEND LONG ! THE ONLY TIME I STOPPED WAS FOR MEALS !
GIVE ME A BREAK ! I KNOW YOU BETTER THAN THAT !
OKAY I CONFESS ...
BATIUK
WESTVIEW HIGH SCHOOL
APR 21 BAND PAPER DRIVE
4-21
© News America Syndicate, 1985
I DIDN'T STOP FOR MEALS !

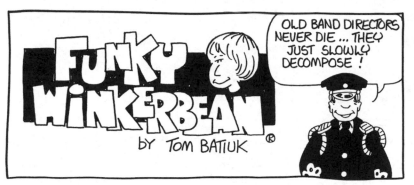

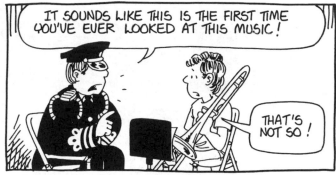

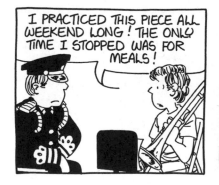

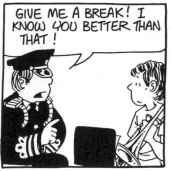

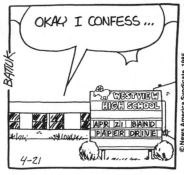

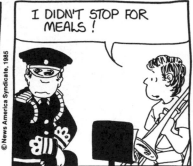

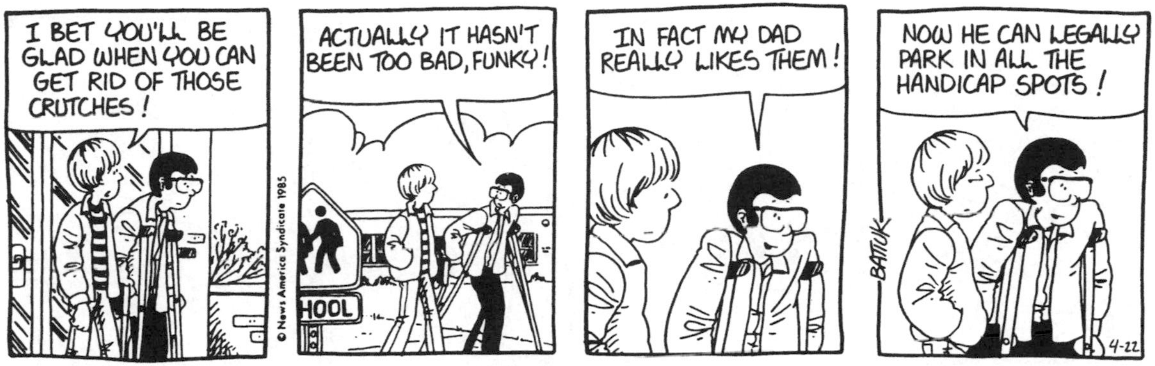
I BET YOU'LL BE GLAD WHEN YOU CAN GET RID OF THOSE CRUTCHES!
ACTUALLY IT HASN'T BEEN TOO BAD, FUNKY!
HOOL
© News America Syndicate 1985
IN FACT MY DAD REALLY LIKES THEM!
NOW HE CAN LEGALLY PARK IN ALL THE HANDICAP SPOTS!
BATIUK
4-22

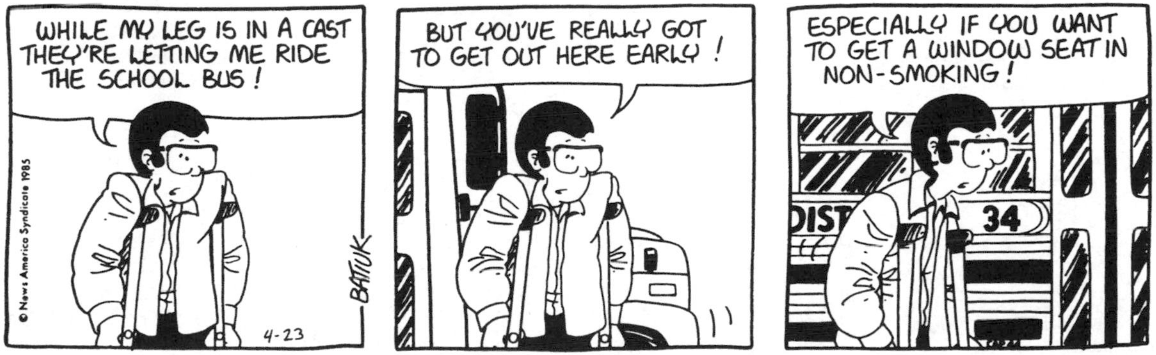
WHILE MY LEG IS IN A CAST THEY'RE LETTING ME RIDE THE SCHOOL BUS!
© News America Syndicate 1985
BATIUK
4-23
BUT YOU'VE REALLY GOT TO GET OUT HERE EARLY!
ESPECIALLY IF YOU WANT TO GET A WINDOW SEAT IN NON-SMOKING!
DIST
34

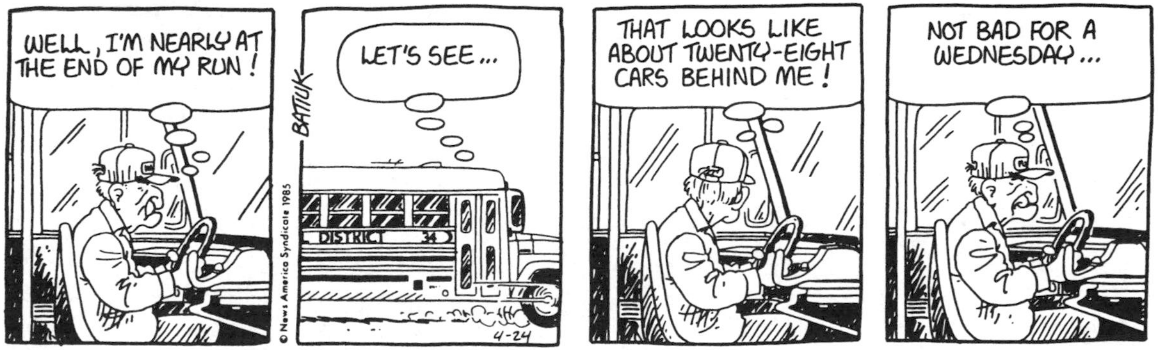
WELL, I'M NEARLY AT THE END OF MY RUN!
LET'S SEE...
BATIUK
DISTRICT 34
© News America Syndicate 1985
4-24
THAT LOOKS LIKE ABOUT TWENTY-EIGHT CARS BEHIND ME!
NOT BAD FOR A WEDNESDAY...

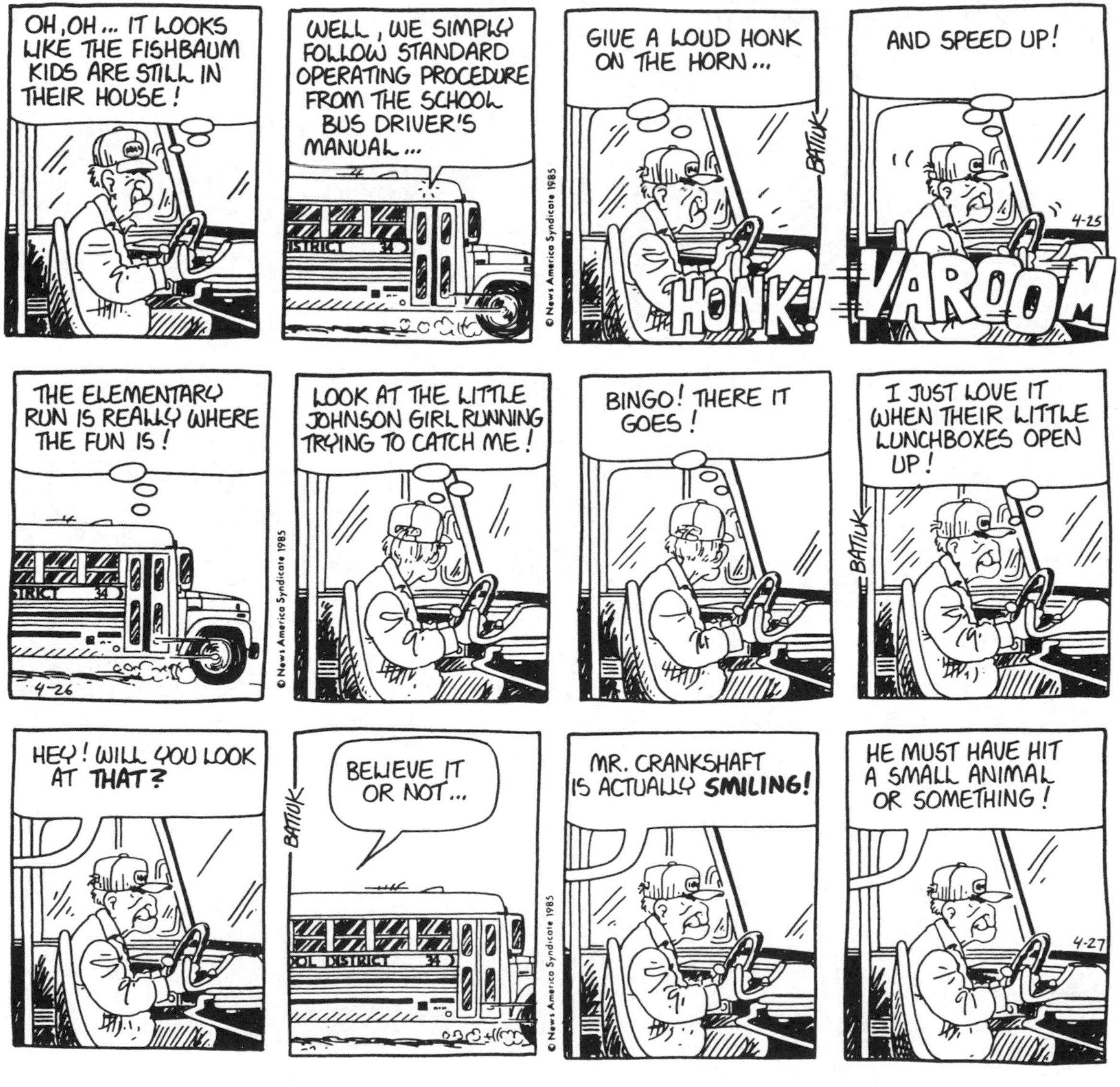
OH, OH... IT LOOKS LIKE THE FISHBAUM KIDS ARE STILL IN THEIR HOUSE!
WELL, WE SIMPLY FOLLOW STANDARD OPERATING PROCEDURE FROM THE SCHOOL BUS DRIVER'S MANUAL...
© News America Syndicate 1985
GIVE A LOUD HONK ON THE HORN...
BATIUK
HONK!
AND SPEED UP!
4-25
VAROOM
THE ELEMENTARY RUN IS REALLY WHERE THE FUN IS!
4-26
© News America Syndicate 1985
LOOK AT THE LITTLE JOHNSON GIRL RUNNING TRYING TO CATCH ME!
BINGO! THERE IT GOES!
I JUST LOVE IT WHEN THEIR LITTLE LUNCHBOXES OPEN UP!
BATIUK
HEY! WILL YOU LOOK AT **THAT?**
BATIUK
BELIEVE IT OR NOT...
© News America Syndicate 1985
MR. CRANKSHAFT IS ACTUALLY **SMILING!**
HE MUST HAVE HIT A SMALL ANIMAL OR SOMETHING!
4-27

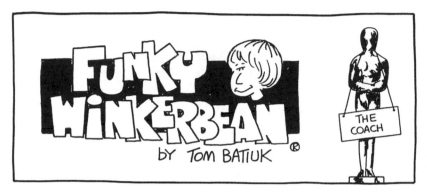

Funky Winkerbean
by Tom Batiuk

THE COACH

THERE GOES A MAN WHO SEES MORE MOVIES IN A YEAR THAN SISKEL AND EBERT COMBINED!

© News America Syndicate, 1985.

COME ON, SERIOUSLY! DOES THE COACH REALLY SHOW THAT MANY MOVIES IN HIS CLASSES?

ARE YOU KIDDING?

FACULTY WORKROOM

4-28

BATIUK

THE LIGHTS IN HIS ROOM BURNED OUT ABOUT SIX YEARS AGO...

AND THEY STILL HAVEN'T BOTHERED TO REPLACE THEM!

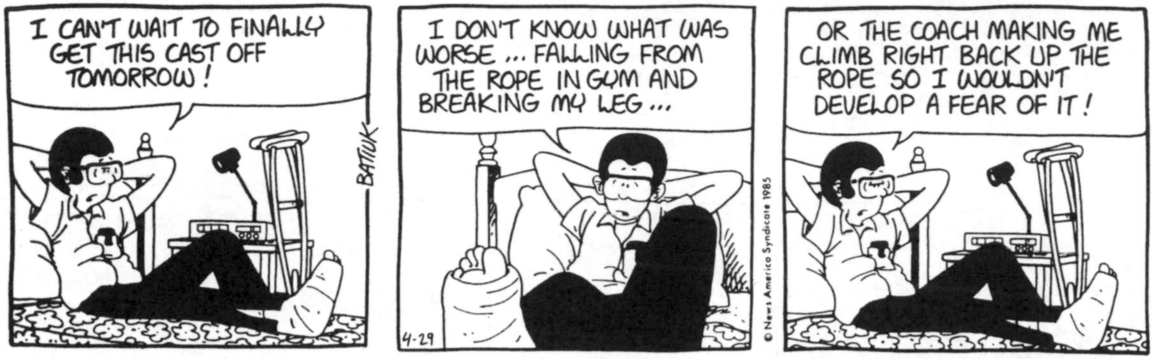
I CAN'T WAIT TO FINALLY GET THIS CAST OFF TOMORROW!
BATIUK
I DON'T KNOW WHAT WAS WORSE ... FALLING FROM THE ROPE IN GYM AND BREAKING MY LEG ...
4-29
OR THE COACH MAKING ME CLIMB RIGHT BACK UP THE ROPE SO I WOULDN'T DEVELOP A FEAR OF IT!
© News America Syndicate 1985

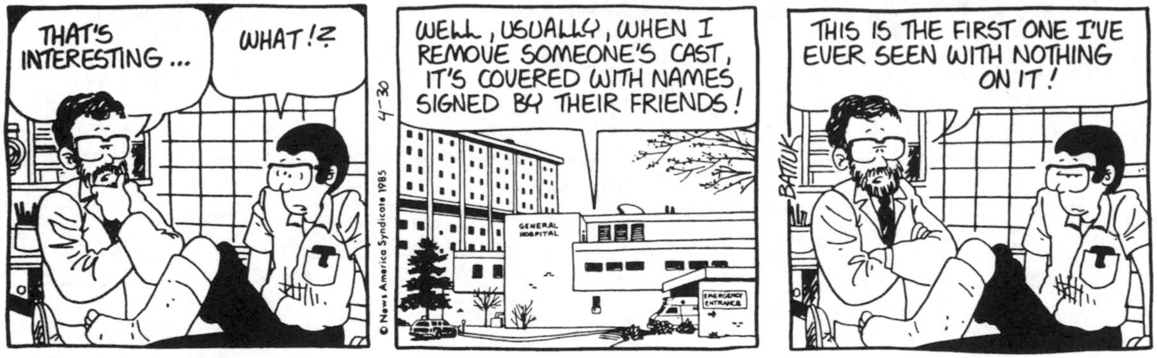
THAT'S INTERESTING ...
WHAT!?
4-30
© News America Syndicate 1985
WELL, USUALLY, WHEN I REMOVE SOMEONE'S CAST, IT'S COVERED WITH NAMES SIGNED BY THEIR FRIENDS!
GENERAL HOSPITAL
EMERGENCY ENTRANCE
BATIUK
THIS IS THE FIRST ONE I'VE EVER SEEN WITH NOTHING ON IT!

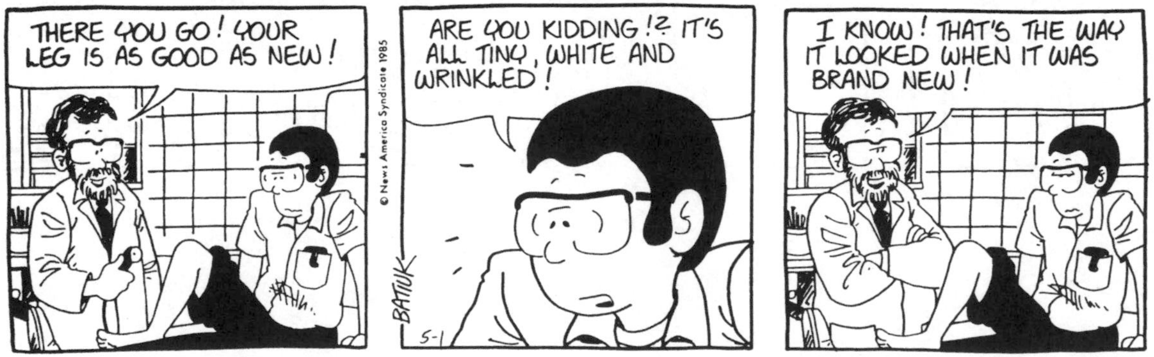
THERE YOU GO! YOUR LEG IS AS GOOD AS NEW!
© News America Syndicate 1985
ARE YOU KIDDING!? IT'S ALL TINY, WHITE AND WRINKLED!
BATIUK
5-1
I KNOW! THAT'S THE WAY IT LOOKED WHEN IT WAS BRAND NEW!

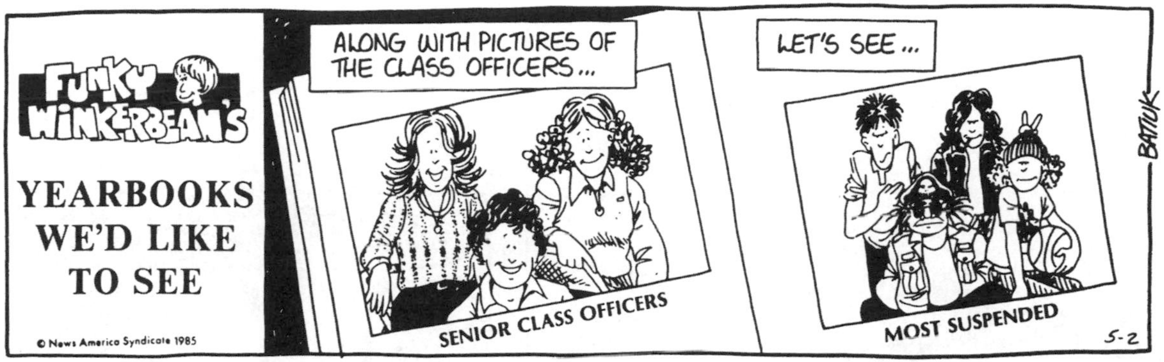
FUNKY WINKERBEAN'S
YEARBOOKS WE'D LIKE TO SEE
© News America Syndicate 1985
ALONG WITH PICTURES OF THE CLASS OFFICERS...
SENIOR CLASS OFFICERS
LET'S SEE...
MOST SUSPENDED
BATIUK
5-2

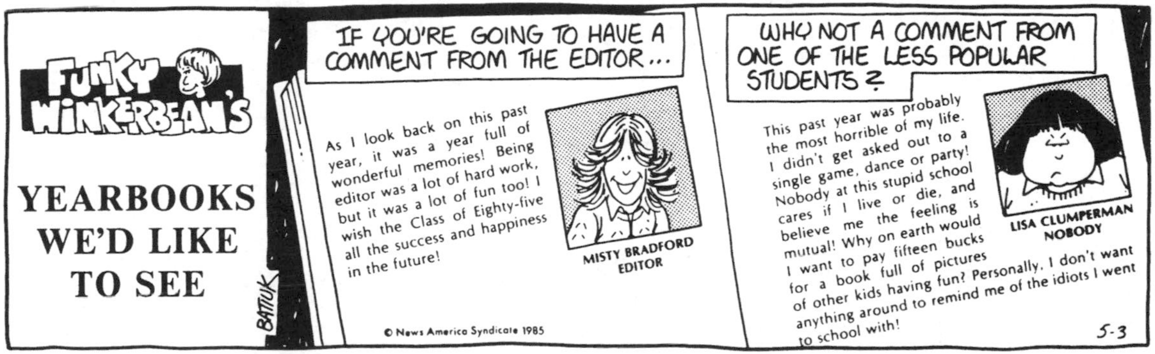
FUNKY WINKERBEAN'S
YEARBOOKS WE'D LIKE TO SEE
BATIUK
IF YOU'RE GOING TO HAVE A COMMENT FROM THE EDITOR...
As I look back on this past year, it was a year full of wonderful memories! Being editor was a lot of hard work, but it was a lot of fun too! I wish the Class of Eighty-five all the success and happiness in the future!
MISTY BRADFORD
EDITOR
© News America Syndicate 1985
WHY NOT A COMMENT FROM ONE OF THE LESS POPULAR STUDENTS?
This past year was probably the most horrible of my life. I didn't get asked out to a single game, dance or party! Nobody at this stupid school cares if I live or die, and believe me the feeling is mutual! Why on earth would I want to pay fifteen bucks for a book full of pictures of other kids having fun? Personally, I don't want anything around to remind me of the idiots I went to school with!
LISA CLUMPERMAN
NOBODY
5-3

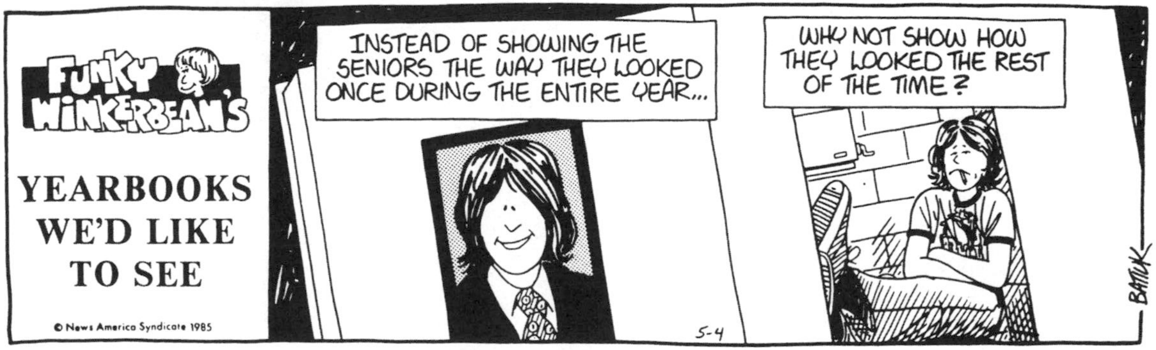
FUNKY WINKERBEAN'S
YEARBOOKS WE'D LIKE TO SEE
© News America Syndicate 1985
INSTEAD OF SHOWING THE SENIORS THE WAY THEY LOOKED ONCE DURING THE ENTIRE YEAR...
5-4
WHY NOT SHOW HOW THEY LOOKED THE REST OF THE TIME?
BATIUK

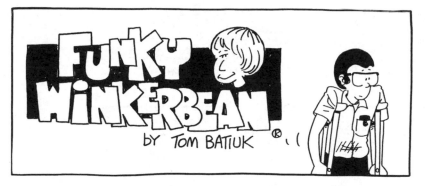

FUNKY WINKERBEAN
BY TOM BATIUK
OH, OH ... HERE COMES LES!
LOOK THE OTHER WAY SO HE DOESN'T TRY TO ASK YOU OUT!
WHY ARE YOU SO WORRIED ABOUT LES ASKING YOU OUT?
DIDN'T YOU HEAR WHAT HAPPENED TO CINDY?
LES ASKED HER OUT AND SHE SHOT HIM DOWN...
BATIUK
5-5
SO HE WENT OUT AND FILED A SEX DISCRIMINATION SUIT!
© News America Syndicate, 1985

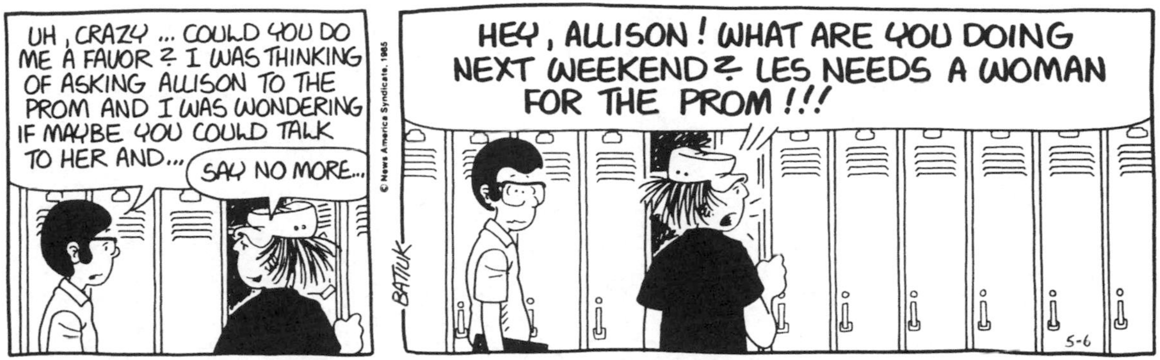
UH, CRAZY ... COULD YOU DO ME A FAVOR? I WAS THINKING OF ASKING ALLISON TO THE PROM AND I WAS WONDERING IF MAYBE YOU COULD TALK TO HER AND...
SAY NO MORE...
© News America Syndicate. 1985
BATIUK
HEY, ALLISON! WHAT ARE YOU DOING NEXT WEEKEND? LES NEEDS A WOMAN FOR THE PROM!!!
5-6

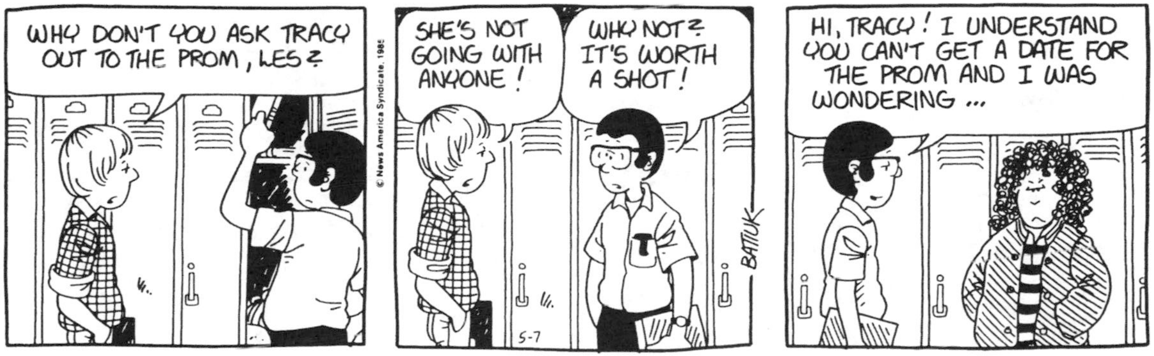
WHY DON'T YOU ASK TRACY OUT TO THE PROM, LES?
© News America Syndicate. 1985
SHE'S NOT GOING WITH ANYONE!
WHY NOT? IT'S WORTH A SHOT!
BATIUK
5-7
HI, TRACY! I UNDERSTAND YOU CAN'T GET A DATE FOR THE PROM AND I WAS WONDERING ...

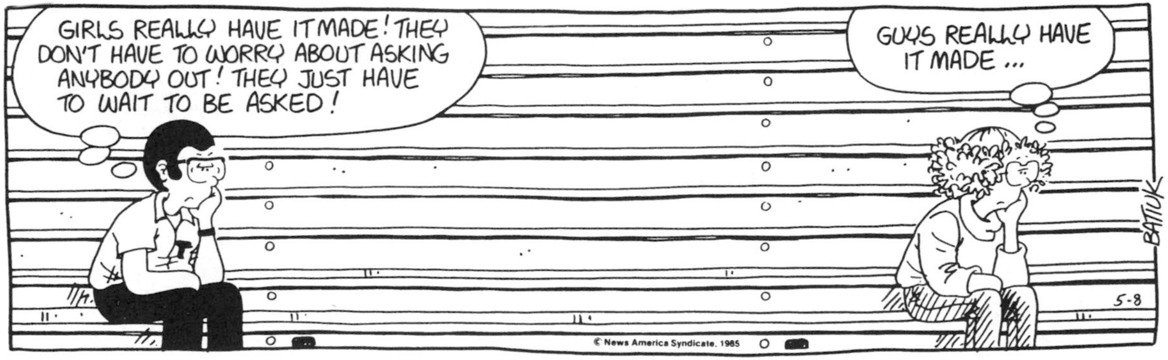
GIRLS REALLY HAVE IT MADE! THEY DON'T HAVE TO WORRY ABOUT ASKING ANYBODY OUT! THEY JUST HAVE TO WAIT TO BE ASKED!
GUYS REALLY HAVE IT MADE ...
BATIUK
5-8
© News America Syndicate. 1985

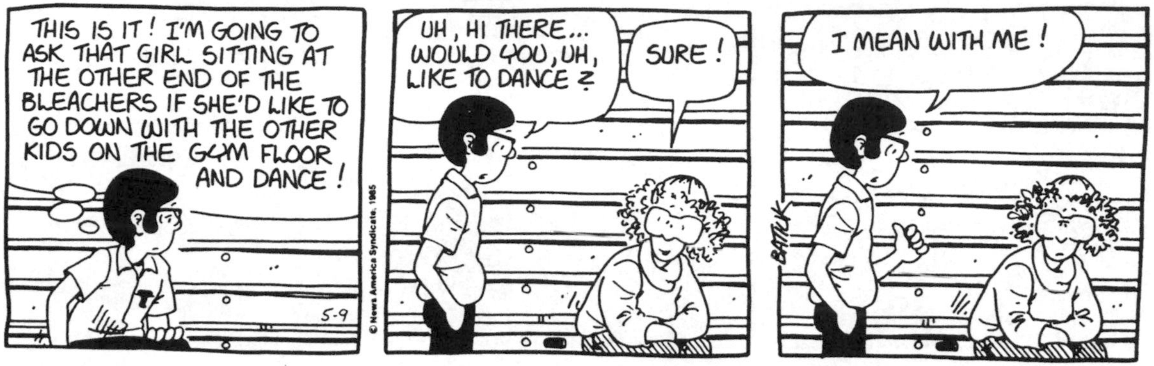
THIS IS IT! I'M GOING TO ASK THAT GIRL SITTING AT THE OTHER END OF THE BLEACHERS IF SHE'D LIKE TO GO DOWN WITH THE OTHER KIDS ON THE GYM FLOOR AND DANCE!
5-9
© News America Syndicate, 1985
UH, HI THERE... WOULD YOU, UH, LIKE TO DANCE?
SURE!
I MEAN WITH ME!
BATIUK

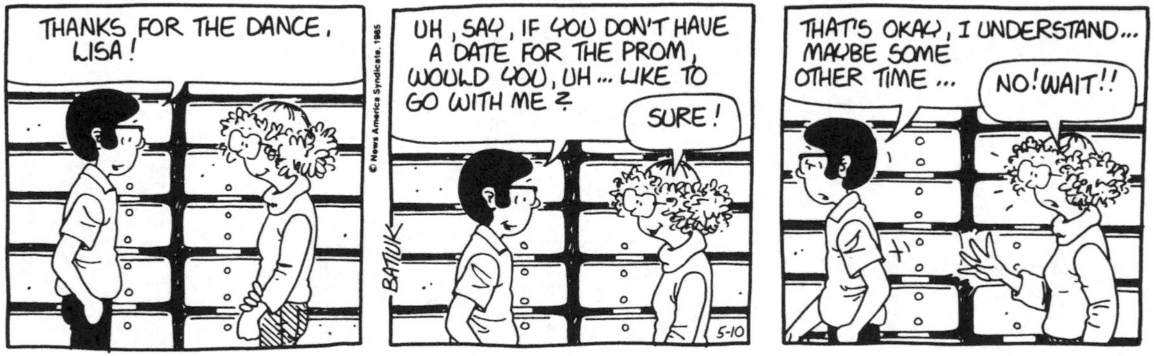
THANKS FOR THE DANCE, LISA!
© News America Syndicate, 1985
UH, SAY, IF YOU DON'T HAVE A DATE FOR THE PROM, WOULD YOU, UH... LIKE TO GO WITH ME?
SURE!
BATIUK
5-10
THAT'S OKAY, I UNDERSTAND... MAYBE SOME OTHER TIME...
NO! WAIT!!

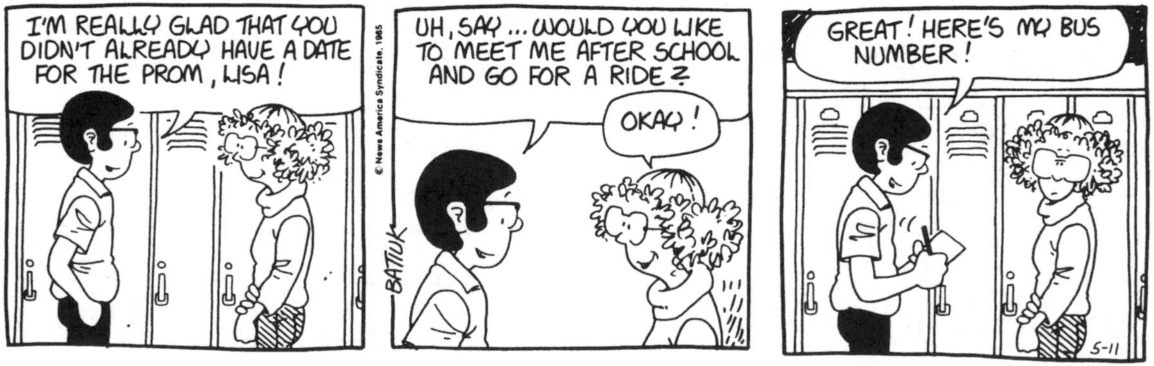
I'M REALLY GLAD THAT YOU DIDN'T ALREADY HAVE A DATE FOR THE PROM, LISA!
© News America Syndicate, 1985
UH, SAY... WOULD YOU LIKE TO MEET ME AFTER SCHOOL AND GO FOR A RIDE?
OKAY!
BATIUK
GREAT! HERE'S MY BUS NUMBER!
5-11

FUNKY WINKERBEAN
BY TOM BATIUK
CLICK! CLICK!
SORRY. WRONG ANSWER.
CLICK!
TRY AGAIN! NYAA! NYAA!
YOU'VE BEEN SWEATING OVER THIS FOR HOURS!
CLICK! CLICK!
BATIUK
WHAT ARE YOU TRYING TO DO? ACCESS THE STRATEGIC AIR COMMAND COMPUTERS AGAIN?
© News America Syndicate, 1985
5-12
NO, EVERYBODY'S DONE THAT! THIS IS A LOT TOUGHER!
CLICK! CLICK!
I'M TRYING TO BALANCE MY MOM'S CHECKBOOK AS A SURPRISE FOR MOTHER'S DAY!

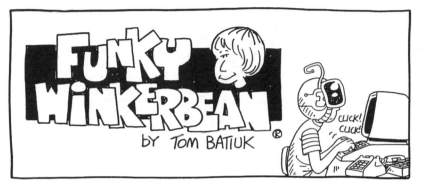

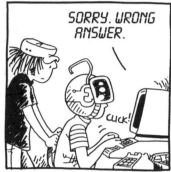

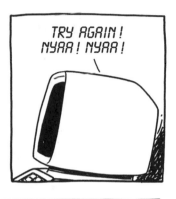

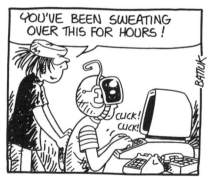

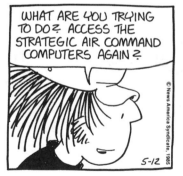

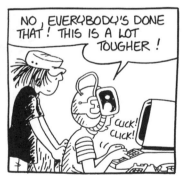

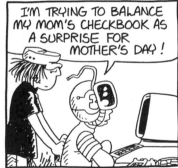

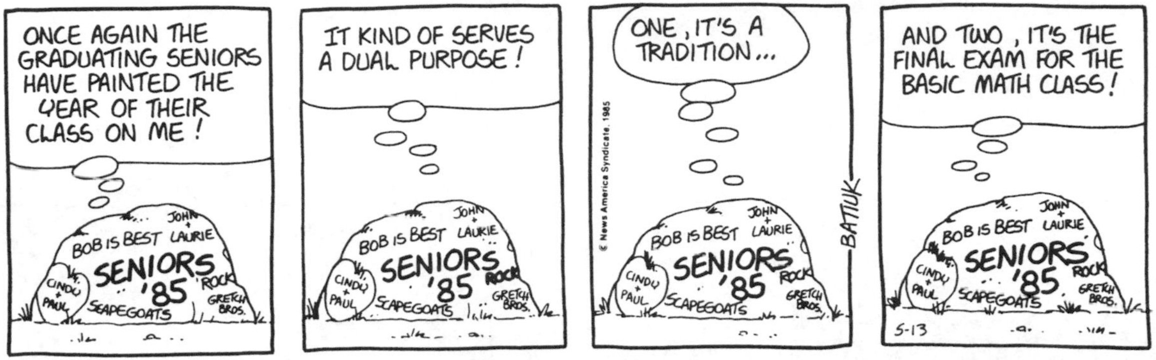

ONCE AGAIN THE GRADUATING SENIORS HAVE PAINTED THE YEAR OF THEIR CLASS ON ME!
JOHN + LAURIE
BOB IS BEST
SENIORS '85
CINDY + PAUL
ROCK
SCAPEGOATS
GRETCH BROS.
IT KIND OF SERVES A DUAL PURPOSE!
ONE, IT'S A TRADITION...
© News America Syndicate, 1985
BATIUK
AND TWO, IT'S THE FINAL EXAM FOR THE BASIC MATH CLASS!
5-13

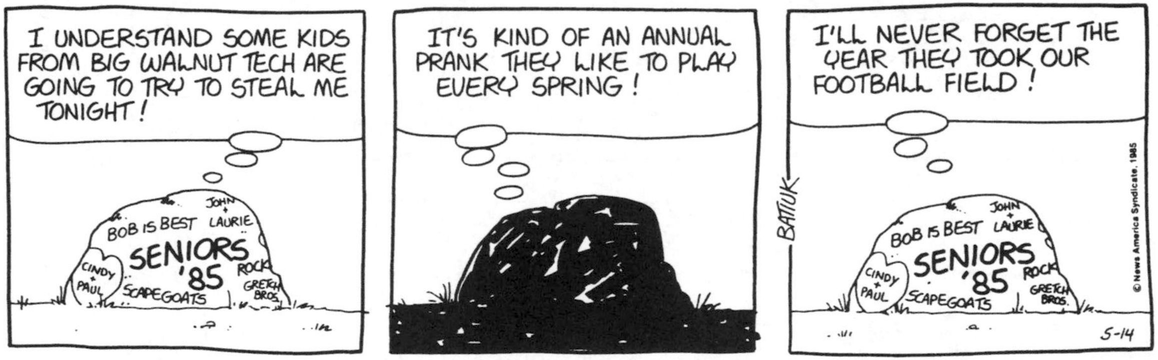

I UNDERSTAND SOME KIDS FROM BIG WALNUT TECH ARE GOING TO TRY TO STEAL ME TONIGHT!
IT'S KIND OF AN ANNUAL PRANK THEY LIKE TO PLAY EVERY SPRING!
BATIUK
I'LL NEVER FORGET THE YEAR THEY TOOK OUR FOOTBALL FIELD!
© News America Syndicate, 1985
5-14

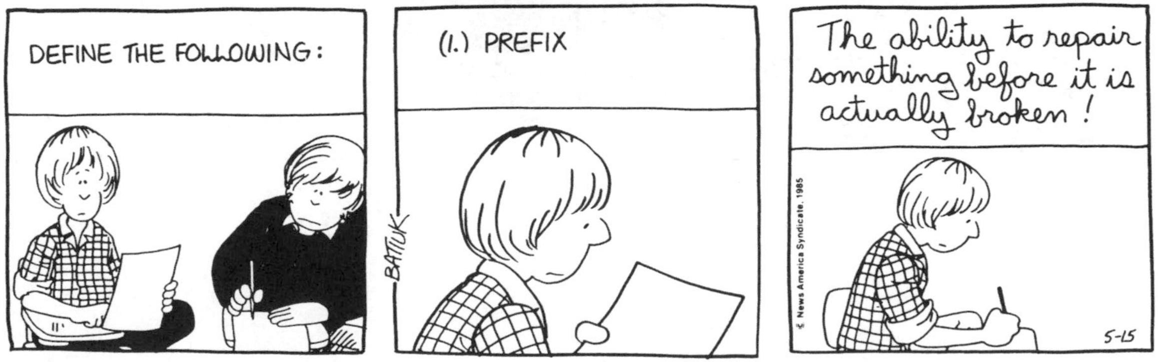

DEFINE THE FOLLOWING:
BATIUK
(1.) PREFIX
The ability to repair something before it is actually broken!
© News America Syndicate, 1985
5-15

DEFINE THE FOLLOWING:	(2.) NECTAR	The worst possible kind of ring around the collar!
		 5-16
DEFINE THE FOLLOWING:	(3.) PARABLES	Two male cattle!
		 5-17
DEFINE THE FOLLOWING:	(4.) TARRAGON	What happened when Scarlett O'Hara lost her home!
		 5-18

BATIUK

237

FUNKY WINKERBEAN

BY Tom Batiuk

I'D LIKE TO WELCOME ALL OF YOU TO THIS YEAR'S BAND AWARDS BANQUET!

WESTVIEW HIGH SCHOOL
BAND AWARDS BANQUET

THIS PAST YEAR'S BAND TURKEY AND FRUITCAKE SALES DIDN'T GO AS WELL AS EXPECTED...

AS I'M SURE YOU'RE AWARE, IF YOU GLANCED AT TONIGHT'S MENU!

OUR FIRST AWARD IS THE GOLDEN SPIT-VALVE AWARD FOR THE MOST CONSCIENTIOUS BAND MEMBER...

WHICH GOES TO MISSY SWIEKERT...

WESTVIEW HIGH SCHOOL
BAND AWARDS BANQUET

BATIUK

© News America Syndicate 1985

WHO TOOK HER MUSIC FOLDER HOME EVERY SINGLE NIGHT!

WHAT SHE DID WITH IT THERE, HEAVEN ONLY KNOWS...

5-19

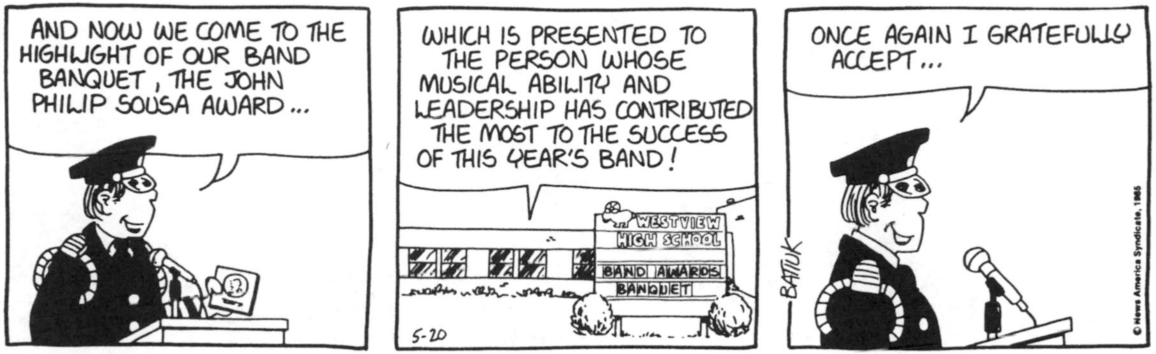
AND NOW WE COME TO THE HIGHLIGHT OF OUR BAND BANQUET, THE JOHN PHILIP SOUSA AWARD...
WHICH IS PRESENTED TO THE PERSON WHOSE MUSICAL ABILITY AND LEADERSHIP HAS CONTRIBUTED THE MOST TO THE SUCCESS OF THIS YEAR'S BAND!
WESTVIEW HIGH SCHOOL
BAND AWARDS BANQUET
5-20
BATIUK
ONCE AGAIN I GRATEFULLY ACCEPT...
© News America Syndicate, 1985

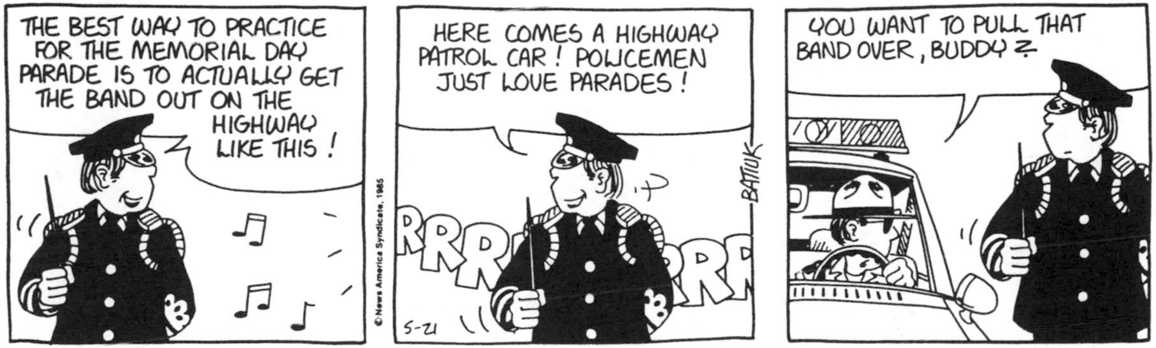
THE BEST WAY TO PRACTICE FOR THE MEMORIAL DAY PARADE IS TO ACTUALLY GET THE BAND OUT ON THE HIGHWAY LIKE THIS!
© News America Syndicate, 1985
HERE COMES A HIGHWAY PATROL CAR! POLICEMEN JUST LOVE PARADES!
RRR
RRR
5-21
BATIUK
YOU WANT TO PULL THAT BAND OVER, BUDDY?

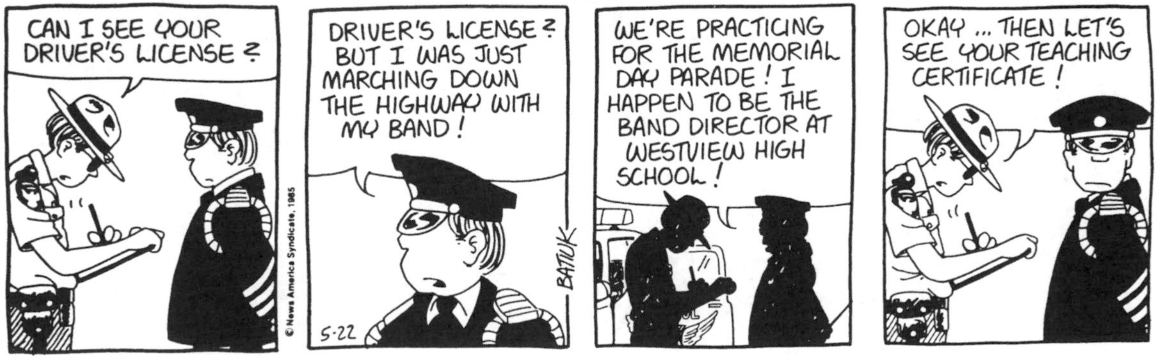
CAN I SEE YOUR DRIVER'S LICENSE?
© News America Syndicate, 1985
DRIVER'S LICENSE? BUT I WAS JUST MARCHING DOWN THE HIGHWAY WITH MY BAND!
5-22
BATIUK
WE'RE PRACTICING FOR THE MEMORIAL DAY PARADE! I HAPPEN TO BE THE BAND DIRECTOR AT WESTVIEW HIGH SCHOOL!
OKAY ... THEN LET'S SEE YOUR TEACHING CERTIFICATE!

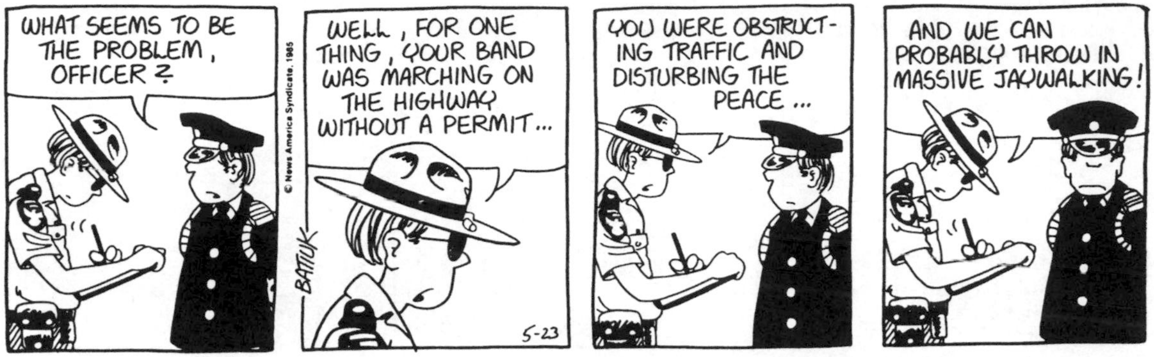
WHAT SEEMS TO BE THE PROBLEM, OFFICER?
© News America Syndicate, 1985
WELL, FOR ONE THING, YOUR BAND WAS MARCHING ON THE HIGHWAY WITHOUT A PERMIT...
BATIUK
5-23
YOU WERE OBSTRUCTING TRAFFIC AND DISTURBING THE PEACE...
AND WE CAN PROBABLY THROW IN MASSIVE JAYWALKING!

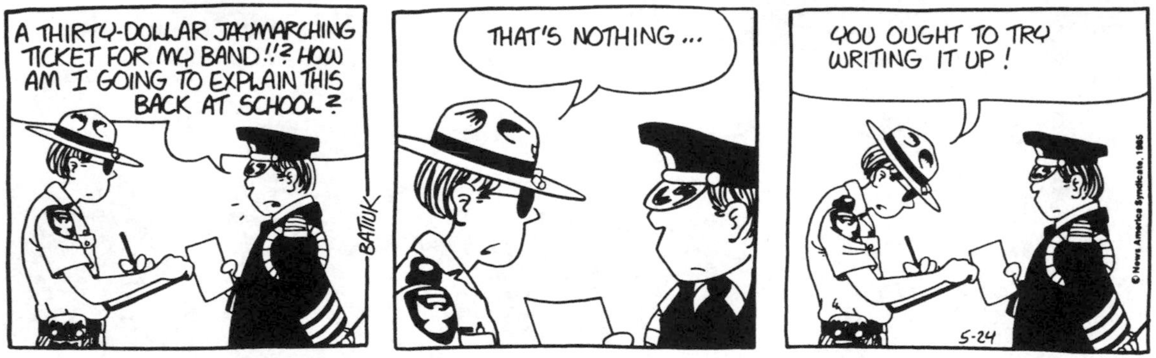
A THIRTY-DOLLAR JAYMARCHING TICKET FOR MY BAND!!? HOW AM I GOING TO EXPLAIN THIS BACK AT SCHOOL?
BATIUK
THAT'S NOTHING...
YOU OUGHT TO TRY WRITING IT UP!
© News America Syndicate, 1985
5-24

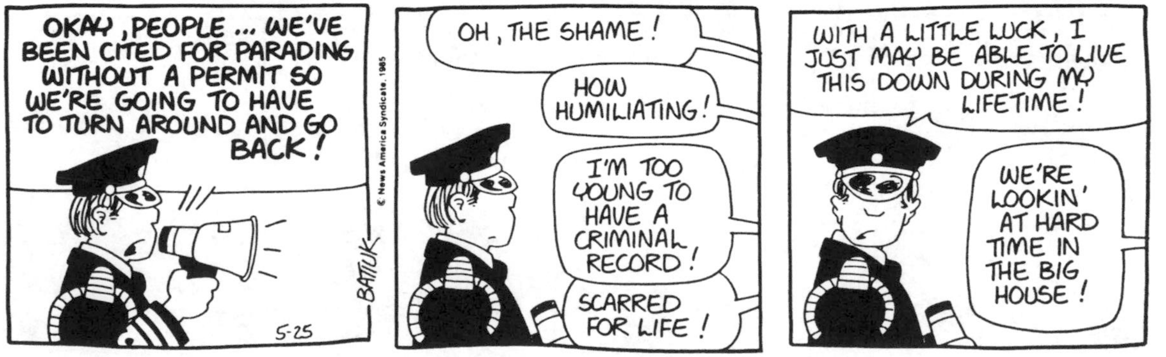
OKAY, PEOPLE... WE'VE BEEN CITED FOR PARADING WITHOUT A PERMIT SO WE'RE GOING TO HAVE TO TURN AROUND AND GO BACK!
© News America Syndicate, 1985
BATIUK
5-25
OH, THE SHAME!
HOW HUMILIATING!
I'M TOO YOUNG TO HAVE A CRIMINAL RECORD!
SCARRED FOR LIFE!
WITH A LITTLE LUCK, I JUST MAY BE ABLE TO LIVE THIS DOWN DURING MY LIFETIME!
WE'RE LOOKIN' AT HARD TIME IN THE BIG HOUSE!

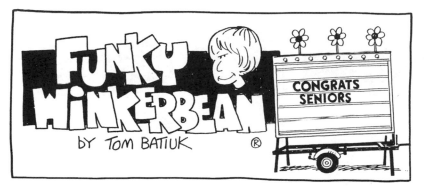

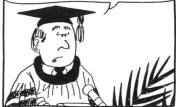

FUNKY WINKERBEAN
BY TOM BATIUK
CONGRATS SENIORS
MANY OF YOU GRADUATING SENIORS WILL BE HEADING OUT INTO THE WORLD TO LOOK FOR A JOB!
OTHERS WILL BE GOING OFF TO COLLEGE... WHILE YOUR PARENTS HEAD OUT TO LOOK FOR A SECOND JOB!
BEING AN EDUCATOR IS A LOT LIKE BEING AN AUTOMAKER!
BATIUK
EACH YEAR WE WATCH THE NEW MODELS ROLL OFF THE LINE...
ZZZZ
© News America Syndicate 1985
5-26
AND WE ONLY SEEM TO RECALL THE ONES THAT GAVE US PROBLEMS!
ZZZZ

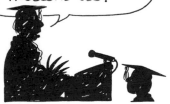

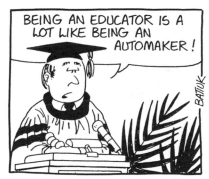

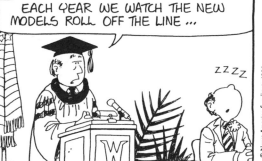

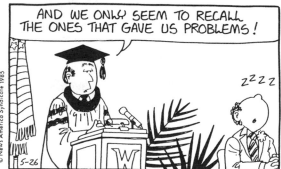

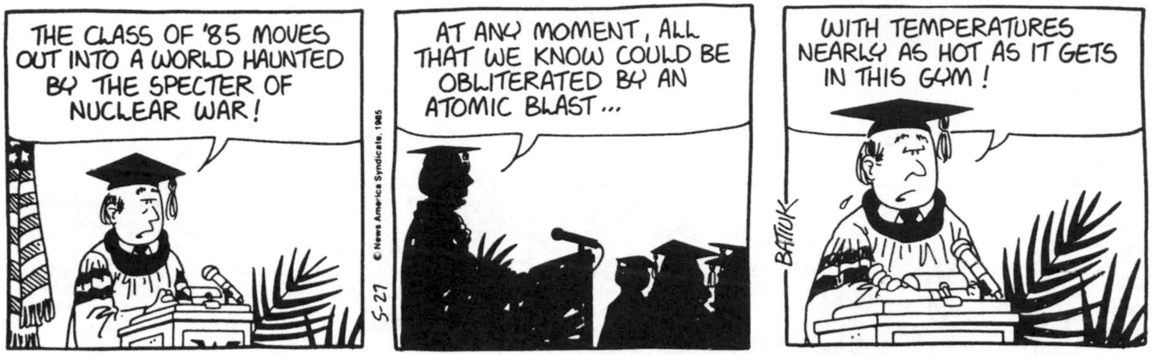
THE CLASS OF '85 MOVES OUT INTO A WORLD HAUNTED BY THE SPECTER OF NUCLEAR WAR!
AT ANY MOMENT, ALL THAT WE KNOW COULD BE OBLITERATED BY AN ATOMIC BLAST...
WITH TEMPERATURES NEARLY AS HOT AS IT GETS IN THIS GYM!
5-27
© News America Syndicate, 1985
BATIUK

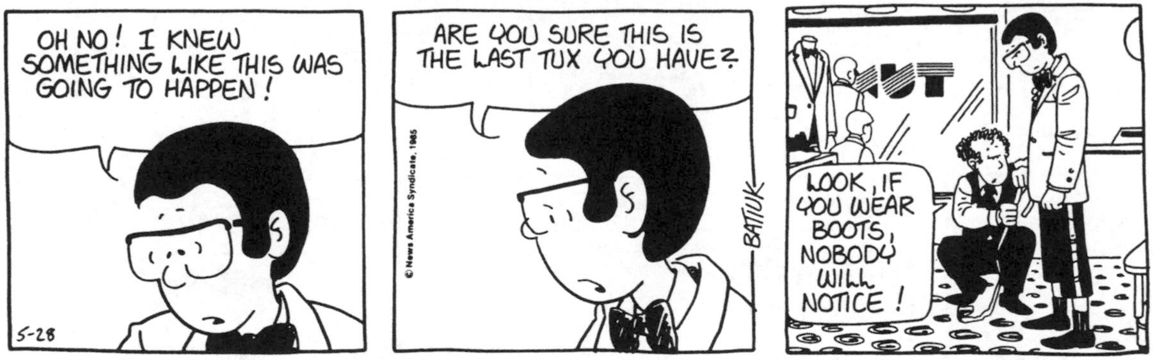
OH NO! I KNEW SOMETHING LIKE THIS WAS GOING TO HAPPEN!
ARE YOU SURE THIS IS THE LAST TUX YOU HAVE?
LOOK, IF YOU WEAR BOOTS, NOBODY WILL NOTICE!
5-28
© News America Syndicate, 1985
BATIUK

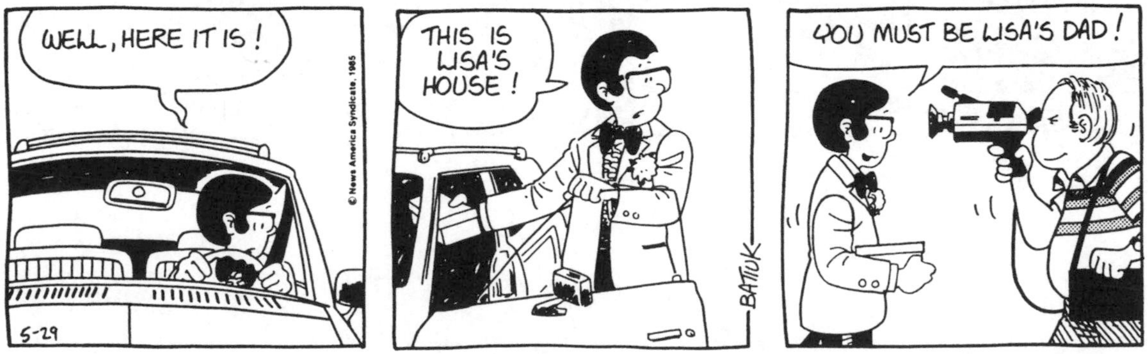
WELL, HERE IT IS!
THIS IS LISA'S HOUSE!
YOU MUST BE LISA'S DAD!
5-29
© News America Syndicate, 1985
BATIUK

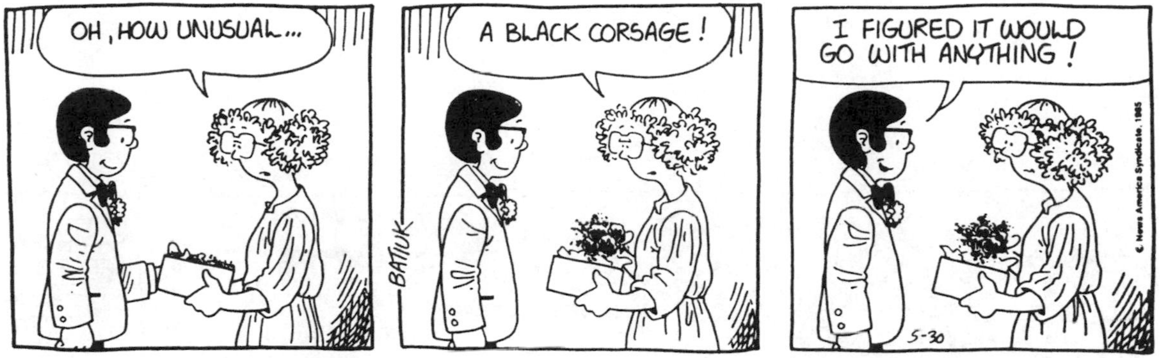
OH, HOW UNUSUAL...
A BLACK CORSAGE!
I FIGURED IT WOULD GO WITH ANYTHING!
BATIUK
© News America Syndicate, 1985
5-30

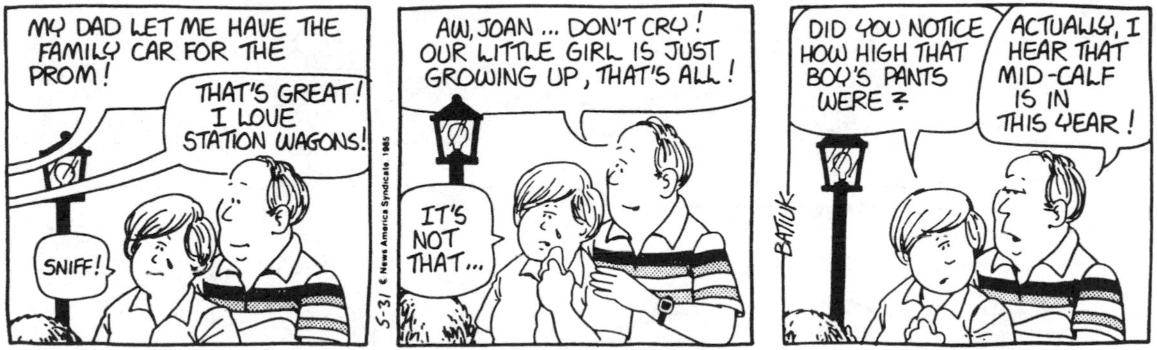
MY DAD LET ME HAVE THE FAMILY CAR FOR THE PROM!
THAT'S GREAT! I LOVE STATION WAGONS!
SNIFF!
5-31 © News America Syndicate, 1985
AW, JOAN ... DON'T CRY! OUR LITTLE GIRL IS JUST GROWING UP, THAT'S ALL!
IT'S NOT THAT...
DID YOU NOTICE HOW HIGH THAT BOY'S PANTS WERE?
ACTUALLY, I HEAR THAT MID-CALF IS IN THIS YEAR!
BATIUK

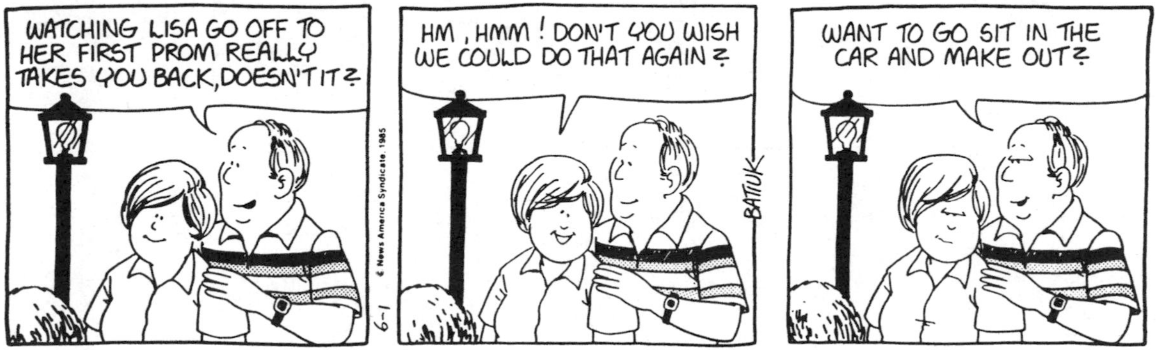
WATCHING LISA GO OFF TO HER FIRST PROM REALLY TAKES YOU BACK, DOESN'T IT?
6-1 © News America Syndicate, 1985
HM, HMM! DON'T YOU WISH WE COULD DO THAT AGAIN?
BATIUK
WANT TO GO SIT IN THE CAR AND MAKE OUT?

FUNKY WINKERBEAN BY TOM BATIUK

DID YOU HAVE ANY TROUBLE FINDING OUR HOUSE?

NO! I SPOTTED IT RIGHT AWAY THE SIXTH TIME I DROVE BY!

IS IT MY IMAGINATION...

OR ARE THESE THE SAME FRUIT CUPS THEY SERVED FOR LUNCH LAST FRIDAY?

WELL, HERE WE ARE!

THIS IS THE PROM!

6-2

I WONDER WHY EVERYONE WANTS TO GO TO THEM SO BADLY...

© News America Syndicate 1985

244

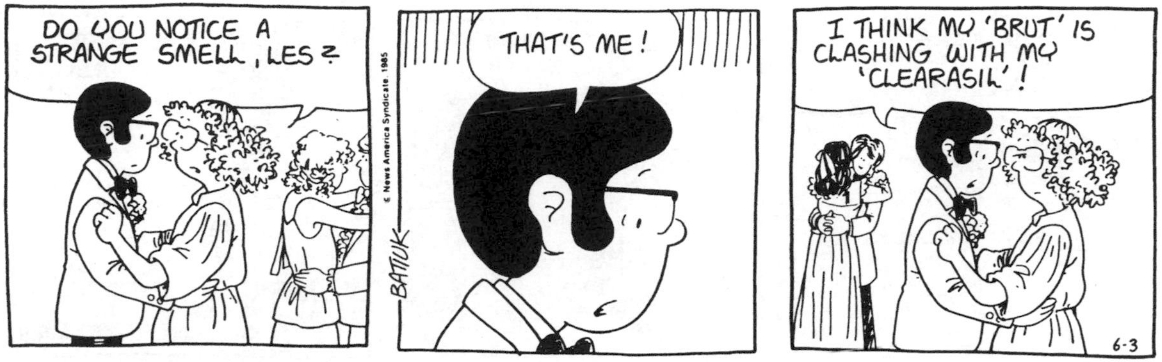
DO YOU NOTICE A STRANGE SMELL, LES?
THAT'S ME!
© News America Syndicate 1985
BATIUK
I THINK MY 'BRUT' IS CLASHING WITH MY 'CLEARASIL'!
6-3

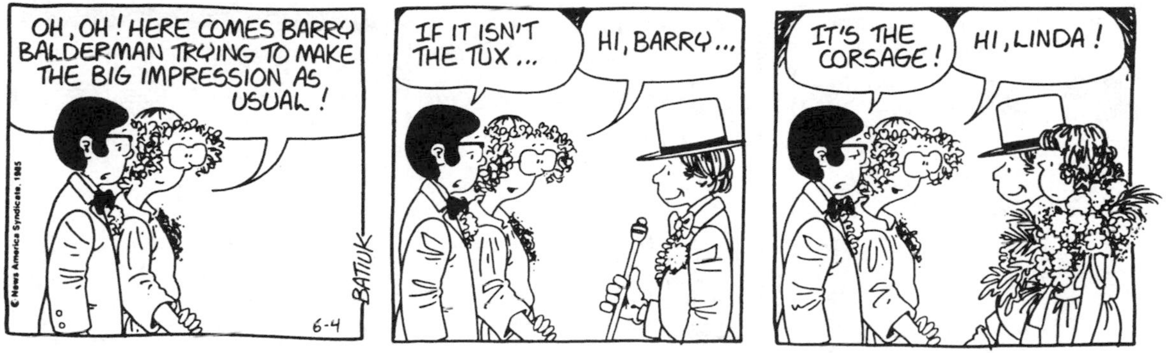
OH, OH! HERE COMES BARRY BALDERMAN TRYING TO MAKE THE BIG IMPRESSION AS USUAL!
© News America Syndicate 1985
BATIUK
6-4
IF IT ISN'T THE TUX...
HI, BARRY...
IT'S THE CORSAGE!
HI, LINDA!

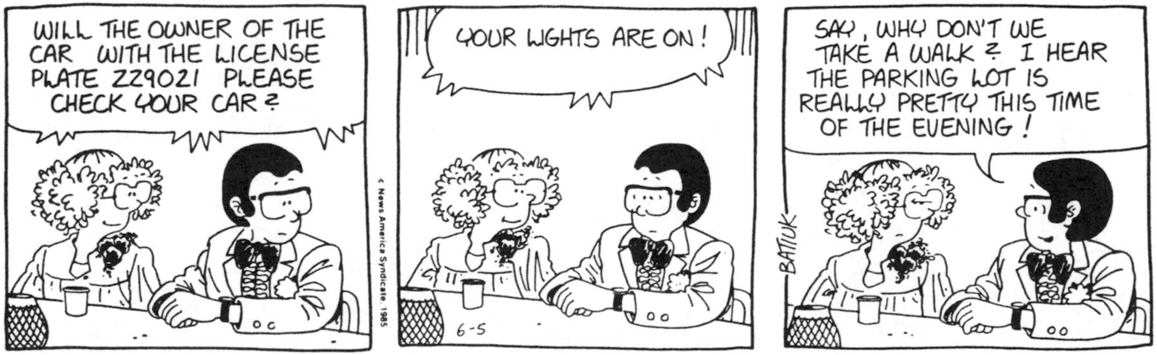
WILL THE OWNER OF THE CAR WITH THE LICENSE PLATE ZZ9021 PLEASE CHECK YOUR CAR?
YOUR LIGHTS ARE ON!
© News America Syndicate 1985
6-5
BATIUK
SAY, WHY DON'T WE TAKE A WALK? I HEAR THE PARKING LOT IS REALLY PRETTY THIS TIME OF THE EVENING!

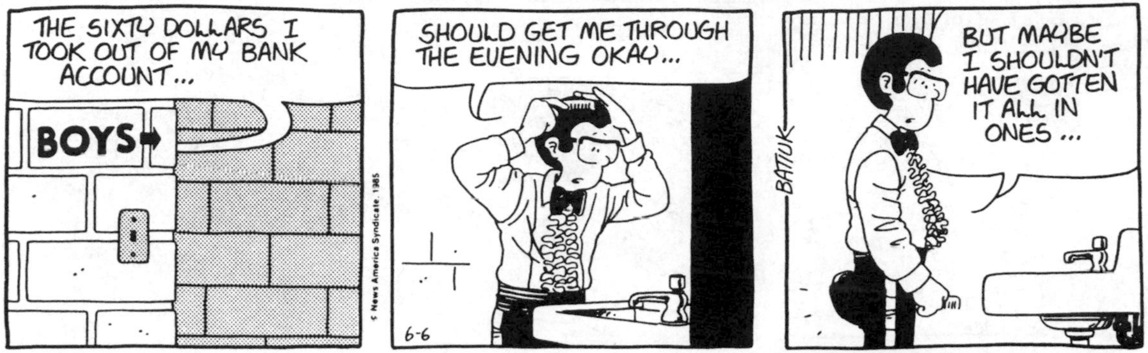
THE SIXTY DOLLARS I TOOK OUT OF MY BANK ACCOUNT...
BOYS
SHOULD GET ME THROUGH THE EVENING OKAY...
© News America Syndicate, 1985
6-6
BUT MAYBE I SHOULDN'T HAVE GOTTEN IT ALL IN ONES ...
BATIUK

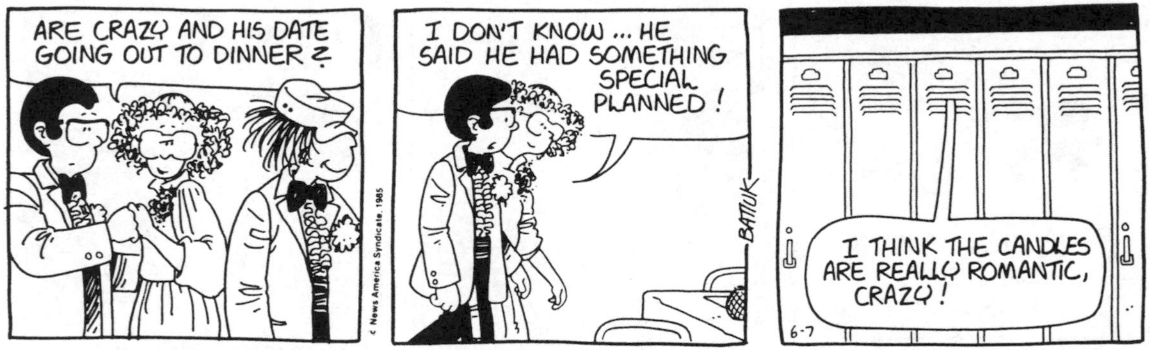
ARE CRAZY AND HIS DATE GOING OUT TO DINNER?
© News America Syndicate, 1985
I DON'T KNOW ... HE SAID HE HAD SOMETHING SPECIAL PLANNED!
BATIUK
I THINK THE CANDLES ARE REALLY ROMANTIC, CRAZY!
6-7

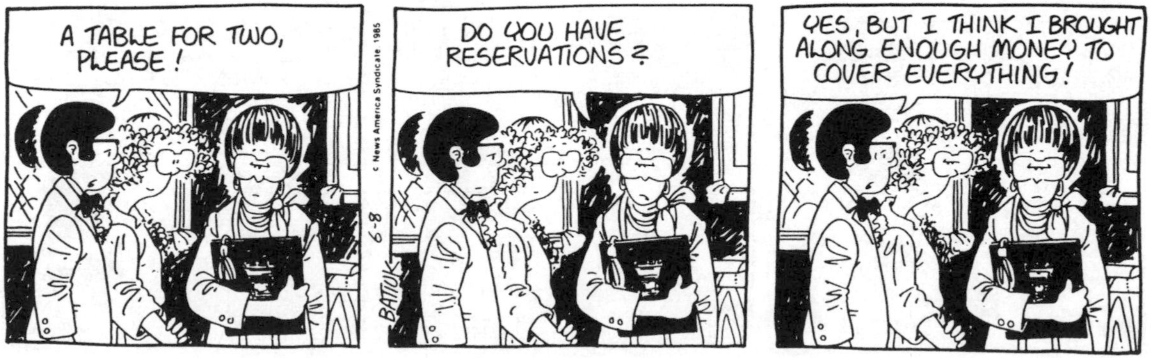
A TABLE FOR TWO, PLEASE!
© News America Syndicate, 1985
6-8
BATIUK
DO YOU HAVE RESERVATIONS?
YES, BUT I THINK I BROUGHT ALONG ENOUGH MONEY TO COVER EVERYTHING!

FUNKY WINKERBEAN
BY TOM BATIUK
I'M SORRY I KEEP STEPPING ON YOUR DRESS!
DON'T WORRY! IT'S A LITTLE TOO LONG!
AT LEAST YOU DON'T HAVE THAT PROBLEM WITH YOUR PANTS!
WELL, GOODNIGHT, LISA...
GOODNIGHT, LES...
6-9
BATIUK
© News America Syndicate. 1985
UH, COULD WE DO THAT AGAIN? I ONLY GOT ONE LIP!

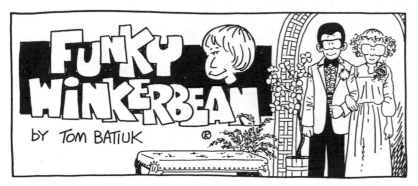

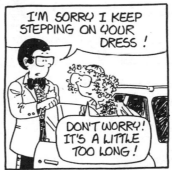

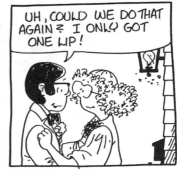

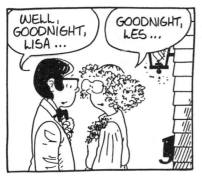

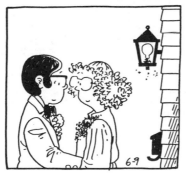

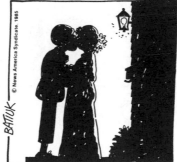

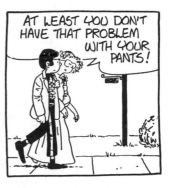

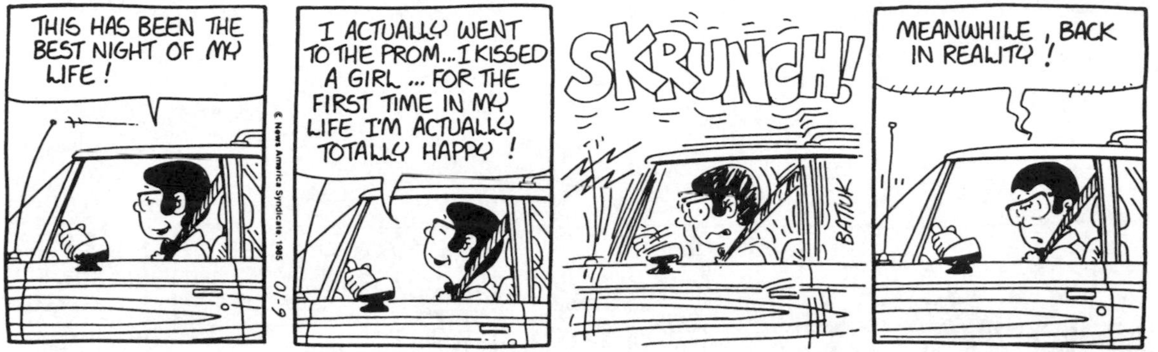
THIS HAS BEEN THE BEST NIGHT OF MY LIFE!
© News America Syndicate 1985
6-10
I ACTUALLY WENT TO THE PROM...I KISSED A GIRL ... FOR THE FIRST TIME IN MY LIFE I'M ACTUALLY TOTALLY HAPPY!
SKRUNCH!
BATIUK
MEANWHILE, BACK IN REALITY!

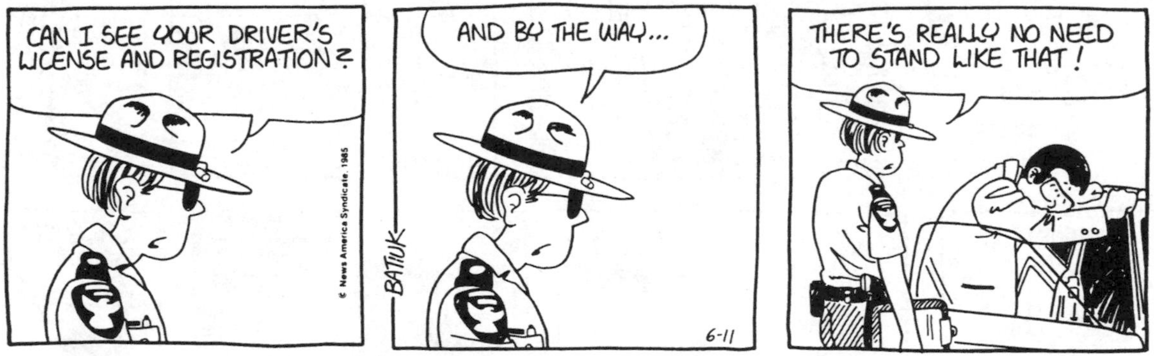
CAN I SEE YOUR DRIVER'S LICENSE AND REGISTRATION?
© News America Syndicate 1985
BATIUK
AND BY THE WAY...
6-11
THERE'S REALLY NO NEED TO STAND LIKE THAT!

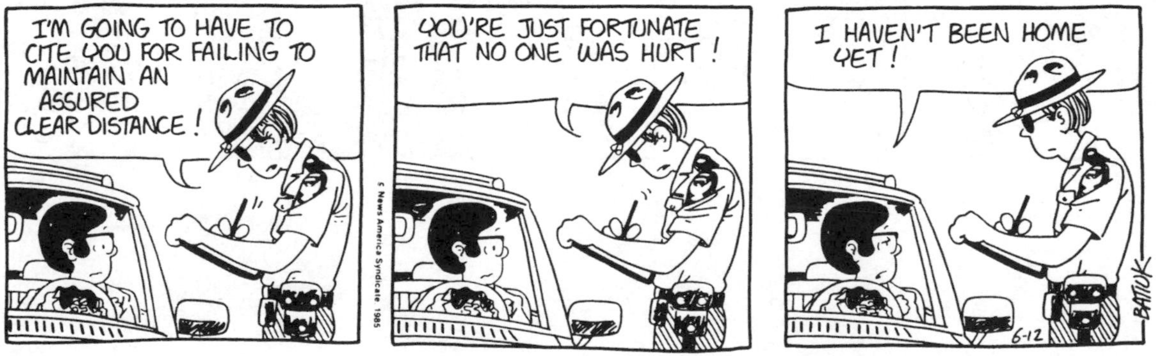
I'M GOING TO HAVE TO CITE YOU FOR FAILING TO MAINTAIN AN ASSURED CLEAR DISTANCE!
© News America Syndicate 1985
YOU'RE JUST FORTUNATE THAT NO ONE WAS HURT!
I HAVEN'T BEEN HOME YET!
BATIUK
6-12

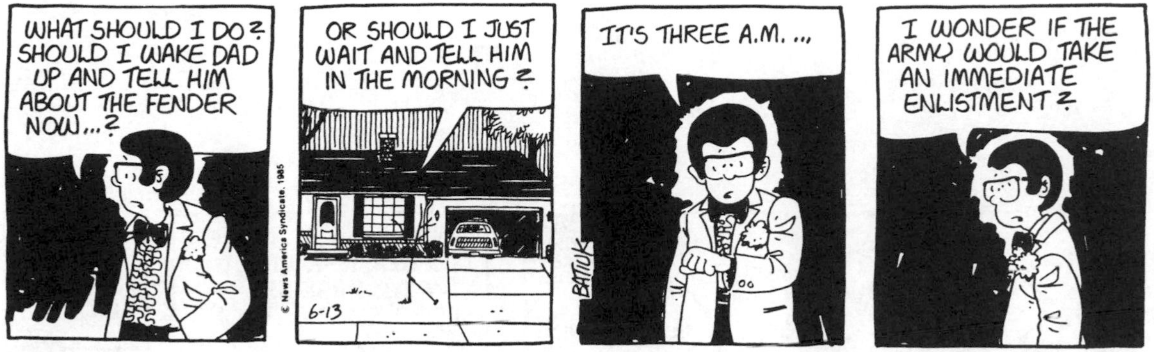
WHAT SHOULD I DO? SHOULD I WAKE DAD UP AND TELL HIM ABOUT THE FENDER NOW...?
OR SHOULD I JUST WAIT AND TELL HIM IN THE MORNING?
IT'S THREE A.M. ...
I WONDER IF THE ARMY WOULD TAKE AN IMMEDIATE ENLISTMENT?
© News America Syndicate. 1985
6-13
BATIUK

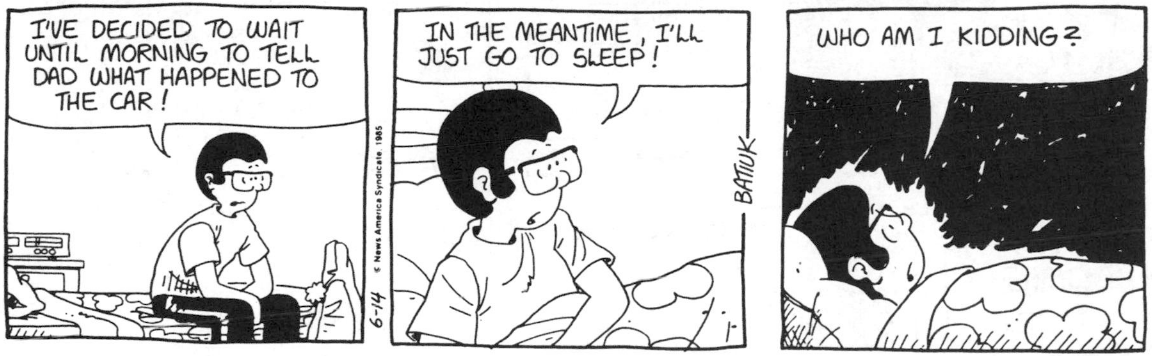
I'VE DECIDED TO WAIT UNTIL MORNING TO TELL DAD WHAT HAPPENED TO THE CAR!
IN THE MEANTIME, I'LL JUST GO TO SLEEP!
WHO AM I KIDDING?
© News America Syndicate. 1985
6-14
BATIUK

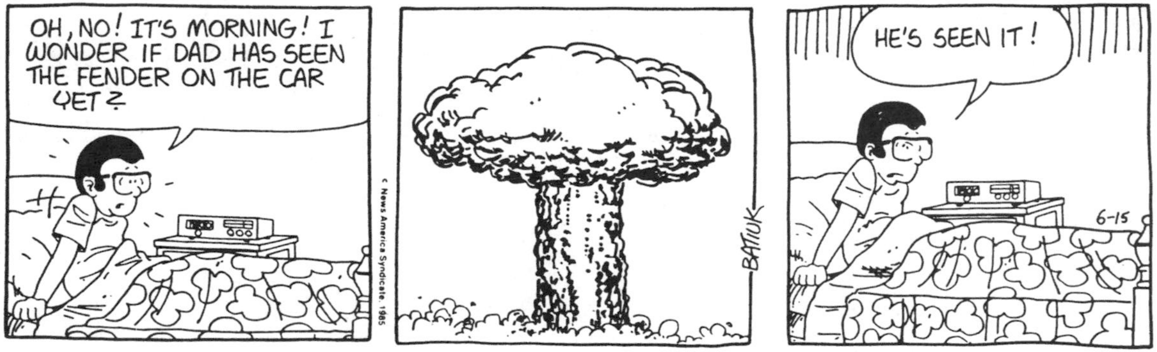
OH, NO! IT'S MORNING! I WONDER IF DAD HAS SEEN THE FENDER ON THE CAR YET?
HE'S SEEN IT!
© News America Syndicate. 1985
BATIUK
6-15

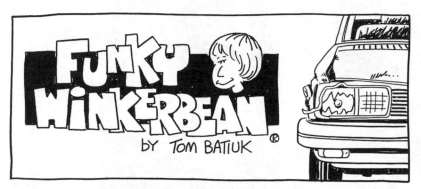

FUNKY WINKERBEAN
BY TOM BATIUK ®
WHO KNOWS? MAYBE DAD WON'T BE UPSET AT ALL WHEN HE SEES THE FENDER ON THE CAR!
THAT'S PRETTY GOOD! MAYBE I SHOULD CONSIDER STAND-UP COMEDY AS A CAREER!
WHAT ON EARTH WERE YOU DOING!!?
6-16
HOW COULD YOU JUST RUN INTO A CAR THAT WAS RIGHT IN FRONT OF YOU LIKE THAT!!?
I DON'T KNOW...
BATIUK
MAYBE IT WAS MAGNETIC!
© News America Syndicate, 1985

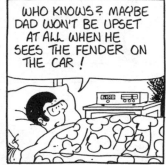

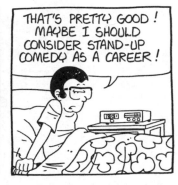

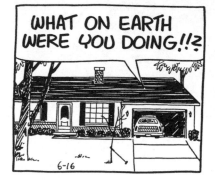

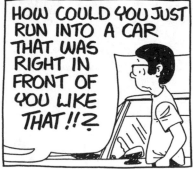

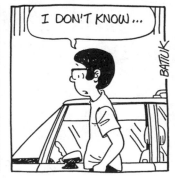

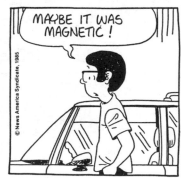

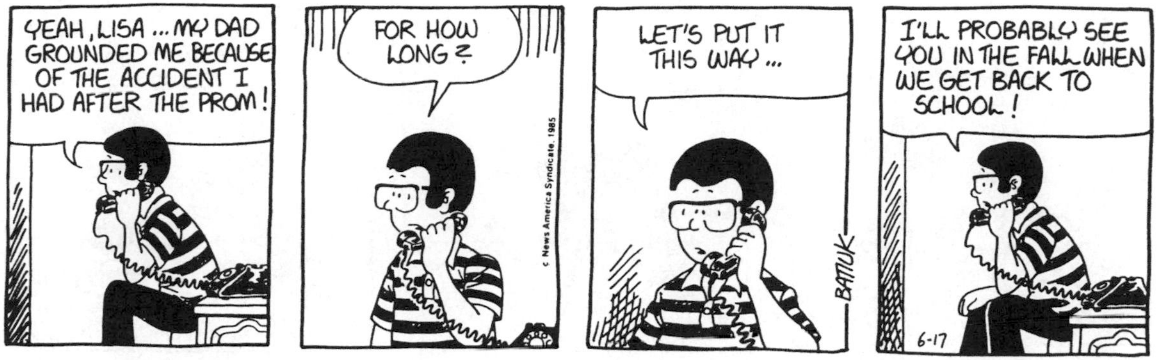
YEAH, LISA ... MY DAD GROUNDED ME BECAUSE OF THE ACCIDENT I HAD AFTER THE PROM!
FOR HOW LONG?
© News America Syndicate, 1985
LET'S PUT IT THIS WAY ...
BATIUK
I'LL PROBABLY SEE YOU IN THE FALL WHEN WE GET BACK TO SCHOOL!
6-17

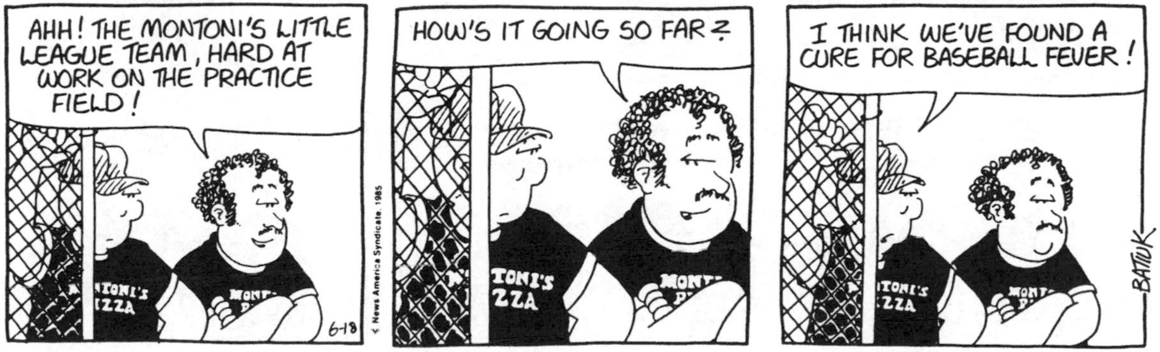
AHH! THE MONTONI'S LITTLE LEAGUE TEAM, HARD AT WORK ON THE PRACTICE FIELD!
6-18
© News America Syndicate, 1985
HOW'S IT GOING SO FAR?
I THINK WE'VE FOUND A CURE FOR BASEBALL FEVER!
BATIUK

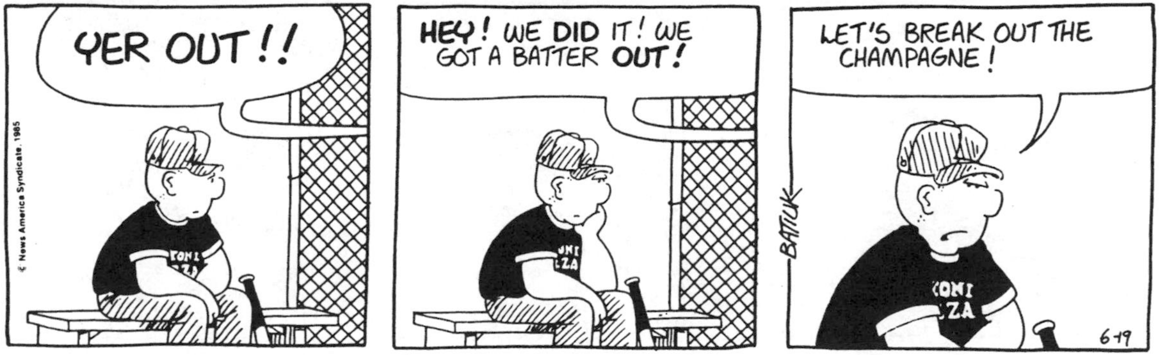
© News America Syndicate, 1985
YER OUT!!
HEY! WE DID IT! WE GOT A BATTER OUT!
BATIUK
LET'S BREAK OUT THE CHAMPAGNE!
6-19

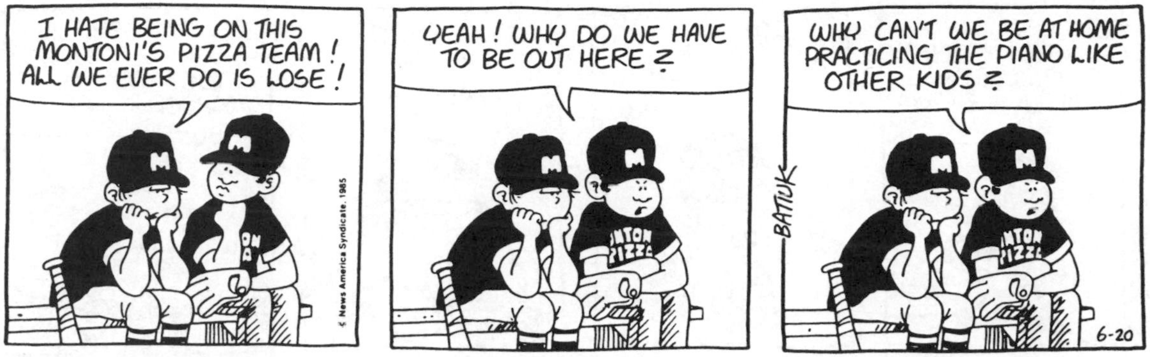
I HATE BEING ON THIS MONTONI'S PIZZA TEAM! ALL WE EVER DO IS LOSE!
YEAH! WHY DO WE HAVE TO BE OUT HERE?
WHY CAN'T WE BE AT HOME PRACTICING THE PIANO LIKE OTHER KIDS?
© News America Syndicate, 1985
BATIUK
6-20

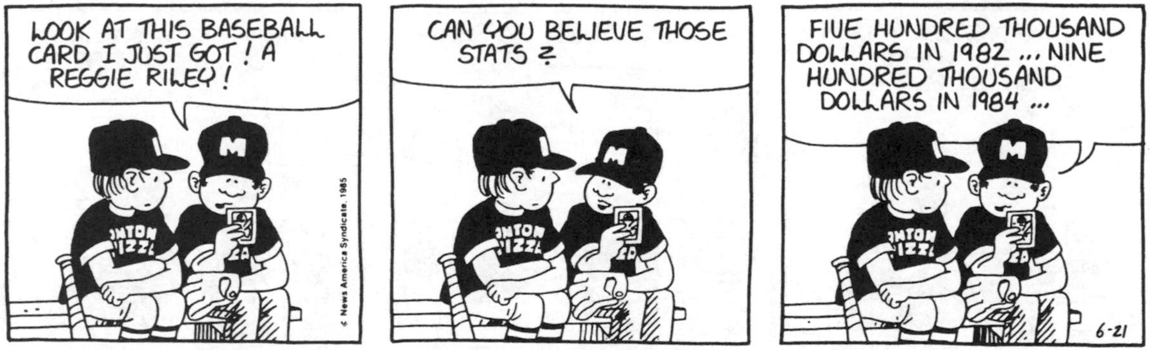
LOOK AT THIS BASEBALL CARD I JUST GOT! A REGGIE RILEY!
CAN YOU BELIEVE THOSE STATS?
FIVE HUNDRED THOUSAND DOLLARS IN 1982 ... NINE HUNDRED THOUSAND DOLLARS IN 1984 ...
© News America Syndicate, 1985
6-21

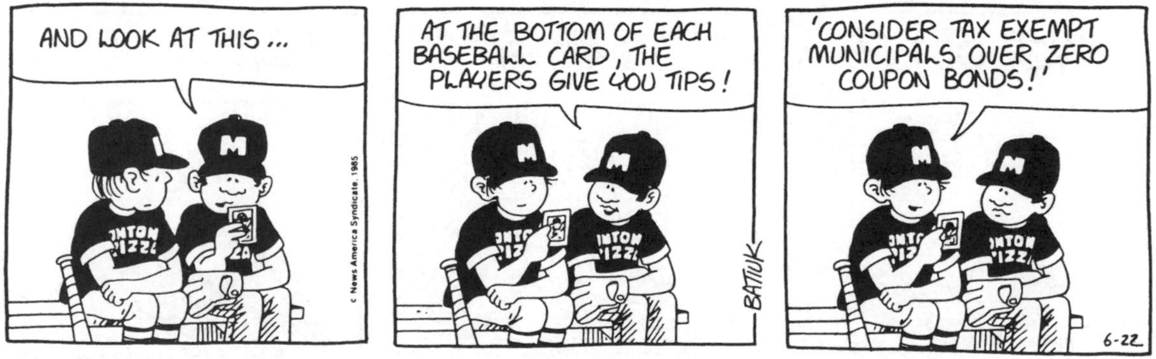
AND LOOK AT THIS ...
AT THE BOTTOM OF EACH BASEBALL CARD, THE PLAYERS GIVE YOU TIPS!
'CONSIDER TAX EXEMPT MUNICIPALS OVER ZERO COUPON BONDS!'
© News America Syndicate, 1985
BATIUK
6-22

FUNKY WINKERBEAN
®
BY TOM BATIUK
AYYYY, BATTER BATTER!
GO AHEAD! HIT ONE OVER THE FENCE! WE'LL FIND IT!!
OUR INFIELD CHATTER DEFINITELY NEEDS WORK!
YOU GUYS STINK!!
YOU'RE A BUNCH OF SORRY LOSERS!
THAT'S A LIE!
THEY'RE NOT SORRY!
BATIUK
© News America Syndicate, 1985
6-23

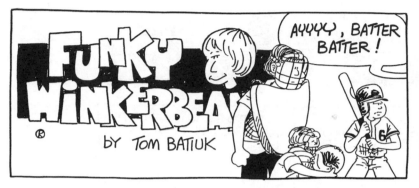

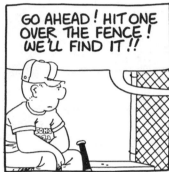

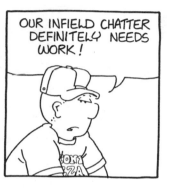

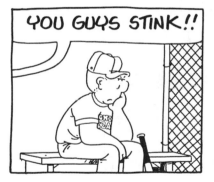

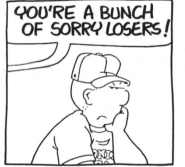

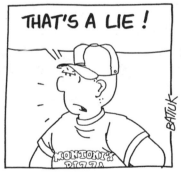

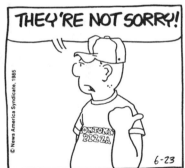

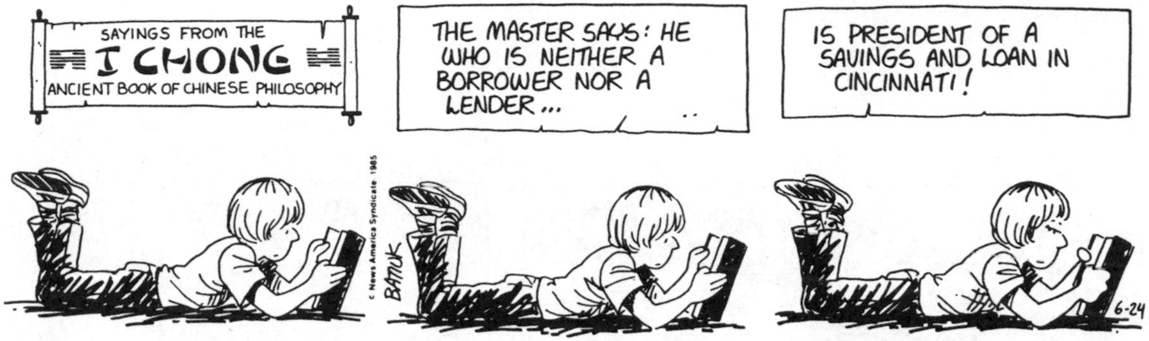
SAYINGS FROM THE I CHONG ANCIENT BOOK OF CHINESE PHILOSOPHY
THE MASTER SAYS: HE WHO IS NEITHER A BORROWER NOR A LENDER...
IS PRESIDENT OF A SAVINGS AND LOAN IN CINCINNATI!
© News America Syndicate 1985
BATIUK
6-24

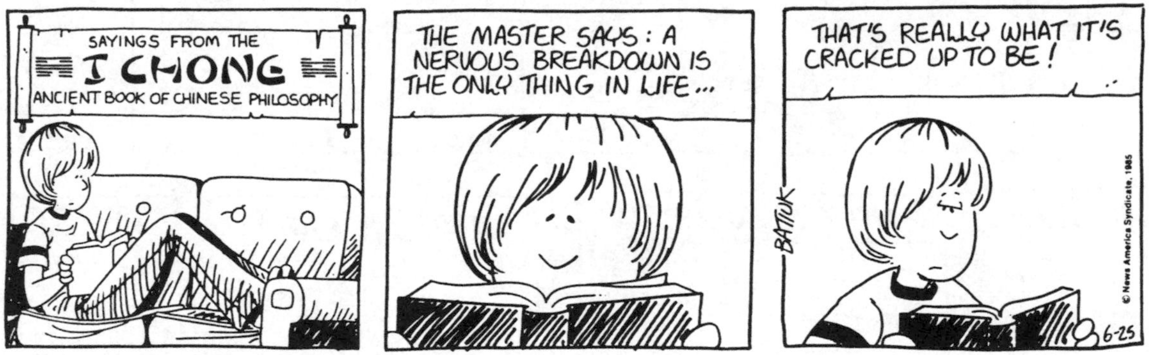
SAYINGS FROM THE I CHONG ANCIENT BOOK OF CHINESE PHILOSOPHY
THE MASTER SAYS: A NERVOUS BREAKDOWN IS THE ONLY THING IN LIFE...
THAT'S REALLY WHAT IT'S CRACKED UP TO BE!
BATIUK
© News America Syndicate, 1985
6-25

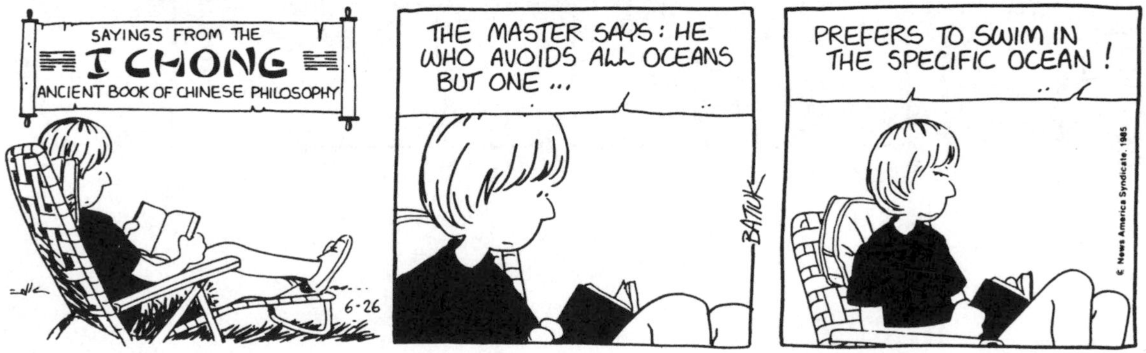
SAYINGS FROM THE I CHONG ANCIENT BOOK OF CHINESE PHILOSOPHY
6-26
THE MASTER SAYS: HE WHO AVOIDS ALL OCEANS BUT ONE...
BATIUK
PREFERS TO SWIM IN THE SPECIFIC OCEAN!
© News America Syndicate, 1985

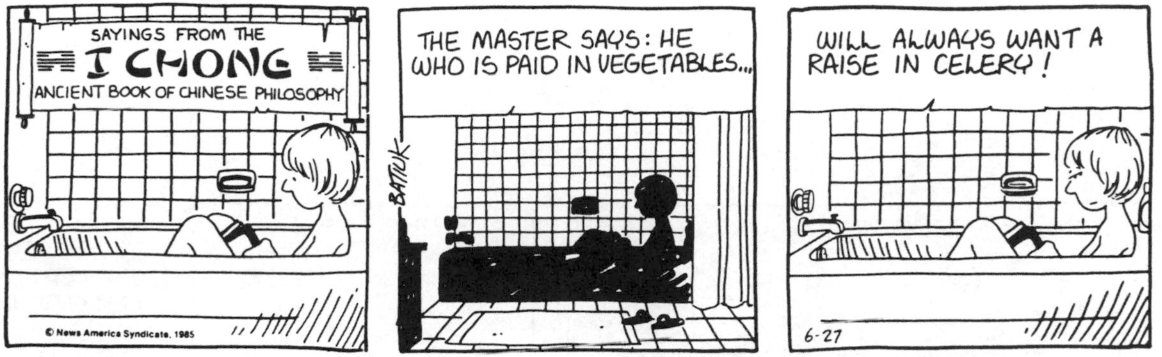
SAYINGS FROM THE
I CHONG
ANCIENT BOOK OF CHINESE PHILOSOPHY
© News America Syndicate, 1985
THE MASTER SAYS: HE WHO IS PAID IN VEGETABLES...
BATIUK
WILL ALWAYS WANT A RAISE IN CELERY!
6-27

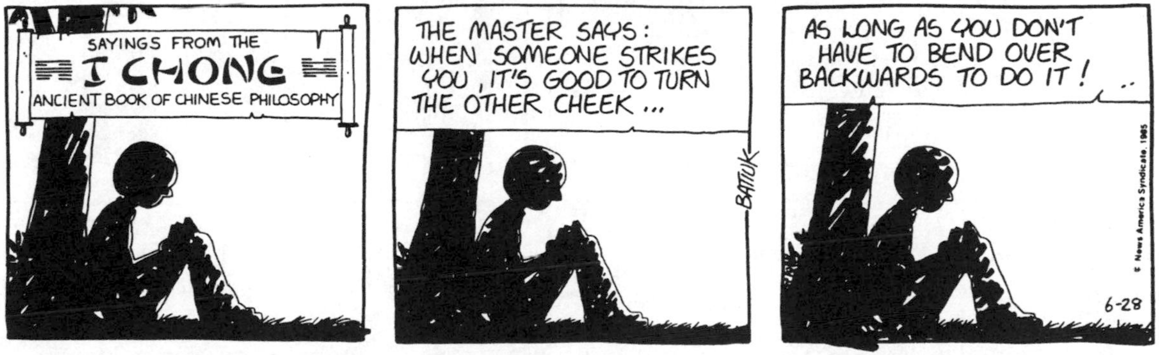
SAYINGS FROM THE
I CHONG
ANCIENT BOOK OF CHINESE PHILOSOPHY
THE MASTER SAYS: WHEN SOMEONE STRIKES YOU, IT'S GOOD TO TURN THE OTHER CHEEK...
BATIUK
AS LONG AS YOU DON'T HAVE TO BEND OVER BACKWARDS TO DO IT!
© News America Syndicate, 1985
6-28

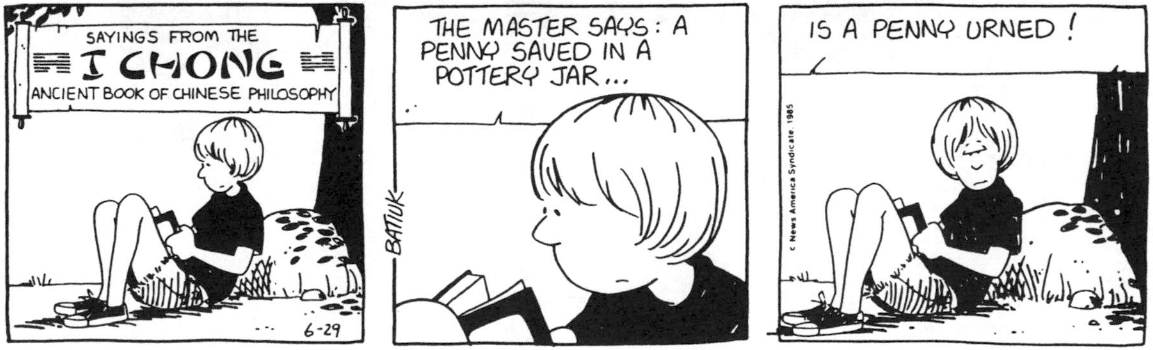
SAYINGS FROM THE
I CHONG
ANCIENT BOOK OF CHINESE PHILOSOPHY
6-29
THE MASTER SAYS: A PENNY SAVED IN A POTTERY JAR...
BATIUK
IS A PENNY URNED!
© News America Syndicate, 1985

Funky Winkerbean
by Tom Batiuk

MONTONI'S PIZZA

SAME DAY DELIVERY!

MY FATHER'S FIRST ATTEMPT AT THE PIZZA BUSINESS WAS A REAL BUST!

TO THIS DAY, HE'S CONVINCED THAT A COMBINATION PIZZERIA-CARWASH WAS THE WAY TO GO!

I ALWAYS FEEL KIND OF PROUD WHEN I SEE THAT FRAMED DOLLAR BILL HANGING ON THE WALL!

MY FATHER VOWED THAT THE VERY FIRST MONEY HE EARNED IN THIS PIZZA BUSINESS...

MONTONI'S PIZZA

24 HR. SERVICE

WOULD HANG ON THE WALL THERE NEXT TO THE STOVE!

YOU CAN'T IMAGINE HOW RELIEVED HE WAS THAT HE WASN'T ASKED TO MAKE CHANGE FOR A TWENTY!

6-30

© News America Syndicate, 1985

BATIUK

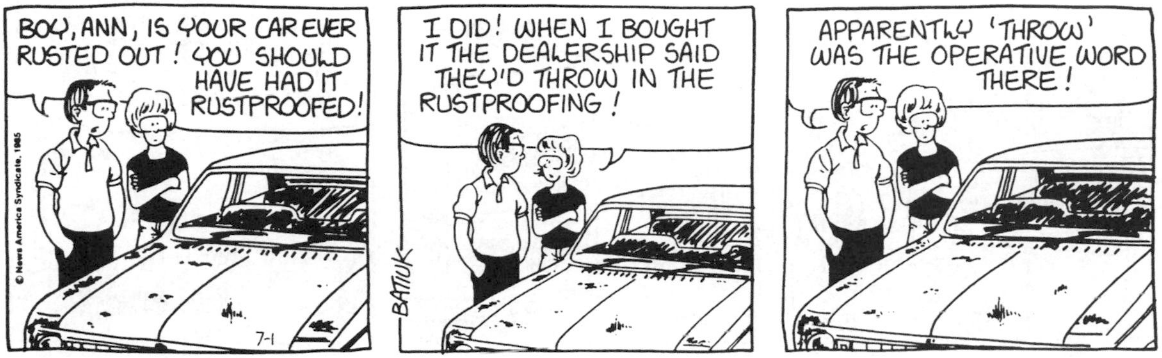
BOY, ANN, IS YOUR CAR EVER RUSTED OUT! YOU SHOULD HAVE HAD IT RUSTPROOFED!
© News America Syndicate, 1985
7-1
I DID! WHEN I BOUGHT IT THE DEALERSHIP SAID THEY'D THROW IN THE RUSTPROOFING!
BATIUK
APPARENTLY 'THROW' WAS THE OPERATIVE WORD THERE!

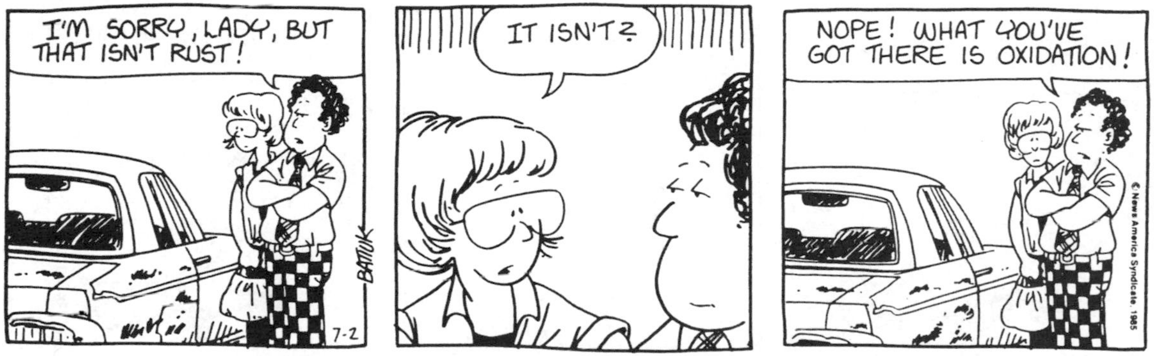
I'M SORRY, LADY, BUT THAT ISN'T RUST!
BATIUK
7-2
IT ISN'T?
NOPE! WHAT YOU'VE GOT THERE IS OXIDATION!
© News America Syndicate, 1985

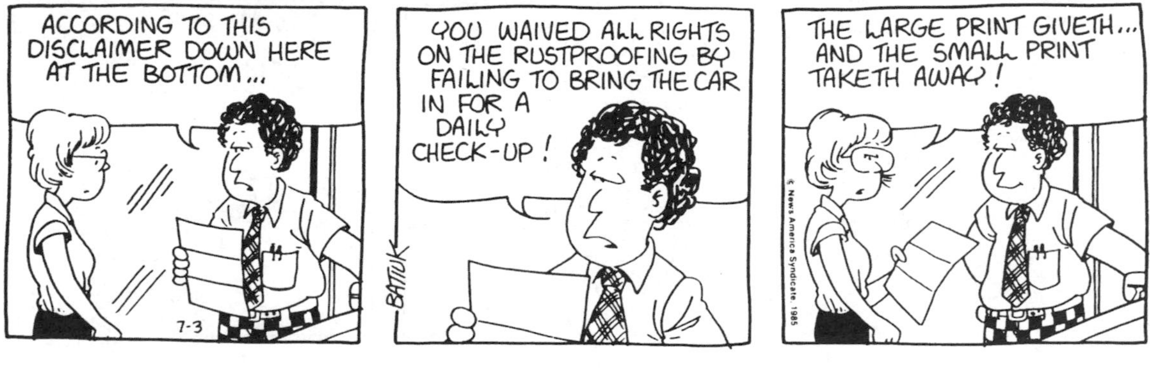
ACCORDING TO THIS DISCLAIMER DOWN HERE AT THE BOTTOM...
7-3
YOU WAIVED ALL RIGHTS ON THE RUSTPROOFING BY FAILING TO BRING THE CAR IN FOR A DAILY CHECK-UP!
BATIUK
THE LARGE PRINT GIVETH... AND THE SMALL PRINT TAKETH AWAY!
© News America Syndicate, 1985

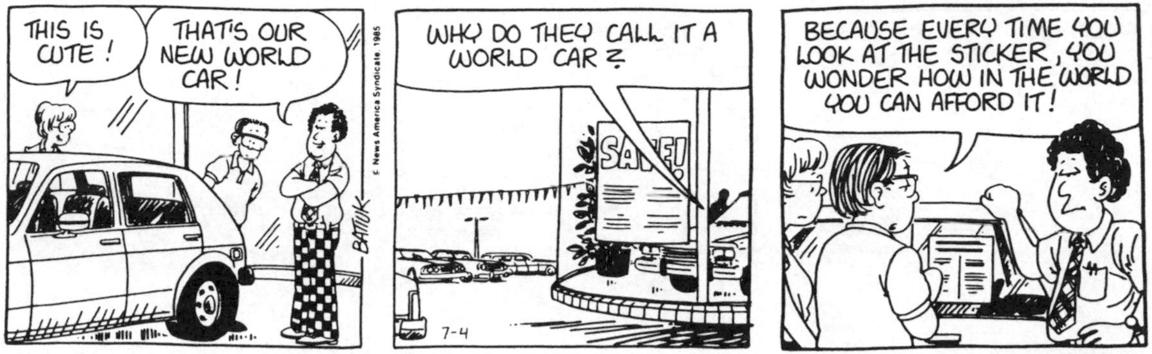
THIS IS CUTE!
THAT'S OUR NEW WORLD CAR!
WHY DO THEY CALL IT A WORLD CAR?
SAVE!
BECAUSE EVERY TIME YOU LOOK AT THE STICKER, YOU WONDER HOW IN THE WORLD YOU CAN AFFORD IT!
BATIUK
© News America Syndicate 1985
7-4

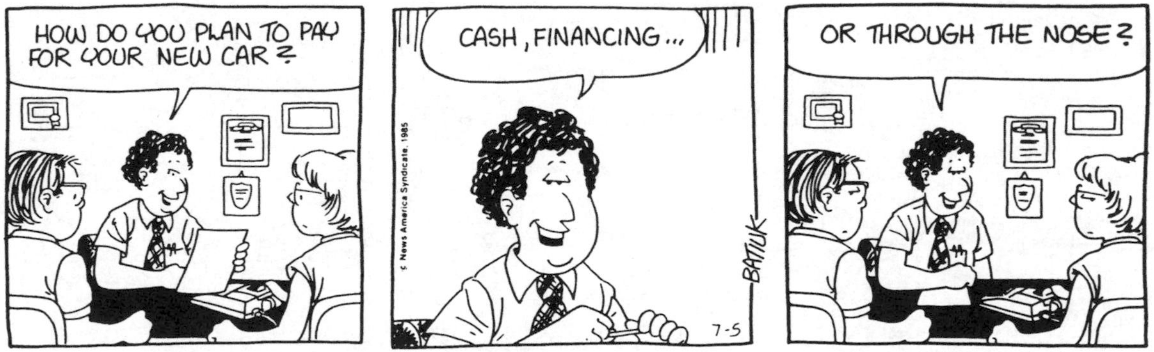
HOW DO YOU PLAN TO PAY FOR YOUR NEW CAR?
CASH, FINANCING...
OR THROUGH THE NOSE?
BATIUK
© News America Syndicate 1985
7-5

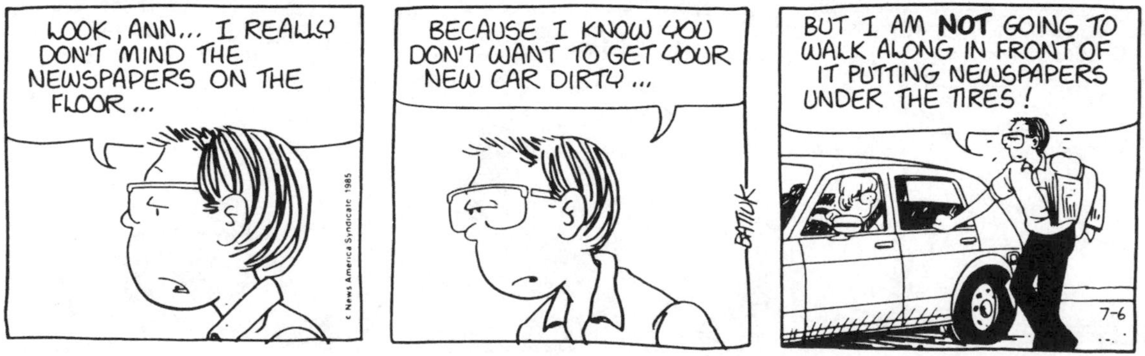
LOOK, ANN... I REALLY DON'T MIND THE NEWSPAPERS ON THE FLOOR...
BECAUSE I KNOW YOU DON'T WANT TO GET YOUR NEW CAR DIRTY...
BUT I AM **NOT** GOING TO WALK ALONG IN FRONT OF IT PUTTING NEWSPAPERS UNDER THE TIRES!
BATIUK
© News America Syndicate 1985
7-6

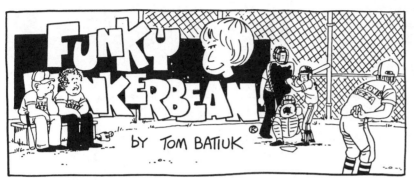

FUNKY WINKERBEAN
BY TOM BATIUK
OUR PITCHER HAS KIND OF A WILD MOVE TO FIRST BASE!
THAT WAS HIS MOVE TO HOME PLATE!
YOU REALLY LIKE TO ROTATE THE PITCHERS ON OUR TEAM, DON'T YOU, COACH?
WELL, YOUNG ARMS CAN GET HURT PRETTY EASILY...
7-7
BATIUK
SO AFTER A KID HAS FACED TWENTY OR MORE BATTERS...
I'LL USUALLY TAKE HIM OUT AND LET SOMEONE ELSE FINISH THE INNING!
© News America Syndicate, 1985

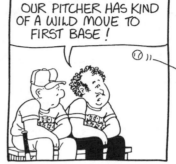

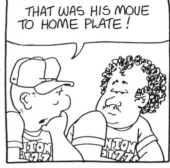

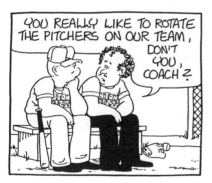

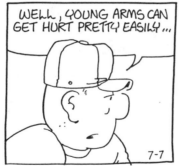

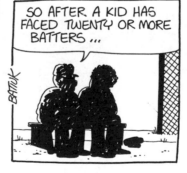

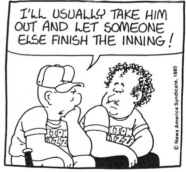

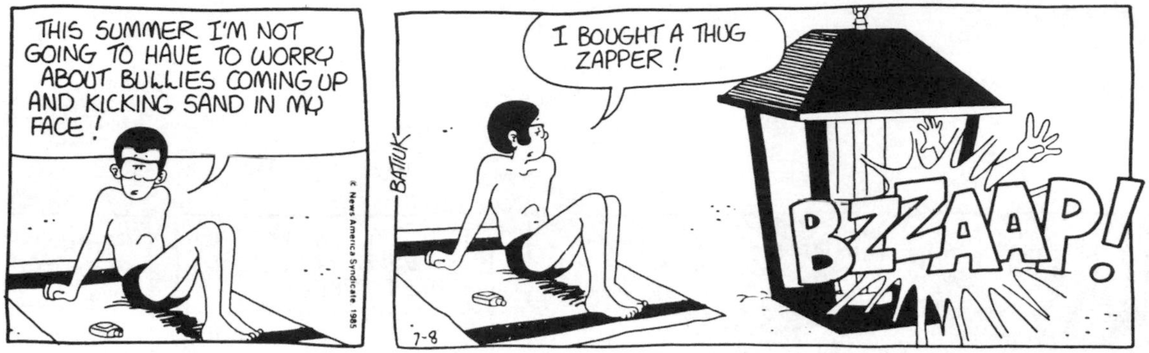
THIS SUMMER I'M NOT GOING TO HAVE TO WORRY ABOUT BULLIES COMING UP AND KICKING SAND IN MY FACE!
© News America Syndicate 1985
BATIUK
I BOUGHT A THUG ZAPPER!
BZZAAP!
7-8

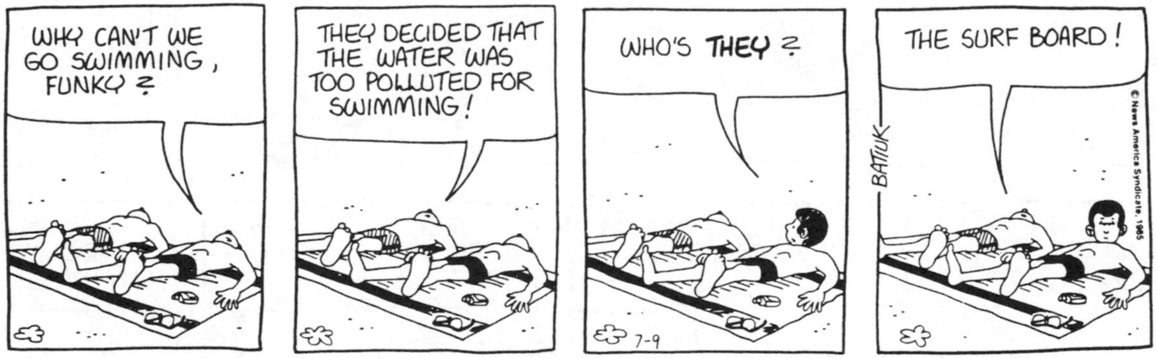
WHY CAN'T WE GO SWIMMING, FUNKY?
THEY DECIDED THAT THE WATER WAS TOO POLLUTED FOR SWIMMING!
WHO'S **THEY**?
7-9
BATIUK
THE SURF BOARD!
© News America Syndicate 1985

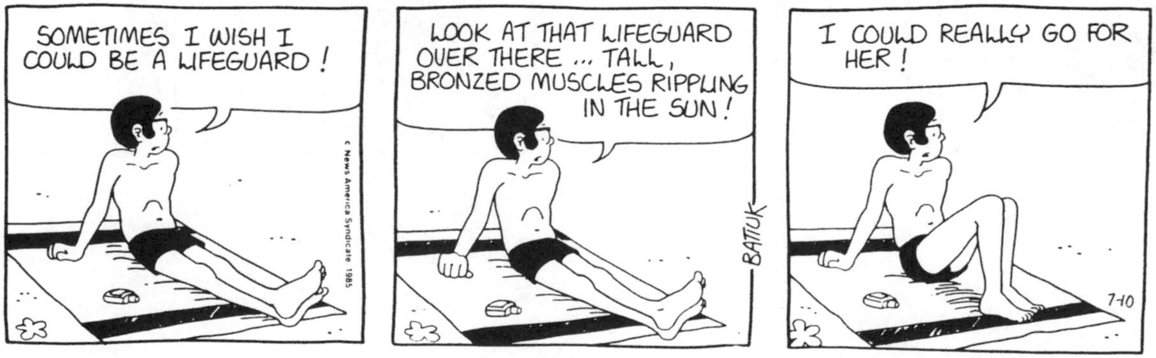
SOMETIMES I WISH I COULD BE A LIFEGUARD!
© News America Syndicate 1985
LOOK AT THAT LIFEGUARD OVER THERE ... TALL, BRONZED MUSCLES RIPPLING IN THE SUN!
BATIUK
I COULD REALLY GO FOR HER!
7-10

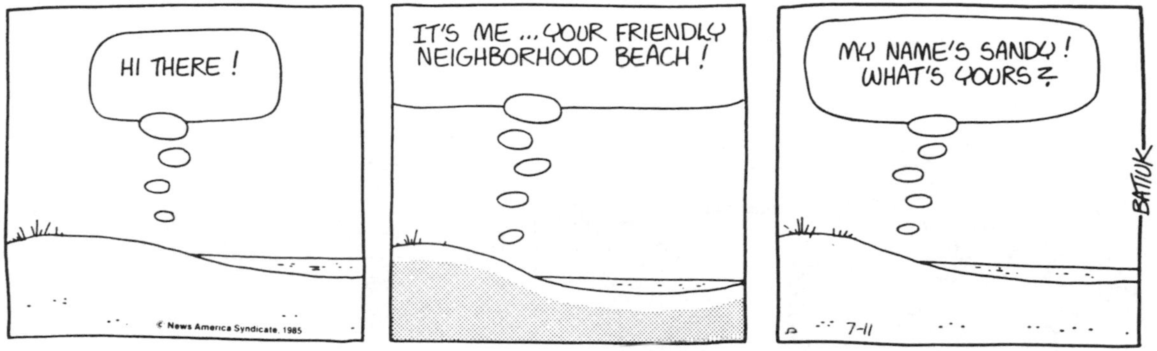
HI THERE !
© News America Syndicate. 1985
IT'S ME ... YOUR FRIENDLY NEIGHBORHOOD BEACH !
MY NAME'S SANDY ! WHAT'S YOURS ?
BATIUK
7-11

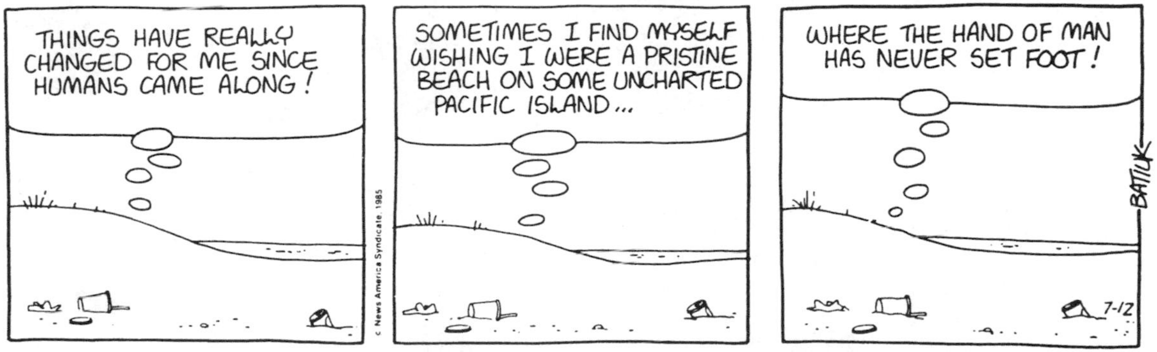
THINGS HAVE REALLY CHANGED FOR ME SINCE HUMANS CAME ALONG !
© News America Syndicate. 1985
SOMETIMES I FIND MYSELF WISHING I WERE A PRISTINE BEACH ON SOME UNCHARTED PACIFIC ISLAND ...
WHERE THE HAND OF MAN HAS NEVER SET FOOT !
BATIUK
7-12

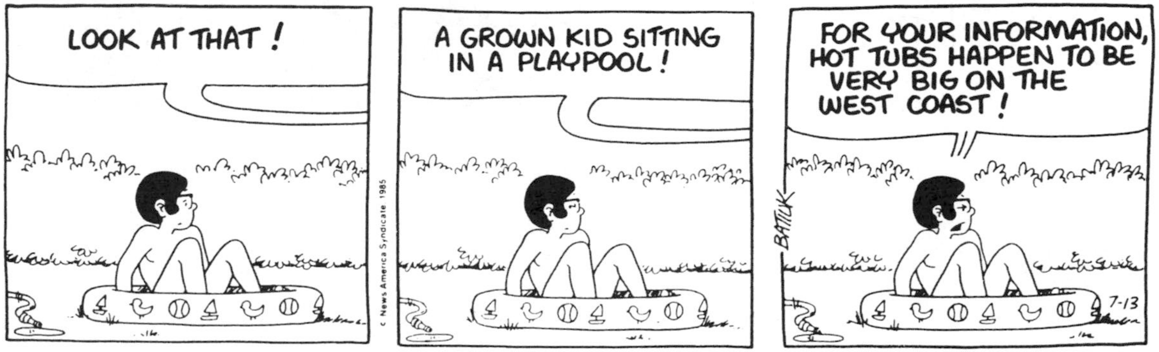
LOOK AT THAT !
© News America Syndicate. 1985
A GROWN KID SITTING IN A PLAYPOOL !
FOR YOUR INFORMATION, HOT TUBS HAPPEN TO BE VERY BIG ON THE WEST COAST !
BATIUK
7-13

Funky Winkerbean
by Tom Batiuk

Claude Barlow
(1543-1627)

FAMOUS COMPOSERS

CHAPTER TEN – CLAUDE BARLOW

TIP! TAP!

THERE'S NO QUESTION THAT CLAUDE BARLOW WAS A MUSICAL VISIONARY!

TAP! TAP!

FOR EXAMPLE, IN HIS MUSIC, HE FORESAW THE DEVELOPMENT OF THE AUTOMOBILE INDUSTRY!

EVIDENCE FOR THIS CAN BE FOUND IN HIS 'SEMI SUITE,' AN ODE TO TRUCKS...

TIP! TAP!

© News America Syndicate, 1985
7-14

AS WELL AS A PIECE HE WROTE FOR AUTOMOBILE HORNS ENTITLED 'TOOT SUITE'!

— BATIUK

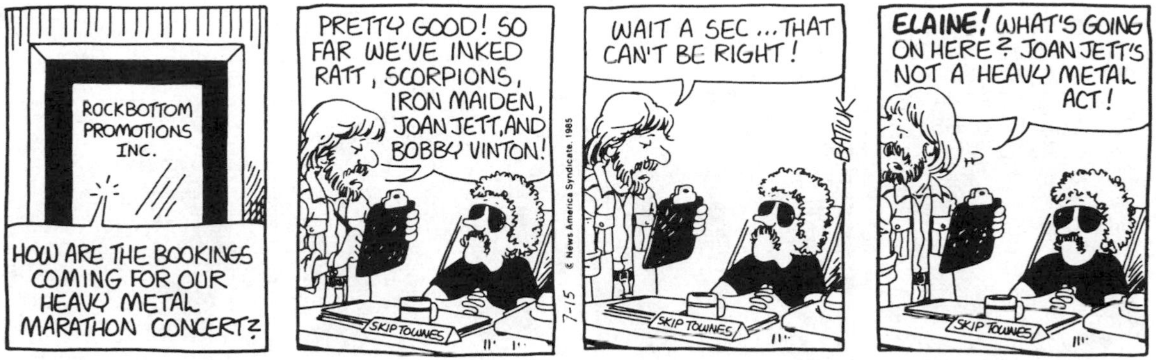
ROCKBOTTOM PROMOTIONS INC.
HOW ARE THE BOOKINGS COMING FOR OUR HEAVY METAL MARATHON CONCERT?
PRETTY GOOD! SO FAR WE'VE INKED RATT, SCORPIONS, IRON MAIDEN, JOAN JETT, AND BOBBY VINTON!
SKIP TOWNES
7-15
© News America Syndicate, 1985
WAIT A SEC... THAT CAN'T BE RIGHT!
BATIUK
ELAINE! WHAT'S GOING ON HERE? JOAN JETT'S NOT A HEAVY METAL ACT!

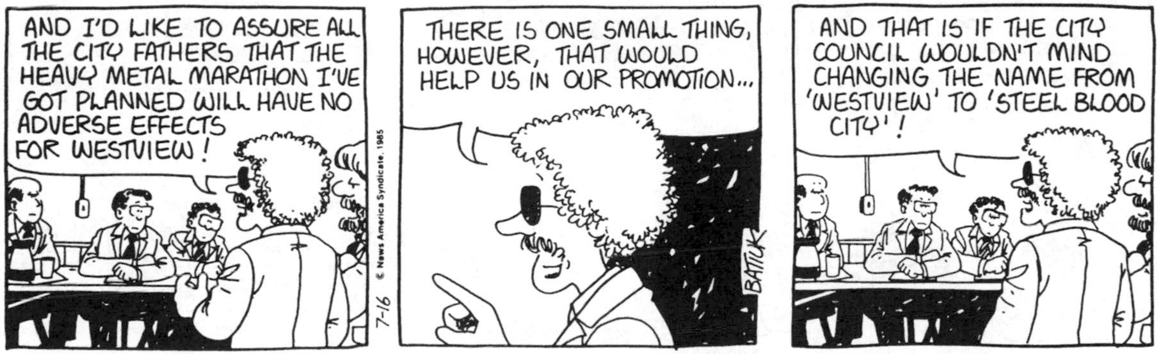
AND I'D LIKE TO ASSURE ALL THE CITY FATHERS THAT THE HEAVY METAL MARATHON I'VE GOT PLANNED WILL HAVE NO ADVERSE EFFECTS FOR WESTVIEW!
7-16
© News America Syndicate, 1985
THERE IS ONE SMALL THING, HOWEVER, THAT WOULD HELP US IN OUR PROMOTION...
BATIUK
AND THAT IS IF THE CITY COUNCIL WOULDN'T MIND CHANGING THE NAME FROM 'WESTVIEW' TO 'STEEL BLOOD CITY'!

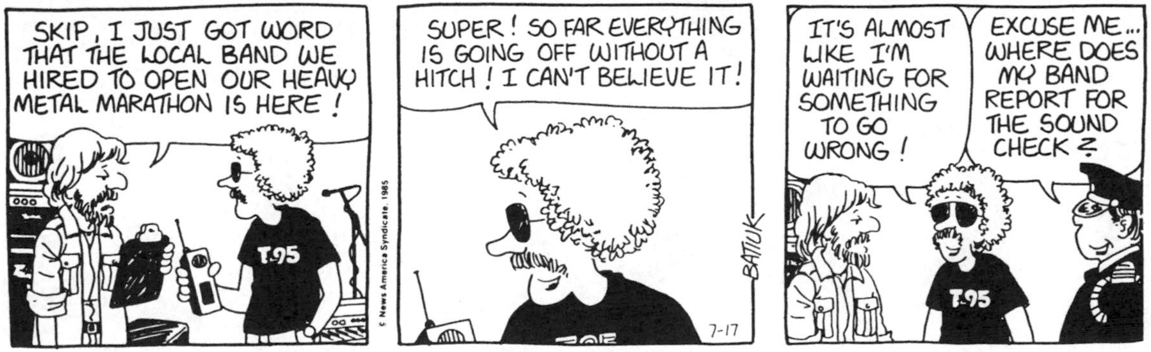
SKIP, I JUST GOT WORD THAT THE LOCAL BAND WE HIRED TO OPEN OUR HEAVY METAL MARATHON IS HERE!
T-95
© News America Syndicate, 1985
SUPER! SO FAR EVERYTHING IS GOING OFF WITHOUT A HITCH! I CAN'T BELIEVE IT!
BATIUK
7-17
IT'S ALMOST LIKE I'M WAITING FOR SOMETHING TO GO WRONG!
EXCUSE ME... WHERE DOES MY BAND REPORT FOR THE SOUND CHECK?
T-95

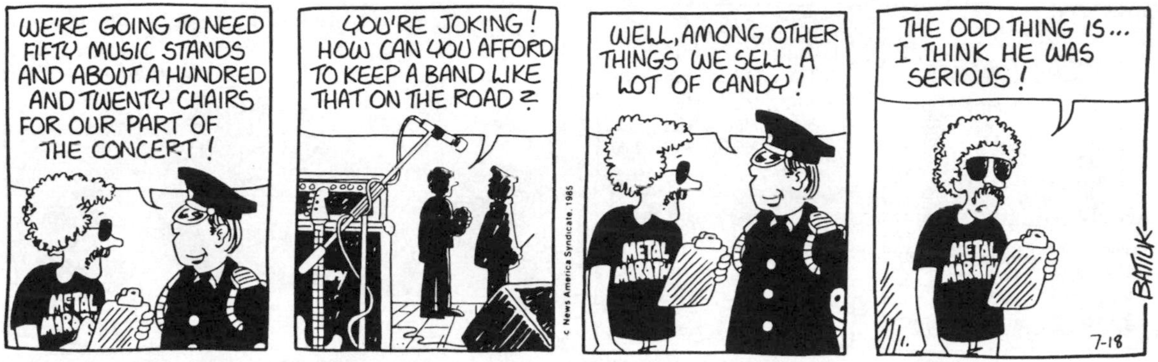
WE'RE GOING TO NEED FIFTY MUSIC STANDS AND ABOUT A HUNDRED AND TWENTY CHAIRS FOR OUR PART OF THE CONCERT!
METAL MARATHON
YOU'RE JOKING! HOW CAN YOU AFFORD TO KEEP A BAND LIKE THAT ON THE ROAD?
© News America Syndicate, 1985
WELL, AMONG OTHER THINGS WE SELL A LOT OF CANDY!
METAL MARATH
THE ODD THING IS... I THINK HE WAS SERIOUS!
METAL MARATH
BATIUK
7-18

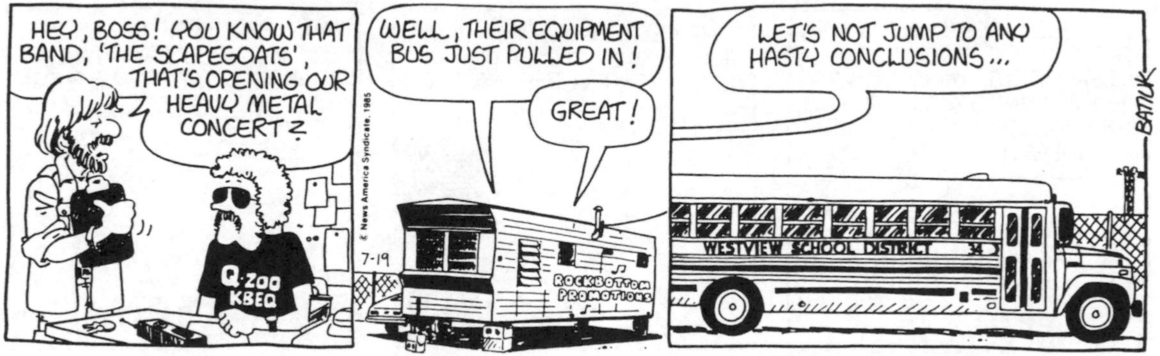
HEY, BOSS! YOU KNOW THAT BAND, 'THE SCAPEGOATS', THAT'S OPENING OUR HEAVY METAL CONCERT?
Q-ZOO KBEQ
© News America Syndicate, 1985
7-19
WELL, THEIR EQUIPMENT BUS JUST PULLED IN!
GREAT!
ROCKBOTTOM PROMOTIONS
LET'S NOT JUMP TO ANY HASTY CONCLUSIONS...
WESTVIEW SCHOOL DISTRICT 34
BATIUK

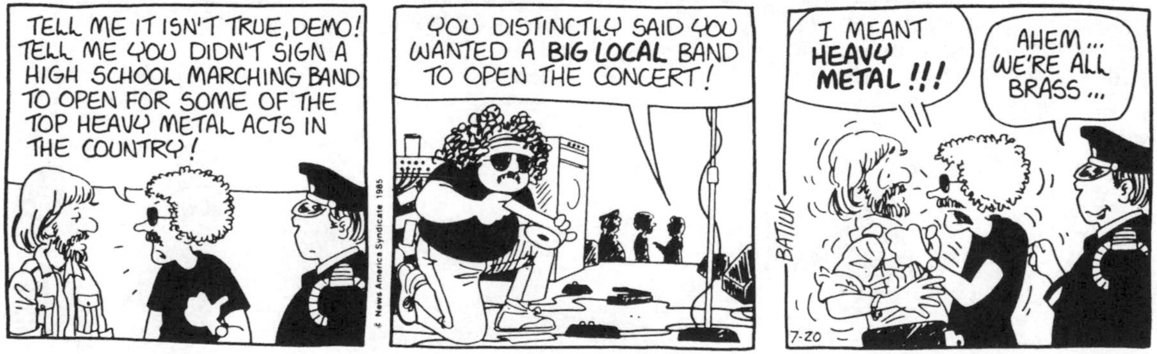
TELL ME IT ISN'T TRUE, DEMO! TELL ME YOU DIDN'T SIGN A HIGH SCHOOL MARCHING BAND TO OPEN FOR SOME OF THE TOP HEAVY METAL ACTS IN THE COUNTRY!
© News America Syndicate 1985
YOU DISTINCTLY SAID YOU WANTED A BIG LOCAL BAND TO OPEN THE CONCERT!
I MEANT HEAVY METAL!!!
AHEM... WE'RE ALL BRASS...
BATIUK
7-20

Funky Winkerbean

by Tom Batiuk

WHAT'S YOUR FAVORITE TV SHOW?

McCLOUD!

BOOM!

DRIP!

ACTUALLY, IT'S PRETTY HARD TO GET ANY RESPECT WHEN YOU'RE A SCATTERED SHOWER!

THE PEOPLE ON THE GROUND LIKE TO LOOK FOR ALL KINDS OF DIFFERENT SHAPES IN CLOUDS!

WELL, THEY'RE NOT GOING TO SEE ANYTHING IN **ME**!

© News America Syndicate, 1985

I DON'T DO IMPRESSIONS!

BATIUK

7-21

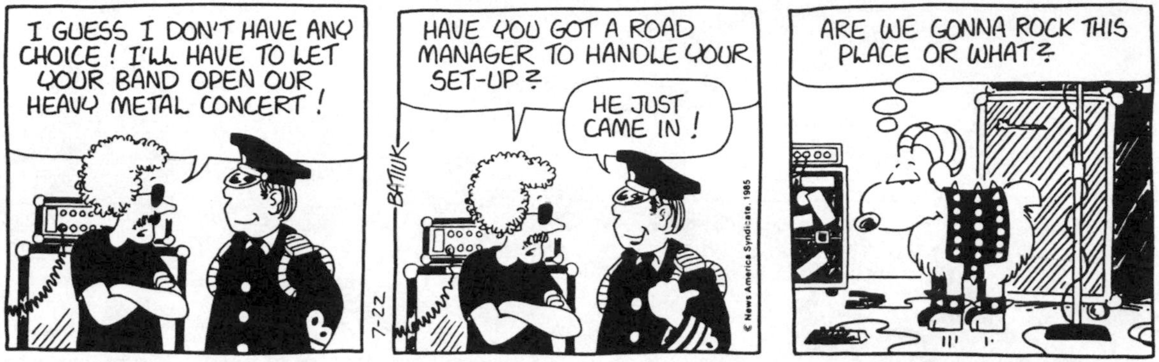
I GUESS I DON'T HAVE ANY CHOICE! I'LL HAVE TO LET YOUR BAND OPEN OUR HEAVY METAL CONCERT!
HAVE YOU GOT A ROAD MANAGER TO HANDLE YOUR SET-UP?
HE JUST CAME IN!
ARE WE GONNA ROCK THIS PLACE OR WHAT?
7-22
BATIUK
© News America Syndicate, 1985

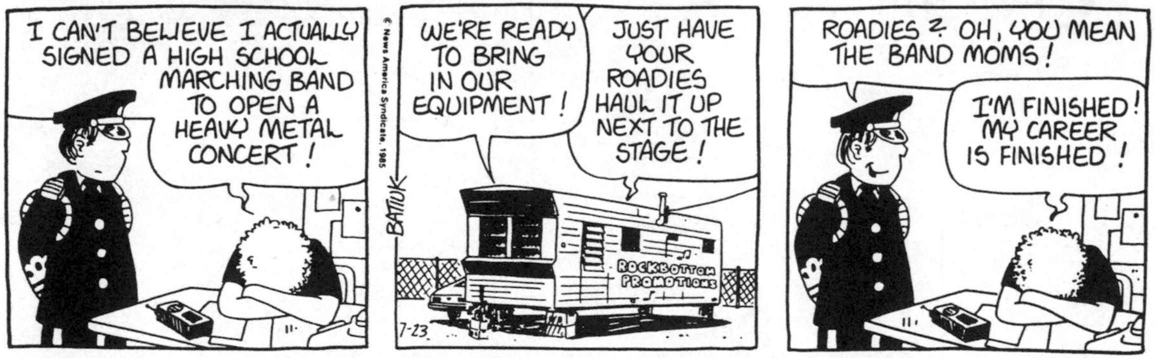
I CAN'T BELIEVE I ACTUALLY SIGNED A HIGH SCHOOL MARCHING BAND TO OPEN A HEAVY METAL CONCERT!
WE'RE READY TO BRING IN OUR EQUIPMENT!
JUST HAVE YOUR ROADIES HAUL IT UP NEXT TO THE STAGE!
ROCKBOTTOM PROMOTIONS
ROADIES? OH, YOU MEAN THE BAND MOMS!
I'M FINISHED! MY CAREER IS FINISHED!
7-23
BATIUK
© News America Syndicate, 1985

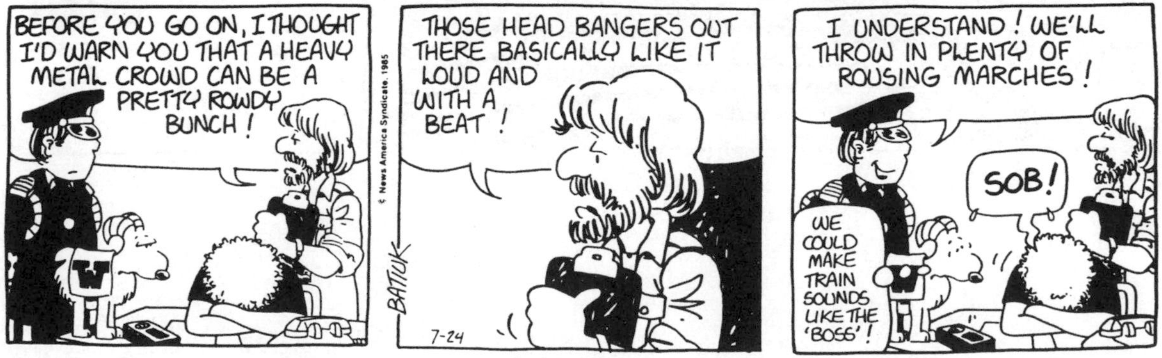
BEFORE YOU GO ON, I THOUGHT I'D WARN YOU THAT A HEAVY METAL CROWD CAN BE A PRETTY ROWDY BUNCH!
THOSE HEAD BANGERS OUT THERE BASICALLY LIKE IT LOUD AND WITH A BEAT!
I UNDERSTAND! WE'LL THROW IN PLENTY OF ROUSING MARCHES!
SOB!
WE COULD MAKE TRAIN SOUNDS LIKE THE 'BOSS'!
7-24
BATIUK
© News America Syndicate, 1985

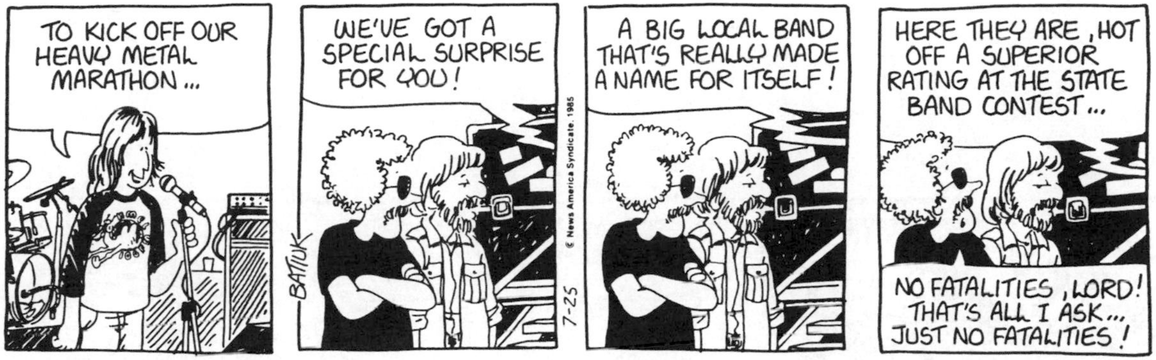
TO KICK OFF OUR HEAVY METAL MARATHON...
WE'VE GOT A SPECIAL SURPRISE FOR YOU!
BATIUK
7-25
© News America Syndicate. 1985
A BIG LOCAL BAND THAT'S REALLY MADE A NAME FOR ITSELF!
HERE THEY ARE, HOT OFF A SUPERIOR RATING AT THE STATE BAND CONTEST...
NO FATALITIES, LORD! THAT'S ALL I ASK... JUST NO FATALITIES!

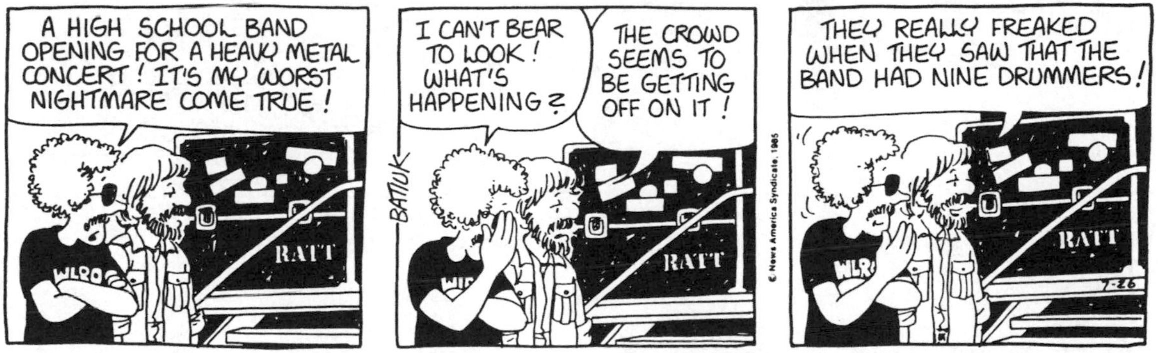
A HIGH SCHOOL BAND OPENING FOR A HEAVY METAL CONCERT! IT'S MY WORST NIGHTMARE COME TRUE!
WLRO
RATT
I CAN'T BEAR TO LOOK! WHAT'S HAPPENING?
THE CROWD SEEMS TO BE GETTING OFF ON IT!
BATIUK
© News America Syndicate. 1985
THEY REALLY FREAKED WHEN THEY SAW THAT THE BAND HAD NINE DRUMMERS!
7-26

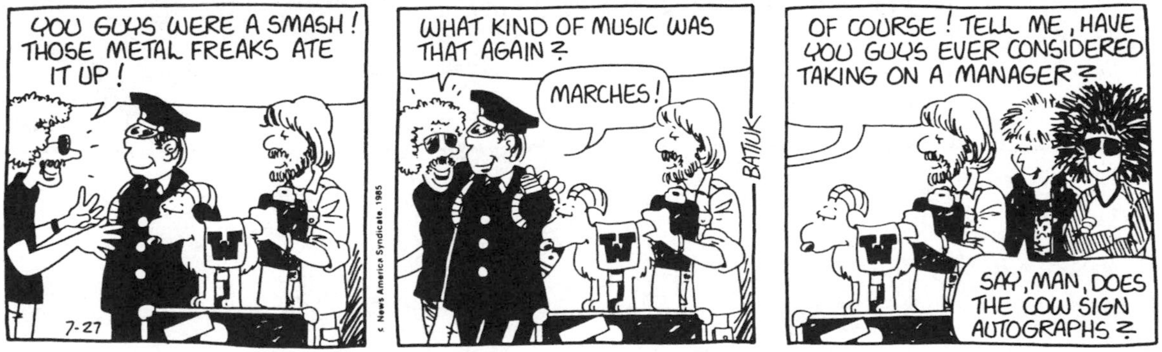
YOU GUYS WERE A SMASH! THOSE METAL FREAKS ATE IT UP!
W
7-27
© News America Syndicate. 1985
WHAT KIND OF MUSIC WAS THAT AGAIN?
MARCHES!
BATIUK
OF COURSE! TELL ME, HAVE YOU GUYS EVER CONSIDERED TAKING ON A MANAGER?
SAY, MAN, DOES THE COW SIGN AUTOGRAPHS?

FUNKY WINKERBEAN
BY TOM BATIUK
SUMMER IS MY FAVORITE SEASON!
I REALLY ENJOY LYING ON THE BEACH!
KICK! KICK! KICK! KICK! KICK! KICK!
AND OCCASIONALLY UNDER IT!
I'VE HAD BULLIES KICK SAND IN MY FACE, STEAL MY GIRL AND MAKE ME THE LAUGHINGSTOCK OF THE BEACH!
© News America Syndicate, 1985
I'D LIKE TO KNOW WHAT ELSE COULD POSSIBLY HAPPEN?
7-28
BATIUK

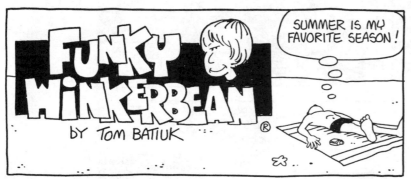

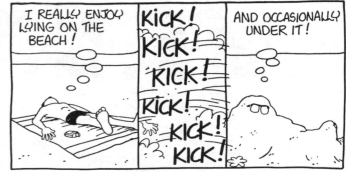

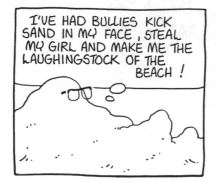

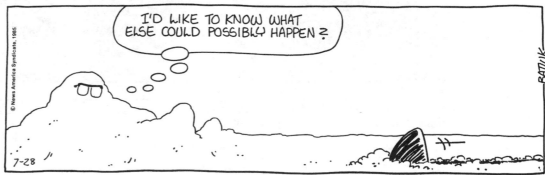

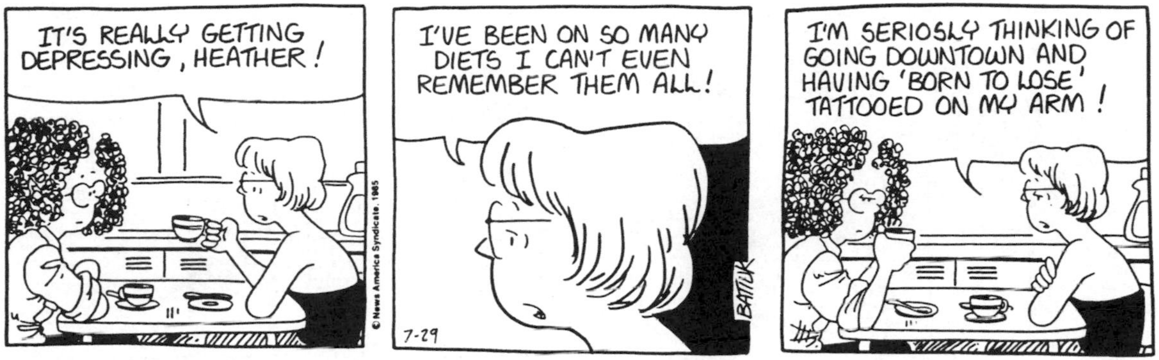
IT'S REALLY GETTING DEPRESSING, HEATHER!
I'VE BEEN ON SO MANY DIETS I CAN'T EVEN REMEMBER THEM ALL!
I'M SERIOSLY THINKING OF GOING DOWNTOWN AND HAVING 'BORN TO LOSE' TATTOOED ON MY ARM!
© News America Syndicate, 1985
7-29
BATIUK

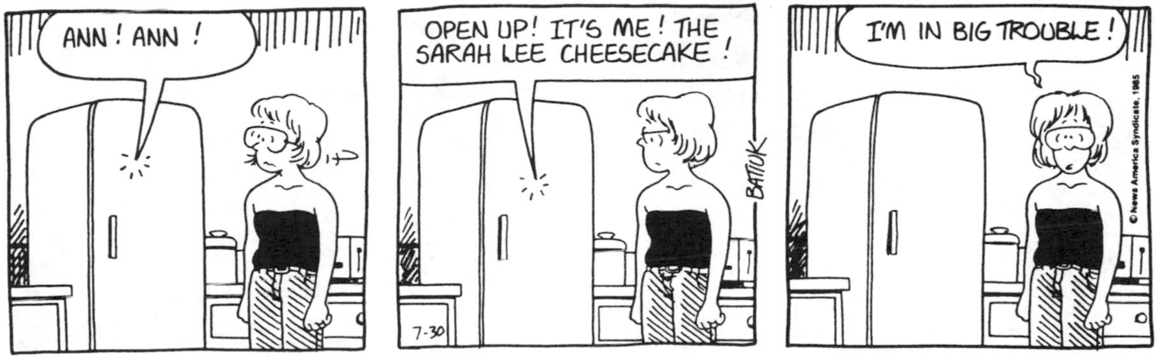
ANN! ANN!
OPEN UP! IT'S ME! THE SARAH LEE CHEESECAKE!
I'M IN BIG TROUBLE!
7-30
BATIUK
© News America Syndicate, 1985

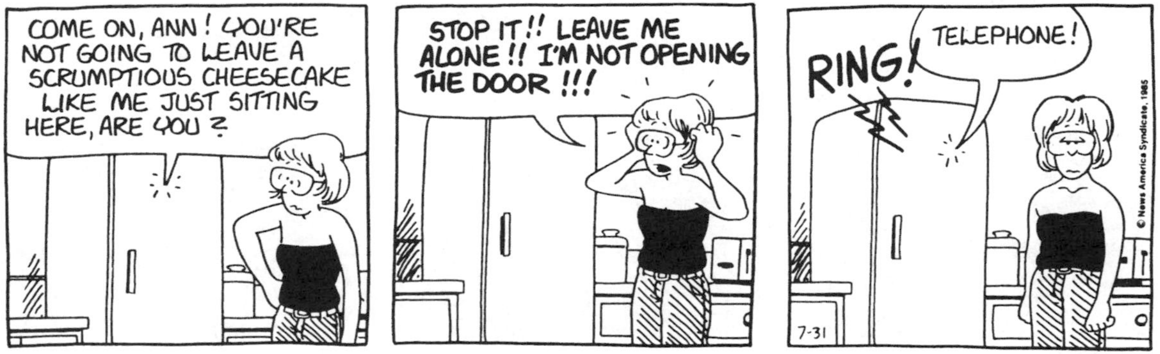
COME ON, ANN! YOU'RE NOT GOING TO LEAVE A SCRUMPTIOUS CHEESECAKE LIKE ME JUST SITTING HERE, ARE YOU?
STOP IT!! LEAVE ME ALONE!! I'M NOT OPENING THE DOOR!!!
RING!
TELEPHONE!
© News America Syndicate, 1985
7-31

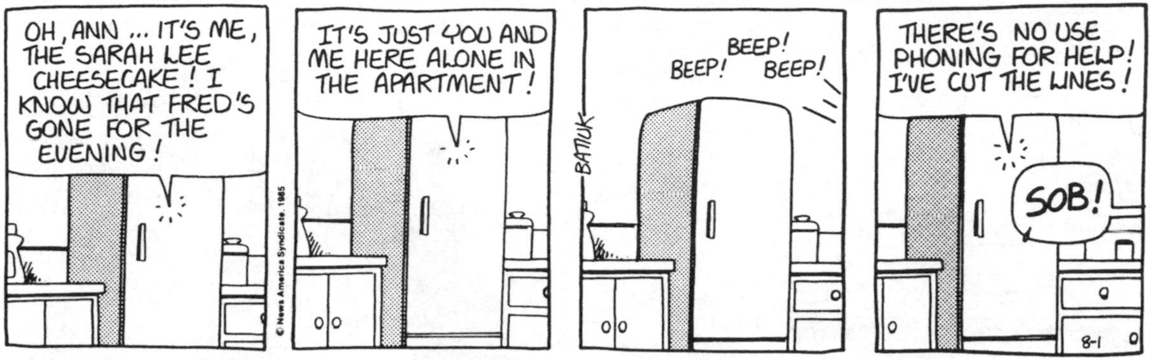
OH, ANN ... IT'S ME, THE SARAH LEE CHEESECAKE! I KNOW THAT FRED'S GONE FOR THE EVENING!
© News America Syndicate, 1985
IT'S JUST YOU AND ME HERE ALONE IN THE APARTMENT!
BATIUK
BEEP! BEEP! BEEP!
THERE'S NO USE PHONING FOR HELP! I'VE CUT THE LINES!
SOB!
8-1

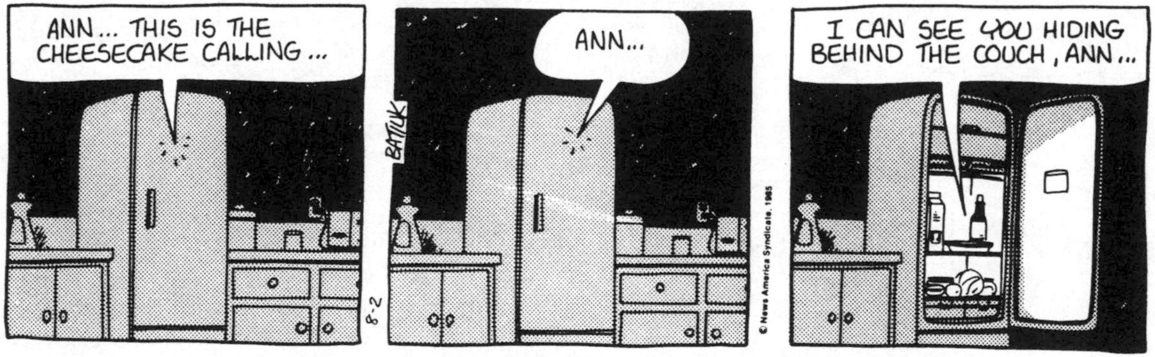
ANN... THIS IS THE CHEESECAKE CALLING...
8-2
BATIUK
ANN...
© News America Syndicate, 1985
I CAN SEE YOU HIDING BEHIND THE COUCH, ANN...

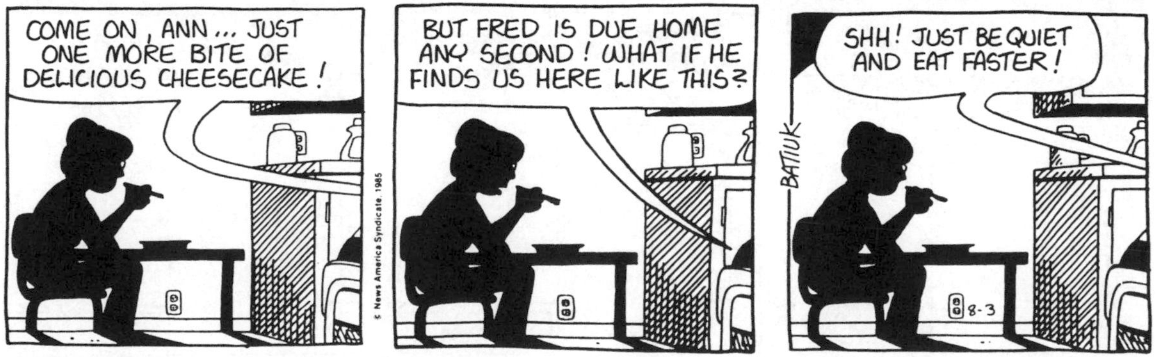
COME ON, ANN... JUST ONE MORE BITE OF DELICIOUS CHEESECAKE!
© News America Syndicate, 1985
BUT FRED IS DUE HOME ANY SECOND! WHAT IF HE FINDS US HERE LIKE THIS?
BATIUK
SHH! JUST BE QUIET AND EAT FASTER!
8-3

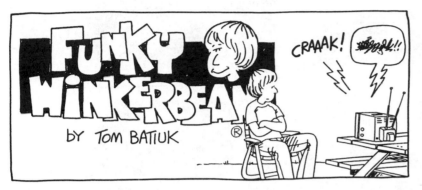

FUNKY WINKERBEAN
by TOM BATIUK
CRAAAK!
CARY, CAN YOU SEE WHERE TOM'S BALL ENDED UP?
YES I CAN...
TOM'S TEE SHOT ON SEVENTEEN KAYOED A LITTLE OLD LADY IN THE CROWD NEXT TO THE FAIRWAY...
AND CAME TO REST ON HER STOMACH!
BATIUK
8-4
IT'S HARD TO TELL FROM HERE...
© News America Syndicate, 1985
BUT HE SEEMS TO HAVE A PRETTY GOOD LIE!

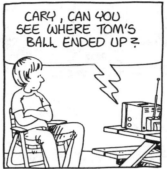

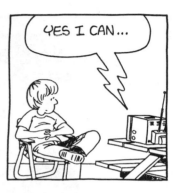

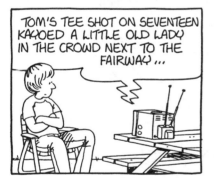

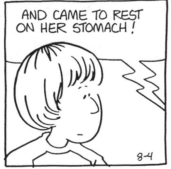

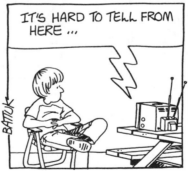

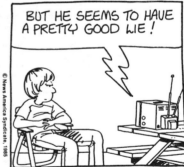

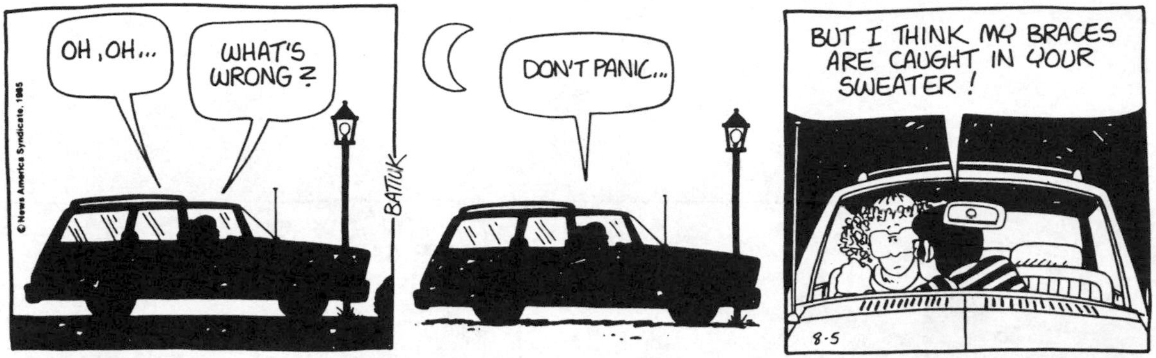
OH, OH...
WHAT'S WRONG?
DON'T PANIC...
BUT I THINK MY BRACES ARE CAUGHT IN YOUR SWEATER!
© News America Syndicate, 1985
BATIUK
8-5

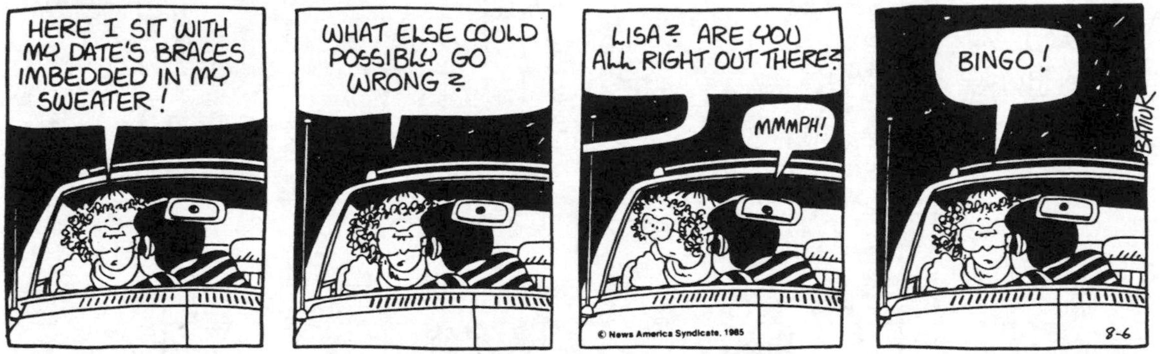
HERE I SIT WITH MY DATE'S BRACES IMBEDDED IN MY SWEATER!
WHAT ELSE COULD POSSIBLY GO WRONG?
LISA? ARE YOU ALL RIGHT OUT THERE?
MMMPH!
BINGO!
© News America Syndicate, 1985
BATIUK
8-6

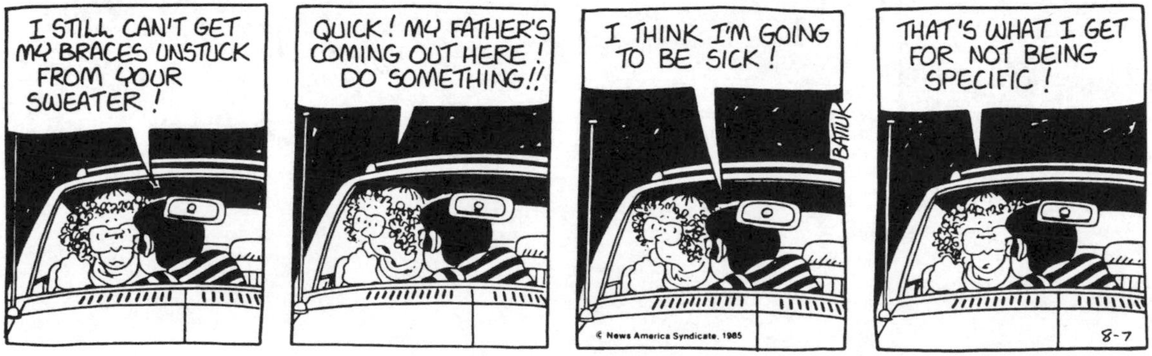
I STILL CAN'T GET MY BRACES UNSTUCK FROM YOUR SWEATER!
QUICK! MY FATHER'S COMING OUT HERE! DO SOMETHING!!
I THINK I'M GOING TO BE SICK!
THAT'S WHAT I GET FOR NOT BEING SPECIFIC!
© News America Syndicate, 1985
BATIUK
8-7

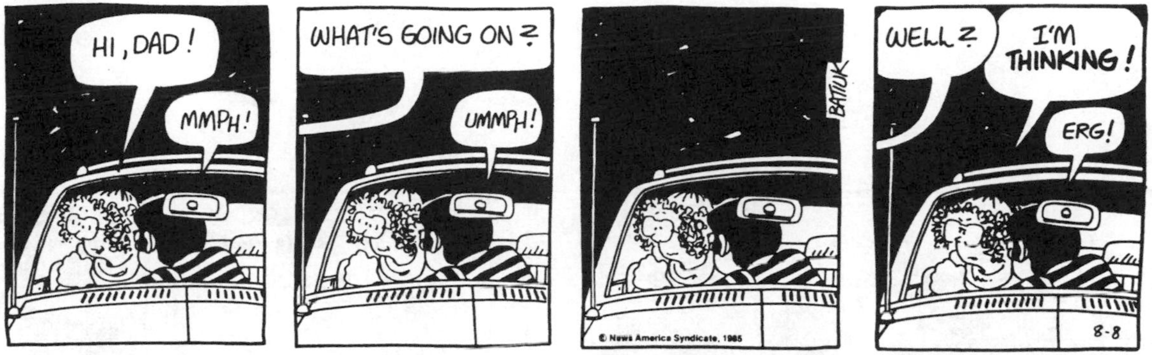
HI, DAD!
MMPH!
WHAT'S GOING ON?
UMMPH!
BATIUK
© News America Syndicate, 1985
WELL?
I'M THINKING!
ERG!
8-8

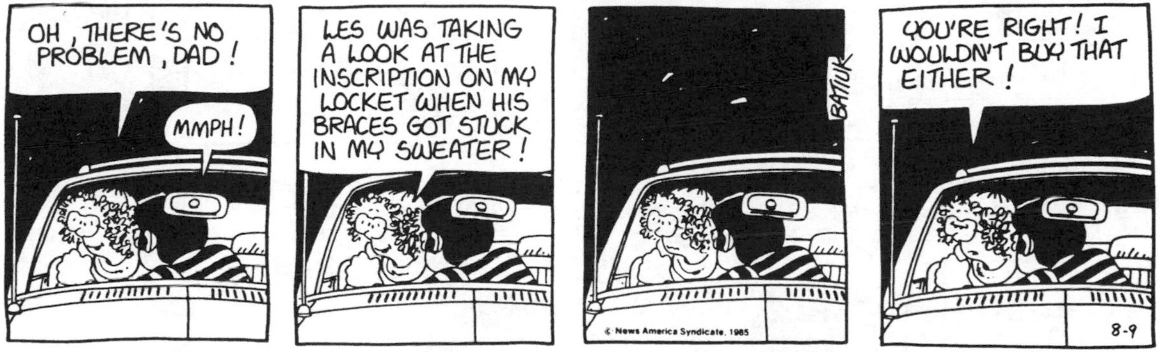
OH, THERE'S NO PROBLEM, DAD!
MMPH!
LES WAS TAKING A LOOK AT THE INSCRIPTION ON MY LOCKET WHEN HIS BRACES GOT STUCK IN MY SWEATER!
BATIUK
© News America Syndicate, 1985
YOU'RE RIGHT! I WOULDN'T BUY THAT EITHER!
8-9

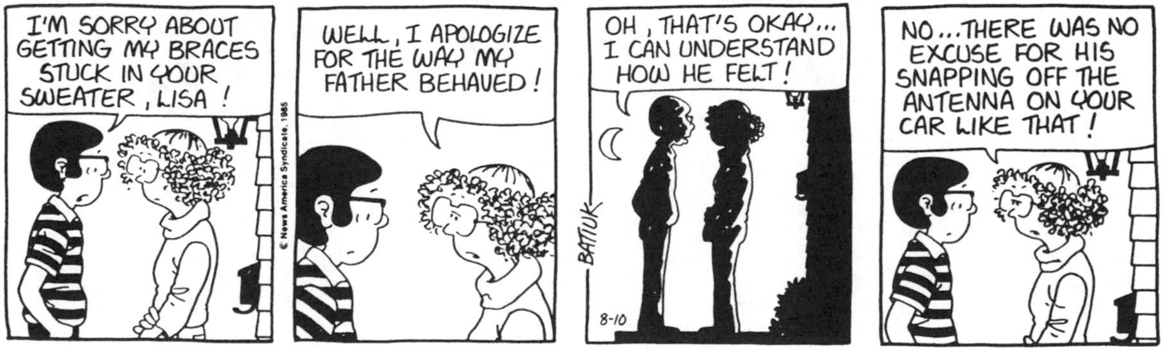
I'M SORRY ABOUT GETTING MY BRACES STUCK IN YOUR SWEATER, LISA!
© News America Syndicate, 1985
WELL, I APOLOGIZE FOR THE WAY MY FATHER BEHAVED!
OH, THAT'S OKAY... I CAN UNDERSTAND HOW HE FELT!
BATIUK
8-10
NO...THERE WAS NO EXCUSE FOR HIS SNAPPING OFF THE ANTENNA ON YOUR CAR LIKE THAT!

FUNKY WINKERBEAN
by TOM BATIUK ®
LISTEN UP, PEOPLE !!
I WISH TOM LANDRY COULD'VE SEEN THAT !
IT WAS THE FINEST EXAMPLE OF BROKEN-FIELD MARCHING I'VE SEEN !
CAN'T YOU PEOPLE TELL YOUR LEFT FOOT FROM YOUR RIGHT!?
© News America Syndicate, 1985
8-11
EVERYBODY RAISE YOUR LEFT FOOT !!
MELODY GROVE BAND CAMP
NOW RAISE YOUR RIGHT FOOT !!
BATIUK
THUMP! THUMP! THUMP! THUMP! THUMP! THUMP! THUMP! THUMP! THUMP! THUMP!

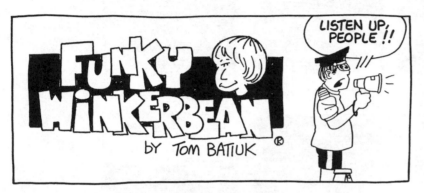

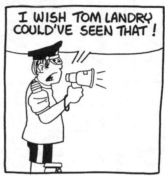

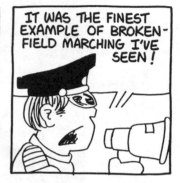

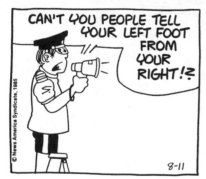

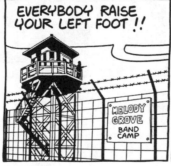

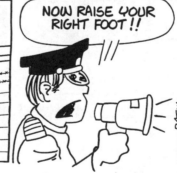

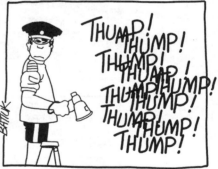

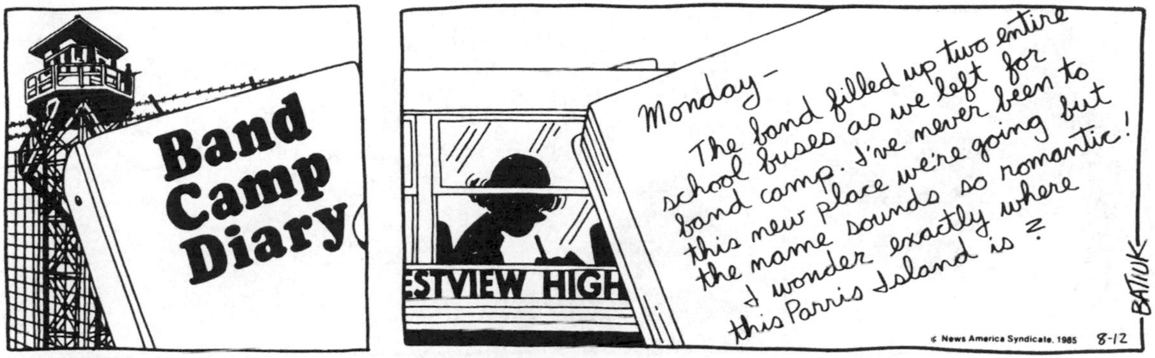
Band Camp Diary
ESTVIEW HIGH
Monday- The band filled up two entire school buses as we left for band camp. I've never been to this new place we're going but the name sounds so romantic! I wonder exactly where this Parris Island is?
BATIUK
© News America Syndicate, 1985
8-12

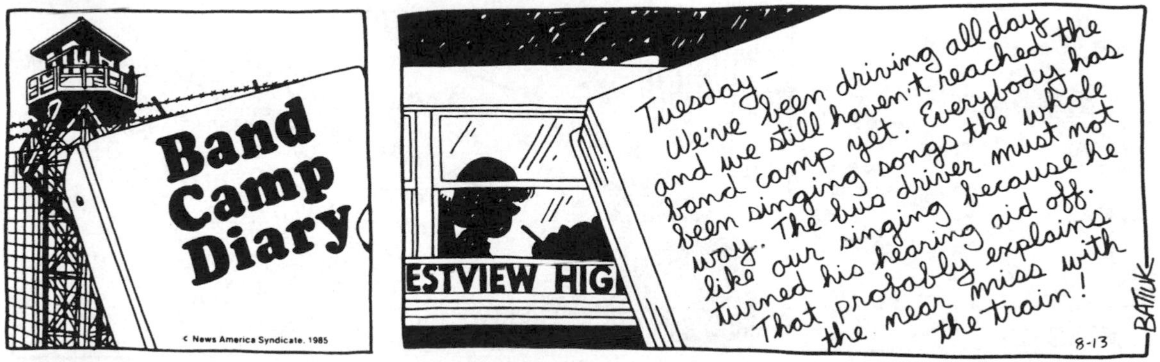
Band Camp Diary
© News America Syndicate, 1985
ESTVIEW HIGH
Tuesday- We've been driving all day and we still haven't reached the band camp yet. Everybody has been singing songs the whole way. The bus driver must not like our singing because he turned his hearing aid off. That probably explains the near miss with the train!
BATIUK
8-13

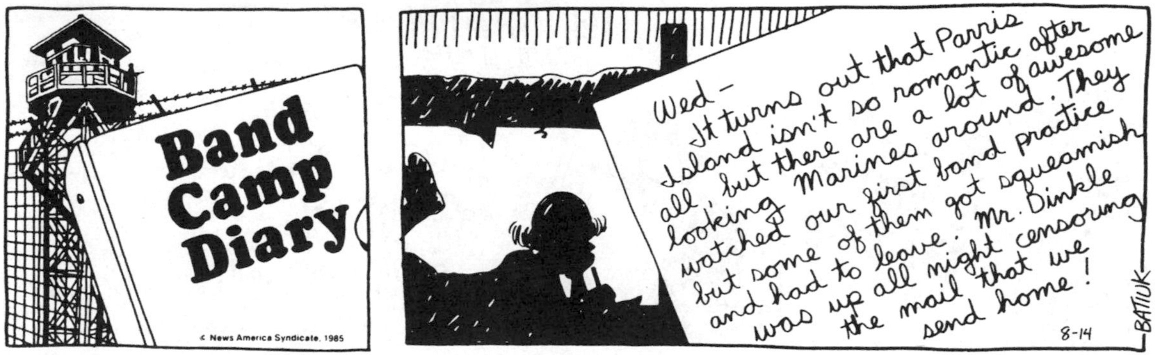
Band Camp Diary
© News America Syndicate, 1985
Wed- It turns out that Parris Island isn't so romantic after all, but there are a lot of awesome looking Marines around. They watched our first band practice but some of them got squeamish and had to leave. Mr. Dinkle was up all night censoring the mail that we send home!
BATIUK
8-14

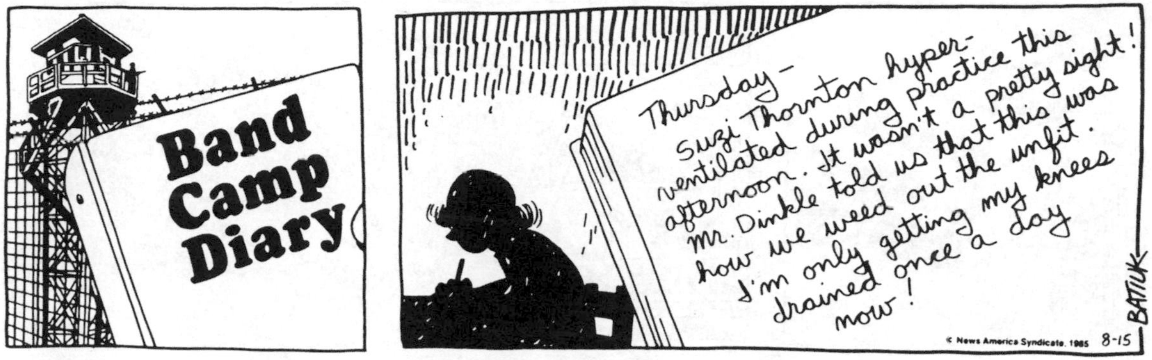
Band Camp Diary
Thursday –
Suzi Thornton hyper-ventilated during practice this afternoon. It wasn't a pretty sight! Mr. Dinkle told us that this was how we weed out the unfit. I'm only getting my knees drained once a day now!
BATIUK
© News America Syndicate, 1985
8-15

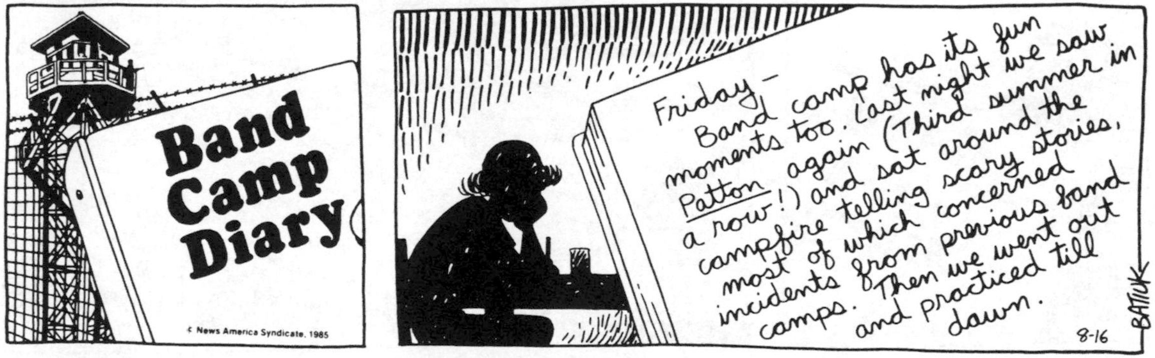
Band Camp Diary
© News America Syndicate, 1985
Friday –
Band camp has its fun moments too. Last night we saw Patton again (Third summer in a row!) and sat around the campfire telling scary stories, most of which concerned incidents from previous band camps. Then we went out and practiced till dawn.
BATIUK
8-16

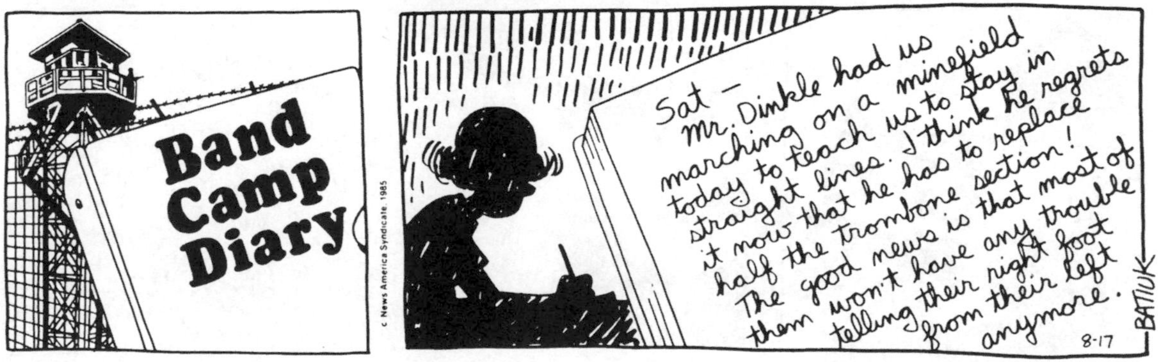
Band Camp Diary
© News America Syndicate, 1985
Sat –
Mr. Dinkle had us marching on a minefield today to teach us to stay in straight lines. I think he regrets it now that he has to replace half the trombone section! The good news is that most of them won't have any trouble telling their right foot from their left anymore.
BATIUK
8-17

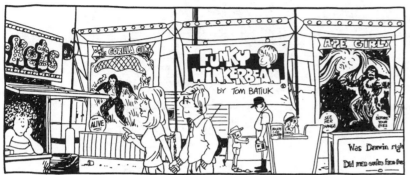

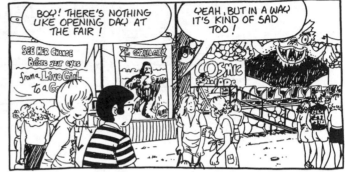

SEE THE GORILLA GIRL
ALIVE
FUNKY WINKERBEAN
BY TOM BATIUK
APE GIRL
SEE HER CHANGE
BEFORE YOUR EYES
Was Darwin righ
BOY! THERE'S NOTHING LIKE OPENING DAY AT THE FAIR!
YEAH, BUT IN A WAY IT'S KIND OF SAD TOO!
SEE HER CHANGE Before your eyes from a Live Girl to a Go
COSMIC
THERE'S ALWAYS SO MUCH TO DO AT A COUNTY FAIR!
THEY ALWAYS REMIND ME THAT SUMMER IS NEARLY OVER...
THERE'S FRENCH FRIES AND SAUSAGE SANDWICHES...
AND THAT SOON WE'LL BE BACK IN SCHOOL WITH WINTER NOT FAR BEHIND!
CH FRIE
D DRINKS
© News America Syndicate, 1985
BATIUK
8-18
RIDES AND GAMES...
IN FACT, THE PASSING OF THE SEASONS ONLY SEEMS TO ECHO OUR OWN MORTALITY!
ZIPPER
I THINK I'LL JUST GO HOME AND GO TO BED...
WHAT DO YOU WANT TO DO FIRST?
TILT-A-WHIRL
DEL FUEGOS

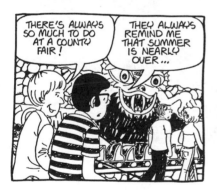

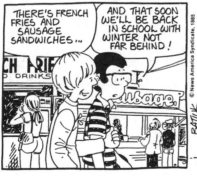

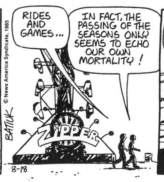

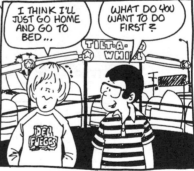

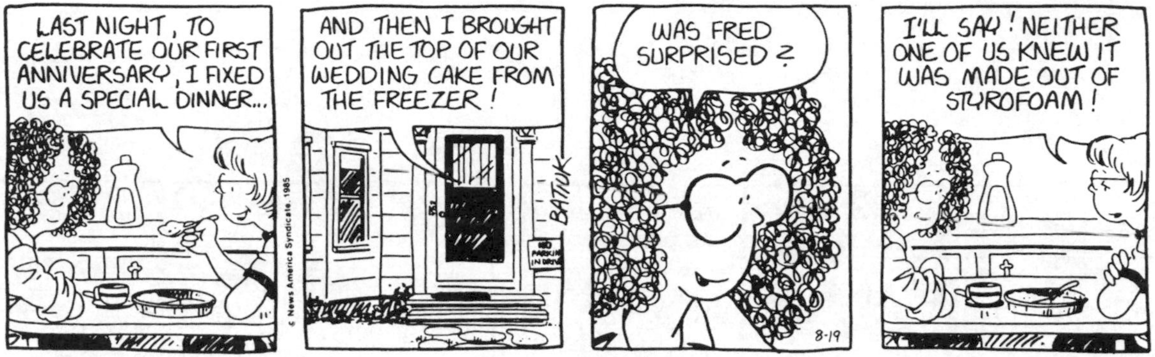
LAST NIGHT, TO CELEBRATE OUR FIRST ANNIVERSARY, I FIXED US A SPECIAL DINNER...
AND THEN I BROUGHT OUT THE TOP OF OUR WEDDING CAKE FROM THE FREEZER!
BATIUK
© News America Syndicate, 1985
WAS FRED SURPRISED?
8-19
I'LL SAY! NEITHER ONE OF US KNEW IT WAS MADE OUT OF STYROFOAM!

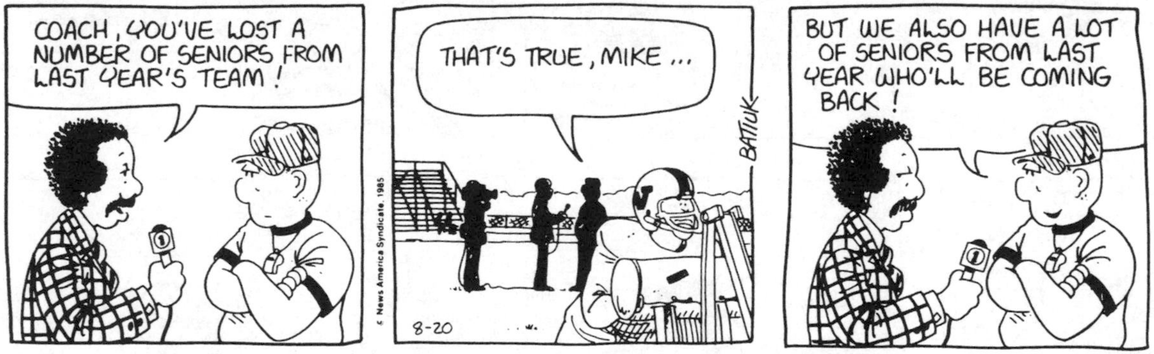
COACH, YOU'VE LOST A NUMBER OF SENIORS FROM LAST YEAR'S TEAM!
© News America Syndicate, 1985
THAT'S TRUE, MIKE...
BATIUK
8-20
BUT WE ALSO HAVE A LOT OF SENIORS FROM LAST YEAR WHO'LL BE COMING BACK!

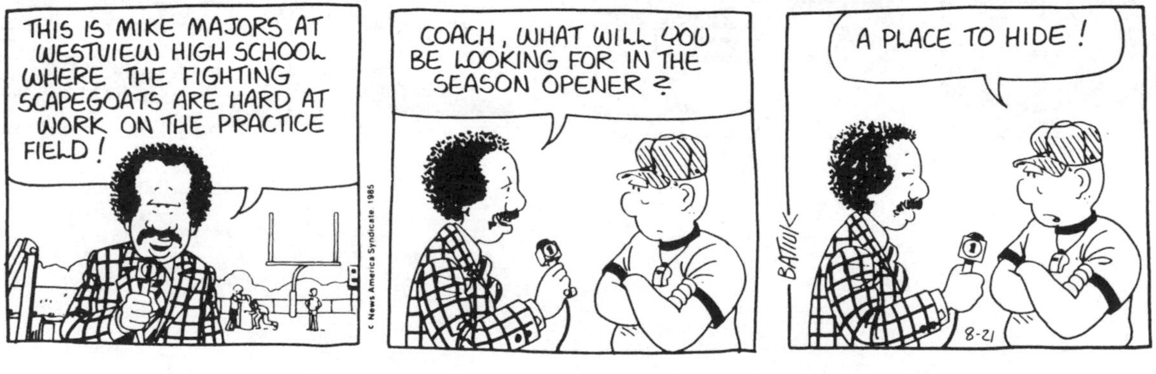
THIS IS MIKE MAJORS AT WESTVIEW HIGH SCHOOL WHERE THE FIGHTING SCAPEGOATS ARE HARD AT WORK ON THE PRACTICE FIELD!
© News America Syndicate 1985
COACH, WHAT WILL YOU BE LOOKING FOR IN THE SEASON OPENER?
A PLACE TO HIDE!
BATIUK
8-21

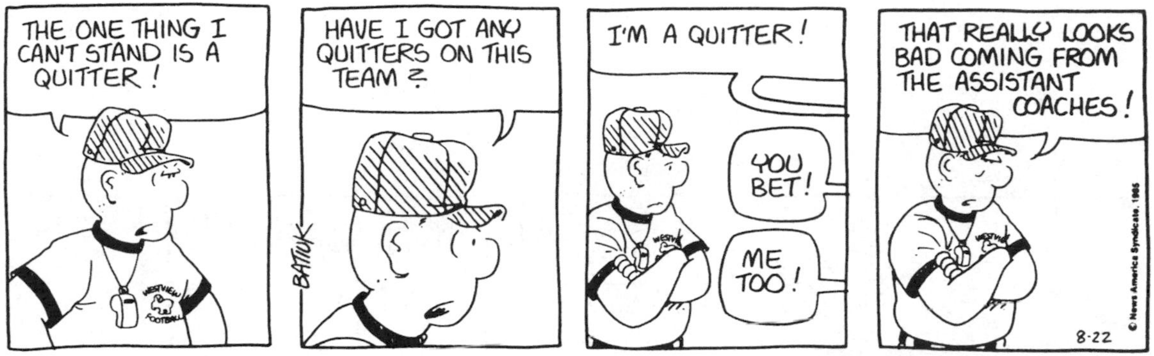
THE ONE THING I CAN'T STAND IS A QUITTER!
HAVE I GOT ANY QUITTERS ON THIS TEAM?
BATIUK
I'M A QUITTER!
YOU BET!
ME TOO!
THAT REALLY LOOKS BAD COMING FROM THE ASSISTANT COACHES!
© News America Syndicate, 1985
8-22

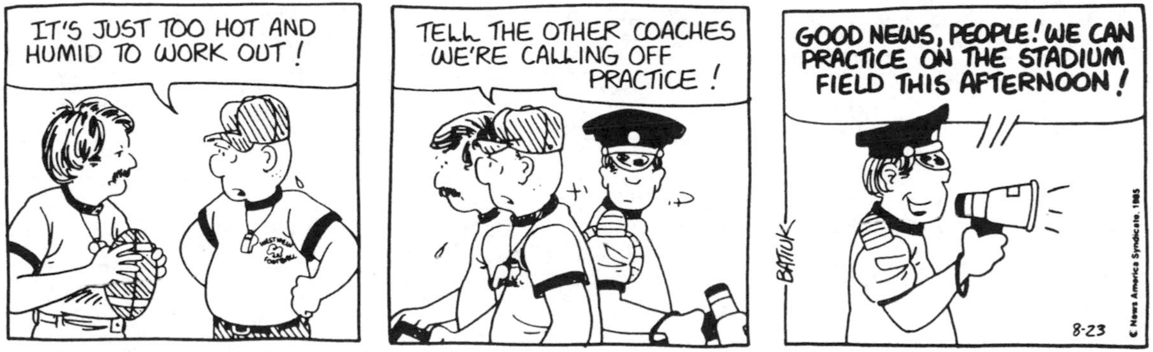
IT'S JUST TOO HOT AND HUMID TO WORK OUT!
TELL THE OTHER COACHES WE'RE CALLING OFF PRACTICE!
GOOD NEWS, PEOPLE! WE CAN PRACTICE ON THE STADIUM FIELD THIS AFTERNOON!
BATIUK
© News America Syndicate, 1985
8-23

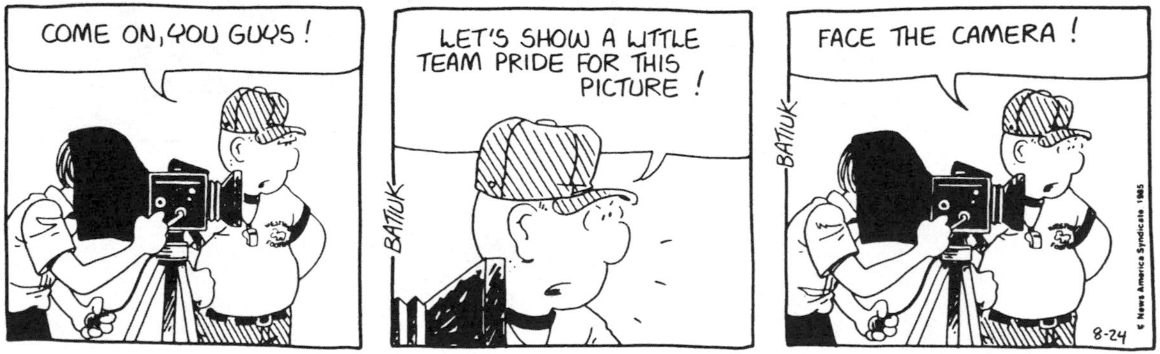
COME ON, YOU GUYS!
LET'S SHOW A LITTLE TEAM PRIDE FOR THIS PICTURE!
BATIUK
FACE THE CAMERA!
BATIUK
© News America Syndicate, 1985
8-24

FUNKY WINKERBEAN
BY TOM BATIUK
WESTVIEW HIGH SCHOOL
AUG 31
H LOWELL
SEPT 7
A McATEER
HERE I SIT COVERED WITH GRAFFITI!
BEAT TECH!
JOHN + LAURIE
SENIORS '86
BUTCH + CAMI
SCAPEGOATS
ROCK DEL FUEGOS
IT'S A LIVING!
ON ONE SIDE OF ME IS THE SCHOOL ROCK THAT SITS AT THE ENTRANCE TO OUR SCHOOL!
ON THE OTHER SIDE IS THE SCHOOL WHERE EACH DAY THE DIFFICULT STRUGGLE TO GET AN EDUCATION GOES ON!
© News America Syndicate, 1985
BATIUK
IT CAN TRULY BE SAID... I'M BETWEEN A ROCK AND A HARD PLACE!
8-25

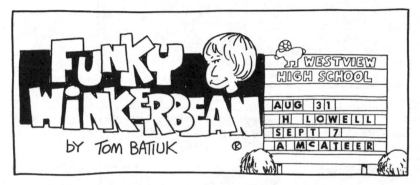

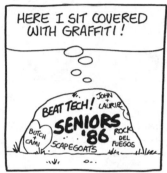

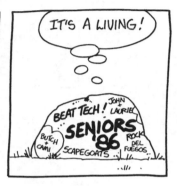

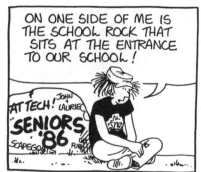

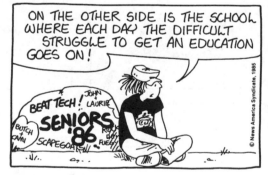

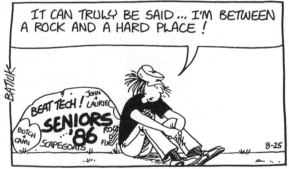

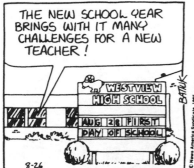

THE NEW SCHOOL YEAR BRINGS WITH IT MANY CHALLENGES FOR A NEW TEACHER!
WESTVIEW HIGH SCHOOL
AUG 28 FIRST DAY OF SCHOOL
BATIUK
© News America Syndicate, 1985
8-26
THERE'S THE CONSTANT SEEKING OF INFORMATION AND TRUTH ... THE LONG DISCUSSIONS, THE HOMEWORK AND THE OCCASIONAL FRUSTRATION AND ANGER...
BUT THEN, NO ONE EVER SAID THAT CONTRACT NEGOTIATIONS WOULD BE EASY!

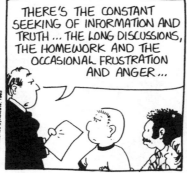

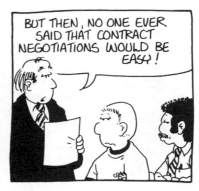

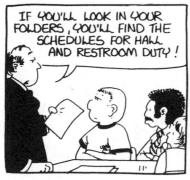

IF YOU'LL LOOK IN YOUR FOLDERS, YOU'LL FIND THE SCHEDULES FOR HALL AND RESTROOM DUTY!
© News America Syndicate, 1985
EXTRA PEOPLE HAVE BEEN ASSIGNED TO THE RESTROOM AT THE SOUTH END OF THE BUILDING...
BATIUK
8-27
WHERE THE TWO FACULTY MEMBERS DISAPPEARED LAST YEAR!

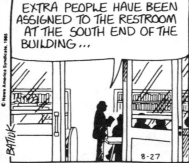

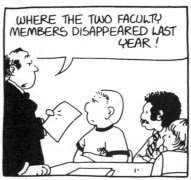

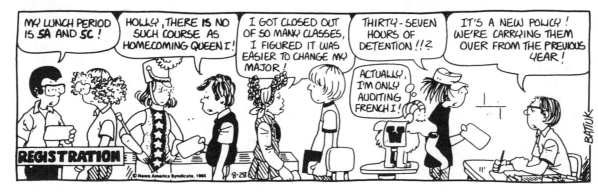

MY LUNCH PERIOD IS 5A AND 5C!
HOLLY, THERE IS NO SUCH COURSE AS HOMECOMING QUEEN I!
I GOT CLOSED OUT OF SO MANY CLASSES, I FIGURED IT WAS EASIER TO CHANGE MY MAJOR!
THIRTY-SEVEN HOURS OF DETENTION!!?
ACTUALLY, I'M ONLY AUDITING FRENCH I!
IT'S A NEW POLICY! WE'RE CARRYING THEM OVER FROM THE PREVIOUS YEAR!
REGISTRATION
© News America Syndicate, 1985
8-28
BATIUK

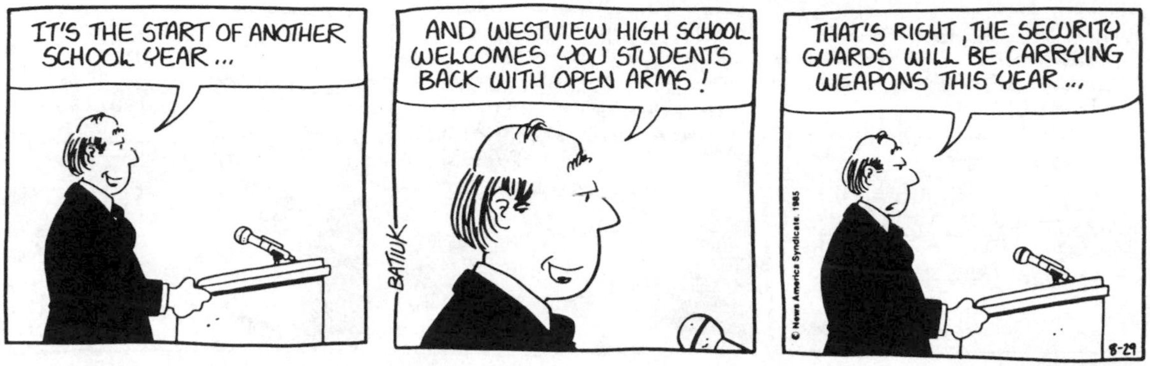
IT'S THE START OF ANOTHER SCHOOL YEAR...
AND WESTVIEW HIGH SCHOOL WELCOMES YOU STUDENTS BACK WITH OPEN ARMS!
BATIUK
THAT'S RIGHT, THE SECURITY GUARDS WILL BE CARRYING WEAPONS THIS YEAR...
© News America Syndicate. 1985
8-29

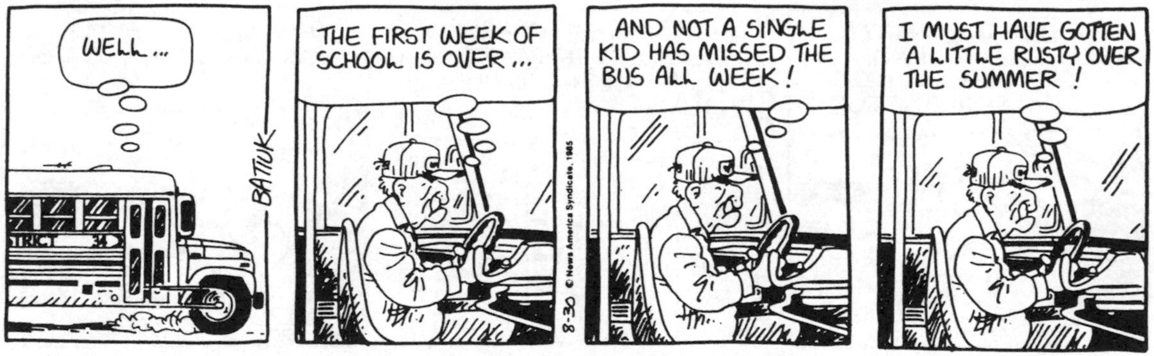
WELL...
BATIUK
THE FIRST WEEK OF SCHOOL IS OVER...
8-30 © News America Syndicate. 1985
AND NOT A SINGLE KID HAS MISSED THE BUS ALL WEEK!
I MUST HAVE GOTTEN A LITTLE RUSTY OVER THE SUMMER!

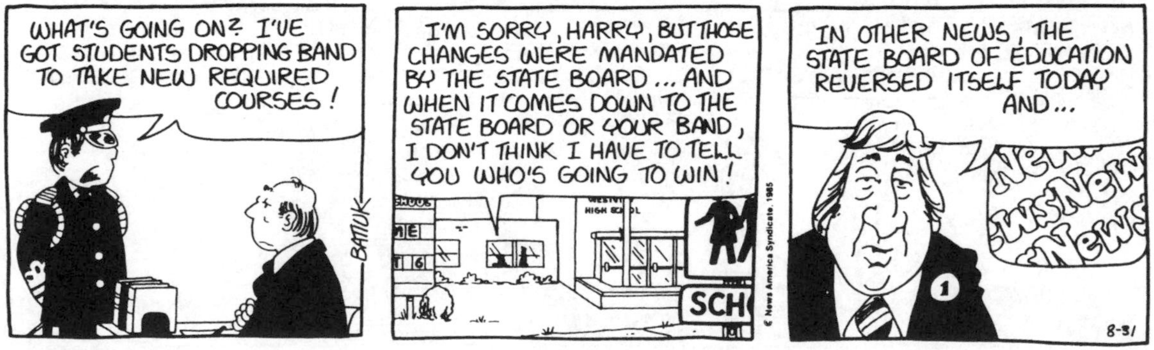
WHAT'S GOING ON?! I'VE GOT STUDENTS DROPPING BAND TO TAKE NEW REQUIRED COURSES!
BATIUK
I'M SORRY, HARRY, BUT THOSE CHANGES WERE MANDATED BY THE STATE BOARD... AND WHEN IT COMES DOWN TO THE STATE BOARD OR YOUR BAND, I DON'T THINK I HAVE TO TELL YOU WHO'S GOING TO WIN!
HIGH SCHOOL
SCH
© News America Syndicate. 1985
IN OTHER NEWS, THE STATE BOARD OF EDUCATION REVERSED ITSELF TODAY AND...
NewsNewsNews
1
8-31

FUNKY WINKERBEAN
BY TOM BATIUK
I DON'T BELIEVE IT!
WE WERE BOTH ASSIGNED TO THE SAME LOCKER!
HMM...
I DON'T SUPPOSE ONE OF YOU WOULD BE INTERESTED IN TRANSFERRING TO A PAROCHIAL SCHOOL?
THIS YEAR I PLAYED IT SAFE AND WROTE MY LOCKER COMBINATION IN THE BACK OF MY BOOK SO I WON'T FORGET IT!
I WISH I'D WRITTEN MY LOCKER NUMBER IN MY NOTEBOOK...
BATIUK
9-1
© News America Syndicate, 1985

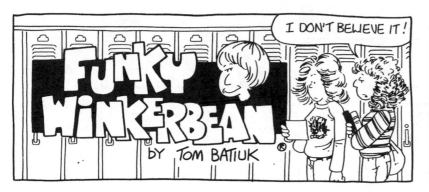

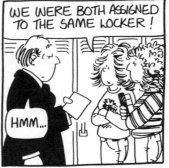

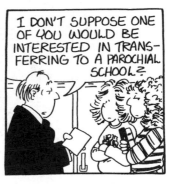

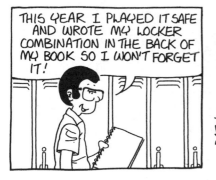

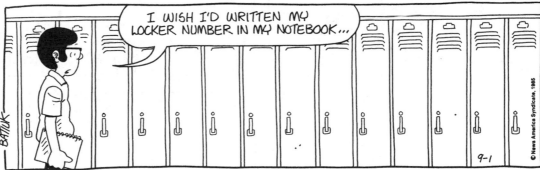

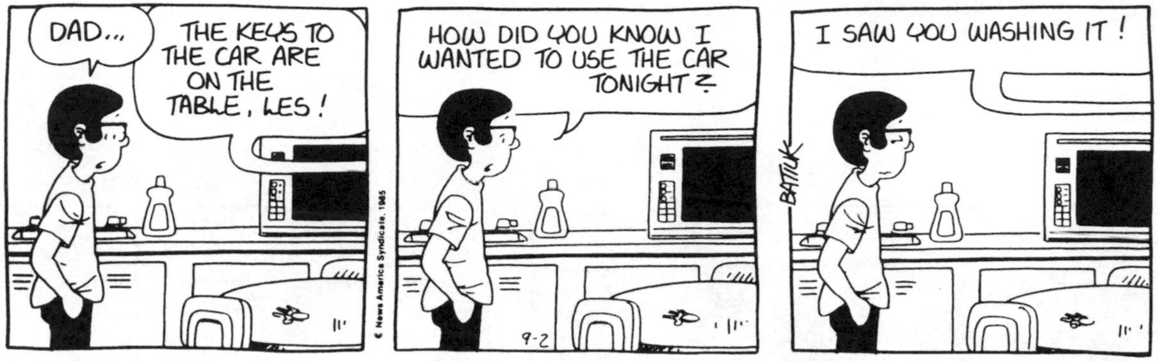
DAD...
THE KEYS TO THE CAR ARE ON THE TABLE, LES!
HOW DID YOU KNOW I WANTED TO USE THE CAR TONIGHT?
I SAW YOU WASHING IT!

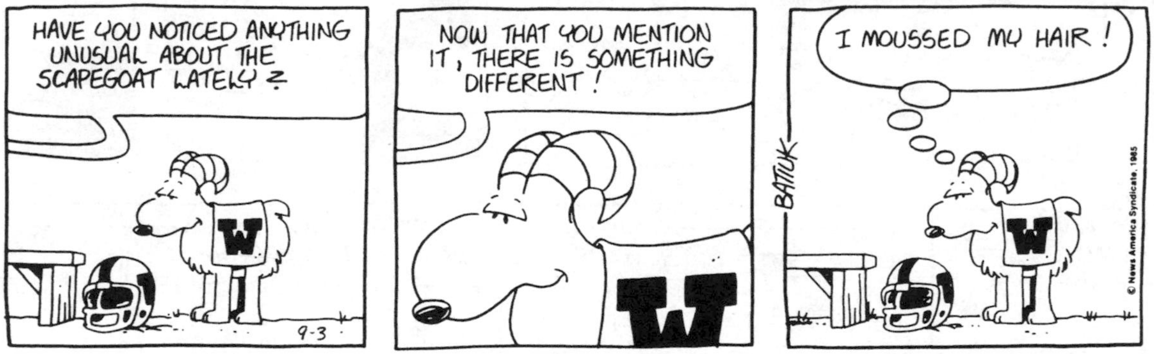
HAVE YOU NOTICED ANYTHING UNUSUAL ABOUT THE SCAPEGOAT LATELY?
NOW THAT YOU MENTION IT, THERE IS SOMETHING DIFFERENT!
I MOUSSED MY HAIR!

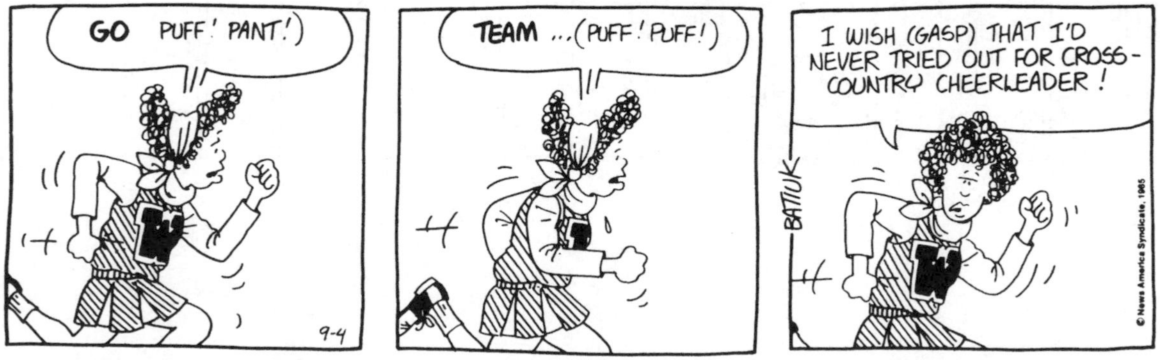
GO PUFF! PANT!)
TEAM ...(PUFF! PUFF!)
I WISH (GASP) THAT I'D NEVER TRIED OUT FOR CROSS-COUNTRY CHEERLEADER!

IF WE'RE GOING TO GO TOGETHER, YOU SHOULD GIVE ME YOUR CLASS RING!

BUT, LISA... I NEVER GOT A CLASS RING!

BATIUK

9-5

© News America Syndicate, 1985

WELL, YOU SHOULD GIVE ME SOMETHING OF YOURS!

OKAY, IT'S THIRD AND ONE, AND WESTVIEW IS ABOUT TO SNAP THE BALL... WAIT A MINUTE!

THE BAND HAS STARTED TO PLAY THE NATIONAL ANTHEM!

ALL THE PLAYERS HAVE STOOD UP AND THE WESTVIEW QUARTERBACK HAS PICKED UP THE BALL AND IS RUNNING FOR A TOUCHDOWN!

HOME OF THE WESTVIEW SCAPEGO

9-6

© News America Syndicate, 1985

THE OLD FAKE NATIONAL ANTHEM PLAY!

BATIUK

COACH, YOUR TEAM FUMBLED THIRTY-SEVEN TIMES TONIGHT!

WHAT DO YOU PLAN TO DO ABOUT IT?

BATIUK

9-7

© News America Syndicate, 1985

WELL, FOR ONE THING, WE'RE GOING TO ELIMINATE THE FUMBLE DRILL!

FUNKY WINKERBEAN
BY TOM BATIUK ®
WE'RE ALWAYS SAYING 'GO TEAM', BUT WE NEVER SAY WHERE !
WHAT IS GOOD AND EVIL ? IS THERE SUCH A THING AS SIN ?
IN THE END, WHAT DOES IT MATTER ... IF WE LOSE OR IF WE WIN ?
OUR FOOTBALL TEAM WORKS VERY HARD ... AND ALL THEY GET IS STRIFE !
IT KIND OF MAKES YOU WONDER ...
WHAT THE PURPOSE IS TO LIFE !
BATIUK
9-8
© News America Syndicate, 1985
EXISTENTIAL FOOTBALL CHEERS ?

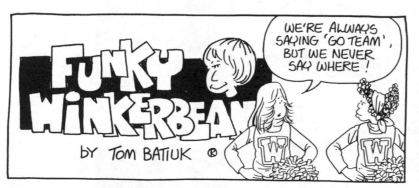

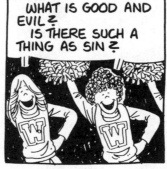

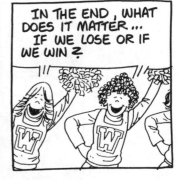

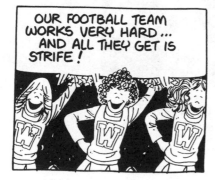

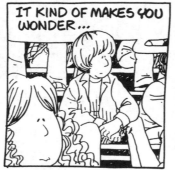

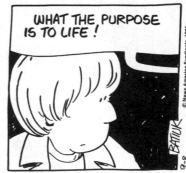

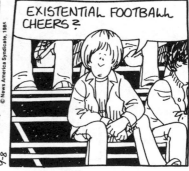

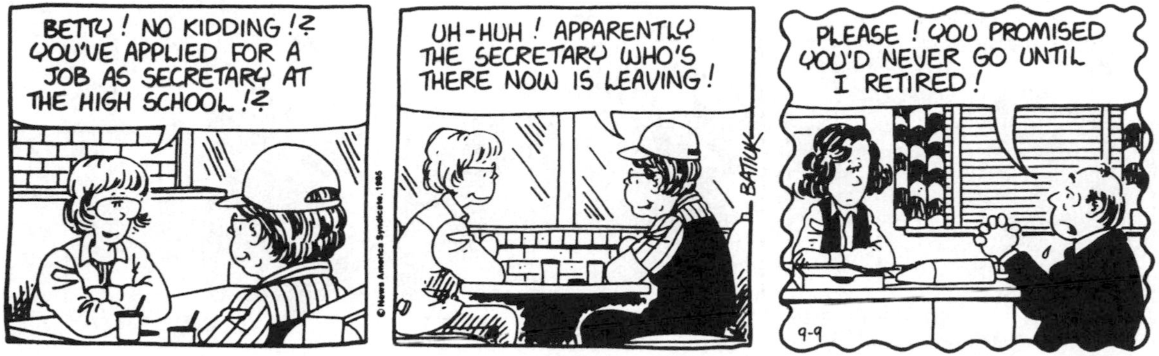
BETTY! NO KIDDING!? YOU'VE APPLIED FOR A JOB AS SECRETARY AT THE HIGH SCHOOL!?
© News America Syndicate, 1985
UH-HUH! APPARENTLY THE SECRETARY WHO'S THERE NOW IS LEAVING!
BATIUK
PLEASE! YOU PROMISED YOU'D NEVER GO UNTIL I RETIRED!
9-9

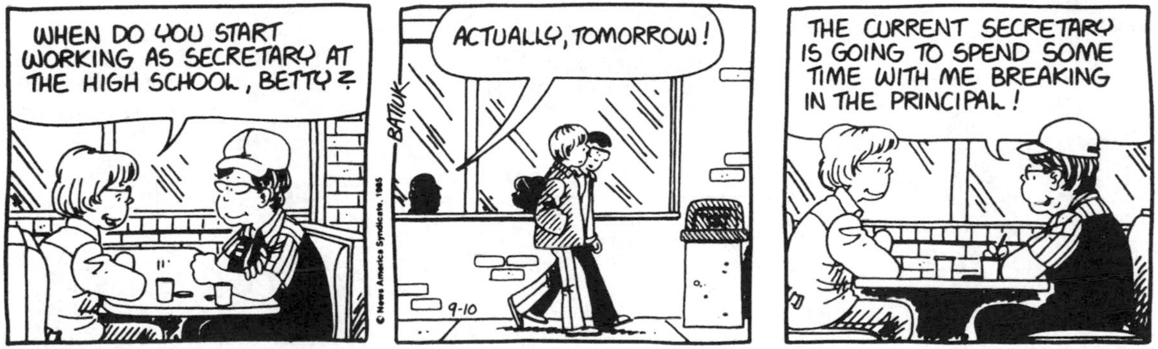
WHEN DO YOU START WORKING AS SECRETARY AT THE HIGH SCHOOL, BETTY?
© News America Syndicate, 1985
BATIUK
ACTUALLY, TOMORROW!
9-10
THE CURRENT SECRETARY IS GOING TO SPEND SOME TIME WITH ME BREAKING IN THE PRINCIPAL!

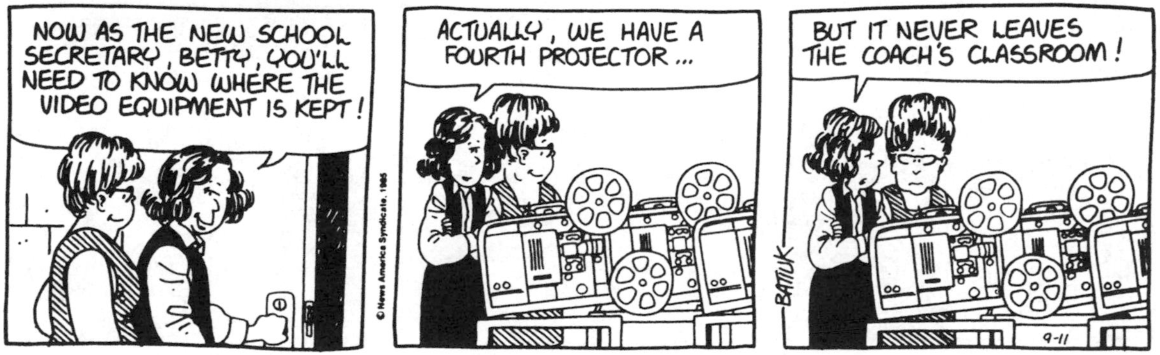
NOW AS THE NEW SCHOOL SECRETARY, BETTY, YOU'LL NEED TO KNOW WHERE THE VIDEO EQUIPMENT IS KEPT!
© News America Syndicate, 1985
ACTUALLY, WE HAVE A FOURTH PROJECTOR...
BUT IT NEVER LEAVES THE COACH'S CLASSROOM!
BATIUK
9-11

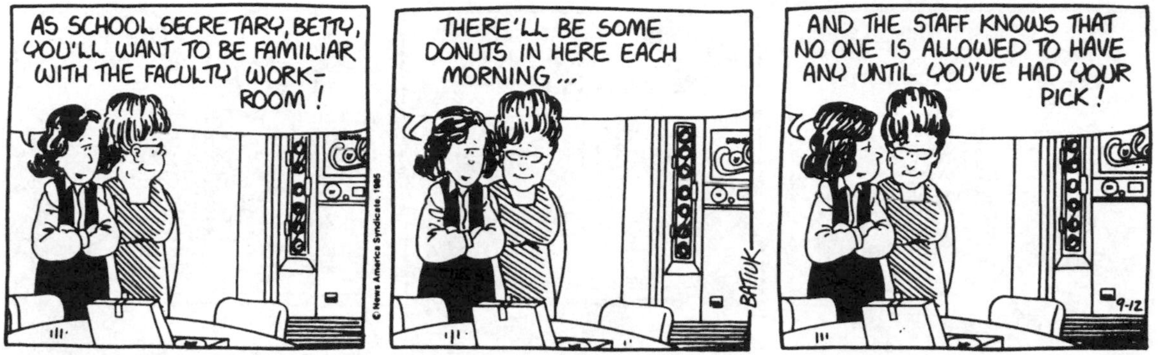
AS SCHOOL SECRETARY, BETTY, YOU'LL WANT TO BE FAMILIAR WITH THE FACULTY WORK-ROOM!
© News America Syndicate. 1985
THERE'LL BE SOME DONUTS IN HERE EACH MORNING...
BATIUK
AND THE STAFF KNOWS THAT NO ONE IS ALLOWED TO HAVE ANY UNTIL YOU'VE HAD YOUR PICK!
9-12

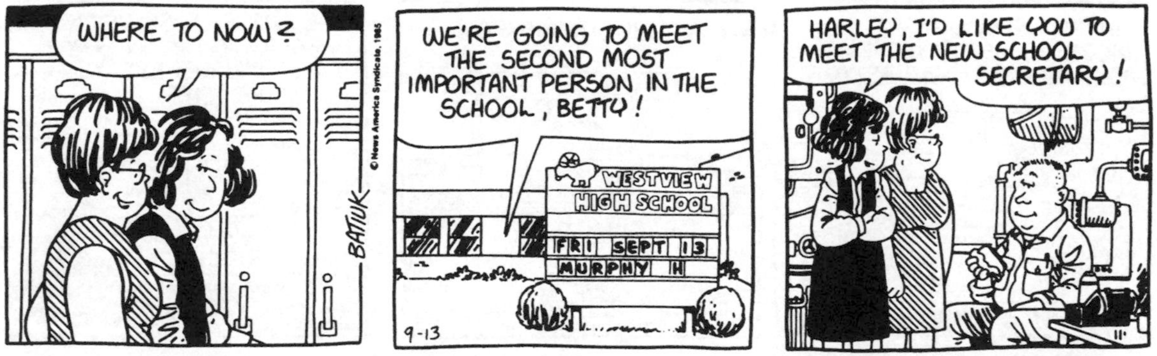
WHERE TO NOW?
BATIUK
© News America Syndicate. 1985
WE'RE GOING TO MEET THE SECOND MOST IMPORTANT PERSON IN THE SCHOOL, BETTY!
WESTVIEW HIGH SCHOOL
FRI SEPT 13
MURPHY H
9-13
HARLEY, I'D LIKE YOU TO MEET THE NEW SCHOOL SECRETARY!

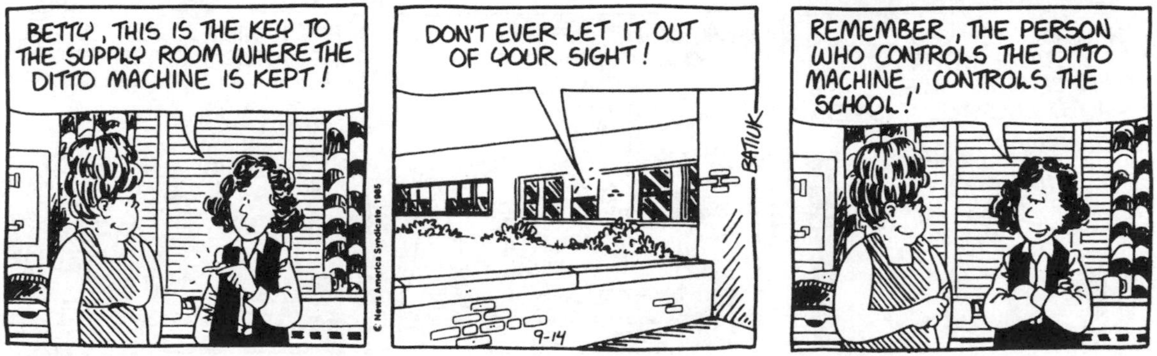
BETTY, THIS IS THE KEY TO THE SUPPLY ROOM WHERE THE DITTO MACHINE IS KEPT!
© News America Syndicate. 1985
DON'T EVER LET IT OUT OF YOUR SIGHT!
BATIUK
9-14
REMEMBER, THE PERSON WHO CONTROLS THE DITTO MACHINE, CONTROLS THE SCHOOL!

FUNKY WINKERBEAN
BY TOM BATIUK ®
I WANT MY EMPTY V!
WOW!
FANTASTIC!
YOU SHOULD SEE THIS VIDEO, FUNKY!
IT'S THE BRAND NEW ONE BY THE 'GRETCH BROTHERS'!
9-15
© News America Syndicate, 1985
BATIUK
FASCINATING...
SOMEHOW I NEVER REALLY PICTURED THAT SONG WITH FLAME THROWERS, BOA CONSTRICTORS AND THREE-WHEEL ALL-TERRAIN VEHICLES BEFORE!

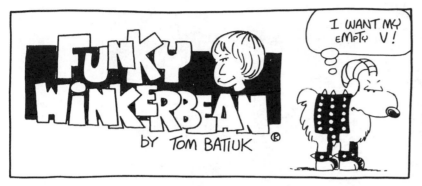

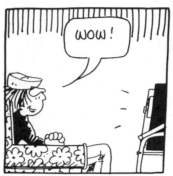

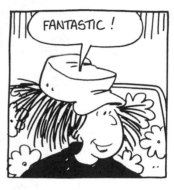

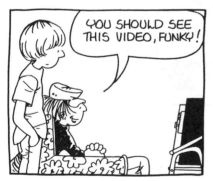

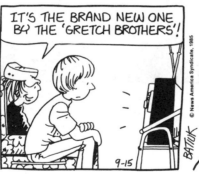

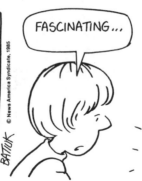

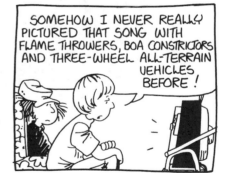

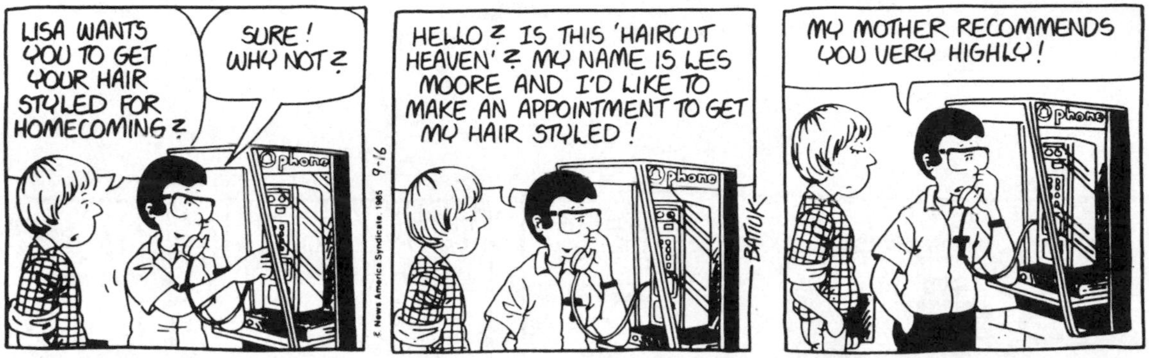
LISA WANTS YOU TO GET YOUR HAIR STYLED FOR HOMECOMING?
SURE! WHY NOT?
HELLO? IS THIS 'HAIRCUT HEAVEN'? MY NAME IS LES MOORE AND I'D LIKE TO MAKE AN APPOINTMENT TO GET MY HAIR STYLED!
MY MOTHER RECOMMENDS YOU VERY HIGHLY!
9-16
© News America Syndicate. 1985
BATIUK

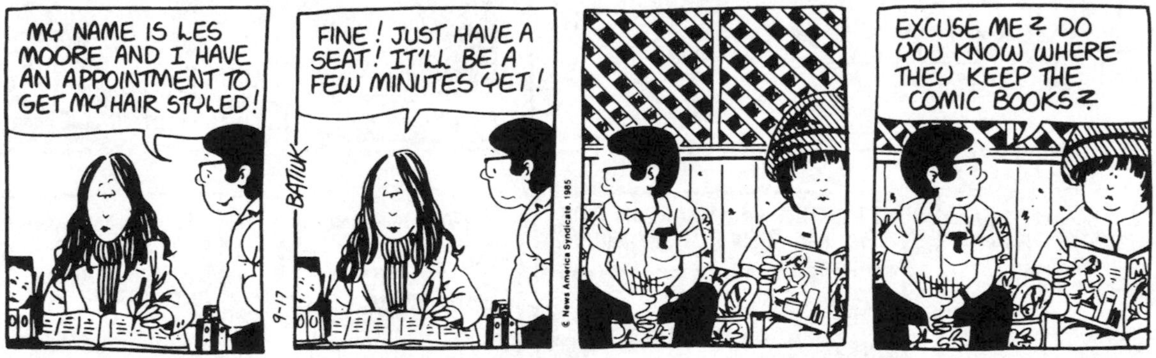
MY NAME IS LES MOORE AND I HAVE AN APPOINTMENT TO GET MY HAIR STYLED!
FINE! JUST HAVE A SEAT! IT'LL BE A FEW MINUTES YET!
EXCUSE ME? DO YOU KNOW WHERE THEY KEEP THE COMIC BOOKS?
9-17
BATIUK
© News America Syndicate. 1985

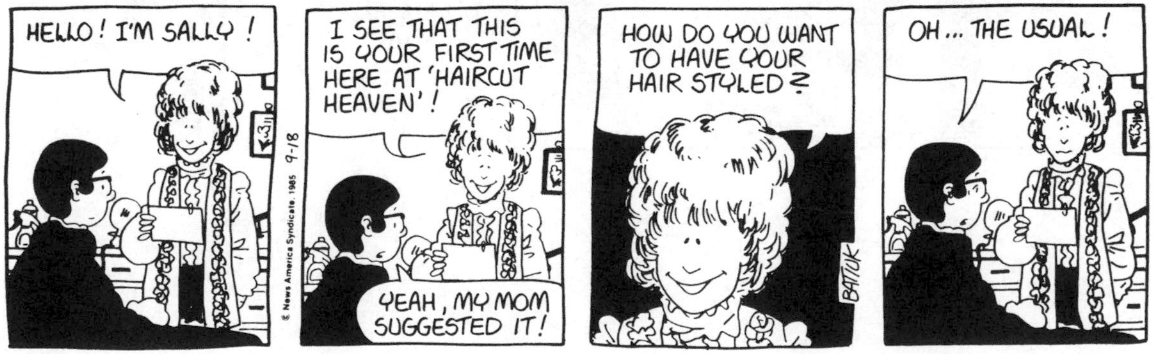
HELLO! I'M SALLY!
I SEE THAT THIS IS YOUR FIRST TIME HERE AT 'HAIRCUT HEAVEN'!
YEAH, MY MOM SUGGESTED IT!
HOW DO YOU WANT TO HAVE YOUR HAIR STYLED?
OH... THE USUAL!
9-18
© News America Syndicate. 1985
BATIUK

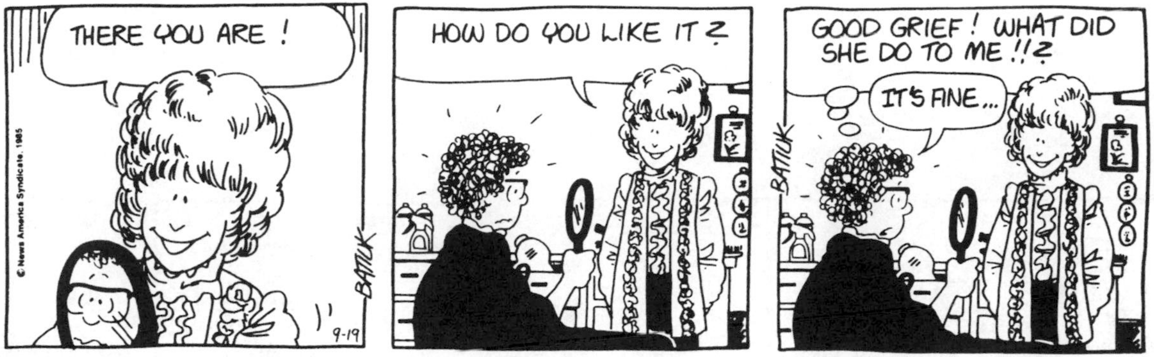
THERE YOU ARE !
HOW DO YOU LIKE IT ?
GOOD GRIEF ! WHAT DID SHE DO TO ME !!?
IT'S FINE...
© News America Syndicate. 1985
BATIUK
9-19

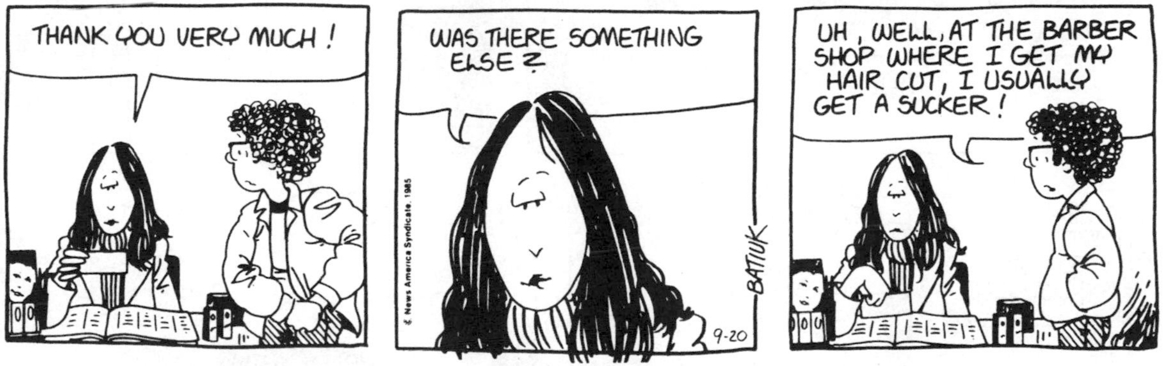
THANK YOU VERY MUCH !
WAS THERE SOMETHING ELSE ?
UH , WELL, AT THE BARBER SHOP WHERE I GET MY HAIR CUT, I USUALLY GET A SUCKER !
© News America Syndicate. 1985
BATIUK
9-20

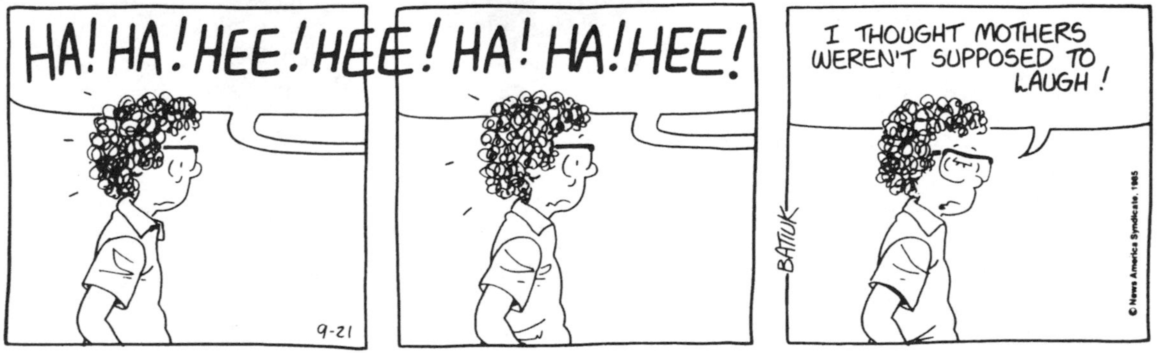
HA! HA! HEE! HEE! HA! HA! HEE!
I THOUGHT MOTHERS WEREN'T SUPPOSED TO LAUGH !
BATIUK
© News America Syndicate. 1985
9-21

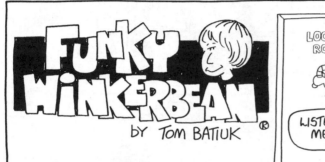

FUNKY WINKERBEAN
BY TOM BATIUK
LOCKER ROOM
LISTEN UP, MEN!
THIS WEEK IS OUR HOMECOMING GAME AND I DON'T THINK I HAVE TO TELL YOU WHAT THAT MEANS! YES! A QUESTION IN THE BACK...
OKAY... TRY BREAKING THE WORD DOWN INTO ITS TWO PARTS, 'HOME' AND 'COMING'...
MEN, FOR THE PAST TWENTY YEARS, WE'VE PLAYED OUR ARCH RIVAL BIG WALNUT TECH AT HOMECOMING...
AND FOR THE PAST TWENTY YEARS THEY'VE BEATEN OUR HEADS IN!
I THINK IT'S HIGH TIME WE DID SOMETHING ABOUT THAT!
BATIUK
© News America Syndicate, 1985 9-22
SO I'D LIKE ALL OF YOU TO SIGN THIS PETITION TO SEE IF WE CAN GET THE SCHEDULE CHANGED NEXT YEAR...

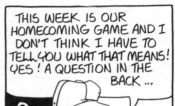

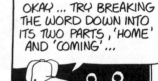

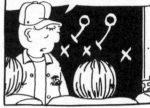

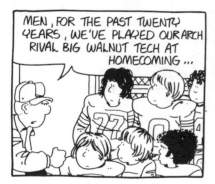

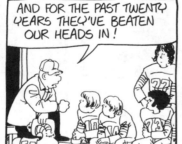

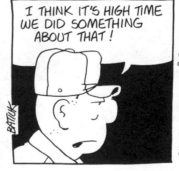

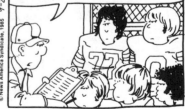

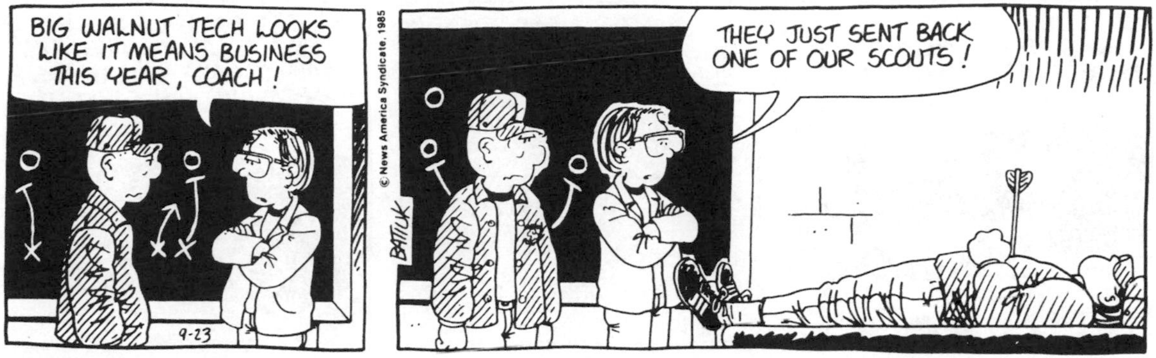
BIG WALNUT TECH LOOKS LIKE IT MEANS BUSINESS THIS YEAR, COACH!
9-23
© News America Syndicate, 1985
BATIUK
THEY JUST SENT BACK ONE OF OUR SCOUTS!

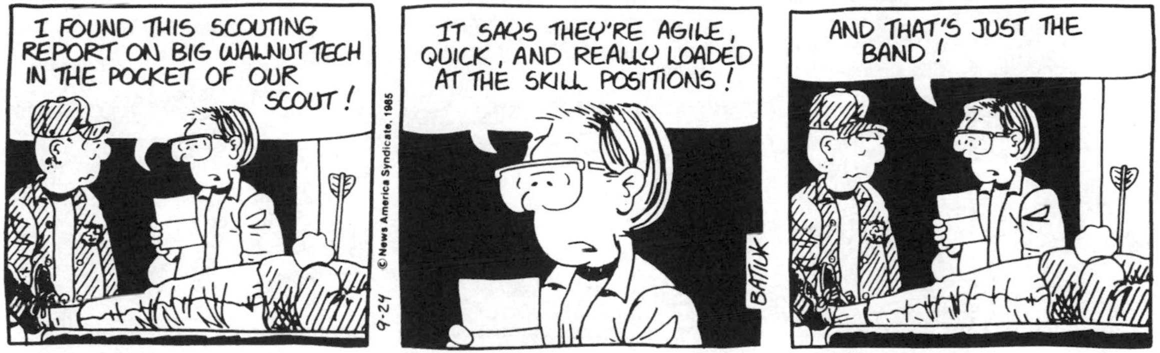
I FOUND THIS SCOUTING REPORT ON BIG WALNUT TECH IN THE POCKET OF OUR SCOUT!
9-24
© News America Syndicate, 1985
IT SAYS THEY'RE AGILE, QUICK, AND REALLY LOADED AT THE SKILL POSITIONS!
BATIUK
AND THAT'S JUST THE BAND!

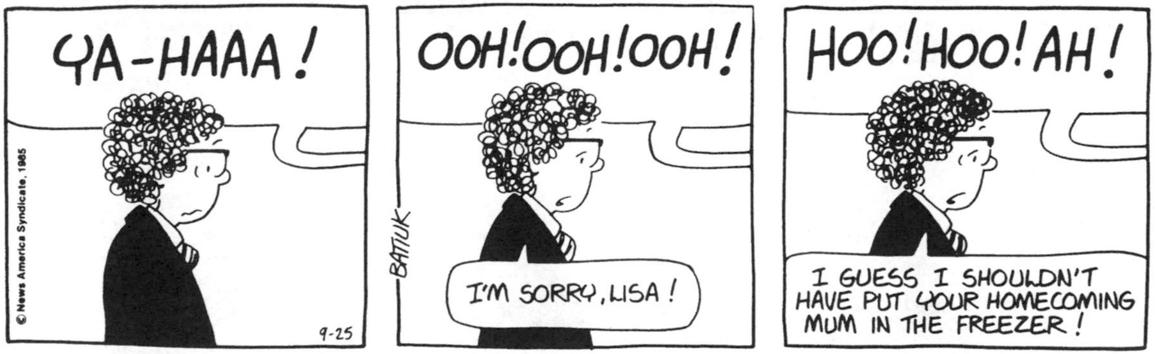
YA-HAAA!
© News America Syndicate, 1985
9-25
BATIUK
OOH! OOH! OOH!
I'M SORRY, LISA!
HOO! HOO! AH!
I GUESS I SHOULDN'T HAVE PUT YOUR HOMECOMING MUM IN THE FREEZER!

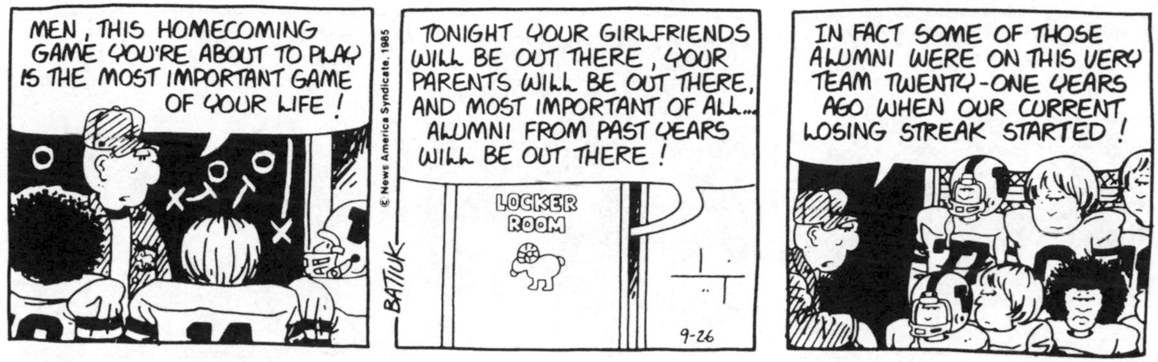
MEN, THIS HOMECOMING GAME YOU'RE ABOUT TO PLAY IS THE MOST IMPORTANT GAME OF YOUR LIFE!
© News America Syndicate, 1985
BATIUK
TONIGHT YOUR GIRLFRIENDS WILL BE OUT THERE, YOUR PARENTS WILL BE OUT THERE, AND MOST IMPORTANT OF ALL... ALUMNI FROM PAST YEARS WILL BE OUT THERE!
LOCKER ROOM
9-26
IN FACT SOME OF THOSE ALUMNI WERE ON THIS VERY TEAM TWENTY-ONE YEARS AGO WHEN OUR CURRENT LOSING STREAK STARTED!

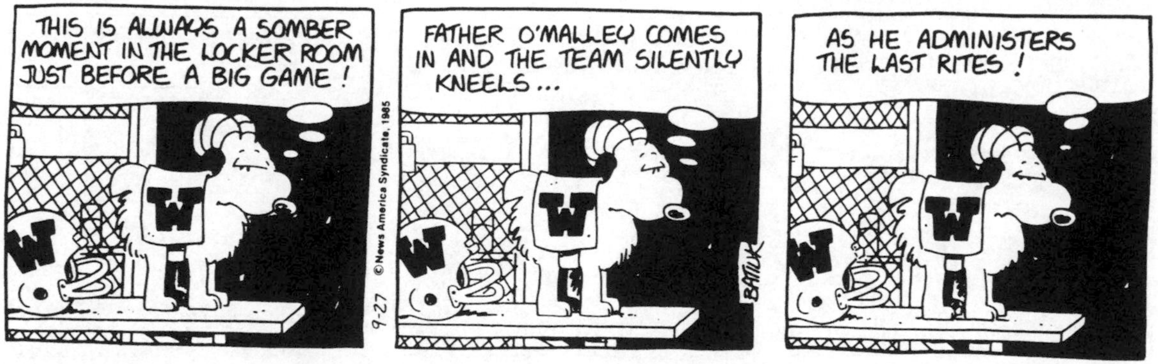
THIS IS ALWAYS A SOMBER MOMENT IN THE LOCKER ROOM JUST BEFORE A BIG GAME!
© News America Syndicate, 1985
9-27
FATHER O'MALLEY COMES IN AND THE TEAM SILENTLY KNEELS...
BATIUK
AS HE ADMINISTERS THE LAST RITES!

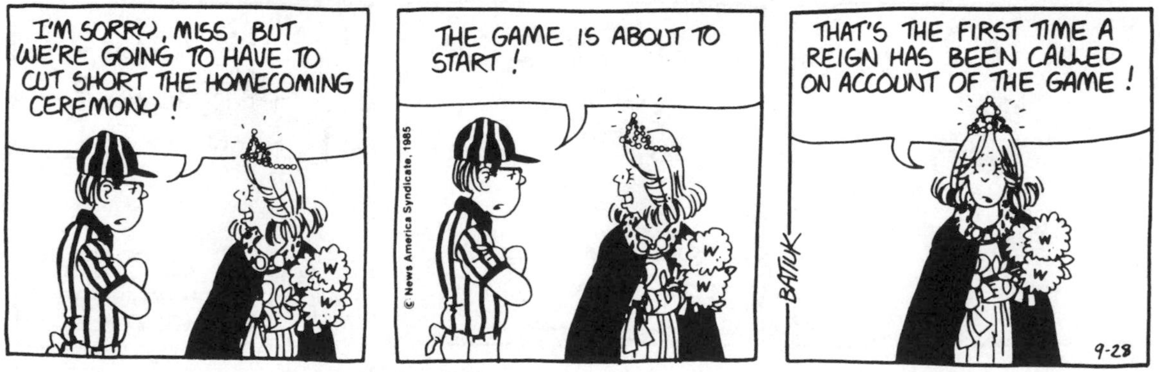
I'M SORRY, MISS, BUT WE'RE GOING TO HAVE TO CUT SHORT THE HOMECOMING CEREMONY!
THE GAME IS ABOUT TO START!
© News America Syndicate, 1985
BATIUK
THAT'S THE FIRST TIME A REIGN HAS BEEN CALLED ON ACCOUNT OF THE GAME!
9-28

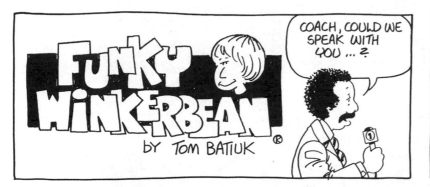

FUNKY WINKERBEAN
BY TOM BATIUK
COACH, COULD WE SPEAK WITH YOU ... ?
OBVIOUSLY YOU'VE GOT SOME PROBLEMS, COACH, SINCE BIG WALNUT TECH RAN FOR A TOUCHDOWN EVERY TIME THEY SNAPPED THE BALL IN THE FIRST HALF!
THAT'S TRUE, MIKE... HOWEVER WE COMPLETELY SHUT DOWN THEIR PASSING GAME!
THIS IS MIKE MAJORS AT WESTVIEW HIGH SCHOOL WHERE THE SCAPEGOATS ARE NOT HAVING A HAPPY HOMECOMING!
THEY'RE ABOUT TO START THE SECOND HALF AGAINST THEIR ARCH-RIVAL, BIG WALNUT TECH, AND THE CROWD HERE PRETTY MUCH TELLS THE WHOLE STORY! LISTEN...
BATIUK
9-29
© News America Syndicate, 1985
THEY SCORED ON A THREE-YARD SCAMPER OFF LEFT TACKLE WITH ONE MINUTE GONE IN THE FIRST QUARTER... AND THEN WE FUMBLED THE ENSUING KICKOFF...

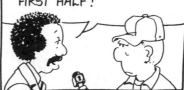

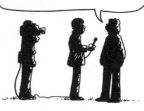

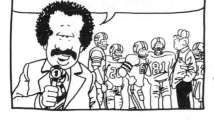

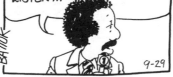

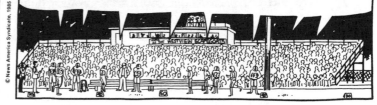

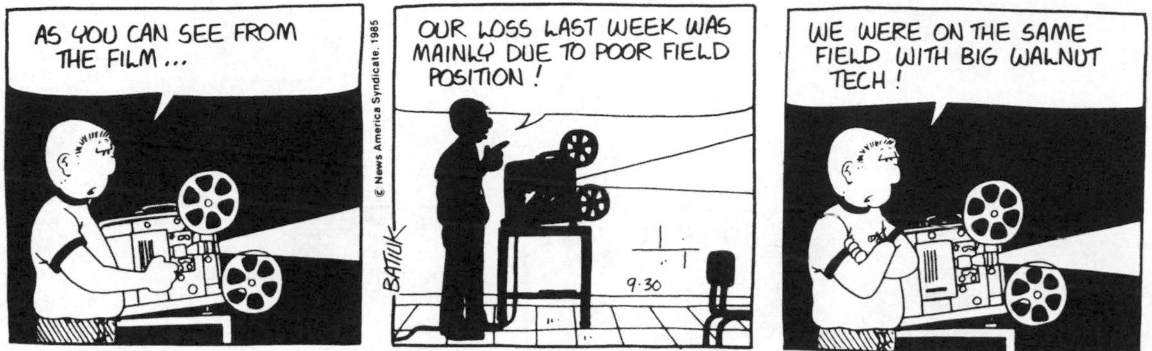
AS YOU CAN SEE FROM THE FILM ...
OUR LOSS LAST WEEK WAS MAINLY DUE TO POOR FIELD POSITION!
© News America Syndicate, 1985
BATIUK
9-30
WE WERE ON THE SAME FIELD WITH BIG WALNUT TECH!

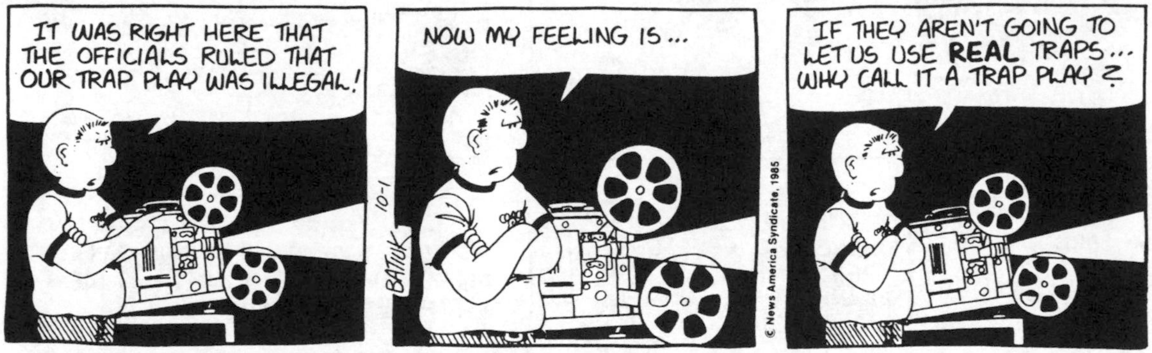
IT WAS RIGHT HERE THAT THE OFFICIALS RULED THAT OUR TRAP PLAY WAS ILLEGAL!
BATIUK
10-1
NOW MY FEELING IS ...
IF THEY AREN'T GOING TO LET US USE **REAL** TRAPS ... WHY CALL IT A TRAP PLAY?
© News America Syndicate, 1985

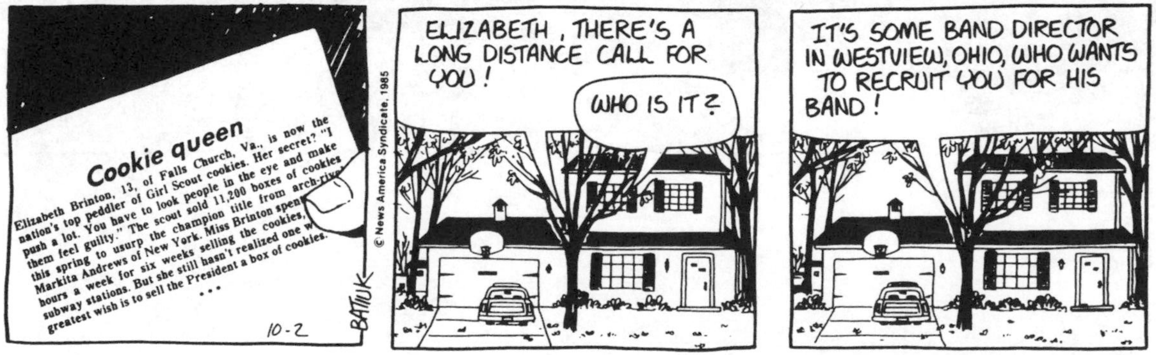
Cookie queen
Elizabeth Brinton, 13, of Falls Church, Va., is now the
nation's top peddler of Girl Scout cookies. Her secret? "I
push a lot. You have to look people in the eye and make
them feel guilty." The scout sold 11,200 boxes of cookies
this spring to usurp the champion title from arch-riv
Markita Andrews of New York. Miss Brinton spen
hours a week for six weeks selling the cookies,
subway stations. But she still hasn't realized one w
greatest wish is to sell the President a box of cookies.
...
10-2
BATIUK
© News America Syndicate, 1985
ELIZABETH, THERE'S A LONG DISTANCE CALL FOR YOU!
WHO IS IT?
IT'S SOME BAND DIRECTOR IN WESTVIEW, OHIO, WHO WANTS TO RECRUIT YOU FOR HIS BAND!

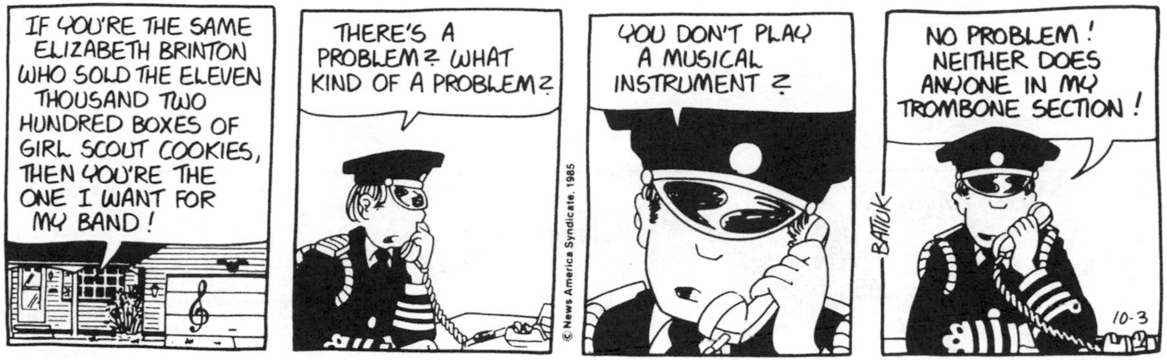
IF YOU'RE THE SAME ELIZABETH BRINTON WHO SOLD THE ELEVEN THOUSAND TWO HUNDRED BOXES OF GIRL SCOUT COOKIES, THEN YOU'RE THE ONE I WANT FOR MY BAND!
THERE'S A PROBLEM? WHAT KIND OF A PROBLEM?
© News America Syndicate, 1985
YOU DON'T PLAY A MUSICAL INSTRUMENT?
BATIUK
NO PROBLEM! NEITHER DOES ANYONE IN MY TROMBONE SECTION!
10-3

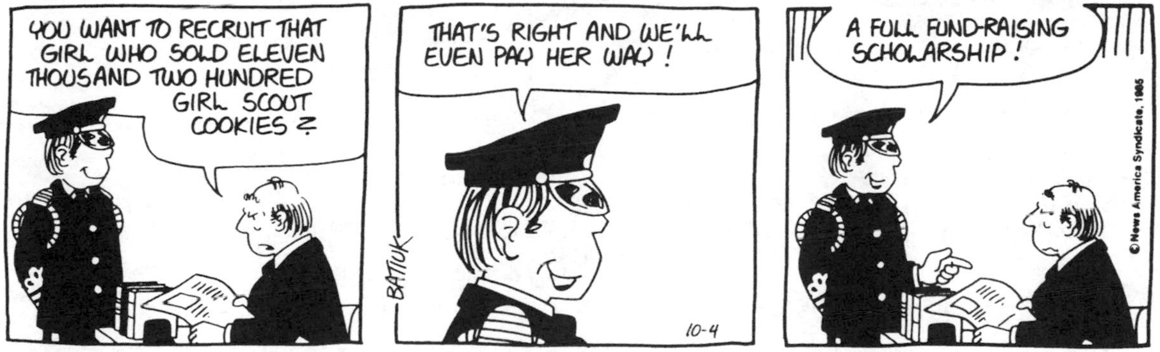
YOU WANT TO RECRUIT THAT GIRL WHO SOLD ELEVEN THOUSAND TWO HUNDRED GIRL SCOUT COOKIES?
BATIUK
THAT'S RIGHT AND WE'LL EVEN PAY HER WAY!
10-4
A FULL FUND-RAISING SCHOLARSHIP!
© News America Syndicate, 1985

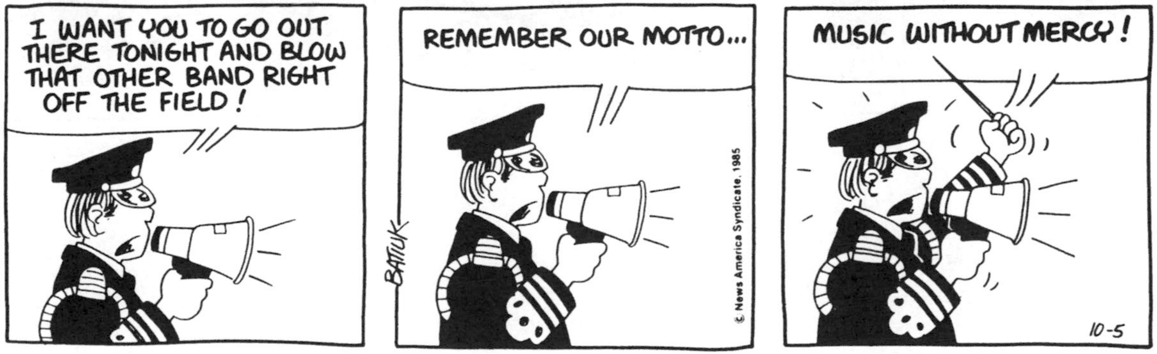
I WANT YOU TO GO OUT THERE TONIGHT AND BLOW THAT OTHER BAND RIGHT OFF THE FIELD!
BATIUK
REMEMBER OUR MOTTO...
© News America Syndicate, 1985
MUSIC WITHOUT MERCY!
10-5

FUNKY WINKERBEAN
BY TOM BATIUK ®
I JUST DON'T UNDERSTAND ANY OF THIS ...
WHY IS IT THAT WE HAVE TO FALL FROM THE TREE AND DIE WHEN AUTUMN COMES?
MAYBE THE WORDS TO THIS SONG WILL HELP YOU UNDERSTAND...
TO EVERYTHING, TURN, TURN, TURN... THERE IS A SEASON, TURN, TURN, TURN... AND A TIME TO EVERY PURPOSE UNDER HEAVEN!
WHO TAUGHT YOU THAT SONG?
THE BIRDS!
BATIUK
10-6
© News America Syndicate, 1985

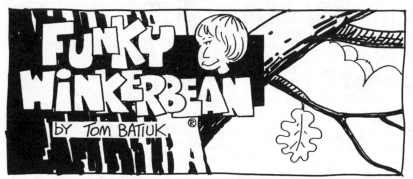

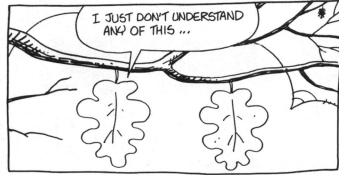

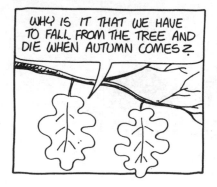

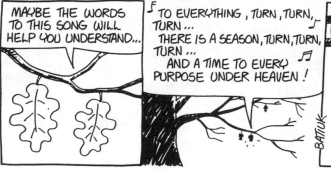

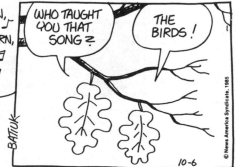

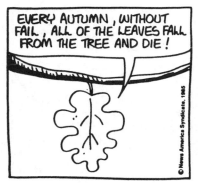

EVERY AUTUMN, WITHOUT FAIL, ALL OF THE LEAVES FALL FROM THE TREE AND DIE!
© News America Syndicate, 1985
AND IF YOU THINK THAT'S DEPRESSING...
BATIUK
YOU SHOULD SEE OUR INSURANCE PREMIUMS!
10-7

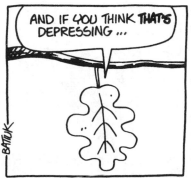

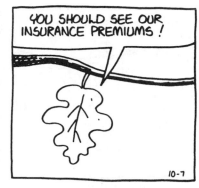

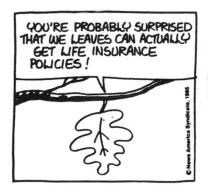

YOU'RE PROBABLY SURPRISED THAT WE LEAVES CAN ACTUALLY GET LIFE INSURANCE POLICIES!
© News America Syndicate, 1985
BASICALLY, WE HAVE A CHOICE BETWEEN TWO KINDS...
BATIUK
SHORT TERM INSURANCE... OR WHOLE LEAF!
10-8

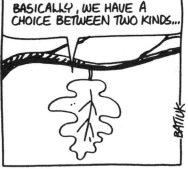

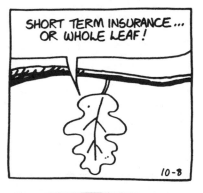

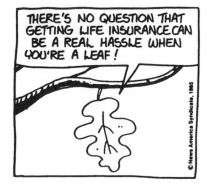

THERE'S NO QUESTION THAT GETTING LIFE INSURANCE CAN BE A REAL HASSLE WHEN YOU'RE A LEAF!
© News America Syndicate, 1985
FORTUNATELY, IT WASN'T QUITE AS DIFFICULT FOR ME!
BATIUK
MY COMPANY, 'MEA CULPA INSURANCE,' HAD A BRANCH OFFICE RIGHT HERE IN OUR TREE!
10-9

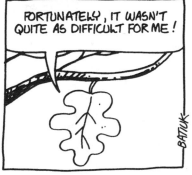

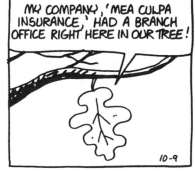

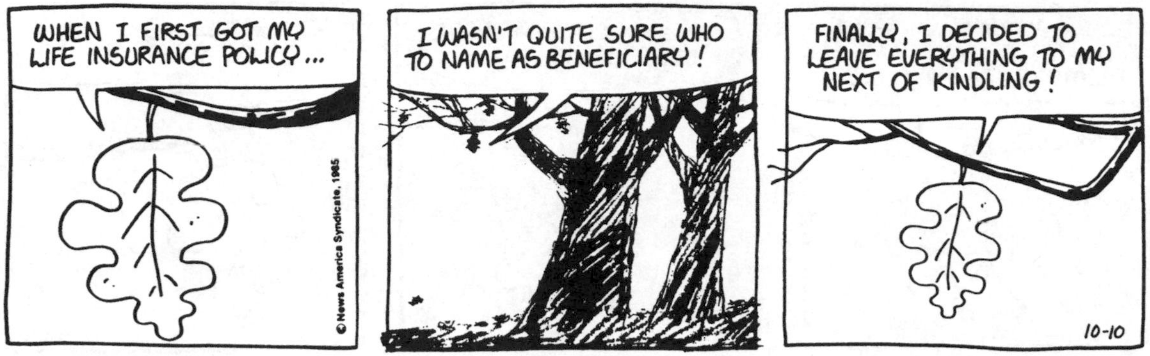
WHEN I FIRST GOT MY LIFE INSURANCE POLICY...
© News America Syndicate, 1985
I WASN'T QUITE SURE WHO TO NAME AS BENEFICIARY!
FINALLY, I DECIDED TO LEAVE EVERYTHING TO MY NEXT OF KINDLING!
10-10

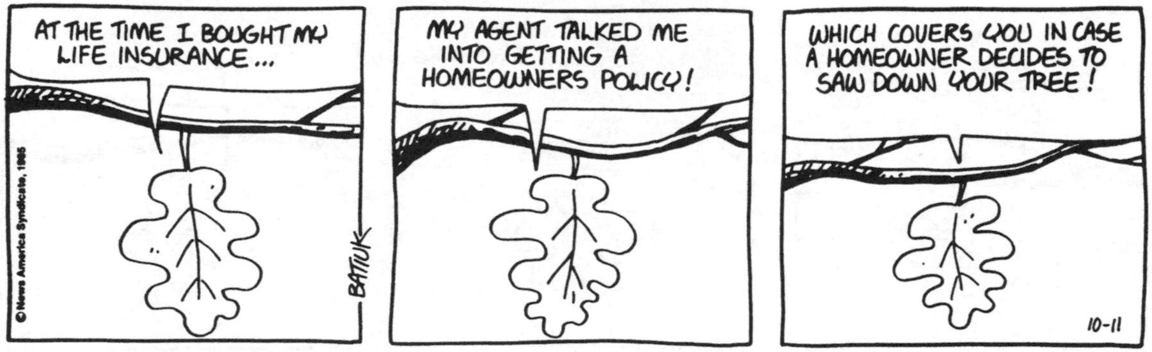
AT THE TIME I BOUGHT MY LIFE INSURANCE...
© News America Syndicate, 1985
BATIUK
MY AGENT TALKED ME INTO GETTING A HOMEOWNERS POLICY!
WHICH COVERS YOU IN CASE A HOMEOWNER DECIDES TO SAW DOWN YOUR TREE!
10-11

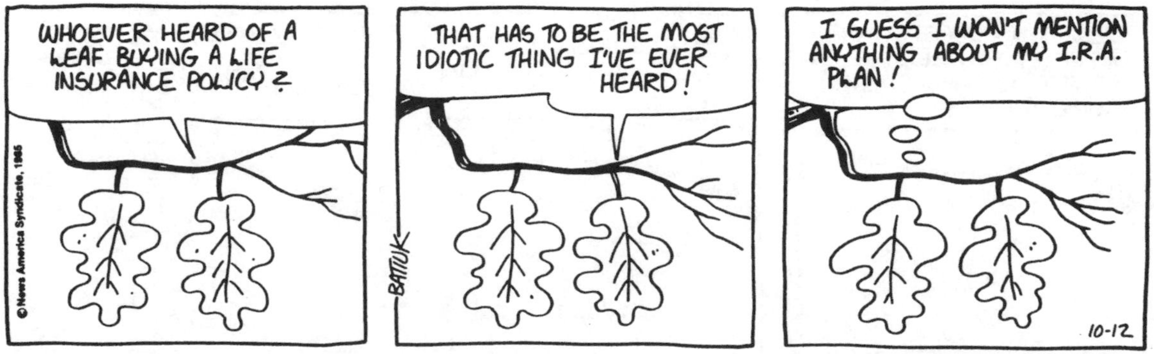
WHOEVER HEARD OF A LEAF BUYING A LIFE INSURANCE POLICY?
© News America Syndicate, 1985
BATIUK
THAT HAS TO BE THE MOST IDIOTIC THING I'VE EVER HEARD!
I GUESS I WON'T MENTION ANYTHING ABOUT MY I.R.A. PLAN!
10-12

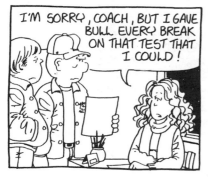

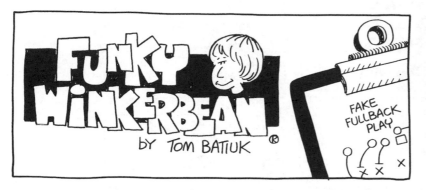

FUNKY WINKERBEAN
BY TOM BATIUK ®
FAKE FULLBACK PLAY
YOUR FAKE FULLBACK PLAY WILL NEVER WORK, COACH!
WHY NOT?
YOUR FULLBACK HAS JUST BEEN DECLARED INELIGIBLE BECAUSE OF GRADES!
I'M SORRY, COACH, BUT I GAVE BULL EVERY BREAK ON THAT TEST THAT I COULD!
WAIT A MINUTE! WHAT ABOUT THESE TWO POINTS HERE?
BATIUK
I TOOK OFF FOR SPELLING BECAUSE BULL MISSPELLED 'RELIEF'!
10-13
© News America Syndicate, 1985
YOU DUMMY... IT'S R...O...L...A...I...D...S!

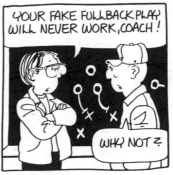

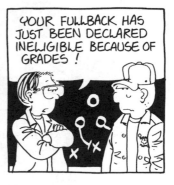

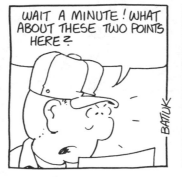

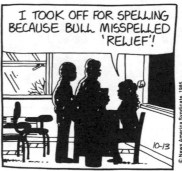

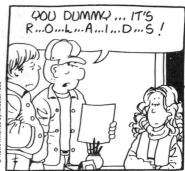

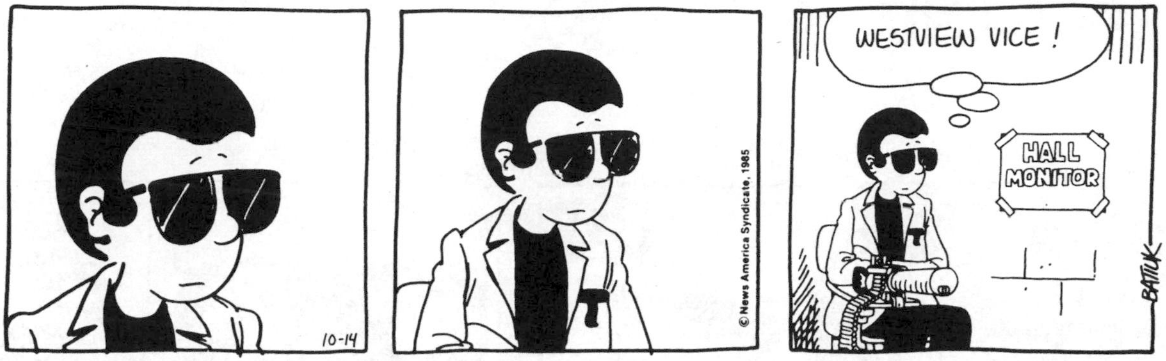
10-14
©News America Syndicate, 1985
WESTVIEW VICE !
HALL MONITOR
BATIUK

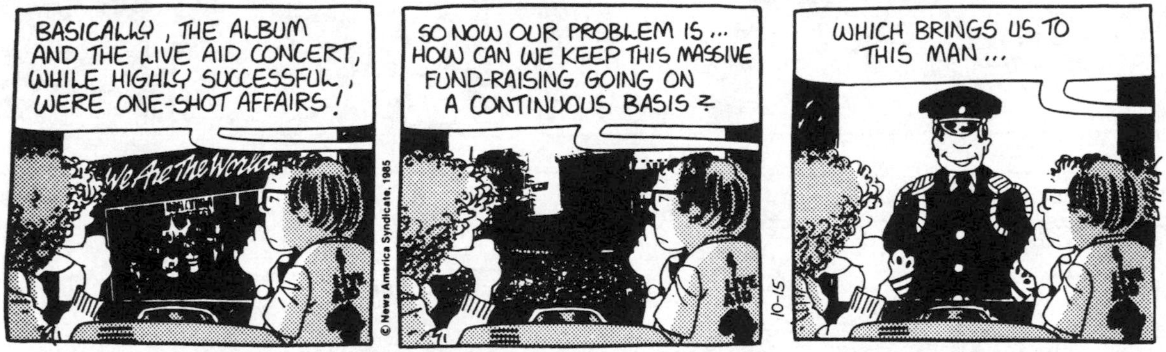
BASICALLY , THE ALBUM AND THE LIVE AID CONCERT, WHILE HIGHLY SUCCESSFUL , WERE ONE-SHOT AFFAIRS !
We Are The World
©News America Syndicate, 1985
SO NOW OUR PROBLEM IS ... HOW CAN WE KEEP THIS MASSIVE FUND-RAISING GOING ON A CONTINUOUS BASIS ?
10-15
WHICH BRINGS US TO THIS MAN ...
BATIUK

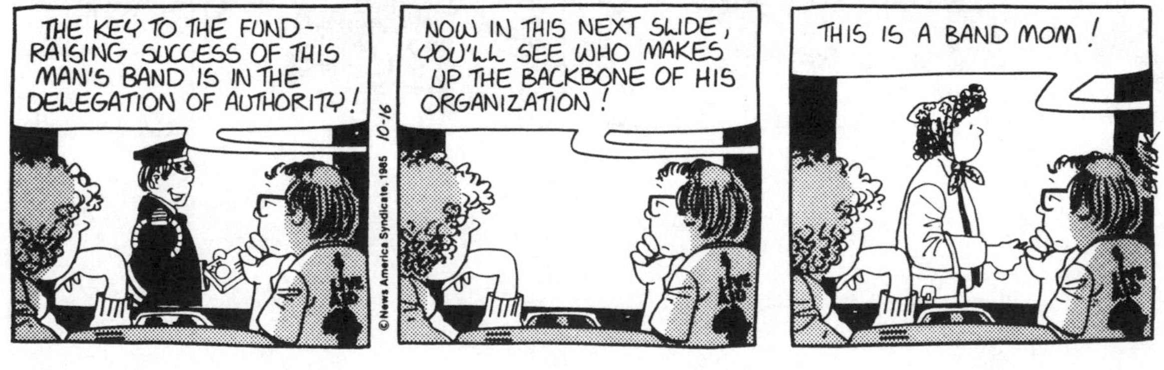
THE KEY TO THE FUND-RAISING SUCCESS OF THIS MAN'S BAND IS IN THE DELEGATION OF AUTHORITY !
10-16
©News America Syndicate, 1985
NOW IN THIS NEXT SLIDE, YOU'LL SEE WHO MAKES UP THE BACKBONE OF HIS ORGANIZATION !
THIS IS A BAND MOM !
BATIUK

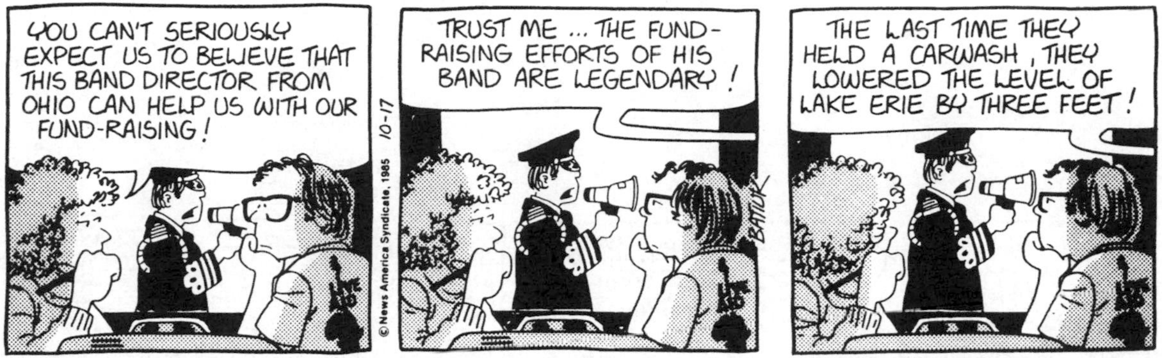
YOU CAN'T SERIOUSLY EXPECT US TO BELIEVE THAT THIS BAND DIRECTOR FROM OHIO CAN HELP US WITH OUR FUND-RAISING!
10-17
© News America Syndicate, 1985
TRUST ME ... THE FUND-RAISING EFFORTS OF HIS BAND ARE LEGENDARY!
BATIUK
THE LAST TIME THEY HELD A CARWASH, THEY LOWERED THE LEVEL OF LAKE ERIE BY THREE FEET!

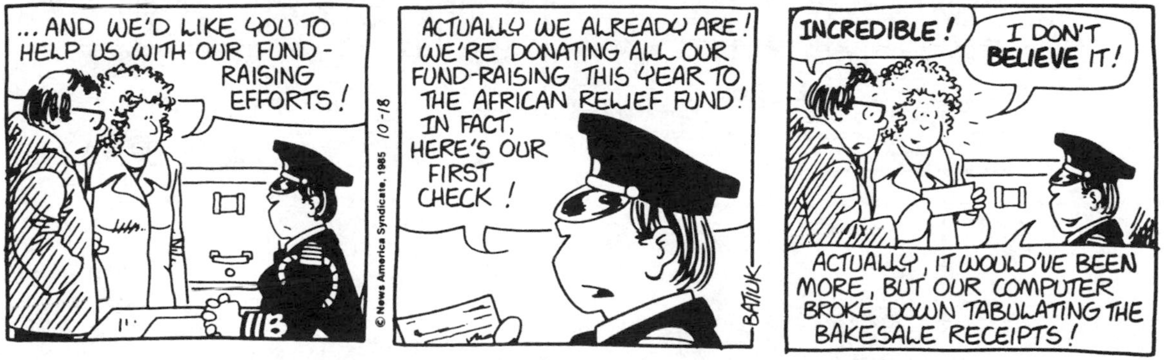
... AND WE'D LIKE YOU TO HELP US WITH OUR FUND-RAISING EFFORTS!
10-18
© News America Syndicate, 1985
ACTUALLY WE ALREADY ARE! WE'RE DONATING ALL OUR FUND-RAISING THIS YEAR TO THE AFRICAN RELIEF FUND! IN FACT, HERE'S OUR FIRST CHECK!
BATIUK
INCREDIBLE!
I DON'T BELIEVE IT!
ACTUALLY, IT WOULD'VE BEEN MORE, BUT OUR COMPUTER BROKE DOWN TABULATING THE BAKESALE RECEIPTS!

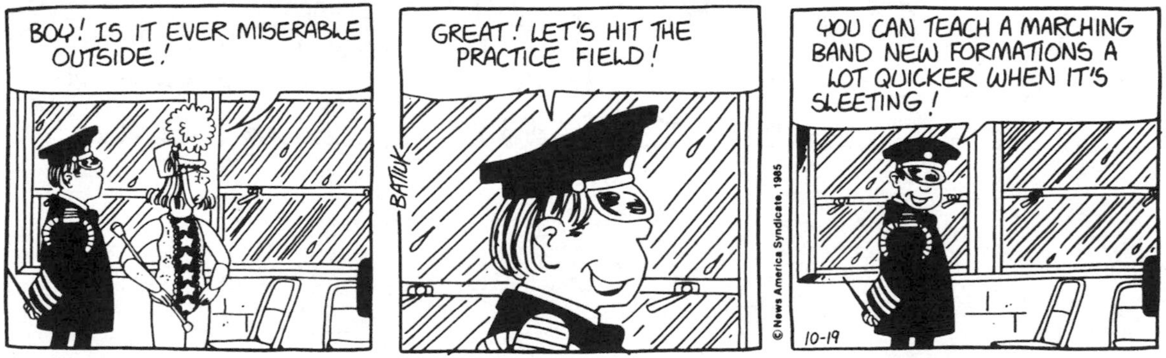
BOY! IS IT EVER MISERABLE OUTSIDE!
BATIUK
GREAT! LET'S HIT THE PRACTICE FIELD!
© News America Syndicate, 1985
10-19
YOU CAN TEACH A MARCHING BAND NEW FORMATIONS A LOT QUICKER WHEN IT'S SLEETING!

FUNKY WINKERBEAN
BY TOM BATIUK ®
NINE HUNDRED AND NINETY-TWO BOTTLES OF BEER ON THE WALL ...
WESTVIEW SCHOOL DISTRICT 34
WHY DID I EVER VOLUNTEER TO DRIVE THE BUS FOR THE BAND?
IT MUST BE BECAUSE I ENJOY FINE MUSIC!
NINE HUNDRED AND NINETY-TWO BOTTLES OF BEER...
I HATE GETTING STUCK DRIVING THE BAND TO AN AWAY GAME!
IF I HAD A CHOICE ...
BATIUK
I'D MUCH RATHER DRIVE THE FOOTBALL TEAM!
© News America Syndicate, 1985
IT'S ALWAYS SO MUCH QUIETER FOLLOWING ANOTHER HUMILIATING LOSS!
10-20
IF ONE OF THOSE BOTTLES SHOULD FALL OFF THE WALL ... THERE'D BE NINE HUNDRED AND NINETY-ONE BOTTLES OF...

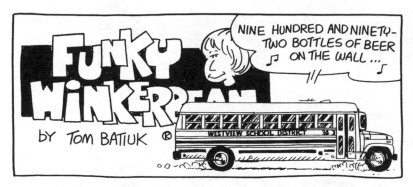

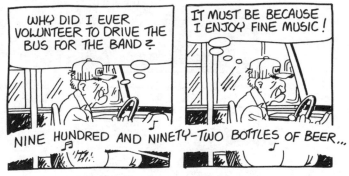

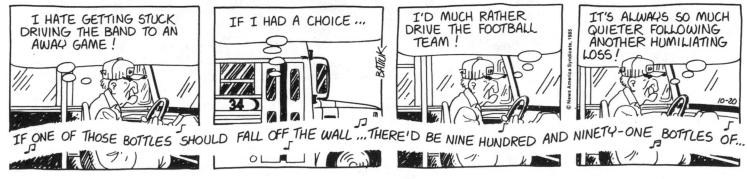

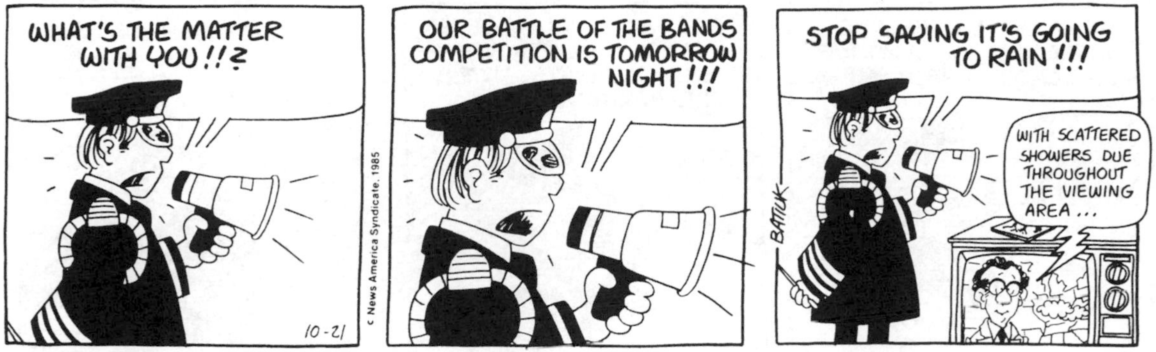
WHAT'S THE MATTER WITH YOU !!?
10-21
c News America Syndicate. 1985
OUR BATTLE OF THE BANDS COMPETITION IS TOMORROW NIGHT !!!
STOP SAYING IT'S GOING TO RAIN !!!
WITH SCATTERED SHOWERS DUE THROUGHOUT THE VIEWING AREA ...
BATIUK

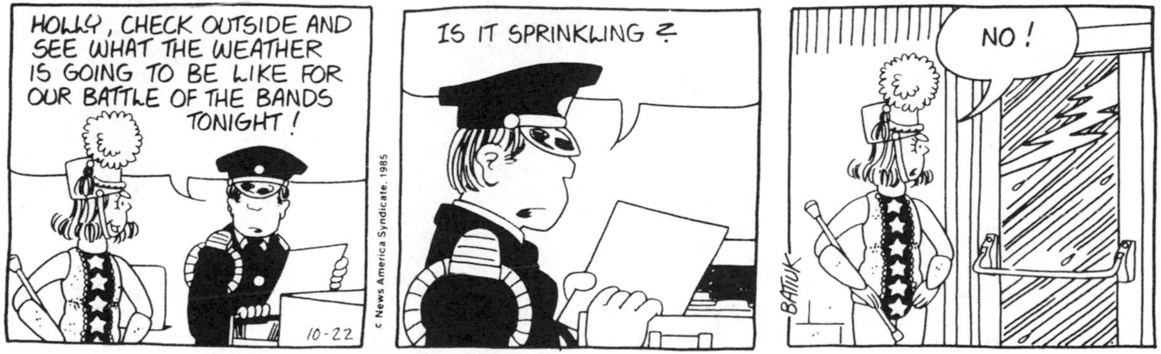
HOLLY, CHECK OUTSIDE AND SEE WHAT THE WEATHER IS GOING TO BE LIKE FOR OUR BATTLE OF THE BANDS TONIGHT !
10-22
c News America Syndicate. 1985
IS IT SPRINKLING ?
NO !
BATIUK

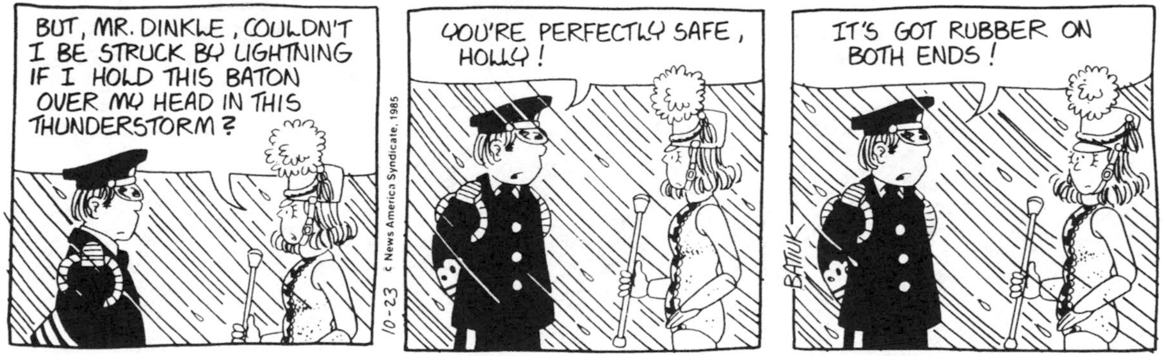
BUT, MR. DINKLE, COULDN'T I BE STRUCK BY LIGHTNING IF I HOLD THIS BATON OVER MY HEAD IN THIS THUNDERSTORM ?
10-23
c News America Syndicate. 1985
YOU'RE PERFECTLY SAFE, HOLLY !
IT'S GOT RUBBER ON BOTH ENDS !
BATIUK

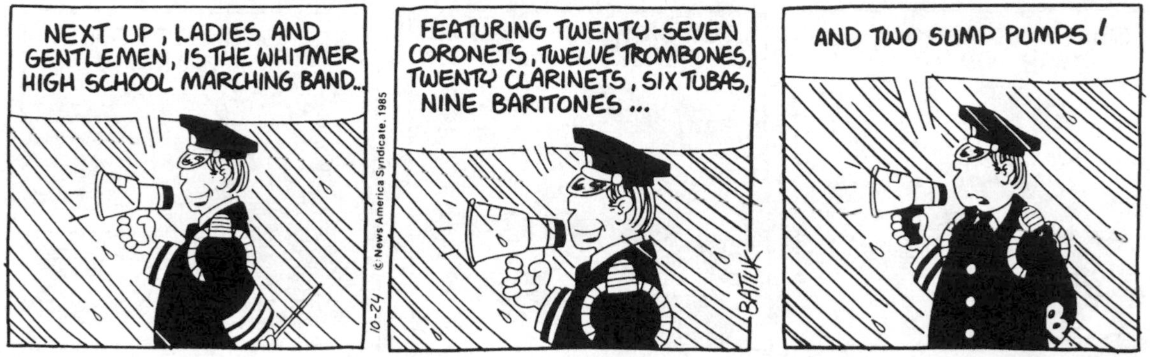
NEXT UP, LADIES AND GENTLEMEN, IS THE WHITMER HIGH SCHOOL MARCHING BAND...
FEATURING TWENTY-SEVEN CORONETS, TWELVE TROMBONES, TWENTY CLARINETS, SIX TUBAS, NINE BARITONES ...
AND TWO SUMP PUMPS!
© News America Syndicate, 1985

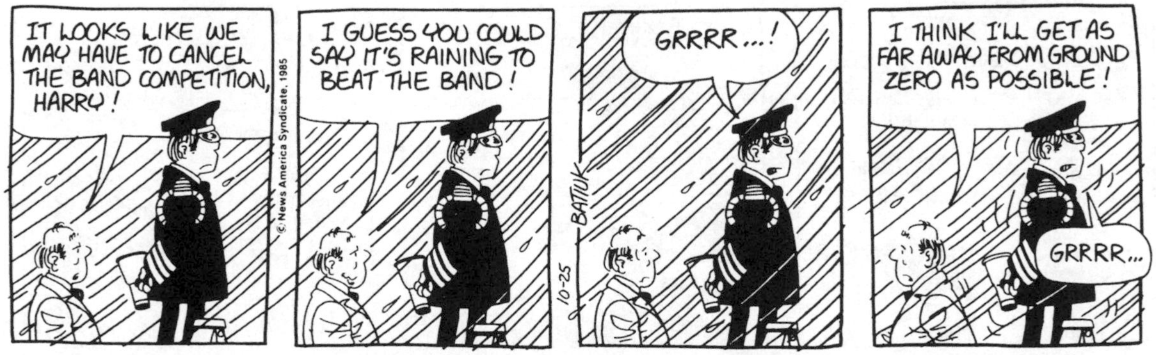
IT LOOKS LIKE WE MAY HAVE TO CANCEL THE BAND COMPETITION, HARRY!
I GUESS YOU COULD SAY IT'S RAINING TO BEAT THE BAND!
GRRRR...!
I THINK I'LL GET AS FAR AWAY FROM GROUND ZERO AS POSSIBLE!
GRRRR...
© News America Syndicate, 1985

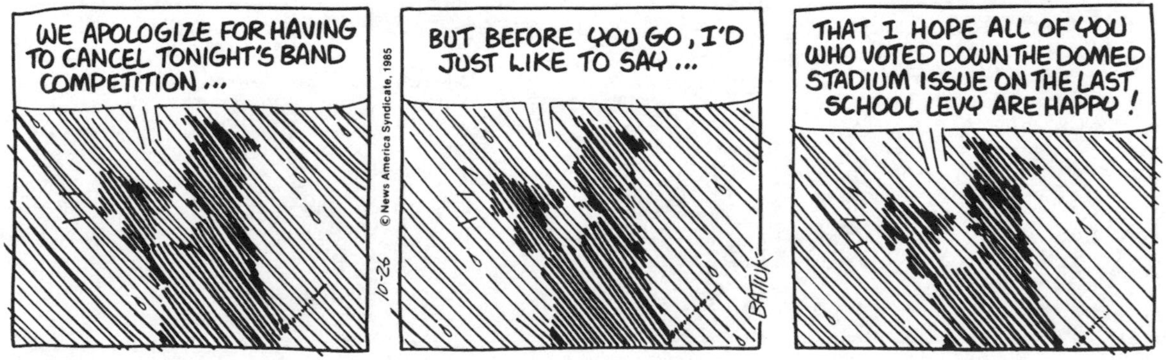
WE APOLOGIZE FOR HAVING TO CANCEL TONIGHT'S BAND COMPETITION...
BUT BEFORE YOU GO, I'D JUST LIKE TO SAY...
THAT I HOPE ALL OF YOU WHO VOTED DOWN THE DOMED STADIUM ISSUE ON THE LAST SCHOOL LEVY ARE HAPPY!
© News America Syndicate, 1985

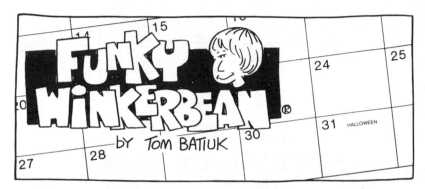

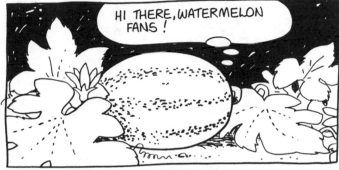

FUNKY WINKERBEAN
BY TOM BATIUK
HALLOWEEN
HI THERE, WATERMELON FANS !
YOU KNOW, WATERMELONS NOT ONLY MAKE GREAT JACK O'LANTERNS ON HALLOWEEN ...
BUT WE'RE SUPER FOR HALLOWEEN TREATS AS WELL !
WHEN THE LITTLE KIDDIES COME TO YOUR DOOR ...
DROP A WATERMELON IN THEIR BAG AND JUST WATCH THEIR EYES LIGHT UP !
BATIUK
10-27
© News America Syndicate. 1985

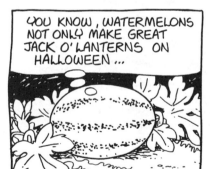

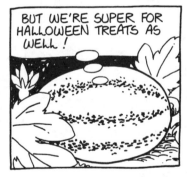

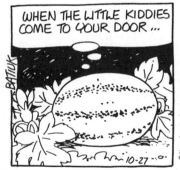

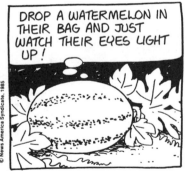

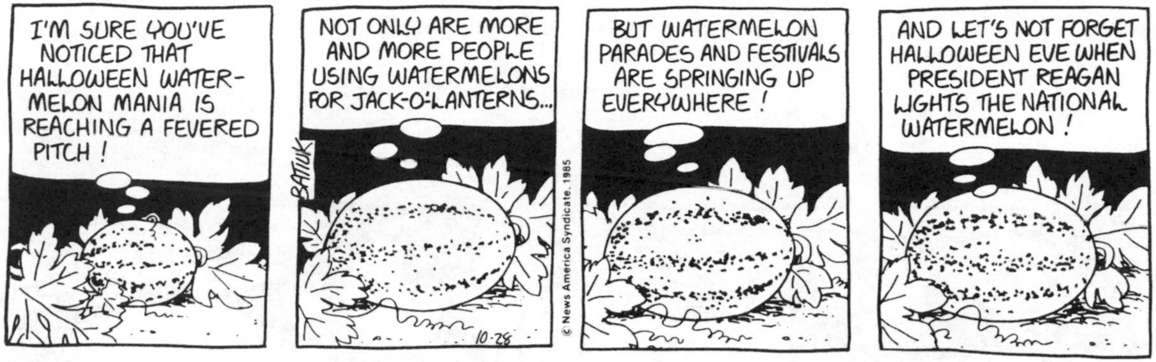
I'M SURE YOU'VE NOTICED THAT HALLOWEEN WATER-MELON MANIA IS REACHING A FEVERED PITCH !
NOT ONLY ARE MORE AND MORE PEOPLE USING WATERMELONS FOR JACK-O'-LANTERNS...
BATIUK
10-28
© News America Syndicate, 1985
BUT WATERMELON PARADES AND FESTIVALS ARE SPRINGING UP EVERYWHERE !
AND LET'S NOT FORGET HALLOWEEN EVE WHEN PRESIDENT REAGAN LIGHTS THE NATIONAL WATERMELON !

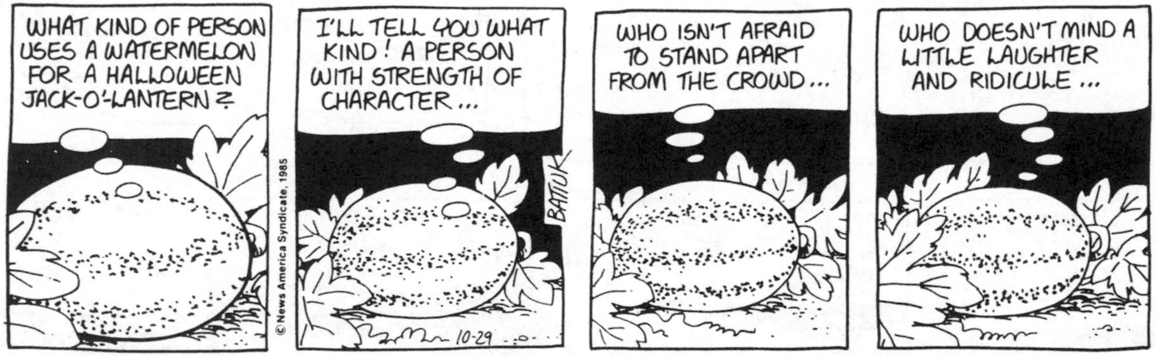
WHAT KIND OF PERSON USES A WATERMELON FOR A HALLOWEEN JACK-O'-LANTERN ?
© News America Syndicate, 1985
I'LL TELL YOU WHAT KIND ! A PERSON WITH STRENGTH OF CHARACTER ...
10-29
BATIUK
WHO ISN'T AFRAID TO STAND APART FROM THE CROWD ...
WHO DOESN'T MIND A LITTLE LAUGHTER AND RIDICULE ...

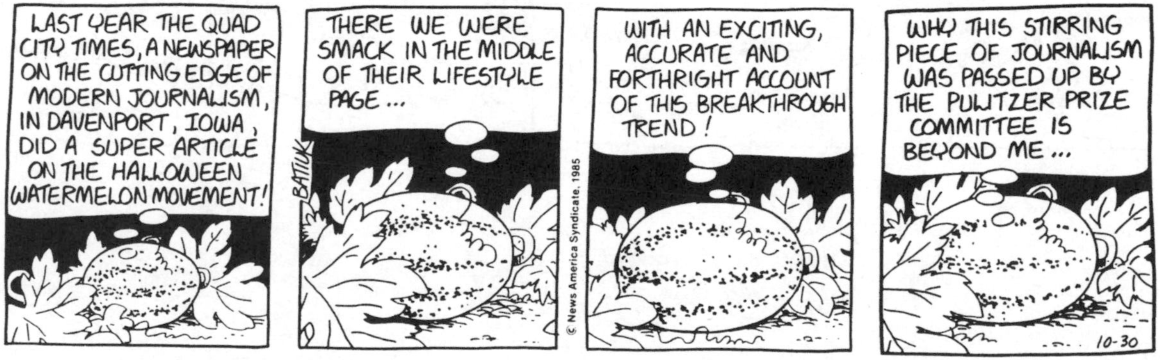
LAST YEAR THE QUAD CITY TIMES, A NEWSPAPER ON THE CUTTING EDGE OF MODERN JOURNALISM, IN DAVENPORT, IOWA, DID A SUPER ARTICLE ON THE HALLOWEEN WATERMELON MOVEMENT!
BATIUK
THERE WE WERE SMACK IN THE MIDDLE OF THEIR LIFESTYLE PAGE ...
© News America Syndicate, 1985
WITH AN EXCITING, ACCURATE AND FORTHRIGHT ACCOUNT OF THIS BREAKTHROUGH TREND !
WHY THIS STIRRING PIECE OF JOURNALISM WAS PASSED UP BY THE PULITZER PRIZE COMMITTEE IS BEYOND ME ...
10-30

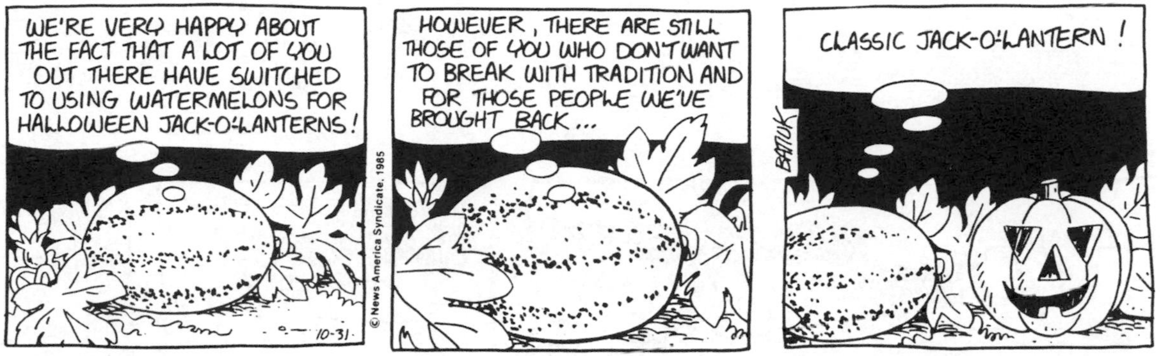
WE'RE VERY HAPPY ABOUT THE FACT THAT A LOT OF YOU OUT THERE HAVE SWITCHED TO USING WATERMELONS FOR HALLOWEEN JACK-O'-LANTERNS!
10-31
© News America Syndicate, 1985
HOWEVER, THERE ARE STILL THOSE OF YOU WHO DON'T WANT TO BREAK WITH TRADITION AND FOR THOSE PEOPLE WE'VE BROUGHT BACK...
CLASSIC JACK-O'-LANTERN!
BATIUK

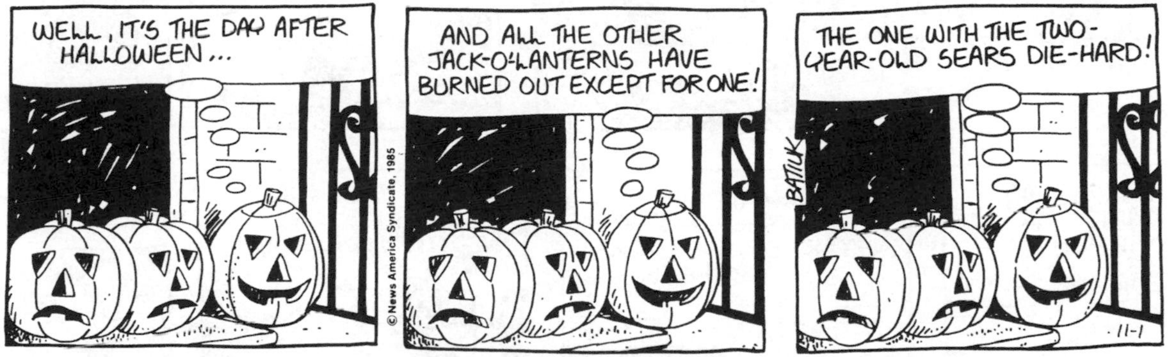
WELL, IT'S THE DAY AFTER HALLOWEEN...
© News America Syndicate, 1985
AND ALL THE OTHER JACK-O'-LANTERNS HAVE BURNED OUT EXCEPT FOR ONE!
THE ONE WITH THE TWO-YEAR-OLD SEARS DIE-HARD!
BATIUK
11-1

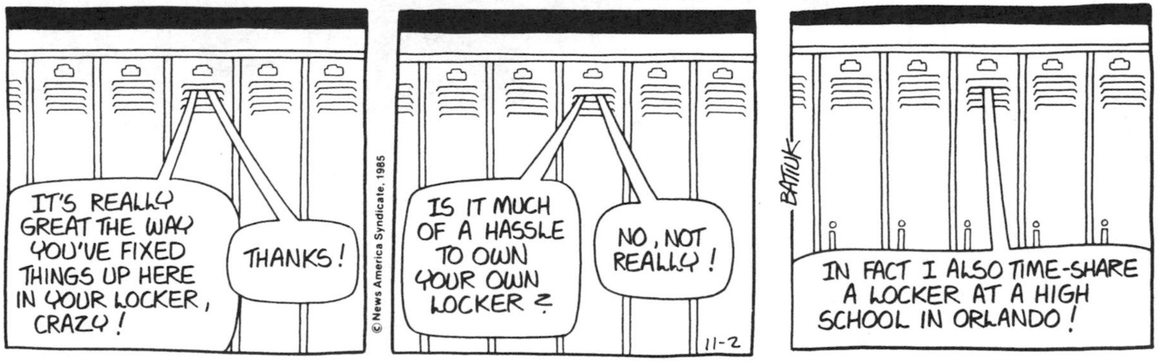
IT'S REALLY GREAT THE WAY YOU'VE FIXED THINGS UP HERE IN YOUR LOCKER, CRAZY!
THANKS!
© News America Syndicate, 1985
IS IT MUCH OF A HASSLE TO OWN YOUR OWN LOCKER?
NO, NOT REALLY!
11-2
BATIUK
IN FACT I ALSO TIME-SHARE A LOCKER AT A HIGH SCHOOL IN ORLANDO!

Funky Winkerbean by Tom Batiuk

RATE-A-RECORD

T. WAITS
RAIN DOGS

THIS NEXT SONG IS FOR ALL OF YOU OUT THERE WHO DIG THINGS THAT ARE FUNKY!

THANK YOU!

RATING A RECORD HAS BECOME AN 'AMERICAN BANDSTAND' TRADITION...

SO TELL ME, WHAT DID YOU THINK OF THIS NEW RECORD BY THE GRETCH BROTHERS?

BATIUK

WELL, DICK... IT HAD A GOOD BEAT AND IT WAS FUN TO DANCE TO...

I'D GIVE IT A PG!

11-3

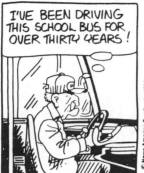

I'VE BEEN DRIVING THIS SCHOOL BUS FOR OVER THIRTY YEARS!
AND IN THOSE THIRTY YEARS...
© News America Syndicate, 1985
DISTRICT 34
11-4
I'VE NEVER BEEN INVOLVED IN A SINGLE ACCIDENT!
BATIUK
THEY WERE ALL ON PURPOSE!

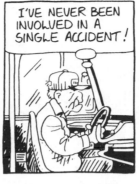

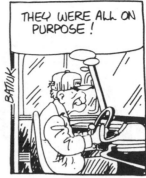

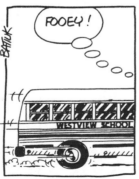

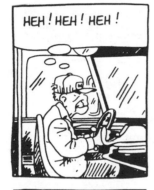

HEH! HEH! HEH!
I MADE LITTLE LAURIE SNYDER WALK RIGHT THROUGH THAT PUDDLE TO GET ON THE BUS!
BATIUK
© News America Syndicate, 1985
NOW SHE'S GOING TO BE WALKING AROUND SCHOOL ALL DAY WITH SOAKING WET FEET!
11-5
PROBABLY WON'T HAVE TO STOP AT HER HOUSE NOW FOR TWO OR THREE DAYS!

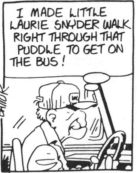

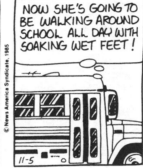

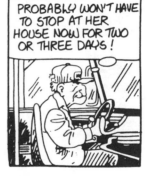

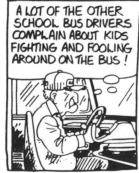

A LOT OF THE OTHER SCHOOL BUS DRIVERS COMPLAIN ABOUT KIDS FIGHTING AND FOOLING AROUND ON THE BUS!
BATIUK
FOOEY!
WESTVIEW SCHOOL DISTRICT 34
I NEVER HAVE ANY TROUBLE!
11-6
© News America Syndicate, 1985
IF YOU GO FAST ENOUGH, THEY JUST STAY PINNED TO THEIR SEATS!

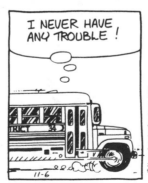

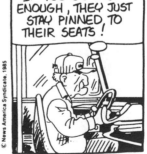

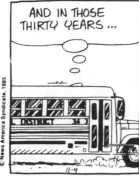

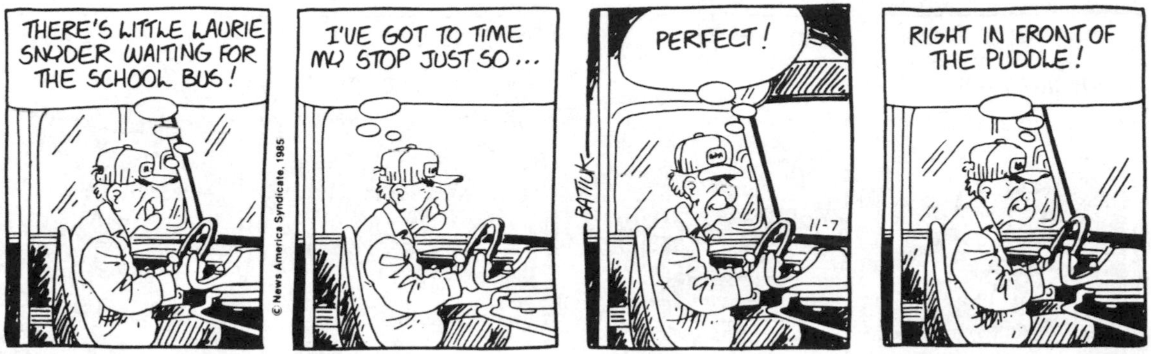
THERE'S LITTLE LAURIE SNYDER WAITING FOR THE SCHOOL BUS!
© News America Syndicate, 1985
I'VE GOT TO TIME MY STOP JUST SO...
BATIUK
PERFECT!
11-7
RIGHT IN FRONT OF THE PUDDLE!

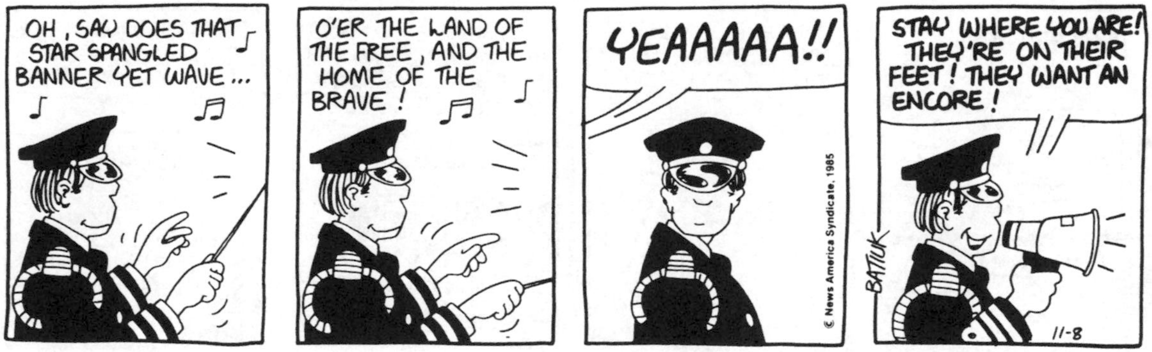
OH, SAY DOES THAT STAR SPANGLED BANNER YET WAVE...
O'ER THE LAND OF THE FREE, AND THE HOME OF THE BRAVE!
YEAAAAA!!
© News America Syndicate, 1985
STAY WHERE YOU ARE! THEY'RE ON THEIR FEET! THEY WANT AN ENCORE!
BATIUK
11-8

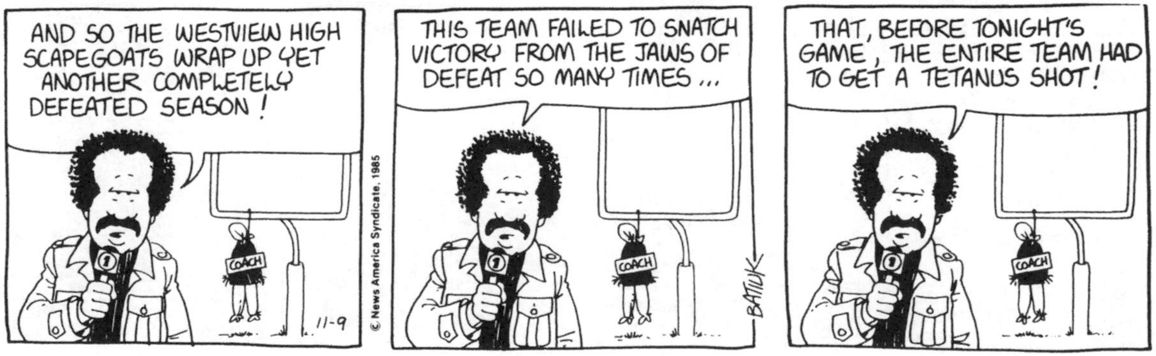
AND SO THE WESTVIEW HIGH SCAPEGOATS WRAP UP YET ANOTHER COMPLETELY DEFEATED SEASON!
COACH
11-9
© News America Syndicate, 1985
THIS TEAM FAILED TO SNATCH VICTORY FROM THE JAWS OF DEFEAT SO MANY TIMES...
COACH
BATIUK
THAT, BEFORE TONIGHT'S GAME, THE ENTIRE TEAM HAD TO GET A TETANUS SHOT!
COACH

FUNKY WINKERBEAN
BY TOM BATIUK
PRINCIPAL
AL, WE'VE GOT A PROBLEM!
THERE'S A FOOD FIGHT IN THE CAFETERIA!
PRINCIPAL
OH, OH! WE'D BETTER GET DOWN THERE!
ACTUALLY THERE'S NO HURRY!
I'VE NEVER QUITE SEEN A FOOD FIGHT LIKE THIS ONE BEFORE!
© News America Syndicate, 1985
11-10
BATIUK
LESS FILLING!!
TASTES GREAT!!

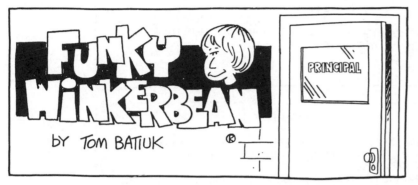

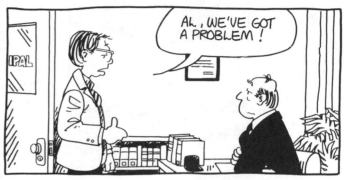

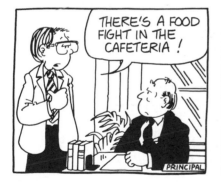

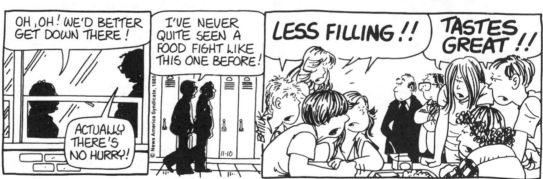

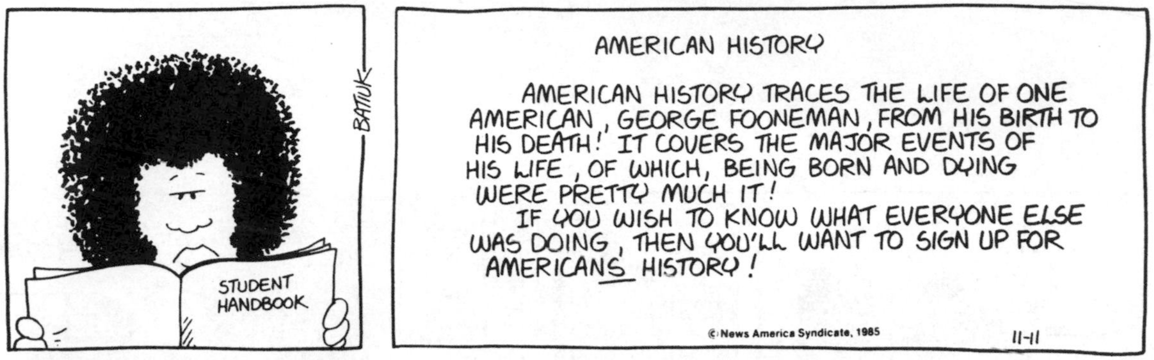
BATIUK
STUDENT HANDBOOK
AMERICAN HISTORY
AMERICAN HISTORY TRACES THE LIFE OF ONE AMERICAN, GEORGE FOONEMAN, FROM HIS BIRTH TO HIS DEATH! IT COVERS THE MAJOR EVENTS OF HIS LIFE, OF WHICH, BEING BORN AND DYING WERE PRETTY MUCH IT!
IF YOU WISH TO KNOW WHAT EVERYONE ELSE WAS DOING, THEN YOU'LL WANT TO SIGN UP FOR AMERICANS HISTORY!
© News America Syndicate, 1985
11-11

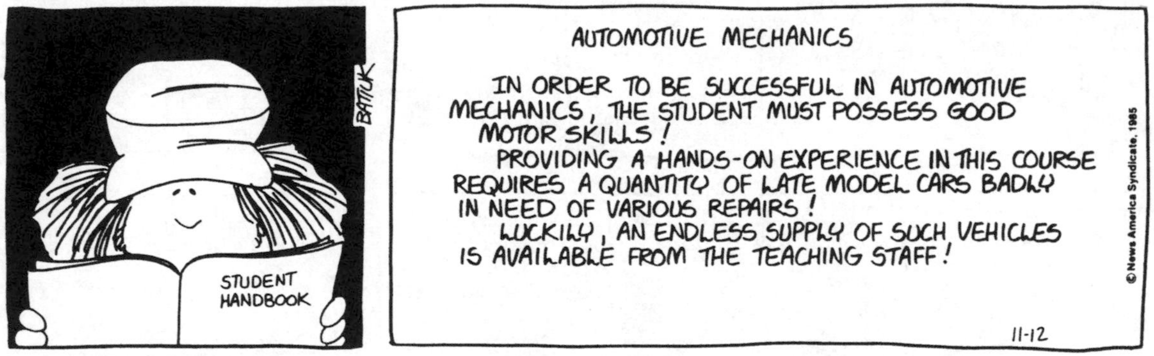
BATIUK
STUDENT HANDBOOK
AUTOMOTIVE MECHANICS
IN ORDER TO BE SUCCESSFUL IN AUTOMOTIVE MECHANICS, THE STUDENT MUST POSSESS GOOD MOTOR SKILLS!
PROVIDING A HANDS-ON EXPERIENCE IN THIS COURSE REQUIRES A QUANTITY OF LATE MODEL CARS BADLY IN NEED OF VARIOUS REPAIRS!
LUCKILY, AN ENDLESS SUPPLY OF SUCH VEHICLES IS AVAILABLE FROM THE TEACHING STAFF!
© News America Syndicate, 1985
11-12

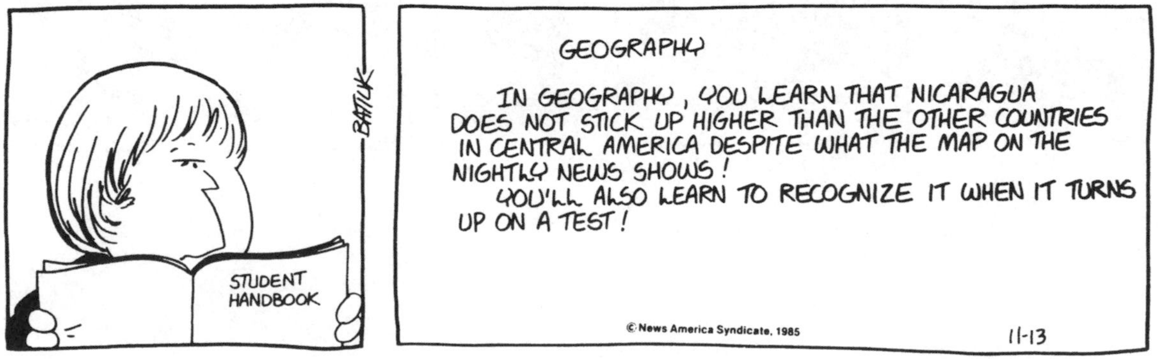
BATIUK
STUDENT HANDBOOK
GEOGRAPHY
IN GEOGRAPHY, YOU LEARN THAT NICARAGUA DOES NOT STICK UP HIGHER THAN THE OTHER COUNTRIES IN CENTRAL AMERICA DESPITE WHAT THE MAP ON THE NIGHTLY NEWS SHOWS!
YOU'LL ALSO LEARN TO RECOGNIZE IT WHEN IT TURNS UP ON A TEST!
© News America Syndicate, 1985
11-13

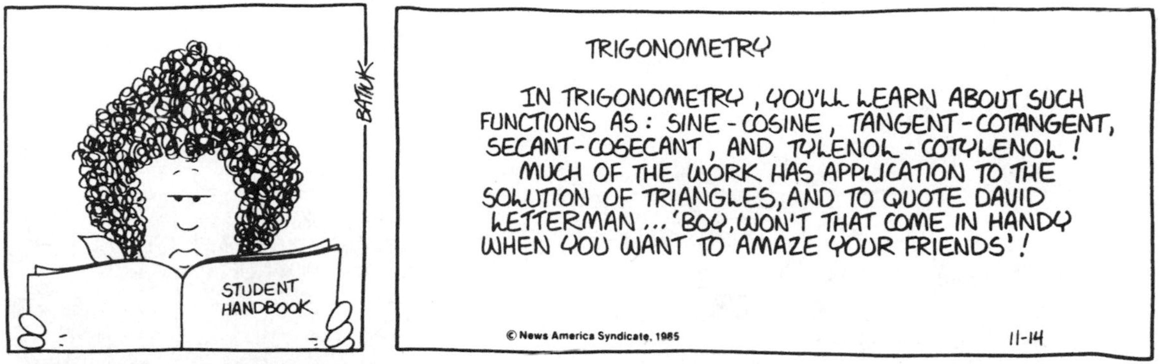
BATIUK
STUDENT HANDBOOK
TRIGONOMETRY
IN TRIGONOMETRY, YOU'LL LEARN ABOUT SUCH FUNCTIONS AS: SINE-COSINE, TANGENT-COTANGENT, SECANT-COSECANT, AND TYLENOL-COTYLENOL!
MUCH OF THE WORK HAS APPLICATION TO THE SOLUTION OF TRIANGLES, AND TO QUOTE DAVID LETTERMAN ...'BOY, WON'T THAT COME IN HANDY WHEN YOU WANT TO AMAZE YOUR FRIENDS'!
© News America Syndicate, 1985
11-14

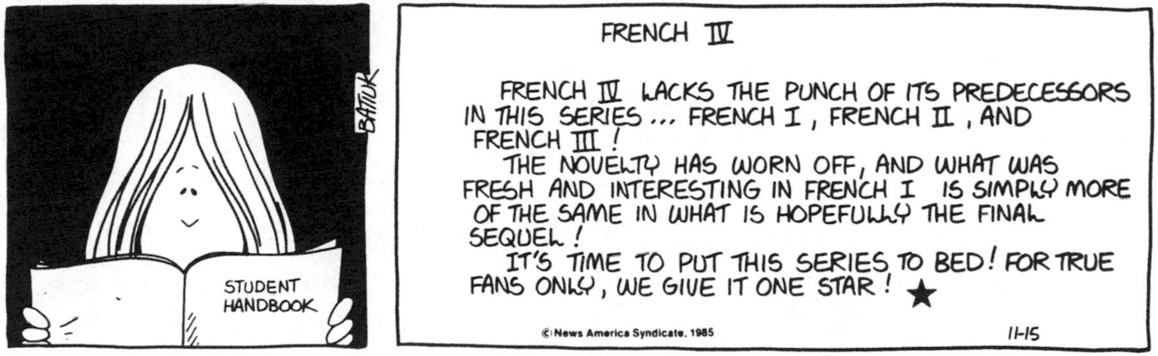
BATIUK
STUDENT HANDBOOK
FRENCH IV
FRENCH IV LACKS THE PUNCH OF ITS PREDECESSORS IN THIS SERIES ... FRENCH I, FRENCH II, AND FRENCH III!
THE NOVELTY HAS WORN OFF, AND WHAT WAS FRESH AND INTERESTING IN FRENCH I IS SIMPLY MORE OF THE SAME IN WHAT IS HOPEFULLY THE FINAL SEQUEL!
IT'S TIME TO PUT THIS SERIES TO BED! FOR TRUE FANS ONLY, WE GIVE IT ONE STAR! ★
© News America Syndicate, 1985
11-15

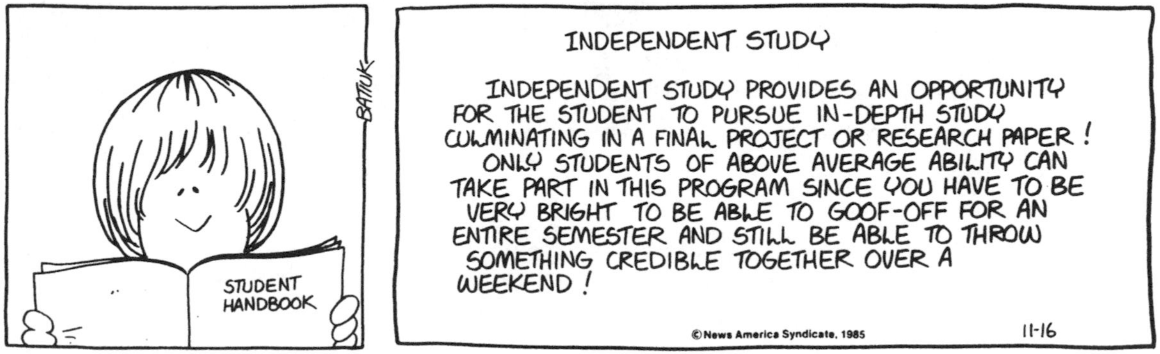
BATIUK
STUDENT HANDBOOK
INDEPENDENT STUDY
INDEPENDENT STUDY PROVIDES AN OPPORTUNITY FOR THE STUDENT TO PURSUE IN-DEPTH STUDY CULMINATING IN A FINAL PROJECT OR RESEARCH PAPER!
ONLY STUDENTS OF ABOVE AVERAGE ABILITY CAN TAKE PART IN THIS PROGRAM SINCE YOU HAVE TO BE VERY BRIGHT TO BE ABLE TO GOOF-OFF FOR AN ENTIRE SEMESTER AND STILL BE ABLE TO THROW SOMETHING CREDIBLE TOGETHER OVER A WEEKEND!
© News America Syndicate, 1985
11-16

FUNKY WINKERBEAN
BY TOM BATIUK
I'VE BEEN DOING THIS FOR A LONG TIME!
EVEN BACK IN ELEMENTARY SCHOOL I WAS A HALL MONITOR!
IN FACT, I WAS THE FIRST ONE IN SCHOOL TO LETTER IN IT!
DO YOU HAVE A HALL PASS?
I SURE DO!
IT SAYS I'VE BEEN EXCUSED FROM STUDY HALL TO GO TO THE RESTROOM AND SMOKE!
BATIUK
SOME OF THE NEWER TEACHERS ARE KIND OF LAX!
© News America Syndicate, 1985
11-17

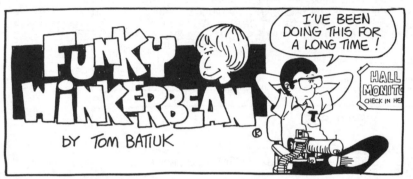

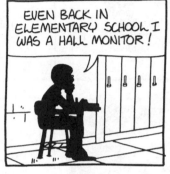

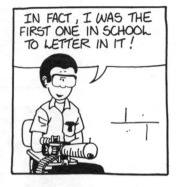

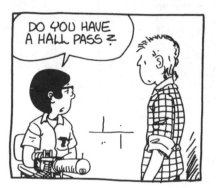

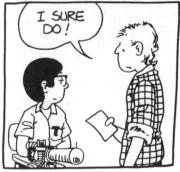

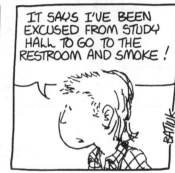

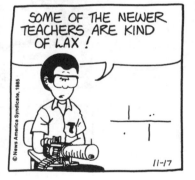

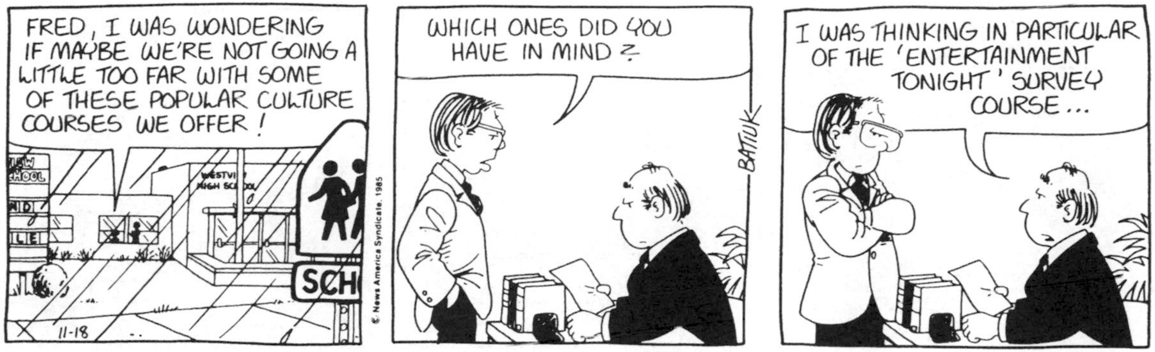
FRED, I WAS WONDERING IF MAYBE WE'RE NOT GOING A LITTLE TOO FAR WITH SOME OF THESE POPULAR CULTURE COURSES WE OFFER!
WHICH ONES DID YOU HAVE IN MIND?
I WAS THINKING IN PARTICULAR OF THE 'ENTERTAINMENT TONIGHT' SURVEY COURSE...
© News America Syndicate, 1985
BATIUK
11-18

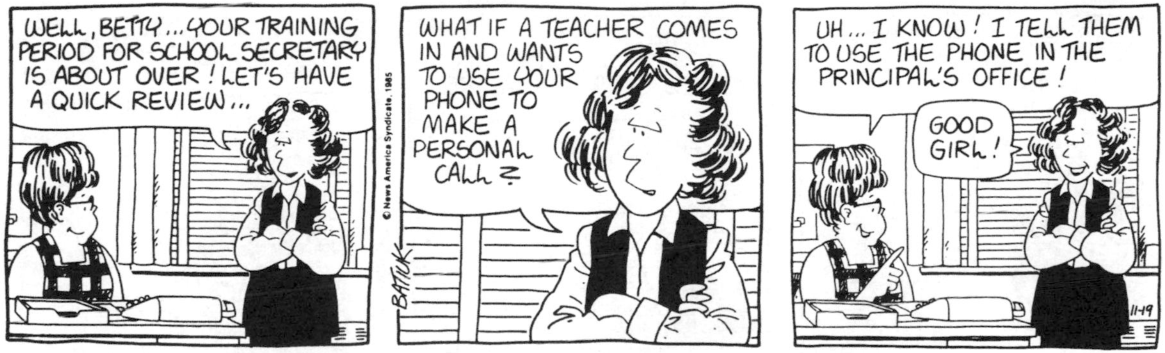
WELL, BETTY... YOUR TRAINING PERIOD FOR SCHOOL SECRETARY IS ABOUT OVER! LET'S HAVE A QUICK REVIEW...
WHAT IF A TEACHER COMES IN AND WANTS TO USE YOUR PHONE TO MAKE A PERSONAL CALL?
UH... I KNOW! I TELL THEM TO USE THE PHONE IN THE PRINCIPAL'S OFFICE!
GOOD GIRL!
© News America Syndicate, 1985
BATIUK
11-19

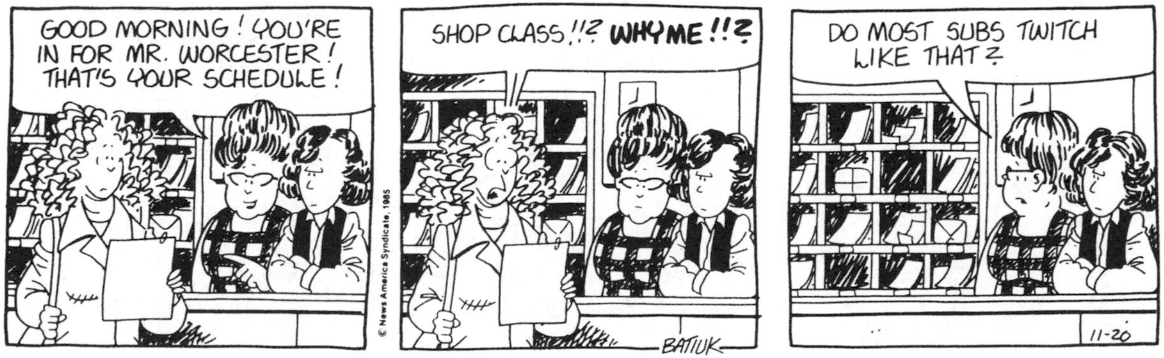
GOOD MORNING! YOU'RE IN FOR MR. WORCESTER! THAT'S YOUR SCHEDULE!
SHOP CLASS!!? WHY ME!!?
DO MOST SUBS TWITCH LIKE THAT?
© News America Syndicate, 1985
BATIUK
11-20

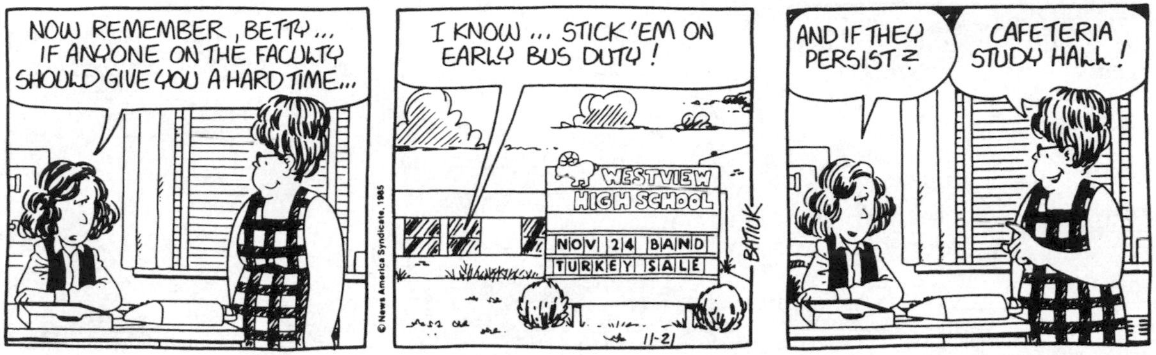
NOW REMEMBER, BETTY... IF ANYONE ON THE FACULTY SHOULD GIVE YOU A HARD TIME...
I KNOW... STICK 'EM ON EARLY BUS DUTY!
WESTVIEW HIGH SCHOOL
NOV 24 BAND TURKEY SALE
BATIUK
11-21
© News America Syndicate, 1985
AND IF THEY PERSIST?
CAFETERIA STUDY HALL!

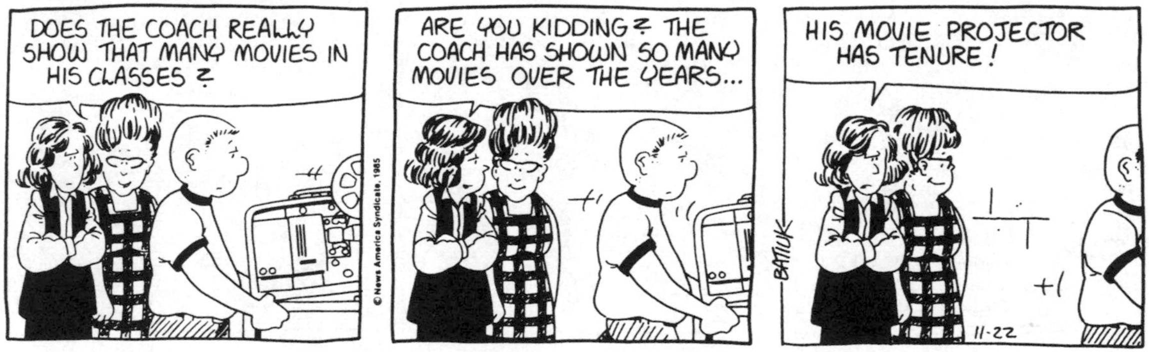
DOES THE COACH REALLY SHOW THAT MANY MOVIES IN HIS CLASSES?
© News America Syndicate, 1985
ARE YOU KIDDING? THE COACH HAS SHOWN SO MANY MOVIES OVER THE YEARS...
HIS MOVIE PROJECTOR HAS TENURE!
BATIUK
11-22

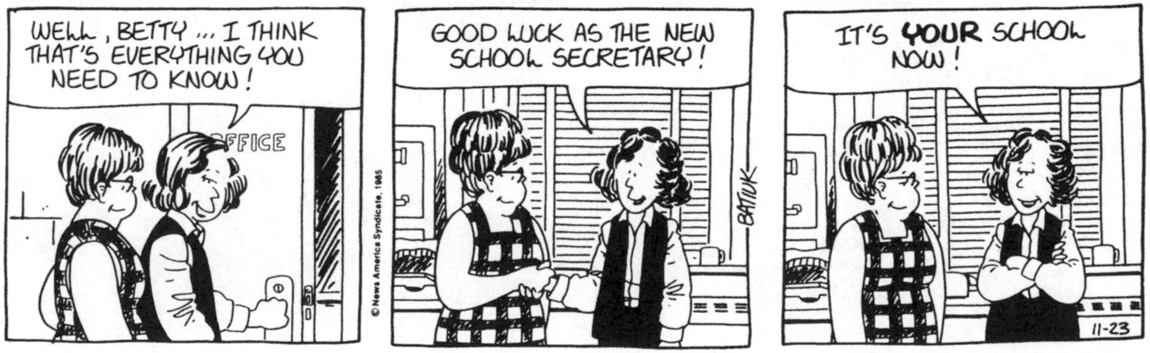
WELL, BETTY... I THINK THAT'S EVERYTHING YOU NEED TO KNOW!
FFICE
© News America Syndicate, 1985
GOOD LUCK AS THE NEW SCHOOL SECRETARY!
BATIUK
IT'S **YOUR** SCHOOL NOW!
11-23

FUNKY WINKERBEAN
BY TOM BATIUK
HELLO THERE...
WOULD YOU LIKE TO BUY A BAND TURKEY FOR THANKSGIVING?
WHAT? AGAIN!? I JUST BOUGHT ONE LAST YEAR!!
ARE THESE BAND TURKEYS FRESH?
ARE YOU KIDDING? LISTEN...
BATIUK
© News America Syndicate, 1985
GOBBLE! GOBBLE! GOBBLE!
WAIT A MINUTE! I SAW YOUR LIPS MOVE!
11-24

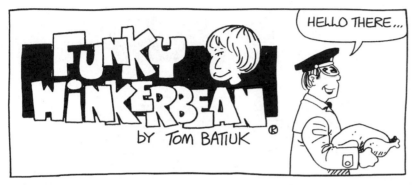

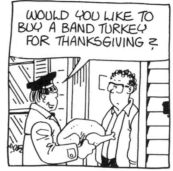

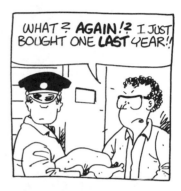

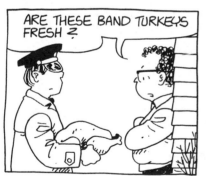

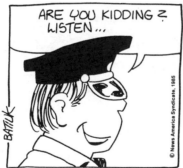

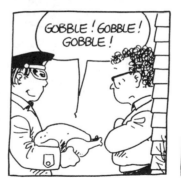

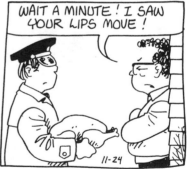

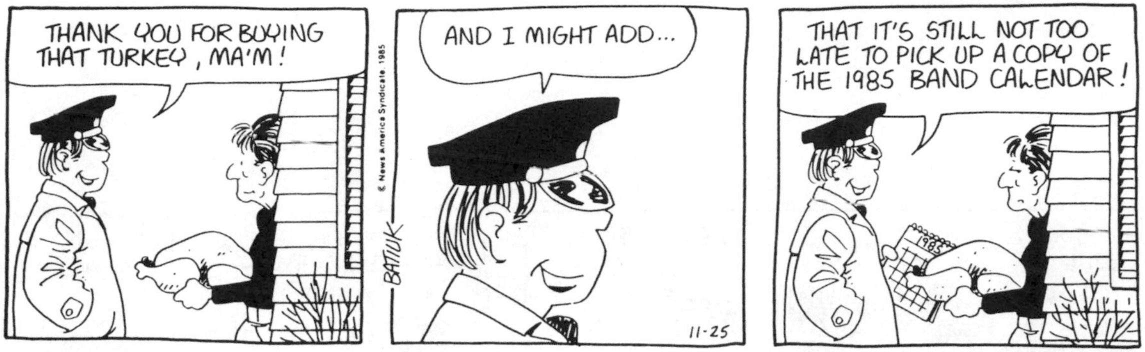
THANK YOU FOR BUYING THAT TURKEY, MA'M!
AND I MIGHT ADD...
THAT IT'S STILL NOT TOO LATE TO PICK UP A COPY OF THE 1985 BAND CALENDAR!
© News America Syndicate, 1985
BATIUK
11-25

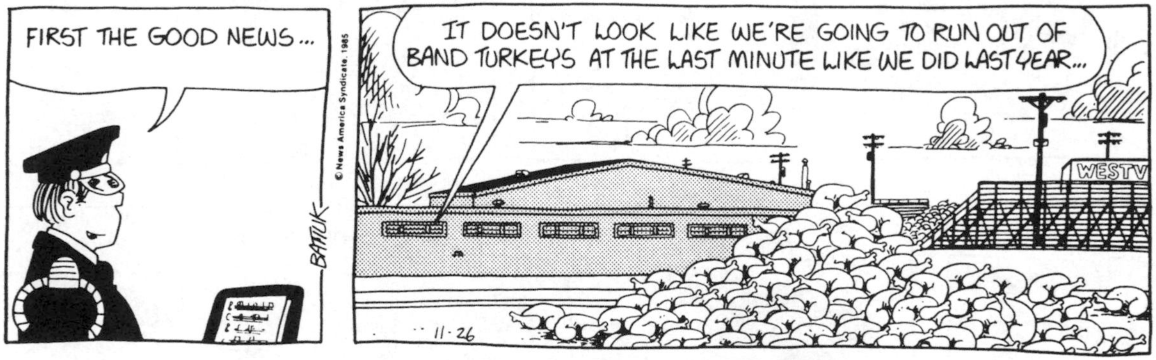
FIRST THE GOOD NEWS...
IT DOESN'T LOOK LIKE WE'RE GOING TO RUN OUT OF BAND TURKEYS AT THE LAST MINUTE LIKE WE DID LAST YEAR...
WESTV
© News America Syndicate, 1985
BATIUK
11-26

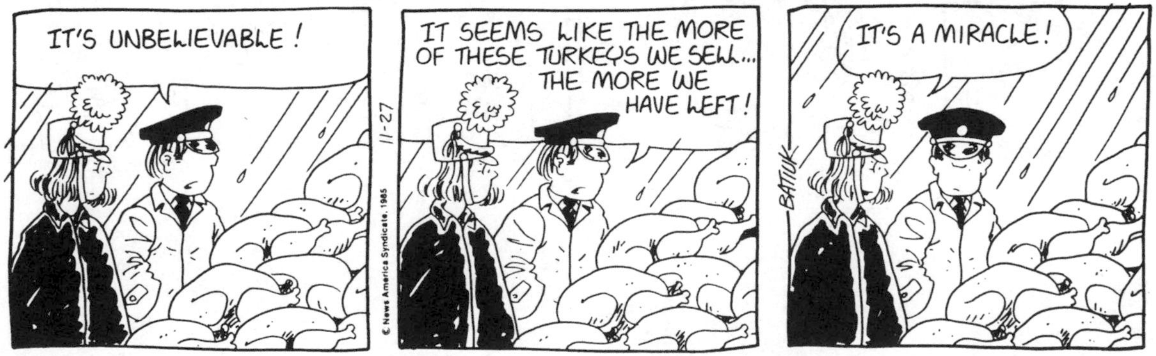
IT'S UNBELIEVABLE!
IT SEEMS LIKE THE MORE OF THESE TURKEYS WE SELL... THE MORE WE HAVE LEFT!
IT'S A MIRACLE!
© News America Syndicate, 1985
BATIUK
11-27

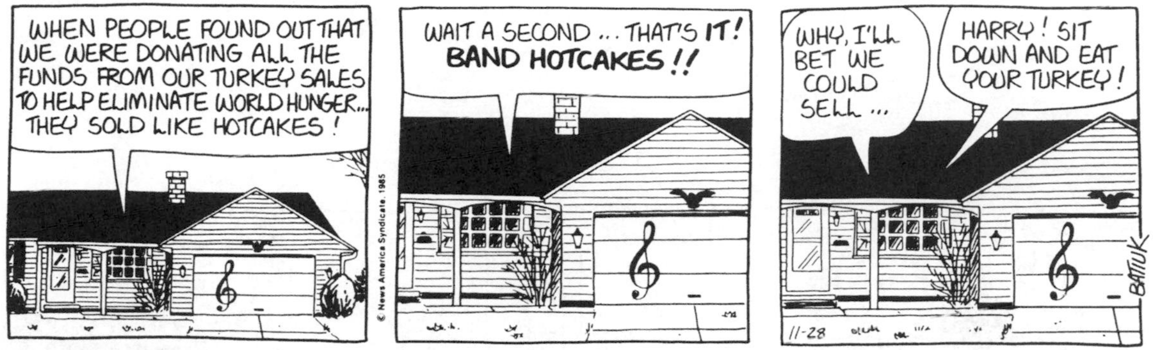
WHEN PEOPLE FOUND OUT THAT WE WERE DONATING ALL THE FUNDS FROM OUR TURKEY SALES TO HELP ELIMINATE WORLD HUNGER... THEY SOLD LIKE HOTCAKES!
© News America Syndicate, 1985
WAIT A SECOND ... THAT'S **IT! BAND HOTCAKES!!**
WHY, I'LL BET WE COULD SELL ...
HARRY! SIT DOWN AND EAT YOUR TURKEY!
BATIUK
11-28

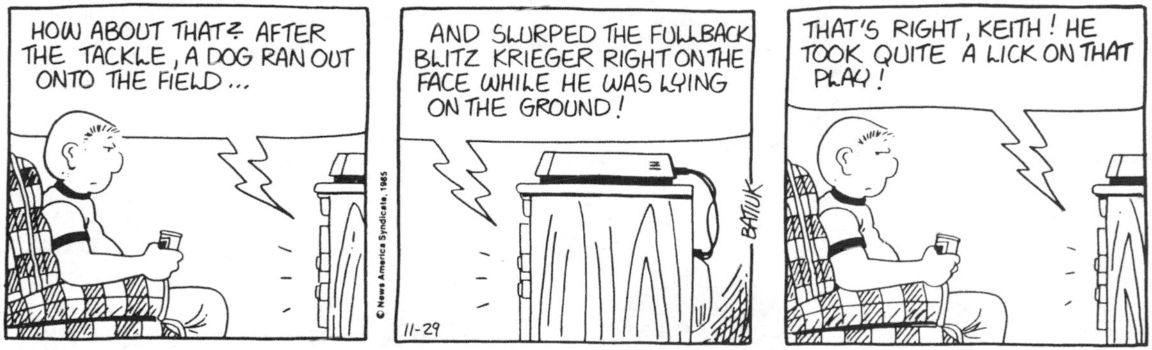
HOW ABOUT THAT? AFTER THE TACKLE, A DOG RAN OUT ONTO THE FIELD ...
© News America Syndicate, 1985
AND SLURPED THE FULLBACK BLITZ KRIEGER RIGHT ON THE FACE WHILE HE WAS LYING ON THE GROUND!
BATIUK
11-29
THAT'S RIGHT, KEITH! HE TOOK QUITE A LICK ON THAT PLAY!

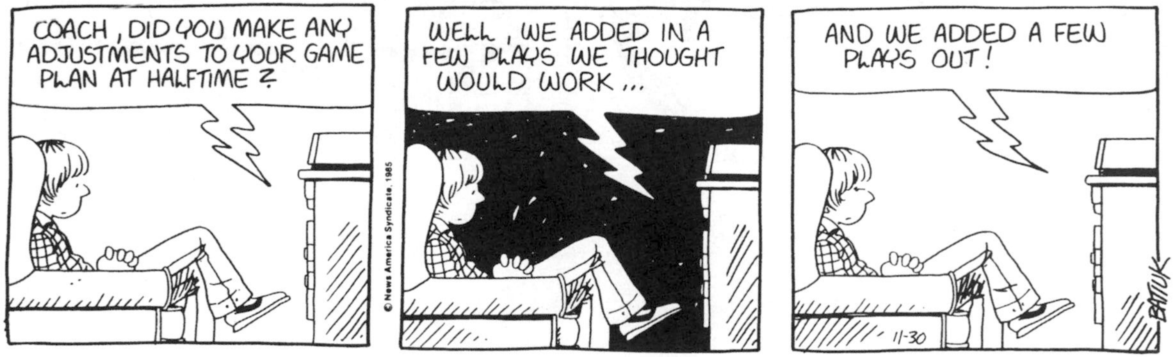
COACH, DID YOU MAKE ANY ADJUSTMENTS TO YOUR GAME PLAN AT HALFTIME?
© News America Syndicate, 1985
WELL, WE ADDED IN A FEW PLAYS WE THOUGHT WOULD WORK ...
AND WE ADDED A FEW PLAYS OUT!
BATIUK
11-30

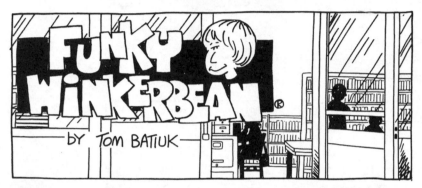

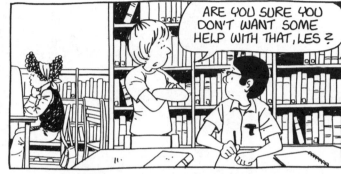

FUNKY WINKERBEAN
BY TOM BATIUK
ARE YOU SURE YOU DON'T WANT SOME HELP WITH THAT, LES?
I APPRECIATE YOUR OFFER, FUNKY...
BUT I THINK I'LL JUST WRITE THIS PAPER MYSELF!
© News America Syndicate, 1985
BATIUK
THE LAST TIME HE WROTE A PAPER FOR ME...
HE WENT IN AFTERWARD AND COMPLAINED ABOUT THE GRADE!
12-1

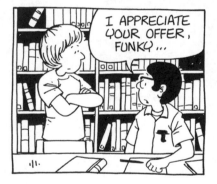

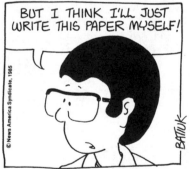

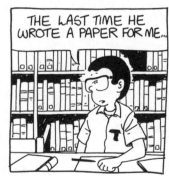

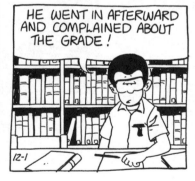

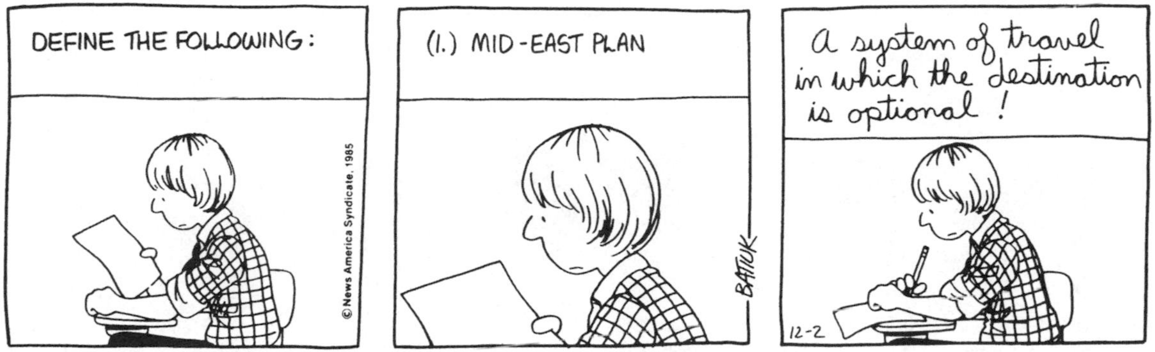
DEFINE THE FOLLOWING:
© News America Syndicate, 1985
(1.) MID-EAST PLAN
BATIUK
A system of travel in which the destination is optional!
12-2

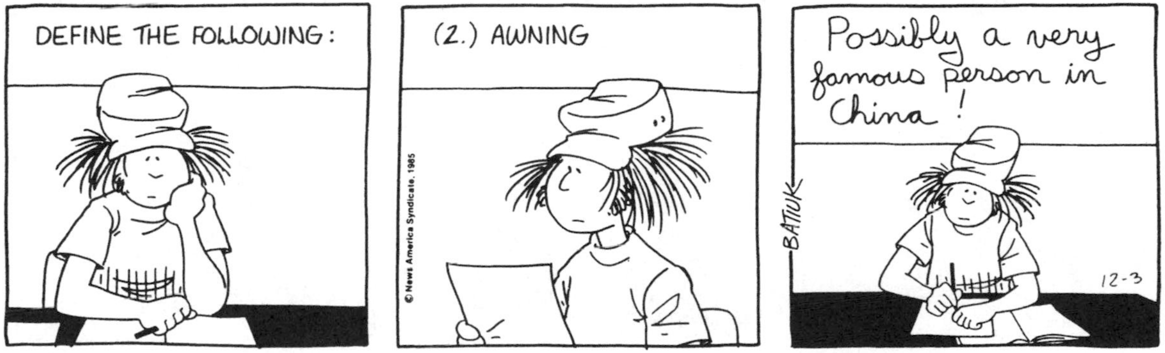
DEFINE THE FOLLOWING:
(2.) AWNING
© News America Syndicate, 1985
Possibly a very famous person in China!
BATIUK
12-3

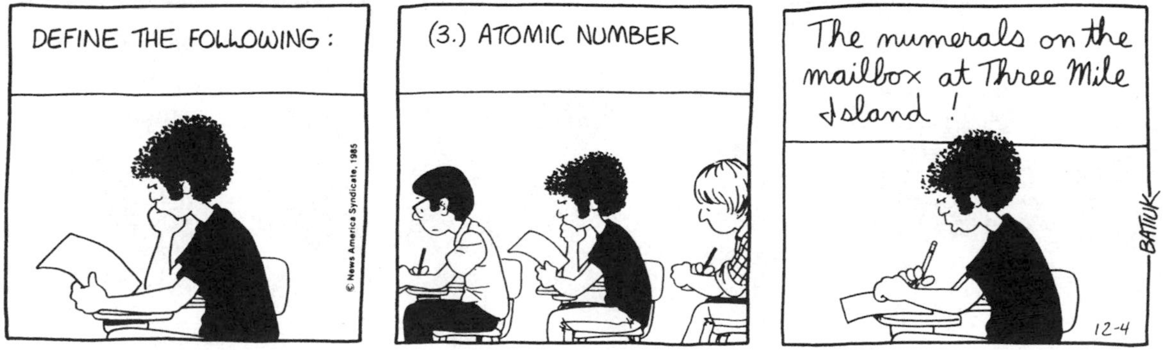
DEFINE THE FOLLOWING:
© News America Syndicate, 1985
(3.) ATOMIC NUMBER
The numerals on the mailbox at Three Mile Island!
BATIUK
12-4

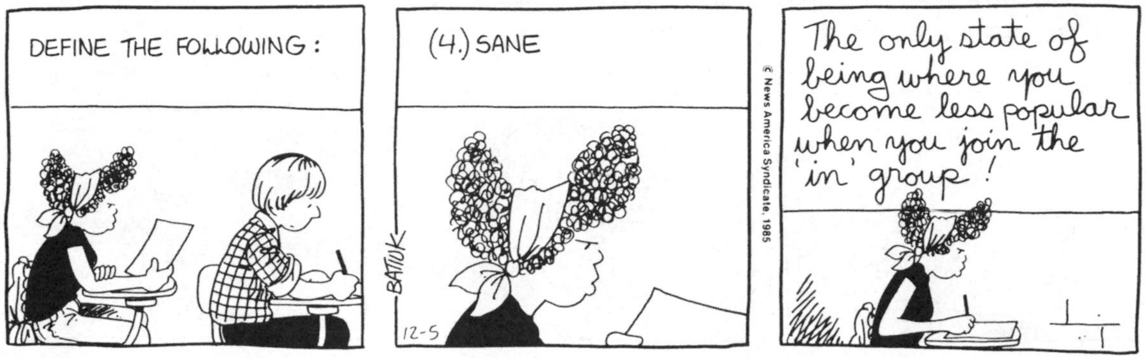
DEFINE THE FOLLOWING:
(4.) SANE
BATIUK
12-5
© News America Syndicate, 1985
The only state of being where you become less popular when you join the 'in' group!

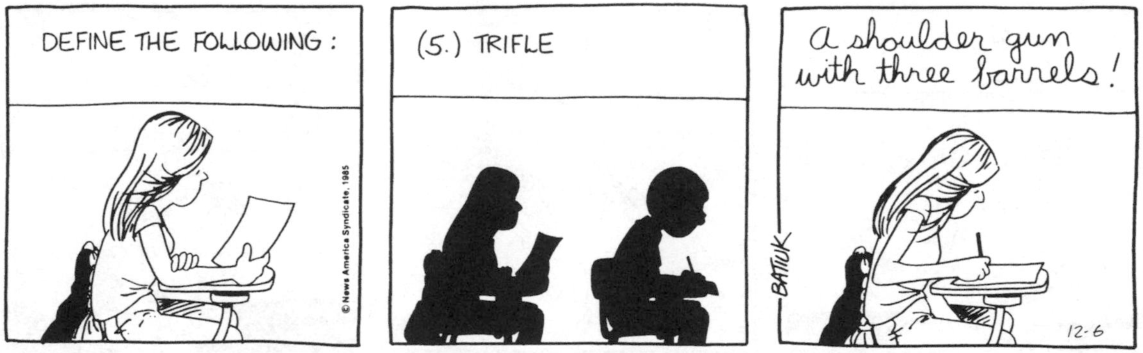
DEFINE THE FOLLOWING:
© News America Syndicate, 1985
(5.) TRIFLE
A shoulder gun with three barrels!
BATIUK
12-6

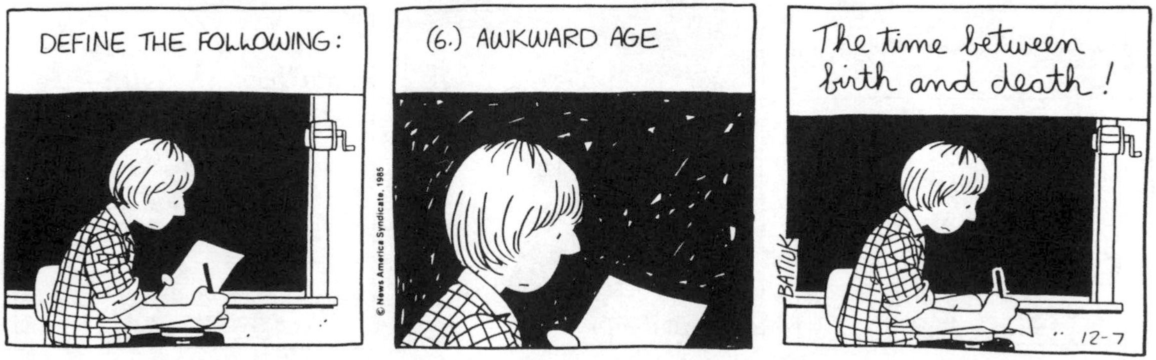
DEFINE THE FOLLOWING:
© News America Syndicate, 1985
(6.) AWKWARD AGE
The time between birth and death!
BATIUK
12-7

FUNKY WINKERBEAN
BY TOM BATIUK ®
NO!
NO!!!
NO!! YOU CAN'T MAKE ME GO BACK THERE!!
I WON'T DO IT!!!!
ANOTHER RESTROOM MONITOR BITES THE DUST!
HALL MONITOR
BATIUK
12-8
© News America Syndicate, 1985

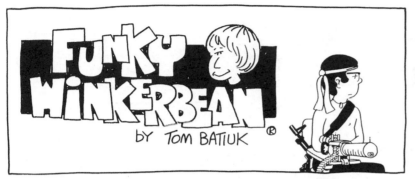

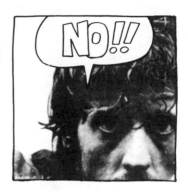

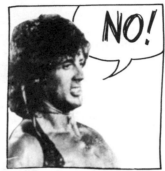

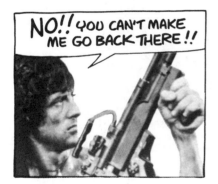

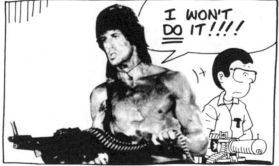

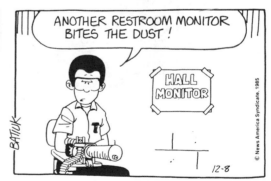

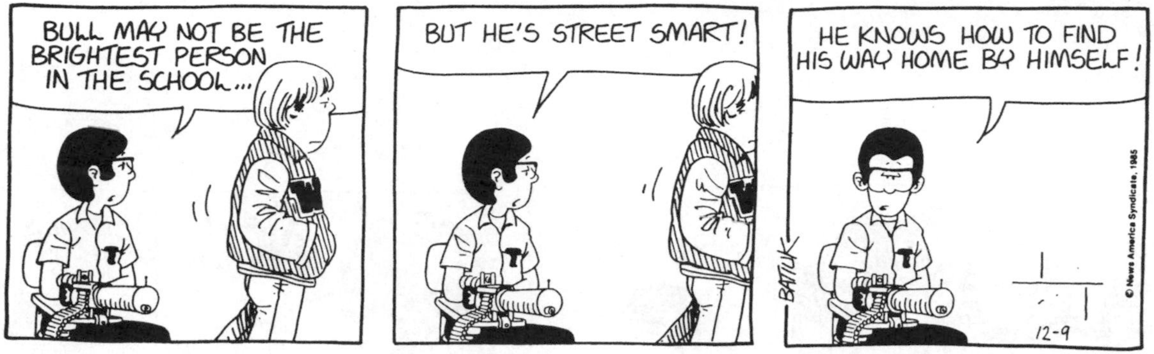
BULL MAY NOT BE THE BRIGHTEST PERSON IN THE SCHOOL...
BUT HE'S STREET SMART!
HE KNOWS HOW TO FIND HIS WAY HOME BY HIMSELF!
BATIUK
© News America Syndicate, 1985
12-9

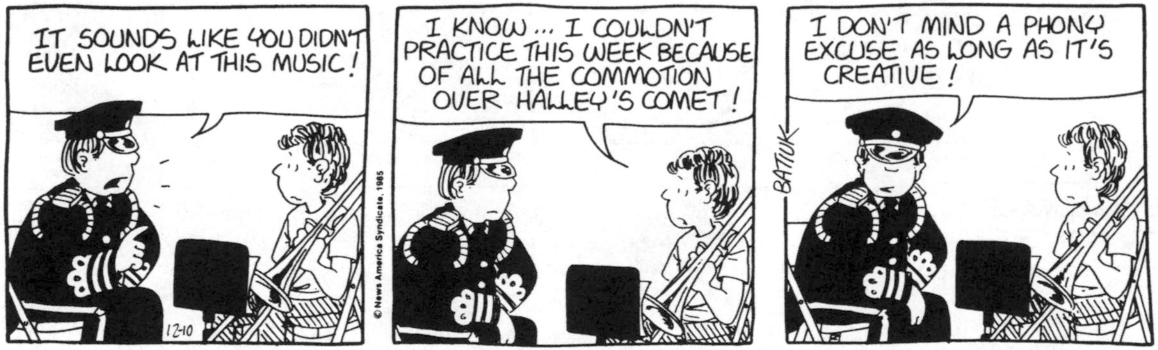
IT SOUNDS LIKE YOU DIDN'T EVEN LOOK AT THIS MUSIC!
12-10
© News America Syndicate, 1985
I KNOW... I COULDN'T PRACTICE THIS WEEK BECAUSE OF ALL THE COMMOTION OVER HALLEY'S COMET!
I DON'T MIND A PHONY EXCUSE AS LONG AS IT'S CREATIVE!
BATIUK

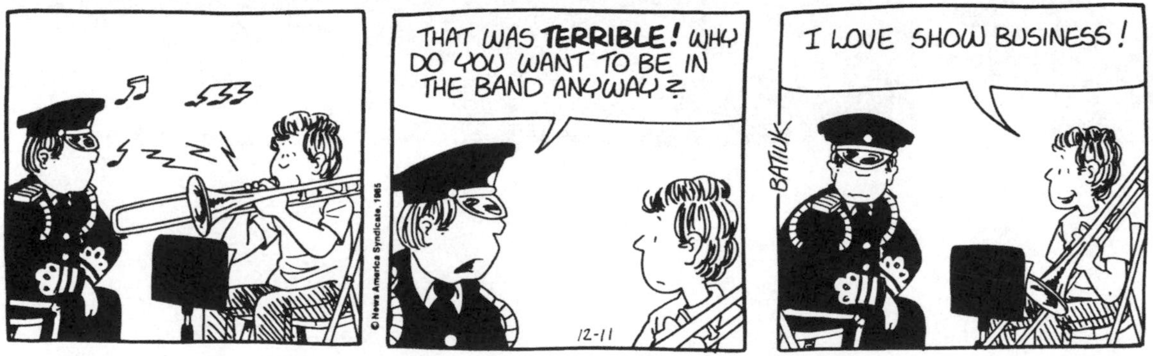
© News America Syndicate, 1985
THAT WAS **TERRIBLE!** WHY DO YOU WANT TO BE IN THE BAND ANYWAY?
12-11
I LOVE SHOW BUSINESS!
BATIUK

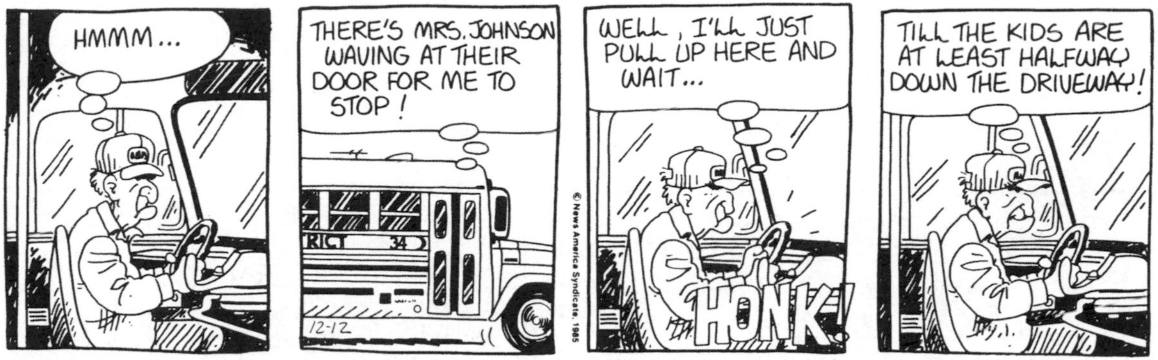
HMMM...
THERE'S MRS. JOHNSON WAVING AT THEIR DOOR FOR ME TO STOP!
WELL, I'LL JUST PULL UP HERE AND WAIT...
HONK!
TILL THE KIDS ARE AT LEAST HALFWAY DOWN THE DRIVEWAY!
12-12
© News America Syndicate, 1985

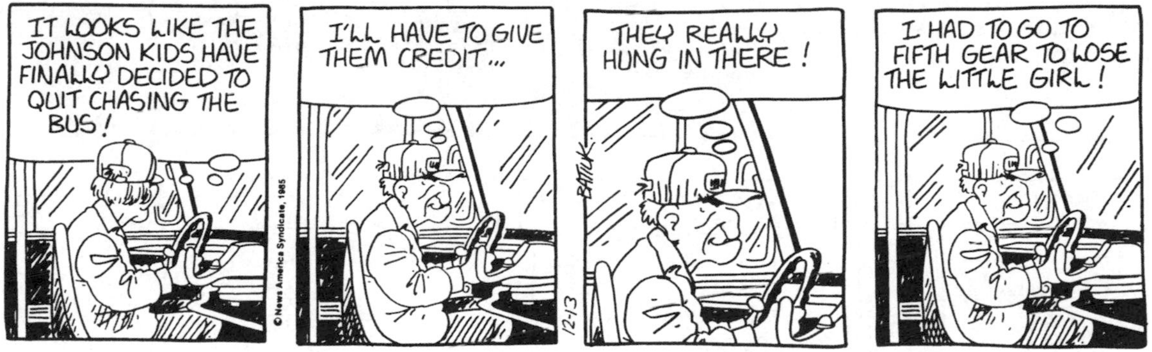
IT LOOKS LIKE THE JOHNSON KIDS HAVE FINALLY DECIDED TO QUIT CHASING THE BUS!
I'LL HAVE TO GIVE THEM CREDIT...
THEY REALLY HUNG IN THERE!
I HAD TO GO TO FIFTH GEAR TO LOSE THE LITTLE GIRL!
© News America Syndicate, 1985
BATIUK
12-13

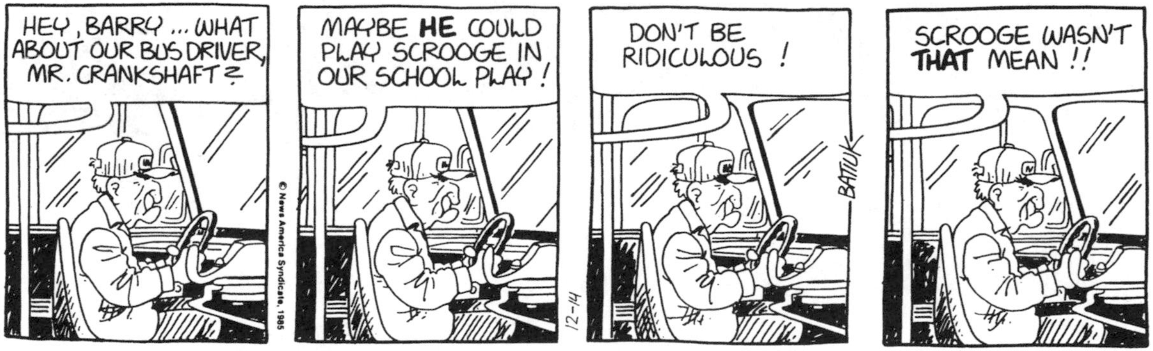
HEY, BARRY... WHAT ABOUT OUR BUS DRIVER, MR. CRANKSHAFT?
MAYBE **HE** COULD PLAY SCROOGE IN OUR SCHOOL PLAY!
DON'T BE RIDICULOUS!
SCROOGE WASN'T **THAT** MEAN!!
© News America Syndicate, 1985
12-14
BATIUK

FUNKY WINKERBEAN
BY TOM BATIUK
LOOK AT THE LITTLE JOHNSON GIRL...
HEH! SHE'S FINALLY GIVEN UP TRYING TO CATCH THE BUS!
I WONDER WHERE SHE LEARNED WORDS LIKE THAT?
I'LL HAVE TO GIVE THAT LITTLE JOHNSON GIRL CREDIT!
SHE ALMOST CAUGHT THE BUS TODAY!
ESPECIALLY WITH THAT LATE BURST OF SPEED SHE PUT ON!
BATIUK
12-15
© News America Syndicate, 1985
SHE PROBABLY COULD'VE MADE IT WITHOUT THE FRENCH HORN!

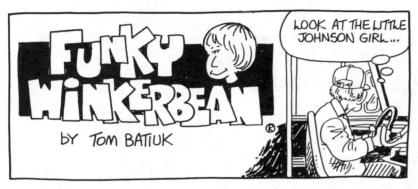

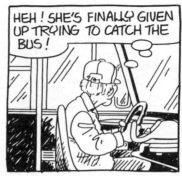

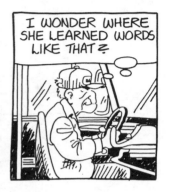

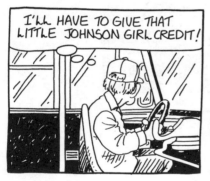

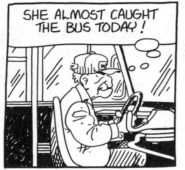

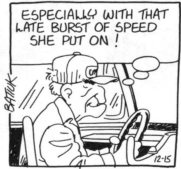

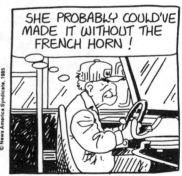

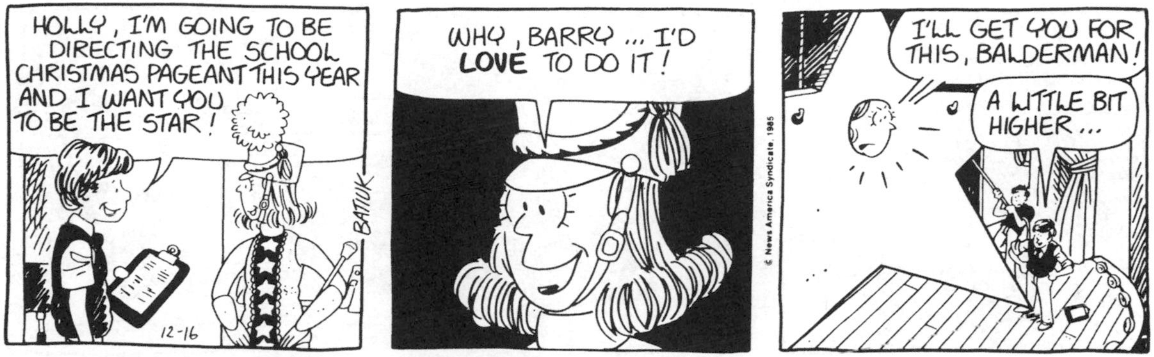
HOLLY, I'M GOING TO BE DIRECTING THE SCHOOL CHRISTMAS PAGEANT THIS YEAR AND I WANT YOU TO BE THE STAR!
BATIUK
12-16
WHY, BARRY ... I'D **LOVE** TO DO IT!
© News America Syndicate, 1985
I'LL GET YOU FOR THIS, BALDERMAN!
A LITTLE BIT HIGHER ...

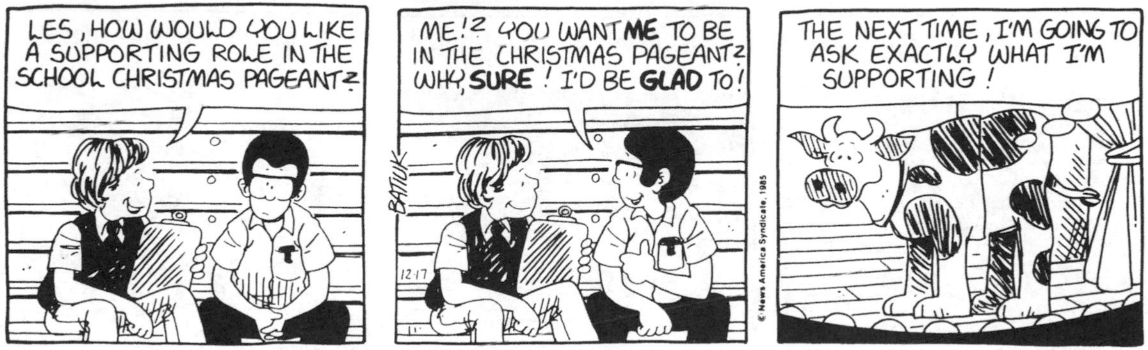
LES, HOW WOULD YOU LIKE A SUPPORTING ROLE IN THE SCHOOL CHRISTMAS PAGEANT?
ME!? YOU WANT **ME** TO BE IN THE CHRISTMAS PAGEANT? WHY, **SURE**! I'D BE **GLAD** TO!
BATIUK
12-17
© News America Syndicate, 1985
THE NEXT TIME, I'M GOING TO ASK EXACTLY WHAT I'M SUPPORTING!

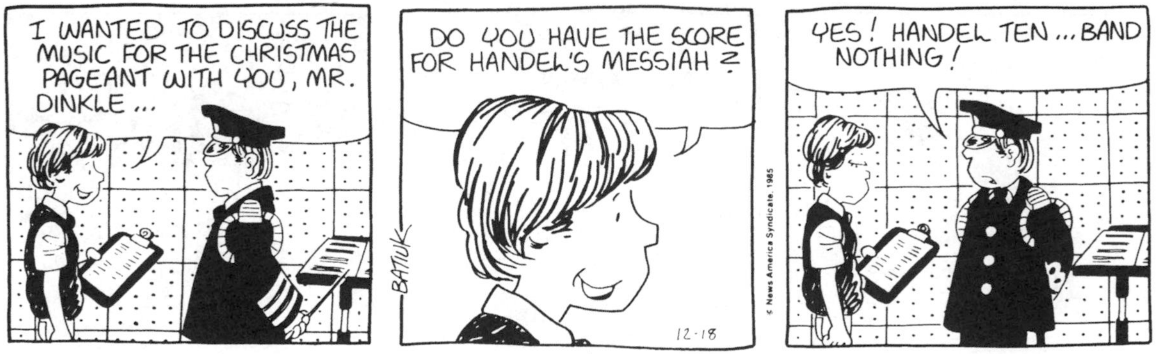
I WANTED TO DISCUSS THE MUSIC FOR THE CHRISTMAS PAGEANT WITH YOU, MR. DINKLE ...
BATIUK
DO YOU HAVE THE SCORE FOR HANDEL'S MESSIAH?
12-18
© News America Syndicate, 1985
YES! HANDEL TEN ... BAND NOTHING!

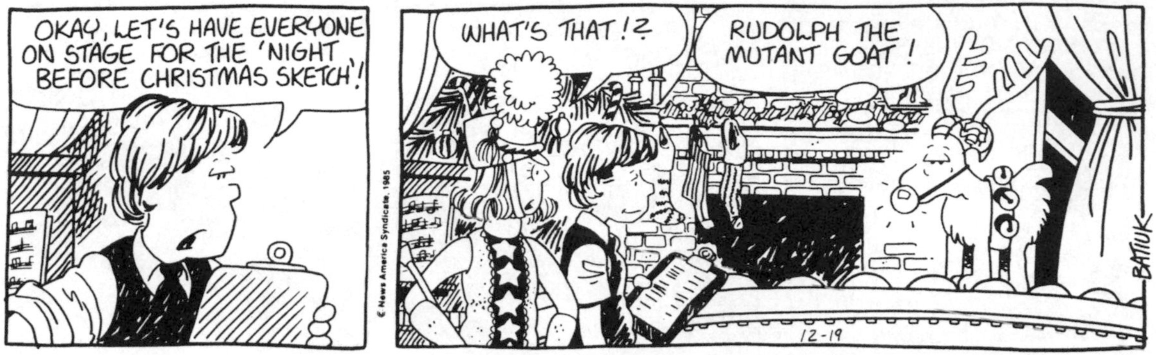
OKAY, LET'S HAVE EVERYONE ON STAGE FOR THE 'NIGHT BEFORE CHRISTMAS SKETCH'!
WHAT'S THAT!?
RUDOLPH THE MUTANT GOAT!
© News America Syndicate 1985
BATIUK
12-19

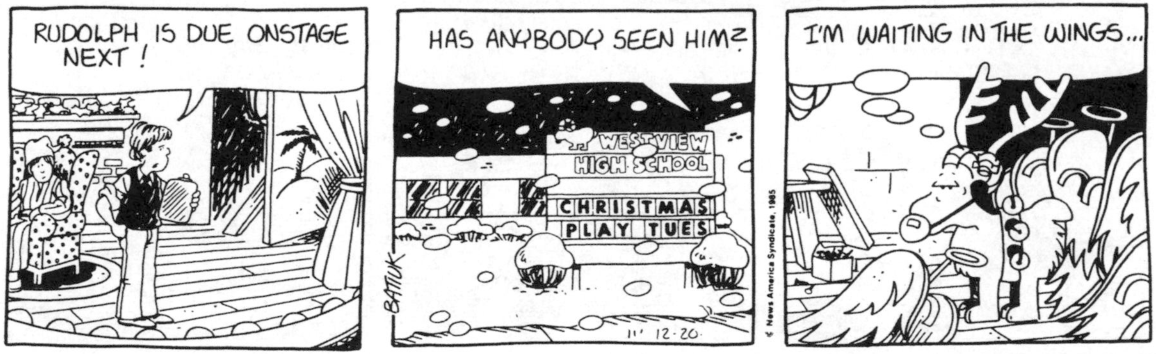
RUDOLPH IS DUE ONSTAGE NEXT!
BATIUK
HAS ANYBODY SEEN HIM?
WESTVIEW HIGH SCHOOL
CHRISTMAS PLAY TUES
12-20
© News America Syndicate 1985
I'M WAITING IN THE WINGS...

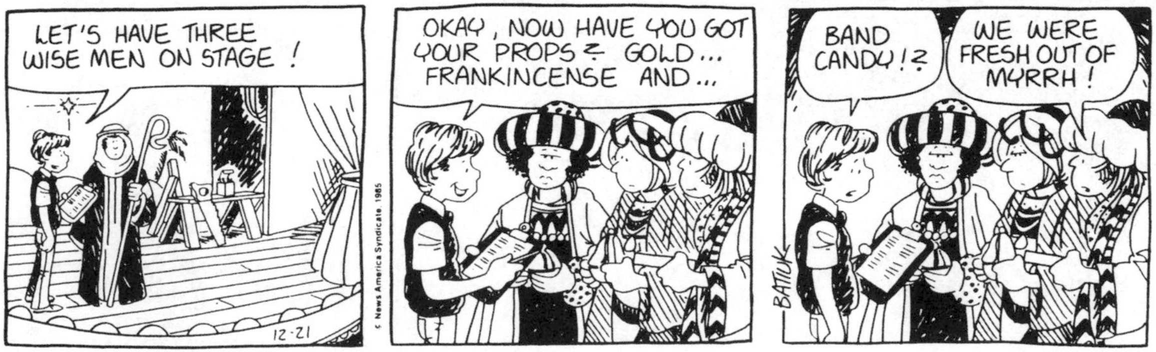
LET'S HAVE THREE WISE MEN ON STAGE!
12-21
© News America Syndicate 1985
OKAY, NOW HAVE YOU GOT YOUR PROPS? GOLD... FRANKINCENSE AND...
BAND CANDY!?
WE WERE FRESH OUT OF MYRRH!
BATIUK

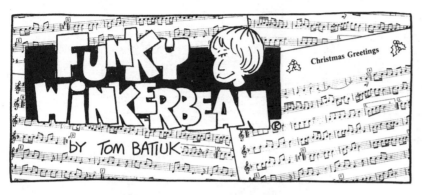

FUNKY WINKERBEAN
BY TOM BATIUK
Christmas Greetings
MERRY CHRISTMAS, MR. DINKLE!
IT'S FROM ALL OF US!
A CHRISTMAS PRESENT FROM THE BAND?
AWW ... YOU REALLY SHOULDN'T HAVE ...
© News America Syndicate, 1985
THEY'RE PILLOW CASES AND BED COVERINGS WITH MUSICAL NOTES ON THEM!
12-22
BATIUK
HOW THOUGHTFUL ... SHEET MUSIC!

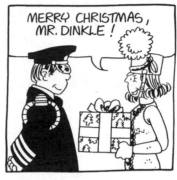

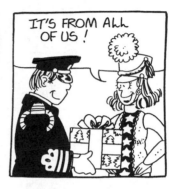

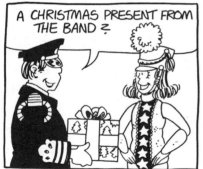

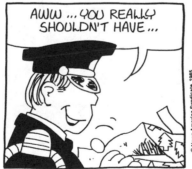

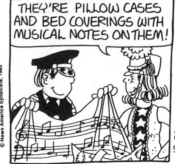

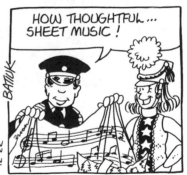

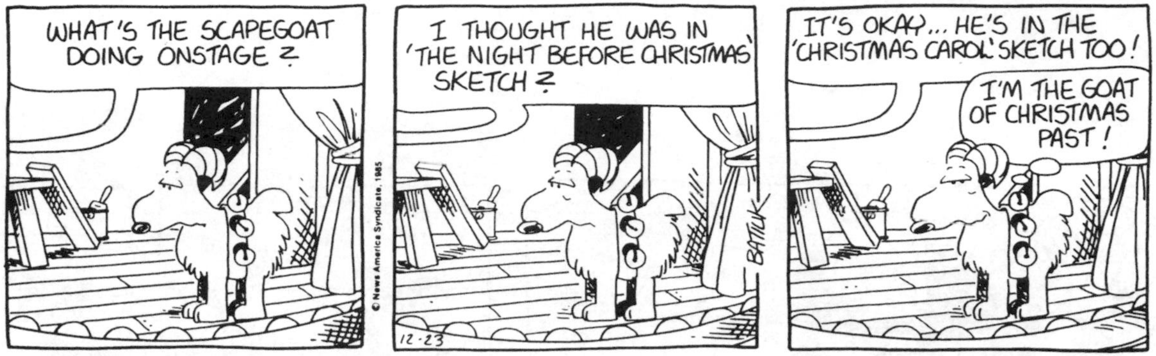
WHAT'S THE SCAPEGOAT DOING ONSTAGE ?
I THOUGHT HE WAS IN 'THE NIGHT BEFORE CHRISTMAS' SKETCH ?
IT'S OKAY... HE'S IN THE 'CHRISTMAS CAROL' SKETCH TOO !
I'M THE GOAT OF CHRISTMAS PAST !
© News America Syndicate, 1985
12-23
BATIUK

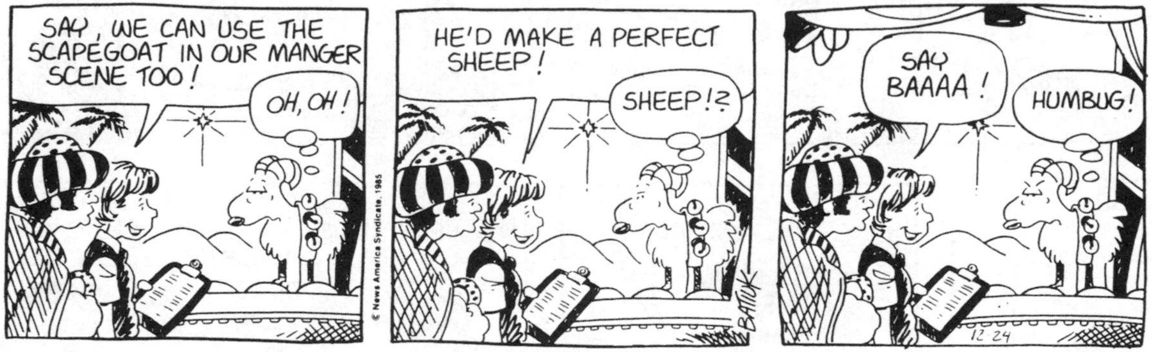
SAY, WE CAN USE THE SCAPEGOAT IN OUR MANGER SCENE TOO !
OH, OH !
HE'D MAKE A PERFECT SHEEP !
SHEEP !?
SAY BAAAA !
HUMBUG !
© News America Syndicate, 1985
BATIUK
12-24

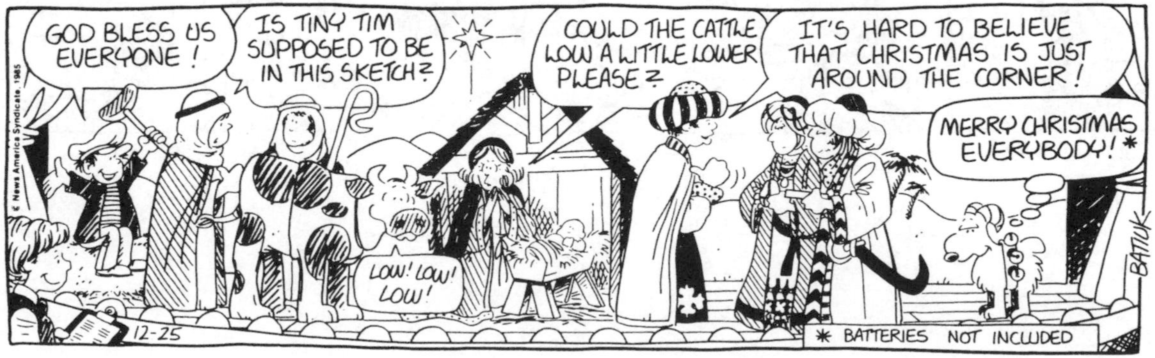
GOD BLESS US EVERYONE !
IS TINY TIM SUPPOSED TO BE IN THIS SKETCH ?
COULD THE CATTLE LOW A LITTLE LOWER PLEASE ?
IT'S HARD TO BELIEVE THAT CHRISTMAS IS JUST AROUND THE CORNER !
MERRY CHRISTMAS EVERYBODY! *
LOW! LOW! LOW!
* BATTERIES NOT INCLUDED
© News America Syndicate, 1985
12-25
BATIUK

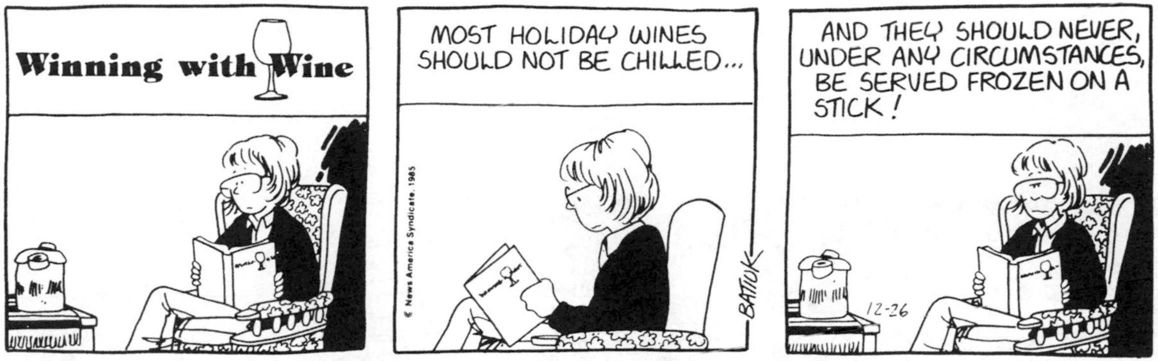
Winning with Wine
MOST HOLIDAY WINES SHOULD NOT BE CHILLED...
AND THEY SHOULD NEVER, UNDER ANY CIRCUMSTANCES, BE SERVED FROZEN ON A STICK!
© News America Syndicate 1985
BATIUK
12-26

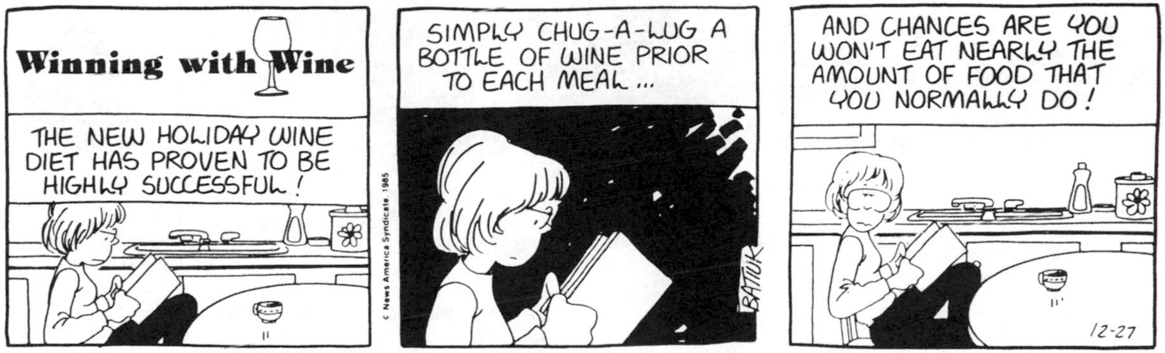
Winning with Wine
THE NEW HOLIDAY WINE DIET HAS PROVEN TO BE HIGHLY SUCCESSFUL!
SIMPLY CHUG-A-LUG A BOTTLE OF WINE PRIOR TO EACH MEAL...
AND CHANCES ARE YOU WON'T EAT NEARLY THE AMOUNT OF FOOD THAT YOU NORMALLY DO!
© News America Syndicate 1985
BATIUK
12-27

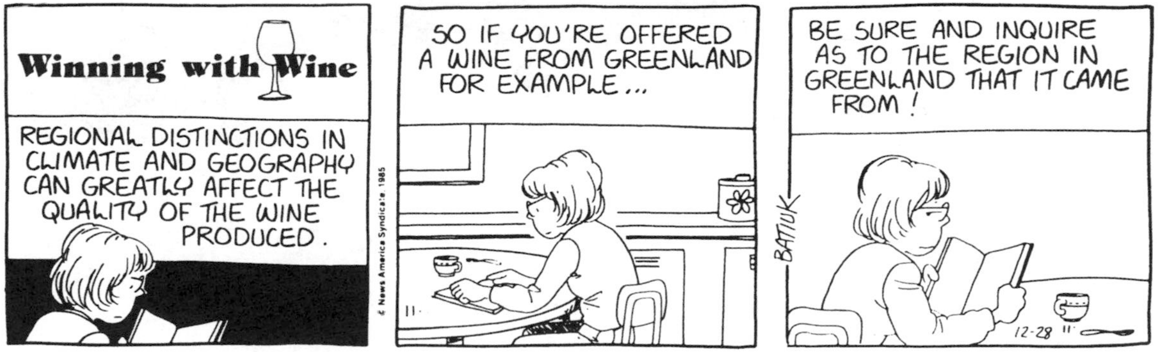
Winning with Wine
REGIONAL DISTINCTIONS IN CLIMATE AND GEOGRAPHY CAN GREATLY AFFECT THE QUALITY OF THE WINE PRODUCED.
SO IF YOU'RE OFFERED A WINE FROM GREENLAND FOR EXAMPLE...
BE SURE AND INQUIRE AS TO THE REGION IN GREENLAND THAT IT CAME FROM!
© News America Syndicate 1985
BATIUK
12-28

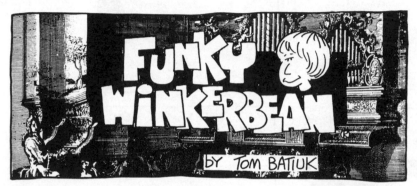

FUNKY WINKERBEAN
BY TOM BATIUK
FAMOUS COMPOSERS
CHAPTER TEN - CLAUDE BARLOW
TAP! TAP!
IN HIS LATER YEARS, THE RENOWNED COMPOSER, CLAUDE BARLOW, BECAME INVOLVED IN AN INTENSE AND BITTER RIVALRY WITH WOLFGANG AMADEUS MOZART!
TAP! TAP!
12-29
IT SEEMS THAT NO MATTER HOW LONG A MUSICAL PIECE BARLOW COMPOSED...
TAP! TAP!
© News America Syndicate, 1985
MOZART ALWAYS WROTE ONE THAT WAS A LITTLE BIT LONGER!
TAP! TAP!
BATIUK
BARLOW SPENT THE REMAINDER OF HIS DAYS CONSTANTLY TRYING TO EVEN THE SCORE!

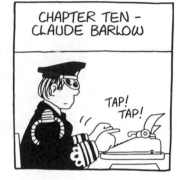

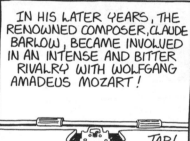

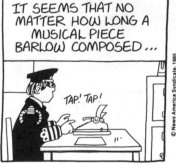

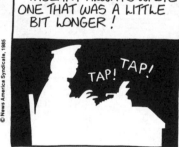

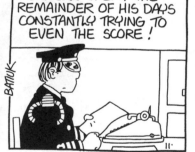

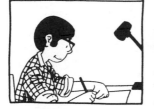

Here comes ol' Halley the Comet,
It looks 'bout as big as a grommet.
There's no need to fear it, Let's hope we get near it,
So we can all run out and glom it!
12-30
BATIUK
© News America Syndicate, 1985

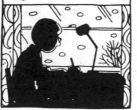

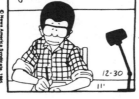

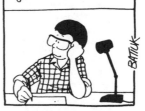

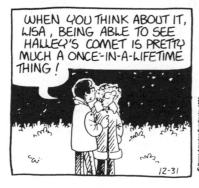

WHEN YOU THINK ABOUT IT, LISA, BEING ABLE TO SEE HALLEY'S COMET IS PRETTY MUCH A ONCE-IN-A-LIFETIME THING!
12-31
© News America Syndicate, 1985
I KNOW... I CAN'T THINK OF ANYBODY WHO'S EVER SEEN IT BEFORE!
BATIUK
I DUNNO... IT SEEMS SMALLER THAN LAST TIME!

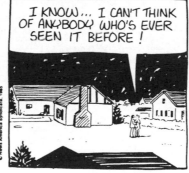

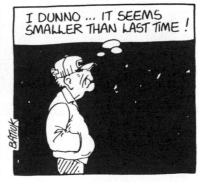

1986

SHOOT!
THERE'S NO SENSE GOING TO BED NOW!
I MIGHT AS WELL STAY UP AND WATCH THE 'SUNRISE BOWL'!
© News America Syndicate, 1986 1-1
BATIUK

HEY, THEY'RE PUTTING UP THE SIGN ON THAT NEW BUSINESS ACROSS THE STREET!
YOU KNOW, CRAZY... I'M REALLY GLAD TO SEE SOMEONE LOCATING HERE!
THE DOWNTOWN AREA CAN REALLY USE ANOTHER...
PIZZA PLACE...
© News America Syndicate, 1986 1-2
BATIUK

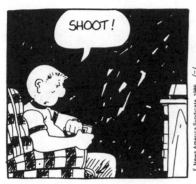

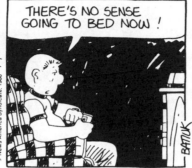

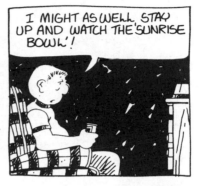

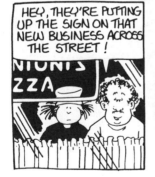

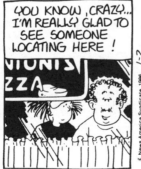

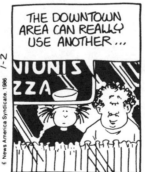

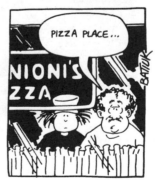

MR. MONTONI, DOMBROWSKI'S PIZZA ACROSS THE STREET IS STEALING ALL OF OUR IDEAS!
KISH!
KISH!
© News America Syndicate, 1986
1-3
THEY'VE EVEN GOT A LITTLE PIZZA ON TOP OF THEIR DELIVERY CAR JUST LIKE WE DO!
KISH!
BATIUK
THAT REMINDS ME... MAYBE WE SHOULD RUN OUR CAR THROUGH THE CARWASH TO SEE IF WE CAN CLEAN THAT PIZZA OFF OF THERE!
KISH!
SQUEE!

IN ORDER TO COMPETE WITH DOMBROWSKI'S PIZZA ACROSS THE STREET...
MONTONI'S PIZZA
TRY OUR 'COMET SPECIAL'!
© News America Syndicate, 1986
I'VE COME UP WITH OUR 'HALLEY'S COMET SPECIAL'!
BATIUK
IT'S A LOT SMALLER THAN YOU THOUGHT IT WAS GOING TO BE!
1-4

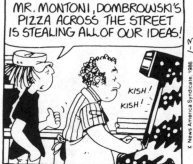

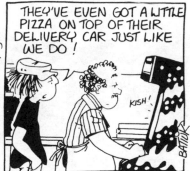

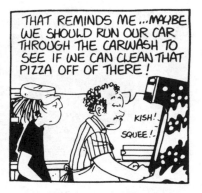

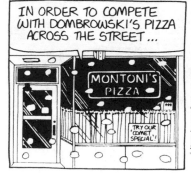

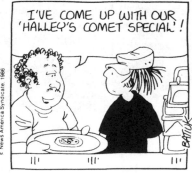

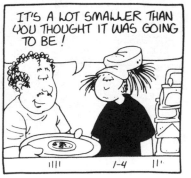

Funky Winkerbean by Tom Batiuk

TAKE OUT A PENCIL AND PAPER FOR A BRIEF QUIZ ON GREAT BRITAIN!

SHOOT! THE ONLY THING I STUDIED ABOUT WAS ENGLAND!

DEFINE THE FOLLOWING:

(1.) BUCCANEER

© News America Syndicate, 1986

An unusually good price for an ear transplant!

1-5

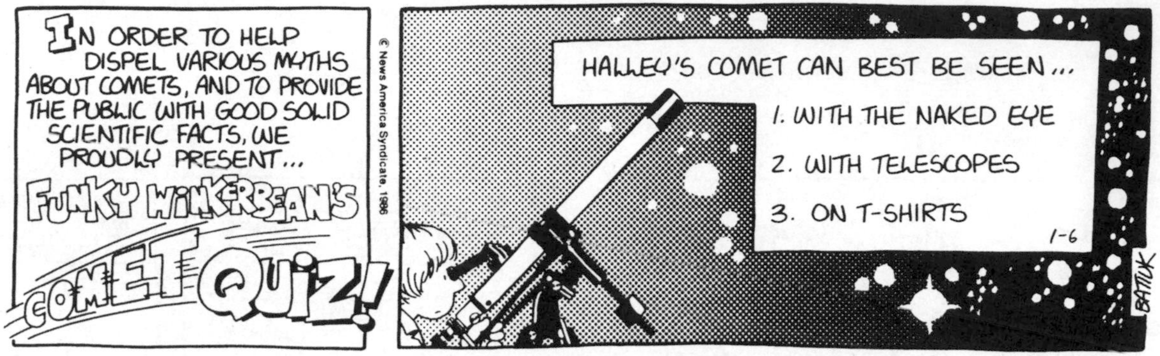
IN ORDER TO HELP DISPEL VARIOUS MYTHS ABOUT COMETS, AND TO PROVIDE THE PUBLIC WITH GOOD SOLID SCIENTIFIC FACTS, WE PROUDLY PRESENT...
FUNKY WINKERBEAN'S
COMET QUIZ!
© News America Syndicate, 1986
HALLEY'S COMET CAN BEST BE SEEN...
1. WITH THE NAKED EYE
2. WITH TELESCOPES
3. ON T-SHIRTS
1-6
BATIUK

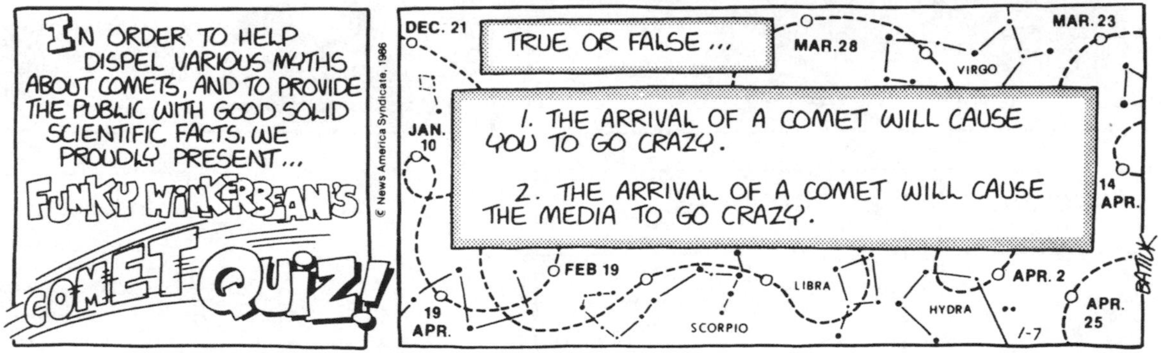
IN ORDER TO HELP DISPEL VARIOUS MYTHS ABOUT COMETS, AND TO PROVIDE THE PUBLIC WITH GOOD SOLID SCIENTIFIC FACTS, WE PROUDLY PRESENT...
FUNKY WINKERBEAN'S
COMET QUIZ!
© News America Syndicate, 1986
TRUE OR FALSE...
1. THE ARRIVAL OF A COMET WILL CAUSE YOU TO GO CRAZY.
2. THE ARRIVAL OF A COMET WILL CAUSE THE MEDIA TO GO CRAZY.
DEC. 21
MAR.28
MAR.23
VIRGO
JAN. 10
14 APR.
FEB 19
LIBRA
HYDRA
SCORPIO
APR. 2
APR. 25
19 APR.
1-7
BATIUK

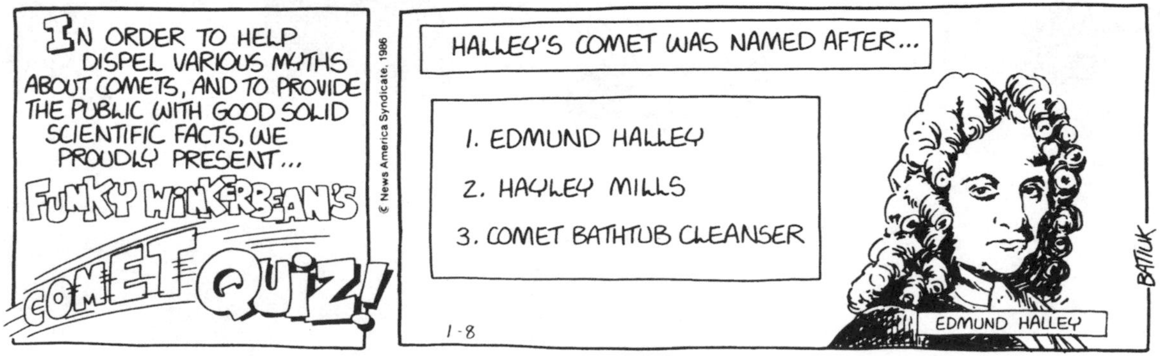
IN ORDER TO HELP DISPEL VARIOUS MYTHS ABOUT COMETS, AND TO PROVIDE THE PUBLIC WITH GOOD SOLID SCIENTIFIC FACTS, WE PROUDLY PRESENT...
FUNKY WINKERBEAN'S
COMET QUIZ!
© News America Syndicate, 1986
HALLEY'S COMET WAS NAMED AFTER...
1. EDMUND HALLEY
2. HAYLEY MILLS
3. COMET BATHTUB CLEANSER
EDMUND HALLEY
1-8
BATIUK

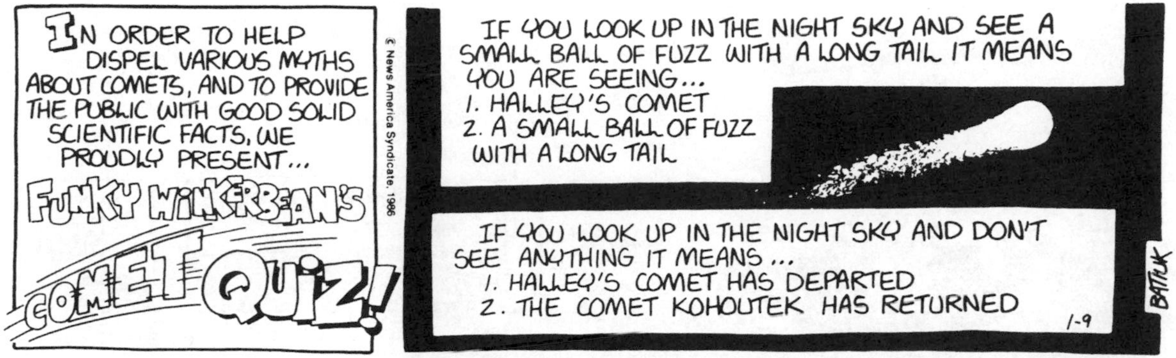
IN ORDER TO HELP DISPEL VARIOUS MYTHS ABOUT COMETS, AND TO PROVIDE THE PUBLIC WITH GOOD SOLID SCIENTIFIC FACTS, WE PROUDLY PRESENT...
FUNKY WINKERBEAN'S
COMET QUIZ!
© News America Syndicate, 1986
IF YOU LOOK UP IN THE NIGHT SKY AND SEE A SMALL BALL OF FUZZ WITH A LONG TAIL IT MEANS YOU ARE SEEING...
1. HALLEY'S COMET
2. A SMALL BALL OF FUZZ WITH A LONG TAIL
IF YOU LOOK UP IN THE NIGHT SKY AND DON'T SEE ANYTHING IT MEANS...
1. HALLEY'S COMET HAS DEPARTED
2. THE COMET KOHOUTEK HAS RETURNED
1-9
BATIUK

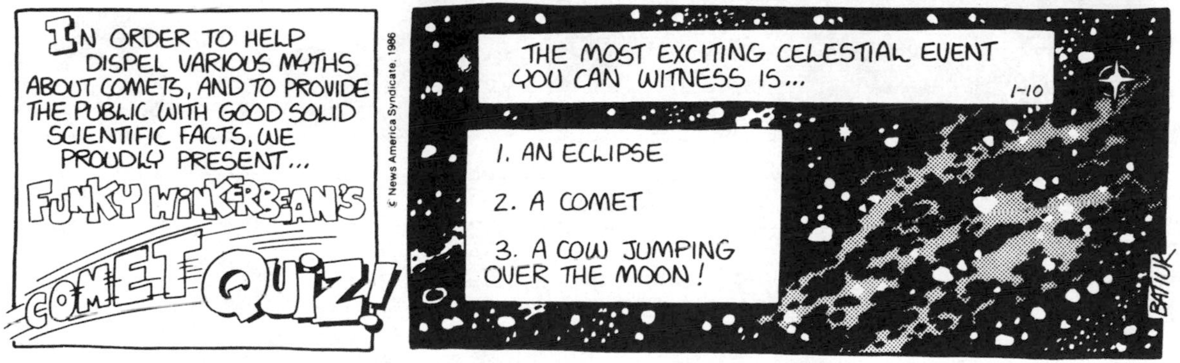
IN ORDER TO HELP DISPEL VARIOUS MYTHS ABOUT COMETS, AND TO PROVIDE THE PUBLIC WITH GOOD SOLID SCIENTIFIC FACTS, WE PROUDLY PRESENT...
FUNKY WINKERBEAN'S
COMET QUIZ!
© News America Syndicate, 1986
THE MOST EXCITING CELESTIAL EVENT YOU CAN WITNESS IS...
1-10
1. AN ECLIPSE
2. A COMET
3. A COW JUMPING OVER THE MOON!
BATIUK

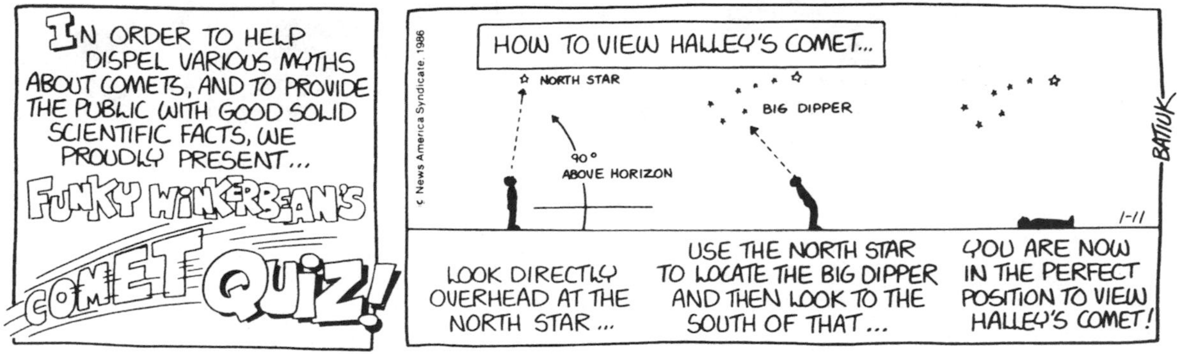
IN ORDER TO HELP DISPEL VARIOUS MYTHS ABOUT COMETS, AND TO PROVIDE THE PUBLIC WITH GOOD SOLID SCIENTIFIC FACTS, WE PROUDLY PRESENT...
FUNKY WINKERBEAN'S
COMET QUIZ!
© News America Syndicate, 1986
HOW TO VIEW HALLEY'S COMET...
NORTH STAR
90° ABOVE HORIZON
BIG DIPPER
BATIUK
1-11
LOOK DIRECTLY OVERHEAD AT THE NORTH STAR...
USE THE NORTH STAR TO LOCATE THE BIG DIPPER AND THEN LOOK TO THE SOUTH OF THAT...
YOU ARE NOW IN THE PERFECT POSITION TO VIEW HALLEY'S COMET!

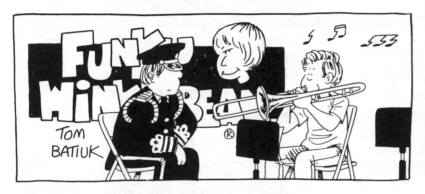

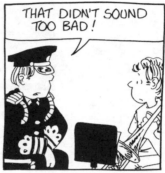

FUNKY WINKERBEAN
TOM BATIUK
THAT DIDN'T SOUND TOO BAD!
YOU'RE USING THE EARPLUGS AGAIN, AREN'T YOU?
MR. DINKLE, I'M NOT SURE I WANT TO BE INVOLVED WITH SOMETHING CREATIVE LIKE PERFORMING MUSIC!
I WAS READING SOMEWHERE THAT CREATIVE PEOPLE OFTEN GO CRAZY!
TRUST ME... YOU'RE PERFECTLY SAFE!
BATIUK
© News America Syndicate, 1986
1-12

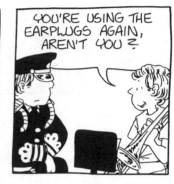

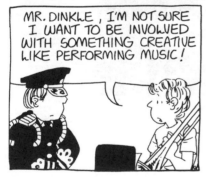

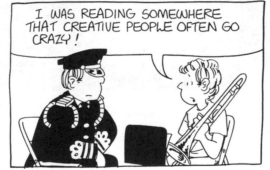

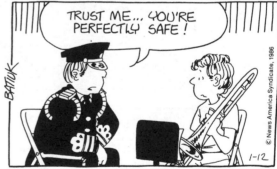

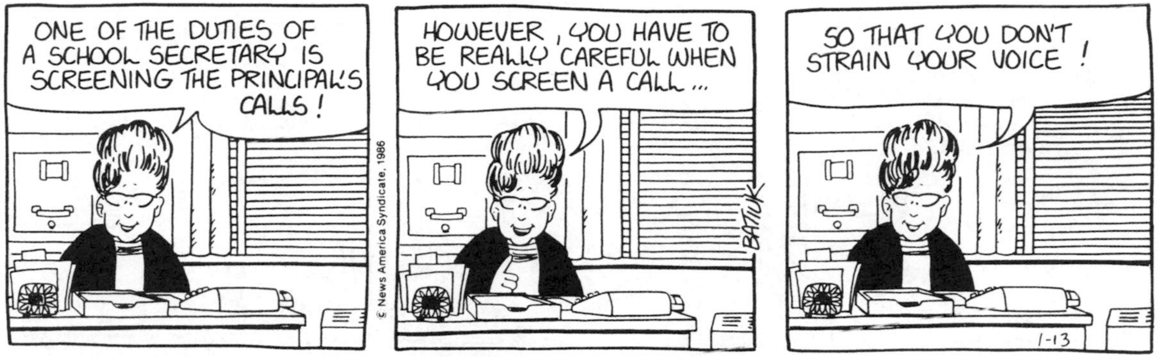
ONE OF THE DUTIES OF A SCHOOL SECRETARY IS SCREENING THE PRINCIPAL'S CALLS!
© News America Syndicate, 1986
HOWEVER, YOU HAVE TO BE REALLY CAREFUL WHEN YOU SCREEN A CALL...
BATIUK
SO THAT YOU DON'T STRAIN YOUR VOICE!
1-13

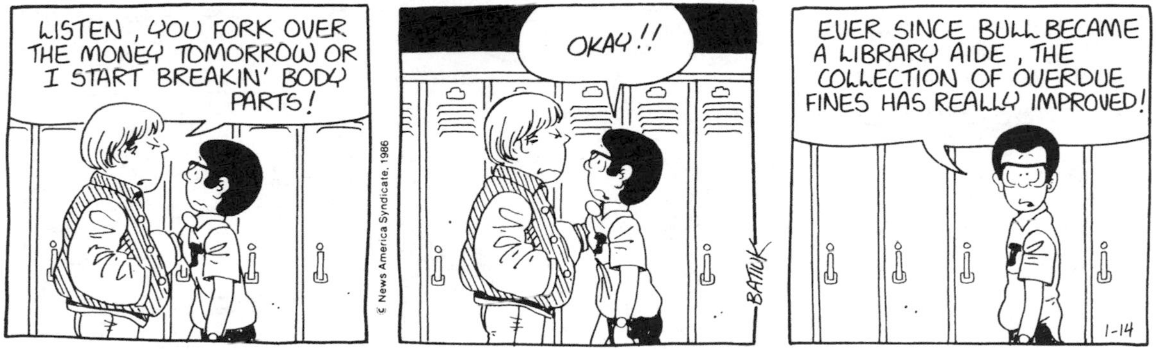
LISTEN, YOU FORK OVER THE MONEY TOMORROW OR I START BREAKIN' BODY PARTS!
© News America Syndicate, 1986
OKAY!!
BATIUK
EVER SINCE BULL BECAME A LIBRARY AIDE, THE COLLECTION OF OVERDUE FINES HAS REALLY IMPROVED!
1-14

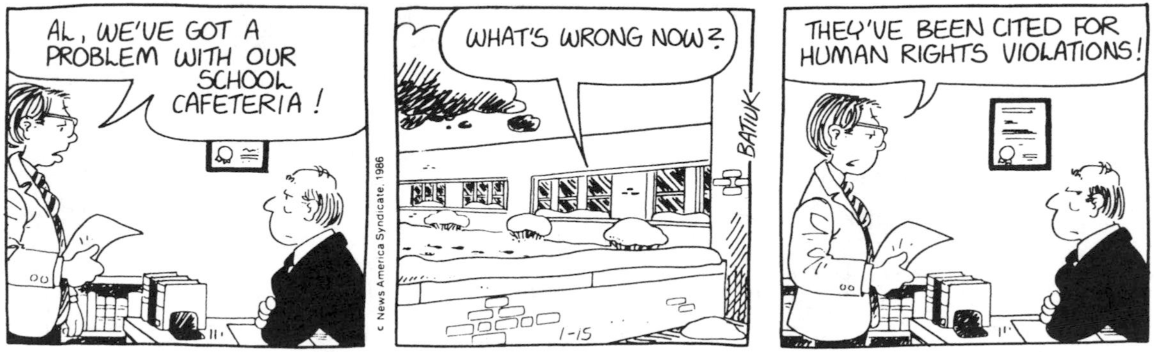
AL, WE'VE GOT A PROBLEM WITH OUR SCHOOL CAFETERIA!
c News America Syndicate, 1986
WHAT'S WRONG NOW?
BATIUK
1-15
THEY'VE BEEN CITED FOR HUMAN RIGHTS VIOLATIONS!

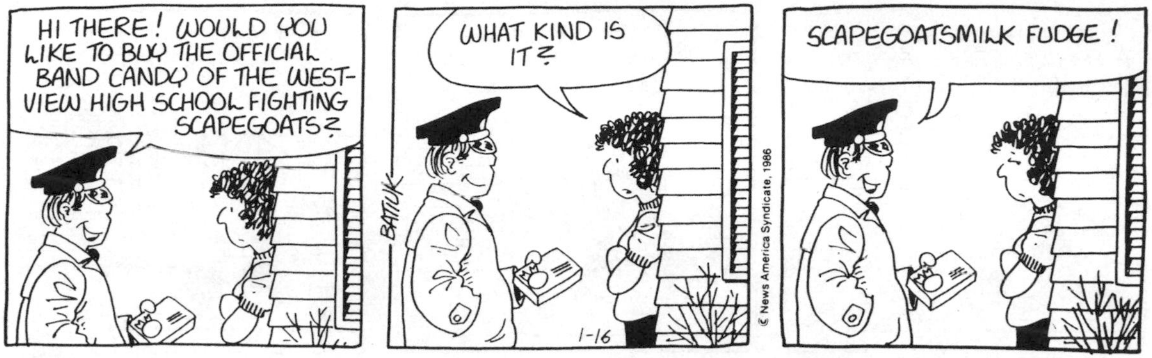
HI THERE! WOULD YOU LIKE TO BUY THE OFFICIAL BAND CANDY OF THE WEST-VIEW HIGH SCHOOL FIGHTING SCAPEGOATS?
WHAT KIND IS IT?
SCAPEGOATSMILK FUDGE!
BATIUK
1-16
© News America Syndicate, 1986

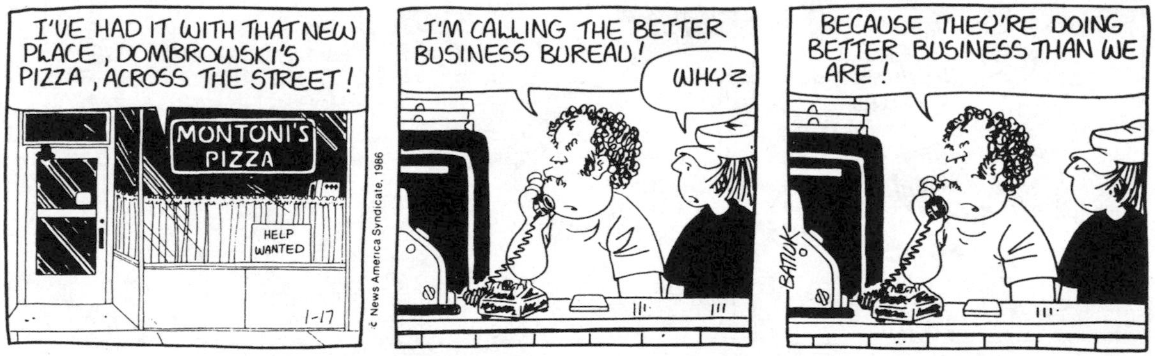
I'VE HAD IT WITH THAT NEW PLACE, DOMBROWSKI'S PIZZA, ACROSS THE STREET!
MONTONI'S PIZZA
HELP WANTED
1-17
© News America Syndicate, 1986
I'M CALLING THE BETTER BUSINESS BUREAU!
WHY?
BECAUSE THEY'RE DOING BETTER BUSINESS THAN WE ARE!
BATIUK

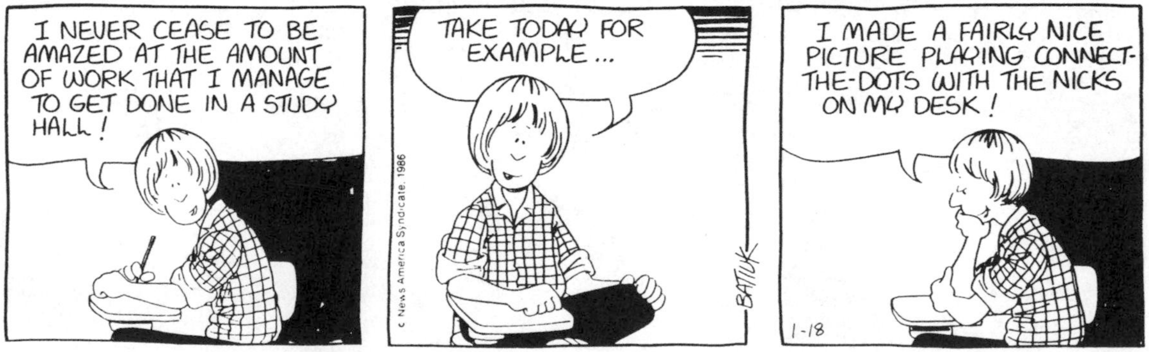
I NEVER CEASE TO BE AMAZED AT THE AMOUNT OF WORK THAT I MANAGE TO GET DONE IN A STUDY HALL!
© News America Syndicate, 1986
TAKE TODAY FOR EXAMPLE...
BATIUK
I MADE A FAIRLY NICE PICTURE PLAYING CONNECT-THE-DOTS WITH THE NICKS ON MY DESK!
1-18

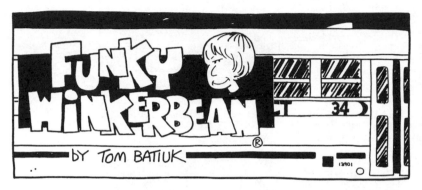

FUNKY WINKERBEAN
BY TOM BATIUK
HERE WE ARE!
LAST STOP!
CHUCKLE ... LOOK AT THAT!
THERE SHE IS ... STANDING THERE SHIVERING IN THE COLD!
WITH LITTLE TEARS TRICKLING DOWN HER CHEEKS AS SHE HUNCHES OVER AGAINST THE GUSTS OF BLOWING SNOW!
I LOVE WATCHING THE TEACHERS ON BUS DUTY!
© News America Syndicate, 1986
BATIUK
1-19

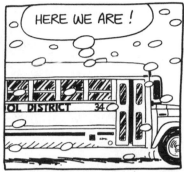

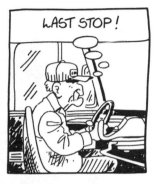

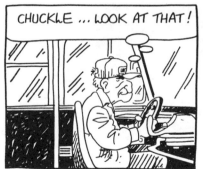

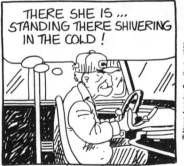

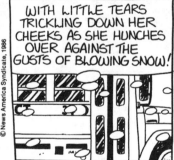

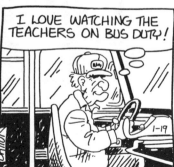

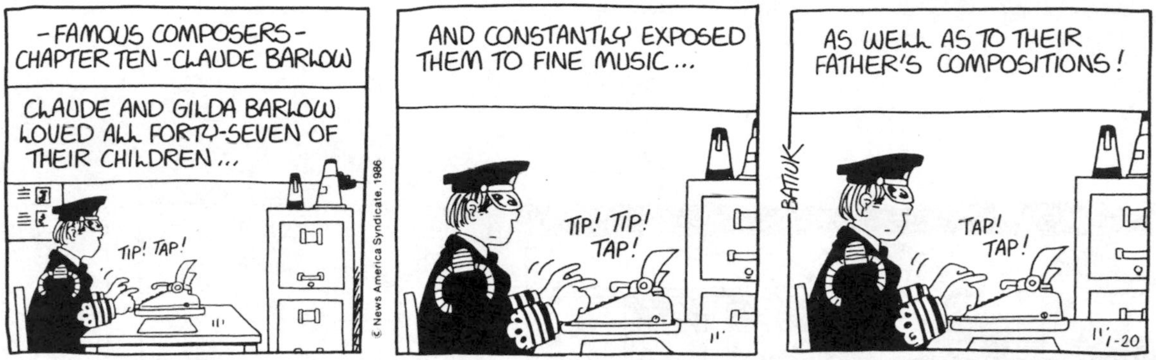
-FAMOUS COMPOSERS-
CHAPTER TEN -CLAUDE BARLOW
CLAUDE AND GILDA BARLOW LOVED ALL FORTY-SEVEN OF THEIR CHILDREN...
TIP! TAP!
© News America Syndicate, 1986
AND CONSTANTLY EXPOSED THEM TO FINE MUSIC...
TIP! TIP! TAP!
AS WELL AS TO THEIR FATHER'S COMPOSITIONS!
BATIUK
TAP! TAP!
1-20

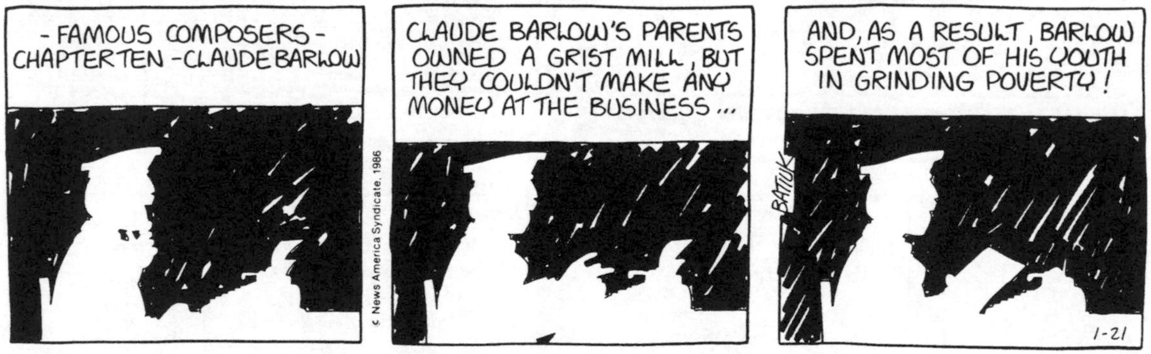
-FAMOUS COMPOSERS-
CHAPTER TEN -CLAUDE BARLOW
© News America Syndicate, 1986
CLAUDE BARLOW'S PARENTS OWNED A GRIST MILL, BUT THEY COULDN'T MAKE ANY MONEY AT THE BUSINESS...
AND, AS A RESULT, BARLOW SPENT MOST OF HIS YOUTH IN GRINDING POVERTY!
BATIUK
1-21

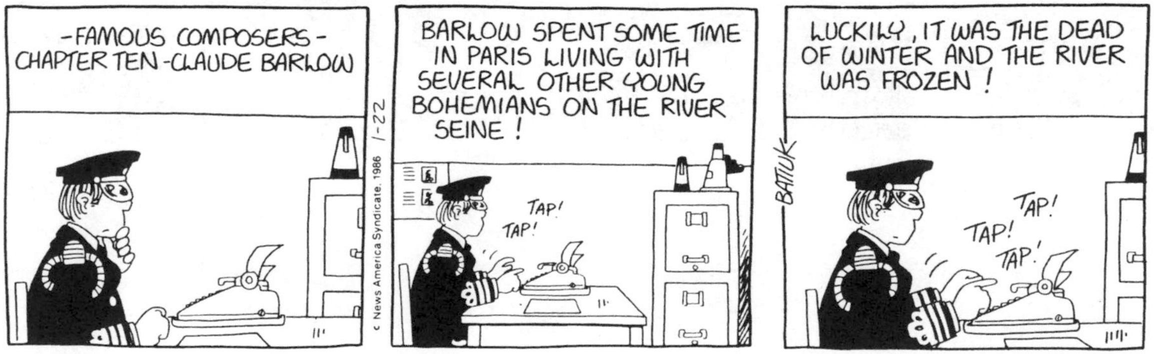
-FAMOUS COMPOSERS-
CHAPTER TEN -CLAUDE BARLOW
© News America Syndicate, 1986
1-22
BARLOW SPENT SOME TIME IN PARIS LIVING WITH SEVERAL OTHER YOUNG BOHEMIANS ON THE RIVER SEINE!
TAP! TAP!
LUCKILY, IT WAS THE DEAD OF WINTER AND THE RIVER WAS FROZEN!
BATIUK
TAP! TAP! TAP!

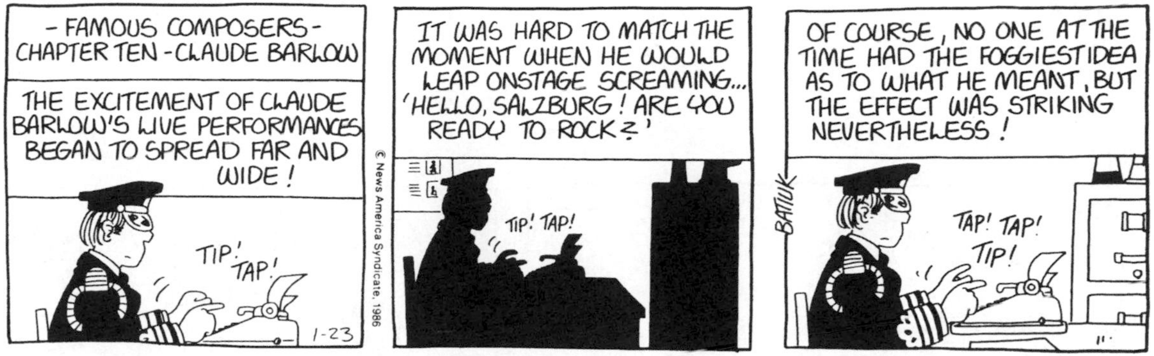
- FAMOUS COMPOSERS -
CHAPTER TEN - CLAUDE BARLOW
THE EXCITEMENT OF CLAUDE BARLOW'S LIVE PERFORMANCES BEGAN TO SPREAD FAR AND WIDE!
TIP! TAP!
1-23
© News America Syndicate, 1986
IT WAS HARD TO MATCH THE MOMENT WHEN HE WOULD LEAP ONSTAGE SCREAMING... 'HELLO, SALZBURG! ARE YOU READY TO ROCK?!'
TIP! TAP!
OF COURSE, NO ONE AT THE TIME HAD THE FOGGIEST IDEA AS TO WHAT HE MEANT, BUT THE EFFECT WAS STRIKING NEVERTHELESS!
BATIUK
TAP! TAP! TIP!

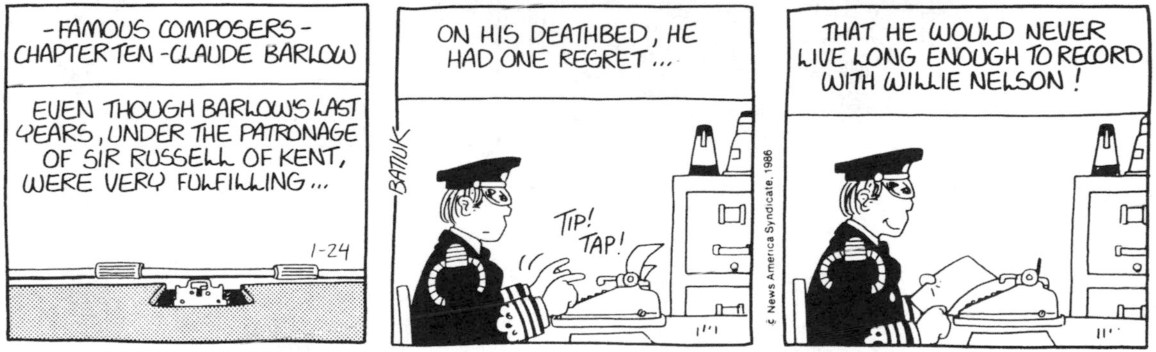
- FAMOUS COMPOSERS -
CHAPTER TEN - CLAUDE BARLOW
EVEN THOUGH BARLOW'S LAST YEARS, UNDER THE PATRONAGE OF SIR RUSSELL OF KENT, WERE VERY FULFILLING...
1-24
ON HIS DEATHBED, HE HAD ONE REGRET...
BATIUK
TIP! TAP!
© News America Syndicate, 1986
THAT HE WOULD NEVER LIVE LONG ENOUGH TO RECORD WITH WILLIE NELSON!

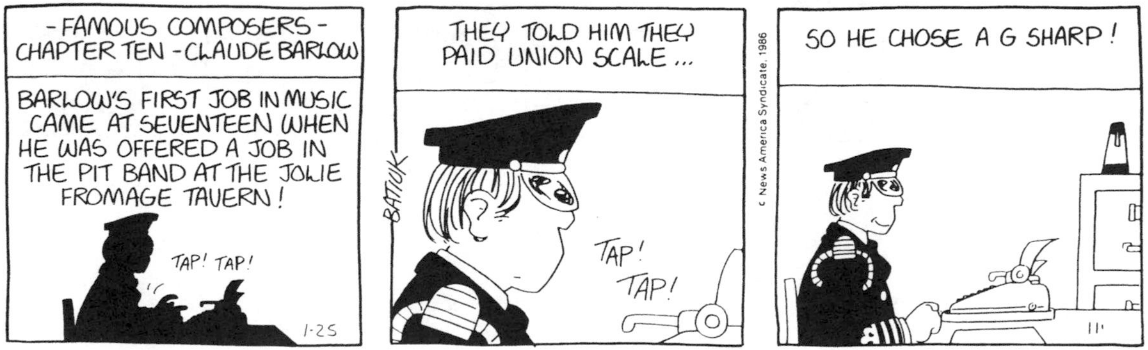
- FAMOUS COMPOSERS -
CHAPTER TEN - CLAUDE BARLOW
BARLOW'S FIRST JOB IN MUSIC CAME AT SEVENTEEN WHEN HE WAS OFFERED A JOB IN THE PIT BAND AT THE JOLIE FROMAGE TAVERN!
TAP! TAP!
1-25
THEY TOLD HIM THEY PAID UNION SCALE...
BATIUK
TAP! TAP!
© News America Syndicate, 1986
SO HE CHOSE A G SHARP!

FUNKY WINKERBEAN
BY TOM BATIUK
EVERYBODY STAND BACK!
OKAY, BRING IT ON THROUGH!
© News America Syndicate, 1986
A BATCH OF SPANISH RICE GOT AWAY FROM THE COOKS!
1-26
BATIUK

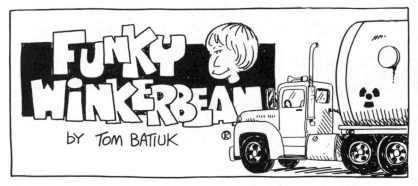

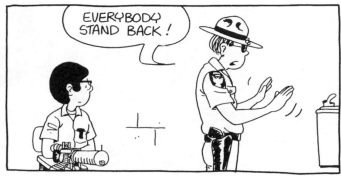

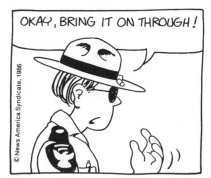

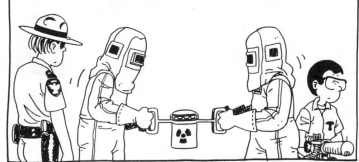

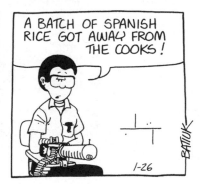

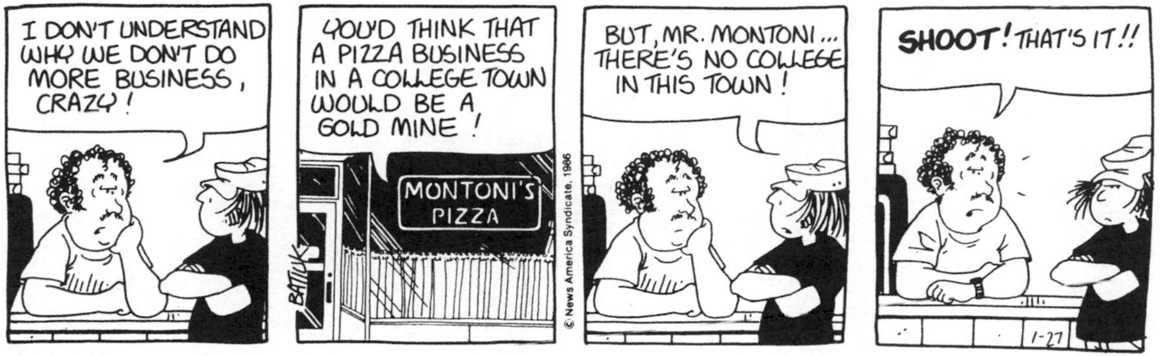
I DON'T UNDERSTAND WHY WE DON'T DO MORE BUSINESS, CRAZY!
YOU'D THINK THAT A PIZZA BUSINESS IN A COLLEGE TOWN WOULD BE A GOLD MINE!
MONTONI'S PIZZA
BATIUK
© News America Syndicate, 1986
BUT, MR. MONTONI... THERE'S NO COLLEGE IN THIS TOWN!
SHOOT! THAT'S IT!!
1-27

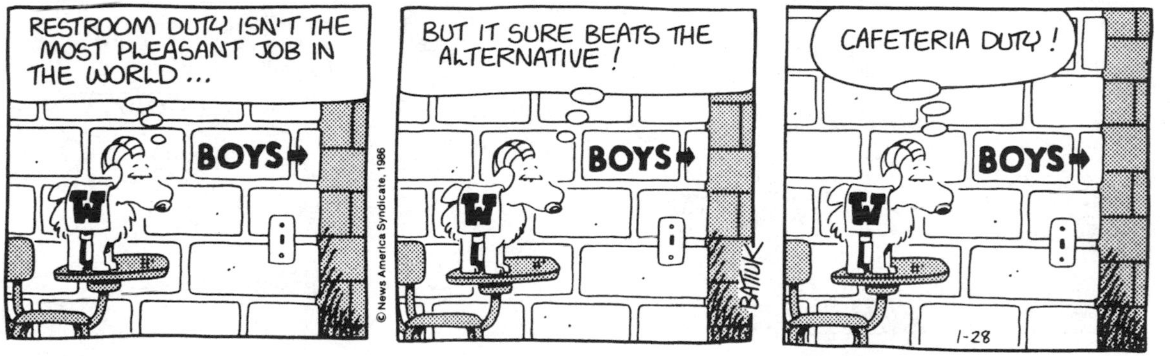
RESTROOM DUTY ISN'T THE MOST PLEASANT JOB IN THE WORLD...
BOYS
W
© News America Syndicate, 1986
BUT IT SURE BEATS THE ALTERNATIVE!
BOYS
BATIUK
CAFETERIA DUTY!
BOYS
1-28

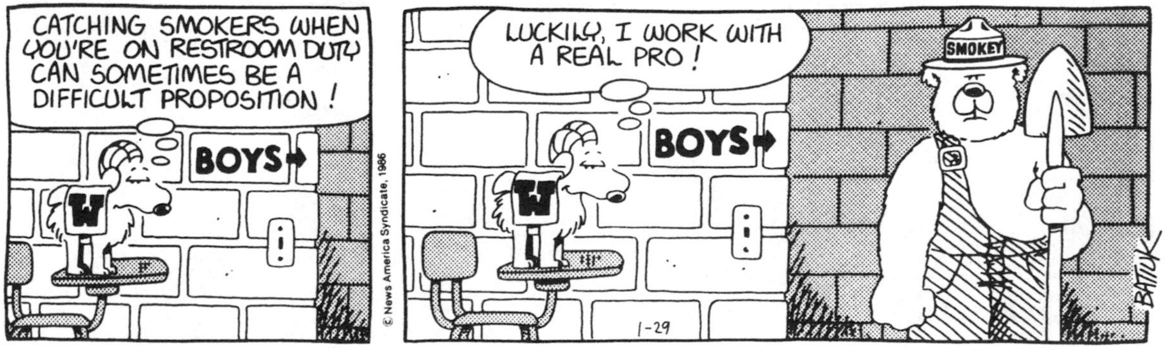
CATCHING SMOKERS WHEN YOU'RE ON RESTROOM DUTY CAN SOMETIMES BE A DIFFICULT PROPOSITION!
BOYS
W
© News America Syndicate, 1986
LUCKILY, I WORK WITH A REAL PRO!
BOYS
SMOKEY
BATIUK
1-29

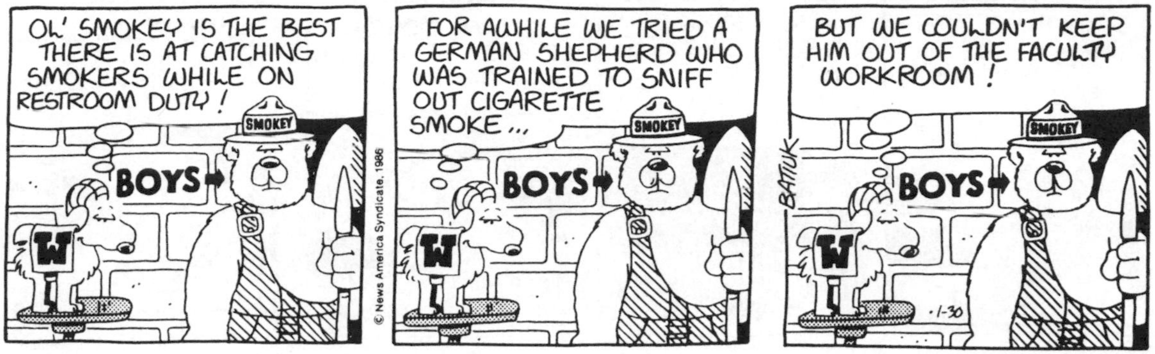
OL' SMOKEY IS THE BEST THERE IS AT CATCHING SMOKERS WHILE ON RESTROOM DUTY!
SMOKEY
BOYS
W
© News America Syndicate, 1986
FOR AWHILE WE TRIED A GERMAN SHEPHERD WHO WAS TRAINED TO SNIFF OUT CIGARETTE SMOKE...
SMOKEY
BOYS
W
BUT WE COULDN'T KEEP HIM OUT OF THE FACULTY WORKROOM!
SMOKEY
BOYS
W
BATIUK
1-30

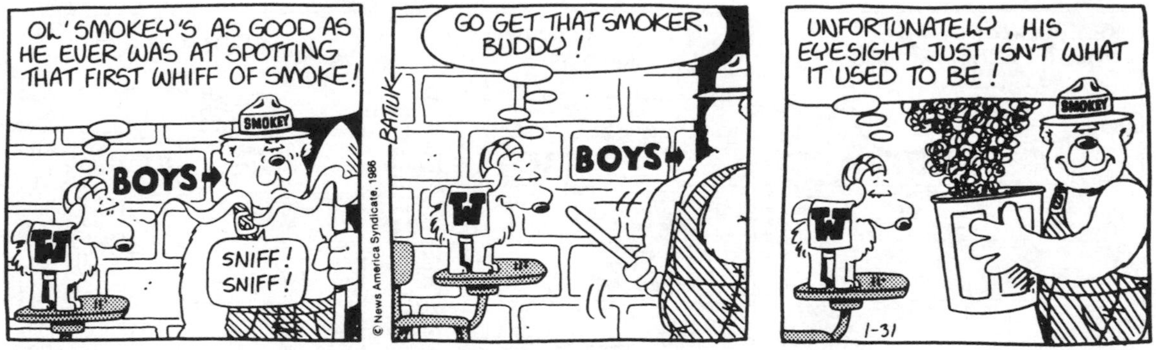
OL' SMOKEY'S AS GOOD AS HE EVER WAS AT SPOTTING THAT FIRST WHIFF OF SMOKE!
SMOKEY
BOYS
W
SNIFF! SNIFF!
BATIUK
© News America Syndicate, 1986
GO GET THAT SMOKER, BUDDY!
BOYS
W
UNFORTUNATELY, HIS EYESIGHT JUST ISN'T WHAT IT USED TO BE!
SMOKEY
W
1-31

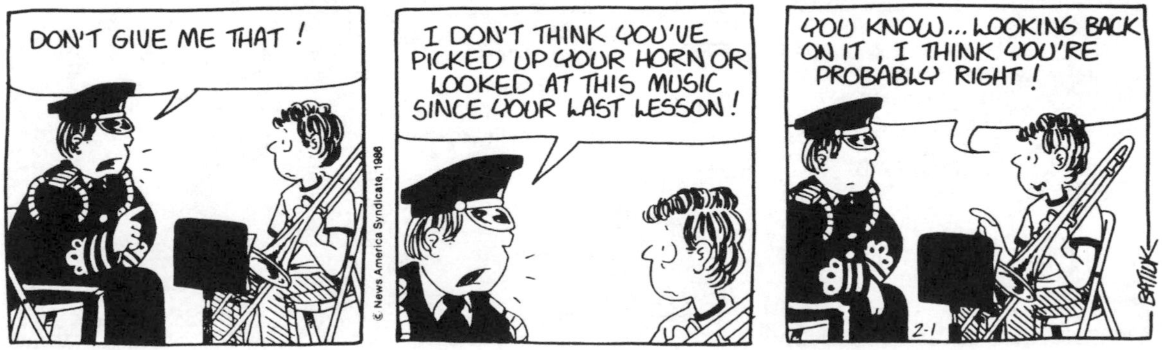
DON'T GIVE ME THAT!
© News America Syndicate, 1986
I DON'T THINK YOU'VE PICKED UP YOUR HORN OR LOOKED AT THIS MUSIC SINCE YOUR LAST LESSON!
YOU KNOW... LOOKING BACK ON IT, I THINK YOU'RE PROBABLY RIGHT!
BATIUK
2-1

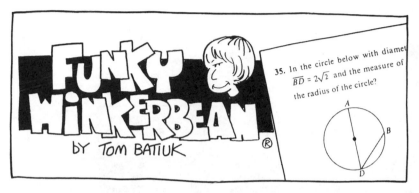

Funky Winkerbean
BY TOM BATIUK

35. In the circle below with diamet $\overline{BD} = 2\sqrt{2}$ and the measure of the radius of the circle?

SHOOT!

I FORGOT ALL ABOUT THAT HOMEWORK WE HAD TO DO FOR ALGEBRA!

HEY, FUNKY! CAN I COPY YOUR ALGEBRA HOMEWORK NEXT PERIOD IN STUDY HALL?

SURE, LES... HERE!

© News America Syndicate, 1986

THANKS!

2-2

ACTUALLY, WE'VE HAD A HOMEWORK ASSISTANCE PROGRAM GOING LONG BEFORE THE SCHOOL SYSTEM STARTED THEIRS!

BATIUK

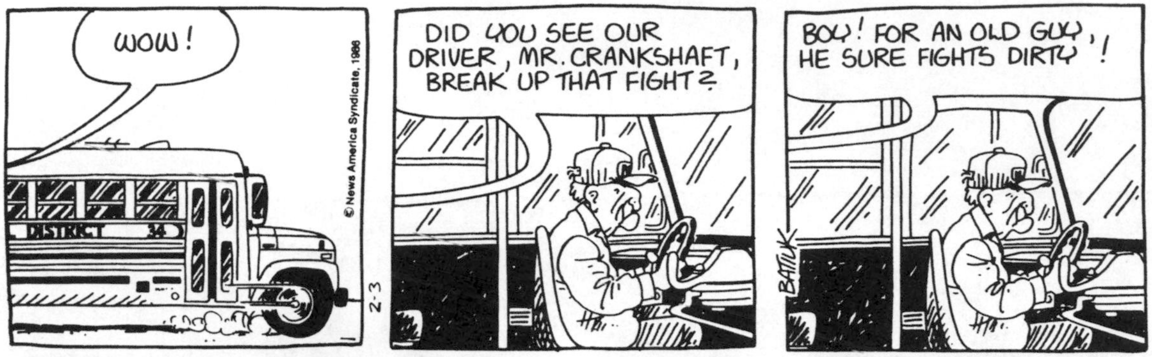
WOW!
© News America Syndicate, 1986
2-3
DID YOU SEE OUR DRIVER, MR. CRANKSHAFT, BREAK UP THAT FIGHT?
BOY! FOR AN OLD GUY, HE SURE FIGHTS DIRTY!
BATIUK

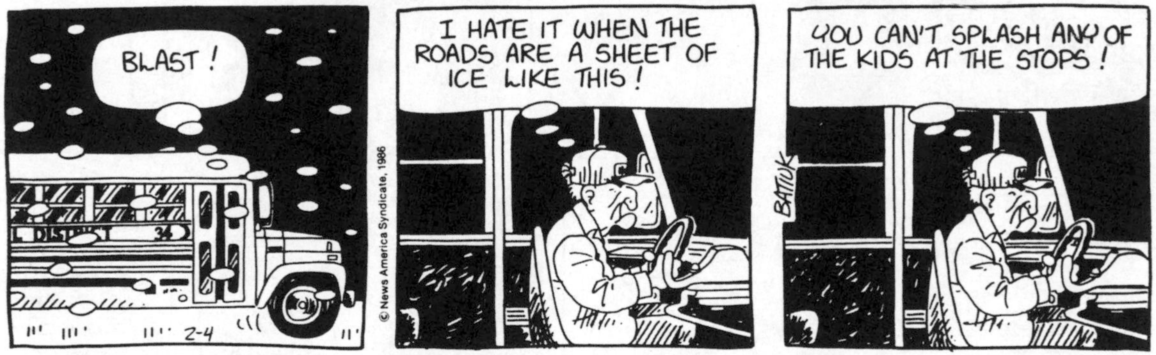
BLAST!
DISTRICT 34
2-4
© News America Syndicate, 1986
I HATE IT WHEN THE ROADS ARE A SHEET OF ICE LIKE THIS!
YOU CAN'T SPLASH ANY OF THE KIDS AT THE STOPS!
BATIUK

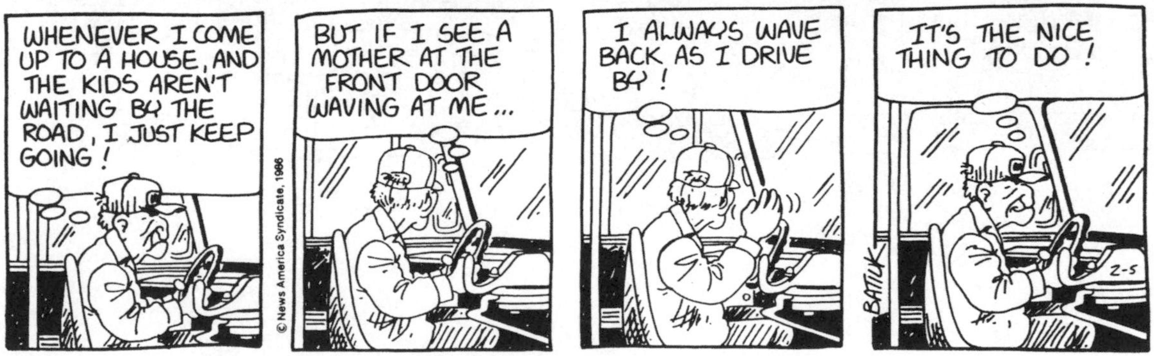
WHENEVER I COME UP TO A HOUSE, AND THE KIDS AREN'T WAITING BY THE ROAD, I JUST KEEP GOING!
© News America Syndicate, 1986
BUT IF I SEE A MOTHER AT THE FRONT DOOR WAVING AT ME...
I ALWAYS WAVE BACK AS I DRIVE BY!
IT'S THE NICE THING TO DO!
BATIUK
2-5

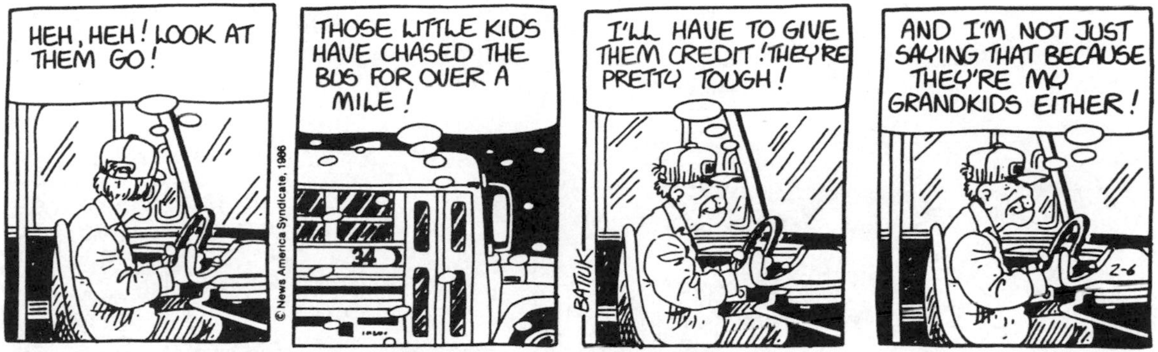
HEH, HEH! LOOK AT THEM GO!
THOSE LITTLE KIDS HAVE CHASED THE BUS FOR OVER A MILE!
© News America Syndicate, 1986
I'LL HAVE TO GIVE THEM CREDIT! THEY'RE PRETTY TOUGH!
BATIUK
AND I'M NOT JUST SAYING THAT BECAUSE THEY'RE MY GRANDKIDS EITHER!
2-6

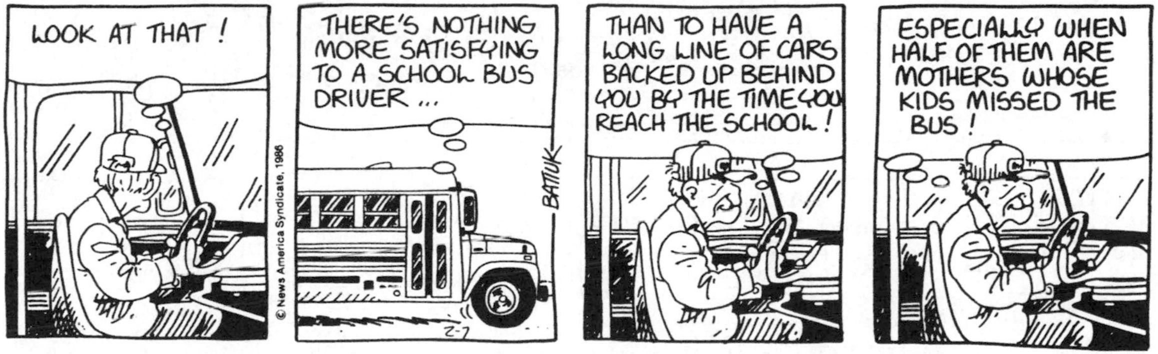
LOOK AT THAT!
© News America Syndicate, 1986
THERE'S NOTHING MORE SATISFYING TO A SCHOOL BUS DRIVER ...
BATIUK
2-7
THAN TO HAVE A LONG LINE OF CARS BACKED UP BEHIND YOU BY THE TIME YOU REACH THE SCHOOL!
ESPECIALLY WHEN HALF OF THEM ARE MOTHERS WHOSE KIDS MISSED THE BUS!

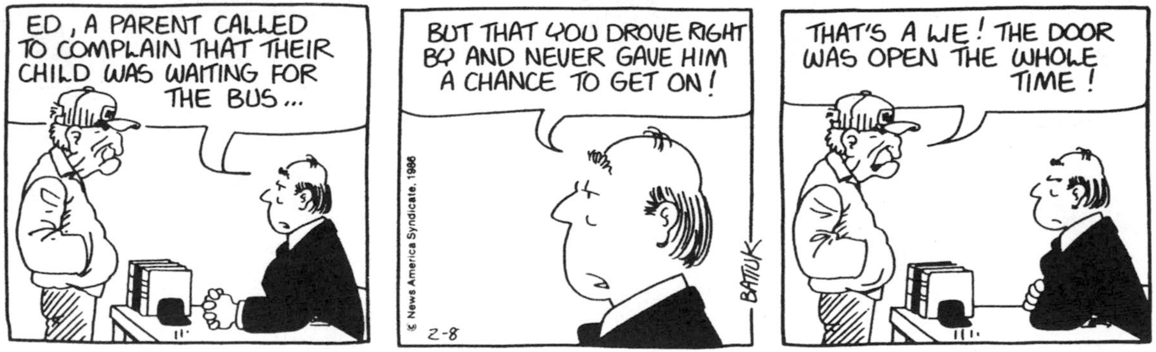
ED, A PARENT CALLED TO COMPLAIN THAT THEIR CHILD WAS WAITING FOR THE BUS ...
© News America Syndicate, 1986
BUT THAT YOU DROVE RIGHT BY AND NEVER GAVE HIM A CHANCE TO GET ON!
BATIUK
2-8
THAT'S A LIE! THE DOOR WAS OPEN THE WHOLE TIME!

FUNKY WINKERBEAN®
LIGHTHOUSE
YOU KNOW...
TEACHING HERE AT THE LIGHTHOUSE'S ALTERNATIVE SCHOOL HAS CERTAIN ADVANTAGES OVER THE PUBLIC SCHOOL!
THE LIGHTHOUSE
FOR ONE THING, YOU DON'T HAVE TO CHAPERONE A LOT OF DANCES!
WELL, GANG, IT LOOKS LIKE WE'VE GOT A NEW RESIDENT WAITING IN THE FOYER!
HIS NAME IS KYLE! APPARENTLY HE RAN AWAY FROM HOME THIS MORNING, TOOK A BUS, AND CAME HERE!
THE LIGHTHOUSE
2-9
© News America Syndicate, 1986
HOW ABOUT IF YOU GUYS HELP KYLE GET SETTLED IN...
BATIUK
WHILE I GO SEE ABOUT RETURNING THE BUS!

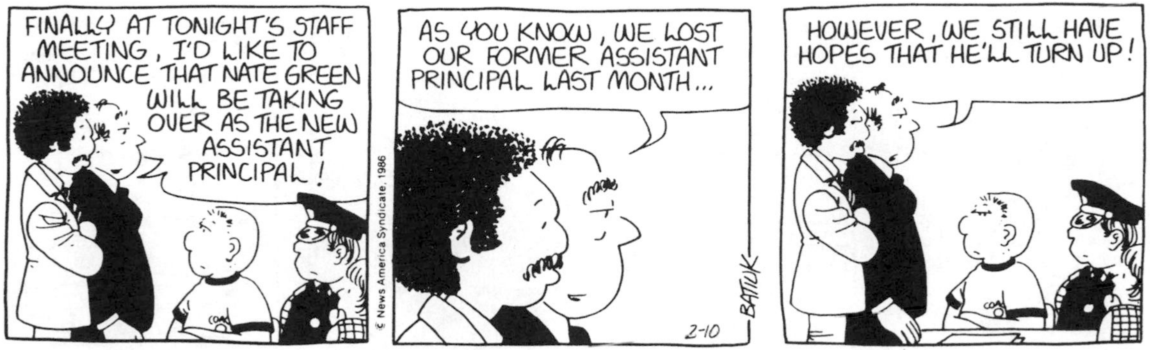
FINALLY AT TONIGHT'S STAFF MEETING, I'D LIKE TO ANNOUNCE THAT NATE GREEN WILL BE TAKING OVER AS THE NEW ASSISTANT PRINCIPAL!
© News America Syndicate, 1986
AS YOU KNOW, WE LOST OUR FORMER ASSISTANT PRINCIPAL LAST MONTH...
BATIUK
2-10
HOWEVER, WE STILL HAVE HOPES THAT HE'LL TURN UP!

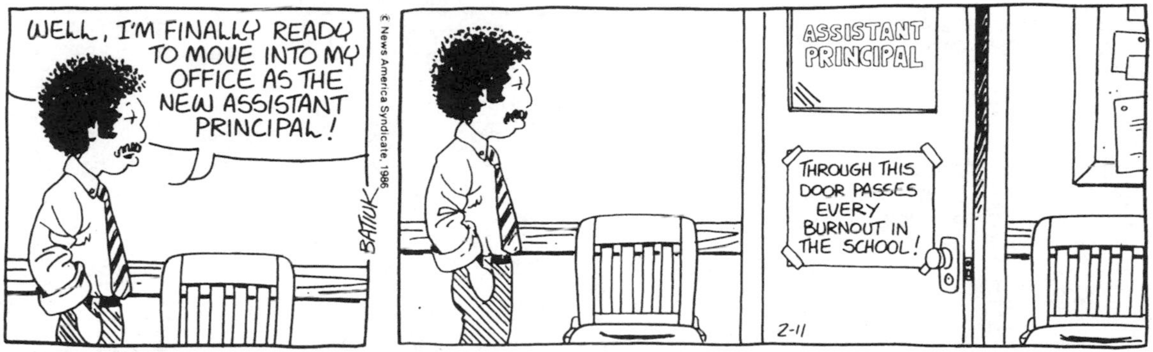
WELL, I'M FINALLY READY TO MOVE INTO MY OFFICE AS THE NEW ASSISTANT PRINCIPAL!
BATIUK
© News America Syndicate, 1986
ASSISTANT PRINCIPAL
THROUGH THIS DOOR PASSES EVERY BURNOUT IN THE SCHOOL!
2-11

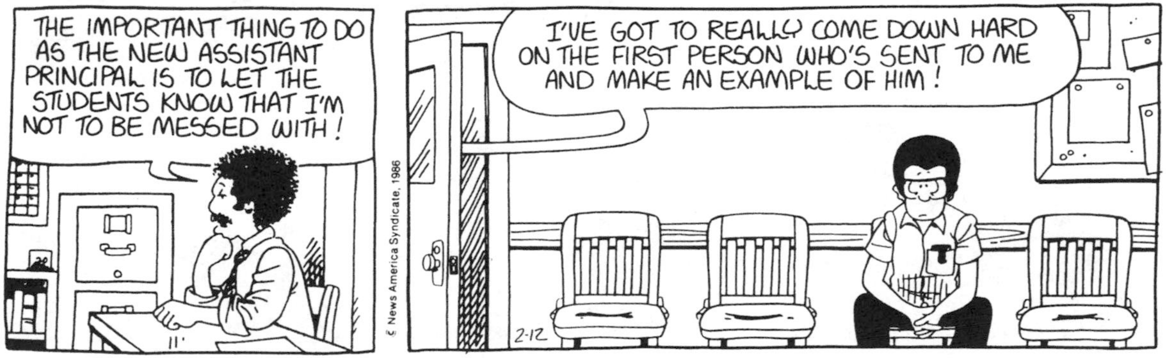
THE IMPORTANT THING TO DO AS THE NEW ASSISTANT PRINCIPAL IS TO LET THE STUDENTS KNOW THAT I'M NOT TO BE MESSED WITH!
© News America Syndicate, 1986
I'VE GOT TO REALLY COME DOWN HARD ON THE FIRST PERSON WHO'S SENT TO ME AND MAKE AN EXAMPLE OF HIM!
2-12

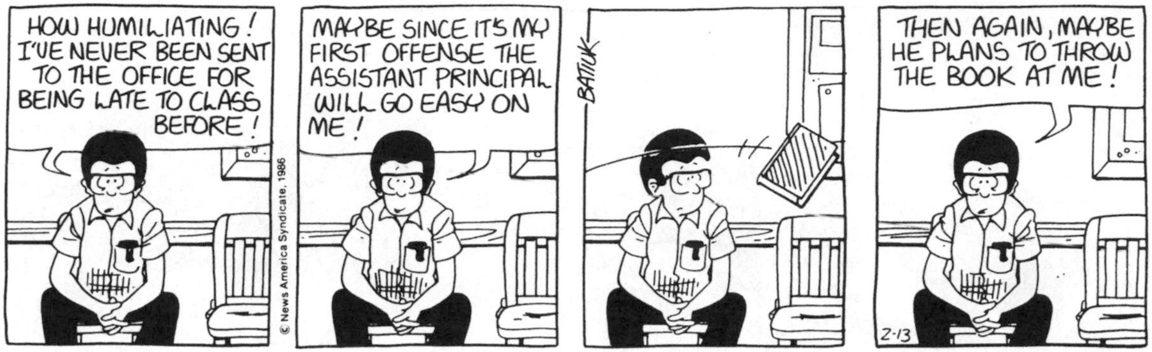
HOW HUMILIATING! I'VE NEVER BEEN SENT TO THE OFFICE FOR BEING LATE TO CLASS BEFORE!
MAYBE SINCE IT'S MY FIRST OFFENSE THE ASSISTANT PRINCIPAL WILL GO EASY ON ME!
BATIUK
THEN AGAIN, MAYBE HE PLANS TO THROW THE BOOK AT ME!
© News America Syndicate, 1986
2-13

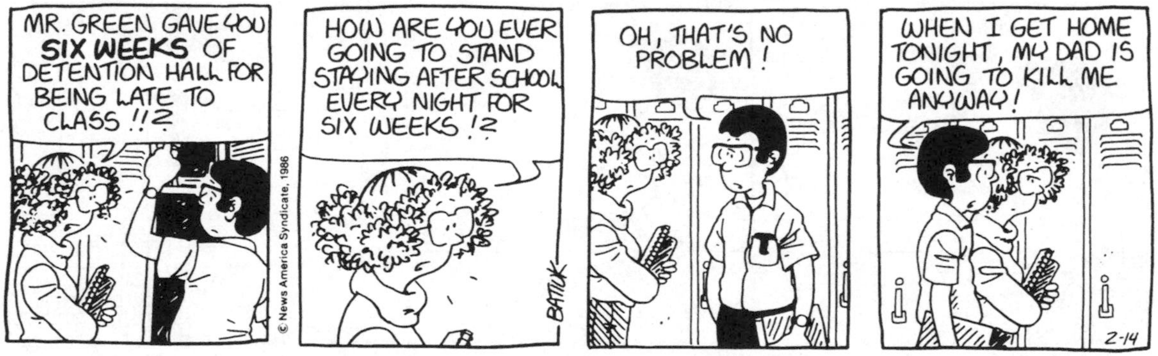
MR. GREEN GAVE YOU **SIX WEEKS** OF DETENTION HALL FOR BEING LATE TO CLASS!!?
HOW ARE YOU EVER GOING TO STAND STAYING AFTER SCHOOL EVERY NIGHT FOR SIX WEEKS!?
BATIUK
OH, THAT'S NO PROBLEM!
WHEN I GET HOME TONIGHT, MY DAD IS GOING TO KILL ME ANYWAY!
© News America Syndicate, 1986
2-14

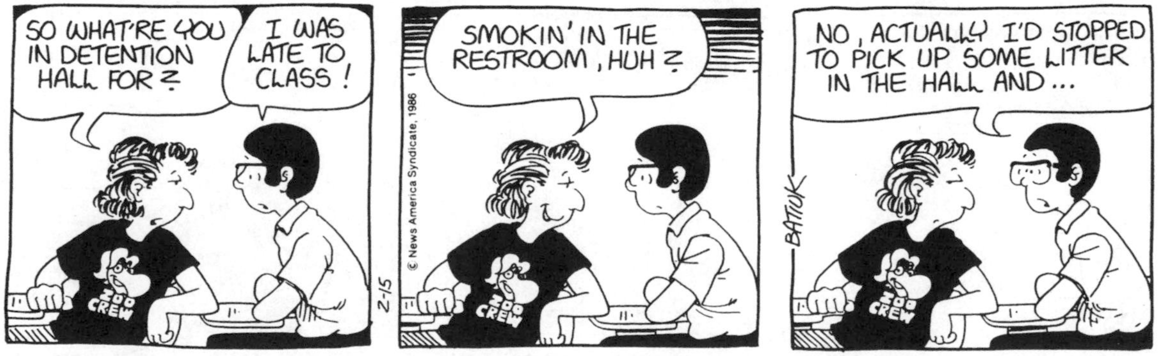
SO WHAT'RE YOU IN DETENTION HALL FOR?
I WAS LATE TO CLASS!
SMOKIN' IN THE RESTROOM, HUH?
NO, ACTUALLY I'D STOPPED TO PICK UP SOME LITTER IN THE HALL AND...
ZOO CREW
BATIUK
© News America Syndicate, 1986
2-15

FUNKY WINKERBEAN
BY TOM BATIUK ®
JUNEBUG!!
WHAT ARE YOU MAD AT ME FOR? PLAYERS FOUL OUT ALL THE TIME!
DURING THE **WARM-UP**?
OKAY, LADIES ... THIS IS A REALLY BIG TOURNAMENT GAME FOR US!
I WANT YOU TO GO OUT THERE TONIGHT AND GIVE IT YOUR ALL!
ALL OUR WHAT?
NO ONE'S EVER ASKED ME THAT BEFORE...
BATIUK
2-16

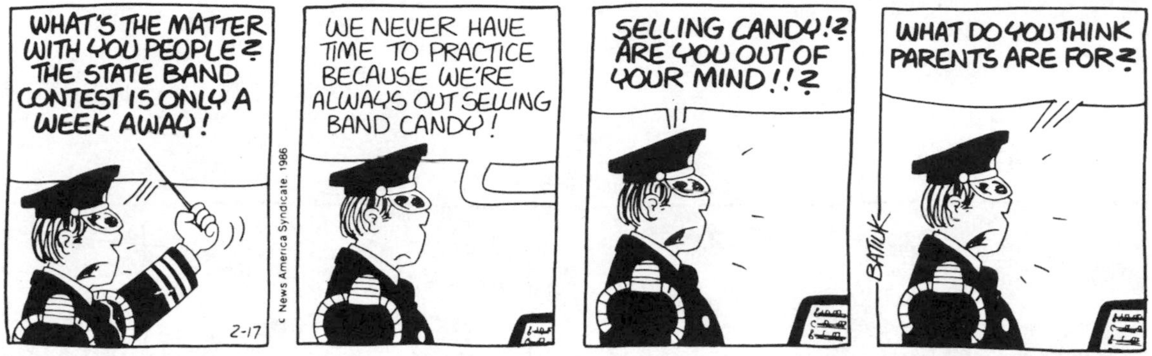
WHAT'S THE MATTER WITH YOU PEOPLE?
THE STATE BAND CONTEST IS ONLY A WEEK AWAY!
WE NEVER HAVE TIME TO PRACTICE BECAUSE WE'RE ALWAYS OUT SELLING BAND CANDY!
SELLING CANDY!? ARE YOU OUT OF YOUR MIND!!?
WHAT DO YOU THINK PARENTS ARE FOR?
2-17
© News America Syndicate, 1986
BATIUK

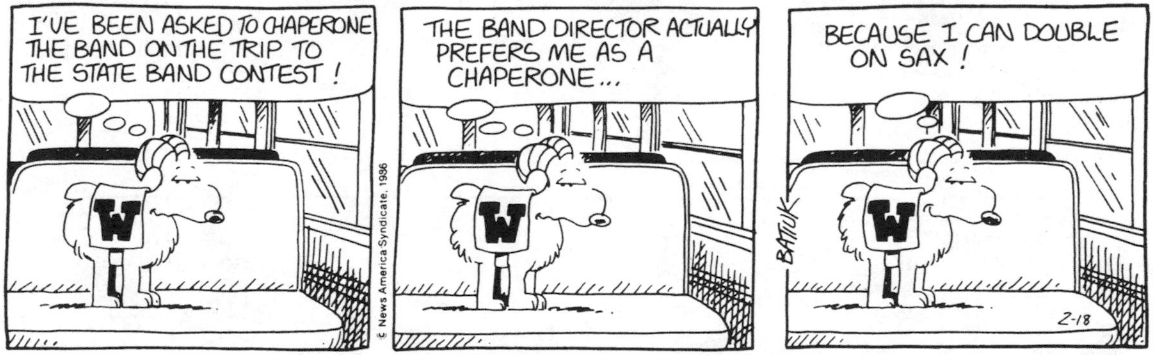
I'VE BEEN ASKED TO CHAPERONE THE BAND ON THE TRIP TO THE STATE BAND CONTEST!
THE BAND DIRECTOR ACTUALLY PREFERS ME AS A CHAPERONE...
BECAUSE I CAN DOUBLE ON SAX!
© News America Syndicate, 1986
BATIUK
2-18

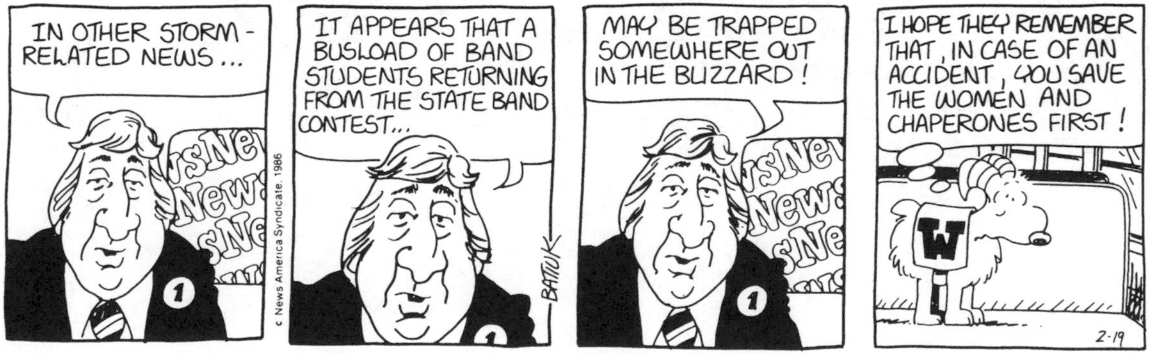
IN OTHER STORM-RELATED NEWS...
IT APPEARS THAT A BUSLOAD OF BAND STUDENTS RETURNING FROM THE STATE BAND CONTEST...
MAY BE TRAPPED SOMEWHERE OUT IN THE BLIZZARD!
I HOPE THEY REMEMBER THAT, IN CASE OF AN ACCIDENT, YOU SAVE THE WOMEN AND CHAPERONES FIRST!
© News America Syndicate, 1986
BATIUK
2-19

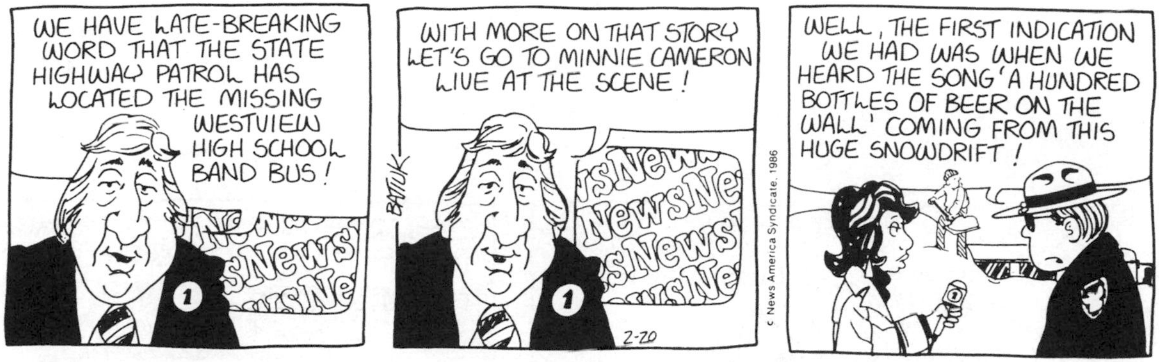
WE HAVE LATE-BREAKING WORD THAT THE STATE HIGHWAY PATROL HAS LOCATED THE MISSING WESTVIEW HIGH SCHOOL BAND BUS!
WITH MORE ON THAT STORY LET'S GO TO MINNIE CAMERON LIVE AT THE SCENE!
BATIUK
2-20
c News America Syndicate, 1986
WELL, THE FIRST INDICATION WE HAD WAS WHEN WE HEARD THE SONG 'A HUNDRED BOTTLES OF BEER ON THE WALL' COMING FROM THIS HUGE SNOWDRIFT!

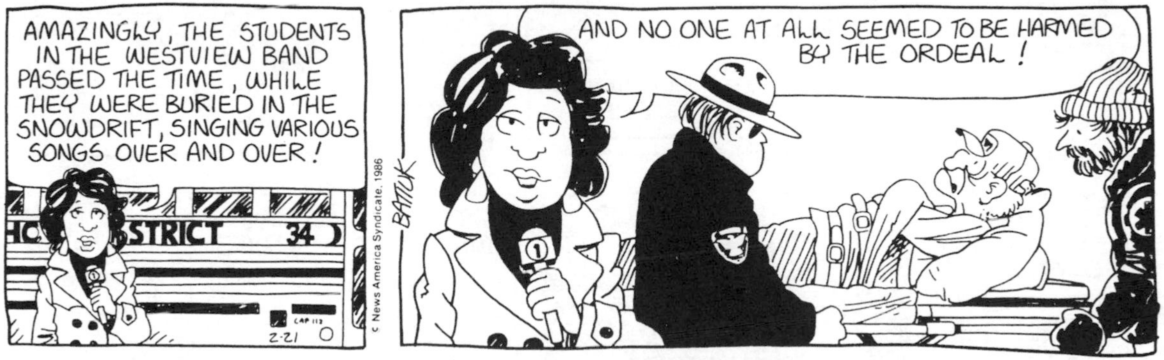
AMAZINGLY, THE STUDENTS IN THE WESTVIEW BAND PASSED THE TIME, WHILE THEY WERE BURIED IN THE SNOWDRIFT, SINGING VARIOUS SONGS OVER AND OVER!
STRICT 34
2-21
c News America Syndicate, 1986
BATIUK
AND NO ONE AT ALL SEEMED TO BE HARMED BY THE ORDEAL!

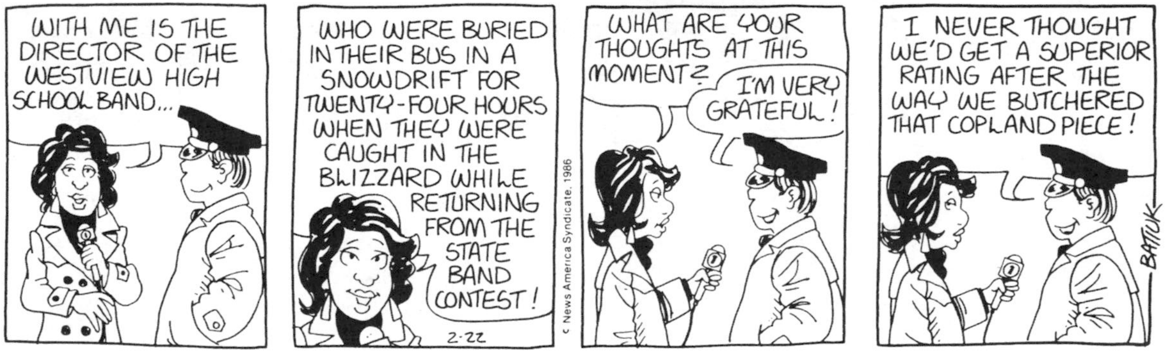
WITH ME IS THE DIRECTOR OF THE WESTVIEW HIGH SCHOOL BAND...
WHO WERE BURIED IN THEIR BUS IN A SNOWDRIFT FOR TWENTY-FOUR HOURS WHEN THEY WERE CAUGHT IN THE BLIZZARD WHILE RETURNING FROM THE STATE BAND CONTEST!
2-22
c News America Syndicate, 1986
WHAT ARE YOUR THOUGHTS AT THIS MOMENT?
I'M VERY GRATEFUL!
I NEVER THOUGHT WE'D GET A SUPERIOR RATING AFTER THE WAY WE BUTCHERED THAT COPLAND PIECE!
BATIUK

FUNKY WINKERBEAN
BY TOM BATIUK
COACH, WHAT DO YOU CALL THAT ZONE YOUR TEAM IS USUALLY IN?
THE TWILIGHT ZONE!
WELCOME TO TONIGHT'S TOURNAMENT ACTION ... AND NOW LADIES AND GENTLEMEN ...
WESTVIEW HIGH SCHOOL
FEB 23
DISTRICT
TOURNAMENT
INTRODUCING THE STARTING FIVE FOR THE WESTVIEW HIGH SCHOOL 'FIGHTING SCAPEGOATS'!
STARTING AT CENTER, 'PEE WEE' HIGGENS ...
AT GUARD, 'TIMMY THE TURTLE WALTERS...
BATIUK
2-23
© News America Syndicate, 1986
AT GUARD, 'POKEY PETE' DOMBROWSKI ...
IT'S BEEN A LONG SEASON!

DEFINE THE FOLLOWING:	(1.) MACROCOSMIC	Referring to the theory that noodles are the building blocks of the universe!

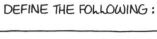

DEFINE THE FOLLOWING:	(2.) HOOD ORNAMENT	An earring worn by one of the school burnouts!

DEFINE THE FOLLOWING:	(3.) UNIVERSE	A poem with a single line in it!

2-24 2-25 2-26

BATIUK

© News America Syndicate, 1986

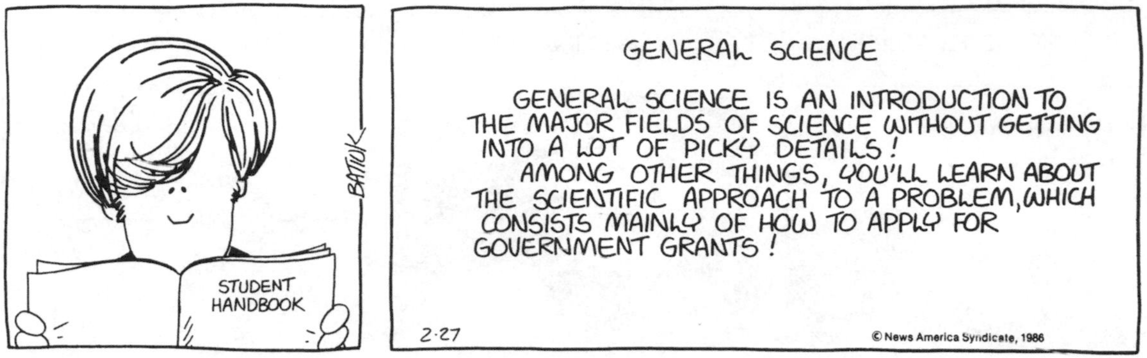
BATIUK
STUDENT HANDBOOK
GENERAL SCIENCE
GENERAL SCIENCE IS AN INTRODUCTION TO THE MAJOR FIELDS OF SCIENCE WITHOUT GETTING INTO A LOT OF PICKY DETAILS!
AMONG OTHER THINGS, YOU'LL LEARN ABOUT THE SCIENTIFIC APPROACH TO A PROBLEM, WHICH CONSISTS MAINLY OF HOW TO APPLY FOR GOVERNMENT GRANTS!
2-27
© News America Syndicate, 1986

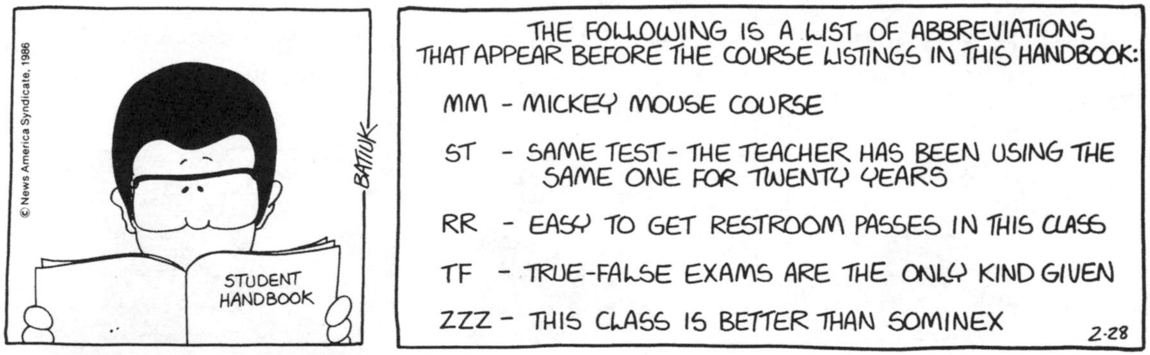
© News America Syndicate, 1986
BATIUK
STUDENT HANDBOOK
THE FOLLOWING IS A LIST OF ABBREVIATIONS THAT APPEAR BEFORE THE COURSE LISTINGS IN THIS HANDBOOK:
MM - MICKEY MOUSE COURSE
ST - SAME TEST - THE TEACHER HAS BEEN USING THE SAME ONE FOR TWENTY YEARS
RR - EASY TO GET RESTROOM PASSES IN THIS CLASS
TF - TRUE-FALSE EXAMS ARE THE ONLY KIND GIVEN
ZZZ - THIS CLASS IS BETTER THAN SOMINEX
2-28

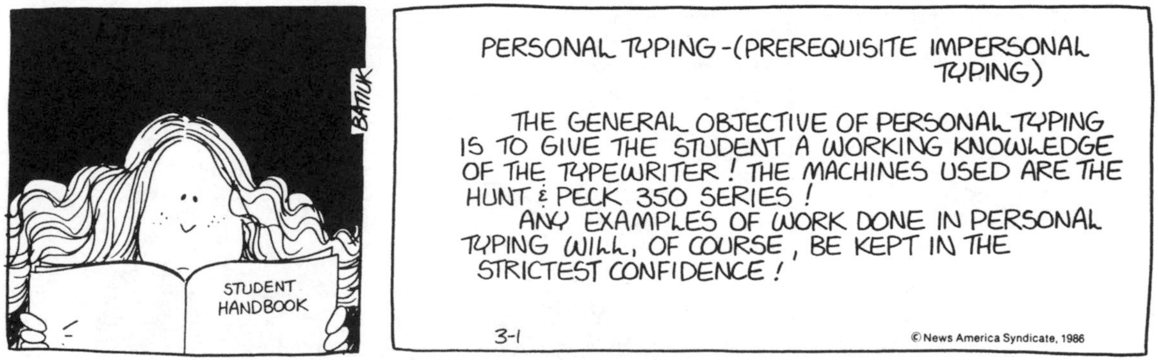
BATIUK
STUDENT HANDBOOK
PERSONAL TYPING - (PREREQUISITE IMPERSONAL TYPING)
THE GENERAL OBJECTIVE OF PERSONAL TYPING IS TO GIVE THE STUDENT A WORKING KNOWLEDGE OF THE TYPEWRITER! THE MACHINES USED ARE THE HUNT & PECK 350 SERIES!
ANY EXAMPLES OF WORK DONE IN PERSONAL TYPING WILL, OF COURSE, BE KEPT IN THE STRICTEST CONFIDENCE!
3-1
© News America Syndicate, 1986

Funky Winkerbean by Tom Batiuk

HAVE YOU GOT A SECOND, AL?

PRINCIPAL

SURE, NATE! WHAT'S THE PROBLEM?

WE'VE SIMPLY GOT TO GET SOME MONEY ALLOCATED FOR NEW SCIENCE BOOKS!

WHY? WHAT'S WRONG WITH THE ONES WE'RE USING?

LET ME QUOTE ... "AND IT'S ENTIRELY POSSIBLE THAT MEN MAY ONE DAY ACTUALLY SET FOOT ON THE MOON."

3-2

OKAY, I'LL BRING IT UP AT THE NEXT BOARD MEETING!

© News America Syndicate, 1986

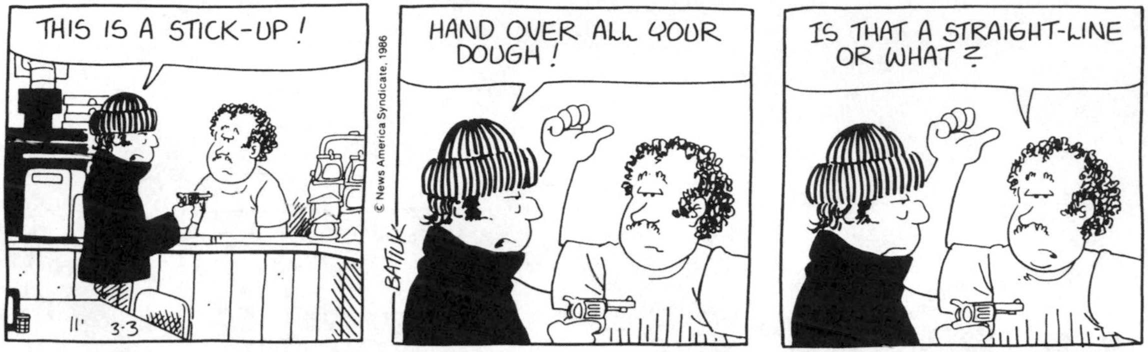
THIS IS A STICK-UP!
© News America Syndicate, 1986
HAND OVER ALL YOUR DOUGH!
IS THAT A STRAIGHT-LINE OR WHAT?

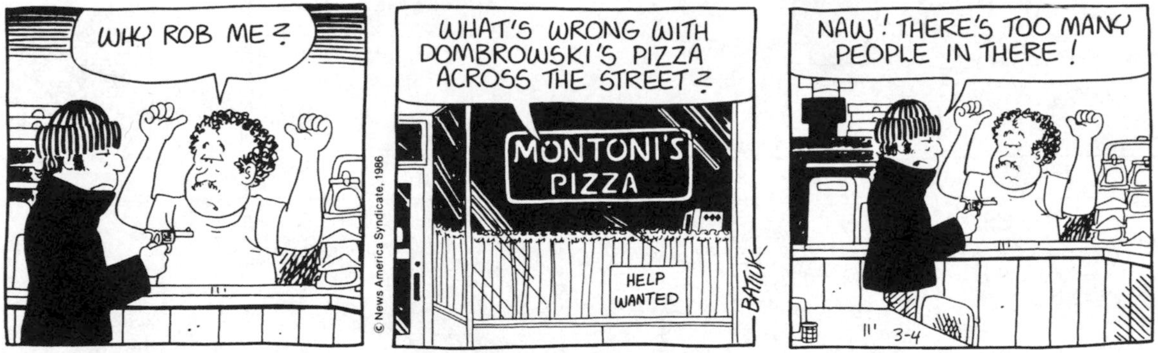
WHY ROB ME?
WHAT'S WRONG WITH DOMBROWSKI'S PIZZA ACROSS THE STREET?
MONTONI'S PIZZA
HELP WANTED
© News America Syndicate, 1986
NAW! THERE'S TOO MANY PEOPLE IN THERE!

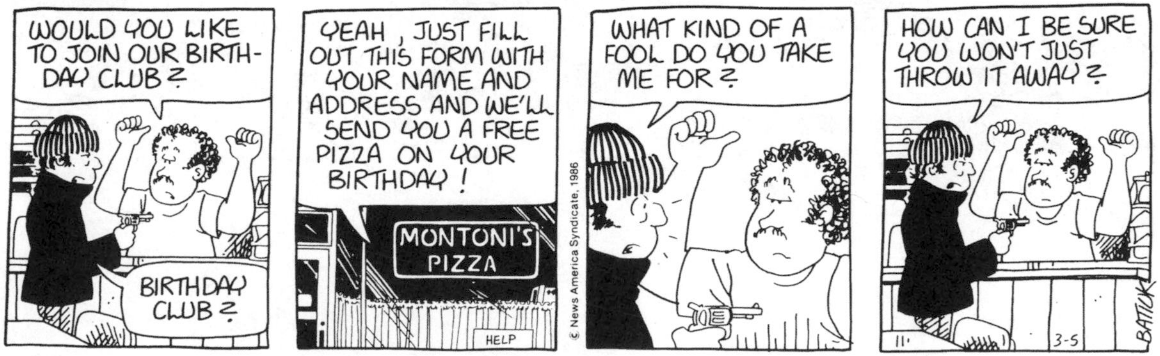
WOULD YOU LIKE TO JOIN OUR BIRTH-DAY CLUB?
BIRTHDAY CLUB?
YEAH, JUST FILL OUT THIS FORM WITH YOUR NAME AND ADDRESS AND WE'LL SEND YOU A FREE PIZZA ON YOUR BIRTHDAY!
MONTONI'S PIZZA
HELP
© News America Syndicate, 1986
WHAT KIND OF A FOOL DO YOU TAKE ME FOR?
HOW CAN I BE SURE YOU WON'T JUST THROW IT AWAY?

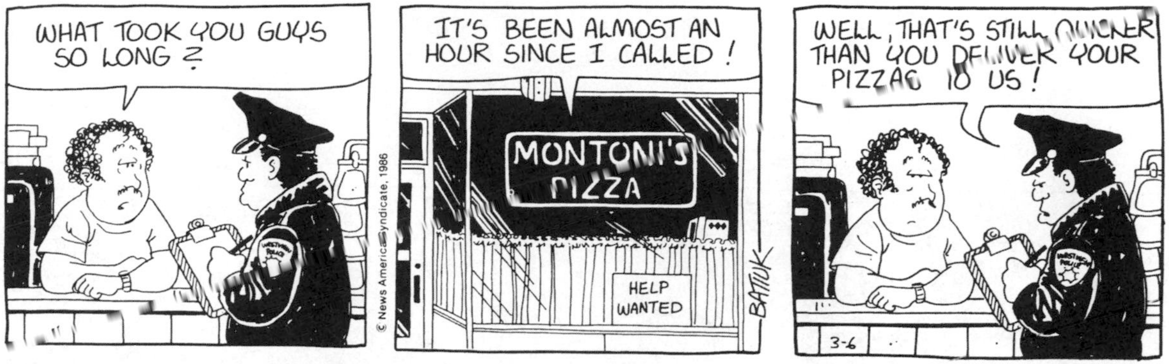
WHAT TOOK YOU GUYS SO LONG?
IT'S BEEN ALMOST AN HOUR SINCE I CALLED!
MONTONI'S PIZZA
HELP WANTED
BATIUK
© News America Syndicate, 1986
WELL, THAT'S STILL QUICKER THAN YOU DELIVER YOUR PIZZAS TO US!
3-6

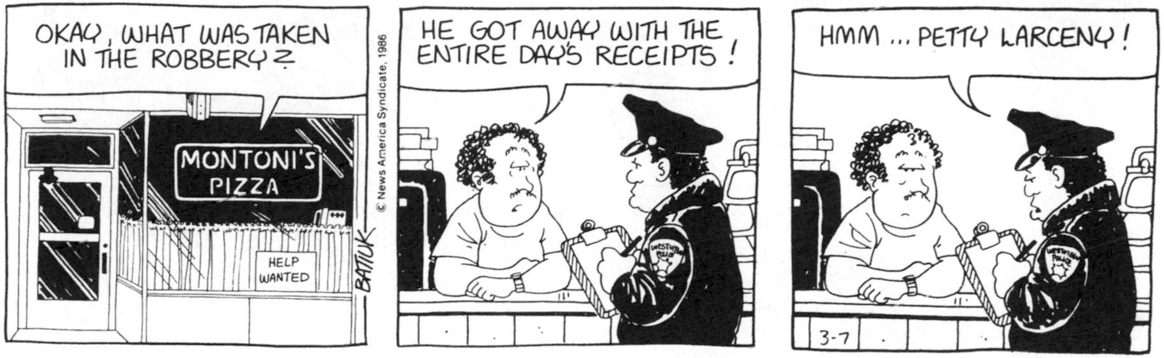
OKAY, WHAT WAS TAKEN IN THE ROBBERY?
MONTONI'S PIZZA
HELP WANTED
BATIUK
© News America Syndicate, 1986
HE GOT AWAY WITH THE ENTIRE DAY'S RECEIPTS!
HMM ... PETTY LARCENY!
3-7

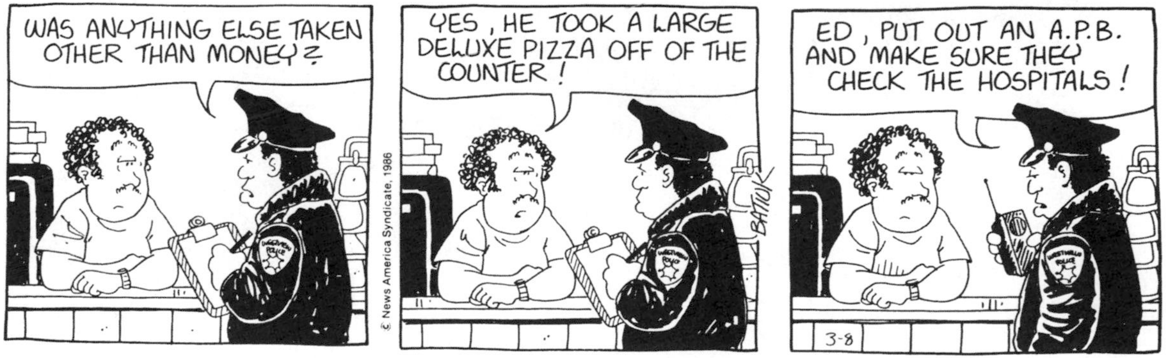
WAS ANYTHING ELSE TAKEN OTHER THAN MONEY?
© News America Syndicate, 1986
YES, HE TOOK A LARGE DELUXE PIZZA OFF OF THE COUNTER!
BATIUK
ED, PUT OUT AN A.P.B. AND MAKE SURE THEY CHECK THE HOSPITALS!
3-8

Funky Winkerbean

by Tom Batiuk

PEN...PAPER... I'M ALL SET!

I'M REALLY PROUD OF MYSELF!

I USUALLY DON'T GET STARTED ON MY CHRISTMAS THANK-YOU NOTES TILL AFTER MEMORIAL DAY!

It was really terrific seeing you over the holidays...

HMM! I'M NOT SURE HOW MANY 'R'S THERE ARE IN TERRIFIC AND I DON'T WANT TO GO LOOK IT UP...

It was really incredible seeing you over the holidays...

I WONDER...IS INCREDIBLE SPELLED I...B...L...E OR A...B...L...E?

It was really nice seeing you over...

3-9

© News America Syndicate, 1986

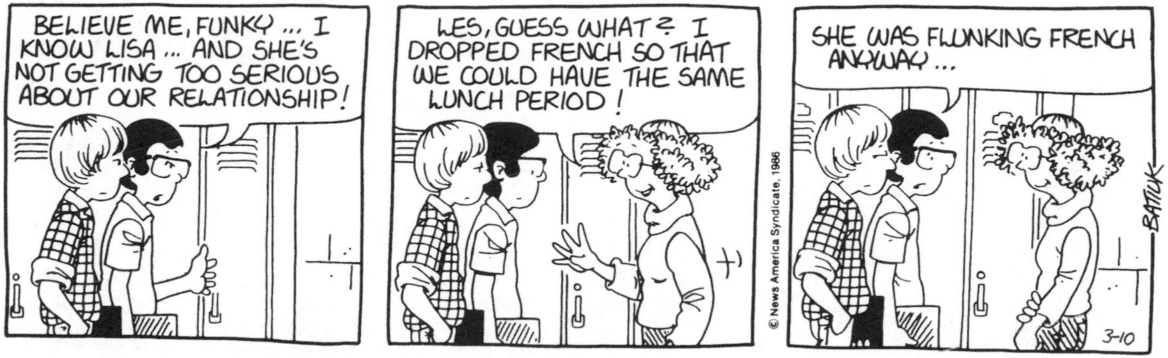
BELIEVE ME, FUNKY ... I KNOW LISA ... AND SHE'S NOT GETTING TOO SERIOUS ABOUT OUR RELATIONSHIP!
LES, GUESS WHAT? I DROPPED FRENCH SO THAT WE COULD HAVE THE SAME LUNCH PERIOD!
© News America Syndicate, 1986
SHE WAS FLUNKING FRENCH ANYWAY ...
BATIUK
3-10

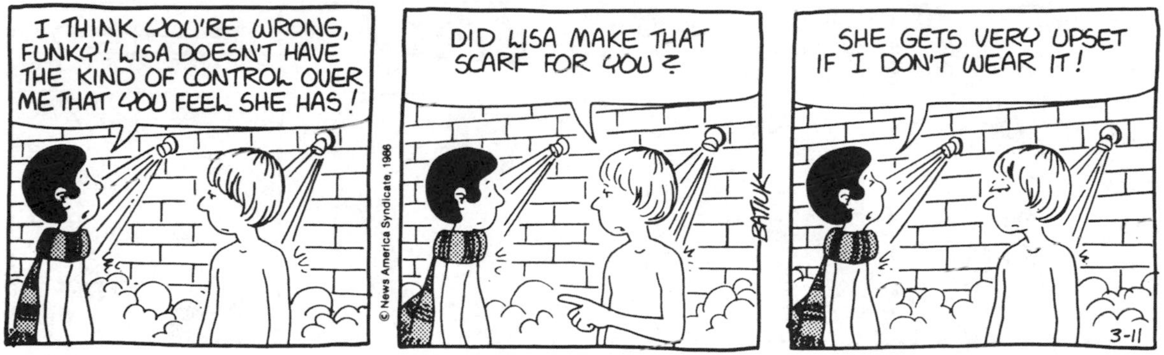
I THINK YOU'RE WRONG, FUNKY! LISA DOESN'T HAVE THE KIND OF CONTROL OVER ME THAT YOU FEEL SHE HAS!
© News America Syndicate, 1986
DID LISA MAKE THAT SCARF FOR YOU?
BATIUK
SHE GETS VERY UPSET IF I DON'T WEAR IT!
3-11

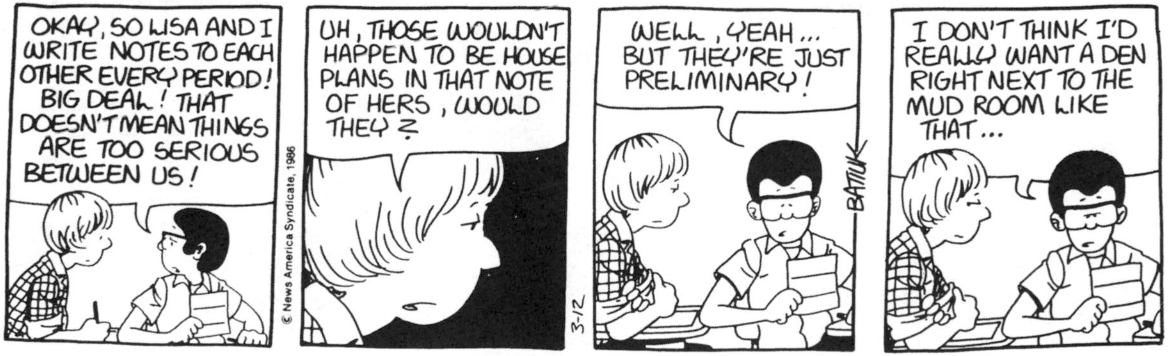
OKAY, SO LISA AND I WRITE NOTES TO EACH OTHER EVERY PERIOD! BIG DEAL! THAT DOESN'T MEAN THINGS ARE TOO SERIOUS BETWEEN US!
© News America Syndicate, 1986
UH, THOSE WOULDN'T HAPPEN TO BE HOUSE PLANS IN THAT NOTE OF HERS, WOULD THEY?
3-12
WELL, YEAH ... BUT THEY'RE JUST PRELIMINARY!
BATIUK
I DON'T THINK I'D REALLY WANT A DEN RIGHT NEXT TO THE MUD ROOM LIKE THAT ...

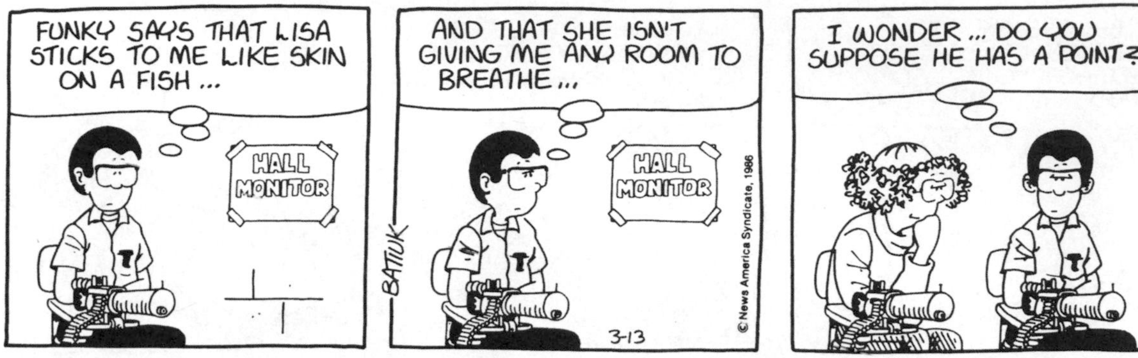
FUNKY SAYS THAT LISA STICKS TO ME LIKE SKIN ON A FISH ...
HALL MONITOR
AND THAT SHE ISN'T GIVING ME ANY ROOM TO BREATHE ...
HALL MONITOR
BATIUK
3-13
© News America Syndicate, 1986
I WONDER ... DO YOU SUPPOSE HE HAS A POINT?

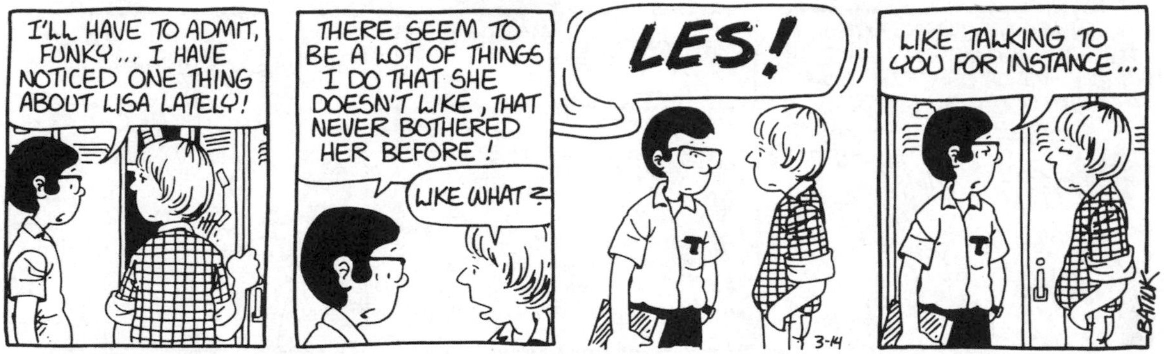
I'LL HAVE TO ADMIT, FUNKY ... I HAVE NOTICED ONE THING ABOUT LISA LATELY!
THERE SEEM TO BE A LOT OF THINGS I DO THAT SHE DOESN'T LIKE, THAT NEVER BOTHERED HER BEFORE!
LIKE WHAT?
LES!
3-14
LIKE TALKING TO YOU FOR INSTANCE ...
BATIUK

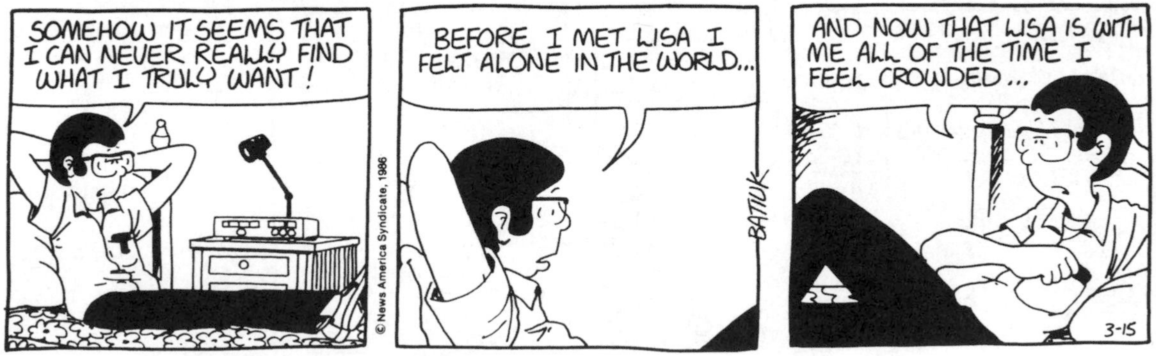
SOMEHOW IT SEEMS THAT I CAN NEVER REALLY FIND WHAT I TRULY WANT!
© News America Syndicate, 1986
BEFORE I MET LISA I FELT ALONE IN THE WORLD ...
BATIUK
AND NOW THAT LISA IS WITH ME ALL OF THE TIME I FEEL CROWDED ...
3-15

FUNKY WINKERBEAN
BY TOM BATIUK ®
WELL, HERE GOES NOTHIN'...
UH...
EXCUSE ME...
HI! MY NAME'S FUNKY WINKERBEAN!
I'VE NOTICED THAT YOU'RE NEW HERE AT SCHOOL... AND I'VE BEEN WANTING TO MEET YOU!
BATIUK
3-16
AND FINALLY ALL OF MY FRIENDS SAID THAT I SHOULD JUST GO OVER AND ASK YOU OUT!
© News America Syndicate, 1986
THOSE ARE MY FRIENDS SITTING OVER AT THAT OTHER TABLE LAUGHING!

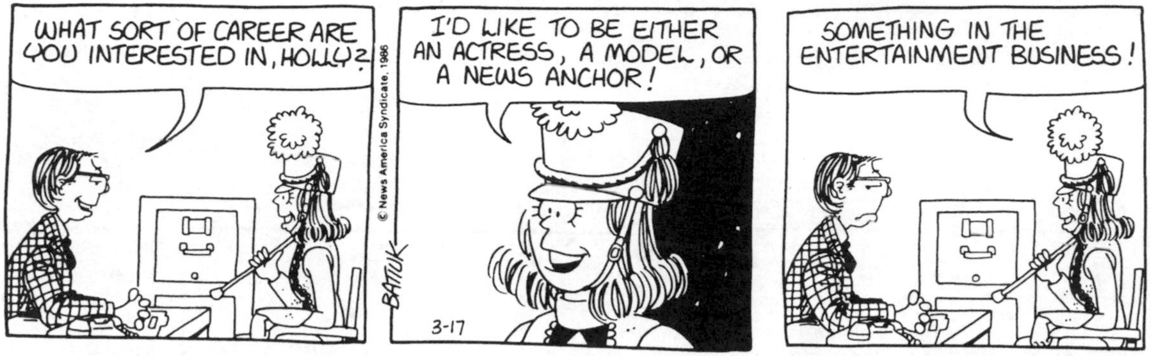
WHAT SORT OF CAREER ARE YOU INTERESTED IN, HOLLY?
© News America Syndicate, 1986
BATIUK
I'D LIKE TO BE EITHER AN ACTRESS, A MODEL, OR A NEWS ANCHOR!
3-17
SOMETHING IN THE ENTERTAINMENT BUSINESS!

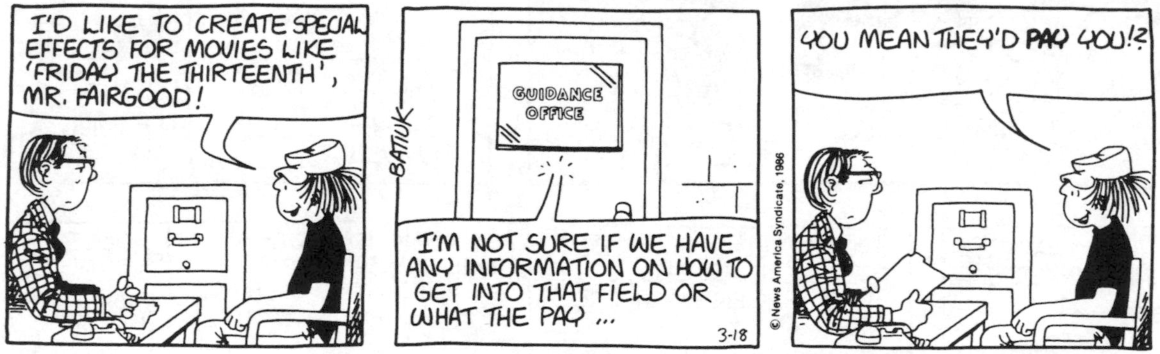
I'D LIKE TO CREATE SPECIAL EFFECTS FOR MOVIES LIKE 'FRIDAY THE THIRTEENTH', MR. FAIRGOOD!
BATIUK
GUIDANCE OFFICE
I'M NOT SURE IF WE HAVE ANY INFORMATION ON HOW TO GET INTO THAT FIELD OR WHAT THE PAY ...
3-18
© News America Syndicate, 1986
YOU MEAN THEY'D PAY YOU!?

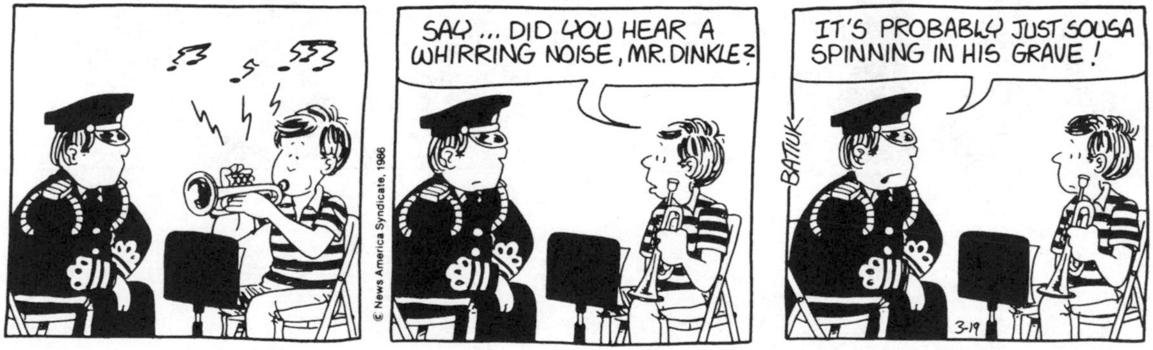
© News America Syndicate, 1986
SAY ... DID YOU HEAR A WHIRRING NOISE, MR. DINKLE?
BATIUK
IT'S PROBABLY JUST SOUSA SPINNING IN HIS GRAVE!
3-19

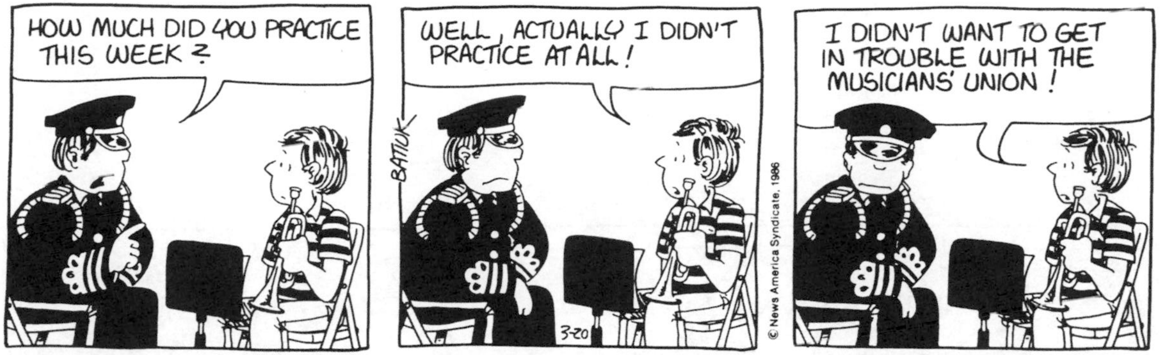
HOW MUCH DID YOU PRACTICE THIS WEEK?
WELL, ACTUALLY I DIDN'T PRACTICE AT ALL!
I DIDN'T WANT TO GET IN TROUBLE WITH THE MUSICIANS' UNION!
BATIUK
3-20
© News America Syndicate, 1986

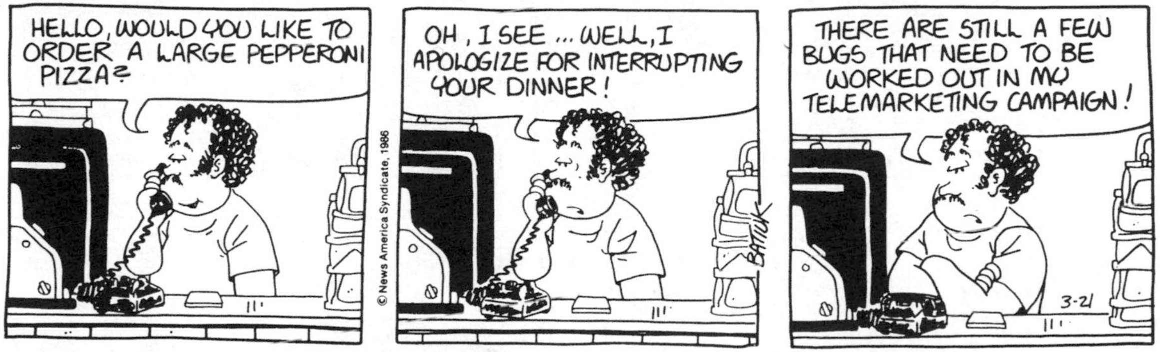
HELLO, WOULD YOU LIKE TO ORDER A LARGE PEPPERONI PIZZA?
OH, I SEE ... WELL, I APOLOGIZE FOR INTERRUPTING YOUR DINNER!
THERE ARE STILL A FEW BUGS THAT NEED TO BE WORKED OUT IN MY TELEMARKETING CAMPAIGN!
© News America Syndicate, 1986
BATIUK
3-21

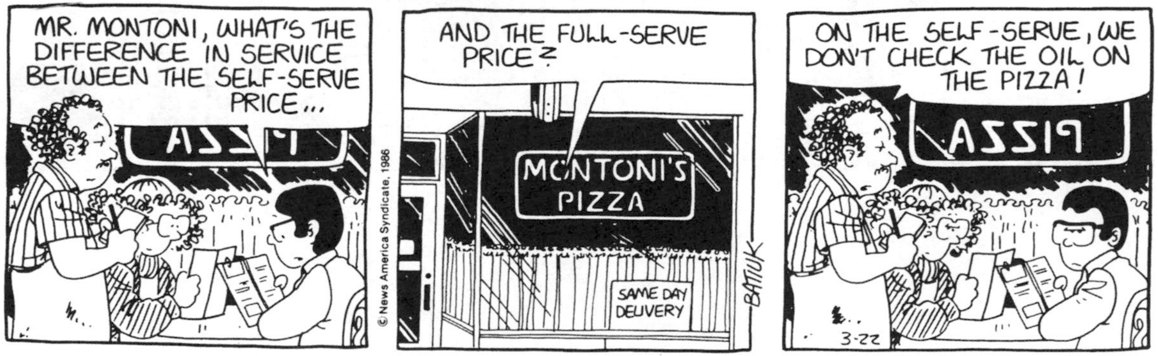
MR. MONTONI, WHAT'S THE DIFFERENCE IN SERVICE BETWEEN THE SELF-SERVE PRICE...
AND THE FULL-SERVE PRICE?
MONTONI'S PIZZA
SAME DAY DELIVERY
ON THE SELF-SERVE, WE DON'T CHECK THE OIL ON THE PIZZA!
PIZZA
© News America Syndicate, 1986
BATIUK
3-22

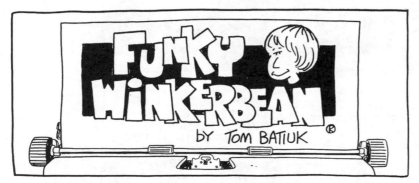

FUNKY WINKERBEAN
BY TOM BATIUK ®
HOW'S YOUR BOOK ON FAMOUS COMPOSERS COMING, HARRY?
NOT TOO BAD, FRED!
TAP! TAP!
I'D ASKED THE RENOWNED COMPOSER ANDREW CLARK TO WRITE A FOREWORD FOR MY BOOK BUT HE WAS TOO BUSY!
TIP! TAP!
HOWEVER, IT WORKED OUT FOR THE BEST BECAUSE THE FOREWORD I HAVE NOW IS EXCEPTIONAL!
TIP! TAP!
IT'S VERY WITTY, INSIGHTFUL, AND GENEROUS IN ITS COMMENTS!
TAP! TAP! TAP!
BATIUK
© News America Syndicate, 1986 3-23
THAT'S NICE... WHO WROTE IT?
I DID!
TIP! TAP!

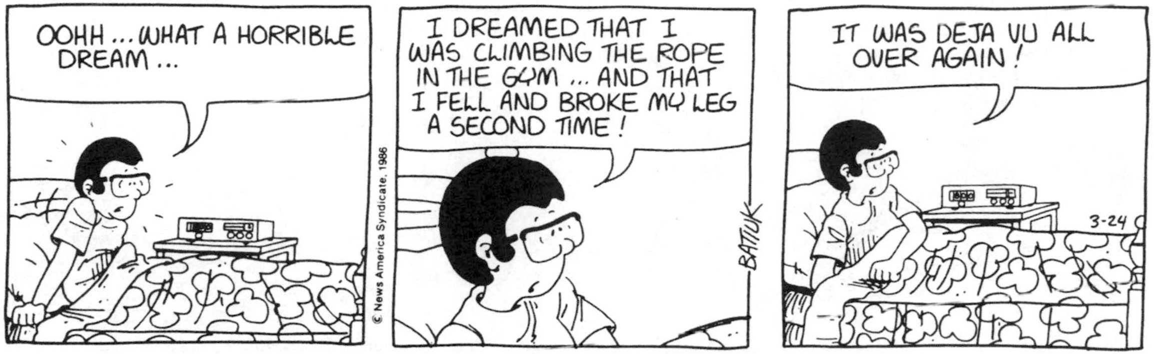
OOHH ... WHAT A HORRIBLE DREAM ...
I DREAMED THAT I WAS CLIMBING THE ROPE IN THE GYM ... AND THAT I FELL AND BROKE MY LEG A SECOND TIME !
IT WAS DEJA VU ALL OVER AGAIN !
© News America Syndicate, 1986
BATIUK
3-24

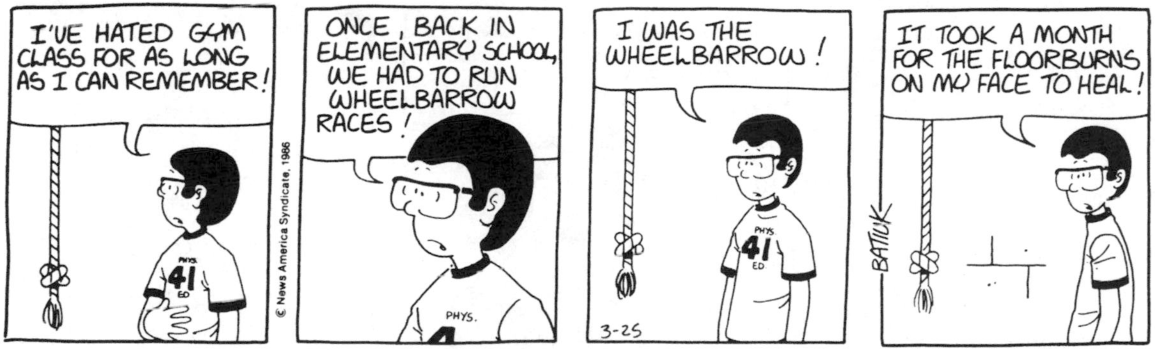
I'VE HATED GYM CLASS FOR AS LONG AS I CAN REMEMBER !
ONCE, BACK IN ELEMENTARY SCHOOL, WE HAD TO RUN WHEELBARROW RACES !
I WAS THE WHEELBARROW !
IT TOOK A MONTH FOR THE FLOORBURNS ON MY FACE TO HEAL !
© News America Syndicate, 1986
3-25
BATIUK

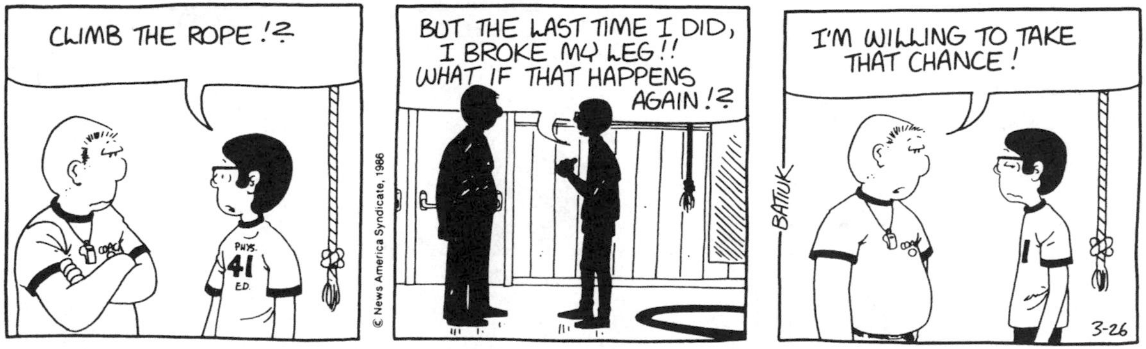
CLIMB THE ROPE !?
BUT THE LAST TIME I DID, I BROKE MY LEG !! WHAT IF THAT HAPPENS AGAIN !?
I'M WILLING TO TAKE THAT CHANCE !
© News America Syndicate, 1986
BATIUK
3-26

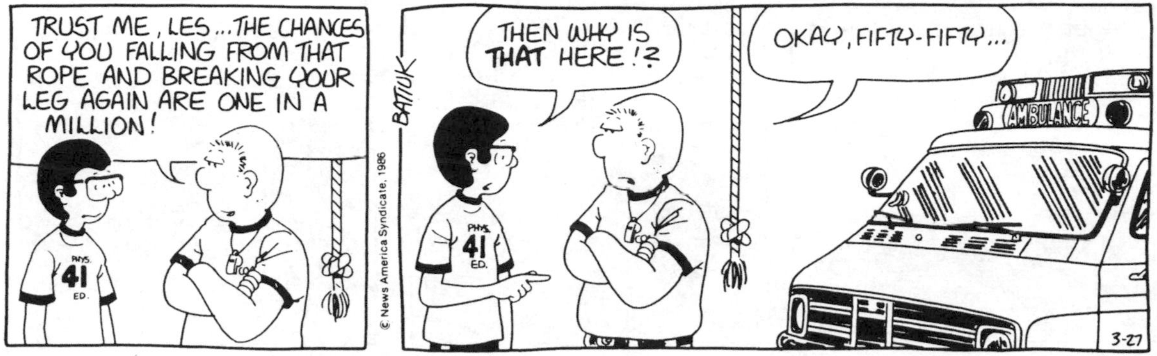
TRUST ME, LES...THE CHANCES OF YOU FALLING FROM THAT ROPE AND BREAKING YOUR LEG AGAIN ARE ONE IN A MILLION!
THEN WHY IS THAT HERE!?
OKAY, FIFTY-FIFTY...
AMBULANCE
BATIUK
© News America Syndicate, 1986
3-27

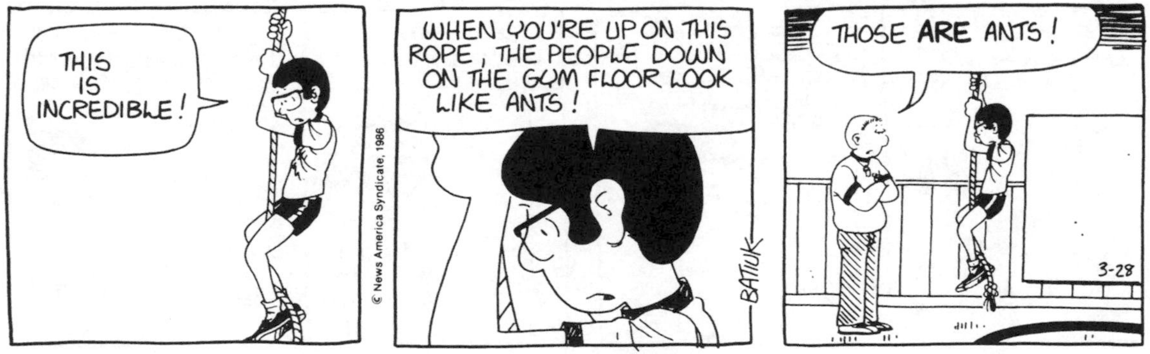
THIS IS INCREDIBLE!
WHEN YOU'RE UP ON THIS ROPE, THE PEOPLE DOWN ON THE GYM FLOOR LOOK LIKE ANTS!
THOSE ARE ANTS!
BATIUK
© News America Syndicate, 1986
3-28

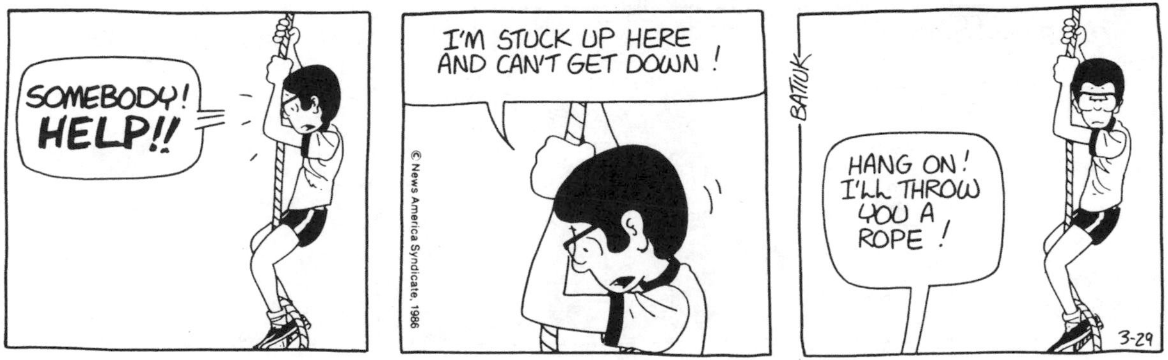
SOMEBODY! HELP!!
I'M STUCK UP HERE AND CAN'T GET DOWN!
HANG ON! I'LL THROW YOU A ROPE!
BATIUK
© News America Syndicate, 1986
3-29

FUNKY WINKERBEAN
BY TOM BATIUK
IS THIS TO GO ?
DRIVE-THRU
WHAT DO YOU SAY WE GO SEE 'ROCKY IV' AT THE MALL ?
3-30
© News America Syndicate, 1986
'ROCKY IV'!? WHY DO YOU ALWAYS GET TO PICK THE MOVIE WE SEE ?
BATIUK
WHY CAN'T WE EVER SEE SOMETHING I'D ENJOY... LIKE 'OUT OF AFRICA' ?
HAMBURGER
DRIVE THRU
WHATEVER HAPPENED TO... 'IT DOESN'T MATTER WHAT WE DO, AS LONG AS I'M WITH YOU' ?

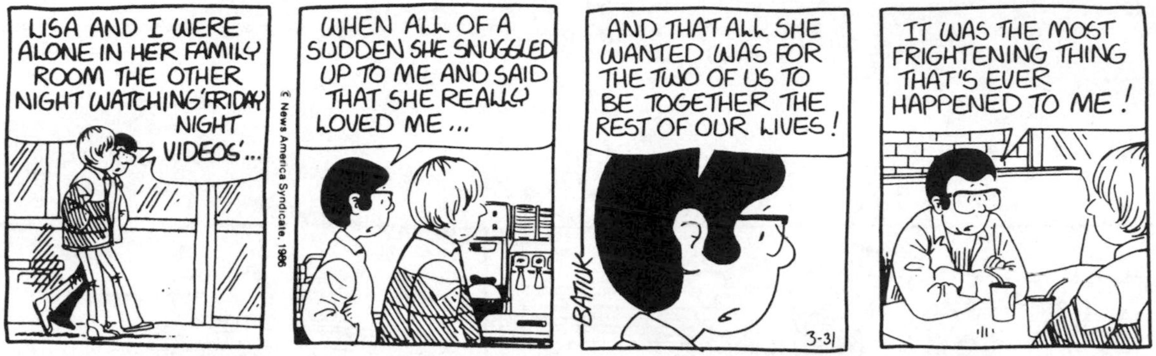
LISA AND I WERE ALONE IN HER FAMILY ROOM THE OTHER NIGHT WATCHING 'FRIDAY NIGHT VIDEOS'...
© News America Syndicate, 1986
WHEN ALL OF A SUDDEN SHE SNUGGLED UP TO ME AND SAID THAT SHE REALLY LOVED ME...
AND THAT ALL SHE WANTED WAS FOR THE TWO OF US TO BE TOGETHER THE REST OF OUR LIVES!
BATIUK
3-31
IT WAS THE MOST FRIGHTENING THING THAT'S EVER HAPPENED TO ME!

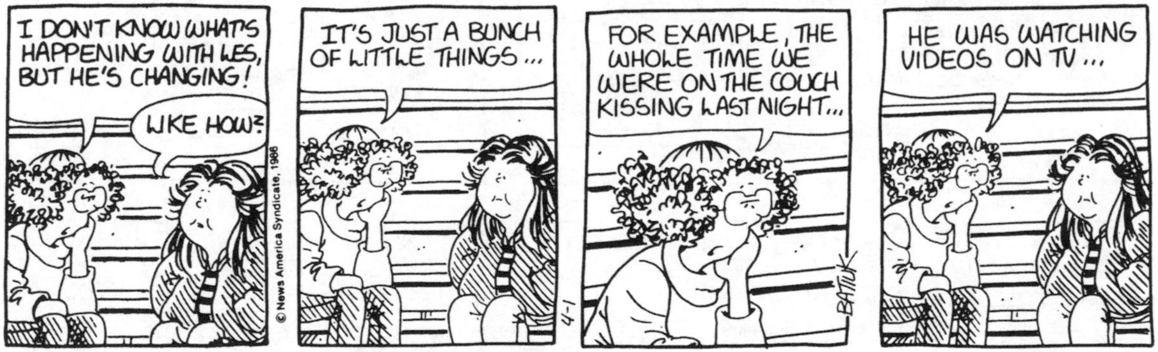
I DON'T KNOW WHAT'S HAPPENING WITH LES, BUT HE'S CHANGING!
LIKE HOW?
© News America Syndicate, 1986
IT'S JUST A BUNCH OF LITTLE THINGS...
4-1
FOR EXAMPLE, THE WHOLE TIME WE WERE ON THE COUCH KISSING LAST NIGHT...
BATIUK
HE WAS WATCHING VIDEOS ON TV...

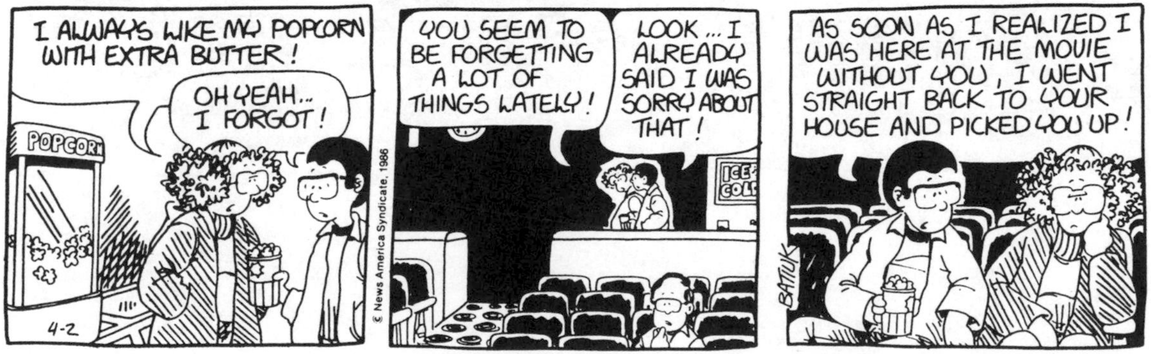
I ALWAYS LIKE MY POPCORN WITH EXTRA BUTTER!
OH YEAH... I FORGOT!
POPCORN
4-2
© News America Syndicate, 1986
YOU SEEM TO BE FORGETTING A LOT OF THINGS LATELY!
LOOK... I ALREADY SAID I WAS SORRY ABOUT THAT!
BATIUK
AS SOON AS I REALIZED I WAS HERE AT THE MOVIE WITHOUT YOU, I WENT STRAIGHT BACK TO YOUR HOUSE AND PICKED YOU UP!

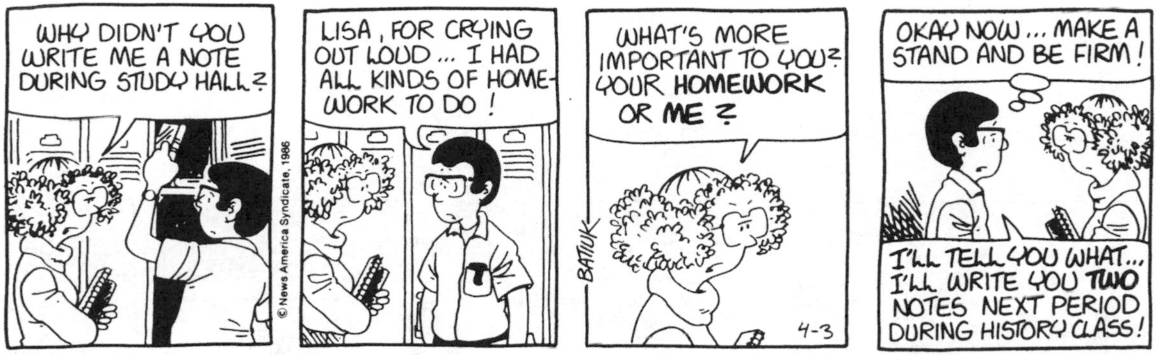
WHY DIDN'T YOU WRITE ME A NOTE DURING STUDY HALL?
LISA, FOR CRYING OUT LOUD ... I HAD ALL KINDS OF HOMEWORK TO DO!
© News America Syndicate, 1986
WHAT'S MORE IMPORTANT TO YOU? YOUR HOMEWORK OR ME?
BATIUK
4-3
OKAY NOW ... MAKE A STAND AND BE FIRM!
I'LL TELL YOU WHAT... I'LL WRITE YOU TWO NOTES NEXT PERIOD DURING HISTORY CLASS!

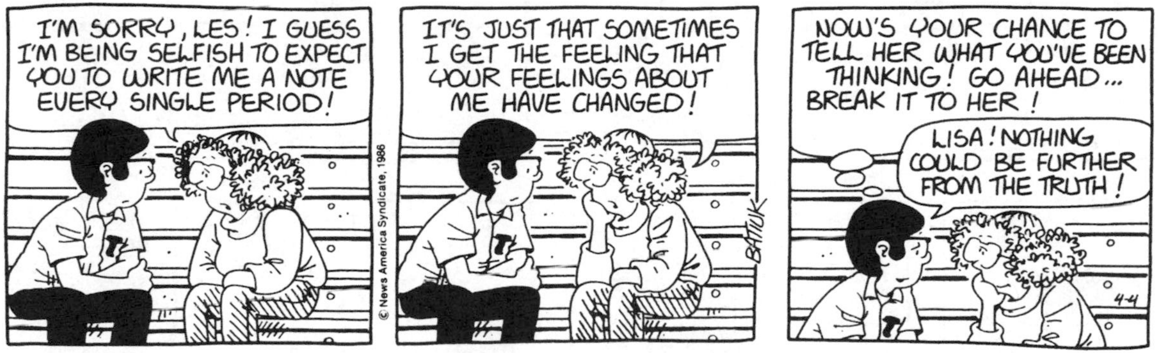
I'M SORRY, LES! I GUESS I'M BEING SELFISH TO EXPECT YOU TO WRITE ME A NOTE EVERY SINGLE PERIOD!
© News America Syndicate, 1986
IT'S JUST THAT SOMETIMES I GET THE FEELING THAT YOUR FEELINGS ABOUT ME HAVE CHANGED!
BATIUK
NOW'S YOUR CHANCE TO TELL HER WHAT YOU'VE BEEN THINKING! GO AHEAD... BREAK IT TO HER!
LISA! NOTHING COULD BE FURTHER FROM THE TRUTH!
4-4

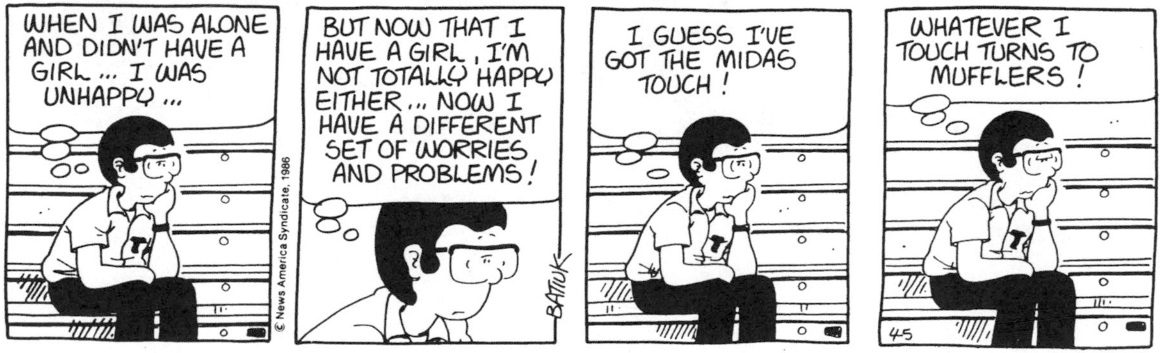
WHEN I WAS ALONE AND DIDN'T HAVE A GIRL ... I WAS UNHAPPY ...
© News America Syndicate, 1986
BUT NOW THAT I HAVE A GIRL, I'M NOT TOTALLY HAPPY EITHER ... NOW I HAVE A DIFFERENT SET OF WORRIES AND PROBLEMS!
BATIUK
I GUESS I'VE GOT THE MIDAS TOUCH!
WHATEVER I TOUCH TURNS TO MUFFLERS!
4-5

FUNKY WINKERBEAN
BY TOM BATIUK
I WONDER WHAT'S FOR LUNCH ?
IT SMELLS LIKE THEY'RE HAVING HOT DOGS AND SAUERKRAUT FOR LUNCH!
NO... IT SMELLS MORE LIKE SAUERKRAUT AND HOT DOGS!
SNIFF! YOU'RE RIGHT!
I DON'T THINK IT'S FAIR!
4-6
HOW COME THE JOCKS ARE ABLE TO GET EXTRA HELPINGS AT THE LUNCH-TIME TRAINING TABLE ?
© News America Syndicate, 1986
BECAUSE THEY'RE ATHLETES!
BATIUK
THEIR BODIES ARE BETTER ABLE TO TOLERATE IT!

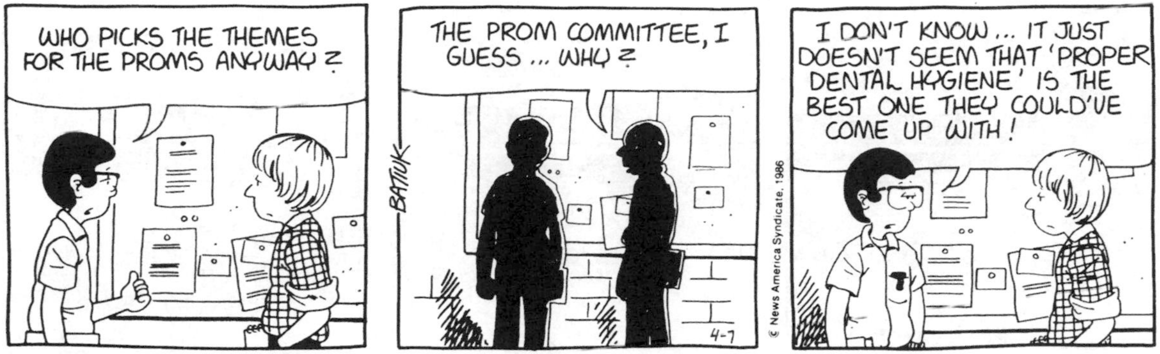
WHO PICKS THE THEMES FOR THE PROMS ANYWAY?
THE PROM COMMITTEE, I GUESS ... WHY?
I DON'T KNOW ... IT JUST DOESN'T SEEM THAT 'PROPER DENTAL HYGIENE' IS THE BEST ONE THEY COULD'VE COME UP WITH!
BATIUK
4-7
© News America Syndicate, 1986

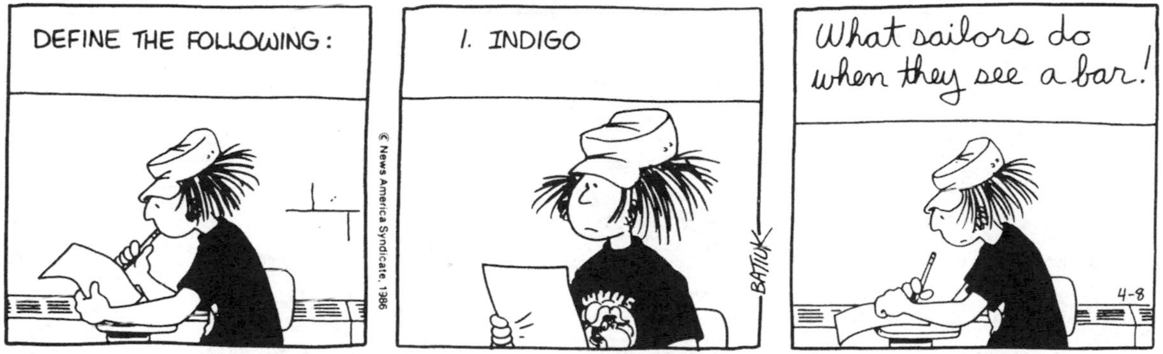
DEFINE THE FOLLOWING:
1. INDIGO
What sailors do when they see a bar!
BATIUK
4-8
© News America Syndicate, 1986

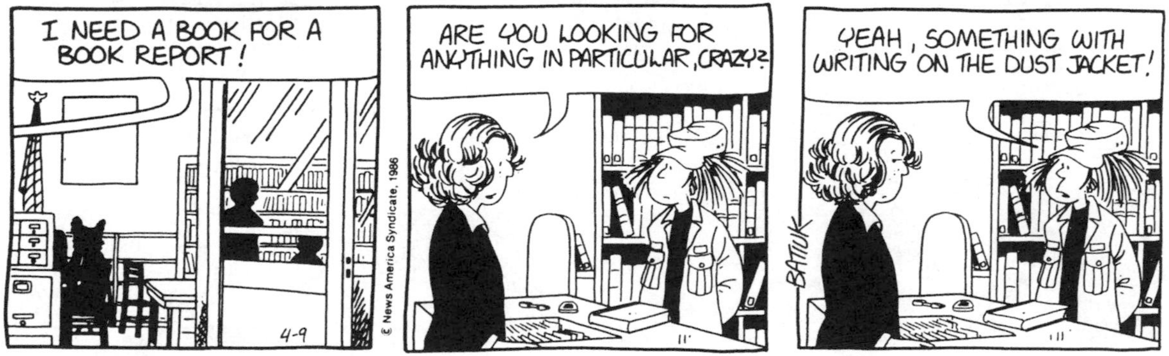
I NEED A BOOK FOR A BOOK REPORT!
ARE YOU LOOKING FOR ANYTHING IN PARTICULAR, CRAZY?
YEAH, SOMETHING WITH WRITING ON THE DUST JACKET!
BATIUK
4-9
© News America Syndicate, 1986

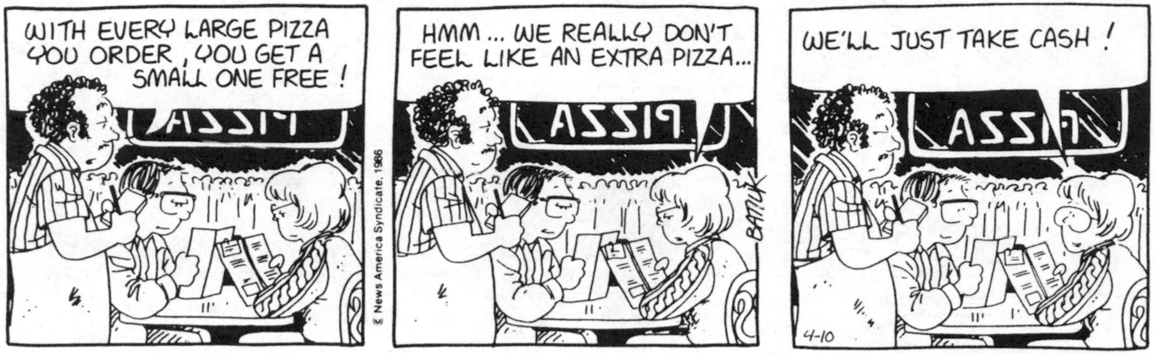
WITH EVERY LARGE PIZZA YOU ORDER, YOU GET A SMALL ONE FREE!
PIZZA
© News America Syndicate, 1986
HMM ... WE REALLY DON'T FEEL LIKE AN EXTRA PIZZA...
PIZZA
BATIUK
WE'LL JUST TAKE CASH!
PIZZA
4-10

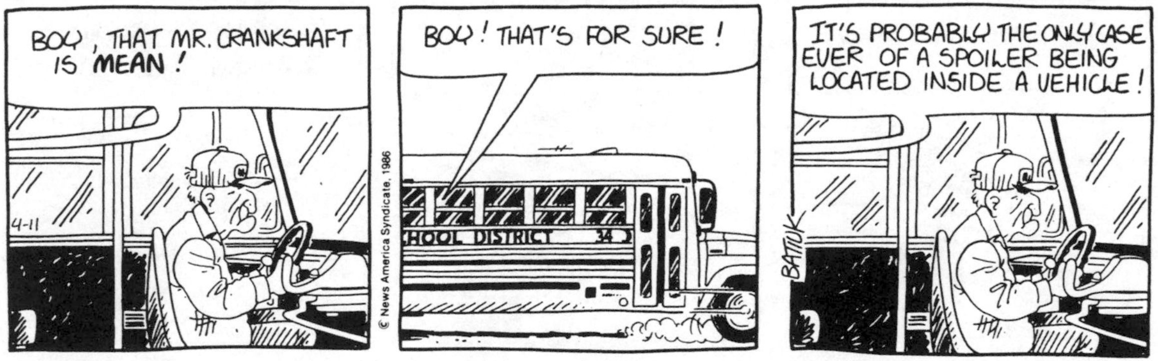
BOY, THAT MR. CRANKSHAFT IS **MEAN**!
4-11
© News America Syndicate, 1986
BOY! THAT'S FOR SURE!
CHOOL DISTRICT 34
IT'S PROBABLY THE ONLY CASE EVER OF A SPOILER BEING LOCATED INSIDE A VEHICLE!
BATIUK

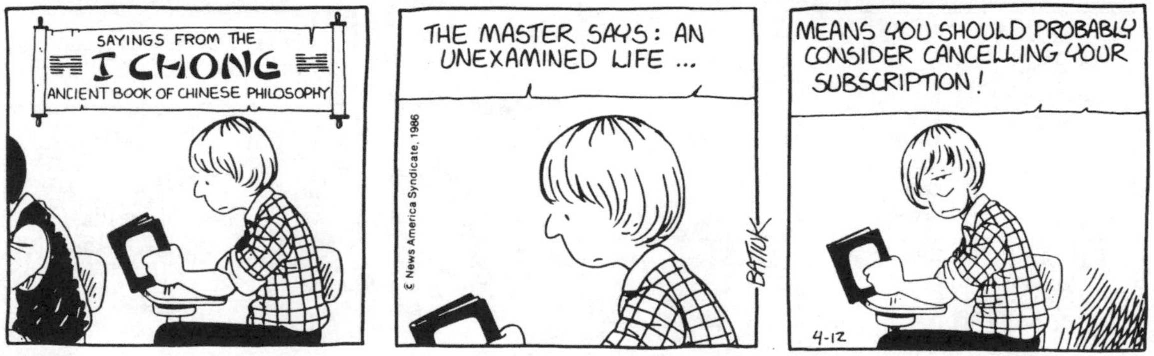
SAYINGS FROM THE
I CHONG
ANCIENT BOOK OF CHINESE PHILOSOPHY
THE MASTER SAYS: AN UNEXAMINED LIFE ...
© News America Syndicate, 1986
BATIUK
MEANS YOU SHOULD PROBABLY CONSIDER CANCELLING YOUR SUBSCRIPTION!
4-12

FUNKY WINKERBEAN
BY TOM BATIUK
THERE GOES THE ONLY PERSON IN THE WORLD WHO SEES MORE MOVIES IN A YEAR THAN SISKEL AND EBERT!
OH NO! NOT AGAIN!!
CLICK!
DO WE HAVE TO SEE ANOTHER MOVIE?
CAN'T WE TAKE A TEST OR SOMETHING?
YEAH, HOW ABOUT A POP QUIZ?
OR A TERM PAPER...
COACH
4-13 © News America Syndicate, 1986
BATIUK

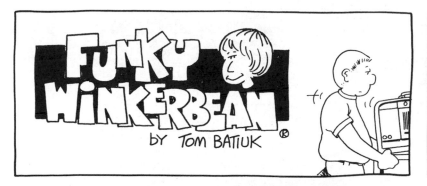

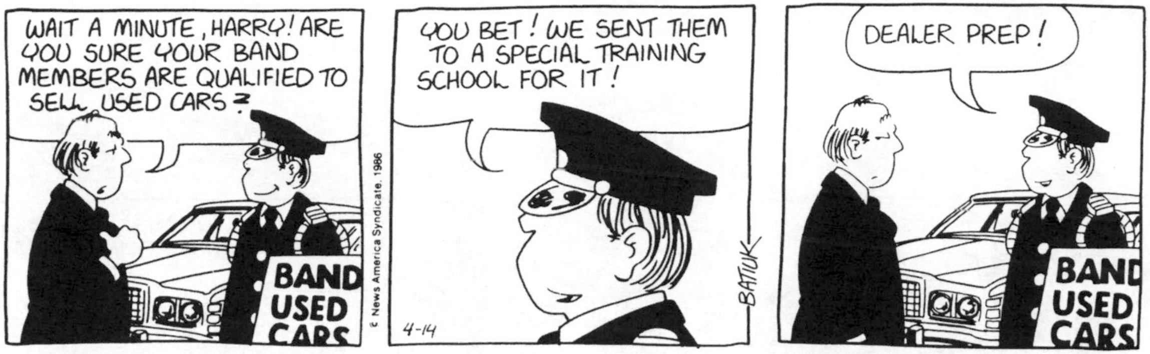
WAIT A MINUTE, HARRY! ARE YOU SURE YOUR BAND MEMBERS ARE QUALIFIED TO SELL USED CARS?
BAND USED CARS
© News America Syndicate, 1986
YOU BET! WE SENT THEM TO A SPECIAL TRAINING SCHOOL FOR IT!
4-14
BATIUK
DEALER PREP!
BAND USED CARS

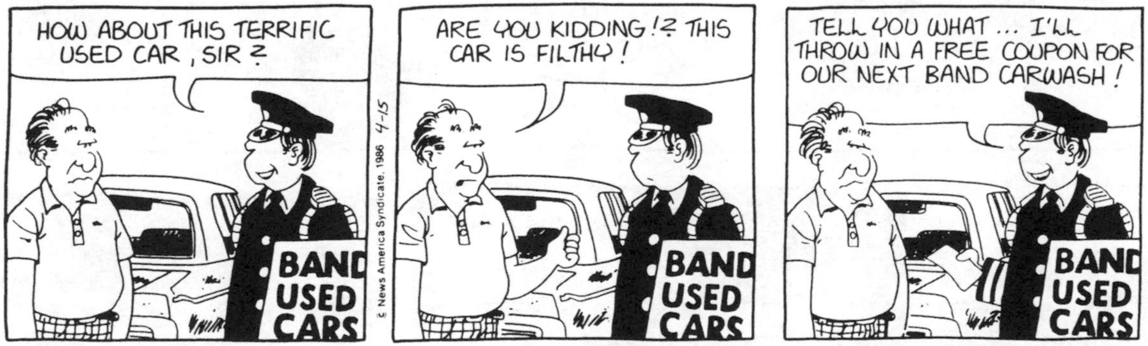
HOW ABOUT THIS TERRIFIC USED CAR, SIR?
BAND USED CARS
© News America Syndicate, 1986
4-15
ARE YOU KIDDING!? THIS CAR IS FILTHY!
BAND USED CARS
TELL YOU WHAT ... I'LL THROW IN A FREE COUPON FOR OUR NEXT BAND CARWASH!
BAND USED CARS

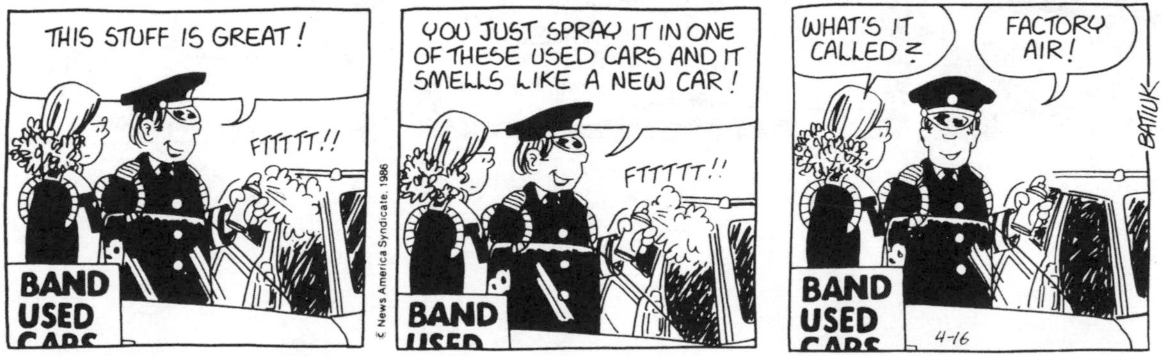
THIS STUFF IS GREAT!
FTTTTT!!
BAND USED
© News America Syndicate, 1986
YOU JUST SPRAY IT IN ONE OF THESE USED CARS AND IT SMELLS LIKE A NEW CAR!
FTTTTT!!
BAND
WHAT'S IT CALLED?
FACTORY AIR!
BATIUK
BAND USED
4-16

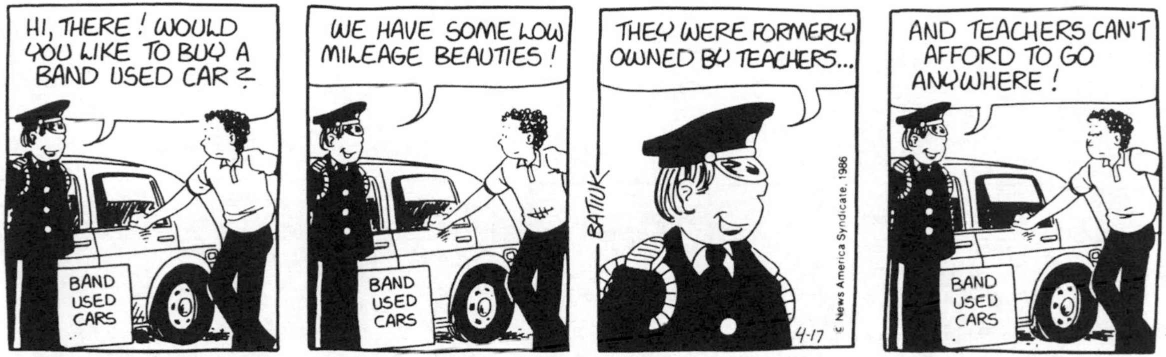
HI, THERE! WOULD YOU LIKE TO BUY A BAND USED CAR?
BAND USED CARS
WE HAVE SOME LOW MILEAGE BEAUTIES!
BAND USED CARS
THEY WERE FORMERLY OWNED BY TEACHERS...
BATIUK
4-17
© News America Syndicate, 1986
AND TEACHERS CAN'T AFFORD TO GO ANYWHERE!
BAND USED CARS

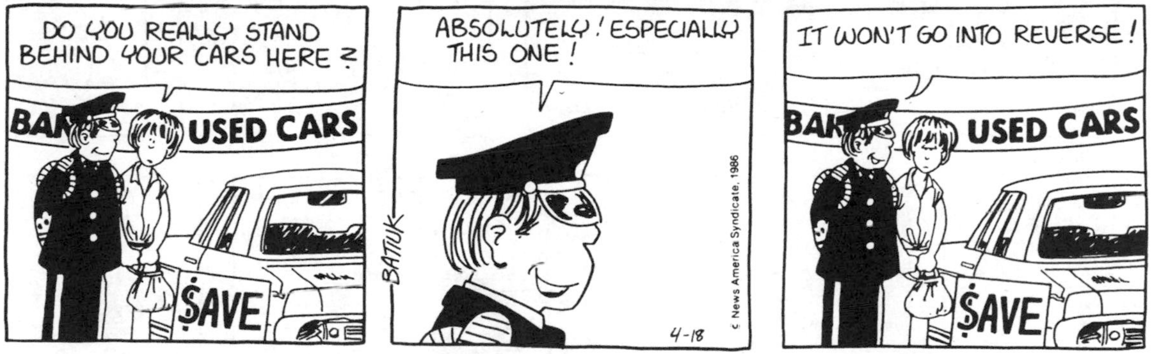
DO YOU REALLY STAND BEHIND YOUR CARS HERE?
USED CARS
$AVE
ABSOLUTELY! ESPECIALLY THIS ONE!
BATIUK
4-18
© News America Syndicate, 1986
IT WON'T GO INTO REVERSE!
USED CARS
$AVE

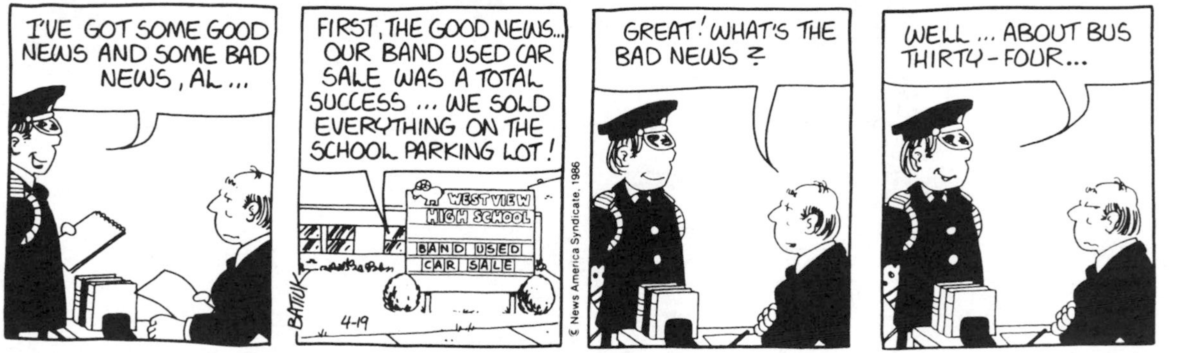
I'VE GOT SOME GOOD NEWS AND SOME BAD NEWS, AL...
FIRST, THE GOOD NEWS... OUR BAND USED CAR SALE WAS A TOTAL SUCCESS ... WE SOLD EVERYTHING ON THE SCHOOL PARKING LOT!
WESTVIEW HIGH SCHOOL
BAND USED CAR SALE
BATIUK
4-19
© News America Syndicate, 1986
GREAT! WHAT'S THE BAD NEWS?
WELL ... ABOUT BUS THIRTY-FOUR...

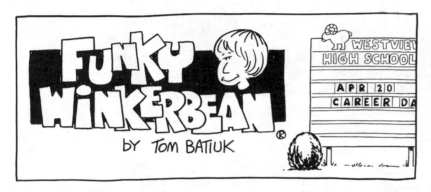

Funky Winkerbean

BY TOM BATIUK

WESTVIEW HIGH SCHOOL

APR 20
CAREER DAY

FRED, I THINK THIS 'CAREER DAY' IDEA OF YOURS IS REALLY GREAT!

I'VE GOTTEN SEVERAL GOOD LEADS SO FAR!

AND ONE FINAL THING I'D LIKE TO ADD HERE ON 'CAREER DAY' IS...

SESSION #3
MR. MONTONI
MONTONI'S
PIZZA

THAT OWNING AND OPERATING YOUR OWN BUSINESS...

© News America Syndicate, 1986

IS A GREAT WAY TO MAKE A SMALL FORTUNE...

BATIUK

OUT OF A MUCH LARGER ONE!

4-20

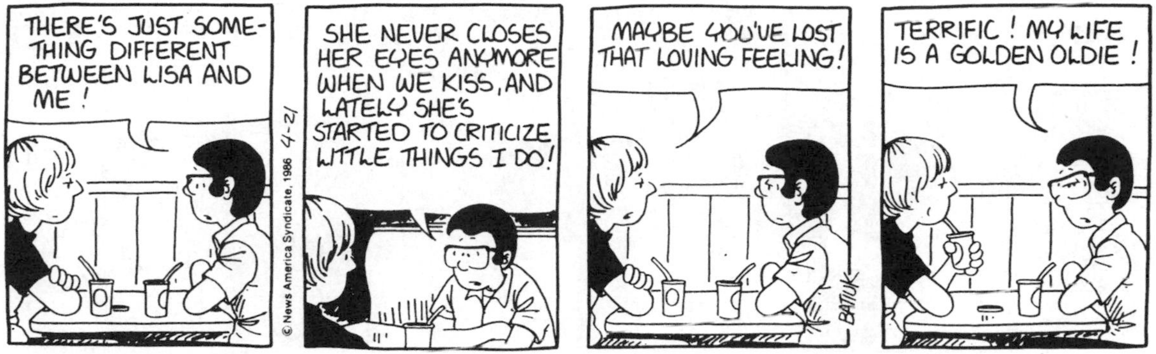
THERE'S JUST SOMETHING DIFFERENT BETWEEN LISA AND ME!
SHE NEVER CLOSES HER EYES ANYMORE WHEN WE KISS, AND LATELY SHE'S STARTED TO CRITICIZE LITTLE THINGS I DO!
MAYBE YOU'VE LOST THAT LOVING FEELING!
TERRIFIC! MY LIFE IS A GOLDEN OLDIE!
4-21
© News America Syndicate, 1986
BATIUK

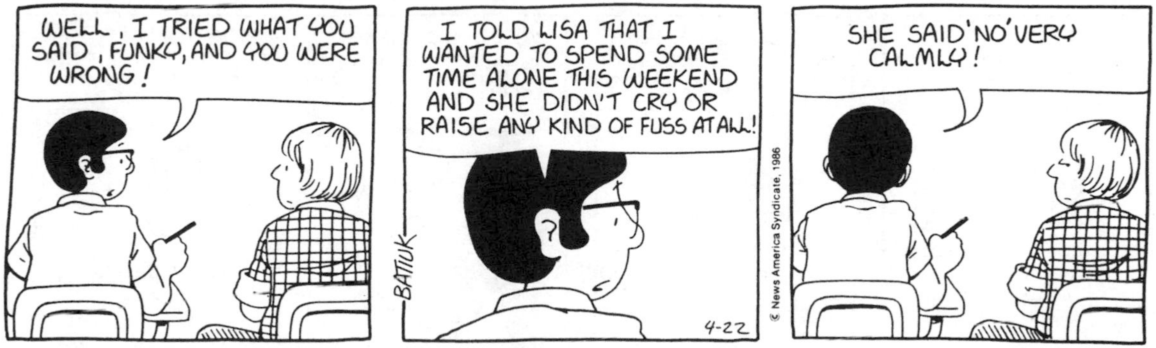
WELL, I TRIED WHAT YOU SAID, FUNKY, AND YOU WERE WRONG!
I TOLD LISA THAT I WANTED TO SPEND SOME TIME ALONE THIS WEEKEND AND SHE DIDN'T CRY OR RAISE ANY KIND OF FUSS AT ALL!
SHE SAID 'NO' VERY CALMLY!
BATIUK
4-22
© News America Syndicate, 1986

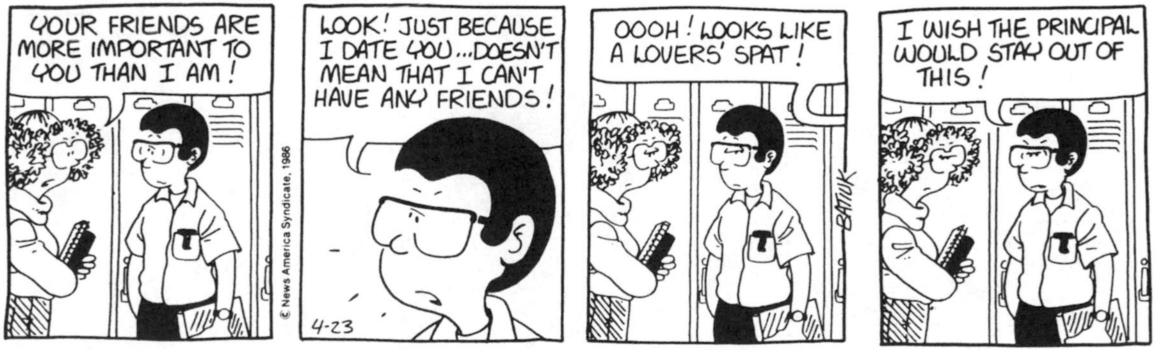
YOUR FRIENDS ARE MORE IMPORTANT TO YOU THAN I AM!
LOOK! JUST BECAUSE I DATE YOU... DOESN'T MEAN THAT I CAN'T HAVE ANY FRIENDS!
OOOH! LOOKS LIKE A LOVERS' SPAT!
I WISH THE PRINCIPAL WOULD STAY OUT OF THIS!
© News America Syndicate, 1986
4-23
BATIUK

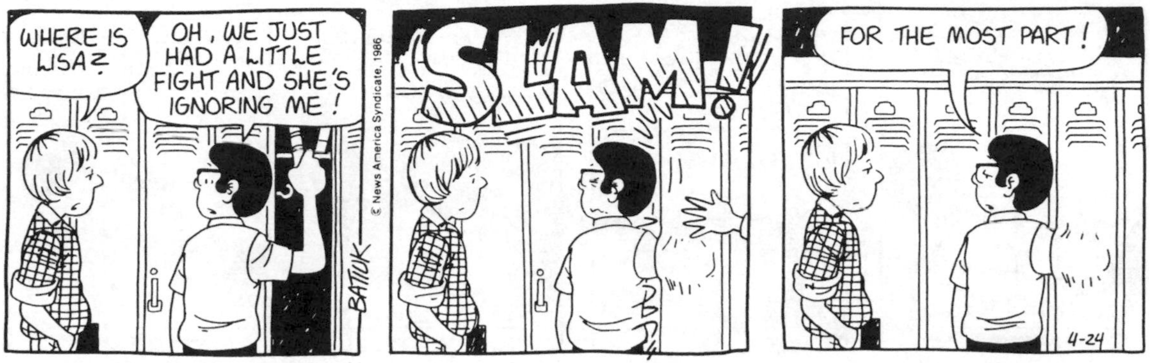
WHERE IS LISA?
OH, WE JUST HAD A LITTLE FIGHT AND SHE'S IGNORING ME!
BATIUK
© News America Syndicate, 1986
SLAM!
FOR THE MOST PART!
4-24

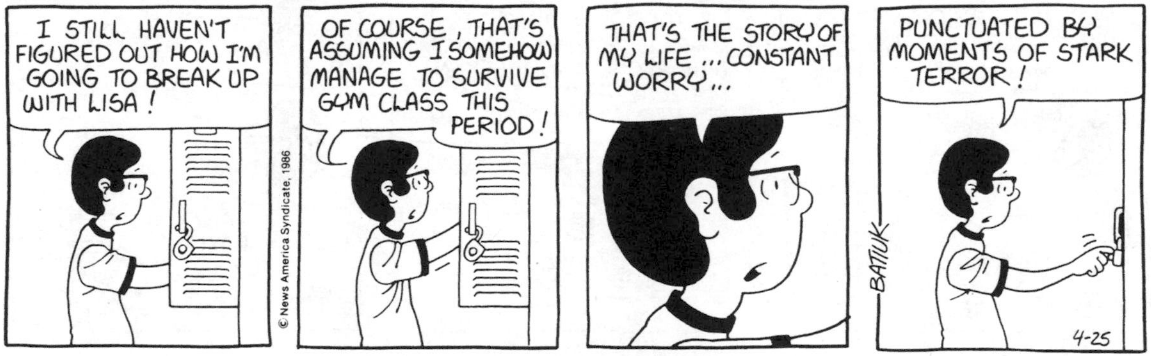
I STILL HAVEN'T FIGURED OUT HOW I'M GOING TO BREAK UP WITH LISA!
© News America Syndicate, 1986
OF COURSE, THAT'S ASSUMING I SOMEHOW MANAGE TO SURVIVE GYM CLASS THIS PERIOD!
THAT'S THE STORY OF MY LIFE... CONSTANT WORRY...
PUNCTUATED BY MOMENTS OF STARK TERROR!
BATIUK
4-25

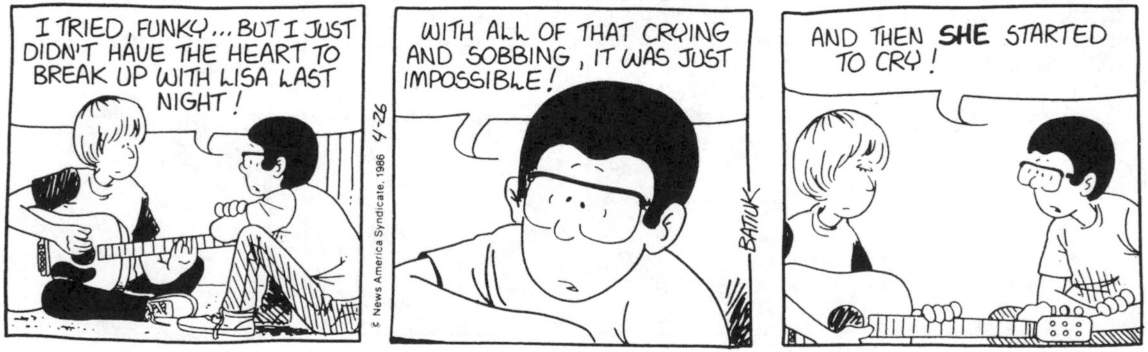
I TRIED, FUNKY... BUT I JUST DIDN'T HAVE THE HEART TO BREAK UP WITH LISA LAST NIGHT!
4-26
© News America Syndicate, 1986
WITH ALL OF THAT CRYING AND SOBBING, IT WAS JUST IMPOSSIBLE!
BATIUK
AND THEN **SHE** STARTED TO CRY!

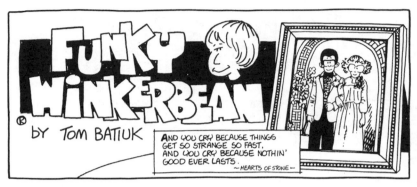

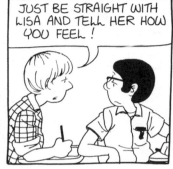

FUNKY WINKERBEAN
® BY TOM BATIUK
AND YOU CRY BECAUSE THINGS GET SO STRANGE SO FAST, AND YOU CRY BECAUSE NOTHIN' GOOD EVER LASTS. ~HEARTS OF STONE~
JUST BE STRAIGHT WITH LISA AND TELL HER HOW YOU FEEL!
BELIEVE ME, LES... HONESTY IS THE BEST GIMMICK!
MAYBE IT WOULD BE EASIER TO BREAK UP WITH LISA BY WRITING HER A NOTE!
Dear Lisa, Chemistry class is as boring as usual.
Crazy Harry keeps trying to break every-body up by making funny noises.
Speaking of breaking up...
BATIUK
© News America Syndicate, 1986
4-27

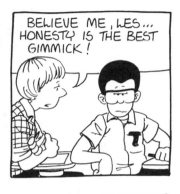

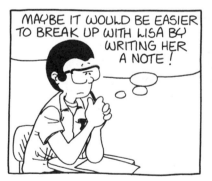

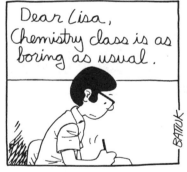

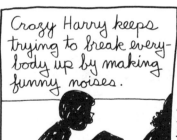

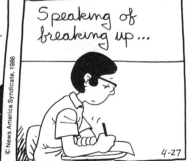

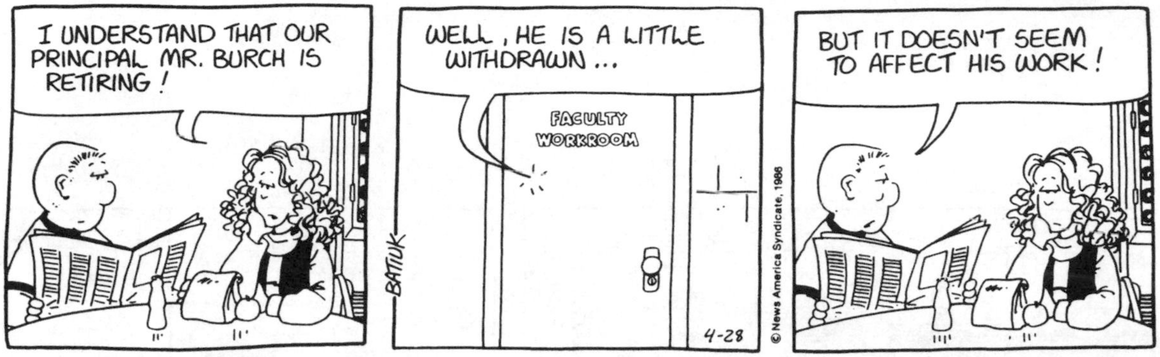
I UNDERSTAND THAT OUR PRINCIPAL MR. BURCH IS RETIRING!
WELL, HE IS A LITTLE WITHDRAWN...
FACULTY WORKROOM
BUT IT DOESN'T SEEM TO AFFECT HIS WORK!
BATIUK
4-28
© News America Syndicate, 1986

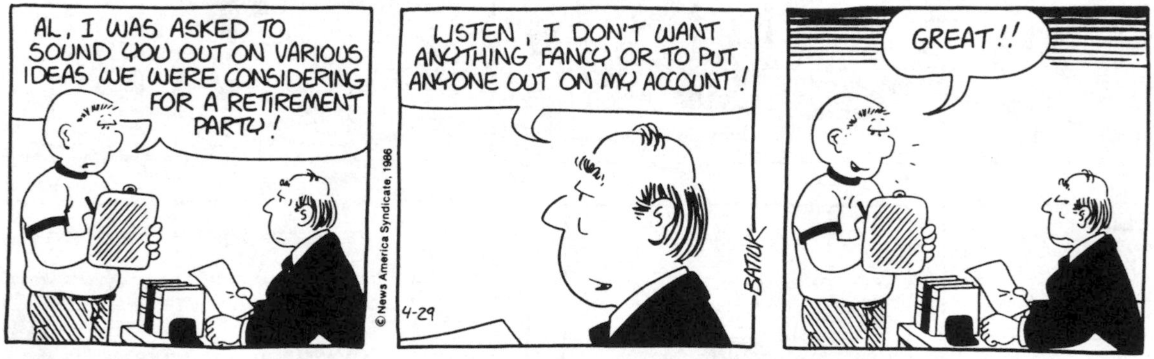
AL, I WAS ASKED TO SOUND YOU OUT ON VARIOUS IDEAS WE WERE CONSIDERING FOR A RETIREMENT PARTY!
LISTEN, I DON'T WANT ANYTHING FANCY OR TO PUT ANYONE OUT ON MY ACCOUNT!
GREAT!!
© News America Syndicate, 1986
4-29
BATIUK

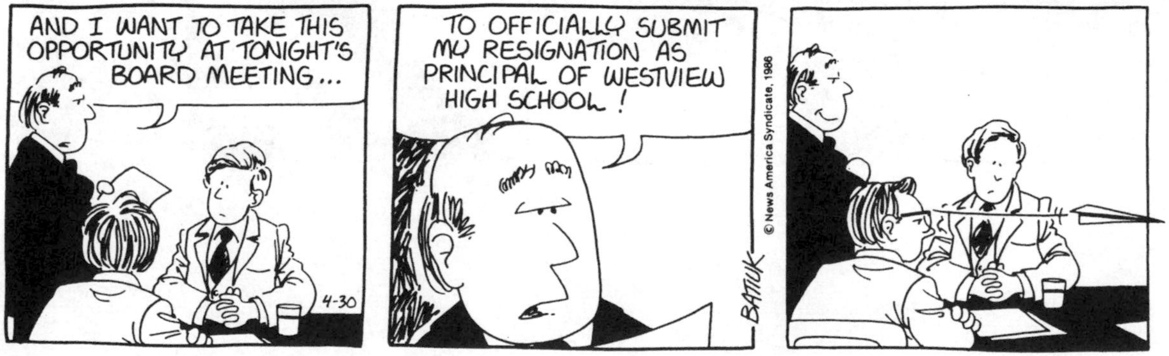
AND I WANT TO TAKE THIS OPPORTUNITY AT TONIGHT'S BOARD MEETING...
TO OFFICIALLY SUBMIT MY RESIGNATION AS PRINCIPAL OF WESTVIEW HIGH SCHOOL!
4-30
BATIUK
© News America Syndicate, 1986

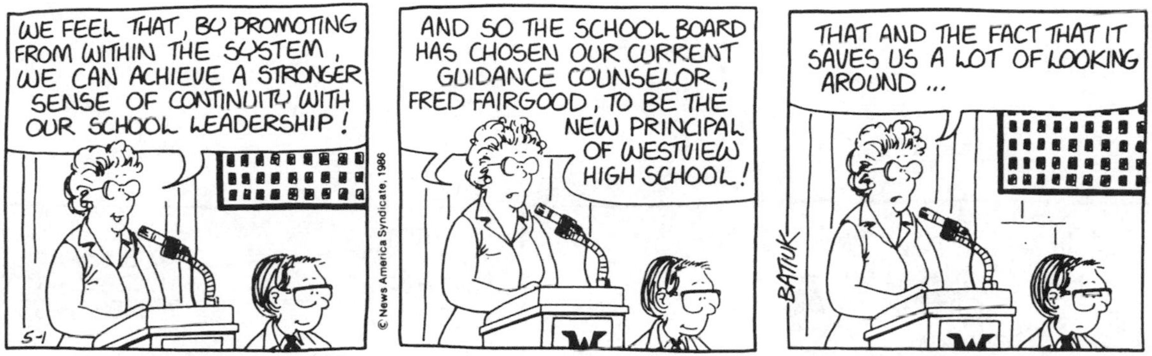
WE FEEL THAT, BY PROMOTING FROM WITHIN THE SYSTEM, WE CAN ACHIEVE A STRONGER SENSE OF CONTINUITY WITH OUR SCHOOL LEADERSHIP!
5-1
© News America Syndicate, 1986
AND SO THE SCHOOL BOARD HAS CHOSEN OUR CURRENT GUIDANCE COUNSELOR, FRED FAIRGOOD, TO BE THE NEW PRINCIPAL OF WESTVIEW HIGH SCHOOL!
THAT AND THE FACT THAT IT SAVES US A LOT OF LOOKING AROUND ...
BATIUK

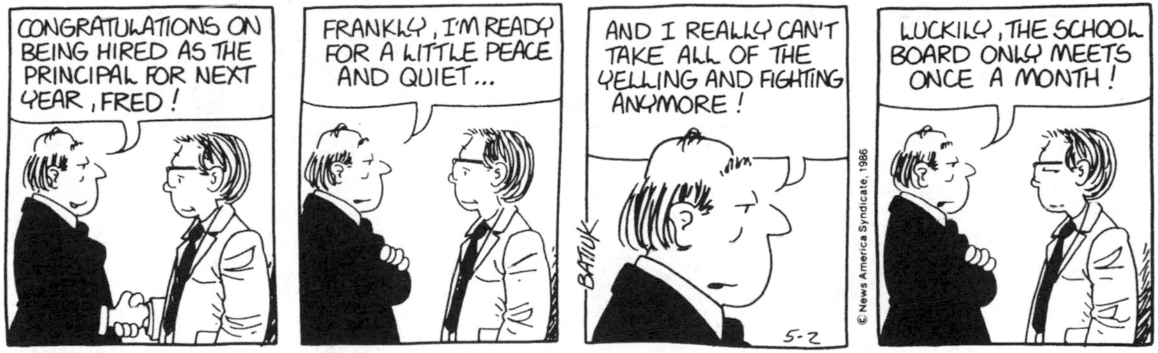
CONGRATULATIONS ON BEING HIRED AS THE PRINCIPAL FOR NEXT YEAR, FRED!
FRANKLY, I'M READY FOR A LITTLE PEACE AND QUIET...
AND I REALLY CAN'T TAKE ALL OF THE YELLING AND FIGHTING ANYMORE!
BATIUK
5-2
© News America Syndicate, 1986
LUCKILY, THE SCHOOL BOARD ONLY MEETS ONCE A MONTH!

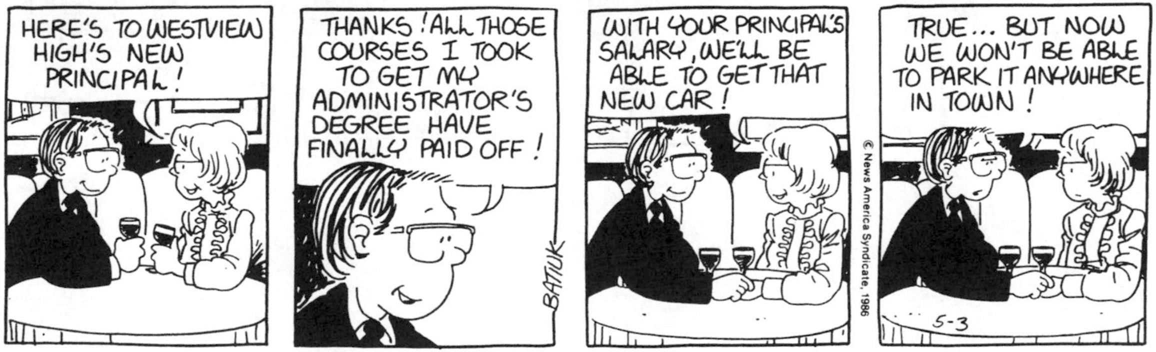
HERE'S TO WESTVIEW HIGH'S NEW PRINCIPAL!
THANKS! ALL THOSE COURSES I TOOK TO GET MY ADMINISTRATOR'S DEGREE HAVE FINALLY PAID OFF!
BATIUK
WITH YOUR PRINCIPAL'S SALARY, WE'LL BE ABLE TO GET THAT NEW CAR!
© News America Syndicate, 1986
TRUE... BUT NOW WE WON'T BE ABLE TO PARK IT ANYWHERE IN TOWN!
5-3

FUNKY WINKERBEAN
BY TOM BATIUK
HE WHO RUNS BECAUSE OF A SPREADING MIDDLE ... PROVES THAT WAIST MAKES HASTE ?
SAYINGS FROM THE I CHONG ANCIENT BOOK OF CHINESE PHILOSOPHY
THE MASTER SAYS:
HE WHO LIVES IN AN EARTHQUAKE ZONE...
SHOULD CONSIDER BUYING NO-FAULT INSURANCE !
© News America Syndicate, 1986
BATIUK
5-4

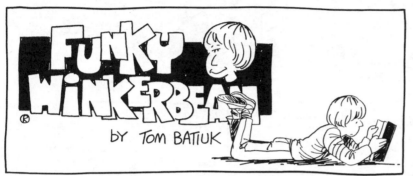

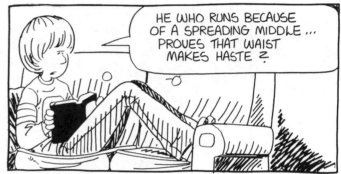

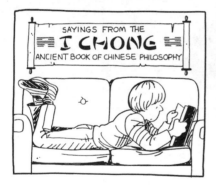

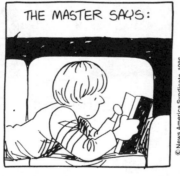

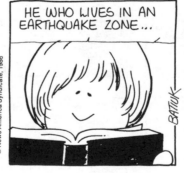

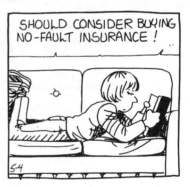

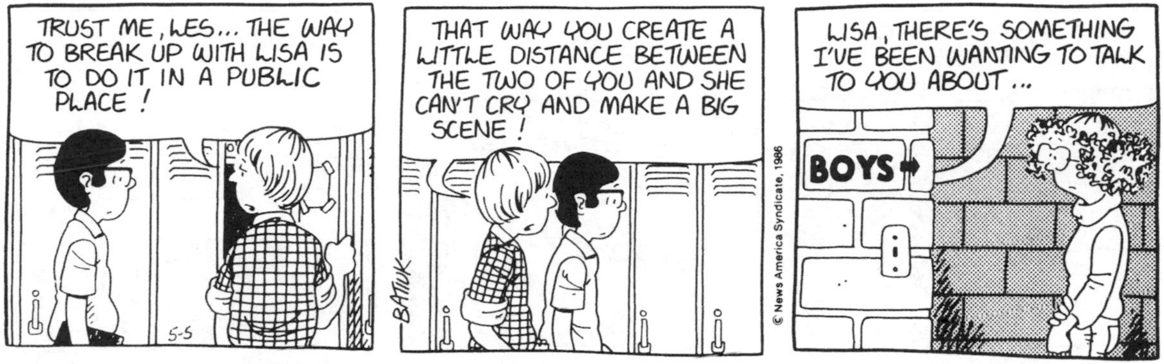
TRUST ME, LES... THE WAY TO BREAK UP WITH LISA IS TO DO IT IN A PUBLIC PLACE !
THAT WAY YOU CREATE A LITTLE DISTANCE BETWEEN THE TWO OF YOU AND SHE CAN'T CRY AND MAKE A BIG SCENE !
LISA, THERE'S SOMETHING I'VE BEEN WANTING TO TALK TO YOU ABOUT...
BOYS
BATIUK
5-5
© News America Syndicate, 1986

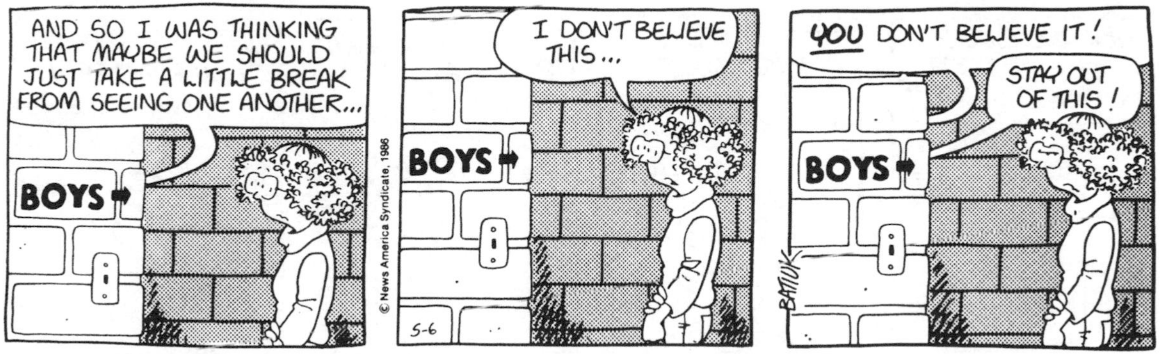
AND SO I WAS THINKING THAT MAYBE WE SHOULD JUST TAKE A LITTLE BREAK FROM SEEING ONE ANOTHER...
I DON'T BELIEVE THIS...
YOU DON'T BELIEVE IT !
STAY OUT OF THIS !
BOYS
BATIUK
5-6
© News America Syndicate, 1986

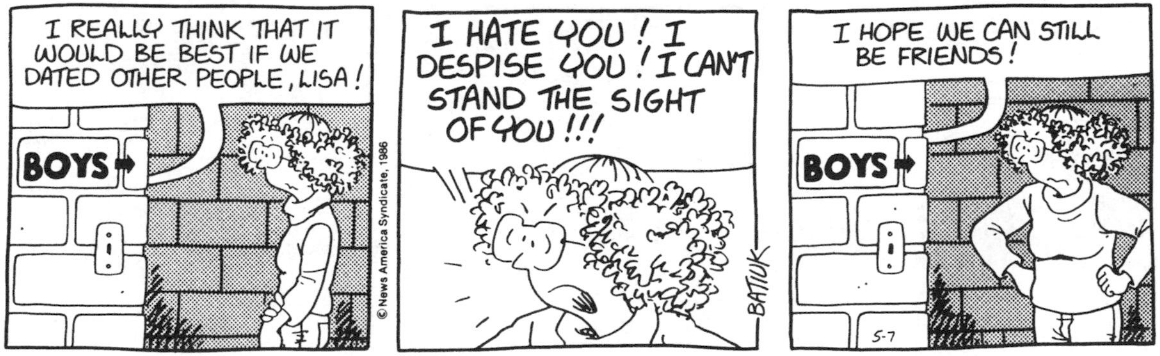
I REALLY THINK THAT IT WOULD BE BEST IF WE DATED OTHER PEOPLE, LISA !
I HATE YOU ! I DESPISE YOU ! I CAN'T STAND THE SIGHT OF YOU !!!
I HOPE WE CAN STILL BE FRIENDS !
BOYS
BATIUK
5-7
© News America Syndicate, 1986

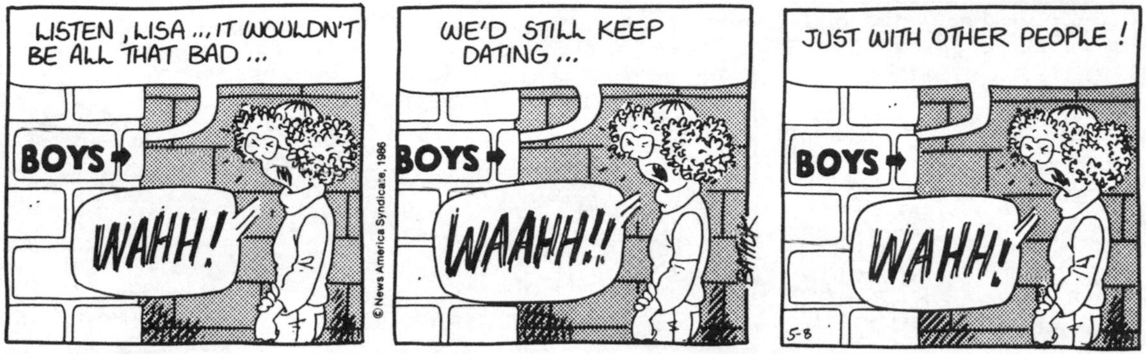
LISTEN, LISA..., IT WOULDN'T BE ALL THAT BAD...
WAHH!
© News America Syndicate, 1986
BOYS
WE'D STILL KEEP DATING...
WAAHH!!
BATIUK
JUST WITH OTHER PEOPLE!
WAHH!
5-8

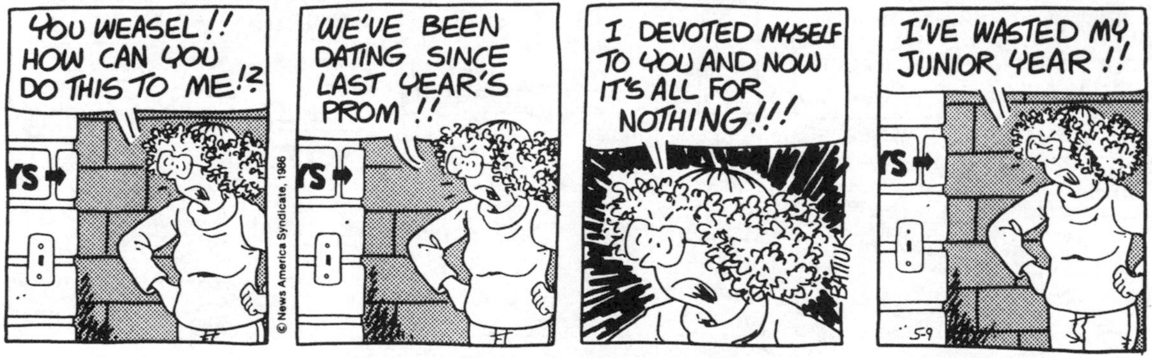
YOU WEASEL!! HOW CAN YOU DO THIS TO ME!?
© News America Syndicate, 1986
WE'VE BEEN DATING SINCE LAST YEAR'S PROM!!
I DEVOTED MYSELF TO YOU AND NOW IT'S ALL FOR NOTHING!!!
BATIUK
I'VE WASTED MY JUNIOR YEAR!!
5-9

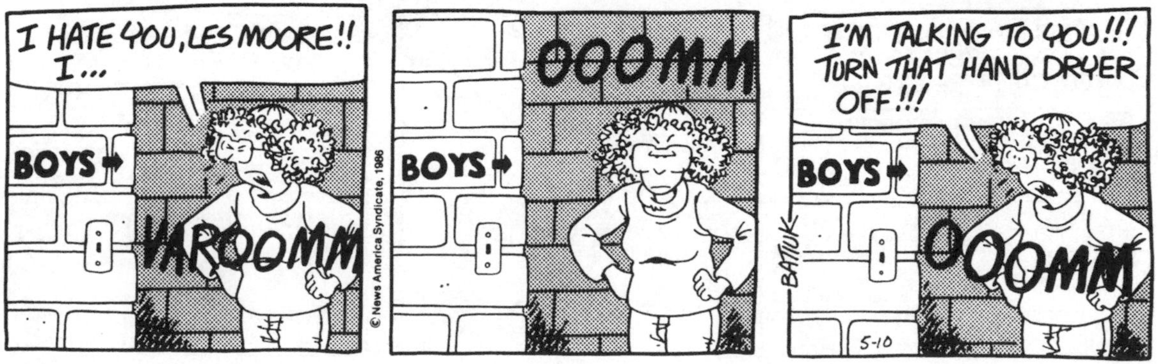
I HATE YOU, LES MOORE!! I...
BOYS
VAROOMM
© News America Syndicate, 1986
OOOMM
I'M TALKING TO YOU!!! TURN THAT HAND DRYER OFF!!!
BATIUK
OOOMM
5-10

Funky Winkerbean by Tom Batiuk

DO YOU GRADE ON THE CURVE, COACH?

NO, I USUALLY DO IT RIGHT HERE IN THE WORKROOM!

WHO WAS THAT?

THE COACH!

OH, I DIDN'T RECOGNIZE HIM WITHOUT HIS MOVIE PROJECTOR!

OKAY MEN, LISTEN UP!

TAKE OUT A SHEET OF PAPER AND NUMBER IT FROM ONE TO TEN!

© News America Syndicate, 1986

SOUNDS LIKE THE COACH IS ABOUT TO GIVE THE TEAM A FINAL EXAM!

5-11

THAT **WAS** THE FINAL EXAM!

395

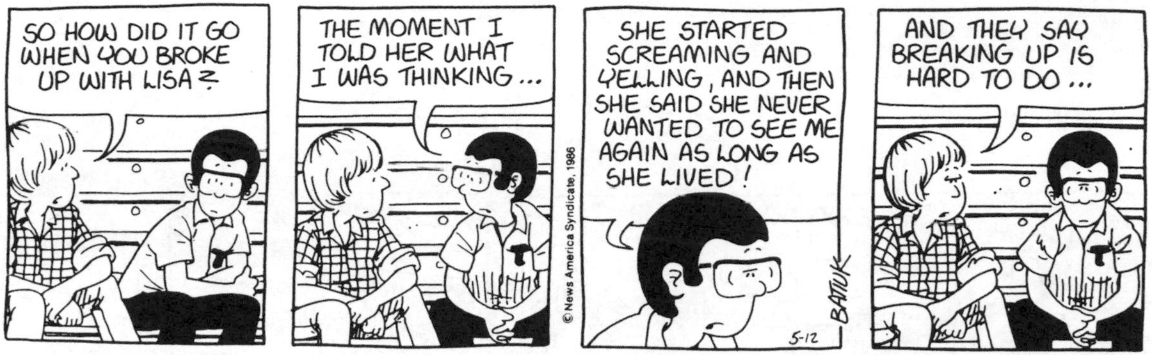
SO HOW DID IT GO WHEN YOU BROKE UP WITH LISA?
THE MOMENT I TOLD HER WHAT I WAS THINKING...
© News America Syndicate, 1986
SHE STARTED SCREAMING AND YELLING, AND THEN SHE SAID SHE NEVER WANTED TO SEE ME AGAIN AS LONG AS SHE LIVED!
5-12
BATIUK
AND THEY SAY BREAKING UP IS HARD TO DO...

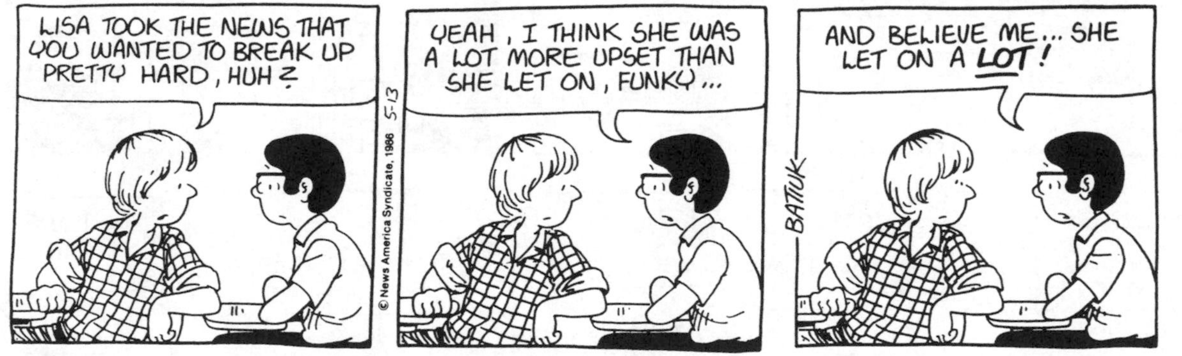
LISA TOOK THE NEWS THAT YOU WANTED TO BREAK UP PRETTY HARD, HUH?
5-13
© News America Syndicate, 1986
YEAH, I THINK SHE WAS A LOT MORE UPSET THAN SHE LET ON, FUNKY...
BATIUK
AND BELIEVE ME... SHE LET ON A LOT!

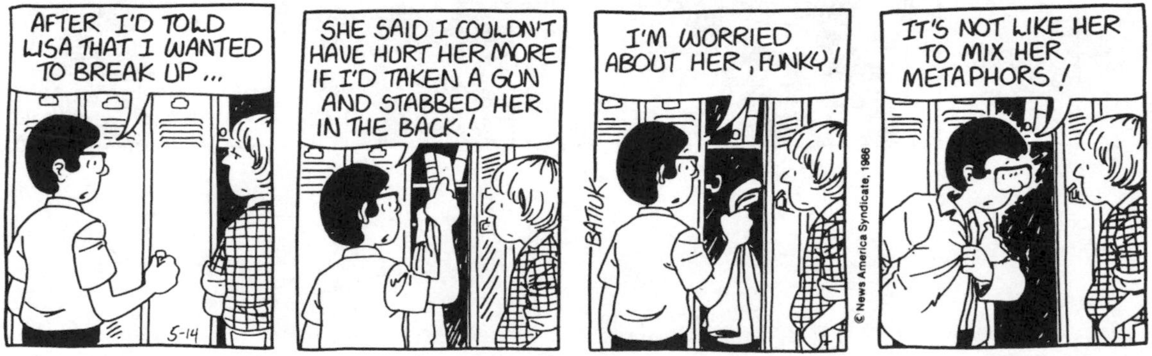
AFTER I'D TOLD LISA THAT I WANTED TO BREAK UP...
5-14
SHE SAID I COULDN'T HAVE HURT HER MORE IF I'D TAKEN A GUN AND STABBED HER IN THE BACK!
I'M WORRIED ABOUT HER, FUNKY!
BATIUK
© News America Syndicate, 1986
IT'S NOT LIKE HER TO MIX HER METAPHORS!

Panel 1: DON'T WORRY, LES... I'M SURE LISA WILL EVENTUALLY GET OVER YOUR BREAKING UP WITH HER!

© News America Syndicate, 1986

Panel 2: YEAH, I GUESS YOU'RE RIGHT, FUNKY...

5-15

Panel 3: SHE PROBABLY JUST FILED THAT PALIMONY SUIT TO SEE HOW YOU'D REACT!

BATIUK

Panel 4: HONEY, LES IS IN HIS ROOM LYING IN THE DARK CRYING!

I KNOW!

© News America Syndicate, 1986

Panel 5: WELL, DON'T YOU THINK YOU SHOULD CHECK IT OUT?

I ALREADY DID!

Panel 6: I LOOKED ALL OVER THE CAR AND THERE'S NOT A SCRATCH ON IT!

BATIUK

5-16

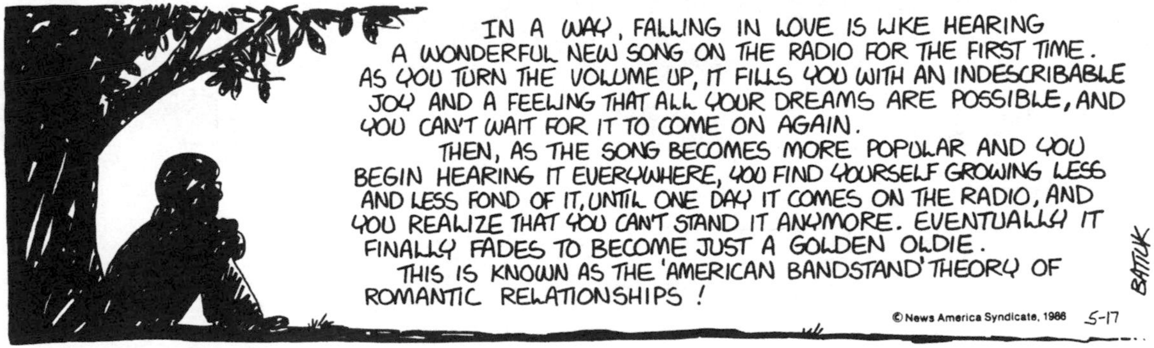

IN A WAY, FALLING IN LOVE IS LIKE HEARING A WONDERFUL NEW SONG ON THE RADIO FOR THE FIRST TIME. AS YOU TURN THE VOLUME UP, IT FILLS YOU WITH AN INDESCRIBABLE JOY AND A FEELING THAT ALL YOUR DREAMS ARE POSSIBLE, AND YOU CAN'T WAIT FOR IT TO COME ON AGAIN.

THEN, AS THE SONG BECOMES MORE POPULAR AND YOU BEGIN HEARING IT EVERYWHERE, YOU FIND YOURSELF GROWING LESS AND LESS FOND OF IT, UNTIL ONE DAY IT COMES ON THE RADIO, AND YOU REALIZE THAT YOU CAN'T STAND IT ANYMORE. EVENTUALLY IT FINALLY FADES TO BECOME JUST A GOLDEN OLDIE.

THIS IS KNOWN AS THE 'AMERICAN BANDSTAND' THEORY OF ROMANTIC RELATIONSHIPS!

BATIUK

© News America Syndicate, 1986   5-17

397

Funky Winkerbean

BY TOM BATIUK

WESTVIEW HIGH SCHOOL

BAND AWARDS BANQUET

WHENEVER THE BAND MAKES A TRIP SOME-WHERE...

WE WOULDN'T BE ABLE TO DO IT WITHOUT SOMEONE WHO'S WILLING TO GIVE UP HIS SPARE TIME AND WEEKENDS TO DRIVE US THERE!

TONIGHT WE'D LIKE TO PRESENT THIS SPECIAL PLAQUE OF APPRECIATION FROM THE BAND TO OUR BUS DRIVER, ED CRANKSHAFT!

THAT'S **IT!?** A CRUMMY LITTLE PLAQUE SOME KID PROBABLY MADE WITH HIS WOODBURNING SET!?

5-18

WHAT ABOUT A PAIR OF LEATHER DRIVING **GLOVES** OR A DECENT **WATCH!!?**

© News America Syndicate, 1986

WHAT'S WRONG WITH SOMETHING **USEFUL!!?**

PLEASE HOLD YOUR APPLAUSE UNTIL ALL THE AWARDS HAVE BEEN GIVEN OUT!

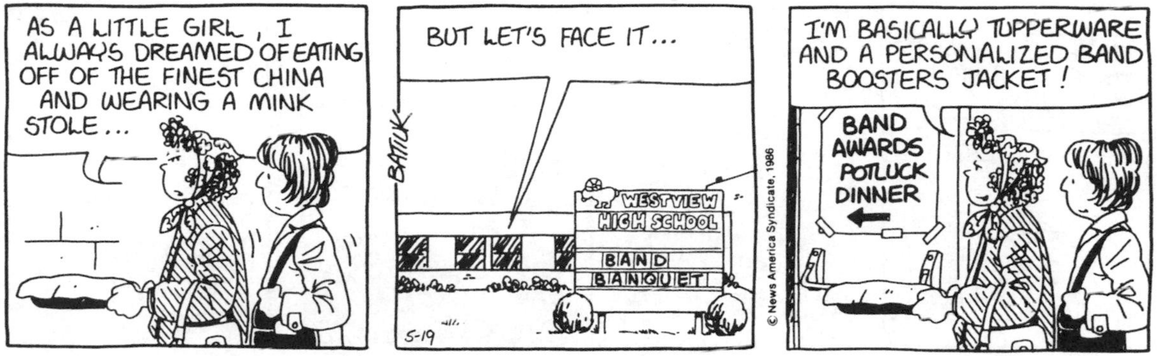
AS A LITTLE GIRL, I ALWAYS DREAMED OF EATING OFF OF THE FINEST CHINA AND WEARING A MINK STOLE...
BUT LET'S FACE IT...
WESTVIEW HIGH SCHOOL
BAND BANQUET
BATIUK
5-19
I'M BASICALLY TUPPERWARE AND A PERSONALIZED BAND BOOSTERS JACKET!
BAND AWARDS POTLUCK DINNER
© News America Syndicate, 1986

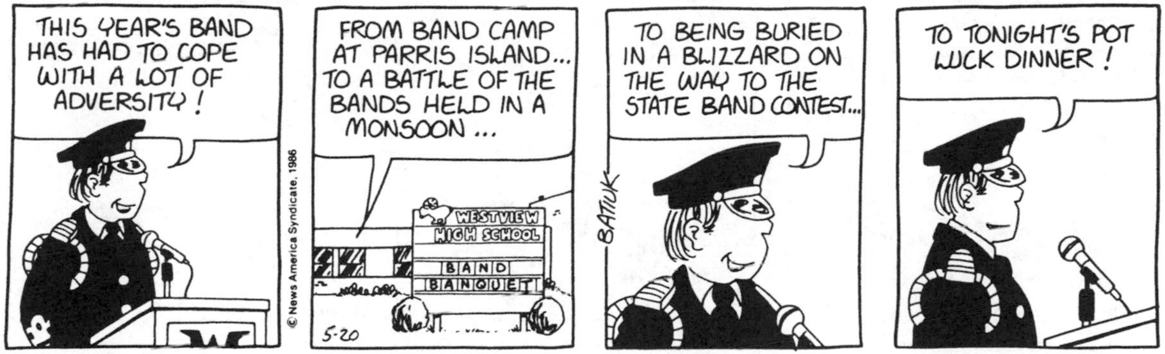
THIS YEAR'S BAND HAS HAD TO COPE WITH A LOT OF ADVERSITY!
© News America Syndicate, 1986
FROM BAND CAMP AT PARRIS ISLAND... TO A BATTLE OF THE BANDS HELD IN A MONSOON...
WESTVIEW HIGH SCHOOL
BAND BANQUET
5-20
TO BEING BURIED IN A BLIZZARD ON THE WAY TO THE STATE BAND CONTEST...
BATIUK
TO TONIGHT'S POT LUCK DINNER!

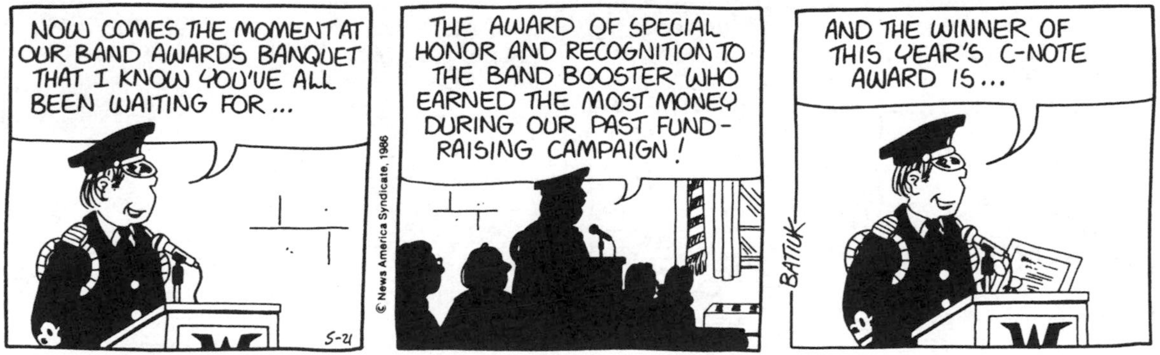
NOW COMES THE MOMENT AT OUR BAND AWARDS BANQUET THAT I KNOW YOU'VE ALL BEEN WAITING FOR...
5-21
© News America Syndicate, 1986
THE AWARD OF SPECIAL HONOR AND RECOGNITION TO THE BAND BOOSTER WHO EARNED THE MOST MONEY DURING OUR PAST FUND-RAISING CAMPAIGN!
BATIUK
AND THE WINNER OF THIS YEAR'S C-NOTE AWARD IS...

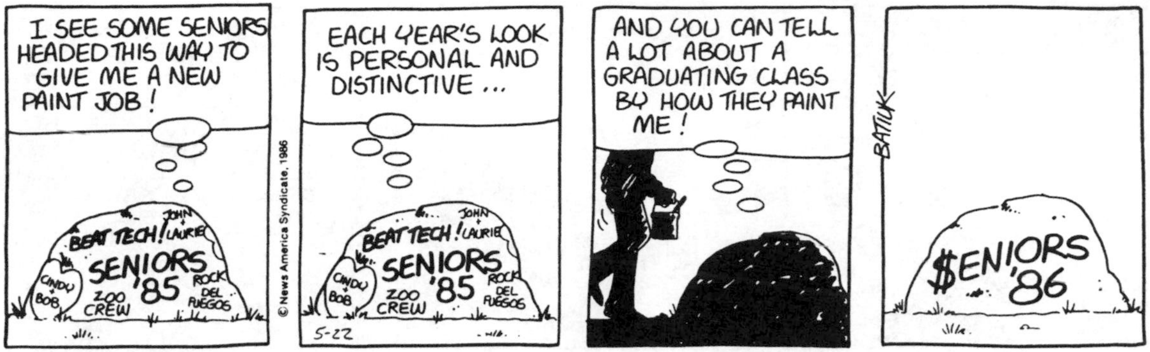
I SEE SOME SENIORS HEADED THIS WAY TO GIVE ME A NEW PAINT JOB!
BEAT TECH!
JOHN + LAURIE
SENIORS '85
CINDY + BOB
ZOO CREW
ROCK DEL FUEGOS
© News America Syndicate, 1986
EACH YEAR'S LOOK IS PERSONAL AND DISTINCTIVE...
5-22
AND YOU CAN TELL A LOT ABOUT A GRADUATING CLASS BY HOW THEY PAINT ME!
BATIUK
$ENIORS '86

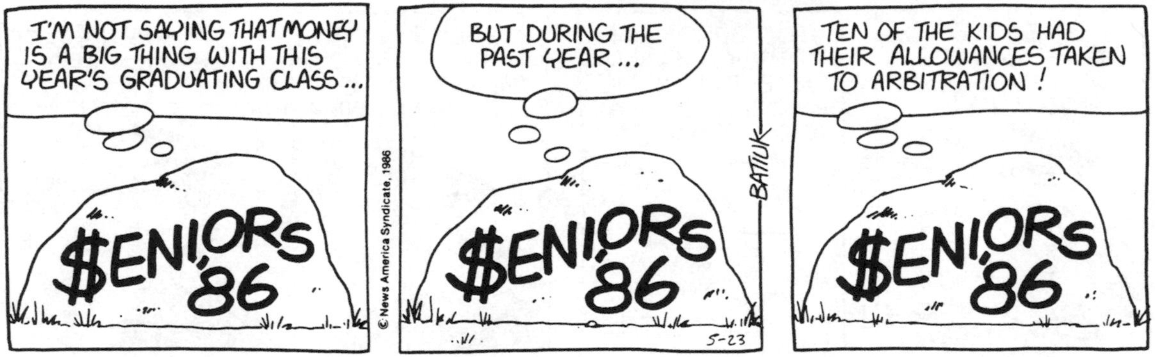
I'M NOT SAYING THAT MONEY IS A BIG THING WITH THIS YEAR'S GRADUATING CLASS...
$ENIORS '86
© News America Syndicate, 1986
BUT DURING THE PAST YEAR...
BATIUK
5-23
TEN OF THE KIDS HAD THEIR ALLOWANCES TAKEN TO ARBITRATION!

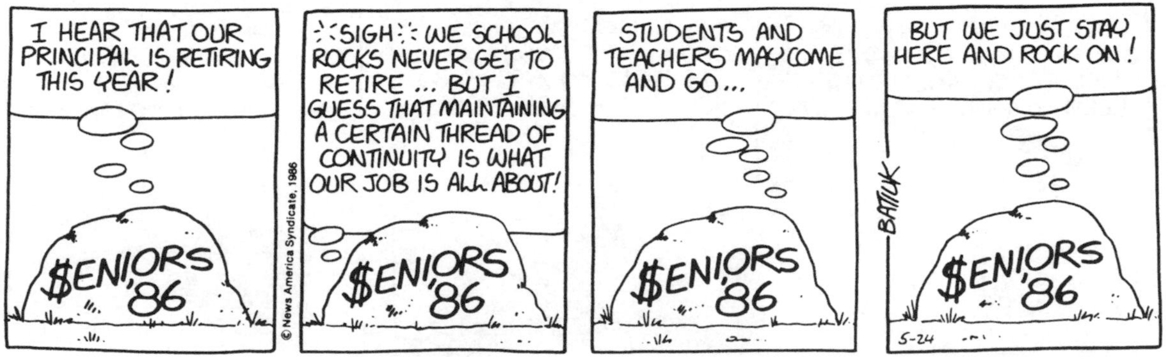
I HEAR THAT OUR PRINCIPAL IS RETIRING THIS YEAR!
$ENIORS '86
© News America Syndicate, 1986
SIGH WE SCHOOL ROCKS NEVER GET TO RETIRE... BUT I GUESS THAT MAINTAINING A CERTAIN THREAD OF CONTINUITY IS WHAT OUR JOB IS ALL ABOUT!
STUDENTS AND TEACHERS MAY COME AND GO...
BATIUK
BUT WE JUST STAY HERE AND ROCK ON!
5-24

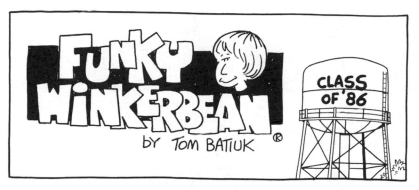

FUNKY WINKERBEAN

BY TOM BATIUK

CLASS OF '86

AS MANY OF YOU MAY BE AWARE...

THIS IS MY LAST GRADUATION CEREMONY!

AS I MOVE FROM BEING PRINCIPAL OF WESTVIEW HIGH SCHOOL AND INTO RETIREMENT, I FIND THAT MY CAREER IN EDUCATION REMINDS ME OF THE GAME OF MARBLES I USED TO PLAY AS A CHILD!

YOU'D HAVE A LITTLE SOCK FULL OF MARBLES AND YOU COULD ALWAYS CONTINUE TO PLAY AS LONG AS YOUR SUPPLY HELD OUT!

© News America Syndicate, 1986

BUT EVENTUALLY, AFTER PLAYING ALL DAY LONG, YOU'D FIND THAT YOU'D LOST ALL OF YOUR MARBLES...

AND THAT'S WHEN YOU KNOW IT'S TIME TO RETIRE!

5-25

401

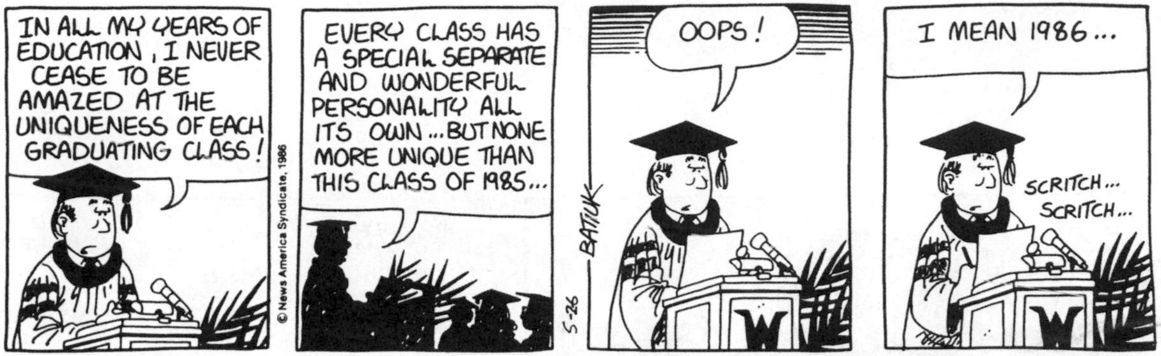
IN ALL MY YEARS OF EDUCATION, I NEVER CEASE TO BE AMAZED AT THE UNIQUENESS OF EACH GRADUATING CLASS!
EVERY CLASS HAS A SPECIAL SEPARATE AND WONDERFUL PERSONALITY ALL ITS OWN ... BUT NONE MORE UNIQUE THAN THIS CLASS OF 1985...
© News America Syndicate, 1986
OOPS!
BATIUK
5-26
I MEAN 1986...
SCRITCH...
SCRITCH...

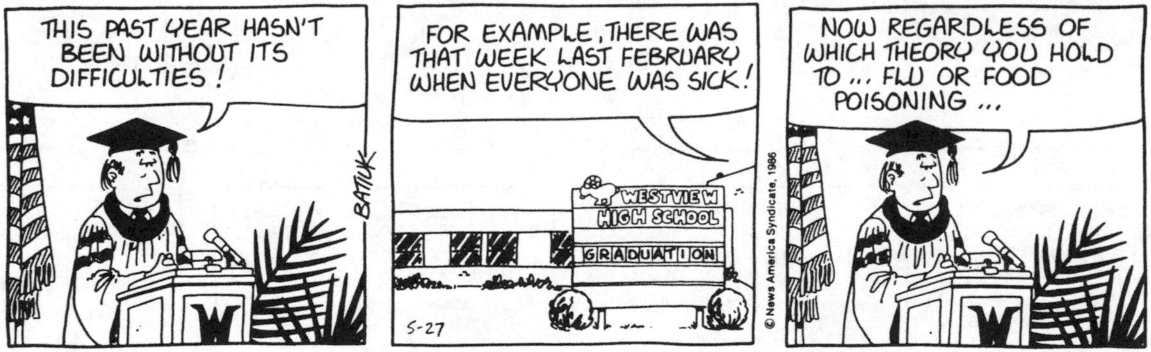
THIS PAST YEAR HASN'T BEEN WITHOUT ITS DIFFICULTIES!
BATIUK
FOR EXAMPLE, THERE WAS THAT WEEK LAST FEBRUARY WHEN EVERYONE WAS SICK!
WESTVIEW
HIGH SCHOOL
GRADUATION
5-27
© News America Syndicate, 1986
NOW REGARDLESS OF WHICH THEORY YOU HOLD TO ... FLU OR FOOD POISONING ...

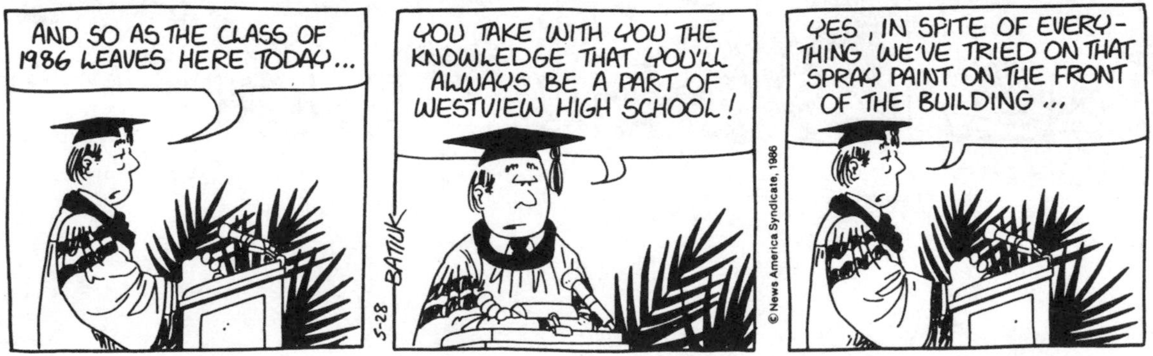
AND SO AS THE CLASS OF 1986 LEAVES HERE TODAY...
BATIUK
5-28
YOU TAKE WITH YOU THE KNOWLEDGE THAT YOU'LL ALWAYS BE A PART OF WESTVIEW HIGH SCHOOL!
© News America Syndicate, 1986
YES, IN SPITE OF EVERYTHING WE'VE TRIED ON THAT SPRAY PAINT ON THE FRONT OF THE BUILDING ...

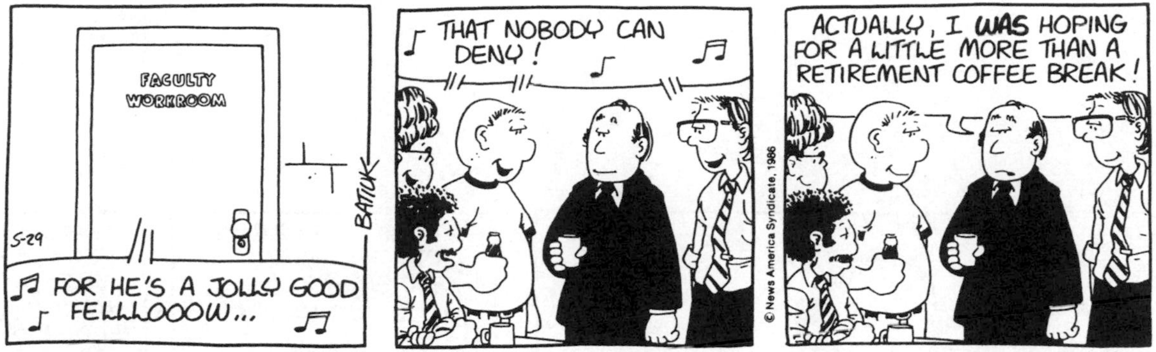
FACULTY WORKROOM
5-29
BATIUK
FOR HE'S A JOLLY GOOD FELLLLOOOW...
THAT NOBODY CAN DENY!
© News America Syndicate, 1986
ACTUALLY, I **WAS** HOPING FOR A LITTLE MORE THAN A RETIREMENT COFFEE BREAK!

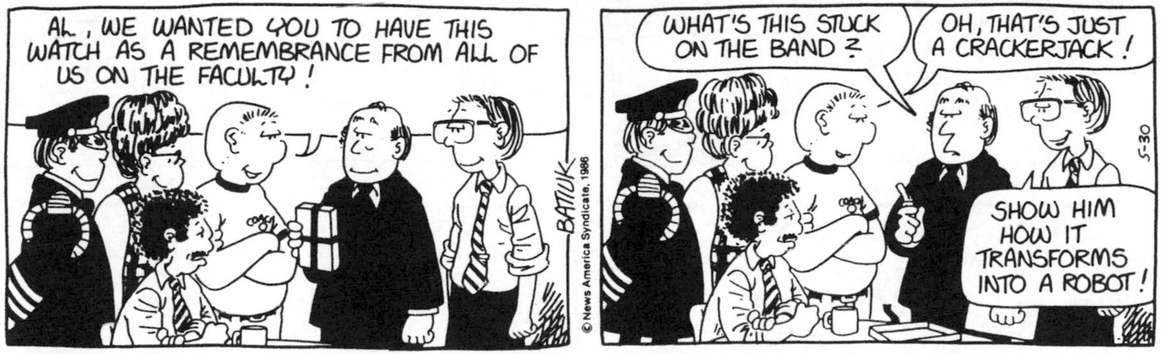
AL, WE WANTED YOU TO HAVE THIS WATCH AS A REMEMBRANCE FROM ALL OF US ON THE FACULTY!
BATIUK
© News America Syndicate, 1986
WHAT'S THIS STUCK ON THE BAND?
OH, THAT'S JUST A CRACKERJACK!
SHOW HIM HOW IT TRANSFORMS INTO A ROBOT!
5-30

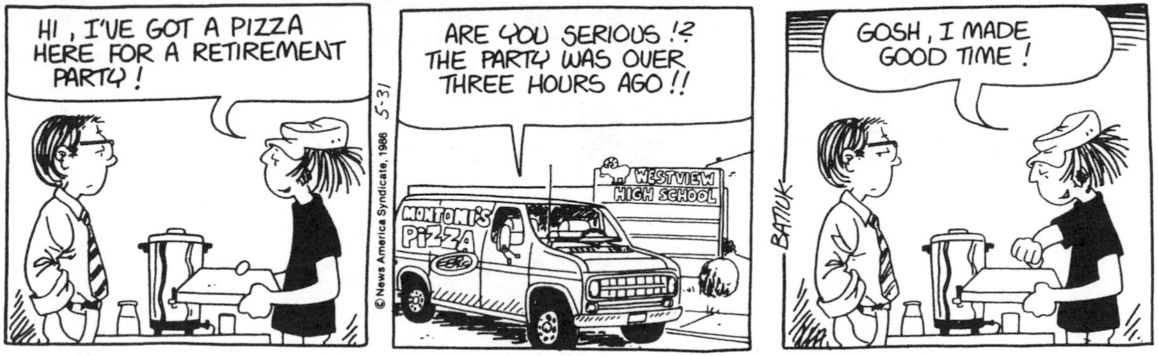
HI, I'VE GOT A PIZZA HERE FOR A RETIREMENT PARTY!
5-31
© News America Syndicate, 1986
ARE YOU SERIOUS!? THE PARTY WAS OVER THREE HOURS AGO!!
MONTONI'S PIZZA
WESTVIEW HIGH SCHOOL
GOSH, I MADE GOOD TIME!
BATIUK

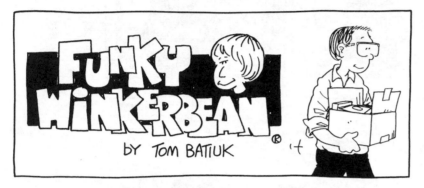

Funky Winkerbean by Tom Batiuk

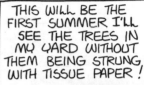

I THINK I'M REALLY GOING TO ENJOY RETIREMENT!

PRINCIPAL

THIS WILL BE THE FIRST SUMMER I'LL SEE THE TREES IN MY YARD WITHOUT THEM BEING STRUNG WITH TISSUE PAPER!

THANKS FOR HELPING ME PACK ALL THIS STUFF, FRED!

PRINCIPAL

© News America Syndicate, 1986

NO PROBLEM, AL!

GEE, I NEVER KNEW YOU HAD MAALOX ON TAP!

BATIUK

YEAH... I GOT A PROFESSIONAL DISCOUNT!

6-1

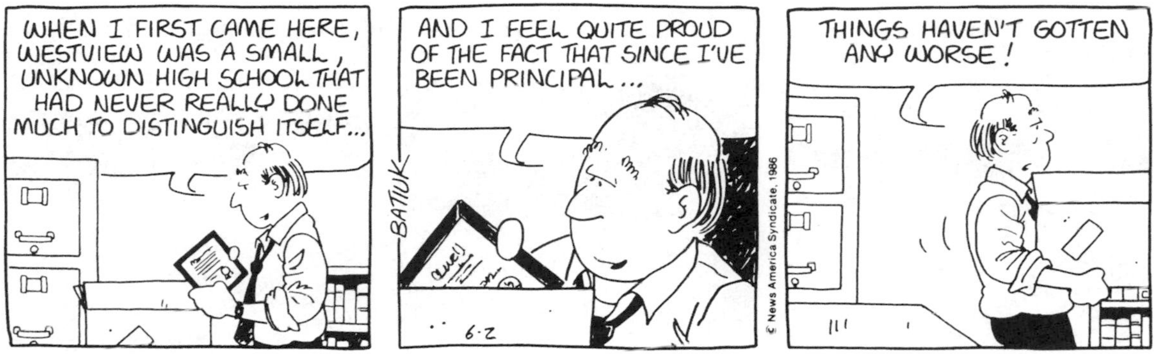
WHEN I FIRST CAME HERE, WESTVIEW WAS A SMALL, UNKNOWN HIGH SCHOOL THAT HAD NEVER REALLY DONE MUCH TO DISTINGUISH ITSELF...
AND I FEEL QUITE PROUD OF THE FACT THAT SINCE I'VE BEEN PRINCIPAL...
THINGS HAVEN'T GOTTEN ANY WORSE!
BATIUK
6-2
© News America Syndicate, 1986

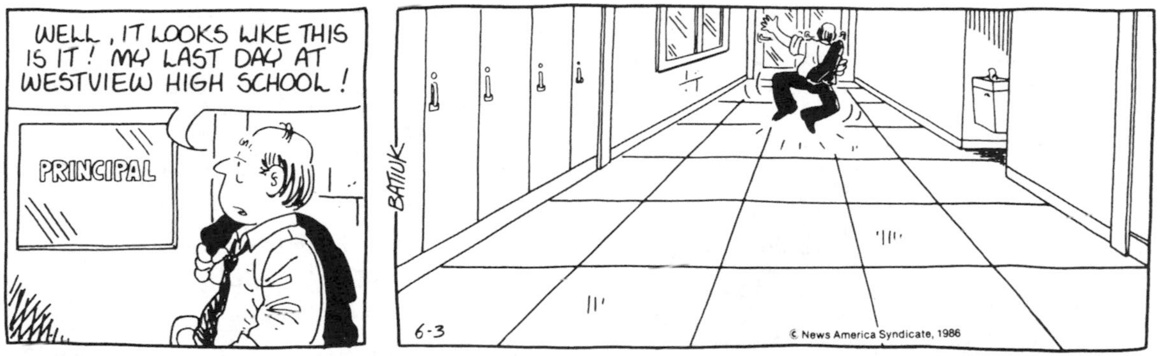
WELL, IT LOOKS LIKE THIS IS IT! MY LAST DAY AT WESTVIEW HIGH SCHOOL!
PRINCIPAL
BATIUK
6-3
© News America Syndicate, 1986

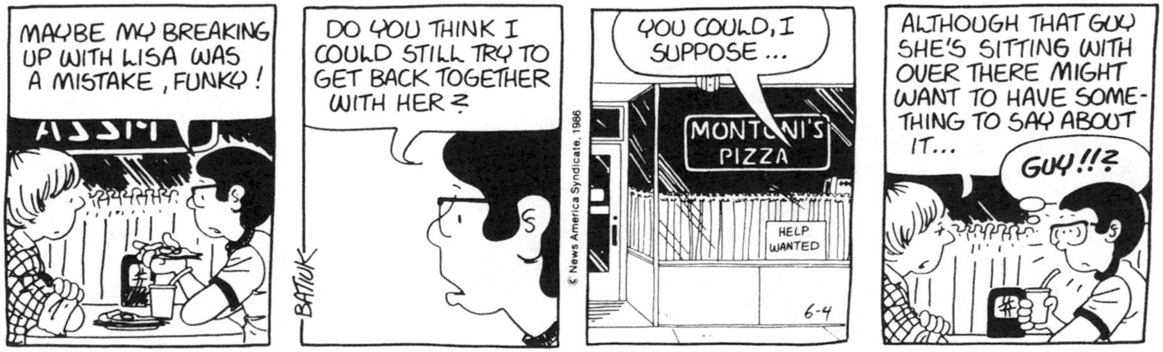
MAYBE MY BREAKING UP WITH LISA WAS A MISTAKE, FUNKY!
DO YOU THINK I COULD STILL TRY TO GET BACK TOGETHER WITH HER?
YOU COULD, I SUPPOSE...
MONTONI'S PIZZA
HELP WANTED
ALTHOUGH THAT GUY SHE'S SITTING WITH OVER THERE MIGHT WANT TO HAVE SOMETHING TO SAY ABOUT IT...
GUY!!?
BATIUK
6-4
© News America Syndicate, 1986

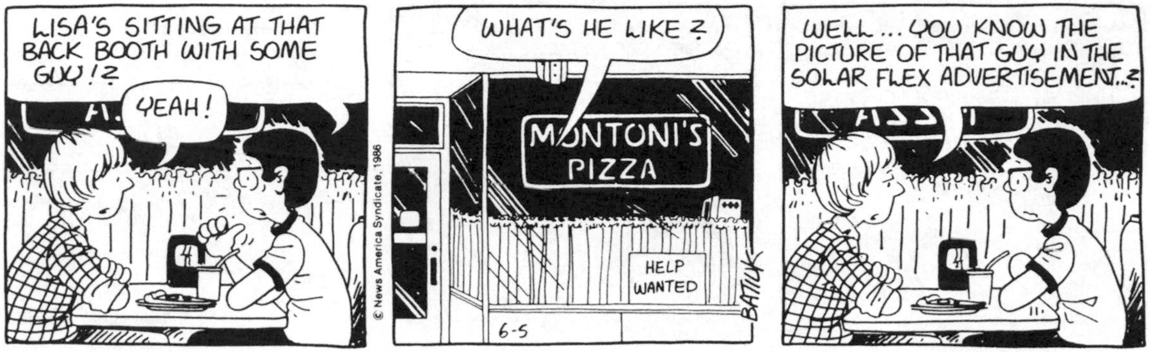
LISA'S SITTING AT THAT BACK BOOTH WITH SOME GUY!?
YEAH!
© News America Syndicate, 1986
WHAT'S HE LIKE?
MONTONI'S PIZZA
HELP WANTED
6-5
BATIUK
WELL... YOU KNOW THE PICTURE OF THAT GUY IN THE SOLAR FLEX ADVERTISEMENT..?

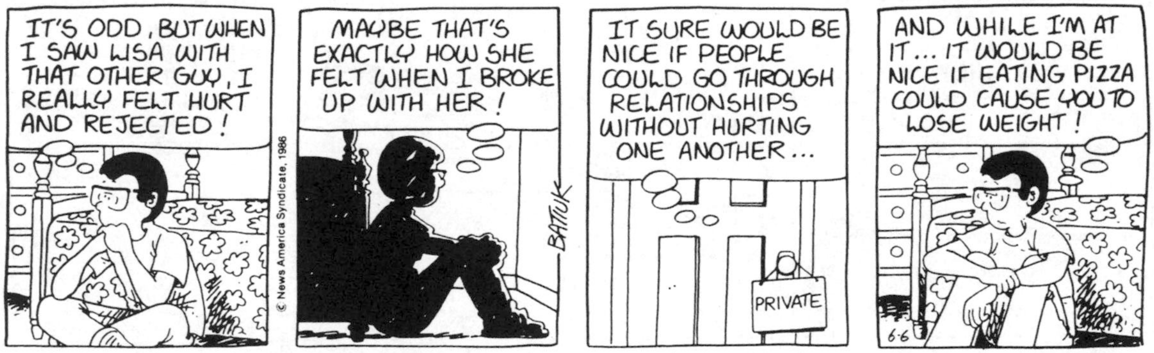
IT'S ODD, BUT WHEN I SAW LISA WITH THAT OTHER GUY, I REALLY FELT HURT AND REJECTED!
© News America Syndicate, 1986
MAYBE THAT'S EXACTLY HOW SHE FELT WHEN I BROKE UP WITH HER!
BATIUK
IT SURE WOULD BE NICE IF PEOPLE COULD GO THROUGH RELATIONSHIPS WITHOUT HURTING ONE ANOTHER...
PRIVATE
AND WHILE I'M AT IT... IT WOULD BE NICE IF EATING PIZZA COULD CAUSE YOU TO LOSE WEIGHT!
6-6

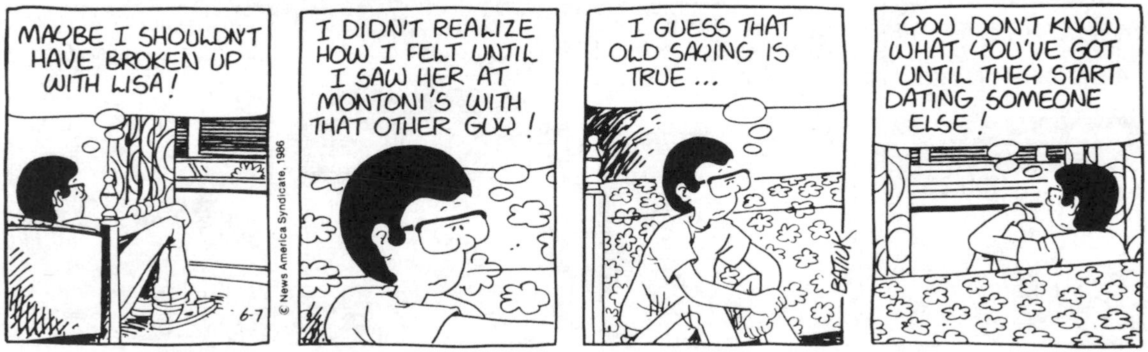
MAYBE I SHOULDN'T HAVE BROKEN UP WITH LISA!
6-7
© News America Syndicate, 1986
I DIDN'T REALIZE HOW I FELT UNTIL I SAW HER AT MONTONI'S WITH THAT OTHER GUY!
I GUESS THAT OLD SAYING IS TRUE...
BATIUK
YOU DON'T KNOW WHAT YOU'VE GOT UNTIL THEY START DATING SOMEONE ELSE!

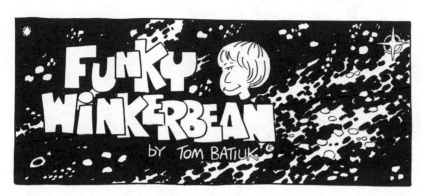

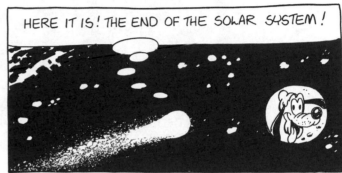

FUNKY WINKERBEAN
BY TOM BATIUK
HERE IT IS! THE END OF THE SOLAR SYSTEM!
WELL, THIS IS YOUR FINAL REPORT FROM HALLEY'S COMET BEFORE I LEAVE THE SOLAR SYSTEM!
I HEARD SOME SCIENTISTS WERE SPECULATING THAT I MAY BE BREAKING APART!
BATIUK
I HOPE I'M STILL IN ONE PIECE WHEN I RETURN!
6-8
© News America Syndicate, 1986
I HOPE YOU ARE TOO!

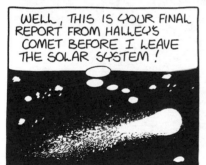

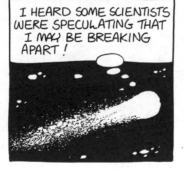

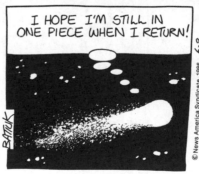

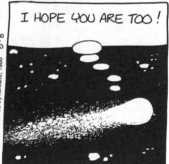

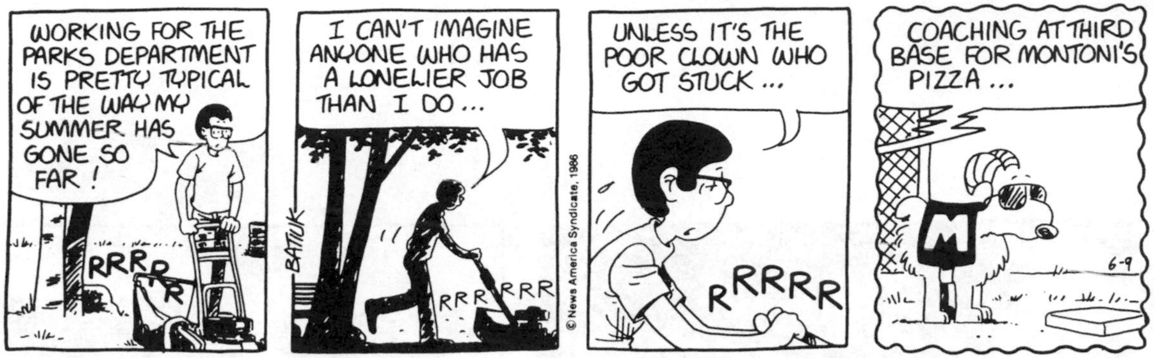
WORKING FOR THE PARKS DEPARTMENT IS PRETTY TYPICAL OF THE WAY MY SUMMER HAS GONE SO FAR!
RRRRR
I CAN'T IMAGINE ANYONE WHO HAS A LONELIER JOB THAN I DO...
BATIUK
RRR RRR
© News America Syndicate, 1986
UNLESS IT'S THE POOR CLOWN WHO GOT STUCK...
RRRRR
COACHING AT THIRD BASE FOR MONTONI'S PIZZA...
M
6-9

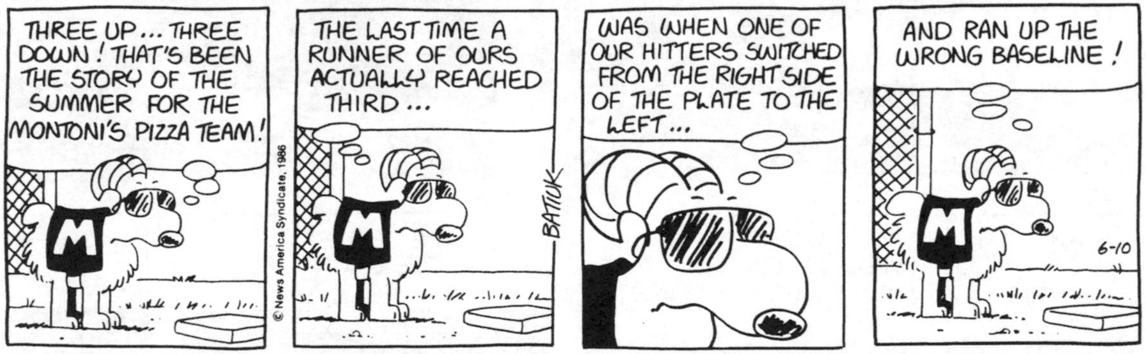
THREE UP... THREE DOWN! THAT'S BEEN THE STORY OF THE SUMMER FOR THE MONTONI'S PIZZA TEAM!
M
© News America Syndicate, 1986
THE LAST TIME A RUNNER OF OURS ACTUALLY REACHED THIRD...
M
BATIUK
WAS WHEN ONE OF OUR HITTERS SWITCHED FROM THE RIGHT SIDE OF THE PLATE TO THE LEFT...
AND RAN UP THE WRONG BASELINE!
M
6-10

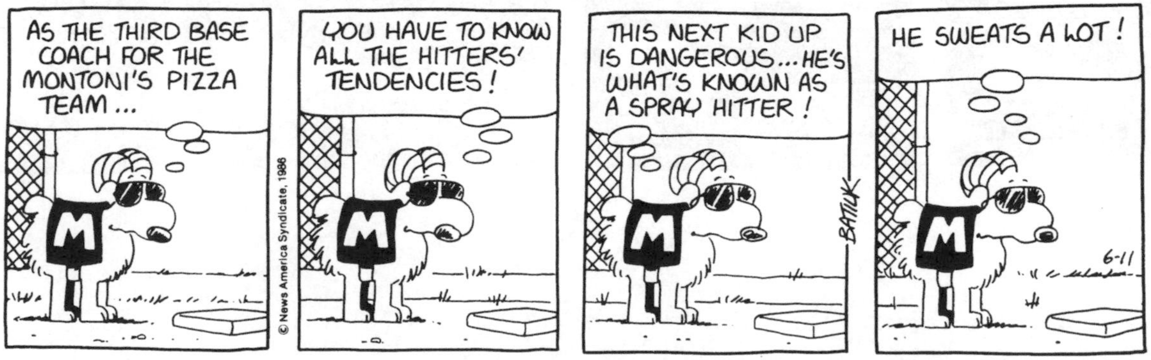
AS THE THIRD BASE COACH FOR THE MONTONI'S PIZZA TEAM...
M
© News America Syndicate, 1986
YOU HAVE TO KNOW ALL THE HITTERS' TENDENCIES!
M
THIS NEXT KID UP IS DANGEROUS... HE'S WHAT'S KNOWN AS A SPRAY HITTER!
M
BATIUK
HE SWEATS A LOT!
M
6-11

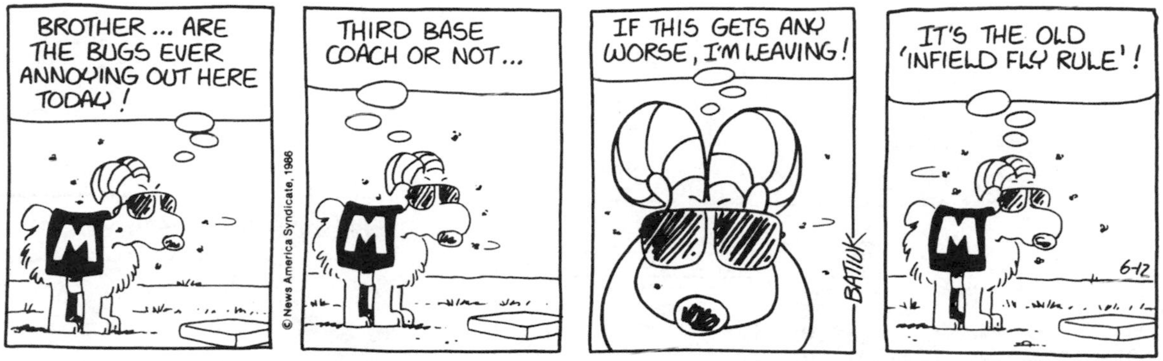
BROTHER ... ARE THE BUGS EVER ANNOYING OUT HERE TODAY!
THIRD BASE COACH OR NOT...
© News America Syndicate, 1986
IF THIS GETS ANY WORSE, I'M LEAVING!
BATIUK
IT'S THE OLD 'INFIELD FLY RULE'!
6-12

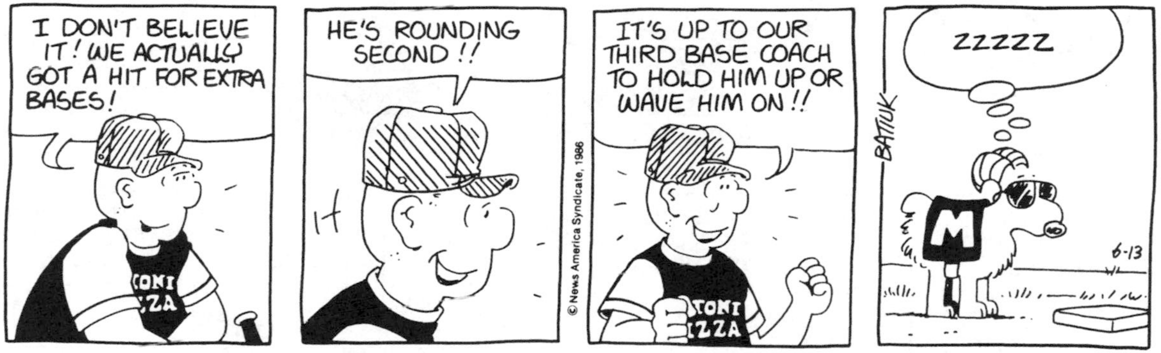
I DON'T BELIEVE IT! WE ACTUALLY GOT A HIT FOR EXTRA BASES!
HE'S ROUNDING SECOND!!
© News America Syndicate, 1986
IT'S UP TO OUR THIRD BASE COACH TO HOLD HIM UP OR WAVE HIM ON!!
BATIUK
ZZZZZ
6-13

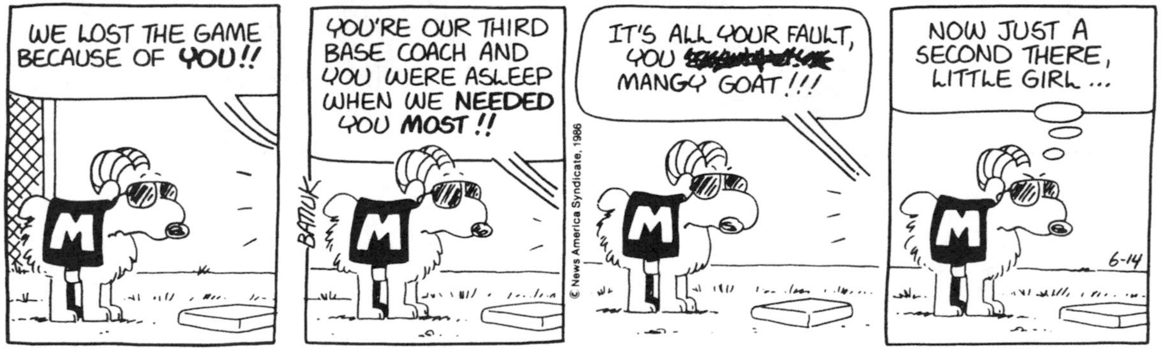
WE LOST THE GAME BECAUSE OF YOU!!
BATIUK
YOU'RE OUR THIRD BASE COACH AND YOU WERE ASLEEP WHEN WE NEEDED YOU MOST!!
© News America Syndicate, 1986
IT'S ALL YOUR FAULT, YOU [redacted] MANGY GOAT!!!
NOW JUST A SECOND THERE, LITTLE GIRL...
6-14

FUNKY WINKERBEAN
BY TOM BATIUK
SCAPEGOAT GAZETTE
DEAR WESTVIEW BAND ALUMNI...
TAP! TAP!
THOSE BAND ALUMNI CONTRIBUTING FIVE HUNDRED DOLLARS OR MORE...
TIP! TAP!
ARE ENTITLED TO RECEIVE ONE OF OUR BEAUTIFULLY LAMINATED EARLY AMERICAN ROCKERS!
TAP! TAP!
© News America Syndicate, 1986
BATIUK
SIMPLY INDICATE WHETHER YOU'D PREFER ELVIS PRESLEY, CHUCK BERRY OR LITTLE RICHARD!
TIP! TAP!
6-15

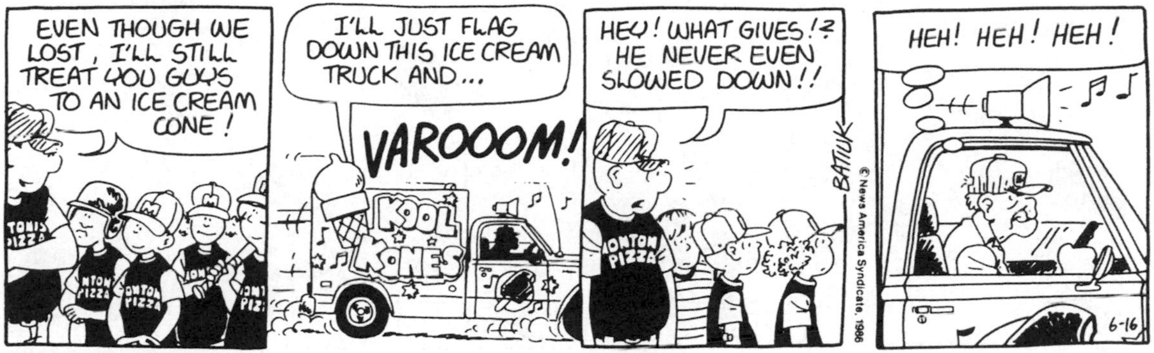
EVEN THOUGH WE LOST, I'LL STILL TREAT YOU GUYS TO AN ICE CREAM CONE!
TONI'S PIZZA
I'LL JUST FLAG DOWN THIS ICE CREAM TRUCK AND...
VAROOOM!
KOOL KONES
HEY! WHAT GIVES!? HE NEVER EVEN SLOWED DOWN!!
MONTON PIZZA
BATIUK
© News America Syndicate, 1986
HEH! HEH! HEH!
6-16

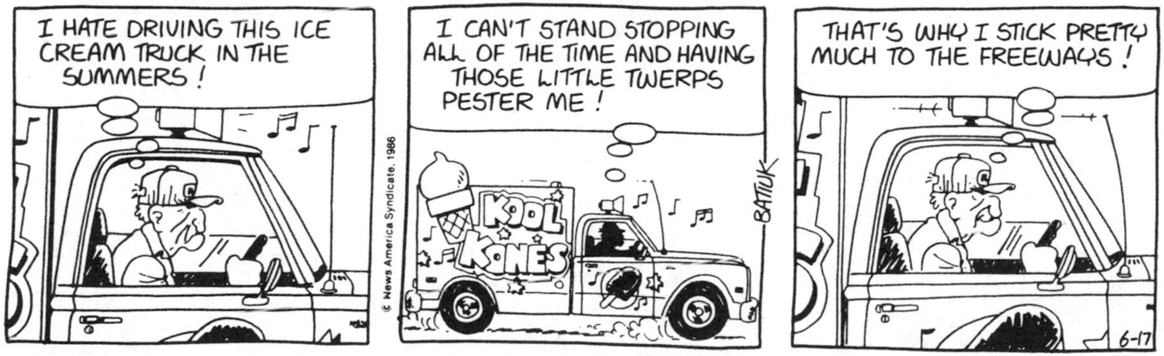
I HATE DRIVING THIS ICE CREAM TRUCK IN THE SUMMERS!
© News America Syndicate, 1986
I CAN'T STAND STOPPING ALL OF THE TIME AND HAVING THOSE LITTLE TWERPS PESTER ME!
KOOL KONES
BATIUK
THAT'S WHY I STICK PRETTY MUCH TO THE FREEWAYS!
6-17

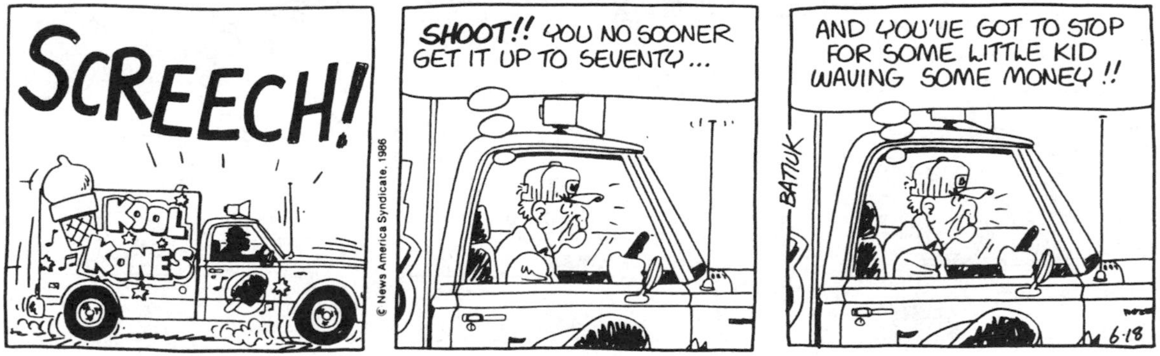
SCREECH!
KOOL KONES
© News America Syndicate, 1986
SHOOT!! YOU NO SOONER GET IT UP TO SEVENTY...
BATIUK
AND YOU'VE GOT TO STOP FOR SOME LITTLE KID WAVING SOME MONEY!!
6-18

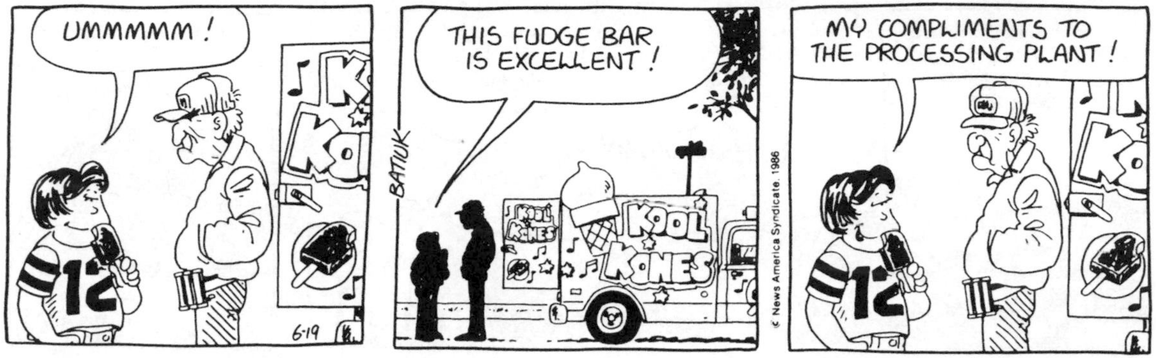
UMMMMM!
THIS FUDGE BAR IS EXCELLENT!
KOOL KONES
MY COMPLIMENTS TO THE PROCESSING PLANT!
BATIUK
6-19
© News America Syndicate, 1986

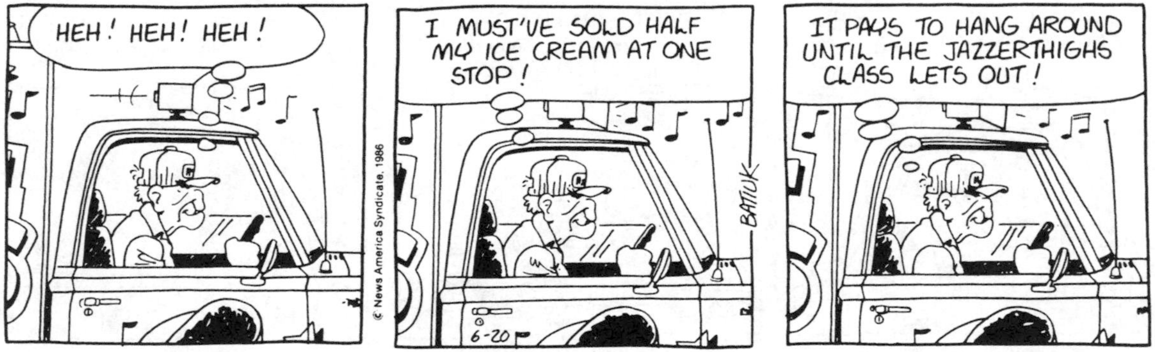
HEH! HEH! HEH!
I MUST'VE SOLD HALF MY ICE CREAM AT ONE STOP!
IT PAYS TO HANG AROUND UNTIL THE JAZZERTHIGHS CLASS LETS OUT!
BATIUK
6-20
© News America Syndicate, 1986

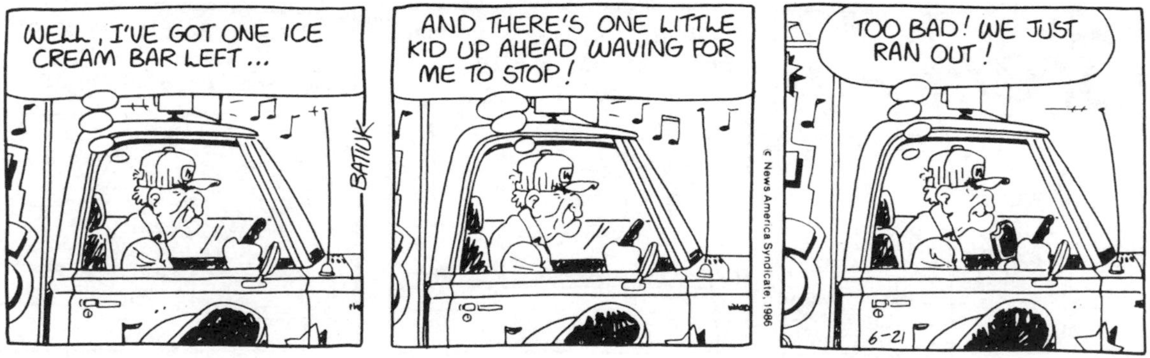
WELL, I'VE GOT ONE ICE CREAM BAR LEFT...
AND THERE'S ONE LITTLE KID UP AHEAD WAVING FOR ME TO STOP!
TOO BAD! WE JUST RAN OUT!
BATIUK
6-21
© News America Syndicate, 1986

FUNKY WINKERBEAN
BY TOM BATIUK
WONDER DOME PARKIN
SIGH ROCK 'N' ROLL HAS CHANGED!
I SUPPOSE IT WAS INEVITABLE!
THE 'STONES' WERE SPONSORED BY JOVAN, THE 'WHO' BY SCHLITZ, TOM PETTY BY LEVIS...
COULD DESIGNER ROCK CONCERTS BE FAR BEHIND...?
Calvin Klein
PRESENTS THE
GRETSCH BROS.
BATIUK
6-22
© News America Syndicate, 1986

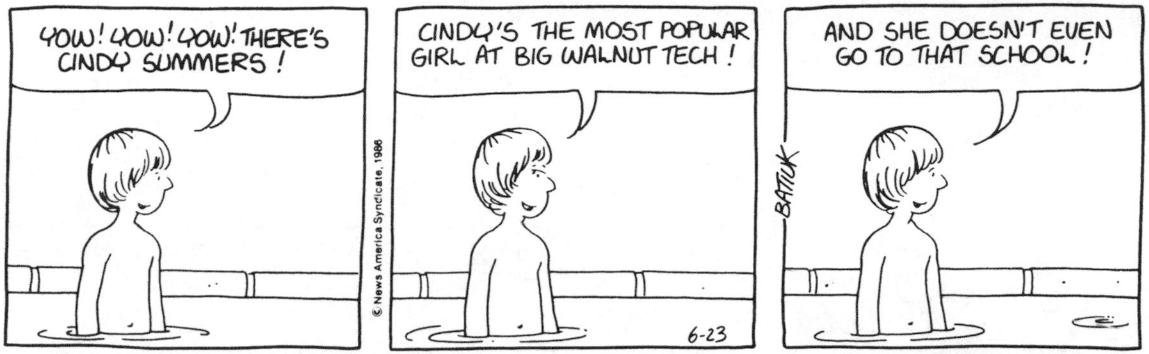
YOW! YOW! YOW! THERE'S CINDY SUMMERS!
CINDY'S THE MOST POPULAR GIRL AT BIG WALNUT TECH!
AND SHE DOESN'T EVEN GO TO THAT SCHOOL!
© News America Syndicate, 1986
BATIUK
6-23

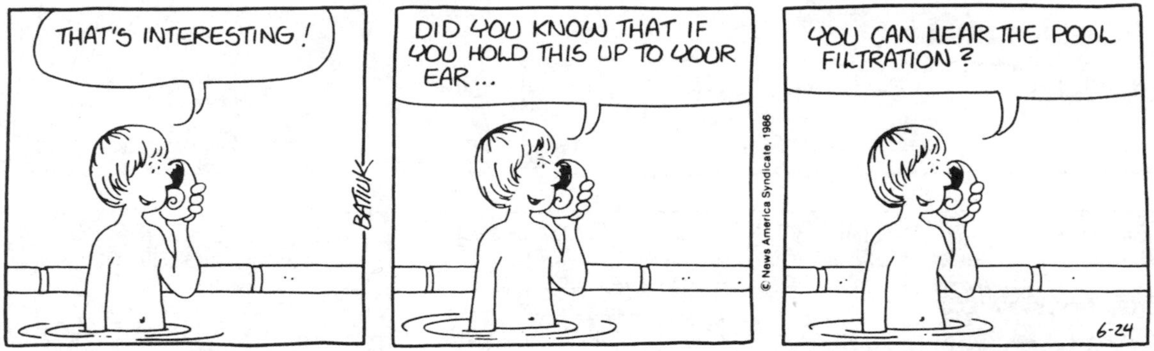
THAT'S INTERESTING!
DID YOU KNOW THAT IF YOU HOLD THIS UP TO YOUR EAR...
YOU CAN HEAR THE POOL FILTRATION?
BATIUK
© News America Syndicate, 1986
6-24

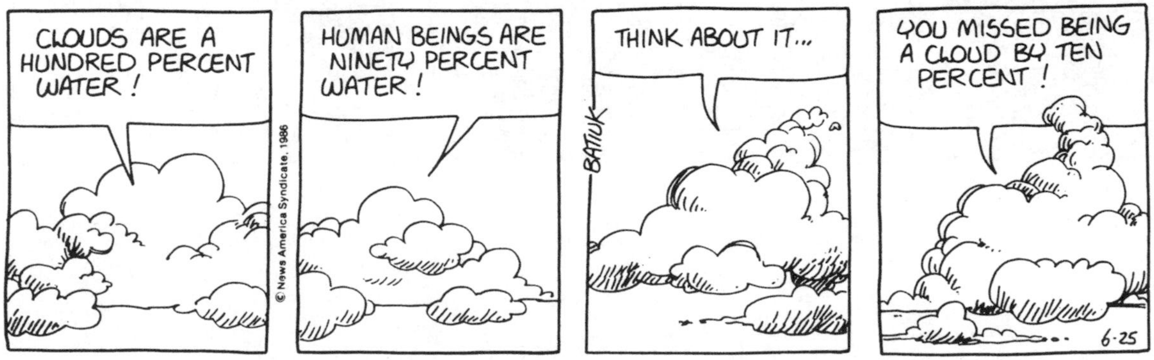
CLOUDS ARE A HUNDRED PERCENT WATER!
HUMAN BEINGS ARE NINETY PERCENT WATER!
THINK ABOUT IT...
YOU MISSED BEING A CLOUD BY TEN PERCENT!
© News America Syndicate, 1986
BATIUK
6-25

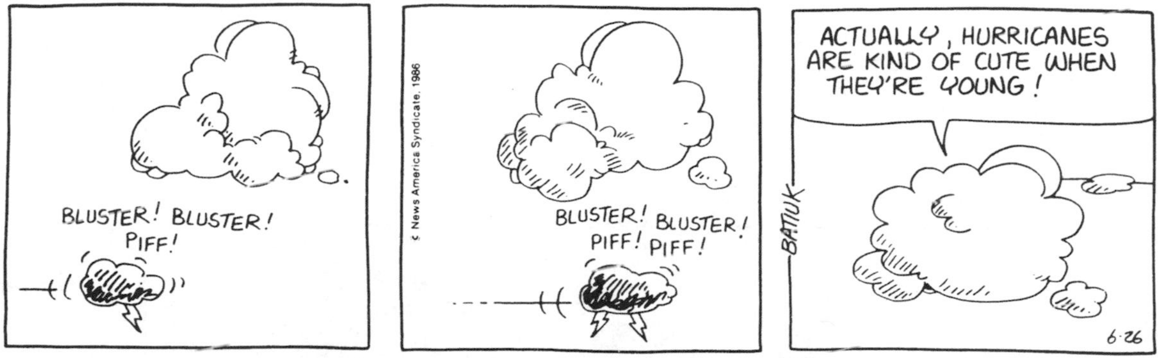
BLUSTER! BLUSTER!
PIFF!
© News America Syndicate. 1986
BLUSTER! BLUSTER!
PIFF! PIFF!
ACTUALLY, HURRICANES ARE KIND OF CUTE WHEN THEY'RE YOUNG!
BATIUK
6-26

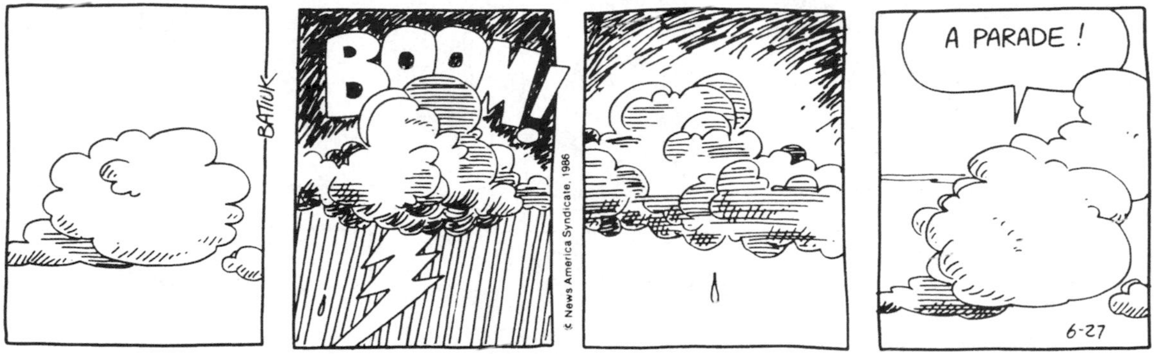
BATIUK
BOOM!
© News America Syndicate. 1986
A PARADE!
6-27

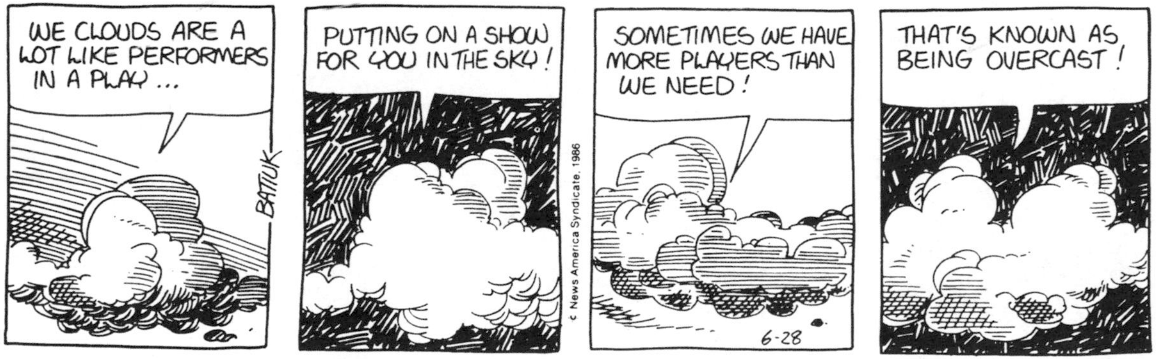
WE CLOUDS ARE A LOT LIKE PERFORMERS IN A PLAY ...
BATIUK
PUTTING ON A SHOW FOR YOU IN THE SKY!
© News America Syndicate. 1986
SOMETIMES WE HAVE MORE PLAYERS THAN WE NEED!
6-28
THAT'S KNOWN AS BEING OVERCAST!

FUNKY WINKERBEAN
BY TOM BATIUK
HEY! I DON'T REMEMBER GIVING ANYONE PERMISSION TO TALK!
YOU'VE GOT TO BE FIRM WITH THOSE BAND MOMS!
WHAT IN THE WORLD IS THAT FORMATION SUPPOSED TO BE?
© News America Syndicate, 1986
IT'S OUR 'SALUTE TO THE STATUE OF LIBERTY'...
HUDDLED MASSES!
BATIUK
6-29

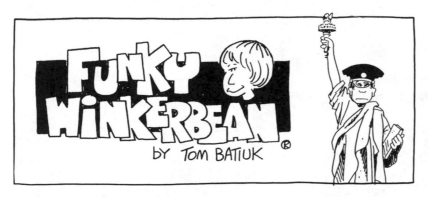

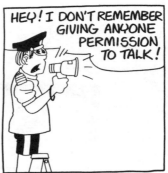

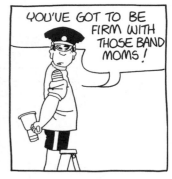

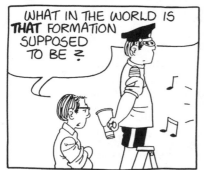

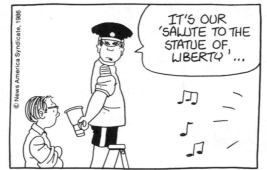

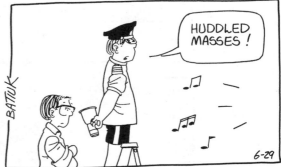

Panel 1: I'M SORRY, BUT THE DEMAND FROM THE MEDIA ALL OVER THE COUNTRY TO DO THEIR SHOWS LIVE AT THE STATUE OF LIBERTY IS SO GREAT, THAT WE JUST CAN'T ACCOMMODATE EVERYONE!

Panel 2: OKAY, WELL, HOW CLOSE CAN YOU GET US TO THE STATUE? 6-30

© News America Syndicate, 1986

Panel 3: IF YOU WERE TO LOOK THROUGH THE VIEWFINDER BEHIND ME... EMPIRE STA OBSERVATIO DECK

Panel 4: I'VE GOT SOME EXCITING NEWS, PEOPLE!

© News America Syndicate, 1986

Panel 5: THE WESTVIEW HIGH SCHOOL MARCHING SCAPEGOATS HAVE BEEN CHOSEN TO PERFORM FOR THE FOURTH OF JULY CELEBRATION IN NEW YORK CITY!

Panel 6: WHEN IS IT? BATIUK

Panel 7: AND PEOPLE WONDER WHY S.A.T. SCORES ARE DROPPING! 6-30

Panel 8: AND AS YOU CAN SEE FROM THESE LIVE SHOTS...

© News America Syndicate, 1986

Panel 9: THE STATUE OF LIBERTY HAS BEEN COMPLETELY REFURBISHED AND IS AS GOOD AS NEW! 7-1

BATIUK/SHAMRAY

Panel 10: CHINK!

417

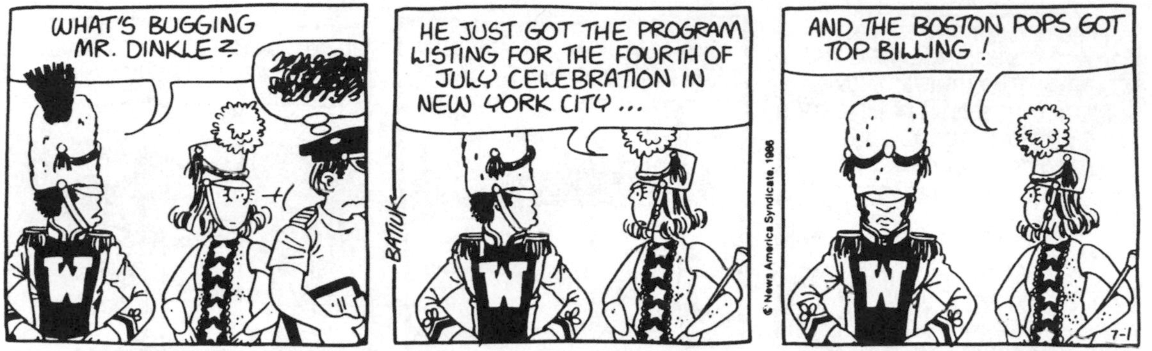
WHAT'S BUGGING MR. DINKLE?
BATIUK
HE JUST GOT THE PROGRAM LISTING FOR THE FOURTH OF JULY CELEBRATION IN NEW YORK CITY...
© News America Syndicate, 1986
AND THE BOSTON POPS GOT TOP BILLING!
7-1

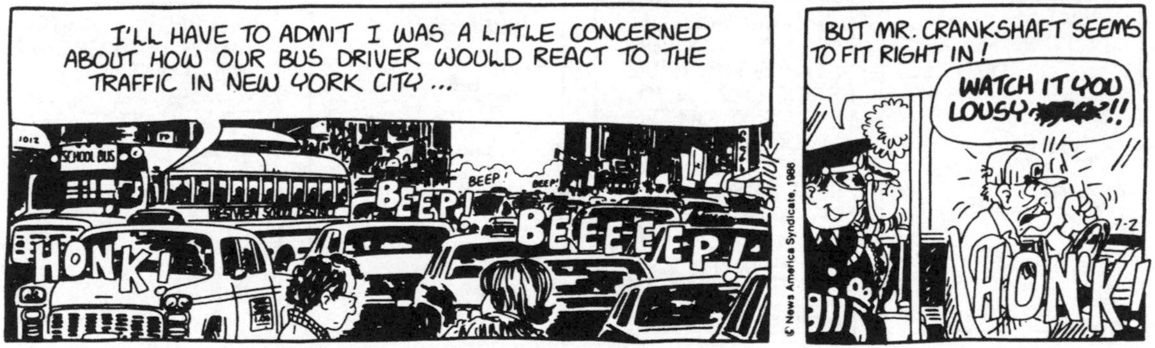
I'LL HAVE TO ADMIT I WAS A LITTLE CONCERNED ABOUT HOW OUR BUS DRIVER WOULD REACT TO THE TRAFFIC IN NEW YORK CITY...
SCHOOL BUS
BEEP!
BEEP!
BEEP!
BEEEEEP!
HONK!
BATIUK
© News America Syndicate, 1986
BUT MR. CRANKSHAFT SEEMS TO FIT RIGHT IN!
WATCH IT YOU LOUSY !!
7-2
HONK!

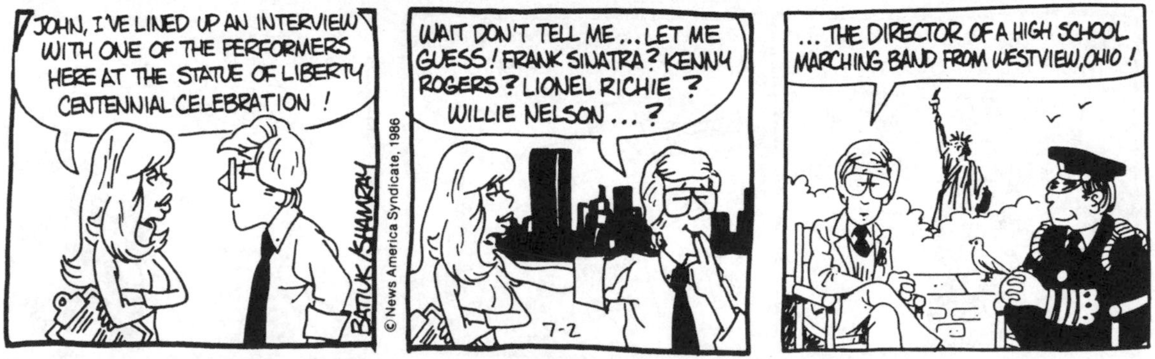
JOHN, I'VE LINED UP AN INTERVIEW WITH ONE OF THE PERFORMERS HERE AT THE STATUE OF LIBERTY CENTENNIAL CELEBRATION!
BATIUK/SHAMRAY
© News America Syndicate, 1986
WAIT DON'T TELL ME... LET ME GUESS! FRANK SINATRA? KENNY ROGERS? LIONEL RICHIE? WILLIE NELSON...?
7-2
...THE DIRECTOR OF A HIGH SCHOOL MARCHING BAND FROM WESTVIEW, OHIO!

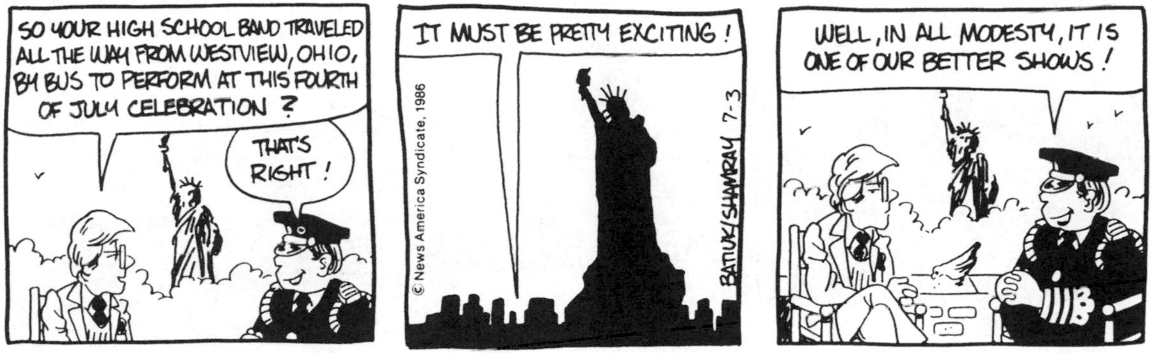
SO YOUR HIGH SCHOOL BAND TRAVELED ALL THE WAY FROM WESTVIEW, OHIO, BY BUS TO PERFORM AT THIS FOURTH OF JULY CELEBRATION ?
THAT'S RIGHT !
IT MUST BE PRETTY EXCITING !
© News America Syndicate, 1986
BATIUK/SHAMRAY 7-3
WELL, IN ALL MODESTY, IT IS ONE OF OUR BETTER SHOWS !

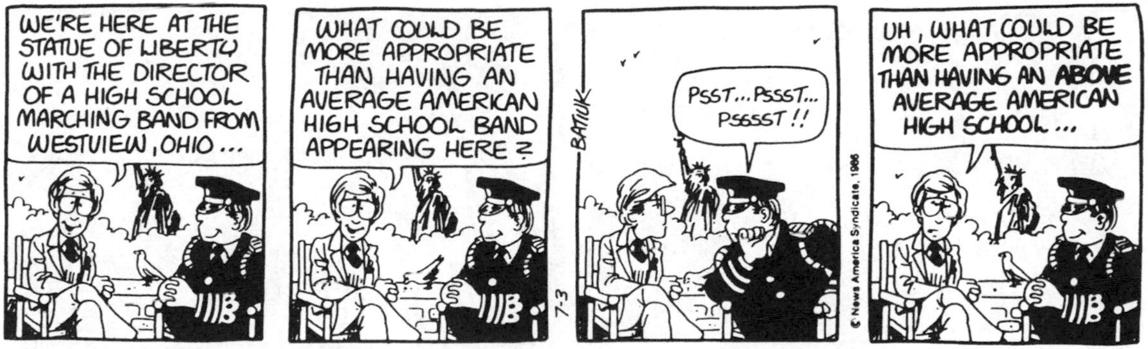
WE'RE HERE AT THE STATUE OF LIBERTY WITH THE DIRECTOR OF A HIGH SCHOOL MARCHING BAND FROM WESTVIEW, OHIO ...
WHAT COULD BE MORE APPROPRIATE THAN HAVING AN AVERAGE AMERICAN HIGH SCHOOL BAND APPEARING HERE ?
BATIUK 7-3
PSST... PSSST... PSSSST !!
© News America Syndicate, 1986
UH, WHAT COULD BE MORE APPROPRIATE THAN HAVING AN **ABOVE** AVERAGE AMERICAN HIGH SCHOOL ...

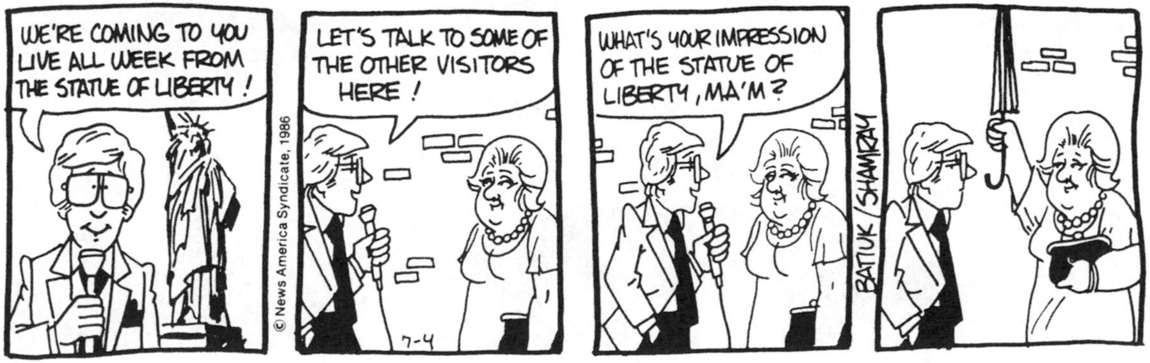
WE'RE COMING TO YOU LIVE ALL WEEK FROM THE STATUE OF LIBERTY !
© News America Syndicate, 1986
LET'S TALK TO SOME OF THE OTHER VISITORS HERE !
7-4
WHAT'S YOUR IMPRESSION OF THE STATUE OF LIBERTY, MA'M ?
BATIUK/SHAMRAY

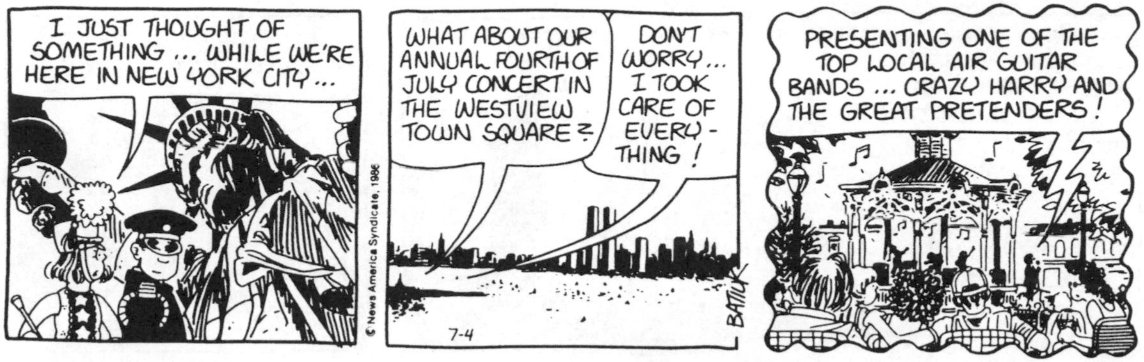
I JUST THOUGHT OF SOMETHING ... WHILE WE'RE HERE IN NEW YORK CITY ...
© News America Syndicate, 1986
WHAT ABOUT OUR ANNUAL FOURTH OF JULY CONCERT IN THE WESTVIEW TOWN SQUARE ?
DON'T WORRY ... I TOOK CARE OF EVERY-THING !
7-4
BATIUK
PRESENTING ONE OF THE TOP LOCAL AIR GUITAR BANDS ... CRAZY HARRY AND THE GREAT PRETENDERS !

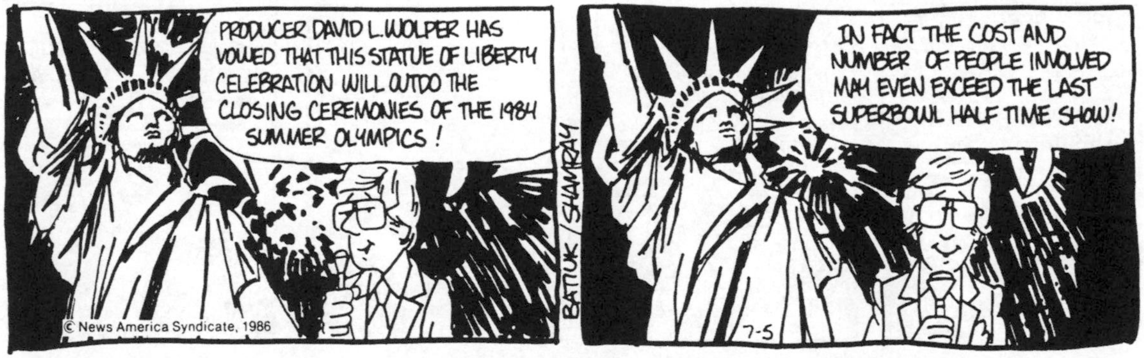
PRODUCER DAVID L. WOLPER HAS VOWED THAT THIS STATUE OF LIBERTY CELEBRATION WILL OUTDO THE CLOSING CEREMONIES OF THE 1984 SUMMER OLYMPICS !
© News America Syndicate, 1986
BATIUK / SHAMRAY
IN FACT THE COST AND NUMBER OF PEOPLE INVOLVED MAY EVEN EXCEED THE LAST SUPERBOWL HALF TIME SHOW!
7-5

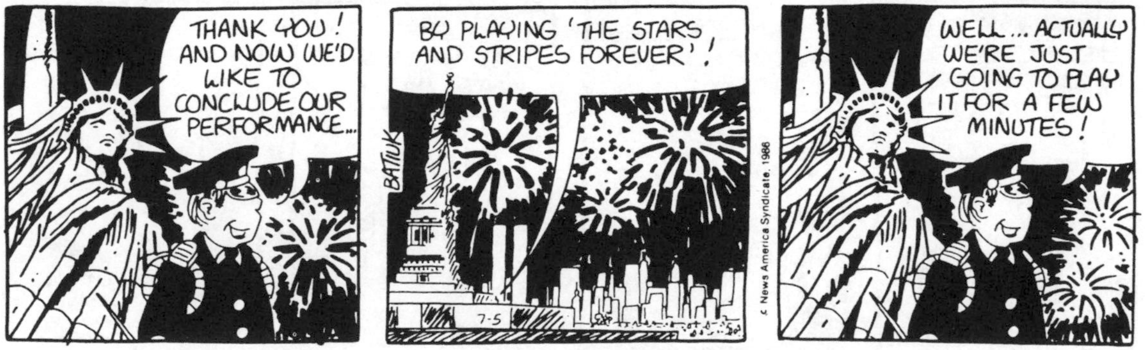
THANK YOU ! AND NOW WE'D LIKE TO CONCLUDE OUR PERFORMANCE...
BATIUK
BY PLAYING 'THE STARS AND STRIPES FOREVER' !
7-5
© News America Syndicate, 1986
WELL ... ACTUALLY WE'RE JUST GOING TO PLAY IT FOR A FEW MINUTES !

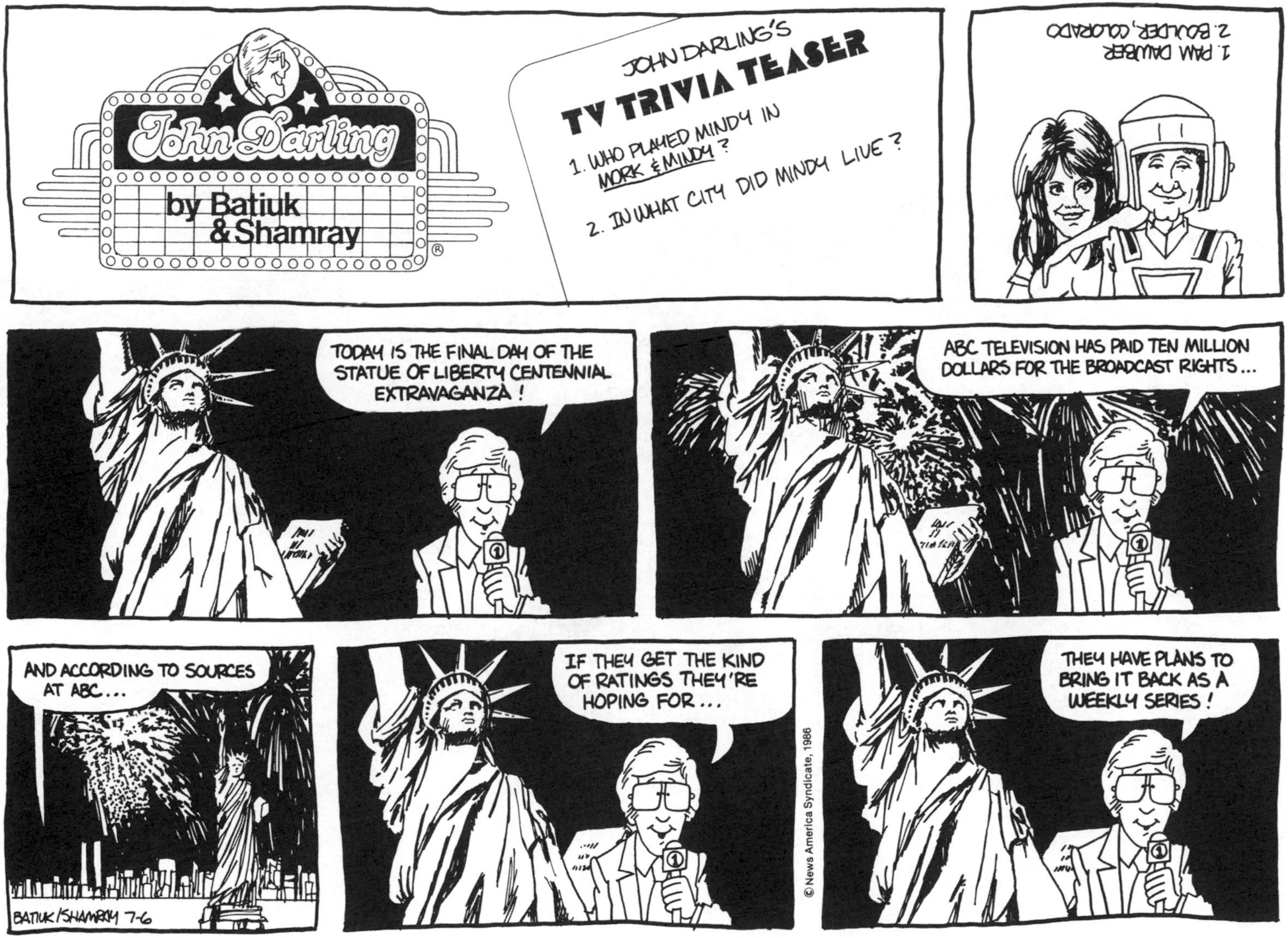
John Darling
by Batiuk & Shamray
JOHN DARLING'S
TV TRIVIA TEASER
1. WHO PLAYED MINDY IN MORK & MINDY ?
2. IN WHAT CITY DID MINDY LIVE ?
1. PAM DAWBER
2. BOULDER, COLORADO
TODAY IS THE FINAL DAY OF THE STATUE OF LIBERTY CENTENNIAL EXTRAVAGANZA !
ABC TELEVISION HAS PAID TEN MILLION DOLLARS FOR THE BROADCAST RIGHTS ...
AND ACCORDING TO SOURCES AT ABC ...
BATIUK/SHAMRAY 7-6
IF THEY GET THE KIND OF RATINGS THEY'RE HOPING FOR ...
© News America Syndicate, 1986
THEY HAVE PLANS TO BRING IT BACK AS A WEEKLY SERIES !

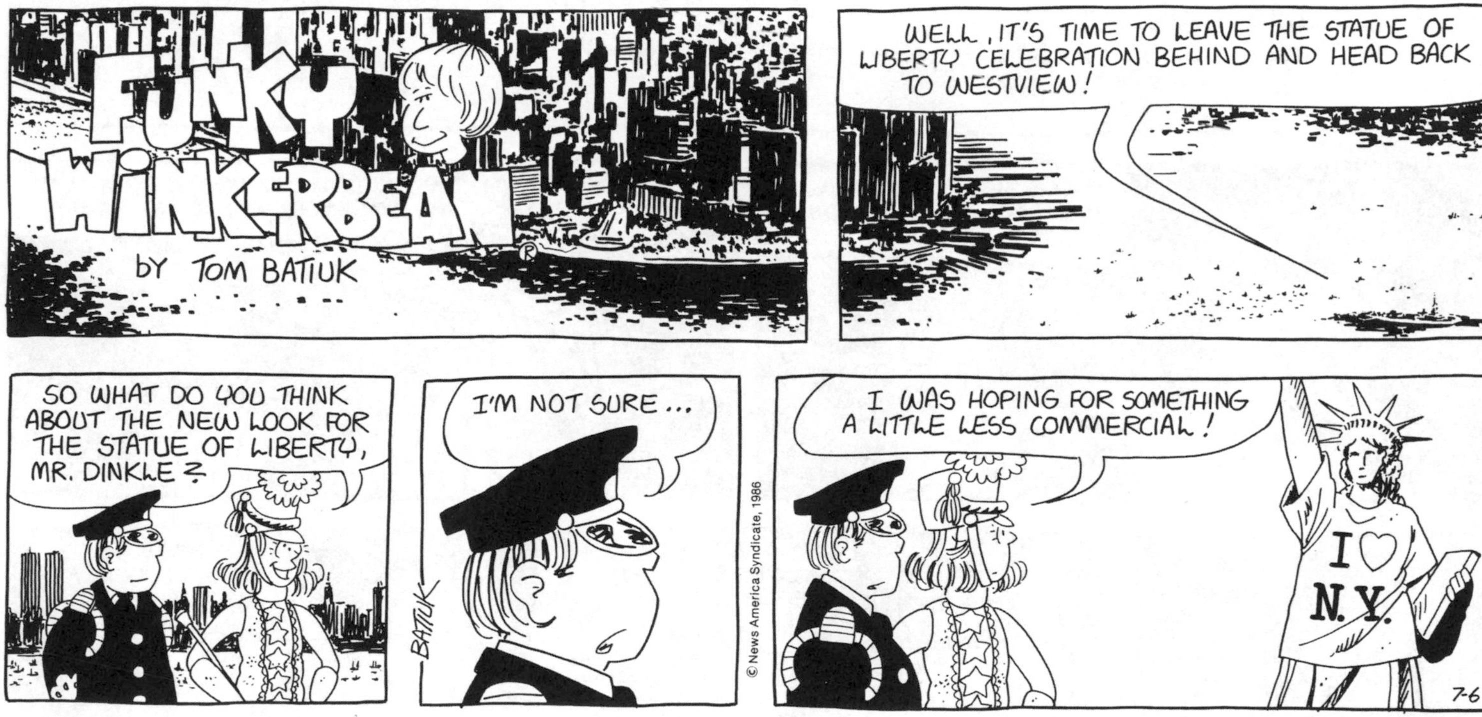
FUNKY WINKERBEAN
BY TOM BATIUK
WELL, IT'S TIME TO LEAVE THE STATUE OF LIBERTY CELEBRATION BEHIND AND HEAD BACK TO WESTVIEW!
SO WHAT DO YOU THINK ABOUT THE NEW LOOK FOR THE STATUE OF LIBERTY, MR. DINKLE?
BATIUK
I'M NOT SURE...
© News America Syndicate, 1986
I WAS HOPING FOR SOMETHING A LITTLE LESS COMMERCIAL!
I ♥ N.Y.
7-6

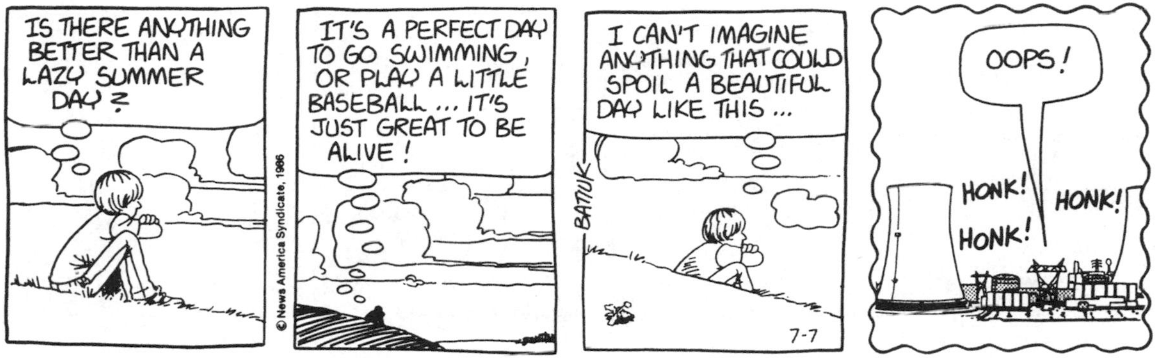
IS THERE ANYTHING BETTER THAN A LAZY SUMMER DAY ?
© News America Syndicate, 1986
IT'S A PERFECT DAY TO GO SWIMMING, OR PLAY A LITTLE BASEBALL ... IT'S JUST GREAT TO BE ALIVE!
BATIUK
I CAN'T IMAGINE ANYTHING THAT COULD SPOIL A BEAUTIFUL DAY LIKE THIS ...
7-7
OOPS!
HONK!
HONK!
HONK!

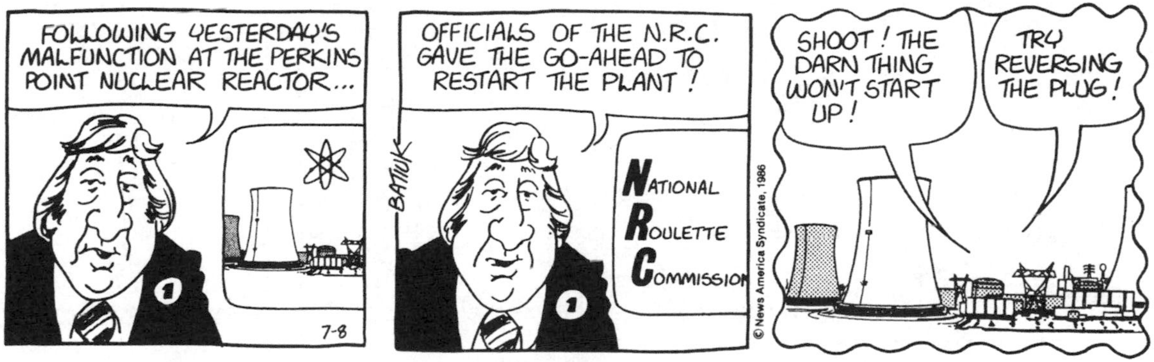
FOLLOWING YESTERDAY'S MALFUNCTION AT THE PERKINS POINT NUCLEAR REACTOR...
7-8
BATIUK
OFFICIALS OF THE N.R.C. GAVE THE GO-AHEAD TO RESTART THE PLANT!
NATIONAL
ROULETTE
COMMISSION
© News America Syndicate, 1986
SHOOT! THE DARN THING WON'T START UP!
TRY REVERSING THE PLUG!

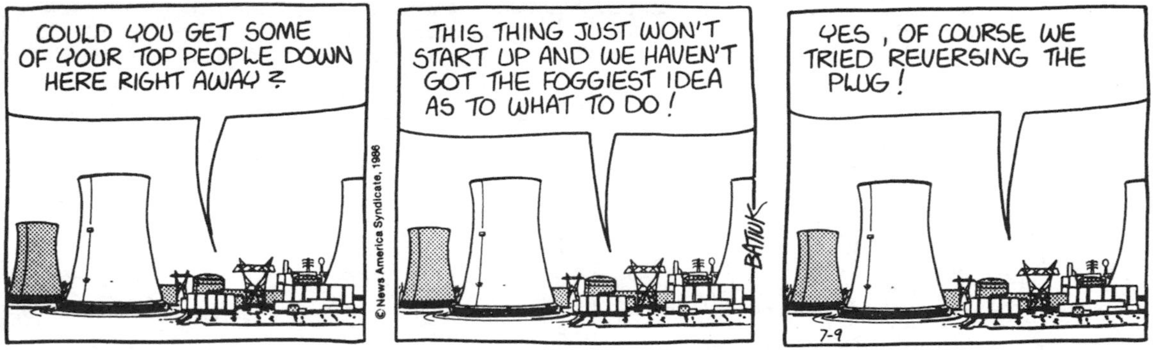
COULD YOU GET SOME OF YOUR TOP PEOPLE DOWN HERE RIGHT AWAY ?
© News America Syndicate, 1986
THIS THING JUST WON'T START UP AND WE HAVEN'T GOT THE FOGGIEST IDEA AS TO WHAT TO DO!
BATIUK
YES, OF COURSE WE TRIED REVERSING THE PLUG!
7-9

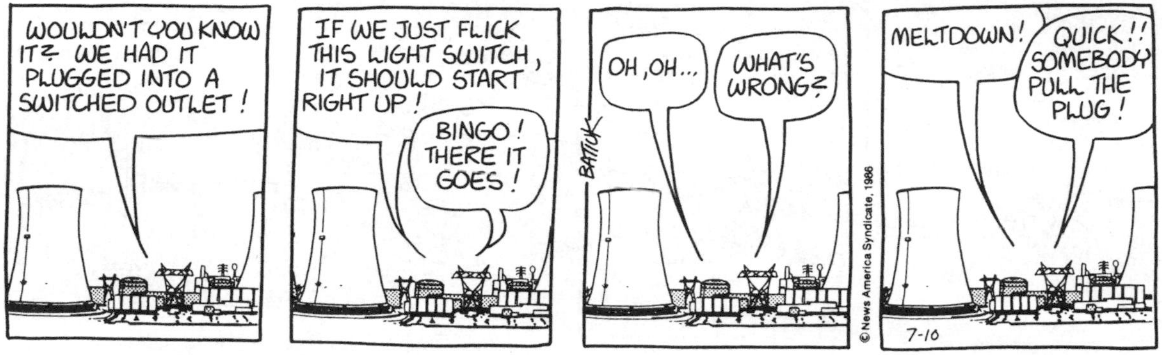
WOULDN'T YOU KNOW IT? WE HAD IT PLUGGED INTO A SWITCHED OUTLET!
IF WE JUST FLICK THIS LIGHT SWITCH, IT SHOULD START RIGHT UP!
BINGO! THERE IT GOES!
BATIUK
OH, OH...
WHAT'S WRONG?
© News America Syndicate, 1986
MELTDOWN!
QUICK!! SOMEBODY PULL THE PLUG!
7-10

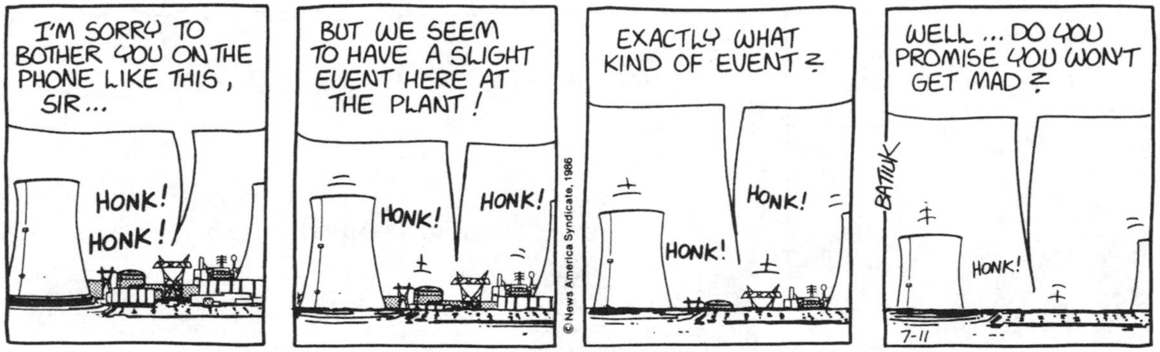
I'M SORRY TO BOTHER YOU ON THE PHONE LIKE THIS, SIR...
HONK!
HONK!
BUT WE SEEM TO HAVE A SLIGHT EVENT HERE AT THE PLANT!
HONK!
HONK!
© News America Syndicate, 1986
EXACTLY WHAT KIND OF EVENT?
HONK!
HONK!
BATIUK
WELL ... DO YOU PROMISE YOU WON'T GET MAD?
HONK!
7-11

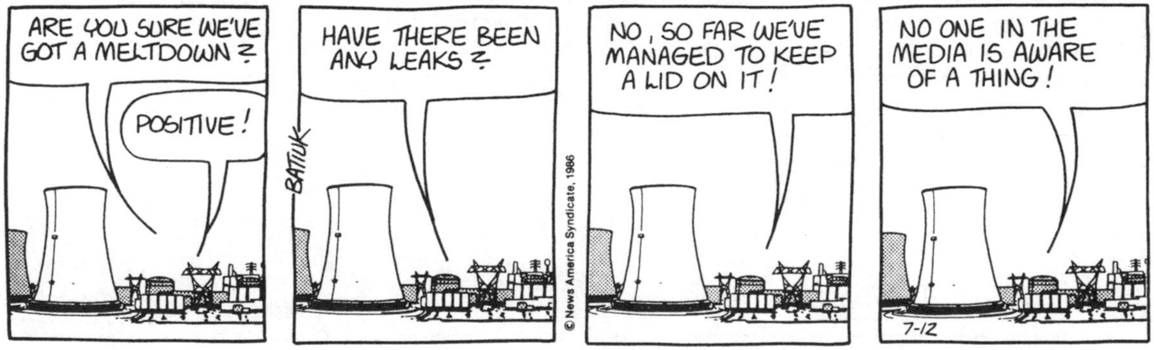
ARE YOU SURE WE'VE GOT A MELTDOWN?
POSITIVE!
BATIUK
HAVE THERE BEEN ANY LEAKS?
© News America Syndicate, 1986
NO, SO FAR WE'VE MANAGED TO KEEP A LID ON IT!
NO ONE IN THE MEDIA IS AWARE OF A THING!
7-12

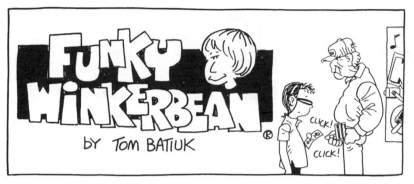

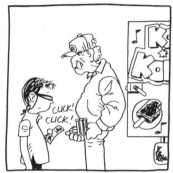

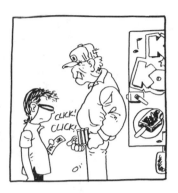

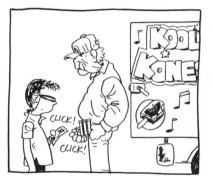

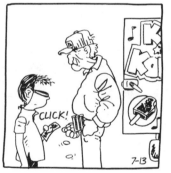

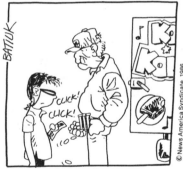

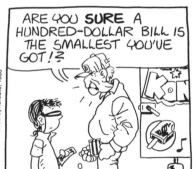

FUNKY WINKERBEAN
by TOM BATIUK
CLICK!
CLICK!
CLICK!
CLICK!
CLICK!
CLICK!
CLICK!
CLICK!
CLICK!
7-13
BATIUK
CLICK!
CLICK!
© News America Syndicate, 1986
ARE YOU **SURE** A HUNDRED-DOLLAR BILL IS THE SMALLEST YOU'VE GOT!?

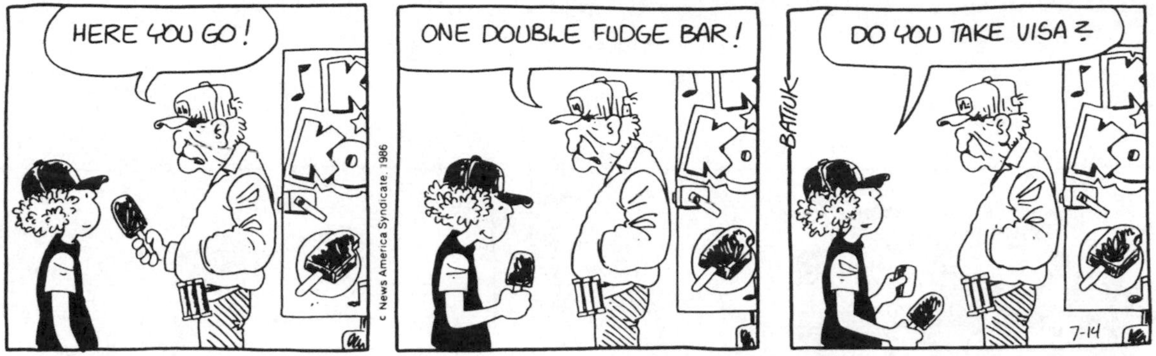
HERE YOU GO!
ONE DOUBLE FUDGE BAR!
DO YOU TAKE VISA?
© News America Syndicate, 1986
BATIUK
7-14

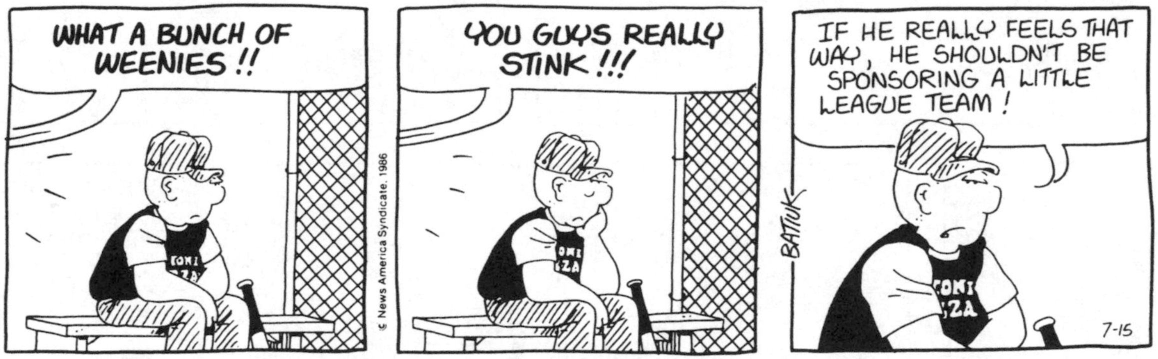
WHAT A BUNCH OF WEENIES!!
YOU GUYS REALLY STINK!!!
IF HE REALLY FEELS THAT WAY, HE SHOULDN'T BE SPONSORING A LITTLE LEAGUE TEAM!
© News America Syndicate, 1986
BATIUK
7-15

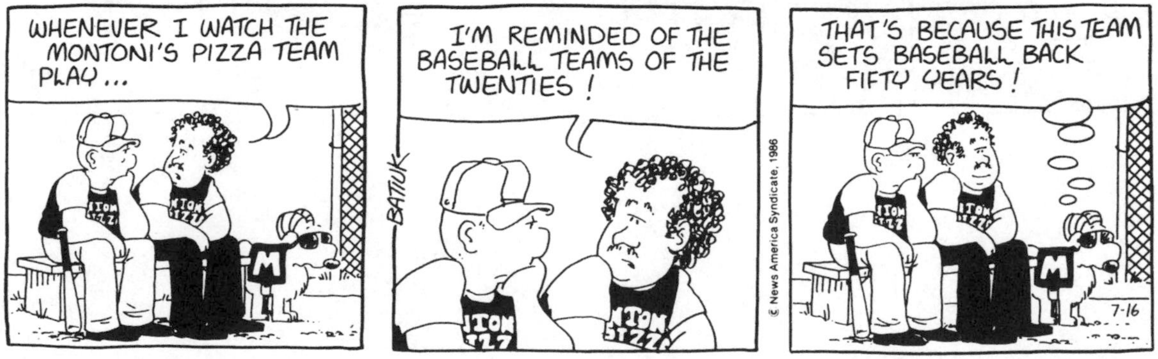
WHENEVER I WATCH THE MONTONI'S PIZZA TEAM PLAY...
I'M REMINDED OF THE BASEBALL TEAMS OF THE TWENTIES!
THAT'S BECAUSE THIS TEAM SETS BASEBALL BACK FIFTY YEARS!
© News America Syndicate, 1986
BATIUK
7-16

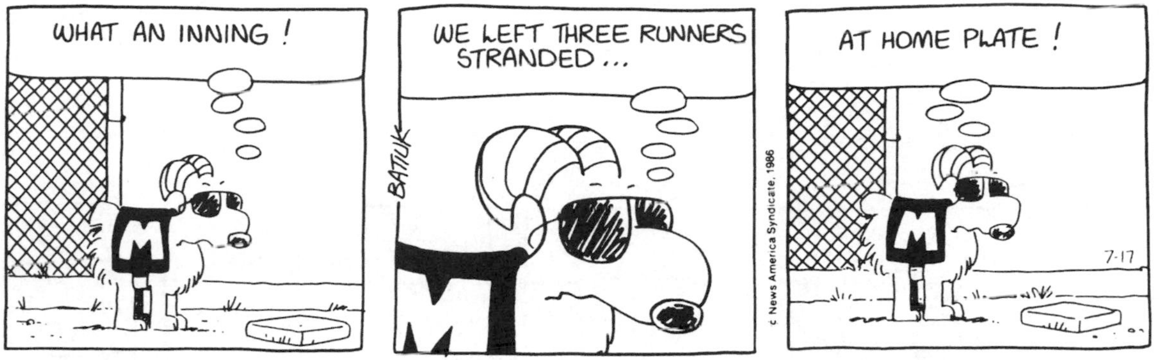
WHAT AN INNING !
WE LEFT THREE RUNNERS STRANDED ...
BATIUK
AT HOME PLATE !
c News America Syndicate, 1986
7-17

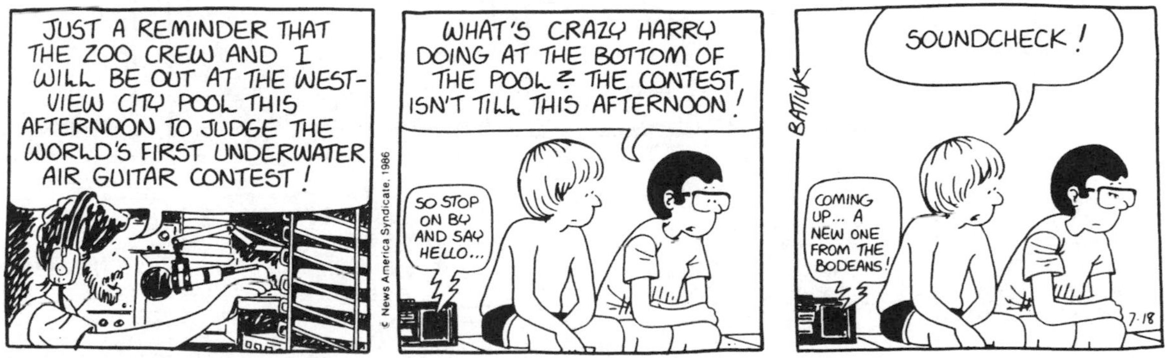
JUST A REMINDER THAT THE ZOO CREW AND I WILL BE OUT AT THE WEST-VIEW CITY POOL THIS AFTERNOON TO JUDGE THE WORLD'S FIRST UNDERWATER AIR GUITAR CONTEST !
c News America Syndicate, 1986
WHAT'S CRAZY HARRY DOING AT THE BOTTOM OF THE POOL ? THE CONTEST ISN'T TILL THIS AFTERNOON !
SO STOP ON BY AND SAY HELLO...
BATIUK
SOUNDCHECK !
COMING UP... A NEW ONE FROM THE BODEANS !
7-18

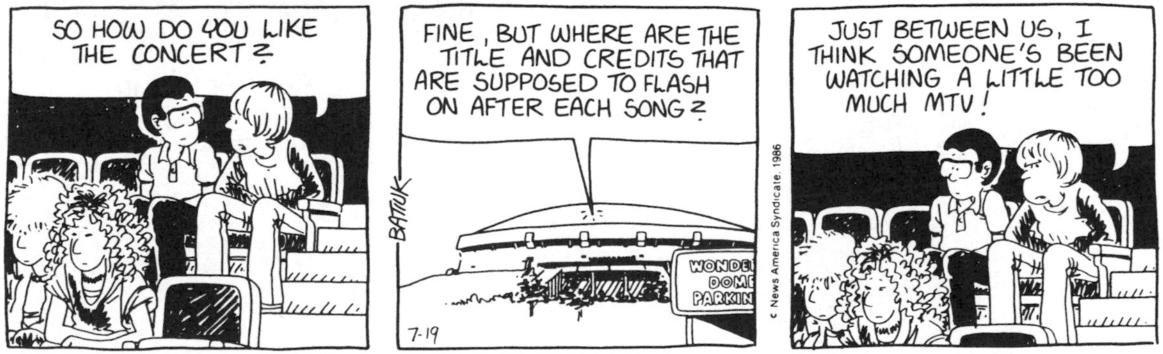
SO HOW DO YOU LIKE THE CONCERT ?
BATIUK
FINE, BUT WHERE ARE THE TITLE AND CREDITS THAT ARE SUPPOSED TO FLASH ON AFTER EACH SONG ?
WONDE
DOME
PARKIN
7-19
c News America Syndicate, 1986
JUST BETWEEN US, I THINK SOMEONE'S BEEN WATCHING A LITTLE TOO MUCH MTV !

Funky Winkerbean

BY TOM BATIUK

SKREEEK!!

WE'LL START THE (SKREEEK!!) PRESS CONFERENCE ...

AS SOON AS WE CAN (SKREEEK!!) FIGURE OUT HOW TO WORK THE MICROPHONE HERE ...

WE CALLED THIS PRESS CONFERENCE, HERE AT THE PERKINS POINT REACTOR, TO REASSURE YOU ABOUT OUR STRONG COMMITMENT TO SAFETY!

WITH THE TYPE OF CONTAINMENT WE HAVE RADIATION LEAKAGE IS VIRTUALLY IMPOSSIBLE!

YES! A QUESTION IN THE BACK...

DO YOU HAVE ANY EXPLANATION FOR THE SIX-HUNDRED-FOOT DANDELION?

WHERE?

7-20

BATIUK

© News America Syndicate, 1986

428

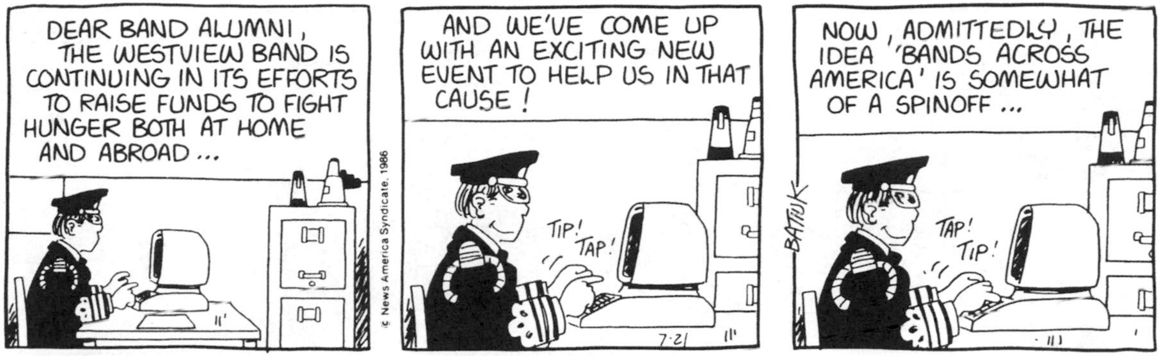
DEAR BAND ALUMNI, THE WESTVIEW BAND IS CONTINUING IN ITS EFFORTS TO RAISE FUNDS TO FIGHT HUNGER BOTH AT HOME AND ABROAD ...
© News America Syndicate. 1986
AND WE'VE COME UP WITH AN EXCITING NEW EVENT TO HELP US IN THAT CAUSE !
TIP! TAP!
7-21
NOW, ADMITTEDLY, THE IDEA 'BANDS ACROSS AMERICA' IS SOMEWHAT OF A SPINOFF ...
BATIUK
TAP! TIP!

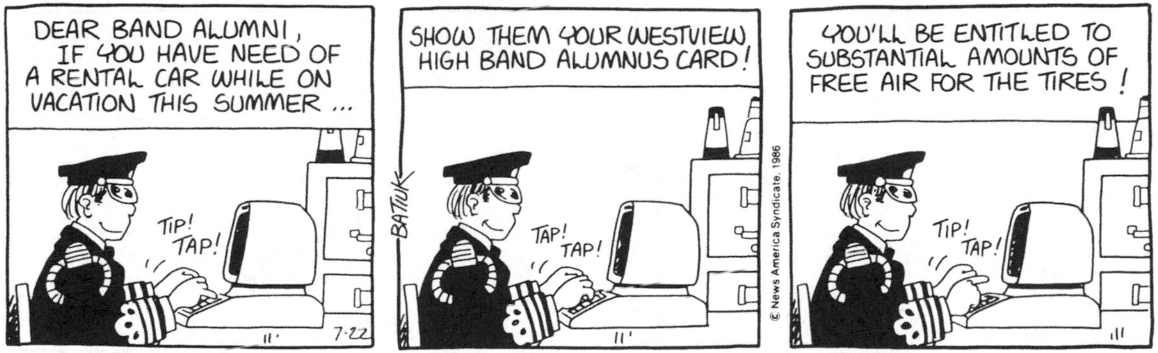
DEAR BAND ALUMNI, IF YOU HAVE NEED OF A RENTAL CAR WHILE ON VACATION THIS SUMMER ...
TIP! TAP!
7-22
BATIUK
SHOW THEM YOUR WESTVIEW HIGH BAND ALUMNUS CARD!
TAP! TAP!
© News America Syndicate. 1986
YOU'LL BE ENTITLED TO SUBSTANTIAL AMOUNTS OF FREE AIR FOR THE TIRES !
TIP! TAP!

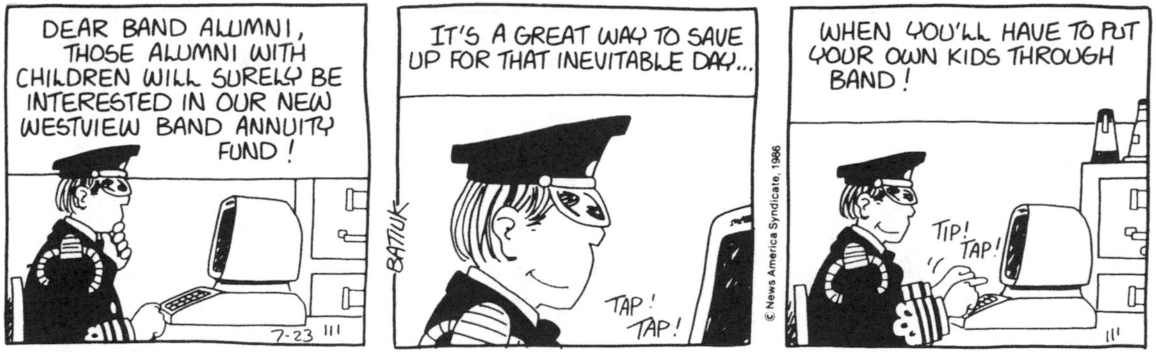
DEAR BAND ALUMNI, THOSE ALUMNI WITH CHILDREN WILL SURELY BE INTERESTED IN OUR NEW WESTVIEW BAND ANNUITY FUND !
7-23
BATIUK
IT'S A GREAT WAY TO SAVE UP FOR THAT INEVITABLE DAY...
TAP! TAP!
© News America Syndicate. 1986
WHEN YOU'LL HAVE TO PUT YOUR OWN KIDS THROUGH BAND !
TIP! TAP!

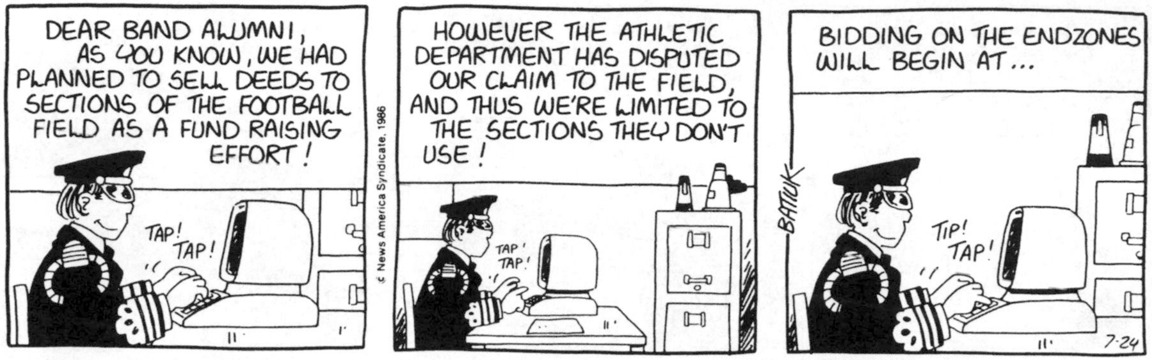
DEAR BAND ALUMNI,
AS YOU KNOW, WE HAD PLANNED TO SELL DEEDS TO SECTIONS OF THE FOOTBALL FIELD AS A FUND RAISING EFFORT!
TAP! TAP!
HOWEVER THE ATHLETIC DEPARTMENT HAS DISPUTED OUR CLAIM TO THE FIELD, AND THUS WE'RE LIMITED TO THE SECTIONS THEY DON'T USE!
TAP! TAP!
BIDDING ON THE ENDZONES WILL BEGIN AT...
TIP! TAP!
© News America Syndicate, 1986
BATIUK
7-24

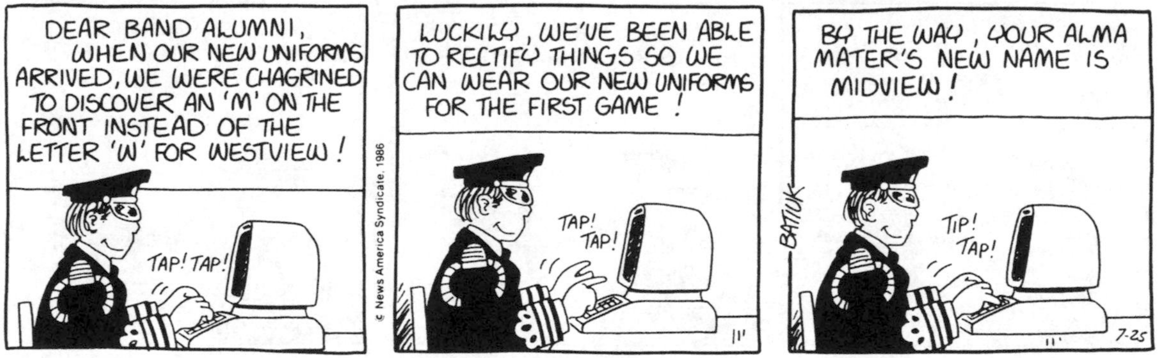
DEAR BAND ALUMNI,
WHEN OUR NEW UNIFORMS ARRIVED, WE WERE CHAGRINED TO DISCOVER AN 'M' ON THE FRONT INSTEAD OF THE LETTER 'W' FOR WESTVIEW!
TAP! TAP!
LUCKILY, WE'VE BEEN ABLE TO RECTIFY THINGS SO WE CAN WEAR OUR NEW UNIFORMS FOR THE FIRST GAME!
TAP! TAP!
BY THE WAY, YOUR ALMA MATER'S NEW NAME IS MIDVIEW!
TIP! TAP!
© News America Syndicate, 1986
BATIUK
7-25

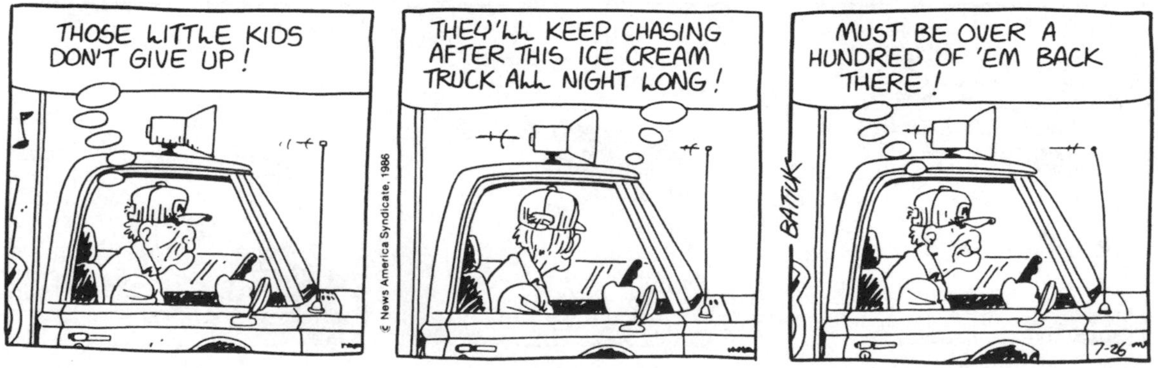
THOSE LITTLE KIDS DON'T GIVE UP!
THEY'LL KEEP CHASING AFTER THIS ICE CREAM TRUCK ALL NIGHT LONG!
MUST BE OVER A HUNDRED OF 'EM BACK THERE!
© News America Syndicate, 1986
BATIUK
7-26

FUNKY WINKERBEAN
I LOVE A CONCERT IN THE PARK ON A SUMMER EVENING! THERE'S JUST SOMETHING IN THE AIR!
YEAH, THEY'RE CALLED MOSQUITOES!
HOW DISAPPOINTING...!
NO ONE SEEMED TO JOIN IN ON THAT LAST SING-A-LONG!
THEN AGAIN, MAYBE THE DEATH SCENE FROM 'LA TRAVIATA' WASN'T THE BEST CHOICE OF MATERIAL!
© News America Syndicate, 1986
7-27
BATIUK

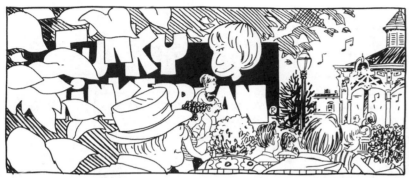

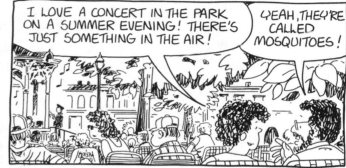

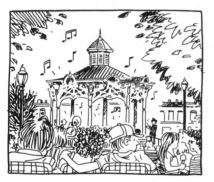

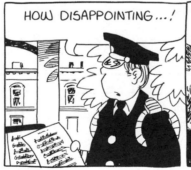

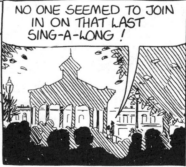

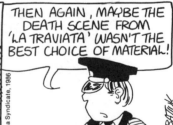

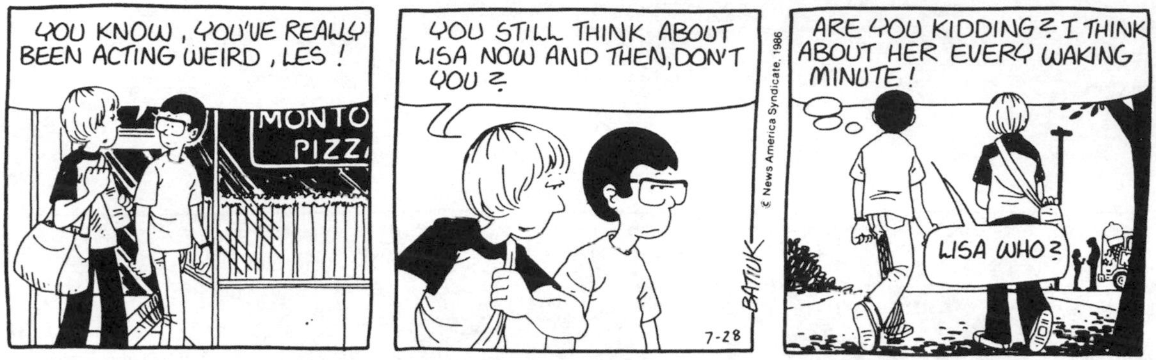
YOU KNOW, YOU'VE REALLY BEEN ACTING WEIRD, LES!
MONTO PIZZ
YOU STILL THINK ABOUT LISA NOW AND THEN, DON'T YOU?
BATIUK
7-28
© News America Syndicate, 1986
ARE YOU KIDDING? I THINK ABOUT HER EVERY WAKING MINUTE!
LISA WHO?

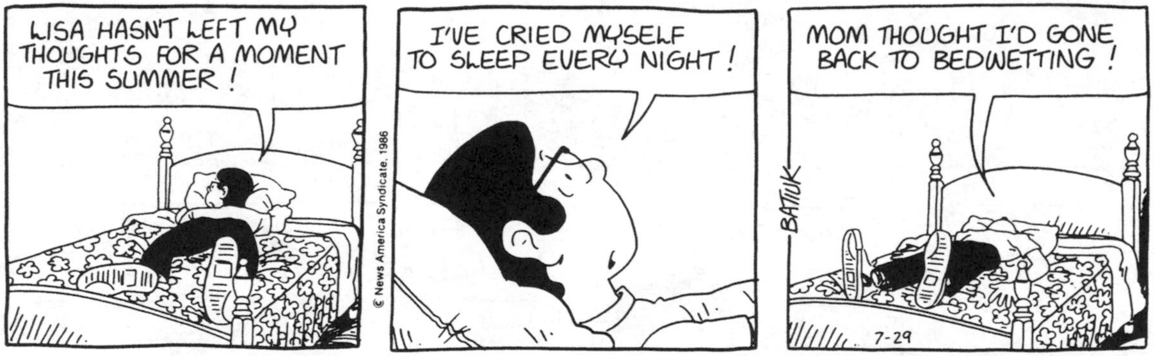
LISA HASN'T LEFT MY THOUGHTS FOR A MOMENT THIS SUMMER!
© News America Syndicate, 1986
I'VE CRIED MYSELF TO SLEEP EVERY NIGHT!
BATIUK
MOM THOUGHT I'D GONE BACK TO BEDWETTING!
7-29

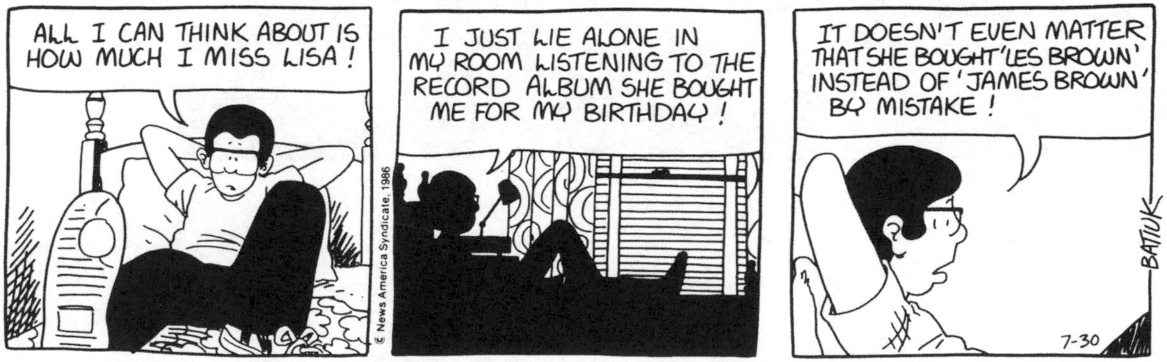
ALL I CAN THINK ABOUT IS HOW MUCH I MISS LISA!
© News America Syndicate, 1986
I JUST LIE ALONE IN MY ROOM LISTENING TO THE RECORD ALBUM SHE BOUGHT ME FOR MY BIRTHDAY!
IT DOESN'T EVEN MATTER THAT SHE BOUGHT 'LES BROWN' INSTEAD OF 'JAMES BROWN' BY MISTAKE!
BATIUK
7-30

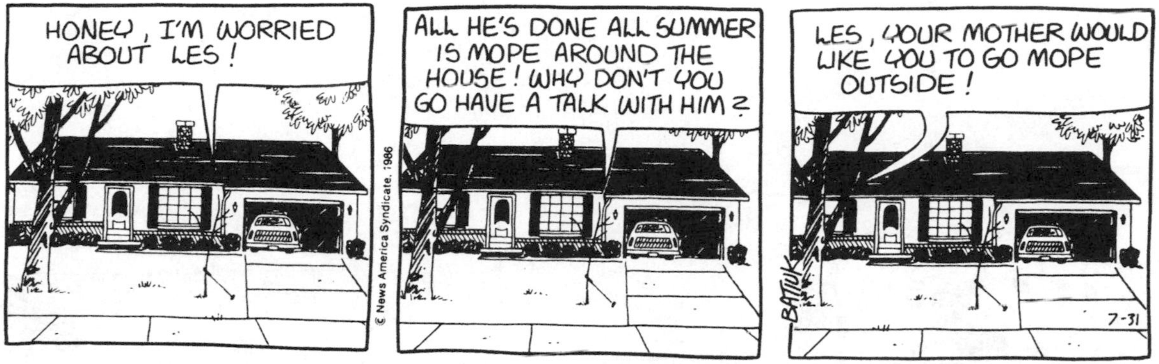
HONEY, I'M WORRIED ABOUT LES!
ALL HE'S DONE ALL SUMMER IS MOPE AROUND THE HOUSE! WHY DON'T YOU GO HAVE A TALK WITH HIM?
LES, YOUR MOTHER WOULD LIKE YOU TO GO MOPE OUTSIDE!
© News America Syndicate, 1986
BATIUK
7-31

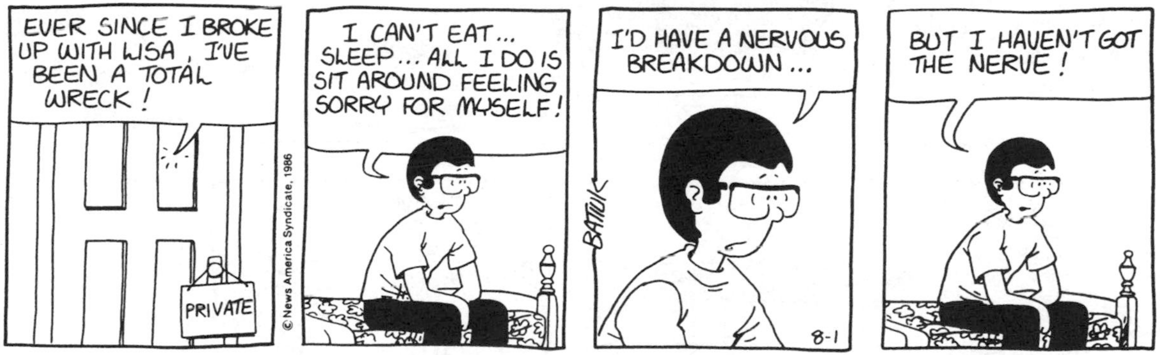
EVER SINCE I BROKE UP WITH LISA, I'VE BEEN A TOTAL WRECK!
PRIVATE
I CAN'T EAT... SLEEP... ALL I DO IS SIT AROUND FEELING SORRY FOR MYSELF!
© News America Syndicate, 1986
I'D HAVE A NERVOUS BREAKDOWN...
BATIUK
8-1
BUT I HAVEN'T GOT THE NERVE!

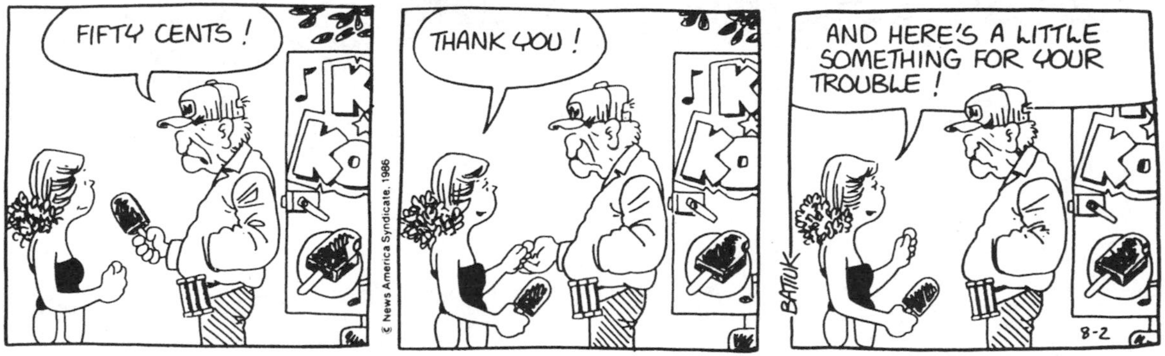
FIFTY CENTS!
THANK YOU!
© News America Syndicate, 1986
AND HERE'S A LITTLE SOMETHING FOR YOUR TROUBLE!
BATIUK
8-2

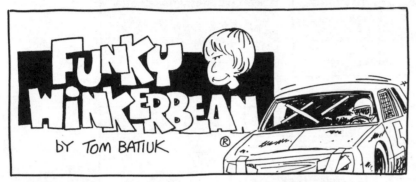

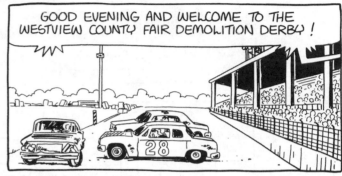

FUNKY WINKERBEAN
BY TOM BATIUK
GOOD EVENING AND WELCOME TO THE WESTVIEW COUNTY FAIR DEMOLITION DERBY!
28
THE PARTICIPANTS IN TONIGHT'S DEMOLITION DERBY ARE ... IN CAR NUMBER ELEVEN ... CRASH CORRIGAN!
11
IN CAR EIGHTY-SEVEN... JIMMY 'BONDO' BARNES!
JIMMY
IN CAR NUMBER SIX ... DAVE 'THE DEMON'!
© News America Syndicate, 1986
8-3
BATIUK
IN BUS THIRTY-FOUR ...

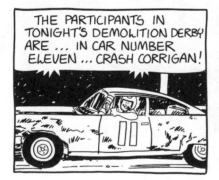

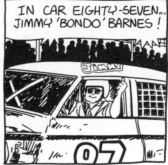

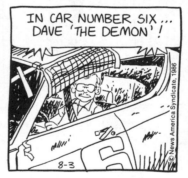

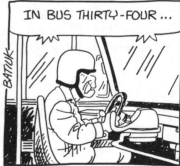

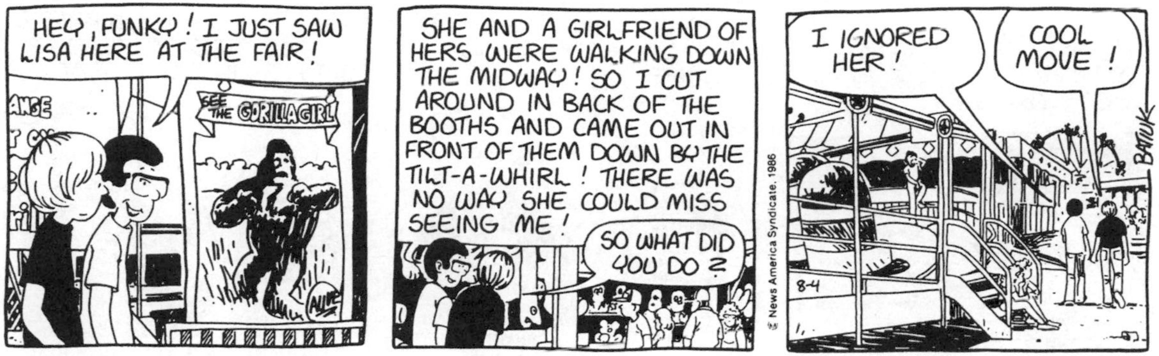
HEY, FUNKY! I JUST SAW LISA HERE AT THE FAIR!
SEE THE GORILLA GIRL
SHE AND A GIRLFRIEND OF HERS WERE WALKING DOWN THE MIDWAY! SO I CUT AROUND IN BACK OF THE BOOTHS AND CAME OUT IN FRONT OF THEM DOWN BY THE TILT-A-WHIRL! THERE WAS NO WAY SHE COULD MISS SEEING ME!
SO WHAT DID YOU DO?
© News America Syndicate, 1986
I IGNORED HER!
COOL MOVE!
BATIUK
8-4

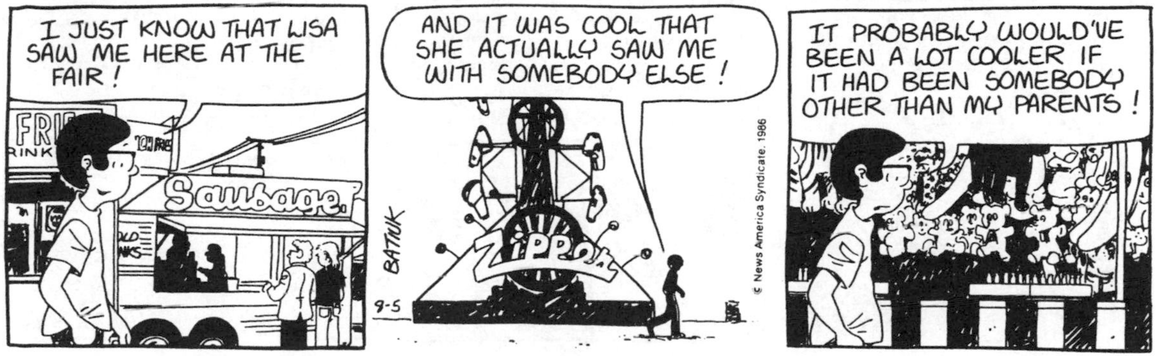
I JUST KNOW THAT LISA SAW ME HERE AT THE FAIR!
Sausage
BATIUK
8-5
AND IT WAS COOL THAT SHE ACTUALLY SAW ME WITH SOMEBODY ELSE!
© News America Syndicate, 1986
IT PROBABLY WOULD'VE BEEN A LOT COOLER IF IT HAD BEEN SOMEBODY OTHER THAN MY PARENTS!

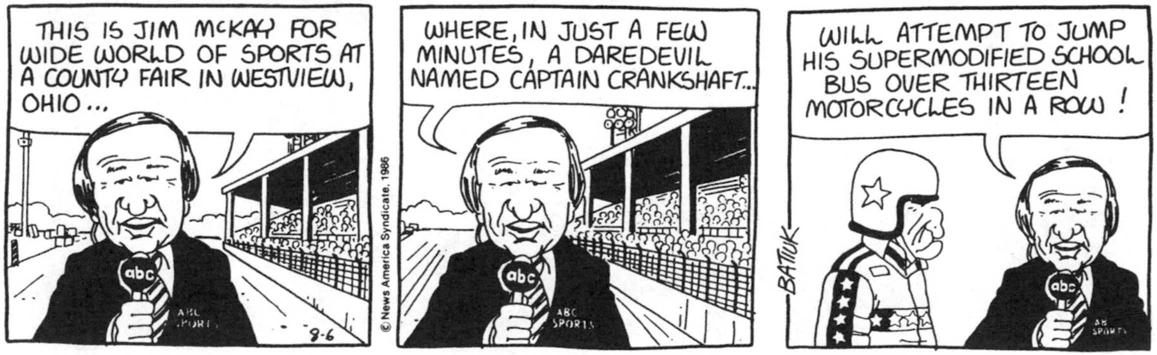
THIS IS JIM McKAY FOR WIDE WORLD OF SPORTS AT A COUNTY FAIR IN WESTVIEW, OHIO...
abc
8-6
© News America Syndicate, 1986
WHERE, IN JUST A FEW MINUTES, A DAREDEVIL NAMED CAPTAIN CRANKSHAFT...
abc
ABC SPORTS
WILL ATTEMPT TO JUMP HIS SUPERMODIFIED SCHOOL BUS OVER THIRTEEN MOTORCYCLES IN A ROW!
BATIUK
abc

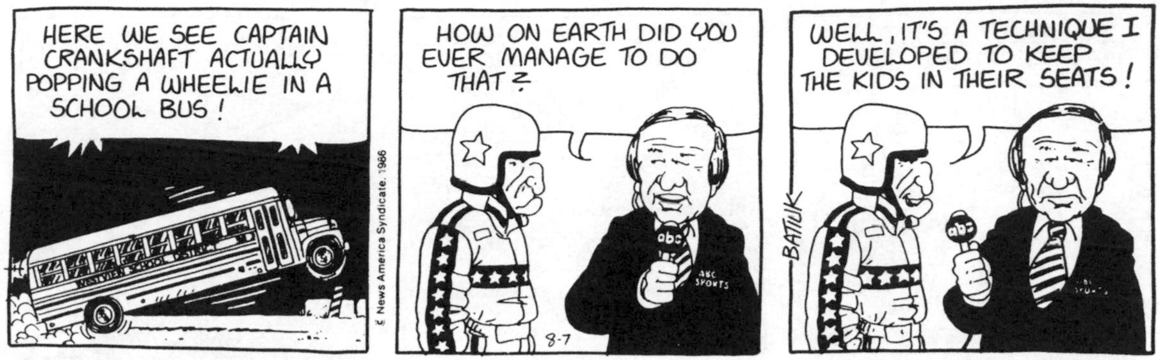
HERE WE SEE CAPTAIN CRANKSHAFT ACTUALLY POPPING A WHEELIE IN A SCHOOL BUS!
© News America Syndicate. 1986
HOW ON EARTH DID YOU EVER MANAGE TO DO THAT?
abc
ABC SPORTS
8-7
BATIUK
WELL, IT'S A TECHNIQUE I DEVELOPED TO KEEP THE KIDS IN THEIR SEATS!

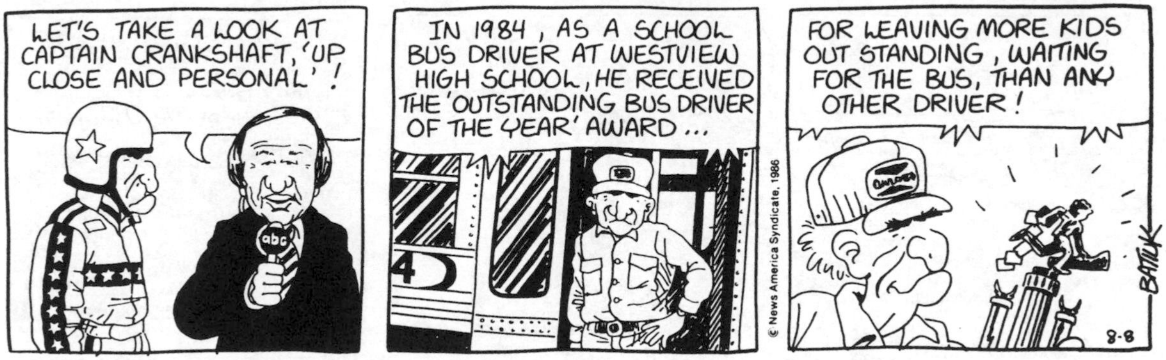
LET'S TAKE A LOOK AT CAPTAIN CRANKSHAFT, 'UP CLOSE AND PERSONAL'!
abc
IN 1984, AS A SCHOOL BUS DRIVER AT WESTVIEW HIGH SCHOOL, HE RECEIVED THE 'OUTSTANDING BUS DRIVER OF THE YEAR' AWARD...
© News America Syndicate. 1986
FOR LEAVING MORE KIDS OUT STANDING, WAITING FOR THE BUS, THAN ANY OTHER DRIVER!
BATIUK
8-8

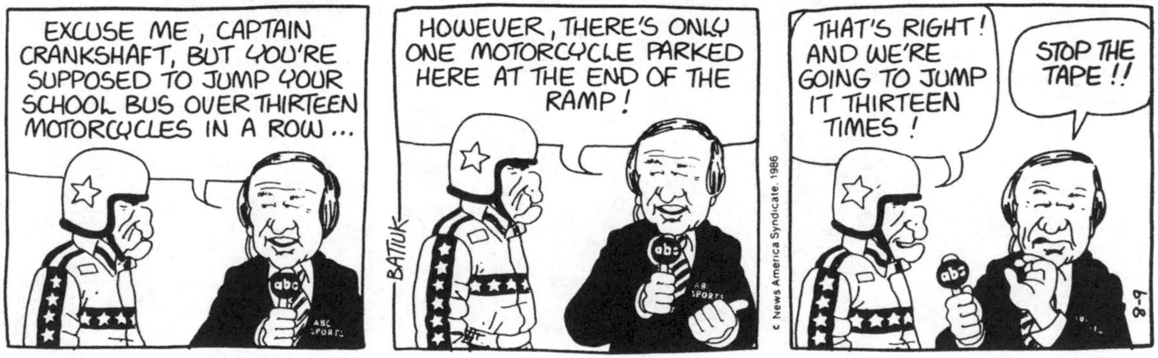
EXCUSE ME, CAPTAIN CRANKSHAFT, BUT YOU'RE SUPPOSED TO JUMP YOUR SCHOOL BUS OVER THIRTEEN MOTORCYCLES IN A ROW...
abc
ABC SPORTS
BATIUK
HOWEVER, THERE'S ONLY ONE MOTORCYCLE PARKED HERE AT THE END OF THE RAMP!
abc
ABC SPORTS
© News America Syndicate. 1986
THAT'S RIGHT! AND WE'RE GOING TO JUMP IT THIRTEEN TIMES!
STOP THE TAPE!!
abc
8-9

Funky Winkerbean BY TOM BATIUK

IN THE SUMMERTIME, THE CITY'S PARKS AND BALL DIAMONDS COME ALIVE WITH YOUNG PEOPLE TAKING PART IN THE NATIONAL PASTIME!

I'M MIKE MAJORS, AND WITH ME TODAY TO TELL US ALL ABOUT PLAYING IN LITTLE LEAGUES...

IS THE COACH AND ONE OF THE PLAYERS FROM THE MONTONI'S PIZZA TEAM!

TELL ME, YOUNG FELLA... HOW LONG HAVE YOU BEEN PLAYING ORGANIZED BALL?

8-10

ARE YOU KIDDING? WE'VE **NEVER** BEEN ORGANIZED!

© News America Syndicate, 1986

437

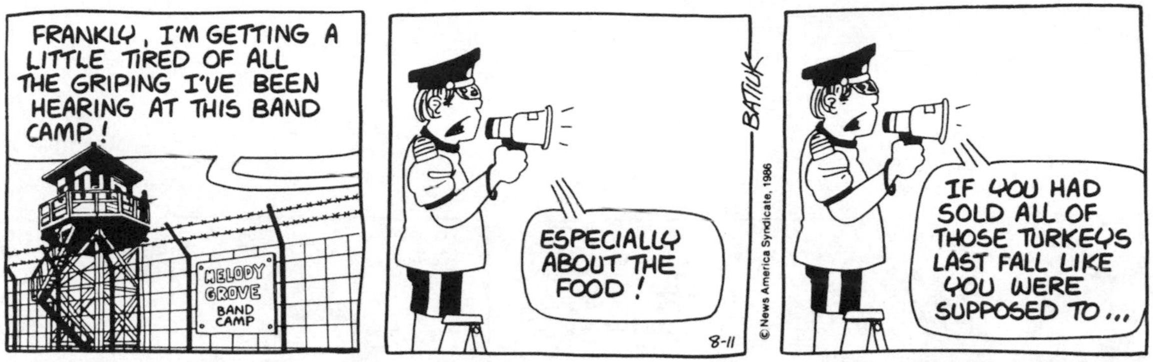
FRANKLY, I'M GETTING A LITTLE TIRED OF ALL THE GRIPING I'VE BEEN HEARING AT THIS BAND CAMP!
MELODY GROVE BAND CAMP
ESPECIALLY ABOUT THE FOOD!
8-11
BATIUK
© News America Syndicate, 1986
IF YOU HAD SOLD ALL OF THOSE TURKEYS LAST FALL LIKE YOU WERE SUPPOSED TO...

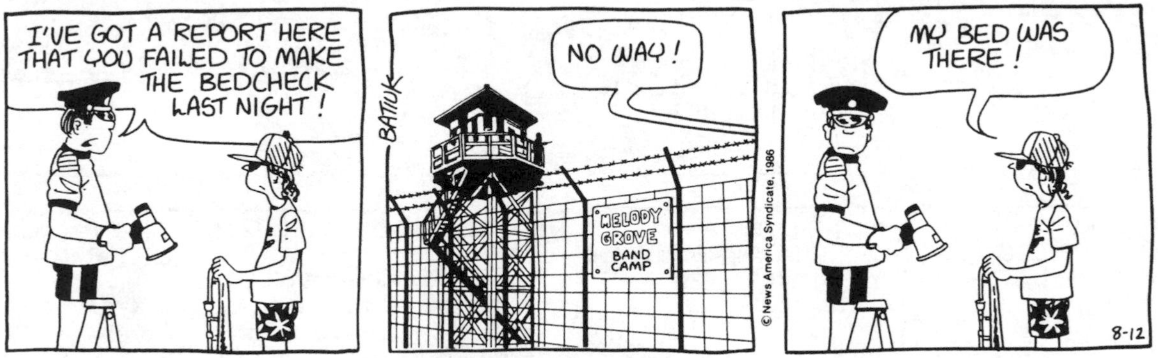
I'VE GOT A REPORT HERE THAT YOU FAILED TO MAKE THE BEDCHECK LAST NIGHT!
BATIUK
NO WAY!
MELODY GROVE BAND CAMP
© News America Syndicate, 1986
MY BED WAS THERE!
8-12

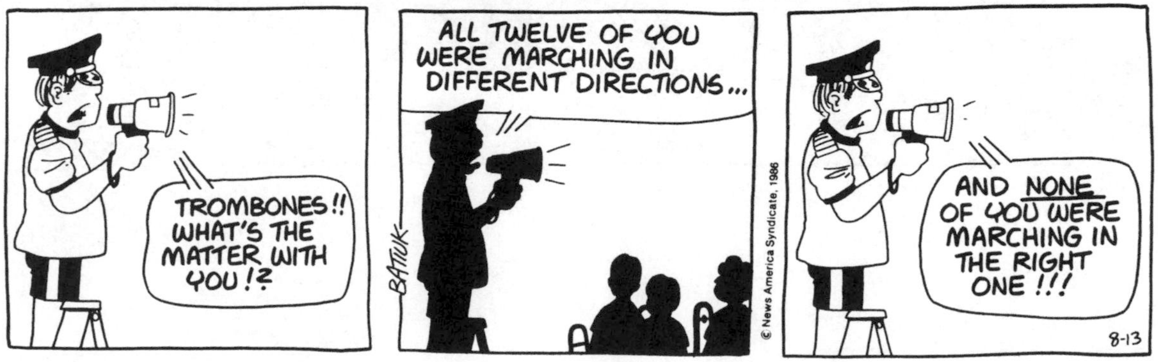
TROMBONES!! WHAT'S THE MATTER WITH YOU!?
ALL TWELVE OF YOU WERE MARCHING IN DIFFERENT DIRECTIONS...
BATIUK
© News America Syndicate, 1986
AND NONE OF YOU WERE MARCHING IN THE RIGHT ONE!!!
8-13

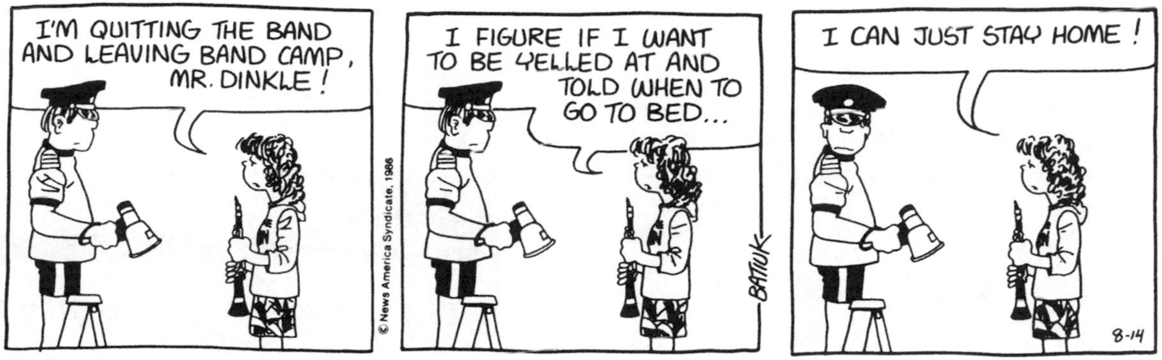
I'M QUITTING THE BAND AND LEAVING BAND CAMP, MR. DINKLE!
© News America Syndicate, 1986
I FIGURE IF I WANT TO BE YELLED AT AND TOLD WHEN TO GO TO BED...
BATIUK
I CAN JUST STAY HOME!
8-14

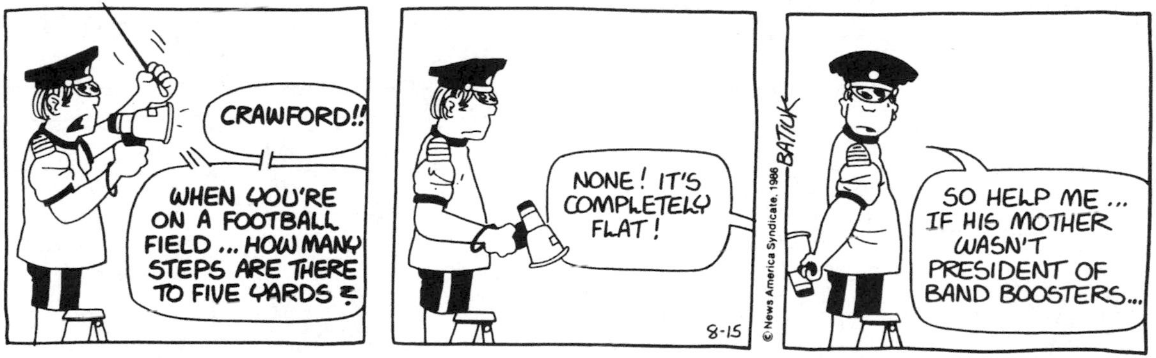
CRAWFORD!!
WHEN YOU'RE ON A FOOTBALL FIELD ... HOW MANY STEPS ARE THERE TO FIVE YARDS?
NONE! IT'S COMPLETELY FLAT!
8-15
© News America Syndicate, 1986
BATIUK
SO HELP ME ... IF HIS MOTHER WASN'T PRESIDENT OF BAND BOOSTERS...

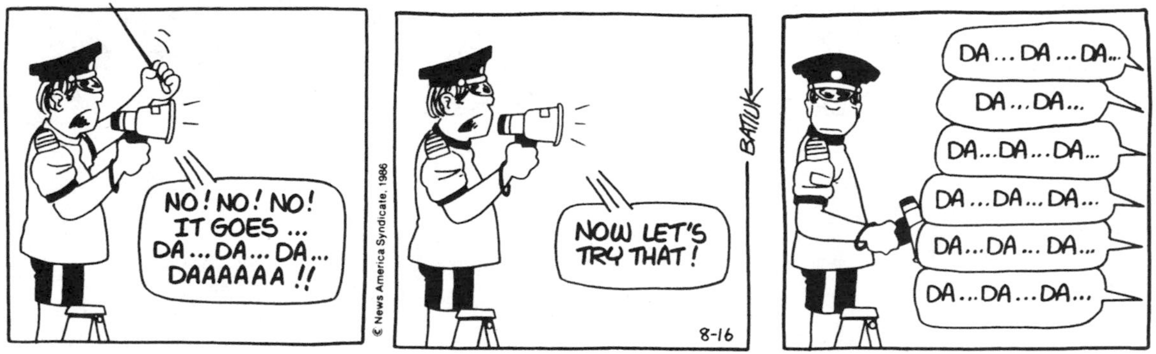
NO! NO! NO! IT GOES ... DA ... DA ... DA ... DAAAAAA!!
© News America Syndicate, 1986
NOW LET'S TRY THAT!
BATIUK
8-16
DA ... DA ... DA...
DA ... DA...
DA...DA...DA...
DA ...DA... DA...
DA...DA ... DA...
DA ... DA ... DA...

FUNKY WINKERBEAN
BY TOM BATIUK
BAND CAMP
I DON'T BELIEVE THIS...!
WESTVIEW SCHOOL DISTRICT 34
THIS ISN'T FAIR!
THE BUS DRIVER IS THE ONLY ONE WHO HAS A DECENT VIEW!
YEAH!
THAT'S RIGHT!
BATIUK
© News America Syndicate, 1986
WHOSE DUMB IDEA WAS IT TO TAKE THE BAND TO A DRIVE-IN MOVIE ANYWAY!?
8-17

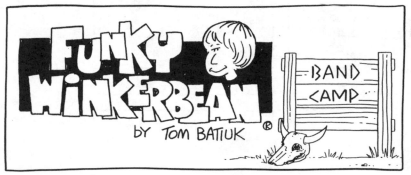

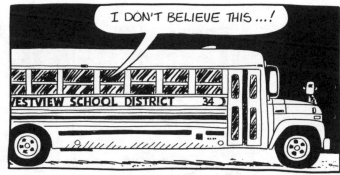

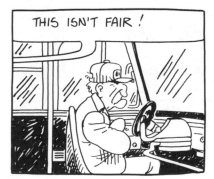

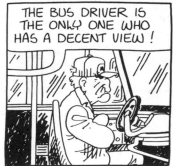

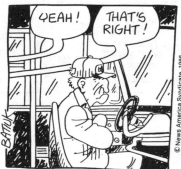

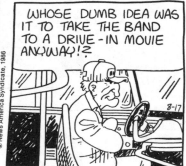

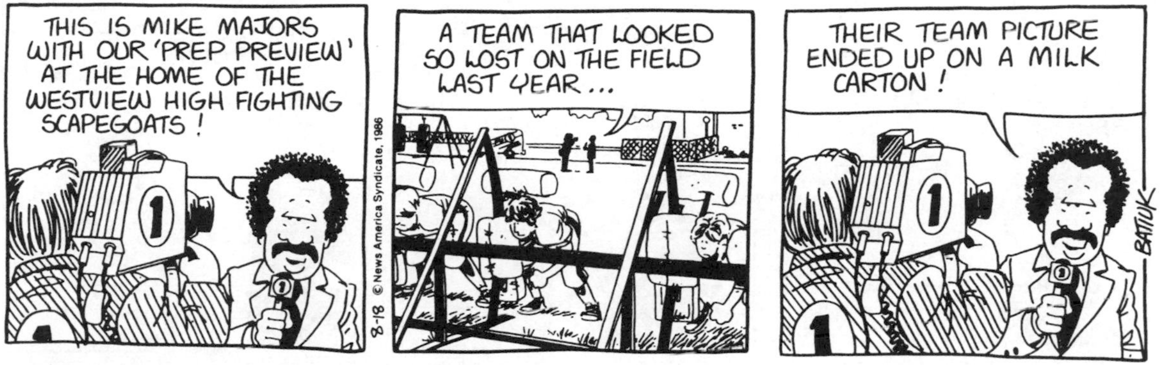
THIS IS MIKE MAJORS WITH OUR 'PREP PREVIEW' AT THE HOME OF THE WESTVIEW HIGH FIGHTING SCAPEGOATS !
8-18 © News America Syndicate, 1986
A TEAM THAT LOOKED SO LOST ON THE FIELD LAST YEAR ...
THEIR TEAM PICTURE ENDED UP ON A MILK CARTON !
BATIUK

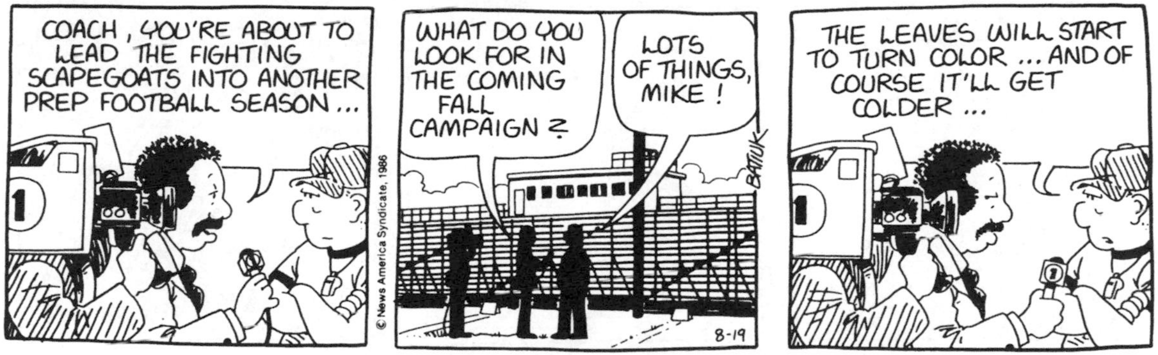
COACH , YOU'RE ABOUT TO LEAD THE FIGHTING SCAPEGOATS INTO ANOTHER PREP FOOTBALL SEASON ...
© News America Syndicate, 1986
WHAT DO YOU LOOK FOR IN THE COMING FALL CAMPAIGN ?
LOTS OF THINGS, MIKE !
BATIUK
8-19
THE LEAVES WILL START TO TURN COLOR ... AND OF COURSE IT'LL GET COLDER ...

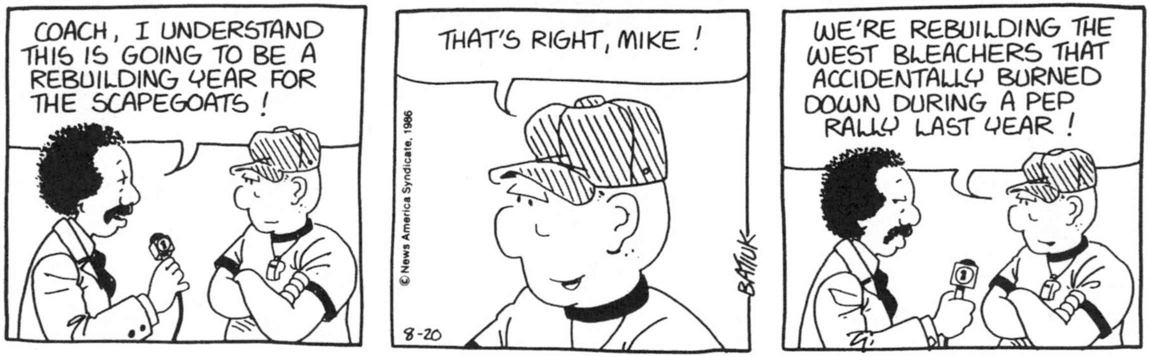
COACH , I UNDERSTAND THIS IS GOING TO BE A REBUILDING YEAR FOR THE SCAPEGOATS !
THAT'S RIGHT, MIKE !
© News America Syndicate, 1986
8-20
BATIUK
WE'RE REBUILDING THE WEST BLEACHERS THAT ACCIDENTALLY BURNED DOWN DURING A PEP RALLY LAST YEAR !

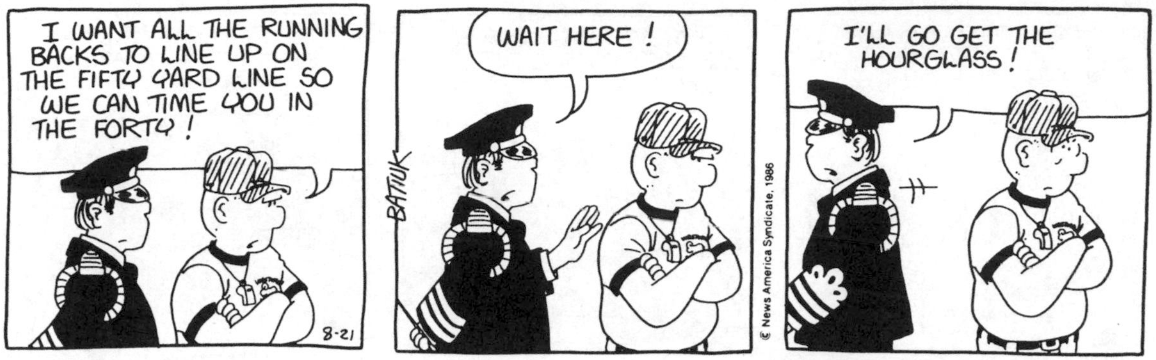
I WANT ALL THE RUNNING BACKS TO LINE UP ON THE FIFTY YARD LINE SO WE CAN TIME YOU IN THE FORTY!
8-21
WAIT HERE!
BATIUK
I'LL GO GET THE HOURGLASS!
© News America Syndicate, 1986

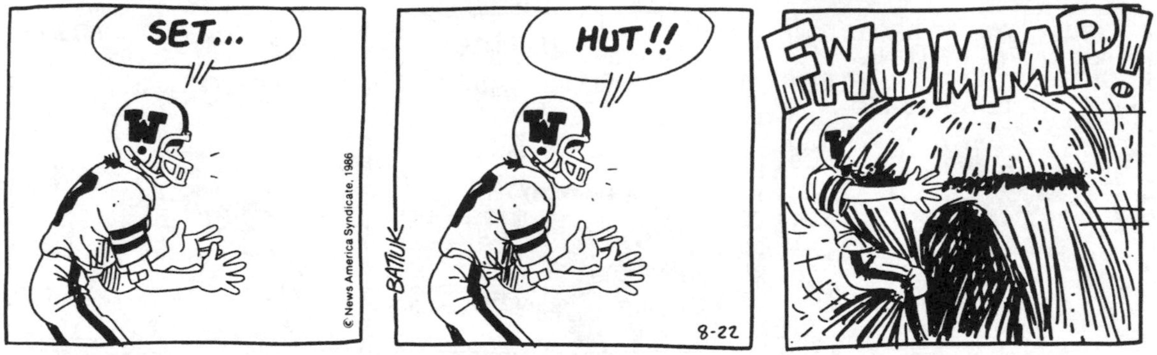
SET...
© News America Syndicate, 1986
HUT!!
BATIUK
8-22
FWUMMP!

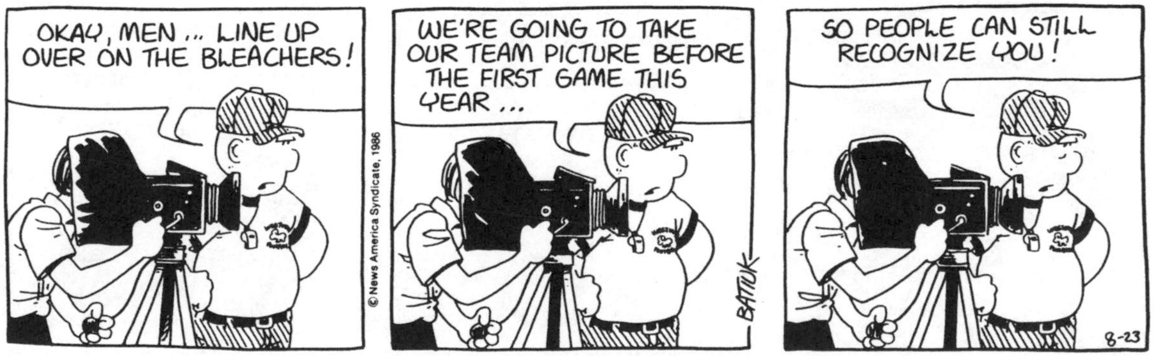
OKAY, MEN... LINE UP OVER ON THE BLEACHERS!
© News America Syndicate, 1986
WE'RE GOING TO TAKE OUR TEAM PICTURE BEFORE THE FIRST GAME THIS YEAR...
BATIUK
SO PEOPLE CAN STILL RECOGNIZE YOU!
8-23

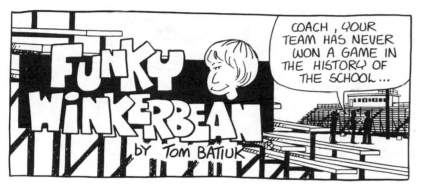

FUNKY WINKERBEAN
BY TOM BATIUK
COACH, YOUR TEAM HAS NEVER WON A GAME IN THE HISTORY OF THE SCHOOL...
HOW ON EARTH DID YOUR SCHOOL EVER GET THE NICKNAME **FIGHTING** SCAPEGOATS?
I THINK IT REFERS MAINLY TO THE SCHOOL BOARD, MIKE!
COACH, I UNDERSTAND YOU LOST YOUR STARTING QUARTER-BACK UNDER SOMEWHAT SHOCKING CIRCUMSTANCES!
YEAH, IT WAS A REAL JOLT TO ALL OF US, MIKE!
OF ALL THE PLAYERS ON THE TEAM...
HE WAS THE LAST ONE IN THE WORLD YOU'D EXPECT TO GO AND DO SOMETHING LIKE GRADUATE!
8-24
BATIUK

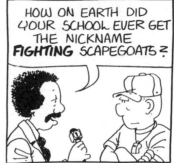

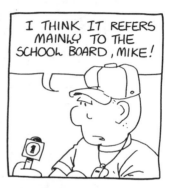

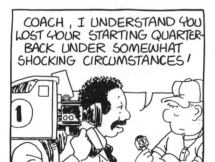

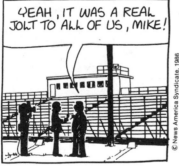

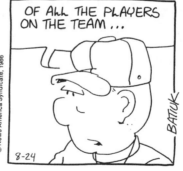

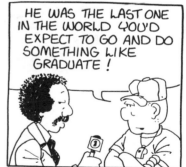

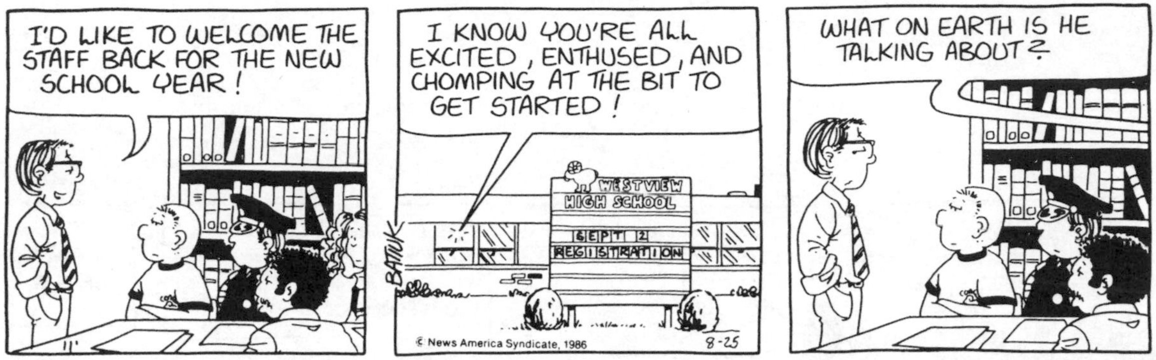
I'D LIKE TO WELCOME THE STAFF BACK FOR THE NEW SCHOOL YEAR!
I KNOW YOU'RE ALL EXCITED, ENTHUSED, AND CHOMPING AT THE BIT TO GET STARTED!
WESTVIEW HIGH SCHOOL
SEPT 2
REGISTRATION
BATIUK
8-25
WHAT ON EARTH IS HE TALKING ABOUT?

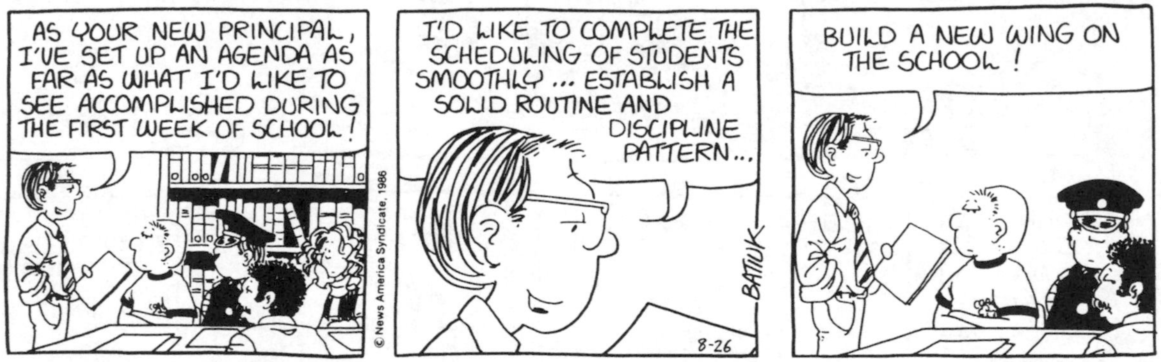
AS YOUR NEW PRINCIPAL, I'VE SET UP AN AGENDA AS FAR AS WHAT I'D LIKE TO SEE ACCOMPLISHED DURING THE FIRST WEEK OF SCHOOL!
I'D LIKE TO COMPLETE THE SCHEDULING OF STUDENTS SMOOTHLY ... ESTABLISH A SOLID ROUTINE AND DISCIPLINE PATTERN...
BATIUK
8-26
BUILD A NEW WING ON THE SCHOOL!

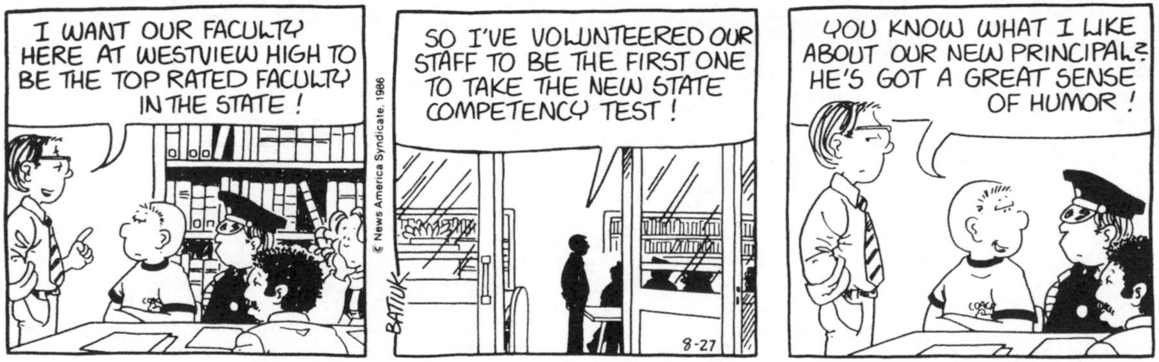
I WANT OUR FACULTY HERE AT WESTVIEW HIGH TO BE THE TOP RATED FACULTY IN THE STATE!
SO I'VE VOLUNTEERED OUR STAFF TO BE THE FIRST ONE TO TAKE THE NEW STATE COMPETENCY TEST!
BATIUK
8-27
YOU KNOW WHAT I LIKE ABOUT OUR NEW PRINCIPAL? HE'S GOT A GREAT SENSE OF HUMOR!

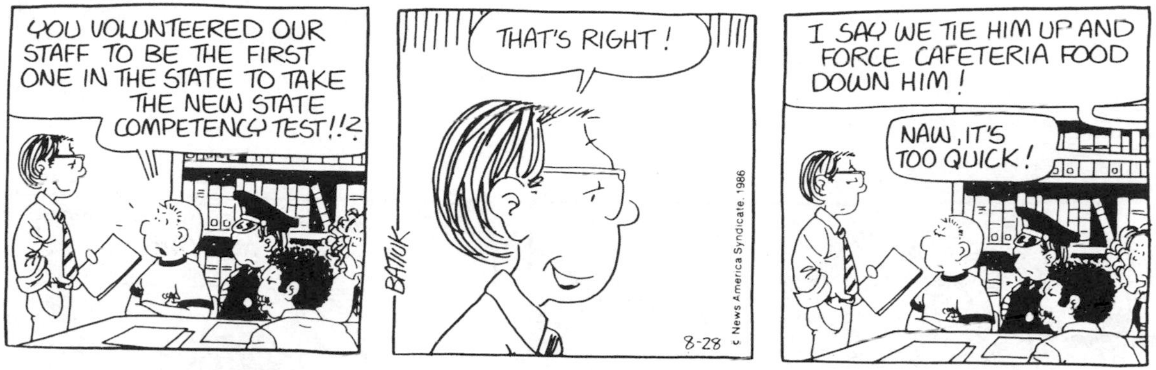
YOU VOLUNTEERED OUR STAFF TO BE THE FIRST ONE IN THE STATE TO TAKE THE NEW STATE COMPETENCY TEST!!?
THAT'S RIGHT!
BATIUK
8-28
© News America Syndicate. 1986
I SAY WE TIE HIM UP AND FORCE CAFETERIA FOOD DOWN HIM!
NAW, IT'S TOO QUICK!

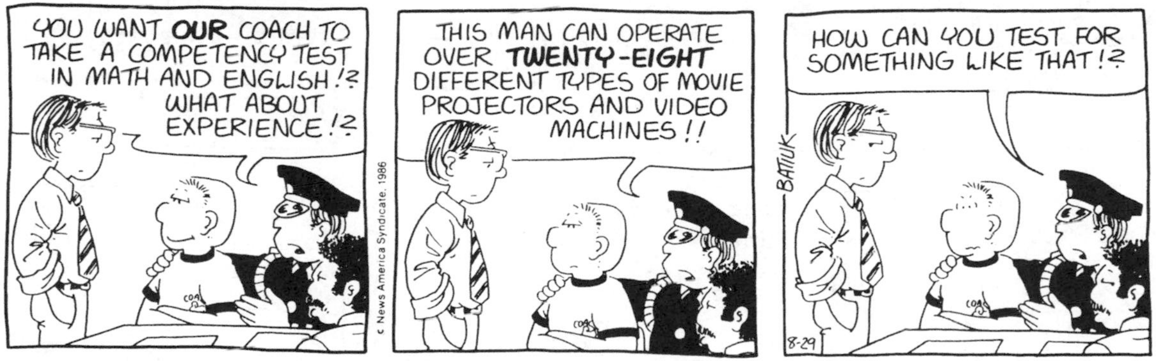
YOU WANT **OUR** COACH TO TAKE A COMPETENCY TEST IN MATH AND ENGLISH!? WHAT ABOUT EXPERIENCE!?
© News America Syndicate. 1986
THIS MAN CAN OPERATE OVER **TWENTY-EIGHT** DIFFERENT TYPES OF MOVIE PROJECTORS AND VIDEO MACHINES!!
BATIUK
HOW CAN YOU TEST FOR SOMETHING LIKE THAT!?
8-29

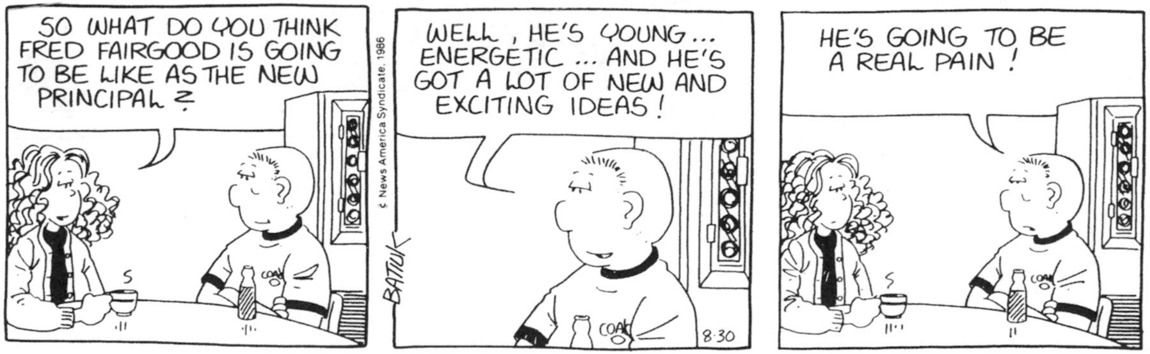
SO WHAT DO YOU THINK FRED FAIRGOOD IS GOING TO BE LIKE AS THE NEW PRINCIPAL?
© News America Syndicate. 1986
BATIUK
WELL, HE'S YOUNG... ENERGETIC ... AND HE'S GOT A LOT OF NEW AND EXCITING IDEAS!
8-30
HE'S GOING TO BE A REAL PAIN!

FUNKY WINKERBEAN
BY TOM BATIUK
WESTVIEW HIGH SCHOOL
SEPT 2
REGISTRATI
BEFORE WE WRAP UP THIS FIRST STAFF MEETING ...
WESTVIEW HIGH SCHOOL
SEPT 2
REGISTRATION
I WANT YOU TO KNOW THAT, AS PRINCIPAL, THE DOOR TO MY OFFICE WILL ALWAYS BE OPEN TO YOU!
8-31
FEEL FREE TO DROP IN IF YOU HAVE ANY QUESTIONS ... A PROBLEM ... OR IF YOU JUST WANT TO TALK!
BATIUK
© News America Syndicate, 1986
WHAT ABOUT IF WE WANT TO USE THE PHONE?

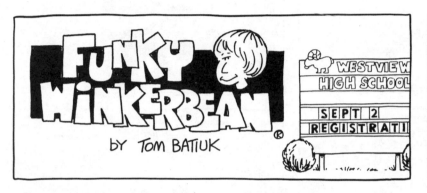

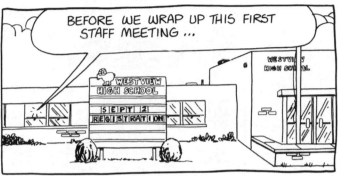

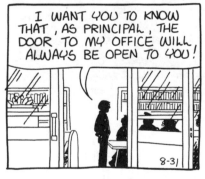

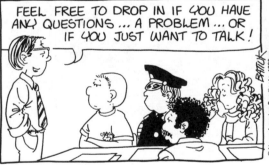

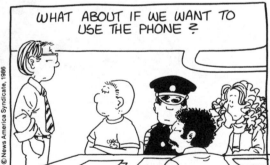

Panel 1: YOU'RE THINKING ABOUT ASKING LISA OUT AGAIN, AREN'T YOU?

POSITIVELY NO SCHEDULE CHANGES

Panel 2: WHY? WHAT MAKES YOU SAY THAT, FUNKY?

© News America Syndicate, 1986

Panel 3: BECAUSE YOU JUST SIGNED HER NAME TO YOUR REGISTRATION CARD!

POSITIVELY NO SCHEDULE CHANGES

9-1

STUDENT REGISTRATION →

BARRY'S THE ONLY KID I KNOW WHO CAMPS OVERNIGHT SO HE CAN BE FIRST IN LINE FOR SCHOOL REGISTRATION!

9-2

© News America Syndicate, 1986

Panel 1: I'D LIKE TO WELCOME ALL OF YOU BACK TO WESTVIEW HIGH!

Panel 2: THERE'S A LOT OF ELECTRICITY IN THE AIR ON THIS FIRST DAY...

BATIUK

9-3

© News America Syndicate, 1986

Panel 3: BUT THE JANITOR ASSURES ME THOSE LOOSE WIRES WILL BE TAKEN CARE OF BEFORE CLASSES ACTUALLY START!

447

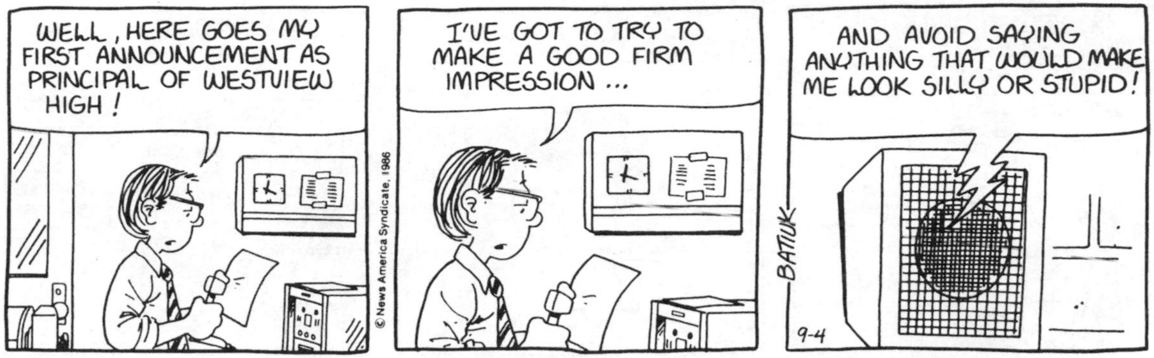
WELL, HERE GOES MY FIRST ANNOUNCEMENT AS PRINCIPAL OF WESTVIEW HIGH!
I'VE GOT TO TRY TO MAKE A GOOD FIRM IMPRESSION ...
AND AVOID SAYING ANYTHING THAT WOULD MAKE ME LOOK SILLY OR STUPID!
© News America Syndicate, 1986
BATIUK
9-4

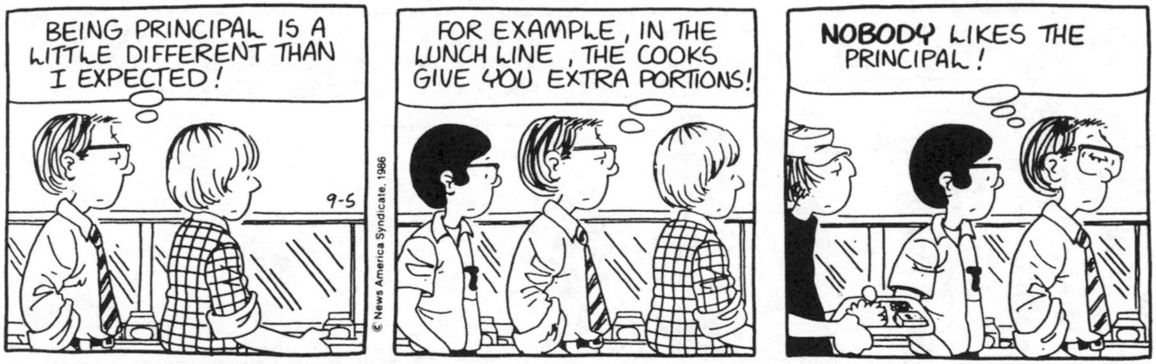
BEING PRINCIPAL IS A LITTLE DIFFERENT THAN I EXPECTED!
9-5
FOR EXAMPLE, IN THE LUNCH LINE, THE COOKS GIVE YOU EXTRA PORTIONS!
© News America Syndicate, 1986
NOBODY LIKES THE PRINCIPAL!

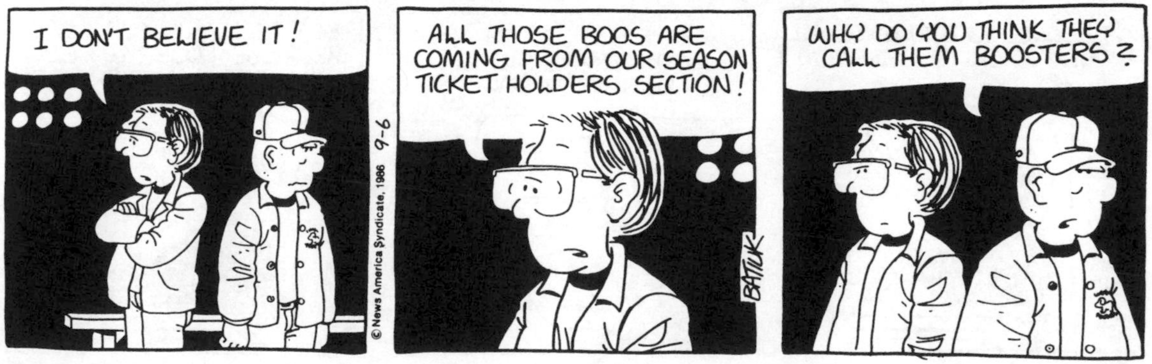
I DON'T BELIEVE IT!
9-6
© News America Syndicate, 1986
ALL THOSE BOOS ARE COMING FROM OUR SEASON TICKET HOLDERS SECTION!
BATIUK
WHY DO YOU THINK THEY CALL THEM BOOSTERS?

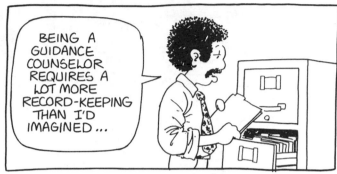

FUNKY WINKERBEAN
BY TOM BATIUK ®
BUSHKA, BULL
BEING A GUIDANCE COUNSELOR REQUIRES A LOT MORE RECORD-KEEPING THAN I'D IMAGINED...
THIS IS INTERESTING...
THE NATIONAL AVERAGE OF THE P.S.A.T. SCORES WENT UP LAST YEAR!
© News America Syndicate, 1986
HMM... OUR SCHOOL'S STAR FULLBACK, BULL BUSHKA, MISSED TAKING THE P.S.A.T. LAST YEAR...
BATIUK
9-7
NAW! IT COULDN'T BE...

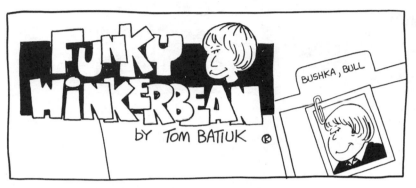

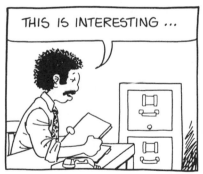

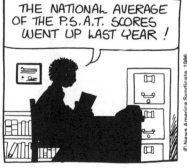

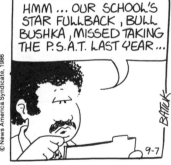

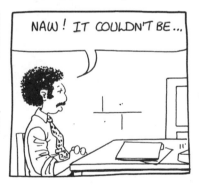

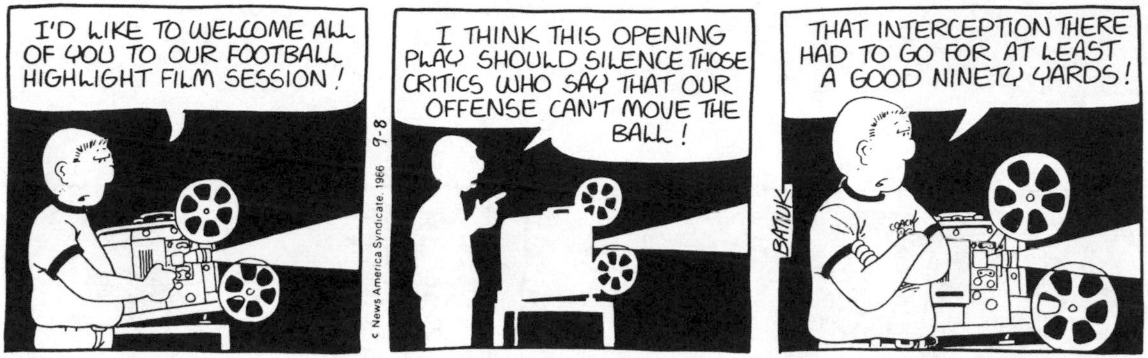
I'D LIKE TO WELCOME ALL OF YOU TO OUR FOOTBALL HIGHLIGHT FILM SESSION!
I THINK THIS OPENING PLAY SHOULD SILENCE THOSE CRITICS WHO SAY THAT OUR OFFENSE CAN'T MOVE THE BALL!
THAT INTERCEPTION THERE HAD TO GO FOR AT LEAST A GOOD NINETY YARDS!
9-8
© News America Syndicate, 1986
BATIUK

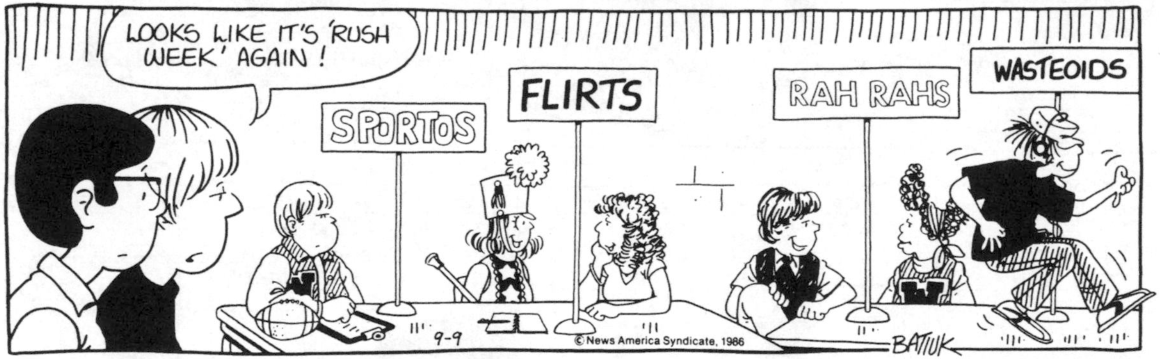
LOOKS LIKE IT'S 'RUSH WEEK' AGAIN!
SPORTOS
FLIRTS
RAH RAHS
WASTEOIDS
9-9
© News America Syndicate, 1986
BATIUK

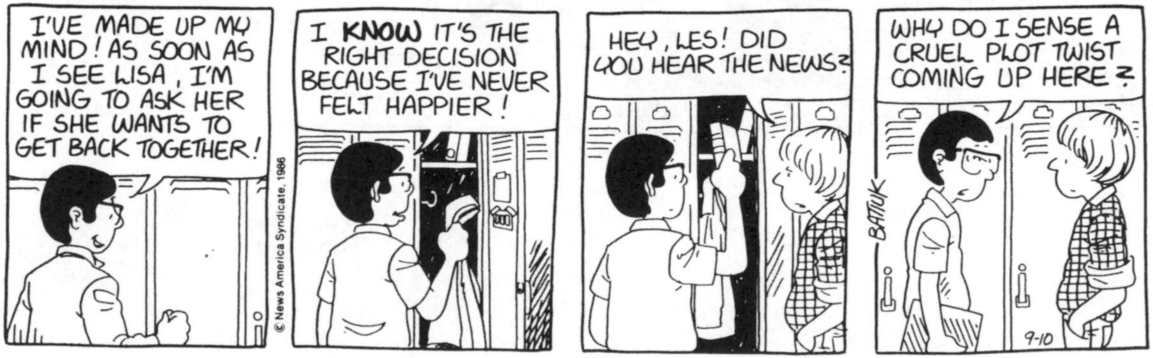
I'VE MADE UP MY MIND! AS SOON AS I SEE LISA, I'M GOING TO ASK HER IF SHE WANTS TO GET BACK TOGETHER!
I KNOW IT'S THE RIGHT DECISION BECAUSE I'VE NEVER FELT HAPPIER!
HEY, LES! DID YOU HEAR THE NEWS?
WHY DO I SENSE A CRUEL PLOT TWIST COMING UP HERE?
© News America Syndicate, 1986
BATIUK
9-10

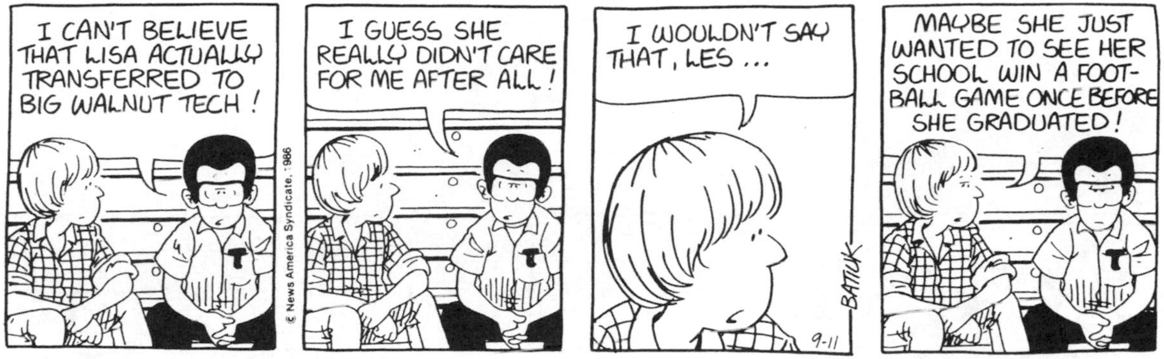
I CAN'T BELIEVE THAT LISA ACTUALLY TRANSFERRED TO BIG WALNUT TECH !
© News America Syndicate, 1986
I GUESS SHE REALLY DIDN'T CARE FOR ME AFTER ALL !
I WOULDN'T SAY THAT, LES ...
BATIUK
9-11
MAYBE SHE JUST WANTED TO SEE HER SCHOOL WIN A FOOT-BALL GAME ONCE BEFORE SHE GRADUATED !

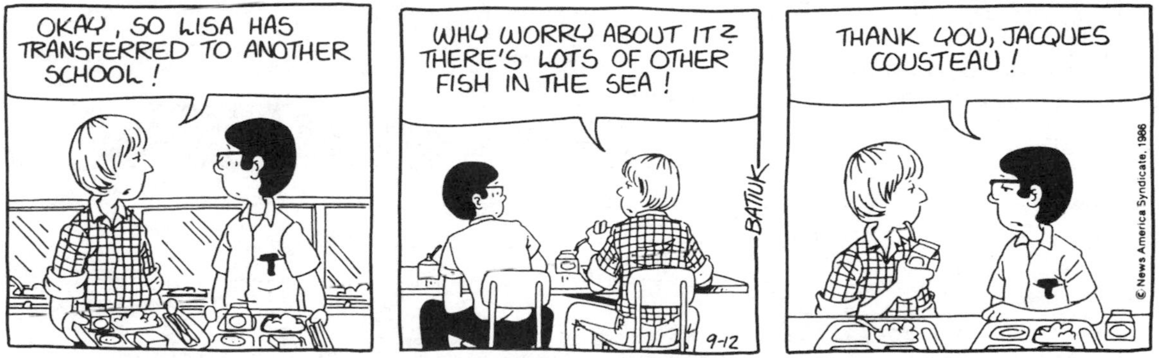
OKAY, SO LISA HAS TRANSFERRED TO ANOTHER SCHOOL !
WHY WORRY ABOUT IT ? THERE'S LOTS OF OTHER FISH IN THE SEA !
BATIUK
9-12
THANK YOU, JACQUES COUSTEAU !
© News America Syndicate, 1986

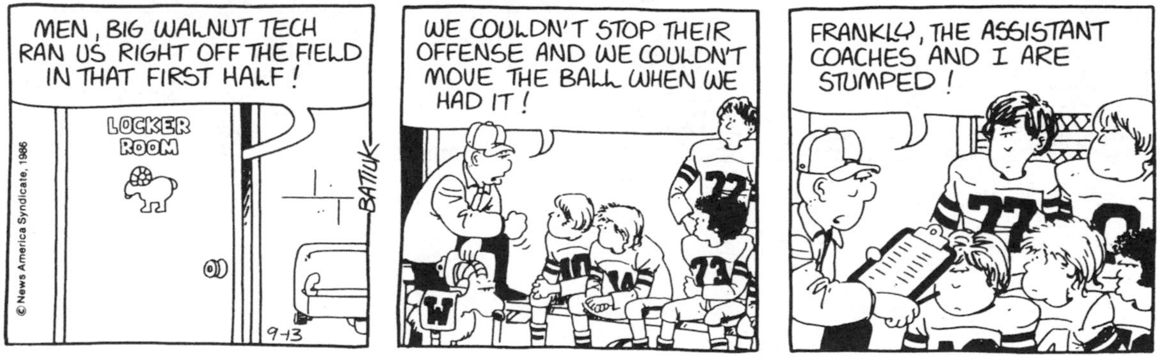
MEN, BIG WALNUT TECH RAN US RIGHT OFF THE FIELD IN THAT FIRST HALF !
LOCKER ROOM
© News America Syndicate, 1986
BATIUK
9-13
WE COULDN'T STOP THEIR OFFENSE AND WE COULDN'T MOVE THE BALL WHEN WE HAD IT !
FRANKLY, THE ASSISTANT COACHES AND I ARE STUMPED !

FUNKY WINKERBEAN
COLD ...
DICK JANE
IPAL
COLD ... COLD ... COLDER ...
COLD ... COLD ... COLD ...
COLDER ... STILL COLDER ...
BATIUK
ICY COLD ...
9-14
© News America Syndicate, 1986
BETTY! FOR HEAVEN'S SAKE ... TELL HIM WHERE THE DITTO MASTERS ARE !!

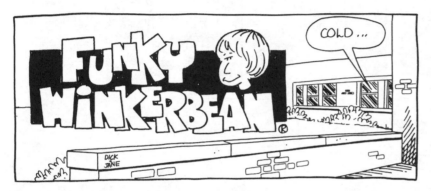

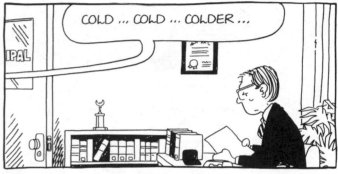

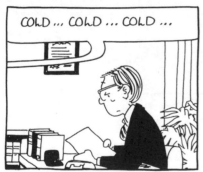

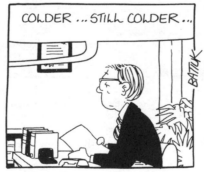

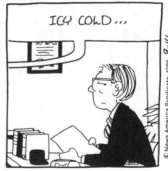

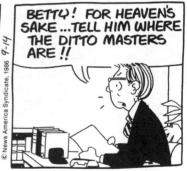

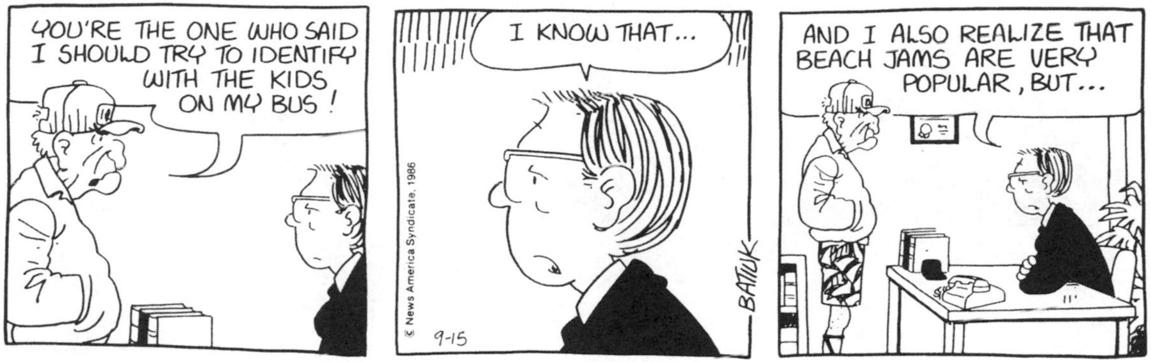
YOU'RE THE ONE WHO SAID I SHOULD TRY TO IDENTIFY WITH THE KIDS ON MY BUS!
I KNOW THAT...
© News America Syndicate, 1986
9-15
BATIUK
AND I ALSO REALIZE THAT BEACH JAMS ARE VERY POPULAR, BUT...

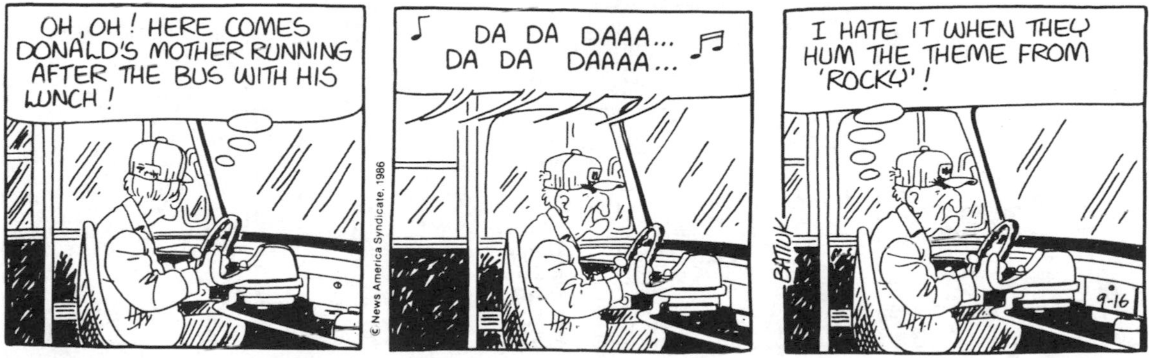
OH, OH! HERE COMES DONALD'S MOTHER RUNNING AFTER THE BUS WITH HIS LUNCH!
DA DA DAAA... DA DA DAAAA...
© News America Syndicate, 1986
I HATE IT WHEN THEY HUM THE THEME FROM 'ROCKY'!
BATIUK
9-16

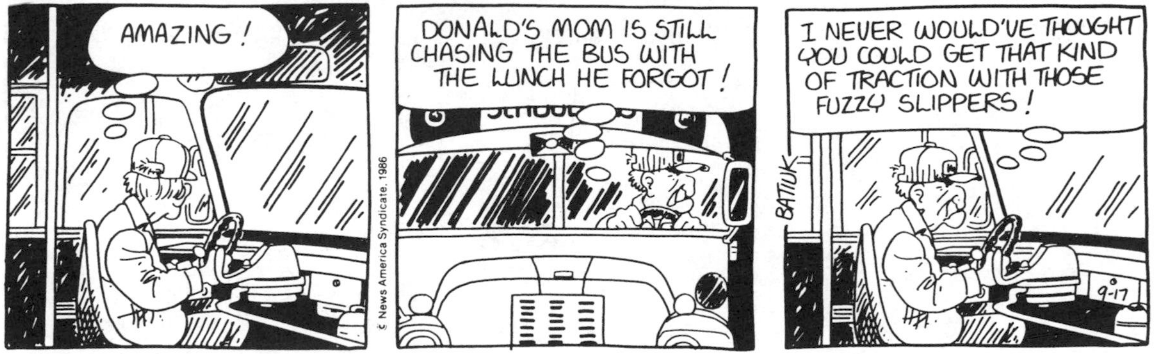
AMAZING!
© News America Syndicate, 1986
DONALD'S MOM IS STILL CHASING THE BUS WITH THE LUNCH HE FORGOT!
I NEVER WOULD'VE THOUGHT YOU COULD GET THAT KIND OF TRACTION WITH THOSE FUZZY SLIPPERS!
BATIUK
9-17

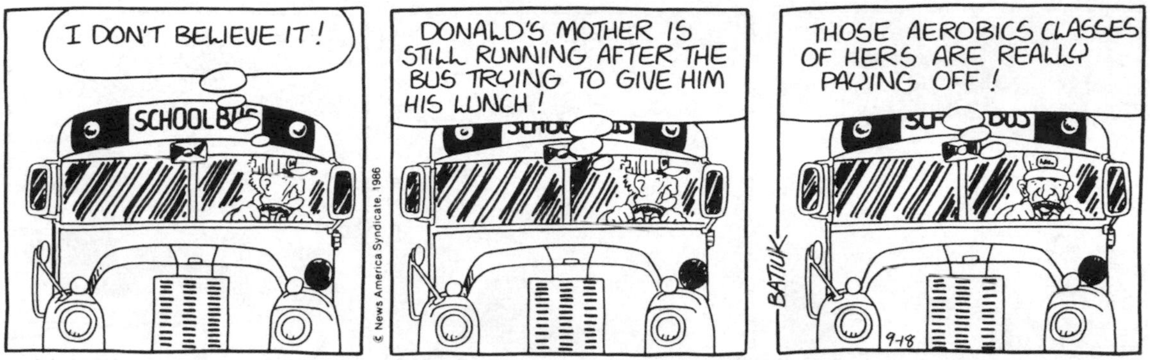
I DON'T BELIEVE IT!
SCHOOLBUS
© News America Syndicate, 1986
DONALD'S MOTHER IS STILL RUNNING AFTER THE BUS TRYING TO GIVE HIM HIS LUNCH!
THOSE AEROBICS CLASSES OF HERS ARE REALLY PAYING OFF!
BATIUK
9-18

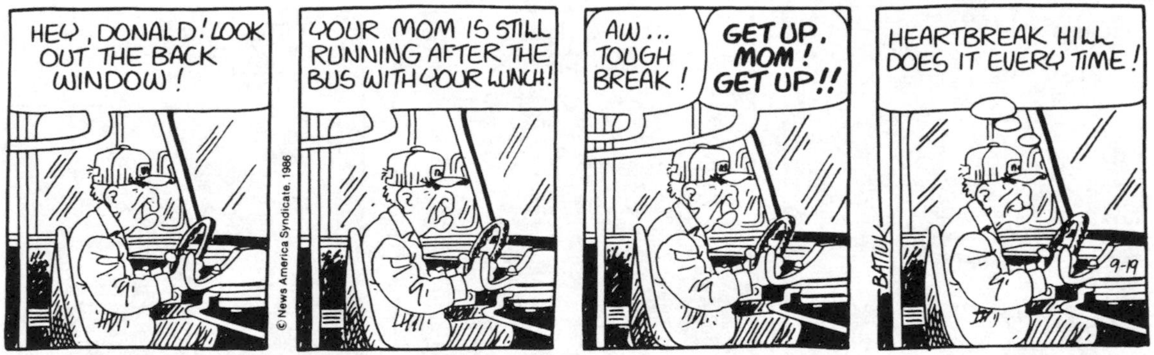
HEY, DONALD! LOOK OUT THE BACK WINDOW!
© News America Syndicate, 1986
YOUR MOM IS STILL RUNNING AFTER THE BUS WITH YOUR LUNCH!
AW... TOUGH BREAK!
GET UP, MOM! GET UP!!
HEARTBREAK HILL DOES IT EVERY TIME!
BATIUK
9-19

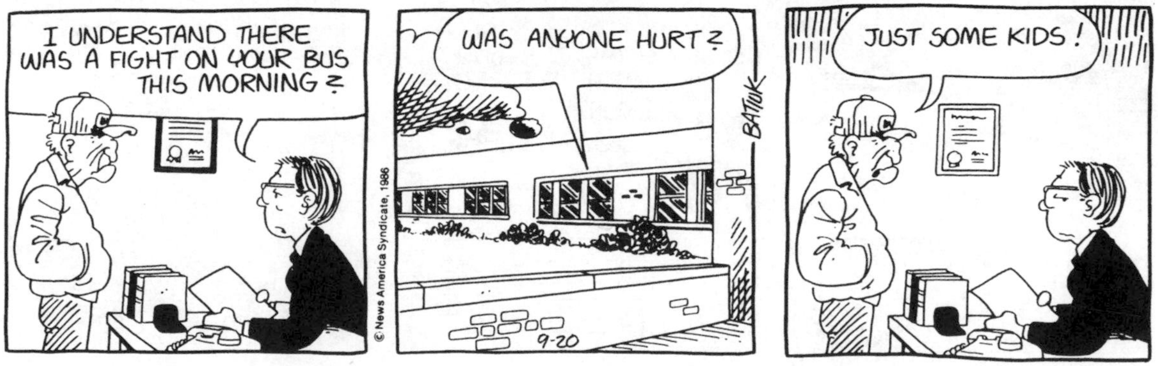
I UNDERSTAND THERE WAS A FIGHT ON YOUR BUS THIS MORNING?
© News America Syndicate, 1986
WAS ANYONE HURT?
BATIUK
9-20
JUST SOME KIDS!

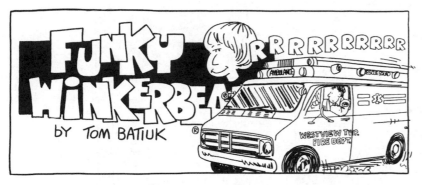

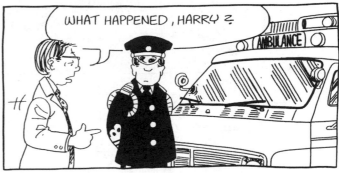

FUNKY WINKERBEAN
by TOM BATIUK
RRRRRRRRRRRR
AMBULANCE
RESCUE SQUAD
WESTVIEW TWP. FIRE DEPT.
WHAT HAPPENED, HARRY?
AMBULANCE
SOME OF THE BAND MEMBERS WERE HORSING AROUND ON THE BLEACHERS...
AND A GIRL FELL OFF WITH HER FRENCH HORN!
©News America Syndicate, 1986 9-21
IS EVERYTHING OKAY?
YEAH... NO PROBLEM!
IT WASN'T A SCHOOL HORN!
BATIUK

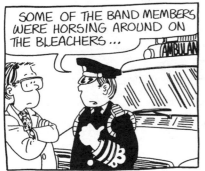

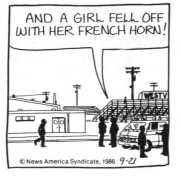

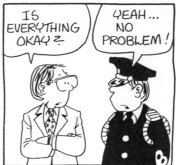

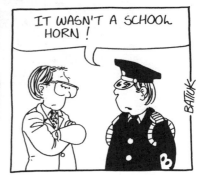

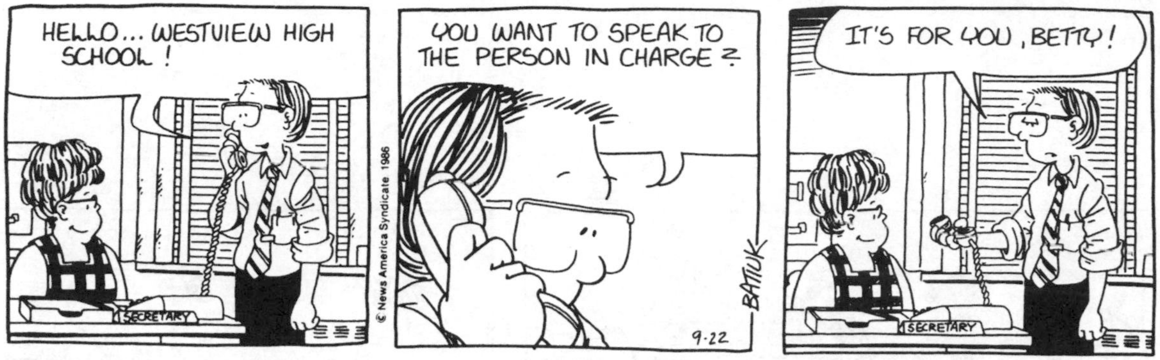
HELLO... WESTVIEW HIGH SCHOOL!
SECRETARY
© News America Syndicate 1986
YOU WANT TO SPEAK TO THE PERSON IN CHARGE?
BATIUK
9-22
IT'S FOR YOU, BETTY!
SECRETARY

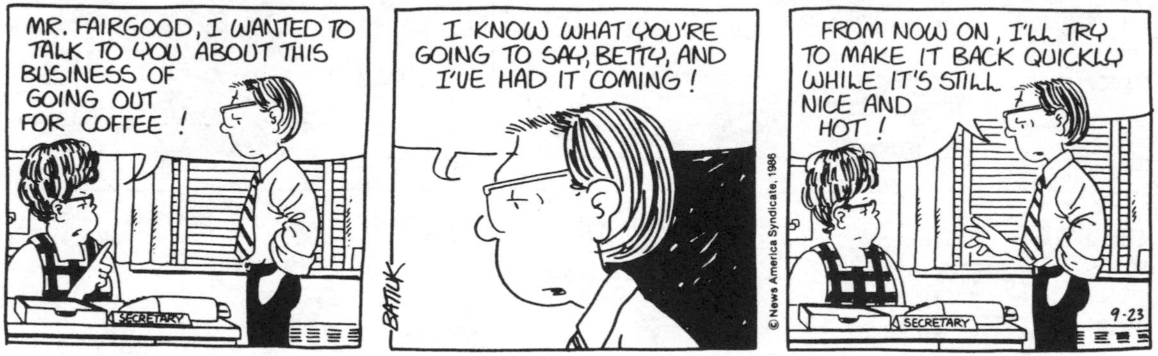
MR. FAIRGOOD, I WANTED TO TALK TO YOU ABOUT THIS BUSINESS OF GOING OUT FOR COFFEE!
SECRETARY
BATIUK
I KNOW WHAT YOU'RE GOING TO SAY, BETTY, AND I'VE HAD IT COMING!
© News America Syndicate, 1986
FROM NOW ON, I'LL TRY TO MAKE IT BACK QUICKLY WHILE IT'S STILL NICE AND HOT!
SECRETARY
9-23

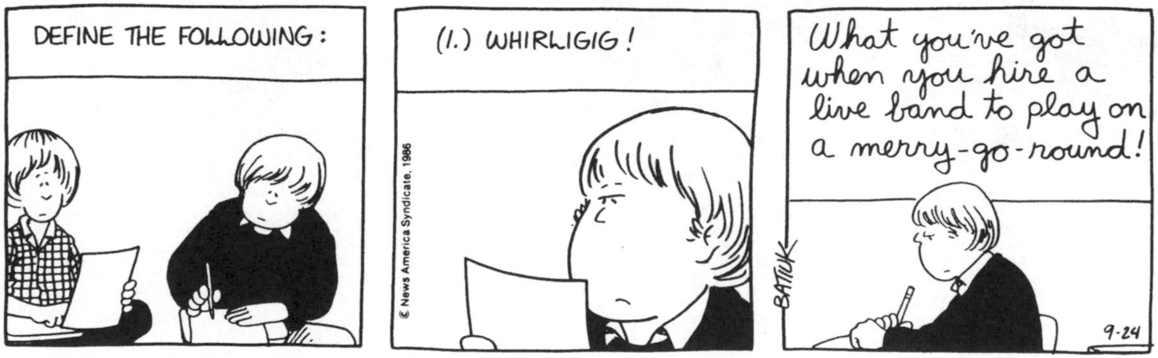
DEFINE THE FOLLOWING:
© News America Syndicate, 1986
(1.) WHIRLIGIG!
What you've got when you hire a live band to play on a merry-go-round!
BATIUK
9-24

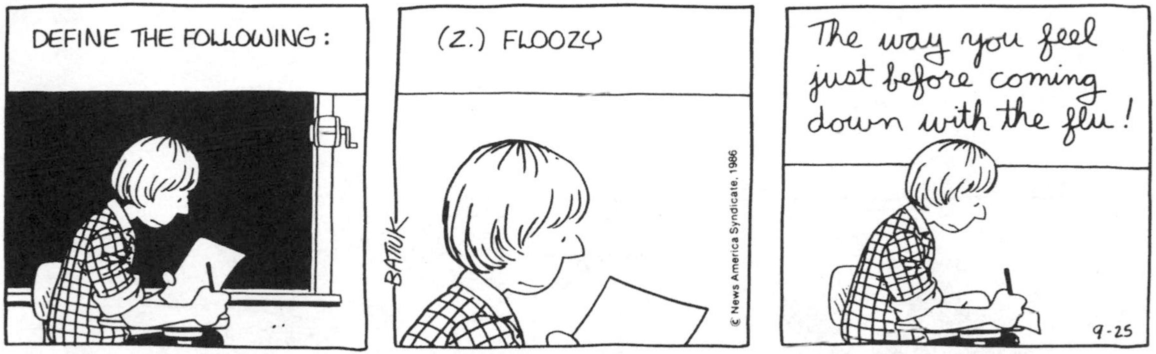
DEFINE THE FOLLOWING:
(2.) FLOOZY
BATIUK
© News America Syndicate, 1986
The way you feel just before coming down with the flu!
9-25

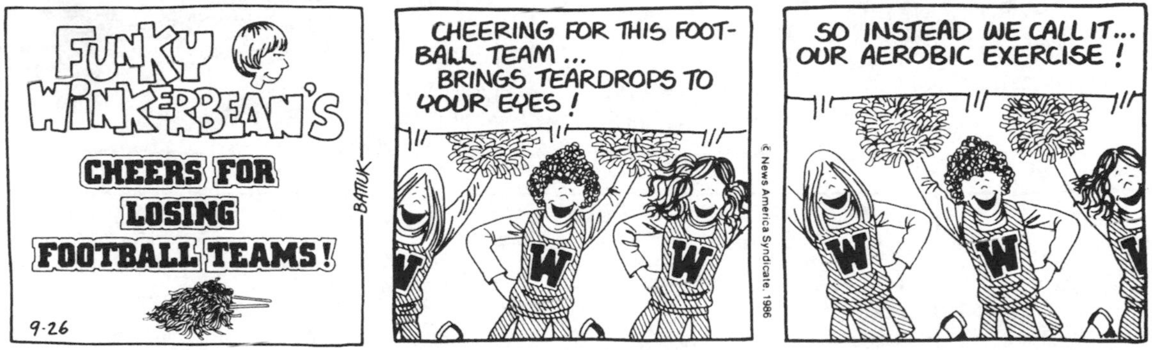
FUNKY WINKERBEAN'S
CHEERS FOR LOSING FOOTBALL TEAMS!
9-26
BATIUK
CHEERING FOR THIS FOOT-BALL TEAM ...
BRINGS TEARDROPS TO YOUR EYES!
© News America Syndicate, 1986
SO INSTEAD WE CALL IT... OUR AEROBIC EXERCISE!

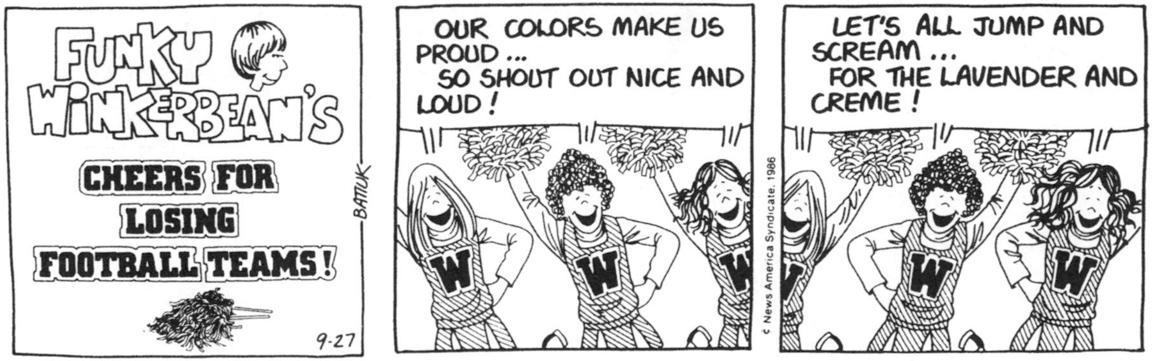
FUNKY WINKERBEAN'S
CHEERS FOR LOSING FOOTBALL TEAMS!
9-27
BATIUK
OUR COLORS MAKE US PROUD ...
SO SHOUT OUT NICE AND LOUD!
© News America Syndicate, 1986
LET'S ALL JUMP AND SCREAM ...
FOR THE LAVENDER AND CREME!

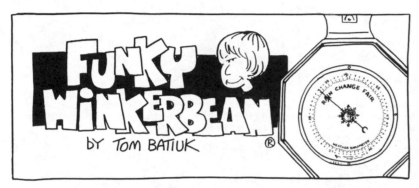

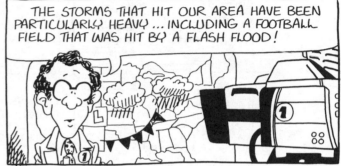

FUNKY WINKERBEAN
BY TOM BATIUK
RAIN CHANGE FAIR
THE STORMS THAT HIT OUR AREA HAVE BEEN PARTICULARLY HEAVY ... INCLUDING A FOOTBALL FIELD THAT WAS HIT BY A FLASH FLOOD!
HARRY! YOU'VE GOT TO CALL OFF THE BATTLE OF THE BANDS!
THE WATER ON THE FIELD IS KNEE DEEP!
NO PROBLEM!
EVERYONE IN THE BAND IS WEARING PUMPS!
©News America Syndicate, 1986
BATIUK
9-28

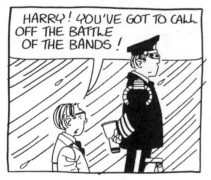

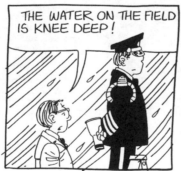

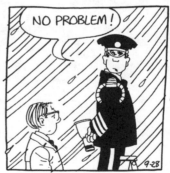

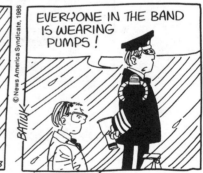

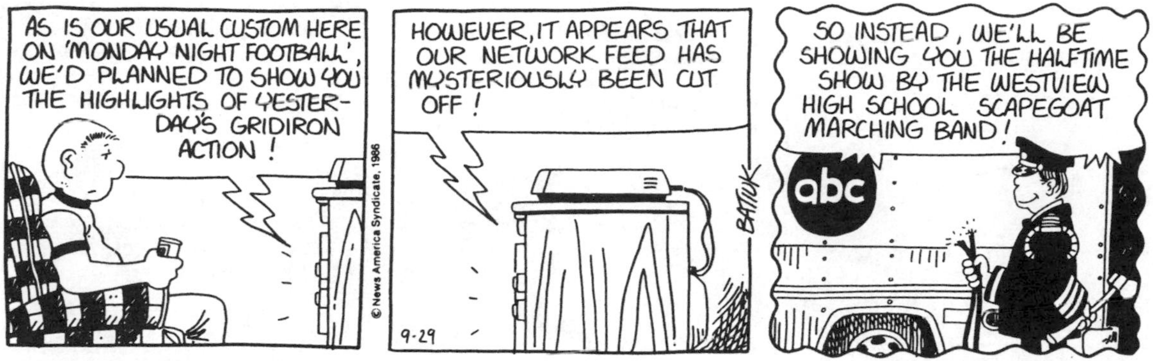
AS IS OUR USUAL CUSTOM HERE ON 'MONDAY NIGHT FOOTBALL', WE'D PLANNED TO SHOW YOU THE HIGHLIGHTS OF YESTER-DAY'S GRIDIRON ACTION !
© News America Syndicate, 1986
HOWEVER, IT APPEARS THAT OUR NETWORK FEED HAS MYSTERIOUSLY BEEN CUT OFF !
9-29
BATIUK
SO INSTEAD, WE'LL BE SHOWING YOU THE HALFTIME SHOW BY THE WESTVIEW HIGH SCHOOL SCAPEGOAT MARCHING BAND !
abc

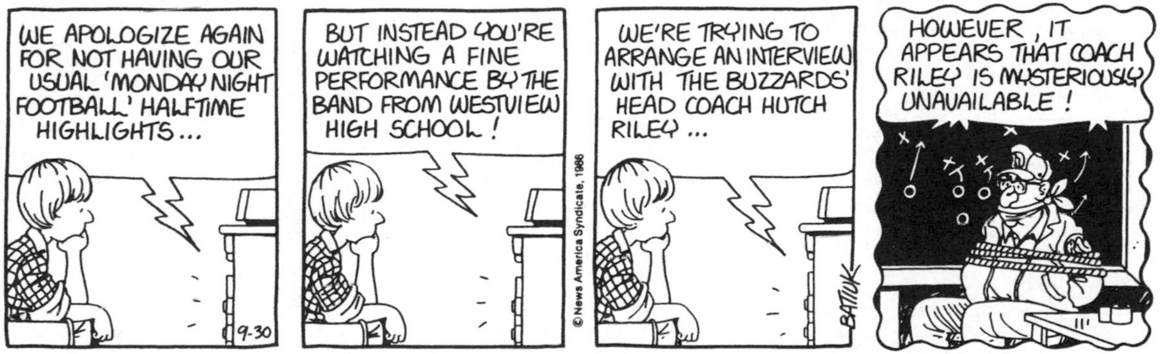
WE APOLOGIZE AGAIN FOR NOT HAVING OUR USUAL 'MONDAY NIGHT FOOTBALL' HALFTIME HIGHLIGHTS ...
9-30
BUT INSTEAD YOU'RE WATCHING A FINE PERFORMANCE BY THE BAND FROM WESTVIEW HIGH SCHOOL !
© News America Syndicate, 1986
WE'RE TRYING TO ARRANGE AN INTERVIEW WITH THE BUZZARDS' HEAD COACH HUTCH RILEY ...
BATIUK
HOWEVER, IT APPEARS THAT COACH RILEY IS MYSTERIOUSLY UNAVAILABLE !

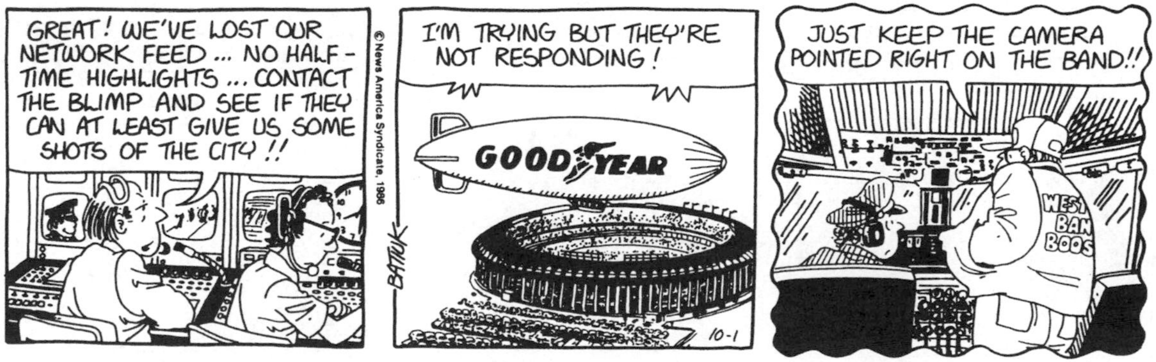
GREAT! WE'VE LOST OUR NETWORK FEED ... NO HALF-TIME HIGHLIGHTS ... CONTACT THE BLIMP AND SEE IF THEY CAN AT LEAST GIVE US SOME SHOTS OF THE CITY !!
© News America Syndicate, 1986
BATIUK
I'M TRYING BUT THEY'RE NOT RESPONDING !
GOODYEAR
10-1
JUST KEEP THE CAMERA POINTED RIGHT ON THE BAND !!

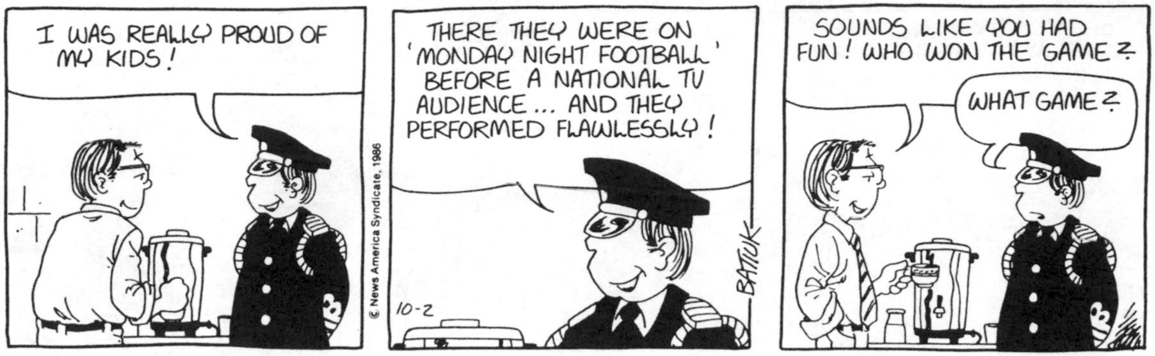
I WAS REALLY PROUD OF MY KIDS!
© News America Syndicate, 1986
THERE THEY WERE ON 'MONDAY NIGHT FOOTBALL' BEFORE A NATIONAL TV AUDIENCE ... AND THEY PERFORMED FLAWLESSLY!
10-2
BATIUK
SOUNDS LIKE YOU HAD FUN! WHO WON THE GAME?
WHAT GAME?

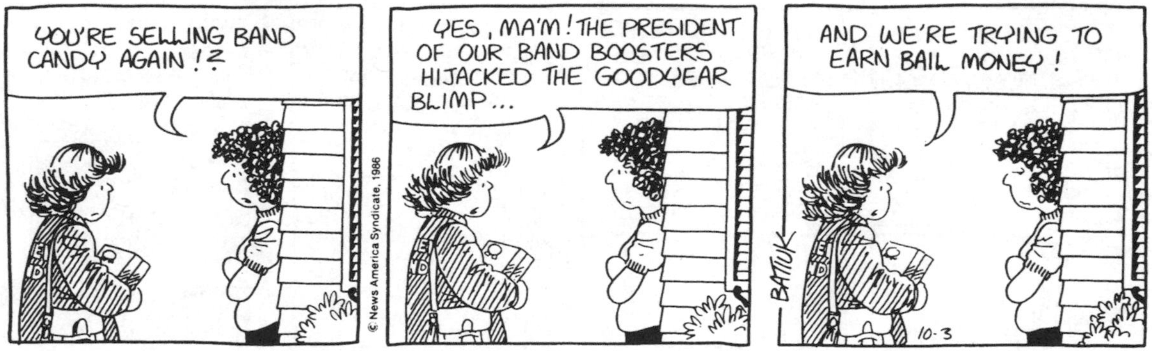
YOU'RE SELLING BAND CANDY AGAIN!?
© News America Syndicate, 1986
YES, MA'M! THE PRESIDENT OF OUR BAND BOOSTERS HIJACKED THE GOODYEAR BLIMP...
AND WE'RE TRYING TO EARN BAIL MONEY!
BATIUK
10-3

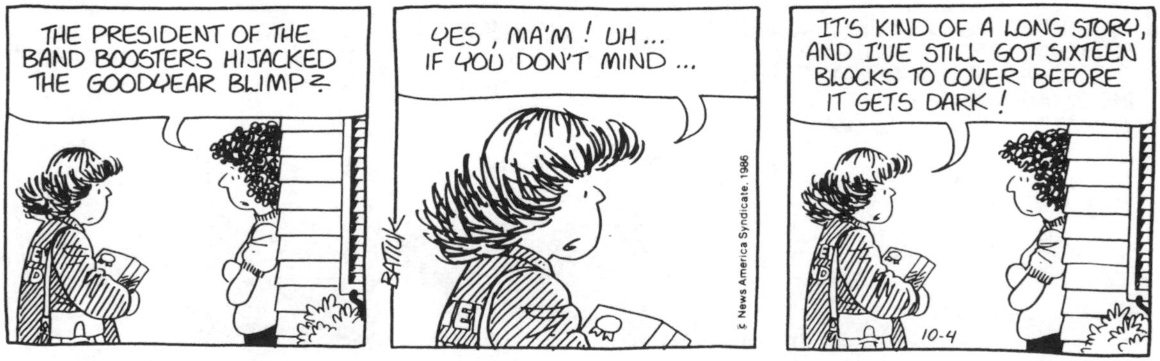
THE PRESIDENT OF THE BAND BOOSTERS HIJACKED THE GOODYEAR BLIMP?
BATIUK
YES, MA'M! UH... IF YOU DON'T MIND...
© News America Syndicate, 1986
IT'S KIND OF A LONG STORY, AND I'VE STILL GOT SIXTEEN BLOCKS TO COVER BEFORE IT GETS DARK!
10-4

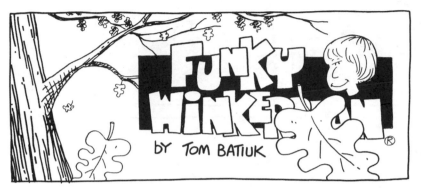

Funky Winkerbean

BY TOM BATIUK

YOU WANT TO KNOW A SECRET?

COME A LITTLE CLOSER AND I'LL WHISPER IT IN THE WIND!

PEOPLE HAVE OFTEN PUZZLED OVER JUST HOW WE LEAVES KNOW WHEN IT'S TIME TO TURN COLOR!

WELL, MOTHER NATURE HAS HER SUBTLE WAYS OF LETTING US KNOW!

© News America Syndicate, 1986

TELEGRAM FROM MOTHER NATURE!! WHO'LL SIGN FOR IT?

THIS COULD BE IT...

BATIUK

10-5

461

WOW, EUGENE !
10-6
ALL THE OTHER LEAVES ON THE TREE HAVE TURNED YELLOW, AND **YOU'RE** STILL GREEN!
NO ONE CAN TELL I USE GRECIAN FORMULA FOR OAK TREES !
BATIUK
© News America Syndicate, 1986

I'VE COME TO THE CONCLUSION THAT LIFE IS AN EMPTY, TEDIOUS EXPERIENCE DEVOID OF ALL MEANING OR HOPE !
© News America Syndicate, 1986
WELL ... IF YOU COULD WISH FOR ONE THING ... WHAT WOULD IT BE ?
IMMORTALITY !
BATIUK
10-7

EUREKA! I'VE **GOT** IT!!
© News America Syndicate, 1986
I'VE FINALLY DISCOVERED THE MEANING OF EXISTENCE!
I ACTUALLY KNOW **WHY** WE'RE PUT HERE FOR A SHORT WHILE AND **WHAT** OUR PURPOSE IS!!
BATIUK
IT'S ... NOW WAIT... I HAD IT A SECOND AGO...
10-8

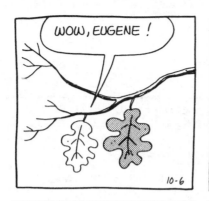

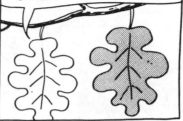

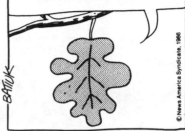

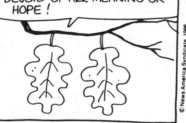

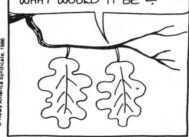

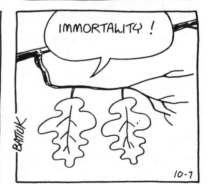

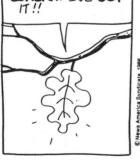

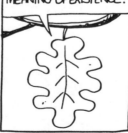

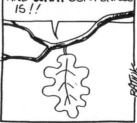

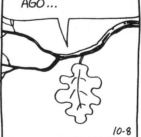

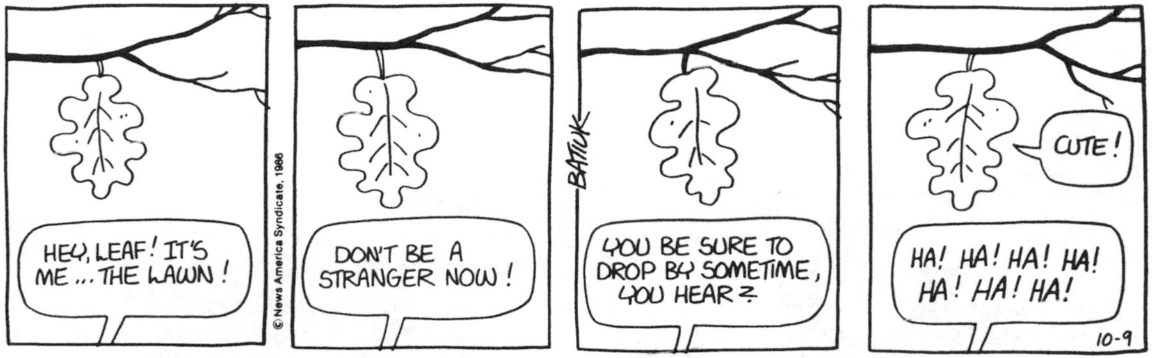
HEY, LEAF! IT'S ME ... THE LAWN!
© News America Syndicate, 1986
DON'T BE A STRANGER NOW!
BATIUK
YOU BE SURE TO DROP BY SOMETIME, YOU HEAR?
CUTE!
HA! HA! HA! HA! HA! HA! HA!
10-9

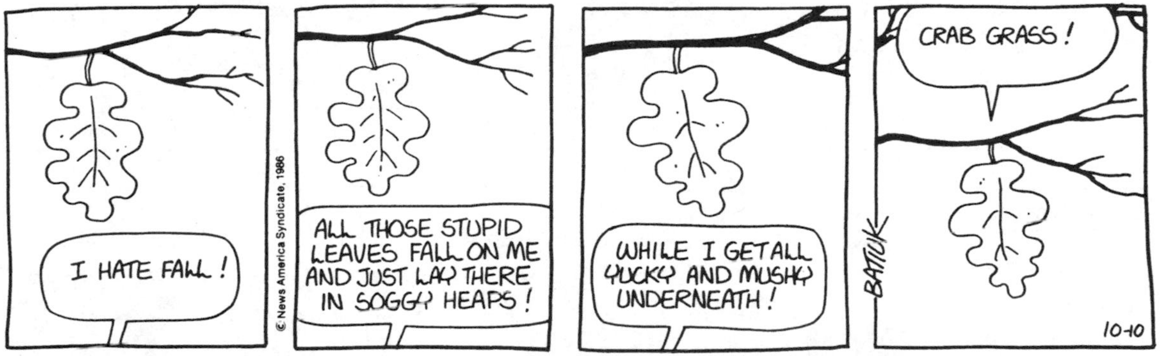
I HATE FALL!
© News America Syndicate, 1986
ALL THOSE STUPID LEAVES FALL ON ME AND JUST LAY THERE IN SOGGY HEAPS!
WHILE I GET ALL YUCKY AND MUSHY UNDERNEATH!
CRAB GRASS!
BATIUK
10-10

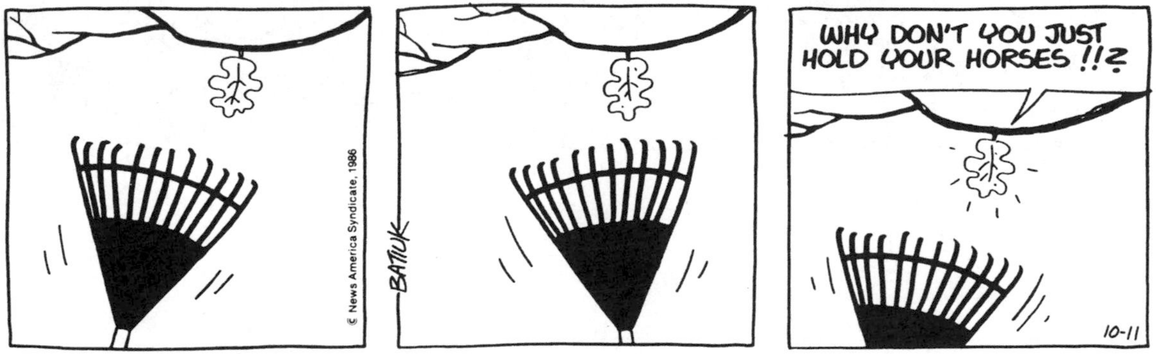
© News America Syndicate, 1986
BATIUK
WHY DON'T YOU JUST HOLD YOUR HORSES!!?
10-11

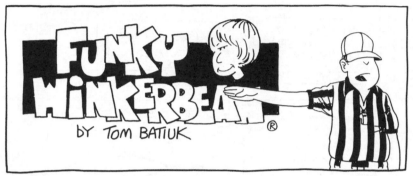

FUNKY WINKERBEAN
BY TOM BATIUK
I'D LIKE A FOOTBALL PROGRAM, PLEASE!
WHEN I'M AT A GAME I ALWAYS BUY A PROGRAM SO I CAN LOOK UP THE VARIOUS SIGNALS THE REFEREES USE!
THAT WAY WHEN I SEE A CALL THAT I'M UNFAMILIAR WITH ... LIKE THAT LAST ONE...
I CAN CHECK AND SEE THAT IT WAS ...
TOO MANY MEN ON THE FIELD ...
© News America Syndicate, 1986
BATIUK
10-12

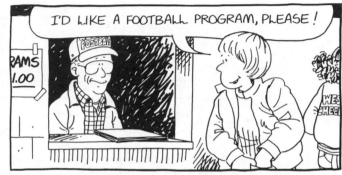

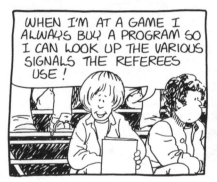

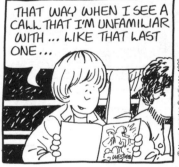

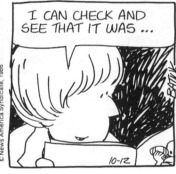

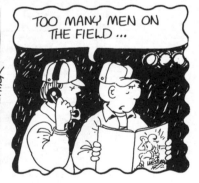

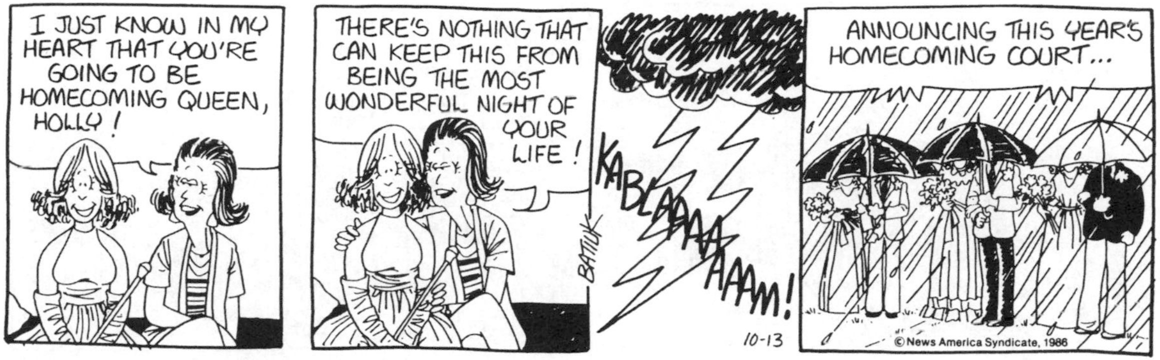
I JUST KNOW IN MY HEART THAT YOU'RE GOING TO BE HOMECOMING QUEEN, HOLLY!
THERE'S NOTHING THAT CAN KEEP THIS FROM BEING THE MOST WONDERFUL NIGHT OF YOUR LIFE!
BATIUK
KABLAAAAAAAAM!
10-13
ANNOUNCING THIS YEAR'S HOMECOMING COURT...
© News America Syndicate, 1986

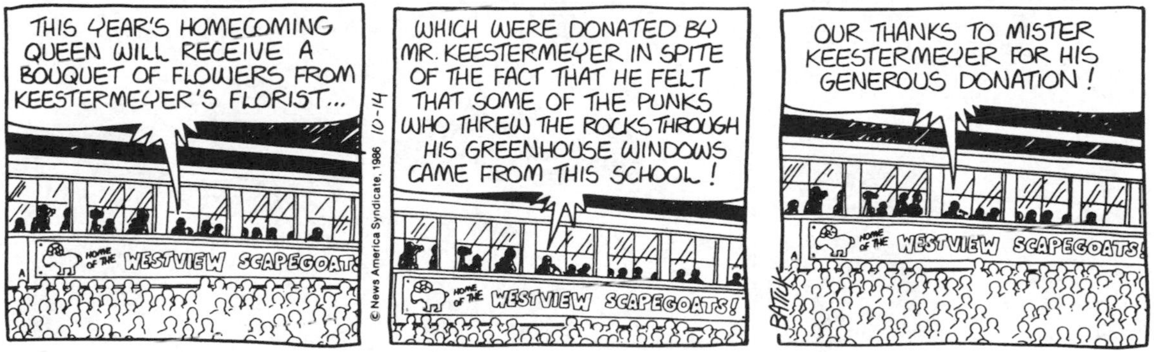
THIS YEAR'S HOMECOMING QUEEN WILL RECEIVE A BOUQUET OF FLOWERS FROM KEESTERMEYER'S FLORIST...
HOME OF THE WESTVIEW SCAPEGOATS!
10-14
© News America Syndicate, 1986
WHICH WERE DONATED BY MR. KEESTERMEYER IN SPITE OF THE FACT THAT HE FELT THAT SOME OF THE PUNKS WHO THREW THE ROCKS THROUGH HIS GREENHOUSE WINDOWS CAME FROM THIS SCHOOL!
HOME OF THE WESTVIEW SCAPEGOATS!
OUR THANKS TO MISTER KEESTERMEYER FOR HIS GENEROUS DONATION!
HOME OF THE WESTVIEW SCAPEGOATS!
BATIUK

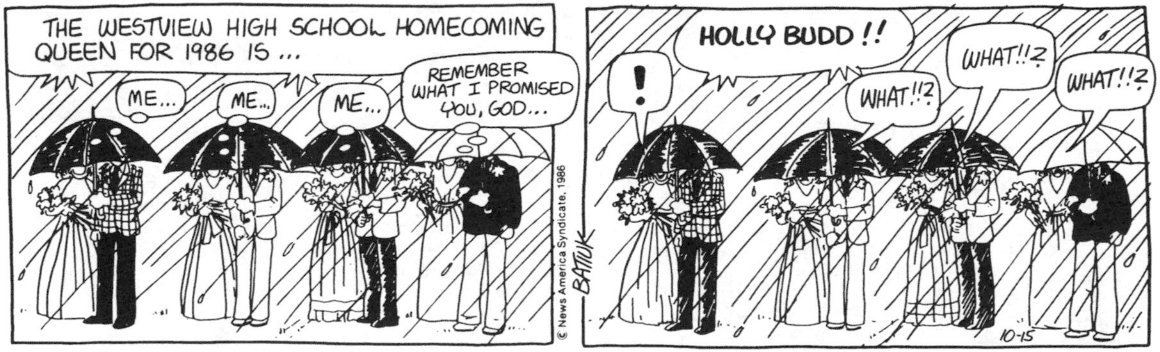
THE WESTVIEW HIGH SCHOOL HOMECOMING QUEEN FOR 1986 IS ...
ME...
ME...
ME...
REMEMBER WHAT I PROMISED YOU, GOD...
© News America Syndicate, 1986
BATIUK
HOLLY BUDD!!
!
WHAT!!?
WHAT!!?
WHAT!!?
10-15

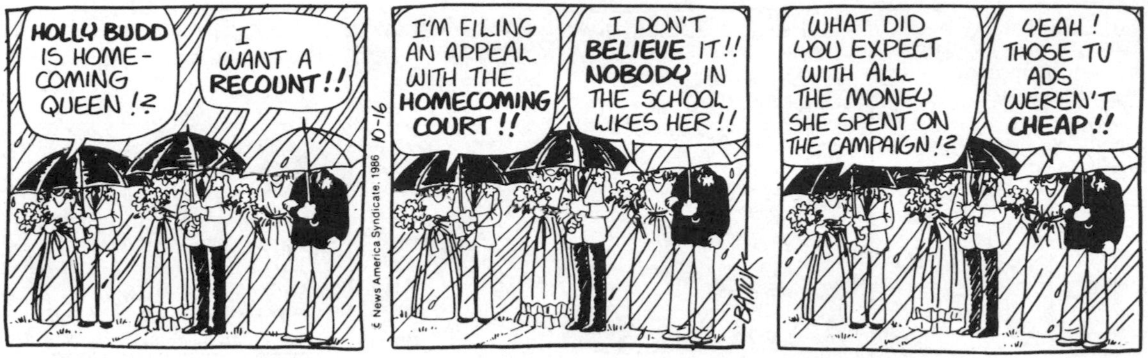
HOLLY BUDD IS HOMECOMING QUEEN !?
I WANT A RECOUNT!!
© News America Syndicate. 1986
10-16
I'M FILING AN APPEAL WITH THE HOMECOMING COURT!!
I DON'T BELIEVE IT!! NOBODY IN THE SCHOOL LIKES HER!!
BATIUK
WHAT DID YOU EXPECT WITH ALL THE MONEY SHE SPENT ON THE CAMPAIGN!?
YEAH! THOSE TV ADS WEREN'T CHEAP!!

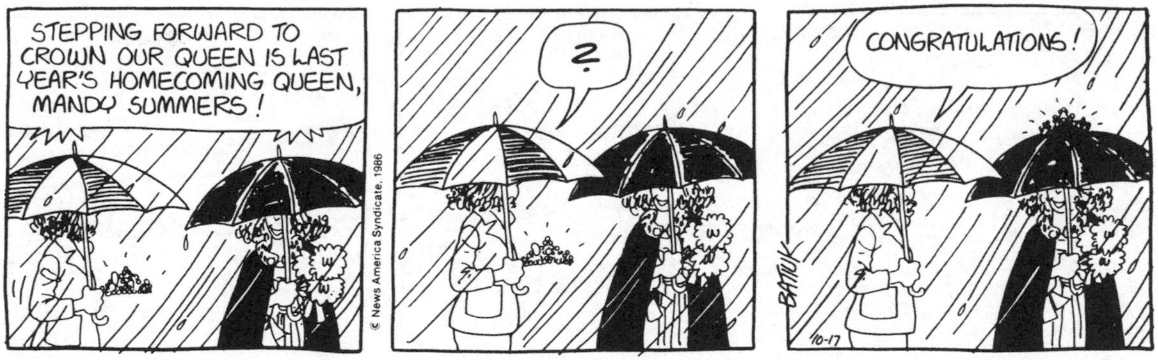
STEPPING FORWARD TO CROWN OUR QUEEN IS LAST YEAR'S HOMECOMING QUEEN, MANDY SUMMERS!
© News America Syndicate. 1986
?
CONGRATULATIONS!
BATIUK
10-17

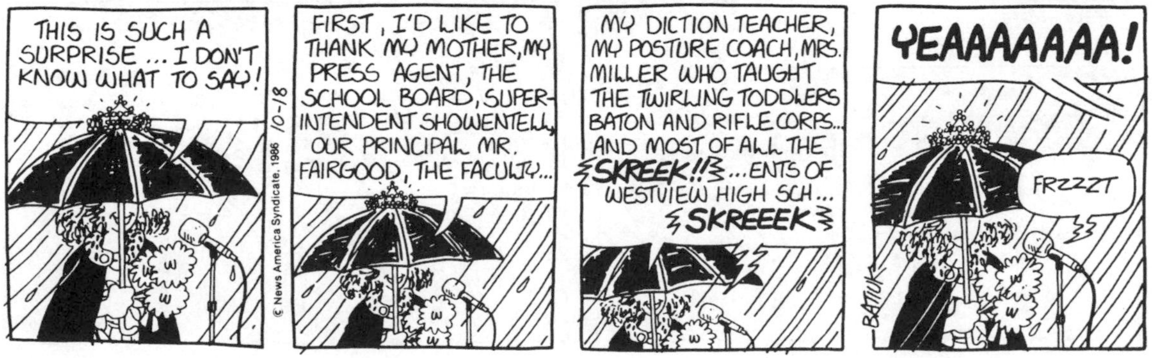
THIS IS SUCH A SURPRISE ... I DON'T KNOW WHAT TO SAY!
10-18
© News America Syndicate. 1986
FIRST, I'D LIKE TO THANK MY MOTHER, MY PRESS AGENT, THE SCHOOL BOARD, SUPERINTENDENT SHOWENTELL, OUR PRINCIPAL MR. FAIRGOOD, THE FACULTY...
MY DICTION TEACHER, MY POSTURE COACH, MRS. MILLER WHO TAUGHT THE TWIRLING TODDLERS BATON AND RIFLE CORPS... AND MOST OF ALL THE SKREEK!! ...ENTS OF WESTVIEW HIGH SCH...
SKREEEK
YEAAAAAAA!
FRZZZT
BATIUK

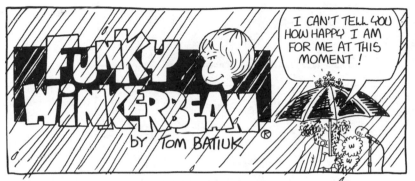

FUNKY WINKERBEAN
BY TOM BATIUK
I CAN'T TELL YOU HOW HAPPY I AM FOR ME AT THIS MOMENT!
I'D LIKE TO THANK MY MOTHER FOR HER ENCOURGEMENT AND FOR PAYING FOR ALL OF MY LESSONS!
PLUS ALL OF THOSE LONG HOURS SHE SPENT WITH ME WHEN I WAS LITTLE, PRACTICING AND REFINING MY ACCEPTANCE SPEECH!
I KNOW THAT MY MOTHER GETS A LOT OF CRITICISM...
BUT I ONLY WISH THAT EVERY GIRL AND HER MOTHER COULD SHARE THE SAME KIND OF CLOSE RELATIONSHIP THAT WE HAVE!
WESTVIEW
©News America Syndicate, 1986
I'LL ADMIT...
BATIUK
10-19
SOMTIMES I DO GET A LITTLE TIRED OF DOUBLE-DATING WITH HER ALL THE TIME...

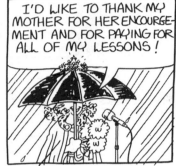

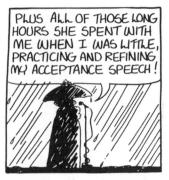

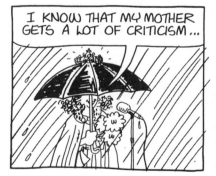

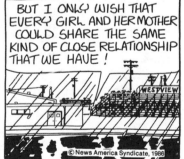

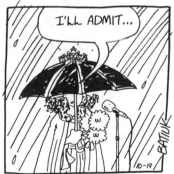

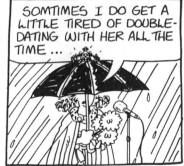

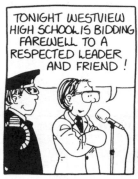

TONIGHT WESTVIEW HIGH SCHOOL IS BIDDING FAREWELL TO A RESPECTED LEADER AND FRIEND!
© News America Syndicate, 1986
10-20
AS MANY OF YOU MAY KNOW, OUR BAND DIRECTOR, HARRY L. DINKLE, IS RETIRING!
WITHOUT HARRY HERE TO LEAD OUR BAND, WESTVIEW HIGH WILL LACK A CERTAIN ENERGY AND SPIRIT... AND, OF COURSE, WITHOUT HIS YEARLY 'BATTLE OF THE BANDS'...
BATIUK
OUR ANNUAL RAINFALL WILL DECREASE MARKEDLY...

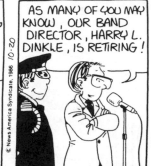

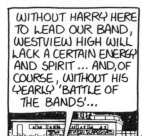

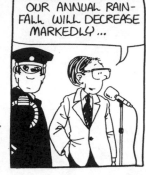

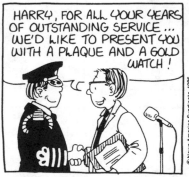

HARRY, FOR ALL YOUR YEARS OF OUTSTANDING SERVICE... WE'D LIKE TO PRESENT YOU WITH A PLAQUE AND A GOLD WATCH!
© News America Syndicate, 1986
ALSO THE KEYS TO THIS BRAND NEW CAR...
BATIUK
GOOD MR.
OOO OOO
AND...
GOODBY MR. 'D'
10-21

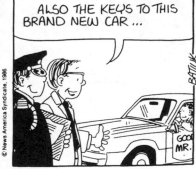

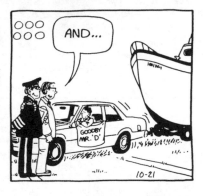

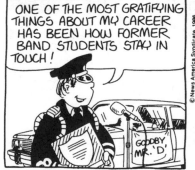

ONE OF THE MOST GRATIFYING THINGS ABOUT MY CAREER HAS BEEN HOW FORMER BAND STUDENTS STAY IN TOUCH!
GOODBY MR. 'D'
© News America Syndicate, 1986
BATIUK
LONG AFTER THEY'VE GRADUATED, THEY KEEP DROPPING BY THE BANDROOM...
10-22
UNTIL THEY FINALLY MEET THEIR ORIGINAL BAND CANDY SALES QUOTA!
GOODBY MR. 'D'

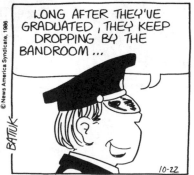

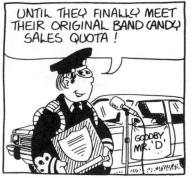

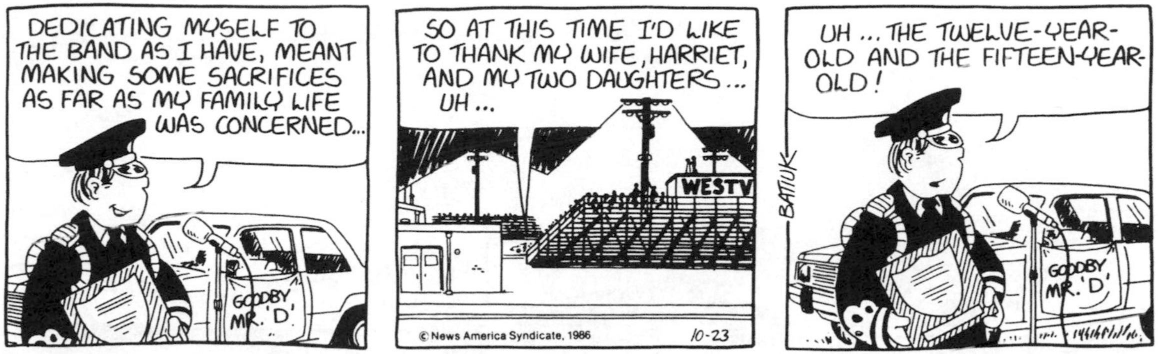
DEDICATING MYSELF TO THE BAND AS I HAVE, MEANT MAKING SOME SACRIFICES AS FAR AS MY FAMILY LIFE WAS CONCERNED...
GOODBY MR. 'D'
SO AT THIS TIME I'D LIKE TO THANK MY WIFE, HARRIET, AND MY TWO DAUGHTERS... UH...
WESTV
© News America Syndicate, 1986
10-23
UH ... THE TWELVE-YEAR-OLD AND THE FIFTEEN-YEAR-OLD!
BATIUK
GOODBY MR. 'D'

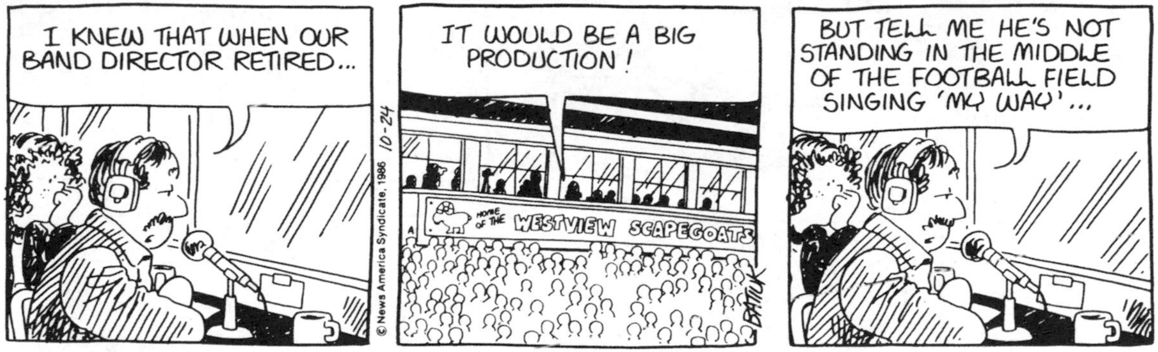
I KNEW THAT WHEN OUR BAND DIRECTOR RETIRED...
© News America Syndicate, 1986
10-24
IT WOULD BE A BIG PRODUCTION!
HOME OF THE WESTVIEW SCAPEGOATS
BATIUK
BUT TELL ME HE'S NOT STANDING IN THE MIDDLE OF THE FOOTBALL FIELD SINGING 'MY WAY'...

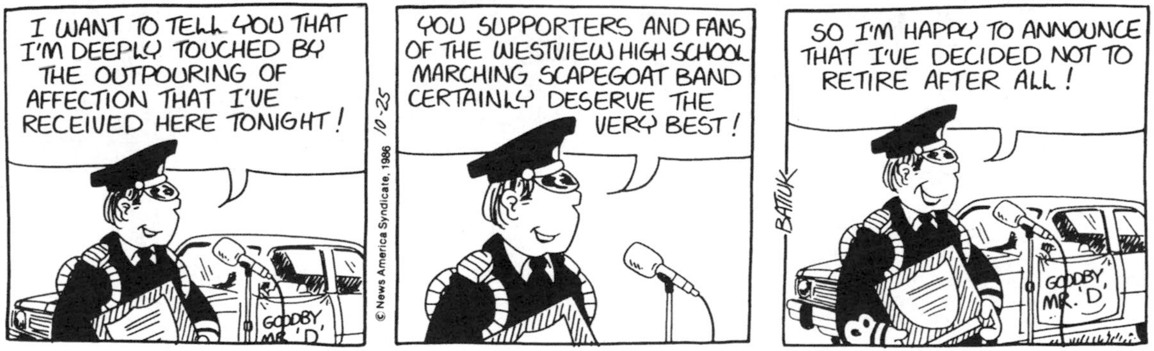
I WANT TO TELL YOU THAT I'M DEEPLY TOUCHED BY THE OUTPOURING OF AFFECTION THAT I'VE RECEIVED HERE TONIGHT!
GOODBY MR. 'D'
© News America Syndicate, 1986
10-25
YOU SUPPORTERS AND FANS OF THE WESTVIEW HIGH SCHOOL MARCHING SCAPEGOAT BAND CERTAINLY DESERVE THE VERY BEST!
SO I'M HAPPY TO ANNOUNCE THAT I'VE DECIDED NOT TO RETIRE AFTER ALL!
BATIUK
GOODBY MR. 'D'

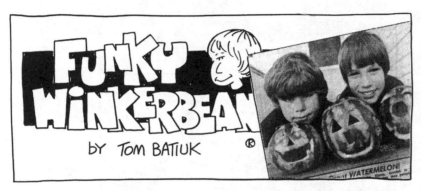

FUNKY WINKERBEAN
BY TOM BATIUK
WATERMELON!
AS THE 1986 HALLOWEEN WATERMELON SPOKESMELON, I'D LIKE TO MAKE THE FOLLOWING ANNOUNCEMENT...
THIS YEAR'S HALLOWEEN WATERMELON SALUTE GOES TO BRIAN EGER AND KENNY NORRIS OF ELYRIA, OHIO...
WHO, TO QUOTE FROM THIS NEWSPAPER CLIPPING... "DECIDED TO CARVE WATERMELONS FOR HALLOWEEN RATHER THAN PUMPKINS!"
10-26
© News America Syndicate, 1986
"THE NEXT DAY AT SCHOOL THE TWO BOYS WERE TAUNTED AND RIDICULED BY CLASSMATES WHO THEN PROCEEDED TO ..."
UH, WELL THE, UH... THE ARTICLE JUST SORT OF GOES ON FROM THERE...
BATIUK
HONORABLE MENTION... THE POINDEXTERS RUTHERFORD, N.J.

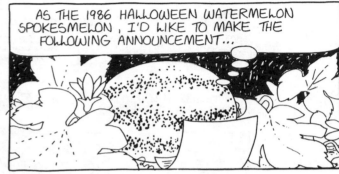

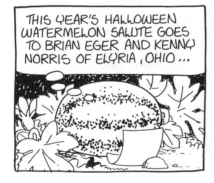

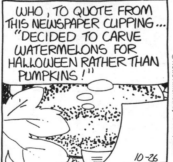

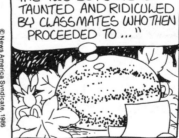

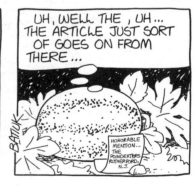

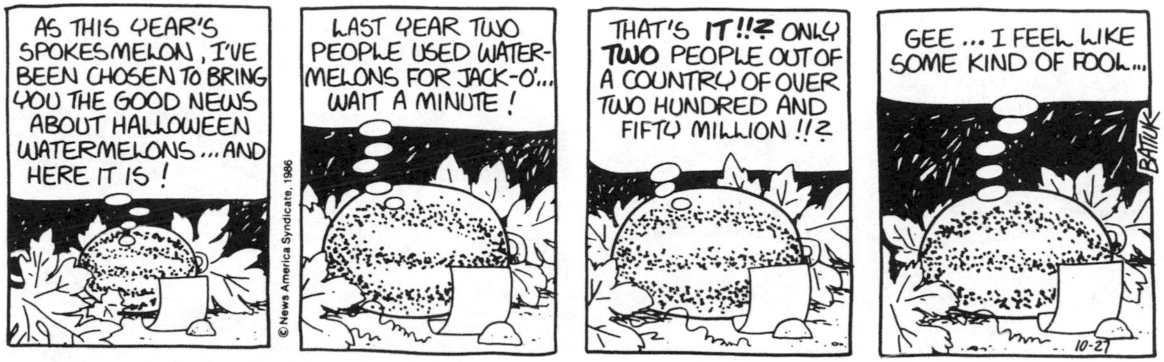
AS THIS YEAR'S SPOKESMELON, I'VE BEEN CHOSEN TO BRING YOU THE GOOD NEWS ABOUT HALLOWEEN WATERMELONS ... AND HERE IT IS!
© News America Syndicate, 1986
LAST YEAR TWO PEOPLE USED WATERMELONS FOR JACK-O'... WAIT A MINUTE!
THAT'S IT!!? ONLY TWO PEOPLE OUT OF A COUNTRY OF OVER TWO HUNDRED AND FIFTY MILLION!!?
GEE ... I FEEL LIKE SOME KIND OF FOOL...
BATIUK
10-27

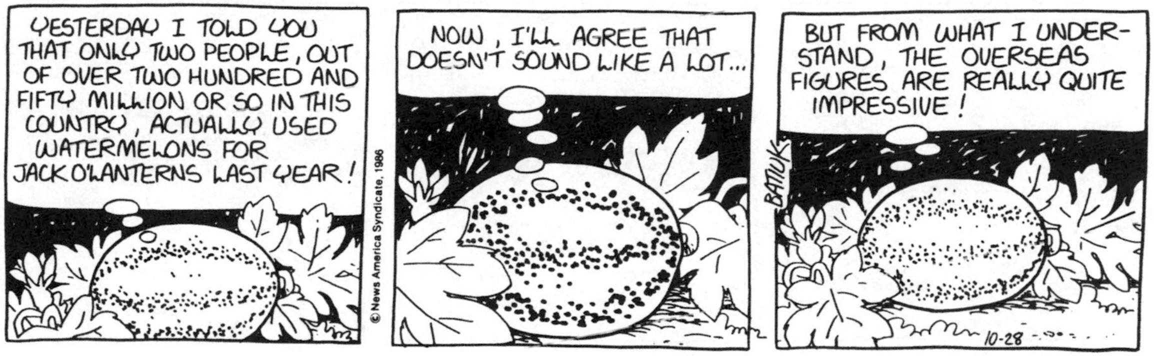
YESTERDAY I TOLD YOU THAT ONLY TWO PEOPLE, OUT OF OVER TWO HUNDRED AND FIFTY MILLION OR SO IN THIS COUNTRY, ACTUALLY USED WATERMELONS FOR JACK O'LANTERNS LAST YEAR!
© News America Syndicate, 1986
NOW, I'LL AGREE THAT DOESN'T SOUND LIKE A LOT...
BATIUK
BUT FROM WHAT I UNDERSTAND, THE OVERSEAS FIGURES ARE REALLY QUITE IMPRESSIVE!
10-28

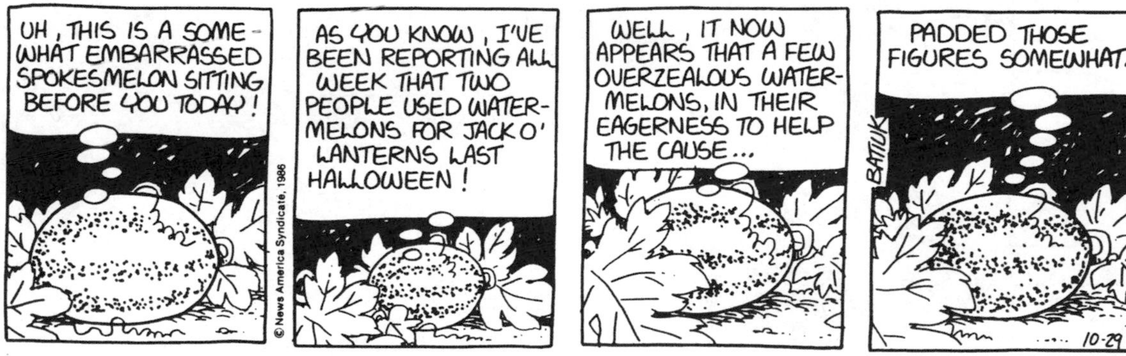
UH, THIS IS A SOMEWHAT EMBARRASSED SPOKESMELON SITTING BEFORE YOU TODAY!
© News America Syndicate, 1986
AS YOU KNOW, I'VE BEEN REPORTING ALL WEEK THAT TWO PEOPLE USED WATERMELONS FOR JACK O' LANTERNS LAST HALLOWEEN!
WELL, IT NOW APPEARS THAT A FEW OVERZEALOUS WATERMELONS, IN THEIR EAGERNESS TO HELP THE CAUSE...
BATIUK
PADDED THOSE FIGURES SOMEWHAT...
10-29

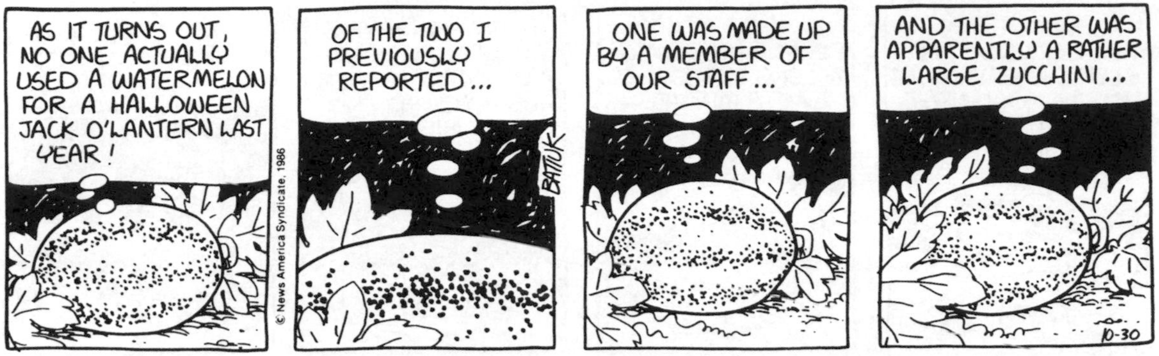
AS IT TURNS OUT, NO ONE ACTUALLY USED A WATERMELON FOR A HALLOWEEN JACK O'LANTERN LAST YEAR!
OF THE TWO I PREVIOUSLY REPORTED...
ONE WAS MADE UP BY A MEMBER OF OUR STAFF...
AND THE OTHER WAS APPARENTLY A RATHER LARGE ZUCCHINI...
© News America Syndicate, 1986
BATIUK
10-30

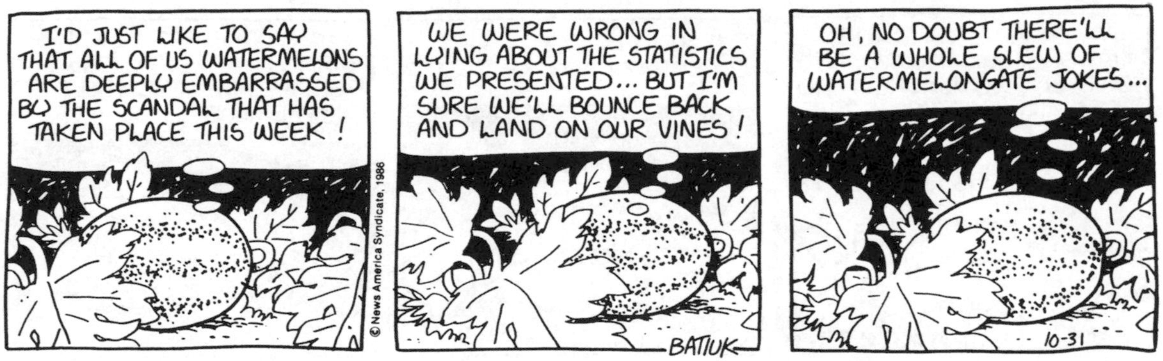
I'D JUST LIKE TO SAY THAT ALL OF US WATERMELONS ARE DEEPLY EMBARRASSED BY THE SCANDAL THAT HAS TAKEN PLACE THIS WEEK!
WE WERE WRONG IN LYING ABOUT THE STATISTICS WE PRESENTED... BUT I'M SURE WE'LL BOUNCE BACK AND LAND ON OUR VINES!
OH, NO DOUBT THERE'LL BE A WHOLE SLEW OF WATERMELONGATE JOKES...
© News America Syndicate, 1986
BATIUK
10-31

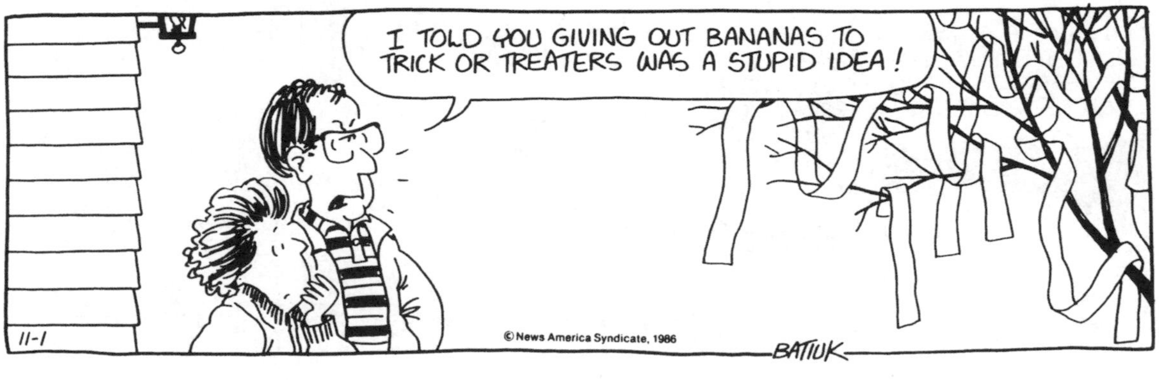
I TOLD YOU GIVING OUT BANANAS TO TRICK OR TREATERS WAS A STUPID IDEA!
11-1
© News America Syndicate, 1986
BATIUK

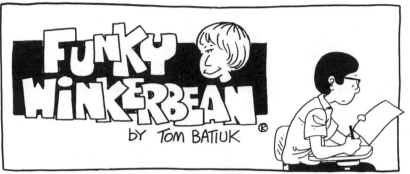

FUNKY WINKERBEAN
BY TOM BATIUK ®
HMM ... EXTRACURRICULAR ACTIVITIES ...
WHAT SORT OF EXTRA-CURRICULAR ACTIVITIES DID YOU MENTION ON YOUR COLLEGE APPLICATIONS, BARRY?
WELL, I SENT A BOUND RÉSUMÉ BOOKLET THAT I HAD PRINTED UP...
BATIUK
AND I ALSO INCLUDED A VIDEO FEATURING SOME OF THE HIGHLIGHTS FROM MY STUDENT ACTIVITIES WITH THE MUSIC FROM MIAMI VICE FOR A SOUND-TRACK!
© News America Syndicate, 1986
MAYBE I'LL JUST SCRATCH OUT THIS PART ABOUT MAKING THIRD BUS PATROL ALTERNATE IN THE THIRD GRADE!
11-2

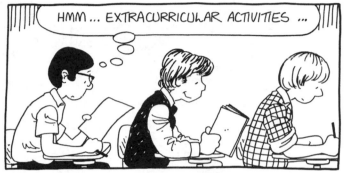

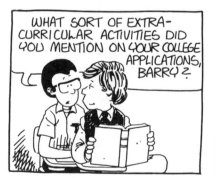

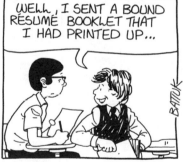

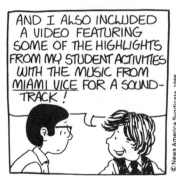

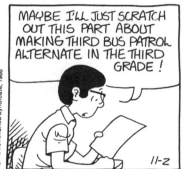

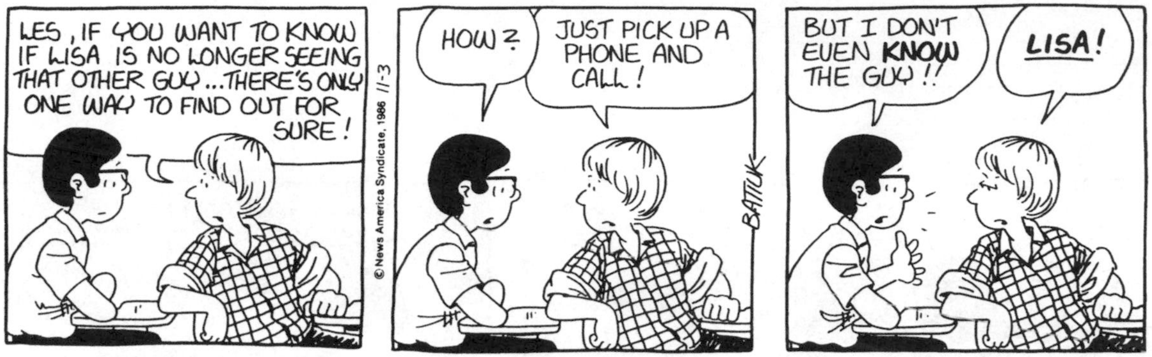
LES, IF YOU WANT TO KNOW IF LISA IS NO LONGER SEEING THAT OTHER GUY... THERE'S ONLY ONE WAY TO FIND OUT FOR SURE!
HOW?
JUST PICK UP A PHONE AND CALL!
BUT I DON'T EVEN **KNOW** THE GUY!!
LISA!
© News America Syndicate, 1986
11-3
BATIUK

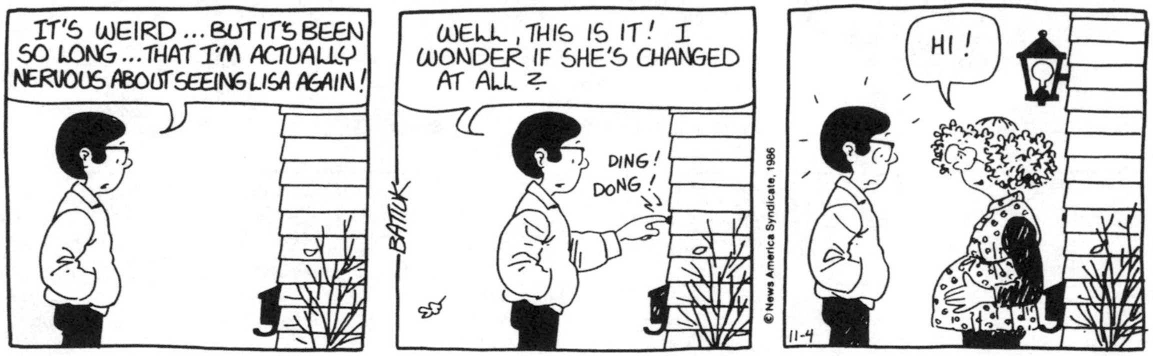
IT'S WEIRD... BUT IT'S BEEN SO LONG... THAT I'M ACTUALLY NERVOUS ABOUT SEEING LISA AGAIN!
BATIUK
WELL, THIS IS IT! I WONDER IF SHE'S CHANGED AT ALL?
DING! DONG!
HI!
© News America Syndicate, 1986
11-4

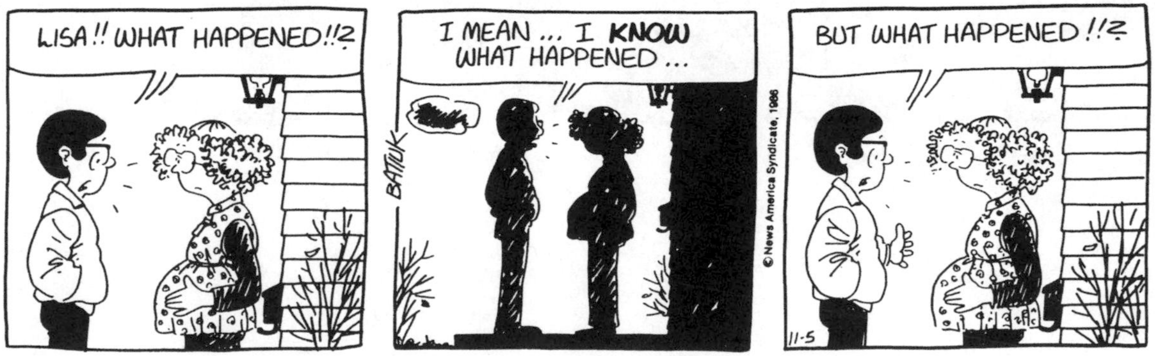
LISA!! WHAT HAPPENED!!?
I MEAN... I **KNOW** WHAT HAPPENED...
BATIUK
BUT WHAT HAPPENED!!?
© News America Syndicate, 1986
11-5

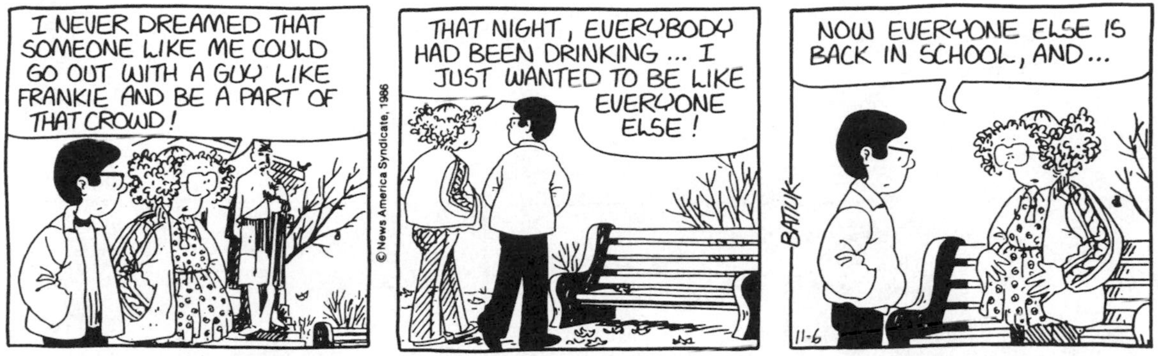
I NEVER DREAMED THAT SOMEONE LIKE ME COULD GO OUT WITH A GUY LIKE FRANKIE AND BE A PART OF THAT CROWD!
© News America Syndicate, 1986
THAT NIGHT, EVERYBODY HAD BEEN DRINKING ... I JUST WANTED TO BE LIKE EVERYONE ELSE!
BATIUK
NOW EVERYONE ELSE IS BACK IN SCHOOL, AND...
11-6

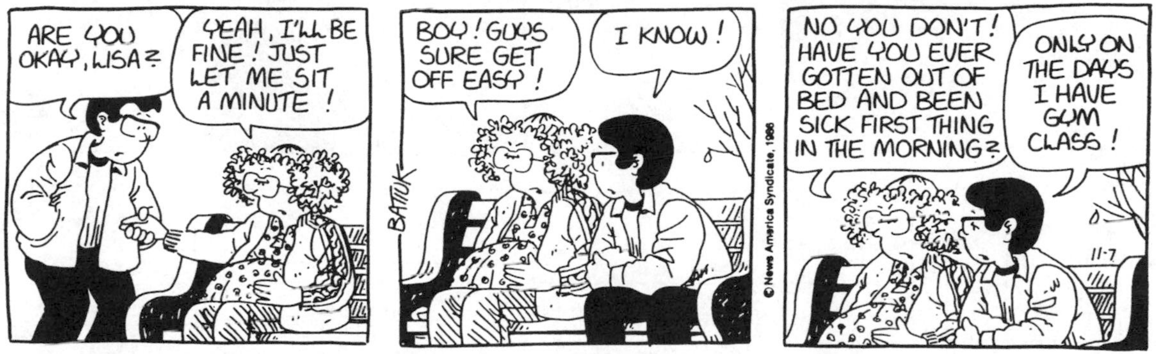
ARE YOU OKAY, LISA?
YEAH, I'LL BE FINE! JUST LET ME SIT A MINUTE!
BATIUK
BOY! GUYS SURE GET OFF EASY!
I KNOW!
© News America Syndicate, 1986
NO YOU DON'T! HAVE YOU EVER GOTTEN OUT OF BED AND BEEN SICK FIRST THING IN THE MORNING?
ONLY ON THE DAYS I HAVE GYM CLASS!
11-7

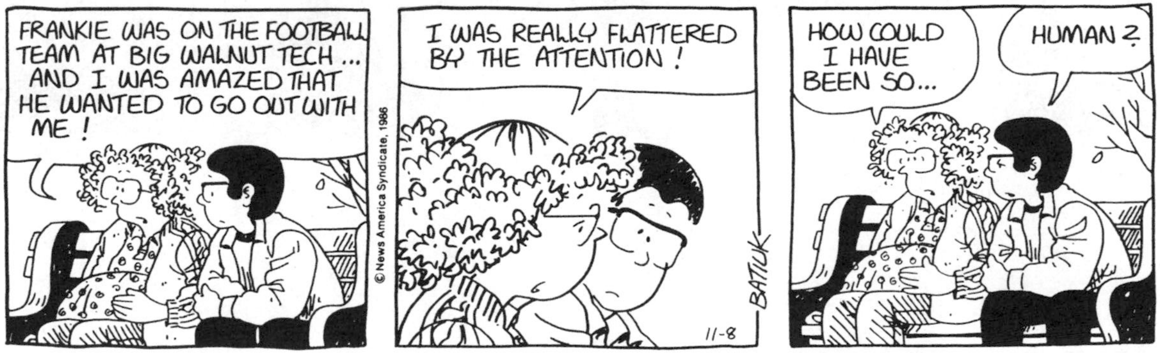
FRANKIE WAS ON THE FOOTBALL TEAM AT BIG WALNUT TECH ... AND I WAS AMAZED THAT HE WANTED TO GO OUT WITH ME!
© News America Syndicate, 1986
I WAS REALLY FLATTERED BY THE ATTENTION!
BATIUK
11-8
HOW COULD I HAVE BEEN SO...
HUMAN?

FUNKY WINKERBEAN
BY TOM BATIUK
1.
YOU'VE GOT FIFTEEN MINUTES FOR THE VOCABULARY TEST!
VOCABULARY TEST? SHOOT! ALL I STUDIED WERE DEFINITIONS!
MAYBE I'LL START WITH THE DIFFICULT ONES FIRST, AND THEN GO BACK AND DO THE IMPOSSIBLE ONES IF I HAVE TIME!
11-9
DEFINE THE FOLLOWING:
© News America Syndicate, 1986
(1.) CLAMMY
BATIUK
The mother of a clam!

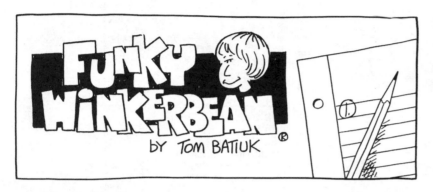

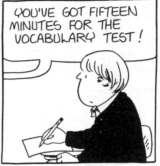

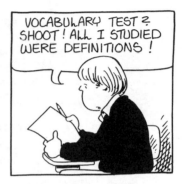

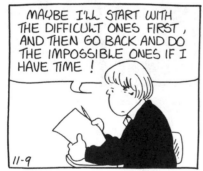

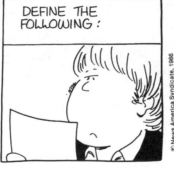

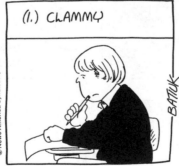

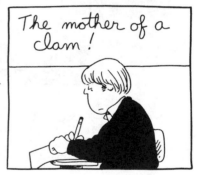

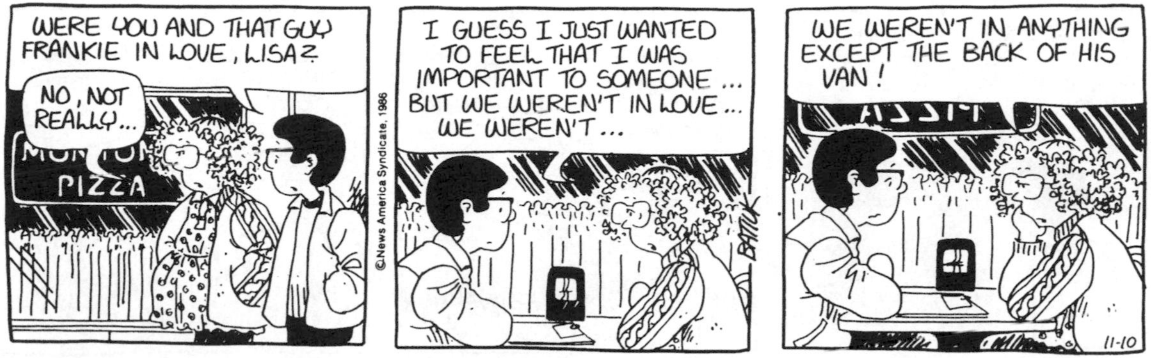
WERE YOU AND THAT GUY FRANKIE IN LOVE, LISA?
NO, NOT REALLY...
MONTONI PIZZA
©News America Syndicate, 1986
I GUESS I JUST WANTED TO FEEL THAT I WAS IMPORTANT TO SOMEONE ... BUT WE WEREN'T IN LOVE... WE WEREN'T...
BATIUK
WE WEREN'T IN ANYTHING EXCEPT THE BACK OF HIS VAN!
11-10

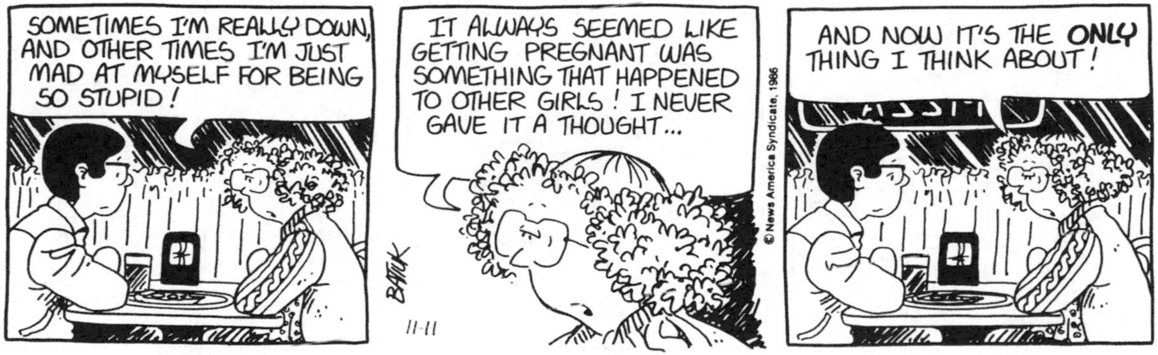
SOMETIMES I'M REALLY DOWN, AND OTHER TIMES I'M JUST MAD AT MYSELF FOR BEING SO STUPID!
BATIUK
11-11
IT ALWAYS SEEMED LIKE GETTING PREGNANT WAS SOMETHING THAT HAPPENED TO OTHER GIRLS! I NEVER GAVE IT A THOUGHT...
©News America Syndicate, 1986
AND NOW IT'S THE **ONLY** THING I THINK ABOUT!

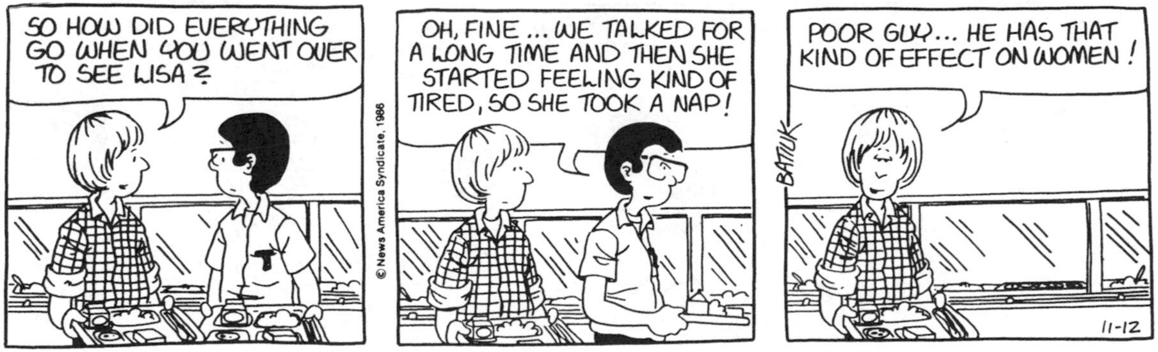
SO HOW DID EVERYTHING GO WHEN YOU WENT OVER TO SEE LISA?
©News America Syndicate, 1986
OH, FINE ... WE TALKED FOR A LONG TIME AND THEN SHE STARTED FEELING KIND OF TIRED, SO SHE TOOK A NAP!
BATIUK
POOR GUY... HE HAS THAT KIND OF EFFECT ON WOMEN!
11-12

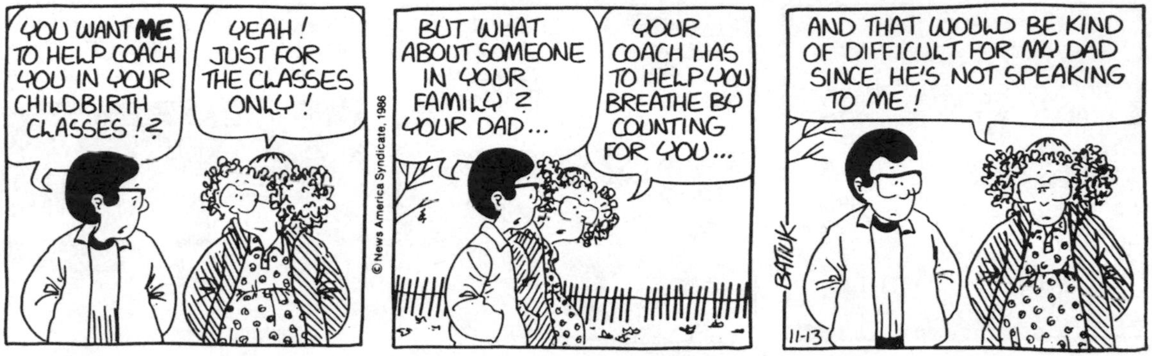
YOU WANT ME TO HELP COACH YOU IN YOUR CHILDBIRTH CLASSES !?
YEAH ! JUST FOR THE CLASSES ONLY !
© News America Syndicate, 1986
BUT WHAT ABOUT SOMEONE IN YOUR FAMILY ? YOUR DAD...
YOUR COACH HAS TO HELP YOU BREATHE BY COUNTING FOR YOU...
AND THAT WOULD BE KIND OF DIFFICULT FOR MY DAD SINCE HE'S NOT SPEAKING TO ME !
BATIUK
11-13

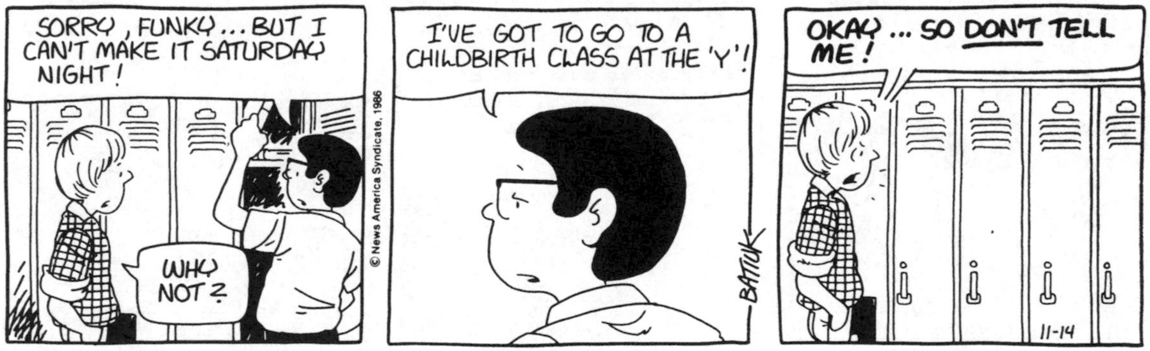
SORRY, FUNKY... BUT I CAN'T MAKE IT SATURDAY NIGHT !
WHY NOT ?
© News America Syndicate, 1986
I'VE GOT TO GO TO A CHILDBIRTH CLASS AT THE 'Y' !
BATIUK
OKAY ... SO DON'T TELL ME !
11-14

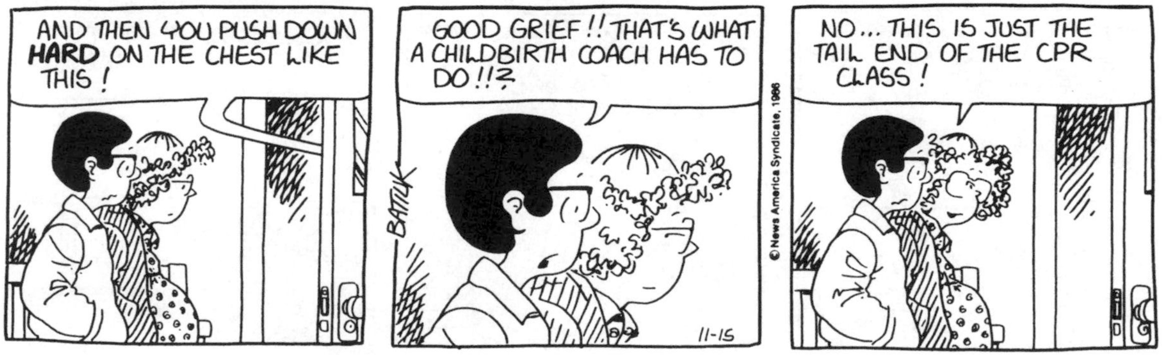
AND THEN YOU PUSH DOWN HARD ON THE CHEST LIKE THIS !
BATIUK
GOOD GRIEF !! THAT'S WHAT A CHILDBIRTH COACH HAS TO DO !!?
11-15
© News America Syndicate, 1986
NO... THIS IS JUST THE TAIL END OF THE CPR CLASS !

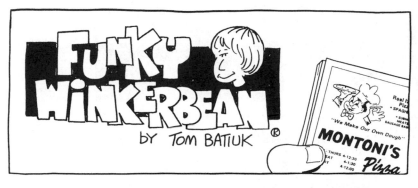

FUNKY WINKERBEAN
BY TOM BATIUK ®
MONTONI'S Pizza
"We Make Our Own Dough"
A LARGE PEPPERONI WITH MUSHROOMS AND DOUBLE CHEESE!
MONTONI'S PIZZA
HELP WANTED
OKAY... WOULD YOU LIKE SOME DOUGH AND TOMATO SAUCE WITH THAT?
OKAY... WILL THERE BE ANYTHING ELSE WITH THAT PIZZA, SIR?
VERY GOOD...
MONTONI'S PIZZA
HELP WANTED
11-16
BATIUK
THAT'LL BE ABOUT TWENTY MINUTES...
© News America Syndicate, 1986
BEFORE WE EVEN GET STARTED!

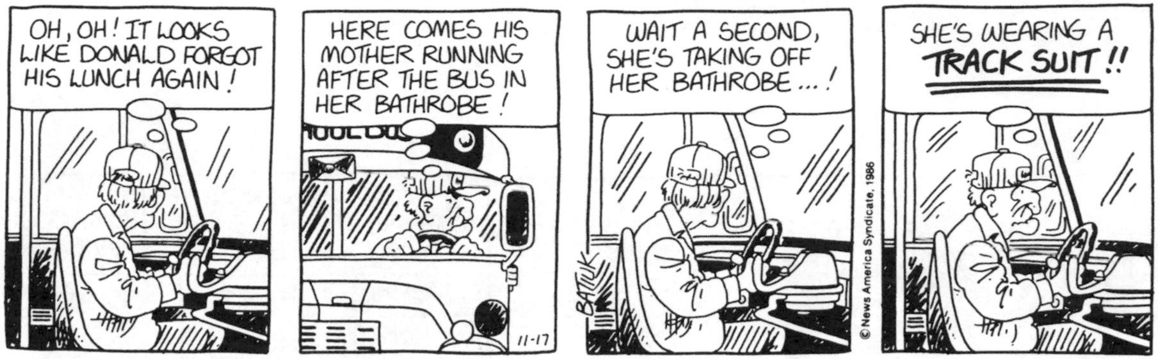
OH, OH! IT LOOKS LIKE DONALD FORGOT HIS LUNCH AGAIN!
HERE COMES HIS MOTHER RUNNING AFTER THE BUS IN HER BATHROBE!
11-17
BATIUK
WAIT A SECOND, SHE'S TAKING OFF HER BATHROBE...!
© News America Syndicate, 1986
SHE'S WEARING A TRACK SUIT!!

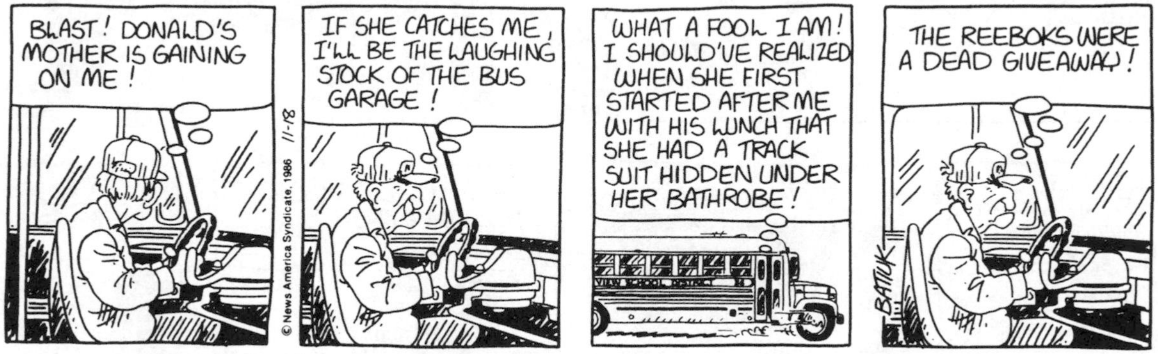
BLAST! DONALD'S MOTHER IS GAINING ON ME!
© News America Syndicate, 1986
11-18
IF SHE CATCHES ME, I'LL BE THE LAUGHING STOCK OF THE BUS GARAGE!
WHAT A FOOL I AM! I SHOULD'VE REALIZED WHEN SHE FIRST STARTED AFTER ME WITH HIS LUNCH THAT SHE HAD A TRACK SUIT HIDDEN UNDER HER BATHROBE!
BATIUK
THE REEBOKS WERE A DEAD GIVEAWAY!

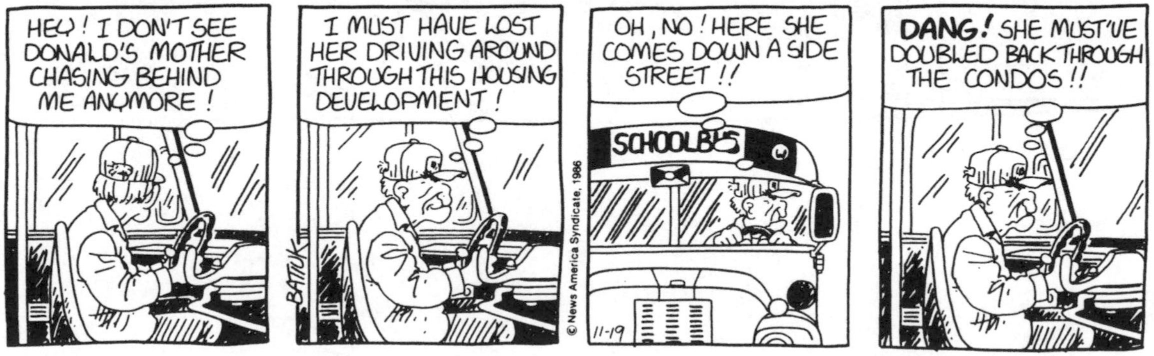
HEY! I DON'T SEE DONALD'S MOTHER CHASING BEHIND ME ANYMORE!
BATIUK
I MUST HAVE LOST HER DRIVING AROUND THROUGH THIS HOUSING DEVELOPMENT!
© News America Syndicate, 1986
OH, NO! HERE SHE COMES DOWN A SIDE STREET!!
SCHOOLBUS
11-19
DANG! SHE MUST'VE DOUBLED BACK THROUGH THE CONDOS!!

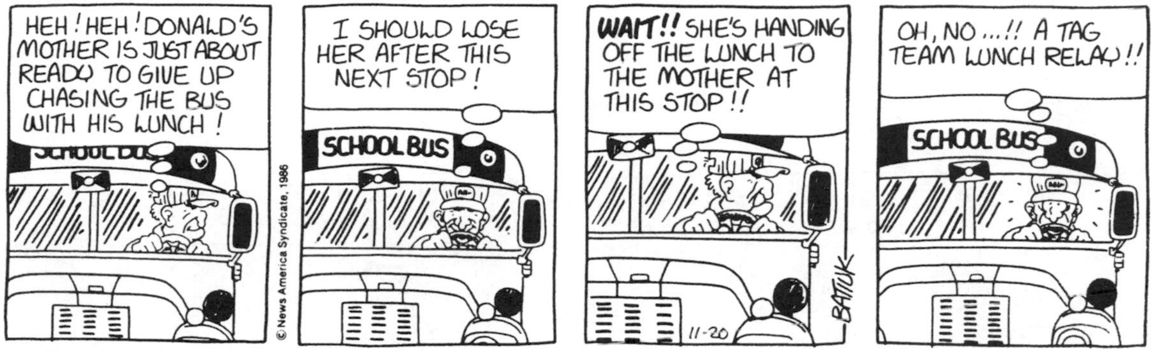
HEH! HEH! DONALD'S MOTHER IS JUST ABOUT READY TO GIVE UP CHASING THE BUS WITH HIS LUNCH!
SCHOOL BUS
© News America Syndicate, 1986
I SHOULD LOSE HER AFTER THIS NEXT STOP!
SCHOOL BUS
WAIT!! SHE'S HANDING OFF THE LUNCH TO THE MOTHER AT THIS STOP!!
11-20
BATIUK
OH, NO...!! A TAG TEAM LUNCH RELAY!!
SCHOOL BUS

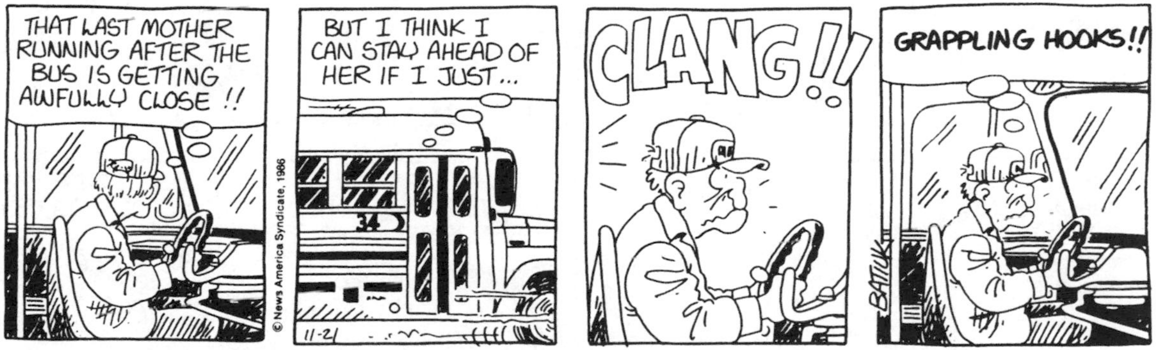
THAT LAST MOTHER RUNNING AFTER THE BUS IS GETTING AWFULLY CLOSE!!
© News America Syndicate, 1986
BUT I THINK I CAN STAY AHEAD OF HER IF I JUST...
34
11-21
CLANG!!
GRAPPLING HOOKS!!
BATIUK

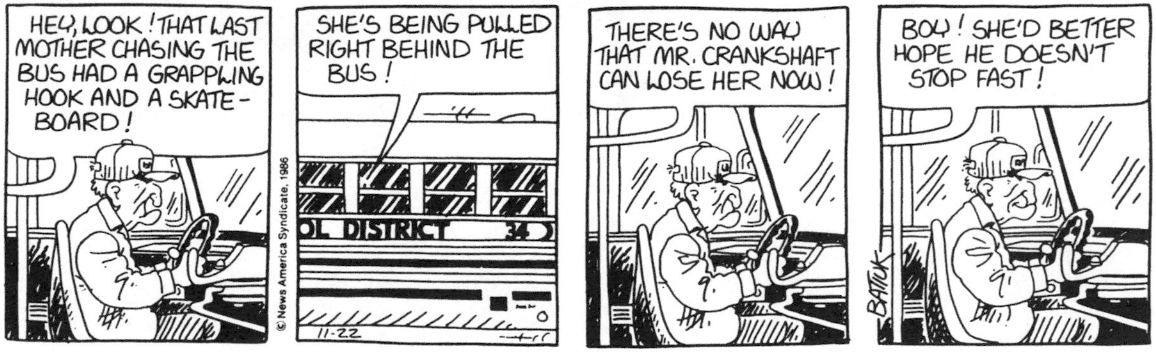
HEY, LOOK! THAT LAST MOTHER CHASING THE BUS HAD A GRAPPLING HOOK AND A SKATE-BOARD!
© News America Syndicate, 1986
SHE'S BEING PULLED RIGHT BEHIND THE BUS!
OL DISTRICT 34
11-22
THERE'S NO WAY THAT MR. CRANKSHAFT CAN LOSE HER NOW!
BATIUK
BOY! SHE'D BETTER HOPE HE DOESN'T STOP FAST!

FUNKY WINKERBEAN
BY TOM BATIUK
WOULD YOU LIKE TO BUY ONE OF OUR TURKEYS?
WHAT KIND OF TURKEYS ARE THEY?
THANKSGIVING TURKEYS!
WE'VE JUST COME OUT WITH OUR 'NEW IMPROVED' BAND TURKEY!
11-23
NEW IMPROVED?
BATIUK
THAT'S RIGHT! IT'S IMPLANTED WITH A SPECIAL TRANSMITTER...
© News America Syndicate, 1986
THAT JAMS THE RECEPTION OF ALL FOOTBALL GAMES!

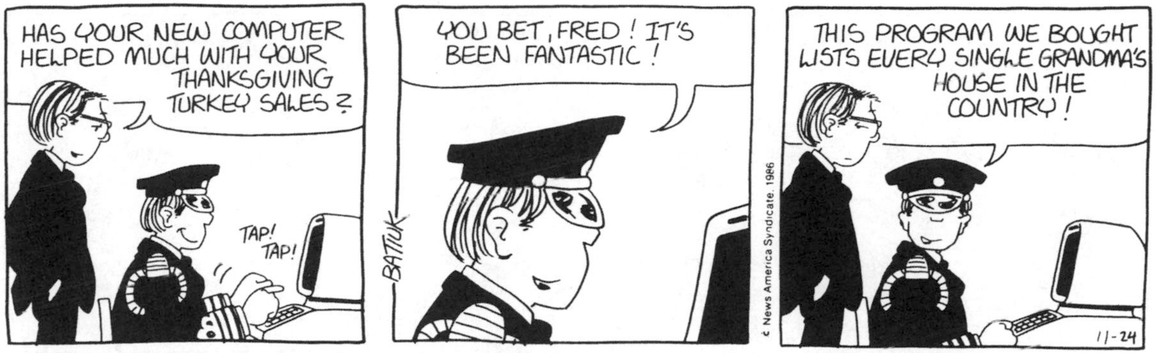
HAS YOUR NEW COMPUTER HELPED MUCH WITH YOUR THANKSGIVING TURKEY SALES ?
TAP! TAP!
YOU BET, FRED! IT'S BEEN FANTASTIC!
BATIUK
© News America Syndicate, 1986
THIS PROGRAM WE BOUGHT LISTS EVERY SINGLE GRANDMA'S HOUSE IN THE COUNTRY!
11-24

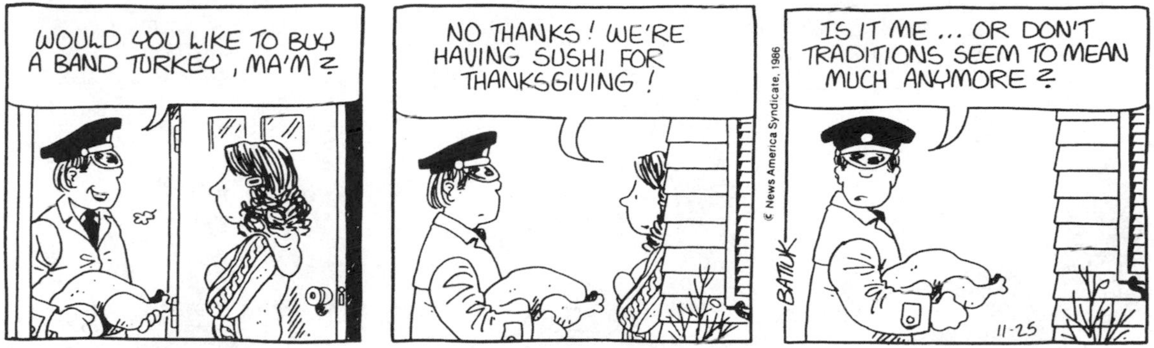
WOULD YOU LIKE TO BUY A BAND TURKEY, MA'M ?
NO THANKS! WE'RE HAVING SUSHI FOR THANKSGIVING!
© News America Syndicate, 1986
BATIUK
IS IT ME ... OR DON'T TRADITIONS SEEM TO MEAN MUCH ANYMORE ?
11-25

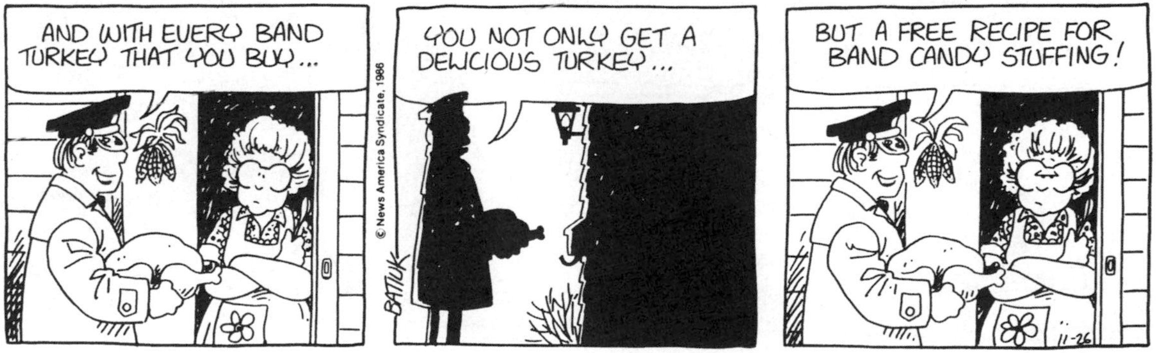
AND WITH EVERY BAND TURKEY THAT YOU BUY...
© News America Syndicate, 1986
BATIUK
YOU NOT ONLY GET A DELICIOUS TURKEY...
BUT A FREE RECIPE FOR BAND CANDY STUFFING!
11-26

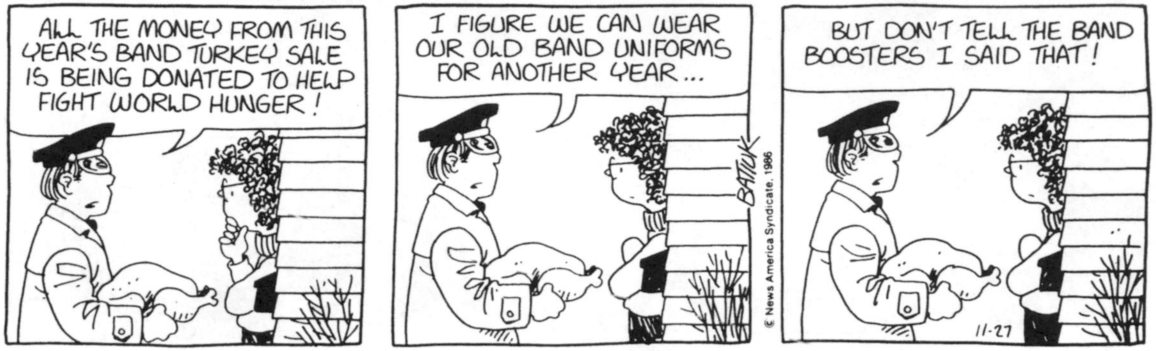
ALL THE MONEY FROM THIS YEAR'S BAND TURKEY SALE IS BEING DONATED TO HELP FIGHT WORLD HUNGER!
I FIGURE WE CAN WEAR OUR OLD BAND UNIFORMS FOR ANOTHER YEAR...
BATIUK
© News America Syndicate, 1986
BUT DON'T TELL THE BAND BOOSTERS I SAID THAT!
11-27

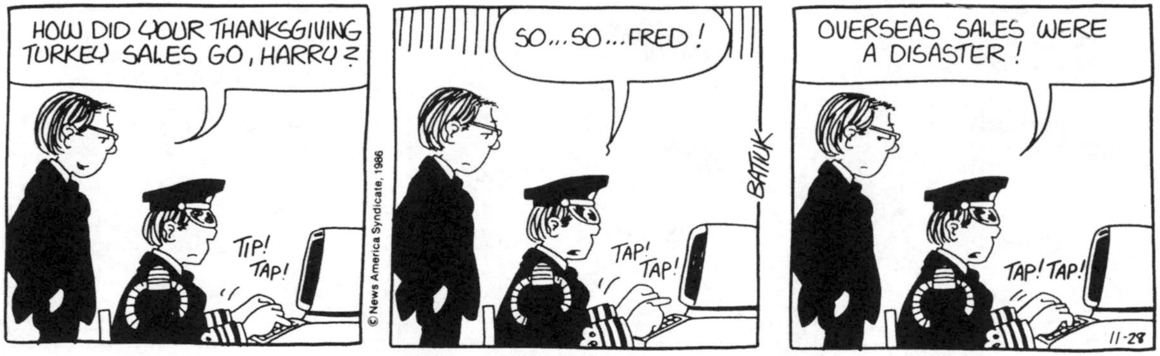
HOW DID YOUR THANKSGIVING TURKEY SALES GO, HARRY?
TIP! TAP!
© News America Syndicate, 1986
SO...SO...FRED!
TAP! TAP!
BATIUK
OVERSEAS SALES WERE A DISASTER!
TAP! TAP!
11-28

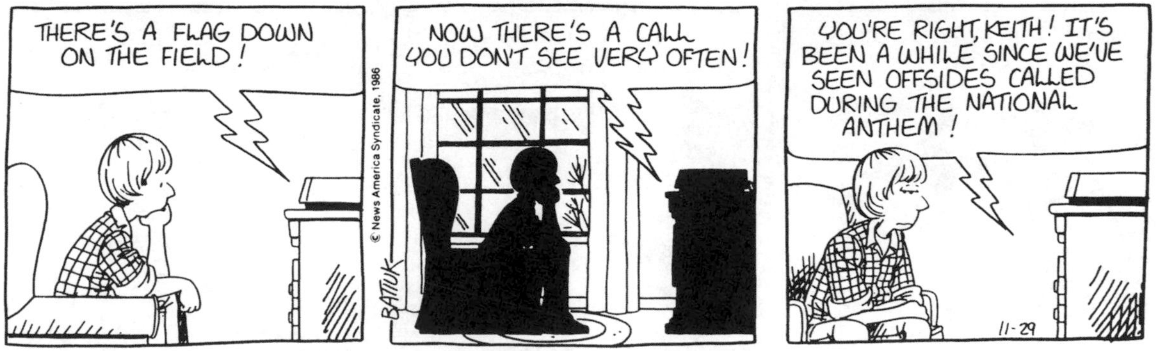
THERE'S A FLAG DOWN ON THE FIELD!
© News America Syndicate, 1986
BATIUK
NOW THERE'S A CALL YOU DON'T SEE VERY OFTEN!
YOU'RE RIGHT, KEITH! IT'S BEEN A WHILE SINCE WE'VE SEEN OFFSIDES CALLED DURING THE NATIONAL ANTHEM!
11-29

FUNKY WINKERBEAN
BY TOM BATIUK
FRENCH FRIED MEATBALLS AGAIN!?
IF YOU DON'T LIKE IT, WHY DO YOU BUY YOUR LUNCH?
WHAT!? AND MISS MY MINIMUM DAILY REQUIREMENT OF JELLO?
THERE'S SOMETHING I'VE ALWAYS WONDERED ABOUT!
WHY IS IT WHEN THE COOKS ARE PASSING OUT THE FOOD...
BATIUK
THEY ALWAYS WEAR THOSE PLASTIC GLOVES?
© News America Syndicate, 1986 11-30
SO THEY CAN'T TRACE THE FINGERPRINTS OF THE PEOPLE RESPONSIBLE!

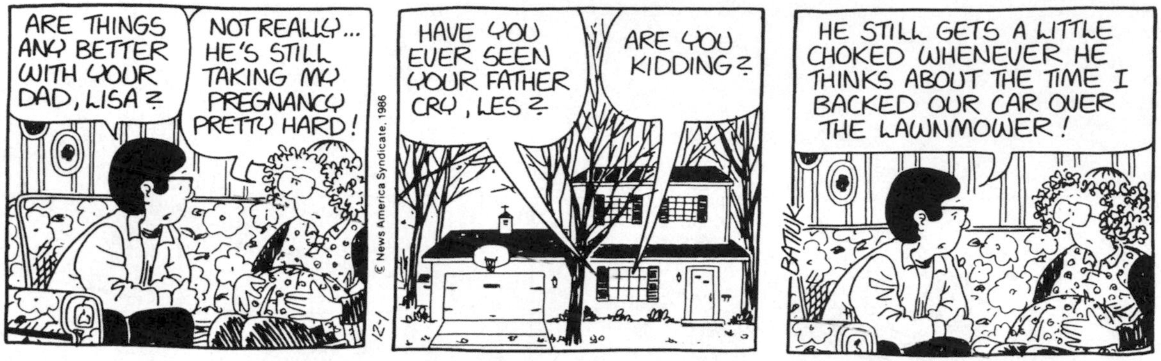
ARE THINGS ANY BETTER WITH YOUR DAD, LISA?
NOT REALLY... HE'S STILL TAKING MY PREGNANCY PRETTY HARD!
© News America Syndicate, 1986
HAVE YOU EVER SEEN YOUR FATHER CRY, LES?
ARE YOU KIDDING?
HE STILL GETS A LITTLE CHOKED WHENEVER HE THINKS ABOUT THE TIME I BACKED OUR CAR OVER THE LAWNMOWER!
BATIUK

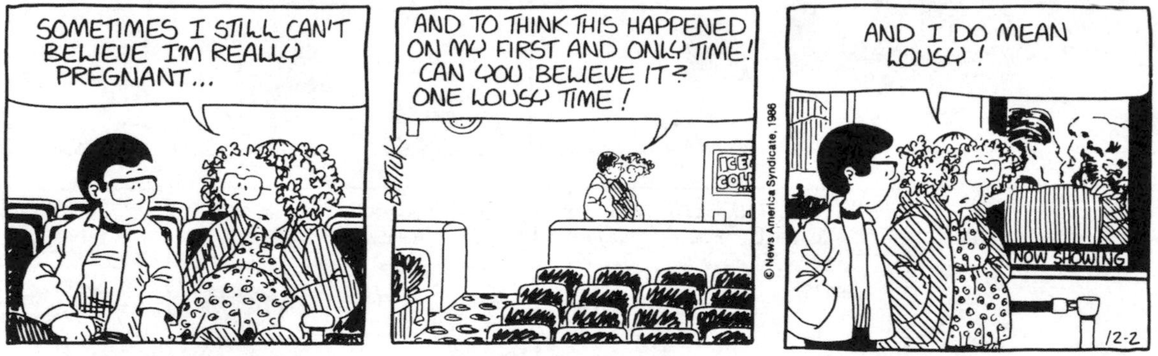
SOMETIMES I STILL CAN'T BELIEVE I'M REALLY PREGNANT...
AND TO THINK THIS HAPPENED ON MY FIRST AND ONLY TIME! CAN YOU BELIEVE IT? ONE LOUSY TIME!
BATIUK
© News America Syndicate, 1986
AND I DO MEAN LOUSY!
NOW SHOWING

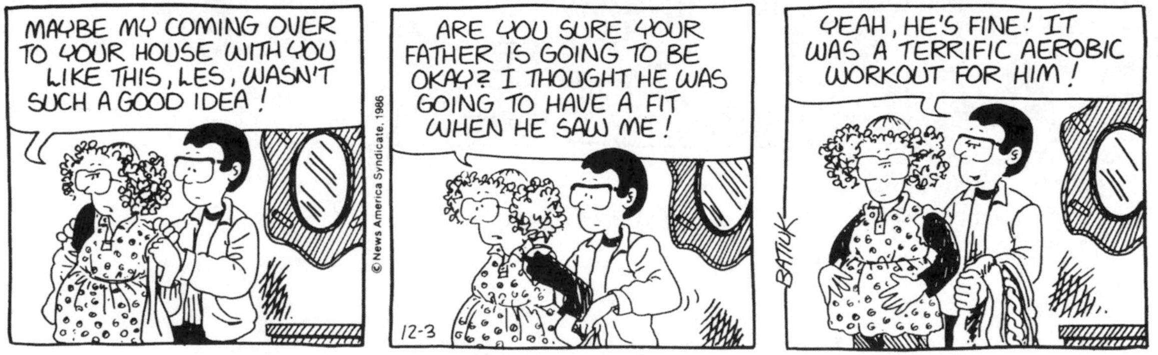
MAYBE MY COMING OVER TO YOUR HOUSE WITH YOU LIKE THIS, LES, WASN'T SUCH A GOOD IDEA!
© News America Syndicate, 1986
ARE YOU SURE YOUR FATHER IS GOING TO BE OKAY? I THOUGHT HE WAS GOING TO HAVE A FIT WHEN HE SAW ME!
YEAH, HE'S FINE! IT WAS A TERRIFIC AEROBIC WORKOUT FOR HIM!
BATIUK

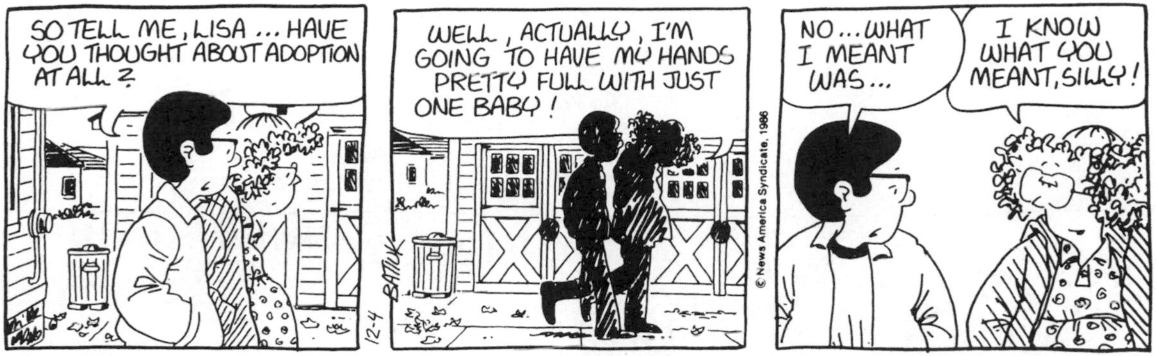
SO TELL ME, LISA ... HAVE YOU THOUGHT ABOUT ADOPTION AT ALL ?
12-4
BATIUK
WELL, ACTUALLY, I'M GOING TO HAVE MY HANDS PRETTY FULL WITH JUST ONE BABY !
© News America Syndicate, 1986
NO ... WHAT I MEANT WAS ...
I KNOW WHAT YOU MEANT, SILLY !

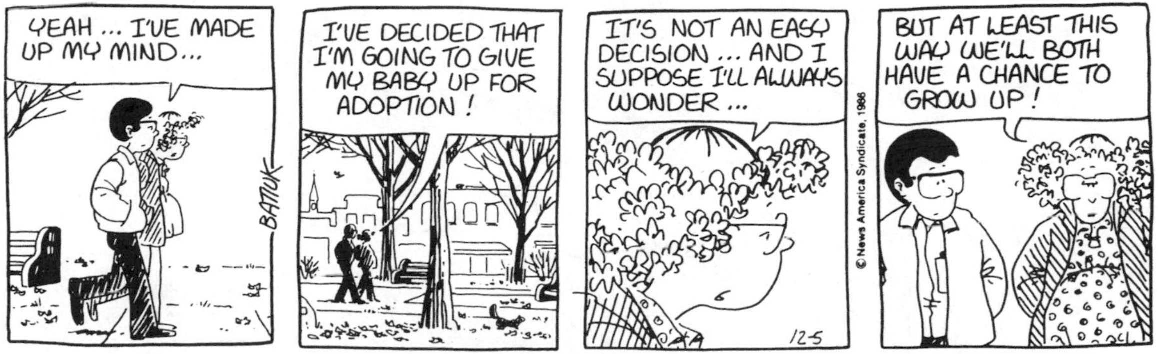
YEAH ... I'VE MADE UP MY MIND ...
BATIUK
I'VE DECIDED THAT I'M GOING TO GIVE MY BABY UP FOR ADOPTION !
IT'S NOT AN EASY DECISION ... AND I SUPPOSE I'LL ALWAYS WONDER ...
12-5
© News America Syndicate, 1986
BUT AT LEAST THIS WAY WE'LL BOTH HAVE A CHANCE TO GROW UP !

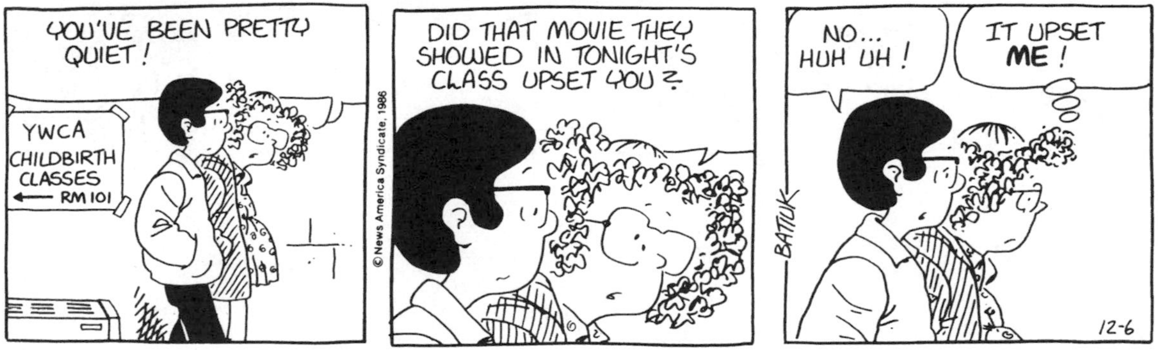
YOU'VE BEEN PRETTY QUIET !
YWCA
CHILDBIRTH CLASSES
RM 101
© News America Syndicate, 1986
DID THAT MOVIE THEY SHOWED IN TONIGHT'S CLASS UPSET YOU ?
BATIUK
NO... HUH UH !
IT UPSET ME !
12-6

FUNKY WINKERBEAN
BY TOM BATIUK
HOLD IT! HOLD IT! STOP!!
WESTVIEW HIGH SCHOOL
FRI DEC 19
CHRISTMAS CONCERT
THAT LAST SECTION YOU JUST PLAYED WAS **HORRIBLE**!!
DID YOU PRACTICE THIS MUSIC FOR THE CONCERT **AT ALL** THIS PAST WEEK!?
BATIUK
12-7
SURE I DID!
© News America Syndicate, 1986
HA! THE NEEDLE MOVED!!
DIOGENES LIE DETECTOR

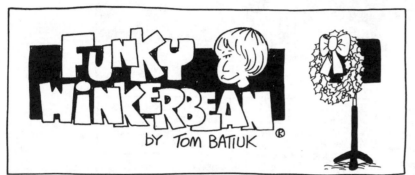

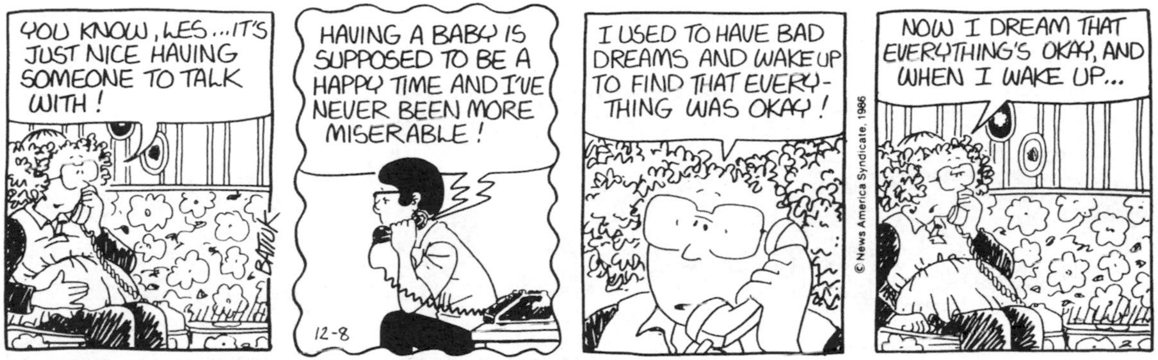
YOU KNOW, LES...IT'S JUST NICE HAVING SOMEONE TO TALK WITH!
HAVING A BABY IS SUPPOSED TO BE A HAPPY TIME AND I'VE NEVER BEEN MORE MISERABLE!
I USED TO HAVE BAD DREAMS AND WAKE UP TO FIND THAT EVERYTHING WAS OKAY!
NOW I DREAM THAT EVERYTHING'S OKAY, AND WHEN I WAKE UP...
BATIUK
12-8
© News America Syndicate, 1986

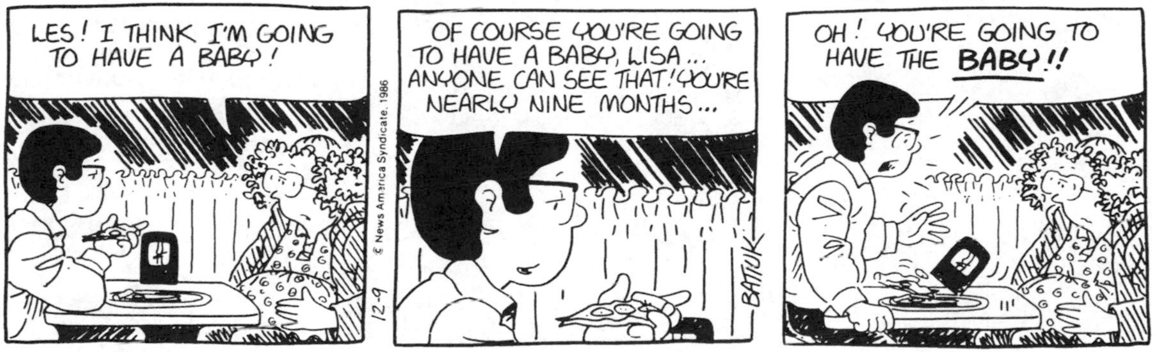
LES! I THINK I'M GOING TO HAVE A BABY!
OF COURSE YOU'RE GOING TO HAVE A BABY, LISA... ANYONE CAN SEE THAT! YOU'RE NEARLY NINE MONTHS...
OH! YOU'RE GOING TO HAVE THE BABY!!
12-9
© News America Syndicate, 1986
BATIUK

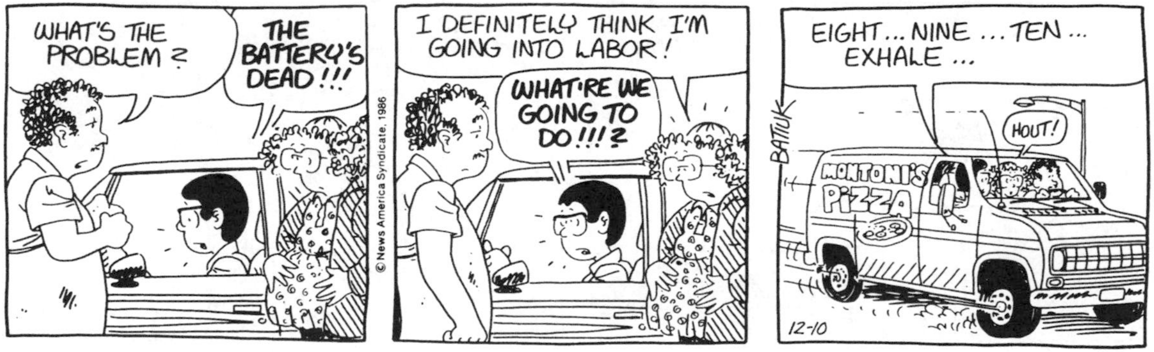
WHAT'S THE PROBLEM?
THE BATTERY'S DEAD!!!
I DEFINITELY THINK I'M GOING INTO LABOR!
WHAT'RE WE GOING TO DO!!!?
EIGHT... NINE ... TEN ... EXHALE ...
HOUT!
MONTONI'S PIZZA
BATIUK
12-10
© News America Syndicate, 1986

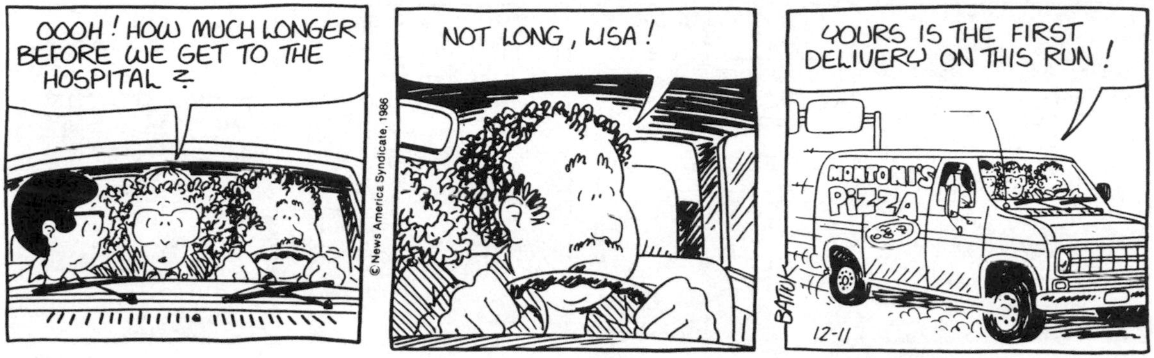
OOOH! HOW MUCH LONGER BEFORE WE GET TO THE HOSPITAL?
© News America Syndicate, 1986
NOT LONG, LISA!
YOURS IS THE FIRST DELIVERY ON THIS RUN!
MONTONI'S PIZZA
BATIUK
12-11

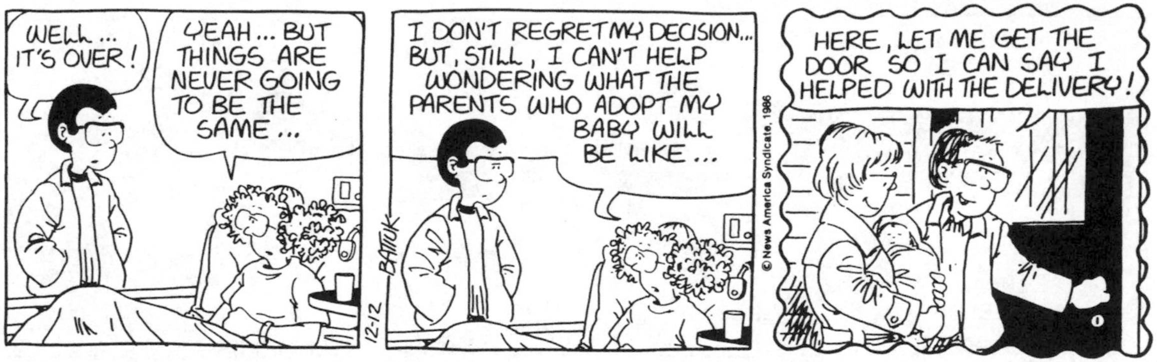
WELL... IT'S OVER!
YEAH... BUT THINGS ARE NEVER GOING TO BE THE SAME...
BATIUK
12-12
I DON'T REGRET MY DECISION... BUT, STILL, I CAN'T HELP WONDERING WHAT THE PARENTS WHO ADOPT MY BABY WILL BE LIKE...
© News America Syndicate, 1986
HERE, LET ME GET THE DOOR SO I CAN SAY I HELPED WITH THE DELIVERY!

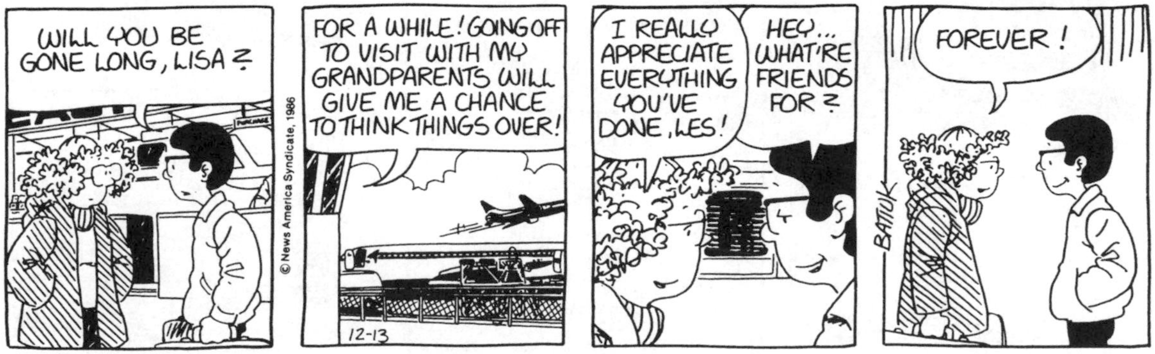
WILL YOU BE GONE LONG, LISA?
© News America Syndicate, 1986
FOR A WHILE! GOING OFF TO VISIT WITH MY GRANDPARENTS WILL GIVE ME A CHANCE TO THINK THINGS OVER!
12-13
I REALLY APPRECIATE EVERYTHING YOU'VE DONE, LES!
HEY... WHAT'RE FRIENDS FOR?
FOREVER!
BATIUK

Funky Winkerbean
by Tom Batiuk ®

DING DONG!

I'M NOT REALLY SURE I WANT ONE OF THOSE BAND FRUITCAKES!

I'M TRYING TO WATCH MY DIET!

DID YOU KNOW THAT BAND FRUITCAKES ARE RECOMMENDED BY THE AMERICAN HEART ASSOCIATION?

NO KIDDING!?

WELL, I'LL TAKE A COUPLE OF BOXES THEN!

© News America Syndicate, 1986

ACTUALLY, THEY RECOMMENDED THAT YOU LAY OFF OF IT IF YOU WANTED TO LOSE WEIGHT!

BATIUK

12-14

491

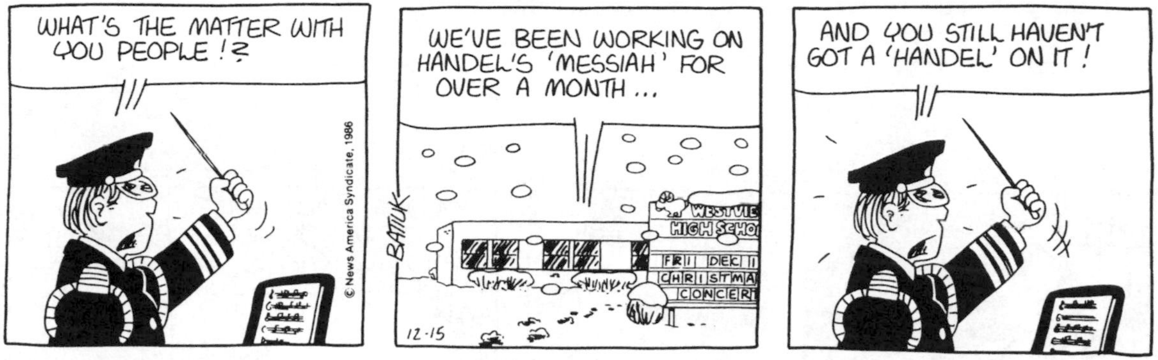
WHAT'S THE MATTER WITH YOU PEOPLE !?
WE'VE BEEN WORKING ON HANDEL'S 'MESSIAH' FOR OVER A MONTH ...
AND YOU STILL HAVEN'T GOT A 'HANDEL' ON IT !
© News America Syndicate, 1986
BATIUK
12-15

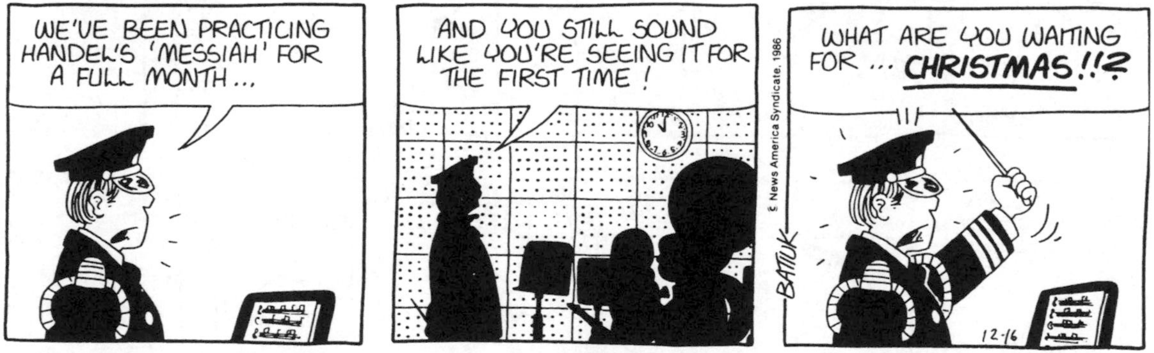
WE'VE BEEN PRACTICING HANDEL'S 'MESSIAH' FOR A FULL MONTH ...
AND YOU STILL SOUND LIKE YOU'RE SEEING IT FOR THE FIRST TIME !
WHAT ARE YOU WAITING FOR ... CHRISTMAS !!?
© News America Syndicate, 1986
BATIUK
12-16

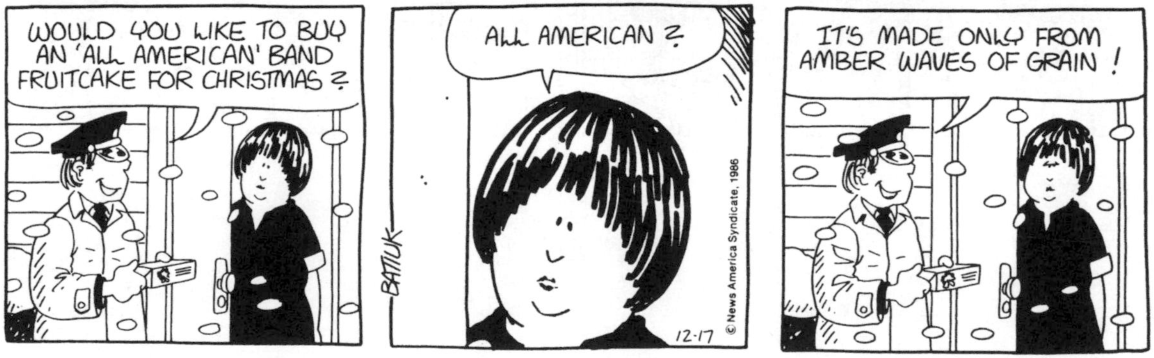
WOULD YOU LIKE TO BUY AN 'ALL AMERICAN' BAND FRUITCAKE FOR CHRISTMAS ?
ALL AMERICAN ?
IT'S MADE ONLY FROM AMBER WAVES OF GRAIN !
© News America Syndicate, 1986
BATIUK
12-17

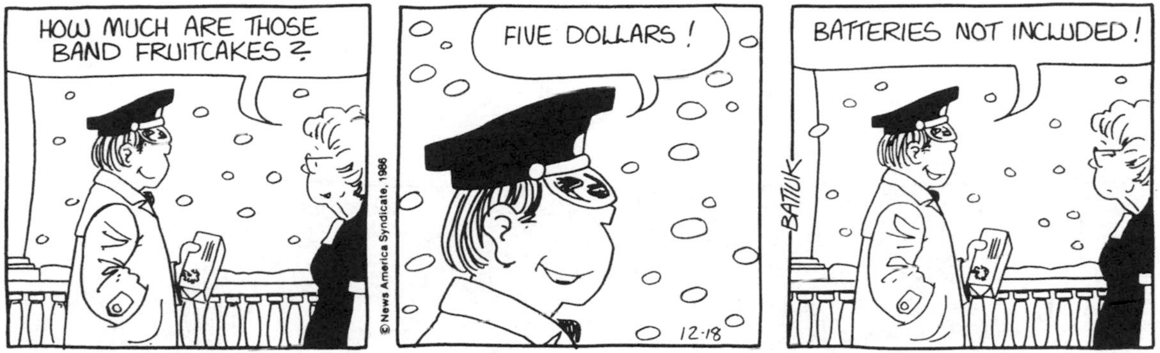
HOW MUCH ARE THOSE BAND FRUITCAKES ?
© News America Syndicate, 1986
FIVE DOLLARS !
12-18
BATTERIES NOT INCLUDED !
BATIUK

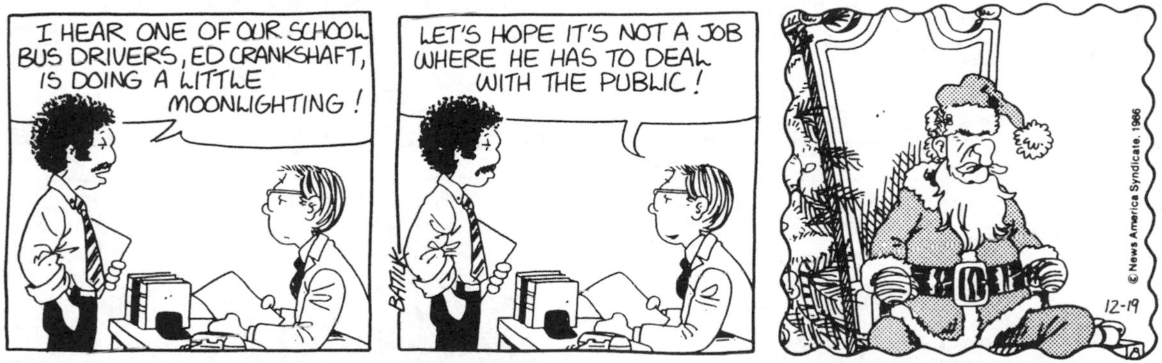
I HEAR ONE OF OUR SCHOOL BUS DRIVERS, ED CRANKSHAFT, IS DOING A LITTLE MOONLIGHTING !
LET'S HOPE IT'S NOT A JOB WHERE HE HAS TO DEAL WITH THE PUBLIC !
BATIUK
© News America Syndicate, 1986
12-19

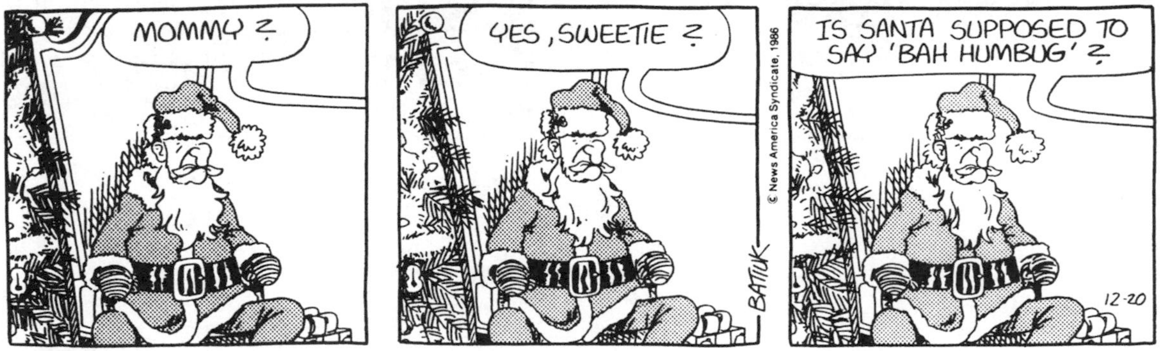
MOMMY ?
YES, SWEETIE ?
BATIUK
© News America Syndicate, 1986
IS SANTA SUPPOSED TO SAY 'BAH HUMBUG' ?
12-20

Funky Winkerbean

by Tom Batiuk

OHH...HERE IT IS!

FRED, DO YOU REMEMBER WHEN WE GOT THIS CHRISTMAS DECORATION?

IS THIS A TEST?

WHAT'S THAT SUPPOSED TO MEAN?

I JUST WANT TO KNOW IF I'M IN TROUBLE IF I DON'T KNOW!

NO...

12-21

© News America Syndicate, 1986

YOU'LL JUST HAVE TO LET ME KNOW IF YOU WANT YOUR CHRISTMAS STOCKING FILLED WITH ANTHRACITE OR BITUMINOUS!

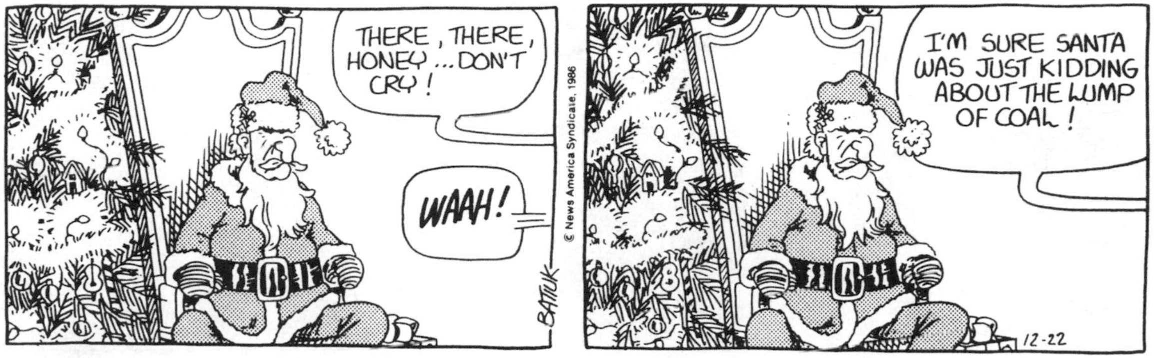
THERE, THERE, HONEY... DON'T CRY!
WAAH!
I'M SURE SANTA WAS JUST KIDDING ABOUT THE LUMP OF COAL!
© News America Syndicate, 1986
BATIUK
12-22

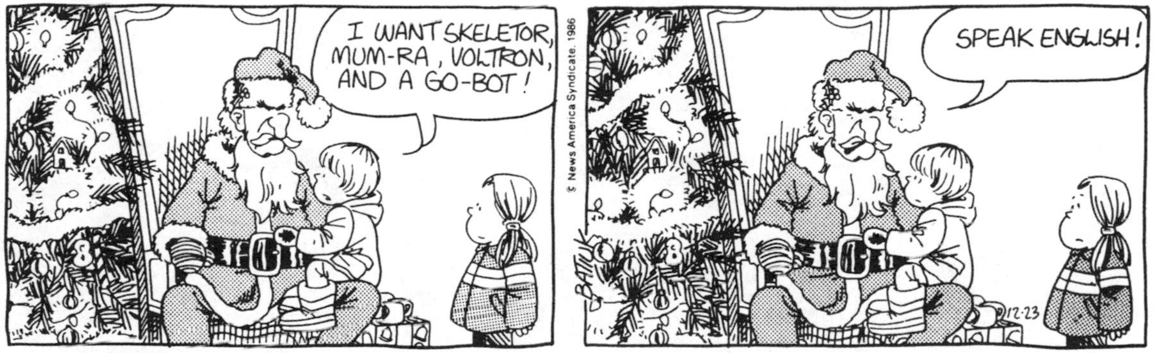
I WANT SKELETOR, MUM-RA, VOLTRON, AND A GO-BOT!
SPEAK ENGLISH!
© News America Syndicate, 1986
BATIUK
12-23

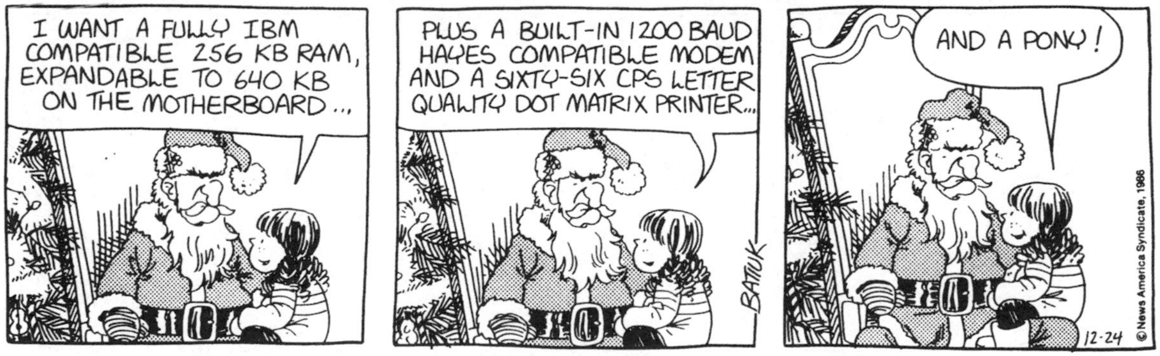
I WANT A FULLY IBM COMPATIBLE 256 KB RAM, EXPANDABLE TO 640 KB ON THE MOTHERBOARD...,
PLUS A BUILT-IN 1200 BAUD HAYES COMPATIBLE MODEM AND A SIXTY-SIX CPS LETTER QUALITY DOT MATRIX PRINTER...
AND A PONY!
BATIUK
© News America Syndicate, 1986
12-24

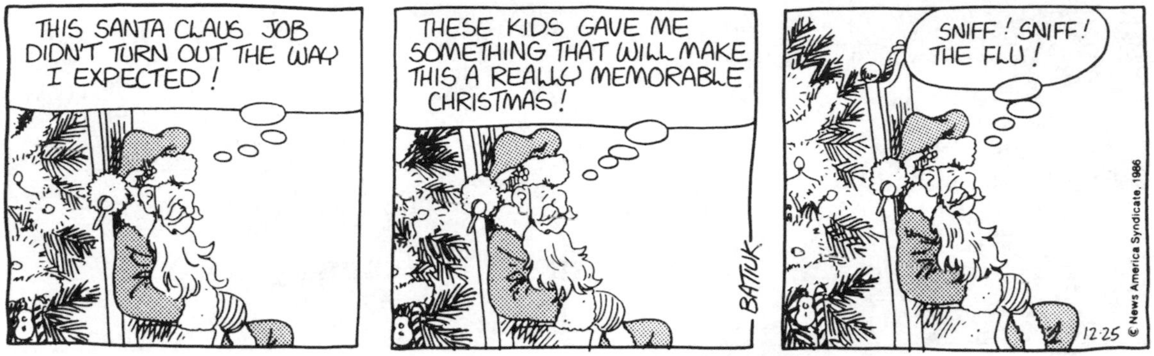
THIS SANTA CLAUS JOB DIDN'T TURN OUT THE WAY I EXPECTED!
THESE KIDS GAVE ME SOMETHING THAT WILL MAKE THIS A REALLY MEMORABLE CHRISTMAS!
BATIUK
SNIFF! SNIFF! THE FLU!
12-25
© News America Syndicate, 1986

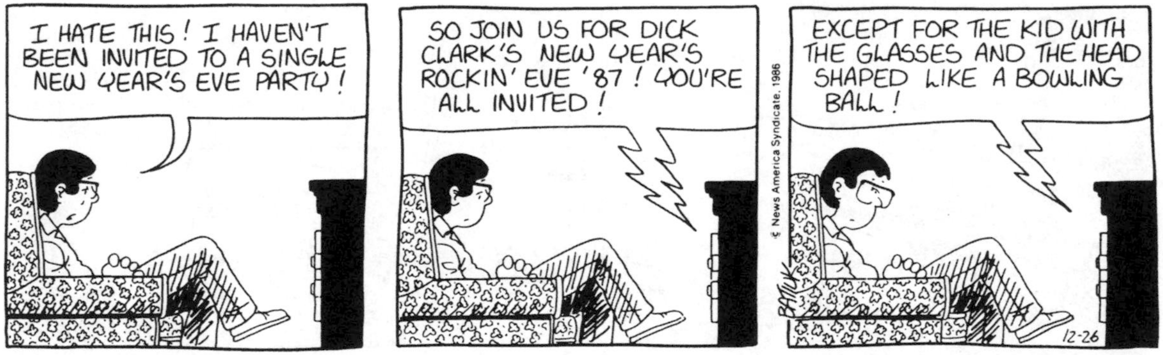
I HATE THIS! I HAVEN'T BEEN INVITED TO A SINGLE NEW YEAR'S EVE PARTY!
SO JOIN US FOR DICK CLARK'S NEW YEAR'S ROCKIN' EVE '87! YOU'RE ALL INVITED!
© News America Syndicate, 1986
BATIUK
EXCEPT FOR THE KID WITH THE GLASSES AND THE HEAD SHAPED LIKE A BOWLING BALL!
12-26

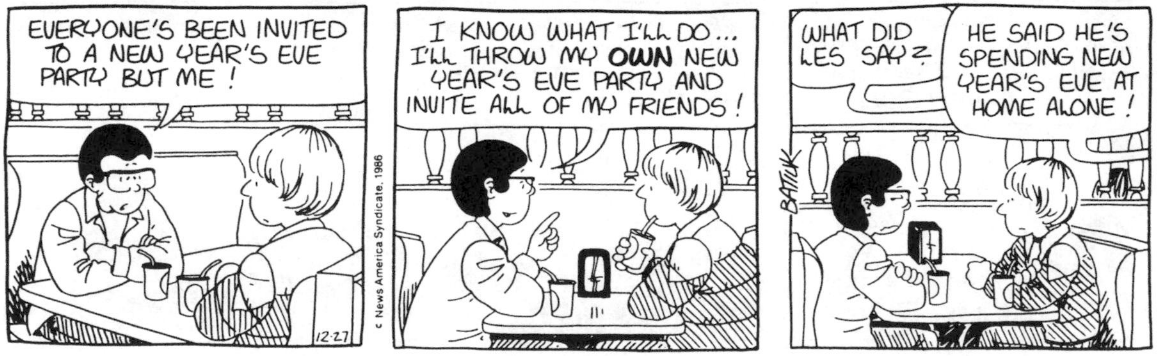
EVERYONE'S BEEN INVITED TO A NEW YEAR'S EVE PARTY BUT ME!
12-27
© News America Syndicate, 1986
I KNOW WHAT I'LL DO... I'LL THROW MY **OWN** NEW YEAR'S EVE PARTY AND INVITE ALL OF MY FRIENDS!
BATIUK
WHAT DID LES SAY?
HE SAID HE'S SPENDING NEW YEAR'S EVE AT HOME ALONE!

FUNKY WINKERBEAN
BY TOM BATIUK
LET'S SEE IF I'VE GOT EVERYTHING FOR MY NEW YEAR'S EVE PARTY!
HATS, NOISEMAKERS, HOT DOGS ... AND FIVE GALLONS OF GENERIC FRUIT PUNCH!
LES, DON'T YOU THINK YOU'RE OVERPLANNING FOR THIS NEW YEAR'S EVE PARTY OF YOURS JUST A BIT?
YOU'VE GOT TO BE PREPARED, FUNKY!
YOU CAN'T JUST WAIT 'TILL THE LAST MINUTE!
BATIUK
12-28
© News America Syndicate, 1986
CAN YOU IMAGINE TRYING TO HIRE SECURITY GUARDS AND PARKING ATTENDANTS ON NEW YEAR'S EVE?

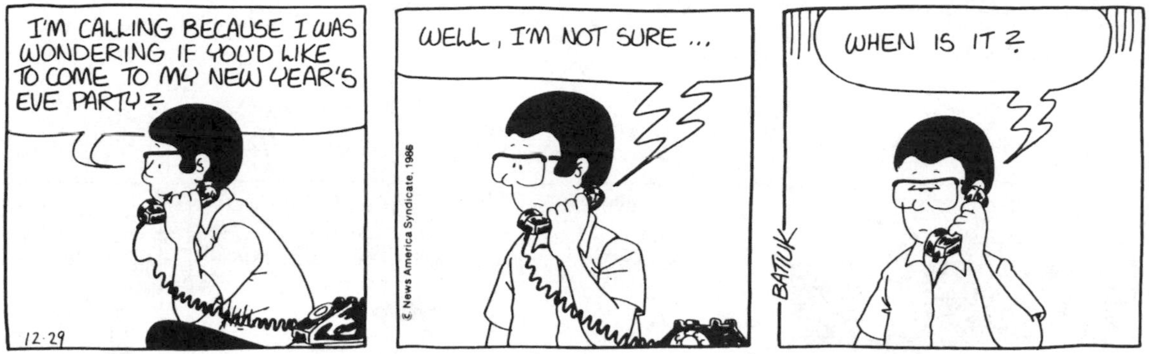
I'M CALLING BECAUSE I WAS WONDERING IF YOU'D LIKE TO COME TO MY NEW YEAR'S EVE PARTY?
WELL, I'M NOT SURE ...
WHEN IS IT?
12-29
© News America Syndicate, 1986
BATIUK

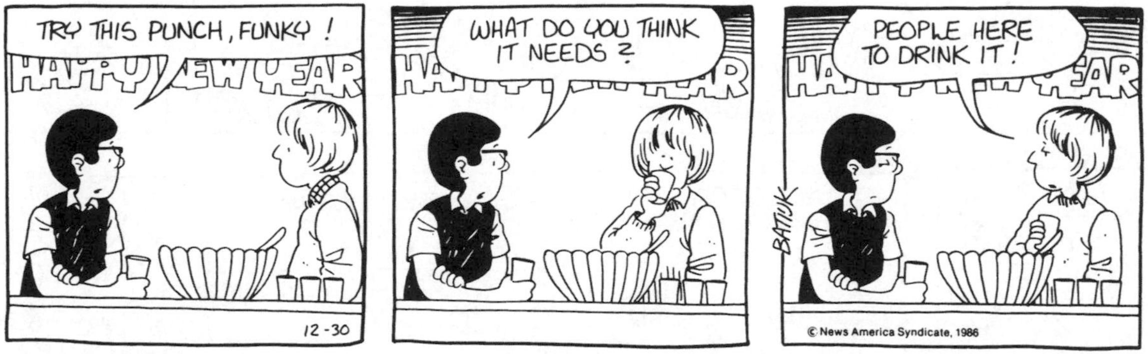
TRY THIS PUNCH, FUNKY!
WHAT DO YOU THINK IT NEEDS?
PEOPLE HERE TO DRINK IT!
12-30
© News America Syndicate, 1986
BATIUK

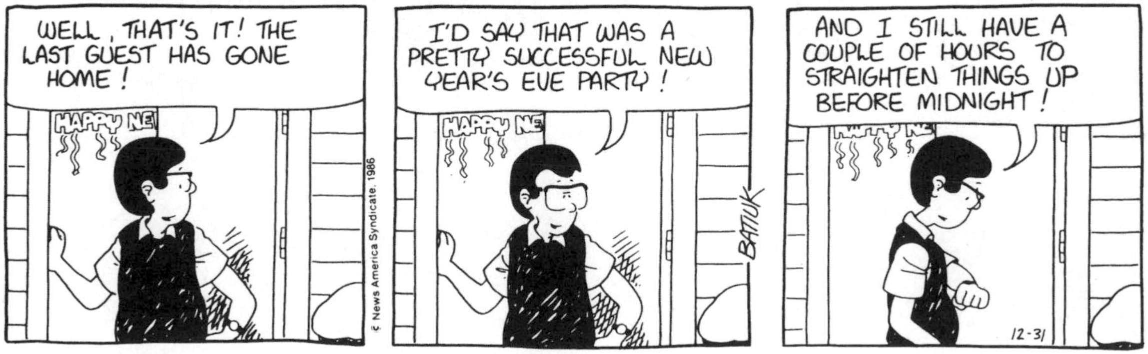
WELL, THAT'S IT! THE LAST GUEST HAS GONE HOME!
I'D SAY THAT WAS A PRETTY SUCCESSFUL NEW YEAR'S EVE PARTY!
AND I STILL HAVE A COUPLE OF HOURS TO STRAIGHTEN THINGS UP BEFORE MIDNIGHT!
12-31
© News America Syndicate, 1986
BATIUK